# Table of Contents

# iOS 7 Programming Cookbook

*Vandad Nahavandipoor*

Beijing • Cambridge • Farnham • Köln • Sebastopol • Tokyo

**iOS 7 Programming Cookbook**
by Vandad Nahavandipoor



Printed in the United States of America.

Published by O'Reilly Media, Inc., 1005 Gravenstein Highway North, Sebastopol, CA 95472.

O'Reilly books may be purchased for educational, business, or sales promotional use. Online editions are also available for most titles (*http://my.safaribooksonline.com*). For more information, contact our corporate/institutional sales department: 800-998-9938 or *corporate@oreilly.com*.

**Editors:** Andy Oram and Rachel Roumeliotis
**Production Editor:** Christopher Hearse
**Copyeditor:** Zyg Group, LLC
**Proofreader:** Julie Van Keuren
**Indexer:** Angela Howard
**Cover Designer:** Randy Comer
**Interior Designer:** David Futato
**Illustrator:** Rebecca Demarest

October 2013: First Edition

**Revision History for the First Edition:**

2013-10-09: First release

See *http://oreilly.com/catalog/errata.csp?isbn=9781449372422* for release details.



ISBN: 978-1-449-37242-2

[QG]

# Preface

This edition of the book is not just an update, but a total remake of the previous edition. iOS 7 changed everything: the look and feel, the way we use our iOS devices, and most importantly, the way we program for iOS devices. This called for a substantial rewrite indeed. I have added roughly 50 new recipes to this book, talking about things such as UIKit dynamics, collection views, the keychain, push notifications, and whatnot. I have also gone through all the example codes and figures and updated them for iOS 7.

iOS 7 is a huge step forward for this amazing operating system that we all, as programmers and users, have grown to love and enjoy programming for. You must have noticed how the focus of iOS 7 is on being *dynamic*: how your UI should adapt to various movements and motions that can be applied to the device. What I mean by that is Apple wants developers to really look at the details of their apps and bring real-world physics and dynamics into them. That's why Apple introduced UIKit Dynamics to the SDK, and that is why this book has a whole chapter dedicated to this concept. The more expensive a high-end device such as the new iPhone becomes, the more demanding the users will get as well. Nobody blames them, though! They have just bought a fantastic and top-of-the-line new iPhone or iPad and they want to see amazing apps running on them, leveraging all the capabilities that those devices have to offer.

That is why now more than ever developers have to get an in-depth knowledge of the SDK and what the SDK has to offer to the developers so that we can create better and faster apps for iOS users. Apple introduced a lot of cool new APIs to the iOS 7 SDK, and we are going to explore them in this book.

The focus of iOS 7 is dynamics!

Before you read about this book, maybe you'd like to know about my background a bit and how I can help you through this journey. I will just briefly let you know who I am and how I got to love iOS. I started out writing Basic code for my Commodore 64 when I was a kid. I then moved on to buy my own PC and started experimenting with Assembly code. At first, it was 8-bit Assembly for DOS. I then moved onto writing my own hobby operating system, which was never really released as a commercial product, for 32-bit Intel x86 CPU architectures.

Among all the programming languages that I have programmed in, Assembly and Objective-C are the two that have really been different from the others, and I've really liked them. Assembly because of the purity of the language: a command does only one thing and does that one thing well. I believe that I like Objective-C for the same reason, and in fact iOS shares the same trait with Assembly and Objective-C. Even though iOS is an operating system and not a programming language, whatever it does, it does it best and better than its rivals. From its simplicity to the sheer power that you can harvest from the software and the hardware combined, using technologies such as GCD, the bar that iOS has set in terms of ease of use and beauty is unprecedented.

This edition of the book has seen all the recipes inside all chapters completely renewed for iOS 7. All screenshots have been updated, and many more recipes—such as those related to security and the keychain, UI dynamics, collection views, push and local notifications, and many more—have exclusively been written for this edition of the book. I really have had a fun time writing this edition of the book, and packed as it is with new features, I hope you'll enjoy reading it. May it be a valuable addition to your tech-book library.

## Audience

I assume you are comfortable with the iOS development environment and know how to create an app for the iPhone or iPad. This book does *not* get novice programmers started but presents useful ways to get things done for iOS programmers ranging from novices to experts.

## Organization of This Book

In this book, we will discuss frameworks and classes that are available in the iOS 7 SDK. This book does its best to teach you the latest and the greatest APIs. As you know, some users of your apps may still be on older versions of iOS, so please consider those users and choose your APIs wisely, depending on the minimum iOS version that you want to target with your apps.

Apple has recommended that you write your apps so that they support and run on iOS 6 and iOS 7. This means you need to use the latest SDK as your base SDK (the SDK that you use to compile your app) and choose iOS 6 as your target, if that's what your business requirements dictate. If you are required to write your app to support only iOS 7, then you are in for a lot of fun, as you can use all the cool APIs that have been introduced in iOS 7 and discussed in this book.

Here is a concise breakdown of the material each chapter covers:

Chapter 1, *Implementing Controllers and Views*
: Explains how Objective-C classes are structured and how objects can be instantiated. The chapter talks about properties and delegates and subscripting by keys and indexes. Even if you are competent in Objective-C, I strongly suggest that you read this chapter, even if you only skim through it, to understand the basic material that is used in the rest of the book. In this chapter, we will also explore the common usage of various UI components, such as alert views, segmented controls, switches, and labels. We will also talk about customizing these components with the latest APIs provided in the SDK.

Chapter 2, *Creating Dynamic and Interactive User Interfaces*
: Talks about UIKit Dynamics, the newest addition to the UIKit framework. These dynamics allow you to add real-life physics and dynamics to your UI components. This will allow you to create even livelier user interfaces with very small effort on your side.

Chapter 3, *Auto Layout and the Visual Format Language*
: Explains how you can take advantage of Auto Layout in the iOS SDK in order to construct your UI in such a way that it can be resized and stretched to pretty much any screen dimension.

Chapter 4, *Constructing and Using Table Views*
: Shows how you can work with table views to create professional-looking iOS applications. Table views are very dynamic in nature, and as a result, programmers sometimes have difficulty understanding how they should work with them. By reading this chapter and trying out the example code, you will gain the knowledge that is required to comfortably work with table views.

Chapter 5, *Building Complex Layouts with Collection Views*
: Collection views have been available to OS X programmers for quite some time now, and Apple decided to provide the same APIs to iOS programmers in the iOS SDK. Collection views are very much like table views, but they are much more configurable and dynamic. Where in table views we have the concept of sections and rows in each section, collection views bring columns to the equation as well, so that you can display many items in one row if you want to. In this chapter we will have a look at all the great user interfaces that you can create using collection views.

Chapter 6, *Storyboards*
: Demonstrates the process of *storyboarding*, the new way to define the connections between different screens in your app. The great thing about storyboarding is that you don't have to know anything about iOS programming to get a simple app running. This helps product analysts, product owners, or designers who work independently of developers to gain knowledge of the UI components iOS offers and to

build more robust products. Programmers can also take advantage of storyboarding to easily create prototypes. Storyboarding is just fun, whether you do it on paper or using Xcode.

Chapter 7, *Concurrency*
: As humans, we can do many things simultaneously without thinking much about it. With advances in computer technology, mobile devices are also able to multitask, and they provide programmers with tools and mechanisms that can accomplish more than one task at the same time. This is called *concurrency*. In this chapter, you will learn about Grand Central Dispatch, Apple's preferred way of achieving concurrency in iOS. You will also learn about timers, threads, and operations.

Chapter 8, *Security*
: iOS is a very secure operating system, and apps that we write for it also have to adhere to certain security standards and practices. In this chapter, we will discuss how you can take advantage of keychain APIs to make your apps more secure. We will also talk about various steps that you can take to make your user interface more secure.

Chapter 9, *Core Location and Maps*
: Describes how you should use Map Kit and Core Location APIs to develop location-aware iOS applications. First you will learn about maps, and then you will learn how to detect a device's location and tailor your maps with custom annotations. You will also learn about geocoding and reverse geocoding, as well as some of the methods of the Core Location framework, which are available only in iOS 7.

Chapter 10, *Implementing Gesture Recognizers*
: Demonstrates how to use gesture recognizers, which enable your users to easily and intuitively manipulate the graphical interface of your iOS applications. In this chapter, you will learn how to use all available gesture recognizers in the iOS SDK, with working examples tested on iOS 7.

Chapter 11, *Networking, JSON, XML, and Sharing*
: Demonstrates the built-in JSON and XML parsers. On top of that, this chapter talks about various networking APIs and how programmers can build social networking into our apps to allow our users to share their creations and data to social networks such as Facebook.

Chapter 12, *Audio and Video*
: Discusses the AV Foundation and Media Player frameworks that are available on the iOS SDK. You will learn how to play audio and video files and how to handle interruptions, such as a phone call, while the audio or video is being played. This chapter also explains how to record audio using an iOS device's built-in microphone(s). At the end of the chapter, you will learn how to access the Music Library and play its media content, all from inside your application.

Chapter 13, *Address Book*
: Explains the Address Book framework and how to retrieve contacts, groups, and their information from the Address Book database on an iOS device. The Address Book framework is composed entirely of C APIs. Because of this, many Objective-C developers find it difficult to use this framework, as compared with frameworks that provide an Objective-C interface. After reading this chapter and trying the examples for yourself, you will feel much more confident using the Address Book framework.

Chapter 14, *Files and Folder Management*
: One of the most important tasks that, as developers, we want to perform in our iOS apps is manipulating files and folders. Whether this means creating, reading from, writing to, or deleting them, this chapter contains enough material to get you up and running with file and folder management in the iOS SDK.

Chapter 15, *Camera and the Photo Library*
: Demonstrates how you can determine the availability of front- and back-facing cameras on an iOS device. You will also learn how to access the photo library using the Assets Library framework. At the end of the chapter, you will learn about editing videos right on an iOS device using a built-in view controller.

Chapter 16, *Multitasking*
: Shows multitasking-aware applications that run beautifully on iOS devices. You will learn about background processing, including how to play audio and retrieve users' locations in the background, as well as how to download content from a URL while your application is running in the background. On top of that, we will explore some of the new APIs that iOS 7 provides to us, in order to enable our apps to download content periodically while in the background or even while our app is not even running.

Chapter 17, *Notifications*
: Notifications are objects that can be composed by a source and delivered to multiple recipients. In this chapter, we will discuss notifications, including local notifications and push notifications, along with how you can use the latest capabilities built into Xcode to easily enable these features in your own apps.

Chapter 18, *Core Data*
: Describes the details of Core Data stacks and what they are made out of. You will then be able to design your own object-oriented data models right into Xcode, using the Core Data model editor, and also create and retrieve your objects in Core Data. On top of that, you will learn how to add your own custom data to Core Data and how to search for data in the background thread, leaving your UI thread ready to process user events.

Chapter 19, *Dates, Calendars, and Events*
: Demonstrates the use of the Event Kit and Event Kit UI frameworks in order to manage calendars and events on an iOS device. You will see how to create, modify, save, and delete events. You will also learn, through examples, how to add alarms to calendar events and how to set up CalDAV calendars so that you can share a single calendar among multiple devices.

Chapter 20, *Graphics and Animations*
: Introduces the Core Graphics framework. You will learn how to draw images and text on a graphics context; draw lines, rectangles, and paths; and much more. You will also learn to use the new iOS SDK APIs to capture your views' contents as screenshots.

Chapter 21, *Core Motion*
: Explains the Core Motion framework. Using Core Motion, you will access the accelerometer and the gyroscope on an iOS device. You will also learn how to detect shakes on a device. Of course, not all iOS devices are equipped with an accelerometer and a gyroscope, so you will also learn how to detect the availability of the required hardware.

Chapter 22, *iCloud*
: Shows how to use the iCloud service, which ties devices together and allows them to share data to provide a seamless user experience as the user moves from one device to another.

Chapter 23, *Pass Kit*
: Describes Passbook: a virtual wallet, if you will, capable of managing your coupons, boarding passes, rail and bus tickets, and much more. In this chapter, you will learn all there is to know in order to be able to create your own digitally signed passes and distribute them to your users easily.

## Additional Resources

From time to time, I refer to official Apple documentation. Some of Apple's descriptions are right on the mark, and there is no point in trying to restate them. Throughout this book, I have listed the most important documents and guides in the official Apple documentation that every professional iOS developer should read.

For starters, I suggest that you have a look at the iOS Human Interface Guidelines (*http://bit.ly/QbdY0B*) for all iOS devices. This document will tell you everything you need to know about developing engaging and intuitive user interfaces for all iOS devices. Every iOS programmer should read this document. In fact, I believe this should be required reading for the product design and development teams of any company that develops iOS applications.

I also suggest that you skim through the "iOS App Programming Guide" in the iOS Developer Library (*http://bit.ly/Qi7JaZ*) for some tips and advice on how to make great iOS applications.

iOS 7 brings with itself quite a lot of changes to how UI components appear on the screen. We will talk at great length about these changes and how you, as the programmer, can use the latest APIs to create great-looking apps for iOS 7. However, I would like to suggest that you have a look at the iOS 7 UI Transition Guide (*http://bit.ly/190XxsL*) provided by Apple, which outlines all the UI changes that have now been made to the latest version of the SDK.

One of the things you will notice when reading Chapter 16 is the use of block objects. This book concisely explains block objects, but if you require further details on the subject, I suggest you read "A Short Practical Guide to Blocks" (*http://bit.ly/TsSMNU*).

Throughout this book, you will see references to "bundles" and loading images and data from bundles. You will read a concise overview about bundles in this book, but if you require further information, head over to the "Bundle Programming Guide" (*http://bit.ly/XdLKE6*).

## Conventions Used in This Book

The following typographical conventions are used in this book:

*Italic*
: Indicates new terms, URLs, email addresses, filenames, and file extensions.

`Constant width`
: Used for program listings, as well as within paragraphs to refer to program elements such as variable or function names, databases, data types, environment variables, statements, and keywords.

**`Constant width bold`**
: Shows commands or other text that should be typed literally by the user.

*`Constant width italic`*
: Shows text that should be replaced with user-supplied values or by values determined by context.

This icon signifies a tip, suggestion, or general note.

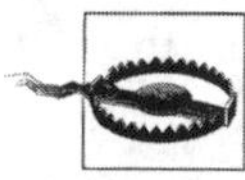

This icon indicates a warning or caution.

## Using Code Examples

Supplemental material (code examples, exercises, etc.) is available for download at *https://github.com/oreillymedia/iOS7_programming_cookbook*.

This book is here to help you get your job done. In general, if example code is offered with this book, you may use it in your programs and documentation. You do not need to contact us for permission unless you're reproducing a significant portion of the code. For example, writing a program that uses several chunks of code from this book does not require permission. Selling or distributing a CD-ROM of examples from O'Reilly books does require permission. Answering a question by citing this book and quoting example code does not require permission. Incorporating a significant amount of example code from this book into your product's documentation does require permission.

We appreciate, but do not require, attribution. An attribution usually includes the title, author, publisher, and ISBN. For example: "*iOS 7 Programming Cookbook* by Vandad Nahavandipoor (O'Reilly). Copyright 2014 Vandad Nahavandipoor, 978-1-4493-7242-2."

If you feel your use of code examples falls outside fair use or the permission given here, feel free to contact us at *permissions@oreilly.com*.

## Safari® Books Online

Safari Books Online (*www.safaribooksonline.com*) is an on-demand digital library that delivers expert content in both book and video form from the world's leading authors in technology and business.

Technology professionals, software developers, web designers, and business and creative professionals use Safari Books Online as their primary resource for research, problem solving, learning, and certification training.

Safari Books Online offers a range of product mixes and pricing programs for organizations, government agencies, and individuals. Subscribers have access to thousands of books, training videos, and prepublication manuscripts in one fully searchable database from publishers like O'Reilly Media, Prentice Hall Professional, Addison-Wesley Professional, Microsoft Press, Sams, Que, Peachpit Press, Focal Press, Cisco Press, John Wiley & Sons, Syngress, Morgan Kaufmann, IBM Redbooks, Packt, Adobe Press, FT Press, Apress, Manning, New Riders, McGraw-Hill, Jones & Bartlett, Course Technology, and dozens more. For more information about Safari Books Online, please visit us online.

## How to Contact Us

Please address comments and questions concerning this book to the publisher:

O'Reilly Media, Inc.
1005 Gravenstein Highway North
Sebastopol, CA 95472
800-998-9938 (in the United States or Canada)
707-829-0515 (international or local)
707-829-0104 (fax)

We have a web page for this book, where we list errata, examples, and any additional information. You can access this page at *http://oreil.ly/iOS7-Programming-Cookbook*.

To comment or ask technical questions about this book, send email to *bookquestions@oreilly.com*.

For more information about our books, courses, conferences, and news, see our website at *http://www.oreilly.com*.

Find us on Facebook: *http://facebook.com/oreilly*

Follow us on Twitter: *http://twitter.com/oreillymedia*

Watch us on YouTube: *http://www.youtube.com/oreillymedia*

## Acknowledgments

Andy Oram, my lovely editor, has again done an amazing job going through all the changes that I made in this edition of the book. In fact, the whole book is updated in this edition, and all example codes and screenshots have also been updated. I'd like to also thank Krzysztof Grobelny and Krzysztof Gutowski, my great friends and colleagues, for tech-reviewing this book. Without their help, this book wouldn't be in your hands.

I'd like to say thank you to Rachel Roumeliotis, for supporting me and Andy, among all the other admin work that she did for us behind the scenes. Rachel, you may be quiet, but we'd have to be blind not to notice your hard work in the background. Also, Meghan Connolly of O'Reilly has been a fantastic sport, listening to my nagging about paperwork, and she has been absolute bliss to work with. A thank-you goes to Jessica Hosman for helping us a great deal with Git issues. Even though I didn't believe the simple solutions that she suggested to me would work, they did, and I looked like a fool.

Last but not least, thank you to Alina Rizzoni, Bruno Packham, and Thomas Packham for being real friends. I feel blessed to know them, and I appreciate their help and support.

CHAPTER 1

# Implementing Controllers and Views

## 1.0. Introduction

iOS 7 has introduced a lot of new features to users, as well as tons of new APIs for us programmers to use and play with. You probably already know that the user interface has drastically changed in iOS 7. This user interface had stayed intact all the way from the first version of iOS till now, and because of this, many apps were coded on the assumption that this user interface would not ever change. Graphic designers are now faced with the challenge of creating the user interface and thinking about the user experience in a way that makes it great for both pre- and post-iOS 7 user interfaces (UIs).

In order to write apps for iOS 7, you need to know some of the basics of the Objective-C programming language that we will use throughout this book. Objective-C, as its name implies, is based on C with extensions that allow it to make use of objects. Objects and classes are fundamental in object-oriented programming (OOP) languages such as Objective-C, Java, C++, and many others. In Objective-C, like any other object-oriented language (OOL), you have not only access to objects, but also to primitives. For instance, the number –20 (minus twenty) can be expressed simply as a primitive in this way:

```
NSInteger myNumber = -20;
```

This simple line of code will define a variable named `myNumber` with the data type of `NSInteger` and sets its value to *`20`*. This is how we define variables in Objective-C. A variable is a simple assignment of a name to a location in memory. In this case, when we set 20 as the value of the `myNumber` variable, we are telling the machine that will eventually run this piece of code to put the aforementioned value in a memory location that belongs to the variable `myNumber`.

All iOS applications essentially use the model-view-controller (MVC) architecture. Model, view, and controller are the three main components of an iOS application from an architectural perspective.

The *model* is the brain of the application. It does the calculations and creates a virtual world for itself that can live without the views and controllers. In other words, think of a model as a virtual copy of your application, without a face!

A *view* is the window through which your users interact with your application. It displays what's inside the model most of the time, but in addition to that, it accepts users' interactions. Any interaction between the user and your application is sent to a view, which then can be captured by a view controller and sent to the model.

The *controller* in iOS programming usually refers to the view controllers I just mentioned. Think of a view controller as a bridge between the model and your views. This controller interprets what is happening on one side and uses that information to alter the other side as needed. For instance, if the user changes some field in a view, the controller makes sure the model changes in response. And if the model gets new data, the controller tells the view to reflect it.

In this chapter, you will learn how to create the structure of an iOS application and how to use views and view controllers to create intuitive applications.

In this chapter, for most of the user interface (UI) components that we create, we are using a Single View Application template in Xcode. To reproduce the examples, follow the instructions in "Creating and Running Our First iOS App" on page 2. Make sure that your app is universal, as opposed to an iPhone or iPad app. A universal app can run on both iPhone and iPad.

## Creating and Running Our First iOS App

Before we dive any deeper into the features of Objective-C, we should have a brief look at how to create a simple iOS app in Xcode. Xcode is Apple's IDE (integrated development environment) that allows you to create, build, and run your apps on iOS Simulator and even on real iOS devices. We will talk more about Xcode and its features as we go along, but for now let's focus on creating and running a simple iOS app. I assume that you've already downloaded Xcode into your computer from the Mac App Store. Once that step is taken care of, please follow these steps to create and run a simple iOS app:

1. Open Xcode if it's not already open.
2. From the File menu, choose New Project...
3. In the New Project window that appears, on the lefthand side under the iOS category, choose Application and then on the righthand side choose Single View Application. Then press the Next button.
4. On the next screen, for the Product Name, enter a name that makes sense for you. For instance, you can set the name of your product as `My First iOS App`. In the

Organization Name section, enter your company's name, or if you don't have a company, enter anything else that makes sense to you. The organization name is quite an important piece of information that you can enter here, but for now, you don't have to worry about it too much. For the Company Identifier field, enter com.*mycompany*. If you really do own a company or you are creating this app for a company that you work with, replace *mycompany* with the actual name of the company in question. If you are just experimenting with development on your own, invent a name. For the Devices section, choose Universal.

5. Once you are done setting the aforementioned values, simply press the Next button.
6. You are now being asked by Xcode to save your project to a suitable place. Choose a suitable folder for your project and press the Create button.
7. As soon as your project is created, you are ready to build and run it. However, before you begin, make sure that you've unplugged all your iOS devices from your computer. The reason behind this is that once an iOS device is plugged in, by default, Xcode will attempt to build and run your project on the device, causing some issues with provisioning profiles (which we haven't talked about yet). So unplug your iOS devices and then press the big Run button on the top-lefthand corner of Xcode. If you cannot find the Run button, go to the Product menu and select the Run menu item.

Voilà! Your first iOS app is running in iOS Simulator now. Even though the app is not exactly impressive, simply displaying a white screen in the simulator, this is just the first step toward our bigger goal of mastering the iOS SDK, so hold on tight as we embark on this journey together.

## Defining and Understanding Variables

All modern programming languages, including Objective-C, have the concept of variables. Variables are simple aliases to locations in the memory. Every variable can have the following properties:

1. A data type, which is either a primitive, such as an integer, or an object
2. A name
3. A value

You don't always have to set a value for a variable, but you need to specify its type and its name. Here are a few data types that you will need to know about when writing any typical iOS app:

**Mutable Versus Immutable**

If a data type is mutable, you can change if after it is initialized. For instance, you can change one of the values in a mutable array, or add or remove values. In contrast, you must provide the values to an immutable data type when you initialize it, and cannot add to them, remove them, or change them later. Immutable types are useful because they are more efficient, and because they can prevent errors when the values are meant to stay the same throughout the life of the data.

*NSInteger and NSUInteger*
: Variables of this type can hold integral values such as 10, 20, etc. The `NSInteger` type allows negative values as well as positive ones, but the NSUInteger data type is the Unsigned type, hence the *U* in its name. Remember, the phrase `unsigned` in programming languages in the context of numbers always means that the number must not be negative. Only a signed data type can hold negative numbers.

*CGFloat*
: Holds floating point variables with decimal points, such as 1.31 or 2.40.

*NSString*
: Allows you to store strings of characters. We will see examples of this later.

*NSNumber*
: Allows you to store numbers as objects.

*id*
: Variables of type `id` can point to any object of any type. These are called *untyped* objects. Whenever you want to pass an object from one place to another but do not wish to specify its type for whatever reason, you can take advantage of this data type.

*NSDictionary and NSMutableDictionary*
: These are immutable and mutable variants of hash tables. A hash table allows you to store a key and to associate a value to that key, such as a key named `phone_num` that has the value `05552487700`. Read the values by referring to the keys associated with them.

*NSArray and NSMutableArray*
: Immutable and mutable arrays of objects. An array is an ordered collection of items. For instance, you may have 10 string objects that you want to store in memory. An array could be a good place for that.

*NSSet, NSMutableSet, NSOrderedSet, NSMutableOrderedSet*
: Sets are like arrays in that they can hold series of objects, but they differ from arrays in that they contain only unique objects. Arrays can hold the same object multiple

times, but a set can contain only one instance of an object. I encourage you to learn the difference between arrays and sets and use them properly.

*NSData and NSMutableData*
: Immutable and mutable containers for any data. These data types are perfect when you want to read the contents of a file, for instance, into memory.

Some of the data types that we talked about are primitive, and some are classes. You'll just have to memorize which is which. For instance, `NSInteger` is a primitive data type, but `NSString` is a class, so objects can be instantiated of it. Objective-C, like C and C++, has the concept of pointers. A pointer is a data type that stores the memory address where the real data is stored. You should know by now that pointers to classes are denoted using an asterisk sign:

```
NSString *myString = @"Objective-C is great!";
```

Thus, when you want to assign a string to a variable of type `NSString` in Objective-C, you simply have to store the data into a pointer of type `NSString *`. However, if you are about to store a floating point value into a variable, you wouldn't specify it as a pointer since the data type for that variable is not a class:

```
/* Set the myFloat variable to PI */
CGFloat myFloat = M_PI;
```

If you wanted to have a pointer to that floating point variable, you could do so as follows:

```
/* Set the myFloat variable to PI */
CGFloat myFloat = M_PI;

/* Create a pointer variable that points to the myFloat variable */
CGFloat *pointerFloat = &myFloat;
```

Getting data from the original float is a simple dereference (`myFloat`), whereas getting the value of through the pointer requires the use of the asterisk (`*pointerFloat`). The pointer can be useful in some situations, such as when you call a function that sets the value of a floating-point argument and you want to retrieve the new value after the function returns.

Going back to classes, we probably have to talk a bit more about classes before things get lost in translation, so let's do that next.

## Creating and Taking Advantage of Classes

A class is a data structure that can have methods, instance variables, and properties, along with many other features, but for now we are just going to talk about the basics. Every class has to follow these rules:

- The class has to be derived from a superclass, apart from a few exceptions such as NSObject and NSProxy classes, which are root classes. Root classes do not have a superclass.
- It has to have a name that conforms to Cocoa's naming convention for methods (*http://bit.ly/19zqpvs*).
- It has to have an interface file that defines the interface of the class.
- It has to have an implementation where you implement the features that you have promised to deliver in the interface of the class.

`NSObject` is the root class from which almost every other class is inherited. For this example, we are going to add a class, named `Person`, to the project we created in "Creating and Running Our First iOS App" on page 2. We are going to then add two properties to this class, named `firstName` and `lastName`, of type `NSString`. Follow these steps to create and add the `Person` class to your project:

1. In Xcode, while your project is open and in front of you, from the File menu, choose New → File...
2. On the lefthand side, ensure that under the iOS main section you have chosen the Cocoa Touch category. Once done, select the Objective-C Class item and press the Next button.
3. In the Class section, enter **`Person`**.
4. In the "Subclass of" section, enter `NSObject`.
5. Once done, press the Next button, at which point Xcode will ask where you would like to save this file. Simply save the new class into the folder where you have placed your project and its files. This is the default selection. Then press the Create button, and you are done.

You now have two files added to your project: *Person.h* and *Person.m*. The former is the interface and the latter is the implementation file for your `Person` class. In Objective-C, *.h* files are headers, where you define the interface of each class, and *.m* files are implementation files where you write the actual implementation of the class.

Now let's go into the header file of our `Person` class and define two properties for the class, of type `NSString`:

```
@interface Person : NSObject

@property (nonatomic, copy) NSString *firstName;
@property (nonatomic, copy) NSString *lastName;

@end
```

Just like a variable, definition of properties has its own format, in this particular order:

1. The definition of the property has to start with the `@property` keyword.
2. You then need to specify the qualifiers of the property. `nonatomic` properties are not thread-safe. We will talk about thread safety in Chapter 16. You can also specify `assign`, `copy`, `weak`, `strong`, or `unsafe_unretained` as the property qualifiers. We will read more about these soon too.
3. You then have to specify the data type of the property, such as `NSInteger` or `NSString`.
4. Last but not least, you have to specify a name for the property. The name of the property has to follow the Apple guidelines (*http://bit.ly/19gFFcX*).

We said that properties can have various qualifiers. Here are the important qualifiers that you need to know about:

`strong`
: Properties of this type will be retained by the runtime. These can only be instances of classes. In other words, you cannot retain a value into a property of type `strong` if the value is a primitive. You can retain objects, but not primitives.

`copy`
: The same as `strong`, but when you assign to properties of this type, the runtime will make a copy of the object on the right side of the assignment. The object on the righthand side of the assignment must conform to the `NSCopying` or `NSMutableCopying` protocol.

`assign`
: Objects or primitive values that are set as the value of a property of type `assign` will not be copied or retained by that property. For primitive properties, this qualifier will create a memory address where you can put the primitive data. For objects, properties of this type will simply point to the object on the righthand side of the equation.

`unsafe_unretained`
: The same as the `assign` qualifier.

`weak`
: The same as the `assign` qualifier with one big difference. In the case of objects, when the object that is assigned to a property of this type is released from memory, the runtime will automatically set the value of this property to `nil`.

We now have a `Person` class with two properties: `firstName` and `lastName`. Let's go back to our app delegate's implementation (*AppDelegate.m*) file and instantiate an object of type `Person`:

```
#import "AppDelegate.h"
#import "Person.h"
```

```
@implementation AppDelegate

- (BOOL)            application:(UIApplication *)application
  didFinishLaunchingWithOptions:(NSDictionary *)launchOptions{

    Person *person = [[Person alloc] init];

    person.firstName = @"Steve";
    person.lastName = @"Jobs";

    self.window = [[UIWindow alloc]
                   initWithFrame:[[UIScreen mainScreen] bounds]];
    self.window.backgroundColor = [UIColor whiteColor];
    [self.window makeKeyAndVisible];
    return YES;
}
```

We are allocating and initializing our instance of the Person class in this example. You may not know what that means yet, but continue to the "Adding Functionality to Classes with Methods" on page 8 section and you will find out.

## Adding Functionality to Classes with Methods

Methods are building blocks of classes. For instance, a class named Person can have logical functionalities such as walk, breathe, eat, and drink. These functionalities are usually encapsulated in methods.

A method can take parameters, which are variables that the caller passes when calling the method and are visible only to the method. For instance, in a simple world, we would have a walk method for our Person class. However, if you want, you can add a parameter or argument to the method and name it `walkingSpeed` of type `CGFloat`, so that when another programmer calls that method on your class, she can specify the speed at which the person has to walk. You, as the programmer of that class, would then write the appropriate code for your class to handle different speeds of walking. Don't worry if this all sounds like too much, but have a look at the following example, where I have added a method to the implementation file we created in "Creating and Taking Advantage of Classes" on page 5 for our Person class:

```
#import "Person.h"

@implementation Person

- (void) walkAtKilometersPerHour:(CGFloat)paramSpeedKilometersPerHour{
    /* Write the code for this method here */
}

- (void) runAt10KilometersPerHour{
    /* Call the walk method in our own class and pass the value of 10 */
```

```
        [self walkAtKilometersPerHour:10.0f];
    }

    @end
```

A typical method has the following qualities in Objective-C:

1. A prefix to tell the compiler whether the method is an instance method (-) or a class method (+). An *instance method* can be accessed only after the programmer allocates and initializes an instance of your class. A *class method* can be accessed by calling it directly from the class itself. Don't worry if this all sounds complicated. We will see examples of these methods in this book, so don't get hung up on this for now.
2. A data type for the method, if the method returns any value. In our example, we have specified `void`, telling the compiler that we are not returning anything.
3. The first part of the method name followed by the first parameter. You don't necessarily have to have any parameters for a method. You can have methods that take no parameters.
4. The list of subsequent parameters following the first parameter.

Let me show you an example of a method with two parameters:

```
- (void) singSong:(NSData *)paramSongData loudly:(BOOL)paramLoudly{
    /* The parameters that we can access here in this method are:

     paramSongData (to access the song's data)
     paramLoudly will tell us if we have to sing the song loudly or not
     */
}
```

It's important to bear in mind that every parameter in every method has an *external* and an *internal* name. The external name is part of the method, whereas the internal part is the actual name or alias of the parameter that can be used inside the method's implementation. In the previous example, the external name of the first parameter is *singSong*, whereas its internal name is *paramSongData*. The external name of the second parameter is *loudly*, but its internal name is *paramLoudly*. The method's name and the external names of its parameters combine to form what is known as the *selector* for the method. The selector for the aforementioned method in this case would be `singSong:loudly:`. A selector, as you will later see in this book, is the runtime identifier of every method. No two methods inside a single class can have the same selector.

In our example, we have defined three methods for our `Person` class, inside its implementation file (*Person.m*):

- `walkAtKilometersPerHour:`
- `runAt10KilometersPerHour`

- `singSong:loudly:`

If we want to be able to use any of these methods from the outside world—for instance, from the app delegate—we should expose those methods in our interface file (*Person.h*):

```
#import <Foundation/Foundation.h>

@interface Person : NSObject

@property (nonatomic, copy) NSString *firstName;
@property (nonatomic, copy) NSString *lastName;

- (void) walkAtKilometersPerHour:(CGFloat)paramSpeedKilometersPerHour;
- (void) runAt10KilometersPerHour;

/* Do not expose the singSong:loudly: method to the outside world.
 That method is internal to our class. So why should we expose it? */

@end
```

Given this interface file, a programmer can call the `walkAtKilometersPerHour:` and the `runAt10KilometersPerHour` methods from outside the `Person` class, but not the `singSong:loudly:` method because it has not been exposed in the file. So let's go ahead and try to call all three of these methods from our app delegate to see what happens!

```
- (BOOL)            application:(UIApplication *)application
  didFinishLaunchingWithOptions:(NSDictionary *)launchOptions{

    Person *person = [[Person alloc] init];

    [person walkAtKilometersPerHour:3.0f];
    [person runAt10KilometersPerHour];

    /* If you uncomment this line of code, the compiler will give
     you an error telling you this method doesn't exist on the Person class */
    //[person singSong:nil loudly:YES];

    self.window = [[UIWindow alloc]
                   initWithFrame:[[UIScreen mainScreen] bounds]];
    self.window.backgroundColor = [UIColor whiteColor];
    [self.window makeKeyAndVisible];
    return YES;
}
```

Now we know how to define and call instance methods, but what about class methods? Let's first find out what class methods are and how they differ from instance methods.

An instance method is a method that relates to an instance of a class. For instance, in our `Person` class, you can instantiate this class twice to create two distinct persons in a hypothetical game that you are working on and have one of those persons walk at the speed of 3 kilometers an hour while the other person walks at 2 kilometers an hour.

Even though you have written the code for the walking instance method only once, when two separate instances of the Person class are created at runtime, the calls to the instance methods will be routed to the appropriate instance of this class.

In contrast, class methods work on the class itself. For instance, in a game where you have instances of a class named Light that light the scenery of your game, you may have a dimAllLights class method on this class that a programmer can call to dim *all* lights in the game, no matter where they are placed. Let's have a look at an example of a class method on our Person class:

```
#import "Person.h"

@implementation Person

+ (CGFloat) maximumHeightInCentimeters{
    return 250.0f;
}

+ (CGFloat) minimumHeightInCentimeters{
    return 40.0f;
}

@end
```

The maximumHeightInCentimeters method is a class method that returns the hypothetical maximum height of *any* person in centimeters. The minimumHeightInCentimeters class method returns the minimum height of *any* person. Here is how we would then expose these methods in the interface of our class:

```
#import <Foundation/Foundation.h>

@interface Person : NSObject

@property (nonatomic, copy) NSString *firstName;
@property (nonatomic, copy) NSString *lastName;
@property (nonatomic, assign) CGFloat currentHeight;

+ (CGFloat) maximumHeightInCentimeters;
+ (CGFloat) minimumHeightInCentimeters;

@end
```

We have also added a new floating point property to our Person class named currentHeight. This allows instances of this class to be able to store their height in memory for later reference, just like their first or last names.

And in our app delegate, we would proceed to use these new methods like so:

```
- (BOOL)            application:(UIApplication *)application
  didFinishLaunchingWithOptions:(NSDictionary *)launchOptions{

    Person *steveJobs = [[Person alloc] init];
    steveJobs.firstName = @"Steve";
    steveJobs.lastName = @"Jobs";
    steveJobs.currentHeight = 175.0f; /* Centimeters */

    if (steveJobs.currentHeight >= [Person minimumHeightInCentimeters] &&
        steveJobs.currentHeight <= [Person maximumHeightInCentimeters]){
        /* The height of this particular person is in the acceptable range */
    } else {
        /* This person's height is not in the acceptable range */
    }

    self.window = [[UIWindow alloc]
                   initWithFrame:[[UIScreen mainScreen] bounds]];
    self.window.backgroundColor = [UIColor whiteColor];
    [self.window makeKeyAndVisible];
    return YES;
}
```

## Conforming to Requirements of Other Classes with Protocols

Objective-C has the concept of a *protocol*. This is a concept found in many other languages (always under a different term, it seems); for instance, it is called an interface in Java. A protocol, as its name implies, is a set of rules that classes can abide by in order to be used in certain ways. A class that follows the rules is said to *conform* to the protocol. Protocols are different from actual classes in that they do not have an implementation. They are just rules. For instance, every car has wheels, doors, and a main body color, among many other things. Let's define these properties in a protocol named Car. Simply follow these steps to create a header file that can contain our Car protocol:

1. In Xcode, while your project is open, from the File menu, select New → File...
2. In the new dialog, on the lefthand side, make sure that you've selected Cocoa Touch under the iOS main category. Once done, on the righthand side of the dialog, choose "Objective-C protocol" and then press the Next button.
3. On the next screen, under the Protocol section, enter **`Car`** as the protocol's name and then press the Next button.
4. You will now be asked to save your protocol on disk. Simply choose a location, usually in your project's folder, and press the Create button.

Xcode will now create a file for you named *Car.h* with content like this:

```
#import <Foundation/Foundation.h>

@protocol Car <NSObject>
```

```
@end
```

So let's go ahead and define the properties for the Car protocol, as we discussed earlier in this section:

```
#import <Foundation/Foundation.h>

@protocol Car <NSObject>

@property (nonatomic, copy) NSArray *wheels;
@property (nonatomic, strong) UIColor *bodyColor;
@property (nonatomic, copy) NSArray *doors;

@end
```

Now that our protocol has been defined, let's create a class for a car, such as `Jaguar`, and then make that class conform to our protocol. Simply follow the steps provided in "Creating and Taking Advantage of Classes" on page 5 to create a class named `Jaguar` and then make it conform to the `Car` protocol like so:

```
#import <Foundation/Foundation.h>
#import "Car.h"

@interface Jaguar : NSObject <Car>

@end
```

If you build your project now, you will notice that the compiler will give you a few warnings such as this:

```
Auto property synthesis will not synthesize property declared in a protocol
```

This is simply telling you that your `Jaguar` class is attempting to conform to the `Car` protocol but is not really implementing the required properties and/or methods in that protocol. So you should now know that a protocol can have required or optional items, and that you denote them by the `@optional` or the `@required` keywords. The default qualifier is `@required`, and since in our `Car` protocol we didn't specify the qualifier explicitly, the compiler has chosen `@required` for us implicitly. Therefore, the `Jaguar` class now *has to* implement everything that is required from it by the `Car` protocol, like so:

```
#import <Foundation/Foundation.h>
#import "Car.h"

@interface Jaguar : NSObject <Car>

@property (nonatomic, copy) NSArray *wheels;
@property (nonatomic, strong) UIColor *bodyColor;
@property (nonatomic, copy) NSArray *doors;

@end
```

Perfect. Now you have an understanding of the basics of protocols and how they work and how you can define them. We will read more about them later in this book, so what you know right now about protocols is quite sufficient.

## Storing Items in and Retrieving Them from Collections

Collections are instances of objects and can hold other objects. One of the primary collections is an array, which instantiates either `NSArray` or `NSMutableArray`. You can store any object in an array, and an array can contain more than one instance of the same object. Here is an example where we create an array of three strings:

```
NSArray *stringsArray = @[
                          @"String 1",
                          @"String 2",
                          @"String 3"
                          ];

__unused NSString *firstString = stringsArray[0];
__unused NSString *secondString = stringsArray[1];
__unused NSString *thirdString = stringsArray[2];
```

The `__unused` macro tells the compiler not to complain when a variable, such as the `firstString` variable in our example, is declared but never used. The default behavior of the compiler is that it throws a warning to the console saying a variable is not used. Our brief example has declared the variables but not used them, so adding the aforementioned macro to the beginning of the variable declaration keeps the compiler and ourselves happy.

A mutable array is an array that can be mutated and changed after it has been created. An immutable array, like we saw, cannot be tampered with after it is created. Here is an example of an immutable array:

```
NSString *string1 = @"String 1";
NSString *string2 = @"String 2";
NSString *string3 = @"String 3";

NSArray *immutableArray = @[string1, string2, string3];

NSMutableArray *mutableArray = [[NSMutableArray alloc]
                                initWithArray:immutableArray];

[mutableArray exchangeObjectAtIndex:0 withObjectAtIndex:1];
[mutableArray removeObjectAtIndex:1];
[mutableArray setObject:string1 atIndexedSubscript:0];
```

```
NSLog(@"Immutable array = %@", immutableArray);
NSLog(@"Mutable Array = %@", mutableArray);
```

The output of this program is as follows:

```
Immutable array = (
    "String 1",
    "String 2",
    "String 3"
)
Mutable Array = (
    "String 1",
    "String 3"
)
```

Another very common collection found throughout iOS programs is a *dictionary*. Dictionaries are like arrays, but every object in a dictionary is assigned to a key so that later you can retrieve the same object using the key. Here is an example:

```
NSDictionary *personInformation =
@{
  @"firstName" : @"Mark",
  @"lastName" : @"Tremonti",
  @"age" : @30,
  @"sex" : @"Male"
  };

NSString *firstName = personInformation[@"firstName"];
NSString *lastName = personInformation[@"lastName"];
NSNumber *age = personInformation[@"age"];
NSString *sex = personInformation[@"sex"];

NSLog(@"Full name = %@ %@", firstName, lastName);
NSLog(@"Age = %@, Sex = %@", age, sex);
```

The output of this program is:

```
Full name = Mark Tremonti
Age = 30, Sex = Male
```

You can also have mutable dictionaries, just as you can have mutable arrays. Mutable dictionaries' contents can be changed after they are instantiated. Here is an example:

```
NSDictionary *personInformation =
@{
  @"firstName" : @"Mark",
  @"lastName" : @"Tremonti",
  @"age" : @30,
  @"sex" : @"Male"
  };

NSMutableDictionary *mutablePersonInformation =
    [[NSMutableDictionary alloc] initWithDictionary:personInformation];
```

```
mutablePersonInformation[@"age"] = @32;

NSLog(@"Information = %@", mutablePersonInformation);
```

The output of this program is:

```
Information = {
    age = 32;
    firstName = Mark;
    lastName = Tremonti;
    sex = Male;
}
```

You can also take advantage of sets. Sets are like arrays but must contain a unique set of objects. You cannot add the same instance of an object twice to the same set. Here is an example:

```
NSSet *shoppingList = [[NSSet alloc] initWithObjects:
                       @"Milk",
                       @"Bananas",
                       @"Bread",
                       @"Milk", nil];

NSLog(@"Shopping list = %@", shoppingList);
```

If you run this program, the output will be:

```
Shopping list = {(
    Milk,
    Bananas,
    Bread
)}
```

Note how *Milk* was mentioned twice in our program but added to the set only once. That's the magic behind sets. You can also use mutable sets like so:

```
NSSet *shoppingList = [[NSSet alloc] initWithObjects:
                       @"Milk",
                       @"Bananas",
                       @"Bread",
                       @"Milk", nil];

NSMutableSet *mutableList = [NSMutableSet setWithSet:shoppingList];

[mutableList addObject:@"Yogurt"];
[mutableList removeObject:@"Bread"];

NSLog(@"Original list = %@", shoppingList);
NSLog(@"Mutable list = %@", mutableList);
```

And the output is:

```
Original list = {(
    Milk,
    Bananas,
```

```
    Bread
)}
Mutable list = {(
    Milk,
    Bananas,
    Yogurt
)}
```

There are two other important classes that you need to know about, now that we are talking about sets and collections:

`NSOrderedSet`
: An immutable set that keeps the order in which objects were added to it

`NSMutableOrderedSet`
: The mutable version of the ordered set

By default, sets do not keep the order in which objects were added to them. Take the following as an example:

```
NSSet *setOfNumbers = [NSSet setWithArray:@[@3, @4, @1, @5, @10]];
NSLog(@"Set of numbers = %@", setOfNumbers);
```

What gets printed to the screen after you run this program is:

```
Set of numbers = {(
    5,
    10,
    3,
    4,
    1
)}
```

But that is not the order in which we created the set. If you want to keep the order intact, simply use the `NSOrderedSet` class instead:

```
NSOrderedSet *setOfNumbers = [NSOrderedSet orderedSetWithArray
                              :@[@3, @4, @1, @5, @10]];

NSLog(@"Ordered set of numbers = %@", setOfNumbers);
```

And, of course, you can use the mutable version of an ordered set:

```
NSMutableOrderedSet *setOfNumbers =
    [NSMutableOrderedSet orderedSetWithArray:@[@3, @4, @1, @5, @10]];

[setOfNumbers removeObject:@5];
[setOfNumbers addObject:@0];
[setOfNumbers exchangeObjectAtIndex:1 withObjectAtIndex:2];

NSLog(@"Set of numbers = %@", setOfNumbers);
```

The results are shown here:

```
Set of numbers = {(
    3,
    1,
    4,
    10,
    0
)}
```

Before we move off the topic of sets, there is one other handy class that you may need to know about. The `NSCountedSet` class can hold a unique instance of an object multiple times. However, the way this is done is different from the way arrays perform the same task. In an array, the same object can appear multiple times. But in a counted set, the object will appear only once, but the set keeps a count of how many times the object was added to the set and will decrement that counter each time you remove an instance of the object. Here is an example:

```
NSCountedSet *setOfNumbers = [NSCountedSet setWithObjects:
                              @10, @20, @10, @10, @30, nil];

[setOfNumbers addObject:@20];
[setOfNumbers removeObject:@10];

NSLog(@"Count for object @10 = %lu",
      (unsigned long)[setOfNumbers countForObject:@10]);

NSLog(@"Count for object @20 = %lu",
      (unsigned long)[setOfNumbers countForObject:@20]);
```

The output is:

```
Count for object @10 = 2
Count for object @20 = 2
```

The `NSCountedSet` class is mutable, despite what its name may lead you to think.

## Adding Object Subscripting Support to Your Classes

Traditionally, when accessing objects in collections such as arrays and dictionaries, programmers had to access a method on the array or the dictionary to get or set that object. For instance, this is the traditional way of creating a mutable dictionary, adding two keys and values to it, and retrieving those values back:

```
NSString *const kFirstNameKey = @"firstName";
NSString *const kLastNameKey = @"lastName";

NSMutableDictionary *dictionary = [[NSMutableDictionary alloc] init];
```

```
[dictionary setValue:@"Tim" forKey:kFirstNameKey];
[dictionary setValue:@"Cook" forKey:kLastNameKey];

__unused NSString *firstName = [dictionary valueForKey:kFirstNameKey];
__unused NSString *lastName = [dictionary valueForKey:kLastNameKey];
```

But with all the advances in the LLVM compiler, this code can now be shortened to this:

```
NSString *const kFirstNameKey = @"firstName";
NSString *const kLastNameKey = @"lastName";

NSDictionary *dictionary = @{
                             kFirstNameKey : @"Tim",
                             kLastNameKey : @"Cook",
                             };

__unused NSString *firstName = dictionary[kFirstNameKey];
__unused NSString *lastName = dictionary[kLastNameKey];
```

You can see that we are initializing the dictionary by providing the keys in curly brackets. The same thing for arrays. Here is how we used to create and use arrays traditionally:

```
NSArray *array = [[NSArray alloc] initWithObjects:@"Tim", @"Cook", nil];
__unused NSString *firstItem = [array objectAtIndex:0];
__unused NSString *secondObject = [array objectAtIndex:1];
```

And now with object subscripting, we can shorten this code, as follows:

```
NSArray *array = @[@"Tim", @"Cook"];
__unused NSString *firstItem = array[0];
__unused NSString *secondObject = array[0];
```

LLVM didn't even stop there. You can add subscripting to your own classes as well. There are two types of subscripting:

*Subscripting by key*
: With this, you can set the value for a specific key inside an object, just like you would in a dictionary. You can also access/read-from values inside the object by providing the key.

*Subscripting by index*
: As with arrays, you can set/get values inside the object by providing an index to that object. This makes sense for array-like classes where the elements lie in a natural order that can be represented by an index.

For the first example, we are going to look at subscripting by key. To do this, we are going to create a class named `Person` with a `firstName` and a `lastName`. Then we are going to allow the programmer to change the first and last names by simply providing the keys to those properties.

The reason you may want to add subscripting by key to a class like this is if your property names are volatile and you want to allow the programmer to set the value of those properties without having to worry about whether the names of those properties will change later; otherwise, the programmer is better off using the properties directly. The other reason for implementing subscripting by key is if you want to hide the exact implementation/declaration of your properties from the programmer and not let her access them directly.

In order to support subscripting by key on your own classes, you must implement the following two methods on your class *and* put the method signatures in your class's header file; otherwise, the compiler won't know that your class supports subscripting by key.

```
#import <Foundation/Foundation.h>

/* We will use these as the keys to our firstName and lastName
 properties so that if our firstName and lastName properties' names
 change in the future in the implementation, we won't break anything
 and our class will still work, as we can simply change the value of
 these constants inside our implementation file */
extern NSString *const kFirstNameKey;
extern NSString *const kLastNameKey;

@interface Person : NSObject

@property (nonatomic, copy) NSString *firstName;
@property (nonatomic, copy) NSString *lastName;

- (id) objectForKeyedSubscript:(id<NSCopying>)paramKey;
- (void) setObject:(id)paramObject forKeyedSubscript:(id<NSCopying>)paramKey;

@end
```

The `objectForKeyedSubscript:` method will be called on your class whenever the programmer provides a key and wants to read the value of that key in your class. The parameter that will be given to you will obviously be the key from which the programmer wants to read the value. To complement this method, the `setObject:forKeyedSubscript:` method will be called on your class whenever the programmer wants to set the value for a specified key. So in our implementation, we want to check whether the given keys are the first name and the last name keys, and if yes, we will set/get the values of the first name and last name in our class:

```
#import "Person.h"

NSString *const kFirstNameKey = @"firstName";
NSString *const kLastNameKey = @"lastName";

@implementation Person

- (id) objectForKeyedSubscript:(id<NSCopying>)paramKey{

    NSObject<NSCopying> *keyAsObject = (NSObject<NSCopying> *)paramKey;
```

```
    if ([keyAsObject isKindOfClass:[NSString class]]){
        NSString *keyAsString = (NSString *)keyAsObject;
        if ([keyAsString isEqualToString:kFirstNameKey] ||
            [keyAsString isEqualToString:kLastNameKey]){
            return [self valueForKey:keyAsString];
        }
    }

    return nil;
}

- (void) setObject:(id)paramObject forKeyedSubscript:(id<NSCopying>)paramKey{
    NSObject<NSCopying> *keyAsObject = (NSObject<NSCopying> *)paramKey;
    if ([keyAsObject isKindOfClass:[NSString class]]){
        NSString *keyAsString = (NSString *)keyAsObject;
        if ([keyAsString isEqualToString:kFirstNameKey] ||
            [keyAsString isEqualToString:kLastNameKey]){
            [self setValue:paramObject forKey:keyAsString];
        }
    }
}

@end
```

So in this code, in the `objectForKeyedSubscript:` method, we are given a key, and we are expected to return the object that is associated in our instance with that key. The key that is given to us is an object that conforms to the `NSCopying` protocol. In other words, it's an object that we can make a copy of, if we want to. We expect the key to be a string so that we can compare it with the predefined keys that we have declared on top of our class, and if it matches, we will set the value of that property in our class. We will then use the `NSObject` method named `valueForKey:` to return the value associated with the given key. But obviously, before we do so, we ensure that the given key is one of the keys that we expect. In the `setObject:forKeyedSubscript:` method we do the exact opposite. We set the values for a given key instead of returning them.

Now, elsewhere in your app, you can instantiate an object of type `Person` and use the predefined keys of `kFirstNameKey` and `kLastNameKey` to change the value of the `firstName` and `lastName` properties like so:

```
Person *person = [Person new];
person[kFirstNameKey] = @"Tim";
person[kLastNameKey] = @"Cook";
__unused NSString *firstName = person[kFirstNameKey];
__unused NSString *lastName = person[kLastNameKey];
```

This code will achieve exactly the same effect as the more direct approach of setting the properties of a class:

```
Person *person = [Person new];
person.firstName = @"Tim";
person.lastName = @"Cook";
```

```
__unused NSString *firstName = person.firstName;
__unused NSString *lastName = person.lastName;
```

You can also support subscripting by index, the same way arrays do. This is useful, as mentioned before, to allow programmers to access objects that have a natural order inside a class. But there are not many data structures besides arrays where it makes sense to order and number elements, unlike subscripting by key, which applies to a wide range of data structures. So the example I'll use to illustrate subscripting by index is a bit contrived. In our previous example, we had the `Person` class with a first and last name. Now if you want to allow programmers to be able to read the first name by providing the index of 0 and the last name by providing the index of 1, all you have to do is declare the `objectAtIndexedSubscript:` and the `setObject:atIndexedSubscript:` methods in the header file of your class, and then write the implementation. Here is how we declare these methods in our `Person` class's header file:

```
- (id) objectAtIndexedSubscript:(NSUInteger)paramIndex;
- (void) setObject:(id)paramObject atIndexedSubscript:(NSUInteger)paramIndex;
```

The implementation is also quite simple. We take the index and act upon it in a way that makes sense to our class. We decided that the first name has to have the index of 0 and the last name the index of 1. So if we get the index of 0 for setting a value, we set the value of the first name to the incoming object, and so on:

```
- (id) objectAtIndexedSubscript:(NSUInteger)paramIndex{

    switch (paramIndex){
        case 0:{
            return self.firstName;
            break;
        }
        case 1:{
            return self.lastName;
            break;
        }
        default:{
            [NSException raise:@"Invalid index" format:nil];
        }
    }

    return nil;
}

- (void) setObject:(id)paramObject atIndexedSubscript:(NSUInteger)paramIndex{
    switch (paramIndex){
        case 0:{
            self.firstName = paramObject;
            break;
        }
        case 1:{
            self.lastName = paramObject;
```

```
                break;
            }
            default:{
                [NSException raise:@"Invalid index" format:nil];
            }
        }
    }
```

Now we can test out what we've written so far, like so:

```
Person *person = [Person new];
person[kFirstNameKey] = @"Tim";
person[kLastNameKey] = @"Cook";
NSString *firstNameByKey = person[kFirstNameKey];
NSString *lastNameByKey = person[kLastNameKey];

NSString *firstNameByIndex = person[0];
NSString *lastNameByIndex = person[1];

if ([firstNameByKey isEqualToString:firstNameByIndex] &&
    [lastNameByKey isEqualToString:lastNameByIndex]){
    NSLog(@"Success");
} else {
    NSLog(@"Something is not right");
}
```

If you've followed all the steps in this recipe, you should see the value `Success` printed to the console now.

# 1.1. Displaying Alerts with UIAlertView

## Problem

You want to display a message to your users in the form of an alert. This could be used to ask them to confirm an action, to ask for their username and password, or simply to let them enter some simple text that you can use in your app.

## Solution

Utilize the `UIAlertView` class.

## Discussion

If you are an iOS user, you have most certainly already seen an alert view. Figure 1-1 depicts an example.

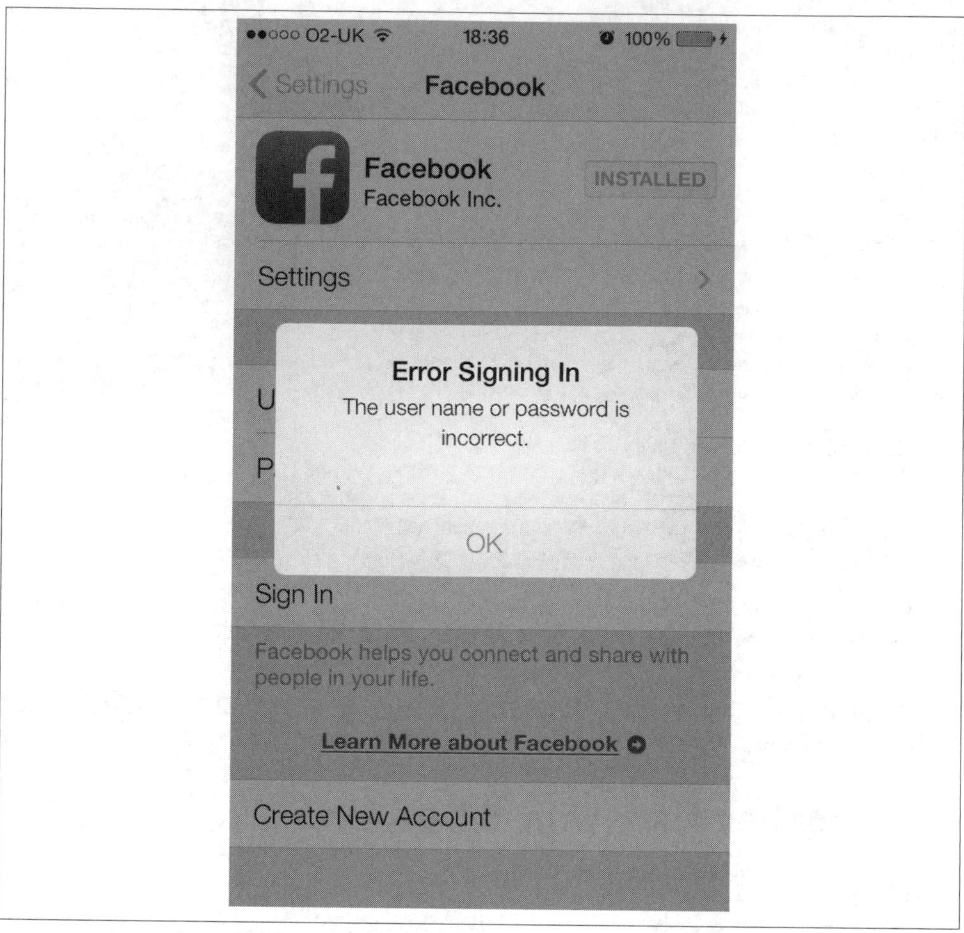


*Figure 1-1. Example of an alert view in iOS*

The best way to initialize an alert view is to use its designated initializer:

```
- (void) viewDidAppear:(BOOL)paramAnimated{

    [super viewDidAppear:paramAnimated];

    UIAlertView *alertView = [[UIAlertView alloc]
                              initWithTitle:@"Alert"
                              message:@"You've been delivered an alert"
                              delegate:nil
                              cancelButtonTitle:@"Cancel"
                              otherButtonTitles:@"Ok", nil];
    [alertView show];

}
```

When this alert view is displayed to the user, she will see something similar to that shown in Figure 1-2.

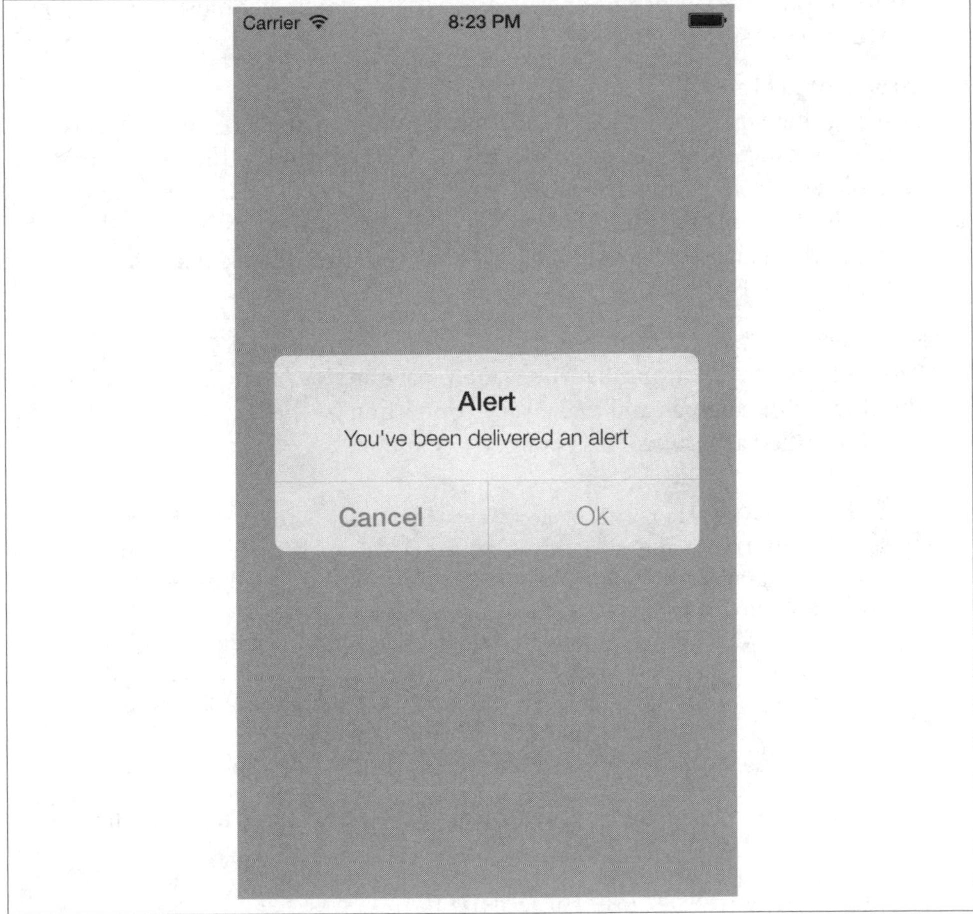


*Figure 1-2. A simple alert view displayed to the user*

In order to display an alert view to the user, we use the alert view's `show` method. Let's have a look at the description for each of the parameters that we passed to the initializer of the alert view:

`title`
: The string that the alert view will display on the top when it is shown to the user. This string is `Title` in Figure 1-2.

`message`
: The actual message that gets displayed to the user. In Figure 1-2, this message is set to `Message`.

`delegate`
: The optional delegate object that we pass to the alert view. This object will get notified whenever the alert's state changes; for instance, when the user taps on a button on the alert view. The object passed to this parameter must conform to the `UIAlertViewDelegate` protocol.

`cancelButtonTitle`
: A string that will get assigned to the cancel button on an alert view. An alert view that has a cancel button usually asks the user for an action. If the user isn't comfortable with performing that action, he will press the cancel button. This button's title does *not* necessarily have to say *`Cancel`*. It is up to you to specify a title for this button. This parameter is optional; you could put up a dialog box with no cancel button.

`otherButtonTitles`
: Titles of any other buttons that you want to have appear on the alert view. Separate the titles with commas and make sure you terminate the list of titles with a `nil`, which is called a *sentinel*. This parameter is optional.

It is possible to create an alert view without any buttons. But the view cannot be dismissed by the user. If you create such a view, you, as the programmer, need to make sure this alert view will get dismissed automatically; for instance, three seconds after it is displayed. An alert view without any buttons that does not dismiss itself automatically gives a really poor user experience. Not only will your app get low ratings on the App Store for blocking the UI from user access, but chances are that your app will get rejected by Apple.

Alert views can take various styles. The `UIAlertView` class has a property called `alertViewStyle` of type `UIAlertViewStyle`:

```
typedef NS_ENUM(NSInteger, UIAlertViewStyle) {
    UIAlertViewStyleDefault = 0,
    UIAlertViewStyleSecureTextInput,
    UIAlertViewStylePlainTextInput,
    UIAlertViewStyleLoginAndPasswordInput
};
```

Here is what each of these styles will do:

`UIAlertViewStyleDefault`
: This is the default style of an alert view, as we saw in Figure 1-2.

`UIAlertViewStyleSecureTextInput`
: With this style, the alert view will contain a secure text field, which hides the actual characters typed by the user. For instance, if you are asking the user for her online banking credentials, you might choose this style of alert view.

`UIAlertViewStylePlainTextInput`
: Under this style, the alert view will display a nonsecure text field to the user. This style is great if you simply want to ask the user for a plain-text entry, such as her phone number.

`UIAlertViewStyleLoginAndPasswordInput`
: With this style, the alert view will display two text fields: a nonsecure one for a username and a secure one for a password.

If you need to get notified when the user interacts with the alert view, specify a delegate object to your alert view. This delegate must conform to the `UIAlertViewDelegate` protocol. The most important method defined in this protocol is the `alertView:clickedButtonAtIndex:` method, which is called as soon as the user taps on one of the buttons in the alert view. The button index is passed to you through the `clickedButtonAtIndex` parameter.

As an example, let's display an alert view to the user and ask whether she would like to visit a website in Safari after having pressed a link to that website available in our UI. We will display two buttons on our alert view: Yes and No. In our alert view delegate, we will detect which button she tapped on and will take action accordingly.

Let's first implement two very simple methods that return the title of our two buttons:

```
- (NSString *) yesButtonTitle{
  return @"Yes";
}

- (NSString *) noButtonTitle{
  return @"No";
}
```

Now we need to make sure that we are conforming to the `UIAlertViewDelegate` protocol in our view controller:

```
#import "ViewController.h"

@interface ViewController () <UIAlertViewDelegate>

@end

@implementation ViewController

...
```

The next step is to create and display our alert view to the user:

```
- (void)viewDidAppear:(BOOL)animated{
  [super viewDidAppear:animated];

  self.view.backgroundColor = [UIColor whiteColor];
```

```
    NSString *message = @"Are you sure you want to open this link in Safari?";
    UIAlertView *alertView = [[UIAlertView alloc]
                              initWithTitle:@"Open Link"
                              message:message
                              delegate:self
                              cancelButtonTitle:[self noButtonTitle]
                              otherButtonTitles:[self yesButtonTitle], nil];
    [alertView show];

}
```

So now, our alert view will look similar to that shown in Figure 1-3.

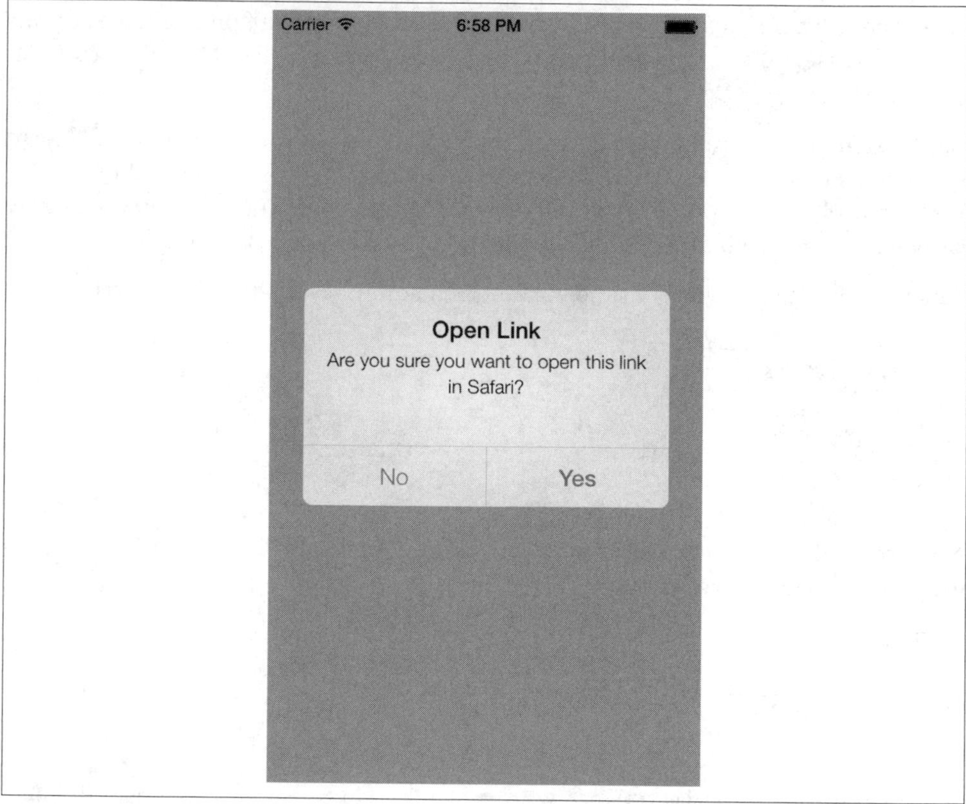


*Figure 1-3. An alert view with Yes and No buttons*

Now we need a way to know whether the user selected the Yes or the No option in our alert view. For this, we will need to implement the `alertView:clickedButtonAtIndex:` method of our alert view delegate:

```
- (void)      alertView:(UIAlertView *)alertView
  clickedButtonAtIndex:(NSInteger)buttonIndex{
```

```
    NSString *buttonTitle = [alertView buttonTitleAtIndex:buttonIndex];

    if ([buttonTitle isEqualToString:[self yesButtonTitle]]){
      NSLog(@"User pressed the Yes button.");
    }
    else if ([buttonTitle isEqualToString:[self noButtonTitle]]){
      NSLog(@"User pressed the No button.");
    }

}
```

Please bear in mind that in big projects where multiple developers work on the same source code, it is usually easier to compare the titles of buttons of alert views to respective strings, rather than picking which button the user selected on an alert view based on the index of that button. For the index solution to work, the programmer has to find out the code that constructed the alert view and, based on the code, find out which button has what index. In our solution, any developer, even without any knowledge as to how the alert view was constructed, can tell which if statement does what.

As you can see, we are using the `buttonTitleAtIndex:` method of `UIAlertView`. We pass the zero-based index of a button inside that alert view to this method and will get back the string that represents the title of that button, if any. Using this method, we can determine which button the user has tapped on. The index of that button will be passed to us as the `buttonIndex` parameter of the `alertView:clickedButtonAtIndex:` method, but if you need the title of that button, you will then need to use the `buttonTitleAtIndex:` method of `UIAlertView`. That is it; job done!

You can also use an alert view for text entry, such as to ask the user for his credit card number or address. For this, as mentioned before, we need to use the `UIAlertViewStylePlainTextInput` alert view style. Here is an example:

```
- (void) viewDidAppear:(BOOL)animated{
    [super viewDidAppear:animated];

    UIAlertView *alertView = [[UIAlertView alloc]
                              initWithTitle:@"Credit Card Number"
                              message:@"Please enter your credit card number:"
                              delegate:self
                              cancelButtonTitle:@"Cancel"
                              otherButtonTitles:@"Ok", nil];
    [alertView setAlertViewStyle:UIAlertViewStylePlainTextInput];

    /* Display a numerical keypad for this text field */
    UITextField *textField = [alertView textFieldAtIndex:0];
    textField.keyboardType = UIKeyboardTypeNumberPad;
```

```
        [alertView show];

    }
```

If you run your app on the simulator now, you will get a result similar to Figure 1-4.

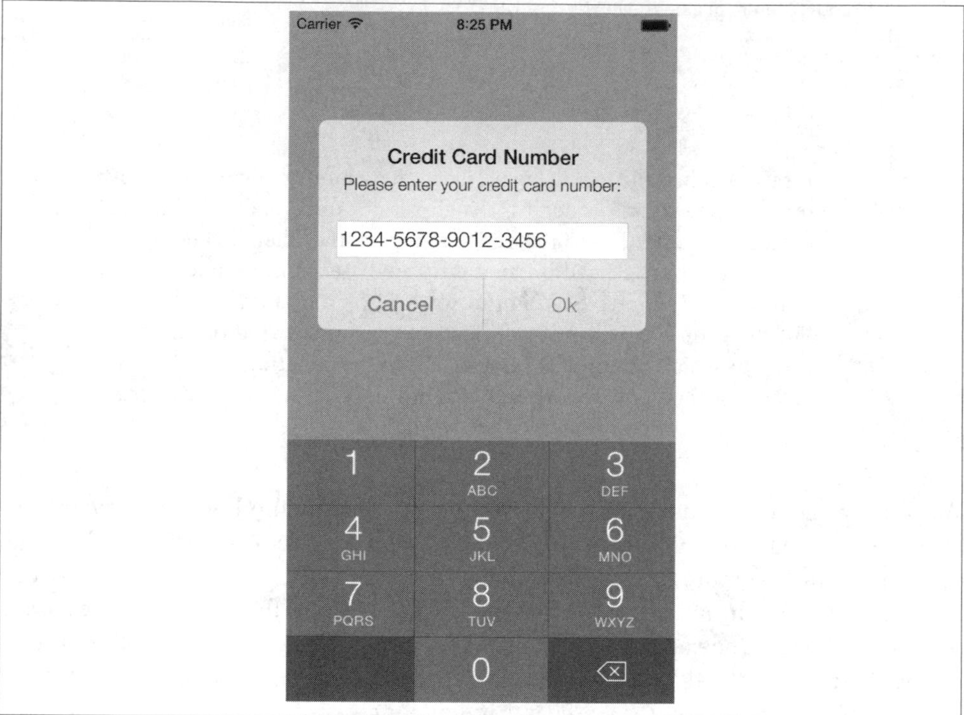


*Figure 1-4. An alert view with plain-text input*

We changed the alert view's style to `UIAlertViewStylePlainTextInput` in this code, but we did something else as well. We retrieved the reference to the first and the only text field that we knew we would have on the alert view and used that text field's reference to change the keyboard type of the text field. For more information about text fields, please refer to Recipe 1.19.

In addition to a plain-text entry, you can ask the user for secure text. You would normally use this if the text that the user is entering is sensitive, such as a password (see Figure 1-5). Here is an example:

```
- (void) viewDidAppear:(BOOL)animated{
    [super viewDidAppear:animated];

    UIAlertView *alertView = [[UIAlertView alloc]
                              initWithTitle:@"Password"
```

```
                                   message:@"Please enter your password:"
                                   delegate:self
                                   cancelButtonTitle:@"Cancel"
                                   otherButtonTitles:@"Ok", nil];

    [alertView setAlertViewStyle:UIAlertViewStyleSecureTextInput];
    [alertView show];

}
```

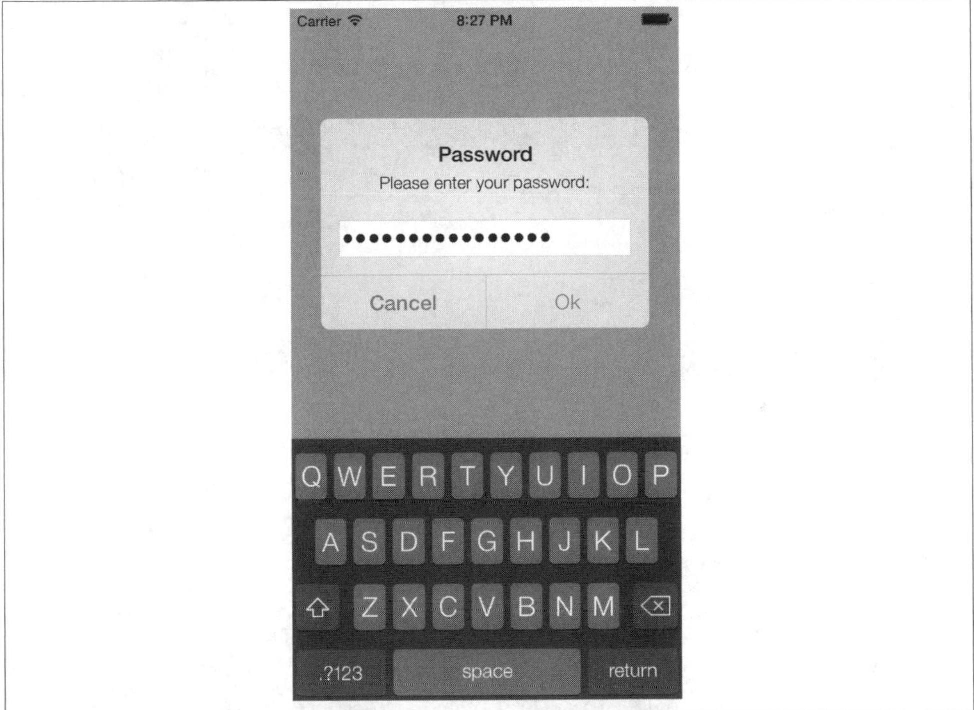


*Figure 1-5. Secure text entry in an alert view*

The `UIAlertViewStyleSecureTextInput` style is very similar to `UIAlertViewStylePlainTextInput`, except that the text field is set to substitute some neutral character for each character of the entered text.

The next style, which is quite useful, displays two text fields, one for a username and the other for a password. The first is a plain-text entry field and the other one is secure:

```
- (void) viewDidAppear:(BOOL)animated{
  [super viewDidAppear:animated];

  UIAlertView *alertView = [[UIAlertView alloc]
                            initWithTitle:@"Password"
```

```
                                        message:@"Please enter your credentials:"
                                        delegate:self
                                        cancelButtonTitle:@"Cancel"
                                        otherButtonTitles:@"Ok", nil];

    [alertView setAlertViewStyle:UIAlertViewStyleLoginAndPasswordInput];
    [alertView show];

}
```

The result will look similar to that shown in Figure 1-6.

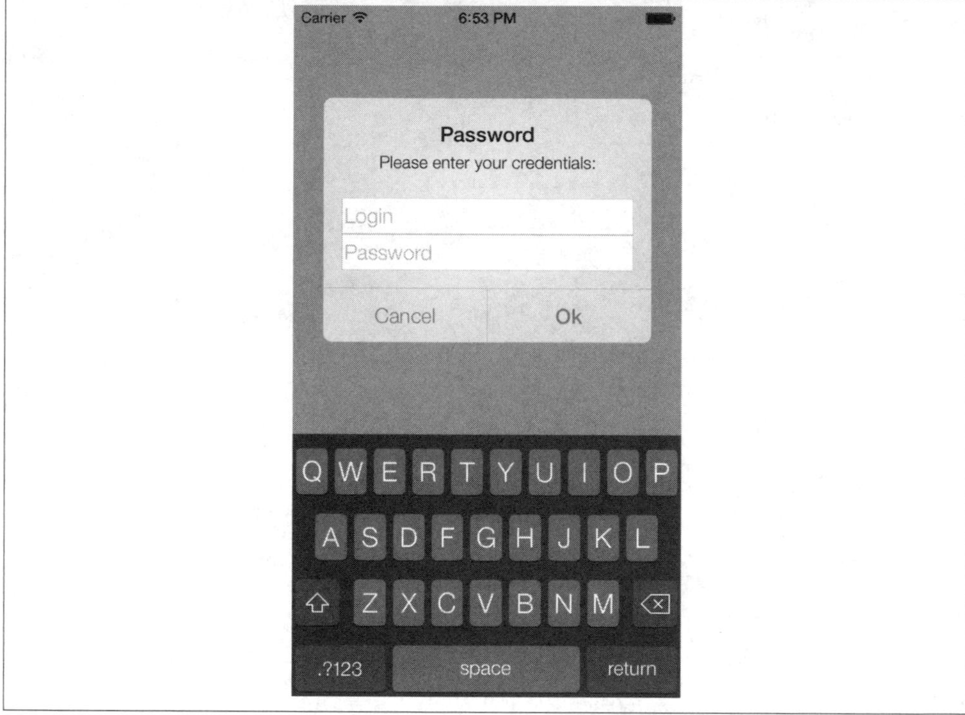


*Figure 1-6. Login and password style of alert view*

## See Also

Recipe 1.19

# 1.2. Creating and Using Switches with UISwitch

## Problem

You would like to give your users the ability to turn an option on or off.

## Solution

Use the `UISwitch` class.

## Discussion

The `UISwitch` class provides an On/Off control like the one shown in Figure 1-7 for Auto-Capitalization, Auto-Correction, and so on.

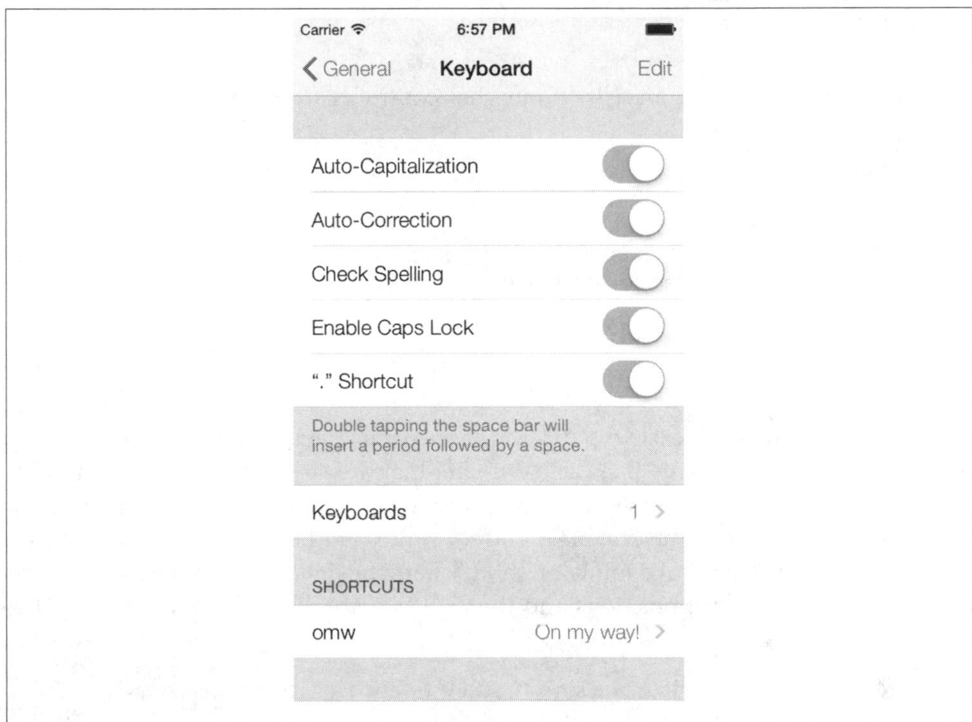


*Figure 1-7. UISwitch used in the Settings app on an iPhone*

In order to create a switch, you can either use Interface Builder or simply create your instance in code. Let's do it through code. So next the challenge is to determine which class to place your code in. It needs to be in a View Controller class, which we haven't discussed yet, but for the single-view application type of app we're creating in this chapter, you can find the view controller's *.m* (implementation) file as *ViewController.m*. Open that file now.

Let's create a property of type `UISwitch` and call it *`mainSwitch`*:

```
#import "ViewController.h"

@interface ViewController ()
```

```
@property (nonatomic, strong) UISwitch *mainSwitch;
@end

@implementation ViewController

...
```

We can go ahead now and create our switch. Find the `viewDidLoad` method in your view controller's implementation file:

```
- (void)viewDidLoad{
  [super viewDidLoad];
}
```

Let's create our switch and place it on our view controller's view:

```
- (void)viewDidLoad{
  [super viewDidLoad];

  /* Create the switch */
  self.mainSwitch = [[UISwitch alloc] initWithFrame:
                     CGRectMake(100, 100, 0, 0)];

  [self.view addSubview:self.mainSwitch];

}
```

So we are allocating an object of type `UISwitch` and using the `initWithFrame:` initializer to initialize our switch. Note that the parameter that we have to pass to this method is of type `CGRect`. A `CGRect` denotes the boundaries of a rectangle using the (*x*,*y*) position of the top-left corner of the rectangle and its width and height. We can construct a `CGRect` using the `CGRectMake` inline method, where the first two parameters passed to this method are the (*x*,*y*) positions and the next two are the width and height of the rectangle.

After we've created the switch, we simply add it to our view controller's view.

Now let's run our app on iOS Simulator. Figure 1-8 shows what happens.

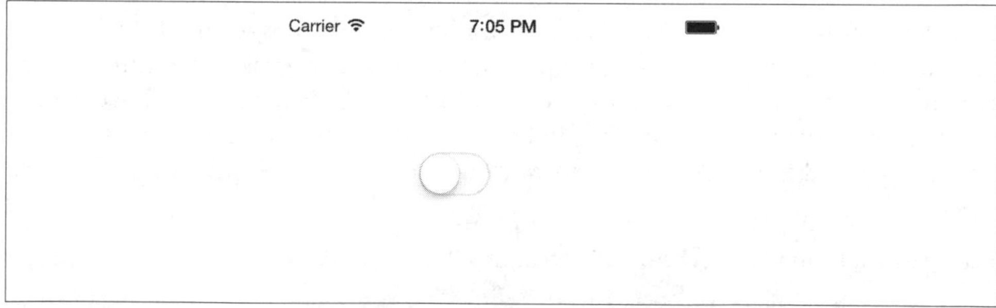


*Figure 1-8. A switch placed on a view*

As you can see, the switch's default state is off. We can change this by changing the value of the on property of the instance of UISwitch. Alternatively, you can call the setOn: method on the switch, as shown here:

```
[self.mainSwitch setOn:YES];
```

You can prettify the user interaction by using the setOn:animated: method of the switch. The animated parameter accepts a Boolean value. If this Boolean value is set to YES, the change in the switch's state (from on to off or off to on) will be animated, just as if the user were interacting with it.

Obviously, you can read from the on property of the switch to find out whether the switch is on or off at the moment. Alternatively, you can use the isOn method of the switch, as shown here:

```
if ([self.mainSwitch isOn]){
  NSLog(@"The switch is on.");
} else {
  NSLog(@"The switch is off.");
}
```

If you want to get notified *when* the switch gets turned on or off, you will need to add your class as the *target* for the switch, using the addTarget:action:forControlEvents: method of UISwitch, as shown here:

```
[self.mainSwitch addTarget:self
                    action:@selector(switchIsChanged:)
          forControlEvents:UIControlEventValueChanged];
```

Then implement the switchIsChanged: method. When the runtime calls this method for the UIControlEventValueChanged event of the switch, it will pass the switch as the parameter to this method, so you can find out which switch has fired this event:

```
- (void) switchIsChanged:(UISwitch *)paramSender{

  NSLog(@"Sender is = %@", paramSender);

  if ([paramSender isOn]){
    NSLog(@"The switch is turned on.");
  } else {
    NSLog(@"The switch is turned off.");
  }

}
```

Now go ahead and run the app on iOS Simulator. You will see messages similar to this in the console window:

```
Sender is = <UISwitch: 0x6e13500;
             frame = (100 100; 79 27);
             layer = <CALayer: 0x6e13700>>
The switch is turned off.
```

```
Sender is = <UISwitch: 0x6e13500;
            frame = (100 100; 79 27);
            layer = <CALayer: 0x6e13700>>
The switch is turned on.
```

## 1.3. Customizing the UISwitch

### Problem

You have placed `UISwitch` instances on your UI and would now like to customize them to match your UI.

### Solution

Use one of the tint/image customization properties of the `UISwitch`, such as the `tintColor` or the `onTintColor`.

### Discussion

Apple has done a fantastic job of bringing customization to UI components such as the `UISwitch`. In previous SDKs, developers were going as far as subclassing `UISwitch` just to change its appearance and color. Now the iOS SDK makes this much simpler.

There are two main ways of customizing a switch:

*Tint Colors*
: Tint colors are colors that you can apply to a UI component such as a `UISwitch`. The tint color will be applied on top of the current color of the component. For instance, in a normal `UISwitch`, you will be able to see different colors. When you apply the tint color on top, the normal color of the control will be mixed with the tint color, giving a *flavor* of the tint color on the UI control.

*Images*
: A switch has two images:

  *On Image*
  : The image that represents the *on* state of the switch. The width of this image is 77 points, and its height is 22.

  *Off Image*
  : The image that represents the switch in its *off* state. This image, like the *on* state of the switch, is 77 points in width and 22 points in height.

Figure 1-9 shows an example of the on and off images of a switch.

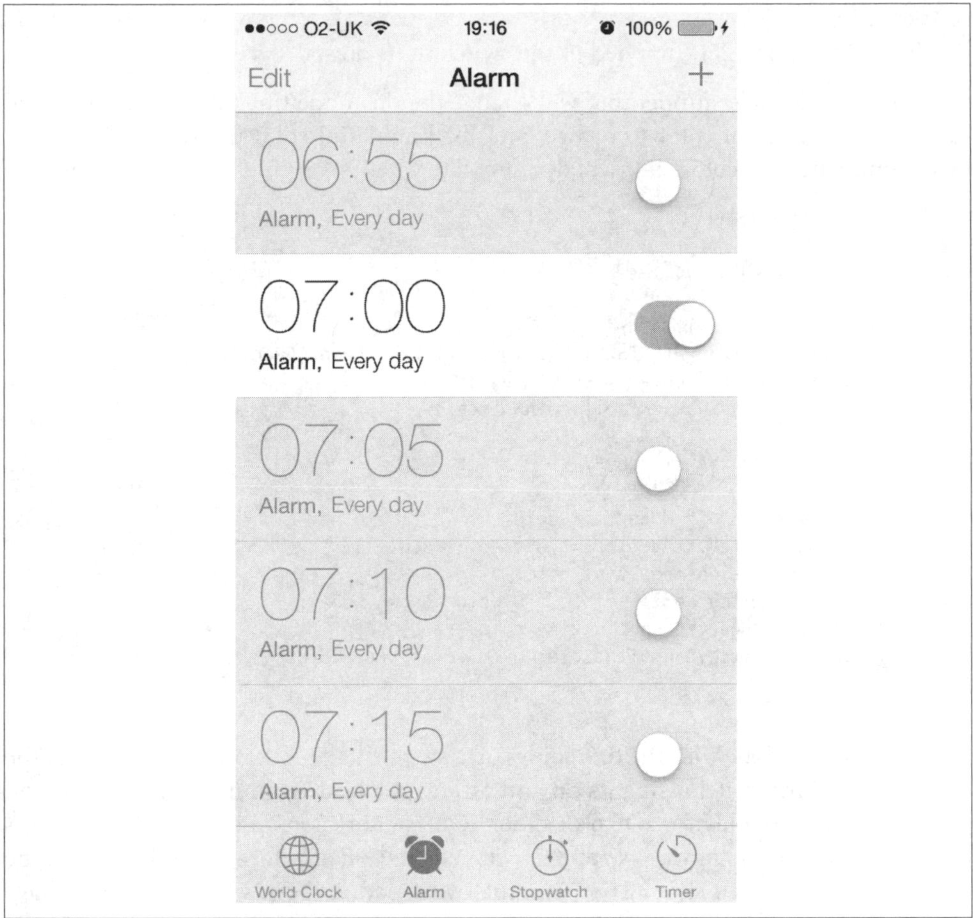


*Figure 1-9. The on and off images on a UISwitch*

Now that we know the two states (on and off) of a switch, let's get started by learning how we can change the tint color of the switch UI component. This can be achieved by the use of three important properties of the `UISwitch` class. Each this property is of type `UIColor`.

`tintColor`
: This is the tint color that will be applied to the off state of the switch. Unfortunately, Apple has not taken the time to name this property `offTintColor` instead of `tintColor` to make it more explicit.

`thumbTintColor`
: This is the tint color that will be applied to the little knob on the switch.

`onTintColor`
: This tint color will be applied to the switch in its on state.

Here is a simple code snippet that will change the on-mode tint color of the switch to red, the off-mode tint color to brown, and the knob's tint color to green. It is not the best combination of colors but will demonstrate what this recipe is trying to explain:

```
- (void)viewDidLoad
{
    [super viewDidLoad];

    /* Create the switch */
    self.mainSwitch = [[UISwitch alloc] initWithFrame:CGRectZero];
    self.mainSwitch.center = self.view.center;
    [self.view addSubview:self.mainSwitch];

    /* Customize the switch */

    /* Adjust the off-mode tint color */
    self.mainSwitch.tintColor = [UIColor redColor];
    /* Adjust the on-mode tint color */
    self.mainSwitch.onTintColor = [UIColor brownColor];
    /* Also change the knob's tint color */
    self.mainSwitch.thumbTintColor = [UIColor greenColor];

}
```

Now that we are done with the tint colors on a switch, let's move on to customizing the appearance of the switch using its on and off images, bearing in mind that custom on and off images are only for iOS 6 or older. iOS 7 ignores on and off images and uses only tint colors to customize its appearance. As mentioned before, both the on and the off images in a switch should be 77 points wide and 22 points tall. For this, I have prepared a new set of on and off images (in both normal and Retina resolutions). I have added them to my Xcode project under the (Retina) names of *On@2x.png* and *Off@2x.png* and I've also placed the non-Retina flavor of the same images in the project. Now we have to construct our switch but assign our custom on and off images to the switch, using the following properties on `UISwitch`:

`onImage`
: As explained before, this will be the image that is displayed when the switch is in its on mode.

`offImage`
: The image that represents the switch when it is in off mode.

And here is our code snippet to achieve this new look:

```
- (void)viewDidLoad
{
    [super viewDidLoad];

    /* Create the switch */
    self.mainSwitch = [[UISwitch alloc] initWithFrame:CGRectZero];
    self.mainSwitch.center = self.view.center;
    /* Make sure the switch won't appear blurry on iOS Simulator */
    self.mainSwitch.frame = [self roundedValuesInRect:self.mainSwitch.frame];
    [self.view addSubview:self.mainSwitch];

    /* Customize the switch */
    self.mainSwitch.onImage = [UIImage imageNamed:@"On"];
    self.mainSwitch.offImage = [UIImage imageNamed:@"Off"];

}
```

## See Also

Recipe 1.2

# 1.4. Picking Values with the UIPickerView

## Problem

You want to allow the users of your app to select from a list of values.

## Solution

Use the `UIPickerView` class.

## Discussion

A picker view is a graphical element that allows you to display a series of values to your users and allow them to pick one. The Timer section of the Clock app on the iPhone is a great example of this (Figure 1-10).

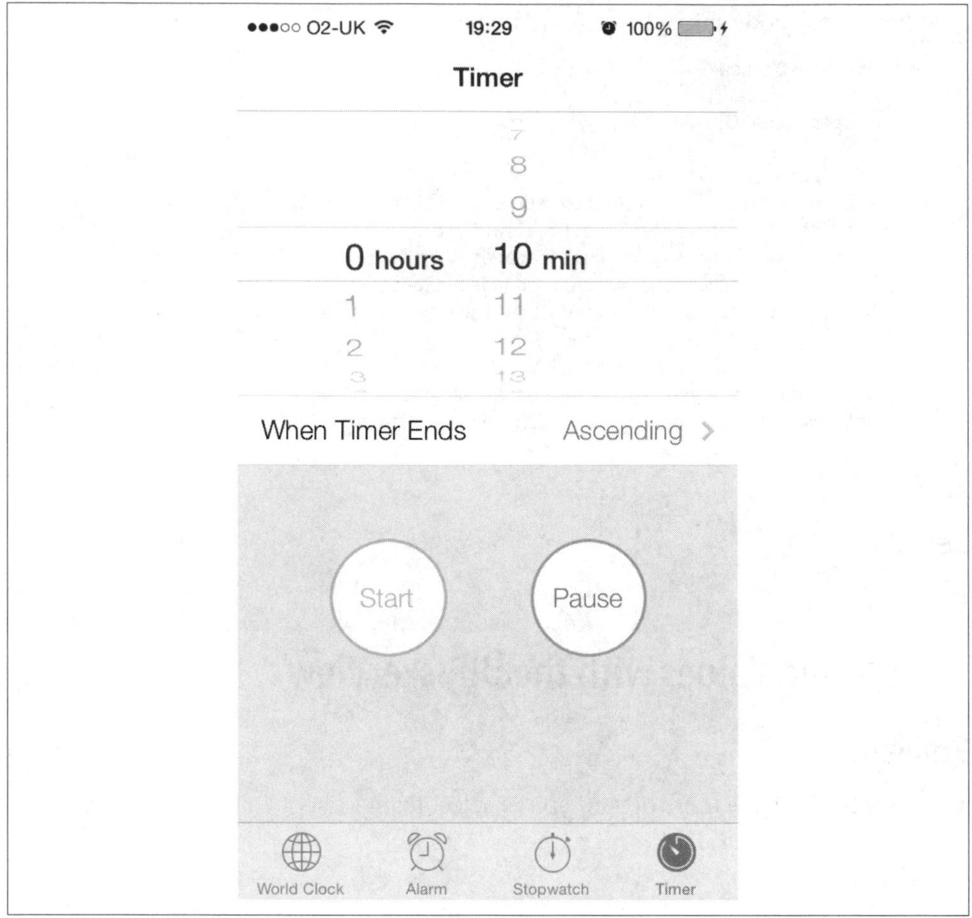


*Figure 1-10. A picker view on top of the screen*

As you can see, this specific picker view has two separate and independent visual elements. One is on the left, and one is on the right. The element on the left is displaying hours (such as 0, 1, 2 hours, etc.) and the one on the right is displaying minutes (such as 10, 11, 12 mins, etc.). These two items are called *components*. Each component has rows. Any item in any of the components is in fact represented by a row, as we will soon see. For instance, in the left component, "0 hours" is a row, "1" is a row, etc.

Let's go ahead and create a picker view on our view controller's view. If you don't know where your view controller's source code is, please have a look at Recipe 1.2, where this subject is discussed.

First let's go to the top of the *.m* (implementation) file of our view controller and define our picker view:

```
@interface ViewController ()
@property (nonatomic, strong) UIPickerView *myPicker;
@end

@implementation ViewController

...
```

Now let's create the picker view in the `viewDidLoad` method of our view controller:

```
- (void)viewDidLoad{
  [super viewDidLoad];

  self.myPicker = [[UIPickerView alloc] init];
  self.myPicker.center = self.view.center;
  [self.view addSubview:self.myPicker];

}
```

It's worth noting that in this example, we are centering our picker view at the center of our view. When you run this app on iOS 7 Simulator, you will see a blank screen because the picker on iOS 7 is white and so is the view controller's background.

The reason this picker view is showing up as a plain white color is that we have not yet populated it with any values. Let's do that. We do that by specifying a data source for the picker view and then making sure that our view controller sticks to the protocol that the data source requires. The data source of an instance of `UIPickerView` must conform to the `UIPickerViewDataSource` protocol, so let's go ahead and make our view controller conform to this protocol in the *.m* file:

```
@interface ViewController () <UIPickerViewDataSource, UIPickerViewDelegate>
@property (nonatomic, strong) UIPickerView *myPicker;
@end

@implementation ViewController

...
```

Good. Let's now change our code in the implementation file to make sure we select the current view controller as the data source of the picker view:

```
- (void)viewDidLoad{
  [super viewDidLoad];

  self.myPicker = [[UIPickerView alloc] init];
  self.myPicker.dataSource = self;
  self.myPicker.center = self.view.center;
  [self.view addSubview:self.myPicker];

}
```

After this, if you try to compile your application, you will get warnings from the compiler telling you that you have *not* yet implemented some of the methods that the `UIPickerViewDataSource` protocol wants you to implement. The way to fix this is to press Command+Shift+O, type in `UIPickerViewDataSource`, and press the Enter key on your keyboard. That will send you to the place in your code where this protocol is defined, where you will see something similar to this:

```
@protocol UIPickerViewDataSource<NSObject>
@required

// returns the number of 'columns' to display.
- (NSInteger)numberOfComponentsInPickerView:(UIPickerView *)pickerView;

// returns the # of rows in each component..
- (NSInteger)pickerView:(UIPickerView *)pickerView
numberOfRowsInComponent:(NSInteger)component;
@end
```

Can you see the `@required` keyword there? That is telling us that whichever class wants to become the data source of a picker view *must* implement these methods. Good deal. Let's go implement them in our view controller's implementation file:

```
- (NSInteger)numberOfComponentsInPickerView:(UIPickerView *)pickerView{

    if ([pickerView isEqual:self.myPicker]){
        return 1;
    }

    return 0;

}

- (NSInteger)   pickerView:(UIPickerView *)pickerView
   numberOfRowsInComponent:(NSInteger)component{

    if ([pickerView isEqual:self.myPicker]){
        return 10;
    }

    return 0;
}
```

So what is happening here? Let's have a look at what each one of these data source methods expects:

`numberOfComponentsInPickerView:`
: This method passes you a picker view object as its parameter and expects you to return an integer, telling the runtime how many components you would like that picker view to render.

`pickerView:numberOfRowsInComponent:`
: For each component that gets added to a picker view, you will need to tell the system how many rows you would like to render in that component. This method passes you an instance of picker view, and you will need to return an integer indicating the number of rows to render for that component.

So in this case, we are asking the system to display 1 component with only 10 rows for a picker view that we have created before, called `myPicker`.

Compile and run your application on iPhone Simulator (Figure 1-11). Ewww, what is that?

*Figure 1-11. A picker view, not knowing what to render*

It looks like our picker view knows how many components it should have and how many rows it should render in that component but doesn't know *what text* to display for each row. That is something we need to do now, and we do that by providing a delegate to the picker view. The delegate of an instance of `UIPickerView` has to conform to the `UIPickerViewDelegate` protocol and must implement all the `@required` methods of that protocol.

There is only one method in the `UIPickerViewDelegate` we are interested in: the `pickerView:titleForRow:forComponent:` method. This method will pass you the index of the current section and the index of the current row in that section for a picker view, and it expects you to return an instance of `NSString`. This string will then get rendered for that specific row inside the component. In here, I would simply like to display the first row as Row 1, and then continue to Row 2, Row 3, etc., till the end. Remember, we also have to set the `delegate` property of our picker view:

```
self.myPicker.delegate = self;
```

And now we will handle the delegate method we just learned about:

```
- (NSString *)pickerView:(UIPickerView *)pickerView
             titleForRow:(NSInteger)row
            forComponent:(NSInteger)component{

    if ([pickerView isEqual:self.myPicker]){

        /* Row is zero-based and we want the first row (with index 0)
         to be rendered as Row 1, so we have to +1 every row index */
        return [NSString stringWithFormat:@"Row %ld", (long)row + 1];

    }

    return nil;

}
```

Now let's run our app and see what happens (Figure 1-12).

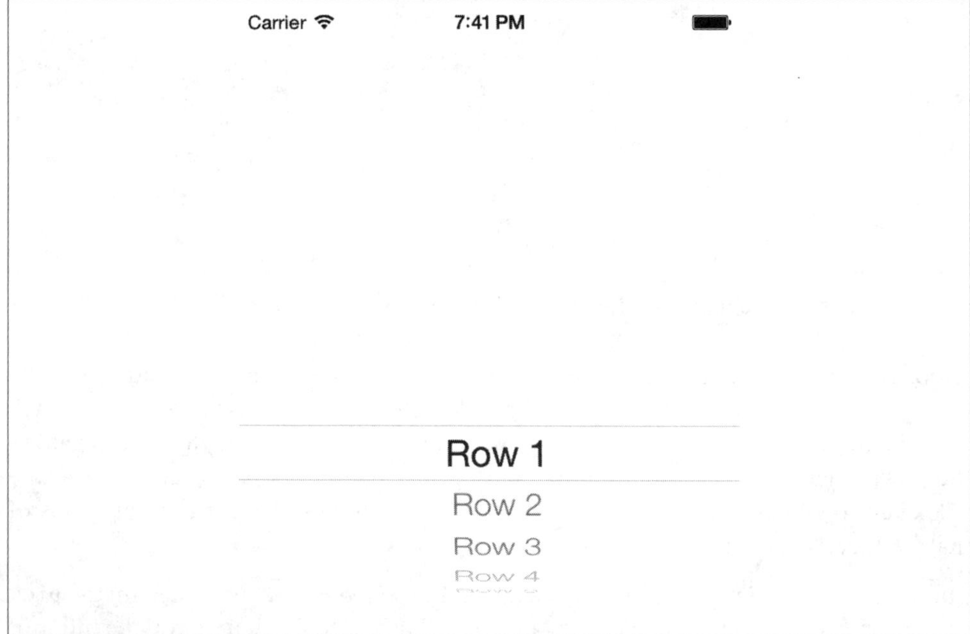


*Figure 1-12. A picker view with one section and a few rows*

Picker views in iOS 6 and older can highlight the current selection using a property called `showsSelectionIndicator`, which by default is set to `NO`. You can either directly set the value of this property to `YES` or use the `setShowsSelectionIndicator:` method of the picker view to turn this indicator on:

```
self.myPicker.showsSelectionIndicator = YES;
```

Now imagine that you have created this picker view in your final application. What is the use of a picker view if we cannot detect what the user has actually selected in each one of its components? Well, it's good that Apple has already thought of that and given us the ability to ask the picker view what is selected. Call the `selectedRowInComponent:` method of a `UIPickerView` and pass the zero-based index of a component. The method will return an integer indicating the zero-based index of the row that is currently selected in that component.

If you need to modify the values in your picker view at runtime, you need to make sure that your picker view reloads its data from its data source and delegate. To do that, you can either force all the components to reload their data, using the `reloadAllComponents` method, or you can ask a specific component to reload its data, using the `reloadComponent:` method and passing the index of the component that has to be reloaded.

### See Also

Recipe 1.2

## 1.5. Picking the Date and Time with UIDatePicker

### Problem

You want to allow the users of your app to select a date and time using an intuitive and ready-made user interface.

### Solution

Use the `UIDatePicker` class.

### Discussion

`UIDatePicker` is very similar to the `UIPickerView` class. The date picker is in fact a prepopulated picker view. A good example of the date picker control is in the Calendar app on the iPhone (Figure 1-13).

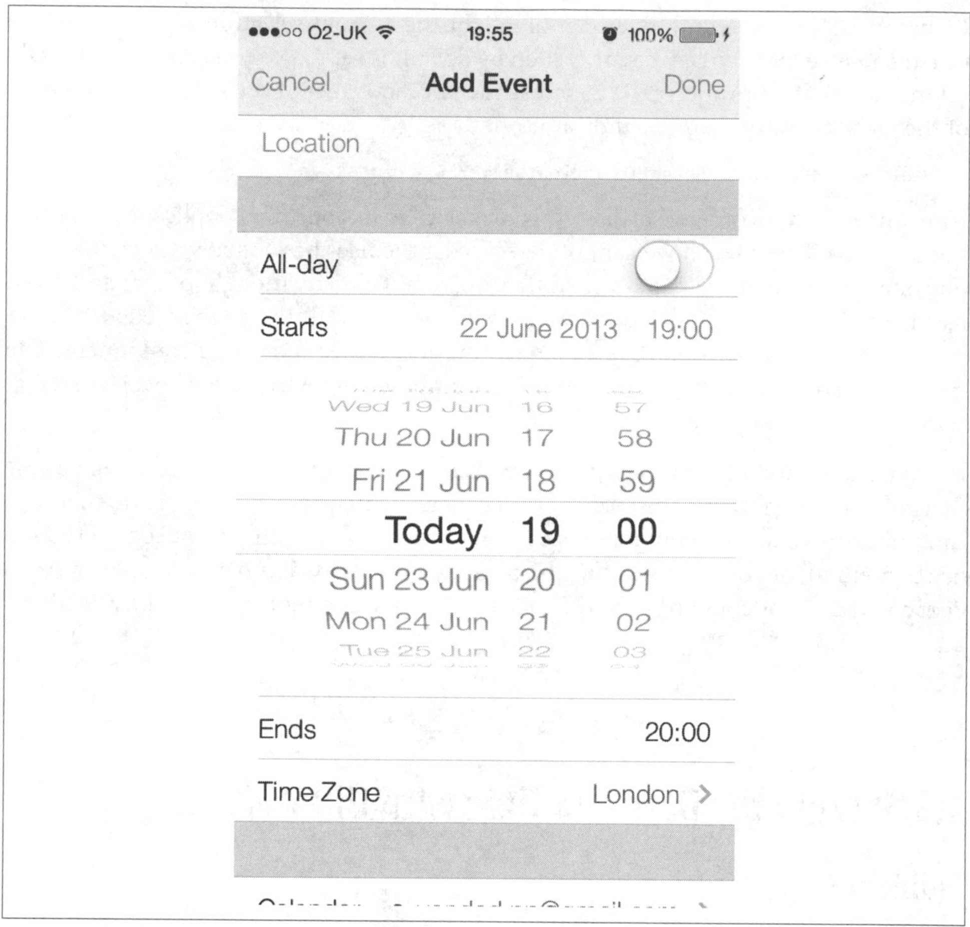


*Figure 1-13. A date picker shown at the center of the screen*

Let's get started by first declaring a property of type `UIDatePicker`. Then we'll allocate and initialize this property and add it to the view of our view controller:

```
#import "ViewController.h"

@interface ViewController ()
@property (nonatomic, strong) UIDatePicker *myDatePicker;
@end

@implementation ViewController

...
```

And now let's instantiate the date picker, as planned:

```
- (void)viewDidLoad{
    [super viewDidLoad];
    self.myDatePicker = [[UIDatePicker alloc] init];
    self.myDatePicker.center = self.view.center;
    [self.view addSubview:self.myDatePicker];
}
```

Now let's run the app and see how it looks in Figure 1-14.

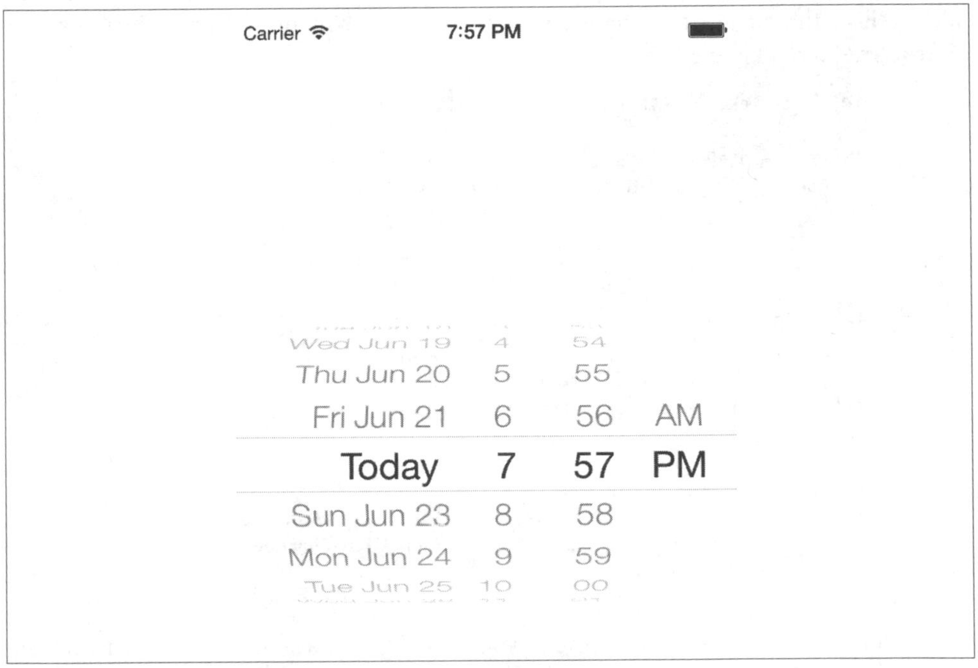

*Figure 1-14. A simple date picker*

You can see that the date picker, by default, has picked today's date. The first thing that we need to know about date pickers is that they can have different styles or modes. This mode can be changed through the `datePickerMode` property, which is of type `UIDatePickerMode`:

```
typedef NS_ENUM(NSInteger, UIDatePickerMode) {
    UIDatePickerModeTime,
    UIDatePickerModeDate,
    UIDatePickerModeDateAndTime,
    UIDatePickerModeCountDownTimer,
};
```

Depending on what you need, you can set the mode of your date picker to any of the values listed in the `UIDatePickerMode` enumeration. I'll show some of these as we go along.

Now that you have successfully displayed a date picker on the screen, you can attempt to retrieve its currently selected date using its `date` property. Alternatively, you can call the `date` method on the date picker, like so:

```
NSDate *currentDate = self.myDatePicker.date;
NSLog(@"Date = %@", currentDate);
```

Just like the `UISwitch` class, a date picker sends action messages to its targets whenever the user has selected a different date. To respond to these messages, the receiver must add itself as the target of the date picker, using the `addTarget:action:forControlEvents:` method, like so:

```
- (void) datePickerDateChanged:(UIDatePicker *)paramDatePicker{

    if ([paramDatePicker isEqual:self.myDatePicker]){
        NSLog(@"Selected date = %@", paramDatePicker.date);
    }

}

- (void)viewDidLoad{
    [super viewDidLoad];
    self.myDatePicker = [[UIDatePicker alloc] init];
    self.myDatePicker.center = self.view.center;
    [self.view addSubview:self.myDatePicker];

    [self.myDatePicker addTarget:self
                          action:@selector(datePickerDateChanged:)
                forControlEvents:UIControlEventValueChanged];

}
```

Now, every time the user changes the date, you will get a message from the date picker.

A date picker also lets you set the minimum and the maximum dates that it can display. For this, let's first switch our date picker mode to `UIDatePickerModeDate` and then, using the `maximumDate` and the `minimumDate` properties, adjust this range:

```
- (void)viewDidLoad{
    [super viewDidLoad];
    self.myDatePicker = [[UIDatePicker alloc] init];
    self.myDatePicker.center = self.view.center;
    self.myDatePicker.datePickerMode = UIDatePickerModeDate;
    [self.view addSubview:self.myDatePicker];


    NSTimeInterval oneYearTime = 365 * 24 * 60 * 60;
    NSDate *todayDate = [NSDate date];

    NSDate *oneYearFromToday = [todayDate
                                dateByAddingTimeInterval:oneYearTime];
```

```
    NSDate *twoYearsFromToday = [todayDate
                                 dateByAddingTimeInterval:2 * oneYearTime];

    self.myDatePicker.minimumDate = oneYearFromToday;
    self.myDatePicker.maximumDate = twoYearsFromToday;
}
```

With these two properties, we can then limit the user's selection on the date to a specific range, as shown in Figure 1-15. In this example code, we have limited the user's input of dates to the range of one year to two years from now.

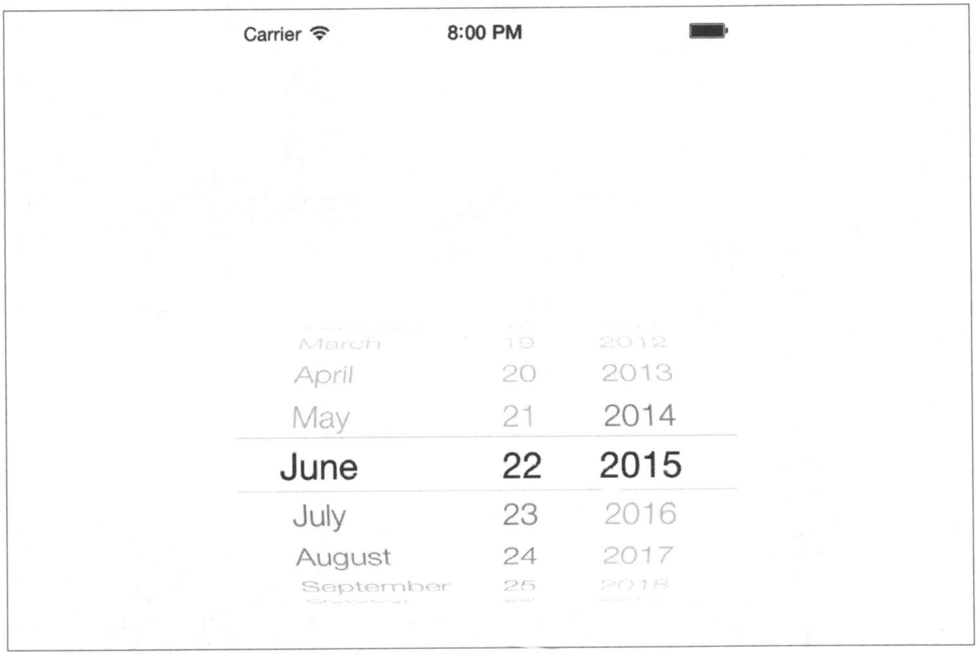

*Figure 1-15. Minimum and maximum dates applied to a date picker*

If you want to use the date picker as a countdown timer, you must set your date picker mode to `UIDatePickerModeCountDownTimer` and use the `countDownDuration` property of the date picker to specify the default countdown duration. For instance, if you want to present a countdown picker to the user and set the default countdown duration to two minutes, write code like this:

```
- (void)viewDidLoad{
    [super viewDidLoad];
    self.myDatePicker = [[UIDatePicker alloc] init];
    self.myDatePicker.center = self.view.center;
    self.myDatePicker.datePickerMode = UIDatePickerModeCountDownTimer;
    [self.view addSubview:self.myDatePicker];
```

```
        NSTimeInterval twoMinutes = 2 * 60;
        [self.myDatePicker setCountDownDuration:twoMinutes];
    }
```

The results are shown in Figure 1-16.

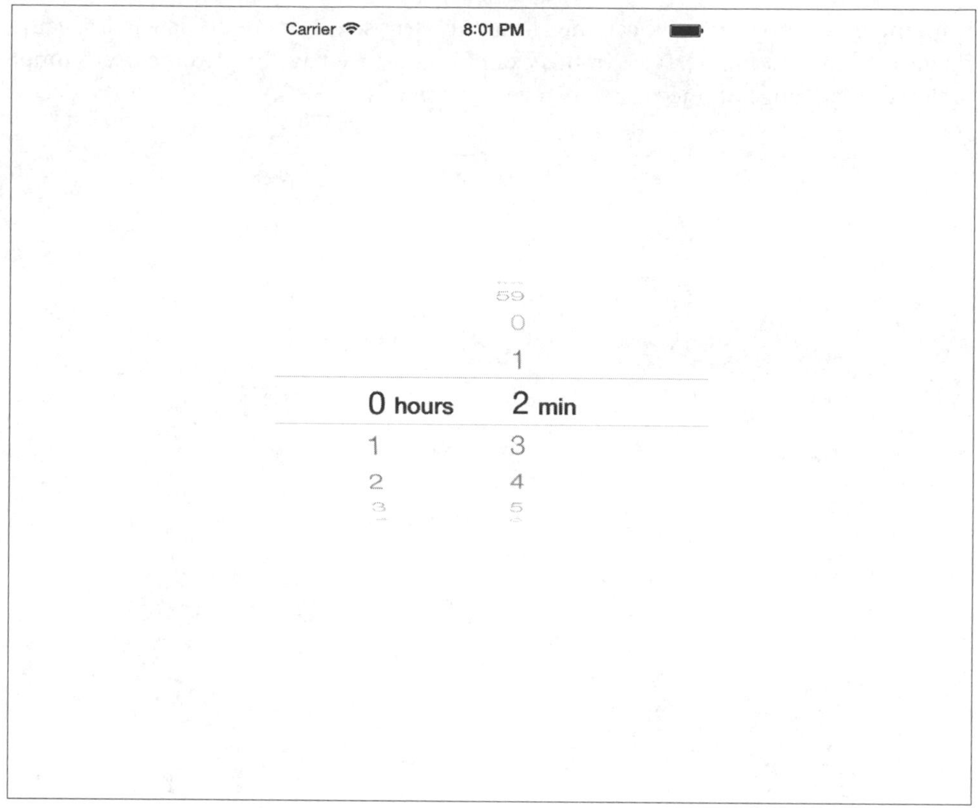


*Figure 1-16. A two-minute countdown duration set on a date picker*

## 1.6. Implementing Range Pickers with UISlider

### Problem

You would like to allow your users to specify a value within a range, using an easy-to-use and intuitive UI.

### Solution

Use the `UISlider` class.

## Discussion

You've certainly seen sliders before. Figure 1-17 shows an example.

*Figure 1-17. The volume slider in Control Center*

To create a slider, instantiate an object of type `UISlider`. Let's dive right in and create a slider and place it on our view controller's view. We'll start with our view controller's implementation file:

```
#import "ViewController.h"

@interface ViewController ()
@property (nonatomic, strong) UISlider *slider;
@end

@implementation ViewController

...
```

And now let's go to the `viewDidLoad` method and create our slider component. In this code, we are going to give our slider a range between 0 and 100 and set its default position to be halfway between start and end.

The range of a slider has *nothing* to do with its appearance. We use the range specifiers of a slider to tell the slider to calculate its value based on the relative position within the range. For instance, if the range of a slider is provided as 0 to 100, when the knob on the slider is on the leftmost part, the `value` property of the slider is 0, and if the knob is to the rightmost side of the slider, the `value` property would be 100.

```
- (void)viewDidLoad{
    [super viewDidLoad];

    self.slider = [[UISlider alloc] initWithFrame:CGRectMake(0.0f,
                                                             0.0f,
                                                             200.0f,
                                                             23.0f)];
    self.slider.center = self.view.center;
    self.slider.minimumValue = 0.0f;
    self.slider.maximumValue = 100.0f;
    self.slider.value = self.slider.maximumValue / 2.0;
    [self.view addSubview:self.slider];
}
```

What do the results look like? You can now run the app on the simulator and you'll get results like those shown in Figure 1-18.

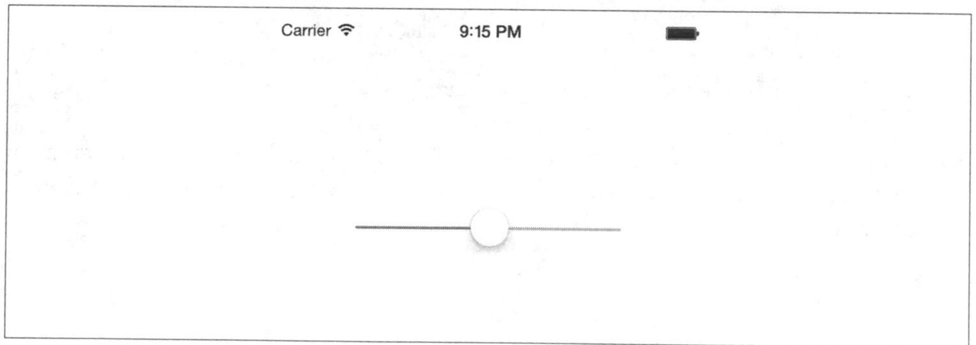


*Figure 1-18. A simple slider at the center of the screen*

We used a few properties of the slider to get the results we wanted. What were they?

`minimumValue`
: Specifies the minimum value of the slider's range.

`maximumValue`
: Specifies the maximum value of the slider's range.

`value`
: The current value of the slider. This is a read/write property, meaning that you can both read from it and write to it. If you want the slider's knob to be moved to this value in an animated mode, you can call the `setValue:animated:` method of the slider and pass `YES` as the `animated` parameter.

The little knob on a slider is called the *thumb*. If you wish to receive an event whenever the slider's thumb has moved, you must add your object as the target of the slider, using the slider's `addTarget:action:forControlEvents:` method:

```
- (void) sliderValueChanged:(UISlider *)paramSender{

    if ([paramSender isEqual:self.slider]){
        NSLog(@"New value = %f", paramSender.value);
    }

}

- (void)viewDidLoad{
    [super viewDidLoad];
    self.slider = [[UISlider alloc] initWithFrame:CGRectMake(0.0f,
                                                             0.0f,
                                                             200.0f,
                                                             23.0f)];
    self.slider.center = self.view.center;
    self.slider.minimumValue = 0.0f;
    self.slider.maximumValue = 100.0f;
    self.slider.value = self.slider.maximumValue / 2.0;
    [self.view addSubview:self.slider];

    [self.slider addTarget:self
                    action:@selector(sliderValueChanged:)
          forControlEvents:UIControlEventValueChanged];
}
```

If you run the application on the simulator now, you will notice that the `sliderValueChanged:` target method gets called *whenever and as soon as* the slider's thumb moves. This might be what you want, but in some cases, you might need to get notified only after the user has let go of the thumb on the slider and let it settle. If you want to wait to be notified, set the `continuous` property of the slider to `NO`. This property, when set to `YES` (its default value), will call the slider's targets continuously *while* the thumb moves.

The iOS SDK also gives you the ability to modify how a slider looks. For instance, the thumb on the slider can have a different image. To change the image of the thumb, simply use the setThumbImage:forState: method and pass an image along with a second parameter that can take any of these values:

UIControlStateNormal
: The normal state of the thumb, with no user finger on this component.

UIControlStateHighlighted
: The image to display for the thumb while the user is moving her finger on this component.

I have prepared two images: one for the normal state of the thumb and the other one for the highlighted (touched) state of the thumb. Let's go ahead and add them to the slider:

```
[self.slider setThumbImage:[UIImage imageNamed:@"ThumbNormal.png"]
                  forState:UIControlStateNormal];
[self.slider setThumbImage:[UIImage imageNamed:@"ThumbHighlighted.png"]
                  forState:UIControlStateHighlighted];
```

And now let's have a look and see how our normal thumb image looks in the simulator (Figure 1-19).

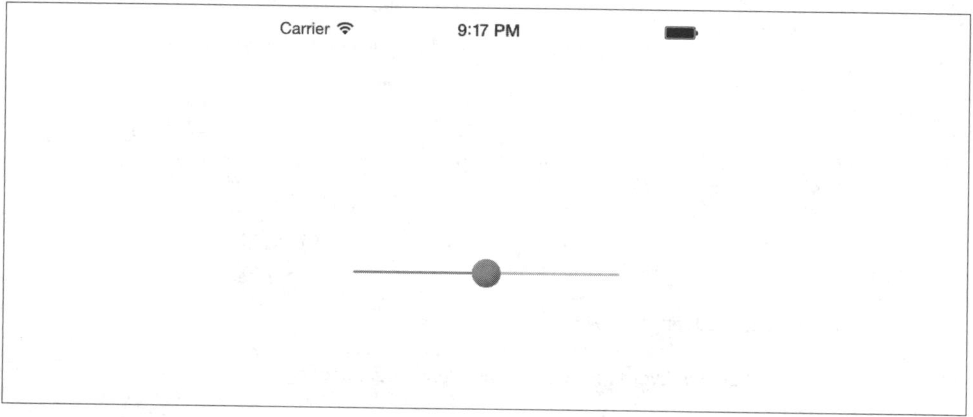


*Figure 1-19. A slider with a custom thumb image*

# 1.7. Customizing the UISlider

## Problem

You are using the default appearance of the UISlider UI component, and now you want to customize this look and feel.

## Solution

Either modify the tint colors of the different parts of the slider or provide your own images for the parts.

## Discussion

Apple has done a great job giving us methods to customize UI components in the iOS SDK. One customization is to modify the tint colors of various parts of the UI component. Let's take a simple `UISlider` as an example. I have broken it down into its different UI components in Figure 1-20.

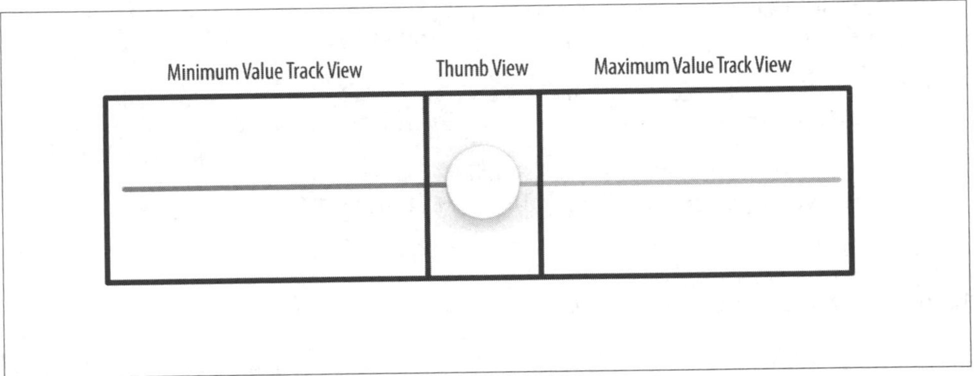


*Figure 1-20. Different components of a UISlider*

For each of these components in `UISlider`, a method and property exist that allow you to change the appearance of the slider. The easiest of these properties to use are the ones that modify the tint color of these components:

`minimumTrackTintColor`
: This property sets the tint color of the minimum value track view.

`thumbTintColor`
: This property, as its name shows, sets the tint color of the thumb view.

`maximumTrackTintColor`
: This property sets the tint color of the maximum value track view.

All these properties are of type `UIColor`.

The following sample code instantiates a `UISlider` and places it at the center of the view of the view controller. It also sets the tint color of the minimum value tracking view of the slider to red, the tint color of the thumb view of the slider to black, and the tint color of the maximum value tracking view of the slider to green:

```
- (void)viewDidLoad{
    [super viewDidLoad];

    /* Create  the slider */
    self.slider = [[UISlider alloc] initWithFrame:CGRectMake(0.0f,
                                                             0.0f,
                                                             118.0f,
                                                             23.0f)];
    self.slider.value = 0.5;
    self.slider.minimumValue = 0.0f;
    self.slider.maximumValue = 1.0f;
    self.slider.center = self.view.center;
    [self.view addSubview:self.slider];

    /* Set the tint color of the minimum value */
    self.slider.minimumTrackTintColor = [UIColor redColor];

    /* Set the tint color of the thumb */
    self.slider.maximumTrackTintColor = [UIColor greenColor];

    /* Set the tint color of the maximum value */
    self.slider.thumbTintColor = [UIColor blackColor];

}
```

If you run the app now, you will see something similar to Figure 1-21.

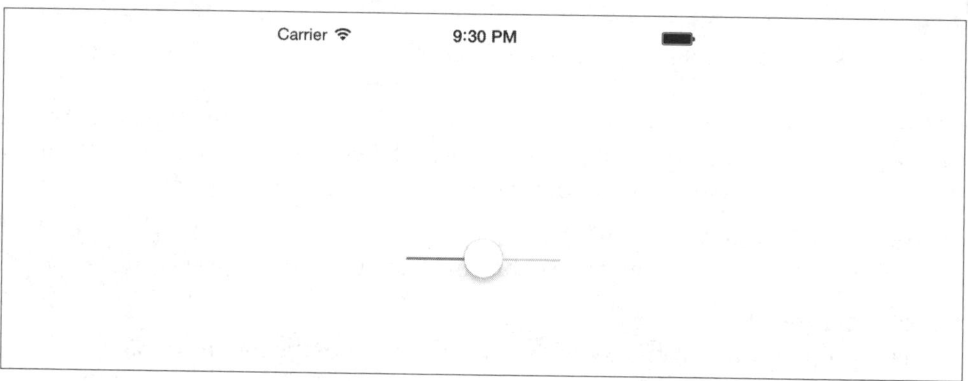


*Figure 1-21. The tint colors of all the different components of a slider are modified*

Sometimes you may want to have more control over how a slider looks on the screen. For this, tint colors may not be sufficient. That's why Apple has provided other ways of modifying the look and feel of a slider, allowing you to provide images for different components in the slider. These images are the following:

*Minimum value image*
: This is the image that will be displayed to the outer-left side of the slider. By default, no image is provided for the minimum value image, so you cannot really see this

if you create a new slider on a view. You can use this image to give your users an indication of what the minimum value in your slider may mean in the context of your app. For instance, in an app where the user is allowed to increase or decrease the brightness of the screen, the minimum value image may display a dim lightbulb, suggesting to users that moving the thumb in the slider to the left (toward the minimum value) will reduce the brightness of the screen further. To change this image, use the `setMinimumValueImage:` instance method of the slider. The image needs to be 23 points wide and 23 points tall. Obviously, for Retina displays, simply provide the same image but twice as big.

*Minimum track image*
: This is the image that will be displayed for the slider's track on the left side of the thumb. To change this image, use the `setMinimumTrackImage:forState:` instance method of the slider. The image needs to be 11 points wide and 9 points tall and be constructed as a resizable image (see Recipe 20.5).

*Thumb image*
: The image for the thumb, the only moving component in the slider. To change this image, use the `setThumbImage:forState:` instance method of the slider. The image needs to be 23 points wide and 23 points tall.

*Maximum track image*
: The image for the track of the slider to the right of the thumb. To change this image, use the `setMaximumTrackImage:forState:` instance method of the slider. The image needs to be 11 points wide and 9 points tall and be constructed as a resizable image (see Recipe 20.5).

*Maximum value image*
: The maximum value image is the image that gets displayed on the outer-right side of the slider. This is similar to the minimum value image but of course depicts the maximum value of the slider instead. To continue the earlier example of a brightness slider, the image for the maximum value can be a bright light with rays emitting from it, suggesting to the user that the farther he moves the slider to the right, the brighter the display gets. To change this image, use the `setMaximumValueImage:` instance method of the slider. The image needs to be 23 points wide and 23 points tall.

The images that you provide for the minimum and the maximum track need to be resizable. For more information about resizable images, see Recipe 20.5.

For the sake of this exercise, I have created five unique images for each one of the components of the slider. I've made sure that the minimum and the maximum track images are resizable images. What I am trying to achieve with the customization of this slider component is to make the user think that she is changing the temperature settings of a room, where moving the slider to the left means less heat and moving to the right means more heat. So here is the code that creates a slider and skins its various components:

```
#import "ViewController.h"

@interface ViewController ()
@property (nonatomic, strong) UISlider *slider;
@end

@implementation ViewController

/*
 This method returns a resizable image for the
 minimum track component of the slider
 */
- (UIImage *) minimumTrackImage{
    UIImage *result = [UIImage imageNamed:@"MinimumTrack"];
    UIEdgeInsets edgeInsets;
    edgeInsets.left = 4.0f;
    edgeInsets.top = 0.0f;
    edgeInsets.right = 0.0f;
    edgeInsets.bottom = 0.0f;
    result = [result resizableImageWithCapInsets:edgeInsets];
    return result;
}

/*
 Similar to the previous method, this one returns the resizable maximum
 track image for the slider
 */
- (UIImage *) maximumTrackImage{
    UIImage *result = [UIImage imageNamed:@"MaximumTrack"];
    UIEdgeInsets edgeInsets;
    edgeInsets.left = 0.0f;
    edgeInsets.top = 0.0f;
    edgeInsets.right = 3.0f;
    edgeInsets.bottom = 0.0f;
    result = [result resizableImageWithCapInsets:edgeInsets];
    return result;
}

- (void)viewDidLoad{
    [super viewDidLoad];

    /* Create  the slider */
    self.slider = [[UISlider alloc] initWithFrame:CGRectMake(0.0f,
                                                             0.0f,
                                                             218.0f,
                                                             23.0f)];
```

```
    self.slider.value = 0.5;
    self.slider.minimumValue = 0.0f;
    self.slider.maximumValue = 1.0f;
    self.slider.center = self.view.center;
    [self.view addSubview:self.slider];

    /* Change the minimum value image */
    [self.slider setMinimumValueImage:[UIImage imageNamed:@"MinimumValue"]];

    /* Change the minimum track image */
    [self.slider setMinimumTrackImage:[self minimumTrackImage]
                             forState:UIControlStateNormal];

    /* Change the thumb image for both untouched and touched states */
    [self.slider setThumbImage:[UIImage imageNamed:@"Thumb"]
                      forState:UIControlStateNormal];
    [self.slider setThumbImage:[UIImage imageNamed:@"Thumb"]
                      forState:UIControlStateHighlighted];

    /* Change the maximum track image */
    [self.slider setMaximumTrackImage:[self maximumTrackImage]
                             forState:UIControlStateNormal];

    /* Change the maximum value image */
    [self.slider setMaximumValueImage:[UIImage imageNamed:@"MaximumValue"]];

}
```

The slider in iOS 7 has a completely new look, as you can guess, very streamlined and slim and thin. The height of the minimum and maximum track images in iOS 7 is only 1 point wide, so setting an image for these components is absolutely useless and won't look very good anyway. Therefore, to skin these components of a `UISlider` in iOS 7, it is recommended that you use the tint colors instead of assigning custom images to it.

## See Also

Recipe 1.6

# 1.8. Grouping Compact Options with UISegmentedControl

## Problem

You would like to present a few options to your users from which they can pick an option, through a UI that is compact, simple, and easy to understand.

## Solution

Use the `UISegmentedControl` class, an example of which is shown in Figure 1-22.

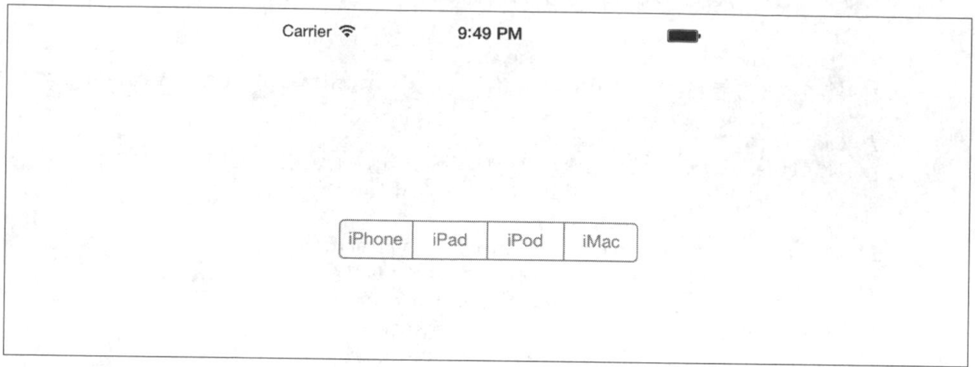


*Figure 1-22. A segmented control displaying four options*

## Discussion

A segmented control is a UI component that allows you to display, in a compact UI, a series of options for the user to choose from. To show a segmented control, create an instance of `UISegmentedControl`. Let's start with our view controller's *.m* file:

```
#import "ViewController.h"

@interface ViewController ()
@property (nonatomic, strong) UISegmentedControl *mySegmentedControl;
@end

@implementation ViewController

...
```

And create the segmented control in the `viewDidLoad` method of your view controller:

```
- (void)viewDidLoad{
    [super viewDidLoad];

    NSArray *segments = [[NSArray alloc] initWithObjects:
                         @"iPhone",
                         @"iPad",
                         @"iPod",
                         @"iMac", nil];

    self.mySegmentedControl = [[UISegmentedControl alloc]
                               initWithItems:segments];
    self.mySegmentedControl.center = self.view.center;
    [self.view addSubview:self.mySegmentedControl];
}
```

We are simply using an array of strings to provide the different options that our segmented control has to display. We initialize our segmented control using the `initWithObjects:` initializer and pass the array of strings and images to the segmented control. The results will look like what we saw in Figure 1-22.

Now the user can pick *one* of the options in the segmented control. Let's say she has picked *iPad*. The segmented control will then change its user interface to show the user what option she has selected, as depicted in Figure 1-23.

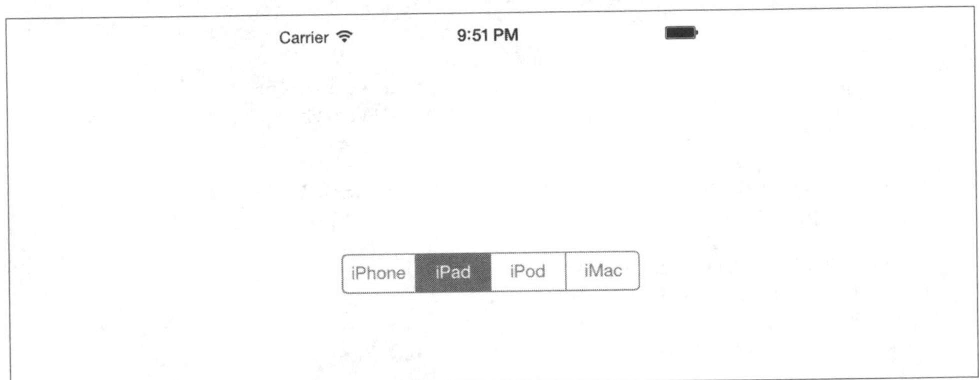


*Figure 1-23. User has selected one of the items in a segmented control*

Now the question is, how do you recognize when the user selects a new option in a segmented control? The answer is simple. Just as with a `UISwitch` or a `UISlider`, use the `addTarget:action:forControlEvents:` method of the segmented control to add a target to it. Provide the value of `UIControlEventValueChanged` for the `forControlEvents` parameter, because that is the event that gets fired when the user selects a new option in a segmented control:

```
- (void) segmentChanged:(UISegmentedControl *)paramSender{

    if ([paramSender isEqual:self.mySegmentedControl]){
        NSInteger selectedSegmentIndex = [paramSender selectedSegmentIndex];

        NSString  *selectedSegmentText =
        [paramSender titleForSegmentAtIndex:selectedSegmentIndex];

        NSLog(@"Segment %ld with %@ text is selected",
              (long)selectedSegmentIndex,
              selectedSegmentText);
    }
}

- (void)viewDidLoad{
    [super viewDidLoad];
```

```
    NSArray *segments = @[
                          @"iPhone",
                          @"iPad",
                          @"iPod",
                          @"iMac"
                          ];

    self.mySegmentedControl = [[UISegmentedControl alloc]
                               initWithItems:segments];
    self.mySegmentedControl.center = self.view.center;
    [self.view addSubview:self.mySegmentedControl];

    [self.mySegmentedControl addTarget:self
                                action:@selector(segmentChanged:)
                      forControlEvents:UIControlEventValueChanged];
}
```

If the user starts from the left side and selects each of the options in Figure 1-22, all the way to the right side of the control, the following text will print out to the console:

```
Segment 0 with iPhone text is selected
Segment 1 with iPad text is selected
Segment 2 with iPod text is selected
Segment 3 with iMac text is selected
```

As you can see, we used the `selectedSegmentIndex` method of the segmented control to find the index of the currently selected item. If no item is selected, this method returns the value –1. We also used the `titleForSegmentAtIndex:` method. Simply pass the index of an option in the segmented control to this method, and the segmented control will return the text for that item. Simple, isn't it?

As you might have noticed, once the user selects an option in a segmented control, that option will get selected and will *remain* selected, as shown in Figure 1-23. If you want the user to be able to select an option but you would like the button for that option to bounce back to its original shape once it has been selected (just like a normal button that bounces back up once it is tapped), you need to set the `momentary` property of the segmented control to `YES`:

```
self.mySegmentedControl.momentary = YES;
```

One of the really neat features of segmented controls is that they can contain images instead of text. To do this, simply use the `initWithObjects:` initializer method of the `UISegmentedControl` class and pass the strings and images that will be used to initialize the segmented UI control:

```
- (void)viewDidLoad{
    [super viewDidLoad];

    NSArray *segments = @[
                          @"iPhone",
                          [UIImage imageNamed:@"iPad"],
```

```
                              @"iPod",
                              @"iMac",
                              ];

    self.mySegmentedControl = [[UISegmentedControl alloc]
                               initWithItems:segments];

    CGRect segmentedFrame = self.mySegmentedControl.frame;
    segmentedFrame.size.height = 128.0f;
    segmentedFrame.size.width = 300.0f;
    self.mySegmentedControl.frame = segmentedFrame;

    self.mySegmentedControl.center = self.view.center;

    [self.view addSubview:self.mySegmentedControl];
}
```

In this example, the *iPad* file is simply an image of an iPad that's been added to our project.

In iOS 7, Apple has deprecated the `segmentedControlStyle` property of the `UISegmentedControl` class, so segmented controls have only a single default style. We can no longer modify this style.

## 1.9. Presenting and Managing Views with UIViewController

### Problem

You want to switch among different views in your application.

### Solution

Use the `UIViewController` class.

### Discussion

Apple's strategy for iOS development was to use the model-view-controller (MVC) division of labor. Views are what get displayed to users, while the model is the data that the app manages, or the engine of the app. The controller is the bridge between the model and the view. The controller, or in this case, the view controller, manages the relationship between the view and the model. Why doesn't the view do that instead? Well, the answer is quite simple: the view's code would get messy, and that design choice would tightly couple our views with the model, which is not a good practice.

View controllers can be loaded from *.xib* files (for use with Interface Builder), or simply be created programmatically. We will first have a look at creating a view controller *without* a *.xib* file.

Xcode helps us create view controllers. Now that you have created an application using the Empty Application template in Xcode, follow these steps to create a new view controller for your app:

1. In Xcode, select the File menu and then choose New → New File...
2. In the New File dialog, make sure iOS is the selected category on the left and that Cocoa Touch is the chosen subcategory. Once you've done that, select the New Objective-C class item on the righthand side and press Next, as shown in Figure 1-24.

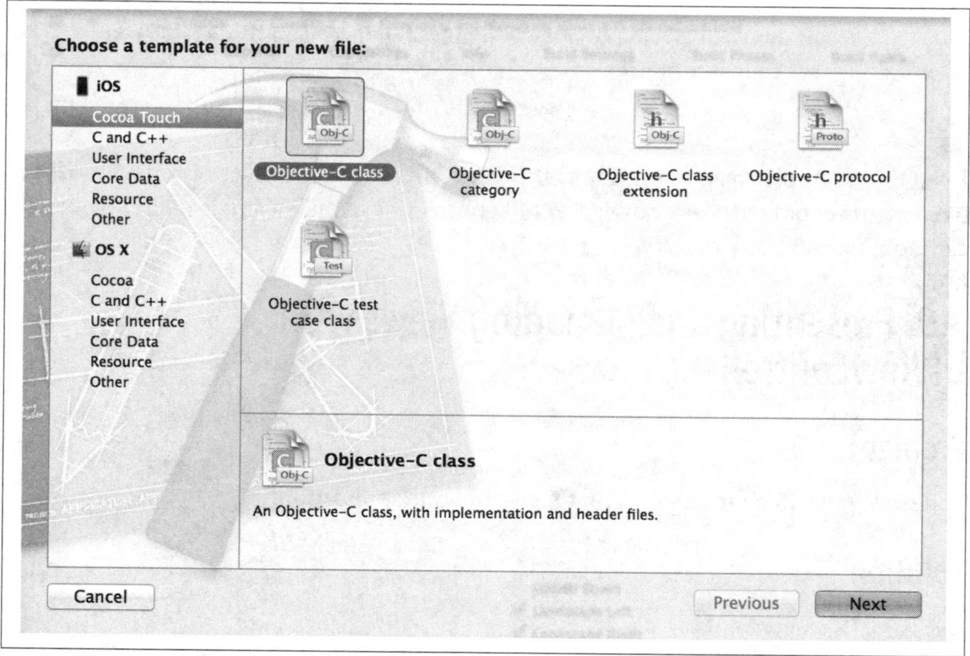


*Figure 1-24. New Objective-C subclass*

3. On the next screen, make sure that the "Subclass of" the text field says `UIViewController`. Also make sure that neither the "Targeted for iPad" nor the "With XIB for user interface" checkboxes is selected, as shown in Figure 1-25. Press Next.

Go ahead and run the app on the simulator. You will now see a plain white view on the screen. Congratulations! You just created a view controller, and now you have access to the view controller and its view object.

While creating the view controller (Figure 1-25), if you had selected the "With XIB for user interface" checkbox, Xcode would have also generated a *.xib* file for you. In that case, you can load your view controller from that *.xib* file by passing the *.xib* file's name (without the extension) to the `initWithNibName` parameter of the `initWithNibName:bundle:` method of the view controller, like so:

```
- (BOOL)            application:(UIApplication *)application
  didFinishLaunchingWithOptions:(NSDictionary *)launchOptions{

    self.viewController = [[ViewController alloc]
                           initWithNibName:@"ViewController"
                           bundle:nil];

    self.window = [[UIWindow alloc]
                   initWithFrame:[[UIScreen mainScreen] bounds]];

    /* Make our view controller the root view controller */
    self.window.rootViewController = self.viewController;

    self.window.backgroundColor = [UIColor whiteColor];
    [self.window makeKeyAndVisible];
    return YES;
}
```

If you *did* create a *.xib* file while creating your view controller, you can now select that file in Xcode and design your user interface with Interface Builder.

### See Also

"Creating and Running Our First iOS App" on page 2

## 1.10. Presenting Sharing Options with UIActivityViewController

### Problem

You want to be able to allow your users to share content inside your apps with their friends, through an interface similar to that shown in Figure 1-27 that provides different sharing options available in iOS, such as Facebook and Twitter.

*Figure 1-27. The activity view controller displayed on an iOS device*

## Solution

Create an instance of the `UIActivityViewController` class and share your content through this class, as we will see in the Discussion section of this recipe.

The instances of `UIActivityViewController` must be presented modally on the iPhone and inside a popover on an iPad. For more information about popovers, refer to Recipe 1.29.

## Discussion

There are many sharing options inside iOS, all built into the core of the OS. For instance, Facebook and Twitter integration is now an integral part of the core of iOS, and you can share pretty much any content from anywhere you want. Third-party apps like ours can also use all the sharing functionalities available in iOS without having to think about the low-level details of these services and how iOS provides these sharing options. The beauty of this whole thing is that you mention *what* you want to share, and iOS will pick the sharing options that are capable of handling those items. For instance, if you want to share images and text, iOS will display many more items to you than if you want to share an audio file.

Sharing data is very easy in iOS. All you have to do is instantiate the `UIActivityView Controller` class using its `initWithActivityItems:applicationActivities:` initializer. Here are the parameters to this method:

`initWithActivityItems`
: The array of items that you want to share. These can be instances of `NSString`, `UIImage`, or instances of any of your custom classes that conform to the `UIActivi tyItemSource` protocol. We will talk about this protocol later in detail.

`applicationActivities`
: An array of instances of `UIActivity` that represent the activities that your own application supports. For instance, you can indicate here whether your application can handle its own sharing of images and strings. We will not go into detail about this parameter for now and will simply pass `nil` as its value, telling iOS that we want to stick to the system sharing options.

So let's say that you have a text field where the user can enter text to be shared, and a Share button right near it. When the user presses the Share button, you will simply pass the text of the text field to your instance of the `UIActivityViewController` class. Here is our code. We are writing this code for iPhone, so we will present our activity view controller as a modal view controller.

Because we are putting a text field on our view controller, we need to make sure that we are handling its delegate messages, especially the `textFieldShouldReturn:` method of the `UITextFieldDelegate` protocol. Therefore, we are going to elect our view controller as the delegate of the text field. Also, we are going to attach an action method to our Share button. Once the button is tapped, we want to make sure there is something in the text field to share. If there isn't, we will simply display an alert to the user telling him why we cannot share the content of the text field. If there is some text in the text field, we will pop up an instance of the `UIActivityViewController` class. So let's begin with the implementation file of our view controller and define our UI components:

```
@interface ViewController () <UITextFieldDelegate>
@property (nonatomic, strong) UITextField *textField;
```

```
@property (nonatomic, strong) UIButton *buttonShare;
@property (nonatomic, strong) UIActivityViewController *activityViewController;
@end

...
```

After this, we will write two methods for our view controller, each of which is able to create one of our UI components and place it on our view controller's view. One will create the text field, and the other will create the button next to it:

```
- (void) createTextField{
    self.textField = [[UITextField alloc] initWithFrame:CGRectMake(20.0f,
                                                                   35.0f,
                                                                   280.0f,
                                                                   30.0f)];
    self.textField.translatesAutoresizingMaskIntoConstraints = NO;
    self.textField.borderStyle = UITextBorderStyleRoundedRect;
    self.textField.placeholder = @"Enter text to share...";
    self.textField.delegate = self;
    [self.view addSubview:self.textField];
}

- (void) createButton{
    self.buttonShare = [UIButton buttonWithType:UIButtonTypeRoundedRect];
    self.buttonShare.translatesAutoresizingMaskIntoConstraints = NO;
    self.buttonShare.frame = CGRectMake(20.0f, 80.0f, 280.0f, 44.0f);
    [self.buttonShare setTitle:@"Share" forState:UIControlStateNormal];

    [self.buttonShare addTarget:self
                         action:@selector(handleShare:)
               forControlEvents:UIControlEventTouchUpInside];

    [self.view addSubview:self.buttonShare];
}
```

Once we are done with that, we just have to call these two methods in the `viewDidLoad` method of our view controller. This will allow the UI components to be placed on the view of our view controller:

```
- (void)viewDidLoad{

    [super viewDidLoad];
    [self createTextField];
    [self createButton];

}
```

In the textFieldShouldReturn: method, all we do is dismiss the keyboard in order to resign the text field's active state. This simply means that when a user has been editing the text field and then presses the Return or Enter button on the keyboard, the keyboard should be dismissed. Bear in mind that the createTextField method that we just coded has set our view controller as the delegate of the text field. So we have to implement the aforementioned method as follows:

```
- (BOOL) textFieldShouldReturn:(UITextField *)textField{
    [textField resignFirstResponder];
    return YES;
}
```

Last but not least is the handler method of our button. As you saw, the createButton method creates the button for us and elects the handleShare: method to handle the touch down inside action of the button. So let's code this method:

```
- (void) handleShare:(id)paramSender{

    if ([self.textField.text length] == 0){
        NSString *message = @"Please enter a text and then press Share";
        UIAlertView *alertView = [[UIAlertView alloc] initWithTitle:nil
                                                            message:message
                                                           delegate:nil
                                                  cancelButtonTitle:@"OK"
                                                  otherButtonTitles:nil];
        [alertView show];
        return;
    }

    self.activityViewController = [[UIActivityViewController alloc]
                                   initWithActivityItems:@[self.textField.text]
                                   applicationActivities:nil];
    [self presentViewController:self.activityViewController
                       animated:YES
                     completion:^{
                         /* Nothing for now */
                     }];

}
```

Now if you run the app, enter some text in the text field, and then press the Share button, you will see something similar to Figure 1-28.

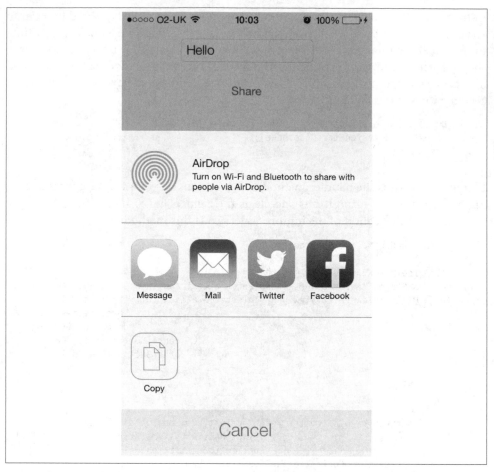

*Figure 1-28. Sharing options displayed for the instance of string that we are trying to share*

You can also have sharing options displayed as soon as your view controller is displayed on the screen. The `viewDidAppear` method of your view controller will be called when the view of your view controller is displayed on the screen and is guaranteed to be in the view hierarchy of your app, meaning that you can now display other views on top of your view controller's view.

Do not attempt to present the activity view controller in the `viewDidLoad` method of your view controller. At that stage in the app, your view controller's view is still not attached to the view hierarchy of the application, so attempting to present a view controller on the view will not work. Your view must be present in the hierarchy of the views for your modal views to work.

For this reason, you need to present the sharing view controller in the `viewDidAppear` method of your view controller.

## See Also

Recipe 1.29

# 1.11. Presenting Custom Sharing Options with UIActivityViewController

## Problem

You want your app to participate in the list of apps that can handle sharing in iOS and appear in the list of available activities displayed in the activity view controller (see Figure 1-27).

You may need something like this, for example, when you have a text-editing app and when the user presses the Share button, you want a custom item that says "Archive" to appear in the activity view controller. When the user presses the Archive button, the text inside your app's editing area will get passed to your custom activity, and your activity can then archive that text into the filesystem on the iOS device.

## Solution

Create a class of type `UIActivity`. In other words, subclass the aforementioned class and give a name (whatever you like) to your new class. Instances of the subclasses of this class can be passed to the `initWithActivityItems:applicationActivities:` initializer of the `UIActivityViewController` class, and if they implement all the required methods of the `UIActivity` class, iOS will display them in the activity view controller.

## Discussion

The `initWithActivityItems:applicationActivities:` method's first parameter accepts values of different types. These values can be strings, numbers, images, etc.—any object, really. When you present an activity controller with an array of arbitrary objects passed to the `initWithActivityItems` parameter, iOS will go through all the available system activities, like Facebook and Twitter, and will ask the user to pick an activity that suits her needs best. After the user picks an activity, iOS will pass the *type* of the objects in your array to the registered system activity that the user picked. Those activities can then check the type of the objects you are trying to share and decide whether they can handle those objects or not. They communicate this to iOS through a specific method that they will implement in their classes.

So let's say that we want to create an activity that can reverse any number of strings that are handed to it. Remember that when your app initializes the activity view controller through the `initWithActivityItems:applicationActivities:` method, it can pass an array of arbitrary objects to the first parameter of this method. So our activity is going to peek at all these objects in this arbitrary array, and if they are all strings, it is going to reverse them and then display all the reversed strings in an alert view.

1. Subclass `UIActivity` as shown here:

   ```
   #import <UIKit/UIKit.h>

   @interface StringReverserActivity : UIActivity

   @end
   ```

2. Since our activity is going to be responsible for displaying an alert view to the user when an array of strings is passed to us, we need to ensure that our activity conforms to the `UIAlertViewDelegate` protocol and marks our activity as "finished" when the user dismisses the alert view, like so:

   ```
   #import "StringReverserActivity.h"

   @interface StringReverserActivity () <UIAlertViewDelegate>
   @property (nonatomic, strong) NSArray *activityItems;
   @end

   @implementation StringReverserActivity

   - (void)             alertView:(UIAlertView *)alertView
       didDismissWithButtonIndex:(NSInteger)buttonIndex{
       [self activityDidFinish:YES];
   }
   ```

3. Next, override the `activityType` method of your activity. The return value of this method is an object of type `NSString` that is a unique identifier of your activity. This value will not be displayed to the user and is just for iOS to keep track of your activity's identifier. There are no specific values that you are asked to return from this method and no guidelines available from Apple, but we will follow the reverse-domain string format and use our app's bundle identifier and append the name of our class to the end of it. So if our bundle identifier is equal to *`com.pixolity.ios.cookbook.myapp`* and our class name is `StringReverserActivity`, we will return *`com.pixolity.ios.cookbook.myapp.StringReverserActivity`* from this method, like so:

   ```
   - (NSString *) activityType{
       return [[NSBundle mainBundle].bundleIdentifier
   ```

```
            stringByAppendingFormat:@".%@", NSStringFromClass([self class])];
}
```

4. The next method to override is the `activityTitle` method, which should return a string to be displayed to the user in the activity view controller. Make sure this string is short enough to fit into the activity view controller:

```
- (NSString *) activityTitle{
    return @"Reverse String";
}
```

5. The next method is `activityImage`, which has to return an instance of `UIImage` that gets displayed in the activity view controller. Make sure that you provide both Retina and non-Retina versions of the image for both iPad and iPhone/iPod. The iPad Retina image has to be 110×110 pixels and the iPhone Retina image has to be 86×86 pixels. Obviously, divide these dimensions by 2 to get the width and the height of the non-Retina images. iOS uses only the alpha channel in this image, so make sure your image's background is transparent and that you illustrate your image with the color white or the color black. I have already created an image in my app's image assets section, and I've named the image "Reverse," as you can see in Figure 1-29. Here is our code, then:

```
- (UIImage *) activityImage{
    return [UIImage imageNamed:@"Reverse"];
}
```

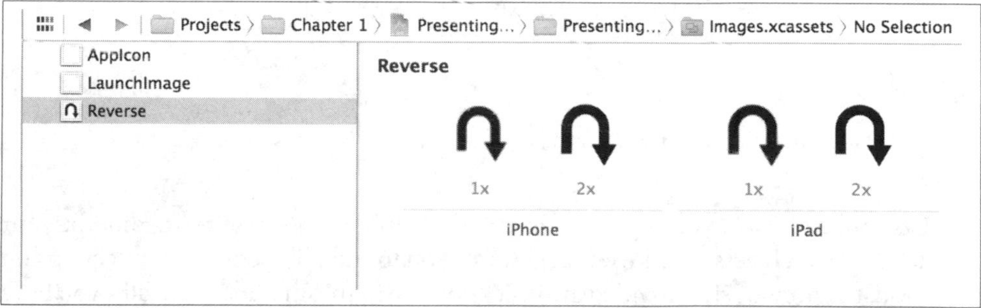


*Figure 1-29. Our asset category contains images for our custom activity*

6. Implement the `canPerformWithActivityItems:` method of your activity. This method's parameter is an array that will be set when an array of activity items is passed to the initializer of the activity view controller. Remember, these are objects of arbitrary type. The return value of your method will be a Boolean indicating whether you can perform your actions on any of the given items or not. For instance, our activity can reverse any number of strings that it is given. So if we find one string in the array, that is good enough for us because we know we will later be able to

reverse that string. If we are given an array of 1,000 objects that contains only 2 strings, we will still accept it. But if we are given an array of 1,000 objects, none of which are of our acceptable type, we will reject this request by returning `NO` from this method:

```
- (BOOL) canPerformWithActivityItems:(NSArray *)activityItems{

    for (id object in activityItems){
        if ([object isKindOfClass:[NSString class]]){
            return YES;
        }
    }

    return NO;

}
```

7. Now implement the `prepareWithActivityItems:` method of your activity, whose parameter is of type `NSArray`. This method gets called if you returned `YES` from the `canPerformWithActivityItems:` method. You have to retain the given array for later use. You don't really actually have to retain the whole array. You may choose to retain only the objects that you need in this array, such as the string objects.

```
- (void) prepareWithActivityItems:(NSArray *)activityItems{

    NSMutableArray *stringObjects = [[NSMutableArray alloc] init];
    for (id object in activityItems){
        if ([object isKindOfClass:[NSString class]]){
            [stringObjects addObject:object];
        }
    }

    self.activityItems = [stringObjects copy];
}
```

8. Last but not least, you need to implement the `performActivity` method of your activity, which gets called when iOS wants you to actually perform your actions on the list of previously-provided arbitrary objects. In this method, basically, you have to perform your work. In our activity, we are going to go through the array of string objects that we extracted from this arbitrary array, reverse all of them, and display them to the user using an alert view:

```
- (NSString *) reverseOfString:(NSString *)paramString{

    NSMutableString *reversed = [[NSMutableString alloc]
                                 initWithCapacity:paramString.length];

    for (NSInteger counter = paramString.length - 1;
         counter >= 0;
```

```
         counter--){
        [reversed appendFormat:@"%c", [paramString characterAtIndex:counter]];
    }

    return [reversed copy];

}

- (void) performActivity{

    NSMutableString *reversedStrings = [[NSMutableString alloc] init];

    for (NSString *string in self.activityItems){
        [reversedStrings appendString:[self reverseOfString:string]];
        [reversedStrings appendString:@"\n"];
    }

    UIAlertView *alertView = [[UIAlertView alloc] initWithTitle:@"Reversed"
                                                        message:reversedStrings
                                                       delegate:self
                                              cancelButtonTitle:@"OK"
                                              otherButtonTitles:nil];

    [alertView show];

}
```

We are done with the implementation of our activity class. Now let's go to our view controller's implementation file and display the activity view controller with our custom activity in the list:

```
#import "ViewController.h"
#import "StringReverserActivity.h"

@implementation ViewController

- (void) viewDidAppear:(BOOL)animated{
    [super viewDidAppear:animated];

    NSArray *itemsToShare = @[
                              @"Item 1",
                              @"Item 2",
                              @"Item 3",
                              ];

    UIActivityViewController *activity =
        [[UIActivityViewController alloc]
         initWithActivityItems:itemsToShare
         applicationActivities:@[[StringReverserActivity new]]];

    [self presentViewController:activity animated:YES completion:nil];
```

```
}
@end
```

When the app runs for the first time, you will see something similar to Figure 1-30 on the screen.

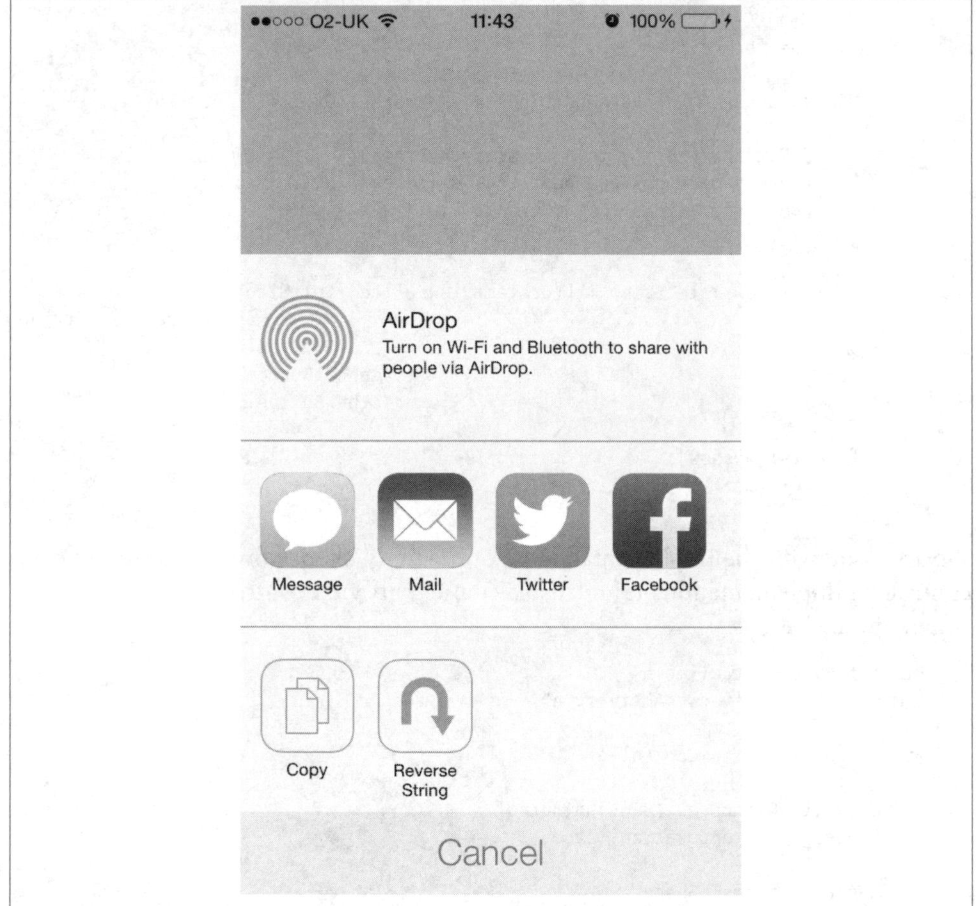


*Figure 1-30. Our custom Reverse String activity is showing in the list of available activities*

If you now tap on the Reverse String item in the list, you should see something similar to that shown in Figure 1-31.

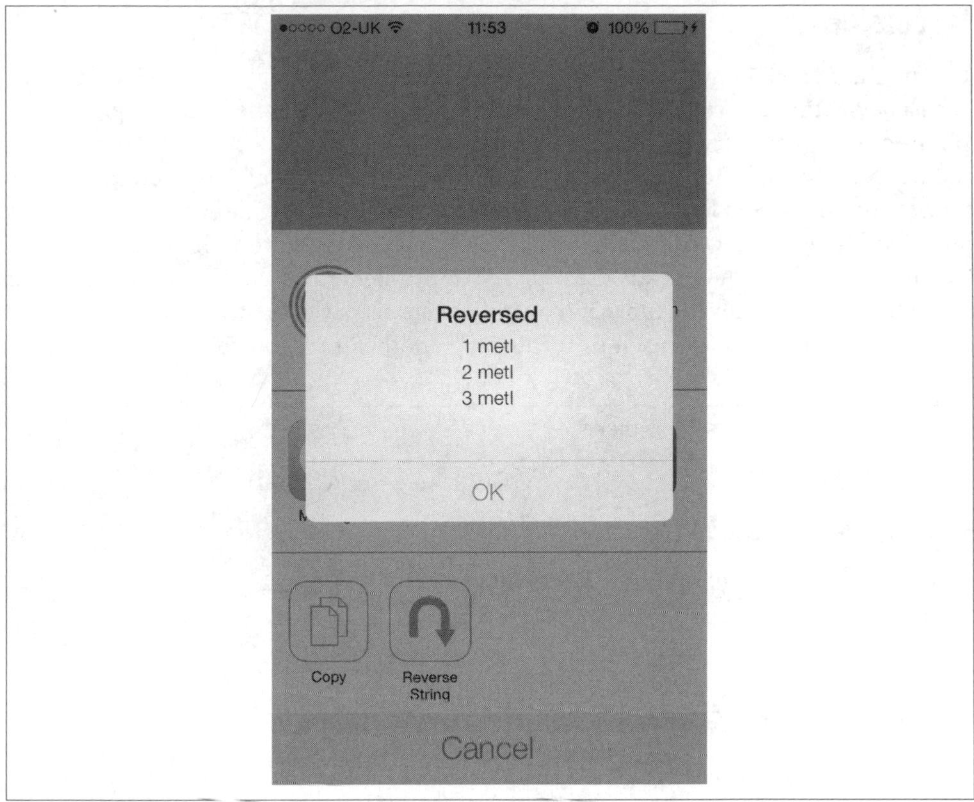


*Figure 1-31. Our string reverser activity in action*

## See Also

Recipe 1.10

# 1.12. Implementing Navigation with UINavigationController

## Problem

You would like to allow your users to move from one view controller to the other with a smooth and built-in animation.

## Solution

Use an instance of `UINavigationController`.

## Discussion

If you've used an iPhone, iPod Touch, or iPad before, chances are that you have already seen a navigation controller in action. For instance, if you go to the Settings app on your phone and then press an option such as Wallpaper (Figure 1-32), you will see the Settings main screen get pulled out of the screen from the left and the Wallpaper screen pushing its way into the screen from the right. That is the magic of navigation controllers. They allow you to *push* view controllers onto a stack and *pop* them from the stack. The view controller on top of the stack is the top view controller and is the one seen by the user at that moment. So only the top view controller gets displayed to the user and is changed either by popping (removing) it or by pushing another view controller onto the stack.

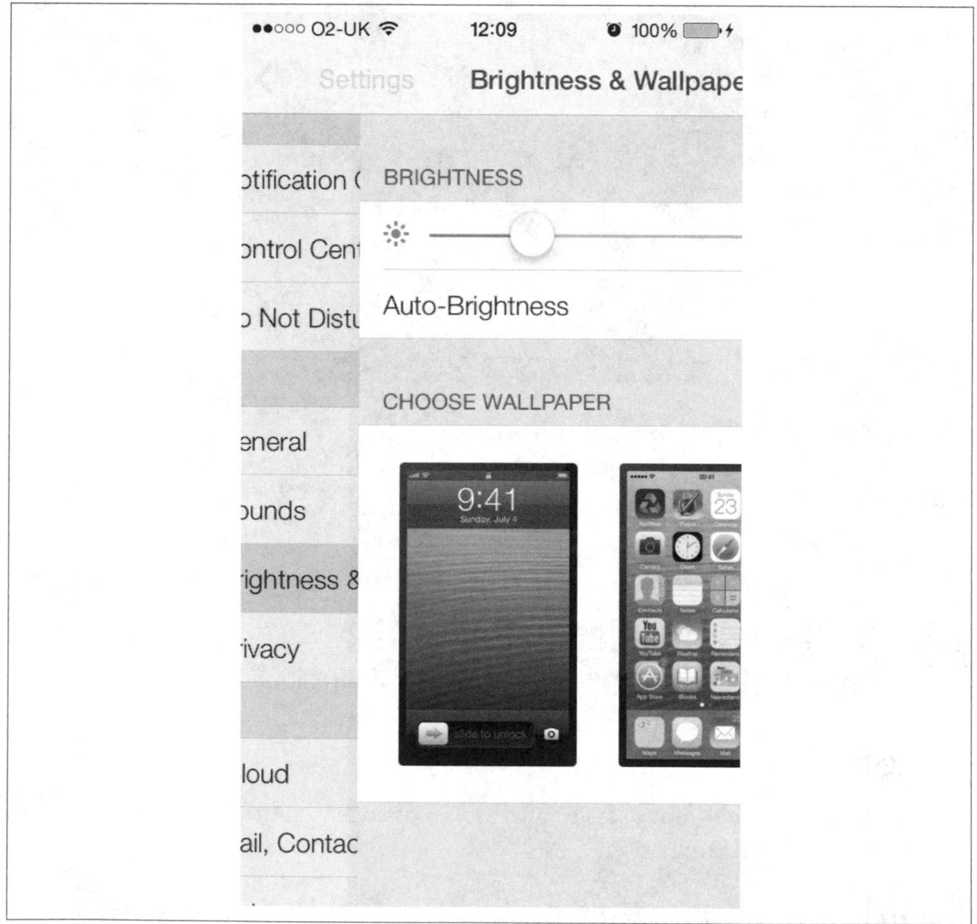


*Figure 1-32. Settings view controller pushing the Wallpaper view controller*

Now we are going to add a navigation controller to our project, but we need a project first. Please follow the instructions in Recipe 1.9 to create an empty application with a simple view controller. In this recipe, we will expand on Recipe 1.9. Let's start with the *.m* file of our app delegate:

```
#import "AppDelegate.h"
#import "FirstViewController.h"

@interface AppDelegate ()
@property (nonatomic, strong) UINavigationController *navigationController;
@end

@implementation AppDelegate

...
```

Now we have to initialize our navigation controller using its `initWithRootViewController:` method and pass our root view controller as its parameter. Then we will set the navigation controller as the root view controller of our window. Don't get confused here. `UINavigationController` is actually a subclass of `UIViewController`, and our window's `rootViewController` property accepts any object of type `UIViewController`, so if we want the root view controller of our window to be a navigation controller, we simply set our navigation controller as the root view controller of the window:

```
- (BOOL)            application:(UIApplication *)application
  didFinishLaunchingWithOptions:(NSDictionary *)launchOptions{

    FirstViewController *viewController = [[FirstViewController alloc]
                                           initWithNibName:nil
                                           bundle:nil];

    self.navigationController = [[UINavigationController alloc]
                                 initWithRootViewController:viewController];

    self.window = [[UIWindow alloc]
                   initWithFrame:[[UIScreen mainScreen] bounds]];

    self.window.rootViewController = self.navigationController;

    self.window.backgroundColor = [UIColor whiteColor];
    [self.window makeKeyAndVisible];
    return YES;
}
```

Now let's run our app in the simulator, as shown in Figure 1-33.

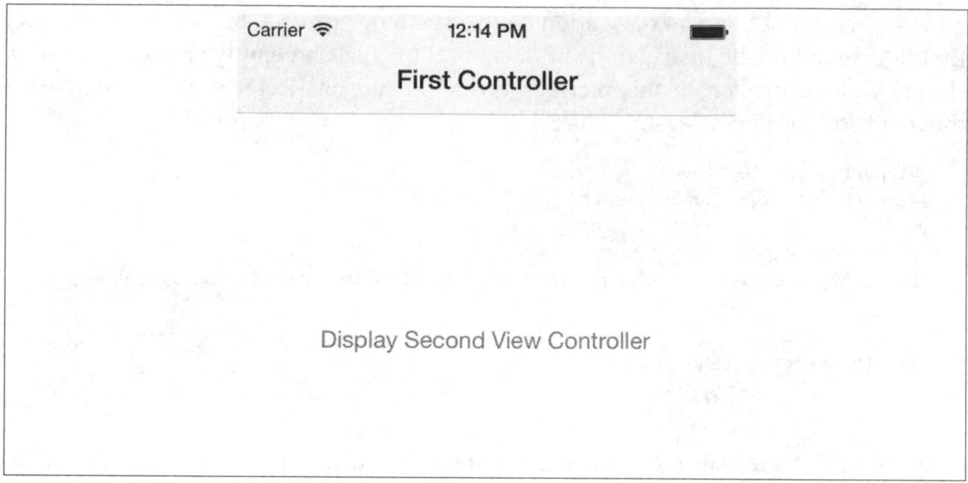


*Figure 1-33. Our root view controller displayed inside a navigation controller*

The root view controller's implementation file is creating the button in the center of the screen (shown in Figure 1-33). We will get to the implementation of that file soon.

The first thing you might notice in Figure 1-33 is the bar on top of the screen. The screen isn't plain white anymore. What's the new widget? A navigation bar. We will be using that bar a lot for navigation, placing buttons there, and so forth. That bar is also capable of displaying a title. Each view controller specifies a title for itself, and the navigation controller will automatically display that title once the view controller is pushed into the stack.

Let's go to our root view controller's implementation file, inside the `viewDidLoad` method, and set the `title` property of our view controller to *`First Controller`*. We'll also create our button there. When the user presses this button, we want to display the second view controller on the screen:

```
#import "FirstViewController.h"
#import "SecondViewController.h"

@interface FirstViewController ()
    @property (nonatomic, strong) UIButton *displaySecondViewController;
@end

@implementation FirstViewController

- (void) performDisplaySecondViewController:(id)paramSender{
    SecondViewController *secondController = [[SecondViewController alloc]
                                              initWithNibName:nil
```

```
                                                    bundle:NULL];
    [self.navigationController pushViewController:secondController
                                          animated:YES];

}

- (void)viewDidLoad{
    [super viewDidLoad];
    self.title = @"First Controller";

    self.displaySecondViewController = [UIButton
                                        buttonWithType:UIButtonTypeSystem];

    [self.displaySecondViewController
    setTitle:@"Display Second View Controller"
    forState:UIControlStateNormal];

    [self.displaySecondViewController sizeToFit];
    self.displaySecondViewController.center = self.view.center;

    [self.displaySecondViewController
    addTarget:self
    action:@selector(performDisplaySecondViewController:)
    forControlEvents:UIControlEventTouchUpInside];

    [self.view addSubview:self.displaySecondViewController];
}

@end
```

Now let's go and create this second view controller, *without* a *.xib* file, and call it `SecondViewController`. Follow the same process that you learned in Recipe 1.9. Once you are done creating this view controller, give it a title of `Second Controller`.

```
#import "SecondViewController.h"

@implementation SecondViewController

- (void)viewDidLoad{
    [super viewDidLoad];
    self.title = @"Second Controller";
}
```

Now what we want to do is "pop" from the second view controller back to the first view controller, five seconds after the second view controller is displayed to the screen. For that we are using the `performSelector:withObject:afterDelay:` method of `NSObject` to call our new method, `goBack`, five seconds after our second view controller successfully displays its view. In the `goBack` method, we are simply using the `navigationController` property of our view controller (this is built into `UIViewController` and is *not* something that we coded) to pop back to the instance of `FirstViewController`, using the `popViewControllerAnimated:` method of our navigation controller that takes a Boolean as a parameter. If this Boolean value is set to `YES`, the transition back to the previous view controller will be animated, and if NO, it won't be. When the second view controller is displayed on the screen, you will see something similar to that shown in Figure 1-34.

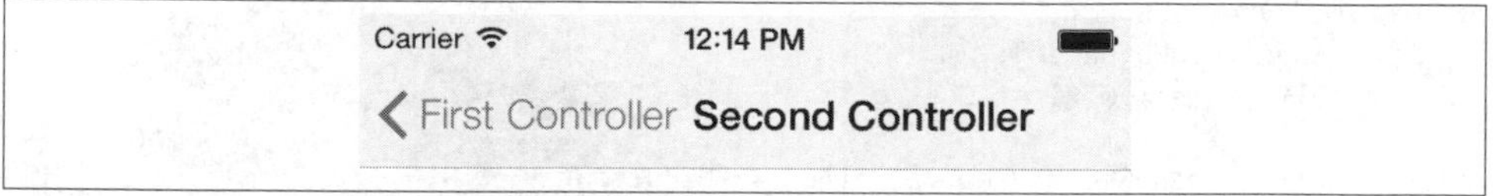


*Figure 1-34. A view controller is pushed on top of another one*

```
#import "SecondViewController.h"

@implementation SecondViewController

- (void)viewDidLoad{
    [super viewDidLoad];
    self.title = @"Second Controller";
}

- (void) goBack{
    [self.navigationController popViewControllerAnimated:YES];
}

- (void) viewDidAppear:(BOOL)paramAnimated{
    [super viewDidAppear:paramAnimated];
    [self performSelector:@selector(goBack)
               withObject:nil
               afterDelay:5.0f];
}

@end
```

You can see that the navigation bar is displaying the title of the top view controller and even sports a back button that will take the user back to the previous view controller. You can push as many view controllers as you like into the stack, and the navigation controller will work the navigation bar to display the relevant back buttons that allow the user to back through your application's UI, all the way to the first screen.

So if you open the app in the simulator now and press the button on the first view controller, you will see that the second view controller will automatically get displayed on the screen. Wait five seconds now on the second view controller and it will automatically go back to the first view controller.

## See Also

Recipe 1.9

# 1.13. Manipulating a Navigation Controller's Array of View Controllers

## Problem

You would like to directly manipulate the array of view controllers associated with a specific navigation controller.

## Solution

Use the `viewControllers` property of the `UINavigationController` class to access and modify the array of view controllers associated with a navigation controller:

```
- (void) goBack{
    /* Get the current array of View Controllers */
    NSArray *currentControllers = self.navigationController.viewControllers;

    /* Create a mutable array out of this array */
    NSMutableArray *newControllers = [NSMutableArray
                                      arrayWithArray:currentControllers];

    /* Remove the last object from the array */
    [newControllers removeLastObject];

    /* Assign this array to the Navigation Controller */
    self.navigationController.viewControllers = newControllers;
}
```

You can call this method inside any view controller in order to pop the last view controller from the hierarchy of the navigation controller associated with the current view controller.

## Discussion

An instance of the `UINavigationController` class holds an array of `UIViewController` objects. After retrieving this array, you can manipulate it in any way you wish. For instance, you can remove a view controller from an arbitrary place in the array.

Manipulating the view controllers of a navigation controller directly by assigning an array to the `viewControllers` property of the navigation controller will commit the operation without a transition/animation. If you wish this operation to be animated, use the `setViewControllers:animated:` method of the `UINavigationController` class, as shown in the following snippet:

```
- (void) goBack{
    /* Get the current array of View Controllers */
    NSArray *currentControllers = self.navigationController.viewControllers;
```

```
    /* Create a mutable array out of this array */
    NSMutableArray *newControllers = [NSMutableArray
                                      arrayWithArray:currentControllers];

    /* Remove the last object from the array */
    [newControllers removeLastObject];

    /* Assign this array to the Navigation Controller with animation */
    [self.navigationController setViewControllers:newControllers
                                         animated:YES];
}
```

## 1.14. Displaying an Image on a Navigation Bar

### Problem

You want to display an image instead of text as the title of the current view controller on the navigation controller.

### Solution

Use the `titleView` property of the view controller's navigation item:

```
- (void)viewDidLoad{
    [super viewDidLoad];

    /* Create an Image View to replace the Title View */
    UIImageView *imageView =
    [[UIImageView alloc]
     initWithFrame:CGRectMake(0.0f, 0.0f, 100.0f, 40.0f)];

    imageView.contentMode = UIViewContentModeScaleAspectFit;

    /* Load an image. Be careful, this image will be cached */
    UIImage *image = [UIImage imageNamed:@"Logo"];

    /* Set the image of the Image View */
    [imageView setImage:image];

    /* Set the Title View */
    self.navigationItem.titleView = imageView;

}
```

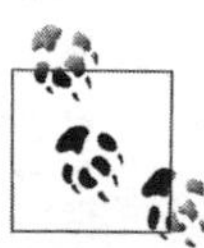

The preceding code must be executed in a view controller that is placed inside a navigation controller.

I have already loaded an image into my project's assets group and I've called this image "Logo". Once you run this app with the given code snippet, you'll see something similar to that shown in Figure 1-35.

*Figure 1-35. An image view in our navigation bar*

## Discussion

The navigation item of every view controller can display two different types of content in the title area of the view controller to which it is assigned:

- Simple text
- A view

If you want to use text, you can use the `title` property of the navigation item. However, if you want more control over the title or if you simply want to display an image or any other view up on the navigation bar, you can use the `titleView` property of the navigation item of a view controller. You can assign any object that is a subclass of the `UIView` class. In our example, we created an image view and assigned an image to it. Then we displayed it as the title of the current view controller on the navigation controller.

The `titleView` property of the navigation bar is just a simple view, but Apple recommends that you limit the height of this view to no more than 128 points. So think about it in terms of the image. If you are loading an image that is 128 *pixels* in height, that will translate to *64 points on a Retina display*, so in that case you are fine. But if you are loading an image that is 300 pixels in height, on a Retina display, that will translate to 150 points in height, so you'll be clearly over the 128-points limit that Apple recommends for the title bar view height. To remedy this situation, you need to ensure that your title view is never taller than 128 points height-wise and set the view's content mode to fill the view, instead of stretching the view to fit the content. This can be done by setting the `contentMode` property of your title bar view to `UIViewContentModeScaleAspectFit`.

# 1.15. Adding Buttons to Navigation Bars Using UIBarButtonItem

## Problem

You want to add buttons to a navigation bar.

## Solution

Use the `UIBarButtonItem` class.

## Discussion

A navigation bar can contain different items. Buttons are often displayed on the left and the right sides. These buttons are of class `UIBarButtonItem` and can take many different shapes and forms. Let's have a look at an example in Figure 1-36.

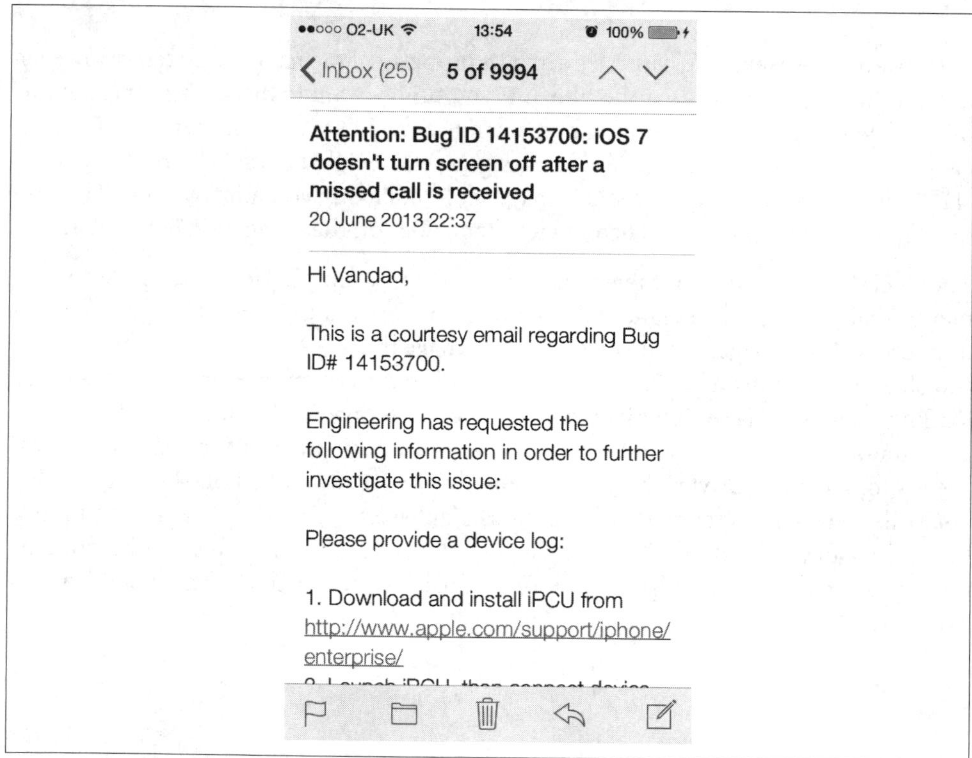


*Figure 1-36. Different buttons displayed on a navigation bar*

Navigation bars are of class UINavigationBar and can be created at any time and added to any view. Just look at all the different buttons with different shapes that have been added to the navigation bar in Figure 1-36. The ones on the top right have up and down arrows, and the one on the top left has an arrow pointing to the left. We will have a look at creating some of these buttons in this recipe.

For this recipe, you must follow the instructions in "Creating and Running Our First iOS App" on page 2 to create an empty application. Then follow the instructions in Recipe 1.12 to add a navigation controller to your app delegate.

In order to create a navigation button, we must do the following:

1. Create an instance of UIBarButtonItem.
2. Add that button to the navigation bar of a view controller using the view controller's navigationItem property. The navigationItem property allows us to interact with the navigation bar. This property has two others on itself: rightBarButtonItem and leftBarButtonItem. Both these properties are of type UIBarButtonItem.

Let's then have a look at an example where we add a button to the right side of our navigation bar. In this button, we will display the text "Add":

```
- (void) performAdd:(id)paramSender{
    NSLog(@"Action method got called.");
}

- (void)viewDidLoad{
    [super viewDidLoad];

    self.title = @"First Controller";

    self.navigationItem.rightBarButtonItem =
    [[UIBarButtonItem alloc] initWithTitle:@"Add"
                                     style:UIBarButtonItemStylePlain
                                    target:self
                                    action:@selector(performAdd:)];

}
```

When we run our app now, we will see something similar to Figure 1-37.

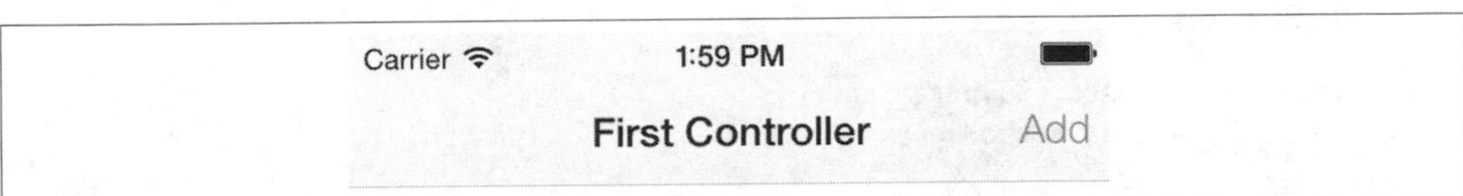


*Figure 1-37. A navigation button added to a navigation bar*

That was easy. But if you are an iOS user, you probably have noticed that the system apps that come preconfigured on iOS have a different Add button. Figure 1-38 shows an example in the Alarm section of the Clock app on the iPhone (notice the + button on the top right of the navigation bar).

*Figure 1-38. The proper way of creating an Add button*

It turns out that the iOS SDK allows us to create *system* buttons on the navigation bar. We do that by using the `initWithBarButtonSystemItem:target:action:` initializer of the `UIBarButtonItem` class:

```
- (void) performAdd:(id)paramSender{
    NSLog(@"Action method got called.");
}

- (void)viewDidLoad{
```

```
    [super viewDidLoad];

    self.title = @"First Controller";

    self.navigationItem.rightBarButtonItem =
    [[UIBarButtonItem alloc]
     initWithBarButtonSystemItem:UIBarButtonSystemItemAdd
     target:self
     action:@selector(performAdd:)];
}
```

And the results are exactly what we were looking for (Figure 1-39).

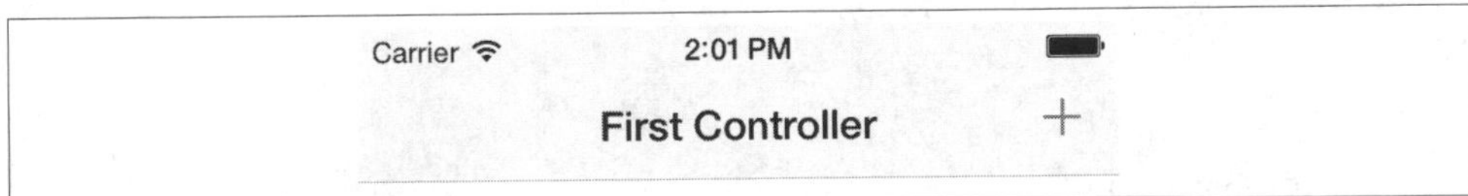


*Figure 1-39. A system Add button*

The first parameter of the `initWithBarButtonSystemItem:target:action:` initializer method of the navigation button can have any of the values listed in the `UIBarButtonSystemItem` enumeration:

```
typedef NS_ENUM(NSInteger, UIBarButtonSystemItem) {
    UIBarButtonSystemItemDone,
    UIBarButtonSystemItemCancel,
    UIBarButtonSystemItemEdit,
    UIBarButtonSystemItemSave,
    UIBarButtonSystemItemAdd,
    UIBarButtonSystemItemFlexibleSpace,
    UIBarButtonSystemItemFixedSpace,
    UIBarButtonSystemItemCompose,
    UIBarButtonSystemItemReply,
    UIBarButtonSystemItemAction,
    UIBarButtonSystemItemOrganize,
    UIBarButtonSystemItemBookmarks,
    UIBarButtonSystemItemSearch,
    UIBarButtonSystemItemRefresh,
    UIBarButtonSystemItemStop,
    UIBarButtonSystemItemCamera,
    UIBarButtonSystemItemTrash,
    UIBarButtonSystemItemPlay,
    UIBarButtonSystemItemPause,
    UIBarButtonSystemItemRewind,
    UIBarButtonSystemItemFastForward,
#if __IPHONE_3_0 <= __IPHONE_OS_VERSION_MAX_ALLOWED
    UIBarButtonSystemItemUndo,
    UIBarButtonSystemItemRedo,
#endif
#if __IPHONE_4_0 <= __IPHONE_OS_VERSION_MAX_ALLOWED
```

```
        UIBarButtonSystemItemPageCurl,
    #endif
    };
```

One of the really great initializers of the `UIBarButtonItem` class is the `initWithCustomView:` method. As its parameter, this method accepts any view. This means we can even add a `UISwitch` (see Recipe 1.2) as a button on the navigation bar. This won't look very good, but let's give it a try:

```
- (void) switchIsChanged:(UISwitch *)paramSender{
    if ([paramSender isOn]){
        NSLog(@"Switch is on.");
    } else {
        NSLog(@"Switch is off.");
    }
}

- (void)viewDidLoad{
    [super viewDidLoad];
    self.view.backgroundColor = [UIColor whiteColor];
    self.title = @"First Controller";

    UISwitch *simpleSwitch = [[UISwitch alloc] init];
    simpleSwitch.on = YES;
    [simpleSwitch addTarget:self
                     action:@selector(switchIsChanged:)
           forControlEvents:UIControlEventValueChanged];

    self.navigationItem.rightBarButtonItem =
    [[UIBarButtonItem alloc] initWithCustomView:simpleSwitch];
}
```

And Figure 1-40 shows the results.

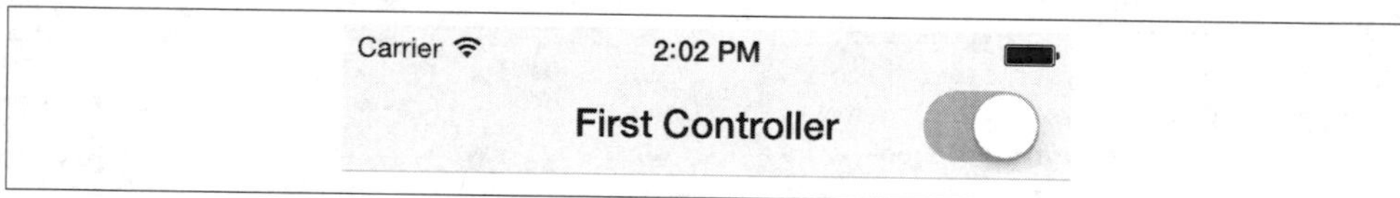


*Figure 1-40. A switch added to a navigation bar*

You can create pretty amazing navigation bar buttons. Just take a look at what Apple has done with the up and down arrows on the top-right corner of Figure 1-36. Let's do the same thing, shall we? Well, it looks like the button actually contains a segmented control (see Recipe 1.8). So we should create a segmented control with two segments, add it to a navigation button, and finally place the navigation button on the navigation bar. Let's get started:

```
- (void) segmentedControlTapped:(UISegmentedControl *)paramSender{
```

```
    switch (paramSender.selectedSegmentIndex){
        case 0:{
            NSLog(@"Up");
            break;
        }
        case 1:{
            NSLog(@"Down");
            break;
        }
    }

}

- (void)viewDidLoad{
    [super viewDidLoad];

    self.title = @"First Controller";

    NSArray *items = @[
                       @"Up",
                       @"Down"
                       ];

    UISegmentedControl *segmentedControl = [[UISegmentedControl alloc]
                                            initWithItems:items];

    segmentedControl.momentary = YES;

    [segmentedControl addTarget:self
                         action:@selector(segmentedControlTapped:)
               forControlEvents:UIControlEventValueChanged];

    self.navigationItem.rightBarButtonItem =
    [[UIBarButtonItem alloc] initWithCustomView:segmentedControl];

}
```

And Figure 1-41 shows what the output looks like.

*Figure 1-41. A segmented control inside a navigation button*

The `navigationItem` of every view controller also has two very interesting methods:

`setRightBarButtonItem:animated:`
: Sets the navigation bar's right button.

`setLeftBarButtonItem:animated:`
: Sets the navigation bar's left button.

Both methods allow you to specify whether you want the placement to be animated. Pass the value of `YES` to the `animated` parameter if you want the placement to be animated. Here is an example:

```
UIBarButtonItem *rightBarButton =
[[UIBarButtonItem alloc] initWithCustomView:segmentedControl];

[self.navigationItem setRightBarButtonItem:rightBarButton
                                  animated:YES];
```

## See Also

"Creating and Running Our First iOS App" on page 2; Recipe 1.2; Recipe 1.8; Recipe 1.12

# 1.16. Presenting Multiple View Controllers with UITabBarController

## Problem

You would like to give your users the option to switch from one section of your app to another, with ease.

## Solution

Use the `UITabBarController` class.

## Discussion

If you use your iPhone as an alarm clock, you have certainly seen a tab bar. Have a look at Figure 1-38. The bottom icons labeled World Clock, Alarm, Stopwatch, and Timer are parts of a tab bar. The whole black bar at the bottom of the screen is a tab bar, and the aforementioned icons are tab bar items.

A tab bar is a container controller. In other words, we create instances of `UITabBarController` and add them to the window of our application. For each tab bar item, we add a navigation controller or a view controller to the tab bar, and those items will appear as tab bar items. A tab bar controller contains a tab bar of type `UITabBar`. We don't create this object manually. We create the tab bar controller, and that will create the tab bar object for us. To make things simple, remember that we instantiate a tab bar controller and set the view controllers of that tab bar to instances of either `UIViewController` or `UINavigationController` if we intend to have navigation controllers for each of the tab bar items (aka, the view controllers set for the tab bar controller). Navigation controllers are of type UINavigationController that are subclasses of UIViewController. Therefore, a navigation controller is a view controller, but view controllers of type UIViewController are not navigation controllers.

So let's assume we have two view controllers with class names FirstViewController and SecondViewController.

```
- (BOOL)            application:(UIApplication *)application
  didFinishLaunchingWithOptions:(NSDictionary *)launchOptions{

    self.window = [[UIWindow alloc] initWithFrame:
                   [[UIScreen mainScreen] bounds]];

    [self.window makeKeyAndVisible];

    FirstViewController *firstViewController = [[FirstViewController alloc]
                                                 initWithNibName:nil
                                                 bundle:NULL];
    SecondViewController *secondViewController = [[SecondViewController alloc]
                                                   initWithNibName:nil
                                                   bundle:NULL];

    UITabBarController *tabBarController = [[UITabBarController alloc] init];
    [tabBarController setViewControllers:@[firstViewController,
                                           secondViewController
                                           ]];

    self.window.rootViewController = tabBarController;

    return YES;

}
```

A tab bar, when displayed on the screen, will display tab bar items just like those we saw in Figure 1-38. The name of each of these tab bar items comes from the title of the view controller that is representing that tab bar item, so let's go ahead and set the title for both of our view controllers.

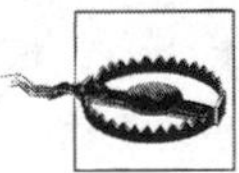

When a tab bar loads up, it loads only the view of the first view controller in its items. All other view controllers will be initialized, but their views won't be loaded. This means that any code that you have written in the viewDidLoad of the second view controller will *not* get executed until after the user taps on the second tab bar item for the first time. So if you assign a title to the second view controller in its viewDidLoad and run your app, you will find that the title in the tab bar item is still empty.

For the first view controller, we choose the title *First*:

```
#import "FirstViewController.h"

@implementation FirstViewController

- (id)initWithNibName:(NSString *)nibNameOrNil
               bundle:(NSBundle *)nibBundleOrNil{

    self = [super initWithNibName:nibNameOrNil
                           bundle:nibBundleOrNil];
    if (self != nil) {
        self.title = @"First";
    }
    return self;

}

- (void)viewDidLoad{
    [super viewDidLoad];
    self.view.backgroundColor = [UIColor whiteColor];
}
```

And for the second view controller, we pick the title *Second*:

```
#import "SecondViewController.h"

@implementation SecondViewController

- (id)initWithNibName:(NSString *)nibNameOrNil
               bundle:(NSBundle *)nibBundleOrNil{

    self = [super initWithNibName:nibNameOrNil
                           bundle:nibBundleOrNil];
    if (self != nil) {
        self.title = @"Second";
    }
    return self;

}

- (void)viewDidLoad{
    [super viewDidLoad];
    self.view.backgroundColor = [UIColor whiteColor];
}
```

Now let's run our app and see what happens (Figure 1-42).

*Figure 1-42. A very simple tab bar populated with two view controllers*

You can see that our view controllers do *not* have a navigation bar. What should we do? It's easy. Remember that a `UINavigationController` is actually a subclass of `UIViewController`. So we can add instances of navigation controllers to a tab bar, and inside each navigation controller, we can load a view controller. What are we waiting for, then?

```
- (BOOL)            application:(UIApplication *)application
  didFinishLaunchingWithOptions:(NSDictionary *)launchOptions{

    // Override point for customization after application launch.
    self.window = [[UIWindow alloc] initWithFrame:
                  [[UIScreen mainScreen] bounds]];

    [self.window makeKeyAndVisible];

    FirstViewController *firstViewController = [[FirstViewController alloc]
```

```
                                                        initWithNibName:nil
                                                        bundle:NULL];

    UINavigationController *firstNavigationController =
        [[UINavigationController alloc]
         initWithRootViewController:firstViewController];

    SecondViewController *secondViewController = [[SecondViewController alloc]
                                                  initWithNibName:nil
                                                  bundle:NULL];

    UINavigationController *secondNavigationController =
        [[UINavigationController alloc]
         initWithRootViewController:secondViewController];

    UITabBarController *tabBarController = [[UITabBarController alloc] init];

    [tabBarController setViewControllers:
        @[firstNavigationController, secondNavigationController]];

    self.window.rootViewController = tabBarController;

    return YES;

}
```

And the results? Exactly what we wanted (Figure 1-43).

As we can see in Figure 1-38, each tab bar item can have text and an image. We've learned that, using the `title` property of a view controller, we can specify this text, but what about the image? It turns out that every view controller has a property called `tabItem`. This property is the tab item for the current view controller, and you can use this property to set the image of the tab bar item through the `image` property of the tab item. I've already designed two images, a rectangle and a circle. I'm going to display them as the tab bar item image for each of my view controllers. Here is code for the first view controller:

```
- (id)initWithNibName:(NSString *)nibNameOrNil
               bundle:(NSBundle *)nibBundleOrNil{

    self = [super initWithNibName:nibNameOrNil
                           bundle:nibBundleOrNil];
    if (self != nil) {
        self.title = @"First";
        self.tabBarItem.image = [UIImage imageNamed:@"FirstTab"];
    }
    return self;

}

- (void)viewDidLoad{
```

```
    [super viewDidLoad];
    self.view.backgroundColor = [UIColor whiteColor];
}
```

And here it is for the second view controller:

```
- (id)initWithNibName:(NSString *)nibNameOrNil
               bundle:(NSBundle *)nibBundleOrNil{

    self = [super initWithNibName:nibNameOrNil
                           bundle:nibBundleOrNil];
    if (self != nil) {
        self.title = @"Second";
        self.tabBarItem.image = [UIImage imageNamed:@"SecondTab"];
    }
    return self;

}

- (void)viewDidLoad{
    [super viewDidLoad];
    self.view.backgroundColor = [UIColor whiteColor];
}
```

Running the app in the simulator, we will see that the images are displayed properly (Figure 1-44).

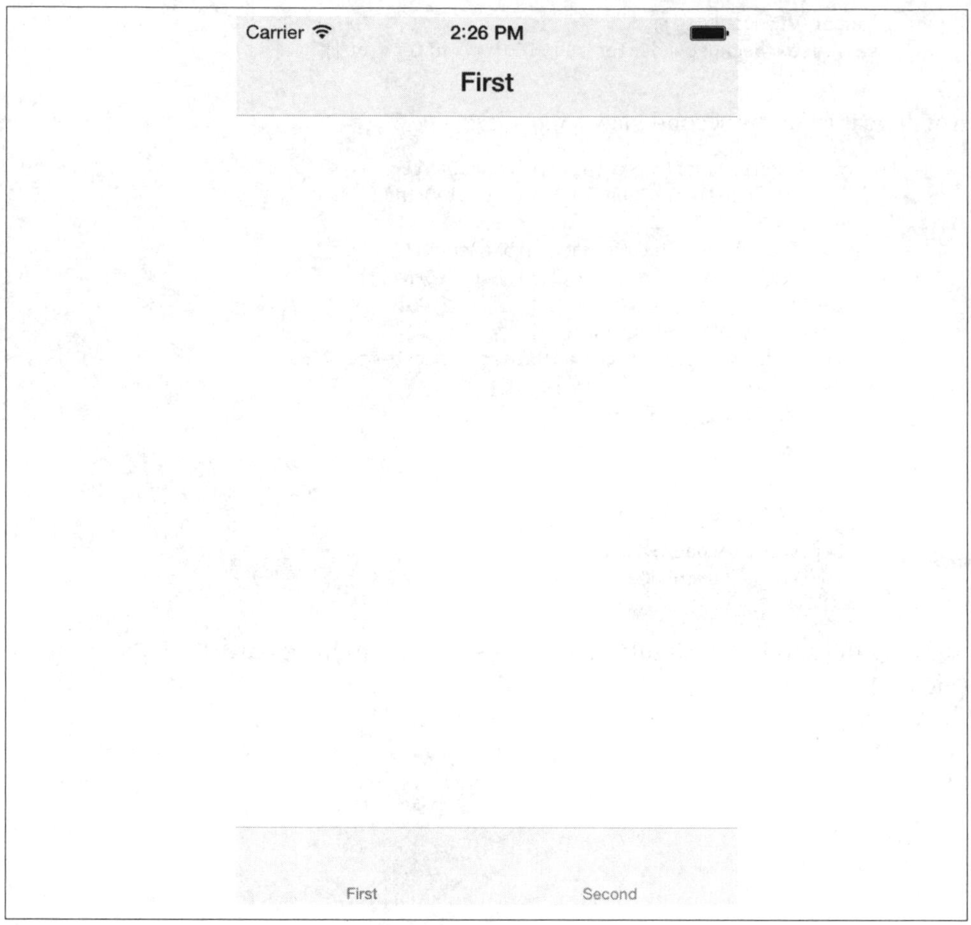


*Figure 1-43. A tab bar displaying view controllers inside navigation controllers*

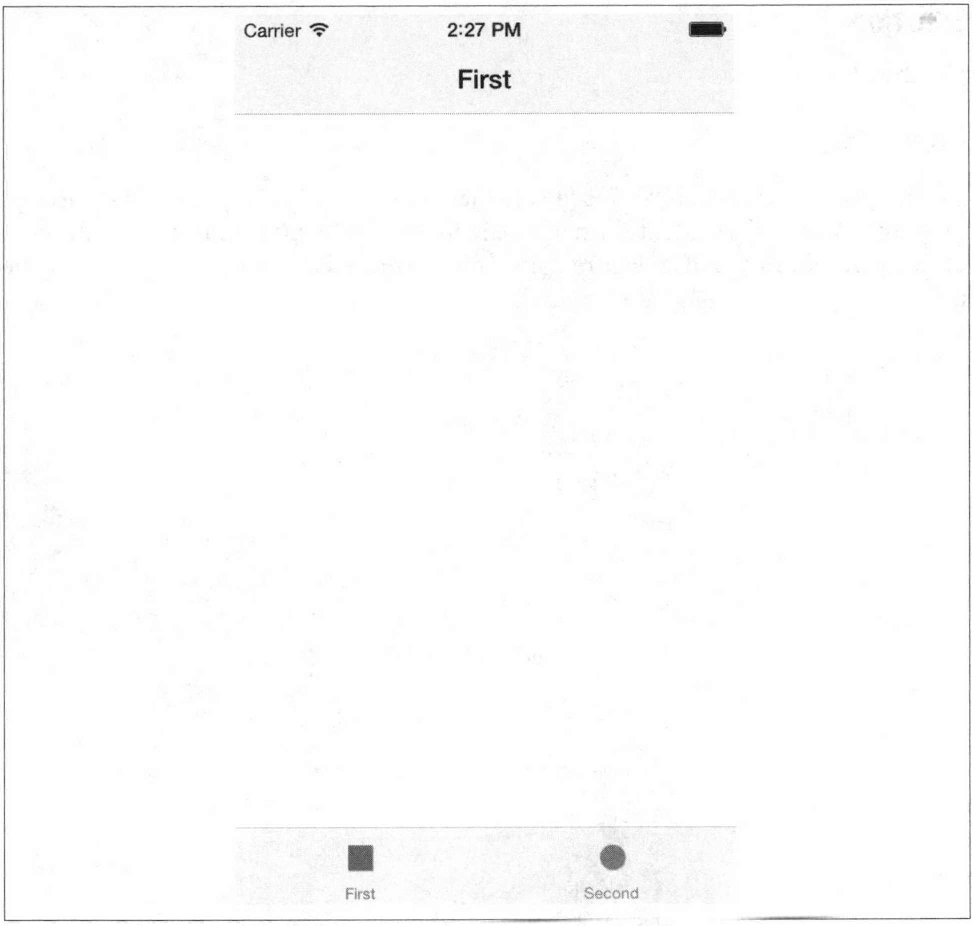

*Figure 1-44. Tab bar items with images*

## 1.17. Displaying Static Text with UILabel

### Problem

You want to display text to your users. You would also like to control the text's font and color.

Static text is text that is not directly changeable by the user at runtime.

## Solution

Use the `UILabel` class.

## Discussion

Labels are everywhere in iOS. You can see them in practically every application, except for games, where the content is usually rendered with OpenGL ES instead of the core drawing frameworks in iOS. Figure 1-45 shows several labels in the Settings app on the iPhone.

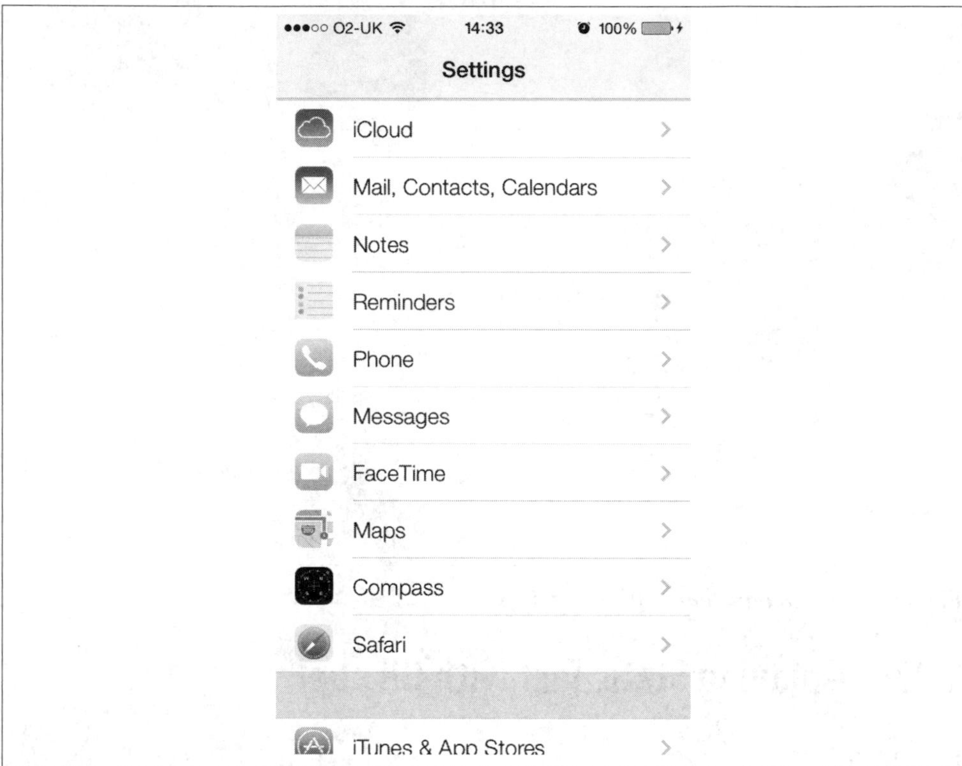


*Figure 1-45. Labels as titles of each one of the settings*

You can see that the labels are displaying text in the Settings app, such as "iCloud," "Phone," "FaceTime," "Safari," etc.

To create a label, instantiate an object of type `UILabel`. Setting or getting the text of a label can be done through its `text` property. So let's first define a label in our view controller's implementation file:

```
#import "ViewController.h"

@interface ViewController ()
@property (nonatomic, strong) UILabel *myLabel;
@end

@implementation ViewController

...
```

Now in the `viewDidLoad` method, instantiate the label and tell the runtime where the label has to be positioned (through its frame property) on the view to which it will be added (in this case, our view controller's view):

```
- (void)viewDidLoad{
    [super viewDidLoad];

    CGRect labelFrame = CGRectMake(0.0f,
                                   0.0f,
                                   100.0f,
                                   23.0f);
    self.myLabel = [[UILabel alloc] initWithFrame:labelFrame];
    self.myLabel.text = @"iOS 7 Programming Cookbook";
    self.myLabel.font = [UIFont boldSystemFontOfSize:14.0f];
    self.myLabel.center = self.view.center;
    [self.view addSubview:self.myLabel];

}
```

Now let's run our app and see what happens (see Figure 1-46).

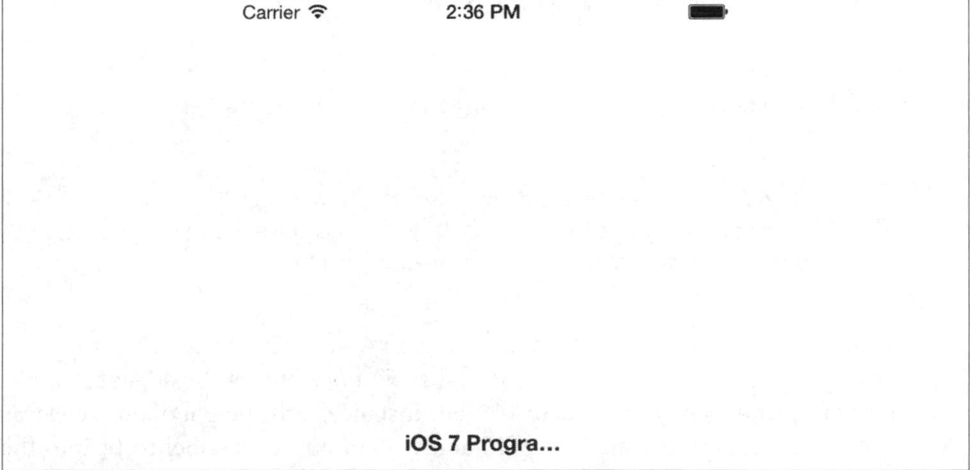


*Figure 1-46. A label that is too small in width to contain its contents*

You can see that the contents of the label are truncated, with a trailing ellipsis, because the width of the label isn't enough to contain the whole contents. One solution would be to make the width longer, but how about the height? What if we wanted the text to wrap to the next line? OK, go ahead and change the height from `23.0f` to `50.0f`:

```
CGRect labelFrame = CGRectMake(0.0f,
                               0.0f,
                               100.0f,
                               50.0f);
```

If you run your app now, you will get *exactly* the same results that you got in Figure 1-46. You might ask, "I increased the height, so why didn't the content wrap to the next line?" It turns out that the `UILabel` class has a property called `numberOfLines` that needs to be adjusted to the number of lines the label has to wrap the text to, in case it runs out of horizontal space. If you set this value to 3, it tells the label that you want the text to wrap to a maximum of three lines if it cannot fit the text into one line:

```
- (void)viewDidLoad{
    [super viewDidLoad];

    CGRect labelFrame = CGRectMake(0.0f,
                                   0.0f,
                                   100.0f,
                                   70.0f);
    self.myLabel = [[UILabel alloc] initWithFrame:labelFrame];
    self.myLabel.numberOfLines = 3;
    self.myLabel.lineBreakMode = NSLineBreakByWordWrapping;
    self.myLabel.text = @"iOS 7 Programming Cookbook";
    self.myLabel.font = [UIFont boldSystemFontOfSize:14.0f];
    self.myLabel.center = self.view.center;
    [self.view addSubview:self.myLabel];

}
```

If you run the app now, you will get the desired results (see Figure 1-47).

In some situations, you might not know how many lines are required to display a certain text in a label. In those instances, you need to set the `numberOfLines` property of your label to 0.

If you want your label's frame to stay static and you want the font inside your label to adjust itself to fit into the boundaries of the label, you need to set the `adjustsFontSizeToFitWidth` property of your label to `YES`. For instance, if the height of our label was `23.0f`, as we see in Figure 1-46, we could adjust the font of the label to fit into the boundaries. Here is how it works:

```
- (void)viewDidLoad{
    [super viewDidLoad];
```

```
    CGRect labelFrame = CGRectMake(0.0f,
                                   0.0f,
                                   100.0f,
                                   23.0f);
    self.myLabel = [[UILabel alloc] initWithFrame:labelFrame];
    self.myLabel.adjustsFontSizeToFitWidth = YES;
    self.myLabel.text = @"iOS 7 Programming Cookbook";
    self.myLabel.font = [UIFont boldSystemFontOfSize:14.0f];
    self.myLabel.center = self.view.center;
    [self.view addSubview:self.myLabel];

}
```

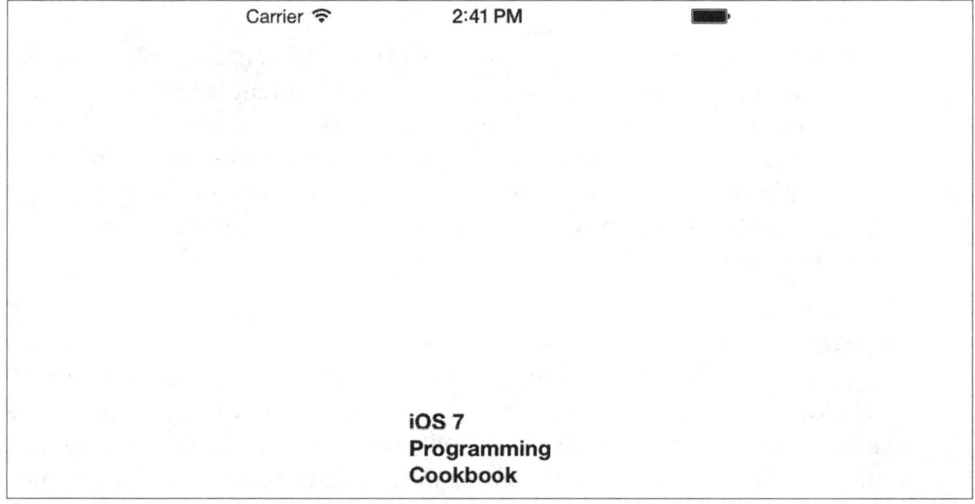


*Figure 1-47. A label wrapping its contents to three lines*

# 1.18. Customizing the UILabel

## Problem

You want to be able to customize the appearance of your labels, from shadow settings to alignment settings.

## Solution

Use the following properties of the `UILabel` class, depending on your requirements:

`shadowColor`
: This property is of type `UIColor` and, as its name shows, it specifies the color of the drop shadow to render for your label. If you are setting this property, you should also set the `shadowOffset` property.

`shadowOffset`
: This property is of type `CGSize`, and it specifies the offset of the drop shadow from the text. For instance, if you set this property to (1, 0), the drop shadow will appear 1 point to the right of the text. If you set this property to (1, 2), the drop shadow will appear 1 point to the right and 2 points down from the text. If you set this property to (–2, –10), the drop shadow will render 2 points to the left and 10 points above the text.

`numberOfLines`
: This property is an integer that specifies how many lines of text the label is able to render. By default, this property's value is set to 1, meaning any label that you create by default can handle 1 line of text. If you want 2 lines of text, for instance, set this property to 2. If you want unlimited lines of text to be rendered in your text field or you simply don't know how many lines of text you will end up displaying, set this property to 0. (I know, it's really strange. Instead of `NSIntegerMax` or something similar, Apple has decided that 0 means unlimited!)

`lineBreakMode`
: This property is of type `NSLineBreakMode` and specifies how you want to line-wrap the text inside your text field. For instance, if you set this property to `NSLineBreakByWordWrapping`, words will be kept together, but the string will be wrapped to the next line if there is not enough space to display it. Alternatively, if you set this property to `NSLineBreakByCharWrapping`, words may be broken across lines when text is wrapped. You would probably use `NSLineBreakByCharWrapping` only if the space is very tight and you need to fit as much information as possible on the screen. I personally do not recommend using this option if you want to keep a consistent and clear user interface.

`textAlignment`
: This property is of type `NSTextAlignment` and sets the horizontal alignment of the text in your label. For instance, you can set the value of this property to `NSTextAlignmentCenter` to horizontally center-align your text.

`textColor`
: This property is of type `UIColor` and defines the color of the text inside the label.

`font`
: This property of type `UIFont` specifies the font with which the text inside your label will get rendered.

`adjustsFontSizeToFitWidth`
: This property is of type `BOOL`. When set to `YES`, it will change the size of the font to fit your label. For instance, if you have a small label and the text you are trying to set in it is too big to fit, if this property is set to `YES`, the runtime will automatically reduce the font size of your label to make sure the text will fit into the label. In contrast, if this property is set to `NO`, the current line/word/character wrapping option is taken into account and your text will be rendered in an incomplete manner with just a few words being displayed.

## Discussion

Labels are one of the easiest UI components we can utilize in our applications. Although labels are simple, they are really powerful. Customization of labels is therefore very important in order to deliver the best user experience. For this reason, Apple has given us plenty of ways to customize the instances of `UILabel`. Let us have a look at an example. We'll create a simple single-view application with one view controller, place a simple label at the center of the screen with a huge font, and write "iOS SDK" in it. We will set the background color of our view to white, the text color of our label to black, and the shadow color of our label to light gray. We will make sure a drop shadow appears at the bottom-right side of our label. Figure 1-48 shows the effect our app should produce.

And here is our code to achieve this:

```
#import "ViewController.h"

@interface ViewController ()
@property (nonatomic, strong) UILabel *label;
@end

@implementation ViewController

- (void)viewDidLoad{
    [super viewDidLoad];

    self.label = [[UILabel alloc] init];
    self.label.backgroundColor = [UIColor clearColor];
    self.label.text = @"iOS SDK";
    self.label.font = [UIFont boldSystemFontOfSize:70.0f];
    self.label.textColor = [UIColor blackColor];
    self.label.shadowColor = [UIColor lightGrayColor];
    self.label.shadowOffset = CGSizeMake(2.0f, 2.0f);
    [self.label sizeToFit];
    self.label.center = self.view.center;
    [self.view addSubview:self.label];

}

@end
```

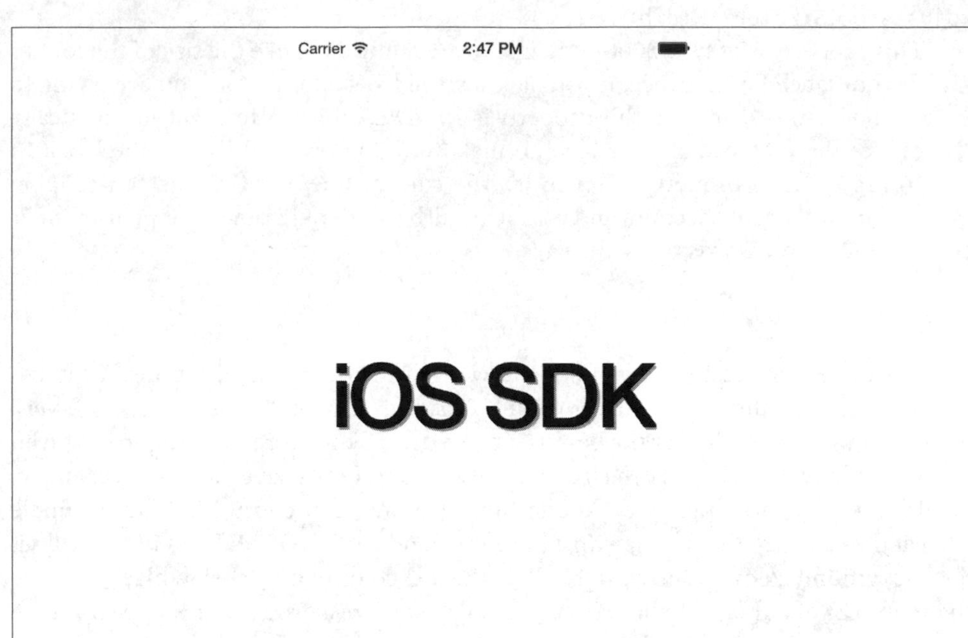


*Figure 1-48. How our label is customized and rendered on the screen*

## See Also

Recipe 1.17; Recipe 1.26

# 1.19. Accepting User Text Input with UITextField

## Problem

You want to accept text input in your user interface.

## Solution

Use the `UITextField` class.

## Discussion

A text field is very much like a label in that it can display text, but a text field can also accept text entry at runtime. Figure 1-49 shows two text fields in the Twitter section of the Settings app on an iPhone.

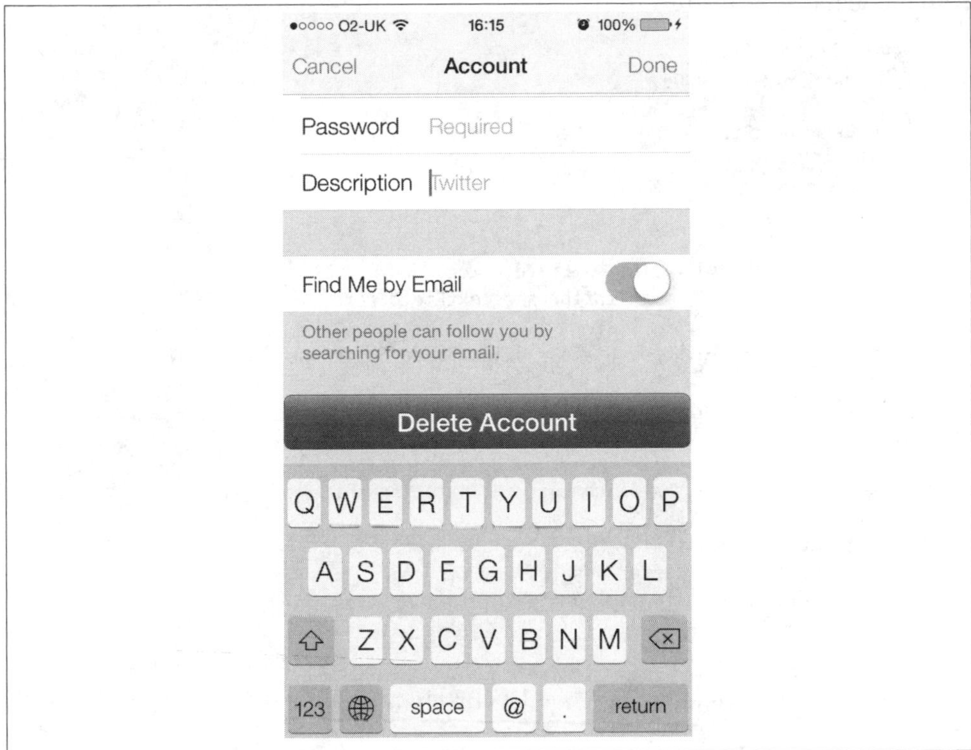


*Figure 1-49. Text fields allowing text entry*

A text field allows only a single line of text to be input/displayed. As a result, the default height of a text field is only 31 points. In Interface Builder, this height cannot be modified, but if you are creating your text field in code, you can change the text field's height. A change in height, though, will *not* change the number of lines you can render in a text field, which is always 1.

Let's start with the implementation file of our view controller to define our text field:

```
#import "ViewController.h"

@interface ViewController ()
```

```
@property (nonatomic, strong) UITextField *myTextField;
@end

@implementation ViewController

...
```

And then let's create the text field:

```
- (void)viewDidLoad{
    [super viewDidLoad];

    CGRect textFieldFrame = CGRectMake(0.0f,
                                       0.0f,
                                       200.0f,
                                       31.0f);

    self.myTextField = [[UITextField alloc]
                        initWithFrame:textFieldFrame];

    self.myTextField.borderStyle = UITextBorderStyleRoundedRect;

    self.myTextField.contentVerticalAlignment =
    UIControlContentVerticalAlignmentCenter;

    self.myTextField.textAlignment = NSTextAlignmentCenter;

    self.myTextField.text = @"Sir Richard Branson";
    self.myTextField.center = self.view.center;
    [self.view addSubview:self.myTextField];

}
```

Before looking at the details of the code, let's first have a look at the results (Figure 1-50).

*Figure 1-50. A simple text field with center aligned text*

In order to create this text field, we used various properties of `UITextField`.

`borderStyle`
: This property is of type `UITextBorderStyle` and specifies how the text field should render its borders.

`contentVerticalAlignment`
: This value is of type `UIControlContentVerticalAlignment` and tells the text field how the text should appear, vertically, in the boundaries of the control. If we didn't center the text vertically, it would appear on the top-left corner of the text field by default.

`textAlignment`
: This property is of type `NSTextAlignment` and specifies the horizontal alignment of the text in a text field. In this example, we have centered the text horizontally.

`text`
: This is a read/write property: you can both read from it and write to it. Reading from it will return the text field's current text, and writing to it will set the text field's text to the value that you specify.

A text field sends delegate messages to its delegate object. These messages get sent, for instance, when the user starts editing the text inside a text field, when the user enters any character into the text field (changing its contents in any way), and when the user finishes editing the field (by leaving the field). To get notified of these events, set the `delegate` property of the text field to your object. The delegate of a text field must conform to the `UITextFieldDelegate` protocol, so let's first take care of this:

```
@interface ViewController () <UITextFieldDelegate>
@property (nonatomic, strong) UITextField *myTextField;
@end

@implementation ViewController
```

Hold down the Command key on your computer and click the `UITextFieldDelegate` protocol in Xcode. You will see all the methods that this protocol gives you control over. Here are those methods with descriptions of when they get called:

`textFieldShouldBeginEditing:`
: A method that returns a `BOOL` telling the text field (the parameter to this method) whether it should start getting edited by the user or not. Return `NO` if you don't want the user to edit your text field. This method gets fired as soon as the user taps on the text field with the goal of editing its content (assuming the text field allows editing).

`textFieldDidBeginEditing:`
: Gets called when the text field starts to get edited by the user. This method gets called when the user has already tapped on the text field and the `textFieldShould`

`BeginEditing:` delegate method of the text field returned `YES`, telling the text field it is OK for the user to edit the content of the text field.

`textFieldShouldEndEditing:`
: Returns a `BOOL` telling the text field whether it should end its current editing session or not. This method gets called when the user is about to leave the text field or the first responder is switching to another data entry field. If you return `NO` from this method, the user will not be able to switch to another text entry field, and the keyboard will stay on the screen.

`textFieldDidEndEditing:`
: Gets called when the editing session of the text field ends. This happens when the user decides to edit some other data entry field or uses a button provided by the supplier of the app to dismiss the keyboard shown for the text field.

`textField:shouldChangeCharactersInRange:replacementString:`
: Gets called whenever the text inside the text field is modified. The return value of this method is a Boolean. If you return `YES`, you say that you allow the text to be changed. If you return `NO`, the change in the text of the text field will *not* be confirmed and will not happen.

`textFieldShouldClear:`
: Each text field has a *clear* button that is usually a circular X button. When the user presses this button, the contents of the text field will automatically get erased. We need to manually enable the clear button, though. If you have enabled the clear button and you return `NO` to this method, that gives the user the impression that your app isn't working, so make sure you know what you are doing. It is a very poor user experience if the user sees a clear button and presses it but doesn't see the text in the text field get erased.

`textFieldShouldReturn:`
: Gets called when the user has pressed the Return/Enter key on the keyboard, trying to dismiss the keyboard. You should assign the text field as the first responder in this method.

Let's mix this recipe with Recipe 1.17 and create a dynamic text label under our text field. We'll also display the total number of characters entered in our text field in the label. Let's start with our implementation file:

```
@interface ViewController () <UITextFieldDelegate>
@property (nonatomic, strong) UITextField *myTextField;
@property (nonatomic, strong) UILabel *labelCounter;
@end

@implementation ViewController
```

Now for the creation of the text field along with the label and the text field delegate methods we require. We skip implementing many of the `UITextFieldDelegate` methods, because we don't need all of them in this example:

```
- (void) calculateAndDisplayTextFieldLengthWithText:(NSString *)paramText{

    NSString *characterOrCharacters = @"Characters";
    if ([paramText length] == 1){
        characterOrCharacters = @"Character";
    }

    self.labelCounter.text = [NSString stringWithFormat:@"%lu %@",
                              (unsigned long)[paramText length],
                              characterOrCharacters];
}

- (BOOL)                textField:(UITextField *)textField
    shouldChangeCharactersInRange:(NSRange)range
                replacementString:(NSString *)string{

    if ([textField isEqual:self.myTextField]){
        NSString *wholeText =
        [textField.text stringByReplacingCharactersInRange:range
                                                withString:string];
        [self calculateAndDisplayTextFieldLengthWithText:wholeText];
    }

    return YES;

}

- (BOOL)textFieldShouldReturn:(UITextField *)textField{
    [textField resignFirstResponder];
    return YES;
}

- (void)viewDidLoad{
    [super viewDidLoad];

    CGRect textFieldFrame = CGRectMake(38.0f,
                                       30.0f,
                                       220.0f,
                                       31.0f);

    self.myTextField = [[UITextField alloc]
                        initWithFrame:textFieldFrame];

    self.myTextField.delegate = self;

    self.myTextField.borderStyle = UITextBorderStyleRoundedRect;

    self.myTextField.contentVerticalAlignment =
```

```
        UIControlContentVerticalAlignmentCenter;

    self.myTextField.textAlignment = NSTextAlignmentCenter;

    self.myTextField.text = @"Sir Richard Branson";

    [self.view addSubview:self.myTextField];

    CGRect labelCounterFrame = self.myTextField.frame;
    labelCounterFrame.origin.y += textFieldFrame.size.height + 10;
    self.labelCounter = [[UILabel alloc] initWithFrame:labelCounterFrame];
    [self.view addSubview:self.labelCounter];

    [self calculateAndDisplayTextFieldLengthWithText:self.myTextField.text];

}
```

One important calculation we are doing is in the `textField:shouldChangeCharactersInRange:replacementString:` method. There, we declare and use a variable called `wholeText`. When this method gets called, the `replacementString` parameter specifies the string that the user has entered into the text field. You might be thinking that the user can enter only one character at a time, so why can't this field be a `char`? But don't forget that the user can paste a whole chunk of text into a text field, so this parameter needs to be a string. The `shouldChangeCharactersInRange` parameter specifies where, in terms of location inside the text field's text, the user is entering the text. So using these two parameters, we will create a string that first reads the whole text inside the text field and then uses the given range to place the new text inside the old text. With this, we will come up with the text that will appear in the text field *after* the `textField:shouldChangeCharactersInRange:replacementString:` method returns `YES`. Figure 1-51 shows how our app looks when it gets run on the simulator.

In addition to displaying text, a text field can also display a *placeholder*. A placeholder is the text displayed *before* the user has entered any text in the text field, while the text field's text property is empty. This can be any string that you wish, and setting it will help give the user an indication as to what this text field is for. Many use this placeholder to tell the user what type of value she can enter in that text field. For instance, in Figure 1-49, the two text fields (password and description) have placeholders that say "Required," etc. You can use the `placeholder` property of the text field to set or get the current placeholder. Here is an example:

```
CGRect textFieldFrame = CGRectMake(38.0f,
                                   30.0f,
                                   220.0f,
                                   31.0f);

self.myTextField = [[UITextField alloc]
                    initWithFrame:textFieldFrame];

self.myTextField.delegate = self;
```

```
self.myTextField.borderStyle = UITextBorderStyleRoundedRect;

self.myTextField.contentVerticalAlignment =
    UIControlContentVerticalAlignmentCenter;

self.myTextField.textAlignment = NSTextAlignmentCenter;

self.myTextField.placeholder = @"Enter text here...";
[self.view addSubview:self.myTextField];
```

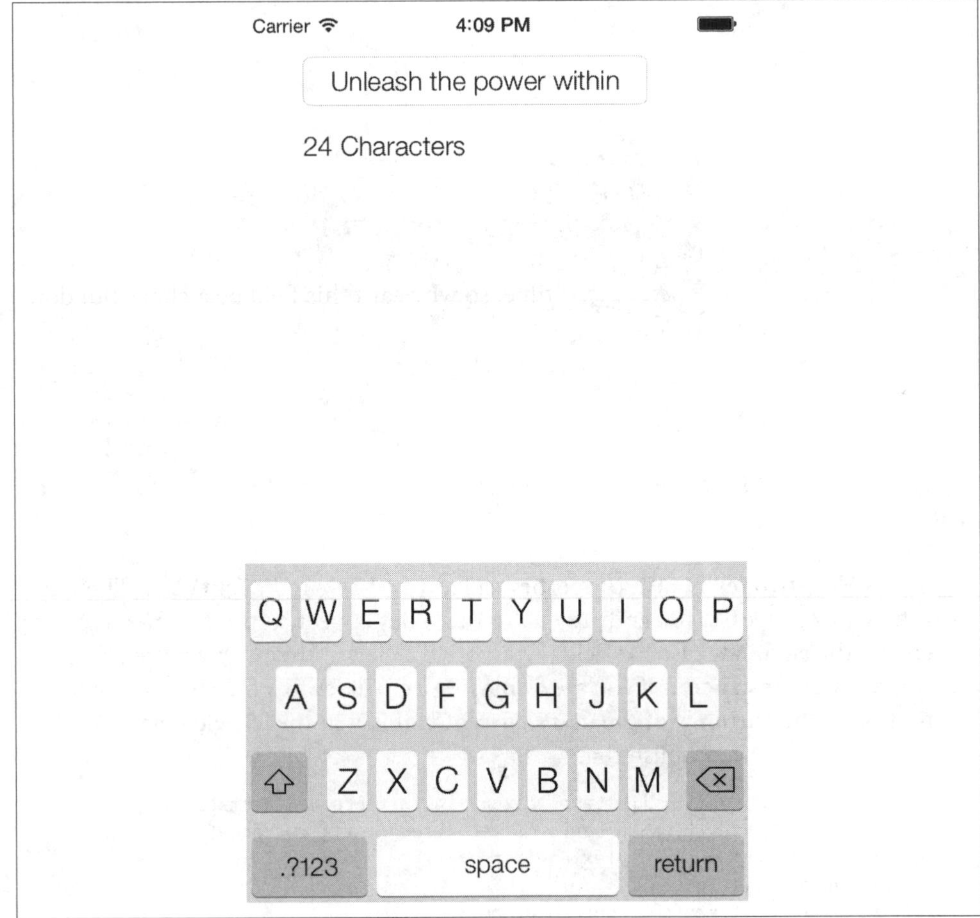


*Figure 1-51. Responding to delegate messages of a text field*

The results are shown in Figure 1-52.

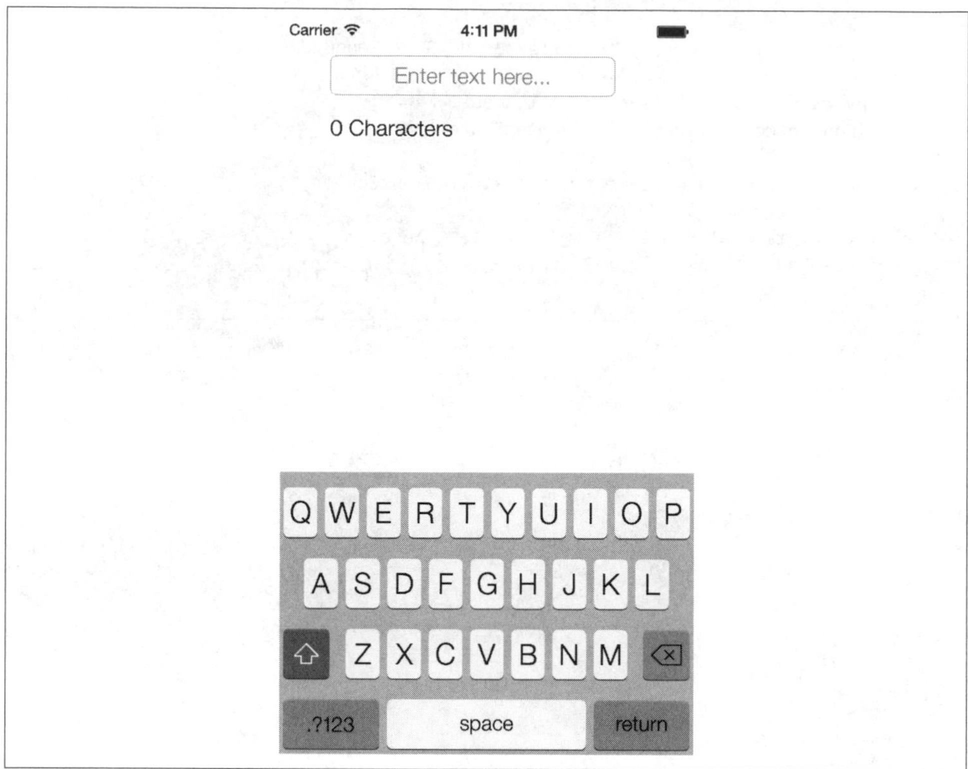


*Figure 1-52. A placeholder is shown when the user has not entered any text in a text field*

Text fields have two really neat properties called `leftView` and `rightView`. These two properties are of type `UIView` and are read/write. They appear, as their names imply, on the left and the right side of a text field if you assign a view to them. One place you might use a left view, for instance, is if you are displaying a currency text field where you would like to display the currency of the user's current country in the left view, as a `UILabel`. Here is how we can accomplish that:

```
UILabel *currencyLabel = [[UILabel alloc] initWithFrame:CGRectZero];
currencyLabel.text = [[[NSNumberFormatter alloc] init] currencySymbol];
currencyLabel.font = self.myTextField.font;
[currencyLabel sizeToFit];
self.myTextField.leftView = currencyLabel;
self.myTextField.leftViewMode = UITextFieldViewModeAlways;
```

If we simply assign a view to the `leftView` or to the `rightView` properties of a text field, those views will not appear automatically by default. When they show up on the screen depends on the mode that governs their appearance, and you can control that mode using the `leftViewMode` and `rightViewMode` properties, respectively. These modes are of type `UITextFieldViewMode`:

```
typedef NS_ENUM(NSInteger, UITextFieldViewMode) {
    UITextFieldViewModeNever,
    UITextFieldViewModeWhileEditing,
    UITextFieldViewModeUnlessEditing,
    UITextFieldViewModeAlways
};
```

So if, for instance, you set the left view mode to `UITextFieldViewModeWhileEditing` and assign a value to it, it will appear only while the user is editing the text field. Conversely, if you set this value to `UITextFieldViewModeUnlessEditing`, the left view will appear only while the user is *not* editing the text field. As soon as editing starts, the left view will disappear. Let's have a look at our code now in the simulator (Figure 1-53).

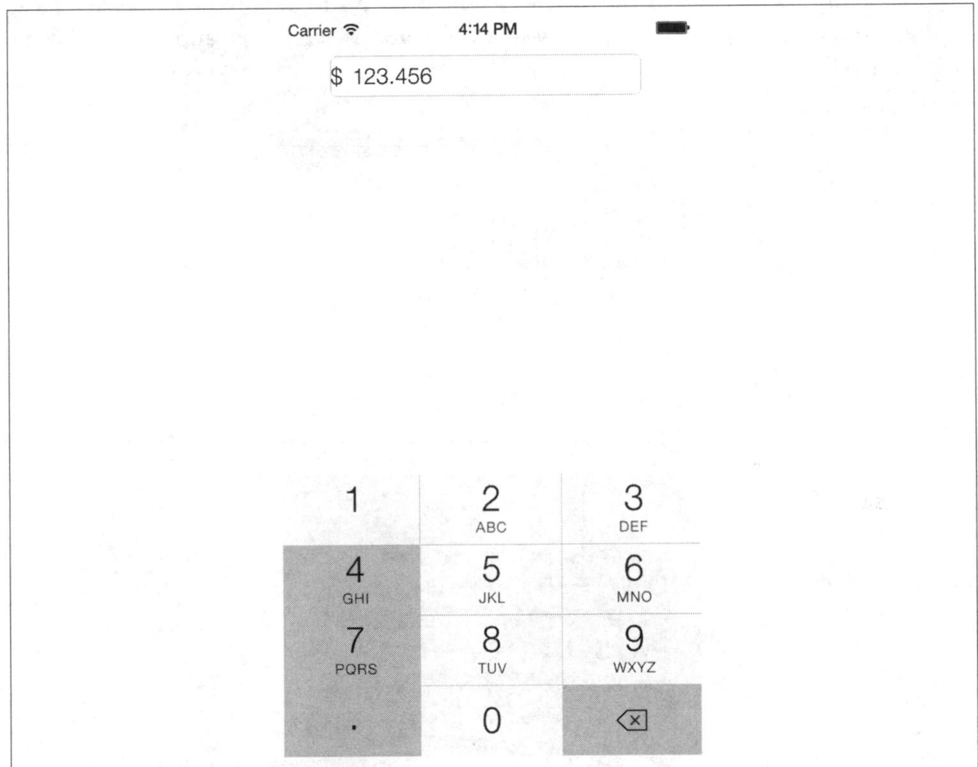


*Figure 1-53. A text field with a left view*

## See Also

Recipe 1.17

# 1.20. Displaying Long Lines of Text with UITextView

## Problem

You want to display multiple lines of text in your UI inside one scrollable view.

## Solution

Use the `UITextView` class.

## Discussion

The `UITextView` class can display multiple lines of text and contain scrollable content, meaning that if the contents run off the boundaries of the text view, the text view's internal components allow the user to scroll the text up and down to see different parts of the text. An example of a text view in an iOS app is the Notes app on the iPhone (Figure 1-54).

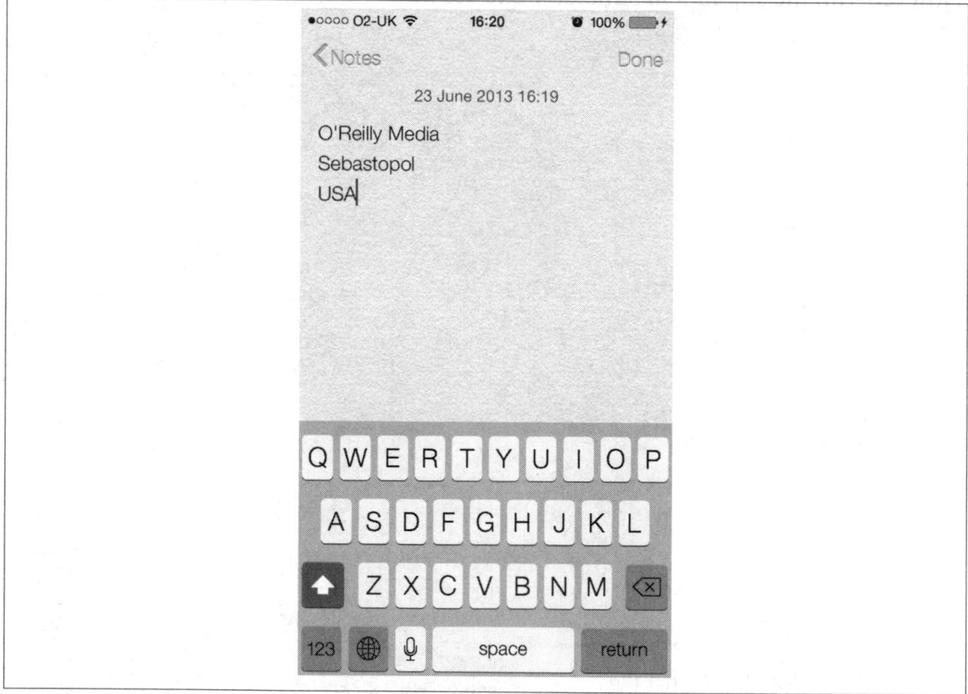


*Figure 1-54. The Notes app on the iPhone uses a text view to render text*

Let's create a text view and see how it works. We start off by declaring the text view in our view controller's implementation file:

```
#import "ViewController.h"

@interface ViewController ()
@property (nonatomic, strong) UITextView *myTextView;
@end

@implementation ViewController
```

Now it's time to create the text view itself. We will make the text view as big as the view controller's view:

```
- (void)viewDidLoad{
    [super viewDidLoad];

    self.myTextView = [[UITextView alloc] initWithFrame:self.view.bounds];
    self.myTextView.text = @"Some text here...";
    self.myTextView.contentInset = UIEdgeInsetsMake(10.0f, 0.0f, 0.0f, 0.0f);
    self.myTextView.font = [UIFont systemFontOfSize:16.0f];
    [self.view addSubview:self.myTextView];

}
```

Now let's run the app in iOS Simulator and see how it looks (Figure 1-55).

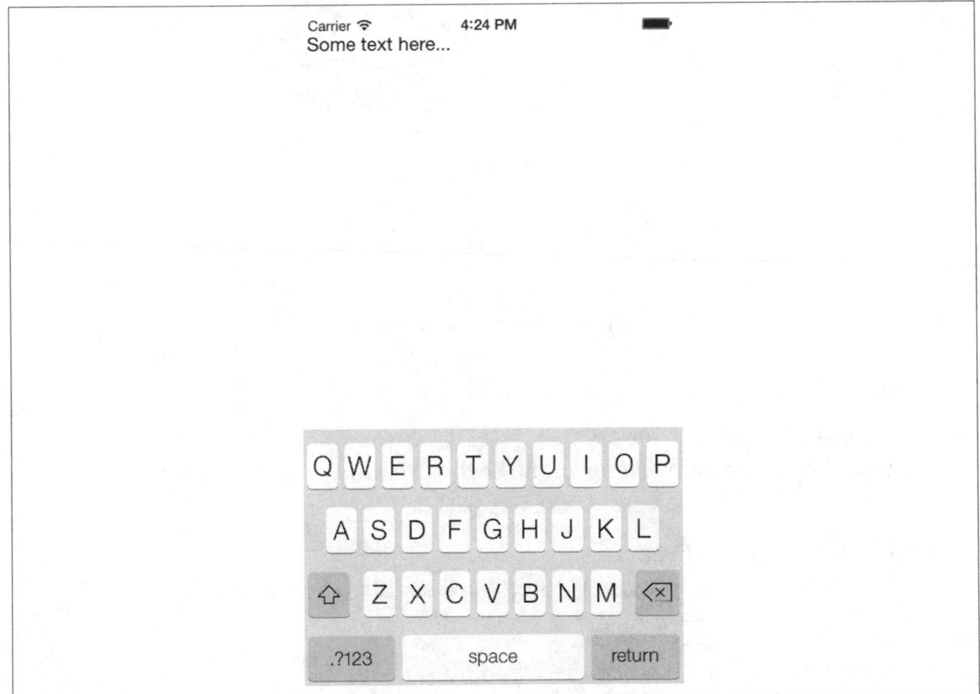


*Figure 1-55. A text view consuming the entire boundary of the screen*

If you tap on the text field, you will notice a keyboard pop up from the bottom of the screen, concealing almost half the entire area of the text view. That means if the user starts typing text and gets to the middle of the text view, the rest of the text that she types will *not* be visible to her (Figure 1-56).

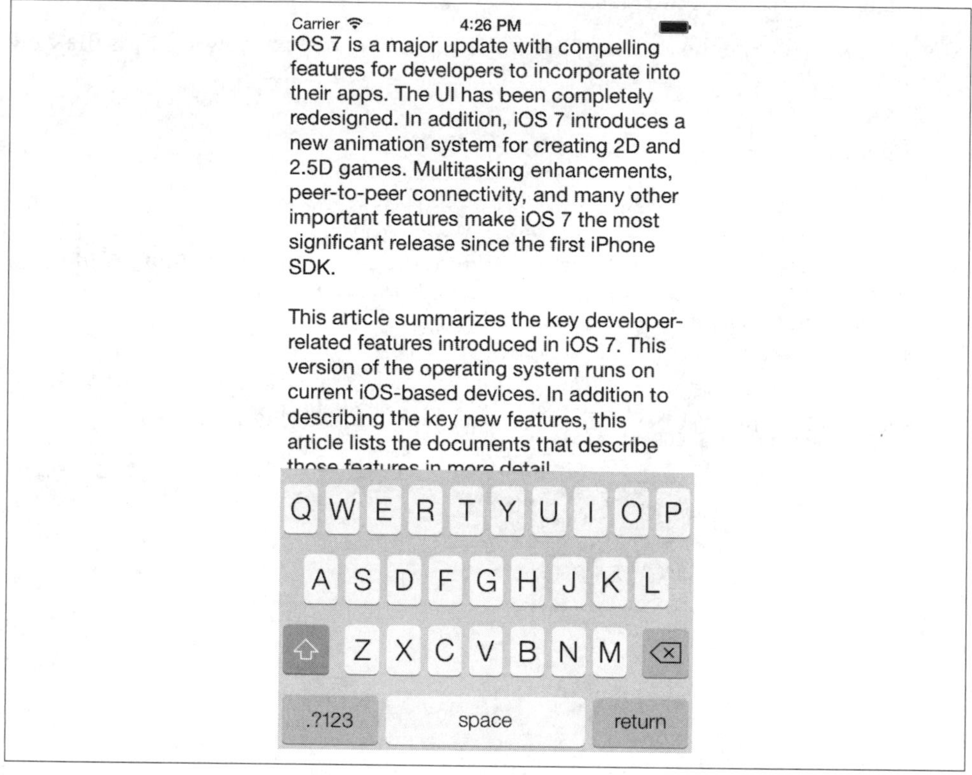


*Figure 1-56. Keyboard concealing half the size of a text view*

To remedy this, we have to listen for certain notifications:

`UIKeyboardWillShowNotification`
: Gets sent by the system whenever the keyboard is brought up on the screen for any component, be it a text field, a text view, etc.

`UIKeyboardDidShowNotification`
: Gets sent by the system when the keyboard has already been displayed.

`UIKeyboardWillHideNotification`
: Gets sent by the system when the keyboard is about to hide.

`UIKeyboardDidHideNotification`
: Gets sent by the system when the keyboard is now fully hidden.

The keyboard notifications contain a dictionary, accessible through the `userInfo` property, that specifies the boundaries of the keyboard on the screen. This property is of type `NSDictionary`. One of the keys in this dictionary is `UIKeyboardFrameEndUserInfoKey`, which contains an object of type `NSValue` that itself contains the rectangular boundaries of the keyboard when it is fully shown. This rectangular area is denoted with a `CGRect`.

So our strategy is to find out when the keyboard is getting displayed and then somehow resize our text view. For this, we will use the `contentInset` property of `UITextView` to specify the margins of contents in the text view from top, left, bottom, and right:

```
- (void) handleKeyboardDidShow:(NSNotification *)paramNotification{

    /* Get the frame of the keyboard */
    NSValue *keyboardRectAsObject =
    [[paramNotification userInfo]
     objectForKey:UIKeyboardFrameEndUserInfoKey];

    /* Place it in a CGRect */
    CGRect keyboardRect = CGRectZero;

    [keyboardRectAsObject getValue:&keyboardRect];

    /* Give a bottom margin to our text view that makes it
     reach to the top of the keyboard */
    self.myTextView.contentInset =
    UIEdgeInsetsMake(0.0f,
                     0.0f,
                     keyboardRect.size.height,
                     0.0f);
}

- (void) handleKeyboardWillHide:(NSNotification *)paramNotification{
    /* Make the text view as big as the whole view again */
    self.myTextView.contentInset = UIEdgeInsetsZero;
}

- (void) viewWillAppear:(BOOL)paramAnimated{
    [super viewWillAppear:paramAnimated];

    [[NSNotificationCenter defaultCenter]
     addObserver:self
     selector:@selector(handleKeyboardDidShow:)
     name:UIKeyboardDidShowNotification
     object:nil];

    [[NSNotificationCenter defaultCenter]
     addObserver:self
```

```
                selector:@selector(handleKeyboardWillHide:)
                name:UIKeyboardWillHideNotification
                object:nil];

    self.myTextView = [[UITextView alloc] initWithFrame:self.view.bounds];
    self.myTextView.text = @"Some text here...";
    self.myTextView.font = [UIFont systemFontOfSize:16.0f];
    [self.view addSubview:self.myTextView];

}

- (void) viewWillDisappear:(BOOL)paramAnimated{
    [super viewWillDisappear:paramAnimated];

    [[NSNotificationCenter defaultCenter] removeObserver:self];
}
```

In this code, we start looking for keyboard notifications in `viewWillAppear:` and we stop listening to keyboard notifications in `viewWillDisappear:`. Removing your view controller as the listener is important, because when your view controller is no longer displayed, you probably don't want to receive keyboard notifications fired by any other view controller. There may be times when a view controller in the background needs to receive notifications, but these are rare, and you must normally make sure to stop listening for notifications in `viewWillDisappear:`. I've seen many programmers break their apps by not taking care of this simple logic.

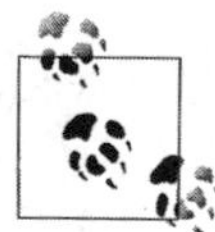

> If you intend to change your UI structure when the keyboard gets displayed and when the keyboard is dismissed, the only method that you can rely on is to use the keyboard notifications. Delegate messages of `UITextField` get fired when the text field is getting edited, whether there is a soft keyboard on the screen or not. Remember, a user can have a Bluetooth keyboard connected to his iOS device and use it to edit the content of text fields and any other data entry in your apps. In the case of a Bluetooth keyboard, no soft keyboard will be displayed on the screen—and if you change your UI when your text fields start to get edited, you might unnecessarily change the UI while the Bluetooth keyboard user is editing text.

Now, if the user tries to enter some text into the text view, the keyboard will pop up, and we take the height of the keyboard and assign that value as the bottom margin of the contents inside the text view. This makes our text view's contents smaller in size and allows the user to enter as much text as she wishes without the keyboard blocking her view.

# 1.21. Adding Buttons to the User Interface with UIButton

## Problem

You want to display a button on your UI and handle the touch events for that button.

## Solution

Use the `UIButton` class.

## Discussion

Buttons allow users to initiate an action in your apps. For instance, the iCloud Settings bundle in the Settings app presents a Delete Account button in Figure 1-57. If you press this button, the iCloud app will take action. The action depends on the app. Not all apps act the same when a Delete button is pressed by the user. Buttons can have images in them as well as text, as we will soon see.

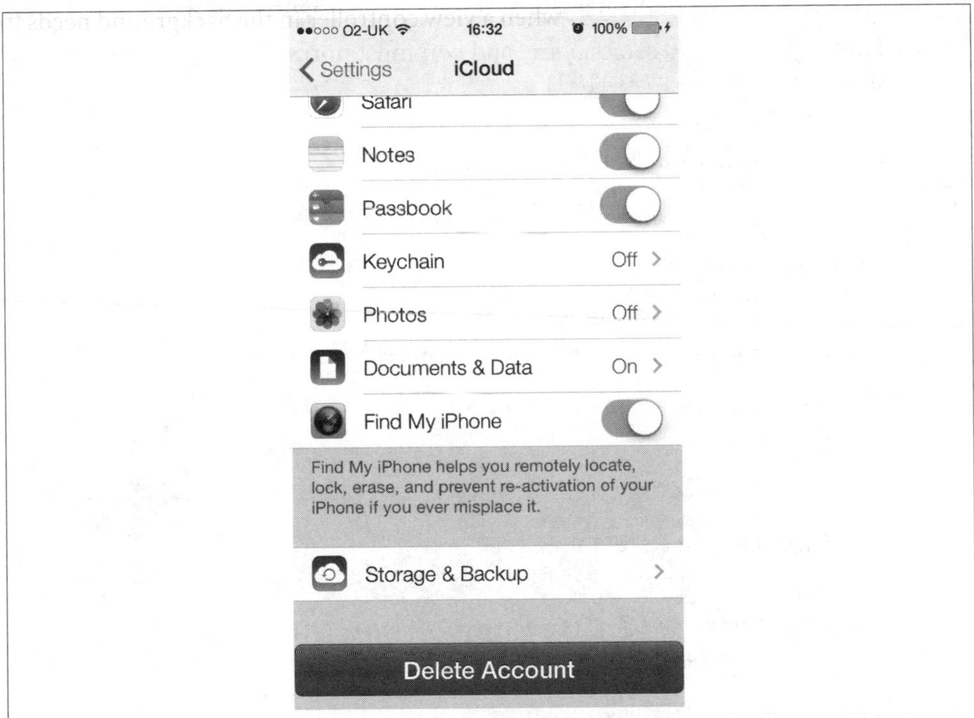


*Figure 1-57. A Delete Account button*

A button can assign actions to different triggers. For instance, a button can fire one action when the user puts her finger down on the button and another action when she lifts her finger off the button. These become actions, and the objects implementing the actions become targets. Let's go ahead and define a button in our view controller's implementation file:

```
#import "ViewController.h"

@interface ViewController ()
@property (nonatomic, strong) UIButton *myButton;
@end

@implementation ViewController
```

The default height of `UIButton` is 44.0f points in iOS 7.

Next, we move on to the implementation of the button (Figure 1-58):

```
- (void) buttonIsPressed:(UIButton *)paramSender{
    NSLog(@"Button is pressed.");
}

- (void) buttonIsTapped:(UIButton *)paramSender{
    NSLog(@"Button is tapped.");
}

- (void)viewDidLoad{
    [super viewDidLoad];

    self.myButton = [UIButton buttonWithType:UIButtonTypeSystem];

    self.myButton.frame = CGRectMake(110.0f,
                                     200.0f,
                                     100.0f,
                                     44.0f);

    [self.myButton setTitle:@"Press Me"
                   forState:UIControlStateNormal];

    [self.myButton setTitle:@"I'm Pressed"
                   forState:UIControlStateHighlighted];

    [self.myButton addTarget:self
                      action:@selector(buttonIsPressed:)
            forControlEvents:UIControlEventTouchDown];

    [self.myButton addTarget:self
```

```
                     action:@selector(buttonIsTapped:)
           forControlEvents:UIControlEventTouchUpInside];

    [self.view addSubview:self.myButton];

}
```

*Figure 1-58. A system button in the middle of the screen*

In this example code, we are using the `setTitle:forState:` method of our button to set two different titles for the button. The title is the text that gets displayed on the button. A button can be in different states at different times—such as normal and highlighted (pressed down)—and can display a different title in each state. So in this case, when the user sees the button for the first time, he will read "Press Me." Once he presses the button, the title of the button will change to "I'm Pressed."

We did a similar thing with the actions that the button fires. We used the `addTarget:action:forControlEvents:` method to specify two actions for our button:

1. An action to be fired when the user presses the button down.
2. Another action to be fired when the user has pressed the button and has lifted his finger off the button. This completes a *touch-up-inside* action.

The other thing that you need to know about `UIButton` is that it must always be assigned a type, which you do by initializing it with a call to the class method `buttonWithType`, as shown in the example code. As the parameter to this method, pass a value of type `UIButtonType`:

```
typedef NS_ENUM(NSInteger, UIButtonType) {
    UIButtonTypeCustom = 0,
    UIButtonTypeSystem NS_ENUM_AVAILABLE_IOS(7_0),
    UIButtonTypeDetailDisclosure,
    UIButtonTypeInfoLight,
    UIButtonTypeInfoDark,
    UIButtonTypeContactAdd,
    UIButtonTypeRoundedRect = UIButtonTypeSystem,
};
```

A button can also render an image. An image will replace the default look and feel of the button. When you have an image or a series of images that you want to assign to different states of a button, make sure your button is of type `UIButtonTypeCustom`. I have prepared two images here: one for the normal state of the button and the other for the highlighted (pressed) state. I will now create my custom button and assign the two images to it.

```
UIImage *normalImage = [UIImage imageNamed:@"NormalBlueButton"];
UIImage *highlightedImage = [UIImage imageNamed:@"HighlightedBlueButton"];

self.myButton = [UIButton buttonWithType:UIButtonTypeCustom];

self.myButton.frame = CGRectMake(110.0f,
                                 200.0f,
                                 100.0f,
                                 44.0f);

[self.myButton setBackgroundImage:normalImage
                         forState:UIControlStateNormal];
[self.myButton setTitle:@"Normal"
               forState:UIControlStateNormal];

[self.myButton setBackgroundImage:highlightedImage
                         forState:UIControlStateHighlighted];
[self.myButton setTitle:@"Pressed"
               forState:UIControlStateHighlighted];
```

Figure 1-59 shows what the app looks like when we run it in iOS Simulator. We are using the `setBackgroundImage:forState:` method of the button to set a background image. With a background image, we can still use the `setTitle:forState:` methods to render text on top of the background image. If your images contain text and you don't need the title for a button, you can instead use the `setImage:forState:` method or simply remove the titles from the button.

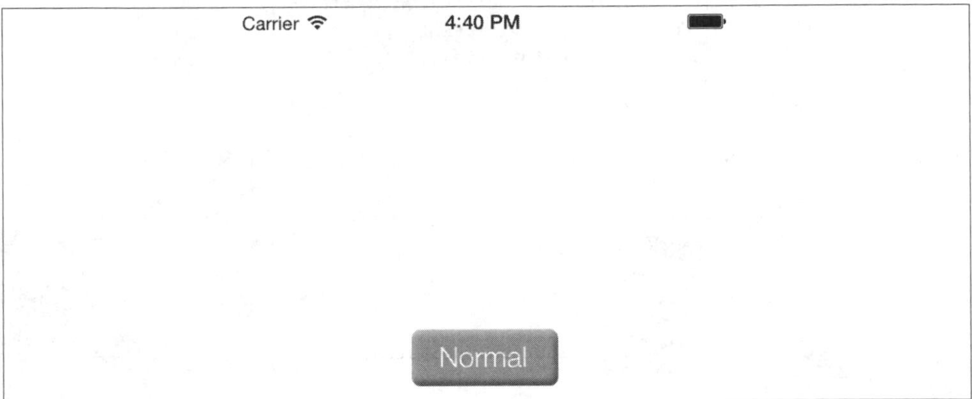


*Figure 1-59. A button with a background image*

# 1.22. Displaying Images with UIImageView

## Problem

You would like to display images to your users on your app's UI.

## Solution

Use the `UIImageView` class.

## Discussion

The `UIImageView` is one of the least-complicated classes in the iOS SDK. As you know, an image view is responsible for displaying images. There are no tips or tricks involved. All you have to do is instantiate an object of type `UIImageView` and add it to your views. Now, I have a picture of a MacBook Air, and I would like to display it in an image view. Let's start with our view controller's implementation file:

```
#import "ViewController.h"

@interface ViewController ()
@property (nonatomic, strong) UIImageView *myImageView;
@end
```

```
@implementation ViewController
```

Go ahead and instantiate the image view and place the image in it:

```
- (void)viewDidLoad{
    [super viewDidLoad];

    UIImage *macBookAir = [UIImage imageNamed:@"MacBookAir"];
    self.myImageView = [[UIImageView alloc] initWithImage:macBookAir];
    self.myImageView.center = self.view.center;
    [self.view addSubview:self.myImageView];

}
```

Now if we run the app, we will see something similar to Figure 1-60.

*Figure 1-60. An image view that is too big to fit on the screen*

I should mention that the MacBook Air image that I'm loading into this image view is 980×519 pixels, and as you can see, it certainly doesn't fit into the iPhone screen. So how do we solve this problem? First, we need to make sure that we are initializing our image view using the `initWithFrame:` method, instead of the `initWithImage:` method, as the latter will set the width and height of the image view to the exact width and height of the image. So let's remedy that first:

```
- (void)viewDidLoad{
    [super viewDidLoad];

    UIImage *macBookAir = [UIImage imageNamed:@"MacBookAir"];
    self.myImageView = [[UIImageView alloc] initWithFrame:self.view.bounds];
    self.myImageView.image = macBookAir;
    self.myImageView.center = self.view.center;
    [self.view addSubview:self.myImageView];
}
```

So how does the app look now? See Figure 1-61.

*Figure 1-61. An image whose width is squished to fit the width of the screen*

This isn't really what we wanted to do, is it? Of course, we got the frame of the image view right, but the way the image is rendered in the image view isn't quite right. So what can we do? We can rectify this by setting the `contentMode` property of the image view. This property is of type `UIContentMode`:

```
typedef NS_ENUM(NSInteger, UIViewContentMode) {
    UIViewContentModeScaleToFill,
    UIViewContentModeScaleAspectFit,
    UIViewContentModeScaleAspectFill,
    UIViewContentModeRedraw,
    UIViewContentModeCenter,
    UIViewContentModeTop,
    UIViewContentModeBottom,
    UIViewContentModeLeft,
    UIViewContentModeRight,
    UIViewContentModeTopLeft,
    UIViewContentModeTopRight,
    UIViewContentModeBottomLeft,
    UIViewContentModeBottomRight,
};
```

Here is an explanation of some of the most useful values in the `UIViewContentMode` enumeration:

`UIViewContentModeScaleToFill`
: This will scale the image inside the image view to fill the entire boundaries of the image view.

`UIViewContentModeScaleAspectFit`
: This will make sure the image inside the image view will have the right aspect ratio and fits inside the image view's boundaries.

`UIViewContentModeScaleAspectFill`
: This will makes sure the image inside the image view will have the right aspect ratio and fills the entire boundaries of the image view. For this value to work properly, make sure that you have set the `clipsToBounds` property of the image view to `YES`.

The `clipsToBounds` property of `UIView` denotes whether the subviews of that view should be clipped if they go outside the boundaries of the view. You use this property if you want to be absolutely certain that the subviews of a specific view will not get rendered outside the boundaries of that view (or that they do get rendered outside the boundaries, depending on your requirements).

So to make sure the image fits into the image view's boundaries and that the aspect ratio of the image is right, we need to use the `UIViewContentModeScaleAspectFit` content mode:

```
- (void)viewDidLoad{
    [super viewDidLoad];

    UIImage *macBookAir = [UIImage imageNamed:@"MacBookAir"];
    self.myImageView = [[UIImageView alloc] initWithFrame:self.view.bounds];
    self.myImageView.contentMode = UIViewContentModeScaleAspectFit;
    self.myImageView.image = macBookAir;
    self.myImageView.center = self.view.center;
    [self.view addSubview:self.myImageView];
}
```

And the results will be exactly what we expected (Figure 1-62).

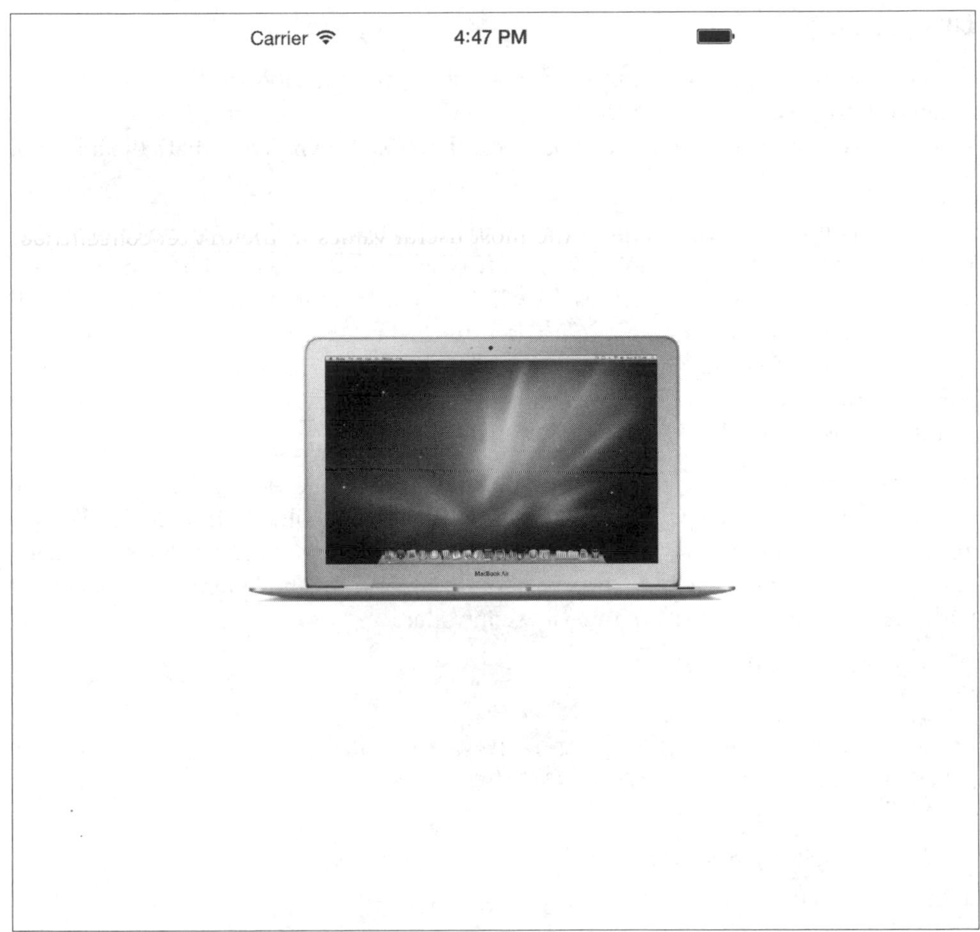


*Figure 1-62. The aspect ratio of image view is absolutely spot on*

# 1.23. Creating Scrollable Content with UIScrollView

## Problem

You have content that needs to get displayed on the screen, but it requires more real estate than what the device's screen allows for.

## Solution

Use the `UIScrollView` class.

## Discussion

Scroll views are one of the features that make iOS a really neat operating system. They are practically everywhere. You've been to the Clock or the Contacts apps, haven't you? Have you seen how the content can be scrolled up and down? Well, that's the magic of scroll views.

There really is one basic concept you need to learn about scroll views: the *content size*, which lets the scroll view conform to the size of what it's displaying. The content size is a value of type `CGSize` that specifies the width and the height of the contents of a scroll view. A scroll view, as its name implies, is a subclass of `UIView`, so you can simply add your views to a scroll view using its `addSubview:` method. However, you need to make sure that the scroll view's content size is set properly; otherwise, the contents inside the scroll view *won't* scroll.

As an example, let's find a big image and load it to an image view. I will add the same image that I used in Recipe 1.22: a MacBook Air image. I will add it to an image view and place it in a scroll view. Then I will use the `contentSize` of the scroll view to make sure this content size is equal to the size of the image (width and height). First, let's start with the implementation file of our view controller:

```
#import "ViewController.h"

@interface ViewController ()
@property (nonatomic, strong) UIScrollView *myScrollView;
@property (nonatomic, strong) UIImageView *myImageView;
@end

@implementation ViewController
```

And let's place the image view inside the scroll view:

```
- (void)viewDidLoad{
    [super viewDidLoad];

    UIImage *imageToLoad = [UIImage imageNamed:@"MacBookAir"];
    self.myImageView = [[UIImageView alloc] initWithImage:imageToLoad];
```

```
    self.myScrollView = [[UIScrollView alloc] initWithFrame:self.view.bounds];
    [self.myScrollView addSubview:self.myImageView];
    self.myScrollView.contentSize = self.myImageView.bounds.size;
    [self.view addSubview:self.myScrollView];

}
```

If you now load up the app in iOS Simulator, you will see that you can scroll the image horizontally and vertically. The challenge here, of course, is to provide an image that is bigger than the screen's boundaries. For example, if you provide an image that is 20×20 pixels, the scroll view won't be of much use to you. In fact, it would be wrong to place such an image into a scroll view, as the scroll view would practically be useless in that scenario. There would be nothing to scroll because the image is smaller than the screen size.

One of the handy features of `UIScrollView` is support for delegation, so that it can report really important events to the app through a delegate. A delegate for a scroll view must conform to the `UIScrollViewDelegate` protocol. Here are some of the methods defined in this protocol:

`scrollViewDidScroll:`
: Gets called whenever the contents of a scroll view get scrolled.

`scrollViewWillBeginDecelerating:`
: Gets called when the user scrolls the contents of a scroll view and lifts his finger off the screen as the scroll view scrolls.

`scrollViewDidEndDecelerating:`
: Gets called when the scroll view has finished scrolling its contents.

`scrollViewDidEndDragging:willDecelerate:`
: Gets called when the user finishes dragging the contents of the scroll view. This method is very similar to the `scrollViewDidEndDecelerating:` method, *but* you need to bear in mind that the user can drag the contents of a scroll view without scrolling the contents. She can simply put her finger on the content, move her finger to any location on the screen and lift her finger, without giving the contents any momentum to move. This is dragging as opposed to scrolling. Scrolling is similar to dragging, but the user will give momentum to the contents' movement by lifting her finger off the screen while the content is being dragged around, and not waiting for the content to stop before lifting her finger off the screen. Dragging is comparable to holding down the accelerator in a car or pedaling on a bicycle, whereas scrolling is comparable to coasting in a car or on a bicycle.

So let's add some fun to our previous app. Now the goal is to set the alpha level of the image inside our image view to 0.50f (half transparent) when the user starts to scroll the scroll view and set this alpha back to 1.0f (opaque) when the user finishes scrolling. Let's begin by conforming to the `UIScrollViewDelegate` protocol:

```
#import "ViewController.h"

@interface ViewController () <UIScrollViewDelegate>
@property (nonatomic, strong) UIScrollView *myScrollView;
@property (nonatomic, strong) UIImageView *myImageView;
@end

@implementation ViewController
```

Then let's implement this functionality:

```
- (void)scrollViewDidScroll:(UIScrollView *)scrollView{
    /* Gets called when user scrolls or drags */
    self.myScrollView.alpha = 0.50f;
}

- (void)scrollViewDidEndDecelerating:(UIScrollView *)scrollView{
    /* Gets called only after scrolling */
    self.myScrollView.alpha = 1.0f;
}

- (void)scrollViewDidEndDragging:(UIScrollView *)scrollView
                  willDecelerate:(BOOL)decelerate{
    /* Make sure the alpha is reset even if the user is dragging */
    self.myScrollView.alpha = 1.0f;
}

- (void)viewDidLoad{
    [super viewDidLoad];

    UIImage *imageToLoad = [UIImage imageNamed:@"MacBookAir"];
    self.myImageView = [[UIImageView alloc] initWithImage:imageToLoad];
    self.myScrollView = [[UIScrollView alloc] initWithFrame:self.view.bounds];
    [self.myScrollView addSubview:self.myImageView];
    self.myScrollView.contentSize = self.myImageView.bounds.size;
    self.myScrollView.delegate = self;
    [self.view addSubview:self.myScrollView];

}
```

As you might have noticed, scroll views have *indicators*. An indicator is the little tracking line that appears on the sides of a scroll view when its contents are getting scrolled and moved. Figure 1-63 shows an example.

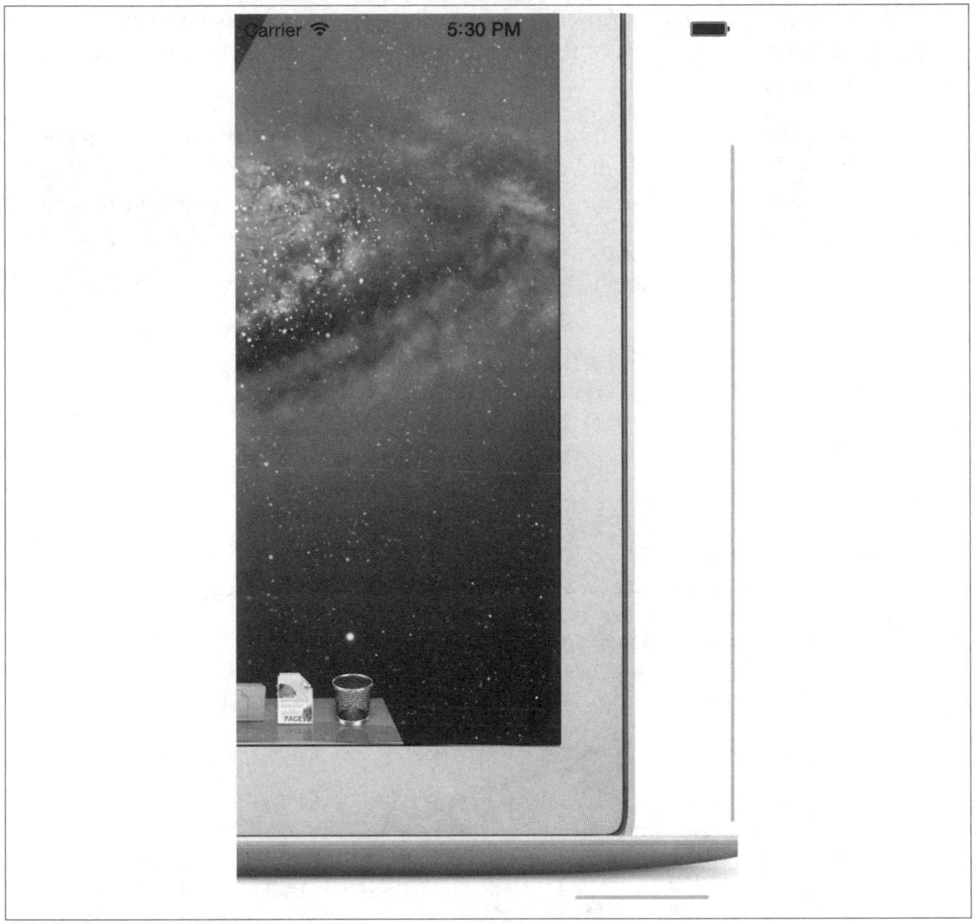


*Figure 1-63. Black indicators appearing on the right and bottom of a scroll view*

Indicators simply show the user where the current view is in relation to the content (top, halfway down, etc.). You can control what the indicators look like by changing the value of the `indicatorStyle` property. For instance, here I have changed the indicator style of my scroll view to white:

```
self.myScrollView.indicatorStyle = UIScrollViewIndicatorStyleWhite;
```

One of the great features of scroll views is that they allow pagination. Pagination is the same as scrolling, but locks the scrolling when the user moves to the next *page*. You have perhaps already seen this if you've ever used the Photos app on the iPhone or iPad. When you are looking at photos, you can swipe between them. Each swipe brings the next or previous photo onto the screen. Your swiping never scrolls all the way to the end or all the way to the start. When the scrolling starts, the scroll view detects the next image to display, scrolls and bounces to that image, and stops the scrolling animation.

That's pagination. If you haven't tried it already, I urge you to do so, because otherwise I could go on and on and none of this would make sense unless you looked at an app that supports pagination.

For this example code, I've prepared three images: an iPhone, an iPad, and a MacBook Air. I've placed them in their individual image views and added them to a scroll view. Then we can enable pagination by setting the value of the `pagingEnabled` property of the scroll view to `YES`:

```
- (UIImageView *) newImageViewWithImage:(UIImage *)paramImage
                                  frame:(CGRect)paramFrame{

    UIImageView *result = [[UIImageView alloc] initWithFrame:paramFrame];
    result.contentMode = UIViewContentModeScaleAspectFit;
    result.image = paramImage;
    return result;

}

- (void)viewDidLoad{
    [super viewDidLoad];

    UIImage *iPhone = [UIImage imageNamed:@"iPhone"];
    UIImage *iPad = [UIImage imageNamed:@"iPad"];
    UIImage *macBookAir = [UIImage imageNamed:@"MacBookAir"];

    CGRect scrollViewRect = self.view.bounds;

    self.myScrollView = [[UIScrollView alloc] initWithFrame:scrollViewRect];
    self.myScrollView.pagingEnabled = YES;
    self.myScrollView.contentSize = CGSizeMake(scrollViewRect.size.width * 3.0f,
                                               scrollViewRect.size.height);
    [self.view addSubview:self.myScrollView];

    CGRect imageViewRect = self.view.bounds;
    UIImageView *iPhoneImageView = [self newImageViewWithImage:iPhone
                                                         frame:imageViewRect];
    [self.myScrollView addSubview:iPhoneImageView];

    /* Go to next page by moving the x position of the next image view */
    imageViewRect.origin.x += imageViewRect.size.width;
    UIImageView *iPadImageView = [self newImageViewWithImage:iPad
                                                       frame:imageViewRect];
    [self.myScrollView addSubview:iPadImageView];

    /* Go to next page by moving the x position of the next image view */
    imageViewRect.origin.x += imageViewRect.size.width;
    UIImageView *macBookAirImageView =
    [self newImageViewWithImage:macBookAir
                          frame:imageViewRect];
    [self.myScrollView addSubview:macBookAirImageView];
}
```

Now we have three pages of scrollable content (Figure 1-64).

*Figure 1-64. Scrolling through pages in a page-enabled scroll view*

# 1.24. Loading Web Pages with UIWebView

## Problem

You want to load a web page dynamically right inside your iOS app.

## Solution

Use the `UIWebView` class.

## Discussion

A web view is what the Safari browser uses on iOS to load web content. You have the whole power of Safari in your iOS apps through the `UIWebView` class. All you have to do is place a web view on your UI and use one of its loading methods:

`loadData:MIMEType:textEncodingName:baseURL:`
: Loads an instance of `NSData` into the web view.

`loadHTMLString:baseURL:`
: Loads an instance of `NSString` into the web view. The string should be a valid HTML, or in other words, something that a web browser can render.

`loadRequest:`
: Loads an instance of `NSURLRequest`. This is useful when you want to load the contents of a remote URL into a web view inside your application.

Let's see an example. We'll start with the implementation file of our view controller:

```
#import "ViewController.h"

@interface ViewController ()
@property(nonatomic, strong) UIWebView *myWebView;
@end

@implementation ViewController
```

Now I would like to load the string *`iOS 7 Programming Cookbook`* into the web view. To prove, things are working as expected and that our web view is capable of rendering rich text, I will go ahead and make the *`Cookbook`* part bold while leaving the rest of the text intact (Figure 1-65):

```
- (void)viewDidLoad{
    [super viewDidLoad];

    self.myWebView = [[UIWebView alloc] initWithFrame:self.view.bounds];
    [self.view addSubview:self.myWebView];

    NSString *htmlString = @"<br/>iOS 7 Programming <strong>Cookbook</strong>";

    [self.myWebView loadHTMLString:htmlString
                           baseURL:nil];
}
```

Carrier 6:14 PM

iOS 7 Programming **Cookbook**

*Figure 1-65. Loading rich text into a web view*

Another way to use a web view is to load a remote URL into it. For this purpose, we can use the `loadRequest:` method. Let's go ahead and look at an example where we will load Apple's main page into a web view in our iOS app (Figure 1-66):

```
- (void)viewDidLoad{
    [super viewDidLoad];

    self.myWebView = [[UIWebView alloc] initWithFrame:self.view.bounds];
    self.myWebView.scalesPageToFit = YES;
    [self.view addSubview:self.myWebView];

    NSURL *url = [NSURL URLWithString:@"http://www.apple.com"];
    NSURLRequest *request = [NSURLRequest requestWithURL:url];

    [self.myWebView loadRequest:request];
}
```

*Figure 1-66. Apple's home page loaded into a web view*

It might take quite a while for a web view to load the contents that you pass to it. You might have noticed that when loading content in Safari, you get a little activity indicator in the top-left corner of the screen telling you that the device is busy loading the contents. Figure 1-67 shows an example.

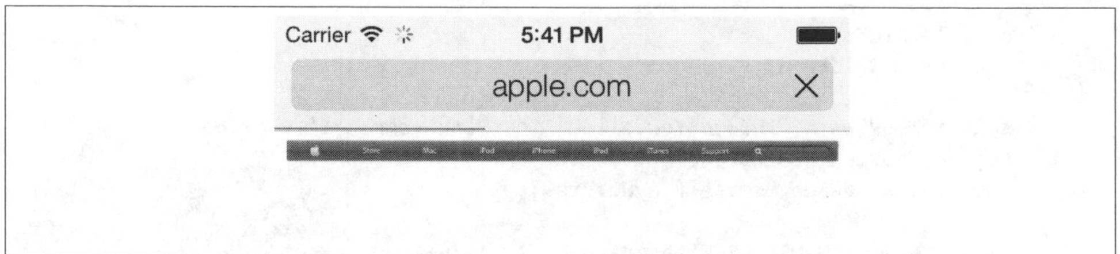


*Figure 1-67. A progress bar indicating a loading process*

iOS accomplishes this through delegation. We will subscribe as the delegate of a web view, and the web view will notify us when it starts to load content. When the content is fully loaded, we get a message from the web view informing us about this. We do this through the `delegate` property of the web view. A delegate of a web view must conform to the `UIWebViewDelegate` protocol.

Let's go ahead and implement the little activity indicator in our view controller. Please bear in mind that the activity indicator is already a part of the application and we don't have to create it. We can control it using the `setNetworkActivityIndicatorVisible:` method of `UIApplication`. So let's start with the implementation file of our view controller:

```
@interface ViewController () <UIWebViewDelegate>
@property(nonatomic, strong) UIWebView *myWebView;
@end

@implementation ViewController
```

Then do the implementation. Here we will use three of the methods declared in the `UIWebViewDelegate` protocol:

`webViewDidStartLoad:`
: This method gets called as soon as the web view starts loading content.

`webViewDidFinishLoad:`
: This method gets called as soon as the web view finishes loading content.

`webView:didFailLoadWithError:`
: This method gets called when the web view stops loading content, for instance because of an error or a broken network connection.

```
- (void)webViewDidStartLoad:(UIWebView *)webView{
    [[UIApplication sharedApplication] setNetworkActivityIndicatorVisible:YES];
}

- (void)webViewDidFinishLoad:(UIWebView *)webView{
    [[UIApplication sharedApplication] setNetworkActivityIndicatorVisible:NO];
}

- (void)webView:(UIWebView *)webView didFailLoadWithError:(NSError *)error{
    [[UIApplication sharedApplication] setNetworkActivityIndicatorVisible:NO];
}

- (void)viewDidLoad{
    [super viewDidLoad];

    self.myWebView = [[UIWebView alloc] initWithFrame:self.view.bounds];
    self.myWebView.delegate = self;
    self.myWebView.scalesPageToFit = YES;
    [self.view addSubview:self.myWebView];

    NSURL *url = [NSURL URLWithString:@"http://www.apple.com"];
    NSURLRequest *request = [NSURLRequest requestWithURL:url];

    [self.myWebView loadRequest:request];

}
```

# 1.25. Displaying Progress with UIProgressView

## Problem

You want to display a progress bar on the screen, depicting the progress of a certain task; for instance, the progress of downloading a file from a URL.

## Solution

Instantiate a view of type `UIProgressView` and place it on another view.

## Discussion

A progress view is what programmers generally call a progress bar. An example of a progress view is depicted in Figure 1-68.

*Figure 1-68. A simple progress view*

Progress views are generally displayed to users to show them the progress of a task that has a well-defined starting and ending point. For instance, downloading 30 files is a well-defined task with a specific starting and ending point. This task obviously finishes when all 30 files have been downloaded. A progress view is an instance of `UIProgressView` and is initialized using the designated initializer of this class, the `initWithProgressViewStyle:` method. This method takes in the style of the progress bar to be created as a parameter. This parameter is of type `UIProgressViewStyle` and can therefore be one of the following values:

`UIProgressViewStyleDefault`
: This is the default style of the progress view. An example of this is the progress view shown in Figure 1-68.

`UIProgressViewStyleBar`
: This is similar to the `UIProgressViewStyleDefault` but is meant to be used for progress views that are to be added to a toolbar.

An instance of `UIProgressView` defines a property called `progress` (of type `float`). This property tells iOS how the bar inside the progress view should be rendered. This value must be in the range +0 to +1.0. If the value of +0 is given, the progress bar won't appear to have started yet. A value of +1.0 shows progress of 100%. The progress depicted in Figure 1-68 is 0.5 (or 50%).

To get used to creating progress views, let's create one similar to what we saw in Figure 1-68. First things first: define a property for your progress view:

```
#import "ViewController.h"

@interface ViewController ()
```

```
@property (nonatomic, strong) UIProgressView *progressView;
@end

@implementation ViewController
```

Then instantiate an object of type `UIProgressView`:

```
- (void)viewDidLoad{

    [super viewDidLoad];

    self.progressView = [[UIProgressView alloc]
                         initWithProgressViewStyle:UIProgressViewStyleBar];
    self.progressView.center = self.view.center;
    self.progressView.progress = 20.0f / 30.0f;
    [self.view addSubview:self.progressView];

}
```

Obviously, creating a progress view is very straightforward. All you really need to do is display your progress correctly, because the `progress` property of a progress view should be in the range +0 to +1.0, which is a normalized value. So if you have 30 tasks to take care of and you have completed 20 of them so far, you need to assign the result of the following equation to the `progress` property of your progress view:

```
self.progressView.progress = 20.0f / 30.0f;
```

The reason the values 20 and 30 are passed to the equation as floating-point values is to tell the compiler that the division has to happen on floating-point values, producing a value with decimal numbers. If you provided the integer division 20/30 to the compiler to place inside the `progress` property of your progress view, you would get the integral value of 0 out of the division, because the compiler will perform integer division that truncates the result to the next lower integer. In short, your progress view would show zero progress all the way to the end, when 30/30 produces the result of 1; not of much value to the user.

# 1.26. Constructing and Displaying Styled Texts

## Problem

You want to be able to display rich formatted text in your UI components without having to create a separate UI component per attribute. For instance, you may want to display one sentence that contains only one of its words written in bold, inside a `UILabel`.

## Solution

Construct an instance of the `NSAttributedString` or the mutable variant of it, the `NSMutableAttributedString`, and either set it as the text of a UI component like the `UILabel` component through its special attributed string property, or simply use the attributed string's built-in methods to draw the text on a canvas.

## Discussion

Rich text is a thing of legend! A lot of us programmers have had the requirement to display mixed-style strings in one line of text on our UI. For instance, in one line of text you may have to display straight and italic text together, where one word is italic and the rest of the words are regular text. Or you may have had to underline a word inside a sentence. For this, some of us had to use Web Views, but that is not the optimal solution because Web Views are quite slow in rendering their content, and that will definitely impact the performance of your app. In iOS 7, we can start using attributed strings. I don't know what took Apple so long to introduce this feature to iOS, as Mac developers have been using attributed strings for a long time now!

Before we begin, I want to clearly show you what I mean by attributed strings, using Figure 1-69. Then we will set out on the journey to write the program to achieve exactly this.

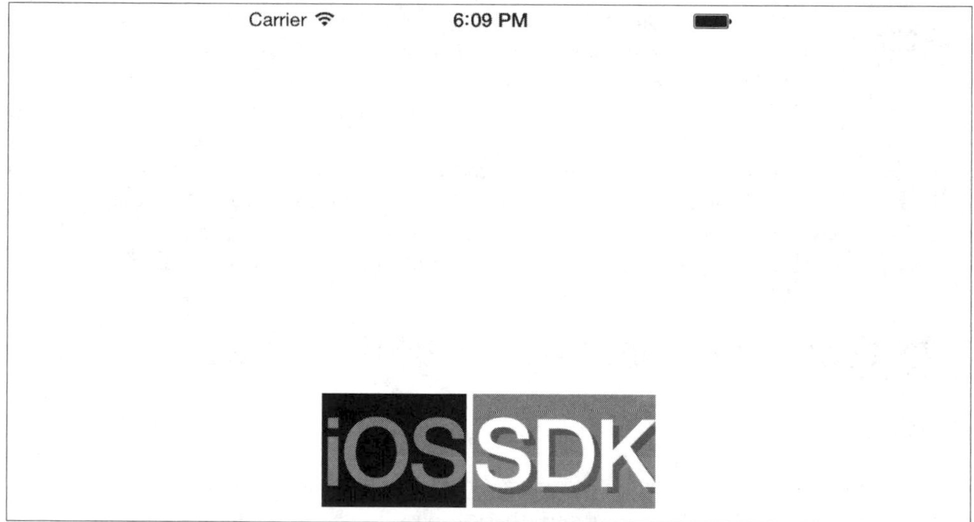


*Figure 1-69. An attributed string is displayed on the screen inside a simple label*

Just to be explicit, this text is rendered inside a *single* instance of the `UILabel` class.

So what do we see in this example? I'll list the pieces:

*The text "iOS" with the following attributes:*

- Bold font with size of 60 points
- Background color of black
- Font color of red

*The text "SDK" with the following attributes:*

- Bold font with size of 60 points
- White text color
- Light-gray shadow
- Red background color

The best way to construct attributed strings is to use the `initWithString:` method of the mutable variant of the `NSMutableAttributedString` class and pass an instance of the `NSString` to this method. This will create our attributed string without any attributes. Then, to assign attributes to different parts of the string, we will use the `setAttributes:range:` method of the `NSMutableAttributedString` class. This method takes in two parameters:

`setAttributes`
: A dictionary whose keys are character attributes and the value of each key depends on the key itself. Here are the most important keys that you can set in this dictionary:

  `NSFontAttributeName`
  : The value of this key is an instance of `UIFont` and defines the font for the specific range of your string.

  `NSForegroundColorAttributeName`
  : The value for this key is of type `UIColor` and defines the color for your text for the specific range of your string.

  `NSBackgroundColorAttributeName`
  : The value of this key is of type `UIColor` and defines the background color on which the specific range of your string has to be drawn.

  `NSShadowAttributeName`
  : The value of this key must be an instance of the `NSShadow` and defines the shadow that you want to use under the specific range of your string.

`range`
: A value of type `NSRange` that defines the starting point and the length of characters to which you want to apply the attributes.

To see all the different keys that you can pass to this method, simply browse the Apple documentation online for the `NSMutableAttributedString` class. I will not put the direct URL to this documentation here as Apple may change the URL at some point, but a simple search online will do the trick.

We'll break our example down into two dictionaries of attributes. The dictionary of attributes for the word "iOS" can be constructed in this way in code:

```
NSDictionary *attributesForFirstWord = @{
                 NSFontAttributeName : [UIFont boldSystemFontOfSize:60.0f],
                 NSForegroundColorAttributeName : [UIColor redColor],
                 NSBackgroundColorAttributeName : [UIColor blackColor]
                 };
```

And the word "SDK" will be constructed using the following attributes:

```
NSShadow *shadow = [[NSShadow alloc] init];
shadow.shadowColor = [UIColor darkGrayColor];
shadow.shadowOffset = CGSizeMake(4.0f, 4.0f);

NSDictionary *attributesForSecondWord = @{
                 NSFontAttributeName : [UIFont boldSystemFontOfSize:60.0f],
                 NSForegroundColorAttributeName : [UIColor whiteColor],
                 NSBackgroundColorAttributeName : [UIColor redColor],
                 NSShadowAttributeName : shadow
                 };
```

Putting it together, we will get the following code that not only creates our label, but also sets its attributed text:

```
#import "ViewController.h"

@interface ViewController ()
@property (nonatomic, strong) UILabel *label;
@end

@implementation ViewController

- (NSAttributedString *) attributedText{

    NSString *string = @"iOS SDK";

    NSMutableAttributedString *result = [[NSMutableAttributedString alloc]
                                         initWithString:string];
```

```
    NSDictionary *attributesForFirstWord = @{
                    NSFontAttributeName : [UIFont boldSystemFontOfSize:60.0f],
                    NSForegroundColorAttributeName : [UIColor redColor],
                    NSBackgroundColorAttributeName : [UIColor blackColor]
                    };

    NSShadow *shadow = [[NSShadow alloc] init];
    shadow.shadowColor = [UIColor darkGrayColor];
    shadow.shadowOffset = CGSizeMake(4.0f, 4.0f);

    NSDictionary *attributesForSecondWord = @{
                     NSFontAttributeName : [UIFont boldSystemFontOfSize:60.0f],
                     NSForegroundColorAttributeName : [UIColor whiteColor],
                     NSBackgroundColorAttributeName : [UIColor redColor],
                     NSShadowAttributeName : shadow
                     };

    /* Find the string "iOS" in the whole string and sets its attribute */
    [result setAttributes:attributesForFirstWord
                   range:[string rangeOfString:@"iOS"]];

    /* Do the same thing for the string "SDK" */
    [result setAttributes:attributesForSecondWord
                   range:[string rangeOfString:@"SDK"]];

    return [[NSAttributedString alloc] initWithAttributedString:result];

}

- (void)viewDidLoad{
    [super viewDidLoad];

    self.label = [[UILabel alloc] init];
    self.label.backgroundColor = [UIColor clearColor];
    self.label.attributedText = [self attributedText];
    [self.label sizeToFit];
    self.label.center = self.view.center;
    [self.view addSubview:self.label];

}

@end
```

## See Also

Recipe 1.17; Recipe 1.18

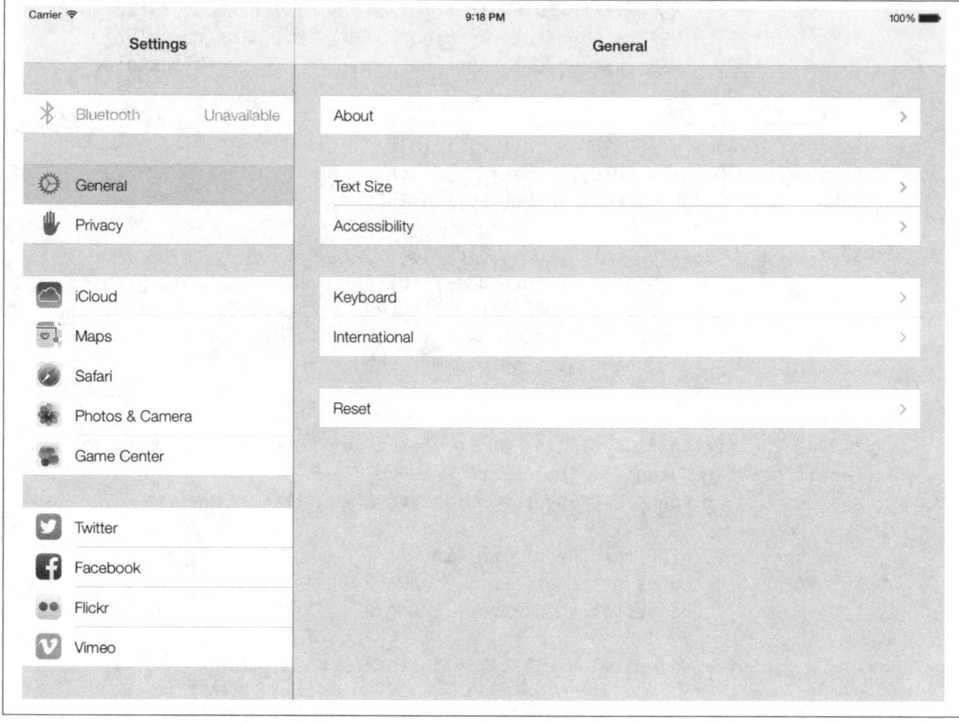


*Figure 1-70. Split view controller in the Settings app on the iPad*

# 1.27. Presenting Master-Detail Views with UISplitViewController

## Problem

You want to take maximum advantage of the iPad's relatively large screen by presenting two side-by-side view controllers.

## Solution

Use the `UISplitViewController` class.

## Discussion

Split view controllers are present only on the iPad. If you've used an iPad, you've probably already seen them. Just open the Settings app in landscape mode and have a look. Can you see the split view controller there in Figure 1-70?

A split view controller has left and right sides. The left side displays the main settings, and tapping on each one of those settings shows the details of that setting item on the right side of the split view controller.

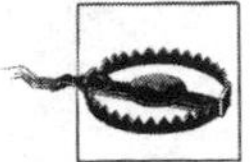

Never attempt to instantiate an object of type `UISplitViewController` on a device other than an iPad. This will raise an exception.

Apple has made it extremely easy to create split view controller based applications. Simply follow these steps to create your app based on split view controllers:

1. In Xcode, navigate to the File menu and choose New → New Project...
2. In the New Project screen, pick iOS → Application on the left side and then pick Master-Detail Application (as shown in Figure 1-71) and press Next.
3. In this screen, pick your product name and make sure your device family is Universal. We want to make sure our app runs both on the iPhone and the iPad. Once you are done, press Next (see Figure 1-72).

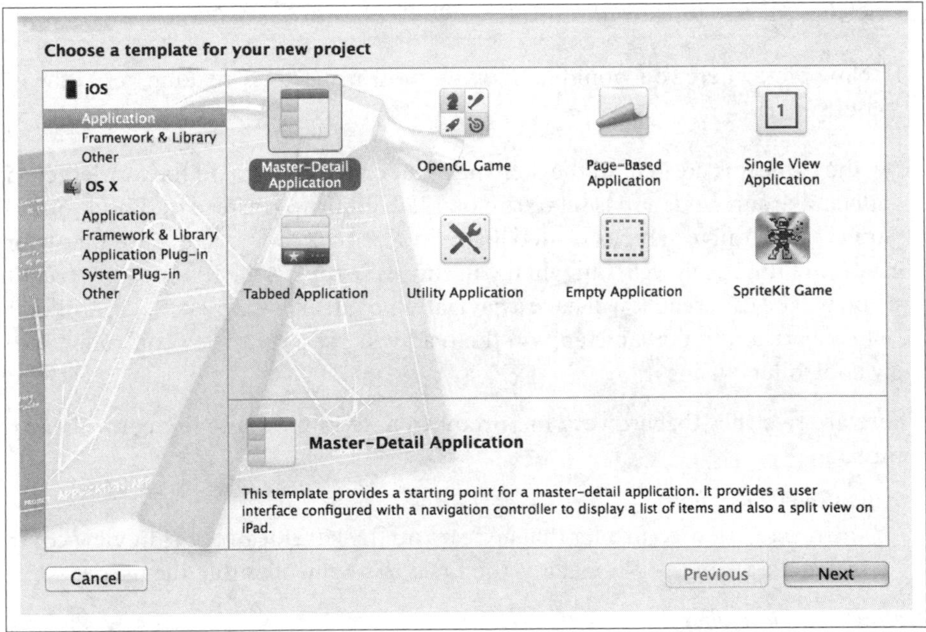


*Figure 1-71. Picking the Master-Detail Application project template in Xcode*

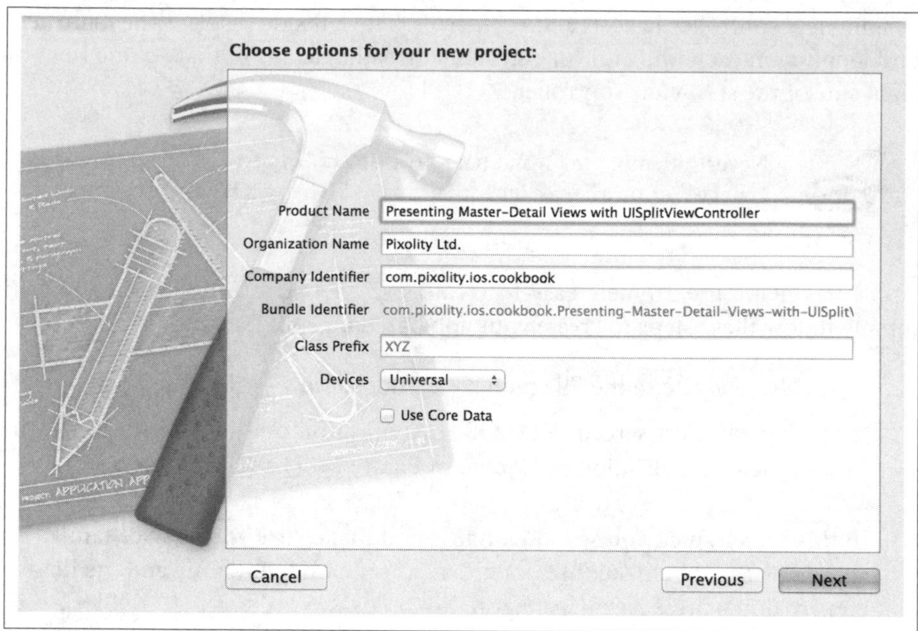


*Figure 1-72. Setting the master-detail project settings in Xcode*

4. Now pick where you would like to save your project. Once done, press the Create button.

Now the project is created. In the Scheme breadcrumb button on the top-left corner of Xcode, make sure your app is set to run on iPad Simulator instead of iPhone Simulator. If you create a universal master-detail app in Xcode, Xcode makes sure that your app runs on the iPhone as well, but when you run your app on the iPhone, the structure of the app will be different. It will have a navigation controller with a view controller inside it, whereas running the same app on the iPad will use a split view controller with two view controllers inside it.

There are two files that are very important to note in the split view controller project template:

*MasterViewController*
: The master view controller that appears on the left side of the split view controller on the iPad. On the iPhone, it is the first view controller that the user sees.

*DetailViewController*
: The detail view controller that appears on the right side of the split view controller on the iPad. On the iPhone, it is the view controller that gets pushed onto the stack once the user taps on any of the items on the root (first, master) view controller.

Now you need to think about communication between the master and the detail view controller. Do you want the communication to be done through the app delegate, or do you want the master view controller to send messages to the detail view controller directly? That's really up to you.

If you run the app in iPad Simulator, you'll notice that in landscape mode, you can see our master and detail view controllers in the split view controller, but as soon as you rotate the orientation to portrait, your master view controller is gone and is replaced with a master navigation button on the top-left side of the navigation bar of the detail view controller. Although this is good, we weren't expecting it, since we were comparing it with the Settings app on the iPad. If you rotate the settings app to portrait on an iPad, you can still see both the master and the detail view controllers. How can we accomplish this? It turns out Apple has exposed an API to us through which we can do it. Simply go to the *DetailViewController.m* file and implement this method:

```
- (BOOL) splitViewController:(UISplitViewController *)svc
    shouldHideViewController:(UIViewController *)vc
               inOrientation:(UIInterfaceOrientation)orientation{
    return NO;
}
```

If you return `NO` from this method, iOS will *not* hide the master view controller in either orientation, and both the master and the detail view controllers will be visible in both landscape and portrait orientations. Now that we have implemented this method, we won't need those two methods anymore:

```
- (void)splitViewController:(UISplitViewController *)splitController
     willHideViewController:(UIViewController *)viewController
          withBarButtonItem:(UIBarButtonItem *)barButtonItem
       forPopoverController:(UIPopoverController *)popoverController{
    barButtonItem.title = NSLocalizedString(@"Master", @"Master");
    [self.navigationItem setLeftBarButtonItem:barButtonItem animated:YES];
    self.masterPopoverController = popoverController;
}

- (void)splitViewController:(UISplitViewController *)splitController
     willShowViewController:(UIViewController *)viewController
  invalidatingBarButtonItem:(UIBarButtonItem *)barButtonItem{
    [self.navigationItem setLeftBarButtonItem:nil animated:YES];
    self.masterPopoverController = nil;
}
```

These methods were there simply to manage the navigation bar button for us, but now that we are not using that button anymore, we can get rid of the methods. You can comment them out or just remove them from the *DetailViewController.m* file.

If you look inside your master view controller's header file, you'll notice something similar to this:

```
#import <UIKit/UIKit.h>

@class DetailViewController;

@interface MasterViewController : UITableViewController

@property (strong, nonatomic) DetailViewController *detailViewController;

@end
```

As you can see, the master view controller has a reference to the detail view controller. Using this connection, we can communicate selections and other values to the detail view controller, as you will soon see.

By default, if you run your app now in iPad Simulator, you will see a UI similar to that shown in Figure 1-73. The default implementation that Apple provides us with in the master view controller has a mutable array that gets populated with instances of `NSDate` every time you press the plus (+) button on the navigation bar of the master view controller. The default implementation is very simple, and you can modify it by learning a bit more about table views. Please refer to Chapter 4 for more details about table views and populating them.

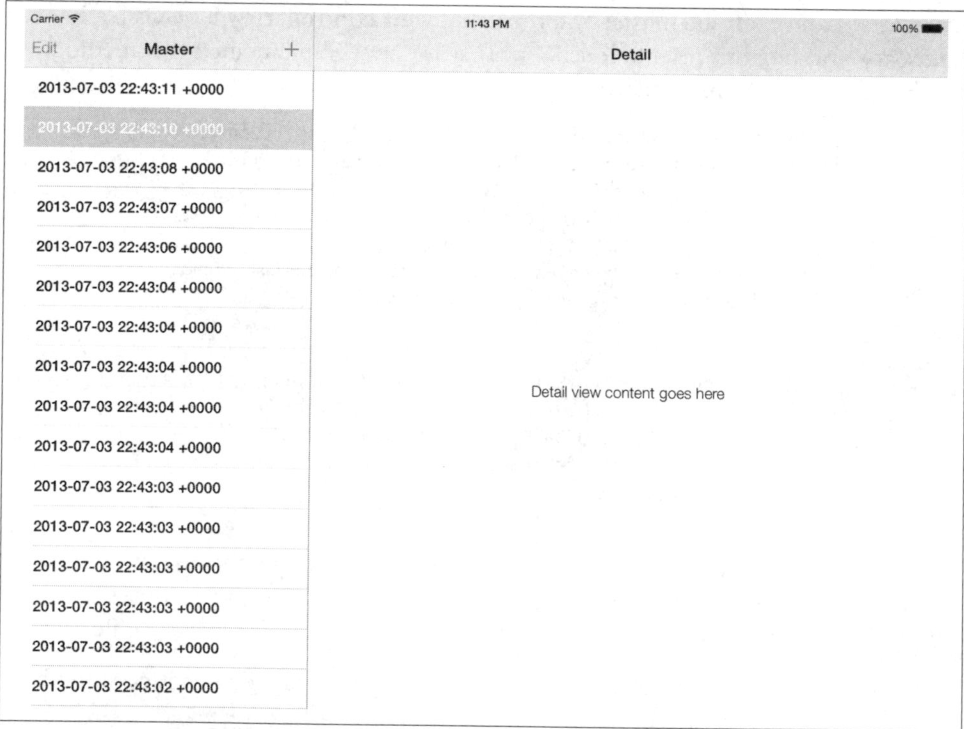


*Figure 1-73. An empty split view controller running on iPad Simulator*

# 1.28. Enabling Paging with UIPageViewController

## Problem

You want to create an app that works similarly to iBooks, where the user can flip through the pages of a book as if it were a real book, to provide an intuitive and real user experience.

## Solution

Use `UIPageViewController`.

## Discussion

Xcode has a template for page view controllers. It's best to first see how they look before reading an explanation of what they actually are. So follow these steps to create your app to use page view controllers:

Page view controllers work on both the iPhone and the iPad.

1. In Xcode, go to the File menu and then choose New → New Project...
2. On the lefthand side of the New Project window, make sure you've selected iOS and then Application. Once that is done, pick the Page-Based Application template from the right side and press Next, as shown in Figure 1-74.
3. Now select a product name and make sure the device family that you've chosen is Universal, as you normally would want your app to run on both the iPhone and the iPad (see Figure 1-75). Once you are done, press Next.
4. Select where you want to save your project. Once you are done, press the Create button. You have now successfully created your project.

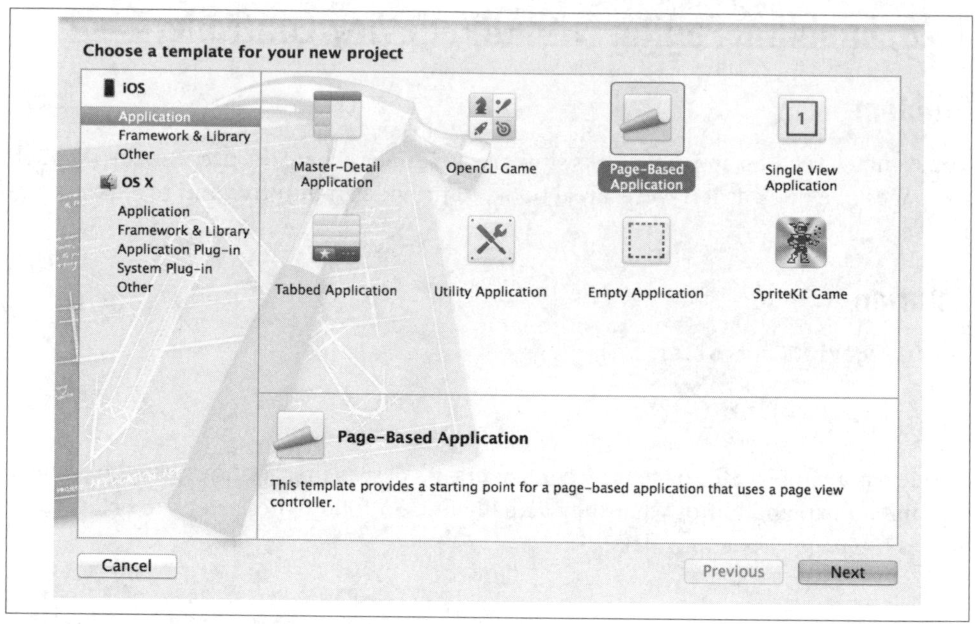


*Figure 1-74. Creating a Page-Based Application in Xcode*

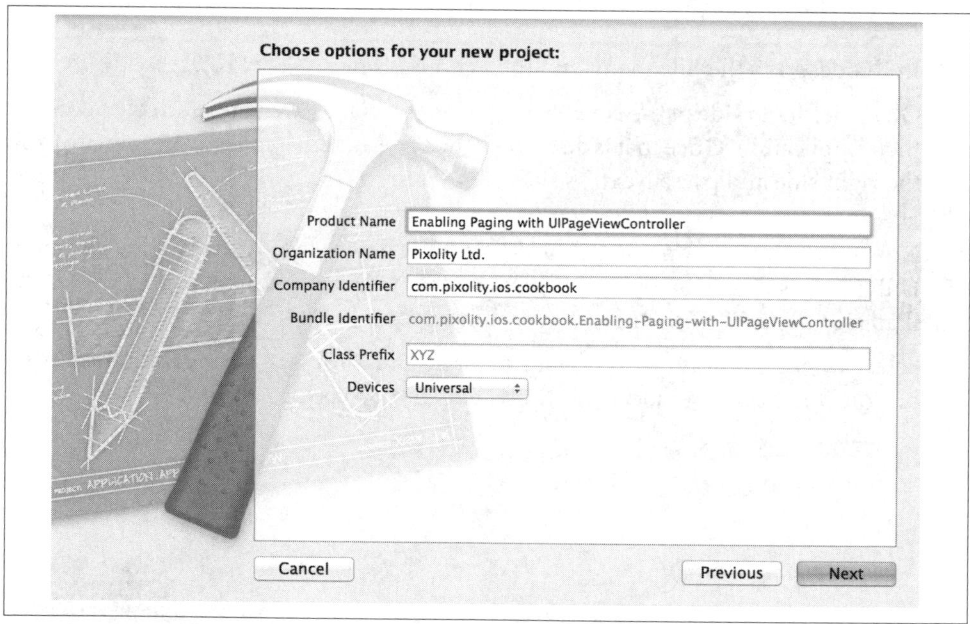


*Figure 1-75. Setting the project settings of a page-based app*

You can now see that Xcode has created quite a few classes in your project. Let's have a quick look at what each one of these classes does:

*Delegate Class*
: The app delegate simply creates an instance of the `RootViewController` class and presents it to the user. There is one *.xib* for iPad and another one for iPhone, but both are using the aforementioned class.

`RootViewController`
: Creates an instance of `UIPageViewController` and adds that view controller to itself. So the UI of this view controller is actually a mix of two view controllers: the `RootViewController` itself and a `UIPageViewController`.

`DataViewController`
: For every page in the page view controller, an instance of this class gets presented to this user. This class is a subclass of `UIViewController`.

`ModelController`
: This is simply a subclass of `NSObject` that conforms to the `UIPageViewController DataSource` protocol. This class is the data source of the page view controller.

So you can see that a page view controller has both a delegate and a data source. With Xcode's default page-based application template, the root view controller becomes the delegate and the model controller becomes the data source of the page view controller. In order to understand how a page view controller really works, we need to understand its delegation and data source protocols. Let's start with the delegate, `UIPageViewControllerDelegate`. This protocol has two important methods:

```
- (void)pageViewController:(UIPageViewController *)pageViewController
       didFinishAnimating:(BOOL)finished
  previousViewControllers:(NSArray *)previousViewControllers
      transitionCompleted:(BOOL)completed;

- (UIPageViewControllerSpineLocation)pageViewController
:(UIPageViewController *)pageViewController
spineLocationForInterfaceOrientation:(UIInterfaceOrientation)orientation;
```

The first method gets called when the user turns to the next or the previous page, *or* if the user initiates the movement from one page to the other but decides against it while the page is moving (in which case, the user gets sent back to the page she was on before). The `transitionCompleted` will get set to `YES` if this was a successful page animation, or set to `NO` if the user decided against the movement and cancelled it in the middle of the animation.

The second method gets called whenever the device orientation changes. You can use this method to specify the location of the spine for the pages by returning a value of type `UIPageViewControllerSpineLocation`:

```
typedef NS_ENUM(NSInteger, UIPageViewControllerSpineLocation) {
    UIPageViewControllerSpineLocationNone = 0,
    UIPageViewControllerSpineLocationMin = 1,
    UIPageViewControllerSpineLocationMid = 2,
    UIPageViewControllerSpineLocationMax = 3
};
```

This might be a bit confusing to you, but let me demonstrate. If we are using a `UIPageViewControllerSpineLocationMin` spine location, the page view controller will require only one view controller to present to the user, and when the user goes to the next page, a new view controller will be presented to him. However, if we set the spine location to `UIPageViewControllerSpineLocationMid`, we will be required to display two view controllers at the same time: one on the left and another on the right, with the spine sitting between them. Let me show you what I mean. In Figure 1-76 you can see an example of a page view controller in landscape mode, with the spine location set to `UIPageViewControllerSpineLocationMin`.

Now if we return the spine location of `UIPageViewControllerSpineLocationMid`, we will get results similar to Figure 1-77.

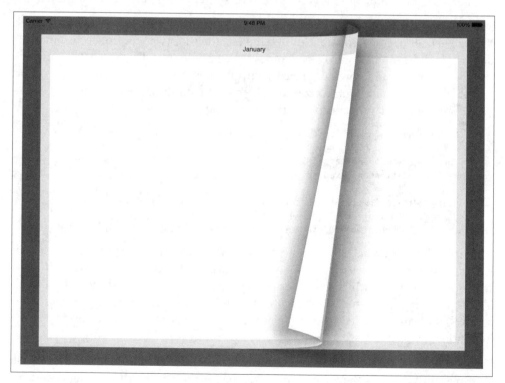

*Figure 1-76. One view controller presented in a page view controller in landscape mode*

As you can see in that image, the spine is located exactly in the center of the screen between two view controllers. Once the user flips a page from right to the left, the page rests on the left and the page view controller reveals a new view controller on the right side. This whole logic is in this delegate method:

```
- (UIPageViewControllerSpineLocation)pageViewController
:(UIPageViewController *)pageViewController
spineLocationForInterfaceOrientation:(UIInterfaceOrientation)orientation;
```

We've now covered the delegate of the page view controller, but how about the data source? The data source of a page view controller must conform to the `UIPageViewControllerDataSource`. This protocol exposes two important methods:

```
- (UIViewController *)pageViewController
:(UIPageViewController *)pageViewController
viewControllerBeforeViewController:(UIViewController *)viewController;

- (UIViewController *)pageViewController
:(UIPageViewController *)pageViewController
viewControllerAfterViewController:(UIViewController *)viewController;
```

The first method gets called when the page view controller already has a view controller on the screen and needs to know which previous view controller to render. This happens when the user decides to flip to the next page. The second method is called when the page view controller needs to figure out which view controller to display after the view controller that is being flipped.

Xcode, as you've already seen, has greatly simplified setting up a page-based application. All you really need to do now is to provide content to the data model (`ModelController`) and off you go. If you need to customize the colors and images in your view controllers, do so by either using the Interface Builder to modify the storyboard files directly or write your own code in the implementation of each of the view controllers.

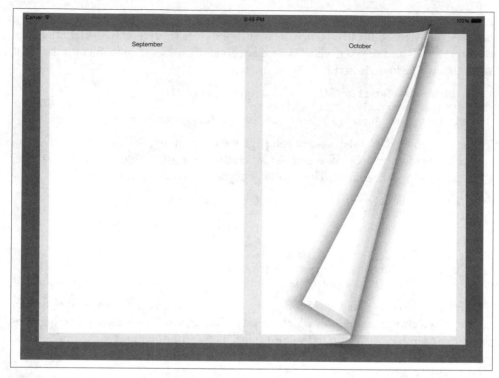

*Figure 1-77. Two view controllers displayed in a page view controller in landscape mode*

# 1.29. Displaying Popovers with UIPopoverController

## Problem

You want to display content on an iPad without blocking the whole screen.

## Solution

Use popovers.

## Discussion

Popovers are used to display additional information on the iPad screen. An example can be seen in the Safari app on the iPad. When the user taps on the Bookmarks button, she will see a popover displaying the bookmarks content on the screen (see Figure 1-78).

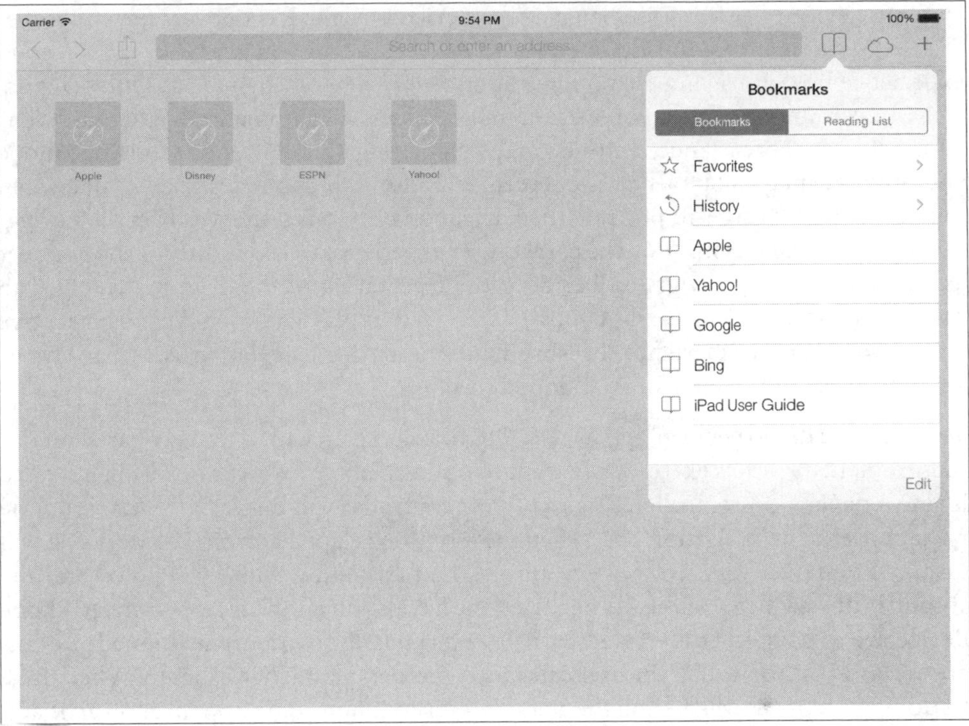


*Figure 1-78. The bookmarks popover in the Safari app on an iPad*

The default behavior of popovers is that when the user taps somewhere outside the region of the popover, the popover will automatically get dismissed. You can ask the popover to not get dismissed if the user taps on specific parts of the screen, as we will see later. Popovers present their content by using a view controller. Note that you can also present navigation controllers inside popovers, because navigation controllers are a subclass of `UIViewController`.

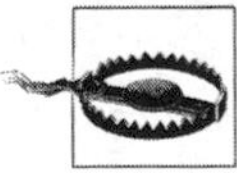

Popovers can be used only on iPad devices. If you have a view controller whose code runs on both an iPad and on an iPhone, you need to make sure that you are not instantiating the popover on a device other than the iPad.

Popovers can be presented to the user in two ways:

1. From inside a navigation button, an instance of `UIBarButtonItem`
2. From inside a rectangular area in a view

When a device orientation is changed (the device is rotated), popovers are either dismissed or hidden temporarily. You need to make sure that you give your users a good experience by redisplaying the popover after the orientation change has settled, if possible. In certain cases, your popover might get dismissed automatically after an orientation change. For instance, if the user taps on a navigation button in landscape mode you might display a popover on the screen. Suppose your app is designed so that when the orientation changes to portrait, the navigation button is removed from the navigation bar for some reason. Now, the correct user experience would be to hide the popover associated with that navigation bar after the orientation of the device is changed to portrait. In some instances, though, you will need to play with popovers a bit to give your users a good experience, because handling device orientation is not always as straightforward as in the aforementioned scenario.

To create the demo popover app, we need to first come up with a strategy based on our requirements. For this example, we want to build an app with a view controller loaded inside a navigation controller. The root view controller will display a + button on the right corner of its navigation bar. When the + button is tapped on an iPad device, it will display a popover with two buttons on it. The first button will say "Photo," and the second button will say "Audio." When the same navigation button is tapped on an iPhone device, we will display an alert view with three buttons: the two aforementioned buttons, and a cancel button so that the user can cancel the alert view if he wishes to. When these buttons are tapped (whether on the alert view on an iPhone or the popover on an iPad), we won't really do anything. We will simply dismiss the alert view or the popover.

Go ahead and create a Single View universal project in Xcode and name the project "Displaying Popovers with UIPopoverController." Then, using the technique shown in Recipe 6.1, add a navigation controller to your storyboard so that your view controllers will have a navigation bar.

After this, we need to go into the definition of our root view controller and define a property of type `UIPopoverController`:

```
#import "ViewController.h"

@interface ViewController () <UIAlertViewDelegate>
@property (nonatomic, strong) UIPopoverController *myPopoverController;
@property (nonatomic, strong) UIBarButtonItem *barButtonAdd;
@end

@implementation ViewController

<# Rest of your code goes here #>
```

You can see that we are also defining a property called `barButtonAdd` in our view controller. This is the navigation button that we will add on our navigation bar. Our plan is to display our popover when the user taps on this button (you can read more about navigation buttons in Recipe 1.15). However, we need to make sure we instantiate the popover only if the device is an iPad. Before we implement our root view controller with the navigation button, let's go ahead and create a subclass of `UIViewController` and name it *`PopoverContentViewController`*. We will display the contents of this view controller inside our popover later. See Recipe 1.9 for information about view controllers and ways of creating them.

The content view controller displayed inside the popover will have two buttons (as per our requirements). However, this view controller will need to have a reference to the popover controller in order to dismiss the popover when the user taps on any of the buttons. For this, we need to define a property in our content view controller to refer to the popover:

```
#import <UIKit/UIKit.h>

@interface PopoverContentViewController : UIViewController

/* We shouldn't define this as strong. That will create a retain cycle
 between the popover controller and the content view controller since the
 popover controller retains the content view controller and the view controller
 will retain the popover controller */
@property (nonatomic, weak) UIPopoverController *myPopoverController;

@end
```

And, also inside the implementation file of our content view controller, we declare our bar buttons:

```
#import "PopoverContentViewController.h"

@interface PopoverContentViewController ()
@property (nonatomic, strong) UIButton *buttonPhoto;
@property (nonatomic, strong) UIButton *buttonAudio;
@end

@implementation PopoverContentViewController

<# Rest of your code goes here #>
```

After this, we'll create our two buttons in the content view controller and link them to their action methods. These methods will take care of dismissing the popover that is displaying this view controller. Remember, the popover controller will be responsible for assigning itself to the `popoverController` property of the content view controller:

```
- (BOOL) isInPopover{

    Class popoverClass = NSClassFromString(@"UIPopoverController");

    if (popoverClass != nil &&
        UI_USER_INTERFACE_IDIOM() == UIUserInterfaceIdiomPad &&
        self.myPopoverController != nil){
        return YES;
```

```
    } else {
        return NO;
    }

}

- (void) gotoAppleWebsite:(id)paramSender{

    if ([self isInPopover]){
        /* Go to website and then dismiss popover */
        [self.myPopoverController dismissPopoverAnimated:YES];
    } else {
        /* Handle case for iPhone */
    }

}

- (void) gotoAppleStoreWebsite:(id)paramSender{

    if ([self isInPopover]){
        /* Go to website and then dismiss popover */
        [self.myPopoverController dismissPopoverAnimated:YES];
    } else {
        /* Handle case for iPhone */
    }

}

- (void)viewDidLoad{
    [super viewDidLoad];

    self.preferredContentSize = CGSizeMake(200.0f, 125.0f);

    CGRect buttonRect = CGRectMake(20.0f,
                                   20.0f,
                                   160.0f,
                                   37.0f);

    self.buttonPhoto = [UIButton buttonWithType:UIButtonTypeSystem];
    [self.buttonPhoto setTitle:@"Photo"
                      forState:UIControlStateNormal];
    [self.buttonPhoto addTarget:self
                         action:@selector(gotoAppleWebsite:)
               forControlEvents:UIControlEventTouchUpInside];

    self.buttonPhoto.frame = buttonRect;

    [self.view addSubview:self.buttonPhoto];


    buttonRect.origin.y += 50.0f;
    self.buttonAudio = [UIButton buttonWithType:UIButtonTypeSystem];
```

```
    [self.buttonAudio setTitle:@"Audio"
                      forState:UIControlStateNormal];
    [self.buttonAudio addTarget:self
                         action:@selector(gotoAppleStoreWebsite:)
               forControlEvents:UIControlEventTouchUpInside];

    self.buttonAudio.frame = buttonRect;

    [self.view addSubview:self.buttonAudio];

}
```

Now in the `viewDidLoad` method of our root view controller, we will create our navigation button. Based on the device type, when the navigation bar is tapped, we will display either a popover (on the iPad) or an alert view (on the iPhone):

```
- (void)viewDidLoad{
    [super viewDidLoad];

    /* See if this class exists on the iOS running the app */
    Class popoverClass = NSClassFromString(@"UIPopoverController");

    if (popoverClass != nil &&
        UI_USER_INTERFACE_IDIOM() == UIUserInterfaceIdiomPad){

        PopoverContentViewController *content =
        [[PopoverContentViewController alloc] initWithNibName:nil
                                                       bundle:nil];

        self.myPopoverController = [[UIPopoverController alloc]
                                    initWithContentViewController:content];

        content.myPopoverController = self.myPopoverController;

        self.barButtonAdd =
        [[UIBarButtonItem alloc]
         initWithBarButtonSystemItem:UIBarButtonSystemItemAdd
         target:self
         action:@selector(performAddWithPopover:)];

    } else {

        self.barButtonAdd =
        [[UIBarButtonItem alloc]
         initWithBarButtonSystemItem:UIBarButtonSystemItemAdd
         target:self
         action:@selector(performAddWithAlertView:)];

    }
```

```
    [self.navigationItem setRightBarButtonItem:self.barButtonAdd
                                      animated:NO];

}
```

The popover controller sets a reference to itself in the content view controller after its initialization. This is very important. A popover controller *cannot* be initialized without a content view controller. Once the popover is initialized with a content view controller, you can go ahead and change the content view controller in the popover controller, but not during the initialization.

We have elected the `performAddWithPopover:` method to be invoked when the + navigation bar button is tapped on an iPad device. If the device isn't an iPad, we've asked the + navigation bar button to invoke the `performAddWithAlertView:` method. Let's go ahead and implement these methods and also take care of the delegate methods of our alert view, so that we know what alert view button the user tapped on an iPhone:

```
- (NSString *) photoButtonTitle{
    return @"Photo";
}

- (NSString *) audioButtonTitle{
    return @"Audio";
}

- (void)          alertView:(UIAlertView *)alertView
  didDismissWithButtonIndex:(NSInteger)buttonIndex{

    NSString *buttonTitle = [alertView buttonTitleAtIndex:buttonIndex];

    if ([buttonTitle isEqualToString:[self photoButtonTitle]]){
        /* Adding a photo ... */
    }
    else if ([buttonTitle isEqualToString:[self audioButtonTitle]]){
        /* Adding an audio... */
    }

}

- (void) performAddWithAlertView:(id)paramSender{

    [[[UIAlertView alloc] initWithTitle:nil
                                message:@"Add..."
                               delegate:self
                      cancelButtonTitle:@"Cancel"
                      otherButtonTitles:
      [self photoButtonTitle],
```

```
        [self audioButtonTitle], nil] show];

}

- (void) performAddWithPopover:(id)paramSender{

    [self.myPopoverController
     presentPopoverFromBarButtonItem:self.barButtonAdd
     permittedArrowDirections:UIPopoverArrowDirectionAny
     animated:YES];

}
```

If you now run your app on iPad Simulator and tap the + button on the navigation bar, you will see an interface similar to Figure 1-79.

*Figure 1-79. Our simple popover displayed when a navigation button was tapped*

If you run the same universal app on iPhone Simulator and tap the + button on the navigation bar, you will see results similar to Figure 1-80.

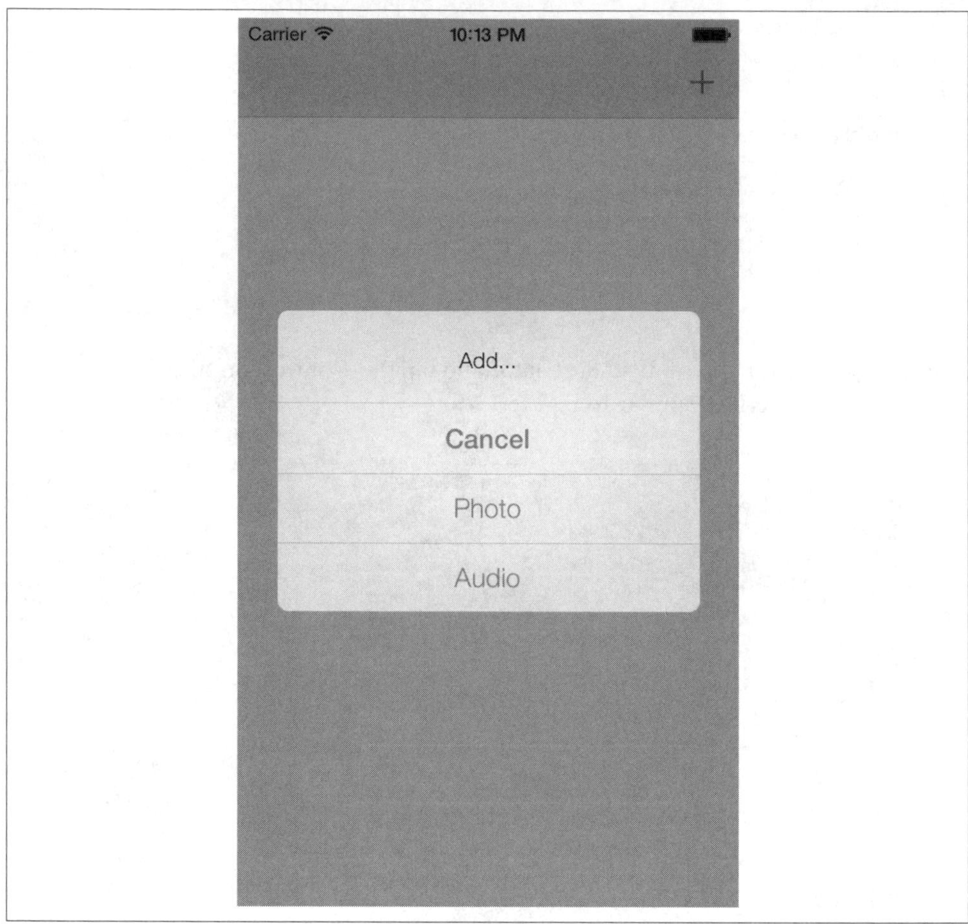


*Figure 1-80. Popovers are replaced by alert view in a universal app*

We used an important property of our content view controller: `preferredContentSize`. The popover, when displaying its content view controller, will read the value of this property automatically and will adjust its width and height to this size. Also, we used the `presentPopoverFromBarButtonItem:permittedArrowDirections:animated:` method of our popover in our root view controller to display the popover over a navigation bar button. The first parameter to this method is the navigation bar button from which the popover controller has to be displayed. The second parameter specifies the direction of the popover when it appears, in relation to the object from which it appears. For example, in Figure 1-79, you can see that our popover's arrow is pointing up toward the navigation bar button. The value that you pass to this parameter must be of type `UIPopoverArrowDirection`:

```
typedef NS_OPTIONS(NSUInteger, UIPopoverArrowDirection) {
    UIPopoverArrowDirectionUp = 1UL << 0,
```

```
    UIPopoverArrowDirectionDown = 1UL << 1,
    UIPopoverArrowDirectionLeft = 1UL << 2,
    UIPopoverArrowDirectionRight = 1UL << 3,
    UIPopoverArrowDirectionAny = UIPopoverArrowDirectionUp |
    UIPopoverArrowDirectionDown |
    UIPopoverArrowDirectionLeft |
    UIPopoverArrowDirectionRight,
    UIPopoverArrowDirectionUnknown = NSUIntegerMax
};
```

## See Also

Recipe 1.9; Recipe 1.15

CHAPTER 2

# Creating Dynamic and Interactive User Interfaces

## 2.0. Introduction

When the iPhone was released, it really set the standard for interactivity in mobile apps. Apps were and still are amazingly interactive, in that you can manipulate various UI components on the go to customize them to your needs. In iOS 7, Apple added a few new classes to the iOS SDK, which you can use to add very interesting physics to your app to make it even more interactive. For instance, if you look at the new iOS, you'll notice that background images that you can use as wallpapers are now more lively than before because they can move and slide around as you move your device to the left, right, etc. These are some of the various behaviors that the new SDK allows you to add to your apps as well.

Let me give you another example. Let's say that you have a photo-sharing application that runs on the iPad. On the lefthand side of the screen, you have some pictures that your app has pulled onto the screen from the user's photo album, and on the right you have a basket-like component where every photo that is placed into the basket will be batch-shared on a social networking service like Facebook. You want to provide interactivity on your UI with an animation so that the user can flick the pictures onto the basket from the left, and the pictures will snap into the basket. This was all possible in the past, but you had to know a fair bit about Core Animation and have a rather good understanding of physics. With UI Dynamics, Apple's new technology, a lot of these things can be attached to your apps very easily. In fact, you can attach very interesting physics and behaviors to your views with a few lines of code.

Apple has categorized these actions into *behavior* classes that you can attach to an *animator*. Behaviors are simple classes that you can configure, while animators group and manage various behaviors. For instance, you can add a *gravity* behavior to a button on your view, and this will cause the button to fall from the top of the screen (if that's where you've placed it) all the way down and even outside the boundaries of your view. Now, if you want to prevent that from happening and you allow your button to fall into the view but snap to the bottom and go no farther than that, you will need to attach a *collision* behavior to your animator as well. The animator will manage all the behaviors that you've added to various views in your app, as well as their interactions. You won't have to worry about that. Here are a few classes that provide different behaviors for your UI components:

`UICollisionBehavior`
: Provides collision detection.

`UIGravityBehavior`
: As its name implies, provides gravity behavior for your views.

`UIPushBehavior`
: Allows you to simulate a push behavior on your views. Imagine yourself placing your finger on the screen and then moving your finger gradually toward the top of the screen. If a button with the push behavior is attached to the view, you can cause it to move up as you move your finger up the screen, as if you are pushing it in the real world.

`UISnapBehavior`
: Allows views to snap to a specific point on the screen.

For every dynamic behavior, as discussed before, we will need an animator of type `UIDynamicAnimator`. This animator needs to be initialized with what Apple calls a *reference view*. The animator uses the reference view's coordinate system to calculate output of various behaviors. For instance, if you pass a view controller's view as the reference view of a dynamic animator, once you add a collision behavior to the animator, you can ask the collision behavior to ensure that the items that are added to it will not go outside the boundaries of the reference view. That means you can put all your UI components within your reference view, even if they have gravity applied to them.

The reference view is also used as the context of the animations that the animator manages. For instance, if the animator wants to figure out whether two squares will collide with each other, it uses Core Graphics methods to find where those two squares overlap with each other in the context of their superview—in this case, the reference view.

In this chapter, we are going to explore the different combinations of these behaviors and how you can add more interactivity to your apps with UIKit behaviors and animators. We will start with simple examples and gradually build on top of what we've learned and dig a bit deeper into more exciting examples.

## 2.1. Adding Gravity to Your UI Components

### Problem

You want your UI components to have gravity, so that if they are dragged up to the top of the screen, they will descend on their own. Combining this with the collision behavior that you will learn later, you can create UI components that fall from their current location until they collide with a path that you'll specify.

### Solution

Initialize an object of type `UIGravityBehavior` and add your UI components that need gravity to this object. After you are done, create an instance of `UIDynamicAnimator`, add your gravity behavior to the animator, and let the animator take care of the rest of the work for you.

### Discussion

For the purpose of this recipe, we are going to create a simple colored square view in our single-view application and place that view at the center of the screen. We will then add gravity to that view and watch it fall from the center all the way down and eventually outside the bounds of the screen.

So let's start by defining our animator and the view:

```
#import "ViewController.h"

@interface ViewController ()
@property (nonatomic, strong) UIView *squareView;
@property (nonatomic, strong) UIDynamicAnimator *animator;
@end

@implementation ViewController

<# Rest of your view controller's code will go here #>
```

Next, we are going to create our little view, assign a color to it, and place it at the center of our view controller's view. Then we will create an instance of the `UIGravityBehav ior` class using its `initWithItems:` initializer. This initializer takes in an array of objects that conform to the `UIDynamicItem` protocol. By default, all instances of `UIView` conform to this protocol, so as long as you have a view, you are good to go.

```
- (void)viewDidAppear:(BOOL)animated{
    [super viewDidAppear:animated];

    /* Create our little square view and add it to self.view */
    self.squareView = [[UIView alloc] initWithFrame:
                       CGRectMake(0.0f, 0.0f, 100.0f, 100.0f)];
```

```
    self.squareView.backgroundColor = [UIColor greenColor];
    self.squareView.center = self.view.center;
    [self.view addSubview:self.squareView];

    /* Create the animator and the gravity */
    self.animator = [[UIDynamicAnimator alloc]
                     initWithReferenceView:self.view];

    UIGravityBehavior *gravity = [[UIGravityBehavior alloc]
                                  initWithItems:@[self.squareView]];

    [self.animator addBehavior:gravity];

}
```

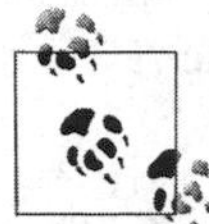

If you don't want to add all your views to the gravity behavior as soon as you initialize the behavior, you can add them later using the `addItem:` instance method of the `UIGravityBehavior` class. This method also accepts any object that conforms to the aforementioned protocol.

Now if you run your app, as soon as your view controller's view appears on screen, you will see the colored view drop from the center of the screen all the way down and out of the screen. It fails to stop because we have not given any collision boundaries to our animator. The gravity behavior, just like real gravity, will pull the items down until they hit a boundary, but since there is no boundary, the items will just keep dropping for all eternity. We will remedy that later in this chapter by adding collision behaviors to our items.

### See Also

Recipe 2.0, "Introduction"

## 2.2. Detecting and Reacting to Collisions Between UI Components

### Problem

You want to specify collision boundaries between your UI components on the screen so that they will not overlap one another.

### Solution

Instantiate an object of type `UICollisionBehavior` and attach it to your animator object. Set the `translatesReferenceBoundsIntoBoundary` property of your collision behavior to YES and ensure that your animator is initialized with your superview as its reference value. This will ensure that the subviews that are the targets of your collision behavior (as will be discussed soon) will not go outside the boundaries of your superview.

## Discussion

A collision behavior of type `UICollisionBehavior` takes in objects that conform to the `UIDynamicItem` protocol. All views of type `UIView` already conform to this protocol, so all you have to do is instantiate your views and add them to the collision behavior. A collision behavior requires you to define the boundaries that the items in the animator will not be able to go past. For instance, if you define a line that runs from the bottom-left edge to the bottom-right edge of your reference view (the bottommost horizontal line of your reference view), and add a gravity behavior to your view as well, those views will be pulled down by gravity to the bottom of the view but will not be able to go further because they will collide with the bottom edge of the view, defined by the collision behavior.

If you want your reference view's boundaries to be considered as the boundaries of your collision detection behavior, just set the `translatesReferenceBoundsIntoBoundary` property of the collision behavior's instance to `YES`. If you want to add custom lines as boundaries to your collision behavior, simply use the `addBoundaryWithIdentifier:fromPoint:toPoint:` instance method of the `UICollisionBehavior` class.

In this recipe, we are going to create two colored views, one on top of the other, and then add gravity to our animator so that the views will fall down from the center of the view controller's view. Then we are going to add a collision behavior to the mix so that the views will not overlap each other. In addition, they won't go outside the boundaries of the reference view (the view controller's view).

So let's begin by defining an array of our views and our animator:

```
#import "ViewController.h"

@interface ViewController ()
@property (nonatomic, strong) NSMutableArray *squareViews;
@property (nonatomic, strong) UIDynamicAnimator *animator;
@end

@implementation ViewController

<# Rest of your code goes here #>
```

Then when our view appears on the screen, we will set up the collision and the gravity behaviors and add them to an animator:

```
- (void)viewDidAppear:(BOOL)animated{
    [super viewDidAppear:animated];


    /* Create the views */
    NSUInteger const NumberOfViews = 2;

    self.squareViews = [[NSMutableArray alloc] initWithCapacity:NumberOfViews];
    NSArray *colors = @[[UIColor redColor], [UIColor greenColor]];

    CGPoint currentCenterPoint = self.view.center;
    CGSize eachViewSize = CGSizeMake(50.0f, 50.0f);
    for (NSUInteger counter = 0; counter < NumberOfViews; counter++){

        UIView *newView =
        [[UIView alloc] initWithFrame:
         CGRectMake(0.0f, 0.0f, eachViewSize.width, eachViewSize.height)];

        newView.backgroundColor = colors[counter];
        newView.center = currentCenterPoint;

        currentCenterPoint.y += eachViewSize.height + 10.0f;

        [self.view addSubview:newView];

        [self.squareViews addObject:newView];

    }

    self.animator = [[UIDynamicAnimator alloc]
                     initWithReferenceView:self.view];

    /* Create gravity */
    UIGravityBehavior *gravity = [[UIGravityBehavior alloc]
                                  initWithItems:self.squareViews];
    [self.animator addBehavior:gravity];

    /* Create collision detection */
    UICollisionBehavior *collision = [[UICollisionBehavior alloc]
                                      initWithItems:self.squareViews];
    collision.translatesReferenceBoundsIntoBoundary = YES;
    [self.animator addBehavior:collision];

}
```

The result will look similar to that shown in Figure 2-1.

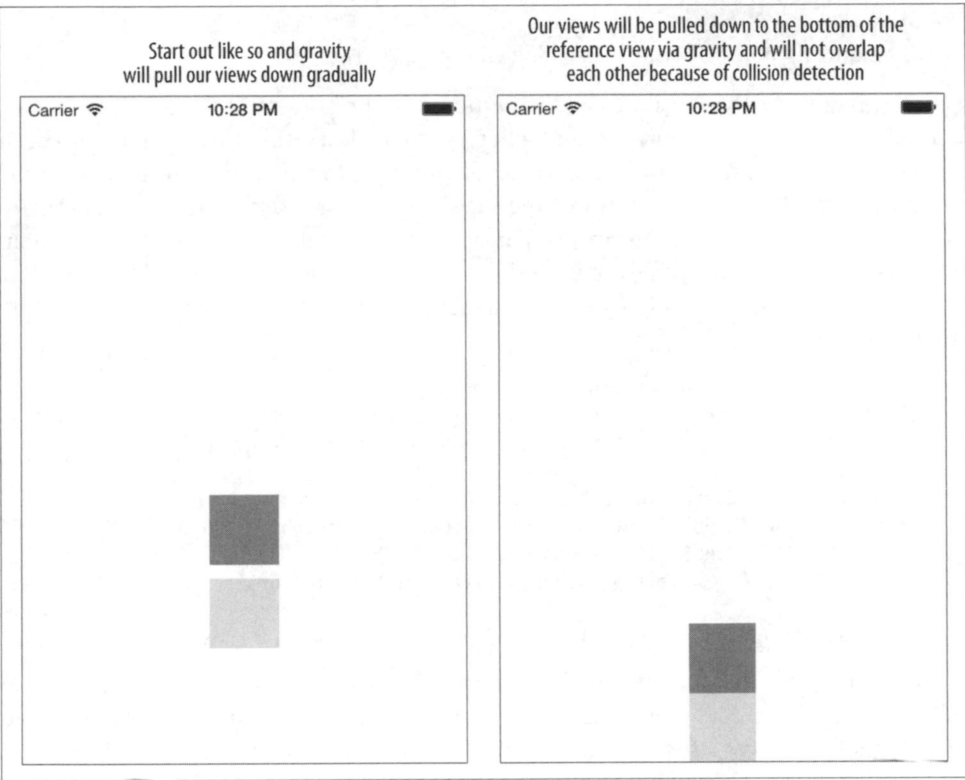

Start out like so and gravity
will pull our views down gradually
Our views will be pulled down to the bottom of the
reference view via gravity and will not overlap
each other because of collision detection
Carrier
10:28 PM
Carrier
10:28 PM


*Figure 2-1. Gravity and collision behaviors working hand in hand*

This example shows that the collision behavior works perfectly when the `translatesReferenceBoundsIntoBoundary` property's value is set to `YES`. But what if we want to specify custom boundaries? This is where we will use the `addBoundaryWithIdentifier:fromPoint:toPoint:` instance method of the collision behavior. Here are the parameters that you should pass to this method:

`addBoundaryWithIdentifier`
: A string identifier for your boundary. This is used so that later, if you want to get the collision behavior back for your boundary, you could pass the same identifier to the `boundaryWithIdentifier:` method and get your boundary object back. The object is of type `UIBezierPath`, which can support quite complicated, curved boundaries. But most programmers are likely to specify simple horizontal or vertical boundaries, which we'll do here.

`fromPoint`
: The starting point of your boundary, of type `CGPoint`.

toPoint
: The ending point of your boundary, of type CGPoint.

So let's imagine that you want to add a boundary to the bottom of your reference view (in this case, the view of our view controller), but you don't want this boundary to be at the bottommost point of your view. Instead, you want this boundary to be 100 points away from the bottommost point of the view. In that case, setting the translatesReferenceBoundsIntoBoundary property of the collision behavior is not going to help you, because you want a different boundary from the boundary provided by the reference view. Instead, we will use the addBoundaryWithIdentifier:fromPoint:toPoint: method like so:

```
/* Create collision detection */
UICollisionBehavior *collision = [[UICollisionBehavior alloc]
                                  initWithItems:self.squareViews];
[collision
 addBoundaryWithIdentifier:@"bottomBoundary"
 fromPoint:CGPointMake(0.0f, self.view.bounds.size.height - 100.0f)
 toPoint:CGPointMake(self.view.bounds.size.width,
                     self.view.bounds.size.height - 100.0f)];

[self.animator addBehavior:collision];
```

Now, when we mix this up with gravity as before, our square views will fall to the bottom of the reference view but won't quite hit the bottom because our boundary is positioned a bit higher. As part of this recipe, I am also going to demonstrate the ability to detect collisions between various items that have been added to your collision behavior. The UICollisionBehavior class has a property called collisionDelegate that will be the delegate whenever a collision is detected on the items that have been added to the collision behavior. This delegate object has to conform to the UICollisionBehaviorDelegate protocol, which has a few methods that you can implement. Here are two of the most important methods in this protocol:

collisionBehavior:beganContactForItem:withBoundaryIdentifier:atPoint:
: Gets called on the delegate when an item in your collision behavior collides with one of the boundaries that you've added to the behavior.

collisionBehavior:endedContactForItem:withBoundaryIdentifier:atPoint:
: Gets called when the item that hit the boundary has bounced off the boundary and is no longer colliding with that boundary.

To demonstrate the delegate's activities to you and show you how you could use it, we are going to expand on our previous example. As soon as our square views hit the bottom of our reference view's boundary, we will set their color to red, enlarge them by 200% in size, and then fade them out to simulate an explosion:

```
NSString *const kBottomBoundary = @"bottomBoundary";

@interface ViewController () <UICollisionBehaviorDelegate>
```

```
@property (nonatomic, strong) NSMutableArray *squareViews;
@property (nonatomic, strong) UIDynamicAnimator *animator;
@end

@implementation ViewController

- (void)collisionBehavior:(UICollisionBehavior*)paramBehavior
      beganContactForItem:(id <UIDynamicItem>)paramItem
   withBoundaryIdentifier:(id <NSCopying>)paramIdentifier
                  atPoint:(CGPoint)paramPoint{

    NSString *identifier = (NSString *)paramIdentifier;

    if ([identifier isEqualToString:kBottomBoundary]){

        [UIView animateWithDuration:1.0f animations:^{
            UIView *view = (UIView *)paramItem;

            view.backgroundColor = [UIColor redColor];
            view.alpha = 0.0f;
            view.transform = CGAffineTransformMakeScale(2.0f, 2.0f);
        } completion:^(BOOL finished) {
            UIView *view = (UIView *)paramItem;
            [paramBehavior removeItem:paramItem];
            [view removeFromSuperview];
        }];

    }

}

- (void)viewDidAppear:(BOOL)animated{
    [super viewDidAppear:animated];

    /* Create the views */
    NSUInteger const NumberOfViews = 2;

    self.squareViews = [[NSMutableArray alloc] initWithCapacity:NumberOfViews];
    NSArray *colors = @[[UIColor redColor], [UIColor greenColor]];

    CGPoint currentCenterPoint = CGPointMake(self.view.center.x, 0.0f);
    CGSize eachViewSize = CGSizeMake(50.0f, 50.0f);
    for (NSUInteger counter = 0; counter < NumberOfViews; counter++){

        UIView *newView =
        [[UIView alloc] initWithFrame:
         CGRectMake(0.0f, 0.0f, eachViewSize.width, eachViewSize.height)];

        newView.backgroundColor = colors[counter];
        newView.center = currentCenterPoint;

        currentCenterPoint.y += eachViewSize.height + 10.0f;
```

```
        [self.view addSubview:newView];

        [self.squareViews addObject:newView];

    }

    self.animator = [[UIDynamicAnimator alloc]
                     initWithReferenceView:self.view];

    /* Create gravity */
    UIGravityBehavior *gravity = [[UIGravityBehavior alloc]
                                  initWithItems:self.squareViews];
    [self.animator addBehavior:gravity];

    /* Create collision detection */
    UICollisionBehavior *collision = [[UICollisionBehavior alloc]
                                      initWithItems:self.squareViews];
    [collision
     addBoundaryWithIdentifier:kBottomBoundary
     fromPoint:CGPointMake(0.0f, self.view.bounds.size.height - 100.0f)
     toPoint:CGPointMake(self.view.bounds.size.width,
                         self.view.bounds.size.height - 100.0f)];
    collision.collisionDelegate = self;

    [self.animator addBehavior:collision];

}
```

I'll explain what is happening in our code here. First, we create two views and place them on top of each other. These views are just two simple, colored squares, the second on top of the first, added to the view of our view controller. As in our previous examples, we are adding gravity to our animator so that once the animation kicks in, our views will be dragged toward the bottom of the screen as if descending to the ground. Then, instead of setting the boundaries of our reference view as the boundaries of collision, we are using the `addBoundaryWithIdentifier:fromPoint:toPoint` method of our collision behavior to create a boundary near the bottom of the screen—specifically, 100 points away from the bottommost point. This will create an invisible line segment that runs from the left side to the right side of the screen, and prevents the views from falling all the way down and out of the reference view.

Also, as you can see, we are setting our view controller as the delegate of the collision behavior. This means that we get updates from the collision behavior telling us when a collision has occurred. Once you learn that one has occurred, you will probably want to find out whether it was with a boundary (such as the one we've created) or an item on the scene. For instance, if you have various virtual walls that you've created on your reference view and your small square views collide with one of those walls, you may want to create a different effect (such as an explosion) based on which boundary they hit. You can find out what the item collided with from the delegate method that gets called on your view controller, which gives you the identifier of the boundary that the item collided with. Knowing what the object is, you can then make a decision about what to do with it.

In our example, we compare the identifier that comes back from the collision behavior with our `kBottomBoundary` constant, which we assigned to our barrier when we created it. We create an animation for the object that moves a square view down the screen, using the gravity and the boundary that we set up. The boundary ensures that the view won't go past the 100-point limit that we have created at the bottom of the screen.

One of the interesting properties of the `UIGravityBehavior` class is `collisionMode`. This property dictates how the collision should be managed in the animator. For instance, in our previous example, we saw a typical collision behavior added to an animator without modifying the value of the `collisionMode`. In this case, the collision behavior was detecting collisions between our small square views and the boundaries that we had set around the reference view. However, this behavior can be changed by modifying the value of the aforementioned property. Here are the values that you can set for this property:

`UICollisionBehaviorModeItems`
: Setting this value means that the collision behavior will detect collisions between dynamic items, such as our small square views.

`UICollisionBehaviorModeBoundaries`
: This tells the collision behavior that it has to detect collisions of dynamic items with the boundaries that we have set up, such as the boundaries around our reference view.

`UICollisionBehaviorModeEverything`
: This dictates to the collision behavior that it has to detect all types of collisions, regardless of whether they are boundaries, items, or something else. This is the default value of this property.

> The values that we just talked about can be mixed together using bitwise OR operators so that you can create a combination of collision modes that comply with your business requirements.

I suggest that you go on and change the value of the `collisionMode` property of the collision behavior in our previous example to `UICollisionBehaviorModeBoundaries` and then run the app. You will see that both of the square views will drop down to the bottom of the screen near the boundaries that we set up, but instead of the items colliding with each other, they will move into each other because the collision behavior doesn't care about or even notice the collision between them.

## See Also

Recipe 2.1

# 2.3. Animating Your UI Components with a Push

## Problem

You want to "flick" your views from one point to another.

## Solution

Initialize a behavior object of type `UIPushBehavior` using its `initWithItems:mode:` method, and for the mode, pass the value of `UIPushBehaviorModeContinuous`. Once you are ready to start pushing the items toward an angle, issue the `setAngle:` method on the push behavior to set the angle (in radians) for the behavior. After that, you will need to set the *magnitude*, or the force behind the push. You can set this force using the `setMagnitude:` method of the push behavior. The magnitude is calculated in this way: each magnitude of 1 point will result in acceleration of 100 points per second squared for your target views.

## Discussion

Push behaviors, especially continuous pushes, are very useful. Let's say you are working on a scrapbook iPad app, and on top of the screen, you have created three slides, each representing one of the scrapbook pages that the user has created. On the bottom of the screen, you have various pictures that the user can drag and drop into the pages. One way to allow the user to do this is to add a tap gesture recognizer (see Recipe 10.5) to your reference view to track the tap and allow the pictures to be moved onto the target slide, which will, in turn, simulate the dragging. The other, and perhaps better, way of doing this is to use the push behavior that Apple has introduced into UIKit.

The push behavior is of type `UIPushBehavior` and has a magnitude and an angle. The angle is measured in radians, and a magnitude of 1 point will result in acceleration of 100 points per second squared. We create push behaviors like we create any other behaviors: we need to initialize them and then add them to an animator of type `UIDynamicAnimator`.

For this example, we are going to create a view and place it at the center of our view controller's view. We are going to incorporate a collision behavior into our animator, which will prevent our little view from going outside the bounds of our view controller's view. You learned this technique in Recipe 2.2. We are then going to add a tap gesture recognizer (see Recipe 10.5) to our view controller's view so that we will be notified whenever a tap occurs.

When a tap is detected, we will calculate the angle between the tap point and the center of our small square view. This will give us the angle, in radians, toward which we can push the small square view. Then we will calculate the distance between the tap point and the center of our small square view, which will then give us a value that can be used as the magnitude of the push. This means that the magnitude will be larger the farther away the tap point and the center of the small square view are.

In this recipe, I'm assuming that you are already familiar with the basics of trigonometry. But if you aren't, that's OK too because all you really need are the formulas that I have described in the example code for this recipe. In Figure 2-2, you can see how the angle between two points is calculated, so I'm hoping that this will give us enough information to write our solution to this problem.

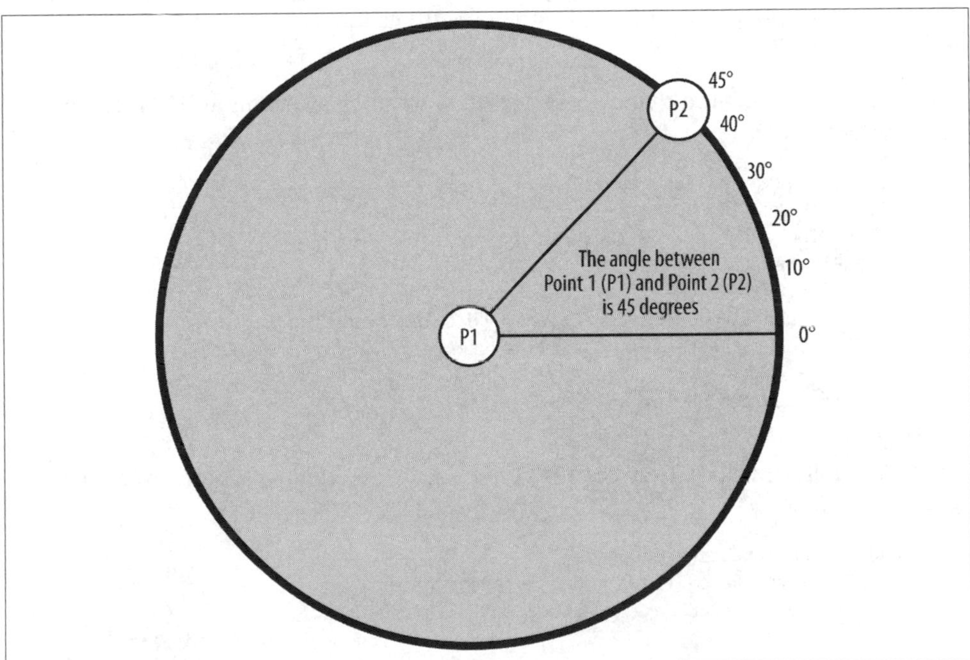


*Figure 2-2. Calculating the angle between two points*

So let's get started by declaring the relevant properties of our view controller:

```
#import "ViewController.h"

@interface ViewController ()
@property (nonatomic, strong) UIView *squareView;
@property (nonatomic, strong) UIDynamicAnimator *animator;
@property (nonatomic, strong) UIPushBehavior *pushBehavior;
@end
```

```
@implementation ViewController

<# Rest of your code goes here #>
```

Our example adds a collision and a push behavior to our animator. The push behavior is added as a property to our class, whereas the collision behavior is just a local variable. The reason behind this is that once we are done adding the collision behavior to our animator, we will leave the animator to calculate all collisions with the boundaries of our reference view and we will no longer need to reference that collision behavior. However, in the case of our push behavior, when we handle taps, we will want to update the push behavior so that it pushes our item toward the tap point. That is why we need to have a reference to the push behavior but not the collision.

The next stop is a method that creates our small square view for us and places it on our view controller's view:

```
- (void) createSmallSquareView{
    self.squareView =
    [[UIView alloc] initWithFrame:
     CGRectMake(0.0f, 0.0f, 80.0f, 80.0f)];

    self.squareView.backgroundColor = [UIColor greenColor];
    self.squareView.center = self.view.center;

    [self.view addSubview:self.squareView];
}
```

Right after that, we will use a tap gesture recognizer to detect taps on our view controller's view:

```
- (void) createGestureRecognizer{
    UITapGestureRecognizer *tapGestureRecognizer =
    [[UITapGestureRecognizer alloc] initWithTarget:self
                                            action:@selector(handleTap:)];
    [self.view addGestureRecognizer:tapGestureRecognizer];
}
```

These methods do all our work for us. Later, when our view gets displayed on the screen, we will call these methods so that they can carry out their work.

And let's not forget a method that will set up our collision and push behaviors:

```
- (void) createAnimatorAndBehaviors{
    self.animator = [[UIDynamicAnimator alloc]
```

```
                               initWithReferenceView:self.view];

    /* Create collision detection */
    UICollisionBehavior *collision = [[UICollisionBehavior alloc]
                                      initWithItems:@[self.squareView]];
    collision.translatesReferenceBoundsIntoBoundary = YES;

    self.pushBehavior = [[UIPushBehavior alloc]
                         initWithItems:@[self.squareView]
                         mode:UIPushBehaviorModeContinuous];

    [self.animator addBehavior:collision];
    [self.animator addBehavior:self.pushBehavior];
}
```

To learn more about collision behaviors, please have a look at Recipe 2.2. Once we set up all these methods, we need to call them when our view appears on the screen:

```
- (void)viewDidAppear:(BOOL)animated{
    [super viewDidAppear:animated];

    [self createGestureRecognizer];
    [self createSmallSquareView];
    [self createAnimatorAndBehaviors];

}
```

Brilliant. Now if you look at our implementation of the `createGestureRecognizer` method, you will notice that we are installing our tap gesture recognizer on a method in our view controller called `handleTap:`. In this method, we will calculate the distance between the center point of the small square view and the point where the user tapped on the reference view. This will give us the magnitude of the push force. We will also calculate the angle between the center of the small square view and the tap point to figure out the angle of the push.

```
- (void) handleTap:(UITapGestureRecognizer *)paramTap{

    /* Get the angle between the center of the square view
     and the tap point */

    CGPoint tapPoint = [paramTap locationInView:self.view];
    CGPoint squareViewCenterPoint = self.squareView.center;

    /* Calculate the angle between the center point of the square view and
     the tap point to find out the angle of the push

     Formula for detecting the angle between two points is:

     arc tangent 2((p1.x - p2.x), (p1.y - p2.y)) */
    CGFloat deltaX = tapPoint.x - squareViewCenterPoint.x;
    CGFloat deltaY = tapPoint.y - squareViewCenterPoint.y;
    CGFloat angle = atan2(deltaY, deltaX);
```

```
    [self.pushBehavior setAngle:angle];

    /* Use the distance between the tap point and the center of our square
     view to calculate the magnitude of the push

     Distance formula is:
     square root of ((p1.x - p2.x)^2 + (p1.y - p2.y)^2) */
    CGFloat distanceBetweenPoints =
    sqrt(pow(tapPoint.x - squareViewCenterPoint.x, 2.0) +
         pow(tapPoint.y - squareViewCenterPoint.y, 2.0));
    [self.pushBehavior setMagnitude:distanceBetweenPoints / 200.0f];

}
```

I am not going to dive into trigonometry here, but this code uses a basic formula taught in high school trigonometry to calculate the angle between two points in radians, along with the Pythagorean theorem to get the distance between two points. You can find these formulas by looking at the comments that I've left in the code, but if you want a deeper understanding of things such as radians and angles, please obtain a basic text on trigonometry.

Now if you run your app, you will first see a green small square view at the center of your screen. Tap anywhere on the area around this view (the white area) to start moving your green view. In this example, I am dividing the distance between the tap point and the center point of the small square view by 200 to get a realistic push magnitude, but you can increase the acceleration of your push behavior, such as by reducing this number from 200 to 100. It's best to experiment with different numbers to get the right feel for *your* app.

## See Also

Recipe 2.2

# 2.4. Attaching Multiple Dynamic Items to Each Other

## Problem

You want to attach dynamic items, such as views, so that the movements in one will cascade to the second view automatically. Alternatively, you want to attach a dynamic item to an anchor point so that when that point moves (because your app or the user moves it), the item will automatically move with it.

## Solution

Instantiate an attachment behavior of type `UIAttachmentBehavior`, using the `initWithItem:point:attachedToAnchor:` instance method of this class. Add this behavior to an animator (see Recipe 2.0, "Introduction"), which will take care of the dynamics and the physics of movement.

## Discussion

The attachment behavior is at first a bit difficult to understand. In simple terms, you can set an anchor and then have a point follow that anchor. But I'd like to give you more details.

Let's say that you have a large photo on a flat desk. Now if you place your index finger on the upper-right corner of the photo and start moving it around, the picture may rotate around your fingertip, and may not go exactly straight toward the direction you are moving it to. But if you move your finger to the center of the photo and move it around, the photo will not rotate around your fingertip. You can create the same real-life behavior using the attachment behavior in UIKit.

In this recipe, we want to create an effect similar to that explained in Figure 2-3.

In Figure 2-3 you can see that we have three views on our screen. The main view is in the center and includes another small view at its top-right corner. The small view is the point that will follow our anchor point, as explained earlier by my photo example. Last but not least, we have the anchor point, which will be moved around the screen with a pan gesture recognizer (see Recipe 10.3). The movements on this view will then cause our view at the center of the screen to move as well. First, let's declare the necessary properties of our view controller:

```
#import "ViewController.h"

@interface ViewController ()
@property (nonatomic, strong) UIView *squareView;
@property (nonatomic, strong) UIView *squareViewAnchorView;
@property (nonatomic, strong) UIView *anchorView;
@property (nonatomic, strong) UIDynamicAnimator *animator;
@property (nonatomic, strong) UIAttachmentBehavior *attachmentBehavior;
@end

@implementation ViewController

<# Rest of your view controller's code goes here #>
```

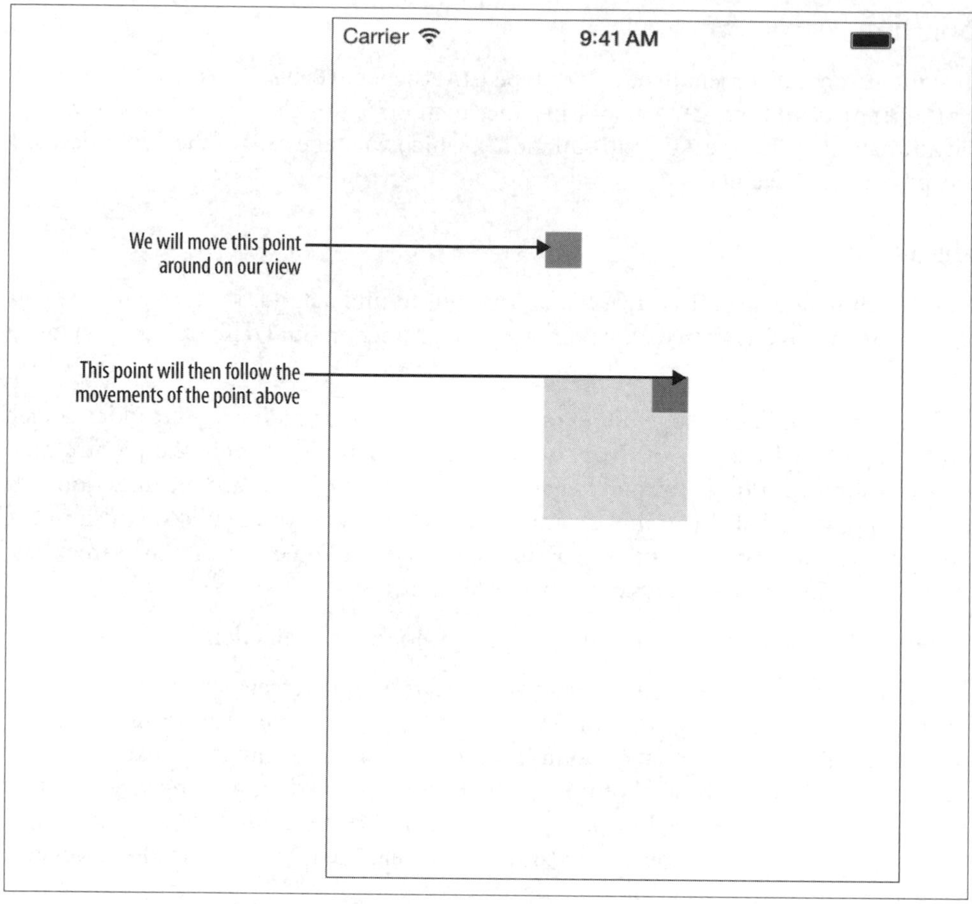


*Figure 2-3. This is what we want to achieve with the attachment behavior in this recipe*

The next thing we have to do is create our small square view. But this time, we are going to put another view inside it. The smaller view, which will be at the top-right corner of the parent view, will be connected virtually to the anchor point of the attachment behavior, just as explained in the photo example:

```
- (void) createSmallSquareView{
    self.squareView =
    [[UIView alloc] initWithFrame:
     CGRectMake(0.0f, 0.0f, 80.0f, 80.0f)];

    self.squareView.backgroundColor = [UIColor greenColor];
    self.squareView.center = self.view.center;

    self.squareViewAnchorView = [[UIView alloc] initWithFrame:
                                 CGRectMake(60.0f, 0.0f, 20.0f, 20.0f)];
    self.squareViewAnchorView.backgroundColor = [UIColor brownColor];
```

```
    [self.squareView addSubview:self.squareViewAnchorView];

    [self.view addSubview:self.squareView];
}
```

Next up, the creation of the anchor point view:

```
- (void) createAnchorView{

    self.anchorView = [[UIView alloc] initWithFrame:
                       CGRectMake(120.0f, 120.0f, 20.0f, 20.0f)];
    self.anchorView.backgroundColor = [UIColor redColor];
    [self.view addSubview:self.anchorView];

}
```

Then we need to create our pan gesture recognizer and the animator, as we have already seen in other recipes in this chapter:

```
- (void) createGestureRecognizer{
    UIPanGestureRecognizer *panGestureRecognizer =
    [[UIPanGestureRecognizer alloc] initWithTarget:self
                                            action:@selector(handlePan:)];
    [self.view addGestureRecognizer:panGestureRecognizer];
}

- (void) createAnimatorAndBehaviors{

    self.animator = [[UIDynamicAnimator alloc]
                     initWithReferenceView:self.view];

    /* Create collision detection */
    UICollisionBehavior *collision = [[UICollisionBehavior alloc]
                                      initWithItems:@[self.squareView]];
    collision.translatesReferenceBoundsIntoBoundary = YES;

    self.attachmentBehavior = [[UIAttachmentBehavior alloc]
                               initWithItem:self.squareView
                               point:self.squareViewAnchorView.center
                               attachedToAnchor:self.anchorView.center];
    [self.animator addBehavior:collision];
    [self.animator addBehavior:self.attachmentBehavior];
}

- (void)viewDidAppear:(BOOL)animated{
    [super viewDidAppear:animated];

    [self createGestureRecognizer];
    [self createSmallSquareView];
    [self createAnchorView];
    [self createAnimatorAndBehaviors];
}
```

You can see how we are initializing our anchor behavior, using its `initWithItem:point:attachedToAnchor:` instance method. This method takes in the following parameters:

`initWithItem`
: The dynamic item, or in our example, the view, that has to be connected to the anchor point.

`point`
: The point inside the dynamic item that has to be connected to the anchor point. This behavior uses the center point of the item to establish a connection to the anchor point. But you can change that by providing a different value to this parameter.

`attachedToAnchor`
: The anchor point itself, measured as a `CGPoint` value.

Now that we have connected the square view's top-right corner to an anchor point (represented by the anchor point view), we need to demonstrate that by moving the anchor point, we will indirectly also move the square view. If you look at the `createGestureRecognizer` method that we wrote earlier, we created a pan gesture recognizer that will track the user's finger movements on the screen. We have elected the `handlePan:` method of our view to handle the gesture recognizer, and we will implement that method like so:

```
- (void) handlePan:(UIPanGestureRecognizer *)paramPan{

    CGPoint tapPoint = [paramPan locationInView:self.view];
    [self.attachmentBehavior setAnchorPoint:tapPoint];
    self.anchorView.center = tapPoint;

}
```

What we are doing here is detecting the point of movement on our view and then moving the anchor point to that point. After we do this, the attachment behavior will then move our small square view as well.

## See Also

Recipe 10.3; Recipe 2.0, "Introduction"

# 2.5. Adding a Dynamic Snap Effect to Your UI Components

## Problem

Using an animation, you want to snap a view in your UI to a specific point on the screen, with the elasticity of a real-world snap effect. This means that when your UI component snaps to the given point, you will feel that it has elasticity built into it.

## Solution

Instantiate an object of type `UISnapBehavior` and add it to an animator of type `UIDynamicAnimator`.

## Discussion

To really understand how the snap dynamic behavior works, think about a small amount of jelly covered in oil with a string attached to it, sitting on a very smooth table. I know that sentence sounds really odd. But bear with me. Now imagine from another point on the table, pulling on that string to get the jelly to move from its initial point to the point you ordered it to move to. With the oil all around it, the jelly will move smoothly from that point to where you want it to go, and because it is jelly, it will wiggle when it snaps to position. This behavior is exactly what you can achieve with the `UISnapBehavior` class.

One of the use cases for this is when you have an app and some views on the screen, such as images, and you want the user to be able to dictate where those views have to be moved to create a customized UI for the user. One way of handling this is using the technique that we learned in Recipe 2.3, but that solution is quite rigid and has its own use cases. Here in this recipe, we have a view on our screen, and we want to allow the user to tap anywhere on the screen to relocate the view. We will then snap that view to the point where that tap originated.

So what we are going to do in this recipe is create a small view in the center of our view controller's view and then attach a tap gesture recognizer (Recipe 10.5) to our view controller's view. Whenever the user taps anywhere on the screen, we will snap the small square view to that point. So let's begin by defining the required properties of our view controller:

```
#import "ViewController.h"

@interface ViewController ()
@property (nonatomic, strong) UIView *squareView;
@property (nonatomic, strong) UIDynamicAnimator *animator;
@property (nonatomic, strong) UISnapBehavior *snapBehavior;
@end
```

```
@implementation ViewController

<# Rest of your code goes here #>
```

The next thing to do is create a method that will create our tap gesture recognizer for us:

```
- (void) createGestureRecognizer{

    UITapGestureRecognizer *tap = [[UITapGestureRecognizer alloc]
                                   initWithTarget:self
                                   action:@selector(handleTap:)];
    [self.view addGestureRecognizer:tap];

}
```

Just like the previous recipes, we also need to create a small view in the center of the screen. I've chosen the center arbitrarily, so you can create it at a different point if you want to. We will then snap this view to where the user taps on the screen. So here is our method for creating this view:

```
- (void) createSmallSquareView{
    self.squareView =
    [[UIView alloc] initWithFrame:
     CGRectMake(0.0f, 0.0f, 80.0f, 80.0f)];

    self.squareView.backgroundColor = [UIColor greenColor];
    self.squareView.center = self.view.center;

    [self.view addSubview:self.squareView];
}
```

The next step is to create our animator (see Recipe 2.0, "Introduction") and attach our snap behavior to it. We will initialize the snap behavior of type `UISnapBehavior` using its `initWithItem:snapToPoint:` method. This method takes two parameters:

`initWithItem`
: The dynamic item (in this case, our view) that the snap behavior has to be applied to. Just like all the other dynamic UI behaviors, this item has to conform to the `UIDynamicItem` protocol. By default, all `UIView` instances conform to this protocol so we are good to go.

`snapToPoint`
: The point on the reference view (see Recipe 2.0, "Introduction") that the dynamic item has to snap to.

There is one very important thing to note about the snap behavior: for it to work on a specific item, you will need to have at least one instance of the snap behavior for that item already added to the animator but snapping the item to its current position. After that, subsequent snaps will work properly. Let me demonstrate this to you. We will now implement a method that will create the snap behavior and the animator and will add the snap behavior to the animator:

```
- (void) createAnimatorAndBehaviors{
    self.animator = [[UIDynamicAnimator alloc]
                     initWithReferenceView:self.view];

    /* Create collision detection */
    UICollisionBehavior *collision = [[UICollisionBehavior alloc]
                                      initWithItems:@[self.squareView]];
    collision.translatesReferenceBoundsIntoBoundary = YES;

    [self.animator addBehavior:collision];

    /* For now, snap the square view to its current center */
    self.snapBehavior = [[UISnapBehavior alloc]
                         initWithItem:self.squareView
                         snapToPoint:self.squareView.center];
    self.snapBehavior.damping = 0.5f; /* Medium oscillation */
    [self.animator addBehavior:self.snapBehavior];
}
```

As you can see, we are currently snapping the small square view to its current center, essentially not moving it at all from its position. Later, when we detect tap gestures on our screen, we will update the snap behavior. Also note that we are setting the `damping` property of our snap behavior. This property will control the elasticity with which your item will snap to place. Higher values mean less elasticity and therefore less wiggle motion. This value can be anything from 0 to 1. Now when our view appears on the screen, we will call all these methods to instantiate our small square view, set up the tap gesture recognizer, and set up the animator and the snap behavior:

```
- (void)viewDidAppear:(BOOL)animated{
    [super viewDidAppear:animated];

    [self createGestureRecognizer];
    [self createSmallSquareView];
    [self createAnimatorAndBehaviors];
}
```

When we created the tap gesture recognizer in the `createGestureRecognizer` method of our view controller, we asked the recognizer to report the taps to the `handleTap:` method of our view controller. In this method, we will get the point where the user tapped on the screen, and we will then update our snap behavior.

The important thing to note here is that you cannot just update the existing behavior without reinstantiating it. So before we instantiate a new instance of the snap behavior, we have to remove the old one (if any) and then add a new one to our animator. Each animator can have only one snap behavior attached to a specific dynamic item, in this case, our small square view. If you add multiple snap behaviors for the same dynamic item to the same animator, the animator will ignore all your snap behaviors for that item, because it won't know which one to execute first. So to make the behavior work, first remove all the snap behaviors for that item from your animator, using its `removeBehavior:` method, and then add a new snap behavior like so:

```
- (void) handleTap:(UITapGestureRecognizer *)paramTap{

    /* Get the angle between the center of the square view
     and the tap point */

    CGPoint tapPoint = [paramTap locationInView:self.view];

    if (self.snapBehavior != nil){
        [self.animator removeBehavior:self.snapBehavior];
    }

    self.snapBehavior = [[UISnapBehavior alloc] initWithItem:self.squareView
                                                 snapToPoint:tapPoint];
    self.snapBehavior.damping = 0.5f; /* Medium oscillation */
    [self.animator addBehavior:self.snapBehavior];
}
```

## See Also

Recipe 10.5; Recipe 2.0, "Introduction"

# 2.6. Assigning Characteristics to Your Dynamic Effects

## Problem

You like the default physics built into the dynamic behaviors of UIKit, but you want to be able to assign different characteristics, such as mass and elasticity, to various items that you control using dynamic behaviors.

## Solution

Instantiate an object of type `UIDynamicItemBehavior` and assign your dynamic items to it. Once instantiated, use the various properties of this class to change the characteristics of your dynamic items. Then add this behavior to your animator (see Recipe 2.0, "Introduction") and let the animator take care of the rest for you.

## Discussion

Dynamic behaviors are great for adding real-life physics to items that conform to the `UIDynamicItem` protocol, such as all views of type `UIView`. In some apps, though, you may wish to explicitly specify the characteristics of a specific item. For instance, in an app where you are using gravity and collision behaviors (see Recipe 2.1 and Recipe 2.2), you may wish to specify that one of the items on your screen affected by this gravity and the collision has to bounce harder than the other item when it collides with a boundary. Another example is when you want to specify that an item, during all the different dynamic animations that will be applied to it with an animator, should not rotate at all.

These are all easily doable when you use instances of the `UIDynamicItemBehavior` class. These instances are dynamic behaviors too, and you can add them to an animator using the `addBehavior:` instance method of the `UIDynamicAnimator` class, as you have already seen in this chapter. When you initialize an instance of this class, you can call the `initWithItems:` initializer and pass your view, or any object that conforms to the `UIDynamicItem` protocol. Alternatively, initialize your dynamic item behavior instance using the `init` method and later add different objects to the behavior using the `addItem:` method.

Instances of the `UIDynamicItemBehavior` have properties that you can adjust in order to customize the behavior of your dynamic items (views, for instance). Some of the most important properties of this class are listed and explained here:

`allowsRotation`
: A Boolean value that, when set to `YES`, as its name implies, allows your dynamic items to get rotated by the animator during the animations that get applied to them. You would ideally want the value of this property to be set to `YES` if you want to mimic real-life physics, but if for any reason in your app you need to ensure that a specific item never rotates, set this property to `NO` and attach the item to this behavior.

`resistance`
: The resistance of the item to movement. This can be from 0 to `CGFLOAT_MAX`. The higher the value, the more resistant that item becomes to forces that you'll apply to it. For instance, if you add a gravity behavior to your animator and create a view in the center of the screen with the resistance of `CGFLOAT_MAX`, the gravity won't be able to force that view down toward its center. The view will just be stuck where you create it.

`friction`
: A floating point value from 0.0 to 1.0 that specifies how much friction should be applied to the edges of this item when other items hit it or slide by its edges. The higher the value, the more friction applied to that item.

  The more friction you put on an item, the more *sticky* that item becomes. This stickiness will be contagious in that, when other items collide with the sticky item, it will feel as if those items are sticking to the target item a bit more than usual. Just think about the friction of tires on a car. The more friction between the tires and the asphalt, the slower the car will move, but the better the grip it will have on slippery roads. This is exactly the type of friction that this property will allow you to assign to your items.

`elasticity`
: A floating point from 0.0 to 1.0 that specifies how elastic an item should be. The higher this value, the more elastic and jelly-like this item will appear to the eyes of the animator. See Recipe 2.5 for an explanation of elasticity.

`density`
: A floating point value between 0 and 1 (the default value is 1) that isn't directly used to affect your dynamic item's behaviors but is used by the animator to calculate the mass of your objects and to find out how that mass will affect your animations. For instance, if you flick two items onto each other (see Recipe 2.3), and one of them has a density of 1 and the other has a density of 0.5, the former item's mass will be more than the latter, given that both items are of the same width and height. The animator calculates the mass of items using their density and size on screen. So if you flick a small view with a high density at a big view with a very low density, the small view may, depending on its size and the value of the density, be seen by your animator as the item with more mass. The animator may push away the item that appears larger on screen harder than the larger item will push the small item.

Let's have a look at an example. This is loosely based on the example that we saw in Recipe 2.2. In this example, we are going to place two views on top of each other, but we are going to make the view on the bottom have a very high elasticity and the view on top have quite a low elasticity. This way, when both views hit the bottom of the screen, where they will collide with the bottom bounds of the screen, the view on the bottom will jump around and bounce much more, due to its high elasticity, than the view on the top. So let's get started by defining the animator and other properties of our view controller:

```
#import "ViewController.h"

@interface ViewController ()
@property (nonatomic, strong) UIDynamicAnimator *animator;
@end

@implementation ViewController

<# Rest of your code goes here #>
```

Next, we will code a handy method that will be able to create views for us with a specific center point and background colors. We will use this method to create two very similar views with different background colors and center points:

```
- (UIView *) newViewWithCenter:(CGPoint)paramCenter
              backgroundColor:(UIColor *)paramBackgroundColor{

    UIView *newView =
    [[UIView alloc] initWithFrame:
     CGRectMake(0.0f, 0.0f, 50.0f, 50.0f)];
```

```
    newView.backgroundColor = paramBackgroundColor;
    newView.center = paramCenter;

    return newView;

}
```

Now when our view gets displayed on the screen, we will create these two views and add them to the screen:

```
UIView *topView = [self newViewWithCenter:CGPointMake(100.0f, 0.0f)
                          backgroundColor:[UIColor greenColor]];
UIView *bottomView = [self newViewWithCenter:CGPointMake(100.0f, 50.0f)
                             backgroundColor:[UIColor redColor]];

[self.view addSubview:topView];
[self.view addSubview:bottomView];
```

Now we are going to add a gravity behavior to our views, as we learned in Recipe 2.1:

```
self.animator = [[UIDynamicAnimator alloc]
                 initWithReferenceView:self.view];

/* Create gravity */
UIGravityBehavior *gravity = [[UIGravityBehavior alloc]
                              initWithItems:@[topView, bottomView]];
[self.animator addBehavior:gravity];
```

We don't want our views to fall off the bottom of the screen, so we are going to use what we learned in Recipe 2.2 to set a boundary and collision behavior for our animator:

```
/* Create collision detection */
UICollisionBehavior *collision = [[UICollisionBehavior alloc]
                                  initWithItems:@[topView, bottomView]];
collision.translatesReferenceBoundsIntoBoundary = YES;

[self.animator addBehavior:collision];
```

Last but not least, we are going to add the dynamic behavior to our views, making the view on top less elastic than the one on the bottom:

```
/* Now specify the elasticity of the items */
UIDynamicItemBehavior *moreElasticItem = [[UIDynamicItemBehavior alloc]
                                          initWithItems:@[bottomView]];
moreElasticItem.elasticity = 1.0f;

UIDynamicItemBehavior *lessElasticItem = [[UIDynamicItemBehavior alloc]
                                          initWithItems:@[topView]];
lessElasticItem.elasticity = 0.5f;
[self.animator addBehavior:moreElasticItem];
[self.animator addBehavior:lessElasticItem];
```

Now you can run your app and see how your views will bounce off the bottom of the screen once they hit it (see Figure 2-4).

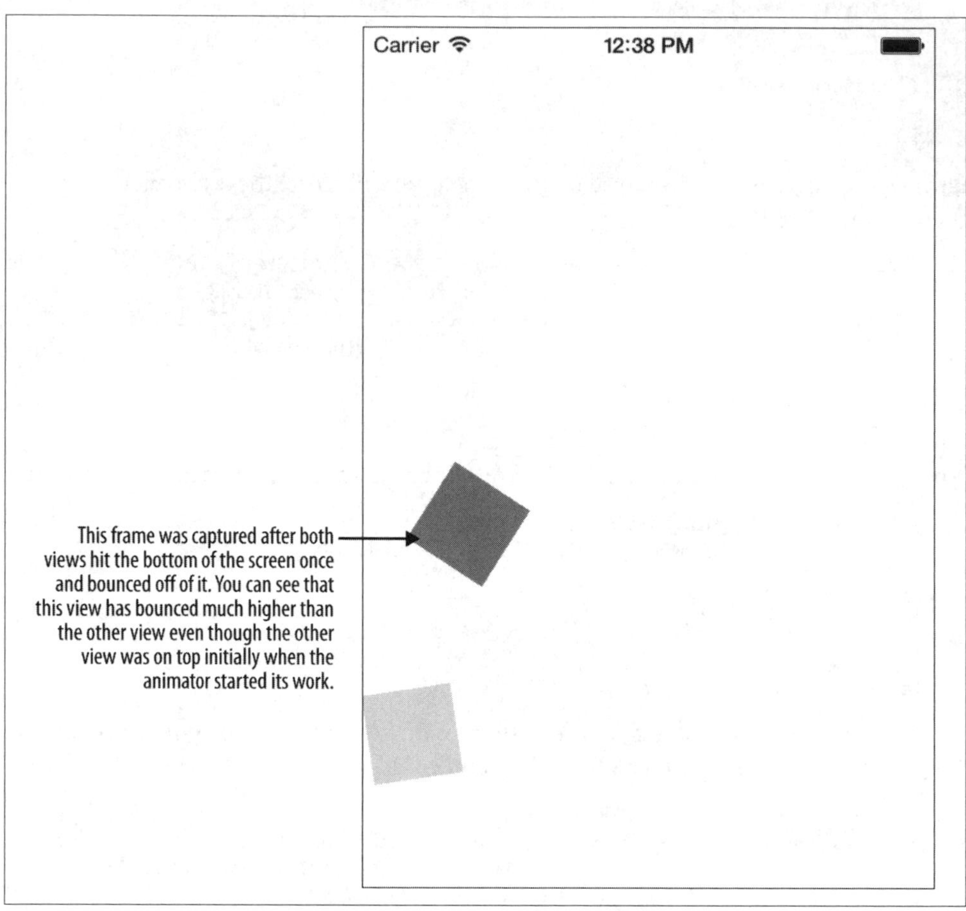


*Figure 2-4. One view is more elastic than the other*

## See Also

Recipe 2.0, "Introduction"

CHAPTER 3

# Auto Layout and the Visual Format Language

## 3.0. Introduction

Aligning UI components has always been a big headache for programmers. Most of the view controllers in complex iOS apps contain a lot of code just to set the frame of UI components on the screen, align components horizontally/vertically, and make sure the components look good on different iOS versions. Not only that, but some programmers also want to use the same view controllers across various devices such as iPhones and iPads. This adds a lot of complexity to the code. Apple has made it easier for us with Auto Layout. It has brought Auto Layout from OS X over to iOS. We will be talking about the details of Auto Layout in a moment, but let me just give you a brief introduction to it and explain what it is for.

Let's say you have a button that you want to keep at the center of the screen. The relation between the center of the button and the center of the view on which it resides can be simply described like so:

- Button's center.x is equal to view's center.x.
- Button's center.y is equal to view's center.y.

Apple noticed that a lot of the positioning of UI components can be solved with a simple formula:

```
object1.property1 = (object2.property2 * multiplier) + constant value
```

For instance, using this formula, I could simply center a button on its superview like so:

```
button.center.x = (button.superview.center.x * 1) + 0
button.center.y = (button.superview.center.y * 1) + 0
```

Using this formula, you can do some really funky things during the UI development of your iOS apps that you could not do before. The aforementioned formula is wrapped inside a class in the iOS SDK called `NSLayoutConstraint`. Every constraint that you create (i.e., every instance of this class) represents only one constraint. For instance, if you want to center your button on the view that owns the button, you have to center the *x* and the *y* position of the button. That means you have to create two constraints. Centering simply cannot be expressed by one constraint. However, later in this chapter we will learn about the Visual Format Language, which is a great addition to the iOS language and simplifies things even further in terms of UI layouts.

Constraints can be created by cross views. For instance, if you have two buttons on one view and you want them to be 100 points apart vertically, you need to create the constraint for this rule but add it to the common ancestor of both the buttons, which is perhaps the view that owns both of them. These are the rules:

- If the constraint is between two views that sit on a common immediate parent view, meaning that both these views have the same superview, add the constraints to the parent view.
- If the constraint is between a view and its parent view, add the constraint to the parent view.
- If the constraint is between two views that do not share the same parent view, add the constraint to the common ancestor of the views.

Figure 3-1 is a graphical demonstration of how these constraints actually work.

Constraints are created using the `constraintWithItem:attribute:relatedBy:toItem:attribute:multiplier:constant:` class method of the `NSLayoutConstraint` class. The parameters to this method are the following:

`constraintWithItem`
: This is a parameter of type `id` and represents *object1* in the formula that I mentioned before.

`attribute`
: This represents *property1* in our formula and should be of type `NSLayoutAttribute`.

`relatedBy`
: This represents the *equals sign* in our formula. The value of this parameter is of type `NSLayoutRelation` and, as you will soon see, you can specify not only an equals sign, but a greater-than or less-than sign here. We will talk about this in detail in this chapter.

`toItem`
: This parameter is of type `id` and represents *object2* in our formula.

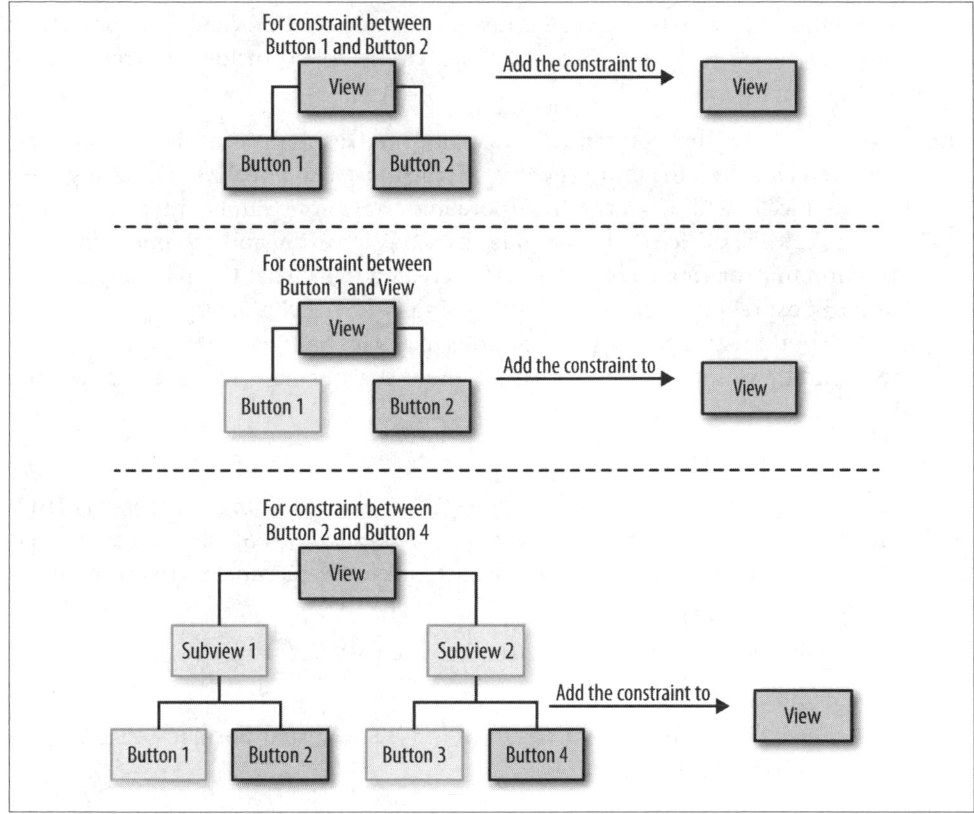


*Figure 3-1. The relationship between constraints and the views they should be added to*

`attribute`
: This parameter is of type `NSLayoutAttribute` and represents *property2* in our formula.

`multiplier`
: This parameter is of type `CGFloat` and represents *multiplier* in our formula.

`constant`
: This parameter is also of type `CGFloat` and represents *constant value* in our formula.

After you create your constraints, you can simply add them to the appropriate view (see Figure 3-1) using either one of these methods of the `UIView` class:

`addConstraint:`
: This method can add a single constraint of type `NSLayoutConstraint` to the view.

`addConstraints:`
: This method allows you to add an array of constraints to the view. The constraints again have to be of type `NSLayoutConstraint` wrapped inside an array of type `NSArray`.

There are many things that you can achieve with Auto Layout, as you will see in the rest of this chapter. However, the more you dive in, the more you'll realize that setting your layout automatically will mean creating more and more constraints of type `NSLayoutConstraint`. You will notice that your code size keeps growing and becomes more difficult to maintain. For this reason, Apple has created the Visual Format Language by which you can express your constraints using simply ASCII characters. For instance, if you have two buttons and you want the buttons to always be 100 points apart from each other horizontally, you would express it using the Visual Format Language code written like this:

```
[button1]-100-[button2]
```

Constraints with the Visual Format Language are created using the `constraintsWithVisualFormat:options:metrics:views:` class method of the `NSLayoutConstraint` class. Here is a brief explanation of each one of the parameters to this method:

`constraintsWithVisualFormat`
: The Visual Format Language expression, written as `NSString`.

`options`
: A parameter of type `NSLayoutFormatOptions`. For Visual Format Language, we usually pass 0 to this parameter.

`metrics`
: A dictionary of constant values that you use in your Visual Format Language expression. For the sake of simplicity, we will pass `nil` to this method for now.

`views`
: This is a dictionary of views that you have written the constraint for in the first parameter of this method. To construct this dictionary, simply use the `NSDictionaryOfVariableBindings` C function and pass your view objects to this method. It will then construct the dictionary for you. The keys in this dictionary are the view names that you should be using in the first parameter to this method. Don't worry if this is all a bit strange right now and doesn't make sense. Soon it will! Once you see a few examples of this, it will all click.

With this basic information in hand, and without bloating our heads with too much information, I believe it is time to dive straight into this chapter's recipes and flex our muscles with constraints a little bit. Are you ready? I know I am!

# 3.1. Placing UI Components in the Center of the Screen

## Problem

You want to be able to place a UI component in the center of the screen. In other words, you want to place a view at the center of its superview, using constraints.

## Solution

Create two constraints: one to align the center.x position of the target view on its superview's center.x position and the other to align the center.y position of the target view on its superview's center.y position.

## Discussion

Let's get started by first creating a simple button, which we will align at the center of the screen. As mentioned in the Solution section of this recipe, all we have to do is make sure the *x* and the *y* of the center of our button are the same as the *x* and *y* of the center of the view on which the button resides. So for this, we will create two constraints and add them to the view that owns the button, called the superview of the button. Here is the simple code that will achieve this:

```
#import "ViewController.h"

@interface ViewController ()
@property (nonatomic, strong) UIButton *button;
@end

@implementation ViewController

- (void)viewDidLoad{
    [super viewDidLoad];

    /* 1) Create our button */
    self.button = [UIButton buttonWithType:UIButtonTypeSystem];
    self.button.translatesAutoresizingMaskIntoConstraints = NO;
    [self.button setTitle:@"Button" forState:UIControlStateNormal];
    [self.view addSubview:self.button];

    UIView *superview = self.button.superview;

    /* 2) Create the constraint to put the button horizontally in the center */
    NSLayoutConstraint *centerXConstraint =
    [NSLayoutConstraint constraintWithItem:self.button
                                 attribute:NSLayoutAttributeCenterX
                                 relatedBy:NSLayoutRelationEqual
                                    toItem:superview
                                 attribute:NSLayoutAttributeCenterX
                                multiplier:1.0f
```

```
                                       constant:0.0f];

    /* 3) Create the constraint to put the button vertically in the center */
    NSLayoutConstraint *centerYConstraint =
    [NSLayoutConstraint constraintWithItem:self.button
                                 attribute:NSLayoutAttributeCenterY
                                 relatedBy:NSLayoutRelationEqual
                                    toItem:superview
                                 attribute:NSLayoutAttributeCenterY
                                multiplier:1.0f
                                  constant:0.0f];


    /* Add the constraints to the superview of the button */
    [superview addConstraints:@[centerXConstraint, centerYConstraint]];

}

@end
```

This view controller is trying to tell iOS that it supports all interface orientations that the device supports, to demonstrate that the button will indeed be placed in the center of the screen regardless of the type of device and its orientation. However, before this method takes over, you need to make sure you have enabled all required orientations inside your project itself. To do this, navigate in Xcode to your target properties, go to the General tab, find the Device Orientation section, and enable all the available orientations, as shown in Figure 3-2.

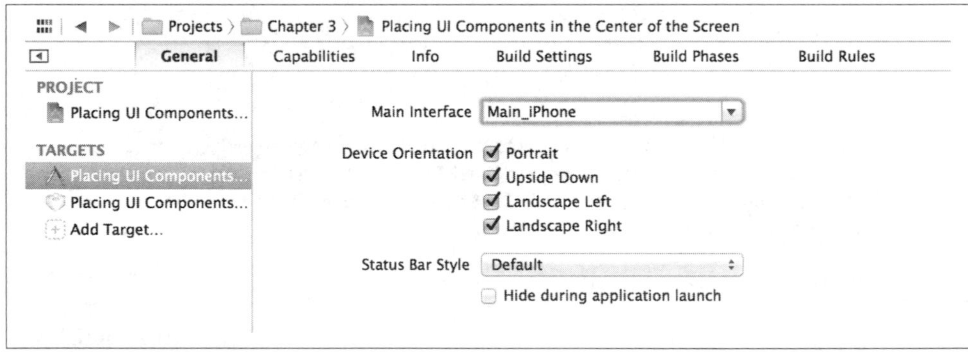


*Figure 3-2. Enabling all supported interface orientations in Xcode for your target*

Now if you run this app on the device or in the simulator, you will notice that a simple button is displayed on the screen. Now rotate the device and note how the button stays at the center of the screen. All of this was achieved without having to write a single line of code for setting the frame of the button or listening to any type of orientation change notification and adjusting the position of the button, thanks to Auto Layout. See Figure 3-3. This approach is better simply because our code now will work on any device in any orientation with any resolution. In contrast, if we were to set the frame of our UI components, we would have to set the frame for each orientation on each device we would want to support, because different iOS devices can have different screen resolutions. For instance, our app now will happily be able to run on an iPad or an iPhone and will retain the button in the center of the screen, regardless of the orientation or the resolution of the device and its display.

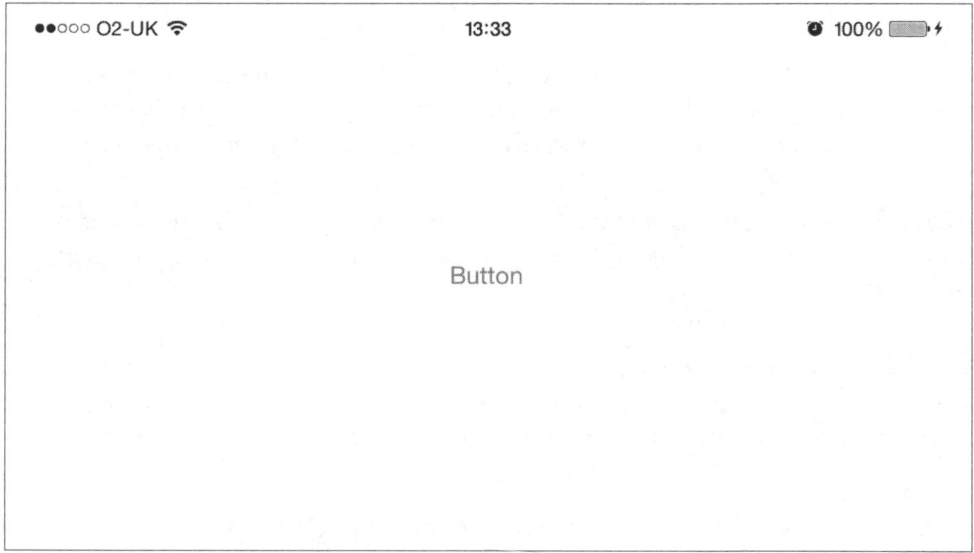


*Figure 3-3. The button is at the center of the screen in every orientation*

## See Also

Recipe 3.2; Recipe 3.0, "Introduction"

# 3.2. Defining Horizontal and Vertical Constraints with the Visual Format Language

## Problem

You want to be able to define constraints that change the way a UI component is horizontally or vertically aligned on its superview.

## Solution

Use the `H:` orientation specifier in the formatting string for your constraint to dictate horizontal alignment and the `V:` orientation specifier to dictate vertical alignment.

## Discussion

I won't pretend the Visual Format Language is easy to understand. It is indeed very cryptic. For this reason, I will give you a few examples that hopefully will clear things up. All of these examples will change the horizontal alignment of a button on the screen:

*The button has to maintain 100 points on each side from its superview's edges.*

```
H:|-100-[_button]-100-|
```

*The button has to have a left distance of less than or equal to 100 points from the left edge of its superview. It also has to have a width that is greater than or equal to 50 points and has to stay 100 points or less away from the right edge of its superview.*

```
H:|-(<=100)-[_button(>=50)]-(<=100)-|
```

*The button has to keep a standard left distance from the left edge of its superview (standard distances are defined by Apple) and has to have a width of at least 100 and at most 200 points.*

```
H:|-[_button(>=100,<=200)]
```

As you can see, the formatting might take you some time to get used to. However, once you get the hang of the basics of it, it will slowly start to make sense. The same rules apply for vertical alignment, which uses the `V:` orientation specifier. For instance:

```
V:[_button]-(>=100)-|
```

This constraint will force the button to stick to the top of its superview (remember, this is a vertical constraint, hence the "V" at its beginning) and keep a distance of at least 100 points from the bottom edge of its superview.

Let's put the things that we have learned so far into practice. How about writing constraints using the Visual Format Language that represent a UI similar to that depicted in Figure 3-4?

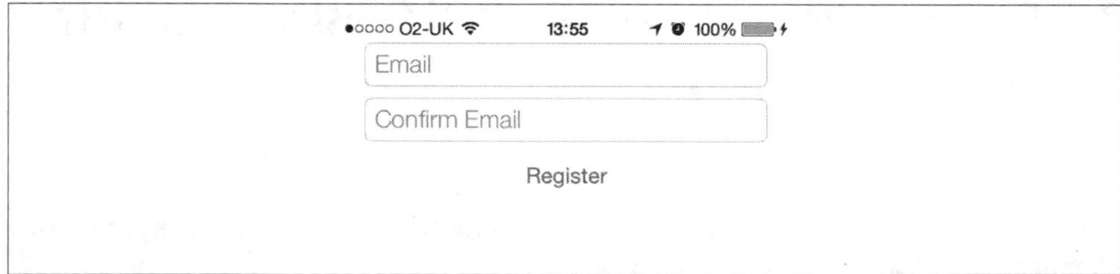


*Figure 3-4. The UI that we want to achieve using constraints and the Visual Format Language*

To help apps look consistent and make decisions easier for the designers of apps, Apple has designed standard distances or spaces between UI components. The standards are described in Apple's iOS Human Interface Guidelines (*http://bit.ly/QkQrtU*).

Before we dive into coding, let's put down the constraints as we can see them in the figure:

- The email field has standard vertical distance to the top of the view.
- The confirm email field has standard vertical distance to the email field.
- The Register button has standard vertical distance to the confirm email field.
- All components are horizontally centered in relation to the parent (super) view.
- Both the email and the confirm email fields have standard horizontal distance from the left- and the righthand side of the superview.
- The width of the button is fixed at 128 points.

Shall we dig into the code now to achieve this? Let's start by actually defining our constraints in plain Visual Format Language on top of our view controller:

```
/* Email Text Field Constraints */
NSString *const kEmailTextFieldHorizontal = @"H:|-[_textFieldEmail]-|";
NSString *const kEmailTextFieldVertical = @"V:|-[_textFieldEmail]";

/* Confirm Email Text Field Constraints */
NSString *const kConfirmEmailHorizontal = @"H:|-[_textFieldConfirmEmail]-|";
NSString *const kConfirmEmailVertical =
@"V:[_textFieldEmail]-[_textFieldConfirmEmail]";

/* Register Button Constraint */
NSString *const kRegisterVertical =
@"V:[_textFieldConfirmEmail]-[_registerButton]";
```

It is immediately obvious that both text fields have both their horizontal and vertical constraints defined in the Visual Format Language, but the Register button has only its vertical constraint defined as a Visual Format Language expression. Why is that? It turns out that center-aligning a UI component horizontally is not possible with the Visual Format Language. For this, we are going to have to use the same technique that we learned in Recipe 3.1. But that's OK. Don't let that stop you from enjoying the Visual Format Language and finding out how powerful it truly is. Obviously nothing is perfect, but that doesn't mean we shouldn't use it.

Now let's define our UI components as private properties in the implementation file of the view controller:

```
@interface ViewController ()
@property (nonatomic, strong) UITextField *textFieldEmail;
@property (nonatomic, strong) UITextField *textFieldConfirmEmail;
@property (nonatomic, strong) UIButton *registerButton;
@end

@implementation ViewController

<# Rest of your code goes here #>
```

What's next? We need to actually construct our UI components in the implementation file of the view controller. So we will write two handy methods that will help us do this. Again, remember, we are not going to set the frame of these UI components. Auto Layout will later help us with this:

```
- (UITextField *) textFieldWithPlaceholder:(NSString *)paramPlaceholder{

    UITextField *result = [[UITextField alloc] init];
    result.translatesAutoresizingMaskIntoConstraints = NO;
    result.borderStyle = UITextBorderStyleRoundedRect;
    result.placeholder = paramPlaceholder;
    return result;

}

- (void) constructUIComponents{

    self.textFieldEmail =
    [self textFieldWithPlaceholder:@"Email"];

    self.textFieldConfirmEmail =
    [self textFieldWithPlaceholder:@"Confirm Email"];

    self.registerButton = [UIButton buttonWithType:UIButtonTypeSystem];
    self.registerButton.translatesAutoresizingMaskIntoConstraints = NO;
    [self.registerButton setTitle:@"Register" forState:UIControlStateNormal];

}
```

The `textFieldWithPlaceholder:` method simply creates text fields that contain a given placeholder text, and the `constructUIComponents` method creates the two text fields using the previously mentioned method and the button. You have probably noticed that we are setting the `translatesAutoresizingMaskIntoConstraints` property of all our UI components to `NO`. This will force UIKit not to think that autoresizing masks have something to do with Auto Layout constraints. As you know, you can set autoresizing masks for your UI components and view controllers in code and Interface Builder, as we learned in Chapter 1. Setting this property to `NO` makes sure that UIKit won't mix things up and won't automatically translate autoresizing masks to Auto Layout constraints. Setting this option is required if you are mixing Auto Layout properties of your components with layout constraints. It is generally a good idea to set this property of all your UI components to NO whenever you are working with Auto Layout constraints, unless you explicitly want UIKit to translate autoresizing masks to Auto Layout constraints.

We are constructing our UI components, but the viewDidLoad method of our view controller obviously needs to add all three UI components to our view, so why not have a little method that will help us with this?

```
- (void) addUIComponentsToView:(UIView *)paramView{

    [paramView addSubview:self.textFieldEmail];
    [paramView addSubview:self.textFieldConfirmEmail];
    [paramView addSubview:self.registerButton];

}
```

We are almost there. The next big task is to create methods that allow us to construct and collect all the constraints into an array. For this, we have three methods that return the constraints of each one of our UI components as an array. We also have a handy fourth method that collects all the constraints from all three UI components and puts them into one big array. Here is how we have implemented it:

```
- (NSArray *) emailTextFieldConstraints{

    NSMutableArray *result = [[NSMutableArray alloc] init];

    NSDictionary *viewsDictionary =
    NSDictionaryOfVariableBindings(_textFieldEmail);

    [result addObjectsFromArray:
     [NSLayoutConstraint constraintsWithVisualFormat:kEmailTextFieldHorizontal
                                              options:0
                                              metrics:nil
                                                views:viewsDictionary]
     ];

    [result addObjectsFromArray:
     [NSLayoutConstraint constraintsWithVisualFormat:kEmailTextFieldVertical
                                              options:0
                                              metrics:nil
                                                views:viewsDictionary]
     ];

    return [NSArray arrayWithArray:result];

}

- (NSArray *) confirmEmailTextFieldConstraints{

    NSMutableArray *result = [[NSMutableArray alloc] init];
```

```
    NSDictionary *viewsDictionary =
    NSDictionaryOfVariableBindings(_textFieldConfirmEmail, _textFieldEmail);

    [result addObjectsFromArray:
     [NSLayoutConstraint constraintsWithVisualFormat:kConfirmEmailHorizontal
                                             options:0
                                             metrics:nil
                                               views:viewsDictionary]
     ];

    [result addObjectsFromArray:
     [NSLayoutConstraint constraintsWithVisualFormat:kConfirmEmailVertical
                                             options:0
                                             metrics:nil
                                               views:viewsDictionary]
     ];

    return [NSArray arrayWithArray:result];

}

- (NSArray *) registerButtonConstraints{

    NSMutableArray *result = [[NSMutableArray alloc] init];

    NSDictionary *viewsDictionary =
    NSDictionaryOfVariableBindings(_registerButton, _textFieldConfirmEmail);

    [result addObject:

     [NSLayoutConstraint constraintWithItem:self.registerButton
                                  attribute:NSLayoutAttributeCenterX
                                  relatedBy:NSLayoutRelationEqual
                                     toItem:self.view
                                  attribute:NSLayoutAttributeCenterX
                                 multiplier:1.0f
                                   constant:0.0f]

     ];

    [result addObjectsFromArray:
     [NSLayoutConstraint constraintsWithVisualFormat:kRegisterVertical
                                             options:0
                                             metrics:nil
                                               views:viewsDictionary]
     ];

    return [NSArray arrayWithArray:result];
}

- (NSArray *)constraints{
    NSMutableArray *result = [[NSMutableArray alloc] init];
```

```
    [result addObjectsFromArray:[self emailTextFieldConstraints]];
    [result addObjectsFromArray:[self confirmEmailTextFieldConstraints]];
    [result addObjectsFromArray:[self registerButtonConstraints]];
    return [NSArray arrayWithArray:result];
}
```

It's in fact the `constraints` instance method of our view controller that collects all the constraints for all three UI components and returns them as one big array. Now for the main part of the controller, the `viewDidLoad` method:

```
- (void)viewDidLoad{

    [super viewDidLoad];

    [self constructUIComponents];
    [self addUIComponentsToView:self.view];
    [self.view addConstraints:[self constraints]];
}
```

This method simply constructs the UI, adding the UI components and their constraints to itself using the methods we wrote before. Great stuff, but how does it look on the screen when we run the program? We have already seen how it looks in the portrait mode of the device (see Figure 3-4) but let's see how it will look once we rotate the device's orientation to landscape (Figure 3-5).

*Figure 3-5. The constraints seem to be working just as fine in landscape as they work in portrait mode*

## See Also

Recipe 3.0, "Introduction"; Recipe 3.1

# 3.3. Utilizing Cross View Constraints

## Problem

You want to align a UI component in relation to another UI component, but these UI components have different parents.

## Solution

Utilizing Figure 3-1, make sure that you find the common UI superview between the two UI components and add your constraint to that superview.

## Discussion

Before going into too much detail, let's first see what cross view constraints are all about. I believe I can demonstrate it to you in a picture better than it can be explained in words, so check out Figure 3-6.

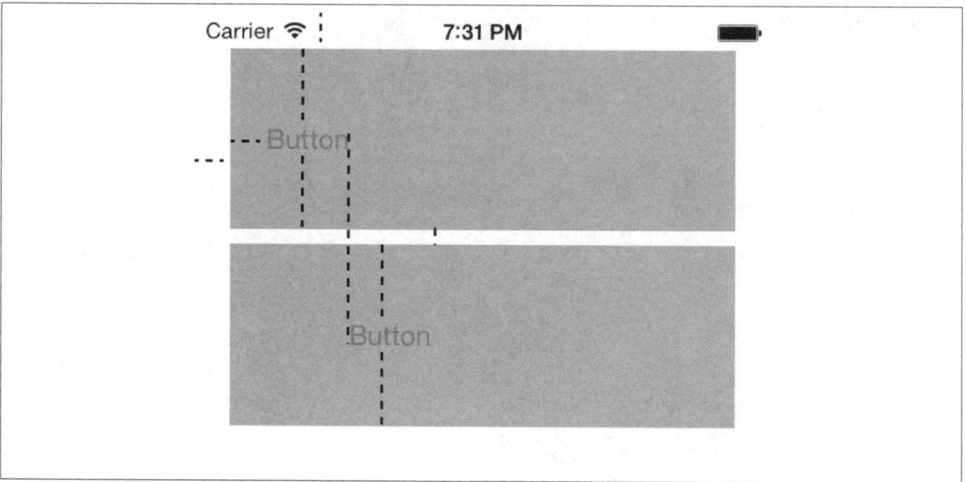


*Figure 3-6. The important cross view constraints between two buttons are depicted in this photo*

Many constraints have been applied to the views in this figure, but let's start one by one and break it down into small chunks:

- We have two gray views on the main view of our view controller. Both should have standard space from the left and the right side of the view of the view controller. There must be standard space from the top of the view to the top of the view on top. There should be standard vertical space between the two gray views.
- There must be a button vertically centered in both gray views.
- The button on the top gray view should have standard space to the left of its superview.
- The button on the bottom gray view should have its lefthand side aligned with the righthand side of the button in the top gray view. This is the cross view constraint that is very important to us.
- The gray views should be able to get resized as the view of the view controller changes orientation.
- The height of both gray views must be 100 points.

OK, let's begin. We are going to do all this by starting from the `viewDidLoad` method of our view controller. It's always best to think of a clean way of putting all your methods together. Obviously, in this example, we are working with quite a few constraints and views, so how can we make the `viewDidLoad` method of our view controller clean? Like this:

```
- (void)viewDidLoad{
    [super viewDidLoad];
    [self createGrayViews];

    [self createButtons];

    [self applyConstraintsToTopGrayView];
    [self applyConstraintsToButtonOnTopGrayView];

    [self applyConstraintsToBottomGrayView];
    [self applyConstraintsToButtonOnBottomGrayView];

}
```

We have simply broken our tasks down into different methods, which we are soon going to implement. Let's go ahead and define our views in the implementation file of our view controller as an extension to our interface:

```
#import "ViewController.h"

@interface ViewController ()
@property (nonatomic, strong) UIView *topGrayView;
@property (nonatomic, strong) UIButton *topButton;
@property (nonatomic, strong) UIView *bottomGrayView;
@property (nonatomic, strong) UIButton *bottomButton;
@end
```

```
@implementation ViewController

<# Rest of your code goes here #>
```

The next step is to implement the `createGrayViews` method. As its name shows, this method is responsible for creating our gray views on the screen:

```
- (UIView *) newGrayView{

    UIView *result = [[UIView alloc] init];
    result.backgroundColor = [UIColor lightGrayColor];
    result.translatesAutoresizingMaskIntoConstraints = NO;
    [self.view addSubview:result];
    return result;

}

- (void) createGrayViews{

    self.topGrayView = [self newGrayView];
    self.bottomGrayView = [self newGrayView];
}
```

Simple enough? Both gray views are getting added to the view of our view controller. Great stuff. What's next? We now need to implement the `createButtons` method, because it is getting called in the `viewDidLoad` method of our view controller. This method should simply create our buttons and place them on their associated gray views:

```
- (UIButton *) newButtonPlacedOnView:(UIView *)paramView{

    UIButton *result = [UIButton buttonWithType:UIButtonTypeSystem];
    result.translatesAutoresizingMaskIntoConstraints = NO;
    [result setTitle:@"Button" forState:UIControlStateNormal];
    [paramView addSubview:result];
    return result;

}

- (void) createButtons{
    self.topButton = [self newButtonPlacedOnView:self.topGrayView];
    self.bottomButton = [self newButtonPlacedOnView:self.bottomGrayView];
}
```

Again, as you can see in the `createButtons` method, after the creation of our gray views and the buttons, we need to start applying the constraints to the gray views and the buttons. We will start by applying the constraints to the top gray view. These constraints must cover the following conditions:

- The top view has to have standard space from the left and the top of the view of the view controller.

• The height of this gray view has to be 100 points.

```
- (void) applyConstraintsToTopGrayView{

    NSDictionary *views = NSDictionaryOfVariableBindings(_topGrayView);

    NSMutableArray *constraints = [[NSMutableArray alloc] init];

    NSString *const kHConstraint = @"H:|-[_topGrayView]-|";
    NSString *const kVConstraint = @"V:|-[_topGrayView(==100)]";

    /* Horizontal constraint(s) */
    [constraints addObjectsFromArray:
     [NSLayoutConstraint constraintsWithVisualFormat:kHConstraint
                                             options:0
                                             metrics:nil
                                               views:views]
     ];

    /* Vertical constraint(s) */
    [constraints addObjectsFromArray:
     [NSLayoutConstraint constraintsWithVisualFormat:kVConstraint
                                             options:0
                                             metrics:nil
                                               views:views]
     ];

    [self.topGrayView.superview addConstraints:constraints];

}
```

It's important to note how we are constructing the vertical constraint of the top gray view. You can see that we are using the `(==100)` format to specify that the height of the top gray view has to be 100 points. The reason that the runtime is interpreting this value as the height is because of the `V:` specifier that tells the runtime that the numbers we are feeding into the system have something to do with the height and the vertical alignment of the target view, rather than the width or the horizontal alignment.

The next thing that we need to take care of is to set the constraints for the button on the top gray view. This is done through the `applyConstraintsToButtonOnTopGrayView` method. This button will have the following constraints, as specified before:

- It should sit vertically in the center of the top gray view.
- It should have standard distance from the left of the top gray view.
- It should have no specific height or width defined and should fit its content, aka the *`Button`* text that we've decided to put in it.

```
- (void) applyConstraintsToButtonOnTopGrayView{
```

```
    NSDictionary *views = NSDictionaryOfVariableBindings(_topButton);

    NSMutableArray *constraints = [[NSMutableArray alloc] init];

    NSString *const kHConstraint = @"H:|-[_topButton]";

    /* Horizontal constraint(s) */
    [constraints addObjectsFromArray:
     [NSLayoutConstraint constraintsWithVisualFormat:kHConstraint
                                             options:0
                                             metrics:nil
                                               views:views]
     ];

    /* Vertical constraint(s) */
    [constraints addObject:
     [NSLayoutConstraint constraintWithItem:self.topButton
                                  attribute:NSLayoutAttributeCenterY
                                  relatedBy:NSLayoutRelationEqual
                                     toItem:self.topGrayView
                                  attribute:NSLayoutAttributeCenterY
                                 multiplier:1.0f
                                   constant:0.0f]
     ];

    [self.topButton.superview addConstraints:constraints];

}
```

We are all done with the top gray view and the button inside it. Time to move on to the bottom gray view and its button. The method we should take care of now is the `applyConstraintsToBottomGrayView` method. This method will be setting the constraints for the bottom gray view. Just to recap, the constraints that we have to create for this view are:

- Must have standard distance from the left of the view of the view controller.
- Must have standard distance from the bottom of the top gray view.
- Must have the height of 100 points.

```
- (void) applyConstraintsToBottomGrayView{

    NSDictionary *views = NSDictionaryOfVariableBindings(_topGrayView,
                                                         _bottomGrayView);

    NSMutableArray *constraints = [[NSMutableArray alloc] init];

    NSString *const kHConstraint = @"H:|-[_bottomGrayView]-|";
    NSString *const kVConstraint =
    @"V:|-[_topGrayView]-[_bottomGrayView(==100)]";
```

```
    /* Horizontal constraint(s) */
    [constraints addObjectsFromArray:
     [NSLayoutConstraint constraintsWithVisualFormat:kHConstraint
                                             options:0
                                             metrics:nil
                                               views:views]
     ];

    /* Vertical constraint(s) */
    [constraints addObjectsFromArray:
     [NSLayoutConstraint constraintsWithVisualFormat:kVConstraint
                                             options:0
                                             metrics:nil
                                               views:views]
     ];

    [self.bottomGrayView.superview addConstraints:constraints];

}
```

The vertical constraints for the bottom gray view may look a bit long in Visual Format Language, but it's very simple indeed. If you have a close look, you'll notice that the constraints are just aligning the top and the bottom gray view on the view of the view controller using standard distance specifiers and the constant height of 100 points.

The next and perhaps the last UI component for which we have to write constraints is the button on the bottom gray view. The method that will take care of this is called `applyConstraintsToButtonOnBottomGrayView`. Before we implement this method, let's talk about the constraint requirements for the bottom button:

- It should be vertically aligned at the center of the bottom gray view.
- Its left side should be aligned with the right side of the button on the top gray view.
- It should have no specific height or width defined and should fit its content, aka the *Button* text that we've decided to put in it.

```
- (void) applyConstraintsToButtonOnBottomGrayView{

    NSDictionary *views = NSDictionaryOfVariableBindings(_topButton,
                                                         _bottomButton);

    NSString *const kHConstraint = @"H:[_topButton][_bottomButton]";

    /* Horizontal constraint(s) */
    [self.bottomGrayView.superview addConstraints:
     [NSLayoutConstraint constraintsWithVisualFormat:kHConstraint
                                             options:0
                                             metrics:nil
                                               views:views]
     ];
```

```
        /* Vertical constraint(s) */
        [self.bottomButton.superview addConstraint:
         [NSLayoutConstraint constraintWithItem:self.bottomButton
                                      attribute:NSLayoutAttributeCenterY
                                      relatedBy:NSLayoutRelationEqual
                                         toItem:self.bottomGrayView
                                      attribute:NSLayoutAttributeCenterY
                                     multiplier:1.0f
                                       constant:0.0f]
         ];

    }
```

Last but not least, we need to make sure our view controller tells the runtime that it is able to handle all orientations, just to demonstrate the point of this recipe, so we should override the `supportedInterfaceOrientations` method of `UIViewController`:

```
- (NSUInteger) supportedInterfaceOrientations{
    return UIInterfaceOrientationMaskAll;
}
```

We are done with this view controller now. Let's run our app and see how it behaves in portrait mode (see Figure 3-7).

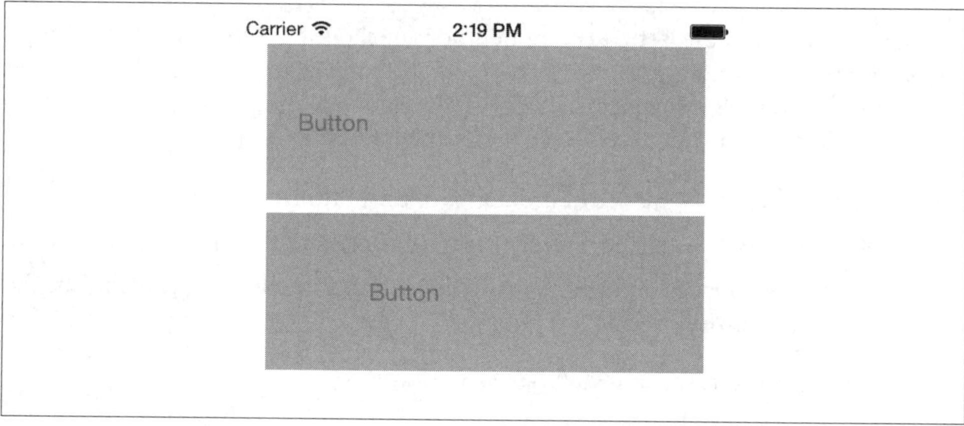


*Figure 3-7. Our app renders the UI components in portrait mode according to the requirements that we set*

The moment of truth! How about in landscape mode? Do we dare run the app in landscape and see whether it behaves as expected? Let's give it a go (see Figure 3-8).

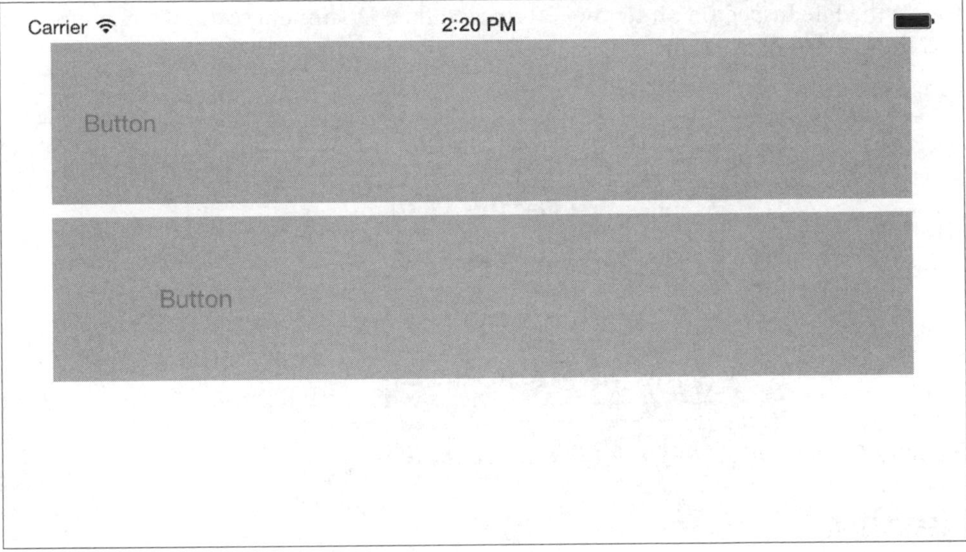


*Figure 3-8. The same code behaves as expected in landscape mode*

Perfect. I think we nailed it.

## See Also

Recipe 3.0, "Introduction"

# 3.4. Configuring Auto Layout Constraints in Interface Builder

## Problem

You want to be able to utilize Interface Builder's power in order to create your UI constraints.

## Solution

Follow these steps:

1. Open the XIB or storyboard file that you want to edit in Interface Builder.
2. In Interface Builder, make sure that you have selected the view object on which you want to enable Auto Layout, simply by clicking on that view object.
3. Click the View → Utilities → Show File Inspector menu item.

4. In the File Inspector, under the Interface Builder Document section, make sure that the Use Autolayout check is enabled, as shown in Figure 3-9.

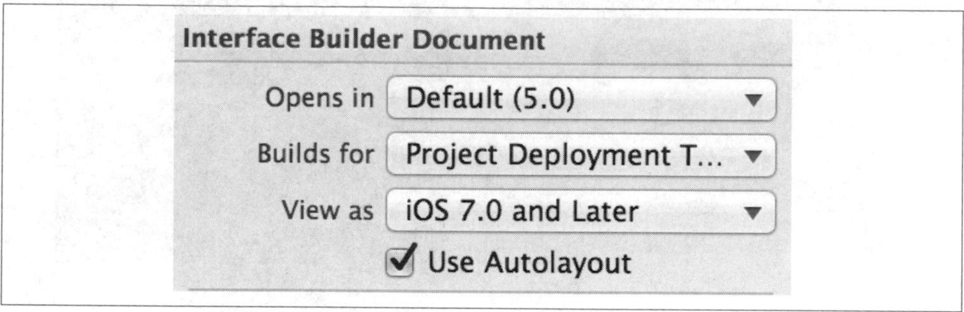


*Figure 3-9. Enabling Auto Layout in Interface Builder*

## Discussion

Interface Builder can help us programmers a lot in creating constraints without much involvement from us. Normally, before the introduction of Auto Layout to iOS, the guideline bars that appeared on the screen while you moved UI components around on a view were related to autosizing masks that you could also create in code, just like Constraints. However, after switching on the Use Auto Layout option in Interface Builder, the guidelines tell you something else. They are telling you about the constraints that Interface Builder is creating for you in the background.

Let's do a little experiment. Create a new Single View Application project in Xcode. This will create an application with a single view controller for you. The class for your view controller will be `ViewController` and the *.xib* file for this view controller will be *View Controller.xib*. Simply click this file to let Interface Builder open it for you. Make sure that the Use Autolayout option is ticked in the File Inspector, as explained in the Solution section of this recipe.

Now from the Object Library, simply drag and drop a *Button* onto the center of the screen until Interface Builder guidelines appear on the screen, telling you that the center of the button is aligned with the center of the screen. From the Edit menu, now choose the Show Document Outline. If you already have the Document Outline section of Interface Builder open, this menu item will read Hide Document Outline, in which case you don't have to take any action. Now in the Document Outline, have a look under a new blue-colored section that has been created for you, named Constraints. Expand the constraints that Interface Builder has created for you for this button. What you see now is quite similar to what is shown in Figure 3-10.

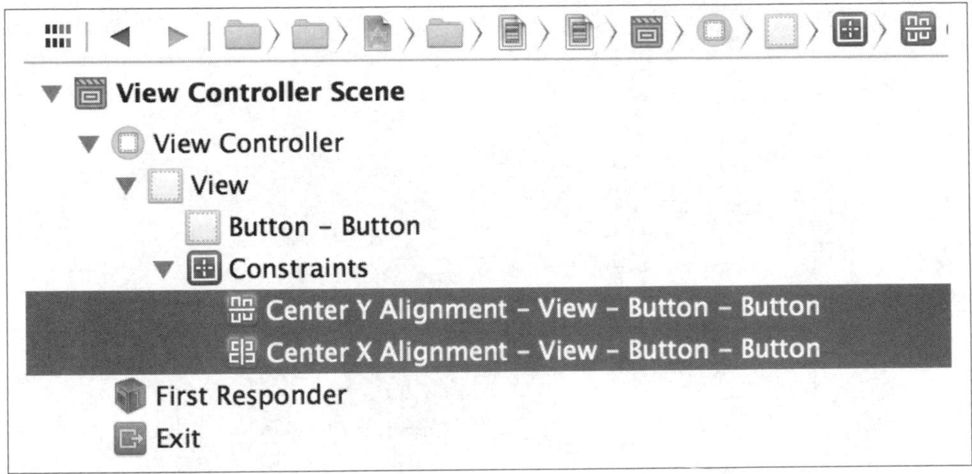


*Figure 3-10. Interface Builder created Layout Constraints for us*

Using Interface Builder, you can create a lot of constraints without having to write a single line of code. There are times when the constraints that you want to define are so complex that they are better off being written in the code. After deciding how you want to lay out your UI components on the screen, you can tell whether it's easier to use Interface Builder, put it in your code, or do a mix of both.

## See Also

Recipe 3.0, "Introduction"

CHAPTER 4

# Constructing and Using Table Views

## 4.0. Introduction

A table view is simply a scrolling view that is separated into sections, each of which is further separated into rows. Each row is an instance of the `UITableViewCell` class, and you can create custom table view rows by *subclassing* this class.

Using table views is an ideal way to present a list of items to users. You can embed images, text, and other objects into your table view cells; you can customize their height, shape, grouping, and much more. The simplicity of the structure of table views is what makes them highly customizable.

A table view can be fed with data using a table view data source, and you can receive various events and control the physical appearance of table views using a table view delegate object. These are defined, respectively, in the `UITableViewDataSource` and `UITableViewDelegate` protocols.

Although an instance of `UITableView` subclasses `UIScrollView`, table views can only scroll vertically. This is more a feature than a limitation. In this chapter, we will discuss the different ways of creating, managing, and customizing table views.

Table views can be utilized in two ways:

- By using the `UITableViewController` class. This class is similar to the `UIViewController` class (see Recipe 1.9) in that it is a view controller, but representing a table instead of a normal view. The beauty of this class is that every instance of it already conforms to the `UITableViewDelegate` and the `UITableViewDataSource` protocols. So the table view controller by default becomes the data source and the delegate of the table view that it controls. Therefore, in order to implement a method of, for instance, the data source of the table view, all you have to do is implement it in the table view controller instead of having to set the data source of your table view manually to your view controller.

- By instantiating the `UITableView` class manually.

Both these methods are valid methods of creating table views. The first method is usually used when you have a table view that fills its container (or the whole screen/window, if the table view controller is the root view controller of the main window of your app). The second method is usually used for situations where you want to display your table view as a smaller part of your UI, perhaps taking half the width and/or height of the screen. But nothing prevents you from using the second method and setting the width and height of your table view to the width and height of your container window, so that your table view fills the whole screen. We will explore both these methods in this chapter.

Let's have a look at an example of creating a table view in our application. We are going to see an example of table view controllers in Recipe 4.9, so for now, we will simply focus on creating table views in code and adding them to an existing view controller.

The way to instantiate `UITableView` is through its `initWithFrame:style:` method. Let's see what parameters we have to pass to this method and what those parameters mean:

`initWithFrame`
: This is a parameter of type `CGRect`. This specifies where the table view has to be positioned in its superview. If you want your table view to simply cover your whole view, pass the value of the `bounds` property of your view controller's view to this parameter.

`style`
: This is a parameter of type `UITableViewStyle` that is defined in this way:

```
typedef NS_ENUM(NSInteger, UITableViewStyle) {
    UITableViewStylePlain,
    UITableViewStyleGrouped
};
```

Figure 4-1 shows the difference between a plain table view and a grouped table view.

We feed data to a table view using its data source, as we will see in Recipe 4.1. Table views also have delegates that receive various events from the table view. Delegate objects have to conform to the `UITableViewDelegate` protocol. There are some methods in this protocol that are quite important to know:

`tableView:viewForHeaderInSection:`
: Gets called on the delegate when the table view wants to render the header view of a section. Each section of a table view can contain a header, some cells, and a footer. We will talk about all these in this chapter. The header and footer are simple instances of `UIView`. This method is optional, but if you want to configure a header for your table view sections, use this method to create that instance of the view and return it as the return value. To read more about headers and footers in table views, refer to Recipe 4.5.

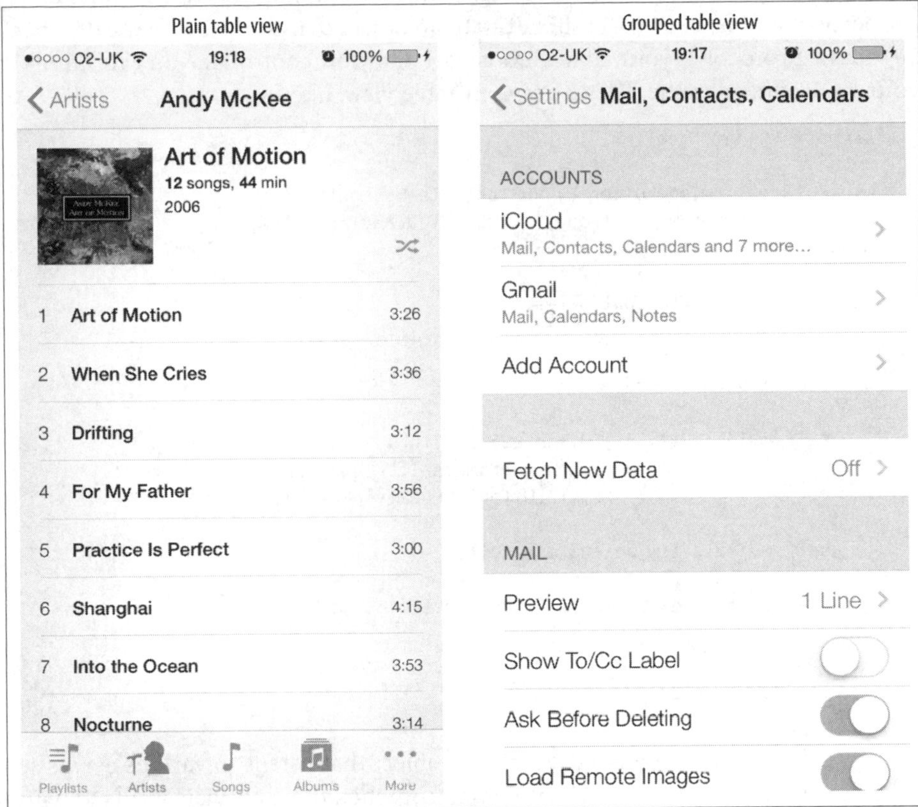


*Figure 4-1. Different types of table views*

`tableView:viewForFooterInSection:`
: Same as the `tableView:viewForHeaderInSection:` delegate method, but returns the footer view. Like the header, the footer is optional but should be created here if you want one. To read more about headers and footers in table views, refer to Recipe 4.5.

`tableView:didEndDisplayingCell:forRowAtIndexPath:`
: Gets called on your delegate object when a cell is scrolled off the screen. This is a really handy method to have called on our delegate because you can delete objects and remove them from memory, if those objects were associated with the cell that is scrolled off the screen and you expect that you may no longer need them.

`tableView:willDisplayCell:forRowAtIndexPath:`
: This method is called on the delegate of a table view whenever a cell is about to be displayed on the screen.

You can set the delegate of a table view simply by setting the value of the `delegate` property of an instance of `UITableView` to an object that conforms to the `UITableViewDelegate` protocol. If your table view is part of a view controller, you can simply make your view controller the delegate of your table view, like so:

```
#import "ViewController.h"

@interface ViewController () <UITableViewDelegate>
@property (nonatomic, strong) UITableView *myTableView;
@end

@implementation ViewController

- (void)viewDidLoad{
    [super viewDidLoad];

    self.myTableView = [[UITableView alloc]
                        initWithFrame:self.view.bounds
                        style:UITableViewStylePlain];

    self.myTableView.delegate = self;

    [self.view addSubview:self.myTableView];

}

@end
```

Think of the delegate of a table view as an object that listens to various events sent by the table view, such as when a cell is selected or when the table view wants to figure out the height of each of its cells.

It is mandatory for the delegate object to respond to messages that are marked as `@required` by the `UITableViewDelegate` protocol. Responding to other messages is optional, but the delegate must respond to any messages you want to affect the table view.

Messages sent to the delegate object of a table view carry a parameter that tells the delegate object which table view has fired that message in its delegate. This is very important to note because you might, under certain circumstances, require more than one table view to be placed on one object (usually a view). Because of this, it is highly recommended that you make your decisions based on which table view has actually sent that specific message to your delegate object, like so:

```
- (CGFloat)     tableView:(UITableView *)tableView
  heightForRowAtIndexPath:(NSIndexPath *)indexPath{
    if ([tableView isEqual:self.myTableView]){
        return 100.0f;
```

```
    }
    return 40.0f;
}
```

The location of a cell in a table view is represented by its index path. An index path is the combination of the section and the row index, where the section index is the zero-based index specifying which grouping or section each cell belongs to, and the cell index is the zero-based index of that particular cell in its section.

# 4.1. Populating a Table View with Data

## Problem

You would like to populate your table view with data.

## Solution

Conform to the `UITableViewDataSource` protocol in an object and assign that object to the `dataSource` property of a table view.

## Discussion

Create an object that conforms to the `UITableViewDataSource` protocol and assign it to a table view instance. Then, by responding to the data source messages, provide information to your table view. For this example, let's go ahead and declare the *.m* file of our view controller, which will later create a table view on its own view, in code:

```
#import "ViewController.h"

static NSString *TableViewCellIdentifier = @"MyCells";

@interface ViewController () <UITableViewDataSource>
@property (nonatomic, strong) UITableView *myTableView;
@end
```

The `TableViewCellIdentifier` contains our cell identifiers as a static string variable. Each cell, as you will learn soon, can have an identifier, which is great for reusing cells. For now, think about this as a unique identifier for all the cells in our table view, nothing more.

In the `viewDidLoad` method of our view controller, we create the table view and assign our view controller as its data source:

```
- (void)viewDidLoad{
    [super viewDidLoad];

    self.myTableView =
    [[UITableView alloc] initWithFrame:self.view.bounds
```

```
                                    style:UITableViewStylePlain];

    [self.myTableView registerClass:[UITableViewCell class]
            forCellReuseIdentifier:TableViewCellIdentifier];

    self.myTableView.dataSource = self;

    /* Make sure our table view resizes correctly */
    self.myTableView.autoresizingMask =
        UIViewAutoresizingFlexibleWidth |
        UIViewAutoresizingFlexibleHeight;

    [self.view addSubview:self.myTableView];

}
```

Everything is very simple in this code snippet except for the `registerClass:forCellReuseIdentifier:` method that we are calling on the instance of our table view. What does this method do, you ask? The `registerClass` parameter of this method simply takes a class name that denotes the type of object that you want your table view to load when it renders each cell. Cells inside a table view all have to be direct or indirect ancestors of the `UITableViewCell` class. This class on its own provides a lot of functionalities to programmers, but if you want to extend this class, you can simply subclass it and add your new functionalities to your own class. So going back to the `registerClass` parameter of the aforementioned method, you have to pass the class name of your cells to this parameter and then pass an identifier to the `forCellReuseIdentifier` parameter. The reason behind associating table view cell classes with identifiers is that later, when you populate your table view, you can simply pass the same identifier to the table view's `dequeueReusableCellWithIdentifier:forIndexPath:` method and have the table view instantiate the cell for you if one cannot be reused. This is great stuff, because in previous versions of the iOS SDK, programmers had to instantiate these cells themselves if a previous and reusable cell could not be retrieved from the table view.

Now we need to make sure our table view responds to the `@required` methods of the `UITableViewDataSource` protocol. Press the Command+Shift+O key combination on your keyboard, type this protocol name in the dialog, and then press the Enter key. This will show you the required methods for this protocol.

The `UITableView` class defines a property called `dataSource`. This is an untyped object that must conform to the `UITableViewDataSource` protocol. Every time a table view is refreshed and reloaded using the `reloadData` method, the table view will call various methods in its data source to find out about the data you intend to populate it with. A table view data source can implement three important methods, two of which are mandatory for every data source:

`numberOfSectionsInTableView:`
: This method allows the data source to inform the table view of the number of sections that must be loaded into the table.

`tableView:numberOfRowsInSection:`
: This method tells the view controller how many cells or rows have to be loaded for each section. The section number is passed to the data source in the `numberOfRowsInSection` parameter. The implementation of this method is mandatory in the data source object.

`tableView:cellForRowAtIndexPath:`
: This method is responsible for returning instances of the `UITableViewCell` class as rows that have to be populated into the table view. The implementation of this method is mandatory in the data source object.

So let's go ahead and implement these methods in our view controller, one by one. First, let's tell the table view that we want it to render three sections:

```
- (NSInteger)numberOfSectionsInTableView:(UITableView *)tableView{

    if ([tableView isEqual:self.myTableView]){
        return 3;
    }

    return 0;

}
```

Then we tell the table view how many rows we want it to render for each section:

```
- (NSInteger)tableView:(UITableView *)tableView
 numberOfRowsInSection:(NSInteger)section{

    if ([tableView isEqual:self.myTableView]){
        switch (section){
            case 0:{
                return 3;
                break;
            }
            case 1:{
                return 5;
                break;
            }
            case 2:{
                return 8;
                break;
            }
        }
    }
    return 0;
}
```

So up to now, we have asked the table view to render three sections with three rows in the first, five rows in the second, and eight rows in the third section. What's next? We have to return instances of `UITableViewCell` to the table view—the cells that we want the table view to render:

```
- (UITableViewCell *)      tableView:(UITableView *)tableView
             cellForRowAtIndexPath:(NSIndexPath *)indexPath{

    UITableViewCell *cell = nil;

    if ([tableView isEqual:self.myTableView]){

        cell = [tableView
                dequeueReusableCellWithIdentifier:TableViewCellIdentifier
                forIndexPath:indexPath];

        cell.textLabel.text = [NSString stringWithFormat:
                               @"Section %ld, Cell %ld",
                               (long)indexPath.section,
                               (long)indexPath.row];

    }

    return cell;

}
```

Now if we run our app in iPhone Simulator, we will see the results of our work (Figure 4-2).

When a table view is reloaded or refreshed, it queries its data source through the `UITableViewDataSource` protocol, asking for various bits of information. Among the important methods previously mentioned, the table view will first ask for the number of sections. Each section is responsible for holding rows or cells. After the data source specifies the number of sections, the table view will ask for the number of rows that have to be loaded into each section. The data source gets the zero-based index of each section and, based on this, can decide how many cells have to be loaded into each section.

The table view, after determining the number of cells in the sections, will continue to ask the data source about the view that will represent each cell in each section. You can allocate instances of the `UITableViewCell` class and return them to the table view. There are, of course, properties that can be set for each cell, including the title, subtitle, and color of each cell, among other properties.

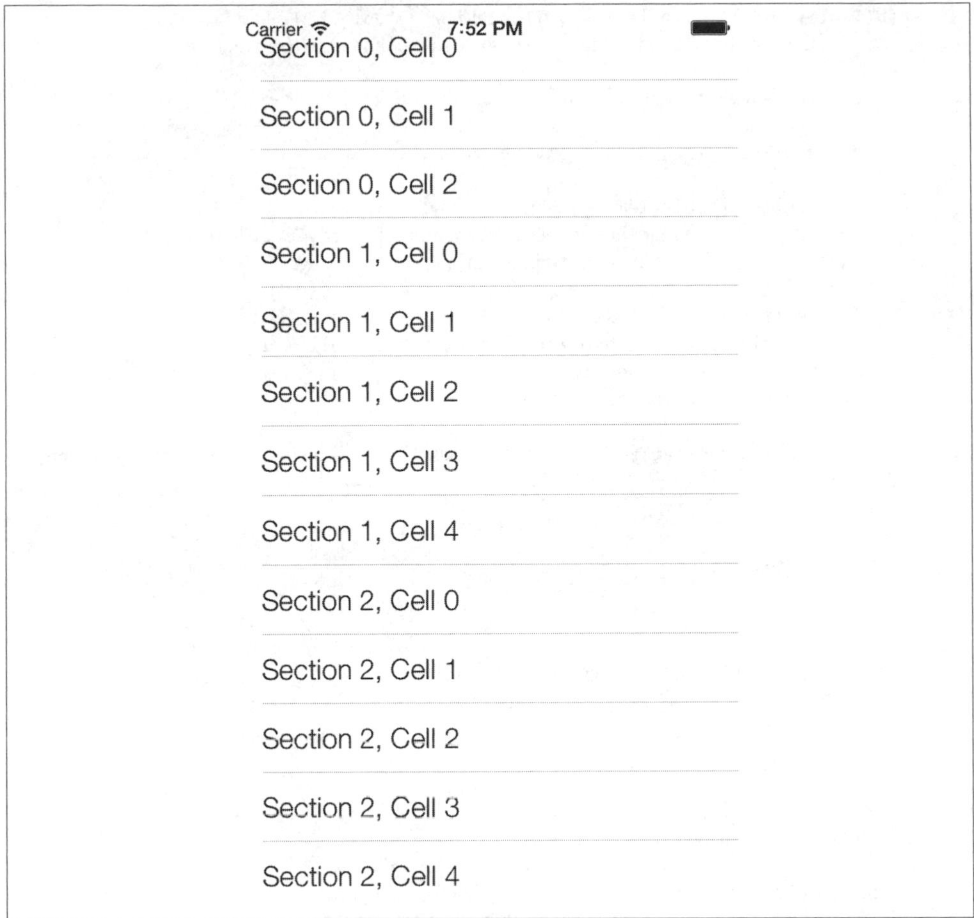


*Figure 4-2. A plain table view with three sections*

# 4.2. Using Different Types of Accessories in a Table View Cell

## Problem

You want to grab users' attention in a table view by displaying accessories and offer different ways to interact with each cell in your table view.

## Solution

Use the `accessoryType` of the `UITableViewCell` class, instances of which you provide to your table view in its data source object:

```
- (UITableViewCell *)tableView:(UITableView *)tableView
         cellForRowAtIndexPath:(NSIndexPath *)indexPath{

    UITableViewCell* result = nil;

    if ([tableView isEqual:self.myTableView]){

        result = [tableView
                  dequeueReusableCellWithIdentifier:MyCellIdentifier
                  forIndexPath:indexPath];

        result.textLabel.text =
        [NSString stringWithFormat:@"Section %ld, Cell %ld",
         (long)indexPath.section,
         (long)indexPath.row];

        result.accessoryType = UITableViewCellAccessoryDetailDisclosureButton;

    }

    return result;

}

- (NSInteger) tableView:(UITableView *)tableView
  numberOfRowsInSection:(NSInteger)section{
    return 10;
}

- (void)viewDidLoad{
    [super viewDidLoad];

    self.myTableView = [[UITableView alloc]
                        initWithFrame:self.view.bounds
                        style:UITableViewStylePlain];

    [self.myTableView registerClass:[UITableViewCell class]
             forCellReuseIdentifier:MyCellIdentifier];

    self.myTableView.dataSource = self;

    self.myTableView.autoresizingMask =
        UIViewAutoresizingFlexibleWidth |
        UIViewAutoresizingFlexibleHeight;

    [self.view addSubview:self.myTableView];

}
```

## Discussion

You can assign any of the values defined in the `UITableViewCellAccessoryType` enumeration to the `accessoryType` property of an instance of the `UITableViewCell` class. Two very useful accessories are the *disclosure indicator* and the *detail disclosure button*. They both display a chevron indicating to users that if they tap on the associated table view cell, a new view or view controller will be displayed. In other words, the users will be taken to a new screen with further information about their current selector. The difference between these two accessories is that the disclosure indicator produces no event, whereas the detail disclosure button fires an event to the delegate when pressed. In other words, pressing the button has a different effect from pressing the cell itself. Thus, the detail disclosure button allows the user to perform two separate but related actions on the same row.

Figure 4-3 shows these two different accessories on a table view. The first row has a disclosure indicator, and the second row has a detail disclosure button.

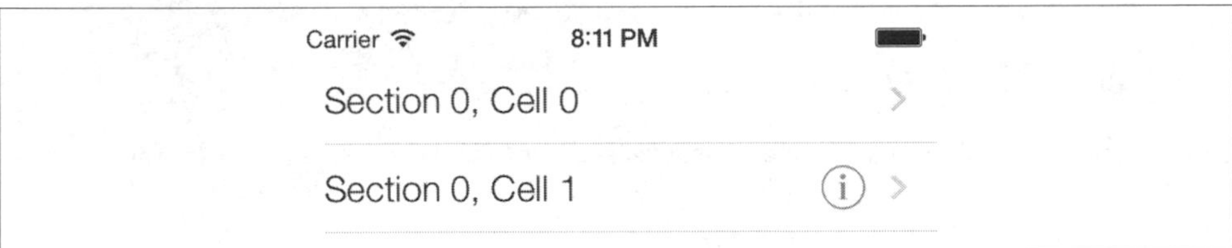


*Figure 4-3. Two table view cells with different accessories*

If you tap any detail disclosure button assigned to a table view cell, you will immediately realize that it truly is a separate button. Now the question is: how does the table view know when the user taps this button?

Table views, as explained before, fire events on their delegate object. The detail disclosure button on a table view cell also fires an event that can be captured by the delegate object of a table view:

```
- (void)                              tableView:(UITableView *)tableView
 accessoryButtonTappedForRowWithIndexPath:(NSIndexPath *)indexPath{

    /* Do something when the accessory button is tapped */
    NSLog(@"Accessory button is tapped for cell at index path = %@", indexPath);

    UITableViewCell *ownerCell = [tableView cellForRowAtIndexPath:indexPath];

    NSLog(@"Cell Title = %@", ownerCell.textLabel.text);

}
```

This code finds the table view cell whose detail disclosure button has been tapped and prints the contents of the text label of that cell into the console screen. As a reminder, you can display the console screen in Xcode by selecting Run → Console.

# 4.3. Creating Custom Table View Cell Accessories

## Problem

The accessories provided to you by the iOS SDK are not sufficient, and you would like to create your own accessories.

## Solution

Assign an instance of the `UIView` class to the `accessoryView` property of any instance of the `UITableViewCell` class:

```
- (UITableViewCell *)tableView:(UITableView *)tableView
        cellForRowAtIndexPath:(NSIndexPath *)indexPath{

    UITableViewCell* cell = nil;

    cell = [tableView dequeueReusableCellWithIdentifier:MyCellIdentifier
                                           forIndexPath:indexPath];

    cell.textLabel.text = [NSString stringWithFormat:@"Section %ld, Cell %ld",
                           (long)indexPath.section,
                           (long)indexPath.row];

    UIButton *button = [UIButton buttonWithType:UIButtonTypeSystem];
    button.frame = CGRectMake(0.0f, 0.0f, 150.0f, 25.0f);

    [button setTitle:@"Expand"
            forState:UIControlStateNormal];

    [button addTarget:self
               action:@selector(performExpand:)
     forControlEvents:UIControlEventTouchUpInside];

    cell.accessoryView = button;

    return cell;

}
```

As you can see, this code uses the `performExpand:` method as the selector for each button. Here is the definition of this method:

```
- (void) performExpand:(UIButton *)paramSender{

    /* Handle the tap event of the button */
```

```
}
```

This example code snippet assigns a custom button to the accessory view of every row in the targeted table. The result is shown in Figure 4-4.

*Figure 4-4. Table view cells with custom accessory views*

## Discussion

An object of type `UITableViewCell` retains a property named `accessoryView`. This is the view you can assign a value to if you are not completely happy with the built-in iOS SDK table view cell accessories. After this property is set, Cocoa Touch will ignore the value of the `accessoryType` property and will use the view assigned to the `accessoryView` property as the accessory assigned to the cell.

The code listed in this recipe's Solution creates buttons for all the cells populated into the table view. When a button is pressed in any cell, the `performExpand:` method gets called, and if you are like me, you have probably already started thinking about how you can determine which cell the sender button belongs to. So now we have to somehow link our buttons with the cells to which they belong.

One way to handle this situation is to take advantage of the `tag` property of the button instance. The tag property is a simple integer that people usually use to associate a view with another object. For instance, if you want to associate the button with the third cell in your table view, set the value of the button's tag property to 3. But there is a problem here: table views have sections, and every section can have *n* number of cells. We, therefore, have to be able to determine the section as well as the cell that owns our button, and since the tag can represent only one integer, this makes things more difficult. Instead of a tag, therefore, we can ask for the superview of the accessory view, going recursively up the chain of views until we find the cell of type `UITableViewCell`, like so:

```
- (UIView *) superviewOfType:(Class)paramSuperviewClass
                     forView:(UIView *)paramView{

    if (paramView.superview != nil){
        if ([paramView.superview isKindOfClass:paramSuperviewClass]){
            return paramView.superview;
        } else {
            return [self superviewOfType:paramSuperviewClass
                                 forView:paramView.superview];
        }
    }

    return nil;

}

- (void) performExpand:(UIButton *)paramSender{

    /* Handle the tap event of the button */
    __unused UITableViewCell *parentCell =
        (UITableViewCell *)[self superviewOfType:[UITableViewCell class]
                                         forView:paramSender];

    /* Now do something with the cell if you want to */

}
```

This is a simple recursive method that accepts a view (in this case our button) and a class name (in this case, `UITableViewCell`), then searches in the view's super view hierarchy to find the super view that is of the given class. So it starts with the super view of the given view, and if that super view is not of the required type, looks at the super view's super view, and so on until it finds the super view of the requested class. You can see that we are using the `Class` structure as the first parameter to the `superviewOfType:forView:` method. This data type can hold any Objective-C class name, and it's great if you are looking for or asking for specific class names from the programmer.

## 4.4. Enabling Swipe Deletion of Table View Cells

### Problem

You want your application users to be able to delete rows from a table view easily.

### Solution

Implement the `tableView:editingStyleForRowAtIndexPath:` selector in the delegate and the `tableView:commitEditingStyle:forRowAtIndexPath:` selector in the data source of your table view:

```
- (UITableViewCellEditingStyle)tableView:(UITableView *)tableView
         editingStyleForRowAtIndexPath:(NSIndexPath *)indexPath{

    return UITableViewCellEditingStyleDelete;

}

- (void) setEditing:(BOOL)editing
         animated:(BOOL)animated{

    [super setEditing:editing
             animated:animated];

    [self.myTableView setEditing:editing
                        animated:animated];


}

- (void)  tableView:(UITableView *)tableView
 commitEditingStyle:(UITableViewCellEditingStyle)editingStyle
  forRowAtIndexPath:(NSIndexPath *)indexPath{

    if (editingStyle == UITableViewCellEditingStyleDelete){

        /* First remove this object from the source */
        [self.allRows removeObjectAtIndex:indexPath.row];

        /* Then remove the associated cell from the Table View */
        [tableView deleteRowsAtIndexPaths:@[indexPath]
                         withRowAnimation:UITableViewRowAnimationLeft];

    }

}
```

The `tableView:editingStyleForRowAtIndexPath:` method can enable deletions. It is called by the table view, and its return value determines what the table view allows the user to do (insertion, deletion, etc.). The `tableView:commitEditingStyle:forRowAtIndexPath:` method carries out the user's requested deletion. The latter method is defined in the delegate, but its functionality is a bit overloaded: not only do you use the method to delete data, but you also have to delete rows from the table here.

## Discussion

The table view responds to the swipe by showing a button on the right side of the targeted row (Figure 4-5). As you can see, the table view is *not* in editing mode, but the button allows the user to delete the row.

This mode is enabled by implementing the `tableView:editingStyleForRowAtIndexPath:` method (declared in the `UITableViewDelegate` protocol), whose return value indicates whether the table should allow insertions, deletions, both, or neither. By implementing the `tableView:commitEditingStyle:forRowAtIndexPath:` method in the data source of a table view, you can then get notified if a user has performed an insertion or deletion.

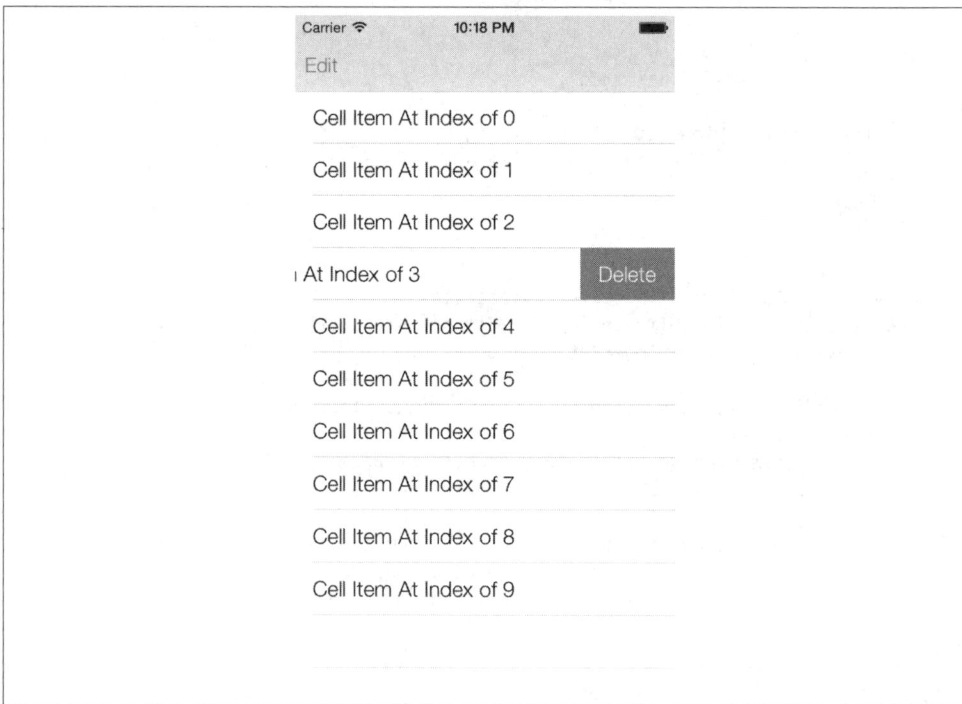


*Figure 4-5. Delete button appearing on a table view cell*

The second parameter of the `deleteRowsAtIndexPaths:withRowAnimation:` method allows you to specify an animation method that will be performed when rows are deleted from a table view. Our example specifies that we want rows to disappear by moving from right to left when deleted.

# 4.5. Constructing Headers and Footers in Table Views

## Problem

You want to create a header and/or a footer for a table view.

## Solution

Create a view (could be a label, image view, etc., anything that directly or indirectly subclasses `UIView`), and assign that view to the header and/or the footer of a section of a table view. You can also allocate a specific number of points in height for a header or a footer, as we will soon see.

## Discussion

A table view can have multiple headers and footers. Each section in a table view can have its own header and footer, so if you have three sections in a table view, you can have a maximum of three headers and a maximum of three footers. You are *not* obliged to provide headers and footers for any of these sections. It is up to you to tell the table view whether you want a header and/or a footer for a section, and you pass these views to the table view through its delegate, should you wish to provide header(s)/footer(s) for section(s) of your table view. Headers and footers in a table view become a part of the table view, meaning that when the table view's contents scroll, so do the header(s) and footer(s) inside that table view. Let's have a look at a sample header and footer in a table view (Figure 4-6).

As you can see, the top section (with items such as "Check Spelling" and "Enable Caps Lock") has a footer that says "Double tapping the space bar will insert a period followed by a space." That is the footer of the top section of that table view. The reason why it is a footer rather than a header is because it is attached to the bottom of that section rather than the top. The last section in this table view also has a header that reads "SHORTCUTS." The reason why this is a header rather than a footer is because it appears on the top of the section rather than the bottom.

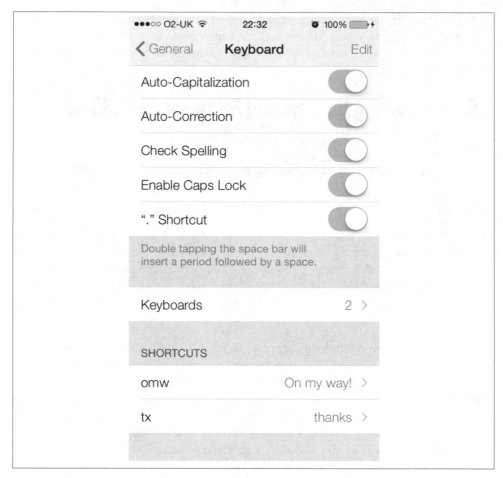

*Figure 4-6. A footer for the top section and the Shortcuts header for the last section of a table view*

Specifying the height of a header and footer in a section inside a table view is done through methods defined in the `UITableViewDataSource`. Specifying the actual view that has to be displayed for the header/footer of a section in a table view is done through methods defined in the `UITableViewDelegate` protocol.

Let's go ahead and create a simple app with one table view in it. Then let's provide two labels, of type `UILabel`, one as the header and the other as the footer of the only section in our table view, and populate this one section with only three cells. In the header we will place the text "Section 1 Header," and in the footer label we will place the text "Section

1 Footer." Starting with the implementation file of our root view controller, we will define a table view:

```
#import "ViewController.h"

static NSString *CellIdentifier = @"CellIdentifier";

@interface ViewController () <UITableViewDelegate, UITableViewDataSource>
@property (nonatomic, strong) UITableView *myTableView;
@end

@implementation ViewController
```

Now we will create a grouped table view and load three cells into it:

```
- (UITableViewCell *) tableView:(UITableView *)tableView
        cellForRowAtIndexPath:(NSIndexPath *)indexPath{

    UITableViewCell *cell = nil;

    cell = [tableView dequeueReusableCellWithIdentifier:CellIdentifier
                                           forIndexPath:indexPath];

    cell.textLabel.text = [[NSString alloc] initWithFormat:@"Cell %ld",
                              (long)indexPath.row];

    return cell;

}

- (NSInteger) tableView:(UITableView *)tableView
  numberOfRowsInSection:(NSInteger)section{
    return 3;
}

- (void)viewDidLoad{
    [super viewDidLoad];

    self.myTableView =
    [[UITableView alloc] initWithFrame:self.view.bounds
                                 style:UITableViewStyleGrouped];

    [self.myTableView registerClass:[UITableViewCell class]
             forCellReuseIdentifier:CellIdentifier];

    self.myTableView.dataSource = self;
    self.myTableView.delegate = self;
    self.myTableView.autoresizingMask = UIViewAutoresizingFlexibleWidth |
    UIViewAutoresizingFlexibleHeight;

    [self.view addSubview:self.myTableView];

}
```

Here is the exciting part. We can now use two important methods (which are defined in `UITableViewDelegate`) to provide a label for the header and another label for the footer of the one section that we have loaded into our table view:

`tableView:viewForHeaderInSection:`
: This method expects a return value of type `UIView`. The view returned from this method will be displayed as the header of the section specified by the `viewForHeaderInSection` parameter.

`tableView:viewForFooterInSection:`
: This method expects a return value of type `UIView`. The view returned from this method will be displayed as the footer of the section specified by the `viewForFooterInSection` parameter.

Our task now is to implement these methods and return an instance of `UILabel`. On the header label we will enter the text "Section 1 Header," and on the footer label the text "Section 1 Footer," as we had planned:

```
- (UILabel *) newLabelWithTitle:(NSString *)paramTitle{
    UILabel *label = [[UILabel alloc] initWithFrame:CGRectZero];
    label.text = paramTitle;
    label.backgroundColor = [UIColor clearColor];
    [label sizeToFit];
    return label;
}

- (UIView *)  tableView:(UITableView *)tableView
 viewForHeaderInSection:(NSInteger)section{

    if (section == 0){
        return [self newLabelWithTitle:@"Section 1 Header"];
    }

    return nil;

}

- (UIView *)  tableView:(UITableView *)tableView
 viewForFooterInSection:(NSInteger)section{

    if (section == 0){
        return [self newLabelWithTitle:@"Section 1 Footer"];
    }

    return nil;

}
```

If you run your app on iOS Simulator now, you will certainly see something strange, as shown in Figure 4-7.

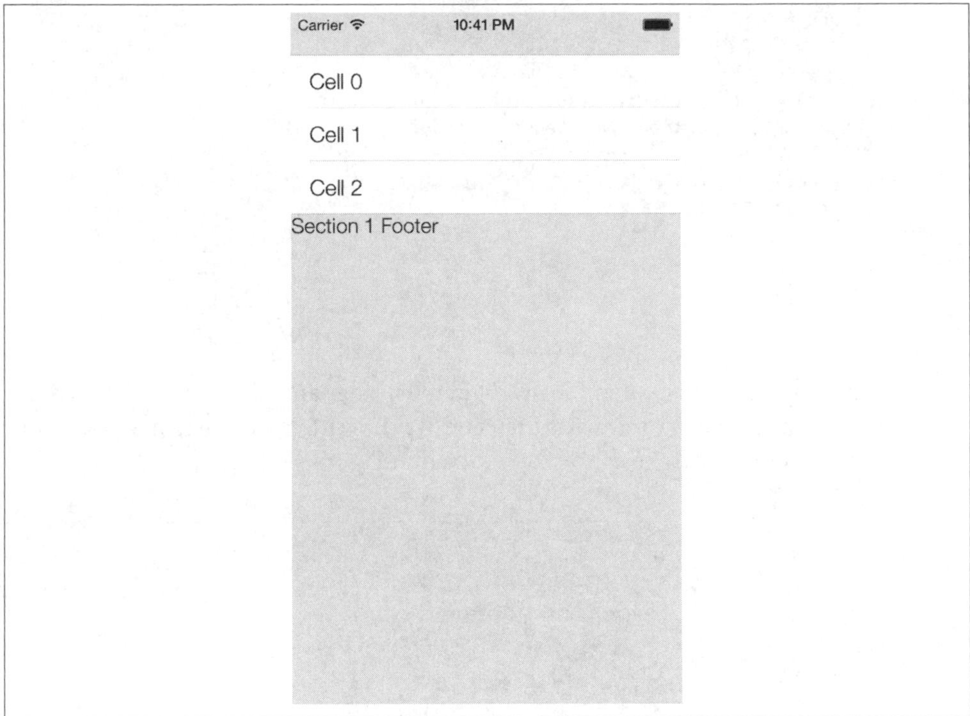


*Figure 4-7. The header and footer labels of a table view are not aligned properly*

The reason for this misalignment of the labels and the omission of the header is that the table view doesn't really know the height of these views. To specify the height of the header and footer views, you need to use the following two methods, which are defined in the `UITableViewDelegate` protocol:

`tableView:heightForHeaderInSection:`
: The return value of this method, of type `CGFloat`, specifies the height of the header for a section in a table view. The section's index is passed through the `heightForHeaderInSection` parameter.

`tableView:heightForFooterInSection:`
: The return value of this method, of type `CGFloat`, specifies the height of the footer for a section in a table view. The section's index is passed through the `heightForHeaderInSection` parameter.

```
- (CGFloat)      tableView:(UITableView *)tableView
 heightForHeaderInSection:(NSInteger)section{

    if (section == 0){
        return 30.0f;
    }
```

```
        return 0.0f;
    }

    - (CGFloat)      tableView:(UITableView *)tableView
     heightForFooterInSection:(NSInteger)section{

        if (section == 0){
            return 30.0f;
        }

        return 0.0f;

    }
```

Running the app, you can see that the height of the header and the footer labels is fixed. There is still something wrong with the code we've written—the left margin of our header and footer labels. Take a look for yourself in Figure 4-8.

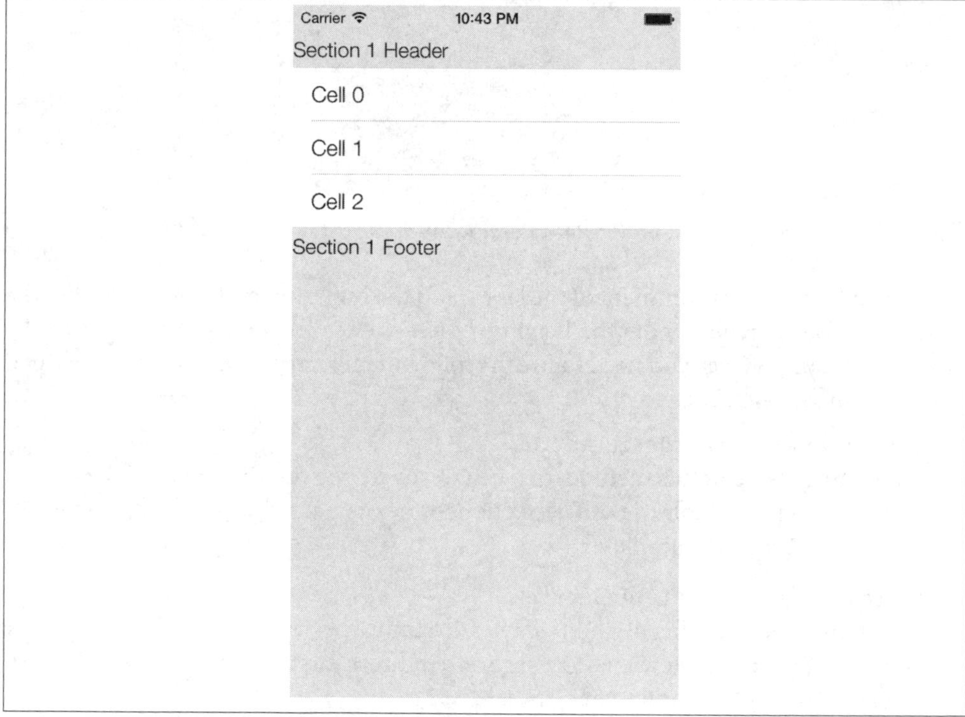


*Figure 4-8. The left margin of our header and footer labels is not correct*

The reason for this is that the table view, by default, places header and footer views at *x* point `0.0f`. You might think that changing the frame of your header and footer labels will fix this issue, but unfortunately it doesn't. The solution to this problem is creating a generic `UIView` and placing your header and footer labels on that view. Return the generic view as the header/footer, but change the *x* position of your labels within the generic view. We now need to modify our implementation of the `tableView:viewForHeaderInSection:` and the `tableView:viewForFooterInSection:` methods:

```
- (UIView *)  tableView:(UITableView *)tableView
 viewForHeaderInSection:(NSInteger)section{

    UIView *header = nil;

    if (section == 0){

        UILabel *label = [self newLabelWithTitle:@"Section 1 Header"];

        /* Move the label 10 points to the right */
        label.frame = CGRectMake(label.frame.origin.x + 10.0f,
                                 5.0f, /* Go 5 points down in y axis */
                                 label.frame.size.width,
                                 label.frame.size.height);

        /* Give the container view 10 points more in width than our label
         because the label needs a 10 extra points left-margin */
        CGRect resultFrame = CGRectMake(0.0f,
                                        0.0f,
                                        label.frame.size.width + 10.0f,
                                        label.frame.size.height);
        header = [[UIView alloc] initWithFrame:resultFrame];
        [header addSubview:label];

    }

    return header;

}

- (UIView *)  tableView:(UITableView *)tableView
 viewForFooterInSection:(NSInteger)section{

    UIView *footer = nil;

    if (section == 0){

        UILabel *label = [[UILabel alloc] initWithFrame:CGRectZero];

        /* Move the label 10 points to the right */
        label.frame = CGRectMake(label.frame.origin.x + 10.0f,
                                 5.0f, /* Go 5 points down in y axis */
                                 label.frame.size.width,
                                 label.frame.size.height);

        /* Give the container view 10 points more in width than our label
```

```
         because the label needs a 10 extra points left-margin */
        CGRect resultFrame = CGRectMake(0.0f,
                                        0.0f,
                                        label.frame.size.width + 10.0f,
                                        label.frame.size.height);
        footer = [[UIView alloc] initWithFrame:resultFrame];
        [footer addSubview:label];

    }

    return footer;
}
```

Now if you run your app, you will get results similar to Figure 4-9.

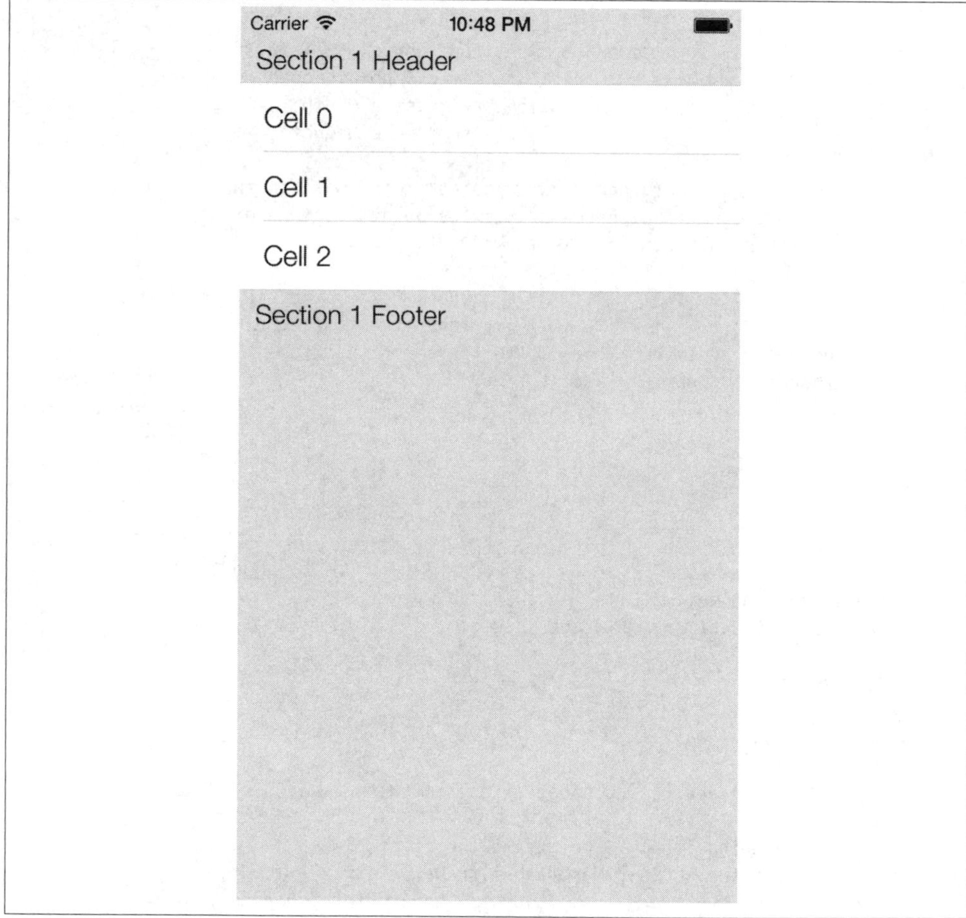


*Figure 4-9. Our header and footer labels displayed in a table view*

With the methods you just learned, you can even place images as the header/footer of your table views. Instances of `UIImageView` have `UIView` as their superclass, so you can easily place your images in image views and return them as headers/footers of a table view. If all you want to place is text as the header/footer of table views, you can use two handy methods defined in the `UITableViewDataSource` protocol, which will save you a lot of hassle. Instead of creating your own labels and returning them as headers/footers of your table view, you can simply use these methods:

`tableView:titleForHeaderInSection:`
: The return value of this method is of type `NSString`. This string will automatically be placed inside a label by the table view and will be displayed as the header of the section, which is specified in the `titleForHeaderInSection` parameter.

`tableView:titleForFooterInSection:`
: The return value of this method is of type `NSString`. This string will automatically be placed inside a label by the table view and will be displayed as the footer of the section, which is specified in the `titleForFooterInSection` parameter.

So to make our app's code simpler, let's get rid of our implementation of the `tableView:viewForHeaderInSection:` and the `tableView:viewForFooterInSection:` methods and replace them with the implementation of the `tableView:titleForHeaderInSection:` and the `tableView:titleForFooterInSection:` methods:

```
- (NSString *) tableView:(UITableView *)tableView
 titleForHeaderInSection:(NSInteger)section{

    if (section == 0){
        return @"Section 1 Header";
    }

    return nil;

}

- (NSString *) tableView:(UITableView *)tableView
 titleForFooterInSection:(NSInteger)section{

    if (section == 0){
        return @"Section 1 Footer";
    }

    return nil;

}
```

Now run your app in iPhone Simulator, and you will see that the table view has automatically created a left-aligned label for the header and the footer of the only section in our table view. In iOS 7, by default, the header and the footer are left-aligned. In earlier versions of iOS, the header is left-aligned but the footer is center-aligned. In every version, the table view can set the alignment of these labels (see Figure 4-10).

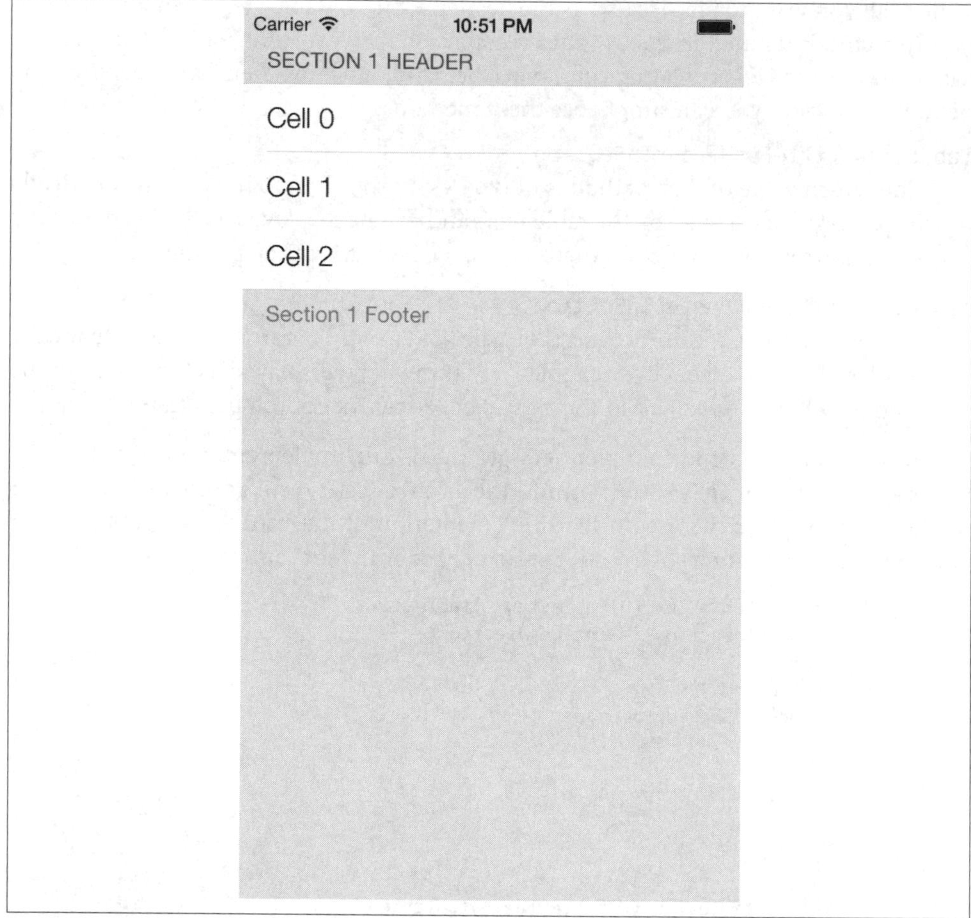


*Figure 4-10. A table view rendering text in headers and footers*

# 4.6. Displaying Context Menus on Table View Cells

## Problem

You want to give your users the ability to use copy/paste options among other operations that they can choose, by holding down one of their fingers on a table view cell in your app.

## Solution

Implement the following three methods of the `UITableViewDelegate` protocol in the delegate object of your table view:

`tableView:shouldShowMenuForRowAtIndexPath:`
: The return value of this method is of type `BOOL`. If you return `YES` from this method, iOS will display the context menu for the table view cell whose index gets passed to you through the `shouldShowMenuForRowAtIndexPath` parameter.

`tableView:canPerformAction:forRowAtIndexPath:withSender:`
: The return value of this method is also of type `BOOL`. Once you allow iOS to display a context menu for a table view cell, iOS will call this method multiple times and pass you the selector of the action that you can choose to display in the context menu or not. So, if iOS wants to ask you whether you would like to show the Copy menu to be displayed to the user, this method will get called in your table view's delegate object and the `canPerformAction` parameter of this method will be equal to `@selector(copy:)`. We will read more information about this in this recipe's Discussion.

`tableView:performAction:forRowAtIndexPath:withSender:`
: Once you allow a certain action to be displayed in the context menu of a table view cell, when the user picks that action from the menu, this method will get called in your table view's delegate object. In here, you must do whatever needs to be done to satisfy the user's request. For instance, if it is the Copy menu that the user has selected, you will need to use a pasteboard to place the chosen table view cell's content into the pasteboard.

## Discussion

A table view can give a yes/no answer to iOS, allowing or disallowing the display of available system menu items for a table view cell. iOS attempts to display a context menu on a table view cell when the user has held down his finger on the cell for a certain period of time, roughly about one second. iOS then asks the table view whose cell was the source of the trigger for the menu. If the table view gives a yes answer, iOS will then tell the table view what options can be displayed in the context menu, and the table view will be able to say yes or no to any of those items. If there are five menu items available, for instance, and the table view says yes to only two of them, then only those two items will be displayed.

After the menu items are displayed to the user, the user can either tap on one of the items or tap outside the context menu to cancel it. Once the user taps on one of the menu items, iOS will send a delegate message to the table view informing it of the menu item that the user has picked. Based on this information, the table view can make a decision as to what to do with the selected action.

I suggest that we first see what actions are actually available for a context menu on a table view cell, so let's create our table view and then display a few cells inside it:

```
- (NSInteger) tableView:(UITableView *)tableView
  numberOfRowsInSection:(NSInteger)section{
    return 3;
}

- (UITableViewCell *) tableView:(UITableView *)tableView
          cellForRowAtIndexPath:(NSIndexPath *)indexPath{

    UITableViewCell *cell = nil;

    cell = [tableView dequeueReusableCellWithIdentifier:CellIdentifier
                                           forIndexPath:indexPath];

    cell.textLabel.text = [[NSString alloc]
                           initWithFormat:@"Section %ld Cell %ld",
                           (long)indexPath.section,
                           (long)indexPath.row];

    return cell;

}

- (void)viewDidLoad{
    [super viewDidLoad];

    self.myTableView = [[UITableView alloc]
                        initWithFrame:self.view.bounds
                        style:UITableViewStylePlain];

    [self.myTableView registerClass:[UITableViewCell class]
             forCellReuseIdentifier:CellIdentifier];

    self.myTableView.autoresizingMask =
        UIViewAutoresizingFlexibleWidth |
        UIViewAutoresizingFlexibleHeight;

    self.myTableView.dataSource = self;
    self.myTableView.delegate = self;

    [self.view addSubview:self.myTableView];

}
```

Now we will implement the three aforementioned methods defined in the `UITableViewDelegate` protocol and simply convert the available actions (of type `SEL`) to strings and print them out to the console:

```
- (BOOL)                tableView:(UITableView *)tableView
  shouldShowMenuForRowAtIndexPath:(NSIndexPath *)indexPath{
```

```
    /* Allow the context menu to be displayed on every cell */
    return YES;

}

- (BOOL) tableView:(UITableView *)tableView
  canPerformAction:(SEL)action
 forRowAtIndexPath:(NSIndexPath *)indexPath
        withSender:(id)sender{

    NSLog(@"%@", NSStringFromSelector(action));

    /* Allow every action for now */
    return YES;
}

- (void) tableView:(UITableView *)tableView
     performAction:(SEL)action
 forRowAtIndexPath:(NSIndexPath *)indexPath
        withSender:(id)sender{

    /* Empty for now */

}
```

Now run your app in the simulator or on the device. You will see three cells loaded into the table view. Hold down your finger (if on a device) or your pointer (if using iOS Simulator) on one of the cells and observe what gets printed out to the console window:

```
cut:
copy:
select:
selectAll:
paste:
delete:
_promptForReplace:
_showTextStyleOptions:
_define:
_addShortcut:
_accessibilitySpeak:
_accessibilitySpeakLanguageSelection:
_accessibilityPauseSpeaking:
makeTextWritingDirectionRightToLeft:
makeTextWritingDirectionLeftToRight:
```

These are all the actions that iOS will allow you to show your users, should you need them. So for instance, if you would like to allow your users to have the Copy option, in the `tableView:canPerformAction:forRowAtIndexPath:withSender:` method, simply find out which action iOS is asking your permission for before displaying it, and either return `YES` or `NO`:

```
- (BOOL) tableView:(UITableView *)tableView
  canPerformAction:(SEL)action
 forRowAtIndexPath:(NSIndexPath *)indexPath
        withSender:(id)sender{

    if (action == @selector(copy:)){
        return YES;
    }

    return NO;
}
```

The next step is to intercept what menu item the user actually selected from the context menu. Based on this information, we can then take appropriate action. For instance, if the user selected the Copy item in the context menu (see Figure 4-11), then we can use `UIPasteBoard` to copy that cell into the pasteboard for later use:

```
- (void) tableView:(UITableView *)tableView
     performAction:(SEL)action
 forRowAtIndexPath:(NSIndexPath *)indexPath
        withSender:(id)sender{

    if (action == @selector(copy:)){

        UITableViewCell *cell = [tableView cellForRowAtIndexPath:indexPath];
        UIPasteboard *pasteBoard = [UIPasteboard generalPasteboard];
        [pasteBoard setString:cell.textLabel.text];

    }

}
```

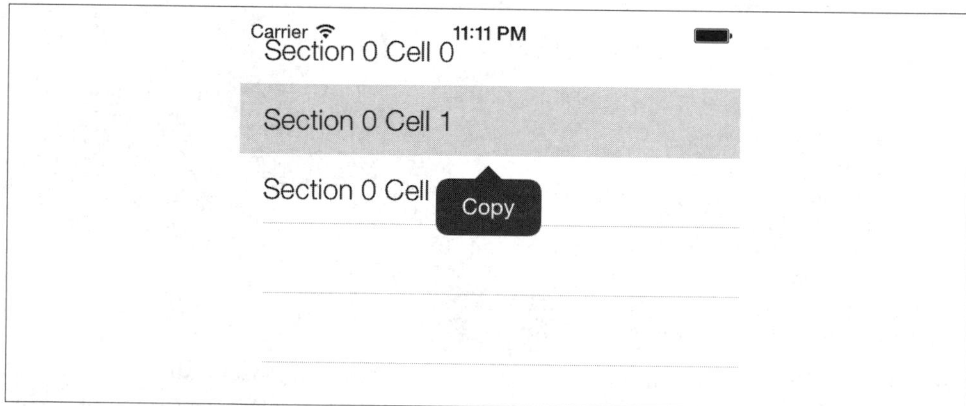


*Figure 4-11. The Copy action displayed inside a context menu on a table view cell*

# 4.7. Moving Cells and Sections in Table Views

## Problem

You want to move and shuffle cells and sections inside a table view, with smooth and intuitive animations.

## Solution

Use the `moveSection:toSection:` method of the table view to move a section to a new position. You can also use the `moveRowAtIndexPath:toIndexPath:` method to move a table view cell from its current place to a new place.

## Discussion

Moving table view cells and sections differs from exchanging them. Let's have a look at an example that will make this easier to understand. Let's say you have three sections in your table view: sections A, B, and C. If you move Section A to Section C, the table view will notice this move and will then shift Section B to the previous position of Section A, and will move Section C to the previous position of Section B. However, if Section B is moved to Section C, the table view will not have to move Section A at all, as it is sitting on top and doesn't interfere with the repositioning of Section B and C. In this case, Section B will be moved to Section C and Section C to Section B. The same logic will be used by the table view when moving cells.

To demonstrate this, let's create a table view and preload it with three sections, each of which contains three cells of its own. Let's start with the implementation file of our view controller:

```
#import "ViewController.h"

static NSString *CellIdentifier = @"CellIdentifier";

@interface ViewController () <UITableViewDelegate, UITableViewDataSource>
@property (nonatomic, strong) UITableView *myTableView;
@property (nonatomic, strong) NSMutableArray *arrayOfSections;
@end
```

Our view controller will become the data source of the table view. The table view has sections, and each section has rows. We will keep an array of arrays; the first array is our array of sections, which will itself contain other arrays that contain our cells. The `arrayOfSections` defined on top of the implementation file of our view controller will bear that responsibility. Let's go ahead and populate this array:

```
- (NSMutableArray *) newSectionWithIndex:(NSUInteger)paramIndex
                               cellCount:(NSUInteger)paramCellCount{
```

```
    NSMutableArray *result = [[NSMutableArray alloc] init];

    NSUInteger counter = 0;
    for (counter = 0;
         counter < paramCellCount;
         counter++){

        [result addObject:[[NSString alloc] initWithFormat:@"Section %lu Cell %lu",
                           (unsigned long)paramIndex,
                           (unsigned long)counter+1]];

    }

    return result;

}

- (NSMutableArray *) arrayOfSections{
    if (_arrayOfSections == nil){
        NSMutableArray *section1 = [self newSectionWithIndex:1
                                                   cellCount:3];
        NSMutableArray *section2 = [self newSectionWithIndex:2
                                                   cellCount:3];
        NSMutableArray *section3 = [self newSectionWithIndex:3
                                                   cellCount:3];

        _arrayOfSections = [[NSMutableArray alloc] initWithArray:@[
                                                                   section1,
                                                                   section2,
                                                                   section3
                                                                   ]
                            ];
    }
    return _arrayOfSections;
}
```

We shall then instantiate our table view and implement the necessary methods in the `UITableViewDataSource` protocol to populate our table view with data:

```
- (NSInteger) numberOfSectionsInTableView:(UITableView *)tableView{

    return self.arrayOfSections.count;

}

- (NSInteger) tableView:(UITableView *)tableView
  numberOfRowsInSection:(NSInteger)section{

    NSMutableArray *sectionArray = self.arrayOfSections[section];
    return sectionArray.count;

}
```

```
- (UITableViewCell *)tableView:(UITableView *)tableView
        cellForRowAtIndexPath:(NSIndexPath *)indexPath{

    UITableViewCell *cell = nil;


    cell = [tableView dequeueReusableCellWithIdentifier:CellIdentifier
                                           forIndexPath:indexPath];


    NSMutableArray *sectionArray = self.arrayOfSections[indexPath.section];

    cell.textLabel.text = sectionArray[indexPath.row];

    return cell;

}

- (void)viewDidLoad{
    [super viewDidLoad];

    self.myTableView =
    [[UITableView alloc] initWithFrame:self.view.bounds
                                 style:UITableViewStyleGrouped];

    [self.myTableView registerClass:[UITableViewCell class]
            forCellReuseIdentifier:CellIdentifier];

    self.myTableView.autoresizingMask =
        UIViewAutoresizingFlexibleWidth |
        UIViewAutoresizingFlexibleHeight;

    self.myTableView.delegate = self;
    self.myTableView.dataSource = self;

    [self.view addSubview:self.myTableView];

}
```

Showtime! Shall we first have a look at how sections can be moved to a new position? Let's write a method that will move Section 1 to Section 3:

```
- (void) moveSection1ToSection3{

    NSMutableArray *section1 = self.arrayOfSections[0];
    [self.arrayOfSections removeObject:section1];
    [self.arrayOfSections addObject:section1];

    [self.myTableView moveSection:0
                       toSection:2];

}
```

I will leave it up to you to decide when you would like to invoke this method, as we don't have a button on our UI at the moment. You can simply create a navigation controller, place a navigation button on it, and then invoke this method.

Once you run the app normally, you will see the sections lined up from 1 to 3, as in Figure 4-12.

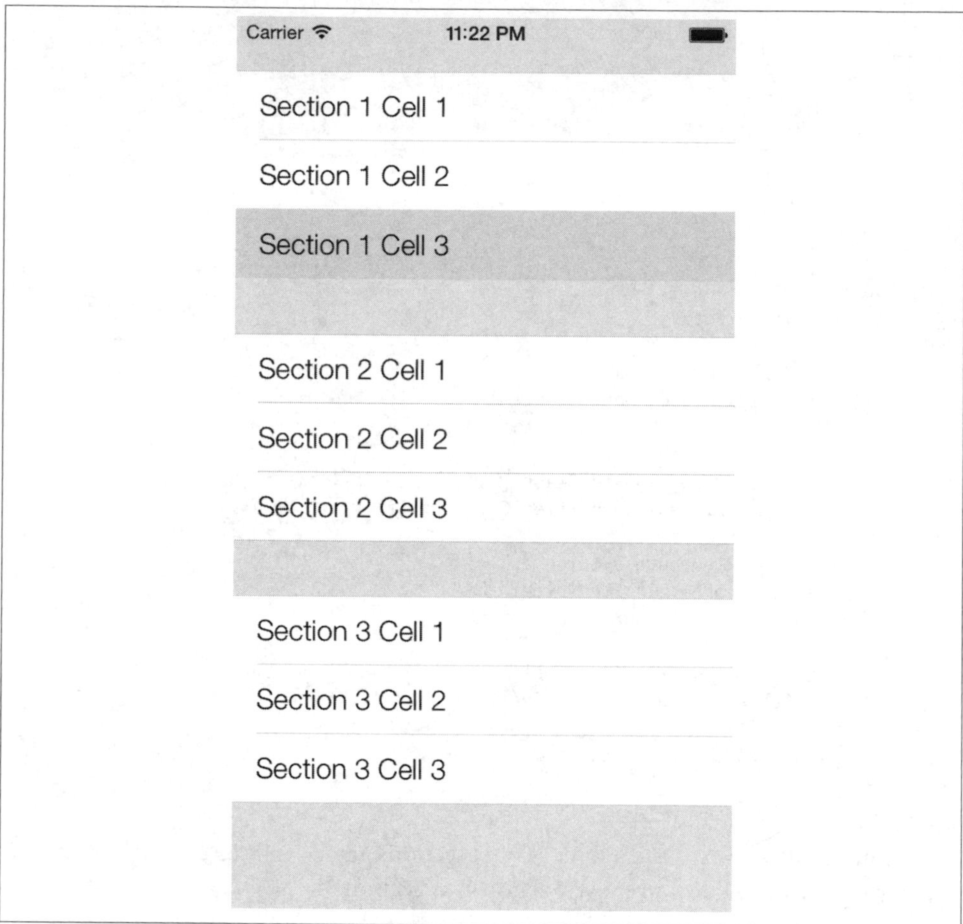


*Figure 4-12. A table view with three sections, each containing three cells*

After you invoke the `moveSection1ToSection3` method, you will see that Section 1 gets moved to Section 3, Section 3 moves to Section 2's previous position, and finally Section 2 moves to Section 1's previous position (Figure 4-13).

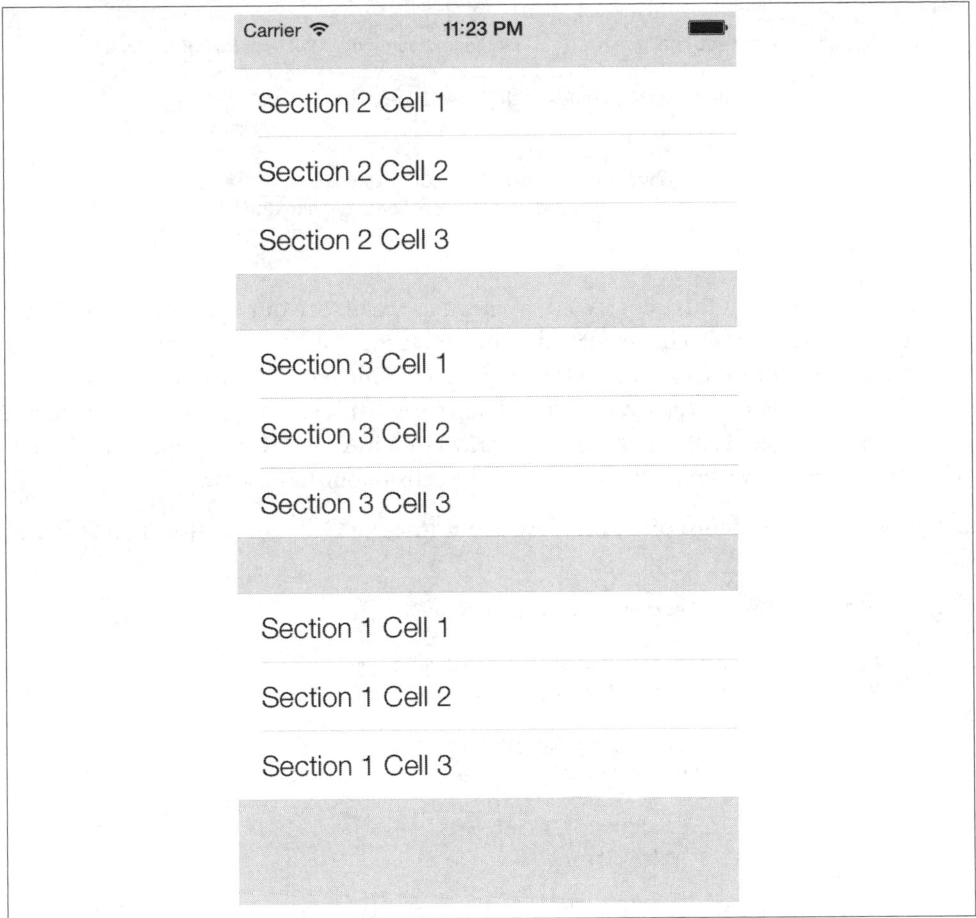


*Figure 4-13. Section 1 is moved to Section 3, and other sections are subsequently moved as well*

Moving cells is very similar to moving sections. To move cells, all we have to do is use the `moveRowAtIndexPath:toIndexPath:` method. Remember that you can move a cell from one section to the same section, or to a new section. Let's make it easy and move Cell 1 in Section 1 to Cell 2 in the same section and see what happens:

```
- (void) moveCell1InSection1ToCell2InSection1{

    NSMutableArray *section1 = self.arrayOfSections[0];
    NSString *cell1InSection1 = section1[0];

    [section1 removeObject:cell1InSection1];

    [section1 insertObject:cell1InSection1
                   atIndex:1];
```

```
    NSIndexPath *sourceIndexPath = [NSIndexPath indexPathForRow:0
                                                      inSection:0];
    NSIndexPath *destinationIndexPath = [NSIndexPath indexPathForRow:1
                                                           inSection:0];

    [self.myTableView moveRowAtIndexPath:sourceIndexPath
                             toIndexPath:destinationIndexPath];

}
```

So what is going on in this code? Well, we need to make sure our data source holds the correct data that needs to be displayed in our table view after we have moved the cells around, so we remove Cell 1 in Section 1 first. That moves Cell 2 to Cell 1, and Cell 3 to Cell 2, with a total of 2 cells in the array. Then we will insert Cell 1 into Index 1 (second object) of the array. That will make our array contain Cell 2, Cell 1, and then Cell 3. After that is done, we have actually moved the cells in our table view.

Let's make this a bit more difficult. How about moving Cell 2 in Section 1 to Cell 1 in Section 2?

```
- (void) moveCell2InSection1ToCell1InSection2{

    NSMutableArray *section1 = self.arrayOfSections[0];
    NSMutableArray *section2 = self.arrayOfSections[1];

    NSString *cell2InSection1 = section1[1];
    [section1 removeObject:cell2InSection1];

    [section2 insertObject:cell2InSection1
                   atIndex:0];

    NSIndexPath *sourceIndexPath = [NSIndexPath indexPathForRow:1
                                                      inSection:0];
    NSIndexPath *destinationIndexPath = [NSIndexPath indexPathForRow:0
                                                           inSection:1];

    [self.myTableView moveRowAtIndexPath:sourceIndexPath
                             toIndexPath:destinationIndexPath];

}
```

The results of this transition are shown in Figure 4-14.

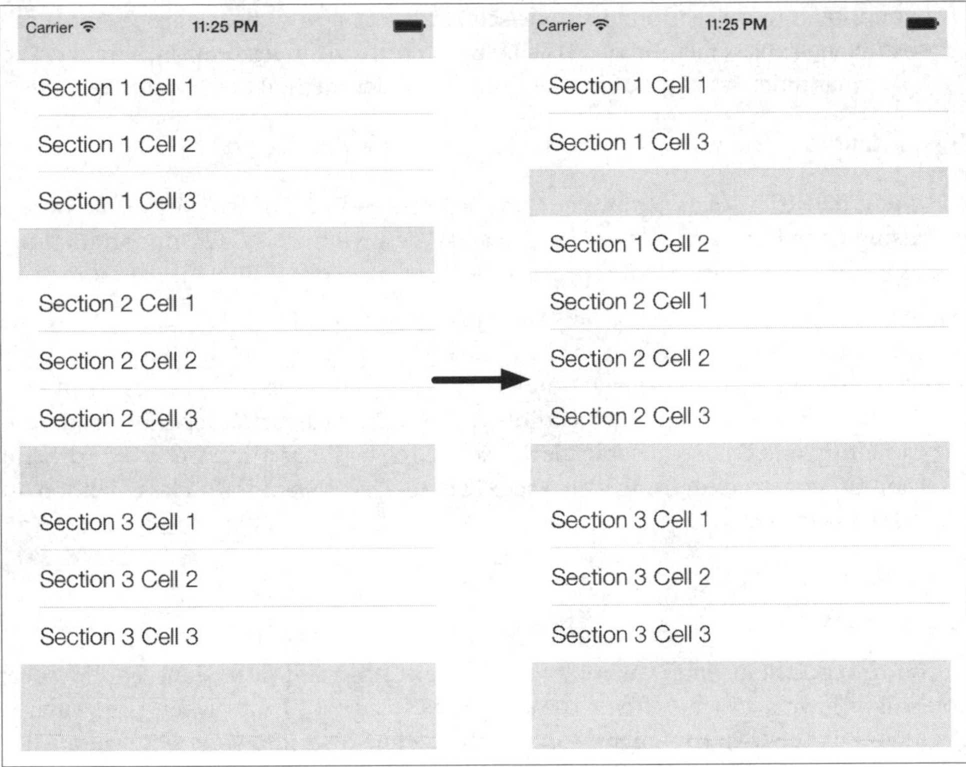


*Figure 4-14. Cell 2 in Section 1 is moved to Cell 1 in Section 2*

# 4.8. Deleting Cells and Sections from Table Views

## Problem

You want to delete sections and/or cells from table views using animations.

## Solution

In order to delete sections from a table view, follow these steps:

1. First delete the section(s) in your data source, whether you are using a data model like Core Data or a dictionary/array.
2. Invoke the `deleteSections:withRowAnimation:` instance method of `UITableView` on your table view. The first parameter that you need to pass to this method is of type `NSIndexSet`, and this object can be instantiated using the `indexSetWithIndex:` class method of `NSIndexSet` class, where the given index is an unsigned integer. Using this approach, you will be able to delete only one section at a time. If

you intend to delete more than one section at a time, use the `indexSetWithIndexesInRange:` class method of `NSIndexSet` to create the index set using a range, and pass that index set to the aforementioned instance method of `UITableView`.

If you want to delete cells from your table view, follow these steps:

1. First, delete the cell(s) from your data source. Again, it doesn't matter if you are using Core Data, a simple dictionary, array, or anything else. The important thing is to delete the objects that represent the table view cells from your data source.
2. Now, in order to delete the cells that correspond to your data objects, invoke the `deleteRowsAtIndexPaths:withRowAnimation:` instance method of your table view. The first parameter that you have to pass to this method is an array of type `NSArray` that must contain objects of type `NSIndexPath`, with each index path representing one cell in the table view. Each index path has a section and a row and can be constructed using the `indexPathForRow:inSection:` class method of `NSIndexPath` class.

## Discussion

In your UI code, sometimes you might need to delete cells and/or sections. For instance, you might have a switch (of type `UISwitch`; see Recipe 1.2), and when the switch is turned on by the user, you might want to insert a few rows into your table view. After the switch is turned off by the user, you will then want to delete those rows. It's not always table view cells (rows) that you have to delete. Sometimes you might need to delete a whole section or a few sections simultaneously from your table view. The key for deleting cells and sections from table views is to first delete the data corresponding to those cells/sections from your data source, and then call the appropriate deletion method on the table view. After the deletion method finishes, the table view will refer back to its data source object. If the number of cells/sections in the data source doesn't match the number of cells/sections in the table view after the deletion is complete, your app will crash. But don't worry—if you ever do make this mistake, the debug text that gets printed to the console is descriptive enough to point you in the right direction.

Let's have a look at how we can delete sections from a table view. For this recipe, we will display a table view on a view controller that is displayed inside a navigation controller. Inside the table view, we will display two sections, one for odd numbers and another for even numbers. We will display only 1, 3, 5, and 7 for odd numbers and 0, 2, 4, and 6 for even numbers. For the first exercise, we are going to place a navigation bar button on our navigation bar and make that button responsible for deleting the section with odd numbers in it. Figure 4-15 shows what we want the results to look like.

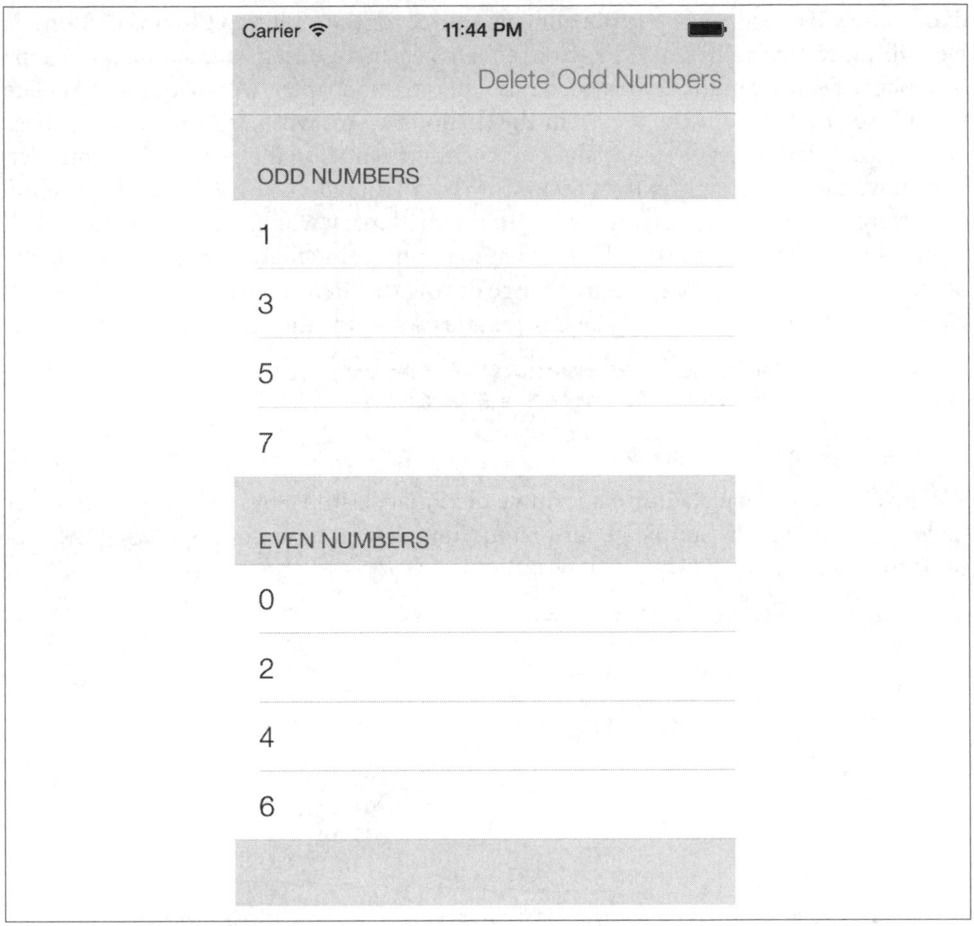

*Figure 4-15. The user interface to display two sections in a table view and a button that will delete the Odd Numbers section*

First things first. Let's define our view controller:

```
#import "ViewController.h"

static NSString *CellIdentifier = @"NumbersCellIdentifier";

@interface ViewController () <UITableViewDataSource, UITableViewDelegate>
@property (nonatomic, strong) UITableView *tableViewNumbers;
@property (nonatomic, strong) NSMutableDictionary *dictionaryOfNumbers;
@property (nonatomic, strong) UIBarButtonItem *barButtonAction;
@end
```

The `tableViewNumbers` property is our table view. The `barButtonAction` property is the bar button that we'll display on the navigation bar. Last but not least, the dictionaryOfNumbers property is our data source for the table view. In this dictionary, we will place two values of type NSMutableArray that contain our numbers of type NSNumber. They are mutable arrays, so that, later in this chapter, we will be able to delete them individually from the arrays in the dictionary. We will keep the keys for these arrays in our dictionary as static values in the implementation file of our view controller, so that we can later simply extract them from the dictionary using the static keys (if the keys were not static, finding our arrays in the dictionary would have to be done with string comparison, which is slightly more time-consuming than simply associating the object with a static key that doesn't change during the lifetime of our view controller). Now let's define the static string keys for our arrays inside the data source dictionary:

```
static NSString *SectionOddNumbers = @"Odd Numbers";
static NSString *SectionEvenNumbers = @"Even Numbers";

@implementation ViewController
```

We now need to populate our data source dictionary with values before we create our table view. Here is the simple getter method that will take care of populating the dictionary for us:

```
- (NSMutableDictionary *) dictionaryOfNumbers{

    if (_dictionaryOfNumbers == nil){
        NSMutableArray *arrayOfEvenNumbers =
        [[NSMutableArray alloc] initWithArray:@[
                                        @0,
                                        @2,
                                        @4,
                                        @6,
                                        ]];

        NSMutableArray *arrayOfOddNumbers =
        [[NSMutableArray alloc] initWithArray:@[
                                        @1,
                                        @3,
                                        @5,
                                        @7,
                                        ]];

        _dictionaryOfNumbers =
        [[NSMutableDictionary alloc]
         initWithDictionary:@{
                              SectionEvenNumbers : arrayOfEvenNumbers,
                              SectionOddNumbers : arrayOfOddNumbers,
                              }];

    }
    return _dictionaryOfNumbers;
}
```

So far, so good? As you can see, we have two arrays, each of which contains some numbers (one odd and the other even numbers) and we associate them with the `SectionEvenNumbers` and `SectionOddNumbers` keys that we declared before in the implementation file of our view controller. Now let's go ahead and instantiate our table view:

```
- (void)viewDidLoad
{
    [super viewDidLoad];

    self.barButtonAction =
    [[UIBarButtonItem alloc]
     initWithTitle:@"Delete Odd Numbers"
     style:UIBarButtonItemStylePlain
     target:self
     action:@selector(deleteOddNumbersSection:)];

    [self.navigationItem setRightBarButtonItem:self.barButtonAction
                                      animated:NO];

    self.tableViewNumbers = [[UITableView alloc]
                             initWithFrame:self.view.frame
                             style:UITableViewStyleGrouped];

    [self.tableViewNumbers registerClass:[UITableViewCell class]
                  forCellReuseIdentifier:CellIdentifier];

    self.tableViewNumbers.autoresizingMask =
        UIViewAutoresizingFlexibleWidth |
        UIViewAutoresizingFlexibleHeight;

    self.tableViewNumbers.delegate = self;
    self.tableViewNumbers.dataSource = self;

    [self.view addSubview:self.tableViewNumbers];

}
```

The next thing we need to do is populate our table view with data inside our data source dictionary:

```
- (NSInteger) numberOfSectionsInTableView:(UITableView *)tableView{

    return self.dictionaryOfNumbers.allKeys.count;

}

- (NSInteger) tableView:(UITableView *)tableView
  numberOfRowsInSection:(NSInteger)section{

    NSString *sectionNameInDictionary =
        self.dictionaryOfNumbers.allKeys[section];
```

```
    NSArray *sectionArray = self.dictionaryOfNumbers[sectionNameInDictionary];
    return sectionArray.count;

}

- (UITableViewCell *) tableView:(UITableView *)tableView
        cellForRowAtIndexPath:(NSIndexPath *)indexPath{

    UITableViewCell *cell = nil;

    cell = [tableView dequeueReusableCellWithIdentifier:CellIdentifier
                                           forIndexPath:indexPath];

    NSString *sectionNameInDictionary =
        self.dictionaryOfNumbers.allKeys[indexPath.section];

    NSArray *sectionArray = self.dictionaryOfNumbers[sectionNameInDictionary];

    NSNumber *number = sectionArray[indexPath.row];

    cell.textLabel.text = [NSString stringWithFormat:@"%lu",
                           (unsigned long)[number unsignedIntegerValue]];

    return cell;

}

- (NSString *) tableView:(UITableView *)tableView
 titleForHeaderInSection:(NSInteger)section{

    return self.dictionaryOfNumbers.allKeys[section];

}
```

Our navigation button is linked to the `deleteOddNumbersSection:` selector. This is a method we are going to code now. The purpose of this method, as its name implies, is to find the section that corresponds to all odd numbers in our data source and the table view and remove that section from both of these. Here is how we will do it:

```
- (void) deleteOddNumbersSection:(id)paramSender{

    /* First remove the section from our data source */
    NSString *key = SectionOddNumbers;
    NSInteger indexForKey = [[self.dictionaryOfNumbers allKeys]
                             indexOfObject:key];

    if (indexForKey == NSNotFound){
        NSLog(@"Could not find the section in the data source.");
        return;
    }
    [self.dictionaryOfNumbers removeObjectForKey:key];
```

```
    /* Then delete the section from the table view */
    NSIndexSet *sectionToDelete = [NSIndexSet indexSetWithIndex:indexForKey];
    [self.tableViewNumbers deleteSections:sectionToDelete
                         withRowAnimation:UITableViewRowAnimationAutomatic];

    /* Finally, remove the button from the navigation bar
     as it is not useful any longer */
    [self.navigationItem setRightBarButtonItem:nil animated:YES];

}
```

Simple enough. Now, when the user presses the navigation bar button, the Odd Numbers section will disappear from the table view. You can note that there is an animation that gets committed on the table view while the section is being deleted. This is because of the `UITableViewRowAnimationAutomatic` animation type that we are passing to the `withRowAnimation:` parameter of the `deleteSections:withRowAnimation:` method of our table view. Now run the app in iOS Simulator and select Debug → Toggle Slow Animations. Then attempt to press the navigation bar button and see what happens. You can see the deletion animation in slow motion. It's neat, isn't it? After the deletion is completed, our app will look similar to Figure 4-16.

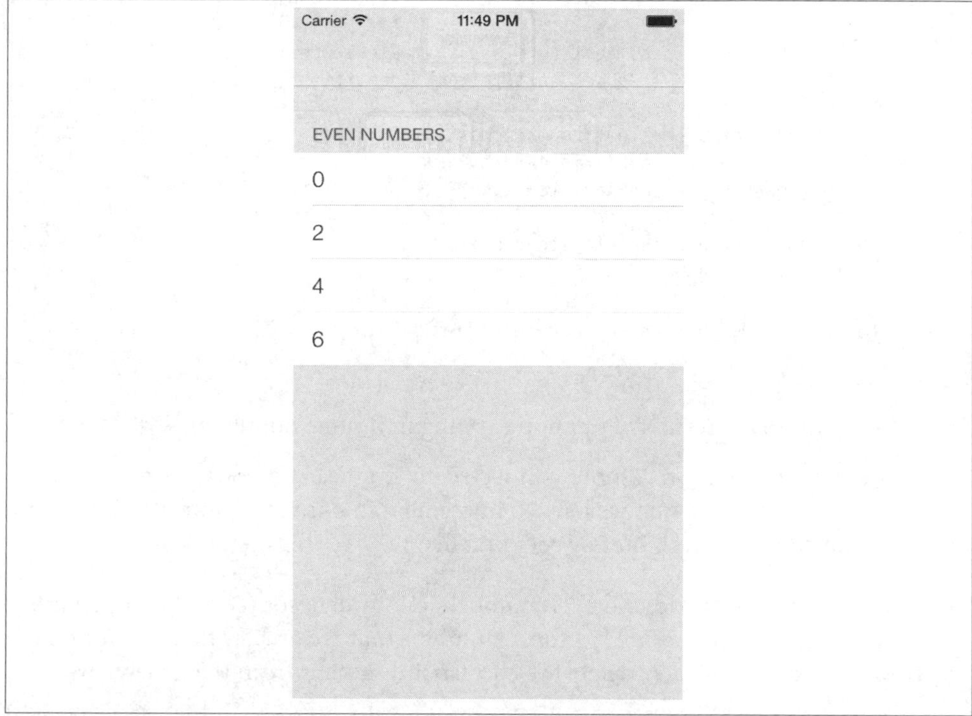


*Figure 4-16. The section containing odd numbers is removed from the table view*

We now know how to delete sections from table views. Let's move to deleting cells. We are going to change the functionality of our navigation bar button so that when it is pressed, it will delete all cells in all sections of our table view with a numerical value greater than 2. That includes all odd and even numbers greater than 2. So let's change our navigation bar button item in the `viewDidLoad` method of our view controller:

```
- (void)viewDidLoad
{
    [super viewDidLoad];

    self.barButtonAction =
    [[UIBarButtonItem alloc]
     initWithTitle:@"Delete Numbers > 2"
     style:UIBarButtonItemStylePlain
     target:self
     action:@selector(deleteNumbersGreaterThan2:)];

    [self.navigationItem setRightBarButtonItem:self.barButtonAction
                                      animated:NO];

    self.tableViewNumbers = [[UITableView alloc]
                             initWithFrame:self.view.frame
                             style:UITableViewStyleGrouped];

    [self.tableViewNumbers registerClass:[UITableViewCell class]
              forCellReuseIdentifier:CellIdentifier];

    self.tableViewNumbers.autoresizingMask =
        UIViewAutoresizingFlexibleWidth |
        UIViewAutoresizingFlexibleHeight;

    self.tableViewNumbers.delegate = self;
    self.tableViewNumbers.dataSource = self;

    [self.view addSubview:self.tableViewNumbers];

}
```

Figure 4-17 shows the results of our app running in iPhone Simulator.

The navigation bar button is now connected to the `deleteNumbersGreaterThan2:` selector. This is a method that we have to implement in our view controller, but before jumping into coding it straightaway, let's first define what this method should do:

1. Find both arrays of odd and even numbers in our data source and grab the index paths (of type `NSIndexPath`) of those numbers that are greater than 2. We will use these index paths to later delete the corresponding cells from the table view.
2. Delete all the numbers greater than 2 from our data source, in both the even and odd number dictionaries.

3. Delete the relevant cells from the table view. We collected the index paths of these cells in the first step.
4. Remove the navigation bar button, since it won't be of any use after the relevant cells have been deleted from the data source and the table view. Alternatively, if you want, you could just disable this button—but I think removing the button provides a better user experience, since a disabled button is really of no use to the user.

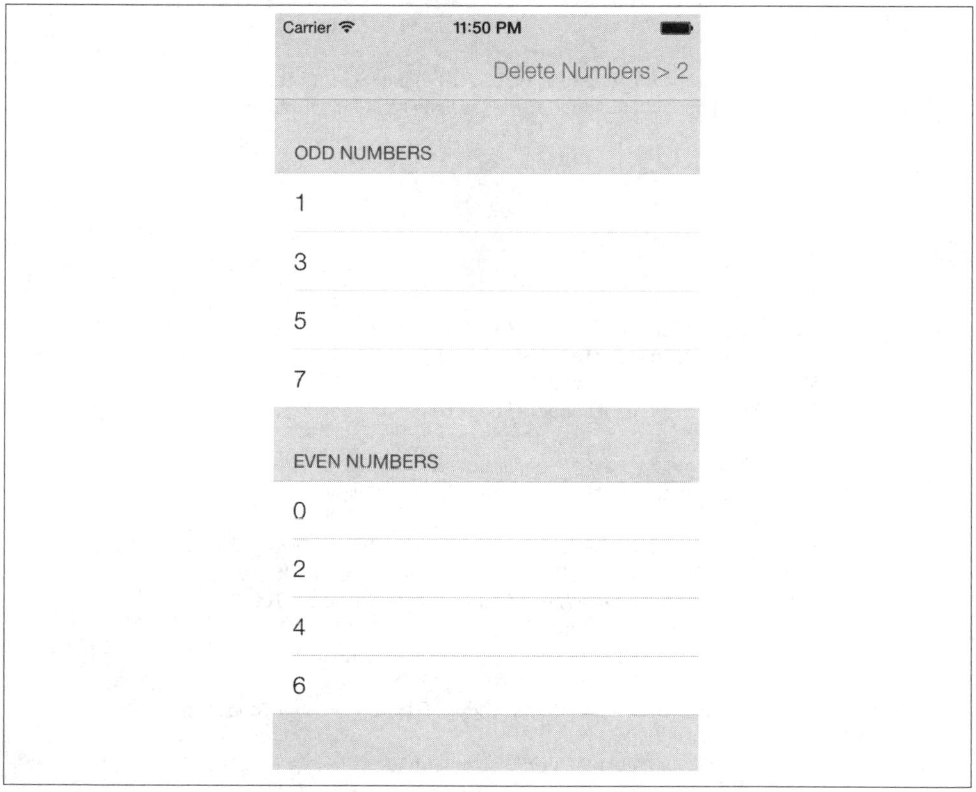

*Figure 4-17. A button that will delete all cells containing a number greater than 2*

```
- (void) deleteNumbersGreaterThan2:(id)paramSender{

    NSMutableArray *arrayOfIndexPathsToDelete =
        [[NSMutableArray alloc] init];

    NSMutableArray *arrayOfNumberObjectsToDelete =
        [[NSMutableArray alloc] init];

    /* Step 1: gather the objects we have to delete from our data source
     and their index paths */
    __block NSUInteger keyIndex = 0;
```

```
    [self.dictionaryOfNumbers enumerateKeysAndObjectsUsingBlock:
     ^(NSString *key, NSMutableArray *object, BOOL *stop) {

         [object enumerateObjectsUsingBlock:
          ^(NSNumber *number, NSUInteger numberIndex, BOOL *stop) {

              if ([number unsignedIntegerValue] > 2){

                  NSIndexPath *indexPath =
                  [NSIndexPath indexPathForRow:numberIndex
                                     inSection:keyIndex];

                  [arrayOfIndexPathsToDelete addObject:indexPath];
                  [arrayOfNumberObjectsToDelete addObject:number];
              }

          }];

         keyIndex++;
     }];

    /* Step 2: delete the objects from the data source */
    if ([arrayOfNumberObjectsToDelete count] > 0){
        NSMutableArray *arrayOfOddNumbers =
            self.dictionaryOfNumbers[SectionOddNumbers];

        NSMutableArray *arrayOfEvenNumbers =
            self.dictionaryOfNumbers[SectionEvenNumbers];

        [arrayOfNumberObjectsToDelete enumerateObjectsUsingBlock:
         ^(NSNumber *numberToDelete, NSUInteger idx, BOOL *stop) {
             if ([arrayOfOddNumbers indexOfObject:numberToDelete]
                    != NSNotFound){
                 [arrayOfOddNumbers removeObject:numberToDelete];
             }
             if ([arrayOfEvenNumbers indexOfObject:numberToDelete]
                    != NSNotFound){
                 [arrayOfEvenNumbers removeObject:numberToDelete];
             }
         }];
    }

    /* Step 3: delete the cells that correspond to the objects */
    [self.tableViewNumbers
     deleteRowsAtIndexPaths:arrayOfIndexPathsToDelete
     withRowAnimation:UITableViewRowAnimationAutomatic];

    [self.navigationItem setRightBarButtonItem:nil animated:YES];

}
```

After the user presses the button on the navigation bar, all cells containing a number greater than 2 will be deleted from our data source, and the table view and our app will look like Figure 4-18.

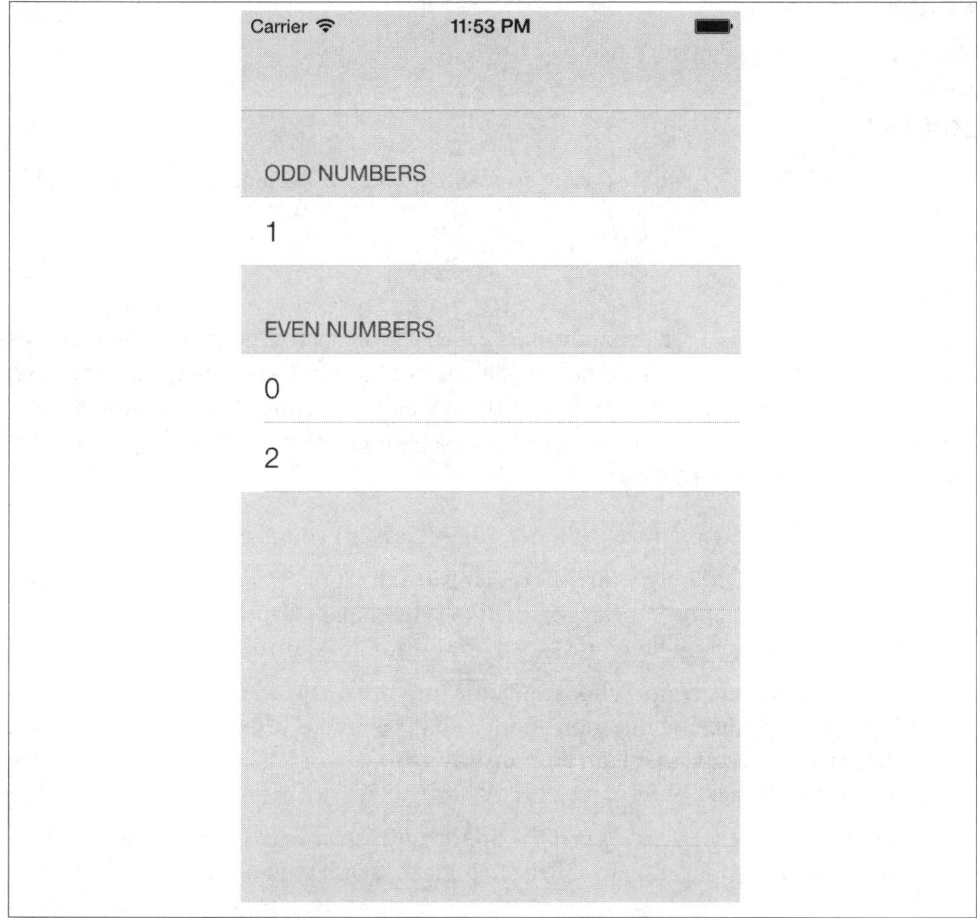


*Figure 4-18. We have deleted all cells with a value greater than 2*

## See Also

Recipe 1.2

# 4.9. Utilizing the UITableViewController for Easy Creation of Table Views

## Problem

You want to be able to create table views quickly.

## Solution

Use the `UITableViewController` view controller, which by default comes with a table view controller.

## Discussion

The iOS SDK contains a really handy class called `UITableViewController` that comes predefined with a table view instance inside it. In order to take advantage of this class, all you have to really do is create a new class that subclasses the aforementioned class. Here, I will walk you through the steps necessary to create a new Xcode project that utilizes the table view controller:

1. In Xcode, from the menu bar, choose File → New → Project...
2. On the lefthand side of the screen, make sure the iOS category is selected. Then choose the Application subcategory. On the righthand side, choose the Empty Application template and then press the Next button, as shown in Figure 4-19.
3. On the next screen, simply choose a name for your project. Also make sure everything except for the Organization Name and the Company Identifier in your dialog is the same as the one that I am demonstrating to you in Figure 4-20. Once you are done, press the Next button.
4. On the next screen, you are given the opportunity to save your application to disk. Simply save the application in a place that makes sense to you, and press the Create button.
5. In Xcode, choose the File → New → File... menu.
6. In the dialog, make sure iOS is the main category on the lefthand side and that Cocoa Touch is the subcategory that is selected. Then on the righthand side of the dialog, choose the Objective-C class as shown in Figure 4-21.
7. On the next screen, you get to choose the superclass of your new class. This step is very important. Make sure that you set your superclass to `UITableViewController`. Also make sure the rest of your settings are the same as those that I am demonstrating in Figure 4-22. After you are done, press the Next button.

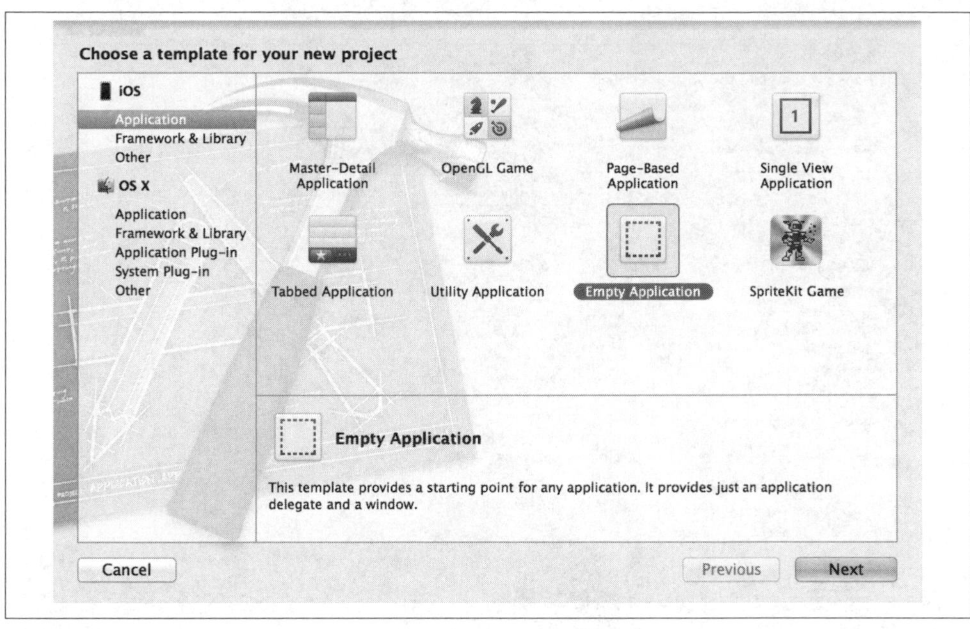


*Figure 4-19. Creating a new empty application that will later contain our table view controller*

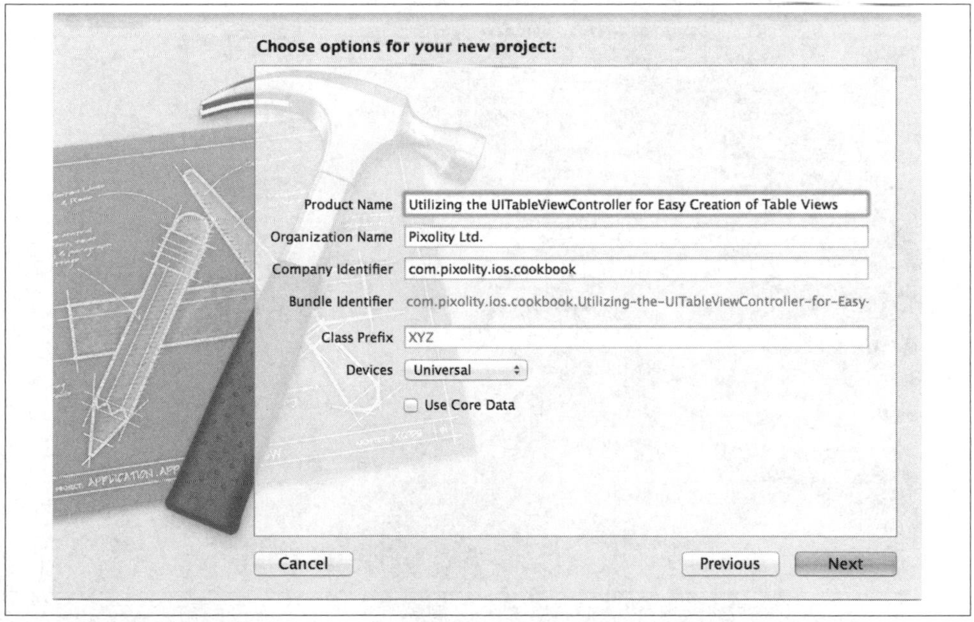


*Figure 4-20. Configuring our new empty application in Xcode*

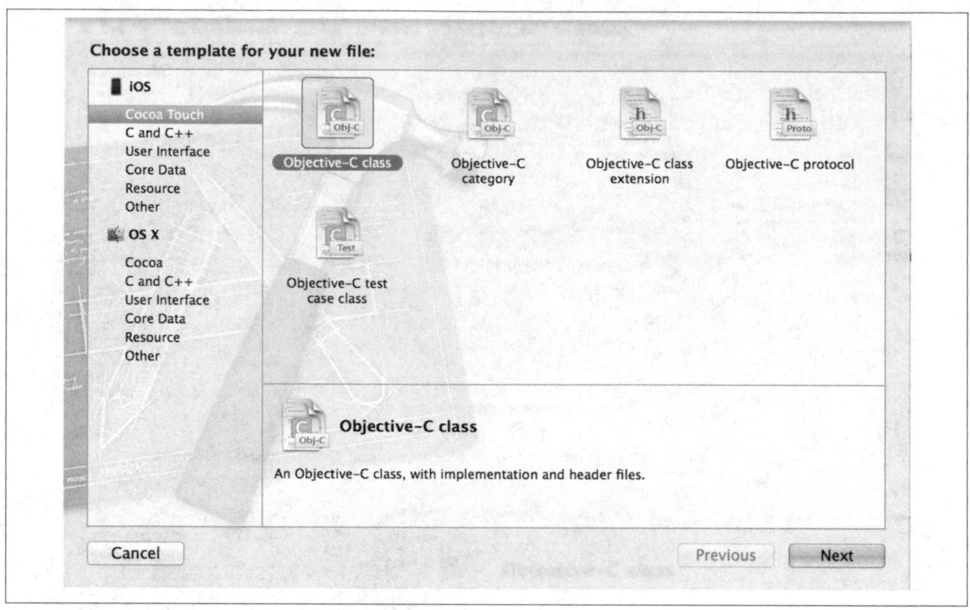


*Figure 4-21. Creating a new class for our table view controller*

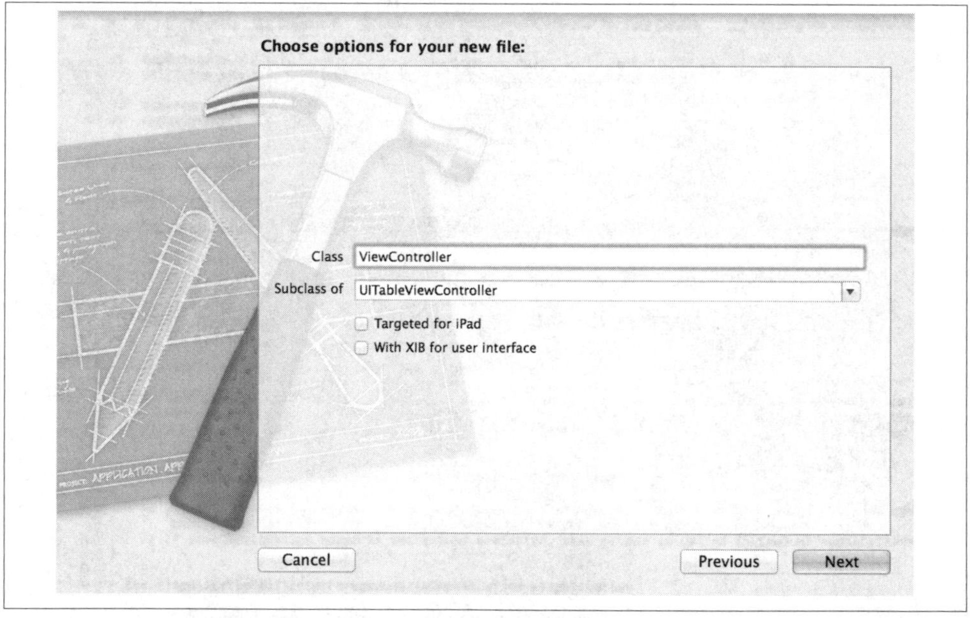


*Figure 4-22. Setting the superclass of our new object that will become the table view controller*

8. On the next screen, you get the chance to save your table view controller in your project. Go on, save it as the ViewController class and press the Create button.
9. In the implementation file of your app delegate, remember to import this view controller's header file and then create an instance of this class and set it as the root view controller of your application, as shown here:

```
#import "AppDelegate.h"
#import "ViewController.h"

@implementation AppDelegate

- (BOOL)            application:(UIApplication *)application
  didFinishLaunchingWithOptions:(NSDictionary *)launchOptions{

    ViewController *controller = [[ViewController alloc]
                                  initWithStyle:UITableViewStylePlain];

    self.window = [[UIWindow alloc]
                   initWithFrame:[[UIScreen mainScreen] bounds]];

    self.window.rootViewController = controller;

    self.window.backgroundColor = [UIColor whiteColor];
    [self.window makeKeyAndVisible];
    return YES;
}
```

Now if you try to compile your project, you will see that the compiler will give you the following warnings:

```
ViewController.m:47:2: Potentially incomplete method implementation.
ViewController.m:54:2: Incomplete method implementation.
```

This simply tells you that there are warnings that you have to take care of in the implementation file of your view controller. If you open this file, you will see that Apple has inserted `#warning` macros in the table view controller class template, which are causing these warnings to be displayed on your screen. One warning is placed inside the `numberOfSectionsInTableView:` method, and the other one is inside the `tableView:numberOfRowsInSection:` method. The reason we are seeing these warnings is that we have not coded the logic for these methods. The minimum information that the table view controller must have is the number of sections to display, the number of rows to display, and the cell object to be displayed for each row. The reason you are not seeing any warnings for the lack of cell object implementation is that Apple by default provides a dummy implementation of this method that creates empty cells for you.

The table view controller by default is the data source and the delegate of the table view. You do not have to specify a delegate or a data source separately to the table view.

Now let's go into the implementation of our table view controller and make sure that we have an array of strings (just as an example) that we can feed into our table view:

```
#import "ViewController.h"

static NSString *CellIdentifier = @"Cell";

@interface ViewController ()
@property (nonatomic, strong) NSArray *allItems;
@end

@implementation ViewController

- (id)initWithStyle:(UITableViewStyle)style
{
    self = [super initWithStyle:style];
    if (self) {
        // Custom initialization
        self.allItems = @[
                       @"Anthony Robbins",
                       @"Steven Paul Jobs",
                       @"Paul Gilbert",
                       @"Yngwie Malmsteen"
                       ];

        [self.tableView registerClass:[UITableViewCell class]
               forCellReuseIdentifier:CellIdentifier];

    }
    return self;
}

- (void) viewDidLoad{
    [super viewDidLoad];
}

- (NSInteger)numberOfSectionsInTableView:(UITableView *)tableView{
    return 1;
}

- (NSInteger)tableView:(UITableView *)tableView
 numberOfRowsInSection:(NSInteger)section{
    return self.allItems.count;
}

- (UITableViewCell *)tableView:(UITableView *)tableView
```

```
        cellForRowAtIndexPath:(NSIndexPath *)indexPath{

    UITableViewCell *cell = [tableView
                             dequeueReusableCellWithIdentifier:CellIdentifier
                             forIndexPath:indexPath];

    cell.textLabel.text = self.allItems[indexPath.row];

    return cell;
}

@end
```

Now if we run our app, we will see something similar to what is shown in Figure 4-23.

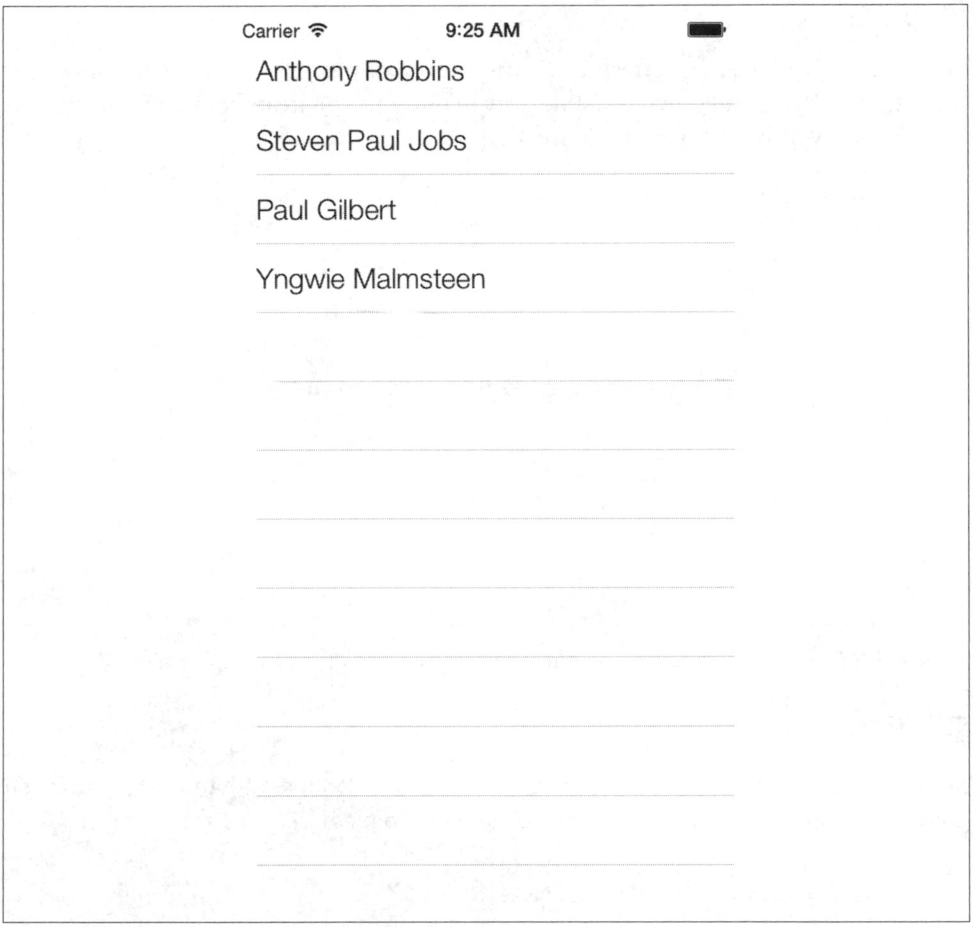

Carrier 9:25 AM

Anthony Robbins

Steven Paul Jobs

Paul Gilbert

Yngwie Malmsteen

*Figure 4-23. Our strings are properly displayed in the table view*

That's pretty much all there is to know about table view controllers. Remember, as mentioned before, that your table view controller is the delegate *and* the data source of your table view now. So you can implement the methods in the `UITableViewDataSource` protocol as well as the `UITableViewDelegate` protocol's methods right in the implementation of your table view controller.

## See Also

Recipe 4.1

# 4.10. Displaying a Refresh Control for Table Views

## Problem

You want to display a nice refresh UI control on top of your table views that allows your users to intuitively pull down the table view in order to update its contents. An example of a refresh control is shown in Figure 4-24.

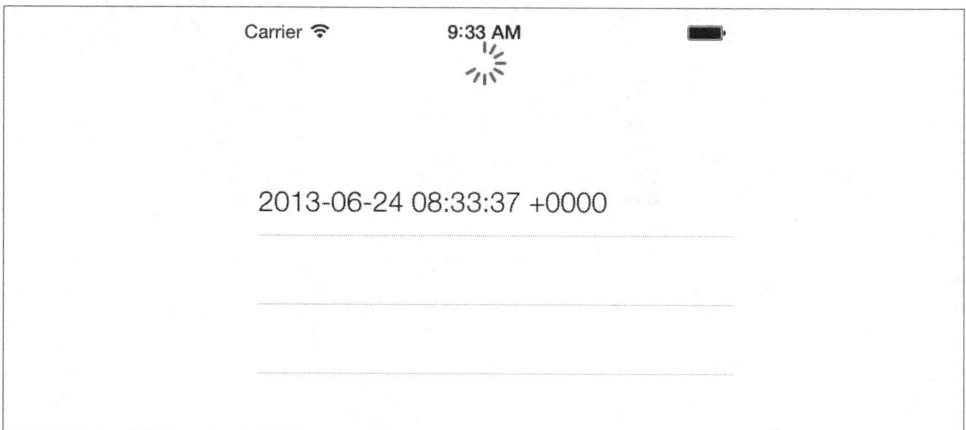


*Figure 4-24. A refresh control is displayed on top of a table view*

## Solution

Simply create a table view controller (as discussed in Recipe 4.9) and set its `refreshControl` property to a new instance of `UIRefreshControl` class, as shown here:

```
- (id)initWithStyle:(UITableViewStyle)style{
    self = [super initWithStyle:style];
    if (self) {

        [self.tableView registerClass:[UITableViewCell class]
               forCellReuseIdentifier:CellIdentifier];
```

```
        self.allTimes = [NSMutableArray arrayWithObject:[NSDate date]];

        /* Create the refresh control */
        self.refreshControl = [[UIRefreshControl alloc] init];
        self.refreshControl = self.refreshControl;
        [self.refreshControl addTarget:self
                                action:@selector(handleRefresh:)
                      forControlEvents:UIControlEventValueChanged];

    }
    return self;
}
```

## Discussion

Refresh controls are simple visual indicators that appear on top of table views and tell the user that something is about to get updated. For instance, prior to iOS 6, in order to refresh your mailbox in the Mail app, you had to press a refresh button. In the new iOS, now you can simply drag the list of your emails down, as if you wanted to see what's above there in the list that you haven't read already. Once iOS detects this gesture of yours, it will trigger a refresh. Isn't that cool? Twitter's iPhone app started this whole thing when they added a refresh control to their apps, so kudos to them for this. Apple has realized that this is in fact a really nice and intuitive way of updating table views and has since added a dedicated component to the SDK to implement it. The class name for this component is `UIRefreshControl`.

Create a new instance of this class simply by calling its `init` method. Once you are done, add this instance to your table view controller, as described in the Solution section of this recipe.

Now you'll want to know when the user has triggered a refresh on your table view. To do this, simply call the `addTarget:action:forControlEvents:` instance method of your refresh control and pass the target object and a selector on that object that takes care of the refresh for you. Pass `UIControlEventValueChanged` to the `forControlEvents` parameter of this method.

Here—I want to demonstrate this to you. In this example, we will have a table view controller that displays the date and time formatted as strings. Once the user refreshes the list by pulling it down, we will add the current date and time again to the list and refresh our table view. This way, every time the user pulls the list down, it triggers a refresh that will allow us to add the current date and time to the list and refresh the table view to display the new date and time. So let's start in the implementation file of our table view controller and define our refresh control and our data source:

```
#import "ViewController.h"

static NSString *CellIdentifier = @"Cell";
```

```
@interface ViewController ()
@property (nonatomic, strong) NSMutableArray *allTimes;
@property (nonatomic, strong) UIRefreshControl *refreshControl;
@end

@implementation ViewController
```

The `allTimes` property is a simple mutable array that will contain all the instances of `NSDate` in it as the user refreshes the table view. We have already seen the initialization of our table view controller in the Solution section of this recipe, so I won't write it again here. But as you saw there, we have hooked the `UIControlEventValueChanged` event of our refresh control to a method called `handleRefresh:`. In this method, all we are going to do is add the current date and time to our array of dates and times and then refresh the table view:

```
- (void) handleRefresh:(id)paramSender{

    /* Put a bit of delay between when the refresh control is released
     and when we actually do the refreshing to make the UI look a bit
     smoother than just doing the update without the animation */
    int64_t delayInSeconds = 1.0f;
    dispatch_time_t popTime =
        dispatch_time(DISPATCH_TIME_NOW, delayInSeconds * NSEC_PER_SEC);

    dispatch_after(popTime, dispatch_get_main_queue(), ^(void){

        /* Add the current date to the list of dates that we have
         so that when the table view is refreshed, a new item will appear
         on the screen so that the user will see the difference between
         the before and the after of the refresh */
        [self.allTimes addObject:[NSDate date]];

        [self.refreshControl endRefreshing];

        NSIndexPath *indexPathOfNewRow =
            [NSIndexPath indexPathForRow:self.allTimes.count-1 inSection:0];

        [self.tableView
             insertRowsAtIndexPaths:@[indexPathOfNewRow]
             withRowAnimation:UITableViewRowAnimationAutomatic];
    });

}
```

Last but not least, we will provide the date to our table view through the table view's delegate and data source methods:

```
- (NSInteger)numberOfSectionsInTableView:(UITableView *)tableView{
    return 1;
}
```

```
- (NSInteger)tableView:(UITableView *)tableView
 numberOfRowsInSection:(NSInteger)section{
    return self.allTimes.count;
}

- (UITableViewCell *)tableView:(UITableView *)tableView
        cellForRowAtIndexPath:(NSIndexPath *)indexPath{


    UITableViewCell *cell = [tableView
                             dequeueReusableCellWithIdentifier:CellIdentifier
                             forIndexPath:indexPath];

    cell.textLabel.text = [NSString stringWithFormat:@"%@",
                           self.allTimes[indexPath.row]];

    return cell;
}
```

Give this a go in either the simulator or the device. Once you open the app, at first you will see only one date/time added to the list. Keep dragging the table view down to get more items in the list (see Figure 4-24).

## See Also

Recipe 4.9

CHAPTER 5

# Building Complex Layouts with Collection Views

## 5.0. Introduction

Table views are great. They really are. However, they are very rigid in that they always render their content vertically. They aren't grids and weren't meant to act like grids. However, as a programmer, you may find yourself in a situation where you want to draw a grid-like component with columns and rows, and put different types of UI objects in each one, or make each one interactive. In a table view, you essentially have one column containing multiple rows. If you want to create an illusion of multiple columns, you will have to provide a custom cell and make that cell look like it is constructed out of multiple columns.

Collection views, just like table views, are based on the concept of cells, with each cell containing an item or view that it renders on the screen. Cells in collection views are reusable, just like in table views, and they can be dequeued and brought back to the screen whenever possible and needed. But the layout can be almost anything you can think of that works in two dimensions.

For this reason, Apple introduced collection views in version 6 of the iOS SDK. A collection view is simply a scroll view on steroids. It has a data source and a delegate, just like a table view, but it has one property that sets it apart from table views or scroll views: the *layout object*.

What the layout object does is essentially calculate where each item in the collection view has to be placed. Apple has made this a *bit* complicated, though, by introducing a concrete layout class for collection views that cannot be used by direct instantiation. Instead, you have to instantiate a subclass of this class named `UICollectionViewFlowLayout`.

The flow layout arranges collection view cells on the screen in sections. Each section is a group of collection view cells, just as in table views. However, in a collection view, a section can be laid out on the screen in many ways, not necessarily vertically. For instance, you might have three rectangles, each containing its own little grid, as in Figure 5-1.

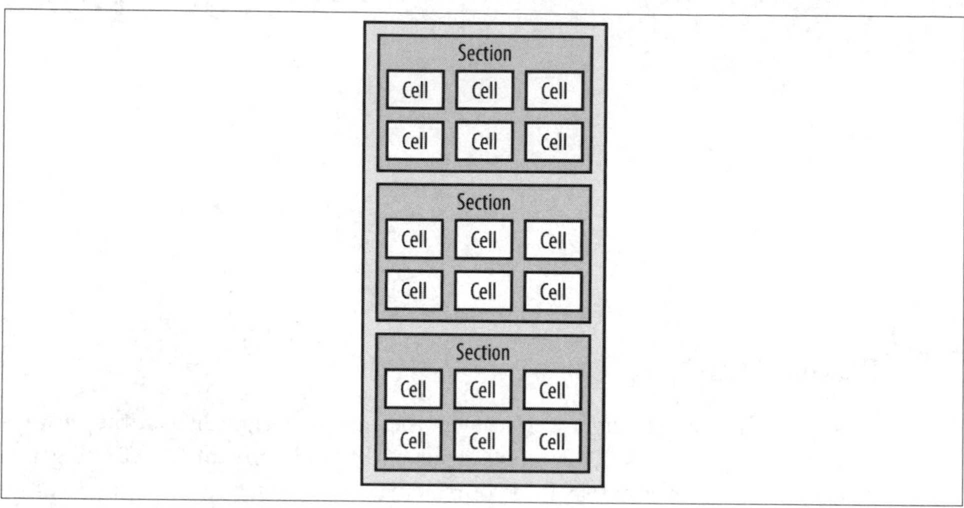


*Figure 5-1. A typical flow layout in a collection view*

A typical way of laying sections out on the screen is in a grid-like fashion with rows and columns, and that's what the flow layout class does. If you want to stretch the limits of the layout further, you have to modify the properties of the flow layout. And if what you want differs quite a lot from what the flow layout provides, you will need to create your own layout class. For instance, you would need a custom layout class to create the collection view in Figure 5-2. Here a custom layout class has laid out three sections and their corresponding cells in quite a different way from a grid.

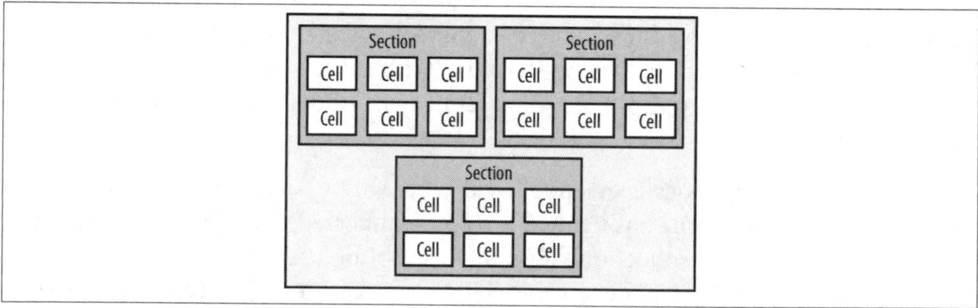


*Figure 5-2. A custom layout in a collection view*

## 5.1. Constructing Collection Views

### Problem

You want to display a collection view on the screen.

### Solution

Either use an instance of the `UICollectionView` as a subview of another view in your app or (if you want a full-screen collection view) use the `UICollectionViewControl ler` class.

### Discussion

Just like table views, a collection view, as its name indicates, is a view and can be added as a subview to other views. So when you are creating your app, think about whether your collection view has to be the main view of a view controller or should appear as a small portion of another view.

Let's explore the full-screen scenario first. Follow these steps to create a simple app that displays a full-screen collection view on the screen:

1. Open Xcode.
2. From the File menu, choose New, and then choose Project.
3. On the left, choose the iOS main category, and under that choose Application. On the righthand side of the screen, choose Empty Application, and then press the Next button.
4. On the next screen, enter your project information and ensure that the Use Automatic Reference Counting box is ticked, as shown in Figure 5-3. Once you are done entering the relevant values, press the Next button.
5. You are now asked to save your project on disk. Choose a suitable place to save your project, and then press the Create button.
6. Now that you have your project set up, create a new class in your project and call it `ViewController`. This class has to subclass `UICollectionViewController`. You won't need a *.xib* file for this view controller, so skip that option, as shown in Figure 5-4.

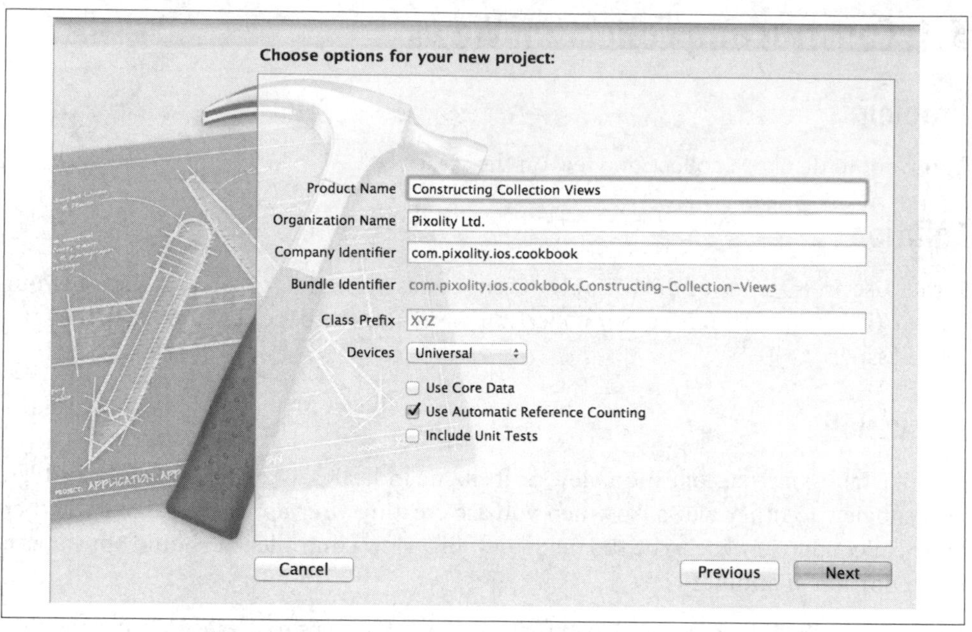


*Figure 5-3. Creating a new Empty Application project for our collection view*

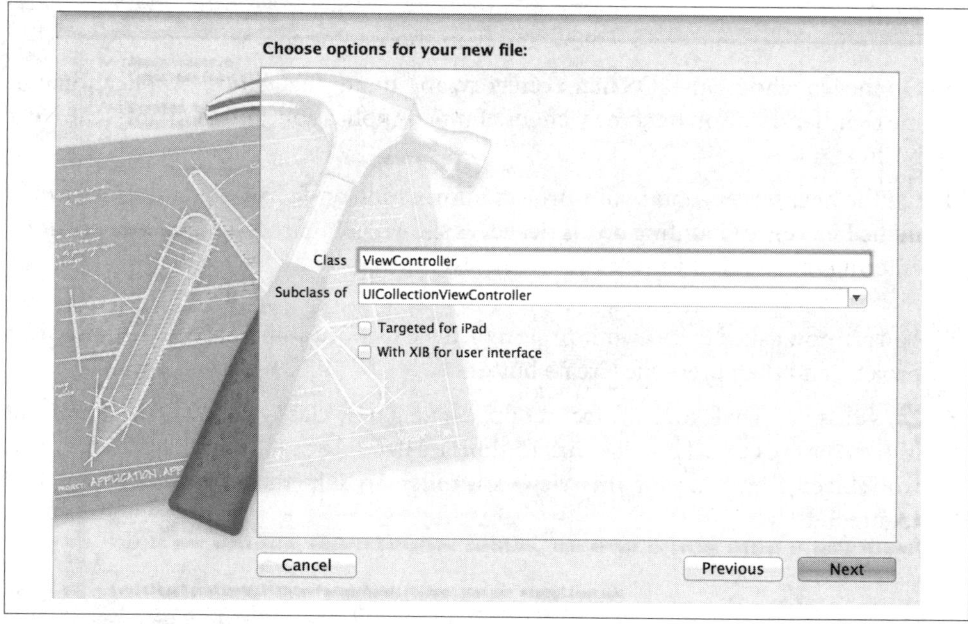


*Figure 5-4. Adding a new collection view class to our project*

7. Find and open the *AppDelegate.m* file in your project (your app delegate's implementation file), create an instance of your collection view, and make that collection view the root view controller of your app, as shown here:

```
- (BOOL)            application:(UIApplication *)application
  didFinishLaunchingWithOptions:(NSDictionary *)launchOptions{

    /* Instantiate the collection view controller with a nil layout object.
     Note: this will throw an exception, but later we will learn how we can
     create layout objects and provide them to our collection views */
    ViewController *viewController = [[ViewController alloc]
                                      initWithCollectionViewLayout:nil];

    self.window = [[UIWindow alloc] initWithFrame:
                   [[UIScreen mainScreen] bounds]];

    self.window.backgroundColor = [UIColor whiteColor];

    /* Set the collection view as the root view controller of our window */
    self.window.rootViewController = viewController;
    [self.window makeKeyAndVisible];
    return YES;
}
```

If you run your app, it will crash with an exception complaining that you have provided a `nil` layout object to your collection view, and the runtime is right. You cannot do this. But I have not yet covered how to instantiate layout objects and pass them to the collection view, so for now, this is the best we can do. You will learn more about collection view layout objects later in this chapter.

So far, we have seen how we can create a collection view controller, and this is good if you want to display a full-screen collection view on the device. However, if you are designing a custom component that is part of another/bigger view, you may simply want to instantiate an object of type `UICollectionView` using its designated initializer, the `initWithFrame:collectionViewLayout:` method.

In order to do that, you can simply instantiate the collection view using the aforementioned initializer, and once initialized, add the collection view as the subview of another view. For instance, if you want to add the collection view to the view of your view controller, simply call the `addSubview:` method of the view of your view controller and pass your collection view instance as the parameter to that method. Also, you will need to ensure that you have set the `delegate` and the `dataSource` properties of your collection view to valid objects that conform to the `UICollectionViewDelegate` and the `UICollectionViewDataSource` protocols, respectively. The rest is really easy and exactly the same as the techniques that you will learn in this chapter to provide data to your collection view through the data source and to react to events through the delegate object.

## See Also

Recipe 5.0, "Introduction"

# 5.2. Assigning a Data Source to a Collection View

## Problem

You want to provide data to a collection view to render the data on the screen.

## Solution

Assign a data source to the collection view using the `dataSource` property of the `UICollectionView` class. Your data source has to be an object that conforms to the `UICollectionViewDataSource` protocol, and it goes without saying that your data source object has to implement the `required` methods/properties of that protocol.

## Discussion

The data source of the collection view, like that in table views, is responsible for providing enough data to the collection view so that it can render its contents on the screen. The way things are rendered on the screen is `not` the data source's job. That is the layout's job. The cells that the layout displays on your collection view will ultimately be provided by your collection view's data source.

Here are the required methods of the `UICollectionViewDataSource` protocol that you have to implement in your data source:

`collectionView:numberOfItemsInSection:`
: This method returns an `NSInteger` that dictates to the collection view the number of items that should be rendered in the given section. The given section is passed to this method as an integer that represents the zero-based index of that section. This is the same in table views.

`collectionView:cellForItemAtIndexPath:`
: Your implementation of this method must return an instance of the `UICollectionViewCell` that represents the cell at a given index path. The `UICollectionViewCell` class subclasses the `UICollectionReusableView` class. In fact, any reusable cell given to a collection view to render must either directly or indirectly subclass `UICollectionReusableView`, as we will see later in this chapter. The index path will

be given to you in the cellForItemAtIndexPath parameter of this method. You can query the section and the row indexes of the item from the index path.

Let's go into the collection view controller's implementation file (*ViewController.m*) that we created in the Recipe 5.1, and implement the aforementioned collection view data source methods:

```
#import "ViewController.h"

@implementation ViewController

/* For now, we won't return any sections */
- (NSInteger)collectionView:(UICollectionView *)collectionView
     numberOfItemsInSection:(NSInteger)section{
    return 0;
}

/* We don't yet know how we can return cells to the collection view so
 let's return nil for now */
- (UICollectionViewCell *)collectionView:(UICollectionView *)collectionView
                  cellForItemAtIndexPath:(NSIndexPath *)indexPath{
    return nil;
}

@end
```

The code is complete *for now*, but if you remember from Recipe 5.1, if you try to run this code, it will crash because the app delegate is setting the layout object of the collection view to nil. This problem is still there and will be solved in Recipe 5.3.

## See Also

Recipe 5.0, "Introduction"; Recipe 5.1

# 5.3. Providing a Flow Layout to a Collection View

## Problem

You want to provide a grid-like layout to your collection view so that your content can render in a way similar to that shown in Figure 5-1.

## Solution

Create an instance of the UICollectionViewFlowLayout class, instantiate your collection view controller using the initWithCollectionViewLayout: designated initializer of the UICollectionViewController class, and pass your layout object to this method.

## Discussion

A flow layout can easily be instantiated, but before it can be passed to a collection view, it has to be configured. Here we are going to discuss the various properties that you can tweak on an instance of the `UICollectionViewFlowLayout` class and how they can affect the rendering of your collection view cells:

`minimumLineSpacing`
: A floating point value that dictates to the flow layout the *minimum* number of points it has to reserve between each row. The layout object may decide to allocate more space in order to make the layout look good, but it must not allocate less. If your collection view is too small for the items to fit into it, your items will be clipped, just like any other view in the iOS SDK.

`minimumInteritemSpacing`
: A floating point value to indicate the minimum number of points that the layout should reserve between cells on the same row. Again, this is the *minimum* number of points, and the layout, depending on the size of the collection view, may decide to increase this number.

`itemSize`
: A `CGSize` that specifies the size of every cell in the collection view.

`scrollDirection`
: A value of type `UICollectionViewScrollDirection` that tells the flow layout how the collection view's contents have to be scrolled. You can have the contents scroll either vertically or horizontally, but not both. The default value of this property is `UICollectionViewScrollDirectionVertical`, but you can change it to `UICollectionViewScrollDirectionHorizontal`.

`sectionInset`
: A value of type `UIEdgeInsets` that specifies the margins around every section. The margins are basically spaces that will not be occupied by any cells. You can use the `UIEdgeInsetsMake` function to create these insets, which are made out of top, left, bottom, and right edges, each of type float. Don't worry if you find this explanation confusing; we will look at an example soon.

For the rest of this recipe, I assume that you have already followed the instructions in Recipe 5.1 and Recipe 5.2, so by now you should have an app that has a collection view controller and an app delegate that displays that collection view controller as the root view controller of the window. Now you are going to modify your app delegate to provide a valid flow layout to our collection view controller:

```
#import "AppDelegate.h"
#import "ViewController.h"

@implementation AppDelegate
```

```
- (UICollectionViewFlowLayout *) flowLayout{

    UICollectionViewFlowLayout *flowLayout =
    [[UICollectionViewFlowLayout alloc] init];

    flowLayout.minimumLineSpacing = 20.0f;
    flowLayout.minimumInteritemSpacing = 10.0f;
    flowLayout.itemSize = CGSizeMake(80.0f, 120.0f);
    flowLayout.scrollDirection = UICollectionViewScrollDirectionVertical;
    flowLayout.sectionInset = UIEdgeInsetsMake(10.0f, 20.0f, 10.0f, 20.0f);

    return flowLayout;
}

- (BOOL)            application:(UIApplication *)application
  didFinishLaunchingWithOptions:(NSDictionary *)launchOptions{

    /* Instantiate the collection view controller with a valid flow layout */
    ViewController *viewController =
    [[ViewController alloc]
     initWithCollectionViewLayout:[self flowLayout]];

    self.window = [[UIWindow alloc] initWithFrame:
                   [[UIScreen mainScreen] bounds]];

    self.window.backgroundColor = [UIColor whiteColor];

    /* Set the collection view as the root view controller of our window */
    self.window.rootViewController = viewController;
    [self.window makeKeyAndVisible];
    return YES;

}
```

Our collection view controller's implementation stays the same as in Recipe 5.2. If you run your app now, all you will see is a black screen because the default implementation of our collection view controller doesn't even set the background color of the collection view to white. That's all right for now. At least our app isn't crashing anymore because of a lack of layout objects.

## See Also

Recipe 5.1; Recipe 5.2

# 5.4. Providing Basic Content to a Collection View

## Problem

You have already set up a flow layout for your collection view, but you don't know how to render cells in your collection view.

## Solution

Either use the `UICollectionViewCell` class directly to present your cells, or subclass this class and provide further implementation on top of that class. In addition, you can have a *.xib* file associated with your cell, as we will soon see.

## Discussion

In this recipe, I assume that you've already gone through Recipe 5.3, Recipe 5.2, and Recipe 5.1 and have already set your project up.

Let's take this one step at a time and start with the fastest and easiest way of creating our cells: instantiate objects of type `UICollectionViewCell` and feed them to our collection view in our data source. The `UICollectionViewCell` class has a content view property named `contentView`, where you can add your own views for display. You can also set various other properties of the cell, such as its background color, which is what we are going to do in this example. But before we begin, let's first set the expectations of what we are going to achieve in this example code and explain the requirements.

We are going to program a collection view with a flow layout that displays three sections, each of which contains anywhere between 20 and 40 cells, with the first section's cells all being red, the second section's cells all being green, and the third section's cells all being blue, as shown in Figure 5-5.

So let's get started. In your collection view controller, create a method that can return an array of three colors, which you will then assign to the cells for each section:

```
/* We will have 3 sections, so for each section, we will define a cell color.
 These are nothing but instances of UIColor that we will later apply to every
 cell in each section. */
- (NSArray *) allSectionColors{

    static NSArray *allSectionColors = nil;

    if (allSectionColors == nil){
        allSectionColors = @[
                             [UIColor redColor],
```

```
                                        [UIColor greenColor],
                                        [UIColor blueColor],
                                        ];
    }

    return allSectionColors;

}
```

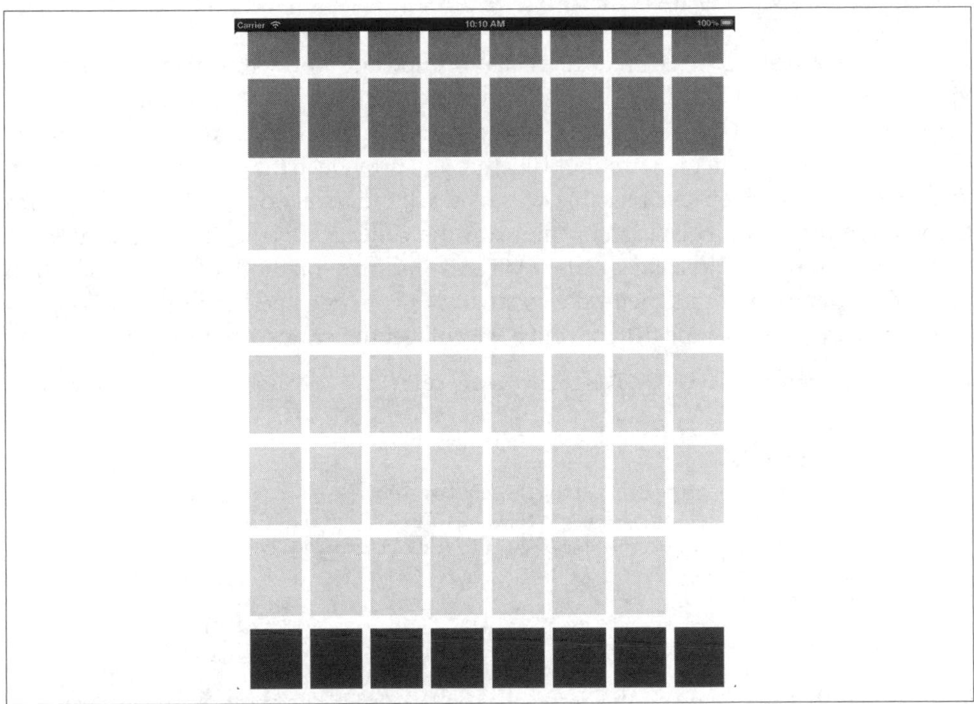

*Figure 5-5. A simple collection view with flow layout displaying three sections with different colors*

After that, override the `initWithCollectionViewLayout:` designated initializer of your collection view controller and register the `UICollectionViewCell` with a specific identifier. Don't worry if this makes no sense yet, but look at it this way: for every cell that your collection view has to render, it will first look into a queue of reusable cells and find out if a reusable cell exists. If so, the collection view will pull the cell from the queue, and if not, it will create a new cell and return that to you for configuration.

In older versions of iOS, you had to manually create cells if the table view (collection views didn't exist in older versions of iOS) could not find a reusable cell. However, with the introduction of newer APIs, what Apple has done with regard to reusable cells is very interesting indeed. It has exposed new APIs for both collection and table views so that you can register a call with the table or the collection view, and when you have to configure a new cell, you simply ask the table or the collection view to give you a new cell of that kind. If the cell exists in the reusable queue, it will be given to you. If not, the table or the collection view will automatically create that cell for you. This is called *registering a reusable cell*, and you can do it in two ways:

- Register a cell using a class name.
- Register a cell using a *.xib* file.

Both these ways of registering reusable cells are good and work perfectly with collection views. To register a new cell with a collection view using the cell's class name, use the `registerClass:forCellWithReuseIdentifier:` method of the `UICollectionView` class, where the identifier is a simple string that you provide to the collection view. When you then attempt to retrieve reusable cells, you ask the collection view for the cell with a given identifier. To register a *.xib* file with the collection view you need to use the `registerNib:forCellWithReuseIdentifier:` instance method of your collection view. The identifier of this method also works, as explained earlier in this paragraph. The nib is an object of type `UINib`, which we will get to use later in this chapter.

```
- (instancetype) initWithCollectionViewLayout:(UICollectionViewLayout *)layout{

    self = [super initWithCollectionViewLayout:layout];
    if (self != nil){
        /* Register the cell with the collection view for easy retrieval */
        [self.collectionView registerClass:[UICollectionViewCell class]
                forCellWithReuseIdentifier:kCollectionViewCellIdentifier];
    }
    return self;

}
```

You can see that we are using the `kCollectionViewCellIdentifier` constant value as the identifier for our cells. We need to define this in our view controller:

```
#import "ViewController.h"

static NSString *kCollectionViewCellIdentifier = @"Cells";

@implementation ViewController
```

The default implementation of your collection view will have one section unless you implement the `numberOfSectionsInCollectionView:` method in your data source. We want three sections for our collection view, so let's implement this method:

```
- (NSInteger)numberOfSectionsInCollectionView
            :(UICollectionView *)collectionView{
    return [self allSectionColors].count;
}
```

Part of the requirement for our application was for each cell to contain at least 20 and at most 40 cells. We can achieve this using the `arc4random_uniform(x)` function. It returns positive integers between 0 and *x*, where *x* is the parameter that you provide to this function. Therefore, to generate a number between 20 and 40, all we have to do is add 20 to the return value of this function while setting *x* to 20 as well. With this knowledge, let's implement the `collectionView:numberOfItemsInSection:` method of our collection view's data source:

```
- (NSInteger)collectionView:(UICollectionView *)collectionView
     numberOfItemsInSection:(NSInteger)section{
    /* Generate between 20 to 40 cells for each section */
    return 20 + arc4random_uniform(21);
}
```

Last but not least, we want to provide the cells to the collection view. For that we need to implement the `collectionView:cellForItemAtIndexPath:` method of our collection view's data source:

```
- (UICollectionViewCell *)collectionView:(UICollectionView *)collectionView
                  cellForItemAtIndexPath:(NSIndexPath *)indexPath{

    UICollectionViewCell *cell =
    [collectionView
     dequeueReusableCellWithReuseIdentifier:kCollectionViewCellIdentifier
     forIndexPath:indexPath];

    cell.backgroundColor = [self allSectionColors][indexPath.section];

    return cell;

}
```

Index paths simply contain a section number and a row number. So an index path of *0, 1* means the first section's second row, since the indexes are zero-based. Or to denote the fifth row of the tenth section, the index path would be *9, 4*. Index paths are extensively used in table and collection views because they intrinsically embody the notion of sections and of cells in each section. Delegates and data sources for tables and collection views work by communicating the target cell to you using its index path. For instance, if the user taps a cell in a collection view, you will receive its index path. Using the index path, you can look at that cell's underlying data structure (the data that was used to construct that cell originally in your class).

As you can see, we are using the `dequeueReusableCellWithReuseIdentifier:forIndexPath:` instance method of our collection view to pull reusable cells out of the queue. This method expects two parameters: the identifier of the cell that you have registered earlier with the collection view, and the index path at which that cell should be rendered. The index path is given to you in the same `collectionView:cellForItemAtIndexPath:` method as a parameter, so the only thing that you do have to provide is the identifier of the cell.

The return value of this method will be a cell of type `UICollectionViewCell`, which you can configure. In this implementation, the only thing we have done is to set the background color of the cell to the background color that we had chosen earlier for all the cells in that section.

One last thing to do before we wrap this up is to set the background color of our collection view to white to make it look a bit better than the default pitch-black color. So implement the `viewDidLoad` method of your collection view controller and set the background color of your collection view right there:

```
- (void) viewDidLoad{
    [super viewDidLoad];
    self.collectionView.backgroundColor = [UIColor whiteColor];
}
```

An instance of `UICollectionViewController` has a view of type `UIView` that can be accessed using its `view` property. Don't confuse this view with the `collectionView` property of your controller, which is where the collection view itself sits.

The great thing about our solution in this recipe is that it works perfectly on both the iPad and the iPhone. We saw how it looks on the iPad in Figure 5-5, and on the iPhone, it looks like what's shown in Figure 5-6.

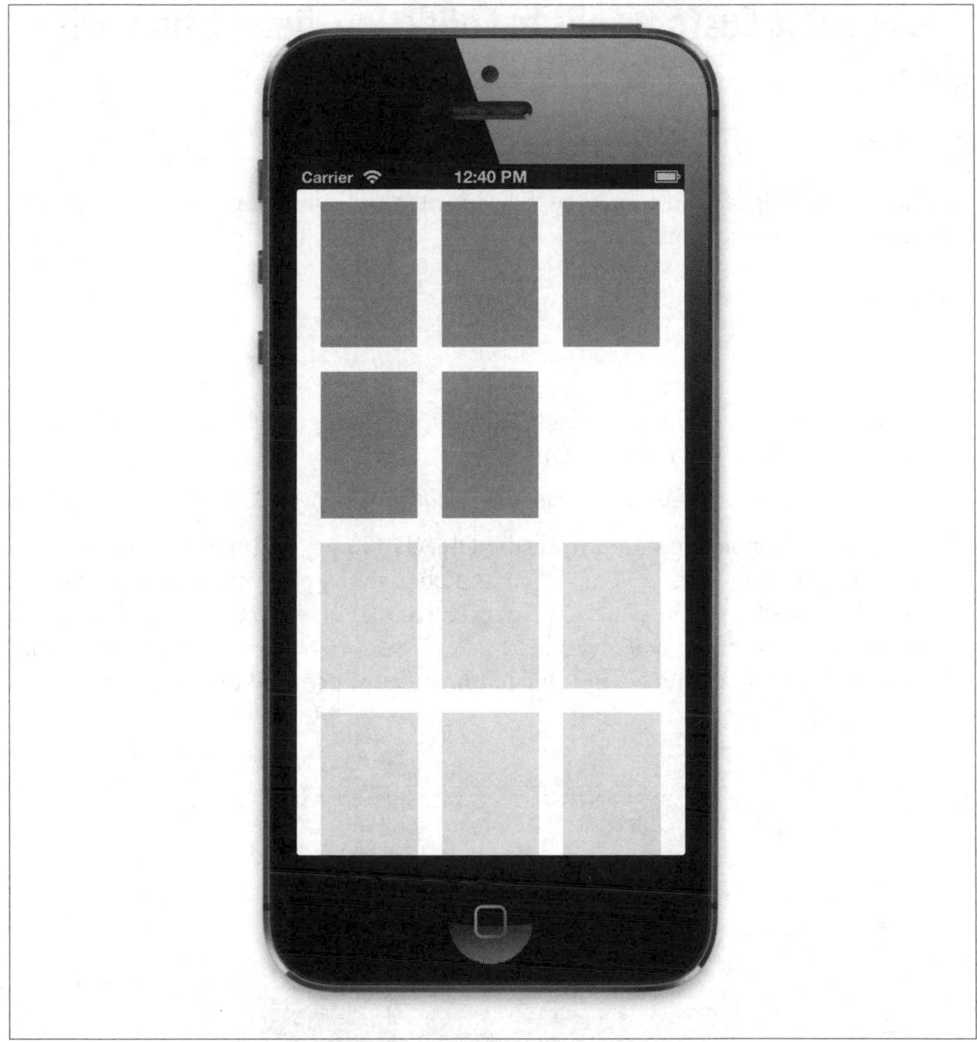


*Figure 5-6. Our simple collection view rendered on iPhone Simulator*

## See Also

Recipe 5.1; Recipe 5.2; Recipe 5.3

# 5.5. Feeding Custom Cells to Collection Views Using .xib Files

## Problem

You want to configure collection view cells in Interface Builder and feed those cells to your collection view for rendering.

## Solution

Follow these steps:

1. Create a subclass of the `UICollectionViewCell` and give it a name (we'll use `MyCollectionViewCell` for this example).
2. Create an *empty .xib* file and name it *MyCollectionViewCell.xib*.
3. Drop a Collection View Cell from the Objects Library in Interface Builder onto your empty *.xib* file (see Figure 5-7) and change the class name of the dropped object in Interface Builder to `MyCollectionViewCell` (see Figure 5-8). Because you make this association, when you load the *.xib* file programmatically, your custom class of `MyCollectionViewCell` will automatically be loaded into memory. This is pure magic!

*Figure 5-7. The Collection View Cell UI object in the Object Library of Interface Builder*

*Figure 5-8. Assigning our custom class to the .xib file of our custom collection view cell*

4. Customize your cell in Interface Builder. For every UI component that you drop on your cell, ensure that you create an associated `IBOutlet` either in the header or the implementation file of your class (`MyCollectionViewCell`).
5. Register your nib with your collection view using the `registerNib:forCellWithReuseIdentifier:` instance method of your collection view. You can load your nib into memory using the `nibWithNibName:bundle:` class method of the `UINib` class, as we will see soon.

## Discussion

As you read earlier in this recipe, you need to create a *.xib* file for your custom cell and call that file *MyCollectionViewCell.xib*. Please do bear in mind that your *.xib* file doesn't necessarily have to be called that. It can be called anything you like. However, for the sake of simplicity and so that readers can follow the same naming convention throughout this chapter, we will use the aforementioned name. So go ahead and create an empty *.xib* file using the following steps:

1. In File → New → File...
2. On the lefthand side, under the iOS category, choose User Interface, and under the righthand side, pick Empty.

3. You are now asked for the device family of your *.xib* file. Simply choose iPhone for device family.
4. You are now asked to save your *.xib* file to disk. Save your file as *MyCollectionView Cell.xib*.

You also need to create a class that you can link to your *.xib* file's contents. The class will be named `MyCollectionViewCell` and will subclass `UICollectionViewCell`. You can do this by following these steps:

1. In Xcode, choose File → New → File...
2. In the new file dialog, under the iOS category, choose Cocoa Touch. On the right-hand side, pick "Objective-C class."
3. Name your class `MyCollectionViewCell` and choose `UICollectionViewCell` as its superclass.
4. When asked to do so, save your file to disk.

Now you have to associate our class with our *.xib* file. To do this, follow these steps:

1. Open your *MyCollectionViewCell.xib* file in Interface Builder. In the Object Library, simply find the Collection View Cell (see Figure 5-7) and drop it into your *.xib* file. By default, this cell will be very small (50×50 points width and height) and will have a black background color.
2. Explicitly select the cell on your *.xib* file by clicking on it. Open the Identity Inspector in Interface Builder and change the Class field's value to `MyCollection ViewCell`, as shown earlier in Figure 5-8.

The next thing you need to do is add some UI components to your cell. Later, when you populate your collection view, we can change the value of those components. The best component for this demonstration would be an image view, so while you have your *MyCollectionViewCell.xib* file open in Interface Builder, drop an instance of `UIImage View` onto it. Connect that image view to the header file of your cell (the *MyCollection ViewCell.h* file) and name it `imageViewBackgroundImage` so that your cell's header file will look like this:

```
#import <UIKit/UIKit.h>

@interface MyCollectionViewCell : UICollectionViewCell

@property (weak, nonatomic) IBOutlet UIImageView *imageViewBackgroundImage;

@end
```

We are going to populate this image view with various images. For this recipe, I have created three simple images that I'm going to use, each one 50×50 points in size. You can use any other image that you wish, simply by doing a quick search on the Internet. Once you've found your images, add them to your project. Ensure that the images are named *1.png*, *2.png*, and *3.png*, and that their @2x Retina counterparts are named *1@2x.png*, *2@2x.png*, and *3@2x.png*.

In this example, we are going to display a user interface similar to that shown in Figure 5-5, but instead of colors for cells, we are going to set the background image view's image to a random image. So it makes sense to base our code on what we wrote for Recipe 5.4 because the output will be very similar.

The first modification that we have to make is to prepare a method in our app that can return a random image to us. We have an array of images, as explained before. So after instantiating the array, we need a handy little method that can grab a random image out of the array for us:

```
- (NSArray *) allImages{

    static NSArray *AllSectionImages = nil;

    if (AllSectionImages == nil){
        AllSectionImages = @[
                             [UIImage imageNamed:@"1"],
                             [UIImage imageNamed:@"2"],
                             [UIImage imageNamed:@"3"]
                             ];
    }

    return AllSectionImages;

}

- (UIImage *) randomImage{
    return [self allImages][arc4random_uniform([self allImages].count)];
}
```

Next, we need to override our collection view controller's designated initializer to register our `MyCollectionViewCell` nib with our collection view:

```
- (instancetype) initWithCollectionViewLayout:(UICollectionViewLayout *)layout{

    self = [super initWithCollectionViewLayout:layout];
    if (self != nil){
        /* Register the nib with the collection view for easy retrieval */
        UINib *nib = [UINib nibWithNibName:
                      NSStringFromClass([MyCollectionViewCell class])
                                    bundle:[NSBundle mainBundle]];

        [self.collectionView registerNib:nib
              forCellWithReuseIdentifier:kCollectionViewCellIdentifier];
  }
```

```
        return self;
    }
```

Also, when asked how many sections we have, we will return a random number between 3 and 6. This is not really required—we could go with one section, but it won't hurt to have more. Also for each section, we want to have between 10 and 15 cells:

```
    - (NSInteger)numberOfSectionsInCollectionView
                :(UICollectionView *)collectionView{
        /* Between 3 to 6 sections */
        return 3 + arc4random_uniform(4);
    }

    - (NSInteger)collectionView:(UICollectionView *)collectionView
      numberOfItemsInSection:(NSInteger)section{
        /* Each section has between 10 to 15 cells */
        return 10 + arc4random_uniform(6);
    }
```

Last but not least, we will ask the collection view for the cells and configure them with a random image:

```
    - (UICollectionViewCell *)collectionView:(UICollectionView *)collectionView
                      cellForItemAtIndexPath:(NSIndexPath *)indexPath{

        MyCollectionViewCell *cell =
        [collectionView
         dequeueReusableCellWithReuseIdentifier:kCollectionViewCellIdentifier
         forIndexPath:indexPath];

        cell.imageViewBackgroundImage.image = [self randomImage];
        cell.imageViewBackgroundImage.contentMode = UIViewContentModeScaleAspectFit;

        return cell;

    }
```

As you can see, we are using our custom `MyCollectionViewCell` class in our collection view controller. For the program to compile successfully, you will need to include the header file for your cell into your view controller's implementation like so:

```
#import "ViewController.h"
#import "MyCollectionViewCell.h"

...
```

Run your app and you will see something similar to that shown in Figure 5-9. Of course if you use different images from the ones I chose, your images will show up instead of mine.

*Figure 5-9. A collection view with custom cells loaded from a nib*

### See Also

Recipe 5.4

## 5.6. Handling Events in Collection Views

### Problem

You want to be able to handle collection view events, such as taps.

### Solution

Assign a delegate to your collection view. In some other cases, you may not even have to do that. All you may need to do is listen for those events in your cell classes and handle them right there.

## Discussion

Collection views have `delegate` properties that have to conform to the `UICollectionViewDelegate` protocol. The delegate object will then receive various delegation calls from the collection view informing the delegate of various events, such as a cell becoming highlighted or selected. You need to know the difference between the highlighted and selected state of a collection view cell. When the user presses her finger down on a cell in a collection view but doesn't lift her finger up, the cell under her finger is *highlighted*. When she presses her finger down and lifts her finger up to say she wants to perform an action on the cell, that cell will then be *selected*.

Collection view cells of type `UICollectionViewCell` have two very useful properties, `highlighted` and `selected`, that get set to `YES` when the cell becomes highlighted or selected.

If all you want to do is change your cell's visual presentation when it becomes selected, you're in luck, because cells of type `UICollectionViewCell` expose a property named `selectedBackgroundView` of type `UIView` that you can set to a valid view. This view will then get displayed on the screen once your cell becomes selected. Let's demonstrate this by building on top of what we created in Recipe 5.5. If you remember, in that example, we created a custom cell that had a background image view property named `imageViewBackgroundImage`, which covered the whole of the cell. We were loading custom image instances into that image view. What we want now is to set the background *color* of our cell to blue once the cell becomes selected. Because the image view is sitting on top of everything else on our collection view, before we set the background color of our cell, we need to ensure that our image view is *see-through* by changing the background color of the image view to a clear color. The reason behind this is that an image view is opaque by default, so if you place it on a view that has a background color, you won't be able to see the color of the view because the opaque image view will not be see-through. Thus, in order for us to see the color of our image view's super view, we will set the image view's background color to a clear and see-through color. So let's get started:

```
#import "MyCollectionViewCell.h"

@implementation MyCollectionViewCell

- (void) awakeFromNib{
    [super awakeFromNib];
    self.imageViewBackgroundImage.backgroundColor = [UIColor clearColor];
    self.selectedBackgroundView = [[UIView alloc] initWithFrame:self.bounds];
    self.selectedBackgroundView.backgroundColor = [UIColor blueColor];
}

@end
```

That's all, really! Now if you tap on any of the cells in your program, you will see that the background color of the cell becomes blue.

There are more things that you may want to do with your collection view by listening to various events that it sends. For instance, you may want to play a sound or an animation once a cell becomes selected. Let's say, when the user taps on a cell, that we want to use an animation to hide the cell momentarily and then show it again, creating a fading-out and fading-in animation. If this is the type of thing you want to do, start by setting the delegate object of your collection view, because that's really where you get a lot of events reported back to you. Your delegate object, as mentioned before, has to conform to the `UICollectionViewDelegate` protocol. This protocol contains a lot of useful methods that you can implement. The following are some of the most important methods in this protocol:

> The `UICollectionViewDelegateFlowLayout` protocol, like the `UITableViewDelegate` protocol that we discussed in Chapter 4, lets you provide information about your items, such as width and height, to the flow layout. You can either provide a generic size for all the flow layout item sizes in one go so that all items will have the same size, or you can respond to the relevant messages that you receive from the flow layout delegate protocol, asking you to provide a size for individual cells in the layout.

`collectionView:didHighlightItemAtIndexPath:`
: Gets called on the delegate when a cell becomes highlighted.

`collectionView:didUnhighlightItemAtIndexPath:`
: Gets called on the delegate when a cell comes out of the highlighted state. This method gets called when the user successfully finishes the tap event (pushes her finger on the item and lifts her finger off it, generating the tap gesture) or it can get called if the user cancels her earlier highlighting of the cell by dragging her finger out of the boundaries of the cell.

`collectionView:didSelectItemAtIndexPath:`
: This method gets called on the delegate object when a given cell becomes selected. The cell is always highlighted before it is selected.

`collectionView:didDeselectItemAtIndexPath:`
: Gets called on the delegate object when the cell comes out of the selected state.

So let's build an app according to our earlier requirements. We want to fade out the cell and fade it back in when it becomes selected. In your `UICollectionViewController` instance, implement the `collectionView:didSelectItemAtIndexPath:` method like so:

Our code is written inside our collection view controller, which by default is automatically chosen by the system as both the data source and the delegate of its collection view. It conforms to both the UICollectionViewDataSource and the UICollectionViewDelegate protocols. Therefore, you can simply implement any of the data source or delegate methods directly in your collection view controller's implementation file.

```
#import "ViewController.h"
#import "MyCollectionViewCell.h"

static NSString *kCollectionViewCellIdentifier = @"Cells";

@implementation ViewController

- (void)    collectionView:(UICollectionView *)collectionView
  didSelectItemAtIndexPath:(NSIndexPath *)indexPath{

    UICollectionViewCell *selectedCell =
        [collectionView cellForItemAtIndexPath:indexPath];

    const NSTimeInterval kAnimationDuration = 0.20;

    [UIView animateWithDuration:kAnimationDuration animations:^{
        selectedCell.alpha = 0.0f;
    } completion:^(BOOL finished) {
        [UIView animateWithDuration:kAnimationDuration animations:^{
            selectedCell.alpha = 1.0f;
        }];
    }];
}

...
```

We are using animations here in our example, but this is not the right place to explain how animations work. If you require more information about composing simple animations in iOS, refer to Chapter 20.

OK! That was easy. How about another example? Let's say you want to make a cell twice as big as its normal size when it becomes highlighted and then take it back to its original size when it loses its highlighted state. That means, when the user presses her finger down on the cell (before releasing her finger), the cell enlarges to twice its size and then, when she releases her finger, the cell goes back to its original size. For this, we have to implement the `collectionView:didHighlightItemAtIndexPath:` and the `collectionView:didUnhighlightItemAtIndexPath:` methods of the `UICollectionViewDelegate` protocol in our collection view controller (remember, collection view controllers, by default, conform to the `UICollectionViewDelegate` and the `UICollectionViewDataSource` protocols):

```
#import "ViewController.h"
#import "MyCollectionViewCell.h"

static NSString *kCollectionViewCellIdentifier = @"Cells";
const NSTimeInterval kAnimationDuration = 0.20;

@implementation ViewController

- (void)        collectionView:(UICollectionView *)collectionView
   didHighlightItemAtIndexPath:(NSIndexPath *)indexPath{

    UICollectionViewCell *selectedCell =
        [collectionView cellForItemAtIndexPath:indexPath];

    [UIView animateWithDuration:kAnimationDuration animations:^{
        selectedCell.transform = CGAffineTransformMakeScale(2.0f, 2.0f);
    }];

}

- (void)        collectionView:(UICollectionView *)collectionView
 didUnhighlightItemAtIndexPath:(NSIndexPath *)indexPath{

    UICollectionViewCell *selectedCell =
        [collectionView cellForItemAtIndexPath:indexPath];

    [UIView animateWithDuration:kAnimationDuration animations:^{
        selectedCell.transform = CGAffineTransformMakeScale(1.0f, 1.0f);
    }];

}
...
```

As you can see, we are using the `CGAffineTransformMakeScale` Core Graphics function to create an affine transformation, and then assigning that to the cell itself to create the visual effect of the cell growing twice as large, before shrinking back to its original size. To learn more about this function, please read through Recipe 20.12.

## See Also

Recipe 5.2; Recipe 5.3; Recipe 5.5; Recipe 20.12

# 5.7. Providing a Header and a Footer in a Flow Layout

## Problem

You want to provide header and footer views for your collection view, just as in table views, while using the flow layout.

## Solution

Follow these steps:

1. Create a *.xib* file for your header and another one for your footer.
2. Drag and drop, from Interface Builder's Object Library, an instance of *Collection Reusable View* into your *.xib* files. Ensure that the collection reusable view that you dropped into your *.xib* file is the only view in your *.xib* file. This makes the reusable view the root view of your *.xib* file, exactly the way that you should provide headers and footers to the collection view.
3. If you want more control over how your *.xib* file behaves, create an Objective-C class and associate your *.xib* file's root view to your class. This ensures that when your *.xib* file's contents are loaded from disk by iOS, the associated class will also be loaded into memory, giving you access to the view hierarchy in the *.xib* file.
4. Instantiate the `registerNib:forSupplementaryViewOfKind:withReuseIdentifier:` instance method of your collection view and register your nib files for the `UICollectionElementKindSectionHeader` and `UICollectionElementKindSectionFooter` view kinds.
5. To customize your header and footer views when they are about to be displayed, implement the `collectionView:viewForSupplementaryElementOfKind:atIndexPath:` method of your collection view's data source, and in there, issue the `dequeueReusableSupplementaryViewOfKind:withReuseIdentifier:forIndexPath:` method of your collection view to dequeue a reusable header/footer of a given kind.
6. Last but not least, ensure that you have set the size for your headers and footers by setting the value of the `headerReferenceSize` and the `footerReferenceSize` properties of your flow layout object. This step is very important: if you forget to do this, you will not see your header or footer.

## Discussion

All right, so now we have to create the *.xib* files for our custom headers and footers. Let's call these *.xib* files *Header.xib* and *Footer.xib*. We create them in the same exact way described in Recipe 5.5, so I won't explain that again here. Ensure that you have also created an Objective-C class for your header and one for your footer. Name those `Header` and `Footer`, respectively, and ensure they subclass `UICollectionReusableView`. Once done, configure a label and a button in Interface Builder, and then drag and drop the label into your Header file and the button into your Footer *.xib* file, and link them up to your classes as shown in Figure 5-10 and Figure 5-11.

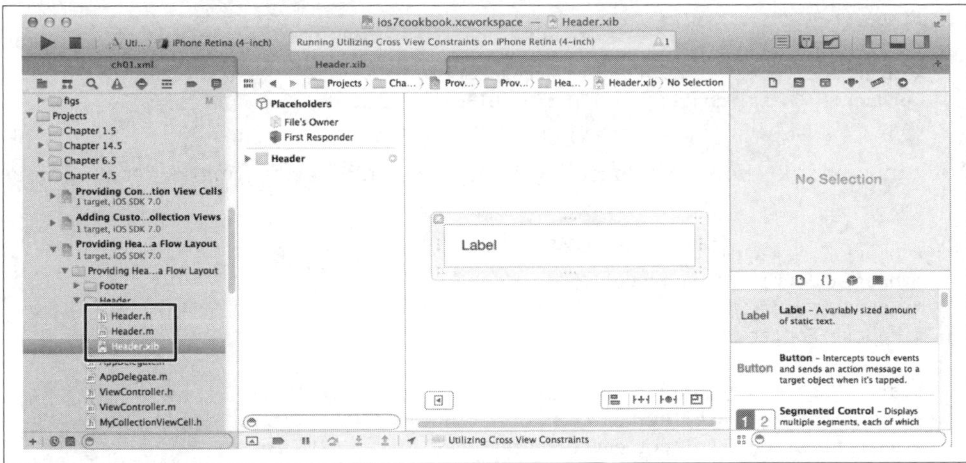


*Figure 5-10. Configuring a header cell for a collection view in Interface Builder*

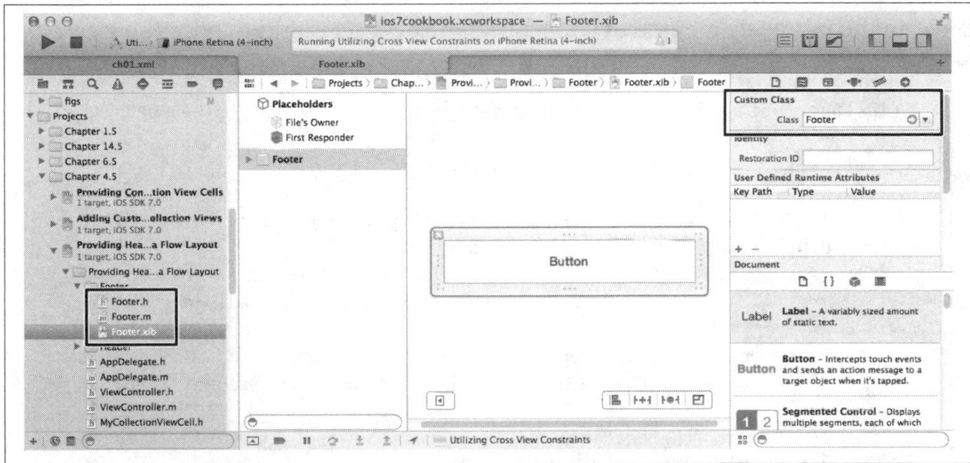


*Figure 5-11. Configuring a footer cell for a collection view in Interface Builder*

I have linked my header's label up to my `Header` class through an outlet property in the *Header.h* file and named the outlet simply *`label`*:

```
#import <UIKit/UIKit.h>

@interface Header : UICollectionReusableView
@property (weak, nonatomic) IBOutlet UILabel *label;
@end
```

I've done the same thing for the footer, linking the button on my Footer *.xib* file to an outlet in my *Footer.h* file and naming the outlet *`button`*:

```
#import <UIKit/UIKit.h>

@interface Footer : UICollectionReusableView
@property (weak, nonatomic) IBOutlet UIButton *button;
@end
```

Now, in your collection view controller, define the identifiers for your header and footer cells:

```
#import "ViewController.h"
#import "MyCollectionViewCell.h"
#import "Header.h"
#import "Footer.h"

static NSString *kCollectionViewCellIdentifier = @"Cells";
static NSString *kCollectionViewHeaderIdentifier = @"Headers";
static NSString *kCollectionViewFooterIdentifier = @"Footers";

@implementation ViewController

...
```

Now, in the initializer method of your collection view, register the collection view's cell, header cell, and footer cell using the nib files that we load into memory:

```
- (instancetype) initWithCollectionViewLayout:(UICollectionViewLayout *)layout{

    self = [super initWithCollectionViewLayout:layout];
    if (self != nil){
        /* Register the nib with the collection view for easy retrieval */
        UINib *nib = [UINib nibWithNibName:
                      NSStringFromClass([MyCollectionViewCell class])
                                     bundle:[NSBundle mainBundle]];

        [self.collectionView registerNib:nib
              forCellWithReuseIdentifier:kCollectionViewCellIdentifier];

        /* Register the header's nib */
        UINib *headerNib = [UINib
                            nibWithNibName:NSStringFromClass([Header class])
                            bundle:[NSBundle mainBundle]];
        [self.collectionView registerNib:headerNib
              forSupplementaryViewOfKind:UICollectionElementKindSectionHeader
                     withReuseIdentifier:kCollectionViewHeaderIdentifier];

        /* Register the footer's nib */
        UINib *footerNib = [UINib
                            nibWithNibName:NSStringFromClass([Footer class])
                            bundle:[NSBundle mainBundle]];
        [self.collectionView registerNib:footerNib
              forSupplementaryViewOfKind:UICollectionElementKindSectionFooter
                     withReuseIdentifier:kCollectionViewFooterIdentifier];
```

```
    }
    return self;

}
```

The next thing you have to do is implement the `collectionView:viewForSupplementaryElementOfKind:atIndexPath:` method of your collection view to configure the headers and footers and provide them back to the collection view:

```
- (UICollectionReusableView *)collectionView:(UICollectionView *)collectionView
          viewForSupplementaryElementOfKind:(NSString *)kind
                                atIndexPath:(NSIndexPath *)indexPath{

    NSString *reuseIdentifier = kCollectionViewHeaderIdentifier;
    if ([kind isEqualToString:UICollectionElementKindSectionFooter]){
        reuseIdentifier = kCollectionViewFooterIdentifier;
    }

    UICollectionReusableView *view =
    [collectionView dequeueReusableSupplementaryViewOfKind:kind
                                       withReuseIdentifier:reuseIdentifier
                                              forIndexPath:indexPath];

    if ([kind isEqualToString:UICollectionElementKindSectionHeader]){
        Header *header = (Header *)view;
        header.label.text = [NSString stringWithFormat:@"Section Header %lu",
                             (unsigned long)indexPath.section + 1];
    }
    else if ([kind isEqualToString:UICollectionElementKindSectionFooter]){
        Footer *footer = (Footer *)view;

        NSString *title = [NSString stringWithFormat:@"Section Footer %lu",
                           (unsigned long)indexPath.section + 1];
        [footer.button setTitle:title forState:UIControlStateNormal];


    }

    return view;

}
```

Last but not least, ensure that your flow layout knows the dimensions of your collection view's header and footer cells. Following what we did in Recipe 5.3, change your app delegate's `flowLayout` method to the following:

```
- (UICollectionViewFlowLayout *) flowLayout{

    UICollectionViewFlowLayout *flowLayout =
    [[UICollectionViewFlowLayout alloc] init];

    flowLayout.minimumLineSpacing = 20.0f;
    flowLayout.minimumInteritemSpacing = 10.0f;
```

```
    flowLayout.itemSize = CGSizeMake(80.0f, 120.0f);
    flowLayout.scrollDirection = UICollectionViewScrollDirectionVertical;
    flowLayout.sectionInset = UIEdgeInsetsMake(10.0f, 20.0f, 10.0f, 20.0f);

    /* Set the reference size for the header and the footer views */
    flowLayout.headerReferenceSize = CGSizeMake(300.0f, 50.0f);
    flowLayout.footerReferenceSize = CGSizeMake(300.0f, 50.0f);

    return flowLayout;
}
```

All ready to go! If you launch your app in iPad Simulator, you will see something similar to that shown in Figure 5-12.

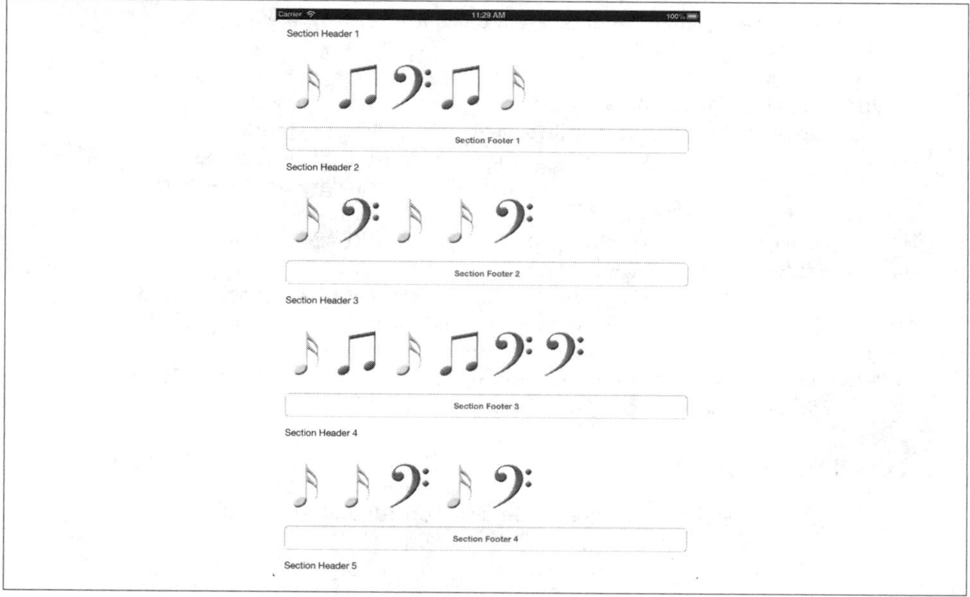


*Figure 5-12. Headers and footers rendered in the collection view*

## See Also

Recipe 5.2; Recipe 5.3; Recipe 5.5

# 5.8. Adding Custom Interactions to Collection Views

## Problem

You want to add your own gesture recognizers, such as pinch gesture recognizers, to a collection view in order to enable custom behaviors on top of the existing ones.

## Solution

Instantiate your gesture recognizer and then go through all the existing collection view gesture recognizers to see whether a gesture recognizer similar to yours already exists. If so, call the `requireGestureRecognizerToFail:` method on the existing gesture recognizer and pass your own recognizer as the parameter to this method. This will ensure that the collection view's gesture recognizer that is similar to yours will grab the gestures only if your gesture recognizer fails to process its data or its requirements/criteria aren't met. That means that if your gesture recognizer can process the gesture, it will, but if it cannot, the gesture will be sent to the collection view's existing gesture recognizers for processing.

Once this is done, add your gesture recognizer to your collection view. Remember, in an instance of `UICollectionViewController`, your collection view object is accessible through the `collectionView` property of the controller and *not* the `view` property.

## Discussion

The iOS API has already added a few gesture recognizers to collection views. So in order to add your own gesture recognizers, on top of the existing collection, you first need to make sure that your gesture recognizers will not interfere with the existing ones. To do that, you have to first instantiate your own gesture recognizers and, as explained before, look through the existing array of gesture recognizers on the collection view and call the `requireGestureRecognizerToFail:` method on the one that is of the same class type of gesture recognizer as the one you are attempting to add to the collection view.

Let's have a look at an example. Our objective for this example is to add pinching for zooming in and zooming out functionality to our collection view. We are going to build this example on top of what we have already done in Recipe 5.5. So the first thing we are going to do is add a pinch gesture recognizer to the collection of gesture recognizers in our collection view, which must be done in the `viewDidLoad` method of the collection view controller:

```
- (void) viewDidLoad{
    [super viewDidLoad];
    self.collectionView.backgroundColor = [UIColor whiteColor];


    UIPinchGestureRecognizer *pinch = [[UIPinchGestureRecognizer alloc]
                                       initWithTarget:self
                                       action:@selector(handlePinches:)];
    for (UIGestureRecognizer *recognizer in
         self.collectionView.gestureRecognizers){
        if ([recognizer isKindOfClass:[pinch class]]){
            [recognizer requireGestureRecognizerToFail:pinch];
        }
    }
```

```
    [self.collectionView addGestureRecognizer:pinch];
}
```

The pinch gesture recognizer is set up to call the `handlePinches:` method of our view controller. We'll write this method now:

```
- (void) handlePinches:(UIPinchGestureRecognizer *)paramSender{

    CGSize DefaultLayoutItemSize = CGSizeMake(80.0f, 120.0f);

    UICollectionViewFlowLayout *layout =
        (UICollectionViewFlowLayout *)self.collectionView.collectionViewLayout;

    layout.itemSize =
    CGSizeMake(DefaultLayoutItemSize.width * paramSender.scale,
               DefaultLayoutItemSize.height * paramSender.scale);

    [layout invalidateLayout];
}
```

There are two very important parts to this code:

1. We are assuming that the default item size on our collection view's flow layout was set to have a width of 80 points and a height of 120 points. That's how we set the collection view's flow layout in Recipe 5.3. We are then taking the scale factor that came back from the pinch gesture recognizer and multiplying the size of the items in our collection view by the pinch scale factor, which can cause our items to become bigger or smaller in dimension, depending on how the user is controlling the pinching on the screen.
2. After we change the default item size in our flow layout, we need to refresh the layout. In table views, we used to refresh the sections, the rows, or the whole table view, but here, we refresh or invalidate the layout that is attached to the collection view in order to ask the collection view to redraw itself after a layout change. Since a collection view can contain only one layout object at a time, invalidating that layout object will force the whole collection view to reload. If we could have one layout per section, we would be able to reload only the section(s) that are linked to that layout, but for now, the whole collection view will be repainted when the layout object is invalidated.

Now if you run your code, you will notice that you can use two fingers on the screen to pinch inward and enlarge the size of the items on your collection view, or pinch outward to make them smaller.

## See Also

Recipe 5.3; Recipe 5.5

## 5.9. Providing Contextual Menus on Collection View Cells

### Problem

You want to provide a menu to the user when she long-presses an item in your collection view. Through this menu, she may then be able to copy an item, move an item, etc.

### Solution

Contextual menus are built into collection views by default. To enable them, all you have to do is implement the following methods from the `UICollectionViewDelegate` protocol:

`collectionView:shouldShowMenuForItemAtIndexPath:`
: The runtime passes the method an index path to an item. The method returns a Boolean value indicating whether you want the collection view to display the contextual menu for that item or not.

`collectionView:canPerformAction:forItemAtIndexPath:withSender:`
: The runtime passes the method a selector of type `SEL`. You can check the selector (usually by converting it to a string and then comparing it to a string representing the action) and find out whether you want to allow that action to happen. Return `YES` to allow the action to happen and `NO` to suppress it. Remember that you can always convert a selector to a string using the `NSStringFromSelector` method. A typical selector could be `copy:` or `paste:` for the copy and the paste contextual menu items.

`collectionView:performAction:forItemAtIndexPath:withSender:`
: Here you will perform the action that you allowed the collection view to display to the user through earlier delegate methods.

### Discussion

Without waiting around, we are going to extend the code that we wrote in Recipe 5.5 and allow a *copy* contextual menu to be displayed on our cells when the user long-presses on them. When the user selects the copy menu item, we will copy the image inside the cell onto the pasteboard so that the user can paste that image into other apps, such as the Mail app.

The first thing we are going to do is implement the `collectionView:shouldShowMenuForItemAtIndexPath:` method in our collection view's delegate. In our example, we are using a collection view controller that is itself the delegate and the data source, so all we have to do, really, is implement the aforementioned method in the collection view controller, like so:

```
- (BOOL)            collectionView:(UICollectionView *)collectionView
  shouldShowMenuForItemAtIndexPath:(NSIndexPath *)indexPath{
    return YES;
}
```

Now we want to allow only the "copy" menu item to be displayed for the cells in our collection view, for the sake of this example, so that you can see how you can filter the available menu items and display only the ones you need:

```
- (BOOL) collectionView:(UICollectionView *)collectionView
       canPerformAction:(SEL)action
     forItemAtIndexPath:(NSIndexPath *)indexPath
             withSender:(id)sender{

    if (action == @selector(copy:)){
        return YES;
    }

    return NO;
}
```

You can see that we are not even converting the selector to a string to compare it with strings such as `copy:`. All we are doing is using the equality operator to check whether the requested selector matches our expectations. If so, we return `YES`, and if not, we return `NO`.

Last but not least, we have to implement the `collectionView:performAction:forItemAtIndexPath:withSender:` method in our delegate to find out when the copy action is called, and then copy the image of the selected cell onto the pasteboard, ready to be pasted into another app by the user:

```
- (void) collectionView:(UICollectionView *)collectionView
          performAction:(SEL)action
     forItemAtIndexPath:(NSIndexPath *)indexPath
             withSender:(id)sender{

    if (action == @selector(copy:)){

        MyCollectionViewCell *cell = (MyCollectionViewCell *)[collectionView
                                      cellForItemAtIndexPath:indexPath];

        [[UIPasteboard generalPasteboard]
         setImage:cell.imageViewBackgroundImage.image];

    }

}
```

Now if you run the app and then long-press on one of the items in the collection view, you will see a result similar to that shown in Figure 5-13.

*Figure 5-13. A contextual menu item displayed for a cell in a collection view*

## See Also

Recipe 5.5

# CHAPTER 6
# Storyboards

## 6.0. Introduction

iOS programmers are all used to view controllers by now. We know how to use navigation controllers in order to push and pop view controllers. But Apple believes this can be done more easily, and that's the whole story behind storyboards. *Storyboarding* is the new way of defining the connections between different screens in your app. For instance, if you have 20 unique view controllers in your app that you coded a year ago and are looking at the source code again *now*, you will need to find your way around the connections between these view controllers and to try to remember what view controller is pushed when a certain action is taken by the user. This can be very difficult, especially if you have not documented your code. Storyboards come to the rescue. With storyboards, you can view/create your entire app's UI and the connections between view controllers in one screen. It's that simple.

To take advantage of storyboarding, you need to get acquainted with Interface Builder. Don't worry; it's all covered in this chapter.

With storyboards, one screen's worth of content is called a *scene*. The relation between a scene and a storyboard on the iPhone can be compared to that between a view and a view controller. In a scene, you put all your content on the screen to be presented to the user at the same time. On the iPad, more than one scene can be presented to the user at the same time because of the bigger screen.

Storyboarding supports transitioning from one scene to another. The equivalent of a navigation controller pushing one view controller on top of another is a *segue* in storyboarding. Another type of transition is a modal view controller that slides a scene from the bottom of the screen up to fill the screen temporarily. On the iPad, modal screens usually appear in the center of the screen and dim the rest of the screen, to point out that they are the main input at that moment.

## 6.1. Adding a Navigation Controller to a Storyboard

### Problem

You want to be able to manage multiple view controllers inside a storyboard-based application.

### Solution

Set a navigation controller as the initial view controller of your storyboard file.

### Discussion

When you create a new universal iOS app using the Single View Application template in Xcode, you will get two storyboard files: *Main_iPhone.storyboard* and *Main_iPad.storyboard*. If you view them in Interface Builder, you'll notice that they contain a view controller as their root controller. Figure 6-1 shows the contents of a simple out-of-the-box iPhone storyboard file.

In order to change the root view controller of your storyboard file into a navigation controller, all you have to do is the following:

1. Select your view controller on the canvas of the storyboard.
2. From the Edit menu, choose Embed In and then Navigation Controller (see Figure 6-2).

Once you are done, you will notice that the root view controller of your storyboard is now a navigation controller, as shown in Figure 6-3.

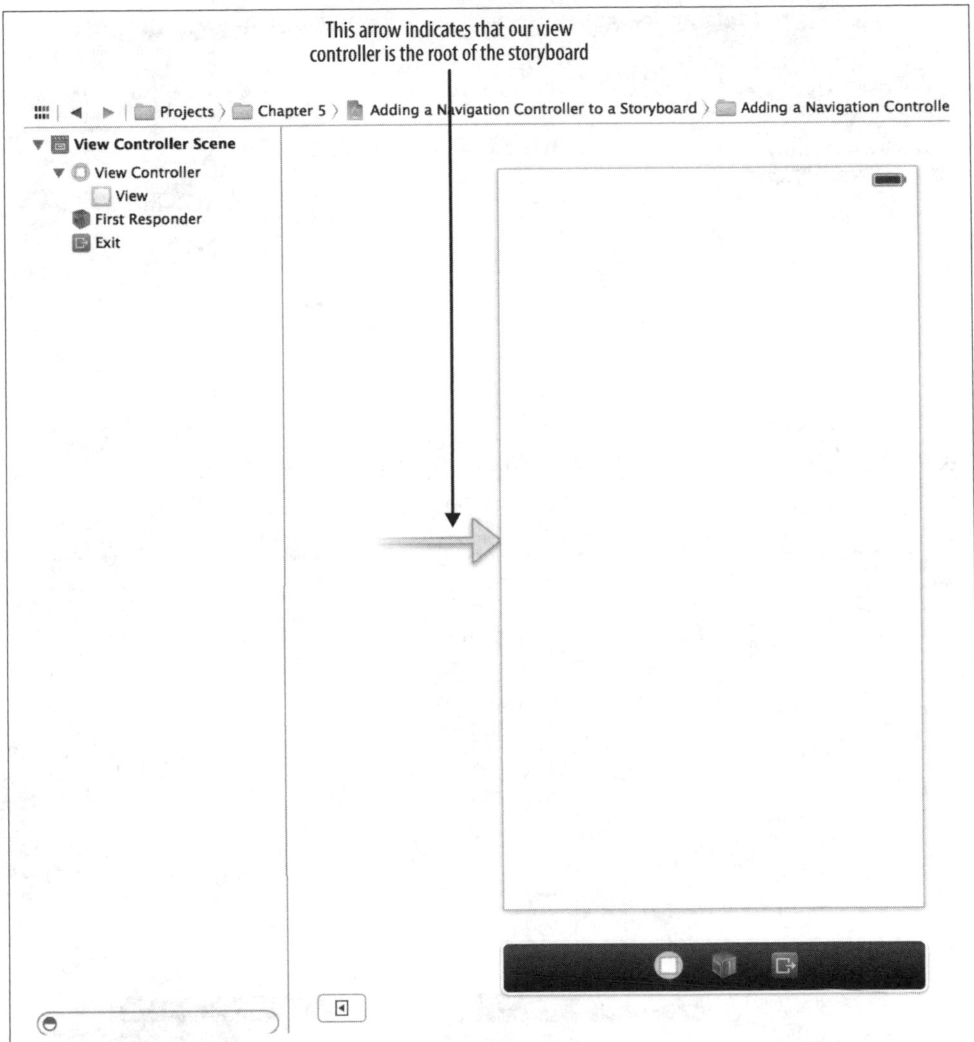


*Figure 6-1. A view controller as the root of a storyboard file*

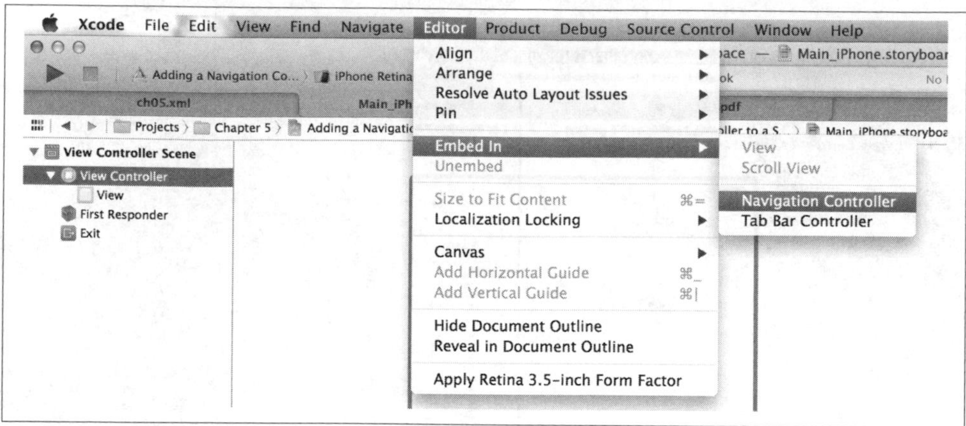


*Figure 6-2. Embedding your view controller in a navigation controller*

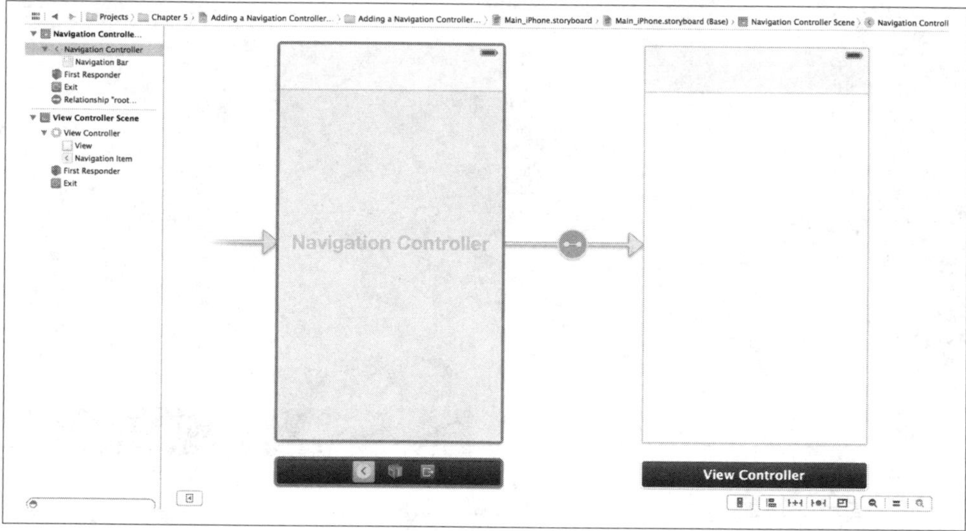


*Figure 6-3. A navigation controller is now the root controller of our storyboard*

## See Also

Recipe 6.0, "Introduction"

# 6.2. Passing Data from One Screen to Another

## Problem

You want to pass data from one scene to another using storyboards.

## Solution

Use segue objects.

## Discussion

A segue is an object, just like any other object in Objective-C. To carry out a transition from one scene to another, the storyboard runtime creates a segue object for that transition. A segue is an instance of class `UIStoryboardSegue`. To start a transition, the current view controller (which will get pushed out of the screen after the segue) receives the `prepareForSegue:sender:` message, where the `prepareForSegue` parameter will be an object of type `UIStoryboardSegue`. If you want to pass any data from the current view controller to the view controller that is about to appear on the screen, you need to do that in the `prepareForSegue:sender:` method.

For this recipe to make sense, you need to have followed the instructions in Recipe 6.1 and created two view controllers inside a navigation controller on your storyboard.

Let's have a look at a real-life example of using segues. In this recipe, we are going to display a view controller similar to that shown in Figure 6-4.

Whatever the user places in our text field will get passed to the second view controller through a segue and will get set as the title of that view controller. The second view controller's canvas will be empty. So using the technique that you learned in Recipe 6.1, place your first view controller inside a navigation controller. Now place another view controller from the Object Library onto your storyboard and place a button and a text field on the first view controller as well. You can make sure that the arrangement of the text field and the button is similar to that shown in Figure 6-4, but that is not required. You can arrange them any way you want. Now hold down the Ctrl key on your keyboard and press your mouse down on the button. Drag and drop the line that will appear on the screen onto the second view controller (Figure 6-5), and from the dialog that appears, select the Push item. By doing this, you just made a connection from your button to the second view controller so that when the button is pressed, the second view controller will be pushed onto the stack of the navigation controller.

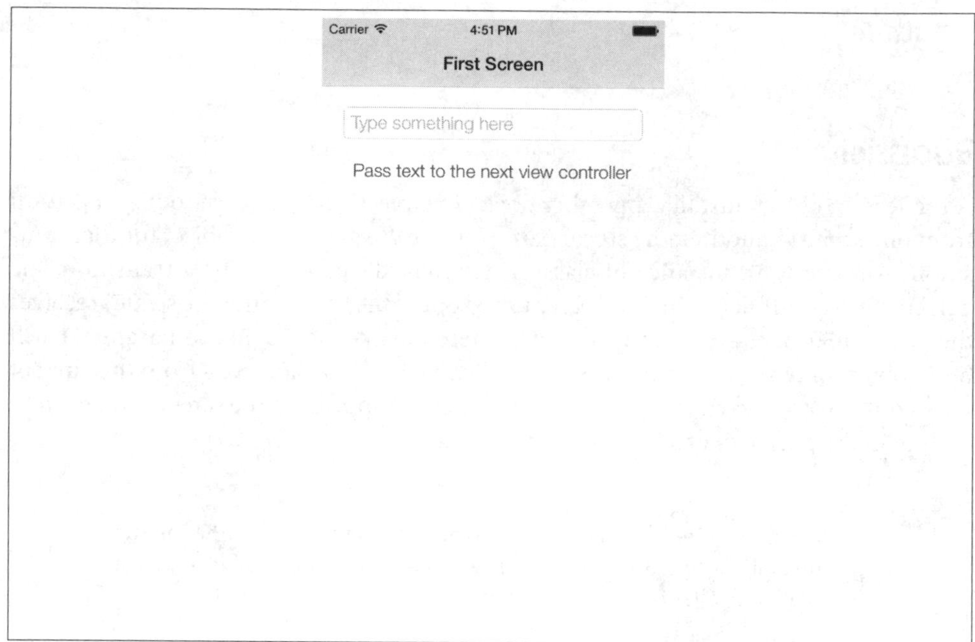


*Figure 6-4. The first view controller in our app with a text field and a button*

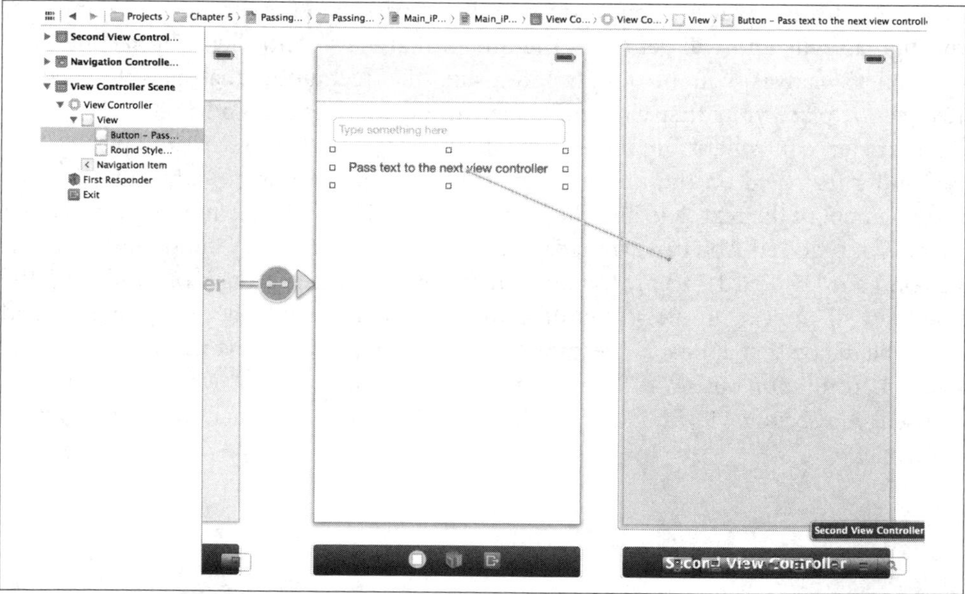


*Figure 6-5. Creating a connection from the press of the button to the second view controller*

You can see that Interface Builder has created a segue between the first and the second view controller. Click that segue, and in the Attributes Inspector, give it an identifier of *pushSecondViewController*, as shown in Figure 6-6.

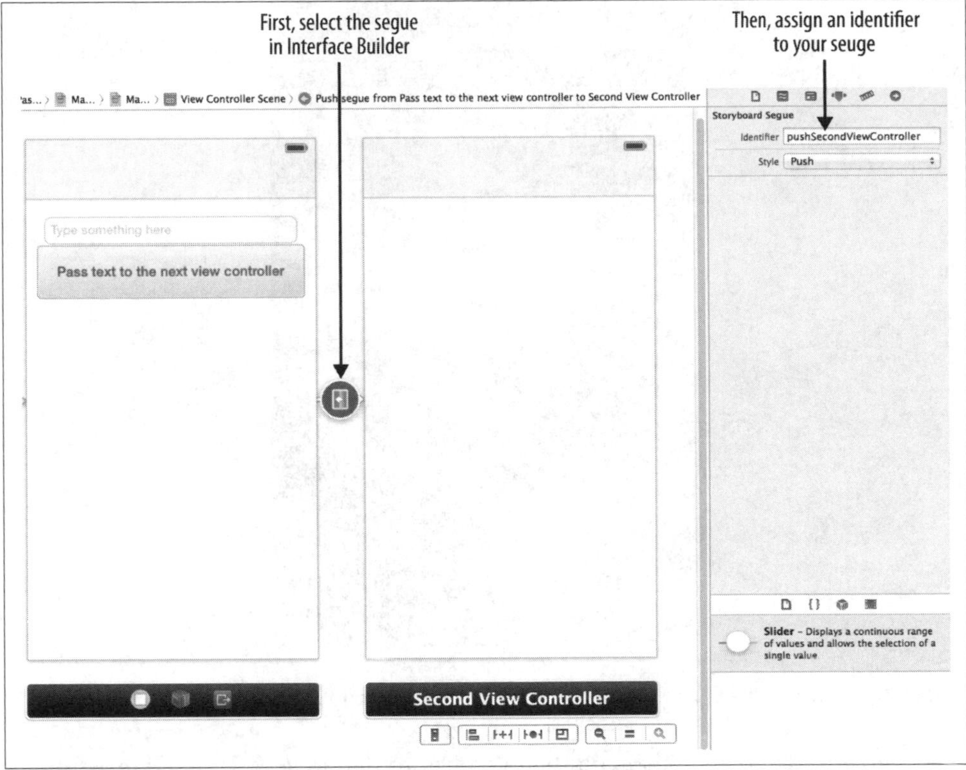


*Figure 6-6. Assigning an identifier to a segue*

You might be asking: why do we need this identifier? The answer is that we will implement a special method of our view controller that will first ask us whether it is OK for a segue to happen or not. In that method we will check the text inside our text field, and if that field is empty, we will not allow the user to go to the next screen. The method that will get called in our view controller is the `shouldPerformSegueWithIdentifier:sender:` method of `UIViewController`. You can use the value that gets sent to its `shouldPerformSegueWithIdentifier` parameter, of type `NSString`, to get the identifier of the segue that is about to trigger. You will then be required to return a value of `YES` if you are happy with the segue that will happen and `NO` if you aren't. Returning `NO` will prevent the segue with that identifier to get fired. But preventing a segue without giving a clue to the user as to why you did so is not a good user experience. Because of this, when the text field is empty and the user attempts to press the button to go to the next screen, we will display the dialog in Figure 6-7.

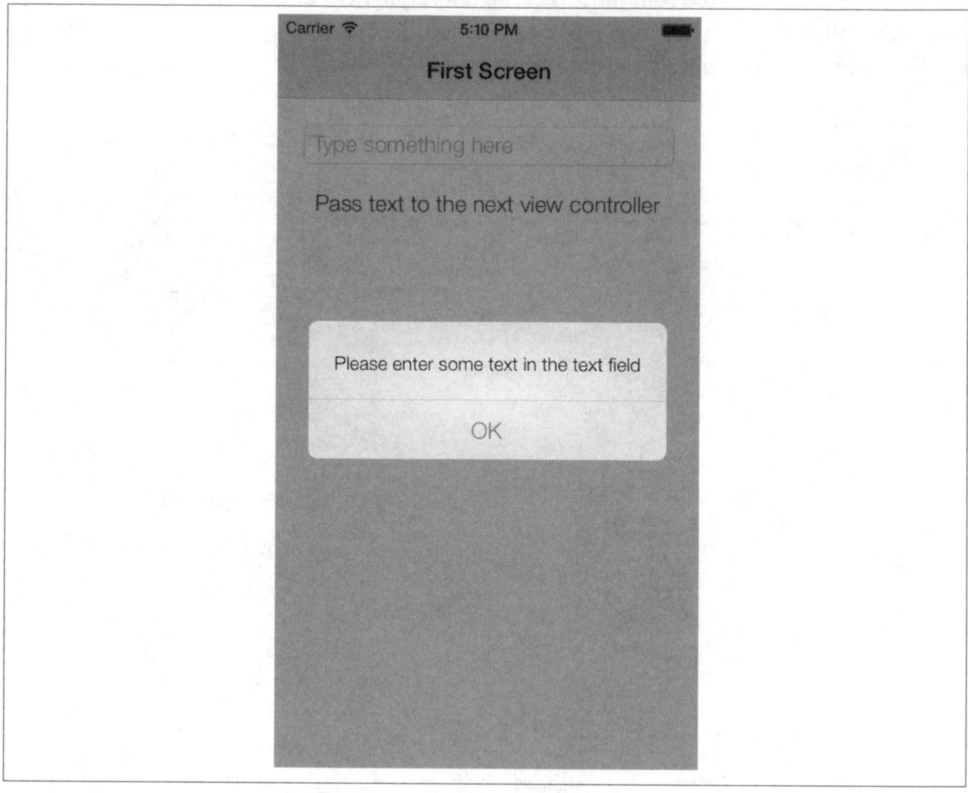


*Figure 6-7. The user cannot go to the next screen without entering some text first*

So let's go ahead and implement our first view controller up to this point. I'm assuming that you have already connected your text field to your view controller as an outlet of the controller so that you can access its `text` property when the segue is about to happen.

```
#import "ViewController.h"
#import "SecondViewController.h"

@interface ViewController () <UITextFieldDelegate>
@property (weak, nonatomic) IBOutlet UITextField *textField;
@end

@implementation ViewController

- (void) viewDidLoad{
    [super viewDidLoad];
    self.title = @"First Screen";
}

- (BOOL) textFieldShouldReturn:(UITextField *)textField{
```

```
    [textField resignFirstResponder];
    return YES;
}

- (void) displayTextIsRequired{

    UIAlertView *alert = [[UIAlertView alloc]
                          initWithTitle:nil
                          message:@"Please enter some text in the text field"
                          delegate:nil
                          cancelButtonTitle:nil
                          otherButtonTitles:@"OK", nil];
    [alert show];

}

- (BOOL) shouldPerformSegueWithIdentifier:(NSString *)identifier
                                   sender:(id)sender{

    /* Check if there is some text and if there isn't, display a message
     to the user and prevent her from going to the next screen */
    if ([identifier isEqualToString:@"pushSecondViewController"]){

        if ([self.textField.text length] == 0){
            [self displayTextIsRequired];
            return NO;
        }
    };

    return YES;

}

- (void) prepareForSegue:(UIStoryboardSegue *)segue sender:(id)sender{

    if ([segue.identifier isEqualToString:@"pushSecondViewController"]){
        SecondViewController *nextController =
        segue.destinationViewController;
        [nextController setText:self.textField.text];
    }

}

@end
```

The `prepareForSegue:sender:` method of our view controller is calling the `setText:` instance method of `SecondViewController`, which is, as its name shows, our second view controller. We will simply implement that method in this way:

```
#import "SecondViewController.h"

@interface SecondViewController ()
```

```
@end

@implementation SecondViewController

- (void) setText:(NSString *)paramText{
    self.title = paramText;
}

@end
```

That's about it. Now if you run your app and enter, for instance, `Hello, World!`, in the text field and press the button, you will see something similar to that shown in Figure 6-8.

*Figure 6-8. Our text is successfully set as the title of the second view controller*

## See Also

Recipe 6.1

## 6.3. Adding a Tab Bar Controller to a Storyboard

### Problem

You want to create an application based on a tab bar controller using storyboards.

### Solution

Create a single-view application in Xcode and embed your first view controller in a tab bar controller. After that, drag and drop more view controllers onto your storyboards and establish a connection between them and the array of view controllers inside your tab bar controller.

### Discussion

So you've created a single-view application project in Xcode and you want to start using tab bar controllers in your app. In order to achieve that, simply follow these steps:

1. Select the view controller on your storyboard in Interface Builder. From the Editor menu, choose Embed In, and then choose Tab Bar Controller, as shown in Figure 6-9.

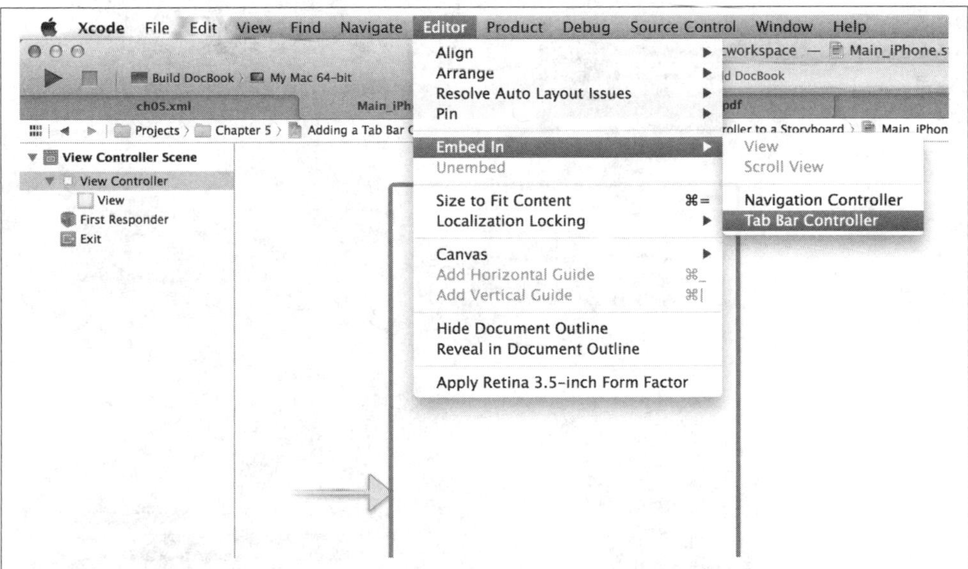


*Figure 6-9. Embedding your root view controller in a tab bar controller*

2. Now, from the Object Library in Interface Builder, drag and drop a new instance of View Controller onto your storyboard.
3. Hold down the Ctrl key on your keyboard and drag and drop your mouse from within the tab bar controller onto the new view controller that you created (Figure 6-10), and in the dialog that appears on the screen, choose *view controllers* under the *Relationship Segues* section (Figure 6-11).

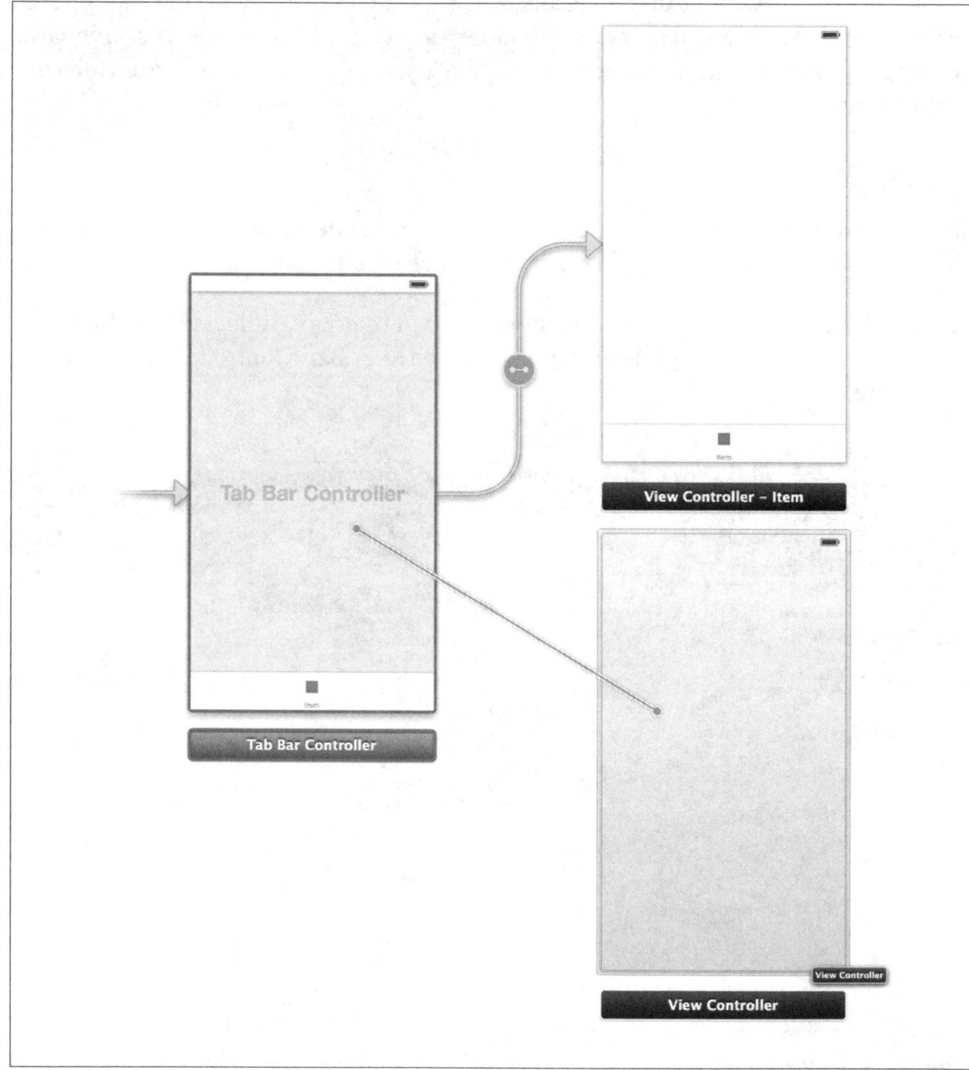


*Figure 6-10. Connecting your view controller to the tab bar controller*

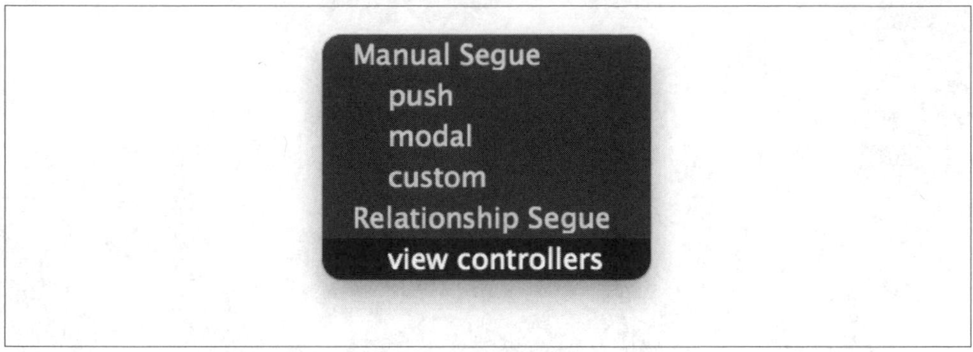


*Figure 6-11. Associating your view controller with the array of view controllers in our tab bar controller*

Now run your app in iOS Simulator. At the bottom of the screen, you will now see two items, as shown in Figure 6-12. Each one of these items represents one of your view controllers. Now, if you are like me, the tab bar controller-based applications that you create usually contain navigation controllers in each of the tab items. If you want to enable that functionality, use the technique that you learned in Recipe 6.1 to embed your view controllers in navigation controllers (see Figure 6-13).

*Figure 6-12. View controllers are successfully showing in the tab bar controller*

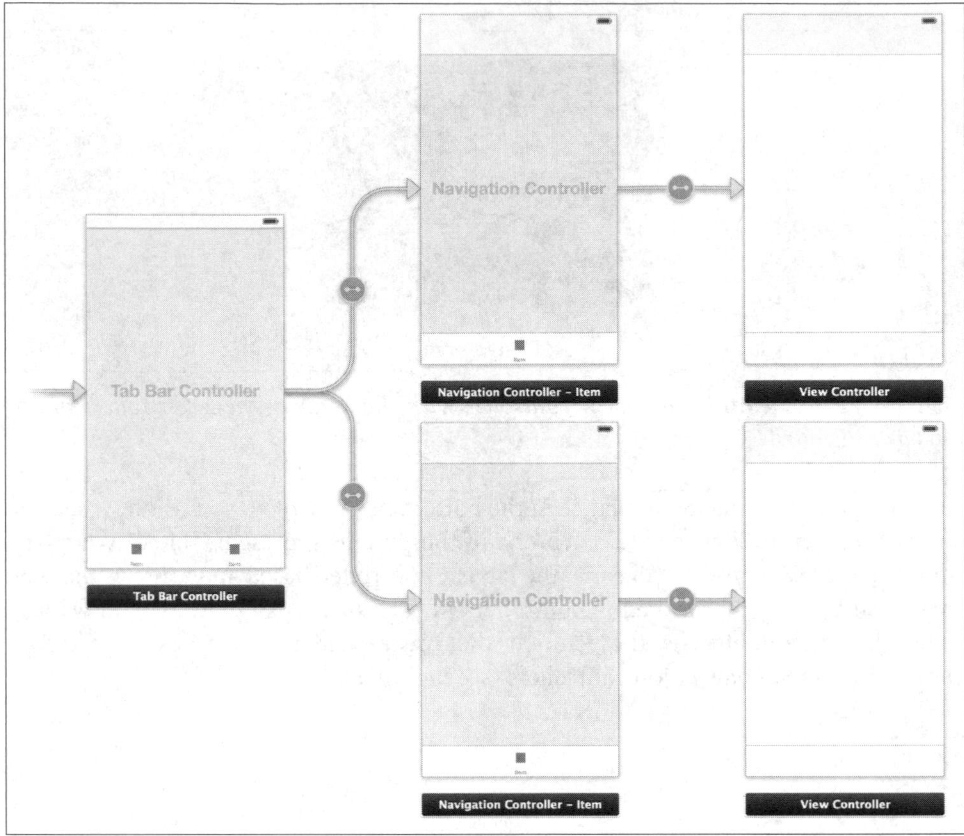


*Figure 6-13. Embedding your view controllers in navigation controllers inside a tab bar controller*

## See Also

Recipe 6.1

# 6.4. Introducing Custom Segue Transitions to Your Storyboard

## Problem

You want to introduce and use a new type of storyboard transition in your storyboard files so that the move from one view controller to another is done in a custom way—for instance, with a custom animation.

## Solution

Subclass `UIStoryboardSegue` and override its `perform` method to do your work.

## Discussion

Storyboards, by default, offer a few useful segue types, such as push and modal. These are great, but sometimes you may wish to perform a custom transition from one view to the other. In these cases, it's best to use a custom segue object. Let's create a segue, then. What we are going to do here is allow the first view controller to display the second view controller with a flip transition. To do this, follow these steps:

1. Create a project based on the Single View Application template in Xcode.
2. In your storyboard file, create a second view controller and place a button in the center of the first view controller. Hold down the Ctrl button on your keyboard and drag and drop from the button onto the second view controller. At this point, a dialog will appear on your screen asking what type of transition you want to associate with this segue. In that dialog, choose "custom" (see Figure 6-14).

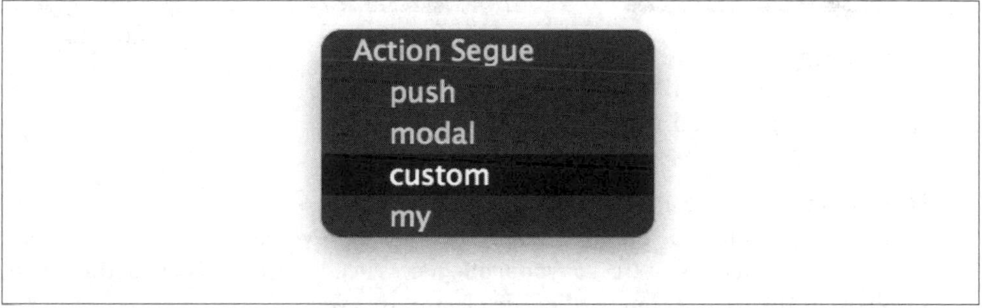


*Figure 6-14. Associating a custom segue with the action of our button*

3. Now select your segue, and in the Attributes Inspector in Interface Builder, change the class name of your segue to *MySegue* (see Figure 6-15). Don't worry if this class doesn't exist already. We are going to code this class in this recipe.

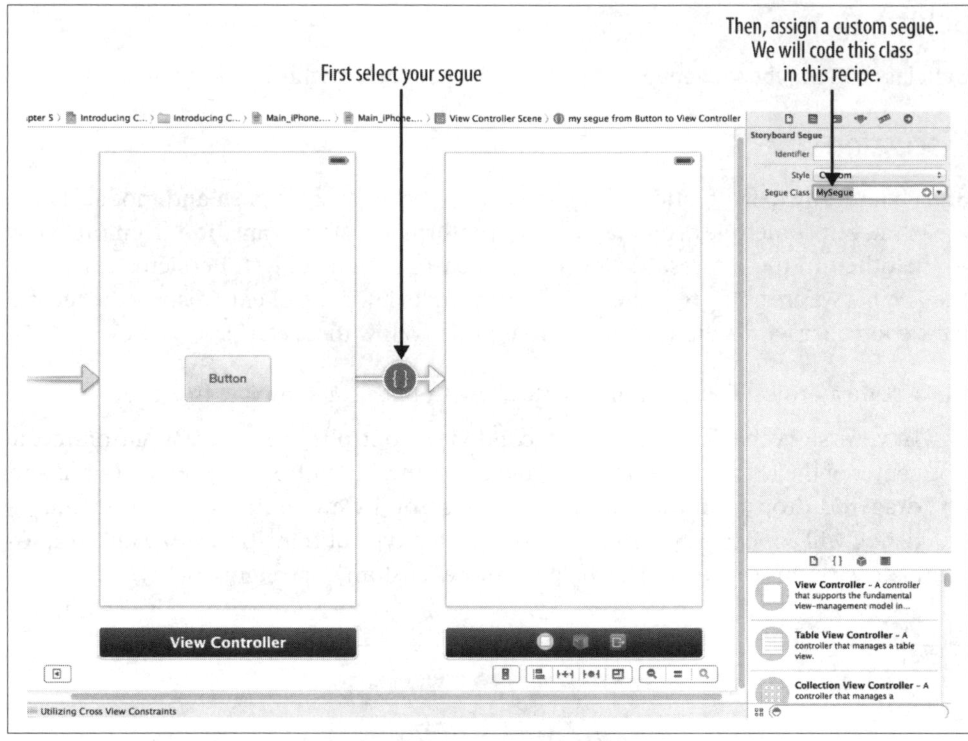


Figure 6-15. Assigning a custom class name to our segue

4. Now in Xcode, create a new Objective-C class inside your project, name that class *MySegue* (matching the name you assigned in the previous step), and ensure that this class is a subclass of `UIStoryboardSegue`. Once your class is created for you, implement the `perform` method of the class in this way:

```
#import "MySegue.h"

@implementation MySegue

- (void) perform{

    UIViewController *source = self.sourceViewController;
    UIViewController *destination = self.destinationViewController;

    [UIView transitionFromView:source.view
                        toView:destination.view
                      duration:0.50f
                       options:UIViewAnimationOptionTransitionFlipFromTop
                    completion:^(BOOL finished) {
                        NSLog(@"Transitioning is finished");
                    }];
```

```
}

@end
```

That's it; we are done. Now you can run your app and see how pressing the button in the first view controller will fire your custom segue, which in turn will flip the second view controller onto the screen. For this recipe, we are using the `transitionFromView:toView:duration:options:completion:` class method of `UIView` to do our transition. This method accepts quite a few parameters, each of which is explained here:

`transitionFromView`
: The view from which the transition has to start. In the context of our segue, this is the source view controller's view.

`toView`
: The view to which the transition has to go. In our segue, this is the destination view controller's view.

`duration`
: The duration of the animation in seconds.

`options`
: The type of animation that you want to perform. This value is of type `UIViewAnimationOptions`. If you want to see all the options available to you, press Command +Shift+O on your keyboard, type **`UIViewAnimationOptions`**, and then press the Enter key.

`completion`
: A completion block that will get called once the transition is finished.

Before we wrap up this recipe, there is one thing to bear in mind. The work that you do (your custom transition) has to be done in the `perform` instance method of your custom segue class. This means that, for instance, you cannot display an alert view to the user in this method and expect her to press a Yes or No button based on her decision, *and then* perform the transition. That won't work. So think about what you want your segue to do and whether subclassing `UIStoryboardSegue` is the best option for you.

## See Also

Recipe 6.0, "Introduction";Recipe 6.1;

# 6.5. Placing Images and Other UI Components on Storyboards

## Problem

You want to be able to place images, buttons, and other UI components onto your storyboard files.

## Solution

Use the Object Library in Interface Builder to look for various UI components. When you are ready to place them on your storyboard files, simply drag and drop them. You can then use the Attributes Inspector to configure those components.

## Discussion

Let's say that you want to place some images on your storyboard. In Interface Builder, while you have your storyboard file open, hold down Ctrl+Alt+Command+3 on your keyboard to get to the Object Library. In the Object Library, find the Image View component (Figure 6-16) and drag and drop it onto your main view controller. Now press Alt+Command+4 simultaneously on your keyboard to open the Attributes Inspector. In this panel, you can now configure your image view. To add an image to this image view, simply add that image to your project. From the Attributes Inspector, while your image view is selected, set its image property, as shown in Figure 6-17.

Every now and then, you may find yourself in a situation where you just cannot find the right UI component in the Object Library but you are sure that the component exists. I know that I have been in that situation. The Object Library gives you a really nice search box where you can just type the name of the component that you are interested in. To get to the search box, make sure that you have already selected the Object Library by pressing its Ctrl+Alt+Command+3 shortcut, and then simply press Command+Alt +L (see Figure 6-18).

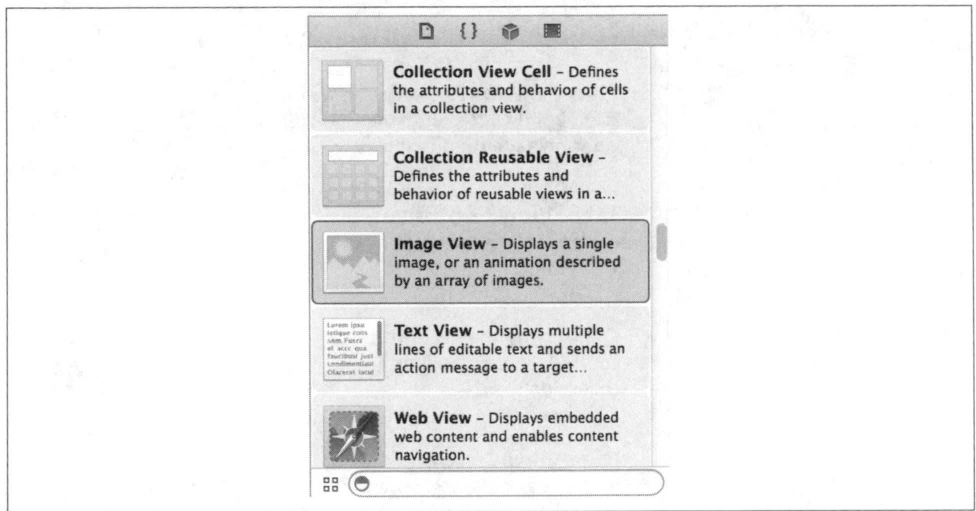


*Figure 6-16. Image view UI component in the Object Library*

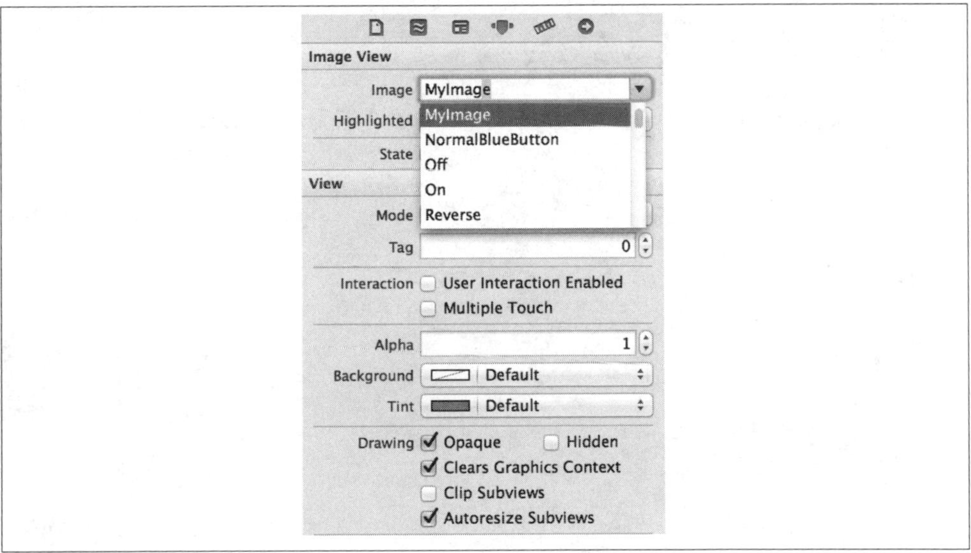


*Figure 6-17. Setting the image property of an image view in the Attributes Inspector in Interface Builder*

The Attributes Inspector allows you to configure most of the very important properties of various UI components that you drop onto your storyboards, but for certain things, you may still need to dive into code.

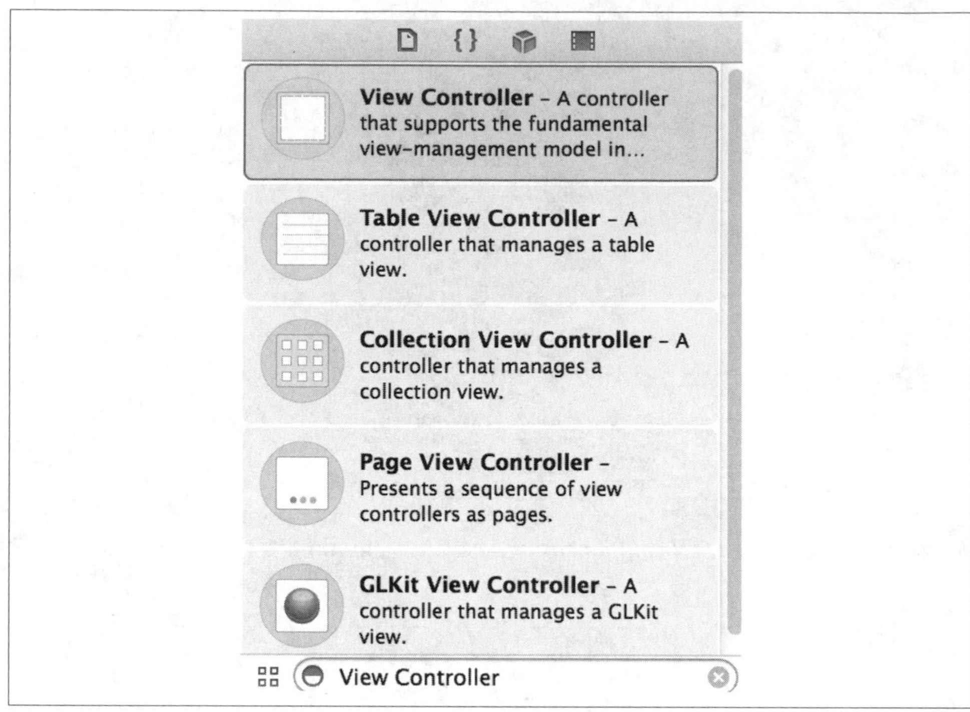


*Figure 6-18. The search box in the Object Library allows you to quickly find the object you are looking for*

## See Also

Recipe 6.0, "Introduction"

CHAPTER 7

# Concurrency

## 7.0. Introduction

Concurrency is achieved when two or more tasks are executed at the same time. Modern operating systems have the ability to run tasks concurrently, even on one CPU. They achieve this by giving every task a certain time slice from the CPU. For instance, if there are 10 tasks to be executed in one second, all with the same priority, the operating system will divide 1,000 milliseconds by 10 (tasks) and will give each task 100 milliseconds of the CPU time. That means all these tasks will then be executed in the same second, and they will appear to have been executed concurrently.

However, with advances in technology, now we have CPUs with more than one core. This means that the CPU is truly capable of executing tasks at the same time. The operating system will dispatch the tasks to the CPU and wait until they are done. It's that simple!

Grand Central Dispatch, or GCD for short, is a low-level C API that works with block objects. The real use for GCD is to dispatch tasks to multiple cores without making you, the programmer, worry about which core is executing which task. On Mac OS X, multicore devices, including laptops, have been available to users for quite some time. With the introduction of multicore devices such as the new iPad, programmers can write amazing multicore-aware multithreaded apps for iOS.

At the heart of GCD are dispatch queues. Dispatch queues, as we will soon see, are pools of threads managed by GCD on the host operating system, whether iOS or Mac OS X. You will not be working with these threads directly. You will just work with dispatch queues, dispatching *tasks* to these queues and asking the queues to invoke your tasks. GCD offers several options for running tasks: synchronously, asynchronously, after a certain delay, etc.

To start using GCD in your apps, you don't have to import any special library into your project. Apple has already incorporated GCD into various frameworks, including Core Foundation and Cocoa/Cocoa Touch. All methods and data types available in GCD start with a *dispatch_* keyword. For instance, `dispatch_async` allows you to dispatch a task on a queue for asynchronous execution, whereas `dispatch_after` allows you to run a block of code after a given delay.

Before GCD and operations, programmers had to create their own threads to perform tasks in parallel. For instance, an iOS developer would create a thread similar to this to perform an operation 1,000 times:

```
- (void) doCalculation{
    /* Do your calculation here */
}

- (void) calculationThreadEntry{

    @autoreleasepool {
        NSUInteger counter = 0;
        while ([[NSThread currentThread] isCancelled] == NO){
            [self doCalculation];
            counter++;
            if (counter >= 1000){
                break;
            }
        }
    }

}

- (BOOL)            application:(UIApplication *)application
  didFinishLaunchingWithOptions:(NSDictionary *)launchOptions{

    /* Start the thread */
    [NSThread detachNewThreadSelector:@selector(calculationThreadEntry)
                             toTarget:self
                           withObject:nil];

    self.window = [[UIWindow alloc] initWithFrame:
                   [[UIScreen mainScreen] bounds]];
    self.window.backgroundColor = [UIColor whiteColor];
    [self.window makeKeyAndVisible];
    return YES;
}
```

The programmer has to start the thread manually and then create the required structure for the thread (entry point, autorelease pool, and thread's main loop). When we write the same code with GCD, we really won't have to do much. We will simply place our code in a block object and dispatch that block object to GCD for execution. Whether that code gets executed on the main thread or any other thread depends on us. Here is an example:

```
dispatch_queue_t queue =
  dispatch_get_global_queue(DISPATCH_QUEUE_PRIORITY_DEFAULT, 0);

size_t numberOfIterations = 1000;dispatch_async(queue, ^(void) {
  dispatch_apply(numberOfIterations, queue, ^(size_t iteration){
    /* Perform the operation here */
  });
});
```

In this chapter, you will learn all there is to know about GCD and how to use it to write modern multithreaded apps for iOS and Mac OS X that will achieve blazing performance on multicore devices such as the iPad 2.

We will be working with dispatch queues a lot, so please make sure that you fully understand the concept behind them. There are three types of dispatch queues:

*Main queue*
: This queue performs all its tasks on the main thread, which is where Cocoa and Cocoa Touch require programmers to call all UI-related methods. Use the `dispatch_get_main_queue` function to retrieve the handle to the main queue.

*Concurrent queues*
: These are queues that you can retrieve from GCD in order to execute asynchronous or synchronous tasks. Multiple concurrent queues can be executing multiple tasks in parallel, without breaking a sweat. No more thread management, yippee! Use the `dispatch_get_global_queue` function to retrieve the handle to a concurrent queue.

*Serial queues*
: These are queues that, no matter whether you submit synchronous or asynchronous tasks to them, will always execute their tasks in a first-in-first-out (FIFO) fashion, meaning that they can only execute one block object at a time. However, they do *not* run on the main thread and therefore are perfect for a series of tasks that have to be executed in strict order without blocking the main thread. Use the `dispatch_queue_create` function to create a serial queue.

There are two ways to submit tasks to dispatch queues:

- Block objects (see Recipe 7.1)
- C functions

Block objects are the best way of utilizing GCD and its enormous power. Some GCD functions have been extended to allow programmers to use C functions instead of block objects. However, the truth is that only a limited set of GCD functions allow programmers to use C functions, so please do read the recipe about block objects (Recipe 7.1) before proceeding any further.

C functions that have to be supplied to various GCD functions should be of type `dispatch_function_t`, which is defined as follows in the Apple libraries:

```
typedef void (*dispatch_function_t)(void *);
```

So if we want to create a function named, for instance, `myGCDFunction`, we would have to implement it in this way:

```
void myGCDFunction(void * paramContext){

    /* Do the work here */

}
```

The `paramContext` parameter refers to the context that GCD allows programmers to pass to their C functions when they dispatch tasks to them. We will learn about this shortly.

Block objects that get passed to GCD functions don't always follow the same structure. Some must accept parameters and some shouldn't, but none of the block objects submitted to GCD return a value.

At any moment during the lifetime of your application, you can use multiple dispatch queues at the same time. Your system has only one main queue, but you can create as many serial dispatch queues as you want (within reason, of course), for whatever functionality you require for your app. You can also retrieve multiple concurrent queues and dispatch your tasks to them. Tasks can be handed to dispatch queues in two forms: block objects or C functions, as was explained earlier.

Block objects are *packages* of code that usually appear in the form of methods in Objective-C. Block objects, together with Grand Central Dispatch (GCD), create a harmonious environment in which you can deliver high-performance multithreaded apps in iOS and Mac OS X. What's so special about block objects and GCD, you might ask? It's simple: no more threads! All you have to do is put your code in block objects and ask GCD to take care of the execution of that code for you.

Perhaps the most important difference between block objects and traditional function pointers is that block objects copy the values of local variables accessed inside the block objects and keep those copies for local use. If the values of those variables change outside the scope of the block object, you can be sure that the block object still keeps its own copy of the variable. We will discuss this in more detail soon.

Block objects in Objective-C are what the programming field calls *first-class objects*. This means you can build code dynamically, pass a block object to a method as a parameter, and return a block object from a method. All of these things make it easier to choose what you want to do at runtime and change the activity of a program. In particular, block objects can be run in individual threads by GCD. Being Objective-C objects, block objects can be treated like any other object.

Block objects are sometimes referred to as *closures*.

Constructing block objects is similar to constructing traditional C functions, as we will see in Recipe 7.1. Block objects can have return values and can accept parameters. Block objects can be defined inline or treated as a separate block of code, similar to a C function. When created inline, the scope of variables accessible to block objects is considerably different from when a block object is implemented as a separate block of code.

GCD works with block objects. When performing tasks with GCD, you can pass a block object whose code can get executed synchronously or asynchronously, depending on which methods you use in GCD. Thus, you can create a block object that is responsible for downloading a URL passed to it as a parameter. That single block object can then be used in various places in your app synchronously or asynchronously, depending on how you would like to run it. You don't have to make the block object synchronous or asynchronous per se; you will simply call it with synchronous or asynchronous GCD methods and the block object will *just work*.

Block objects are quite new to programmers writing iOS and OS X apps. In fact, block objects are not as popular as threads yet, perhaps because their syntax is a bit different from pure Objective-C methods and more complicated. Nonetheless, block objects are enormously powerful, and Apple is making a big push toward incorporating them into Apple libraries. You can already see these additions in classes such as `NSMutableArray`, where programmers can sort the array using a block object.

This chapter is dedicated entirely to constructing and using block objects in iOS and Mac OS X apps, using GCD for dispatching tasks to the operating system, threads and timers. I would like to stress that the only way to get used to block objects' syntax is to write a few of them for yourself. Have a look at the sample code in this chapter and try implementing your own block objects.

Here, you will learn the basics of block objects, followed by some more advanced subjects, such as Grand Central Dispatch, Threads, Timers, Operations, and Operation Queues. You will understand everything you need to know about block objects before moving to the Grand Central Dispatch material. From my experience, the best way to learn block objects is through examples, so you will see a lot of them in this chapter. Make sure you try the examples for yourself in Xcode to really *get* the syntax of block objects.

Operations can be configured to run a block of code synchronously or asynchronously. You can manage operations manually or place them on *operation queues*, which facilitate concurrency so that you do not need to think about the underlying thread management. In this chapter, you will see how to use operations and operation queues, as well as basic threads and timers, to synchronously and asynchronously execute tasks in applications.

Cocoa provides three different types of operations:

*Block operations*
: These facilitate the execution of one or more block objects.

*Invocation operations*
: These allow you to invoke a method in another, currently existing object.

*Plain operations*
: These are plain operation classes that need to be subclassed. The code to be executed will be written inside the `main` method of the operation object.

Operations, as mentioned before, can be managed with operation queues, which have the data type `NSOperationQueue`. After instantiating any of the aforementioned operation types (block, invocation, or plain operation), you can add them to an operation queue and have the queue manage the operation.

An operation object can have dependencies on other operation objects and be instructed to wait for the completion of one or more operations before executing the task associated with it. Unless you add a dependency, you have no control over the order in which operations run. For instance, adding them to a queue in a certain order does not guarantee that they will execute in that order, despite the use of the term *queue*.

There are a few important things to bear in mind while working with operation queues and operations:

- Operations, by default, run on the thread that starts them, using their `start` instance method. If you want the operations to work asynchronously, you will have to use either an operation queue or a subclass `NSOperation` and detach a new thread on the `main` instance method of the operation.
- An operation can wait for the execution of another operation to finish before it starts itself. Be careful not to create interdependent operations, a common mistake known as a *deadlock*. In other words, do not tell operation A to depend on operation B if B already depends on A; this will cause both to wait forever, taking up memory and possibly hanging your application.

- Operations can be cancelled. So, if you have subclassed `NSOperation` to create custom operation objects, you have to make sure to use the `isCancelled` instance method to check whether the operation has been cancelled before executing the task associated with the operation. For instance, if your operation's task is to check for the availability of an Internet connection every 20 seconds, it must call the `isCancelled` instance method at the beginning of each run to make sure it has not been cancelled before attempting to check for an Internet connection again. If the operation takes more than a few seconds (such as when you download a file), you should also check `isCancelled` periodically while running the task.
- Operation objects are key-value observing (KVO) compliant on various key paths such as `isFinished`, `isReady`, and `isExecuting`. We will be discussing Key Value Coding and Key Value Observing in a later chapter.
- If you plan to subclass `NSOperation` and provide a custom implementation for the operation, you must create your own autorelease pool in the `main` method of the operation, which gets called from the `start` method. We will discuss this in detail later in this chapter.
- Always keep a reference to the operation objects you create. The concurrent nature of operation queues might make it impossible for you to retrieve a reference to an operation after it has been added to the queue.

Threads and timers are objects, subclassing `NSObject`. Spawning a thread requires more work than creating timers, and setting up a thread loop itself is more difficult than simply listening for a timer firing on a selector. When an application runs under iOS, the operating system creates at least one thread for that application, called the main thread. Every thread and timer must be added to a run loop. A run loop, as its name implies, is a loop during which different events can occur, such as a timer firing or a thread running. Discussion of run loops is beyond the scope of this chapter, but we will refer to them here and there in recipes.

Think of a run loop as a kind of loop that has a starting point, a condition for finishing, and a series of events to process during its lifetime. A thread or timer is attached to a `run` loop and in fact requires a run loop to function.

The main thread of an application is the thread that handles the UI events. If you perform a long-running task on the main thread, you will notice that the UI of your application will become unresponsive or slow to respond. To avoid this, you can create separate threads and/or timers, each of which performs its own task (even if it is a long-running task) but will not block the main thread.

# 7.1. Constructing Block Objects

## Problem

You want to be able to write your own block objects or use block objects with iOS SDK classes.

## Solution

You just need to understand the basic differences between the syntax of block objects and classic C functions. These differences are explained in the Discussion section.

## Discussion

Block objects can either be inline or coded as independent blocks of code. Let's start with the latter type. Suppose you have a method in Objective-C that accepts two integer values of type `NSInteger` and returns the difference of the two values, by subtracting one from the other, as an `NSInteger`:

```
- (NSInteger) subtract:(NSInteger)paramValue
                  from:(NSInteger)paramFrom{

    return paramFrom - paramValue;

}
```

That was very simple, wasn't it? Now let's translate this Objective-C code to a pure C function that provides the same functionality to get one step closer to learning the syntax of block objects:

```
NSInteger subtract(NSInteger paramValue, NSInteger paramFrom){

    return paramFrom - paramValue;

}
```

You can see that the C function is quite different in syntax from its Objective-C counterpart. Now let's have a look at how we could code the same function as a block object:

```
NSInteger (^subtract)(NSInteger, NSInteger) = ^(NSInteger paramValue,
                                                NSInteger paramFrom){

    return paramFrom - paramValue;

};
```

Before I go into details about the syntax of block objects, let me show you a few more examples. Suppose we have a function in C that takes a parameter of type `NSUInteger` (an unsigned integer) and returns it as a string of type NSString. Here is how we implement this in C:

```
NSString* intToString (NSUInteger paramInteger){

    return [NSString stringWithFormat:@"%lu",
            (unsigned long)paramInteger];

}
```

To learn about formatting strings with system-independent format specifiers in Objective-C, please refer to the String Programming Guide in the iOS Developer Library (*http://bit.ly/1bHamO2*) on Apple's website.

The block object equivalent of this C function is shown in Example 7-1.

*Example 7-1. Example block object defined as function*

```
NSString* (^intToString)(NSUInteger) = ^(NSUInteger paramInteger){

    NSString *result = [NSString stringWithFormat:@"%lu",
                        (unsigned long)paramInteger];

    return result;

};
```

The simplest form of an independent block object would be a block object that returns void and does not take in any parameters:

```
void (^simpleBlock)(void) = ^{
    /* Implement the block object here */
};
```

Block objects can be invoked in the exact same way as C functions. If they have any parameters, you pass those as you would for a C function, and any return value can be retrieved exactly as you would retrieve a C function's return value. Here is an example:

```
NSString* (^intToString)(NSUInteger) = ^(NSUInteger paramInteger){

    NSString *result = [NSString stringWithFormat:@"%lu",
                        (unsigned long)paramInteger];

    return result;

};

- (void) callIntToString{
```

```
        NSString *string = intToString(10);
        NSLog(@"string = %@", string);

    }
```

The `callIntToString` Objective-C method is calling the `intToString` block object by passing the value 10 as the only parameter to this block object and placing the return value of this block object in the `string` local variable.

Now that we know how to write block objects as independent blocks of code, let's have a look at passing block objects as parameters to Objective-C methods. We will have to think a bit abstractly to understand the goal of the following example.

Suppose we have an Objective-C method that accepts an integer and performs some kind of transformation on it, which may change depending on what else is happening in the program. We know that we'll have an integer as input and a string as output, but we'll leave the exact transformation up to a block object that can be different each time the method runs. This method, therefore, will accept as parameters both the integer to be transformed and the block that will transform it.

For the block object, we'll use the same `intToString` block object that we implemented earlier in Example 7-1. Now we need an Objective-C method that will accept an unsigned integer parameter and a block object as its parameter. The unsigned integer parameter is easy, but how do we tell the method that it has to accept a block object *of the same type* as the `intToString` block object? First we `typedef` the signature of the `intToString` block object, which tells the compiler what parameters the block object should accept:

```
typedef NSString* (^IntToStringConverter)(NSUInteger paramInteger);
```

This `typedef` just tells the compiler that block objects that accept an integer parameter and return a string can simply be represented by an identifier named `IntToStringConverter`. Now let's go ahead and write the Objective-C method that accepts both an integer and a block object of type `IntToStringConverter`:

```
- (NSString *) convertIntToString:(NSUInteger)paramInteger
               usingBlockObject:(IntToStringConverter)paramBlockObject{

    return paramBlockObject(paramInteger);

}
```

All we have to do now is call the `convertIntToString:` method with the block object of choice (Example 7-2).

*Example 7-2. Calling the block object in another method*

```
- (void) doTheConversion{

    NSString *result = [self convertIntToString:123
```

```
                                usingBlockObject:intToString];

    NSLog(@"result = %@", result);

}
```

Now that we know something about independent block objects, let's turn to inline block objects. In the `doTheConversion` method we just saw, we passed the `intToString` block object as the parameter to the `convertIntToString:usingBlockObject:` method. What if we didn't have a block object ready to be passed to this method? Well, that wouldn't be a problem. As mentioned before, block objects are first-class functions and can be constructed at runtime. Let's have a look at an alternative implementation of the `doTheConversion` method (Example 7-3).

*Example 7-3. Example block object defined as a function*

```
- (void) doTheConversion{

    IntToStringConverter inlineConverter = ^(NSUInteger paramInteger){
        NSString *result = [NSString stringWithFormat:@"%lu",
                            (unsigned long)paramInteger];
        return result;
    };

    NSString *result = [self convertIntToString:123
                               usingBlockObject:inlineConverter];

    NSLog(@"result = %@", result);
```

Compare Example 7-3 to Example 7-1. I have removed the initial code that provided the block object's signature, which consisted of a name and argument, `(^intToString)(NSUInteger)`. I left the rest of the block object intact; it is now an anonymous object. But this doesn't mean I have no way to refer to the block object. I assign it using an equals sign to a type and a name: `IntToStringConverter inlineConverter`. Now I can use the data type to enforce proper use in methods and use the name to actually pass the block object.

In addition to constructing block objects inline as just shown, we can construct a block object *while* passing it as a parameter:

```
- (void) doTheConversion{

    NSString *result =
    [self convertIntToString:123
            usingBlockObject:^NSString *(NSUInteger paramInteger) {

                NSString *result = [NSString stringWithFormat:@"%lu",
                                    (unsigned long)paramInteger];
                return result;
```

```
            }];

        NSLog(@"result = %@", result);

    }
```

Compare this example with Example 7-2. Both methods use a block object through the `usingBlockObject` syntax. But whereas the earlier version referred to a previously declared block object by name (`intToString`), this one simply creates a block object on the fly. In this code, we constructed an inline block object that gets passed to the `convertIntToString:usingBlockObject:` method as the second parameter.

# 7.2. Accessing Variables in Block Objects

## Problem

You want to understand the difference between accessing variables in Objective-C methods and accessing those variables in block objects.

## Solution

Here is a brief summary of what you must know about variables in block objects:

- Local variables in block objects work exactly the same as in Objective-C methods.
- For inline block objects, local variables constitute not only variables defined within the block, but also the variables that have been defined in the method that implements that block object. (Examples will come shortly.)
- You *cannot* refer to `self` in independent block objects implemented in an Objective-C class. If you need to access `self`, you must pass that object to the block object as a parameter. We will see an example of this soon.
- You can refer to `self` in an inline block object only if `self` is present in the lexical scope inside which the block object is created.
- For inline block objects, local variables that are defined *inside* the block object's implementation can be read from and written to. In other words, the block object has read/write access to variables defined inside the block object's body.
- For inline block objects, variables local to the Objective-C method that implement that block can only be read from, not written to. There is an exception, though: a block object can write to such variables if they are defined with the `__block` storage type. We will see an example of this as well.
- Suppose you have an object of type `NSObject` and inside that object's implementation you are using a block object in conjunction with GCD. Inside this block object,

you will have read/write access to declared properties of that `NSObject` inside which your block is implemented.

- You can access declared properties of your `NSObject` inside independent block objects *only if* you use the setter and getter methods of these properties. You cannot access declared properties of an object using dot notation inside an independent block object.

## Discussion

Let's first see how we can use variables that are local to the implementation of two block objects. One is an inline block object and the other an independent block object:

```
void (^independentBlockObject)(void) = ^(void){

    NSInteger localInteger = 10;

    NSLog(@"local integer = %ld", (long)localInteger);

    localInteger = 20;

    NSLog(@"local integer = %ld", (long)localInteger);

};
```

Invoking this block object, the values we assigned are printed to the console window:

```
local integer = 10
local integer = 20
```

So far, so good. Now let's have a look at inline block objects and variables that are local to them:

```
- (void) simpleMethod{

    NSUInteger outsideVariable = 10;

    NSMutableArray *array = [[NSMutableArray alloc]
                             initWithObjects:@"obj1",
                             @"obj2", nil];

    [array sortUsingComparator:^NSComparisonResult(id obj1, id obj2) {
        NSUInteger insideVariable = 20;

        NSLog(@"Outside variable = %lu", (unsigned long)outsideVariable);
        NSLog(@"Inside variable = %lu", (unsigned long)insideVariable);

        /* Return value for our block object */
        return NSOrderedSame;
    }];
}
```

The `sortUsingComparator:` instance method of `NSMutableArray` attempts to sort a mutable array. The goal of this example code is just to demonstrate the use of local variables, so you don't have to know what this method actually does.

The block object can read and write its own `insideVariable` local variable. However, the block object has read-only access to the `outsideVariable` variable by default. In order to allow the block object to write to `outsideVariable`, we must prefix `outsideVariable` with the `__block` storage type:

```
- (void) simpleMethod{

    __block NSUInteger outsideVariable = 10;

    NSMutableArray *array = [[NSMutableArray alloc]
                             initWithObjects:@"obj1",
                             @"obj2", nil];


    [array sortUsingComparator:^NSComparisonResult(id obj1, id obj2) {

        NSUInteger insideVariable = 20;
        outsideVariable = 30;

        NSLog(@"Outside variable = %lu", (unsigned long)outsideVariable);
        NSLog(@"Inside variable = %lu", (unsigned long)insideVariable);

        /* Return value for our block object */
        return NSOrderedSame;

    }];

}
```

Accessing `self` in inline block objects is fine as long as `self` is defined in the lexical scope inside which the inline block object is created. For instance, in this example, the block object will be able to access `self`, since `simpleMethod` is an instance method of an Objective-C class:

```
- (void) simpleMethod{

    NSMutableArray *array = [[NSMutableArray alloc]
                             initWithObjects:@"obj1",
                             @"obj2", nil];

    [array sortUsingComparator:^NSComparisonResult(id obj1, id obj2) {

        NSLog(@"self = %@", self);

        /* Return value for our block object */
```

```
            return NSOrderedSame;

        }];

    }
```

You cannot, without a change in your block object's implementation, access `self` in an independent block object. Attempting to compile this code will give you a compile-time error:

```
void (^incorrectBlockObject)(void) = ^{
  NSLog(@"self = %@", self); /* self is undefined here */
};
```

If you want to access `self` in an independent block object, simply pass the object that `self` represents as a parameter to your block object:

```
void (^correctBlockObject)(id) = ^(id self){

  NSLog(@"self = %@", self);

};

- (void) callCorrectBlockObject{

  correctBlockObject(self);

}
```

You don't have to assign the name `self` to this parameter. You can simply call this parameter anything else. However, if you call this parameter `self`, you can simply grab your block object's code later and place it in an Objective-C method's implementation without having to change every instance of your variable's name to `self` for it to be understood by the compiler.

Let's have a look at declared properties and how block objects can access them. For inline block objects, you can use dot notation to read from or write to declared properties of `self`. For instance, let's say we have a declared property of type `NSString` called `stringProperty` in the class:

```
#import "AppDelegate.h"

@interface AppDelegate()
@property (nonatomic, copy) NSString *stringProperty;
@end

@implementation AppDelegate
```

Now we can simply access this property in an inline block object like so:

```
- (void) simpleMethod{

    NSMutableArray *array = [[NSMutableArray alloc]
                             initWithObjects:@"obj1",
                             @"obj2", nil];

    [array sortUsingComparator:^NSComparisonResult(id obj1, id obj2) {

        NSLog(@"self = %@", self);

        self.stringProperty = @"Block Objects";

        NSLog(@"String property = %@", self.stringProperty);

        /* Return value for our block object */
        return NSOrderedSame;

    }];

}
```

In an independent block object, however, you cannot use dot notation to read from or write to a declared property:

```
void (^incorrectBlockObject)(id) = ^(id self){

    NSLog(@"self = %@", self);

    /* Should use setter method instead of this */
    self.stringProperty = @"Block Objects"; /* Compile-time Error */

    /* Should use getter method instead of this */
    NSLog(@"self.stringProperty = %@",
          self.stringProperty); /* Compile-time Error */

};
```

Instead of dot notation in this scenario, use the getter and the setter methods of this property:

```
void (^correctBlockObject)(id) = ^(id self){

    NSLog(@"self = %@", self);

    /* This will work fine */
    [self setStringProperty:@"Block Objects"];

    /* This will work fine as well */
    NSLog(@"self.stringProperty = %@",
          [self stringProperty]);
};
```

When it comes to inline block objects, there is one *very* important rule that you have to remember: inline block objects copy the value for the variables in their lexical scope. If you don't understand what that means, don't worry. Let's have a look at an example:

```
typedef void (^BlockWithNoParams)(void);

- (void) scopeTest{

    NSUInteger integerValue = 10;

    BlockWithNoParams myBlock = ^{
        NSLog(@"Integer value inside the block = %lu",
              (unsigned long)integerValue);
    };

    integerValue = 20;

    /* Call the block here after changing the
     value of the integerValue variable */
    myBlock();

    NSLog(@"Integer value outside the block = %lu",
          (unsigned long)integerValue);

}
```

We are declaring an integer local variable and initially assigning the value of 10 to it. We then implement the block object, but *don't call the block object yet*. After the block object is *implemented*, we simply change the value of the local variable that the block object will later try to read when we call it. Right after changing the local variable's value to 20, we call the block object. You would expect the block object to print the value 20 for the variable, but it won't. It will print 10, as you can see here:

```
Integer value inside the block = 10
Integer value outside the block = 20
```

What's happening here is that the block object is keeping a read-only copy of the `integerValue` variable for itself right where the block is implemented. You might be thinking: why is the block object capturing a *read-only* value of the local variable `integerValue`? The answer is simple, and we've already learned it in this section. Unless prefixed with storage type `__block`, local variables in the lexical scope of a block object are just passed to the block object as read-only variables. Therefore, to change this behavior, we could change the implementation of the `scopeTest` method to prefix the `integerValue` variable with `__block` storage type, like so:

```
- (void) scopeTest{

    __block NSUInteger integerValue = 10;

    BlockWithNoParams myBlock = ^{
```

```
        NSLog(@"Integer value inside the block = %lu",
              (unsigned long)integerValue);
    };

    integerValue = 20;

    /* Call the block here after changing the
     value of the integerValue variable */
    myBlock();

    NSLog(@"Integer value outside the block = %lu",
          (unsigned long)integerValue);

}
```

Now if we get the results from the console window after the `scopeTest` method is called, we will see this:

```
Integer value inside the block = 20
Integer value outside the block = 20
```

This section should have given you sufficient information about using variables with block objects. I suggest that you write a few block objects and use variables inside them, assigning to them and reading from them, to get a better understanding of how block objects use variables. Keep coming back to this section if you forget the rules that govern variable access in block objects.

# 7.3. Invoking Block Objects

## Problem

You've learned how to construct block objects, and now you want to execute your block objects to get results.

## Solution

Execute your block objects the same way you execute a C function, as shown in the Discussion section.

## Discussion

We've seen examples of invoking block objects in Recipes 7.1 and 7.2. This section contains more concrete examples.

If you have an independent block object, you can simply invoke it just like you would invoke a C function:

```
void (^simpleBlock)(NSString *) = ^(NSString  *paramString){
    /* Implement the block object here and use the
```

```
        paramString parameter */
};

- (void) callSimpleBlock{

    simpleBlock(@"O'Reilly");

}
```

If you want to invoke an independent block object within another independent block object, follow the same instructions by invoking the new block object just as you would invoke a C method:

```
NSString *(^trimString)(NSString *) = ^(NSString *inputString){

    NSString *result = [inputString stringByTrimmingCharactersInSet:
                        [NSCharacterSet whitespaceCharacterSet]];
    return result;

};

NSString *(^trimWithOtherBlock)(NSString *) = ^(NSString *inputString){
    return trimString(inputString);
};

- (void) callTrimBlock{

    NSString *trimmedString = trimWithOtherBlock(@"   O'Reilly     ");
    NSLog(@"Trimmed string = %@", trimmedString);

}
```

In this example, go ahead and invoke the `callTrimBlock` Objective-C method:

```
[self callTrimBlock];
```

The `callTrimBlock` method will call the `trimWithOtherBlock` block object, and the `trimWithOtherBlock` block object will call the `trimString` block object in order to trim the given string. Trimming a string is easy and can be done in one line of code, but this example code shows how you can call block objects within block objects.

## See Also

Recipe 7.1; Recipe 7.2

# 7.4. Performing UI-Related Tasks with GCD

## Problem

You are using GCD for concurrency, and you would like to know the best way of working with UI-related APIs.

## Solution

Use the `dispatch_get_main_queue` function.

## Discussion

UI-related tasks have to be performed on the main thread, so the main queue is the only candidate for UI task execution in GCD. We can use the `dispatch_get_main_queue` function to get the handle to the main dispatch queue.

There are two ways of dispatching tasks to the main queue. Both are asynchronous, letting your program continue even when the task is not yet executed:

`dispatch_async` *function*
: Executes a block object on a dispatch queue.

`dispatch_async_f` *function*
: Executes a C function on a dispatch queue.

The `dispatch_sync` method *cannot* be called on the main queue because it will block the thread indefinitely and cause your application to deadlock. All tasks submitted to the main queue through GCD must be submitted asynchronously.

Let's have a look at using the `dispatch_async` function. It accepts two parameters:

*Dispatch queue handle*
: The dispatch queue on which the task has to be executed

*Block object*
: The block object to be sent to the dispatch queue for asynchronous execution

Here is an example. This code will display an alert in iOS to the user, using the main queue:

```
dispatch_queue_t mainQueue = dispatch_get_main_queue();

dispatch_async(mainQueue, ^(void) {

    [[[UIAlertView alloc] initWithTitle:@"GCD"
```

```
                              message:@"GCD is amazing!"
                             delegate:nil
                    cancelButtonTitle:@"OK"
                    otherButtonTitles:nil, nil] show];

});
```

As you've noticed, the `dispatch_async` GCD function has no parameters or return value. The block object that is submitted to this function must gather its own data in order to complete its task. In the code snippet that we just saw, the alert view has all the values that it needs to finish its task. However, this might not always be the case. In such instances, you must make sure the block object submitted to GCD has access in its scope to all the values that it requires.

Running this app in iOS Simulator, the user will get results similar to those shown in Figure 7-1.

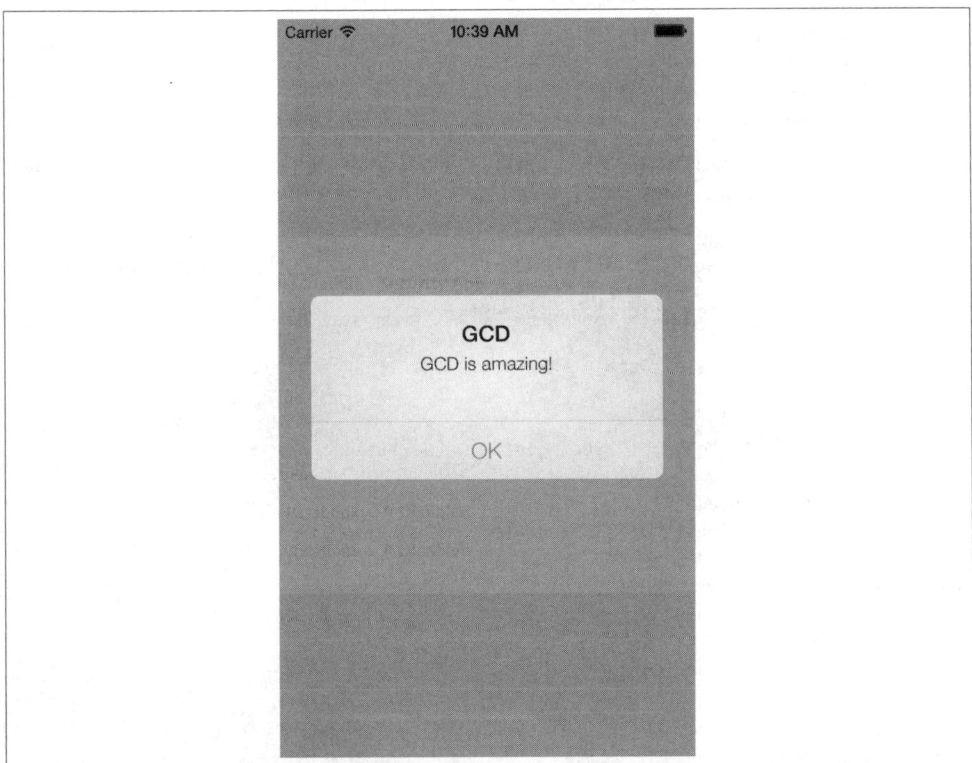


*Figure 7-1. An alert displayed using asynchronous GCD calls*

This might not seem very impressive, if you think about it. So what makes the main queue truly interesting? The answer is simple: when you are getting the maximum performance from GCD to do some heavy calculation on concurrent or serial threads, you might want to display the results to your user or move a component on the screen. For that, you *must* use the main queue, because it is UI-related work. The functions shown in this section are the *only* ways to get out of a serial or a concurrent queue while still utilizing GCD to update your UI, so you can imagine how important they are.

Instead of submitting a block object for execution on the main queue, you can submit a C function object. Submit all UI-related C functions for execution in GCD to the `dispatch_async_f` function. We can get the same results as we got in Figure 7-1, using C functions instead of block objects, with a few adjustments to the code.

As mentioned before, with the `dispatch_async_f` function, we can submit a pointer to an application-defined context, which can then be used by the C function that gets called. So let's create a structure that holds values such as an alert view's title and message, and a cancel button's title. When the app starts, we will put all the values in this structure and pass it to the C function to display. Here is how we define the structure:

```
typedef struct{
    char *title;
    char *message;
    char *cancelButtonTitle;
} AlertViewData;
```

Now let's go and implement a C function that we will later call with GCD. This C function should expect a parameter of type `void *`, which we will then typecast to `AlertViewData *`. In other words, we expect the caller of this function to pass us a reference to the data for the alert view, encapsulated inside the `AlertViewData` structure:

```
void displayAlertView(void *paramContext){

    AlertViewData *alertData = (AlertViewData *)paramContext;

    NSString *title =
    [NSString stringWithUTF8String:alertData->title];

    NSString *message =
    [NSString stringWithUTF8String:alertData->message];

    NSString *cancelButtonTitle =
    [NSString stringWithUTF8String:alertData->cancelButtonTitle];

    [[[UIAlertView alloc] initWithTitle:title
                                message:message
                               delegate:nil
                      cancelButtonTitle:cancelButtonTitle
                      otherButtonTitles:nil, nil] show];
```

```
        free(alertData);
}
```

The reason we are freeing the context passed to us in here instead of in the caller is that the caller is going to execute this C function asynchronously and cannot know when the C function will finish executing. Therefore, the caller has to malloc enough space for the AlertViewData context, and the displayAlertView C function has to free that space.

And now let's call the displayAlertView function on the main queue and pass the context (the structure that holds the alert view's data) to it:

```
- (BOOL)            application:(UIApplication *)application
  didFinishLaunchingWithOptions:(NSDictionary *)launchOptions{

    dispatch_queue_t mainQueue = dispatch_get_main_queue();

    AlertViewData *context = (AlertViewData *)
    malloc(sizeof(AlertViewData));

    if (context != NULL){
        context->title = "GCD";
        context->message = "GCD is amazing.";
        context->cancelButtonTitle = "OK";

        dispatch_async_f(mainQueue,
                         (void *)context,
                         displayAlertView);
    }

    self.window = [[UIWindow alloc] initWithFrame:
                   [[UIScreen mainScreen] bounds]];

    self.window.backgroundColor = [UIColor whiteColor];
    [self.window makeKeyAndVisible];
    return YES;
}
```

If you invoke the currentThread class method of the NSThread class, you will find out that the block objects or the C functions you dispatch to the main queue are indeed running on the main thread:

```
- (BOOL)            application:(UIApplication *)application
  didFinishLaunchingWithOptions:(NSDictionary *)launchOptions{

    dispatch_queue_t mainQueue = dispatch_get_main_queue();

    dispatch_async(mainQueue, ^(void) {
```

```
        NSLog(@"Current thread = %@", [NSThread currentThread]);
        NSLog(@"Main thread = %@", [NSThread mainThread]);
    });

    self.window = [[UIWindow alloc] initWithFrame:
                   [[UIScreen mainScreen] bounds]];
    self.window.backgroundColor = [UIColor whiteColor];
    [self.window makeKeyAndVisible];
    return YES;
}
```

The output of this code would be similar to that shown here:

```
Current thread = <NSThread: 0x4b0e4e0>{name = (null), num = 1}
Main thread = <NSThread: 0x4b0e4e0>{name = (null), num = 1}
```

Now that you know how to perform UI-related tasks using GCD, it is time we moved to other subjects, such as performing tasks in parallel using concurrent queues (see Recipes 7.5 and 7.6) and mixing the code with UI-related code if need be.

## 7.5. Executing Non-UI Related Tasks Synchronously with GCD

### Problem

You want to perform synchronous tasks that do not involve any UI-related code.

### Solution

Use the `dispatch_sync` function.

### Discussion

There are times when you want to perform tasks that have nothing to do with the UI or that interact with the UI as well as doing other tasks that take up a lot of time. For instance, you might want to download an image and display it to the user after it is downloaded. The downloading process has absolutely nothing to do with the UI.

For any task that doesn't involve the UI, you can use global concurrent queues in GCD. These allow either synchronous or asynchronous execution. But synchronous execution does *not* mean your program waits for the code to finish before continuing. It simply means that the concurrent queue will wait until your task has finished before it continues to the next block of code on the queue. When you put a block object on a concurrent queue, your own program *always* continues right away without waiting for the queue to execute the code. This is because concurrent queues, as their name implies, run their code on threads other than the main thread. (There is one exception to this: when a task is submitted to a concurrent or a serial queue using the `dispatch_sync` function, iOS will, if possible, run the task on the *current* thread, which *might* be the main thread, depending on where the code path is at the moment. This is an optimization that has been programmed on GCD, as we shall soon see.)

If you submit a task to a concurrent queue synchronously, and at the same time submit another synchronous task to *another* concurrent queue, these two synchronous tasks will run asynchronously in relation to each other because they are running two *different concurrent queues*. It's important to understand this because sometimes, as we'll see, you want to make sure task A finishes before task B starts. To ensure that, submit them synchronously to the *same* queue.

You can perform synchronous tasks on a dispatch queue using the `dispatch_sync` function. All you have to do is provide it with the handle of the queue that has to run the task and a block of code to execute on that queue.

Let's look at an example. It prints the integers 1 to 1,000 twice, one complete sequence after the other, without blocking the main thread. We can create a block object that does the counting for us and synchronously call the same block object twice:

```
void (^printFrom1To1000)(void) = ^{

    NSUInteger counter = 0;
    for (counter = 1;
         counter <= 1000;
         counter++){

        NSLog(@"Counter = %lu - Thread = %@",
              (unsigned long)counter,
              [NSThread currentThread]);

    }

};
```

Now let's go and invoke this block object using GCD:

```
- (BOOL)            application:(UIApplication *)application
    didFinishLaunchingWithOptions:(NSDictionary *)launchOptions{

    dispatch_queue_t concurrentQueue =
    dispatch_get_global_queue(DISPATCH_QUEUE_PRIORITY_DEFAULT, 0);

    dispatch_sync(concurrentQueue, printFrom1To1000);
    dispatch_sync(concurrentQueue, printFrom1To1000);

    // Override point for customization after application launch.
    [self.window makeKeyAndVisible];
    return YES;
}
```

If you run this code, you might notice the counting taking place on the main thread, even though you've asked a concurrent queue to execute the task. It turns out this is an optimization by GCD. The `dispatch_sync` function will use the current thread—the thread you're using when you dispatch the task—whenever possible, as a part of an optimization that has been programmed into GCD. Here is what Apple says about it:

> As an optimization, this function invokes the block on the current thread when possible.
>
> —Grand Central Dispatch (GCD) Reference

To execute a C function instead of a block object, synchronously, on a dispatch queue, use the `dispatch_sync_f` function. Let's simply translate the code we've written for the `printFrom1To1000` block object to its equivalent C function, like so:

```
void printFrom1To1000(void *paramContext){

    NSUInteger counter = 0;
    for (counter = 1;
         counter <= 1000;
         counter++){

        NSLog(@"Counter = %lu - Thread = %@",
              (unsigned long)counter,
              [NSThread currentThread]);

    }

}
```

And now we can use the `dispatch_sync_f` function to execute the `printFrom1To1000` function on a concurrent queue, as demonstrated here:

```
- (BOOL)            application:(UIApplication *)application
  didFinishLaunchingWithOptions:(NSDictionary *)launchOptions{

    dispatch_queue_t concurrentQueue =
    dispatch_get_global_queue(DISPATCH_QUEUE_PRIORITY_DEFAULT, 0);

    dispatch_sync_f(concurrentQueue,
                    NULL,
                    printFrom1To1000);

    dispatch_sync_f(concurrentQueue,
                    NULL,
                    printFrom1To1000);

    self.window = [[UIWindow alloc]
                   initWithFrame:[[UIScreen mainScreen] bounds]];
    self.window.backgroundColor = [UIColor whiteColor];
    [self.window makeKeyAndVisible];
    return YES;
}
```

The first parameter of the `dispatch_get_global_queue` function specifies the priority of the concurrent queue that GCD has to retrieve for the programmer. The higher the priority, the more CPU timeslices will be provided to the code getting executed on that queue. You can use any of these values for the first parameter to the `dispatch_get_glob al_queue` function:

`DISPATCH_QUEUE_PRIORITY_LOW`
: Fewer timeslices will be applied to your task than normal tasks.

`DISPATCH_QUEUE_PRIORITY_DEFAULT`
: The default system priority for code execution will be applied to your task.

`DISPATCH_QUEUE_PRIORITY_HIGH`
: More timeslices will be applied to your task than normal tasks.

The second parameter of the `dispatch_get_global_queue` function is reserved, and you should always pass the value 0 to it.

In this section you saw how you can dispatch tasks to concurrent queues for synchronous execution. The next section shows asynchronous execution on concurrent queues, while Recipe 7.10 will show you how to execute tasks synchronously and asynchronously on serial queues that you create for your applications.

### See Also

Recipe 7.6; Recipe 7.10

## 7.6. Executing Non-UI Related Tasks Asynchronously with GCD

### Problem

You want to be able to execute non-UI related tasks asynchronously, with the help of GCD.

### Solution

This is where GCD can show its true power: executing blocks of code asynchronously on the main, serial, or concurrent queues. I promise that, by the end of this section, you will be completely convinced that GCD is the future of multithread applications, completely replacing threads in modern apps.

In order to execute asynchronous tasks on a dispatch queue, you must use one of these functions:

`dispatch_async`
: Submits a block object to a dispatch queue (both specified by parameters) for asynchronous execution.

`dispatch_async_f`
: Submits a C function to a dispatch queue, along with a context reference (all three specified by parameters), for asynchronous execution.

## Discussion

Let's have a look at a real example. We'll write an iOS app that is able to download an image from a URL on the Internet. After the download is finished, the app should display the image to the user. Here is the plan and how we will use what we've learned so far about GCD in order to accomplish it:

1. We are going to launch a block object asynchronously on a concurrent queue.
2. Once in this block, we will launch another block object *synchronously*, using the `dispatch_sync` function, to download the image from a URL. We do this because we want the rest of the code in this concurrent queue to wait until the image is downloaded. Therefore, we are only making the concurrent queue wait; not the rest of the queues. Synchronously downloading a URL from an asynchronous code block holds up just the queue running the synchronous function, not the main thread. The whole operation is still asynchronous when we look at it from the main thread's perspective. All we care about is that we are not blocking the main thread while downloading the image.
3. Right after the image is downloaded, we will synchronously execute a block object on the *main queue* (see Recipe 7.4) in order to display the image to the user on the UI.

The skeleton for the plan is as simple as this:

```
- (void) viewDidAppear:(BOOL)animated{
    [super viewDidAppear:animated];

    dispatch_queue_t concurrentQueue =
    dispatch_get_global_queue(DISPATCH_QUEUE_PRIORITY_DEFAULT, 0);

    dispatch_async(concurrentQueue, ^{

        __block UIImage *image = nil;

        dispatch_sync(concurrentQueue, ^{
            /* Download the image here */
        });
```

```
            dispatch_sync(dispatch_get_main_queue(), ^{
                /* Show the image to the user here on the main queue */
            });

        });

    }
```

The second `dispatch_sync` call, which displays the image, will be executed on the queue after the first synchronous call, which downloads the image. That's exactly what we want, because we *have* to wait for the image to be fully downloaded before we can display it to the user. So after the image is downloaded, we execute the second block object, but this time on the main queue.

Let's download the image and display it to the user now. We will do this in the `viewDidAppear:` instance method of a view controller displayed in an iPhone app:

```
- (void) viewDidAppear:(BOOL)paramAnimated{

    [super viewDidAppear:paramAnimated];

    dispatch_queue_t concurrentQueue =
    dispatch_get_global_queue(DISPATCH_QUEUE_PRIORITY_DEFAULT, 0);

    dispatch_async(concurrentQueue, ^{

        __block UIImage *image = nil;

        dispatch_sync(concurrentQueue, ^{
            /* Download the image here */

            /* iPad's image from Apple's website. Wrap it into two
             lines as the URL is too long to fit into one line */
            NSString *urlAsString =
            @"http://images.apple.com/mobileme/features"\
            "/images/ipad_findyouripad_20100518.jpg";

            NSURL *url = [NSURL URLWithString:urlAsString];

            NSURLRequest *urlRequest = [NSURLRequest requestWithURL:url];

            NSError *downloadError = nil;
            NSData *imageData = [NSURLConnection
                                 sendSynchronousRequest:urlRequest
                                 returningResponse:nil
                                 error:&downloadError];

            if (downloadError == nil &&
                imageData != nil){

                image = [UIImage imageWithData:imageData];
```

```
                /* We have the image. We can use it now */

            }
            else if (downloadError != nil){
                NSLog(@"Error happened = %@", downloadError);
            } else {
                NSLog(@"No data could get downloaded from the URL.");
            }

        });

        dispatch_sync(dispatch_get_main_queue(), ^{
            /* Show the image to the user here on the main queue*/

            if (image != nil){
                /* Create the image view here */
                UIImageView *imageView = [[UIImageView alloc]
                                          initWithFrame:self.view.bounds];

                /* Set the image */
                [imageView setImage:image];

                /* Make sure the image is not scaled incorrectly */
                [imageView setContentMode:UIViewContentModeScaleAspectFit];

                /* Add the image to this view controller's view */
                [self.view addSubview:imageView];

            } else {
                NSLog(@"Image isn't downloaded. Nothing to display.");
            }

        });

    });

}
```

As you can see in Figure 7-2, we have successfully downloaded the image and also created an image view to display the image to the user on the UI.

Let's move on to another example. Let's say that we have an array of 10,000 random numbers that have been stored in a file on disk and we want to load this array into memory, sort the numbers in an ascending fashion (with the smallest number appearing first in the list), and then display the list to the user. The control used for the display depends on whether you are coding this for iOS (ideally, you'd use an instance of `UITableView`) or Mac OS X (`NSTableView` would be a good candidate). Since we don't have an array, why don't we create the array first, then load it, and finally display it?

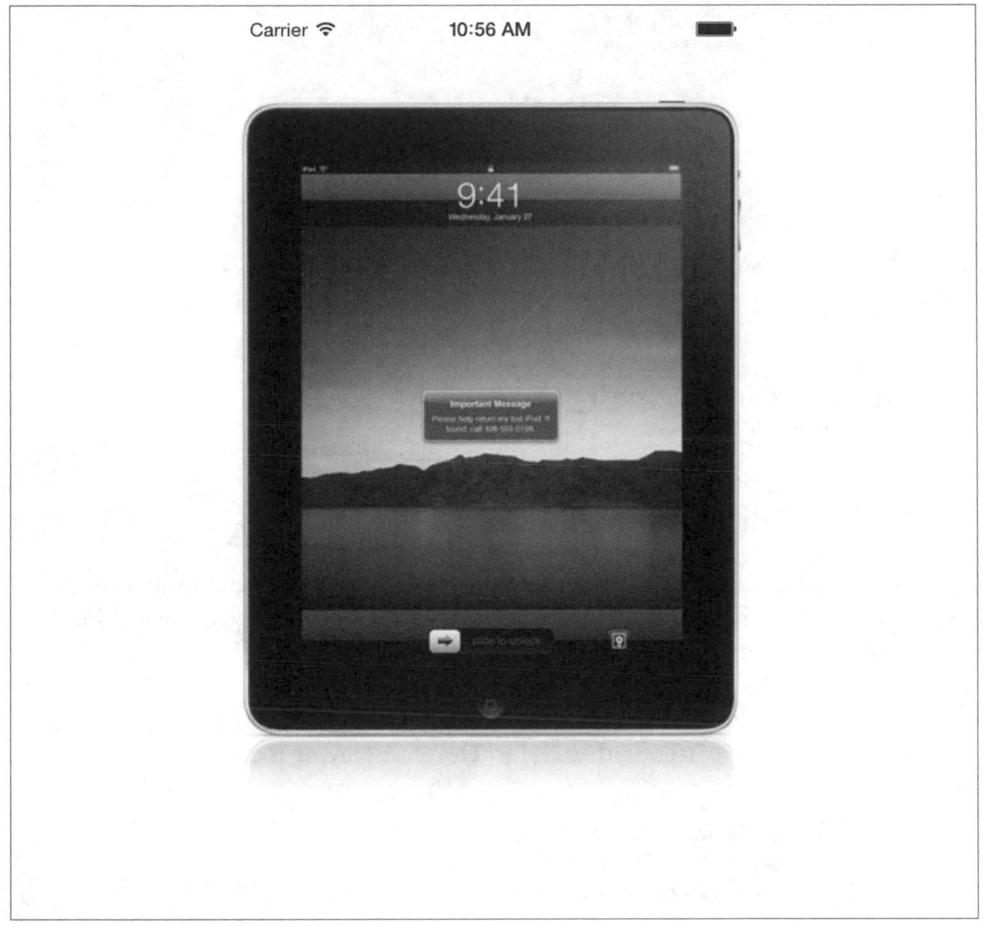


*Figure 7-2. Downloading and displaying images to users, using GCD*

Here are two methods that will help us find the location where we want to save the array of 10,000 random numbers on disk on the device:

```
- (NSString *) fileLocation{

    /* Get the document folder(s) */
    NSArray *folders =
    NSSearchPathForDirectoriesInDomains(NSDocumentDirectory,
                                        NSUserDomainMask,
                                        YES);

    /* Did we find anything? */
    if ([folders count] == 0){
        return nil;
    }
```

```
    /* Get the first folder */
    NSString *documentsFolder = folders[0];

    /* Append the filename to the end of the documents path */
    return [documentsFolder
            stringByAppendingPathComponent:@"list.txt"];

}

- (BOOL) hasFileAlreadyBeenCreated{

    BOOL result = NO;

    NSFileManager *fileManager = [[NSFileManager alloc] init];
    if ([fileManager fileExistsAtPath:[self fileLocation]]){
        result = YES;
    }

    return result;
}
```

Now the important part: we want to save an array of 10,000 random numbers to disk *if and only if* we have not created this array before on disk. If we have, we will load the array from disk immediately. If we have not created this array before on disk, we will first create it and then move on to loading it from disk. At the end, if the array was successfully read from disk, we will sort the array in an ascending fashion and finally display the results to the user on the UI. I will leave displaying the results to the user up to you:

```
- (void) viewDidAppear:(BOOL)paramAnimated{

    [super viewDidAppear:paramAnimated];

    dispatch_queue_t concurrentQueue =
    dispatch_get_global_queue(DISPATCH_QUEUE_PRIORITY_DEFAULT, 0);

    /* If we have not already saved an array of 10,000
     random numbers to the disk before, generate these numbers now
     and then save them to the disk in an array */
    dispatch_async(concurrentQueue, ^{

        NSUInteger numberOfValuesRequired = 10000;

        if ([self hasFileAlreadyBeenCreated] == NO){
            dispatch_sync(concurrentQueue, ^{

                NSMutableArray *arrayOfRandomNumbers =
                [[NSMutableArray alloc]
                 initWithCapacity:numberOfValuesRequired];

                NSUInteger counter = 0;
                for (counter = 0;
```

```
                 counter < numberOfValuesRequired;
                 counter++){
                unsigned int randomNumber =
                arc4random() % ((unsigned int)RAND_MAX + 1);

                [arrayOfRandomNumbers addObject:
                 [NSNumber numberWithUnsignedInt:randomNumber]];
            }

            /* Now let's write the array to disk */
            [arrayOfRandomNumbers writeToFile:[self fileLocation]
                                   atomically:YES];

        });
    }

    __block NSMutableArray *randomNumbers = nil;

    /* Read the numbers from disk and sort them in an
     ascending fashion */
    dispatch_sync(concurrentQueue, ^{

        /* If the file has now been created, we have to read it */
        if ([self hasFileAlreadyBeenCreated]){
            randomNumbers = [[NSMutableArray alloc]
                             initWithContentsOfFile:[self fileLocation]];

            /* Now sort the numbers */
            [randomNumbers sortUsingComparator:
             ^NSComparisonResult(id obj1, id obj2) {

                 NSNumber *number1 = (NSNumber *)obj1;
                 NSNumber *number2 = (NSNumber *)obj2;
                 return [number1 compare:number2];

             }];
        }
    });


    dispatch_async(dispatch_get_main_queue(), ^{
        if ([randomNumbers count] > 0){
            /* Refresh the UI here using the numbers in the
             randomNumbers array */
        }
    });

});

}
```

There is a lot more to GCD than synchronous and asynchronous block or function execution. In Recipe 7.9, you will learn how to group block objects together and prepare them for execution on a dispatch queue. I also suggest that you have a look at Recipes 7.7 and 7.8 to learn about other functionalities that GCD can provide to programmers.

### See Also

Recipe 7.4; Recipe 7.7; Recipe 7.8

## 7.7. Performing Tasks after a Delay with GCD

### Problem

You want to be able to execute code, but after a certain amount of delay, which you would like to specify using GCD.

### Solution

Use the `dispatch_after` and `dispatch_after_f` functions.

### Discussion

With Core Foundation, you can invoke a selector in an object after a given period of time, using the `performSelector:withObject:afterDelay:` method of the `NSObject` class. Here is an example:

```
- (void) printString:(NSString *)paramString{
    NSLog(@"%@", paramString);
}

- (BOOL)            application:(UIApplication *)application
  didFinishLaunchingWithOptions:(NSDictionary *)launchOptions{

    [self performSelector:@selector(printString:)
               withObject:@"Grand Central Dispatch"
               afterDelay:3.0];

    self.window = [[UIWindow alloc] initWithFrame:
                   [[UIScreen mainScreen] bounds]];

    // Override point for customization after application launch.
    self.window.backgroundColor = [UIColor whiteColor];
    [self.window makeKeyAndVisible];
    return YES;
}
```

In this example, we are asking the runtime to call the `printString:` method after three seconds of delay. We can do the same thing in GCD using the `dispatch_after` and `dispatch_after_f` functions, each of which is described here:

`dispatch_after`
: Dispatches a block object to a dispatch queue after a given period of time, specified in nanoseconds. These are the parameters that this function requires:

  *Delay in nanoseconds*
  : The number of nanoseconds GCD has to wait on a given dispatch queue (specified by the second parameter) before it executes the given block object (specified by the third parameter).

  *Dispatch queue*
  : The dispatch queue on which the block object (specified by the third parameter) has to be executed after the given delay (specified by the first parameter).

  *Block object*
  : The block object to be invoked after the specified number of nanoseconds on the given dispatch queue. This block object should have no return value and should accept no parameters (see Recipe 7.1).

`dispatch_after_f`
: Dispatches a C function to GCD for execution after a given period of time, specified in nanoseconds. This function accepts four parameters:

  *Delay in nanoseconds*
  : The number of nanoseconds GCD has to wait on a given dispatch queue (specified by the second parameter) before it executes the given function (specified by the fourth parameter).

  *Dispatch queue*
  : The dispatch queue on which the C function (specified by the fourth parameter) has to be executed after the given delay (specified by the first parameter).

  *Context*
  : The memory address of a value in the heap to be passed to the C function (for an example, see Recipe 7.4).

  *C function*
  : The address of the C function that has to be executed after a certain period of time (specified by the first parameter) on the given dispatch queue (specified by the second parameter).

Although the delays are in nanoseconds, it is up to iOS to decide the granularity of dispatch delay, and this delay might not be as precise as what you hope when you specify a value in nanoseconds.

Let's have a look at an example for `dispatch_after` first:

```
- (BOOL)            application:(UIApplication *)application
  didFinishLaunchingWithOptions:(NSDictionary *)launchOptions{

    double delayInSeconds = 2.0;

    dispatch_time_t delayInNanoSeconds =
    dispatch_time(DISPATCH_TIME_NOW, delayInSeconds * NSEC_PER_SEC);

    dispatch_queue_t concurrentQueue =
    dispatch_get_global_queue(DISPATCH_QUEUE_PRIORITY_DEFAULT, 0);

    dispatch_after(delayInNanoSeconds, concurrentQueue, ^(void){
        /* Perform your operations here */
    });

    self.window = [[UIWindow alloc] initWithFrame:
                   [[UIScreen mainScreen] bounds]];

    // Override point for customization after application launch.
    self.window.backgroundColor = [UIColor whiteColor];
    [self.window makeKeyAndVisible];
    return YES;
}
```

As you can see, the nanoseconds delay parameter for both the `dispatch_after` and `dispatch_after_f` functions has to be of type `dispatch_time_t`, which is an abstract representation of absolute time. To get the value for this parameter, you can use the `dispatch_time` function as demonstrated in this sample code. Here are the parameters that you can pass to the `dispatch_time` function:

*Base time*
: If this value was denoted with *B* and the delta parameter was denoted with *D*, the resulting time from this function would be equal to *B* + *D*. You can set this parameter's value to `DISPATCH_TIME_NOW` to denote *now* as the base time and then specify the delta from now using the delta parameter.

*Delta to add to base time*
: This parameter is the nanoseconds that will get added to the base time parameter to create the result of this function.

For example, to denote a time three seconds from now, you could write your code like so:

```
dispatch_time_t delay =
dispatch_time(DISPATCH_TIME_NOW, 3.0f * NSEC_PER_SEC);
```

Or to denote half a second from now:

```
dispatch_time_t delay =
dispatch_time(DISPATCH_TIME_NOW, (1.0 / 2.0f) * NSEC_PER_SEC);
```

Now let's have a look at how we can use the `dispatch_after_f` function:

```
void processSomething(void *paramContext){
    /* Do your processing here */
    NSLog(@"Processing...");
}

- (BOOL)            application:(UIApplication *)application
  didFinishLaunchingWithOptions:(NSDictionary *)launchOptions{

    double delayInSeconds = 2.0;

    dispatch_time_t delayInNanoSeconds =
    dispatch_time(DISPATCH_TIME_NOW, delayInSeconds * NSEC_PER_SEC);

    dispatch_queue_t concurrentQueue =
    dispatch_get_global_queue(DISPATCH_QUEUE_PRIORITY_DEFAULT, 0);

    dispatch_after_f(delayInNanoSeconds,
                     concurrentQueue,
                     NULL,
                     processSomething);

    self.window = [[UIWindow alloc] initWithFrame:
                   [[UIScreen mainScreen] bounds]];

    // Override point for customization after application launch.
    self.window.backgroundColor = [UIColor whiteColor];
    [self.window makeKeyAndVisible];
    return YES;
}
```

## See Also

Recipe 7.1; Recipe 7.4

# 7.8. Performing a Task Only Once with GCD

## Problem

You want to make sure a piece of code gets executed only once during the lifetime of your application, even if it gets called more than once from different places in your code (such as the initializer for a singleton).

## Solution

Use the dispatch_once function.

## Discussion

Allocating and initializing a singleton is one of the tasks that has to happen exactly once during the lifetime of an app. I am sure you know of other scenarios where you had to make sure a piece of code was executed only once during the lifetime of your application.

GCD lets you specify an identifier for a piece of code when you attempt to execute it. If GCD detects that this identifier has been passed to the framework before, it won't execute that block of code again. The function that allows you to do this is dispatch_once, which accepts two parameters:

*Token*
: A token of type dispatch_once_t that holds the token generated by GCD when the block of code is executed for the first time. If you want a piece of code to be executed at most once, you must specify the same token to this method whenever it is invoked in the app. We will see an example of this soon.

*Block object*
: The block object to get executed at most once. This block object returns no values and accepts no parameters.

dispatch_once always executes its task on the current queue being used by the code that issues the call, be it a serial queue, a concurrent queue, or the main queue.

Here is an example:

```
static dispatch_once_t onceToken;

void (^executedOnlyOnce)(void) = ^{

    static NSUInteger numberOfEntries = 0;
    numberOfEntries++;
    NSLog(@"Executed %lu time(s)", (unsigned long)numberOfEntries);

};


- (BOOL)            application:(UIApplication *)application
  didFinishLaunchingWithOptions:(NSDictionary *)launchOptions{

    dispatch_queue_t concurrentQueue =
    dispatch_get_global_queue(DISPATCH_QUEUE_PRIORITY_DEFAULT, 0);
```

```
    dispatch_once(&onceToken, ^{
        dispatch_async(concurrentQueue,
                       executedOnlyOnce);
    });

    dispatch_once(&onceToken, ^{
        dispatch_async(concurrentQueue,
                       executedOnlyOnce);
    });

    self.window = [[UIWindow alloc] initWithFrame:
                   [[UIScreen mainScreen] bounds]];

    self.window.backgroundColor = [UIColor whiteColor];
    [self.window makeKeyAndVisible];
    return YES;

}
```

As you can see, although we are attempting to invoke the `executedOnlyOnce` block object twice, using the `dispatch_once` function, in reality GCD is executing this block object only once, since the identifier passed to the `dispatch_once` function is the same both times.

Apple, in its Cocoa Fundamentals Guide (*http://bit.ly/18PYUvs*), shows programmers how to create a singleton. This source code is quite old and has *not yet been updated* to use GCD and Automatic Reference Counting. We can change this model to make use of GCD and the `dispatch_once` function in order to initialize a shared instance of an object, like so:

```
#import "MySingleton.h"

@implementation MySingleton

- (instancetype) sharedInstance{
    static MySingleton *SharedInstance = nil;
    static dispatch_once_t onceToken;
    dispatch_once(&onceToken, ^{
        SharedInstance = [MySingleton new];
    });
    return SharedInstance;
}
@end
```

## 7.9. Grouping Tasks Together with GCD

### Problem

You want to group blocks of code together and ensure that all of them get executed by GCD one by one, as dependencies of one another.

### Solution

Use the `dispatch_group_create` function to create groups in GCD.

### Discussion

GCD lets us create *groups*, which allow you to place your tasks in one place, run all of them, and get a notification at the end from GCD. This has many valuable applications. For instance, suppose you have a UI-based app and want to reload the components on your UI. You have a table view, a scroll view, and an image view. You want to reload the contents of these components using these methods:

```
- (void) reloadTableView{
    /* Reload the table view here */
    NSLog(@"%s", __FUNCTION__);
}

- (void) reloadScrollView{
    /* Do the work here */
    NSLog(@"%s", __FUNCTION__);
}

- (void) reloadImageView{
    /* Reload the image view here */
    NSLog(@"%s", __FUNCTION__);
}
```

At the moment these methods are empty, but you can put the relevant UI code in them later. Now we want to call these three methods, one after the other, and we want to know when GCD has finished calling these methods so that we can display a message to the user. For this, we should be using a group. You should know about three functions when working with groups in GCD:

`dispatch_group_create`
: Creates a group handle.

`dispatch_group_async`
: Submits a block of code for execution on a group. You must specify the dispatch queue on which the block of code has to be executed *as well as* the group to which this block of code belongs.

`dispatch_group_notify`
: Allows you to submit a block object that should be executed once all tasks added to the group for execution have finished their work. This function also allows you to specify the dispatch queue on which that block object has to be executed.

Let's have a look at an example. As explained, in the example we want to invoke the `reloadTableView`, `reloadScrollView`, and `reloadImageView` methods one after the other and then display a message to the user once we are done. We can utilize GCD's powerful grouping facilities in order to accomplish this:

```
- (BOOL)            application:(UIApplication *)application
  didFinishLaunchingWithOptions:(NSDictionary *)launchOptions{

    dispatch_group_t taskGroup =  dispatch_group_create();
    dispatch_queue_t mainQueue =  dispatch_get_main_queue();

    /* Reload the table view on the main queue */
    dispatch_group_async(taskGroup, mainQueue, ^{
        [self reloadTableView];
    });

    /* Reload the scroll view on the main queue */
    dispatch_group_async(taskGroup, mainQueue, ^{
        [self reloadScrollView];
    });

    /* Reload the image view on the main queue */
    dispatch_group_async(taskGroup, mainQueue, ^{
        [self reloadImageView];
    });

    /* At the end when we are done, dispatch the following block */
    dispatch_group_notify(taskGroup, mainQueue, ^{
        /* Do some processing here */
        [[[UIAlertView alloc] initWithTitle:@"Finished"
                                    message:@"All tasks are finished"
                                   delegate:nil
                          cancelButtonTitle:@"OK"
                          otherButtonTitles:nil, nil] show];

    });

    self.window = [[UIWindow alloc] initWithFrame:
                   [[UIScreen mainScreen] bounds]];

    self.window.backgroundColor = [UIColor whiteColor];
    [self.window makeKeyAndVisible];
    return YES;
}
```

In addition to dispatch_group_async, you can also dispatch asynchronous C functions to a dispatch group using the dispatch_group_async_f function.

GCDAppDelegate is simply the name of the class from which this example is taken. We have to use this class name in order to typecast a context object so that the compiler will understand the commands.

Like so:

```
void reloadAllComponents(void *context){

    AppDelegate *self = (__bridge AppDelegate *)context;

    [self reloadTableView];
    [self reloadScrollView];
    [self reloadImageView];

}

- (BOOL)              application:(UIApplication *)application
    didFinishLaunchingWithOptions:(NSDictionary *)launchOptions{

    dispatch_group_t taskGroup =  dispatch_group_create();
    dispatch_queue_t mainQueue =  dispatch_get_main_queue();

    dispatch_group_async_f(taskGroup,
                           mainQueue,
                           (__bridge void *)self,
                           reloadAllComponents);

    /* At the end when we are done, dispatch the following block */
    dispatch_group_notify(taskGroup, mainQueue, ^{
        /* Do some processing here */
        [[[UIAlertView alloc] initWithTitle:@"Finished"
                                    message:@"All tasks are finished"
                                   delegate:nil
                          cancelButtonTitle:@"OK"
                          otherButtonTitles:nil, nil] show];

    });

    self.window = [[UIWindow alloc] initWithFrame:
                   [[UIScreen mainScreen] bounds]];

    self.window.backgroundColor = [UIColor whiteColor];
    [self.window makeKeyAndVisible];
    return YES;
}
```

Since the `dispatch_group_async_f` function accepts a C function as the block of code to be executed, the C function must have a reference to `self` to be able to invoke instance methods of the current object in which the C function is implemented. That is the reason behind passing `self` as the context pointer in the `dispatch_group_async_f` function. For more information about contexts and C functions, please refer to Recipe 7.4.

Once all the given tasks are finished, the user will see a result similar to that shown in Figure 7-3.

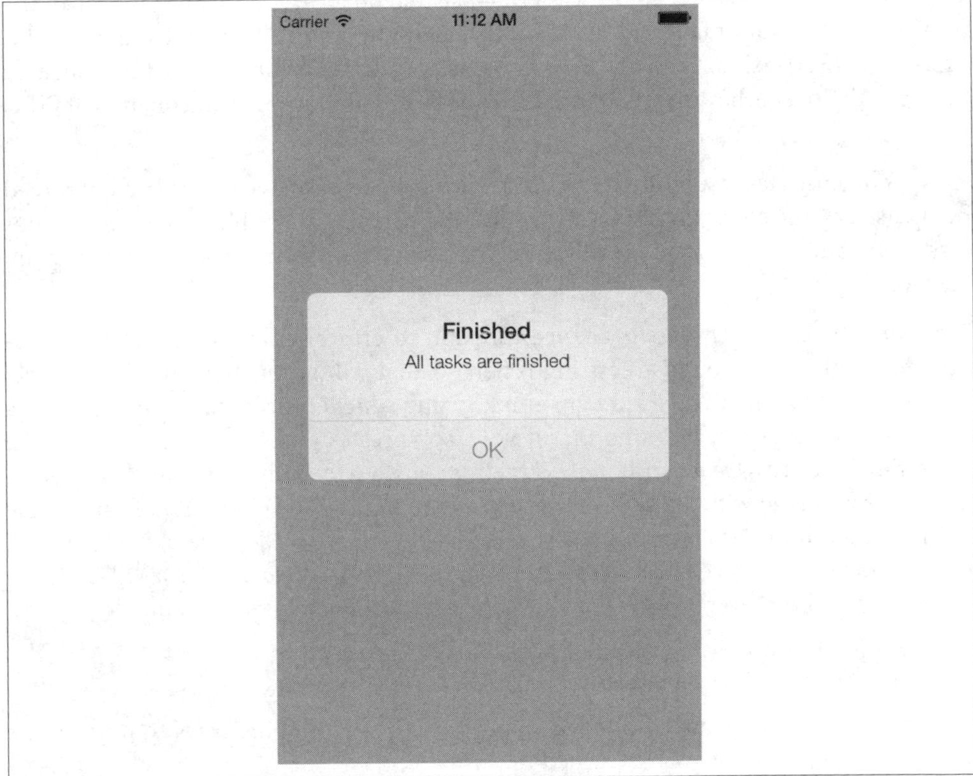


*Figure 7-3. Managing a group of tasks with GCD*

## See Also

Recipe 7.4

## 7.10. Constructing Your Own Dispatch Queues with GCD

### Problem

You want to create your own uniquely named dispatch queues.

### Solution

Use the `dispatch_queue_create` function.

### Discussion

With GCD, you can create your own serial dispatch queues (see Recipe 7.0, "Introduction" to read about serial queues). Serial dispatch queues run their tasks in a first-in-first-out (FIFO) fashion. The asynchronous tasks on serial queues will *not* be performed on the main thread, however, making serial queues highly desirable for concurrent FIFO tasks.

All synchronous tasks submitted to a serial queue will be executed on the current thread being used by the code that is submitting the task, whenever possible. But asynchronous tasks submitted to a serial queue will always be executed on a thread other than the main thread.

We'll use the `dispatch_queue_create` function to create serial queues. The first parameter in this function is a C string (`char *`) that will uniquely identify that serial queue in the *system*. The reason I am emphasizing *system* is because this identifier is a system-wide identifier, meaning that if your app creates a new serial queue with the identifier of *`serialQueue1`* and somebody else's app does the same, the results of creating a new serial queue with the same name are undefined by GCD. Because of this, Apple strongly recommends that you use a reverse DNS format for identifiers. Reverse DNS identifiers are usually constructed in this way: `com.`*`COMPANY. PRODUCT. IDENTIFIER`*. For instance, I could create two serial queues and assign these names to them:

```
com.pixolity.GCD.serialQueue1
com.pixolity.GCD.serialQueue2
```

After you've created your serial queue, you can start dispatching tasks to it using the various GCD functions you've learned in this book.

Would you like to see an example? I thought so!

```
- (BOOL)            application:(UIApplication *)application
  didFinishLaunchingWithOptions:(NSDictionary *)launchOptions{

    dispatch_queue_t firstSerialQueue =
    dispatch_queue_create("com.pixolity.GCD.serialQueue1", 0);

    dispatch_async(firstSerialQueue, ^{
```

```
        NSUInteger counter = 0;
        for (counter = 0;
             counter < 5;
             counter++){
            NSLog(@"First iteration, counter = %lu", (unsigned long)counter);
        }
    });

    dispatch_async(firstSerialQueue, ^{
        NSUInteger counter = 0;
        for (counter = 0;
             counter < 5;
             counter++){
            NSLog(@"Second iteration, counter = %lu", (unsigned long)counter);
        }
    });

    dispatch_async(firstSerialQueue, ^{
        NSUInteger counter = 0;
        for (counter = 0;
             counter < 5;
             counter++){
            NSLog(@"Third iteration, counter = %lu", (unsigned long)counter);
        }
    });

    self.window = [[UIWindow alloc] initWithFrame:
                   [[UIScreen mainScreen] bounds]];
    self.window.backgroundColor = [UIColor whiteColor];
    [self.window makeKeyAndVisible];
    return YES;
}
```

If you run this code and have a look at the output printed to the console window, you will see results similar to these:

```
First iteration, counter = 0
First iteration, counter = 1
First iteration, counter = 2
First iteration, counter = 3
First iteration, counter = 4
Second iteration, counter = 0
Second iteration, counter = 1
Second iteration, counter = 2
Second iteration, counter = 3
Second iteration, counter = 4
Third iteration, counter = 0
Third iteration, counter = 1
Third iteration, counter = 2
Third iteration, counter = 3
Third iteration, counter = 4
```

It's obvious that, although we dispatched the block objects asynchronously to the serial queue, the queue has executed their code in a FIFO fashion. We can modify the same sample code to make use of `dispatch_async_f` function instead of the `dispatch_async` function, like so:

```
void firstIteration(void *paramContext){

    NSUInteger counter = 0;
    for (counter = 0;
         counter < 5;
         counter++){
        NSLog(@"First iteration, counter = %lu", (unsigned long)counter);
    }
}

void secondIteration(void *paramContext){

    NSUInteger counter = 0;
    for (counter = 0;
         counter < 5;
         counter++){
        NSLog(@"Second iteration, counter = %lu", (unsigned long)counter);
    }
}

void thirdIteration(void *paramContext){

    NSUInteger counter = 0;
    for (counter = 0;
         counter < 5;
         counter++){
        NSLog(@"Third iteration, counter = %lu", (unsigned long)counter);
    }
}

- (BOOL)            application:(UIApplication *)application
  didFinishLaunchingWithOptions:(NSDictionary *)launchOptions{

    dispatch_queue_t firstSerialQueue =
    dispatch_queue_create("com.pixolity.GCD.serialQueue1", 0);

    dispatch_async_f(firstSerialQueue, NULL, firstIteration);
    dispatch_async_f(firstSerialQueue, NULL, secondIteration);
    dispatch_async_f(firstSerialQueue, NULL, thirdIteration);

    self.window = [[UIWindow alloc] initWithFrame:
                   [[UIScreen mainScreen] bounds]];
    self.window.backgroundColor = [UIColor whiteColor];
    [self.window makeKeyAndVisible];
    return YES;
}
```

# 7.11. Running Tasks Synchronously with Operations

## Problem

You want to run a series of tasks synchronously.

## Solution

Create operations and start them manually:

```
@interface AppDelegate ()
@property (nonatomic, strong) NSInvocationOperation *simpleOperation;
@end
```

The implementation of the application delegate is as follows:

```
- (void) simpleOperationEntry:(id)paramObject{

    NSLog(@"Parameter Object = %@", paramObject);
    NSLog(@"Main Thread = %@", [NSThread mainThread]);
    NSLog(@"Current Thread = %@", [NSThread currentThread]);

}

- (BOOL)            application:(UIApplication *)application
  didFinishLaunchingWithOptions:(NSDictionary *)launchOptions{

    NSNumber *simpleObject = [NSNumber numberWithInteger:123];

    self.simpleOperation = [[NSInvocationOperation alloc]
                            initWithTarget:self
                            selector:@selector(simpleOperationEntry:)
                            object:simpleObject];

    [self.simpleOperation start];

    self.window = [[UIWindow alloc] initWithFrame:
                   [[UIScreen mainScreen] bounds]];
    self.window.backgroundColor = [UIColor whiteColor];
    [self.window makeKeyAndVisible];
    return YES;
}
```

The output of this program (in the console window) will be similar to this:

```
Parameter Object = 123
Main Thread = <NSThread: 0x6810280>{name = (null), num = 1}
Current Thread = <NSThread: 0x6810280>{name = (null), num = 1}
```

As the name of this class implies (`NSInvocationOperation`), the main responsibility of an object of this type is to invoke a method in an object. This is the most straightforward way to invoke a method inside an object using operations.

## Discussion

An invocation operation, as described in this chapter's Introduction, is able to invoke a method inside an object. "What is so special about this?" you might ask. The invocation operation's power can be demonstrated when it is added to an operation queue. With an operation queue, an invocation operation can invoke a method in a target object asynchronously and in parallel to the thread that started the operation. If you have a look at the output printed to the console (in this recipe's Solution), you will notice that the current thread inside the method invoked by the invocation operation is the same as the main thread since the main thread in the `application:didFinishLaunchingWithOptions:` method started the operation using its `start` method. In Recipe 7.12, we will learn how to take advantage of operation queues to run tasks asynchronously.

In addition to invocation operations, you can use block or plain operations to perform tasks synchronously. Here is an example using a block operation to count numbers from 0 to 999 (inside the *.m* file of the application delegate):

```
@interface AppDelegate ()
@property (nonatomic, strong) NSBlockOperation *simpleOperation;
@end

@implementation AppDelegate
```

Here is the implementation of the application delegate (*.m* file):

```
- (BOOL)            application:(UIApplication *)application
  didFinishLaunchingWithOptions:(NSDictionary *)launchOptions{

    self.simpleOperation = [NSBlockOperation blockOperationWithBlock:^{
        NSLog(@"Main Thread = %@", [NSThread mainThread]);
        NSLog(@"Current Thread = %@", [NSThread currentThread]);
        NSUInteger counter = 0;
        for (counter = 0;
             counter < 1000;
             counter++){
            NSLog(@"Count = %lu", (unsigned long)counter);
        }
    }];

    /* Start the operation */
    [self.simpleOperation start];

    /* Print something out just to test if we have to wait
     for the block to execute its code or not */
    NSLog(@"Main thread is here");

    self.window = [[UIWindow alloc] initWithFrame:
                   [[UIScreen mainScreen] bounds]];
    self.window.backgroundColor = [UIColor whiteColor];
    [self.window makeKeyAndVisible];
```

```
    return YES;
}
```

If we run the application, we will see the values 0 to 999 printed out to the screen followed by the "Main thread is here" message, like this:

```
Main Thread = <NSThread: 0x6810280>{name = (null), num = 1}
Current Thread = <NSThread: 0x6810280>{name = (null), num = 1}
...
Count = 991
Count = 992
Count = 993
Count = 994
Count = 995
Count = 996
Count = 997
Count = 998
Count = 999
Main thread is here
```

This proves that since the block operation was started in the `application:didFinishLaunchingWithOptions:` method, which itself runs on the main thread, the code inside the block was also running on the main thread. The main point to take from the log messages is that the operation blocked the main thread and the main thread's code continued to be executed after the work for the block operation was done. This is a very bad programming practice. In fact, iOS developers must perform any trick and use any technique they know of to keep the main thread responsive so that it can do the key job of processing users' input. Here is what Apple has to say about this:

> You should be careful what work you perform from the main thread of your application. The main thread is where your application handles touch events and other user input. To ensure that your application is always responsive to the user, you should never use the main thread to perform long-running tasks or to perform tasks with a potentially unbounded end, such as tasks that access the network. Instead, you should always move those tasks onto background threads. The preferred way to do so is to wrap each task in an operation object and add it to an operation queue, but you can also create explicit threads yourself.

To read more about this subject, browse through the "Performance Tuning" document in the iOS Reference Library, available at this URL (*http://bit.ly/RGuYIJ*).

In addition to invocation and block operations, you can also subclass `NSOperation` and perform your task in that class. Before getting started, you must keep a few things in mind while subclassing `NSOperation`:

- If you are not planning on using an operation queue, you have to detach a new thread of your own in the `start` method of the operation. If you do not want to use an operation queue and you do not want your operation to run asynchronously from other operations that you start manually, you can simply call the `main` method of your operation inside the `start` method.

- Two important methods in an instance of `NSOperation` must be overridden by your own implementation of the operation: `isExecuting` and `isFinished`. These can be called from any other object. In these methods, you must return a thread-safe value that you can manipulate from inside the operation. As soon as your operation starts, you must, through KVO, inform any listeners that you are changing the values that these two methods return. We will see how this works in the example code.
- You must provide your own autorelease pool inside the `main` method of the operation in case your operation will be added to an operation queue at some point in the future. You must make sure your operations work in both ways: whether you start them manually or they get started by an operation queue.
- You must have an initialization method for your operations. There must be only one designated initializer method per operation. All other initializer methods, including the default `init` method of an operation, must call the designated initializer that has the greatest number of parameters. Other initializer methods must make sure they pass appropriate parameters (if any) to the designated initializer.

Here is the declaration of the operation object (*.h* file):

```
#import <Foundation/Foundation.h>

@interface CountingOperation : NSOperation

/* Designated Initializer */
- (instancetype) initWithStartingCount:(NSUInteger)paramStartingCount
                           endingCount:(NSUInteger)paramEndingCount;

@end
```

The implementation (*.m* file) of the operation might be a bit long, but hopefully it's easy to understand:

```
#import "CountingOperation.h"

@interface CountingOperation ()
@property (nonatomic, unsafe_unretained) NSUInteger startingCount;
@property (nonatomic, unsafe_unretained) NSUInteger endingCount;
@property (nonatomic, unsafe_unretained, getter=isFinished) BOOL finished;
@property (nonatomic, unsafe_unretained, getter=isExecuting) BOOL executing;
@end

@implementation CountingOperation

- (instancetype) init {
    return([self initWithStartingCount:0
                           endingCount:1000]);
}

- (instancetype) initWithStartingCount:(NSUInteger)paramStartingCount
```

```
                        endingCount:(NSUInteger)paramEndingCount{

    self = [super init];

    if (self != nil){

        /* Keep these values for the main method */
        _startingCount = paramStartingCount;
        _endingCount = paramEndingCount;

    }

    return(self);

}

- (void) main {

    @try {
        /* Here is our autorelease pool */
        @autoreleasepool {
            /* Keep a local variable here that must get set to YES
             whenever we are done with the task */
            BOOL taskIsFinished = NO;

            /* Create a while loop here that only exists
             if the taskIsFinished variable is set to YES or
             the operation has been cancelled */
            while (taskIsFinished == NO &&
                   [self isCancelled] == NO){

                /* Perform the task here */
                NSLog(@"Main Thread = %@", [NSThread mainThread]);
                NSLog(@"Current Thread = %@", [NSThread currentThread]);
                NSUInteger counter = _startingCount;
                for (counter = _startingCount;
                     counter < _endingCount;
                     counter++){
                    NSLog(@"Count = %lu", (unsigned long)counter);
                }
                /* Very important. This way we can get out of the
                 loop and we are still complying with the cancellation
                 rules of operations */
                taskIsFinished = YES;

            }

            /* KVO compliance. Generate the
             required KVO notifications */
            [self willChangeValueForKey:@"isFinished"];
            [self willChangeValueForKey:@"isExecuting"];
            _finished = YES;
```

```
            _executing = NO;
            [self didChangeValueForKey:@"isFinished"];
            [self didChangeValueForKey:@"isExecuting"];
        }
    }
    @catch (NSException * e) {
        NSLog(@"Exception %@", e);
    }

}
@end
```

We can start this operation like so:

```
@interface AppDelegate ()
@property (nonatomic, strong) CountingOperation *simpleOperation;
@end

@implementation AppDelegate

- (BOOL)            application:(UIApplication *)application
  didFinishLaunchingWithOptions:(NSDictionary *)launchOptions{

    self.simpleOperation = [[CountingOperation alloc]
                             initWithStartingCount:0
                             endingCount:1000];

    [self.simpleOperation start];

    NSLog(@"Main thread is here");

    self.window = [[UIWindow alloc] initWithFrame:
                   [[UIScreen mainScreen] bounds]];
    self.window.backgroundColor = [UIColor whiteColor];
    [self.window makeKeyAndVisible];
    return YES;
}
```

If we run the code, we will see the following results in the console window, just as we did when we used a block operation:

```
Main Thread = <NSThread: 0x6810260>{name = (null), num = 1}
Current Thread = <NSThread: 0x6810260>{name = (null), num = 1}
...
Count = 993
Count = 994
Count = 995
Count = 996
Count = 997
Count = 998
Count = 999
Main thread is here
```

## See Also

Recipe 7.12

# 7.12. Running Tasks Asynchronously with Operations

## Problem

You want to execute operations concurrently.

## Solution

Use operation queues. Alternatively, subclass `NSOperation` and detach a new thread on the `main` method.

## Discussion

As mentioned in Recipe 7.11, operations, by default, run on the thread that calls the `start` method. Usually we start operations on the main thread, but at the same time we expect the operations to run on their own threads and not take the main thread's time slice. The best solution for us would be to use operation queues. However, if you want to manage your operations manually, which I do not recommend, you can subclass `NSOperation` and detach a new thread on the main method. Please refer to Recipe 7.15 for more information about detached threads.

Let's go ahead and use an operation queue and add two simple invocation operations to it. (For more information about invocation operations, please refer to this chapter's Introduction. For additional example code on invocation operations, please refer to Recipe 7.11.) Here is the declaration (*.m* file) of the application delegate that utilizes an operation queue and two invocation operations:

```
@interface AppDelegate ()
@property (nonatomic, strong) NSOperationQueue *operationQueue;
@property (nonatomic, strong) NSInvocationOperation *firstOperation;
@property (nonatomic, strong) NSInvocationOperation *secondOperation;
@end

@implementation AppDelegate
```

The inside of the implementation (*.m* file) of the application delegate is as follows:

```
- (void) firstOperationEntry:(id)paramObject{

    NSLog(@"%s", __FUNCTION__);
    NSLog(@"Parameter Object = %@", paramObject);
    NSLog(@"Main Thread = %@", [NSThread mainThread]);
    NSLog(@"Current Thread = %@", [NSThread currentThread]);
```

```
}

- (void) secondOperationEntry:(id)paramObject{

    NSLog(@"%s", __FUNCTION__);
    NSLog(@"Parameter Object = %@", paramObject);
    NSLog(@"Main Thread = %@", [NSThread mainThread]);
    NSLog(@"Current Thread = %@", [NSThread currentThread]);

}

- (BOOL)            application:(UIApplication *)application
  didFinishLaunchingWithOptions:(NSDictionary *)launchOptions{

    NSNumber *firstNumber = @111;
    NSNumber *secondNumber = @222;

    self.firstOperation =[[NSInvocationOperation alloc]
                          initWithTarget:self
                          selector:@selector(firstOperationEntry:)
                          object:firstNumber];

    self.secondOperation = [[NSInvocationOperation alloc]
                            initWithTarget:self
                            selector:@selector(secondOperationEntry:)
                            object:secondNumber];

    self.operationQueue = [[NSOperationQueue alloc] init];

    /* Add the operations to the queue */
    [self.operationQueue addOperation:self.firstOperation];
    [self.operationQueue addOperation:self.secondOperation];

    NSLog(@"Main thread is here");

    self.window = [[UIWindow alloc] initWithFrame:
                   [[UIScreen mainScreen] bounds]];
    self.window.backgroundColor = [UIColor whiteColor];
    [self.window makeKeyAndVisible];
    return YES;
}
```

Here is what is happening in the implementation of the code:

- We have two methods: `firstOperationEntry:` and `secondOperationEntry:`. Each method accepts an object as a parameter and prints out the current thread, the main thread, and the parameter to the console window. These are the entry methods of the invocation operations that will be added to an operation queue.
- We initialize two objects of type `NSInvocationOperation` and set the target selector to each operation entry point described previously.

- We then initialize an object of type `NSOperationQueue`. (It could also be created before the entry methods.) The queue object will be responsible for managing the concurrency in the operation objects.
- We invoke the `addOperation:` instance method of `NSOperationQueue` to add each invocation operation to the operation queue. At this point, the operation queue may or may not immediately start the invocation operations through their `start` methods. However, it is very important to bear in mind that after adding operations to an operation queue, you must not start the operations manually. You must leave this to the operation queue.

Now let's run the example code once and see the results in the console window:

```
[Running_Tasks_Asynchronously_with_OperationsAppDelegate firstOperationEntry:]
Main thread is here
Parameter Object = 111
[Running_Tasks_Asynchronously_with_OperationsAppDelegate secondOperationEntry:]
Main Thread = <NSThread: 0x6810260>{name = (null), num = 1}
Parameter Object = 222
Current Thread = <NSThread: 0x6805c20>{name = (null), num = 3}
Main Thread = <NSThread: 0x6810260>{name = (null), num = 1}
Current Thread = <NSThread: 0x6b2d1d0>{name = (null), num = 4}
```

Brilliant! This proves that the invocation operations are running on their own threads in parallel to the main thread without blocking the main thread at all. Now let's run the same code a couple more times and observe the output in the console window. If you do this, chances are that you will get a completely different result, such as this:

```
Main thread is here
[Running_Tasks_Asynchronously_with_OperationsAppDelegate firstOperationEntry:]
[Running_Tasks_Asynchronously_with_OperationsAppDelegate secondOperationEntry:]
Parameter Object = 111
Main Thread = <NSThread: 0x6810260>{name = (null), num = 1}
Current Thread = <NSThread: 0x68247c0>{name = (null), num = 3}
Parameter Object = 222
Main Thread = <NSThread: 0x6810260>{name = (null), num = 1}
Current Thread = <NSThread: 0x6819b00>{name = (null), num = 4}
```

You can clearly observe that the main thread is not blocked and that both invocation operations are running in parallel with the main thread. This just proves the concurrency in the operation queue when two nonconcurrent operations are added to it. The operation queue manages the threads required to run the operations.

If we were to subclass `NSOperation` and add the instances of the new class to an operation queue, we would do things slightly differently. Keep a few things in mind:

- Plain operations that subclass `NSOperation`, when added to an operation queue, will run asynchronously. For this reason, you must override the `isConcurrent` instance method of `NSOperation` and return the value `YES`.

- You must prepare your operation for cancellation by checking the value of the `isCancelled` method periodically while performing the main task of the operation and in the `start` method before you even run the operation. The `start` method will get called by the operation queue in this case after the operation is added to the queue. In this method, check whether the operation is cancelled using the `isCancelled` method. If the operation is cancelled, simply return from the `start` method. If not, call the `main` method from inside the `start` method.
- Override the `main` method with your own implementation of the main task that is to be carried out by the operation. Make sure to allocate and initialize your own autorelease pool in this method and to release the pool just before returning.
- Override the `isFinished` and `isExecuting` methods of your operation and return appropriate `BOOL` values to reveal whether the operation is finished or is executing at the time.

Here is the declaration (*.h* file) of the operation:

```
#import <Foundation/Foundation.h>

@interface SimpleOperation : NSOperation

/* Designated Initializer */
- (instancetype) initWithObject:(NSObject *)paramObject;

@end
```

The implementation of the operation is as follows:

```
#import "SimpleOperation.h"

@interface SimpleOperation ()
@property (nonatomic, strong) NSObject *givenObject;
@property (nonatomic, unsafe_unretained, getter=isFinished) BOOL finished;
@property (nonatomic, unsafe_unretained, getter=isExecuting) BOOL executing;
@end

@implementation SimpleOperation

- (instancetype) init {
    return([self initWithObject:@123]);
}

- (instancetype) initWithObject:(NSObject *)paramObject{
    self = [super init];
    if (self != nil){
        /* Keep these values for the main method */
        _givenObject = paramObject;
    }
    return(self);
}
```

```
- (void) main {

    @try {
        @autoreleasepool {
            /* Keep a local variable here that must get set to YES
             whenever we are done with the task */
            BOOL taskIsFinished = NO;

            /* Create a while loop here that only exists
             if the taskIsFinished variable is set to YES or
             the operation has been cancelled */
            while (taskIsFinished == NO &&
                   [self isCancelled] == NO){

                /* Perform the task here */
                NSLog(@"%s", __FUNCTION__);
                NSLog(@"Parameter Object = %@", _givenObject);
                NSLog(@"Main Thread = %@", [NSThread mainThread]);
                NSLog(@"Current Thread = %@", [NSThread currentThread]);

                /* Very important. This way we can get out of the
                 loop and we are still complying with the cancellation
                 rules of operations */
                taskIsFinished = YES;

            }

            /* KVO compliance. Generate the
             required KVO notifications */
            [self willChangeValueForKey:@"isFinished"];
            [self willChangeValueForKey:@"isExecuting"];
            _finished = YES;
            _executing = NO;
            [self didChangeValueForKey:@"isFinished"];
            [self didChangeValueForKey:@"isExecuting"];
        }
    }
    @catch (NSException * e) {
        NSLog(@"Exception %@", e);
    }

}

- (BOOL)  isConcurrent{
    return YES;
}

@end
```

You can now use this operation class in any other class, such as your application delegate. Here is the declaration of the application delegate to utilize this new operation class and add it in an operation queue:

```
@interface AppDelegate ()
@property (nonatomic, strong) NSOperationQueue *operationQueue;
@property (nonatomic, strong) SimpleOperation *firstOperation;
@property (nonatomic, strong) SimpleOperation *secondOperation;
@end

@implementation AppDelegate
```

The implementation of the application delegate is as follows:

```
- (BOOL)            application:(UIApplication *)application
  didFinishLaunchingWithOptions:(NSDictionary *)launchOptions{

    NSNumber *firstNumber = @111;
    NSNumber *secondNumber = @222;

    self.firstOperation = [[SimpleOperation alloc]
                           initWithObject:firstNumber];
    self.secondOperation = [[SimpleOperation alloc]
                            initWithObject:secondNumber];

    self.operationQueue = [[NSOperationQueue alloc] init];

    /* Add the operations to the queue */
    [self.operationQueue addOperation:self.firstOperation];
    [self.operationQueue addOperation:self.secondOperation];

    NSLog(@"Main thread is here");

    self.window = [[UIWindow alloc] initWithFrame:
                   [[UIScreen mainScreen] bounds]];
    self.window.backgroundColor = [UIColor whiteColor];
    [self.window makeKeyAndVisible];
    return YES;
}
```

The results printed to the console window will be similar to what we saw earlier when we used concurrent invocation operations:

```
Main thread is here
-[SimpleOperation main]
-[SimpleOperation main]
Parameter Object = 222
Parameter Object = 222
Main Thread = <NSThread: 0x6810260>{name = (null), num = 1}
Main Thread = <NSThread: 0x6810260>{name = (null), num = 1}
Current Thread = <NSThread: 0x6a10b90>{name = (null), num = 3}
Current Thread = <NSThread: 0x6a13f50>{name = (null), num = 4}
```

## See Also

Recipe 7.11; Recipe 7.15

# 7.13. Creating Dependency Between Operations

## Problem

You want to start a certain task only after another task has finished executing.

## Solution

If operation B has to wait for operation A before it can run the task associated with it, operation B has to add operation A as its dependency using the `addDependency:` instance method of `NSOperation`, as shown here:

```
[self.firstOperation addDependency:self.secondOperation];
```

Both the `firstOperation` and the `secondOperation` properties are of type `NSInvocationOperation`, as we will see in this recipe's Discussion. In this example code, the first operation will not be executed by the operation queue until after the second operation's task is finished.

## Discussion

An operation will not start executing until all the operations on which it depends have successfully finished executing the tasks associated with them. By default, an operation, after initialization, has no dependency on other operations.

If we want to introduce dependencies to the example code described in Recipe 7.12, we can slightly modify the application delegate's implementation and use the `addDependency:` instance method to have the first operation wait for the second operation:

```
#import "AppDelegate.h"

@interface AppDelegate ()
@property (nonatomic, strong) NSInvocationOperation *firstOperation;
@property (nonatomic, strong) NSInvocationOperation *secondOperation;
@property (nonatomic, strong) NSOperationQueue *operationQueue;
@end

@implementation AppDelegate

- (void) firstOperationEntry:(id)paramObject{

    NSLog(@"First Operation - Parameter Object = %@",
          paramObject);
```

```
    NSLog(@"First Operation - Main Thread = %@",
          [NSThread mainThread]);

    NSLog(@"First Operation - Current Thread = %@",
          [NSThread currentThread]);

}

- (void) secondOperationEntry:(id)paramObject{

    NSLog(@"Second Operation - Parameter Object = %@",
          paramObject);

    NSLog(@"Second Operation - Main Thread = %@",
          [NSThread mainThread]);

    NSLog(@"Second Operation - Current Thread = %@",
          [NSThread currentThread]);

}

- (BOOL)            application:(UIApplication *)application
  didFinishLaunchingWithOptions:(NSDictionary *)launchOptions{

    NSNumber *firstNumber = @111;
    NSNumber *secondNumber = @222;

    self.firstOperation = [[NSInvocationOperation alloc]
                           initWithTarget:self
                           selector:@selector(firstOperationEntry:)
                           object:firstNumber];

    self.secondOperation = [[NSInvocationOperation alloc]
                            initWithTarget:self
                            selector:@selector(secondOperationEntry:)
                            object:secondNumber];

    [self.firstOperation addDependency:self.secondOperation];

    self.operationQueue = [[NSOperationQueue alloc] init];

    /* Add the operations to the queue */
    [self.operationQueue addOperation:self.firstOperation];
    [self.operationQueue addOperation:self.secondOperation];

    NSLog(@"Main thread is here");

    self.window = [[UIWindow alloc] initWithFrame:
                   [[UIScreen mainScreen] bounds]];
    self.window.backgroundColor = [UIColor whiteColor];
    [self.window makeKeyAndVisible];
```

```
    return YES;
}
```

Now if you execute the program, you will see a result similar to this in the console window:

```
Second Operation - Parameter Object = 222
Main thread is here
Second Operation - Main Thread = <NSThread: 0x6810250>{name = (null), num = 1}
Second Operation - Current Thread = <NSThread: 0x6836ab0>{name = (null), num = 3}
First Operation - Parameter Object = 111
First Operation - Main Thread = <NSThread: 0x6810250>{name = (null), num = 1}
First Operation - Current Thread = <NSThread: 0x6836ab0>{name = (null), num = 3}
```

It's quite obvious that although the operation queue attempted to run both operations in parallel, the first operation had a dependency on the second operation, and therefore the second operation had to finish before the first operation could run.

If at any time you want to break the dependency between two operations, you can use the `removeDependency:` instance method of an operation object.

## See Also

Recipe 7.12

# 7.14. Creating Timers

## Problem

You would like to perform a specific task repeatedly with a certain delay. For instance, you want to update a view on your screen every second that your application is running.

## Solution

Use a timer:

```
- (void) paint:(NSTimer *)paramTimer{
    /* Do something here */
    NSLog(@"Painting");
}

- (void) startPainting{

    self.paintingTimer = [NSTimer
                          scheduledTimerWithTimeInterval:1.0
                          target:self
                          selector:@selector(paint:)
                          userInfo:nil
                          repeats:YES];
```

```
}

- (void) stopPainting{
    if (self.paintingTimer != nil){
        [self.paintingTimer invalidate];
    }
}

- (void)applicationWillResignActive:(UIApplication *)application{
    [self stopPainting];
}

- (void)applicationDidBecomeActive:(UIApplication *)application{
    [self startPainting];
}
```

The `invalidate` method will also release the timer, so that we don't have to do that manually. As you can see, we have defined a property called `paintingTimer` that is declared in this way in the implementation file (*.m* file):

```
#import "AppDelegate.h"

@interface AppDelegate ()
@property (nonatomic, strong) NSTimer *paintingTimer;
@end

@implementation AppDelegate
```

## Discussion

A timer is an object that fires an event at specified intervals. A timer must be scheduled in a run loop. Defining an `NSTimer` object creates a nonscheduled timer that does nothing but is available to the program when you want to schedule it. Once you issue a call, e.g. `scheduledTimerWithTimeInterval:target:selector:userInfo:repeats:`, the time becomes a scheduled timer and will fire the event you request. A scheduled timer is a timer that is added to a run loop. To get any timer to fire its target event, we must schedule that timer on a run loop. This is demonstrated in a later example where we create a nonscheduled timer and then manually schedule it on the main run loop of the application.

Once a timer is created and added to a `run` loop, either explicitly or implicitly, the timer will start calling a method in its target object (as specified by the programmer) every *n* seconds (*n* is specified by the programmer as well). Because *n* is floating-point, you can specify a fraction of a second.

There are various ways to create, initialize, and schedule timers. One of the easiest ways is through the `scheduledTimerWithTimeInterval:target:selector:userInfo:repeats:` class method of `NSTimer`. Here are the different parameters of this method:

`scheduledTimerWithTimeInterval`
: This is the number of seconds the timer has to wait before it fires an event. For example, if you want the timer to call a method in its target object twice per second, you have to set this parameter to 0.5 (1 second divided by 2); if you want the target method to be called four times per second, this parameter should be set to 0.25 (1 second divided by 4).

`target`
: This is the object that will receive the event.

`selector`
: This is the method signature in the target object that will receive the event.

`userInfo`
: This is the object that will be retained in the timer for later reference (in the target method of the target object).

`repeats`
: This specifies whether the timer must call its target method repeatedly (in which case this parameter has to be set to `YES`), or just once and then stop (in which case this parameter has to be set to `NO`).

Once a timer is created and added to a run loop, you can stop and release that timer using the `invalidate` instance method of the `NSTimer` class. This not only will release the timer, but also will release the object, if any, that was passed for the timer to retain during its lifetime (e.g., the object passed to the `userInfo` parameter of the `scheduledTimerWithTimeInterval:target:selector:userInfo:repeats:` class method of `NSTimer`). If you pass `NO` to the `repeats` parameter, the timer will invalidate itself after the first pass and subsequently will release the object it had retained (if any).

There are other methods you can use to create a scheduled timer. One of them is the `scheduledTimerWithTimeInterval:invocation:repeats:` class method of `NSTimer`:

```
- (void) paint:(NSTimer *)paramTimer{
    /* Do something here */
    NSLog(@"Painting");
}

- (void) startPainting{

    /* Here is the selector that we want to call */
    SEL selectorToCall = @selector(paint:);

    /* Here we compose a method signature out of the selector. We
     know that the selector is in the current class so it is easy
```

```
     to construct the method signature */
    NSMethodSignature *methodSignature =
    [[self class] instanceMethodSignatureForSelector:selectorToCall];

    /* Now base our invocation on the method signature. We need this
     invocation to schedule a timer */
    NSInvocation *invocation =
    [NSInvocation invocationWithMethodSignature:methodSignature];
    [invocation setTarget:self];
    [invocation setSelector:selectorToCall];

    /* Start a scheduled timer now */
    self.paintingTimer = [NSTimer scheduledTimerWithTimeInterval:1.0
                                                      invocation:invocation
                                                         repeats:YES];

}

- (void) stopPainting{
    if (self.paintingTimer != nil){
        [self.paintingTimer invalidate];
    }
}

- (void)applicationWillResignActive:(UIApplication *)application{
    [self stopPainting];
}

- (void)applicationDidBecomeActive:(UIApplication *)application{
    [self startPainting];
}
```

Scheduling a timer can be compared to starting a car's engine. A scheduled timer is a running car engine. A nonscheduled timer is a car engine that is ready to be started but is not running yet. We can schedule and unschedule timers whenever we want in the application, just like we might need the engine of a car to be on or off depending on the situation we are in. If you want to schedule a timer manually at a certain time in your application, you can use the `timerWithTimeInterval:target:selector:userInfo:repeats:` class method of `NSTimer`, and when you are ready, you can add the timer to your run loop of choice:

```
- (void) startPainting{

    self.paintingTimer = [NSTimer timerWithTimeInterval:1.0
                                                 target:self
                                               selector:@selector(paint:)
                                               userInfo:nil
                                                repeats:YES];

    /* Do your processing here and whenever you are ready,
     use the addTimer:forMode instance method of the NSRunLoop class
```

```
     in order to schedule the timer on that run loop */

    [[NSRunLoop currentRunLoop] addTimer:self.paintingTimer
                                 forMode:NSDefaultRunLoopMode];
}
```

The currentRunLoop and mainRunLoop class methods of NSRunLoop return the current and main run loops of the application, as their names imply.

Just like you can use the scheduledTimerWithTimeInterval:invocation:repeats: variant of creating scheduled timers using invocations, you can also use the timerWithTimeInterval:invocation:repeats: class method of NSTimer to create an unscheduled timer using an invocation:

```
- (void) paint:(NSTimer *)paramTimer{
    /* Do something here */
    NSLog(@"Painting");
}

- (void) startPainting{

    /* Here is the selector that we want to call */
    SEL selectorToCall = @selector(paint:);

    /* Here we compose a method signature out of the selector. We
     know that the selector is in the current class so it is easy
     to construct the method signature */
    NSMethodSignature *methodSignature =
    [[self class] instanceMethodSignatureForSelector:selectorToCall];

    /* Now base our invocation on the method signature. We need this
     invocation to schedule a timer */
    NSInvocation *invocation =
    [NSInvocation invocationWithMethodSignature:methodSignature];

    [invocation setTarget:self];
    [invocation setSelector:selectorToCall];

    self.paintingTimer = [NSTimer timerWithTimeInterval:1.0
                                             invocation:invocation
                                                repeats:YES];;

    /* Do your processing here and whenever you are ready,
     use the addTimer:forMode instance method of the NSRunLoop class
     in order to schedule the timer on that run loop */

    [[NSRunLoop currentRunLoop] addTimer:self.paintingTimer
                                 forMode:NSDefaultRunLoopMode];
```

```
}

- (void) stopPainting{
    if (self.paintingTimer != nil){
        [self.paintingTimer invalidate];
    }
}

- (void)applicationWillResignActive:(UIApplication *)application{
    [self stopPainting];
}

- (void)applicationDidBecomeActive:(UIApplication *)application{
    [self startPainting];
}
```

The target method of a timer receives the instance of the timer that calls it as its parameter. For instance, the `paint:` method introduced initially in this recipe demonstrates how the timer gets passed to its target method, by default, as the target method's one and only parameter:

```
- (void) paint:(NSTimer *)paramTimer{
  /* Do something here */
  NSLog(@"Painting");
}
```

This parameter provides you with a reference to the timer that is firing this method. You can, for instance, prevent the timer from running again using the `invalidate` method, if needed. You can also invoke the `userInfo` method of the `NSTimer` instance in order to retrieve the object being retained by the timer (if any). This object is just an object passed to the initialization methods of `NSTimer`, and it gets directly passed to the timer for future reference.

# 7.15. Creating Concurrency with Threads

## Problem

You would like to have maximum control over how separate tasks run in your application. For instance, you would like to run a long calculation requested by the user while freeing the main UI thread to interact with the user and do other things.

## Solution

Utilize threads in your application, like so:

```
- (void) downloadNewFile:(id)paramObject{

    @autoreleasepool {
```

```
        NSString *fileURL = (NSString *)paramObject;

        NSURL    *url = [NSURL URLWithString:fileURL];

        NSURLRequest *request = [NSURLRequest requestWithURL:url];

        NSURLResponse *response = nil;
        NSError       *error = nil;

        NSData *downloadedData =
        [NSURLConnection sendSynchronousRequest:request
                              returningResponse:&response
                                          error:&error];

        if ([downloadedData length] > 0){
            /* Fully downloaded */
        } else {
            /* Nothing was downloaded. Check the Error value */
        }
    }

}

- (void)viewDidLoad {
    [super viewDidLoad];

    NSString *fileToDownload = @"http://www.OReilly.com";

    [NSThread detachNewThreadSelector:@selector(downloadNewFile:)
                             toTarget:self
                           withObject:fileToDownload];

}
```

## Discussion

Any iOS application is made out of one or more threads. In iOS, a normal application with one view controller could initially have up to four or five threads created by the system libraries to which the application is linked. At least one thread will be created for your application whether you use multiple threads or not. It is called the "main UI thread" attached to the main run loop.

To understand how useful threads are, let's do an experiment. Suppose we have three loops:

```
- (void) firstCounter{

    NSUInteger counter = 0;
    for (counter = 0;
         counter < 1000;
         counter++){
```

```
        NSLog(@"First Counter = %lu", (unsigned long)counter);
    }

}

- (void) secondCounter{

    NSUInteger counter = 0;
    for (counter = 0;
         counter < 1000;
         counter++){
        NSLog(@"Second Counter = %lu", (unsigned long)counter);
    }

}

- (void) thirdCounter{

    NSUInteger counter = 0;
    for (counter = 0;
         counter < 1000;
         counter++){
        NSLog(@"Third Counter = %lu", (unsigned long)counter);
    }

}
```

Very simple, aren't they? All they do is go from 0 to 1,000, printing their counter numbers. Now suppose you want to run these counters as we would normally do:

```
- (void) viewDidLoad{
    [super viewDidLoad];
    [self firstCounter];
    [self secondCounter];
    [self thirdCounter];
}
```

This code does not necessarily have to be in a view controller's `viewDidLoad` method.

Now open the console window and run this application. You will see the first counter's complete run, followed by the second counter and then the third counter. This means these loops are being run on the same thread. Each one blocks the rest of the thread's code from being executed until it finishes its loop.

What if we wanted all these counters to run at the same time? Of course, we would have to create separate threads for each one. But wait a minute! We already learned that the application creates threads for us when it loads and that whatever code we have been writing so far in the application, wherever it was, was being executed in a thread. So we just have to create two threads for the first and second counters and leave the third counter to do its job in the main thread:

```
- (void) firstCounter{

    @autoreleasepool {
        NSUInteger counter = 0;
        for (counter = 0;
             counter < 1000;
             counter++){
            NSLog(@"First Counter = %lu", (unsigned long)counter);
        }
    }

}

- (void) secondCounter{

    @autoreleasepool {
        NSUInteger counter = 0;
        for (counter = 0;
             counter < 1000;
             counter++){
            NSLog(@"Second Counter = %lu", (unsigned long)counter);
        }
    }

}

- (void) thirdCounter{

    NSUInteger counter = 0;
    for (counter = 0;
         counter < 1000;
         counter++){
        NSLog(@"Third Counter = %lu", (unsigned long)counter);
    }

}

- (void)viewDidLoad {

    [super viewDidLoad];

    [NSThread detachNewThreadSelector:@selector(firstCounter)
                             toTarget:self
                           withObject:nil];


    [NSThread detachNewThreadSelector:@selector(secondCounter)
                             toTarget:self
```

```
                                    withObject:nil];

        /* Run this on the main thread */
        [self thirdCounter];

    }
```

The `thirdCounter` method does not have an autorelease pool since it is not run in a new detached thread. This method will be run in the application's main thread, which has an autorelease pool created for it automatically at the startup of every Cocoa Touch application.

The calls to `detachNewThreadSelector` near the end of the code run the first and second counters as separate threads. Now if you run the application, you will notice output such as the following, in the console window:

```
Second Counter = 921
Third Counter = 301
Second Counter = 922
Second Counter = 923
Second Counter = 924
First Counter = 956
Second Counter = 925
First Counter = 957
Second Counter = 926
First Counter = 958
Third Counter = 302
Second Counter = 927
Third Counter = 303
Second Counter = 928
```

In other words, all three counters run at once and interleave their output randomly.

Every thread must create an autorelease pool. An autorelease pool internally keeps a reference to objects that are being autoreleased before the pool itself is released. This is a very important mechanism in a reference-counted memory management environment such as Cocoa Touch, where objects can be autoreleased. Whenever we allocate instances of objects, the retain count of the objects gets set to 1. If we mark the objects as autorelease, the retain count remains at 1, but when the autorelease pool in which the object was created is released, the autorelease object is also sent a `release` message. If its retain count is still 1 at that point, the object gets deallocated.

Every thread requires an autorelease pool to be created for it as the first object that is allocated in that thread. If you don't do this, any object that you allocate in your thread will leak when the thread exists. To understand this better, let's have a look at the following code:

```
- (void) autoreleaseThread:(id)paramSender{

    NSBundle *mainBundle = [NSBundle mainBundle];
    NSString *filePath = [mainBundle pathForResource:@"MacBookAir"
                                              ofType:@"png"];

    UIImage *image = [UIImage imageWithContentsOfFile:filePath];

    /* Do something with the image */
    NSLog(@"Image = %@", image);

}

- (void)viewDidLoad {

    [super viewDidLoad];

    [NSThread detachNewThreadSelector:@selector(autoreleaseThread:)
                             toTarget:self
                           withObject:self];

}
```

If you run this code and keep an eye on the console window, you *might* receive a message similar to this:

```
*** __NSAutoreleaseNoPool(): Object 0x5b2c990 of
class NSCFString autoreleased with no pool in place - just leaking
*** __NSAutoreleaseNoPool(): Object 0x5b2ca30 of
class NSPathStore2 autoreleased with no pool in place - just leaking
*** __NSAutoreleaseNoPool(): Object 0x5b205c0 of
class NSPathStore2 autoreleased with no pool in place - just leaking
*** __NSAutoreleaseNoPool(): Object 0x5b2d650 of
class UIImage autoreleased with no pool in place - just leaking
```

This shows that the autorelease `UIImage` instance we created is creating a memory leak—and, in addition, so is the `NSString` instance called `FilePath` and other objects that would normally "magically" get deallocated. This is because in the thread, we forgot to allocate and initialize an autorelease pool as the first thing we did. The following is the correct code, which you can test for yourself to make sure it doesn't leak:

```
- (void) autoreleaseThread:(id)paramSender{

    @autoreleasepool {
        NSBundle *mainBundle = [NSBundle mainBundle];
        NSString *filePath = [mainBundle pathForResource:@"MacBookAir"
                                                  ofType:@"png"];

        UIImage *image = [UIImage imageWithContentsOfFile:filePath];

        /* Do something with the image */
        NSLog(@"Image = %@", image);
```

```
    }

}

- (void)viewDidLoad {

    [super viewDidLoad];

    [NSThread detachNewThreadSelector:@selector(autoreleaseThread:)
                             toTarget:self
                           withObject:self];

}
```

# 7.16. Invoking Background Methods

## Problem

You want to know an easy way to create threads without having to deal with threads directly.

## Solution

Use the `performSelectorInBackground:withObject:` instance method of `NSObject`:

```
- (BOOL)            application:(UIApplication *)application
  didFinishLaunchingWithOptions:(NSDictionary *)launchOptions{

    [self performSelectorInBackground:@selector(firstCounter)
                           withObject:nil];

    [self performSelectorInBackground:@selector(secondCounter)
                           withObject:nil];

    [self performSelectorInBackground:@selector(thirdCounter)
                           withObject:nil];

    self.window = [[UIWindow alloc] initWithFrame:
                   [[UIScreen mainScreen] bounds]];
    self.window.backgroundColor = [UIColor whiteColor];
    [self.window makeKeyAndVisible];
    return YES;
}
```

The counter methods are implemented in this way:

```
- (void) firstCounter{

    @autoreleasepool {
        NSUInteger counter = 0;
        for (counter = 0;
```

```
            counter < 1000;
            counter++){
           NSLog(@"First Counter = %lu", (unsigned long)counter);
        }
    }

}

- (void) secondCounter{

    @autoreleasepool {
        NSUInteger counter = 0;
        for (counter = 0;
             counter < 1000;
             counter++){
            NSLog(@"Second Counter = %lu", (unsigned long)counter);
        }
    }

}

- (void) thirdCounter{

    @autoreleasepool {
        NSUInteger counter = 0;
        for (counter = 0;
             counter < 1000;
             counter++){
            NSLog(@"Third Counter = %lu", (unsigned long)counter);
        }
    }

}
```

## Discussion

The `performSelectorInBackground:withObject:` method creates a new thread in the background for us. This is equivalent to creating a new thread for the selectors. The most important thing we have to keep in mind is that since this method creates a thread on the given selector, the selector must have an autorelease pool just like any other thread in a reference-counted memory environment.

# 7.17. Exiting Threads and Timers

## Problem

You would like to stop a thread or a timer, or prevent one from firing again.

## Solution

For timers, use the `invalidate` instance method of `NSTimer`. For threads, use the `cancel` method. Avoid using the `exit` method of threads, as it does not give the thread a chance to clean up after itself, and your application will end up leaking resources:

```
NSThread *thread = /* Get the reference to your thread here */;
[thread cancel];

NSTimer *timer = /* Get the reference to your timer here */;
[timer invalidate];
```

## Discussion

Exiting a timer is quite straightforward; you can simply call the timer's `invalidate` instance method. After you call that method, the timer will not fire any more events to its target object.

However, threads are a bit more complicated to exit. When a thread is sleeping and its `cancel` method is called, the thread's loop will still perform its task fully before exiting. Let me demonstrate this for you:

```
- (void) threadEntryPoint{

    @autoreleasepool {
        NSLog(@"Thread Entry Point");
        while ([[NSThread currentThread] isCancelled] == NO){
            [NSThread sleepForTimeInterval:4];
            NSLog(@"Thread Loop");
        }
        NSLog(@"Thread Finished");
    }

}

- (void) stopThread{

    NSLog(@"Cancelling the Thread");
    [self.myThread cancel];
    NSLog(@"Releasing the thread");
    self.myThread = nil;

}

- (BOOL)            application:(UIApplication *)application
  didFinishLaunchingWithOptions:(NSDictionary *)launchOptions{

    self.myThread = [[NSThread alloc]
                     initWithTarget:self
                     selector:@selector(threadEntryPoint)
                     object:nil];
```

```
    [self performSelector:@selector(stopThread)
               withObject:nil
               afterDelay:3.0f];

    [self.myThread start];

    self.window = [[UIWindow alloc] initWithFrame:
                   [[UIScreen mainScreen] bounds]];
    self.window.backgroundColor = [UIColor whiteColor];
    [self.window makeKeyAndVisible];
    return YES;
}
```

This code creates an instance of NSThread and starts the thread immediately. The thread sleeps for four seconds in every loop before performing its task. However, before the thread is started, we are calling the stopThread method of the view controller (which we have written) with a three-second delay. This method calls the cancel method of the thread in an attempt to make the thread exit its loop. Now let's run the application and see what gets printed to the console screen:

```
...
Thread Entry Point
Cancelling the Thread
Releasing the thread
Thread Loop
Thread Finished
```

You can clearly see that the thread finished its current loop before exiting, even though the request to cancel it was fired in the middle of the loop. This is a very common pitfall that can be avoided simply by checking whether the thread is cancelled before attempting to perform a task with external side effects inside the thread's loop. We can rewrite the example as follows so that the operation with an external effect (writing to the log) checks first to make sure the thread hasn't been cancelled:

```
- (void) threadEntryPoint{

    @autoreleasepool {
        NSLog(@"Thread Entry Point");
        while ([[NSThread currentThread] isCancelled] == NO){
            [NSThread sleepForTimeInterval:4];
            if ([[NSThread currentThread] isCancelled] == NO){
                NSLog(@"Thread Loop");
            }
        }
        NSLog(@"Thread Finished");
    }

}

- (void) stopThread{
```

```
    NSLog(@"Cancelling the Thread");
    [self.myThread cancel];
    NSLog(@"Releasing the thread");
    self.myThread = nil;

}

- (BOOL)            application:(UIApplication *)application
  didFinishLaunchingWithOptions:(NSDictionary *)launchOptions{

    self.myThread = [[NSThread alloc]
                     initWithTarget:self
                     selector:@selector(threadEntryPoint)
                     object:nil];

    [self performSelector:@selector(stopThread)
               withObject:nil
               afterDelay:3.0f];

    [self.myThread start];

    self.window = [[UIWindow alloc] initWithFrame:
                   [[UIScreen mainScreen] bounds]];
    self.window.backgroundColor = [UIColor whiteColor];
    [self.window makeKeyAndVisible];
    return YES;
}
```

# CHAPTER 8
# Security

## 8.0. Introduction

Security is at the heart of iOS and OS X. You can use security functions in iOS to store data or files securely in different storage spaces. For instance, you can ask iOS to lock and secure your app's data files stored on disk if the user has enabled a passcode for her device and her device is locked. If you do not explicitly ask for this, iOS will not use any secure storage for your app, and your app data will be available to be read by a process that has access to read your device's filesystem. There are a variety of Mac applications out there that can explore an iOS device's filesystem *without* the iOS device being jailbroken.

*Jailbreaking* is the process of enabling root access and removing many protection layers built on top of an operating system, such as iOS. For instance, on a jailbroken device, an application can execute an unsigned binary. However, on a normal iOS device, for an app to be able to get executed on the device, it has to be signed either by Apple through the App Store, or through a verified iOS developer portal.

Apple has had Keychain Access in OS X for a long time. Keychain Access is a program that allows OS X users to store data securely on their computers. Built on top of the Common Data Security Architecture, or CDSA, the Keychain Access and other security functionalities in OS X are available to programmers like us. Keychain Access can manage various keychains. Every keychain itself can contain secure data such as passwords. For instance, on your OS X machine, when you log into a website using Safari, you will be prompted to either request for your password to be remembered by Safari or ignore that request. If you ask Safari to remember your password, Safari will then store the given password securely in your default keychain.

The OS X and iOS keychains differ in various ways, as listed here:

- In OS X, the user can have multiple keychains. In iOS, there is a single global keychain.
- In OS X, a keychain can be locked by the user. In iOS, the default keychain gets locked and unlocked as the device gets locked and unlocked.
- OS X has the concept of a *default keychain* that gets automatically unlocked by OS X when the user logs in, as long as the default keychain has the same password as the user's account password. iOS, as just mentioned, has only one keychain and this keychain, is unlocked by iOS by default.

To get a better understanding of the keychain on OS X, before we dig deeper into the keychain and security concepts in iOS, I would like to demonstrate something to you. Open Terminal on your Mac, type the following command, and press Enter:

```
security list-keychains
```

The output, depending on your machine's setup and your username, may be very similar to that shown here:

```
"/Users/vandadnp/Library/Keychains/login.keychain"
"/Library/Keychains/System.keychain"
```

You can see that I have two keychains, the first being the login keychain and the second being the system keychain. To find out which keychain is the default keychain, type the following command in Terminal, and then press Enter:

```
security default-keychain
```

On a typical OS X installation, this command will return a result similar to this:

```
"/Users/vandadnp/Library/Keychains/login.keychain"
```

The output indicates that my default keychain is the login keychain. So by default, all passwords that I have asked various programs in my OS X installation to remember will get stored in the default keychain unless the app in question decides that it needs to store the password in a different keychain. The app will have to create that keychain if it's not already there.

Now let's try something exciting. To find out what passwords are already stored in your default keychain, assuming that the default keychain as we found out earlier was the `login.keychain`, type the following command in Terminal and press Enter:

```
security dump-keychain login.keychain | grep "password" -i
```

The `dump-keychain` argument to the `security` command in Terminal will dump the whole contents of a keychain to the standard output. We used the `grep` command to search for the passwords. The output of this command may be similar to the following, depending on your computer's remembered passwords:

```
"desc"<blob>="AirPort network password"
"desc"<blob>="AirPort network password"
"desc"<blob>="AirPort network password"
"desc"<blob>="AirPort network password"
"desc"<blob>="AirPort network password"
"desc"<blob>="AirPort network password"
"desc"<blob>="AirPort network password"
"desc"<blob>="AirPort network password"
"desc"<blob>="Web form password"
"desc"<blob>="Web form password"
"desc"<blob>="Web form password"
"desc"<blob>="Web form password"
```

OK, well, this is all great, but why am I talking about it, and how is it related to iOS? It turns out that the architecture of the keychain in iOS is *very* similar to OS X, because iOS was based on OS X's source code. A lot of the concepts in iOS are similar to those in OS X, and the keychain is no exception. There are some really important things to note about the keychain in iOS, such as access groups and services. To ease you into the subject, I will demonstrate how they apply to OS X, and then I will talk more about the iOS implementation of the keychain.

On your Mac, press Command+space to open the Spotlight, or simply click the Spotlight icon on the top menu bar on your screen. The Spotlight icon is shown in Figure 8-1.

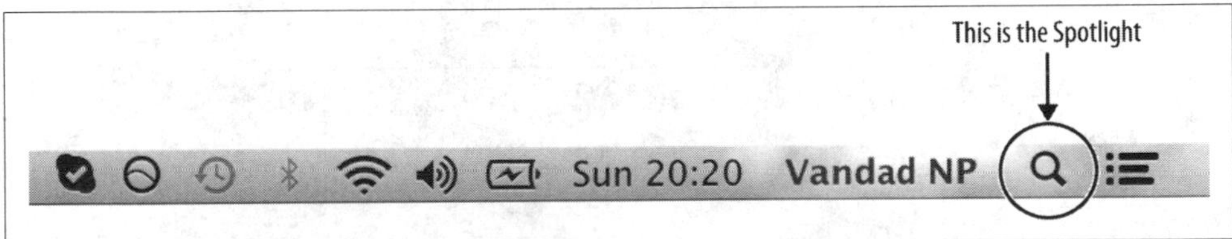


*Figure 8-1. Click the Spotlight icon on the menu bar in OS X*

When the Spotlight opens, type in "Keychain Access" and press the Enter key to open Keychain Access. On the lefthand side of Keychain Access, under the Keychains section, click the *login* keychain and then, under the Category section on the lefthand side, choose *Passwords*. Now you should be seeing an interface similar to that shown in Figure 8-2.

*Figure 8-2. The Keychain Access on Mac OS X*

Keychain Access is the graphical user interface that sits on top of the keychain and security APIs in OS X, giving you a nice, clean interface that hides a lot of the complexity underneath the security frameworks in OS X. Now, if you have any passwords remembered by apps such as Safari, I need you to double-click one of the password items on the righthand side of the Keychain Access screen to open a dialog similar to that shown in Figure 8-3.

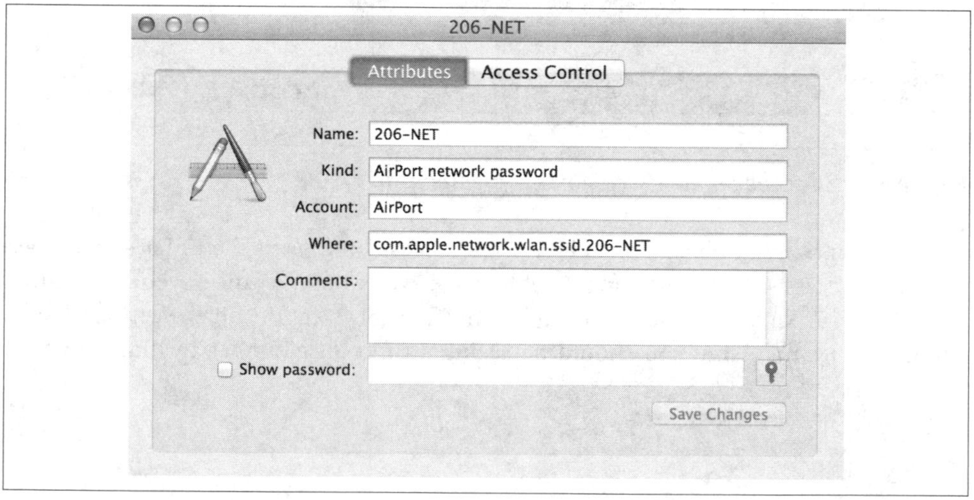

*Figure 8-3. Keychain Access dialog displaying information for a saved password*

We need to know some of the properties of the password shown in Figure 8-3:

*Name*
: The name of the password, which was assigned by the application that stored the item. For instance, this one is a WiFi password for a network named *`206-NET`*. This name is also sometimes referred to as the *label*.

*Kind*
: The kind of item that this is. In this case, the kind is *AirPort network password*. This is a plain string and can be used to query the keychain later, as we will see.

*Account*
: This is usually the key for the value that we want to store. The keychain uses a key-value store, just as dictionaries do in Objective-C. The key is an arbitrary string, and most applications that store items in the keychain store the key of the value in this section.

*Where*
: Often referred to as the *service*, this is the identifier of the service that stored this item in the keychain. This identifier is something for you to remember, and the keychain doesn't really care about it too much as long as it makes sense to you. In iOS, we usually set this service name to the bundle identifier of our apps to distinguish our app's stored values from other apps' stored data. We will talk about this in a short while.

You can also see the *Show password* checkbox in Figure 8-3. Pressing this checkbox will ask for your permission to display the password for the item in question. If you enter your password and give permission to display the password for this item, Keychain Access will retrieve the secure password for you and display it on-screen.

We can use the `security` command in Terminal to fetch the exact same information. If you type in Terminal the following command:

```
security find-generic-password -help
```

You will get an output similar to this:

```
Usage: find-generic-password [-a account] [-s service]
        [options...] [-g] [keychain...]
    -a  Match "account" string
    -c  Match "creator" (four-character code)
    -C  Match "type" (four-character code)
    -D  Match "kind" string
    -G  Match "value" string (generic attribute)
    -j  Match "comment" string
    -l  Match "label" string
    -s  Match "service" string
    -g  Display the password for the item found
    -w  Display only the password on stdout
```

```
If no keychains are specified to search, the default search list is used.
        Find a generic password item.
```

So if you pass the required parameters one by one to the `security` command, you will be able to retrieve the properties of the password in question (Figure 8-3):

```
security find-generic-password
        -a "AirPort"
        -s "com.apple.network.wlan.ssid.206-NET"
        -D "AirPort network password"
        -l "206-NET"
        -g
        login.keychain
```

The `-g` command will, as you saw before, ask the `security` command to display the password associated with the given item, if any. Therefore, when you type this command in Terminal, you will be prompted to enter your account's password before proceeding, just as we were asked to put in our account's password to show the password in Figure 8-3.

In iOS, even though the whole operating system has one global keychain area, an application can still just read from and write to a sandboxed area of the global keychain. Two apps that have been written by the same developer (signed by a provision profile from the same iOS Developer Portal) can access a shared area of the keychain, but they still maintain their own sandboxed access to their own keychain. Therefore, two apps, named App X and App Y, developed by the same iOS developer, can access the following keychain areas:

1. App X can access App X's keychain area.
2. App Y can access App Y's keychain area.
3. App X and App Y can both access a shared keychain area (using access groups, if the programmer configures the app's entitlements appropriately).
4. App X cannot read App Y's keychain data, and App Y cannot read App X's keychain data.

iOS looks at an app's *entitlements* to figure out what type of access it requires. Entitlements of an app are encoded inside the provision profile that is used to sign the app. Let's assume we have just created a new provision profile called *KeychainTest_Dev.mobileprovision* and placed it on our desktop. Using the following command, you can extract the entitlements inside the profile, as follows:

```
cd ~/Desktop
```

That command will take you to your desktop, where you can issue the following command to read the entitlements of your provision profile:

```
security cms -D -i KeychainTest_Dev.mobileprovision |  grep -A12 "Entitlements"
```

The `security` command shown here will decode the whole provision profile, after which the `grep` command will look for the Entitlements section in the profile and will read 12 lines of text after the start of the Entitlements section. If your entitlements contain more or less text, you may need to adjust the `-A12` argument to read more lines or fewer.

The output of that command will potentially look like this, depending on your profile:

```
<key>Entitlements</key>
<dict>
    <key>application-identifier</key>
    <string>F3FU372W5M.com.pixolity.ios.cookbook.KeychainTest</string>
    <key>com.apple.developer.default-data-protection</key>
    <string>NSFileProtectionComplete</string>
    <key>get-task-allow</key>
    <true/>
    <key>keychain-access-groups</key>
    <array>
        <string>F3FU372W5M.*</string>
    </array>
</dict>
```

The important section that we are looking for is the *keychain-access-groups* section that specifies the access groups for our keychain items. This is the group identifier of the shared keychain for all apps developed by the same developer. In this case, the *F3FU372W5M* is my iOS portal's team ID, and the asterisk after that shows what access groups in the keychain I can place my securely stored items in later. The asterisk in this case means *any group*, so by default, this app will be able to access the keychain items for any app that belongs to the aforementioned team. Don't worry if this doesn't make that much sense for now. I can guarantee that by reading more about this subject in this chapter, you will get to know all a programmer needs to use keychain in iOS.

It is absolutely crucial that you add the Security framework to your app before continuing to read the recipes in this chapter. Most of the recipes in this chapter work with the keychain services in iOS, which require the presence of the Security framework. The iOS SDK 7 introduced the idea of modules, so that if you simply import the security framework's umbrella header into your project, LLVM will link your application to the relevant security module; you won't have to do the link manually. All you have to do is ensure that the Enable Modules feature is enabled in your build settings and that you import the following header file into your project:

```
#import <Security/Security.h>
```

Xcode 5 also added support for Capabilities, a new tab near the Build Settings tab. There, you can easily add entitlements to your app or even enable the keychain without much hassle. However, this hides almost every detail from you and doesn't allow you to create your own provision profiles. All you will be able to use are Wildcard provision profiles, which is not what we usually use when adding push notifications and other capabilities to our apps. I suggest that you have a look at this new tab simply by clicking on your project file in Xcode, looking to the righthand side of the screen, and selecting Capabilities. You can then easily turn on or off features such as iCloud and Keychain Access.

# 8.1. Enabling Security and Protection for Your Apps

## Problem

You want to store values in the keychain and enable secure file storage for your app.

## Solution

Create a provision profile for your app that has file protection enabled.

## Discussion

Provision profiles, as discussed earlier in Recipe 8.0, "Introduction", contain entitlements that dictate to iOS how your app utilizes the security functionalities in the operating system. On iOS Simulator, apps do not get codesigned and, therefore, these concepts will not make sense, but for debugging your app on a device or submitting your app to the App Store, you need to ensure that your app is signed with the correct provision profile, for both the Debug and the Release schemes.

I will show you the steps required to create a valid provision profile for your development, as well as Ad Hoc and the App Store. Follow these steps to create a valid development provision profile (with debugging enabled) for the apps that we are going to be working on in this chapter of the book. We start by creating an App ID:

I am assuming that you have already created valid development and distribution certificates for yourself.

1. Navigate to the iOS Dev Center (*https://developer.apple.com/devcenter/ios/index.action*) and sign in with your username and password.
2. After you are signed in, find the iOS Developer Program section and choose Certificates, Identifiers & Profiles.
3. On the lefthand side of the screen, find and navigate to the App IDs section of the portal and press the plus button (+) to create a new App ID.

4. In the Name section, enter the name "Security App." You can actually enter anything you want, but to avoid confusion in this chapter, it's best to stick with the aforementioned name, which I will be using in examples.
5. Under the App Services section, check the Data Protection box and ensure that the Complete Protection option is selected. Leave the rest of the settings intact.
6. Under the App ID Suffix section, ensure that the Explicit App ID option is selected, and in the Bundle ID box, enter the dot-separated name of a service. I recommend `com.`*`NAME`*`.ios.cookbook.SecurityApp`, where *`NAME`* is your company's name. If you don't have a company, make up a name! I am using `com.pixolity.ios.cookbook.SecurityApp` in examples, but you need a unique name, so you can't use mine.
7. After you are done, press the Continue button.
8. You should now be asked to confirm your settings before your App ID is created, similar to the screen depicted in Figure 8-4.

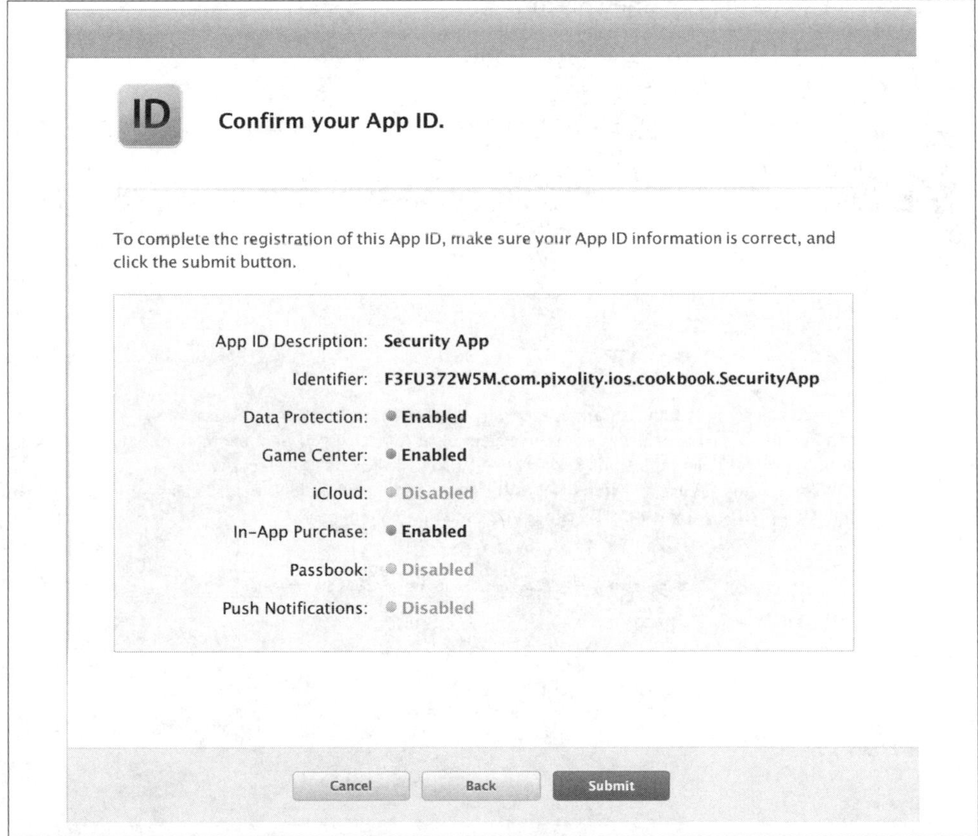


*Figure 8-4. Confirming your App ID settings before creating the App ID*

9. When you are happy with your settings, press the Submit button to create your App ID.

Beautiful! Now we have an App ID, but we still need to create our provision profiles. I am going to walk you through creating your development provision profile, and I will let you create the Ad Hoc and your App Store profiles on your own because the process is almost identical. Follow these steps to create your development provision profile:

1. In the Certificates, Identifiers & Profiles section of the Developer Portal, choose the Development section of the Provisioning Profiles category and press the plus button (+).
2. In the screen that appears, under the Development section, choose the iOS App Development option and press the Continue button.
3. When asked to choose your App ID, select the App ID that you created earlier. For me, this would be the App ID shown in Figure 8-5. Once you are happy with your selection, press the Continue button.

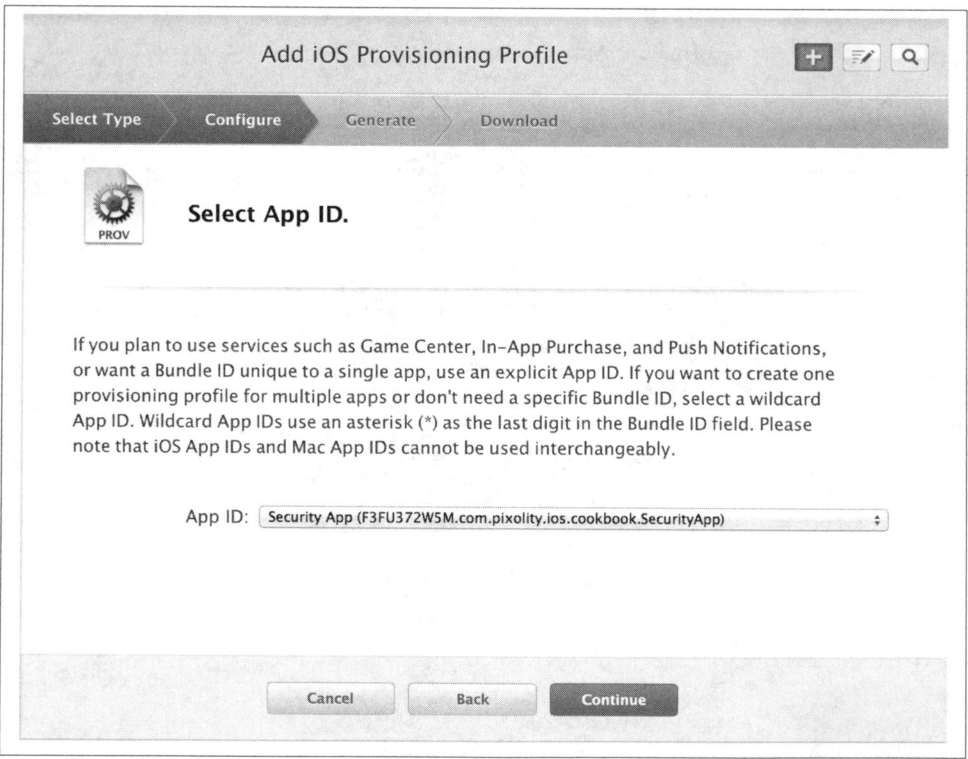


*Figure 8-5. Choosing our new App ID for the new development provision profile*

4. Choose the development certificate(s) to which you want to link your profile. Then press the Continue button.
5. Choose the list of devices on which your profile is allowed to be installed (only for Development and Ad Hoc profiles, not for App Store). Press the Continue button.
6. On the next screen, where you are asked to specify a name for your profile, enter something along the lines of "SecurityApp Dev Profile" and then press the Generate button to create your provision profile.
7. Your profile is now ready to be downloaded (see Figure 8-6). Press the Download button to download your profile.

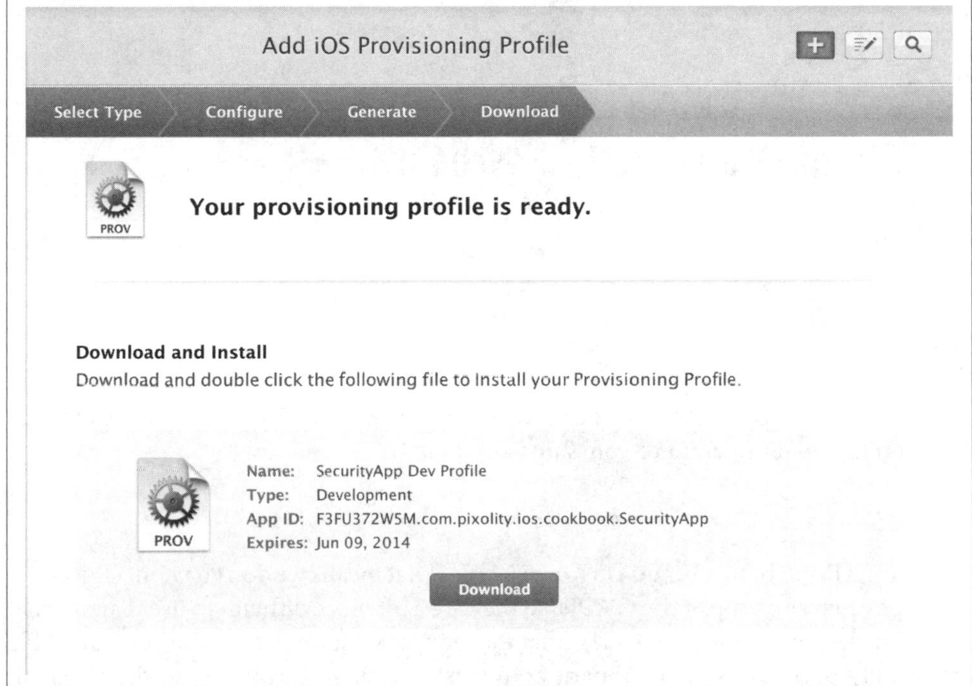


*Figure 8-6. A development profile is generated and ready to be downloaded*

8. To install the profile, drag and drop the downloaded profile into iTunes. This will install the profile with its original name into the *~/Library/MobileDevice/Provisioning Profiles/* folder. I have seen many iOS developers install a provision profile by double-clicking on it. While this does work, in that it installs the profile into the aforementioned folder, it will destroy the original profile's filename and will install the profile using the SHA1 hash of the profile. If you later go into the aforementioned folder, you won't be able to tell which profile is which unless you look inside

the profiles for their names, so I strongly discourage this way of installing profiles. It's best to either drag and drop the downloaded profiles into iTunes or manually paste the profiles into the aforementioned folder.

Brilliant. You now have the provision profile installed on your computer. Use the build settings of your project to make sure that the correct profile is selected for the Debug scheme. After you follow the same process for creating your Ad Hoc and App Store profiles, you can ensure that your app is built with the correct Ad Hoc or App Store profile for the Release scheme.

The provision profile that you created now will allow you to debug your apps on an iOS device and store data onto the disk or into the keychain with ease.

## See Also

Recipe 8.0, "Introduction"

# 8.2. Storing Values in the Keychain

## Problem

You want to securely store sensitive data in the keychain.

## Solution

Ensure that your app is linked against the Security framework. Then use the `SecItemAdd` function to add a new item to your app's keychain.

## Discussion

Keychain APIs in both iOS and OS X are C APIs. That means we don't have an Objective-C bridge or layer on top of the C APIs, so they are a bit more difficult to use than normal APIs. The key to learning the APIs is that the requests that we send to the keychain APIs are usually packed inside dictionaries. For instance, if you want to ask the keychain services to securely store a piece of data, you put your request—including the data that you want to store, the key for that data, the identifier of your app, etc.—inside a dictionary and submit that dictionary to an API such as the `SecItemAdd` function. To store a piece of value in the keychain, construct a dictionary with the following keys:

`kSecClass`
: The value of this key is usually equal to `kSecClassGenericPassword` for storage of secure pieces of data, such as strings.

`kSecAttrService`
: The value of this key is usually a string. This string usually is our app bundle identifier.

`kSecAttrAccount`
: The value of this key is a string that specifies the key to the value that we want to store. This is an arbitrary string that should make sense to you and your app.

`kSecValueData`
: The value of this key is an instance of `NSData` that you want to store for a given key (`kSecAttrAccount`.)

The return value of the `SecItemAdd` function is of type `OSStatus`. The different values that you can receive from this function are defined inside the *SecBase.h* file in your SDK, so simply press the Command+Shift+O keys on your keyboard while in Xcode, type in *SecBase.h*, and try to find the value `errSecSuccess`. After you find `errSecSuccess` in an enumeration, you will be able to see the rest of the values that can be returned inside a value of type `OSStatus`:

```
enum
{
    errSecSuccess                 = 0,
    errSecUnimplemented           = -4,
    errSecParam                   = -50,
    errSecAllocate                = -108,
    errSecNotAvailable            = -25291,
    errSecDuplicateItem           = -25299,
    errSecItemNotFound            = -25300,
    errSecInteractionNotAllowed   = -25308,
    errSecDecode                  = -26275,
    errSecAuthFailed              = -25293,
};
```

If the `SecItemAdd` function succeeds, you will receive the `errSecSuccess` value as the return value of this function. Otherwise, this function is indicating failure. So let's put all this together and write a small piece of code that can write a string value to the keychain:

```
#import "AppDelegate.h"
#import <Security/Security.h>

@implementation AppDelegate

- (BOOL)            application:(UIApplication *)application
  didFinishLaunchingWithOptions:(NSDictionary *)launchOptions{

    NSString *key = @"Full Name";
    NSString *value = @"Steve Jobs";
    NSData *valueData = [value dataUsingEncoding:NSUTF8StringEncoding];
    NSString *service = [[NSBundle mainBundle] bundleIdentifier];
```

```
    NSDictionary *secItem = @{
              (__bridge id)kSecClass : (__bridge id)kSecClassGenericPassword,
              (__bridge id)kSecAttrService : service,
              (__bridge id)kSecAttrAccount : key,
              (__bridge id)kSecValueData : valueData,
              };

    CFTypeRef result = NULL;
    OSStatus status = SecItemAdd((__bridge CFDictionaryRef)secItem, &result);

    if (status == errSecSuccess){
        NSLog(@"Successfully stored the value");
    } else {
        NSLog(@"Failed to store the value with code: %ld", (long)status);
    }

    self.window = [[UIWindow alloc]
                   initWithFrame:[[UIScreen mainScreen] bounds]];
    self.window.backgroundColor = [UIColor whiteColor];
    [self.window makeKeyAndVisible];
    return YES;
}
```

If you run this app for the first time, assuming that you have followed the advice in previous sections of this chapter to set up your profile correctly, you will receive the `errSecSuccess` value from the `SecItemAdd` function. However, if you run the same app again, you will receive the `errSecDuplicateItem` value. This is iOS's way of telling you that you cannot overwrite the existing value. In the world of keychain security, you cannot overwrite an existing value. What you *can* do, though, is update the existing value, as we will see later in this chapter.

## See Also

Recipe 8.1

# 8.3. Finding Values in the Keychain

## Problem

You want to query the keychain to find an existing item.

## Solution

Use the `SecItemCopyMatching` function. Follow these steps:

1. Construct a dictionary to pass to the aforementioned function. Add the kSecClass key to the dictionary. Set the key's value to reflect the type of item that you are looking for. Usually the value should be kSecClassGenericPassword.
2. Add the kSecAttrService key to the dictionary. Set the key's value to the service string of the item you are looking for. In this chapter, for service names, we use our app's bundle identifier and we are setting the bundle identifiers of all our apps to the same string, so that one can write to the keychain, another can read the same data, etc.
3. Add the kSecAttrAccount key to the dictionary and set its value to the actual key of the value that you previously stored in the keychain. If you followed the example that we wrote in Recipe 8.2, the account name in this case would be the string "Full Name."
4. Add the kSecReturnAttributes attribute to the dictionary and set its value to kCFBooleanTrue if you want to retrieve the attributes, such as the creation and modification date, of the existing value in the keychain. If you want to retrieve the actual value of the item you stored in the keychain, instead of the kSecReturnAttributes key, add the kSecReturnData key to your dictionary and set its value to kCFBooleanTrue.

Once your dictionary is ready, you can pass it as the first parameter to the SecItemCopyMatching function. The second parameter is a pointer to an object that will be returned by this function. This pointer must be of type CFTypeRef *. This is a generic data type, and the type depends on what you pass as the first parameter to the SecItemCopyMatching function. For instance, if your dictionary contains the kSecReturnAttributes key, the second parameter to this function must be either NULL or a pointer to a CFDictionaryRef opaque type. If you instead pass the kSecReturnData key to your dictionary, the second parameter to this function must be of type CFDataRef, which is an opaque type that will receive the actual data of the existing item. You can then convert this data to an instance of NSString and work with it.

## Discussion

Suppose you want to read the *properties* of the string that you wrote to the keychain in Recipe 8.2. You can write your code in this way:

```
- (BOOL)            application:(UIApplication *)application
didFinishLaunchingWithOptions:(NSDictionary *)launchOptions{

    NSString *keyToSearchFor = @"Full Name";
    NSString *service = [[NSBundle mainBundle] bundleIdentifier];

    NSDictionary *query = @{
              (__bridge id)kSecClass : (__bridge id)kSecClassGenericPassword,
              (__bridge id)kSecAttrService : service,
```

```
                (__bridge id)kSecAttrAccount : keyToSearchFor,
                (__bridge id)kSecReturnAttributes : (__bridge id)kCFBooleanTrue,
                };

    CFDictionaryRef valueAttributes = NULL;
    OSStatus results = SecItemCopyMatching((__bridge CFDictionaryRef)query,
                                           (CFTypeRef *)&valueAttributes);

    NSDictionary *attributes =
        (__bridge_transfer NSDictionary *)valueAttributes;

    if (results == errSecSuccess){

        NSString *key, *accessGroup, *creationDate, *modifiedDate, *service;

        key = attributes[(__bridge id)kSecAttrAccount];
        accessGroup = attributes[(__bridge id)kSecAttrAccessGroup];
        creationDate = attributes[(__bridge id)kSecAttrCreationDate];
        modifiedDate = attributes[(__bridge id)kSecAttrModificationDate];
        service = attributes[(__bridge id)kSecAttrService];

        NSLog(@"Key = %@\n \
              Access Group = %@\n \
              Creation Date = %@\n \
              Modification Date = %@\n \
              Service = %@", key, accessGroup, creationDate,
              modifiedDate, service);


    } else {
        NSLog(@"Error happened with code: %ld", (long)results);
    }

    self.window = [[UIWindow alloc]
                   initWithFrame:[[UIScreen mainScreen] bounds]];
    self.window.backgroundColor = [UIColor whiteColor];
    [self.window makeKeyAndVisible];
    return YES;
}
```

When you run the app, results similar to the following will print to the console:

```
Key = Full Name
Access Group = F3FU372W5M.com.pixolity.ios.cookbook.SecurityApp
Creation Date = 2013-06-09 10:44:55 +0000
Modification Date = 2013-06-09 10:44:55 +0000
Service = com.pixolity.ios.cookbook.SecurityApp
```

That is great, but how can you now read the actual data of the value? The Solution section of this recipe already answered this: you have to include the `kSecReturnData` in your query. Once you do that, the second parameter to the `SecItemCopyMatching` function will need to either be `NULL` or a pointer to a `CFDataRef` opaque variable, like so:

```
#import "AppDelegate.h"
#import <Security/Security.h>

@implementation AppDelegate

- (BOOL)            application:(UIApplication *)application
  didFinishLaunchingWithOptions:(NSDictionary *)launchOptions{

    NSString *keyToSearchFor = @"Full Name";
    NSString *service = [[NSBundle mainBundle] bundleIdentifier];

    NSDictionary *query = @{
            (__bridge id)kSecClass : (__bridge id)kSecClassGenericPassword,
            (__bridge id)kSecAttrService : service,
            (__bridge id)kSecAttrAccount : keyToSearchFor,
            (__bridge id)kSecReturnData : (__bridge id)kCFBooleanTrue,
            };

    CFDataRef cfValue = NULL;
    OSStatus results = SecItemCopyMatching((__bridge CFDictionaryRef)query,
                                           (CFTypeRef *)&cfValue);

    if (results == errSecSuccess){

        NSString *value = [[NSString alloc]
                           initWithData:(__bridge_transfer NSData *)cfValue
                           encoding:NSUTF8StringEncoding];

        NSLog(@"Value = %@", value);

    } else {
        NSLog(@"Error happened with code: %ld", (long)results);
    }

    self.window = [[UIWindow alloc]
                   initWithFrame:[[UIScreen mainScreen] bounds]];
    self.window.backgroundColor = [UIColor whiteColor];
    [self.window makeKeyAndVisible];
    return YES;
}
```

By default, the `SecItemCopyMatching` function looks for the first match in the keychain. Let's say that you have stored 10 secure items of class `kSecClassGenericPassword` in the keychain and you want to query them all. How can you do that? The answer is simple. Just add the `kSecMatchLimit` key into your query dictionary and provide the maximum number of matching items that the keychain services have to look for in the keychain or, alternatively, set the value of this key to `kSecMatchLimitAll` to find all matching items. Once you include the `kSecMatchLimit` key into your query dictionary to the `SecItemCopyMatching` function, the second parameter to this method will then require a pointer to a `CFArrayRef` opaque type, and the items in this array will then be the items that you asked for. If you include the `kSecReturnData` key in your dictionary with the value of `@YES`, the items in this array will be of type `CFDataRef`. However, if instead of the `kSecReturnData` key, you included the `kSecReturnAttributes` key in your query dictionary with the value of `@YES`, the items in your array will be of type `CFDictionaryRef` containing the dictionary object that describes the found item.

Let's have a look at an example that attempts to find *all* items in the keychain that match a certain criteria:

```
#import "AppDelegate.h"
#import <Security/Security.h>

@implementation AppDelegate

- (BOOL)            application:(UIApplication *)application
  didFinishLaunchingWithOptions:(NSDictionary *)launchOptions{

    NSString *keyToSearchFor = @"Full Name";
    NSString *service = [[NSBundle mainBundle] bundleIdentifier];

    NSDictionary *query = @{
            (__bridge id)kSecClass : (__bridge id)kSecClassGenericPassword,
            (__bridge id)kSecAttrService : service,
            (__bridge id)kSecAttrAccount : keyToSearchFor,
            (__bridge id)kSecReturnData : (__bridge id)kCFBooleanTrue,
            (__bridge id)kSecMatchLimit : (__bridge id)kSecMatchLimitAll
            };

    CFArrayRef allCfMatches = NULL;
    OSStatus results = SecItemCopyMatching((__bridge CFDictionaryRef)query,
                                           (CFTypeRef *)&allCfMatches);

    if (results == errSecSuccess){

        NSArray *allMatches = (__bridge_transfer NSArray *)allCfMatches;

        for (NSData *itemData in allMatches){
            NSString *value = [[NSString alloc]
                               initWithData:itemData
                               encoding:NSUTF8StringEncoding];
            NSLog(@"Value = %@", value);
        }

    } else {
        NSLog(@"Error happened with code: %ld", (long)results);
    }

    self.window = [[UIWindow alloc]
                   initWithFrame:[[UIScreen mainScreen] bounds]];
    self.window.backgroundColor = [UIColor whiteColor];
    [self.window makeKeyAndVisible];
```

```
    return YES;
}
```

## See Also

Recipe 8.2

# 8.4. Updating Existing Values in the Keychain

## Problem

You have already stored a value in the keychain but now want to update it to a new value.

## Solution

Given that you have been able to find the value in the keychain (see Recipe 8.3), you can issue the `SecItemUpdate` function with your query dictionary as its first parameter and a dictionary describing the change that you want to make to the existing value as its second parameter. Usually this update dictionary (the second parameter to the method) contains just one key (`kSecValueData`) and the value of this dictionary key is the data to set for the existing key in the keychain.

## Discussion

Let's assume that, following the advice given in Recipe 8.2, you have stored the string *`Steve Jobs`* with the key of *`Full Name`* in your app's keychain but want to update that value now. The first thing that you have to do is find out whether the existing value is already in the keychain. For that, construct a simple query, as we have seen earlier in this chapter:

```
NSString *keyToSearchFor = @"Full Name";
NSString *service = [[NSBundle mainBundle] bundleIdentifier];

NSDictionary *query = @{
        (__bridge id)kSecClass : (__bridge id)kSecClassGenericPassword,
        (__bridge id)kSecAttrService : service,
        (__bridge id)kSecAttrAccount : keyToSearchFor,
        };
```

Then query for that dictionary and see whether you can find the existing item in the keychain:

```
OSStatus found = SecItemCopyMatching((__bridge CFDictionaryRef)query,
                                     NULL);
```

You don't necessarily have to check for an existing value before attempting to update it. You can just attempt to update the value, and if the item doesn't exist, the `SecItemUpdate` function returns the value of `errSecItemNotFound` to you. The choice is whether to search in the keychain yourself or let `SecItemUpdate` do the check for you.

If this function returns the value of `errSecSuccess`, you know that your value is already there. Note that we passed `NULL` as the second parameter. The reason behind this is that we are not interested in retrieving the old value from the keychain. We just want to find out whether the value exists, and we can find that out by checking the function's return value. If the return value is `errSecSuccess`, then we know the value has already been stored and can be updated. So all we have to do is update it like so:

```
NSData *newData = [@"Mark Tremonti"
                   dataUsingEncoding:NSUTF8StringEncoding];

NSDictionary *update = @{
                         (__bridge id)kSecValueData : newData,
                         };

OSStatus updated = SecItemUpdate((__bridge CFDictionaryRef)query,
                                 (__bridge CFDictionaryRef)update);

if (updated == errSecSuccess){
    NSLog(@"Successfully updated the existing value");
} else {
    NSLog(@"Failed to update the value. Error = %ld", (long)updated);
}
```

The update dictionary that we pass to the second parameter of the `SecItemUpdate` function can contain more keys than the `kSecValueData` key that we used in our example. This dictionary can indeed contain any update to the existing item. For instance, if you want to add a comment to the existing value (a comment is a string), you can issue your update like so:

```
#import "AppDelegate.h"
#import <Security/Security.h>

@implementation AppDelegate

- (void) readExistingValue{

    NSString *keyToSearchFor = @"Full Name";
    NSString *service = [[NSBundle mainBundle] bundleIdentifier];

    NSDictionary *query = @{
            (__bridge id)kSecClass : (__bridge id)kSecClassGenericPassword,
            (__bridge id)kSecAttrService : service,
            (__bridge id)kSecAttrAccount : keyToSearchFor,
```

```
            (__bridge id)kSecReturnAttributes : (__bridge id)kCFBooleanTrue,
            };

    CFDictionaryRef cfAttributes = NULL;
    OSStatus found = SecItemCopyMatching((__bridge CFDictionaryRef)query,
                                         (CFTypeRef *)&cfAttributes);

    if (found == errSecSuccess){

        NSDictionary *attributes =
            (__bridge_transfer NSDictionary *)cfAttributes;

        NSString *comments = attributes[(__bridge id)kSecAttrComment];
        NSLog(@"Comments = %@", comments);

    } else {
        NSLog(@"Error happened with code: %ld", (long)found);
    }

}

- (BOOL)            application:(UIApplication *)application
  didFinishLaunchingWithOptions:(NSDictionary *)launchOptions{

    NSString *keyToSearchFor = @"Full Name";
    NSString *service = [[NSBundle mainBundle] bundleIdentifier];

    NSDictionary *query = @{
            (__bridge id)kSecClass : (__bridge id)kSecClassGenericPassword,
            (__bridge id)kSecAttrService : service,
            (__bridge id)kSecAttrAccount : keyToSearchFor,
            };

    OSStatus found = SecItemCopyMatching((__bridge CFDictionaryRef)query,
                                          NULL);

    if (found == errSecSuccess){

        NSData *newData = [@"Mark Tremonti"
                           dataUsingEncoding:NSUTF8StringEncoding];

        NSDictionary *update = @{
                                 (__bridge id)kSecValueData : newData,
                                 (__bridge id)kSecAttrComment : @"My Comments",
                                 };

        OSStatus updated = SecItemUpdate((__bridge CFDictionaryRef)query,
                                         (__bridge CFDictionaryRef)update);

        if (updated == errSecSuccess){
            [self readExistingValue];
        } else {
```

```
            NSLog(@"Failed to update the value. Error = %ld", (long)updated);
        }


    } else {
        NSLog(@"Error happened with code: %ld", (long)found);
    }

    self.window = [[UIWindow alloc]
                   initWithFrame:[[UIScreen mainScreen] bounds]];

    self.window.backgroundColor = [UIColor whiteColor];
    [self.window makeKeyAndVisible];
    return YES;
}
```

The important thing to note about this example code is the inclusion of the `kSecAttrComment` key in our update dictionary. Once the update is done, we are reading our comment back using the same reading technique that we learned in Recipe 8.3.

## See Also

Recipe 8.3; Recipe 8.2

# 8.5. Deleting Exiting Values in the Keychain

## Problem

You want to delete a keychain item.

## Solution

Use the `SecItemDelete` function.

## Discussion

In Recipe 8.2, we learned how to store values in the keychain. In order to delete those values, you will need to use the `SecItemDelete` function. This function takes only one parameter: a dictionary of type `CFDictionaryRef`. You can take a normal dictionary and bridge-convert it to an instance of `CFDictionaryRef`, as we have done in other recipes in this chapter. The dictionary that you'll pass to this method has to contain the following keys:

`kSecClass`
: The type of item that you want to delete. For instance `kSecClassGenericPassword`.

`kSecAttrService`
: The service that this item is hooked to. When you stored the item, you chose the service for it, so you'll need to provide the same service here. For instance, in previous examples, we set the value of this key to our app's bundle identifier. If that's what you did as well, simply provide your app's bundle identifier for the value of this key.

`kSecAttrAccount`
: The value of this key is the key that has to be deleted.

Assuming you have followed Recipe 8.2, the keychain now has a generic password (`kSecClassGenericPassword`) with the service name (`kSecAttrService`) equal to our app's bundle ID and the key (`kSecAttrAccount`) equal to *`Full Name`*. To delete this key, here is what you'll have to do:

```
#import "AppDelegate.h"
#import <Security/Security.h>

@implementation AppDelegate

- (BOOL)            application:(UIApplication *)application
  didFinishLaunchingWithOptions:(NSDictionary *)launchOptions{

    NSString *key = @"Full Name";
    NSString *service = [[NSBundle mainBundle] bundleIdentifier];

    NSDictionary *query = @{
                (__bridge id)kSecClass : (__bridge id)kSecClassGenericPassword,
                (__bridge id)kSecAttrService : service,
                (__bridge id)kSecAttrAccount : key
                };

    OSStatus foundExisting =
        SecItemCopyMatching((__bridge CFDictionaryRef)query, NULL);

    if (foundExisting == errSecSuccess){
        OSStatus deleted = SecItemDelete((__bridge CFDictionaryRef)query);
        if (deleted == errSecSuccess){
            NSLog(@"Successfully deleted the item");
        } else {
            NSLog(@"Failed to delete the item.");
        }
    } else {
        NSLog(@"Did not find the existing value.");
    }

    self.window = [[UIWindow alloc]
                   initWithFrame:[[UIScreen mainScreen] bounds]];
    self.window.backgroundColor = [UIColor whiteColor];
    [self.window makeKeyAndVisible];
```

```
        return YES;
    }
```

After you run this program, assuming that you've followed the instructions in Recipe 8.2, you should see the `NSLog` on the console for a successful deletion. If not, you can always read the return value of the `SecItemDelete` function to determine what the issue was.

### See Also

Recipe 8.2

## 8.6. Sharing Keychain Data Between Multiple Apps

### Problem

You want two of your apps to be able to share keychain storage.

### Solution

When storing your keychain data, specify the `kSecAttrAccessGroup` key in the dictionary that gets passed to the `SecItemAdd` function. The value of this key has to be the access group, which you can find in the Entitlements section of your provision profile, as explained in this chapter's Introduction.

### Discussion

Multiple apps from the same developer portal can share a keychain area. To avoid complications, we are going to limit our thoughts to only two apps for now, but this same technique applies for any number of apps.

In order for two apps to be able to share a keychain area, the following criteria must be met:

1. Both apps must have been signed using a provision profile originated from the same iOS Developer Portal.
2. Both apps have to have the same Group ID in their provision profile. This is usually the Team ID as selected by Apple. I suggest that you *don't* change this group ID when you create your own provision profiles.
3. The first app that stores the value in the keychain must specify the `kSecAttrAccessGroup` attribute for the keychain item that is getting stored. This access group must be the same access group that is mentioned in your provision profile. Have a look at this chapter's Introduction to learn how to extract this value from your provision profiles.

4. The value stored in the keychain should have been stored with the `kSecAttrService` attribute set to a value that the two apps know about. This is usually the bundle identifier of the app that actually stored the value. If both apps are created by you, you know the bundle identifier of the app that stored the value. So you can read the value in your other app by providing the bundle identifier of the first app for the aforementioned key.
5. Both apps have to have a codesigning identity. This is a *plist* that contains the exact same contents from the Entitlements section of your provision profile. You will then have to set the path of this file in the Code Signing Entitlements of your build settings. We will talk about this in greater detail in a short while.

Even though your app is signed with provision profiles that have entitlements in them (please see this chapter's Introduction), you will still need to explicitly tell Xcode about your entitlements. The entitlements are nothing but a *plist* file with contents similar to these, which I took from the Entitlements that I showed you how to print in the Introduction:

```
<plist version="1.0">
    <dict>
        <key>application-identifier</key>
        <string>F3FU372W5M.com.pixolity.ios.cookbook.SecondSecurityApp</string>
        <key>com.apple.developer.default-data-protection</key>
        <string>NSFileProtectionComplete</string>
        <key>get-task-allow</key>
        <true/>
        <key>keychain-access-groups</key>
        <array>
            <string>F3FU372W5M.*</string>
        </array>
    </dict>
</plist>
```

Note the `keychain-access-groups` key. That key's value specifies the keychain group to which the current app has access: `F3FU372W5M.*`. You will have to find your own keychain access group in your Entitlements and use it in the example code in this recipe. We are going to write two apps. The first will write information to the keychain, referring to the keychain access group, and the second will read that information. The apps are going to have different bundle identifiers and are generally two completely separate apps, yet they will be able to share a keychain area.

The *F3FU372W5M.** access group is my team ID's keychain access group. This value will certainly be different for you. Use the technique that you learned in the Introduction section of this chapter to extract the entitlements of your provision profiles.

I am going to use the following settings for the first iOS app. You should replace them with your own:

*Bundle identifier*
: `com.pixolity.ios.cookbook.SecurityApp`

*Keychain access group*
: `F3FU372W5M.*`

*Provision profile*
: A provision profile specifically created for the bundle ID of this app

And here are my settings for the second app, or the app that can read the values stored in the keychain by the first app:

*Bundle identifier*
: `com.pixolity.ios.cookbook.SecondSecurityApp`

*Keychain access group*
: `F3FU372W5M.*`

*Provision profile*
: A provision profile specifically created for the bundle ID of this app, which differs from the provision profile that was created for the first app

The most important thing that differentiates the first app (the keychain storing app) from the second app (the keychain reading app) is the bundle identifiers. The first app will use its own bundle identifier to store a value in the keychain and the second app will use the first app's bundle identifier to read that same value back from the keychain. So let's write the code for the first app. This code is very similar to what we saw in Recipe 8.2. The only difference is that this new code will specify a keychain access group when storing the data to the keychain:

```
#import "AppDelegate.h"
#import <Security/Security.h>

@implementation AppDelegate

- (BOOL)            application:(UIApplication *)application
  didFinishLaunchingWithOptions:(NSDictionary *)launchOptions{

    NSString *key = @"Full Name";
    NSString *service = [[NSBundle mainBundle] bundleIdentifier];
    NSString *accessGroup = @"F3FU372W5M.*";

    /* First delete the existing one if one exists. We don't have to do this
     but SecItemAdd will fail if an existing value is in the keychain. */
    NSDictionary *queryDictionary = @{
              (__bridge id)kSecClass : (__bridge id)kSecClassGenericPassword,
              (__bridge id)kSecAttrService : service,
              (__bridge id)kSecAttrAccessGroup : accessGroup,
```

```
            (__bridge id)kSecAttrAccount : key,
            };

    SecItemDelete((__bridge CFDictionaryRef)queryDictionary);

    /* Then write the new value in the keychain */
    NSString *value = @"Steve Jobs";
    NSData *valueData = [value dataUsingEncoding:NSUTF8StringEncoding];

    NSDictionary *secItem = @{
            (__bridge id)kSecClass : (__bridge id)kSecClassGenericPassword,
            (__bridge id)kSecAttrService : service,
            (__bridge id)kSecAttrAccessGroup : accessGroup,
            (__bridge id)kSecAttrAccount : key,
            (__bridge id)kSecValueData : valueData,
            };

    CFTypeRef result = NULL;
    OSStatus status = SecItemAdd((__bridge CFDictionaryRef)secItem, &result);

    if (status == errSecSuccess){
        NSLog(@"Successfully stored the value");
    } else {
        NSLog(@"Failed to store the value with code: %ld", (long)status);
    }

    self.window = [[UIWindow alloc]
                   initWithFrame:[[UIScreen mainScreen] bounds]];
    self.window.backgroundColor = [UIColor whiteColor];
    [self.window makeKeyAndVisible];
    return YES;
}
```

This starts by querying the keychain to find an existing item with a given key, service name and keychain access group. If one exists, it deletes it from the keychain. We are doing this just to ensure that later we can add the new value successfully. The `SecItemAdd` fails if you attempt to overwrite an existing value. So we delete the existing value (if it exists) and write a new one. You could just as well attempt to find an existing value, update it if it exists, and write a new one if it doesn't exist. The latter approach is more complicated and not necessary for our demonstration.

Before you can run this app, though, you need to set up your code signing entitlements. To set the code signing entitlements of an app, follow these steps:

1. Use the technique that you learned in this chapter's Introduction to extract the entitlements of your provision profile.
2. Create a new plist in your app and call it *Entitlements.plist*. Paste the *contents* of the entitlements of your provision profile, exactly as they are, into the *Entitlements.plist* file and save.

3. Go to your build settings and look for Code Signing Entitlements. Set the value of this section to `$(TARGET_NAME)/Entitlements.plist`. This means that Xcode has to find the *Entitlements.plist* file in a folder that has the name of your target.

> The reason behind this value is that if you create a project named MyProject, Xcode will create a root directory (or SRCROOT) called *MyProject*. Under that, it will create another folder called *MyProject* under which your source codes will reside. Under SRCROOT (or the top-level MyProject), it will create another folder called *MyProjectTests* that will contain your unit/integration/UI tests. Under this structure, your *Entitlements.plist* file will be under *MyProject/MyProject/Entitlements.plist*. The Code Signing Entitlements looks for the given plist file under SRCROOT, so if you provide the value of *MyProject/Entitlements.plist* to it, it will be happy! The `$(TARGET_NAME)` is a variable in Xcode that resolves to the name of your target, which, by default, is the name of your project. Therefore, in the case of MyProject, the value `$(TARGET_NAME)/Entitlements.plist` will resolve to *MyProject/Entitlements.plist*.

4. Build your app to ensure that everything is working fine.

If you get an error similar to this:

```
error: The data couldn't be read because it isn't in the correct format.
```

it means that your entitlements are in the wrong format. The common error that a lot of iOS programmers make is to populate their entitlements file like so:

```
<plist version="1.0">
    <key>Entitlements</key>
    <dict>
        <key>application-identifier</key>
        <string>F3FU372W5M.com.pixolity.ios.cookbook.SecurityApp</string>
        <key>com.apple.developer.default-data-protection</key>
        <string>NSFileProtectionComplete</string>
        <key>get-task-allow</key>
        <true/>
        <key>keychain-access-groups</key>
        <array>
            <string>F3FU372W5M.*</string>
        </array>
    </dict>
</plist>
```

Note that this entitlements file is invalid because it contains an orphan `Entitlements` key on top. You will need to remove that key to make your entitlements file look like this:

```
<plist version="1.0">
    <dict>
        <key>application-identifier</key>
        <string>F3FU372W5M.com.pixolity.ios.cookbook.SecurityApp</string>
        <key>com.apple.developer.default-data-protection</key>
        <string>NSFileProtectionComplete</string>
        <key>get-task-allow</key>
        <true/>
        <key>keychain-access-groups</key>
        <array>
            <string>F3FU372W5M.*</string>
        </array>
    </dict>
</plist>
```

Now that we have the writing app done, we can focus on the iOS app that can read the data. These two are completely separate signed apps, each with its own provision profile:

```
#import "AppDelegate.h"
#import <Security/Security.h>

@implementation AppDelegate

- (BOOL)            application:(UIApplication *)application
  didFinishLaunchingWithOptions:(NSDictionary *)launchOptions{

    NSString *key = @"Full Name";
    /* This is the bundle ID of the app that wrote the data to the keychain.
     This is NOT this app's bundle ID. This app's bundle ID is
     com.pixolity.ios.cookbook.SecondSecurityApp. */
    NSString *service = @"com.pixolity.ios.cookbook.SecurityApp";
    NSString *accessGroup = @"F3FU372W5M.*";

    NSDictionary *queryDictionary = @{
              (__bridge id)kSecClass : (__bridge id)kSecClassGenericPassword,
              (__bridge id)kSecAttrService : service,
              (__bridge id)kSecAttrAccessGroup : accessGroup,
              (__bridge id)kSecAttrAccount : key,
              (__bridge id)kSecReturnData : (__bridge id)kCFBooleanTrue,
              };


    CFDataRef data = NULL;
    OSStatus found =
        SecItemCopyMatching((__bridge CFDictionaryRef)queryDictionary,
                            (CFTypeRef *)&data);

    if (found == errSecSuccess){
```

```
        NSString *value = [[NSString alloc]
                           initWithData:(__bridge_transfer NSData *)data
                           encoding:NSUTF8StringEncoding];

        NSLog(@"Value = %@", value);

    } else {
        NSLog(@"Failed to read the value with error = %ld", (long)found);
    }

    self.window = [[UIWindow alloc]
                   initWithFrame:[[UIScreen mainScreen] bounds]];
    self.window.backgroundColor = [UIColor whiteColor];
    [self.window makeKeyAndVisible];
    return YES;
}
```

Getting used to how the keychain works takes a while, but don't worry if things don't work right out the box. Simply read the instructions given in this chapter, especially this chapter's Introduction, to get a better understanding of the keychain access group and how that relates to your app's entitlements.

### See Also

Recipe 8.0, "Introduction"; Recipe 8.2

## 8.7. Writing to and Reading Keychain Data from iCloud

### Problem

You want to store data in the keychain and have that data stored in the user's iCloud keychain so that it will be available on all her devices.

### Solution

When adding your item to the keychain using the `SecItemAdd` function, add the `kSecAttrSynchronizable` key to the dictionary that you pass to that function. For the value of this key, pass `kCFBooleanTrue`.

### Discussion

When items are stored in the keychain with their `kSecAttrSynchronizable` key set to `kCFBooleanTrue`, they will be stored in the user's iCloud keychain. This means that the items will be available on all the user's devices as long as she is logged into them using her iCloud account. If you want to simply read a value that you know is synchronized to the user's iCloud keychain, you need to specify the aforementioned key and the kCFBooleanTrue for this key as well, so that iOS will retrieve that value from the cloud if it hasn't already done so.

The example that we are going to see here is 99% similar to the example code that we saw in Recipe 8.6. The difference is that, when we store or try to read from the keychain, we specify the kSecAttrSynchronizable in our dictionary and set the value of this key to kCFBooleanTrue. So let's have a look at how we can store the value in the keychain first:

```
#import "AppDelegate.h"
#import <Security/Security.h>

@implementation AppDelegate

- (BOOL)            application:(UIApplication *)application
  didFinishLaunchingWithOptions:(NSDictionary *)launchOptions{

    NSString *key = @"Full Name";
    NSString *service = [[NSBundle mainBundle] bundleIdentifier];
    NSString *accessGroup = @"F3FU372W5M.*";

    /* First delete the existing one if one exists. We don't have to do this
     but SecItemAdd will fail if an existing value is in the keychain. */
    NSDictionary *queryDictionary = @{
              (__bridge id)kSecClass : (__bridge id)kSecClassGenericPassword,
              (__bridge id)kSecAttrService : service,
              (__bridge id)kSecAttrAccessGroup : accessGroup,
              (__bridge id)kSecAttrAccount : key,
              (__bridge id)kSecAttrSynchronizable : (__bridge id)kCFBooleanTrue
              };

    SecItemDelete((__bridge CFDictionaryRef)queryDictionary);

    /* Then write the new value in the keychain */
    NSString *value = @"Steve Jobs";
    NSData *valueData = [value dataUsingEncoding:NSUTF8StringEncoding];

    NSDictionary *secItem = @{
              (__bridge id)kSecClass : (__bridge id)kSecClassGenericPassword,
              (__bridge id)kSecAttrService : service,
              (__bridge id)kSecAttrAccessGroup : accessGroup,
              (__bridge id)kSecAttrAccount : key,
              (__bridge id)kSecValueData : valueData,
              (__bridge id)kSecAttrSynchronizable : (__bridge id)kCFBooleanTrue
              };

    CFTypeRef result = NULL;
    OSStatus status = SecItemAdd((__bridge CFDictionaryRef)secItem, &result);

    if (status == errSecSuccess){
        NSLog(@"Successfully stored the value");
    } else {
```

```
        NSLog(@"Failed to store the value with code: %ld", (long)status);
    }

    self.window = [[UIWindow alloc]
                   initWithFrame:[[UIScreen mainScreen] bounds]];
    self.window.backgroundColor = [UIColor whiteColor];
    [self.window makeKeyAndVisible];
    return YES;
}
```

Please read the notes in Recipe 8.6. You should now know that the access group that has been provided in all these examples will be different from developer to developer. This is usually the team ID that Apple's iOS Developer Portal will generate for each developer, which is a random ID for that development team. You will need to change this for your app to make sure it matches *your* team ID.

That's the code for the app that stores values in the iCloud keychain. Now we have to write the app that reads this data:

```
#import "AppDelegate.h"
#import <Security/Security.h>

@implementation AppDelegate

- (BOOL)            application:(UIApplication *)application
  didFinishLaunchingWithOptions:(NSDictionary *)launchOptions{

    NSString *key = @"Full Name";
    /* This is the bundle ID of the app that wrote the data to the
     iCloud keychain. This is NOT this app's bundle ID. This app's bundle ID is
     com.pixolity.ios.cookbook.SecondSecurityApp */
    NSString *service = @"com.pixolity.ios.cookbook.SecurityApp";
    NSString *accessGroup = @"F3FU372W5M.*";

    NSDictionary *queryDictionary = @{
              (__bridge id)kSecClass : (__bridge id)kSecClassGenericPassword,
              (__bridge id)kSecAttrService : service,
              (__bridge id)kSecAttrAccessGroup : accessGroup,
              (__bridge id)kSecAttrAccount : key,
              (__bridge id)kSecReturnData : (__bridge id)kCFBooleanTrue,
              (__bridge id)kSecAttrSynchronizable : (__bridge id)kCFBooleanTrue
              };

    CFDataRef data = NULL;
    OSStatus found =
        SecItemCopyMatching((__bridge CFDictionaryRef)queryDictionary,
                            (CFTypeRef *)&data);
```

```
    if (found == errSecSuccess){
        NSString *value = [[NSString alloc]
                           initWithData:(__bridge_transfer NSData *)data
                           encoding:NSUTF8StringEncoding];

        NSLog(@"Value = %@", value);

    } else {
        NSLog(@"Failed to read the value with error = %ld", (long)found);
    }

    self.window = [[UIWindow alloc]
                   initWithFrame:[[UIScreen mainScreen] bounds]];
    self.window.backgroundColor = [UIColor whiteColor];
    [self.window makeKeyAndVisible];
    return YES;
}
```

There are a few things that you have to note about working with the iCloud keychain:

- Only passwords can be stored.
- The iCloud keychain is ubiquitous, meaning that it appears on multiple devices belonging to the same iCloud user. If you write to one iCloud keychain, the same item will be synchronized to all her devices. Similarly, if you delete an item, it will be deleted from all her devices, so take extra caution.

It's worth mentioning that all the other techniques that you learned in this chapter (such as updating an existing keychain item; see Recipe 8.4) work with the iCloud keychain as well.

### See Also

Recipe 8.0, "Introduction";Recipe 8.6

## 8.8. Storing Files Securely in the App Sandbox

### Problem

You want iOS to protect the files in your app sandbox from being read without permission, perhaps by iOS file explorers available on the Internet.

### Solution

Follow these steps:

1. Follow the steps in this chapter's Introduction to create a provision profile that is linked to an App ID that has Data Protection enabled.

2. Sign your app with the provision profile.
3. Set the Code Signing Entitlements of your app by following the instructions given in Recipe 8.6.
4. Use the `createFileAtPath:contents:attributes:` method of an instance of `NSFileManager` to store your file. For the `attributes` property, pass a dictionary that contains the `NSFileProtectionKey` key. The value of this key can be one of the following:

   `NSFileProtectionNone`
   : This dictates that there should be no file protection on the stored file. A file that is stored using this protection will be available to the app that writes it to disk and to any free or commercially accessible file explorer apps on the Internet that can expose the filesystem of an iOS device, even if the user's device is locked with a passcode. If you specify this key, you will be able to read from and write to your file, even if the user's device is locked.

   `NSFileProtectionComplete`
   : This is the strongest protection that you can give to your files. By doing so, your app will be able to read from and write to this file as long as the device is unlocked. As soon as the device is locked, you won't be able to read from or write to the file. When you use this type of protection, free or commercial file system explorers will not be able to read the contents of your files, even if the user's device is unlocked.

   `NSFileProtectionCompleteUnlessOpen`
   : Very similar to `NSFileProtectionComplete`. The only difference is that, as its name suggests, you will be able to access the file if you have already opened it, even if the user subsequently locks the device. So after you first open the file, you will be ensured access to it as long as your app doesn't exit.

   `NSFileProtectionCompleteUntilFirstUserAuthentication`
   : This means that your app will be able to read from and write to the file as soon as the user unlocks her device for the first time. After that, you can continue accessing the file, even if the user subsequently locks her device again.

Here is an example:

```
- (NSString *) filePath{
    NSFileManager *fileManager = [[NSFileManager alloc] init];

    NSError *error = nil;
    NSURL *documentFolderUrl = [fileManager URLForDirectory:NSDocumentDirectory
                                                   inDomain:NSUserDomainMask
                                          appropriateForURL:nil
                                                     create:YES
                                                      error:&error];
```

```
    if (error == nil && documentFolderUrl != nil){
        NSString *fileName = @"MyFile.txt";
        NSString *filePath = [documentFolderUrl.path
                              stringByAppendingPathComponent:fileName];
        return filePath;
    }

    return nil;
}

- (BOOL)            application:(UIApplication *)application
  didFinishLaunchingWithOptions:(NSDictionary *)launchOptions{

    /*
     Prerequisites:

        1) Sign with a valid provision profile
        2) Your profile has to have complete-file-protection enabled.
        3) Add Code Signing Entitlements to your project
     */

    NSFileManager *fileManager = [[NSFileManager alloc] init];

    if ([self filePath] != nil){

        NSData *dataToWrite = [@"Hello, World"
                               dataUsingEncoding:NSUTF8StringEncoding];

        NSDictionary *fileAttributes = @{
                                 NSFileProtectionKey : NSFileProtectionComplete
                                 };

        BOOL wrote = [fileManager createFileAtPath:[self filePath]
                                          contents:dataToWrite
                                        attributes:fileAttributes];

        if (wrote){
            NSLog(@"Successfully and securely stored the file");
        } else {
            NSLog(@"Failed to write the file");
        }
    }

    self.window = [[UIWindow alloc]
                   initWithFrame:[[UIScreen mainScreen] bounds]];

    self.window.backgroundColor = [UIColor whiteColor];
    [self.window makeKeyAndVisible];
    return YES;
}
```

## Discussion

Your users trust your apps. That means that if you ask them for information such as their first name and last name, they expect you, if storing those values, to store them in a secure place and protect them from being retrieved by a hacker or somebody who may have temporary access to their iOS devices.

Let's imagine that you are working on a photo-editing application where the user can hook up her camera to her iOS device, import her photos into your app, and use your app to edit, save, and share those photos. You can do what a lot of app developers do, which is import those photos into the Documents folder of your app, ready for editing. The issue with this approach is that any freely available iOS device explorer on the Internet can read the contents of the Documents folder on any app, even if the device is locked. In order to protect the user's data, you are expected to enable file protection on the files that you store in your app's sandbox. The file protection goes hand in hand with the user's device security, specifically her device's passcode/password. If she has set a passcode for her device, even if it is a simple passcode, and she locks her device, the files that have been stored in your app sandbox with the `NSFileProtectionComplete` key will not be accessible to outsiders, even those who may try to read the file using an iOS device explorer.

So, when shipping your application, or even while developing it, set up your development and distribution provision profiles with file protection enabled and ensure that the files that you store on disk are protected. Obviously, you don't want to protect *every* file if there is no need to. Just find out which files need to be protected from prying eyes, apply your file protections on those files, and leave the rest of the files unprotected on disk.

## See Also

Recipe 8.0, "Introduction"; Recipe 8.6

# 8.9. Securing Your User Interface

## Problem

You want to ensure that your UI conforms to some of the most common security guidelines in iOS.

## Solution

Follow these guidelines:

- Ensure that all passwords and secure fields are entered, by the user, into instances of `UITextField` with their `secureTextEntry` properties set to `YES`.
- If the user is on a screen that contains personal information, such as the user's credit card number or home address, set the `hidden` property of your app's main window to `YES` in the `applicationWillResignActive:` method of your app delegate, and set the same property to `NO` (to show the window) in the `applicationDidBecomeActive:` app delegate method. This will ensure that the screenshot that iOS takes of your app's UI when going to the background will not contain any of your window's contents in it. This method is recommended by Apple.
- Ensure that you validate the user's input in your text fields/views before sending them to a server.
- Using the mechanisms that you've learned in this chapter, secure the user's entry if you are storing it in files on disk or in the keychain.
- On screens where you accept a password or a numerical code for authentication, once the view controller is no longer on the screen, clear those password/code fields because the user won't need them anymore. If you are not relinquishing ownership of those view controllers, their contents will stay in the memory. This includes the secure text field entries on those view controllers. It's best to dispose of memory that contains sensitive information as soon as you are done with that data.

## Discussion

The only item in the list that requires more explanation is the second. When the user is looking at an app on the screen of her iOS device and sends the app to the background by pressing the Home screen, iOS puts the app into the inactive state and sends it to the background. When the app is sent to the background, iOS takes a screenshot of the app's user interface as it appears on the screen and saves that file in the *Library/Caches/Snapshots/* folder inside your app's sandbox. Once the user brings the app back to the foreground, iOS momentarily displays that screenshot to the user until the app comes back alive and takes control of the screen. This makes the transition from background to foreground look very smooth. Even though this adds value from the UX point of view, it raises a security concern that if the screen that was in the screenshot contained sensitive information, that information will be present in the screenshot and subsequently saved on disk. We cannot really disable this functionality in iOS, but we can neutralize its negative security aspects for our app. The way to do this, and the way Apple recommends we do it, is to cover our app's main window with another view or to hide our app's window by setting its `hidden` property to `YES` when our app becomes inactive and setting this property back to `NO` (to make the window visible again) when our app becomes active.

A common mistake made by iOS developers trying to meet this security requirement is to attempt to set the value of the `hidden` property of the `keyWindow` of their application to `YES` or `NO`. Even though the `keyWindow` of your application instance will be a valid window when your app is becoming inactive, it will be `nil` (or pointing to nothing) when your app becomes active. Therefore, to avoid this mistake, simply use the `window` property of your app delegate to hide or show the window.

The other security concern raised was the lingering personal data in our view controllers. Suppose you have a login view controller where the user can enter her username and password. Once the Login button is tapped (for instance), you send the user's credentials to a server using HTTPS network connections, and once the user is authenticated, you push another view controller on the screen. The problem with this approach is that the username and the password that the user entered on the previous screen are still in memory because the view controller is still in memory (remember, it is in the stack of view controllers of your navigation controller).

The way to solve this and increase the security of your UI is to set the `text` property of your (secure) text fields to `nil` just as you are pushing the second view controller on the screen. Alternatively, override the `viewWillDisappear:` instance method of your login view controller and set the text fields' `text` property to `nil` right there. However, you should be careful with this approach because the aforementioned instance method of your view controller gets called *anytime* your view controller disappears—for instance, when the user switches from the tab on which your view controller sits into another tab, and then comes back to your tab. That means your view controller disappeared and then reappeared. So if you clear your text fields in this case, when the user switches from the second tab back to the tab that contains your view controller, all the values that she may have entered into your text fields will disappear and she will have to type them all over again. You need to develop against your business requirements, and there is no single right way of handling this situation.

## See Also

Recipe 8.2; Recipe 8.8

CHAPTER 9

# Core Location and Maps

## 9.0. Introduction

The Core Location and Map Kit frameworks can be used to create location-aware and map-based applications. The Core Location framework uses the device's internal hardware to determine the current location of the device. The Map Kit framework enables your application to display maps to your users, put custom annotations on the maps, and so on. The availability of location services from a pure programming perspective depends on the availability of hardware on the device; if the hardware is there, it must be enabled and switched on for the Map Kit and Core Location frameworks to work. An iOS device with GPS services can use 2G, EDGE, 3G, 4G, and other technologies to determine the user's location. Presently, almost all iOS devices support location services, but it is good programming practice to check the availability of location services before starting to use them, as we cannot predict whether in the future Apple will release a device with all hardware required to support location services.

In the new LLVM compiler shipped with Xcode for iOS 7, Apple has introduced modules. In older versions of the SDK and Xcode, to be able to use the Core Location and Map Kit frameworks, you had to import those frameworks into your target manually. But with the introduction of modules, all you have to do to use these frameworks is to import their header files into your project's classes like so:

```
#import <CoreLocation/CoreLocation.h>
#import <MapKit/MapKit.h>
```

This will then import the Core Location and the Map Kit frameworks into your projects for you.

# 9.1. Creating a Map View

## Problem

You want to instantiate and display a map on a view.

## Solution

Create an instance of the `MKMapView` class and add it to a view or assign it as a subview of your view controller. Here is the declaration part of the implementation of our view controller that creates an instance of `MKMapView` and displays it full-screen on its view:

```
#import "ViewController.h"
#import <MapKit/MapKit.h>

@interface ViewController ()
@property (nonatomic, strong) MKMapView *myMapView;
@end

@implementation ViewController
```

This is a simple root view controller with a variable of type `MKMapView`. Later in the implementation of this view controller (*.m* file), we will initialize the map and set its type to `Satellite`, like so:

```
- (void)viewDidLoad{
    [super viewDidLoad];

    self.view.backgroundColor = [UIColor whiteColor];

    self.myMapView = [[MKMapView alloc]
                      initWithFrame:self.view.bounds];
    /* Set the map type to Satellite */
    self.myMapView.mapType = MKMapTypeSatellite;

    self.myMapView.autoresizingMask =
        UIViewAutoresizingFlexibleWidth |
        UIViewAutoresizingFlexibleHeight;

    /* Add it to our view */
    [self.view addSubview:self.myMapView];

}
```

## Discussion

Creating an instance of the `MKMapView` class is quite straightforward. We can simply assign a frame to it using its constructor, and after the map is created, add it as a subview of the view on the screen just so that we can see it.

MKMapView is a subclass of UIView, so you can manipulate any map view the way you manipulate an instance of UIView. We use a UIView property, for instance, in setting the backgroundColor property of our view.

If you haven't already noticed, the MKMapView class has a property called mapType that can be set to satellite, standard, or hybrid. In this example, we are using the satellite map type (see Figure 9-1).

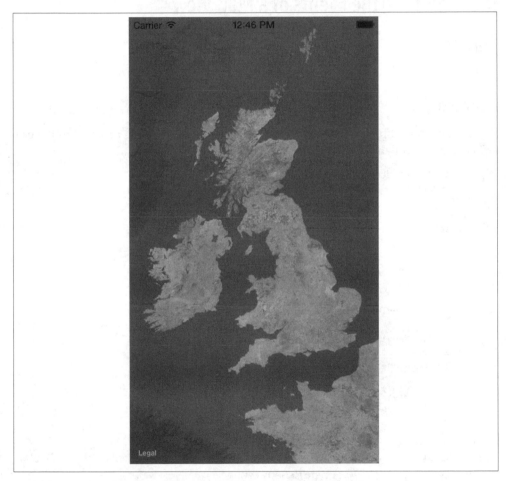

*Figure 9-1. A satellite map view*

You can change the visual representation type of a map view using the mapType property of the MKMapView instance. Here are the different values you can use for this property:

`MKMapTypeStandard`
: Use this map type to display a standard map (this is the default).

`MKMapTypeSatellite`
: Use this map type to display a satellite image map (as depicted in Figure 9-1).

`MKMapTypeHybrid`
: Use this map type to display a standard map overlaid on a satellite image map.

# 9.2. Handling the Events of a Map View

## Problem

You want to handle various events that a map view can send to its delegate.

## Solution

Assign a delegate object that conforms to the `MKMapViewDelegate` protocol to the `delegate` property of an instance of the `MKMapView` class:

```
- (void)viewDidLoad{
    [super viewDidLoad];

    /* Create a map as big as our view */
    self.myMapView = [[MKMapView alloc]
                      initWithFrame:self.view.bounds];

    /* Set the map type to Satellite */
    self.myMapView.mapType = MKMapTypeSatellite;

    self.myMapView.delegate = self;

    self.myMapView.autoresizingMask =
    UIViewAutoresizingFlexibleWidth |
    UIViewAutoresizingFlexibleHeight;

    /* Add it to our view */
    [self.view addSubview:self.myMapView];

}
```

This code can easily run in the `viewDidLoad` method of a view controller object that has a property named `MapView` of type `MKMapView`:

```
#import "ViewController.h"
#import <MapKit/MapKit.h>

@interface ViewController () <MKMapViewDelegate>
@property (nonatomic, strong) MKMapView *myMapView;
@end
```

```
@implementation ViewController
```

## Discussion

The delegate object of an instance of the `MKMapView` class must implement the methods defined in the `MKMapViewDelegate` protocol in order to receive various messages from the map view and, as we will see later, to provide information to the map view. Various methods are defined in the `MKMapViewDelegate` protocol, such as the `mapViewWillStartLoadingMap:` method that will get called in the delegate object whenever the map loading process starts. Bear in mind that a delegate for a map view is not a required object, meaning that you can create map views without assigning delegates to them; these views simply won't respond to user manipulation.

Here is a list of *some* of the methods declared in the `MKMapViewDelegate` protocol and what they are meant to report to the delegate object of an instance of `MKMapView`:

`mapViewWillStartLoadingMap:`
: This method is called on the delegate object whenever the map view starts to load the data that visually represents the map to the user.

`mapView:viewForAnnotation:`
: This method is called on the delegate object whenever the map view is asking for an instance of `MKAnnotationView` to visually represent an annotation on the map. For more information about this, please refer to Recipe 9.4.

`mapViewWillStartLocatingUser:`
: This method, as its name implies, gets called on the delegate object whenever the map view starts to detect the user's location. For information about finding a user's location, please refer to Recipe 9.3.

`mapView:regionDidChangeAnimated:`
: This method gets called on the delegate object whenever the region displayed by the map changes.

## See Also

Recipe 9.3; Recipe 9.4

# 9.3. Pinpointing the Location of a Device

## Problem

You want to find the latitude and longitude of a device.

## Solution

Use the CLLocationManager class:

```
- (void)viewDidLoad {
    [super viewDidLoad];

    if ([CLLocationManager locationServicesEnabled]){
        self.myLocationManager = [[CLLocationManager alloc] init];
        self.myLocationManager.delegate = self;


        [self.myLocationManager startUpdatingLocation];
    } else {
        /* Location services are not enabled.
         Take appropriate action: for instance, prompt the
         user to enable the location services */
        NSLog(@"Location services are not enabled");
    }

}
```

In this code, myLocationManager is a property of type CLLocationManager. The current class is also the delegate of the location manager in this sample code.

## Discussion

The Core Location framework in the SDK provides functionality for programmers to detect the current spatial location of an iOS device. Because in iOS, the user is allowed to disable location services using Settings, before instantiating an object of type CLLocationManager, it is best to first determine whether location services are enabled on the device.

The delegate object of an instance of CLLocationManager must conform to the CLLocationManagerDelegate protocol.

This is how we will declare our location manager object in our view controller (the object creating an instance of CLLocationManager does not necessarily have to be a view controller):

```
#import "ViewController.h"
#import <CoreLocation/CoreLocation.h>

@interface ViewController () <CLLocationManagerDelegate>
@property (nonatomic, strong) CLLocationManager *myLocationManager;
@end
```

```
@implementation ViewController
```

The implementation of our view controller is as follows:

```
- (void)locationManager:(CLLocationManager *)manager
    didUpdateToLocation:(CLLocation *)newLocation
           fromLocation:(CLLocation *)oldLocation{

    /* We received the new location */

    NSLog(@"Latitude = %f", newLocation.coordinate.latitude);
    NSLog(@"Longitude = %f", newLocation.coordinate.longitude);

}

- (void)locationManager:(CLLocationManager *)manager
       didFailWithError:(NSError *)error{

    /* Failed to receive user's location */

}

- (void)viewDidLoad {
    [super viewDidLoad];

    if ([CLLocationManager locationServicesEnabled]){
        self.myLocationManager = [[CLLocationManager alloc] init];
        self.myLocationManager.delegate = self;


        [self.myLocationManager startUpdatingLocation];
    } else {
        /* Location services are not enabled.
         Take appropriate action: for instance, prompt the
         user to enable the location services */
        NSLog(@"Location services are not enabled");
    }

}
```

The `startUpdateLocation` instance method of `CLLocationManager` reports the success or failure of retrieving the user's location to its delegate through the `locationManag er:didUpdateToLocation:fromLocation:` method and the `locationManager:did FailWithError:` method of its delegate object, in that order.

# 9.4. Displaying Pins on a Map View

## Problem

You want to point out a specific location on a map to the user.

## Solution

Use built-in map view annotations. Follow these steps:

1. Create a new class and call it `MyAnnotation`.
2. Make sure this class conforms to the `MKAnnotation` protocol.
3. Define a property for this class of type `CLLocationCoordinate2D` and name it `coordinate`. Make sure you set it as a `readonly` property since the `coordinate` property is defined as `readonly` in the `MKAnnotation` protocol.
4. Optionally, define two properties of type `NSString`, namely `title` and `subtitle`, which will be able to carry the title and the subtitle information for your annotation view. Both of these properties are `readonly` as well.
5. Create an initializer method for your class that will accept a parameter of type `CLLocationCoordinate2D`. In this method, assign the passed location parameter to the property that we defined in step 3. Since this property is `readonly`, it cannot be assigned by code outside the scope of this class. Therefore, the initializer of this class acts as a bridge here and allows us to indirectly assign a value to this property. We will do the same thing for the `title` and `subtitle` properties.
6. Instantiate the `MyAnnotation` class and add it to your map using the `addAnnotation:` method of the `MKMapView` class.

## Discussion

As explained in this recipe's Solution, we must create an object that conforms to the `MKAnnotation` protocol and later instantiate this object and pass it to the map to be displayed. We will declare the header of this object like so:

```
#import <Foundation/Foundation.h>
#import <MapKit/MapKit.h>

@interface MyAnnotation : NSObject <MKAnnotation>

@property (nonatomic, readonly) CLLocationCoordinate2D coordinate;
@property (nonatomic, copy, readonly) NSString *title;
@property (nonatomic, copy, readonly) NSString *subtitle;

- (instancetype) initWithCoordinates:(CLLocationCoordinate2D)paramCoordinates
                               title:(NSString *)paramTitle
                            subTitle:(NSString *)paramSubTitle;

@end
```

The *.m* file of the `MyAnnotation` class sets up the class to display location information as follows:

```
#import "MyAnnotation.h"

@implementation MyAnnotation

- (instancetype) initWithCoordinates:(CLLocationCoordinate2D)paramCoordinates
                               title:(NSString *)paramTitle
                            subTitle:(NSString *)paramSubTitle{

    self = [super init];

    if (self != nil){
        _coordinate = paramCoordinates;
        _title = paramTitle;
        _subtitle = paramSubTitle;
    }

    return self;

}

@end
```

Later, we will instantiate this class and add it to our map, for instance, in the *.m* file of a view controller that creates and displays a map view:

```
#import "ViewController.h"
#import "MyAnnotation.h"
#import <MapKit/MapKit.h>

@interface ViewController () <MKMapViewDelegate>
@property (nonatomic, strong) MKMapView *myMapView;
@end

@implementation ViewController

- (void)viewDidLoad {
    [super viewDidLoad];

    /* Create a map as big as our view */
    self.myMapView = [[MKMapView alloc]
                      initWithFrame:self.view.bounds];

    self.myMapView.delegate = self;

    /* Set the map type to Standard */
    self.myMapView.mapType = MKMapTypeStandard;

    self.myMapView.autoresizingMask =
        UIViewAutoresizingFlexibleWidth |
        UIViewAutoresizingFlexibleHeight;

    /* Add it to our view */
    [self.view addSubview:self.myMapView];
```

```
        /* This is just a sample location */
        CLLocationCoordinate2D location =
        CLLocationCoordinate2DMake(50.82191692907181, -0.13811767101287842);

        /* Create the annotation using the location */
        MyAnnotation *annotation =
        [[MyAnnotation alloc] initWithCoordinates:location
                                            title:@"My Title"
                                         subTitle:@"My Sub Title"];

        /* And eventually add it to the map */
        [self.myMapView addAnnotation:annotation];

    }

    @end
```

Figure 9-2 depicts the output of the program when run in iPhone Simulator.

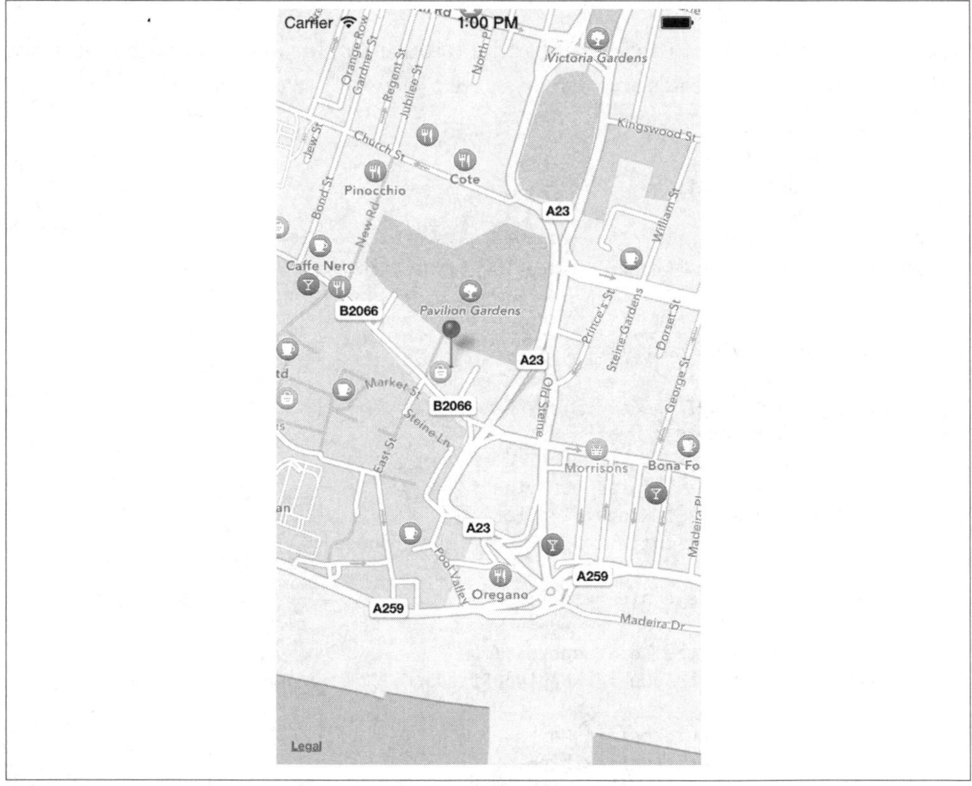


*Figure 9-2. A built-in pin dropped on a map*

# 9.5. Displaying Pins with Different Colors on a Map View

## Problem

The default color for pins dropped on a map view is red. You want to be able to display pins in different colors in addition to the default color.

## Solution

Return instances of `MKPinAnnotationView` to your map view through the `mapView:viewForAnnotation:` delegate method.

Every annotation that is added to an instance of `MKMapView` has a corresponding view that gets displayed on the map view. These views are called *annotation views*. An annotation view is an object of type `MKAnnotationView`, which is a subclass of `UIView`. If the delegate object of a map view implements the `mapView:viewForAnnotation:` delegate method, the delegate object will have to return instances of the `MKAnnotationView` class to represent (and optionally, customize) the annotation views to be displayed on a map view.

## Discussion

To set up our program so we can customize the color (choosing from the default SDK pin colors) of the annotation view that gets dropped on a map view to represent the annotation, we must return an instance of the `MKPinAnnotationView` class instead of an instance of `MKAnnotationView` in the `mapView:viewForAnnotation:` delegate method. Bear in mind that the `MKPinAnnotationView` class is a subclass of the `MKAnnotationView` class.

```
- (MKAnnotationView *)mapView:(MKMapView *)mapView
          viewForAnnotation:(id <MKAnnotation>)annotation{

    MKAnnotationView *result = nil;

    if ([annotation isKindOfClass:[MyAnnotation class]] == NO){
        return result;
    }

    if ([mapView isEqual:self.myMapView] == NO){
        /* We want to process this event only for the Map View
         that we have created previously */
        return result;
    }

    /* First typecast the annotation for which the Map View has
     fired this delegate message */
    MyAnnotation *senderAnnotation = (MyAnnotation *)annotation;
```

```
    /* Using the class method we have defined in our custom
     annotation class, we will attempt to get a reusable
     identifier for the pin we are about
     to create */
    NSString *pinReusableIdentifier =
    [MyAnnotation
     reusableIdentifierforPinColor:senderAnnotation.pinColor];

    /* Using the identifier we retrieved above, we will
     attempt to reuse a pin in the sender Map View */
    MKPinAnnotationView *annotationView = (MKPinAnnotationView *)
    [mapView
     dequeueReusableAnnotationViewWithIdentifier:pinReusableIdentifier];

    if (annotationView == nil){
        /* If we fail to reuse a pin, then we will create one */
        annotationView =  [[MKPinAnnotationView alloc]
                           initWithAnnotation:senderAnnotation
                           reuseIdentifier:pinReusableIdentifier];

        /* Make sure we can see the callouts on top of
         each pin in case we have assigned title and/or
         subtitle to each pin */
        [annotationView setCanShowCallout:YES];
    }

    /* Now make sure, whether we have reused a pin or not, that
     the color of the pin matches the color of the annotation */
    annotationView.pinColor = senderAnnotation.pinColor;

    result = annotationView;

    return result;
}
```

An annotation view must be reused by giving it an identifier (an `NSString`). By determining which type of pin you would like to display on a map view and setting a unique identifier for each type of pin (e.g., blue pins can be treated as one type of pin and red pins as another), you must reuse the proper type of pin using the `dequeueReusableAnnotationViewWithIdentifier:` instance method of `MKMapView` as demonstrated in the code.

We have set the mechanism of retrieving the unique identifiers of each pin in our custom `MyAnnotation` class. Here is the *.h* file of the `MyAnnotation` class:

```
#import <Foundation/Foundation.h>
#import <MapKit/MapKit.h>

/* These are the standard SDK pin colors. We are setting
 unique identifiers per color for each pin so that later we
 can reuse the pins that have already been created with the same
 color */
```

```
extern NSString *const kReusablePinRed;
extern NSString *const kReusablePinGreen;
extern NSString *const kReusablePinPurple;

@interface MyAnnotation : NSObject <MKAnnotation>

/* unsafe_unretained since this is not an object. We can skip this and leave
 it to the compiler to decide. weak or strong won't work as this is not
 an object */
@property (nonatomic, unsafe_unretained, readonly)
  CLLocationCoordinate2D coordinate;

@property (nonatomic, copy) NSString  *title;
@property (nonatomic, copy) NSString  *subtitle;

/* unsafe_unretained for the same reason as the coordinate property */
@property (nonatomic, unsafe_unretained) MKPinAnnotationColor  pinColor;

- (instancetype) initWithCoordinates:(CLLocationCoordinate2D)paramCoordinates
                               title:(NSString*)paramTitle
                            subTitle:(NSString*)paramSubTitle;

+ (NSString *) reusableIdentifierforPinColor:(MKPinAnnotationColor)paramColor;

@end
```

Annotations are not the same as annotation views. An annotation is the location that you want to show on a map, and an annotation view is the view that represents that annotation on the map. The `MyAnnotation` class is the annotation, not the annotation view. When we create an annotation by instantiating the `MyAnnotation` class, we can assign a color to it using the `pinColor` property that we have defined and implemented. When the time comes for a map view to display an annotation, the map view will call the `mapView:viewForAnnotation:` delegate method and ask its delegate for an annotation view. The `forAnnotation` parameter of this method passes the annotation that needs to be displayed. By getting a reference to the annotation, we can typecast the annotation to an instance of `MyAnnotation`, retrieve its `pinColor` property, and based on that, create an instance of `MKPinAnnotationView` with the given pin color and return it to the map view.

This is the *.m* file of `MyAnnotation`:

```
#import "MyAnnotation.h"

NSString *const kReusablePinRed = @"Red";
NSString *const kReusablePinGreen = @"Green";
NSString *const kReusablePinPurple = @"Purple";

@implementation MyAnnotation

+ (NSString *) reusableIdentifierforPinColor:(MKPinAnnotationColor)paramColor{
```

```
    NSString *result = nil;

    switch (paramColor){
        case MKPinAnnotationColorRed:{
            result = kReusablePinRed;
            break;
        }
        case MKPinAnnotationColorGreen:{
            result = kReusablePinGreen;
            break;
        }
        case MKPinAnnotationColorPurple:{
            result = kReusablePinPurple;
            break;
        }
    }

    return result;
}

- (instancetype) initWithCoordinates:(CLLocationCoordinate2D)paramCoordinates
                               title:(NSString*)paramTitle
                            subTitle:(NSString*)paramSubTitle{

    self = [super init];

    if (self != nil){
        _coordinate = paramCoordinates;
        _title = paramTitle;
        _subtitle = paramSubTitle;
        _pinColor = MKPinAnnotationColorGreen;
    }

    return self;

}

@end
```

After implementing the MyAnnotation class, it's time to use it in our application (in this example, we will use it in a view controller). Here is the top of the implementation file of the view controller:

```
#import "ViewController.h"
#import "MyAnnotation.h"
#import <MapKit/MapKit.h>

@interface ViewController () <MKMapViewDelegate>
@property (nonatomic, strong) MKMapView *myMapView;
@end
```

```
@implementation ViewController
```

The implementation is in the *.m* file like so:

```
- (MKAnnotationView *)mapView:(MKMapView *)mapView
          viewForAnnotation:(id <MKAnnotation>)annotation{

    MKAnnotationView *result = nil;

    if ([annotation isKindOfClass:[MyAnnotation class]] == NO){
        return result;
    }

    if ([mapView isEqual:self.myMapView] == NO){
        /* We want to process this event only for the Map View
         that we have created previously */
        return result;
    }

    /* First typecast the annotation for which the Map View has
     fired this delegate message */
    MyAnnotation *senderAnnotation = (MyAnnotation *)annotation;

    /* Using the class method we have defined in our custom
     annotation class, we will attempt to get a reusable
     identifier for the pin we are about
     to create */
    NSString *pinReusableIdentifier =
    [MyAnnotation
     reusableIdentifierforPinColor:senderAnnotation.pinColor];

    /* Using the identifier we retrieved above, we will
     attempt to reuse a pin in the sender Map View */
    MKPinAnnotationView *annotationView = (MKPinAnnotationView *)
    [mapView
     dequeueReusableAnnotationViewWithIdentifier:pinReusableIdentifier];

    if (annotationView == nil){
        /* If we fail to reuse a pin, then we will create one */
        annotationView =  [[MKPinAnnotationView alloc]
                           initWithAnnotation:senderAnnotation
                           reuseIdentifier:pinReusableIdentifier];

        /* Make sure we can see the callouts on top of
         each pin in case we have assigned title and/or
         subtitle to each pin */
        [annotationView setCanShowCallout:YES];
    }

    /* Now make sure, whether we have reused a pin or not, that
     the color of the pin matches the color of the annotation */
    annotationView.pinColor = senderAnnotation.pinColor;
```

```
        result = annotationView;

        return result;
    }

    - (void)viewDidLoad {
        [super viewDidLoad];

        /* Create a map as big as our view */
        self.myMapView = [[MKMapView alloc]
                          initWithFrame:self.view.bounds];

        self.myMapView.delegate = self;

        /* Set the map type to Standard */
        self.myMapView.mapType = MKMapTypeStandard;

        self.myMapView.autoresizingMask =
        UIViewAutoresizingFlexibleWidth |
        UIViewAutoresizingFlexibleHeight;

        /* Add it to our view */
        [self.view addSubview:self.myMapView];

        /* This is just a sample location */
        CLLocationCoordinate2D location;
        location.latitude = 50.82191692907181;
        location.longitude = -0.13811767101287842;

        /* Create the annotation using the location */
        MyAnnotation *annotation =
        [[MyAnnotation alloc] initWithCoordinates:location
                                            title:@"My Title"
                                         subTitle:@"My Sub Title"];

        annotation.pinColor = MKPinAnnotationColorPurple;

        /* And eventually add it to the map */
        [self.myMapView addAnnotation:annotation];

    }
```

The results are shown in Figure 9-3.

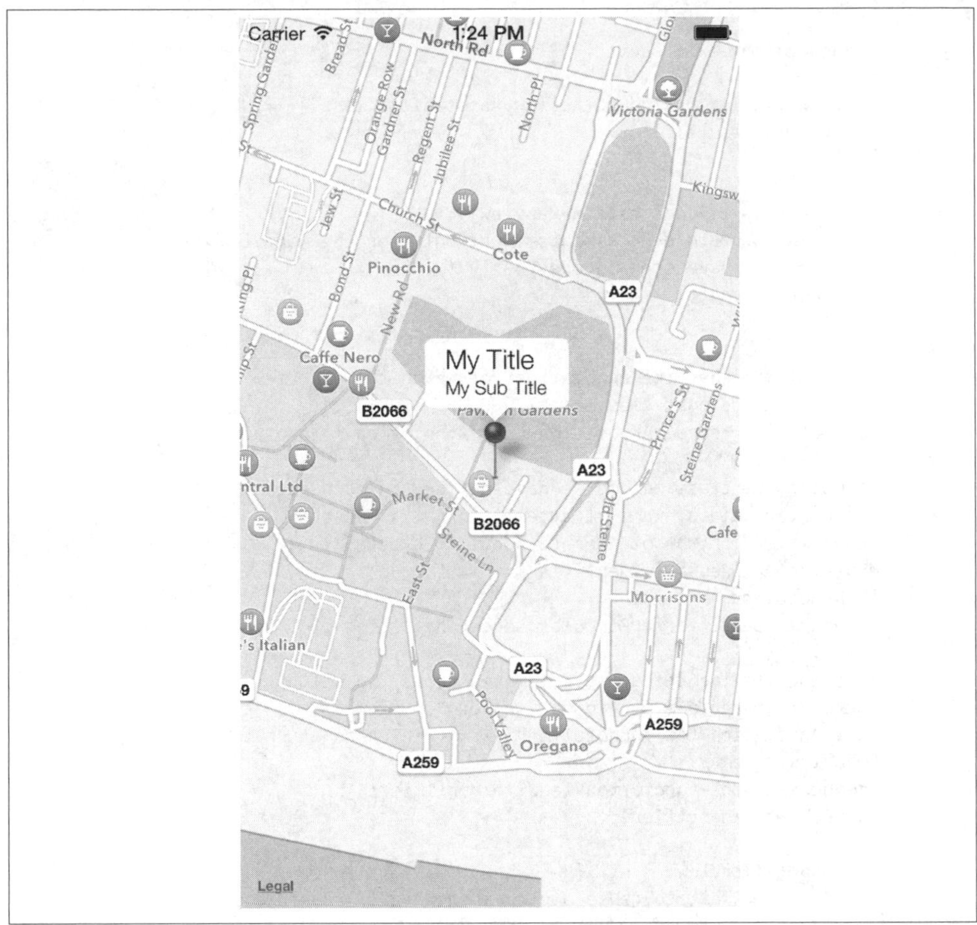


*Figure 9-3. A pin with an alternative color displayed on a map view*

# 9.6. Displaying Custom Pins on a Map View

## Problem

Instead of the default iOS SDK pins, you would like to display your own images as pins on a map view.

## Solution

Load an arbitrary image into an instance of the `UIImage` class and assign it to the `image` property of the `MKAnnotationView` instance that you return to your map view as a pin:

```
- (MKAnnotationView *)mapView:(MKMapView *)mapView
          viewForAnnotation:(id <MKAnnotation>)annotation{
```

```
MKAnnotationView *result = nil;

if ([annotation isKindOfClass:[MyAnnotation class]] == NO){
    return result;
}

if ([mapView isEqual:self.myMapView] == NO){
    /* We want to process this event only for the Map View
     that we have created previously */
    return result;
}

/* First typecast the annotation for which the Map View has
 fired this delegate message */
MyAnnotation *senderAnnotation = (MyAnnotation *)annotation;

/* Using the class method we have defined in our custom
 annotation class, we will attempt to get a reusable
 identifier for the pin we are about to create */
NSString *pinReusableIdentifier =
[MyAnnotation
 reusableIdentifierforPinColor:senderAnnotation.pinColor];

/* Using the identifier we retrieved above, we will
 attempt to reuse a pin in the sender Map View */
MKPinAnnotationView *annotationView = (MKPinAnnotationView *)
[mapView
 dequeueReusableAnnotationViewWithIdentifier:
 pinReusableIdentifier];

if (annotationView == nil){
    /* If we fail to reuse a pin, then we will create one */
    annotationView =
    [[MKPinAnnotationView alloc] initWithAnnotation:senderAnnotation
                                     reuseIdentifier:pinReusableIdentifier];

    /* Make sure we can see the callouts on top of
     each pin in case we have assigned title and/or
     subtitle to each pin */
    annotationView.canShowCallout = YES;

}

UIImage *pinImage = [UIImage imageNamed:@"BluePin"];
if (pinImage != nil){
    annotationView.image = pinImage;
}

result = annotationView;
```

```
        return result;
    }
```

In this code, we are displaying an image named *BluePin.png* (in our application bundle) for any pin that is dropped on the map. For the definition and the implementation of the `MyAnnotation` class, refer to Recipe 9.5.

## Discussion

The delegate object of an instance of the `MKMapView` class must conform to the `MKMapViewDelegate` protocol and implement the `mapView:viewForAnnotation:` method. The return value of this method is an instance of the `MKAnnotationView` class. Any object that subclasses the aforementioned class, by default, inherits a property called `image`. Assigning a value to this property will replace the default image provided by the Map Kit framework, as shown in Figure 9-4.

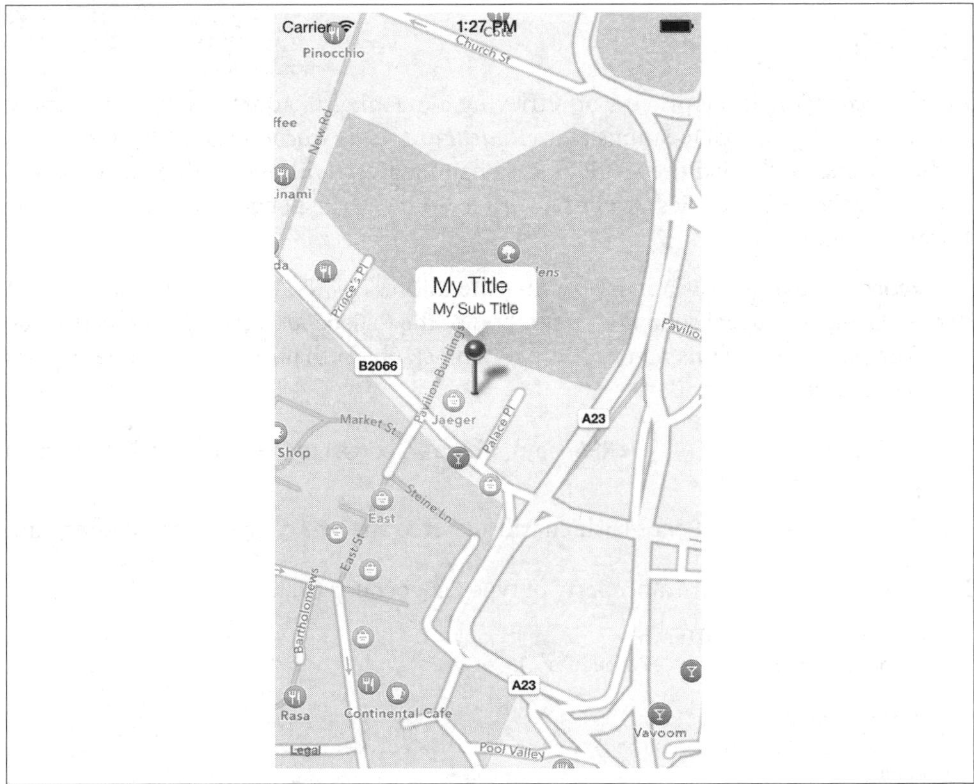


*Figure 9-4. A custom image displayed on a map view*

## See Also

Recipe 9.5

# 9.7. Converting Meaningful Addresses to Longitude and Latitude

## Problem

You have an address of a location and you want to find the spatial location (*longitude, latitude*) of that address.

## Solution

Use the `geocodeAddressString:completionHandler:` method of the `CLGeocoder` class.

## Discussion

*Reverse geocoding* is the process of retrieving a meaningful address, city and country, and so on, using spatial locations (*Longitude, Latitude*). *Geocoding*, on the other hand, is the process of finding the spatial locations of a given address. Both geocoding and reverse geocoding facilities are encapsulated into the `CLGeocoder` class in the Core Location framework.

We geocode spatial locations by passing the address as `NSString` to the `geocodeAddressString:completionHandler:` method of the `CLGeocoder` class. The `completionHandler` parameter of this method accepts a block object that returns no value and has two parameters:

1. A placemarks array (of type `NSArray`), which will be set to the locations that matched your search.
2. An error (of type `NSError`), which will get set to an error code if the geocoding fails.

Let's go ahead and declare a property of type `CLGeocoder` first:

```
#import "ViewController.h"
#import <CoreLocation/CoreLocation.h>

@interface ViewController ()
@property (nonatomic, strong) CLGeocoder *myGeocoder;
@end

@implementation ViewController
```

Now, let's go ahead and implement the code to geocode an address:

```
- (void)viewDidLoad{
    [super viewDidLoad];

    /* We have our address */
    NSString *oreillyAddress =
        @"1005 Gravenstein Highway North, Sebastopol, CA 95472, USA";

    self.myGeocoder = [[CLGeocoder alloc] init];

    [self.myGeocoder
     geocodeAddressString:oreillyAddress
     completionHandler:^(NSArray *placemarks, NSError *error) {

         if (placemarks.count > 0 && error == nil){

             NSLog(@"Found %lu placemark(s).",
                   (unsigned long)[placemarks count]);

             CLPlacemark *firstPlacemark = placemarks[0];

             NSLog(@"Longitude = %f",
                   firstPlacemark.location.coordinate.longitude);
             NSLog(@"Latitude = %f",
                   firstPlacemark.location.coordinate.latitude);
         }
         else if (placemarks.count == 0 &&
                  error == nil){
             NSLog(@"Found no placemarks.");
         }
         else if (error != nil){
             NSLog(@"An error occurred = %@", error);
         }

     }];

}
```

Once the program is run, even in the simulator, you will get the following values printed to the console window if you have a working and active network connection:

```
Found 1 placemark(s).
Longitude = -122.84159
Latitude = 38.410924
```

## See Also

Recipe 9.8

# 9.8. Converting Longitude and Latitude to a Meaningful Address

## Problem

You have the latitude and longitude of a spatial location, and you want to retrieve the address of this location.

## Solution

Retrieving a meaningful address using spatial *x* and *y* coordinates is called *reverse geocoding*. To do this, create and use an instance of the `CLGeocoder` class and provide a completion block object, making sure that the block object has no return value and accepts two parameters:

1. A placemarks array (of type `NSArray`), which will be set to the locations that matched your search.
2. An error (of type `NSError`), which will get set to an error code if the reverse geocoding fails.

After instantiating an object of type `CLGeocoder`, we will use its `reverseGeocodeLocation:completionHandler:` method to do the reverse geocoding.

The top of the *.m* file of a simple view controller for this purpose is defined like so:

```
#import "ViewController.h"
#import <CoreLocation/CoreLocation.h>

@interface ViewController ()
@property (nonatomic, strong) CLGeocoder *myGeocoder;
@end

@implementation ViewController
```

You can do the reverse geocoding when your view loads:

```
- (void)viewDidLoad{
    [super viewDidLoad];

    CLLocation *location = [[CLLocation alloc]
                            initWithLatitude:+38.4112810
                            longitude:-122.8409780f];

    self.myGeocoder = [[CLGeocoder alloc] init];

    [self.myGeocoder
     reverseGeocodeLocation:location
     completionHandler:^(NSArray *placemarks, NSError *error) {
```

```
            if (error == nil && placemarks.count > 0){
                CLPlacemark *placemark = placemarks[0];
                /* We received the results */
                NSLog(@"Country = %@", placemark.country);
                NSLog(@"Postal Code = %@", placemark.postalCode);
                NSLog(@"Locality = %@", placemark.locality);
            }
            else if (error == nil && placemarks.count == 0){
                NSLog(@"No results were returned.");
            }
            else if (error != nil){
                NSLog(@"An error occurred = %@", error);
            }

        }];
    }
```

The `placemarks` array, if the operation is successful, will contain objects of type `CLPlacemark`, which mark the addresses that match the longitude and latitude we passed to the `reverseGeocodeLocation:completionHandler:` method. So all we have to do is make sure that there were no errors, and that the array of placemarks contains at least one placemark.

The `NSLog` methods in the preceding code write the reverse geocoded address to the console window:

```
Country = United States
Postal Code = 95472
Locality = Sebastopol
```

## Discussion

Each application has a limit on the number of reverse geocoding requests that it can make each day. The amount depends on the backend provider for the location services in iOS. There are various paid online services that expose third-party APIs to developers. I cannot promote any of these services, but feel free to browse the Internet for them if you would like to get rid of limitations that currently exist in the iOS SDK for reverse geocoding spatial coordinates. To perform a reverse geocoding request, you must create an instance of the `CLGeocoder` class. This class requires an active network connection in order to process requests successfully. The reverse geocoded values are reported to the completion handler block that is passed to the `reverseGeocodeLocation:completionHandler:` method.

## See Also

Recipe 9.7

## 9.9. Searching on a Map View

### Problem

You want to be able to provide search functionality to your users while they are viewing a map view. For instance, you may want to allow your users to search for all restaurants or gyms in a given region inside the map. So if the person is in the center of the town and she can see her location on the map, she can simply type "restaurants" in the search box and get your app to do the search for her.

### Solution

Instantiate an object of type `MKLocalSearchRequest` and provide your search query, such as "restaurants," for the request. Then you can submit your request to the iOS SDK using the `MKLocalSearch` class. The response that you get will be of type `MKLocalSearchResponse`.

### Discussion

Map views are great, they really are. But what use do they have for the user if all she can see is just the map itself? The user may as well buy a traditional map on a piece of paper. Users like their smartphones' map capabilities because they are interactive. The user can find things, search for locations, and get directions to an address. Apple has included three really handy classes in the iOS SDK that allow us to search for locations on the map. The searching is really easy. All you have to do is provide a text of what you are actually looking for, such as "restaurants" or "cafes," and the SDK will do the rest of the job for you. For the purpose of this recipe, we are going to display a map view on our view controller, ask the map view to display the user's location, and track the user as she moves around so that the center of the map is always the location of where the user is right now.

Once our map view finds the user's location (assuming that the user gives us permission to find her location), we will issue a call to the `MKLocalSearch` class to fetch all the restaurants around the user's location. So let's begin by creating a map view on the screen and start tracking the user's location. The first thing to do is define the map view:

```
#import "ViewController.h"
#import <MapKit/MapKit.h>

@interface ViewController () <MKMapViewDelegate>
@property (nonatomic, strong) MKMapView *myMapView;
@end

@implementation ViewController
```

Next, we have to create the map view:

```
- (void)viewDidLoad {
    [super viewDidLoad];

    /* Create a map as big as our view */
    self.myMapView = [[MKMapView alloc]
                      initWithFrame:self.view.bounds];

    self.myMapView.delegate = self;

    /* Set the map type to Standard */
    self.myMapView.mapType = MKMapTypeStandard;

    self.myMapView.autoresizingMask =
        UIViewAutoresizingFlexibleWidth |
        UIViewAutoresizingFlexibleHeight;

    self.myMapView.showsUserLocation = YES;
    self.myMapView.userTrackingMode = MKUserTrackingModeFollow;

    /* Add it to our view */
    [self.view addSubview:self.myMapView];}
```

We are using the `showsUserLocation` property of the map view. It's a Boolean value, which, when set to `YES`, makes the map view find the user's location, assuming that she has given us permission to. That is all good, but the default behavior of the map view is to find the location and display an annotation on the map, but not to move the map's center location to zoom on the user's location. In other words, if the current view on the map view is on the United Kingdom and the user's current location is somewhere in New York, the user will still see her view of the United Kingdom on the map. We can remedy this by setting the value of the `userTrackingMode` property of our map view to `MKUserTrackingModeFollow`, which forces the map view to always keep the center of the map view as the user's location and adjust the map as the user moves.

Now that we have asked the map view to track the user's location, we need to implement the following map view delegates' methods:

`mapView:didFailToLocateUserWithError:`
: Gets called on the delegate when the map view has trouble finding the user's location. In this method, we are going to display an alert to the user to let her know that we had trouble finding her location.

`mapView:didUpdateUserLocation:`
: Gets called on the delegate of the map whenever the user's location is updated. So this is always the successful path of our logic, and we can implement our local search functionality in this method.

Let's implement the `mapView:didFailToLocateUserWithError:` method first:

```
- (void)                mapView:(MKMapView *)mapView
  didFailToLocateUserWithError:(NSError *)error{
```

```
    UIAlertView *alertView = [[UIAlertView alloc]
                              initWithTitle:@"Failed"
                              message:@"Could not get the user's location"
                              delegate:nil cancelButtonTitle:@"OK"
                              otherButtonTitles:nil];
    [alertView show];
}
```

Plain and simple. Next up, the `mapView:didUpdateUserLocation:` method:

```
- (void)        mapView:(MKMapView *)mapView
  didUpdateUserLocation:(MKUserLocation *)userLocation{

    MKLocalSearchRequest *request = [[MKLocalSearchRequest alloc] init];
    request.naturalLanguageQuery = @"restaurants";

    MKCoordinateSpan span = MKCoordinateSpanMake(0.01, 0.01);

    request.region =
    MKCoordinateRegionMake(userLocation.location.coordinate, span);

    MKLocalSearch *search = [[MKLocalSearch alloc] initWithRequest:request];

    [search startWithCompletionHandler:
     ^(MKLocalSearchResponse *response, NSError *error) {

         for (MKMapItem *item in response.mapItems){

             NSLog(@"Item name = %@", item.name);
             NSLog(@"Item phone number = %@", item.phoneNumber);
             NSLog(@"Item url = %@", item.url);
             NSLog(@"Item location = %@", item.placemark.location);

         }

    }];

}
```

What we are doing in this method is simple. We are creating a local search request and setting its `naturalLanguageQuery` property to the actual items that we want to find on the map, in this case restaurants. Then, we are retrieving the user's location and creating a region of type `MKCoordinateRegion` out of that. The purpose of this is that we want to find the region around the user and do our local search in there. The region tells the location search engines that we want to limit our search to the given region. Once the region is created, we will set that as the `region` property of the local search. As soon as that is done, we can begin the search by sending our local search request to the `startWithCompletionHandler:` instance method of the `MKLocalSearch` class. This method accepts a block as a parameter. This block will get called when the search results come back or an error occurs.

The items that are found will be in the `mapItems` property of the response parameter of your block object, and these map items will be of type `MKMapItem`. Each item has properties such as `name`, `phoneNumber`, and `url` that will help you plot those points of interest on the map, using the techniques that you learned in this chapter for displaying pins on the map (see Recipe 9.4).

### See Also

Recipe 9.4; Recipe 9.5; Recipe 9.6

## 9.10. Displaying Directions on the Map

### Problem

You want to display directions on a map to show the user how to get from point A to point B.

### Solution

Instantiate an object of type `MKDirections` and issue the `calculateDirectionsWithCompletionHandler:` instance method of that object. The completion handler will get called and will pass you an object of type `MKDirectionsResponse`. Use the directions response object to open the Maps app on your device, as you will soon learn.

### Discussion

Directions to walk or drive can be displayed only in the Maps app on a device, so you cannot display them inside an instance of a map view in your app. The way we will go about displaying directions is very straightforward. In order to display the directions on the Maps app, we need to create an instance of the `MKDirections` class. This class will require us to have already prepared an instance of the `MKDirectionsRequest`.

In addition, to create the directions request, you need to create instances of the `MKMapItem`. Every map item will represent a point on the map. So the bottom line is that if you want to display directions from point A to point B on the map, you need to represent them as map items, create a request out of that, and then use the `MKDirections` class to receive the directions. After receiving the directions, you have two choices:

- Process the directions yourself. For instance, using the technique that you learned earlier in this chapter (see Recipe 9.4), you may want to retrieve all the gas stations (placemarks) that are along the way from point A to point B and drop pins for those gas stations on the map.
- Send the directions to the Maps app for rendering.

In this recipe, we are going to explore the second option. So let's assume that we want to get *driving directions* from our current location to an arbitrary location on the map. For the purpose of this recipe, I am going to set the destination address as *`Churchill Square Shopping Center, Brighton, United Kingdom`*. Using the technique that you learned in Recipe 9.7, you can convert this meaningful address to its latitude and longitude, and then use that information to create an instance of the `MKPlacemark` class, as we shall soon see.

So let's get started. The first thing that we have to do is import the Core Location framework so that we can translate the aforementioned address to its raw coordinates (latitude, longitude). We will also import the MapKit framework so that we can create the directions request. Using LLVM's Modules feature, all we have to do is import these frameworks into our app:

```
#import "AppDelegate.h"
#import <CoreLocation/CoreLocation.h>
#import <MapKit/MapKit.h>

@implementation AppDelegate

<# Rest of your code goes here #>
```

Now we use what we learned in Recipe 9.7 to convert our destination address to latitude and longitude:

```
- (BOOL)            application:(UIApplication *)application
  didFinishLaunchingWithOptions:(NSDictionary *)launchOptions{

    NSString *destination = @"Churchill Square Shopping Center, \
    Brighton, United Kingdom";

    [[CLGeocoder new]
     geocodeAddressString:destination
     completionHandler:^(NSArray *placemarks, NSError *error) {

         <# Now we have the coordinates for the address #>

     }];

    self.window = [[UIWindow alloc] initWithFrame:[[UIScreen mainScreen] bounds]];
    // Override point for customization after application launch.
    self.window.backgroundColor = [UIColor whiteColor];
    [self.window makeKeyAndVisible];
    return YES;
}
```

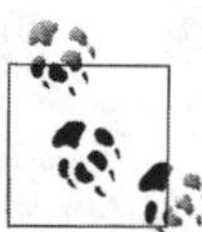

All the code that we write from here in this recipe will go inside the completion block object of the `geocodeAddressString:completionHandler:` method of the `CLGeocoder` class that we just wrote.

The completion block will give us a reference to an error object. You need to read this error object and, if an error comes back, handle it appropriately. I will leave that part to you. So now let's go and tell MapKit that we want the source of the directions to be where we currently are. We will use the `MKDirectionsRequest` class to create a directions request and set the value of the request's `source` property to the value of the `mapItemForCurrentLocation` class method of the `MKMapItem` class:

```
if (error != nil){
    /* Handle the error here perhaps by displaying an alert */
    return;
}

MKDirectionsRequest *request = [[MKDirectionsRequest alloc] init];
request.source = [MKMapItem mapItemForCurrentLocation];
```

Earlier on, we created a string object that contained our destination address. Now that we have its `CLPlacemark` instance, we need to convert it to an instance of `MKPlacemark` that can be set as the value of the `Destination` property of our directions request, like so:

```
/* Convert the CoreLocation destination
 placemark to a MapKit placemark */
/* Get the placemark of the destination address */
CLPlacemark *placemark = placemarks[0];
CLLocationCoordinate2D destinationCoordinates =
placemark.location.coordinate;
MKPlacemark *destination = [[MKPlacemark alloc]
                            initWithCoordinate:destinationCoordinates
                            addressDictionary:nil];

request.destination = [[MKMapItem alloc]
                       initWithPlacemark:destination];
```

The `MKDirectionsRequest` class has a property named `transportType` that is of type `MKDirectionsTransportType`:

```
typedef NS_OPTIONS(NSUInteger, MKDirectionsTransportType) {
    MKDirectionsTransportTypeAutomobile     = 1 << 0,
    MKDirectionsTransportTypeWalking        = 1 << 1,
    MKDirectionsTransportTypeAny            = 0x0FFFFFFF
} NS_ENUM_AVAILABLE(10_9, 7_0);
```

Since we want to display driving directions from our source to the destination, we are going to use the `MKDirectionsTransportTypeAutomobile` value in our recipe:

```
/* Set the transportation method to automobile */
request.transportType = MKDirectionsTransportTypeAutomobile;
```

Eventually, we will create an instance of the `MKDirections` class using its `initWithRequest:` initializer, which takes in as a parameter an instance of the `MKDirectionsRe` quest class. We already created and prepared this object with a map item indicating the source and destination.

We will then use the calculateDirectionsWithCompletionHandler: instance method of our directions class to get the directions from our source to destination map items. This method takes in as a parameter a block object that will provide us with an object of type MKDirectionsResponse and an error of type NSError that we can use to determine whether an error occurred. The response object that will get passed to us will have two very important properties: source and destination. These will be the same source and destination map items that we set before. Once in this block, you can either use the direction response and handle it manually, as explained before, or pass the source and destination to the Maps app for rendering like so:

```
/* Get the directions */
MKDirections *directions = [[MKDirections alloc]
                            initWithRequest:request];
[directions calculateDirectionsWithCompletionHandler:
 ^(MKDirectionsResponse *response, NSError *error) {

     /* You can manually parse the response, but in here we will take
      a shortcut and use the Maps app to display our source and
      destination. We didn't have to make this API call at all,
      as we already had the map items before, but this is to
      demonstrate that the directions response contains more
      information than just the source and the destination. */

     /* Display the directions on the Maps app */
     [MKMapItem
      openMapsWithItems:@[response.source, response.destination]
      launchOptions:@{
                      MKLaunchOptionsDirectionsModeKey :
                          MKLaunchOptionsDirectionsModeDriving}];
 }];
```

If we put all our code together now, we will get to a compact piece of code like this:

```
#import "AppDelegate.h"
#import <CoreLocation/CoreLocation.h>
#import <MapKit/MapKit.h>

@implementation AppDelegate

- (BOOL)            application:(UIApplication *)application
  didFinishLaunchingWithOptions:(NSDictionary *)launchOptions{

    NSString *destination = <# Place your destination address here #>;

    [[CLGeocoder new]
     geocodeAddressString:destination
     completionHandler:^(NSArray *placemarks, NSError *error) {
```

```
        if (error != nil){
            /* Handle the error here perhaps by displaying an alert */
            return;
        }

        MKDirectionsRequest *request = [[MKDirectionsRequest alloc] init];
        request.source = [MKMapItem mapItemForCurrentLocation];

        /* Convert the CoreLocation destination
         placemark to a MapKit placemark */
        /* Get the placemark of the destination address */
        CLPlacemark *placemark = placemarks[0];
        CLLocationCoordinate2D destinationCoordinates =
        placemark.location.coordinate;
        MKPlacemark *destination = [[MKPlacemark alloc]
                                    initWithCoordinate:destinationCoordinates
                                    addressDictionary:nil];

        request.destination = [[MKMapItem alloc]
                               initWithPlacemark:destination];

        /* Set the transportation method to automobile */
        request.transportType = MKDirectionsTransportTypeAutomobile;

        /* Get the directions */
        MKDirections *directions = [[MKDirections alloc]
                                    initWithRequest:request];
        [directions calculateDirectionsWithCompletionHandler:
         ^(MKDirectionsResponse *response, NSError *error) {

             /* You can manually parse the response, but in here we will take
              a shortcut and use the Maps app to display our source and
              destination. We didn't have to make this API call at all
              as we already had the map items before, but this is to
              demonstrate that the directions response contains more
              information than just the source and the destination. */

             /* Display the directions on the Maps app */
             [MKMapItem
              openMapsWithItems:@[response.source, response.destination]
              launchOptions:@{
                              MKLaunchOptionsDirectionsModeKey :
                                  MKLaunchOptionsDirectionsModeDriving}];
         }];

    }];

    self.window = [[UIWindow alloc] initWithFrame:[[UIScreen mainScreen] bounds]];
    // Override point for customization after application launch.
    self.window.backgroundColor = [UIColor whiteColor];
    [self.window makeKeyAndVisible];
```

```
    return YES;
}
```

Once I run this app in the iOS simulator, because my current location is very close to the destination location that I've chosen, I will see a result similar to that shown in Figure 9-5.

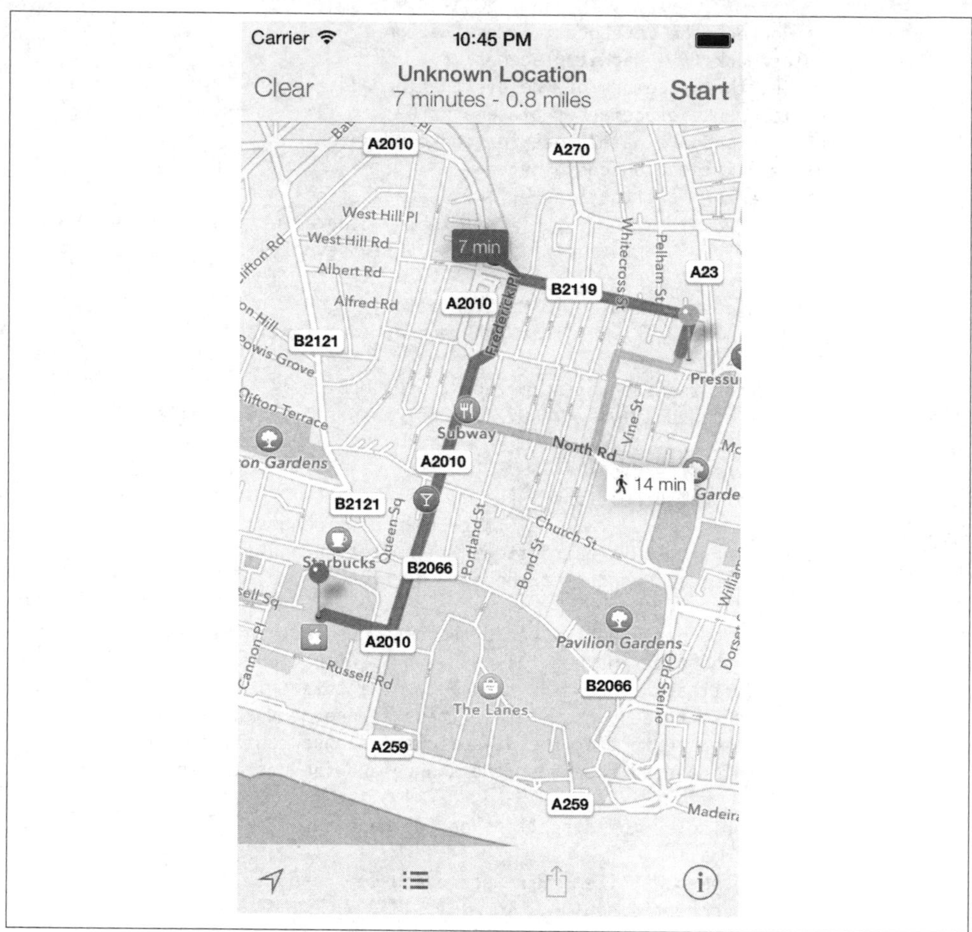


*Figure 9-5. Displaying directions on the map*

## See Also

Recipe 9.3

CHAPTER 10

# Implementing Gesture Recognizers

## 10.0. Introduction

Gestures are a combination of touch events. An example of a gesture can be found in the default iOS Photo application, which allows the user to zoom into and out of a photo while "pinching" the photo in and out using two fingers. Some of the most common gesture event detection code is encapsulated into reusable classes built into the iOS SDK. These classes can be used to detect swipe, pinch, pan, tap, drag, long-press, and rotation gestures.

Gesture recognizers must be added to instances of the `UIView` class. A single view can have more than one gesture recognizer. Once a view catches the gesture, that view will be responsible for passing down the same gesture to other views in the hierarchy, if needed.

Some touch events required by an application might be complicated to process and might require the same event to be detectable in other views in the same application. This introduces the requirements for reusable gesture recognizers. There are six gesture recognizers in iOS SDK 5 and above:

- Swipe
- Rotation
- Pinch
- Pan
- Long-press
- Tap

The basic framework for handling a gesture through a built-in gesture recognizer is as follows:

1. Create an object of the right data type for the gesture recognizer you want.
2. Add this object as a gesture recognizer to the view that will receive the gesture.
3. Write a method that is called when the gesture occurs and that takes the action you want.

The method associated as the target method of any gesture recognizer must follow these rules:

- It must return `void`.
- It must either accept no parameters, or accept a single parameter of type `UIGestureRecognizer` in which the system will pass the gesture recognizer that calls this method.

Here are two examples:

```
- (void) tapRecognizer:(UITapGestureRecognizer *)paramSender{
    /* */
}

- (void) tapRecognizer{
    /* */
}
```

Gesture recognizers are divided into two categories: *discrete* and *continuous*. Discrete gesture recognizers detect their gesture events and, once detected, call a method in their respective owners. Continuous gesture recognizers keep their owner objects informed of the events as they happen and will call the method in their target object repeatedly as the event happens and until it ends.

For instance, a double-tap event is discrete. Even though it consists of two taps, the system recognizes that the taps occurred close enough together to be treated as a single event. The double-tap gesture recognizer calls the method in its target object once the double-tap event is detected.

An example of a continuous gesture recognizer is rotation. This gesture starts as soon as the user starts the rotation and only finishes when the user lifts his fingers off the screen. The method provided to the rotation gesture recognizer class gets called at short intervals until the event is finished.

Gesture recognizers can be added to any instance of the `UIView` class using the `addGestureRecognizer:` method of the view, and when needed, they can be removed from the view using the `removeGestureRecognizer:` method.

The `UIGestureRecognizer` class has a property named `state`. The `state` property represents the different states the gesture recognizer can have throughout the recognition process. Discrete and continuous gesture recognizers go through different sets of states.

Discrete gesture recognizers can pass through the following states:

1. `UIGestureRecognizerStatePossible`
2. `UIGestureRecognizerStateRecognized`
3. `UIGestureRecognizerStateFailed`

Depending on the situation, a discrete gesture recognizer might send the `UIGestureRecognizerStateRecognized` state to its target, or it might send the `UIGestureRecognizerStateFailed` state if an error occurs during the recognition process.

Continuous gesture recognizers take a different path in the states they send to their targets:

1. `UIGestureRecognizerStatePossible`
2. `UIGestureRecognizerStateBegan`
3. `UIGestureRecognizerStateChanged`
4. `UIGestureRecognizerStateEnded`
5. `UIGestureRecognizerStateFailed`

A gesture recognizer's state is changed to `UIGestureRecognizerStatePossible` when it is gathering information about touch events on a view and *might* at any point detect the relevant gesture. In addition to the aforementioned states of a continuous gesture recognizer, the `UIGestureRecognizerStateCancelled` state can also be generated if anything interrupts the gesture. For instance, an incoming phone call can interrupt a pan gesture. In that case, the state of the gesture recognizer will be changed to `UIGestureRecognizerStateCancelled` and no further messages will be called on the receiver object by that gesture recognizer unless the user restarts the gesture sequence.

Again, if the continuous gesture recognizer stumbles upon a situation that cannot be fixed internally, it will end with the `UIGestureRecognizerStateFailed` state instead of `UIGestureRecognizerStateEnded`.

# 10.1. Detecting Swipe Gestures

## Problem

You want to be able to detect when the user performs a swipe gesture on a view—for instance, swiping a picture out of the window.

## Solution

Instantiate an object of type `UISwipeGestureRecognizer` and add it to an instance of `UIView`:

```
#import "ViewController.h"

@interface ViewController ()
@property (nonatomic, strong)
    UISwipeGestureRecognizer *swipeGestureRecognizer;
@end

@implementation ViewController

- (void)viewDidLoad {
    [super viewDidLoad];

    /* Instantiate our object */
    self.swipeGestureRecognizer = [[UISwipeGestureRecognizer alloc]
                                   initWithTarget:self
                                   action:@selector(handleSwipes:)];

    /* Swipes that are performed from right to
     left are to be detected */
    self.swipeGestureRecognizer.direction =
    UISwipeGestureRecognizerDirectionLeft;

    /* Just one finger needed */
    self.swipeGestureRecognizer.numberOfTouchesRequired = 1;

    /* Add it to the view */
    [self.view addGestureRecognizer:self.swipeGestureRecognizer];

}
```

A gesture recognizer could be created as a standalone object, but here, because we are using it for just one view, we have created it as a property of the view controller that will receive the gesture (`self.swipeGestureRecognizer`). This recipe's Discussion shows the `handleSwipes:` method used in this code as the target for the swipe gesture recognizer.

## Discussion

The swipe gesture is one of the most straightforward motions that built-in iOS SDK gesture recognizers will register. It is a simple movement of one or more fingers on a view from one direction to another. The `UISwipeGestureRecognizer`, like other gesture recognizers, inherits from the `UIGestureRecognizer` class and adds various functionalities to this class, such as properties that allow us to specify the direction in which the swipe gestures have to be performed in order to be detected, or how many fingers the user has to hold on the screen to be able to perform a swipe gesture. Please bear in mind that swipe gestures are discrete gestures.

The `handleSwipes:` method that we used for the gesture recognizer instance can be implemented in this way:

```
- (void) handleSwipes:(UISwipeGestureRecognizer *)paramSender{

    if (paramSender.direction & UISwipeGestureRecognizerDirectionDown){
        NSLog(@"Swiped Down.");
    }
    if (paramSender.direction & UISwipeGestureRecognizerDirectionLeft){
        NSLog(@"Swiped Left.");
    }
    if (paramSender.direction & UISwipeGestureRecognizerDirectionRight){
        NSLog(@"Swiped Right.");
    }
    if (paramSender.direction & UISwipeGestureRecognizerDirectionUp){
        NSLog(@"Swiped Up.");
    }

}
```

You can combine more than one direction in the `direction` property of an instance of the `UISwipeGestureRecognizer` class by using the bitwise OR operand. In Objective-C, this is done with the pipe (`|`) character. For instance, to detect diagonal swipes to the bottom-left corner of the screen, you can combine the `UISwipeGestureRecognizerDirectionLeft` and `UISwipeGestureRecognizerDirectionDown` values using the pipe character when constructing your swipe gesture recognizer. In the example, we are attempting to detect only swipes from the right side to the left.

Although swipe gestures are usually performed with one finger, the number of fingers required for the swipe gesture to be recognized can also be specified with the `numberOfTouchesRequired` property of the `UISwipeGestureRecognizer` class.

# 10.2. Detecting Rotation Gestures

## Problem

You want to detect when a user is attempting to rotate an element on the screen using her fingers.

## Solution

Create an instance of the UIRotationGestureRecognizer class and attach it to your target view:

```
- (void)viewDidLoad {
    [super viewDidLoad];

    self.helloWorldLabel = [[UILabel alloc] initWithFrame:CGRectZero];
    self.helloWorldLabel.text = @"Hello, World!";
    self.helloWorldLabel.font = [UIFont systemFontOfSize:16.0f];
    [self.helloWorldLabel sizeToFit];
    self.helloWorldLabel.center = self.view.center;
    [self.view addSubview:self.helloWorldLabel];

    self.rotationGestureRecognizer = [[UIRotationGestureRecognizer alloc]
                                      initWithTarget:self
                                      action:@selector(handleRotations:)];

    [self.view addGestureRecognizer:self.rotationGestureRecognizer];

}
```

## Discussion

The UIRotationGestureRecognizer, as its name implies, is the perfect candidate among gesture recognizers to detect rotation gestures and to help you build more intuitive graphical user interfaces. For instance, when the user encounters an image on the screen in your application in full-screen mode, it is quite intuitive for him to attempt to correct the orientation by rotating the image.

The UIRotationGestureRecognizer class implements a property named rotation that specifies the total amount and direction of rotation requested by the user's gesture, in radians. The rotation is determined from the fingers' initial position (UIGestureRecognizerStateBegan) and final position (UIGestureRecognizerStateEnded).

To rotate UI elements that inherit from UIView class, you can pass the rotation property of the rotation gesture recognizer to the CGAffineTransformMakeRotation function to make an affine transform, as shown in the example.

The code in this recipe's Solution passes the current object, in this case a view controller, to the target of the rotation gesture recognizer. The target selector is specified as handleRotations:, a method we have to implement. But before we do that, let's have a look at the top of the implementation file of the view controller:

```
#import "ViewController.h"

@interface ViewController ()
@property (nonatomic, strong)
    UIRotationGestureRecognizer *rotationGestureRecognizer;
```

```
@property (nonatomic, strong)
    UILabel *helloWorldLabel;

/* We can remove the nonatomic and the unsafe_unretained marks from this
 property declaration. On a float value, the compiler will generate both
 these for us automatically */
@property (nonatomic, unsafe_unretained)
    CGFloat rotationAngleInRadians;
@end

@implementation ViewController
```

Before we carry on, let's have a look at what each one of these properties does and why it is declared:

`helloWorldLabel`
: This is a label we must create on the view of the view controller. Then we will write the code to rotate this label whenever the user attempts to perform rotation gestures on the view that owns this label (in this case, the view of the view controller).

`rotationGestureRecognizer`
: This is the instance of the rotation gesture recognizer that we will later allocate and initialize.

`rotationAngleInRadians`
: This is the value we will query as the exact rotation angle of our label. Initially we will set this to zero. Since the rotation angles reported by a rotation gesture recognizer are reset every time the rotation gesture is started again, we can keep the value of the rotation gesture recognizer whenever it goes into the `UIGestureRecognizerStateEnded` state. The next time the gesture is started, we will add the previous value to the new value to get an overall rotation angle.

The size and the origin of the label does not matter much. Even the position of the label isn't that important, as we will only attempt to rotate the label around its center, no matter where on the view the label is positioned. The only important thing to remember is that in universal applications, the position of a label on a view controller used in different targets (devices) must be calculated dynamically using the size of its parent view. Otherwise, on different devices such as the iPad or the iPhone, it might appear in different places on the screen.

Using the `center` property of the label, and setting that center location to the center of the containing view, we will center-align the contents of the label. The rotation transformation that we will apply to this label rotates the label around its center—and left-aligned or right-aligned labels whose actual frame is bigger than the minimum frame required to hold their contents without truncation will appear to be rotating in an unnatural way and not on the center. If you are curious, go ahead and left- or right-align the contents of the label and see what happens.

As we saw in this recipe's Solution, the rotation gesture recognizer that we created will send its events to a method called `handleRotations:`. Here is the implementation for this method:

```
- (void) handleRotations:(UIRotationGestureRecognizer *)paramSender{

    if (self.helloWorldLabel == nil){
        return;
    }

    /* Take the previous rotation and add the current rotation to it */
    self.helloWorldLabel.transform =
    CGAffineTransformMakeRotation(self.rotationAngleInRadians +
                                  paramSender.rotation);

    /* At the end of the rotation, keep the angle for later use */
    if (paramSender.state == UIGestureRecognizerStateEnded){
        self.rotationAngleInRadians += paramSender.rotation;
    }

}
```

The way a rotation gesture recognizer sends us the rotation angles is very interesting. This gesture recognizer is continuous, which means it starts finding the angles as soon as the user begins her rotation gesture and sends updates to the handler method at frequent intervals until the user is done. Each message treats the starting angle as zero and reports the difference between the message's starting point (which is the angle where the previous message left off) and its ending point. Thus, the complete effect of the gesture can be discovered only by adding up the angles reported by the different events. Clockwise movement produces a positive angular value, whereas counterclockwise movement produces a negative value.

> If you are using iPhone Simulator instead of a real device, you can still simulate the rotation gesture by holding down the Option key in the simulator. You will see two circles appear on the simulator at the same distance from the center of the screen, representing two fingers. If you want to shift these fingers from the center to another location while holding down the Alt key, press the Shift key and point somewhere else on the screen. Where you leave your pointer will become the new center for these two fingers.

Now we will simply assign this angle to the rotation angle of the label. But can you imagine what will happen once the rotation is finished and another one starts? The second rotation gesture's angle will replace that of the first rotation in the `rotation` value reported to the handler. For this reason, whenever a rotation gesture is finished, we must keep the current rotation of the label. The value in each rotation gesture's angle must be added in turn, and we must assign the result to the label's rotation transformation as we saw before.

As we saw earlier, we used the `CGAffineTransformMakeRotation` function to create an affine transformation. Functions in the iOS SDK that start with "CG" refer to the Core Graphics framework. For programs that use Core Graphics to compile and link successfully, you must make sure the Core Graphics framework is added to the list of frameworks. New versions of Xcode link a default project against the Core Graphics framework automatically, so you don't really have to worry about that.

Now that we are sure Core Graphics is added to the target, we can compile and run the app.

## See Also

Recipe 10.6

# 10.3. Detecting Panning and Dragging Gestures

## Problem

You want the users of your application to be able to move GUI elements around using their fingers.

Pan gestures are continuous movements of fingers on the screen; recall that swipe gestures were discrete gestures. This means the method set as the target method of a pan gesture recognizer gets called repeatedly from the beginning to the end of the recognition process.

## Solution

Use the `UIPanGestureRecognizer` class:

```
- (void)viewDidLoad {
    [super viewDidLoad];

    /* Let's first create a label */
    CGRect labelFrame = CGRectMake(0.0f,     /* X */
                                   0.0f,     /* Y */
                                   150.0f,   /* Width */
                                   100.0f); /* Height */

    self.helloWorldLabel = [[UILabel alloc] initWithFrame:labelFrame];
    self.helloWorldLabel.text = @"Hello World";
    self.helloWorldLabel.backgroundColor = [UIColor blackColor];
    self.helloWorldLabel.textColor = [UIColor whiteColor];
```

```
    self.helloWorldLabel.textAlignment = NSTextAlignmentCenter;

    /* Make sure to enable user interaction; otherwise, tap events
     won't be caught on this label */
    self.helloWorldLabel.userInteractionEnabled = YES;

    /* And now make sure this label gets displayed on our view */
    [self.view addSubview:self.helloWorldLabel];

    /* Create the Pan Gesture Recognizer */
    self.panGestureRecognizer = [[UIPanGestureRecognizer alloc]
                                 initWithTarget:self
                                 action:@selector(handlePanGestures:)];

    /* At least and at most we need only one finger to activate
     the pan gesture recognizer */
    self.panGestureRecognizer.minimumNumberOfTouches = 1;
    self.panGestureRecognizer.maximumNumberOfTouches = 1;

    /* Add it to our view */
    [self.helloWorldLabel addGestureRecognizer:self.panGestureRecognizer];

}
```

The pan gesture recognizer will call the `handlePanGestures:` method as its target method. This method is described in this recipe's Discussion.

## Discussion

The `UIPanGestureRecognizer`, as its name implies, can detect *pan gestures*. The pan gesture recognizer will go through the following states while recognizing the pan gesture:

1. `UIGestureRecognizerStateBegan`
2. `UIGestureRecognizerStateChanged`
3. `UIGestureRecognizerStateEnded`

We can implement the gesture recognizer target method as follows. The code will continuously move the center of the label along with the user's finger as `UIGestureRecognizerStateChanged` events are reported:

```
- (void) handlePanGestures:(UIPanGestureRecognizer*)paramSender{

    if (paramSender.state != UIGestureRecognizerStateEnded &&
        paramSender.state != UIGestureRecognizerStateFailed){

        CGPoint location = [paramSender
                            locationInView:paramSender.view.superview];
```

```
        paramSender.view.center = location;
    }

}
```

To be able to move the label on the view of the view controller, we need the position of the finger on the view, not the label. For this reason, we are calling the `locationInView:` method of the pan gesture recognizer and passing the superview of the label as the target view.

Use the `locationInView:` method of the pan gesture recognizer to find the point of the current panning finger(s). To detect multiple finger locations, use the `locationOfTouch:inView:` method. Using the `minimumNumberOfTouches` and `maximumNumberOfTouches` properties of the `UIPanGestureRecognizer`, you can detect more than one panning touch at a time. In the example, for the sake of simplicity, we are trying to detect only one finger.

During the `UIGestureRecognizerStateEnded` state, the reported *x* and *y* values might not be a number; in other words, they could be equal to `NAN`. That is why we need to avoid using the reported values during this particular state.

# 10.4. Detecting Long-Press Gestures

## Problem

You want to be able to detect when the user taps and holds his finger on a view for a certain period of time.

## Solution

Create an instance of the `UILongPressGestureRecognizer` class and add it to the view that has to detect long-tap gestures:

```
#import "ViewController.h"

@interface ViewController ()
@property (nonatomic, strong)
    UILongPressGestureRecognizer *longPressGestureRecognizer;
@property (nonatomic, strong) UIButton *dummyButton;
@end

@implementation ViewController
```

Here is the `viewDidLoad` instance method of the view controller that uses the long-press gesture recognizer that we defined in the *.m* file:

```
- (void)viewDidLoad {
    [super viewDidLoad];

    self.dummyButton = [UIButton buttonWithType:UIButtonTypeRoundedRect];
    self.dummyButton.frame = CGRectMake(0.0f,
                                        0.0f,
                                        72.0f,
                                        37.0f);
    [self.dummyButton setTitle:@"My button" forState:UIControlStateNormal];
    self.dummyButton.center = self.view.center;
    [self.view addSubview:self.dummyButton];

    /* First create the gesture recognizer */
    self.longPressGestureRecognizer =
    [[UILongPressGestureRecognizer alloc]
     initWithTarget:self
     action:@selector(handleLongPressGestures:)];

    /* The number of fingers that must be present on the screen */
    self.longPressGestureRecognizer.numberOfTouchesRequired = 2;

    /* Maximum 100 points of movement allowed before the gesture
     is recognized */
    self.longPressGestureRecognizer.allowableMovement = 100.0f;

    /* The user must press 2 fingers (numberOfTouchesRequired) for
     at least 1 second for the gesture to be recognized */
    self.longPressGestureRecognizer.minimumPressDuration = 1.0;

    /* Add this gesture recognizer to our view */
    [self.view addGestureRecognizer:self.longPressGestureRecognizer];

}
```

If the long-press gesture recognizer is firing events to the receiver object while the gesture is continuing on the user's end, and a phone call or any other interruption comes in, the state of the gesture recognizer will be changed to `UIGestureRecognizerStateCancelled`. No further messages will be sent to the receiver object from that gesture recognizer until the user initiates the actions required to start the recognition process again; in this example, holding two fingers for at least one second on the view of our view controller.

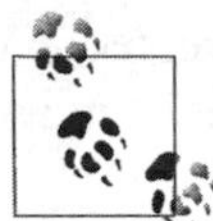

Our code runs on a view controller with a property named `longPressGestureRecognizer` of type `UILongPressGestureRecognizer`. For more information, refer to this recipe's Discussion.

## Discussion

The iOS SDK comes with a long-tap gesture recognizer class named `UILongTapGestureRecognizer`. A long-tap gesture is triggered when the user presses one or more fingers (configurable by the programmer) on a `UIView` and holds the finger(s) for a specific amount of time. Furthermore, you can narrow the detection of gestures down to only those long-tap gestures that are performed after a certain number of fingers are tapped on a view for a certain number of times and are then kept on the view for a specified number of seconds. Bear in mind that long taps are continuous events.

Four important properties can change the way the long-tap gesture recognizer performs.

`numberOfTapsRequired`
: This is the number of taps the user has to perform on the target view before the gesture can be triggered. Bear in mind that a tap is *not* merely a finger positioned on a screen. A tap is the movement of putting a finger down on the screen and lifting the finger off. The default value of this property is `0`.

`numberOfTouchesRequired`
: This property specifies the number of fingers that must be touching the screen before the gesture can be recognized. You must specify the same number of fingers to detect the taps, if the `numberOfTapsRequired` property is set to a value larger than `0`.

`allowableMovement`
: This is the maximum number of pixels that the fingers on the screen can be moved before the gesture recognition is aborted.

`minimumPressDuration`
: This property dictates how long, measured in seconds, the user must press his finger(s) on the screen before the gesture event can be detected.

In the example, these properties are set as follows:

- `numberOfTapsRequired`: Default (we are not changing this value)
- `numberOfTouchesRequired`: 2
- `allowableMovement`: 100
- `minimumPressDuration`: 1

With these values, the long-tap gesture will be recognized only if the user presses on the screen and holds both fingers for 1 second (`minimumPressDuration`) without moving her fingers more than 100 pixels around (`allowableMovement`).

Now when the gesture is recognized, it will call the `handleLongPressGestures:` method, which we can implement in this way:

```
- (void) handleLongPressGestures:(UILongPressGestureRecognizer *)paramSender{

    /* Here we want to find the mid point of the two fingers
     that caused the long press gesture to be recognized. We configured
     this number using the numberOfTouchesRequired property of the
     UILongPressGestureRecognizer that we instantiated in the
     viewDidLoad instance method of this View Controller. If we
     find that another long press gesture recognizer is using this
     method as its target, we will ignore it */

    if ([paramSender isEqual:self.longPressGestureRecognizer]){

        if (paramSender.numberOfTouchesRequired == 2){

            CGPoint touchPoint1 =
            [paramSender locationOfTouch:0
                                  inView:paramSender.view];

            CGPoint touchPoint2 =
            [paramSender locationOfTouch:1
                                  inView:paramSender.view];

            CGFloat midPointX = (touchPoint1.x + touchPoint2.x) / 2.0f;
            CGFloat midPointY = (touchPoint1.y + touchPoint2.y) / 2.0f;

            CGPoint midPoint = CGPointMake(midPointX, midPointY);

            self.dummyButton.center = midPoint;

        } else {
            /* This is a long press gesture recognizer with more
             or less than 2 fingers */

        }
    }

}
```

One of the applications in iOS that uses long-tap gesture recognizers is the Maps application. In this application, when you are looking at different locations, press your finger on a specific location and hold it for a while without lifting it off the screen. This will drop a pin on that specific location.

# 10.5. Detecting Tap Gestures

## Problem

You want to be able to detect when users tap on a view.

## Solution

Create an instance of the `UITapGestureRecognizer` class and add it to the target view, using the `addGestureRecognizer:` instance method of the `UIView` class. Let's have a look at the definition of the view controller:

```
#import "ViewController.h"

@interface ViewController ()
@property (nonatomic, strong)
    UITapGestureRecognizer *tapGestureRecognizer;
@end

@implementation ViewController
```

The implementation of the `viewDidLoad` instance method of the view controller is as follows:

```
- (void)viewDidLoad {
    [super viewDidLoad];

    /* Create the Tap Gesture Recognizer */
    self.tapGestureRecognizer = [[UITapGestureRecognizer alloc]
                                 initWithTarget:self
                                 action:@selector(handleTaps:)];

    /* The number of fingers that must be on the screen */
    self.tapGestureRecognizer.numberOfTouchesRequired = 2;

    /* The total number of taps to be performed before the
     gesture is recognized */
    self.tapGestureRecognizer.numberOfTapsRequired = 3;

    /* Add this gesture recognizer to our view */
    [self.view addGestureRecognizer:self.tapGestureRecognizer];
}
```

## Discussion

The tap gesture recognizer is the best candidate among gesture recognizers to detect plain tap gestures. A tap event is the event triggered by the user touching and lifting his finger(s) off the screen. A tap gesture is a discrete gesture.

The locationInView: method of the UITapGestureRecognizer class can be used to detect the location of the tap event. If the tap gesture requires more than one touch, the locationOfTouch:inView: method of the UITapGestureRecognizer class can be called to determine individual touch points. In the code, we have set the numberOfTouchesRequired property of the tap gesture recognizer to 2. With this value set, the gesture recognizer will require two fingers to be on the screen on each tap event. The number of taps that are required for the gesture recognizer to recognize this gesture is set to 3, using the numberOfTapsRequired property. We have provided the handleTaps: method as the target method of the tap gesture recognizer:

```
- (void) handleTaps:(UITapGestureRecognizer*)paramSender{

    NSUInteger touchCounter = 0;
    for (touchCounter = 0;
         touchCounter < paramSender.numberOfTouchesRequired;
         touchCounter++){
        CGPoint touchPoint =
        [paramSender locationOfTouch:touchCounter
                              inView:paramSender.view];
        NSLog(@"Touch #%lu: %@",
              (unsigned long)touchCounter+1,
              NSStringFromCGPoint(touchPoint));
    }

}
```

In this code, we are going through the number of touches that the tap gesture recognizer was asked to look for. Based on that number, we are finding the location of each tap. Depending on where you tap on the view on your simulator, you will get results similar to this in the console window:

```
Touch #1: {107, 186}
Touch #2: {213, 254}
```

If you are using the simulator, you can simulate two touches at the same time by holding down the Option key and moving your mouse on the simulator's screen. You will now have two concentric touch points on the screen.

One function worth noting is the NSStringFromCGPoint method, which, as its name implies, can convert a CGPoint structure to NSString. We use this function to convert the CGPoint of each touch on the screen to an NSString, so that we can log it to the console window using NSLog. You can bring up the console window with Run → Console.

# 10.6. Detecting Pinch Gestures

## Problem

You want your users to be able to perform pinch gesture on a view.

## Solution

Create an instance of the `UIPinchGestureRecognizer` class and add it to your target view, using the `addGestureRecognizer:` instance method of the `UIView` class:

```
- (void)viewDidLoad {
    [super viewDidLoad];

    CGRect labelRect = CGRectMake(0.0f,      /* X */
                                  0.0f,      /* Y */
                                  200.0f,    /* Width */
                                  200.0f);   /* Height */

    self.myBlackLabel = [[UILabel alloc] initWithFrame:labelRect];
    self.myBlackLabel.center = self.view.center;
    self.myBlackLabel.backgroundColor = [UIColor blackColor];

    /* Without this line, our pinch gesture recognizer
     will not work */
    self.myBlackLabel.userInteractionEnabled = YES;
    [self.view addSubview:self.myBlackLabel];

    /* Create the Pinch Gesture Recognizer */
    self.pinchGestureRecognizer =  [[UIPinchGestureRecognizer alloc]
                                    initWithTarget:self
                                    action:@selector(handlePinches:)];

    /* Add this gesture recognizer to our view */
    [self.myBlackLabel
     addGestureRecognizer:self.pinchGestureRecognizer];

}
```

The view controller is defined in this way:

```
#import "ViewController.h"

@interface ViewController ()
@property (nonatomic, strong)
    UIPinchGestureRecognizer *pinchGestureRecognizer;
@property (nonatomic, strong) UILabel *myBlackLabel;
@property (nonatomic, unsafe_unretained) CGFloat currentScale;
@end
```

## Discussion

Pinching allows users to scale GUI elements up and down easily. For instance, the Safari web browser on iOS allows users to pinch on a web page in order to zoom into the contents being displayed. Pinching works in two ways: scaling up and scaling down. It is a continuous gesture that must always be performed using two fingers on the screen.

The state of this gesture recognizer changes in this order:

1. `UIGestureRecognizerStateBegan`
2. `UIGestureRecognizerStateChanged`
3. `UIGestureRecognizerStateEnded`

Once the pinch gesture is recognized, the action method in the target object will be called (and will continue to be called until the pinch gesture ends). Inside the action method, you can access two very important properties of the pinch gesture recognizer: `scale` and `velocity`. `scale` is the factor by which you should scale the *x*- and *y*-axes of a GUI element to reflect the size of the user's gesture. `velocity` is the velocity of the pinch in pixels per second. The velocity is a negative value if the touch points are getting closer to each other and a positive value if they are getting farther away from each other.

The value of the `scale` property can be provided to the `CGAffineTransformMakeScale` Core Graphics function in order to retrieve an affine transformation. This affine transformation can be applied to the transform property of any instance of the `UIView` class in order to change its transformation. We are using this function in this way:

```
- (void) handlePinches:(UIPinchGestureRecognizer*)paramSender{

    if (paramSender.state == UIGestureRecognizerStateEnded){
        self.currentScale = paramSender.scale;
    } else if (paramSender.state == UIGestureRecognizerStateBegan &&
               self.currentScale != 0.0f){
        paramSender.scale = self.currentScale;
    }

    if (paramSender.scale != NAN &&
        paramSender.scale != 0.0){
        paramSender.view.transform =
        CGAffineTransformMakeScale(paramSender.scale,
                                   paramSender.scale);
    }

}
```

Since the `scale` property of a pinch gesture recognizer is reset every time a new pinch gesture is recognized, we are storing the last value of this property in an instance property of the view controller called `currentScale`. The next time a new gesture is recognized, we start the scale factor from the previously reported scale factor, as demonstrated in the code.

CHAPTER 11

# Networking, JSON, XML, and Sharing

## 11.0. Introduction

iOS apps, when connected to the Internet, become more lively. For example, imagine an app that brings high-quality wallpapers to its users. The user can pick from a big list of wallpapers and assign any of those images as his iOS background. Now consider an app that does the same thing but adds to its list of wallpapers every day, week, or month. The user comes back to the app, and voilà! Tons of new wallpapers are dynamically added to the app. That is the magic of web services and the Internet. This can easily be achieved with basic knowledge of networking, XML, JSON, and sharing options, along with some creativity on the app developer's part.

The iOS SDK allows us to connect to the Internet and retrieve and send data using the `NSURLConnection` class. JSON serialization and deserialization will all be done using the `NSJSONSerialization` class. XML parsing will be done using `NSXMLParser`, and the Twitter connectivity will be done using the Twitter framework.

The iOS 7 SDK brings along new classes that we can take advantage of in this chapter. One of these classes is the `NSURLSession`, which manages the connectivity to web services in a more thorough way than the `NSURLConnection` class does, as we shall see later in this chapter.

## 11.1. Downloading Asynchronously with NSURLConnection

### Problem

You want to download a file from a URL, asynchronously.

## Solution

Use the `NSURLConnection` class with an asynchronous request.

## Discussion

There are two ways of using the `NSURLConnection` class. One is asynchronous, and the other is synchronous. An asynchronous connection will create a new thread and does its downloading process on the new thread. A synchronous connection will block the *calling thread* while downloading content and doing its communication.

Many developers think that a synchronous connection blocks the *main thread*, but that is incorrect. A synchronous connection will always block the thread from which it is fired. If you fire a synchronous connection from the main thread, yes, the main thread will be blocked. But if you fire a synchronous connection from a thread other than the main thread, it will be like an asynchronous connection in that it won't block your main thread. In fact, the only difference between a synchronous and an asynchronous connection is that the runtime will create a thread for the asynchronous connection, while it won't do the same for a synchronous connection.

In order to create an asynchronous connection, we need to do the following:

1. Have our URL in an instance of `NSString`.
2. Convert our string to an instance of `NSURL`.
3. Place our URL in a URL Request of type `NSURLRequest`, or in the case of mutable URLs, in an instance of `NSMutableURLRequest`.
4. Create an instance of `NSURLConnection` and pass the URL request to it.

We can create an asynchronous URL connection using the `sendAsynchronousRequest:queue:completionHandler:` class method of `NSURLConnection`. Here are the parameters to this method:

`sendAsynchronousRequest`
: A request of type `NSURLRequest`, as we already discussed.

`queue`
: An operation queue. We can simply allocate and initialize a new operation queue and pass it to this method, if we wish.

`completionHandler`
: A block object to be executed when the asynchronous connection finishes its work either successfully or unsuccessfully. This block object should accept three parameters:

    1. An object of type `NSURLResponse`, which encapsulates the response that the server sent us, if any.

2. Data of type `NSData`, if any. This data will be the data that the connection fetched from the URL.
3. Error of type `NSError` if an error occurs.

The `sendAsynchronousRequest:queue:completionHandler:` method doesn't get called on the main thread, so make sure that, if you want to perform a UI-related task, you are back on the main thread.

Enough talk. Let's have a look at an example. In this example, we will try to fetch the HTML contents of Apple's home page and then print the contents as a string to the console window:

```
NSString *urlAsString = @"http://www.apple.com";
NSURL *url = [NSURL URLWithString:urlAsString];
NSURLRequest *urlRequest = [NSURLRequest requestWithURL:url];
NSOperationQueue *queue = [[NSOperationQueue alloc] init];

[NSURLConnection
sendAsynchronousRequest:urlRequest
queue:queue
completionHandler:^(NSURLResponse *response,
                    NSData *data,
                    NSError *error) {

  if ([data length] >0  &&
      error == nil){
    NSString *html = [[NSString alloc] initWithData:data
                                           encoding:NSUTF8StringEncoding];
    NSLog(@"HTML = %@", html);
  }
  else if ([data length] == 0 &&
           error == nil){
    NSLog(@"Nothing was downloaded.");
  }
  else if (error != nil){
    NSLog(@"Error happened = %@", error);
  }

}];
```

It's as simple as that. If you wanted to save the data that the connection downloaded for us to disk, you could simply do so using the appropriate methods of the `NSData` that we get from the completion block:

```
NSString *urlAsString = @"http://www.apple.com";
NSURL *url = [NSURL URLWithString:urlAsString];
NSURLRequest *urlRequest = [NSURLRequest requestWithURL:url];
NSOperationQueue *queue = [[NSOperationQueue alloc] init];
```

```
[NSURLConnection
 sendAsynchronousRequest:urlRequest
 queue:queue
 completionHandler:^(NSURLResponse *response,
                     NSData *data,
                     NSError *error) {

    if ([data length] >0  &&
        error == nil){

        /* Append the filename to the documents directory */
        NSURL *filePath =
        [[self documentsFolderUrl]
         URLByAppendingPathComponent:@"apple.html"];

        [data writeToURL:filePath atomically:YES];

        NSLog(@"Successfully saved the file to %@", filePath);

    }
    else if ([data length] == 0 &&
             error == nil){
        NSLog(@"Nothing was downloaded.");
    }
    else if (error != nil){
        NSLog(@"Error happened = %@", error);
    }

}];
```

It's that simple, really. In older versions of iOS SDK, URL connections used the delegation model, but now it's all simply block-based, and you no longer have to worry about implementing delegate methods.

# 11.2. Handling Timeouts in Asynchronous Connections

## Problem

You want to set a wait limit—in other words, a timeout—on an asynchronous connection.

## Solution

Set the timeout on the URL request that you pass to the `NSURLConnection` class.

## Discussion

When instantiating an object of type `NSURLRequest` to pass to your URL connection, you can use its `requestWithURL:cachePolicy:timeoutInterval:` class method and pass the desired number of seconds of your timeout as the `timeoutInterval` parameter.

For instance, if you want to wait a maximum of 30 seconds to download the contents of Apple's home page using a synchronous connection, create your URL request like so:

```
- (BOOL)            application:(UIApplication *)application
  didFinishLaunchingWithOptions:(NSDictionary *)launchOptions{

    NSString *urlAsString = @"http://www.apple.com";
    NSURL *url = [NSURL URLWithString:urlAsString];

    NSURLRequest *urlRequest =
    [NSURLRequest
     requestWithURL:url
     cachePolicy:NSURLRequestReloadIgnoringLocalAndRemoteCacheData
     timeoutInterval:30.0f];

    NSOperationQueue *queue = [[NSOperationQueue alloc] init];

    [NSURLConnection
     sendAsynchronousRequest:urlRequest
     queue:queue
     completionHandler:^(NSURLResponse *response,
                         NSData *data,
                         NSError *error) {

         if ([data length] >0  && error == nil){
             NSString *html =
             [[NSString alloc] initWithData:data
                                   encoding:NSUTF8StringEncoding];
             NSLog(@"HTML = %@", html);
         }
         else if ([data length] == 0 && error == nil){
             NSLog(@"Nothing was downloaded.");
         }
         else if (error != nil){
             NSLog(@"Error happened = %@", error);
         }

     }];

    self.window = [[UIWindow alloc]
                   initWithFrame:[[UIScreen mainScreen] bounds]];
    self.window.backgroundColor = [UIColor whiteColor];
    [self.window makeKeyAndVisible];
    return YES;
}
```

What will happen here is that the runtime will try to retrieve the contents of the provided URL. If this can be done before 30 seconds have elapsed and the connection is established before the timeout occurs, then fine. If not, the runtime will provide you with a timeout error in the error parameter of the completion block.

## 11.3. Downloading Synchronously with NSURLConnection

### Problem

You want to download the contents of a URL, synchronously.

### Solution

Use the `sendSynchronousRequest:returningResponse:error:` class method of `NSURLConnection`. The return value of this method is data of type `NSData`.

### Discussion

Using the `sendSynchronousRequest:returningResponse:error:` class method of `NSURLConnection`, we can send a synchronous request to a URL. Now, remember: synchronous connections do *not* necessarily block the main thread! Synchronous connections block the *current thread*, and if the current thread is the main thread, then the main thread will be blocked. If you go on a global concurrent queue with GCD and then initiate a synchronous connection, then you are *not* blocking the main thread.

Let's go ahead and initiate our first synchronous connection and see what happens. In this example, we will try to retrieve the home page of Yahoo!'s US website:

```
- (BOOL)            application:(UIApplication *)application
  didFinishLaunchingWithOptions:(NSDictionary *)launchOptions{

    NSLog(@"We are here...");

    NSString *urlAsString = @"http://www.yahoo.com";
    NSURL *url = [NSURL URLWithString:urlAsString];

    NSURLRequest *urlRequest = [NSURLRequest requestWithURL:url];

    NSURLResponse *response = nil;
    NSError *error = nil;

    NSLog(@"Firing synchronous url connection...");
    NSData *data = [NSURLConnection sendSynchronousRequest:urlRequest
                                         returningResponse:&response
                                                     error:&error];

    if ([data length] > 0 && error == nil){
        NSLog(@"%lu bytes of data was returned.",
```

```
                (unsigned long)[data length]);
    }
    else if ([data length] == 0 && error == nil){
        NSLog(@"No data was returned.");
    }
    else if (error != nil){
        NSLog(@"Error happened = %@", error);
    }

    NSLog(@"We are done.");

    self.window = [[UIWindow alloc] initWithFrame:
                   [[UIScreen mainScreen] bounds]];

    self.window.backgroundColor = [UIColor whiteColor];
    [self.window makeKeyAndVisible];
    return YES;
}
```

If you run this app and then look at the console window, you will see something similar to this printed out:

```
We are here...
Firing synchronous url connection...
252117 bytes of data was returned.
We are done.
```

So it's obvious that the current thread printed the string We are here... to the console window, waited for the connection to finish (as it was a synchronous connection that blocks the current thread), and then printed the We are done. text to the console window. Now let's do an experiment. Let's place the same exact synchronous connection inside a global concurrent queue in GCD, which guarantees concurrency, and see what happens:

```
- (BOOL)            application:(UIApplication *)application
  didFinishLaunchingWithOptions:(NSDictionary *)launchOptions{

    NSLog(@"We are here...");

    NSString *urlAsString = @"http://www.yahoo.com";

    NSLog(@"Firing synchronous url connection...");

    dispatch_queue_t dispatchQueue =
    dispatch_get_global_queue(DISPATCH_QUEUE_PRIORITY_DEFAULT, 0);

    dispatch_async(dispatchQueue, ^(void) {

        NSURL *url = [NSURL URLWithString:urlAsString];
        NSURLRequest *urlRequest = [NSURLRequest requestWithURL:url];
        NSURLResponse *response = nil;
        NSError *error = nil;
```

```
        NSData *data = [NSURLConnection sendSynchronousRequest:urlRequest
                                            returningResponse:&response
                                                        error:&error];

        if ([data length] > 0 && error == nil){
            NSLog(@"%lu bytes of data was returned.",
                  (unsigned long)[data length]);
        }
        else if ([data length] == 0 && error == nil){
            NSLog(@"No data was returned.");
        }
        else if (error != nil){
            NSLog(@"Error happened = %@", error);
        }
    });

    NSLog(@"We are done.");

    self.window = [[UIWindow alloc] initWithFrame:
                   [[UIScreen mainScreen] bounds]];

    self.window.backgroundColor = [UIColor whiteColor];
    [self.window makeKeyAndVisible];
    return YES;
}
```

The output will be similar to this:

```
We are here...
Firing synchronous url connection...
We are done.
252450 bytes of data was returned.
```

So in this example, the current thread carried on to print the `We are done.` text to the console window without having to wait for the synchronous connection to finish reading from its URL. That is interesting, isn't it? So this proves that a synchronous URL connection won't necessarily block the main thread, if managed properly. Synchronous connections are guaranteed to block the *current thread*, though.

# 11.4. Modifying a URL Request with NSMutableURLRequest

## Problem

You want to adjust various HTTP headers and settings of a URL request before passing it to a URL connection.

## Solution

This technique is the basis of many useful recipes shown later in this chapter. Use `NSMutableURLRequest` instead of `NSURLRequest`.

## Discussion

A URL request can be either *mutable* or *immutable*. A mutable URL request can be changed after it has been allocated and initialized, whereas an immutable URL request cannot. Mutable URL requests are the target of this recipe. You can create them using the `NSMutableURLRequest` class.

Let's have a look at an example where we will change the timeout interval of a URL request *after* we have allocated and initialized it:

```
NSString *urlAsString = @"http://www.apple.com";
NSURL *url = [NSURL URLWithString:urlAsString];

NSMutableURLRequest *urlRequest =
    [NSMutableURLRequest requestWithURL:url];

[urlRequest setTimeoutInterval:30.0f];
```

Now let's have a look at another example where we set the URL and the timeout of a URL request after it has been allocated and initialized:

```
NSString *urlAsString = @"http://www.apple.com";
NSURL *url = [NSURL URLWithString:urlAsString];
NSMutableURLRequest *urlRequest = [NSMutableURLRequest new];
[urlRequest setTimeoutInterval:30.0f];
[urlRequest setURL:url];
```

In other recipes in this chapter, we will have a look at some of the really neat tricks that we can perform using mutable URL requests.

# 11.5. Sending HTTP GET Requests with NSURLConnection

## Problem

You want to send a GET request over the HTTP protocol and perhaps pass parameters along your request to the receiver.

## Solution

By convention, GET requests allow parameters through query strings of the familiar form:

```
http://example.com/?param1=value1&param2=value2...
```

You can use strings to provide the parameters in the conventional format.

## Discussion

A GET request is a request to a web server to retrieve data. The request usually carries some parameters, which are sent in a query string as part of the URL.

In order to test a GET call, you need to find a web server that accepts the GET method and can send you some data back. This is simple. You may already know that when you open a web page in your browser, your browser by default sends a GET request to that end point, so you can use this recipe on any website of your liking.

To simulate sending query string parameters in a GET request to the same web service using `NSURLConnection`, use a mutable URL request and explicitly specify your HTTP method to `GET` using the `setHTTPMethod:` method of `NSMutableURLRequest` and put your parameters as part of the URL, like so:

```
- (BOOL)            application:(UIApplication *)application
  didFinishLaunchingWithOptions:(NSDictionary *)launchOptions{

    NSString *urlAsString = <# Place the URL of the web server here #>;
    urlAsString = [urlAsString stringByAppendingString:@"?param1=First"];
    urlAsString = [urlAsString stringByAppendingString:@"&param2=Second"];

    NSURL *url = [NSURL URLWithString:urlAsString];

    NSMutableURLRequest *urlRequest =
        [NSMutableURLRequest requestWithURL:url];

    [urlRequest setTimeoutInterval:30.0f];
    [urlRequest setHTTPMethod:@"GET"];

    NSOperationQueue *queue = [[NSOperationQueue alloc] init];

    [NSURLConnection
     sendAsynchronousRequest:urlRequest
     queue:queue
     completionHandler:^(NSURLResponse *response,
                         NSData *data,
                         NSError *error) {

         if ([data length] >0  && error == nil){
             NSString *html =
             [[NSString alloc] initWithData:data
                                   encoding:NSUTF8StringEncoding];
             NSLog(@"HTML = %@", html);
         }
         else if ([data length] == 0 && error == nil){
             NSLog(@"Nothing was downloaded.");
         }
         else if (error != nil){
```

```
                NSLog(@"Error happened = %@", error);
            }

        }];

    self.window = [[UIWindow alloc] initWithFrame:
                   [[UIScreen mainScreen] bounds]];

    self.window.backgroundColor = [UIColor whiteColor];
    [self.window makeKeyAndVisible];
    return YES;
}
```

The `urlAsString` variable in this code is an Xcode variable template. If you copy and paste this code into your Xcode project, the variable will get displayed as shown in Figure 11-1. Before running this example code, ensure that you have assigned a valid URL to the aforementioned variable.

```
NSString *urlAsString = Place the URL of the web server here ;
urlAsString = [urlAsString stringByAppendingString:@"?param1=First"];
urlAsString = [urlAsString stringByAppendingString:@"&param2=Second"];
```

*Figure 11-1. A replaceable variable in Xcode*

The only thing that you have to bear in mind is that the first parameter is prefixed with a question mark, and any subsequent parameter is prefixed with an ampersand. That's really about it! Now you are using the HTTP GET method, and you know how to send parameters as a query string.

# 11.6. Sending HTTP POST Requests with NSURLConnection

## Problem

You want to call a web service using the HTTP POST method, and perhaps pass parameters (as part of the HTTP body or in the query string) to the web service.

## Solution

Just as with the GET method, we can use the POST method using `NSURLConnection`. We must explicitly set our URL's method to POST.

## Discussion

Let's write a simple app that can create an asynchronous connection and send a few parameters as a query string and a few parameters in the HTTP body to a URL:

```
- (BOOL)            application:(UIApplication *)application
  didFinishLaunchingWithOptions:(NSDictionary *)launchOptions{

    NSString *urlAsString = <# Place the URL of the web server here #>;
    urlAsString = [urlAsString stringByAppendingString:@"?param1=First"];
    urlAsString = [urlAsString stringByAppendingString:@"&param2=Second"];

    NSURL *url = [NSURL URLWithString:urlAsString];

    NSMutableURLRequest *urlRequest = [NSMutableURLRequest requestWithURL:url];
    [urlRequest setTimeoutInterval:30.0f];
    [urlRequest setHTTPMethod:@"POST"];

    NSString *body = @"bodyParam1=BodyValue1&bodyParam2=BodyValue2";
    [urlRequest setHTTPBody:[body dataUsingEncoding:NSUTF8StringEncoding]];

    NSOperationQueue *queue = [[NSOperationQueue alloc] init];

    [NSURLConnection
     sendAsynchronousRequest:urlRequest
     queue:queue
     completionHandler:^(NSURLResponse *response,
                         NSData *data,
                         NSError *error) {

         if ([data length] >0  && error == nil){
             NSString *html =
             [[NSString alloc] initWithData:data
                                   encoding:NSUTF8StringEncoding];
             NSLog(@"HTML = %@", html);
         }
         else if ([data length] == 0 &&
                  error == nil){
             NSLog(@"Nothing was downloaded.");
         }
         else if (error != nil){
             NSLog(@"Error happened = %@", error);
         }

     }];

    self.window = [[UIWindow alloc] initWithFrame:
                   [[UIScreen mainScreen] bounds]];

    self.window.backgroundColor = [UIColor whiteColor];
    [self.window makeKeyAndVisible];
```

```
    return YES;
}
```

The first parameter sent in the HTTP body does not have to be prefixed with a question mark, unlike the first parameter in a query string.

# 11.7. Sending HTTP DELETE Requests with NSURLConnection

## Problem

You want to call a web service using the HTTP DELETE method to delete a resource from a URL, and perhaps pass parameters, as part of the HTTP body or in the query string, to the web service.

## Solution

Just as with the GET and POST methods, you can use the DELETE method using `NSURLConnection`. You must explicitly set your URL's method to DELETE.

## Discussion

Let's write a simple app that can create an asynchronous connection and send a few parameters as a query string and a few parameters in the HTTP body to the aforementioned URL, using the DELETE HTTP method:

```
- (BOOL)            application:(UIApplication *)application
  didFinishLaunchingWithOptions:(NSDictionary *)launchOptions{

    NSString *urlAsString = <# Place the URL of the web server here #>;
    urlAsString = [urlAsString stringByAppendingString:@"?param1=First"];
    urlAsString = [urlAsString stringByAppendingString:@"&param2=Second"];

    NSURL *url = [NSURL URLWithString:urlAsString];

    NSMutableURLRequest *urlRequest =
        [NSMutableURLRequest requestWithURL:url];

    [urlRequest setTimeoutInterval:30.0f];
    [urlRequest setHTTPMethod:@"DELETE"];

    NSString *body = @"bodyParam1=BodyValue1&bodyParam2=BodyValue2";
    [urlRequest setHTTPBody:[body dataUsingEncoding:NSUTF8StringEncoding]];

    NSOperationQueue *queue = [[NSOperationQueue alloc] init];
```

```
    [NSURLConnection
     sendAsynchronousRequest:urlRequest
     queue:queue
     completionHandler:^(NSURLResponse *response,
                         NSData *data,
                         NSError *error) {

         if ([data length] >0  && error == nil){
             NSString *html =
             [[NSString alloc] initWithData:data
                                   encoding:NSUTF8StringEncoding];
             NSLog(@"HTML = %@", html);
         }
         else if ([data length] == 0 && error == nil){
             NSLog(@"Nothing was downloaded.");
         }
         else if (error != nil){
             NSLog(@"Error happened = %@", error);
         }

     }];

    self.window = [[UIWindow alloc] initWithFrame:
                   [[UIScreen mainScreen] bounds]];

    self.window.backgroundColor = [UIColor whiteColor];
    [self.window makeKeyAndVisible];
    return YES;
}
```

This example is very similar to what we have already read about in Recipe 11.5 and Recipe 11.6. All we are doing differently here is setting the HTTP method of our connection to DELETE. The rest is really similar to what you already learned in the aforementioned recipes.

# 11.8. Sending HTTP PUT Requests with NSURLConnection

## Problem

You want to call a web service using the HTTP PUT method to place a resource into the web server, and perhaps pass parameters as part of the HTTP body or in the query string, to the web service.

## Solution

Just as with the GET, POST, and DELETE methods, we can use the PUT method using NSURLConnection. We must explicitly set our URL's method to PUT.

## Discussion

Let's write a simple app that can create an asynchronous connection and send a few parameters as a query string and a few parameters in the HTTP body to the aforementioned URL using the PUT method:

```
- (BOOL)            application:(UIApplication *)application
  didFinishLaunchingWithOptions:(NSDictionary *)launchOptions{

    NSString *urlAsString = <# Place the URL of the web server here #>;
    urlAsString = [urlAsString stringByAppendingString:@"?param1=First"];
    urlAsString = [urlAsString stringByAppendingString:@"&param2=Second"];

    NSURL *url = [NSURL URLWithString:urlAsString];

    NSMutableURLRequest *urlRequest =
        [NSMutableURLRequest requestWithURL:url];

    [urlRequest setTimeoutInterval:30.0f];
    [urlRequest setHTTPMethod:@"PUT"];

    NSString *body = @"bodyParam1=BodyValue1&bodyParam2=BodyValue2";
    [urlRequest setHTTPBody:[body dataUsingEncoding:NSUTF8StringEncoding]];

    NSOperationQueue *queue = [[NSOperationQueue alloc] init];

    [NSURLConnection
     sendAsynchronousRequest:urlRequest
     queue:queue
     completionHandler:^(NSURLResponse *response,
                         NSData *data,
                         NSError *error) {

         if ([data length] >0  && error == nil){
             NSString *html =
             [[NSString alloc] initWithData:data
                                   encoding:NSUTF8StringEncoding];
             NSLog(@"HTML = %@", html);
         }
         else if ([data length] == 0 && error == nil){
             NSLog(@"Nothing was downloaded.");
         }
         else if (error != nil){
             NSLog(@"Error happened = %@", error);
         }

     }];

    self.window = [[UIWindow alloc] initWithFrame:
                   [[UIScreen mainScreen] bounds]];

    self.window.backgroundColor = [UIColor whiteColor];
```

```
    [self.window makeKeyAndVisible];
    return YES;
}
```

The first parameter sent in the HTTP body does not have to be prefixed with a question mark, unlike the first parameter in a query string.

# 11.9. Serializing Arrays and Dictionaries into JSON

## Problem

You want to serialize a dictionary or an array into a JSON object that you can transfer over the network or simply save to disk.

## Solution

Use the `dataWithJSONObject:options:error:` method of the `NSJSONSerialization` class.

## Discussion

The `dataWithJSONObject:options:error:` method of the `NSJSONSerialization` class can serialize dictionaries and arrays that contain only instances of `NSString`, `NSNumber`, `NSArray`, `NSDictionary` variables, or `NSNull` for nil values. As mentioned, the object that you pass to this method should be either an array or a dictionary.

Now let's go ahead and create a simple dictionary with a few keys and values:

```
NSDictionary *dictionary =
@{
  @"First Name" : @"Anthony",
  @"Last Name" : @"Robbins",
  @"Age" : @51,
  @"children" : @[
          @"Anthony's Son 1",
          @"Anthony's Daughter 1",
          @"Anthony's Son 2",
          @"Anthony's Son 3",
          @"Anthony's Daughter 2"
          ],
  };
```

As you can see, this dictionary contains the first name, last name, and age of Anthony Robbins. A key in the dictionary named children contains the names of Anthony's children. This is an array of strings with each string representing one child. So by this time, the `dictionary` variable contains all the values that we want it to contain. It is now time to serialize it into a JSON object:

```
NSError *error = nil;
NSData *jsonData = [NSJSONSerialization
                    dataWithJSONObject:dictionary
                    options:NSJSONWritingPrettyPrinted
                    error:&error];

if ([jsonData length] > 0 && error == nil){
    NSLog(@"Successfully serialized the dictionary into data = %@",
          jsonData);
}
else if ([jsonData length] == 0 && error == nil){
    NSLog(@"No data was returned after serialization.");
}
else if (error != nil){
    NSLog(@"An error happened = %@", error);
}
```

The return value of the `dataWithJSONObject:options:error:` method is data of type `NSData`. However, you can simply turn this data into a string and print it to the console using the `initWithData:encoding:` initializer of `NSString`. Here is the complete example that serializes a dictionary into a JSON object, converts that object into a string, and prints the string out to the console window:

```
- (BOOL)            application:(UIApplication *)application
  didFinishLaunchingWithOptions:(NSDictionary *)launchOptions{

    NSDictionary *dictionary =
    @{
      @"First Name" : @"Anthony",
      @"Last Name" : @"Robbins",
      @"Age" : @51,
      @"children" : @[
              @"Anthony's Son 1",
              @"Anthony's Daughter 1",
              @"Anthony's Son 2",
              @"Anthony's Son 3",
              @"Anthony's Daughter 2"
              ],
      };

    NSError *error = nil;
    NSData *jsonData = [NSJSONSerialization
                        dataWithJSONObject:dictionary
                        options:NSJSONWritingPrettyPrinted
                        error:&error];

    if ([jsonData length] > 0 && error == nil){

        NSLog(@"Successfully serialized the dictionary into data.");
```

```
        NSString *jsonString =
        [[NSString alloc] initWithData:jsonData
                              encoding:NSUTF8StringEncoding];
        NSLog(@"JSON String = %@", jsonString);

    }
    else if ([jsonData length] == 0 && error == nil){
        NSLog(@"No data was returned after serialization.");
    }
    else if (error != nil){
        NSLog(@"An error happened = %@", error);
    }

    self.window = [[UIWindow alloc]
                   initWithFrame:[[UIScreen mainScreen] bounds]];
    // Override point for customization after application launch.
    self.window.backgroundColor = [UIColor whiteColor];
    [self.window makeKeyAndVisible];
    return YES;
}
```

When you run this app, the following results will get printed to the console window:

```
Successfully serialized the dictionary into data.
JSON String = {
  "Last Name" : "Robbins",
  "First Name" : "Anthony",
  "children" : [
    "Anthony's Son 1",
    "Anthony's Daughter 1",
    "Anthony's Son 2",
    "Anthony's Son 3",
    "Anthony's Daughter 2"
  ],
  "Age" : 51
}
```

# 11.10. Deserializing JSON into Arrays and Dictionaries

## Problem

You have JSON data, and you want to deserialize it into a dictionary or an array.

## Solution

Use the `JSONObjectWithData:options:error:` method of the `NSJSONSerialization` class.

## Discussion

If you already have serialized your dictionary or array into a JSON object (encapsulated inside an instance of `NSData`; see Recipe 11.9), you should be able to deserialize them back into a dictionary or an array, using the `JSONObjectWithData:options:error:` method of the `NSJSONSerialization` class. The object that is returned back by this method will be either a dictionary or an array, depending on the data that we pass to it. Here is an example:

```
/* Now try to deserialize the JSON object into a dictionary */
        error = nil;
        id jsonObject = [NSJSONSerialization
                         JSONObjectWithData:jsonData
                         options:NSJSONReadingAllowFragments
                         error:&error];

        if (jsonObject != nil && error == nil){

            NSLog(@"Successfully deserialized...");

            if ([jsonObject isKindOfClass:[NSDictionary class]]){

                NSDictionary *deserializedDictionary = jsonObject;
                NSLog(@"Deserialized JSON Dictionary = %@",
                      deserializedDictionary);

            }
            else if ([jsonObject isKindOfClass:[NSArray class]]){

                NSArray *deserializedArray = (NSArray *)jsonObject;
                NSLog(@"Deserialized JSON Array = %@", deserializedArray);

            }
            else {
                /* Some other object was returned. We don't know how to
                 deal with this situation as the deserializer only
                 returns dictionaries or arrays */
            }
        }
        else if (error != nil){
            NSLog(@"An error happened while deserializing the JSON data.");
        }
```

If now we mix this code with the code from Recipe 11.9, we can first serialize our dictionary into a JSON object, deserialize that JSON object back into a dictionary, and print out the results to make sure things went fine:

```
- (BOOL)            application:(UIApplication *)application
  didFinishLaunchingWithOptions:(NSDictionary *)launchOptions{

    NSDictionary *dictionary =
```

```
@{
  @"First Name" : @"Anthony",
  @"Last Name" : @"Robbins",
  @"Age" : @51,
  @"Children" : @[
          @"Anthony's Son 1",
          @"Anthony's Daughter 1",
          @"Anthony's Son 2",
          @"Anthony's Son 3",
          @"Anthony's Daughter 2",
          ],
  };

NSError *error = nil;
NSData *jsonData = [NSJSONSerialization
                    dataWithJSONObject:dictionary
                    options:NSJSONWritingPrettyPrinted
                    error:&error];

if ([jsonData length] > 0 && error == nil){

    NSLog(@"Successfully serialized the dictionary into data.");

    /* Now try to deserialize the JSON object into a dictionary */
    error = nil;
    id jsonObject = [NSJSONSerialization
                     JSONObjectWithData:jsonData
                     options:NSJSONReadingAllowFragments
                     error:&error];

    if (jsonObject != nil && error == nil){

        NSLog(@"Successfully deserialized...");

        if ([jsonObject isKindOfClass:[NSDictionary class]]){

            NSDictionary *deserializedDictionary = jsonObject;
            NSLog(@"Deserialized JSON Dictionary = %@",
                  deserializedDictionary);

        }
        else if ([jsonObject isKindOfClass:[NSArray class]]){

            NSArray *deserializedArray = (NSArray *)jsonObject;
            NSLog(@"Deserialized JSON Array = %@", deserializedArray);

        }
        else {
            /* Some other object was returned. We don't know how to
             deal with this situation as the deserializer only
             returns dictionaries or arrays */
        }
```

```
            }
            else if (error != nil){
                NSLog(@"An error happened while deserializing the JSON data.");
            }

        }
        else if ([jsonData length] == 0 && error == nil){
            NSLog(@"No data was returned after serialization.");
        }
        else if (error != nil){
            NSLog(@"An error happened = %@", error);
        }


        self.window = [[UIWindow alloc] initWithFrame:
                       [[UIScreen mainScreen] bounds]];
        // Override point for customization after application launch.
        self.window.backgroundColor = [UIColor whiteColor];
        [self.window makeKeyAndVisible];
        return YES;
    }
```

The `options` parameter of the `JSONObjectWithData:options:error:` method accepts one or a mixture of the following values:

`NSJSONReadingMutableContainers`
: The dictionary or the array returned by the `JSONObjectWithData:options:error:` method will be mutable. In other words, this method will return either an instance of `NSMutableArray` or `NSMutableDictionary`, as opposed to an immutable array or dictionary.

`NSJSONReadingMutableLeaves`
: Leaf values will be encapsulated into instances of `NSMutableString`.

`NSJSONReadingAllowFragments`
: Allows the deserialization of JSON data whose root top-level object is not an array or a dictionary.

## See Also

Recipe 11.9

# 11.11. Integrating Social Sharing into Your Apps

## Problem

You want to provide sharing capabilities in your app so that your user can compose a tweet or a Facebook status update on her device.

## Solution

Incorporate the `Social` framework into your app and use the `SLComposeViewController` class to compose social sharing messages, such as tweets.

## Discussion

The `SLComposeViewController` class is available in the `Social` framework and with the Modules feature in the LLVM compiler. All you have to do to start using this framework is import its umbrella header file into your project like so:

```
#import "ViewController.h"
#import <Social/Social.h>

@implementation ViewController
```

As Apple adds new social sharing options to the SDK, you can query the `Social` framework to find out, at runtime, which one of the services is available on the device that runs your app. Because the particular services vary from device to device, you should not try to use one until you make sure it is running. In order to query iOS for that, you need to use the `isAvailableForServiceType:` class method of the `SLComposeViewController` class. The parameter that you pass to this method is of type `NSString`, and here is a list of some of the valid parameters that you may pass to this method:

```
SOCIAL_EXTERN NSString *const SLServiceTypeTwitter;
SOCIAL_EXTERN NSString *const SLServiceTypeFacebook;
SOCIAL_EXTERN NSString *const SLServiceTypeSinaWeibo;
SOCIAL_EXTERN NSString *const SLServiceTypeTencentWeibo;
SOCIAL_EXTERN NSString *const SLServiceTypeLinkedIn;
```

Once you know a service is available, you can use the `composeViewControllerForServiceType:` class method of the `SLComposeViewController` class to get a new instance of your social sharing view controller. After that, things are super easy. All you have to do is use one or more of the following methods on your social sharing view controller:

`setInitialText:`
: Sets the string that you want to share with others.

`addImage:`
: Adds an image that has to be attached to your post.

`addURL:`
: Adds a URL that you can share along with your text and image.

The instance of the `SLComposeViewController` will also have a very handy property called `completionHandler`, which is a block object of type `SLComposeViewController CompletionHandler`. This completion handler will be called whenever the user finishes the sharing process successfully (meaning that she sends the sharing post out to be delivered by iOS to Twitter, Facebook, etc.) or if she cancels the dialog. A parameter of type `SLComposeViewControllerResult` will be delivered to this method to denote the type of event that happened, such as success or cancellation.

OK, enough talking. Let's get to the real juicy stuff. Here we are going to look at a code snippet that tries to find out whether the current device has Twitter sharing capabilities. If it does, the code composes a simple tweet with a picture and URL and displays the tweet dialog to the user, ready for tweeting:

```
- (void) viewDidAppear:(BOOL)animated{
    [super viewDidAppear:animated];

    if ([SLComposeViewController
         isAvailableForServiceType:SLServiceTypeTwitter]){

        SLComposeViewController *controller =
        [SLComposeViewController
         composeViewControllerForServiceType:SLServiceTypeTwitter];

        [controller setInitialText:@"MacBook Airs are amazingly thin!"];
        [controller addImage:[UIImage imageNamed:@"MacBookAir"]];
        [controller addURL:[NSURL URLWithString:@"http://www.apple.com/"]];

        controller.completionHandler = ^(SLComposeViewControllerResult result){
            NSLog(@"Completed");
        };

        [self presentViewController:controller animated:YES completion:nil];

    } else {
        NSLog(@"The twitter service is not available");
    }
}
```

Once you run this app on a device that has Twitter integration enabled in the iOS settings, the user will see something similar to that shown in Figure 11-2.

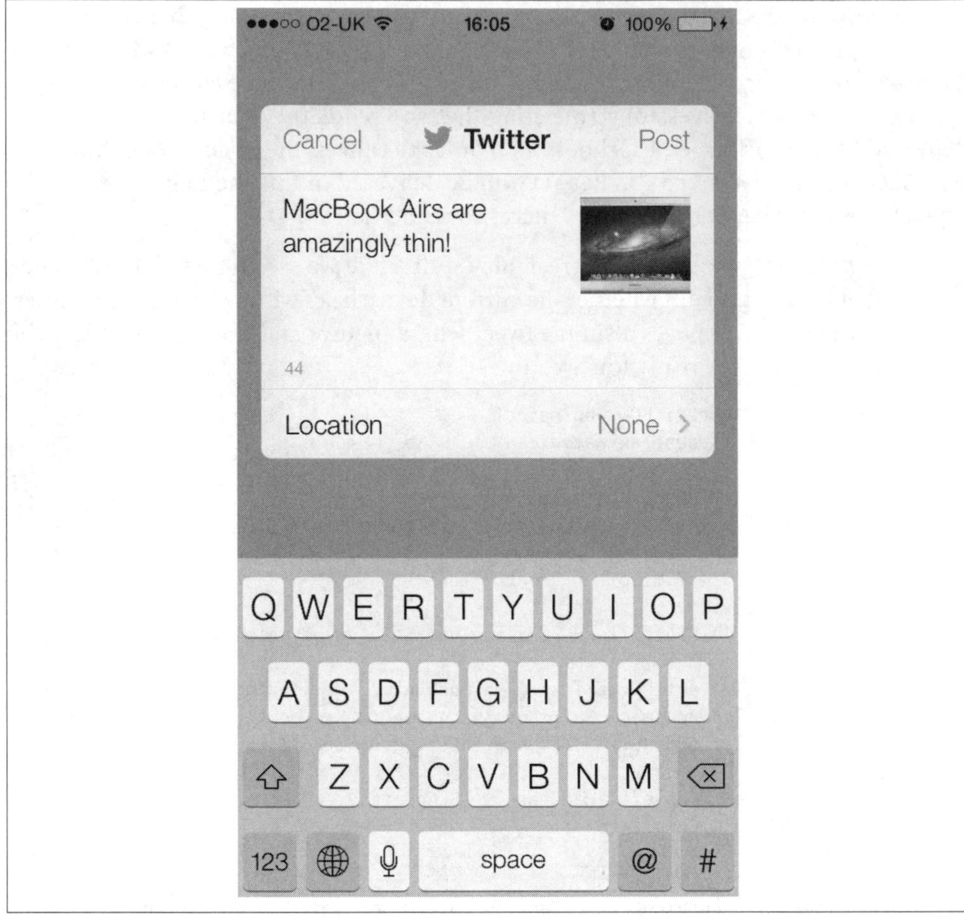


*Figure 11-2. Composing a simple tweet with the Social framework*

With this information, you can then compose various other messages, such as Facebook updates. All you have to do, really, as explained earlier, is to find out at runtime whether the given service is enabled and then attempt to use it by adding text, images, and URLs to your request.

One last thing to keep in mind is that the completion handler for your composer view controllers *may* be called on a different thread from the one that you used to create the controller. So remember that and use the techniques that you learned in Chapter 7 to switch to the main thread inside the completion handler if you want to do something UI related.

## See Also

Recipe 11.0, "Introduction"

# 11.12. Parsing XML with NSXMLParser

## Problem

You want to parse an XML snippet or document.

## Solution

Use the `NSXMLParser` class.

## Discussion

The `NSXMLParser` uses a delegate model to parse XML content. Let's go ahead and create a simple XML file that contains the following data (save this file as *MyXML.xml* in your project):

```
<?xml version="1.0" encoding="UTF-8"?>
<root>

    <person id="1">
        <firstName>Anthony</firstName>
        <lastName>Robbins</lastName>
        <age>51</age>
    </person>

    <person id="2">
        <firstName>Richard</firstName>
        <lastName>Branson</lastName>
        <age>61</age>
    </person>

</root>
```

Now define a property of type `NSXMLParser`:

```
#import "AppDelegate.h"

@interface AppDelegate () <NSXMLParserDelegate>
@property (nonatomic, strong) NSXMLParser *xmlParser;
@end

@implementation AppDelegate
```

You can also see that I have defined my app delegate as an XML parser delegate by conforming to the `NSXMLParserDelegate` protocol, which is required for a delegate object of an XML parser of type `NSXMLParser`. Now let's read the *MyXML.xml* file from the disk and pass it to your XML parser:

```
- (BOOL)            application:(UIApplication *)application
  didFinishLaunchingWithOptions:(NSDictionary *)launchOptions{
```

```
    NSString *xmlFilePath = [[NSBundle mainBundle] pathForResource:@"MyXML"
                                                            ofType:@"xml"];

    NSData *xml = [[NSData alloc] initWithContentsOfFile:xmlFilePath];

    self.xmlParser = [[NSXMLParser alloc] initWithData:xml];
    self.xmlParser.delegate = self;
    if ([self.xmlParser parse]){
        NSLog(@"The XML is parsed.");
    } else{
        NSLog(@"Failed to parse the XML");
    }

    self.window = [[UIWindow alloc] initWithFrame:
                   [[UIScreen mainScreen] bounds]];

    self.window.backgroundColor = [UIColor whiteColor];
    [self.window makeKeyAndVisible];
    return YES;
}
```

We first read the contents of our file into an instance of `NSData` and then initialize our XML parser with the `initWithData:`, using the data that we read from the XML file. We then call the `parse` method of the XML parser to start the parsing process. This method will block the current thread until the parsing process is finished. If you have big XML files to parse, it is highly recommended that you use a global dispatch queue to do the parsing.

To parse the XML file, we need to know the delegate methods defined in the `NSXMLParserDelegate` protocol and their responsibilities:

`parserDidStartDocument:`
: Called when the parsing starts.

`parserDidEndDocument:`
: Called when the parsing ends

`parser:didStartElement:namespaceURI:qualifiedName:attributes:`
: Called when the parser encounters and parses a new element in the XML document

`parser:didEndElement:namespaceURI:qualifiedName:`
: Called when the parser has finished parsing the current element

`parser:foundCharacters:`
: Called when the parser parses string contents of elements

Using these delegate methods, we can go ahead and define an object model for our XML objects. Let's first define an object to represent an XML element, in a class called `XMLElement`:

```
#import <Foundation/Foundation.h>

@interface XMLElement : NSObject

@property (nonatomic, copy) NSString *name;
@property (nonatomic, copy) NSString *text;
@property (nonatomic, copy) NSDictionary *attributes;
@property (nonatomic, strong) NSMutableArray *subElements;
@property (nonatomic, weak) XMLElement *parent;

@end
```

Now let's implement our `XMLElement` class:

```
#import "XMLElement.h"

@implementation XMLElement

- (NSMutableArray *) subElements{
    if (_subElements == nil){
        _subElements = [[NSMutableArray alloc] init];
    }
    return _subElements;
}

@end
```

We want the `subElements` mutable array to be created only if it is nil when it is accessed, so we place our allocation and initialization code for the `subElements` property of the `XMLElement` class in its own getter method. If an XML element doesn't have subelements and we never use that property, there is no point allocating and initializing a mutable array for that element. This technique is known as lazy allocation.

So now let's go ahead and define an instance of `XMLElement` and call it *`rootElement`*. Our plan is to start the parsing process and drill down the XML file as we parse it with our delegate methods, until we have successfully parsed the whole file:

```
#import "AppDelegate.h"
#import "XMLElement.h"

@interface AppDelegate () <NSXMLParserDelegate>
@property (nonatomic, strong) NSXMLParser *xmlParser;
@property (nonatomic, strong) XMLElement *rootElement;
@property (nonatomic, strong) XMLElement *currentElementPointer;
@end

@implementation AppDelegate
```

The `currentElementPointer` will be the XML element that we are parsing at the moment in our XML structure, so it can move up and down the structure as we parse the file. Unlike the constantly changing `currentElementPointer` pointer, the `rootElement` pointer will always be the root element of our XML, and its value will not change during the course of parsing the XML file.

Let's start the parsing process. The first method we want to take care of is the `parserDidStartDocument:` method. In this method, we will simply reset everything:

```
- (void)parserDidStartDocument:(NSXMLParser *)parser{
    self.rootElement = nil;
    self.currentElementPointer = nil;
}
```

The next method is the `parser:didStartElement:namespaceURI:qualifiedName:attributes:` method. In this method, we will create the root element (if it has not been created already). If any new element in the XML file is getting parsed, we will calculate where in the structure of the XML we are and then add a new element object to our current element object:

```
- (void)        parser:(NSXMLParser *)parser
       didStartElement:(NSString *)elementName
          namespaceURI:(NSString *)namespaceURI
         qualifiedName:(NSString *)qName
            attributes:(NSDictionary *)attributeDict{

    if (self.rootElement == nil){
        /* We don't have a root element. Create it and point to it */
        self.rootElement = [[XMLElement alloc] init];
        self.currentElementPointer = self.rootElement;
    } else {
        /* Already have root. Create new element and add it as one of
         the subelements of the current element */
        XMLElement *newElement = [[XMLElement alloc] init];
        newElement.parent = self.currentElementPointer;
        [self.currentElementPointer.subElements addObject:newElement];
        self.currentElementPointer = newElement;
    }

    self.currentElementPointer.name = elementName;
    self.currentElementPointer.attributes = attributeDict;

}
```

Next up is the `parser:foundCharacters:` method. This method can get called multiple times for the current element, so you need to make sure we are ready for multiple entries into this method. For instance, if the text of an element is 4,000 characters long, the parser might parse a maximum of 1,000 characters in the first go, then the next 1,000, and so on. In that case, the parser would call your `parser:foundCharacters:` method for the current element four times. You probably want to just accumulate the results that get returned into a string:

```
- (void)        parser:(NSXMLParser *)parser
       foundCharacters:(NSString *)string{
```

```
    if ([self.currentElementPointer.text length] > 0){
        self.currentElementPointer.text =
        [self.currentElementPointer.text stringByAppendingString:string];
    } else {
        self.currentElementPointer.text = string;
    }

}
```

The next method to take care of is the `parser:didEndElement:namespaceURI:qualifiedName:` method, which gets called when the parser encounters the end of an element. Here you just need to point our XML element pointer back one level to the parent of the current element—it's as simple as this:

```
- (void)        parser:(NSXMLParser *)parser
         didEndElement:(NSString *)elementName
          namespaceURI:(NSString *)namespaceURI
         qualifiedName:(NSString *)qName{

    self.currentElementPointer = self.currentElementPointer.parent;

}
```

Last but not least, you need to handle the `parserDidEndDocument:` method and dispose of your `currentElementPointer` property:

```
- (void)parserDidEndDocument:(NSXMLParser *)parser{
    self.currentElementPointer = nil;
}
```

That is all. Now let's go ahead and parse our document:

```
- (BOOL)            application:(UIApplication *)application
  didFinishLaunchingWithOptions:(NSDictionary *)launchOptions{

    NSString *xmlFilePath = [[NSBundle mainBundle] pathForResource:@"MyXML"
                                                            ofType:@"xml"];

    NSData *xml = [[NSData alloc] initWithContentsOfFile:xmlFilePath];

    self.xmlParser = [[NSXMLParser alloc] initWithData:xml];
    self.xmlParser.delegate = self;
    if ([self.xmlParser parse]){
        NSLog(@"The XML is parsed.");

        /* self.rootElement is now the root element in the XML */
        XMLElement *element = self.rootElement.subElements[1];
        NSLog(@"%@", element.subElements);

    } else{
        NSLog(@"Failed to parse the XML");
    }
```

```
    self.window = [[UIWindow alloc] initWithFrame:
                   [[UIScreen mainScreen] bounds]];

    self.window.backgroundColor = [UIColor whiteColor];
    [self.window makeKeyAndVisible];
    return YES;
}
```

Now you can use the `rootElement` property to traverse the structure of your XML.

# CHAPTER 12
# Audio and Video

## 12.0. Introduction

The AV Foundation (Audio and Video Foundation) framework in the iOS SDK allows developers to play and/or record audio and video with ease. In addition, the Media Player framework allows developers to play audio and video files.

Before you can run the code in this chapter, you must add the *AVFoundation.framework* and *MediaPlayer.framework* frameworks to your Xcode project. With the new LLVM compiler, all you have to do in order to include these frameworks into your app is to import their umbrella header files into your app like so:

```
#import "AppDelegate.h"
#import <AVFoundation/AVFoundation.h>
#import <MediaPlayer/MediaPlayer.h>

@implementation AppDelegate

<# Rest of your app delegate code goes here #>
```

## 12.1. Playing Audio Files

### Problem

You want to be able to play an audio file in your application.

### Solution

Use the AV Foundation framework's `AVAudioPlayer` class.

## Discussion

The AVAudioPlayer class in the AV Foundation framework can play back all audio formats supported by iOS. The delegate property of an instance of AVAudioPlayer allows you to get notified by events, such as when the audio playback is interrupted or when an error occurs as a result of playing an audio file. Let's have a look at a simple example that demonstrates how we can play an audio file from the application's bundle:

```
- (void)audioPlayerDidFinishPlaying:(AVAudioPlayer *)player
                       successfully:(BOOL)flag{

    NSLog(@"Finished playing the song");

    /* The [flag] parameter tells us if the playback was successfully
     finished or not */

    if ([player isEqual:self.audioPlayer]){
        self.audioPlayer = nil;
    } else {
        /* Which audio player is this? We certainly didn't allocate
         this instance! */
    }

}

- (void)viewDidLoad {
    [super viewDidLoad];

    dispatch_queue_t dispatchQueue =
    dispatch_get_global_queue(DISPATCH_QUEUE_PRIORITY_DEFAULT, 0);

    dispatch_async(dispatchQueue, ^(void) {
        NSBundle *mainBundle = [NSBundle mainBundle];

        NSString *filePath = [mainBundle pathForResource:@"MySong"
                                                  ofType:@"mp3"];

        NSData   *fileData = [NSData dataWithContentsOfFile:filePath];

        NSError  *error = nil;

        /* Start the audio player */
        self.audioPlayer = [[AVAudioPlayer alloc] initWithData:fileData
                                                         error:&error];

        /* Did we get an instance of AVAudioPlayer? */
        if (self.audioPlayer != nil){
            /* Set the delegate and start playing */
            self.audioPlayer.delegate = self;
            if ([self.audioPlayer prepareToPlay] &&
                [self.audioPlayer play]){
                /* Successfully started playing */
```

```
            } else {
                /* Failed to play */
            }
        } else {
            /* Failed to instantiate AVAudioPlayer */
        }
    });

}
```

As you can see, the file's data is loaded into an instance of `NSData` and then passed on to `AVAudioPlayer`'s `initWithData:error:` method. Because we need the actual, absolute path of the MP3 file to extract the data from that file, we invoke the `mainBundle` class method of `NSBundle` to retrieve the information from the application's configuration. The `pathForResource:ofType:` instance method of `NSBundle` can then be used to retrieve the absolute path to a resource of a specific type, as demonstrated in the example code.

The `audioPlayerDidFinishPlaying:successfully:` delegate method of the audio player will get called on the delegate object of the player whenever, as the method's name indicates, the audio player finishes playing the audio file. Now, this does not necessarily mean that the audio playback was finished after the whole audio file was finished playing. There could have been an interruption—for instance, the audio channel may have gotten occupied by another app that came to the foreground, causing your app to stop playing. In this case, the aforementioned method gets called. This is a great place to release your audio player if you no longer need it.

In the `viewDidLoad` method, we are using GCD to asynchronously load the song's data into an instance of `NSData` and use that as a feed to the audio player. We do this because loading the data of an audio file can take a long time (depending on the length of the audio file), and if we do this on the main thread, we run the risk of stalling the UI experience. Because of this, we are using a global concurrent queue to ensure that the code does *not* run on the main thread.

Since we are assigning the instance of `AVAudioPlayer` to a property named `audioPlayer`, we must also see how this property is defined:

```
#import "ViewController.h"
#import <AVFoundation/AVFoundation.h>

@interface ViewController () <AVAudioPlayerDelegate>
@property (nonatomic, strong) AVAudioPlayer *audioPlayer;
@end

@implementation ViewController
```

As you can see, we have made the view controller the delegate of the audio player. This way, we can receive messages from the system whenever the audio player, for instance, is interrupted or has finished playing the song. With this information in hand, we can make appropriate decisions in the application, such as starting to play another audio file.

## See Also

Recipe 12.2; Recipe 12.5; Chapter 7

# 12.2. Handling Interruptions While Playing Audio

## Problem

You want your `AVAudioPlayer` instance to resume playing after an interruption on an iOS device, such as an incoming call.

## Solution

Implement the `audioPlayerBeginInterruption:` and `audioPlayerEndInterruption:withOptions:` methods of the `AVAudioPlayerDelegate` protocol in the delegate object of your `AVAudioPlayer` instance:

```
- (void)audioPlayerBeginInterruption:(AVAudioPlayer *)player{

    /* Audio Session is interrupted. The player will be paused here */

}

- (void) audioPlayerEndInterruption:(AVAudioPlayer *)player
                        withOptions:(NSUInteger)flags{

    if (flags == AVAudioSessionInterruptionOptionShouldResume &&
        player != nil){
        [player play];
    }

}
```

## Discussion

On an iOS device, such as an iPhone, a phone call could interrupt the execution of the foreground application. In that case, the audio session(s) associated with the application will be deactivated, and audio files will not be played until the interruption has ended. At the beginning and the end of an interruption, we receive delegate messages from the `AVAudioPlayer` informing us of the different states the audio session is passing through. After the end of an interruption, we can simply resume the playback of audio.

Incoming phone calls cannot be simulated with iPhone Simulator. You must always test your applications on a real device.

When an interruption occurs, the `audioPlayerBeginInterruption:` delegate method of an `AVAudioPlayer` instance will be called. Here your audio session has been deactivated. In case of a phone call, the user can just hear his ringtone. When the interruption ends (the phone call is finished or the user rejects the call), the `audioPlayerEndInterruption:withOptions:` delegate method of your `AVAudioPlayer` will be invoked. If the `withOptions` parameter contains the value `AVAudioSessionInterruptionOptionShouldResume`, you can immediately resume the playback of your audio player using the `play` instance method of `AVAudioPlayer`.

The playback of audio files using `AVAudioPlayer` might show memory leaks in Instruments when the application is being run on iPhone Simulator. Testing the same application on an iOS device proves that the memory leaks are unique to the simulator, not the device. I strongly suggest that you run, test, debug, and optimize your applications on real devices before releasing them to the App Store.

# 12.3. Recording Audio

## Problem

You want to be able to record audio files on an iOS device.

## Solution

Use the `AVAudioRecorder` class in the AV Foundation framework.

## Discussion

The `AVAudioRecorder` class in the AV Foundation framework facilitates audio recording in iOS applications. To start a recording, you need to pass various pieces of information to the `initWithURL:settings:error:` instance method of `AVAudioRecorder`:

*The URL of the file where the recording should be saved*
: This is a local URL. The AV Foundation framework will decide which audio format should be used for the recording based on the file extension provided in this URL, so choose the extension carefully.

*The settings that must be used before and while recording*
: Examples include the sampling rate, channels, and other information that will help the audio recorder start the recording. This is a dictionary object.

*The address of an instance of* `NSError` *where any initialization errors should be saved to*
: The error information could be valuable later, and you can retrieve it from this instance method in case something goes wrong.

The `settings` parameter of the `initWithURL:settings:error:` method is particularly interesting. There are many keys that could be saved in the `settings` dictionary, but we will discuss only some of the most important ones in this recipe:

`AVFormatIDKey`
: The format of the recorded audio. Some of the values that can be specified for this key are the following:

  - `kAudioFormatLinearPCM`
  - `kAudioFormatAppleLossless`

`AVSampleRateKey`
: The sample rate that needs to be used for the recording.

`AVNumberOfChannelsKey`
: The number of channels that must be used for the recording.

`AVEncoderAudioQualityKey`
: The quality with which the recording must be made. Here are some of the values that can be specified for this key:

  - `AVAudioQualityMin`
  - `AVAudioQualityLow`
  - `AVAudioQualityMedium`
  - `AVAudioQualityHigh`
  - `AVAudioQualityMax`

With all this information in hand, we can go on and write an application that can record audio input into a file and then play it using `AVAudioPlayer`. What we want to do, specifically, is this:

1. Start recording audio in Apple Lossless format.
2. Save the recording into a file named *Recording.m4a* in the application's *Documents* directory.

3. Five seconds after the recording starts, finish the recording process and immediately start playing the file into which we recorded the audio input.

We will start by declaring the required properties in our view controller:

```
#import "ViewController.h"
#import <AVFoundation/AVFoundation.h>

@interface ViewController () <AVAudioPlayerDelegate, AVAudioRecorderDelegate>
@property (nonatomic, strong) AVAudioRecorder *audioRecorder;
@property (nonatomic, strong) AVAudioPlayer *audioPlayer;
@end

@implementation ViewController
```

When the view inside the view controller is loaded for the first time, we will attempt to start the recording process and then stop the process, if successfully started, after five seconds:

```
- (void) startRecordingAudio{

    NSError   *error = nil;

    NSURL *audioRecordingURL = [self audioRecordingPath];

    self.audioRecorder = [[AVAudioRecorder alloc]
                          initWithURL:audioRecordingURL
                          settings:[self audioRecordingSettings]
                          error:&error];

    if (self.audioRecorder != nil){

        self.audioRecorder.delegate = self;
        /* Prepare the recorder and then start the recording */

        if ([self.audioRecorder prepareToRecord] &&
            [self.audioRecorder record]){
            NSLog(@"Successfully started to record.");

            /* After 5 seconds, let's stop the recording process */
            [self performSelector:@selector(stopRecordingOnAudioRecorder:)
                       withObject:self.audioRecorder
                       afterDelay:5.0f];

        } else {
            NSLog(@"Failed to record.");
            self.audioRecorder = nil;
        }

    } else {
        NSLog(@"Failed to create an instance of the audio recorder.");
    }
```

```
}

- (void)viewDidLoad {
    [super viewDidLoad];

    /* Ask for permission to see if we can record audio */
    AVAudioSession *session = [AVAudioSession sharedInstance];

    [session setCategory:AVAudioSessionCategoryPlayAndRecord
             withOptions:AVAudioSessionCategoryOptionDuckOthers
                   error:nil];

    if ([session requestRecordPermission]){
        [self startRecordingAudio];
    } else {
        NSLog(@"We don't have permission to record audio.");
    }

}
```

In iOS 7, users have to give permissions to apps that want to access the microphone. This is why we are using `AVAudioSession` in our code snippet to ask the user for permission before attempting to use the microphone. The permission dialog that iOS will display to the user will be similar to that shown in Figure 12-1.

In the `startRecordingAudio` method of the view controller, we attempt to instantiate an object of type `AVAudioRecorder` and assign it to the `audioRecorder` property that we declared in the same view controller earlier.

We are using an instance method called `audioRecordingPath` to determine the local URL where we want to store the recording. This method is implemented like so:

```
- (NSURL *) audioRecordingPath{

    NSFileManager *fileManager = [[NSFileManager alloc] init];

    NSURL *documentsFolderUrl =
    [fileManager URLForDirectory:NSDocumentDirectory
                        inDomain:NSUserDomainMask
               appropriateForURL:nil
                          create:NO
                           error:nil];

    return [documentsFolderUrl
            URLByAppendingPathComponent:@"Recording.m4a"];

}
```

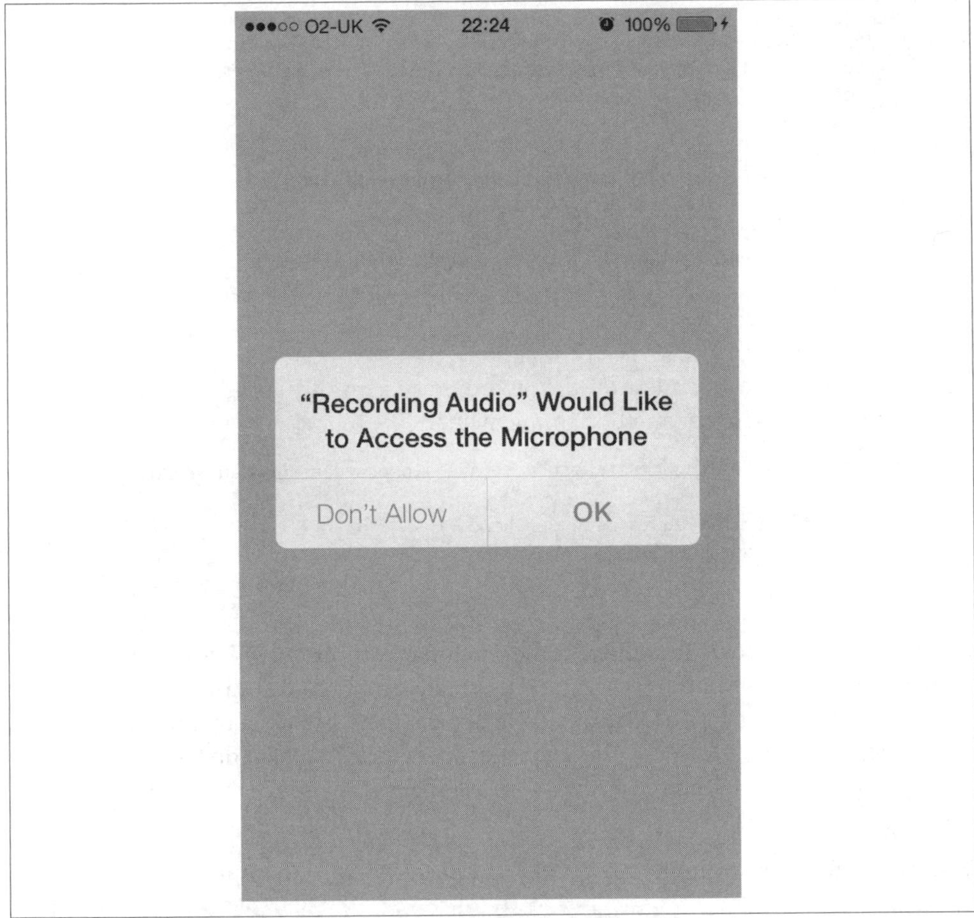


*Figure 12-1. iOS requires permission from the user for apps to access the microphone*

The return value of this function is the document path of your application with the name of the destination file appended to it. For instance, if the document path of your application is:

```
/var/mobile/Applications/<# Your Application ID #>/Documents/
```

the destination audio recording path will be:

```
/var/mobile/Applications/<# Your Application ID #>/Documents/Recording.m4a
```

When instantiating the `AVAudioRecorder`, we are using a dictionary for the settings parameter of the initialization method of the audio recorder, as explained before. This dictionary is constructed using the `audioRecordingSettings` instance method, implemented in this way:

```
- (NSDictionary *) audioRecordingSettings{

    /* Let's prepare the audio recorder options in the dictionary.
     Later we will use this dictionary to instantiate an audio
     recorder of type AVAudioRecorder */

    return @{
             AVFormatIDKey : @(kAudioFormatAppleLossless),
             AVSampleRateKey : @(44100.0f),
             AVNumberOfChannelsKey : @1,
             AVEncoderAudioQualityKey : @(AVAudioQualityLow),
             };

}
```

You can see that five seconds after the recording successfully starts, we call the `stopRecordingOnAudioRecorder` method, implemented like so:

```
- (void) stopRecordingOnAudioRecorder:(AVAudioRecorder *)paramRecorder{

    /* Just stop the audio recorder here */
    [paramRecorder stop];

}
```

Now that we have asked the audio recorder to stop recording, we will wait for its delegate messages to tell us when the recording has actually stopped. You shouldn't assume that the `stop` instance method of `AVAudioRecorder` instantly stops the recording. Instead, I recommend that you wait for the `audioRecorderDidFinishRecording:successfully:` delegate method (declared in the `AVAudioRecorderDelegate` protocol) before proceeding.

When the audio recording has actually stopped, we will attempt to play what was recorded:

```
- (void)audioRecorderDidFinishRecording:(AVAudioRecorder *)recorder
                           successfully:(BOOL)flag{

    if (flag){

        NSLog(@"Successfully stopped the audio recording process.");

        /* Let's try to retrieve the data for the recorded file */
        NSError *playbackError = nil;

        NSError *readingError = nil;
        NSData  *fileData =
        [NSData dataWithContentsOfURL:[self audioRecordingPath]
                              options:NSDataReadingMapped
                                error:&readingError];

        /* Form an audio player and make it play the recorded data */
```

```
        self.audioPlayer = [[AVAudioPlayer alloc] initWithData:fileData
                                                          error:&playbackError];

        /* Could we instantiate the audio player? */
        if (self.audioPlayer != nil){
            self.audioPlayer.delegate = self;

            /* Prepare to play and start playing */
            if ([self.audioPlayer prepareToPlay] &&
                [self.audioPlayer play]){
                NSLog(@"Started playing the recorded audio.");
            } else {
                NSLog(@"Could not play the audio.");
            }

        } else {
            NSLog(@"Failed to create an audio player.");
        }

    } else {
        NSLog(@"Stopping the audio recording failed.");
    }

    /* Here we don't need the audio recorder anymore */
    self.audioRecorder = nil;

}
```

After the audio player is finished playing the song (if it does so successfully), the `audioPlayerDidFinishPlaying:successfully:` delegate method will be called in the delegate object of the audio player. We will implement this method like so (this method is defined in the `AVAudioPlayerDelegate` protocol):

```
- (void)audioPlayerDidFinishPlaying:(AVAudioPlayer *)player
                       successfully:(BOOL)flag{

    if (flag){
        NSLog(@"Audio player stopped correctly.");
    } else {
        NSLog(@"Audio player did not stop correctly.");
    }

    if ([player isEqual:self.audioPlayer]){
        self.audioPlayer = nil;
    } else {
        /* This is not our player */
    }

}
```

As explained in Recipe 12.2, when playing audio files using AVAudioPlayer, we also need to handle interruptions (such as incoming phone calls) when deploying the application on an iOS device and before releasing the application to the App Store:

```
- (void)audioPlayerBeginInterruption:(AVAudioPlayer *)player{

    /* The audio session has been deactivated here */

}

- (void)audioPlayerEndInterruption:(AVAudioPlayer *)player
                        withOptions:(NSUInteger)flags{

    if (flags == AVAudioSessionInterruptionOptionShouldResume){
        [player play];
    }

}
```

Instances of AVAudioRecorder must also handle interruptions, just like instances of AVAudioPlayer. These interruptions can be handled as explained in Recipe 12.4.

## See Also

Recipe 12.2; Recipe 12.4

# 12.4. Handling Interruptions While Recording Audio

## Problem

You want your AVAudioRecorder instance to be able to resume recording after an interruption, such as an incoming phone call.

## Solution

Implement the audioRecorderBeginInterruption: and audioRecorderEndInterruption:withOptions: methods of the AVAudioRecorderDelegate protocol in the delegate object of your audio recorder, and resume the recording process by invoking the record instance method of your AVAudioRecorder when the interruption has ended:

```
- (void)audioRecorderBeginInterruption:(AVAudioRecorder *)recorder{

    NSLog(@"Recording process is interrupted");

}

- (void)audioRecorderEndInterruption:(AVAudioRecorder *)recorder
                          withOptions:(NSUInteger)flags{
```

```
        if (flags == AVAudioSessionInterruptionOptionShouldResume){
            NSLog(@"Resuming the recording...");
            [recorder record];
        }

}
```

## Discussion

Just like audio players (instances of `AVAudioPlayer`), audio recorders of type `AVAudioRecorder` also receive delegate messages whenever the audio session associated with them is deactivated because of an interruption. The two methods mentioned in this recipe's Solution are the best places to handle such interruptions. In the case of an interruption to the audio recorder, you can invoke the `record` instance method of `AVAudioRecorder` after the interruption to continue the recording process. However, the recording will overwrite the previous recording, and all data recorded before the interruption will be lost.

It is very important to bear in mind that when the delegate of your audio recorder receives the `audioRecorderBeginInterruption:` method, the audio session has already been deactivated, and invoking the `resume` instance method will not work on your audio recorder. After the interruption has ended, you must invoke the `record` instance method of your `AVAudioRecorder` to resume recording.

# 12.5. Playing Audio over Other Active Sounds

## Problem

You either want to put other applications in silent mode while you play audio or play audio on top of other applications' audio playback (if any).

## Solution

Use audio sessions to set the type of audio category your application uses.

## Discussion

The `AVAudioSession` class was introduced in the AV Foundation framework. Every iOS application has one audio session. This audio session can be accessed using the `sharedInstance` class method of the `AVAudioSession` class, like so:

```
AVAudioSession *audioSession = [AVAudioSession sharedInstance];
```

After retrieving an instance of the `AVAudioSession` class, you can invoke the `setCategory:error:` instance method of the audio session object to choose among the different categories available to iOS applications. Different values that can be set as the audio session category of an application are listed here:

`AVAudioSessionCategoryAmbient`
: This category will not stop the audio from other applications, but it will allow you to play audio over the audio being played by other applications, such as the Music app. The main UI thread of your application will function normally. The `prepareToPlay` and `play` instance methods of `AVAudioPlayer` will return with the value `YES`. The audio being played by your application will stop when the user locks the screen. The silent mode silences the audio playback of your application only if your application is the only application playing an audio file. If you start playing audio while the Music app is playing a song, putting the device in silent mode does not stop your audio playback.

`AVAudioSessionCategorySoloAmbient`
: This category is exactly like the `AVAudioSessionCategoryAmbient` category, except that this category will stop the audio playback of all other applications, such as the Music app. When the device is put into silent mode, your audio playback will be paused. This also happens when the screen is locked. This is the default category that iOS chooses for an application.

`AVAudioSessionCategoryRecord`
: This stops other applications' audio (e.g., the music) and also will not allow your application to initiate an audio playback (e.g., using `AVAudioPlayer`). You can only record audio in this mode. Using this category, calling the `prepareToPlay` instance method of `AVAudioPlayer` will return `YES`, and the `play` instance method will return `NO`. The main UI interface will function as usual. The recording of your application will continue even if the iOS device's screen is locked by the user.

`AVAudioSessionCategoryPlayback`
: This category will silence other applications' audio playback (such as the audio playback of music applications). You can then use the `prepareToPlay` and `play` instance methods of `AVAudioPlayer` to play a sound in your application. The main UI thread will function as normal. The audio playback will continue even if the screen is locked by the user or if the device is in silent mode.

`AVAudioSessionCategoryPlayAndRecord`
: This category allows audio to be played and recorded at the same time in your application. This will stop the audio playback of other applications when your audio recording or playback begins. The main UI thread of your application will function as normal. The playback and the recording will continue even if the screen is locked or the device is in silent mode.

`AVAudioSessionCategoryAudioProcessing`
: This category can be used for applications that do audio processing, but not audio playback or recording. By setting this category, you cannot play or record any audio in your application. Calling the `prepareToPlay` and `play` instance methods of `AVAudioPlayer` will return `NO`. Audio playback of other applications, such as the Music app, will also stop if this category is set.

To give you an example of using `AVAudioSession`, let's start an audio player that will play its audio file over other applications' audio playback. We will begin with the declarations:

```
#import "ViewController.h"
#import <AVFoundation/AVFoundation.h>

@interface ViewController () <AVAudioPlayerDelegate>
@property (nonatomic, strong) AVAudioPlayer *audioPlayer;
@end

@implementation ViewController
```

Here is how we will alter the audio session and then load a song into the memory and into an audio player for playing. We will do this in the `viewDidLoad` method of the view controller:

```
- (void)viewDidLoad {
    [super viewDidLoad];

    NSError *audioSessionError = nil;
    AVAudioSession *audioSession = [AVAudioSession sharedInstance];
    if ([audioSession setCategory:AVAudioSessionCategoryAmbient
                            error:&audioSessionError]){
        NSLog(@"Successfully set the audio session.");
    } else {
        NSLog(@"Could not set the audio session");
    }

    dispatch_queue_t dispatchQueue =
    dispatch_get_global_queue(DISPATCH_QUEUE_PRIORITY_DEFAULT, 0);

    dispatch_async(dispatchQueue, ^(void) {
        NSBundle *mainBundle = [NSBundle mainBundle];

        NSString *filePath = [mainBundle pathForResource:@"MySong"
                                                  ofType:@"mp3"];

        NSData *fileData = [NSData dataWithContentsOfFile:filePath];

        NSError *audioPlayerError = nil;

        self.audioPlayer = [[AVAudioPlayer alloc]
                            initWithData:fileData
```

```
                                        error:&audioPlayerError];

        if (self.audioPlayer != nil){

            self.audioPlayer.delegate = self;

            if ([self.audioPlayer prepareToPlay] &&
                [self.audioPlayer play]){
                NSLog(@"Successfully started playing.");

            } else {
                NSLog(@"Failed to play the audio file.");
                self.audioPlayer = nil;
            }

        } else {
            NSLog(@"Could not instantiate the audio player.");
        }
    });

}
```

Next, we will move on to handling the `AVAudioPlayerDelegate` protocol's methods:

```
- (void)audioPlayerBeginInterruption:(AVAudioPlayer *)player{
    /* The audio session has been deactivated here */
}

- (void)audioPlayerEndInterruption:(AVAudioPlayer *)player
                       withOptions:(NSUInteger)flags{
    if (flags == AVAudioSessionInterruptionOptionShouldResume){
        [player play];
    }
}

- (void)audioPlayerDidFinishPlaying:(AVAudioPlayer *)player
                       successfully:(BOOL)flag{

    if (flag){
        NSLog(@"Audio player stopped correctly.");
    } else {
        NSLog(@"Audio player did not stop correctly.");
    }

    if ([player isEqual:self.audioPlayer]){
        self.audioPlayer = nil;
    } else {
        /* This is not our audio player */
    }

}
```

You can see that we are using the shared instance of the `AVAudioSession` class in the `viewDidLoad` instance method of the view controller to set the audio category of the application to `AVAudioSessionCategoryAmbient` in order to allow the application to play audio files over other applications' audio playback.

# 12.6. Playing Video Files

## Problem

You would like to be able to play video files in your iOS application.

## Solution

Use an instance of the `MPMoviePlayerController` class.

If you simply want to display a full-screen movie player, you can use the `MPMoviePlayerViewController` class and push your movie player view controller into the stack of view controllers of a navigation controller (for instance), or simply present your movie player view controller as a modal controller on another view controller using the `presentMoviePlayerViewControllerAnimated:` instance method of `UIViewController`. In this recipe, we will use `MPMoviePlayerController` instead of `MPMoviePlayerViewController` in order to get full access to various settings that a movie player view controller does not offer, such as windowed-mode video playback (not full-screen).

## Discussion

The Media Player framework in the iOS SDK allows programmers to play audio and video files, among other interesting things. To be able to play a video file, we will instantiate an object of type `MPMoviePlayerController` like so:

```
MPMoviePlayerController *newMoviePlayer =
[[MPMoviePlayerController alloc] initWithContentURL:url];

self.moviePlayer = newMoviePlayer;
```

In this code, `moviePlayer` is a property of type `MPMoviePlayerController` defined for the current view controller. In older iOS SDKs, programmers had very little control over how movies were played using the Media Player framework. With the introduction of the iPad, the whole framework changed drastically to give more control to programmers and allow them to present their contents with more flexibility than before.

An instance of `MPMoviePlayerController` has a property called `view`. This view is of type `UIView` and is the view in which the media, such as video, will be played. As a programmer, you are responsible for inserting this view into your application's view hierarchy to present your users with the content being played. Since you get a reference to an object of type `UIView`, you can shape this view however you want. For instance, you can simply change the background color of this view to a custom color.

Many multimedia operations depend on the notification system. For instance, `MPMoviePlayerController` does not work with delegates; instead, it relies on notifications. This allows for a very flexible decoupling between the system libraries and the applications that iOS programmers write. For classes such as `MPMoviePlayerController`, we start listening for notifications that get sent by instances of that class. We use the default notification center and add ourselves as an observer for a notification.

To be able to test the recipe, we need a sample *.mov* file to play with the movie player. You can download an Apple-provided sample file from *http://bit.ly/TtfcP7*. Make sure you download the H.264 file format. If this file is zipped, unzip it and rename it to *Sample.m4v*. Now drag and drop this file into your application bundle in Xcode.

After doing this, we can go ahead and write a simple program that attempts to play the video file for us. Here are the declarations:

```
#import "ViewController.h"
#import <MediaPlayer/MediaPlayer.h>

@interface ViewController ()
@property (nonatomic, strong) MPMoviePlayerController *moviePlayer;
@property (nonatomic, strong) UIButton *playButton;
@end

@implementation ViewController
```

Here is the implementation of the `startPlayingVideo:` method:

```
- (void) startPlayingVideo:(id)paramSender{

    /* First let's construct the URL of the file in our application bundle
     that needs to get played by the movie player */
    NSBundle *mainBundle = [NSBundle mainBundle];

    NSURL *url = [mainBundle URLForResource:@"Sample"
                              withExtension:@"m4v"];

    /* If we have already created a movie player before,
     let's try to stop it */
    if (self.moviePlayer != nil){
        [self stopPlayingVideo:nil];
    }

    /* Now create a new movie player using the URL */
    self.moviePlayer = [[MPMoviePlayerController alloc] initWithContentURL:url];

    if (self.moviePlayer != nil){
```

```
        /* Listen for the notification that the movie player sends us
         whenever it finishes playing an audio file */
        [[NSNotificationCenter defaultCenter]
         addObserver:self
         selector:@selector(videoHasFinishedPlaying:)
         name:MPMoviePlayerPlaybackDidFinishNotification
         object:self.moviePlayer];

        NSLog(@"Successfully instantiated the movie player.");

        /* Scale the movie player to fit the aspect ratio */
        self.moviePlayer.scalingMode = MPMovieScalingModeAspectFit;

        [self.view addSubview:self.moviePlayer.view];

        [self.moviePlayer setFullscreen:YES
                               animated:NO];

        /* Let's start playing the video in full screen mode */
        [self.moviePlayer play];

    } else {
        NSLog(@"Failed to instantiate the movie player.");
    }

}
```

As you can see, we manage the movie player's view ourselves. If we add the view of the movie player to the view controller's view, we have to remove the view manually. This view will not get removed from the view controller's view even if we release the movie player. The following method stops the video and then removes the associated view:

```
- (void) stopPlayingVideo:(id)paramSender {

    if (self.moviePlayer != nil){

        [[NSNotificationCenter defaultCenter]
         removeObserver:self
         name:MPMoviePlayerPlaybackDidFinishNotification
         object:self.moviePlayer];

        [self.moviePlayer stop];

        [self.moviePlayer.view removeFromSuperview];
    }

}
```

In the `startPlayingVideo:` instance method of the view controller, we are listening for the `MPMoviePlayerPlaybackDidFinishNotification` notification that `MKMoviePlayerViewController` will send to the default notification center. We listen to this notification on the videoHasFinishedPlaying: instance method of the view controller. Here we can be notified when the movie playback has finished and perhaps dispose of the movie player object:

```
- (void) videoHasFinishedPlaying:(NSNotification *)paramNotification{

    /* Find out what the reason was for the player to stop */
    NSNumber *reason =
    paramNotification.userInfo
    [MPMoviePlayerPlaybackDidFinishReasonUserInfoKey];

    if (reason != nil){
        NSInteger reasonAsInteger = [reason integerValue];

        switch (reasonAsInteger){
            case MPMovieFinishReasonPlaybackEnded:{
                /* The movie ended normally */
                break;
            }
            case MPMovieFinishReasonPlaybackError:{
                /* An error happened and the movie ended */
                break;
            }
            case MPMovieFinishReasonUserExited:{
                /* The user exited the player */
                break;
            }
        }

        NSLog(@"Finish Reason = %ld", (long)reasonAsInteger);
        [self stopPlayingVideo:nil];
    }

}
```

You might have already noticed that we are invoking the stopPlayingVideo: instance method that we implemented in the videoHasFinishedPlaying: notification handler. We do this because the stopPlayingVideo: instance method takes care of unregistering the object from the notifications received by the media player and removes the media player from the superview. In other words, when the video stops playing, it does not necessarily mean that the resources we allocated for that player have been deallocated. We need to take care of that manually.

## See Also

Recipe 12.7

# 12.7. Capturing Thumbnails from Video Files

## Problem

You are playing a video file using an instance of the `MPMoviePlayerController` class and would like to capture a screenshot from the movie at a certain time.

## Solution

Use the `requestThumbnailImagesAtTimes:timeOption:` instance method of `MPMovie PlayerController` like so:

```
/* Capture the frame at the third second into the movie */
NSNumber *thirdSecondThumbnail = @3.0f;

/* We can ask to capture as many frames as we
 want. But for now, we are just asking to capture one frame */

/* Ask the movie player to capture this frame for us */
[self.moviePlayer
 requestThumbnailImagesAtTimes:@[thirdSecondThumbnail]
 timeOption:MPMovieTimeOptionExact];
```

## Discussion

An instance of `MPMoviePlayerController` is able to capture thumbnails from the currently playing movie, synchronously and asynchronously. In this recipe, we are going to focus on asynchronous image capture for this class.

We can use the `requestThumbnailImagesAtTimes:timeOption:` instance method of `MPMoviePlayerController` to asynchronously access thumbnails. When I say "asynchronously," I mean that during the time the thumbnail is being captured and reported to your designated object (as we will soon see), the movie player will continue its work and will not block the playback. We must observe the `MPMoviePlayerThumbnail ImageRequestDidFinishNotification` notification message the movie player sends to the default notification center in order to find out when the thumbnails are available:

```
- (void) startPlayingVideo:(id)paramSender{

    /* First let's construct the URL of the file in our application bundle
     that needs to get played by the movie player */
    NSBundle *mainBundle = [NSBundle mainBundle];

    NSURL *url = [mainBundle URLForResource:@"Sample"
                              withExtension:@"m4v"];

    /* If we have already created a movie player before,
     let's try to stop it */
    if (self.moviePlayer != nil){
```

```
        [self stopPlayingVideo:nil];
    }

    /* Now create a new movie player using the URL */
    self.moviePlayer = [[MPMoviePlayerController alloc]
                        initWithContentURL:url];

    if (self.moviePlayer != nil){

        /* Listen for the notification that the movie player sends us
         whenever it finishes playing an audio file */
        [[NSNotificationCenter defaultCenter]
         addObserver:self
         selector:@selector(videoHasFinishedPlaying:)
         name:MPMoviePlayerPlaybackDidFinishNotification
         object:self.moviePlayer];

        [[NSNotificationCenter defaultCenter]
         addObserver:self
         selector:@selector(videoThumbnailIsAvailable:)
         name:MPMoviePlayerThumbnailImageRequestDidFinishNotification
         object:self.moviePlayer];

        NSLog(@"Successfully instantiated the movie player.");

        /* Scale the movie player to fit the aspect ratio */
        self.moviePlayer.scalingMode = MPMovieScalingModeAspectFit;

        /* Let's start playing the video in full screen mode */
        [self.moviePlayer play];

        [self.view addSubview:self.moviePlayer.view];

        [self.moviePlayer setFullscreen:YES
                               animated:YES];

        /* Capture the frame at the third second into the movie */
        NSNumber *thirdSecondThumbnail = @3.0f;

        /* We can ask to capture as many frames as we
         want. But for now, we are just asking to capture one frame */

        /* Ask the movie player to capture this frame for us */
        [self.moviePlayer
         requestThumbnailImagesAtTimes:@[thirdSecondThumbnail]
         timeOption:MPMovieTimeOptionExact];

    } else {
        NSLog(@"Failed to instantiate the movie player.");
    }

}
```

You can see that we are asking the movie player to capture the frame at the third second into the movie. Once this task is completed, the `videoThumbnailIsAvailable:` instance method of the view controller will be called. Here is how we can access the captured image:

```
- (void) videoThumbnailIsAvailable:(NSNotification *)paramNotification{

    MPMoviePlayerController *controller = [paramNotification object];

    if ([controller isEqual:self.moviePlayer]){
        NSLog(@"Thumbnail is available");

        /* Now get the thumbnail out of the user info dictionary */
        UIImage *thumbnail =
        [paramNotification.userInfo
         objectForKey:MPMoviePlayerThumbnailImageKey];

        if (thumbnail != nil){
            /* We got the thumbnail image. You can now use it here */
        }
    }

}
```

Since we started listening to the `MPMoviePlayerThumbnailImageRequestDidFinishNotification` notifications when we instantiated the movie player object in the `startPlayingVideo:` method, we must also stop listening for this notification whenever we stop the movie player (or whenever you believe is appropriate, depending on your application architecture):

```
- (void) stopPlayingVideo:(id)paramSender {

    if (self.moviePlayer != nil){

        [[NSNotificationCenter defaultCenter]
         removeObserver:self
         name:MPMoviePlayerPlaybackDidFinishNotification
         object:self.moviePlayer];

        [[NSNotificationCenter defaultCenter]
         removeObserver:self
         name:MPMoviePlayerThumbnailImageRequestDidFinishNotification
         object:self.moviePlayer];

        [self.moviePlayer stop];

            [self.moviePlayer.view removeFromSuperview];
    }

}
```

When calling the `requestThumbnailImagesAtTimes:timeOption:` instance method of `MPMoviePlayerController`, we can specify one of two values for `timeOption`: `MPMovieTimeOptionExact` or `MPMovieTimeOptionNearestKeyFrame`. The former gives us the frame playing at the exact point we requested in the timeline of the video, whereas the latter is less exact but uses fewer system resources and offers better performance when capturing thumbnails from a video. `MPMovieTimeOptionNearestKeyFrame` is usually adequate in terms of precision because it is just a couple of frames off.

# 12.8. Accessing the Music Library

## Problem

You want to access an item that your user picks from her music library.

## Solution

Use the `MPMediaPickerController` class:

```
MPMediaPickerController *mediaPicker = [[MPMediaPickerController alloc]
                                        initWithMediaTypes:MPMediaTypeAny];
```

## Discussion

`MPMediaPickerController` is a view controller that the Music app displays to the user. By instantiating `MPMediaPickerController`, you can present a standard view controller to your users to allow them to select whatever item they want from the library and then transfer the control to your application. This is particularly useful in games, for instance, where the user plays the game and can have your application play his favorite tracks in the background.

You can get information from the media picker controller by becoming its delegate (conforming to `MPMediaPickerControllerDelegate`):

```
#import "ViewController.h"
#import <MediaPlayer/MediaPlayer.h>

@interface ViewController () <MPMediaPickerControllerDelegate>
@property (nonatomic, strong) MPMediaPickerController *mediaPicker;
@end

@implementation ViewController
```

Inside your `displayMediaPicker:` selector, implement the code required to display an instance of the media picker controller and present it to the user as a modal view controller:

```
- (void) displayMediaPicker{
```

```
    self.mediaPicker = [[MPMediaPickerController alloc]
                         initWithMediaTypes:MPMediaTypeAny];

    if (self.mediaPicker != nil){

        NSLog(@"Successfully instantiated a media picker.");
        self.mediaPicker.delegate = self;
        self.mediaPicker.allowsPickingMultipleItems = NO;

        [self.navigationController presentViewController:self.mediaPicker
                                                animated:YES
                                              completion:nil];

    } else {
        NSLog(@"Could not instantiate a media picker.");
    }

}
```

The `allowsPickingMultipleItems` property of the media picker controller lets you specify whether users can pick more than one item from their library before dismissing the media picker controller. This takes a `BOOL` value, so for now we just set it to `NO`; we will later see what this looks like. Now let's implement the various delegate messages defined in the `MPMediaPickerControllerDelegate` protocol:

```
- (void) mediaPicker:(MPMediaPickerController *)mediaPicker
   didPickMediaItems:(MPMediaItemCollection *)mediaItemCollection{

    NSLog(@"Media Picker returned");

    for (MPMediaItem *thisItem in mediaItemCollection.items){

        NSURL     *itemURL =
        [thisItem valueForProperty:MPMediaItemPropertyAssetURL];

        NSString  *itemTitle =
        [thisItem valueForProperty:MPMediaItemPropertyTitle];

        NSString  *itemArtist =
        [thisItem valueForProperty:MPMediaItemPropertyArtist];

        MPMediaItemArtwork *itemArtwork =
        [thisItem valueForProperty:MPMediaItemPropertyArtwork];

        NSLog(@"Item URL = %@", itemURL);
        NSLog(@"Item Title = %@", itemTitle);
        NSLog(@"Item Artist = %@", itemArtist);
        NSLog(@"Item Artwork = %@", itemArtwork);
    }

    [mediaPicker dismissViewControllerAnimated:YES completion:nil];
}
```

You can access different properties of each selected item using the `valueForProperty:` instance method of `MPMediaItem`. Instances of this class will be returned to your application through the `mediaItemCollection` parameter of the `mediaPicker:didPickMediaItems:` delegate message.

Now let's write a program with a very simple GUI that allows us to ask the user to pick one music item from his Music library. After he picks the music file, we will attempt to play it using an `MPMusicPlayerController` instance. The GUI has two simple buttons: Pick and Play, and Stop Playing. The first button will ask the user to pick an item from his Music library to play, and the second button will stop the audio playback (if we are already playing the song). We will start with the design of the UI of the application. Let's create it in a simple way, as shown in Figure 12-2.

*Figure 12-2. A very simple UI for the media picker and AV Audio Player*

Now let's go ahead and define these two buttons in our view controller:

```
@interface ViewController ()
<MPMediaPickerControllerDelegate,AVAudioPlayerDelegate>
```

```
@property (nonatomic, strong) MPMusicPlayerController *myMusicPlayer;
@property (nonatomic, strong) UIButton *buttonPickAndPlay;
@property (nonatomic, strong) UIButton *buttonStopPlaying;
@property (nonatomic, strong) MPMediaPickerController *mediaPicker;
@end

@implementation ViewController
```

When the view loads up, we will then instantiate these two buttons and place them on the view:

```
- (void)viewDidLoad {
    [super viewDidLoad];

    self.title = @"Media picker...";

    self.buttonPickAndPlay = [UIButton buttonWithType:UIButtonTypeSystem];
    self.buttonPickAndPlay.frame = CGRectMake(0.0f,
                                              0.0f,
                                              200,
                                              37.0f);
    self.buttonPickAndPlay.center = CGPointMake(self.view.center.x,
                                                self.view.center.y - 50);
    [self.buttonPickAndPlay setTitle:@"Pick and Play"
                            forState:UIControlStateNormal];
    [self.buttonPickAndPlay addTarget:self
                               action:@selector(displayMediaPickerAndPlayItem)
                     forControlEvents:UIControlEventTouchUpInside];
    [self.view addSubview:self.buttonPickAndPlay];

    self.buttonStopPlaying = [UIButton buttonWithType:UIButtonTypeSystem];
    self.buttonStopPlaying.frame = CGRectMake(0.0f,
                                              0.0f,
                                              200,
                                              37.0f);
    self.buttonStopPlaying.center = CGPointMake(self.view.center.x,
                                                self.view.center.y + 50);
    [self.buttonStopPlaying setTitle:@"Stop Playing"
                            forState:UIControlStateNormal];
    [self.buttonStopPlaying addTarget:self
                               action:@selector(stopPlayingAudio)
                     forControlEvents:UIControlEventTouchUpInside];
    [self.view addSubview:self.buttonStopPlaying];

}
```

The two most important methods in the view controller are the `displayMediaPickerAndPlayItem` and `stopPlayingAudio`:

```
- (void) stopPlayingAudio{

    if (self.myMusicPlayer != nil){
```

```
        [[NSNotificationCenter defaultCenter]
         removeObserver:self
         name:MPMusicPlayerControllerPlaybackStateDidChangeNotification
         object:self.myMusicPlayer];

        [[NSNotificationCenter defaultCenter]
         removeObserver:self
         name:MPMusicPlayerControllerNowPlayingItemDidChangeNotification
         object:self.myMusicPlayer];

        [[NSNotificationCenter defaultCenter]
         removeObserver:self
         name:MPMusicPlayerControllerVolumeDidChangeNotification
         object:self.myMusicPlayer];

        [self.myMusicPlayer stop];
    }

}

- (void) displayMediaPickerAndPlayItem{

    self.mediaPicker =
    [[MPMediaPickerController alloc]
     initWithMediaTypes:MPMediaTypeAnyAudio];

    if (self.mediaPicker != nil){

        NSLog(@"Successfully instantiated a media picker.");
        self.mediaPicker.delegate = self;
        self.mediaPicker.allowsPickingMultipleItems = YES;
        self.mediaPicker.showsCloudItems = YES;
        self.mediaPicker.prompt = @"Pick a song please...";

        [self.view addSubview:self.mediaPicker.view];

        [self.navigationController presentViewController:self.mediaPicker
                                                animated:YES
                                              completion:nil];

    } else {
        NSLog(@"Could not instantiate a media picker.");
    }

}
```

When the media picker controller succeeds, the `mediaPicker:didPickMediaItems` message will be called in the delegate object (in this case, the view controller). On the other hand, if the user cancels the media player, we'll get the `mediaPicker:mediaPickerDidCancel` message. The following code implements the method that will be called in each case:

```
- (void) mediaPicker:(MPMediaPickerController *)mediaPicker
  didPickMediaItems:(MPMediaItemCollection *)mediaItemCollection{

    NSLog(@"Media Picker returned");

    /* First, if we have already created a music player, let's
     deallocate it */
    self.myMusicPlayer = nil;

    self.myMusicPlayer = [[MPMusicPlayerController alloc] init];

    [self.myMusicPlayer beginGeneratingPlaybackNotifications];

    /* Get notified when the state of the playback changes */
    [[NSNotificationCenter defaultCenter]
     addObserver:self
     selector:@selector(musicPlayerStateChanged:)
     name:MPMusicPlayerControllerPlaybackStateDidChangeNotification
     object:self.myMusicPlayer];

    /* Get notified when the playback moves from one item
     to the other. In this recipe, we are only going to allow
     our user to pick one music file */
    [[NSNotificationCenter defaultCenter]
     addObserver:self
     selector:@selector(nowPlayingItemIsChanged:)
     name:MPMusicPlayerControllerNowPlayingItemDidChangeNotification
     object:self.myMusicPlayer];

    /* And also get notified when the volume of the
     music player is changed */
    [[NSNotificationCenter defaultCenter]
     addObserver:self
     selector:@selector(volumeIsChanged:)
     name:MPMusicPlayerControllerVolumeDidChangeNotification
     object:self.myMusicPlayer];

    /* Start playing the items in the collection */
    [self.myMusicPlayer setQueueWithItemCollection:mediaItemCollection];
    [self.myMusicPlayer play];

    /* Finally dismiss the media picker controller */
    [mediaPicker dismissViewControllerAnimated:YES completion:nil];

}

- (void) mediaPickerDidCancel:(MPMediaPickerController *)mediaPicker{

    /* The media picker was cancelled */
    NSLog(@"Media Picker was cancelled");
    [mediaPicker dismissViewControllerAnimated:YES completion:nil];
```

```
}
```

We are listening for the events the music player generates through the notifications that it sends. Here are the three methods that are going to be responsible for handling the notifications we are listening to for the music player:

```
- (void) musicPlayerStateChanged:(NSNotification *)paramNotification{

    NSLog(@"Player State Changed");

    /* Let's get the state of the player */
    NSNumber *stateAsObject =
    [paramNotification.userInfo
     objectForKey:@"MPMusicPlayerControllerPlaybackStateKey"];

    NSInteger state = [stateAsObject integerValue];

    /* Make your decision based on the state of the player */
    switch (state){
        case MPMusicPlaybackStateStopped:{
            /* Here the media player has stopped playing the queue. */
            break;
        }
        case MPMusicPlaybackStatePlaying:{
            /* The media player is playing the queue. Perhaps you
             can reduce some processing that your application
             that is using to give more processing power
             to the media player */
            break;
        }
        case MPMusicPlaybackStatePaused:{
            /* The media playback is paused here. You might want
             to indicate by showing graphics to the user */
            break;
        }
        case MPMusicPlaybackStateInterrupted:{
            /* An interruption stopped the playback of the media queue */
            break;
        }
        case MPMusicPlaybackStateSeekingForward:{
            /* The user is seeking forward in the queue */
            break;
        }
        case MPMusicPlaybackStateSeekingBackward:{
            /* The user is seeking backward in the queue */
            break;
        }
    } /* switch (State){ */

}
```

```
- (void) nowPlayingItemIsChanged:(NSNotification *)paramNotification{

    NSLog(@"Playing Item Is Changed");

    NSString *persistentID =
    [paramNotification.userInfo
     objectForKey:@"MPMusicPlayerControllerNowPlayingItemPersistentIDKey"];

    /* Do something with Persistent ID */
    NSLog(@"Persistent ID = %@", persistentID);

}

- (void) volumeIsChanged:(NSNotification *)paramNotification{
    NSLog(@"Volume Is Changed");
    /* The userInfo dictionary of this notification is normally empty */
}
```

By running the application and pressing the Pick and Play button on the view controller, we will be presented with the media picker controller. Once the picker view controller is displayed, the same Music UI will be presented to the user. After the user picks an item (or cancels the whole dialog), we will get appropriate delegate messages called in the view controller (since the view controller is the delegate of the media picker). After the items are picked (we allow only one item in this recipe, though), we will start the music player and start playing the whole collection.

If you want to allow your users to pick more than one item at a time, simply set the `allowsPickingMultipleItems` property of your media picker controller to `YES`:

```
mediaPicker.allowsPickingMultipleItems = YES;
```

Sometimes when working with the media picker controller (`MPMediaPickerController`), the "MPMediaPicker: Lost connection to iPod library" message will be printed to the console screen. This is because the media picker has been interrupted by an event, such as syncing with iTunes while the picker was being displayed to the user. Immediately, your `mediaPickerDidCancel:` delegate message will be called as well.

# CHAPTER 13
# Address Book

## 13.0. Introduction

On an iOS device, the Contacts application allows users to add contacts to, remove contacts from, and manipulate their address books. An address book can be a collection of people and groups. Each person can have properties such as first name, last name, phone number, and email address. Some properties can have a single value, and some can have multiple values. For instance, the first name of a person is one value, but the phone number can be multiple values (e.g., if the user has two home phone numbers).

The AddressBook.framework framework in the iOS SDK allows you to interact with the address book database on the device. You can get the array of all entities in the user's address book, insert and change values, and much more.

To use the address book-related functions in your application, using the latest LLVM compiler features, all you have to do is import the following header file into your source code:

```
#import "AppDelegate.h"
#import <AddressBook/AddressBook.h>

@implementation AppDelegate

<# Rest of your code goes here #>
```

You can use the Address Book framework on iOS Simulator, and you will be happy to know that Apple has already prepopulated the Contacts database on the simulator so that you don't have to do that by yourself (see Figure 13-1).

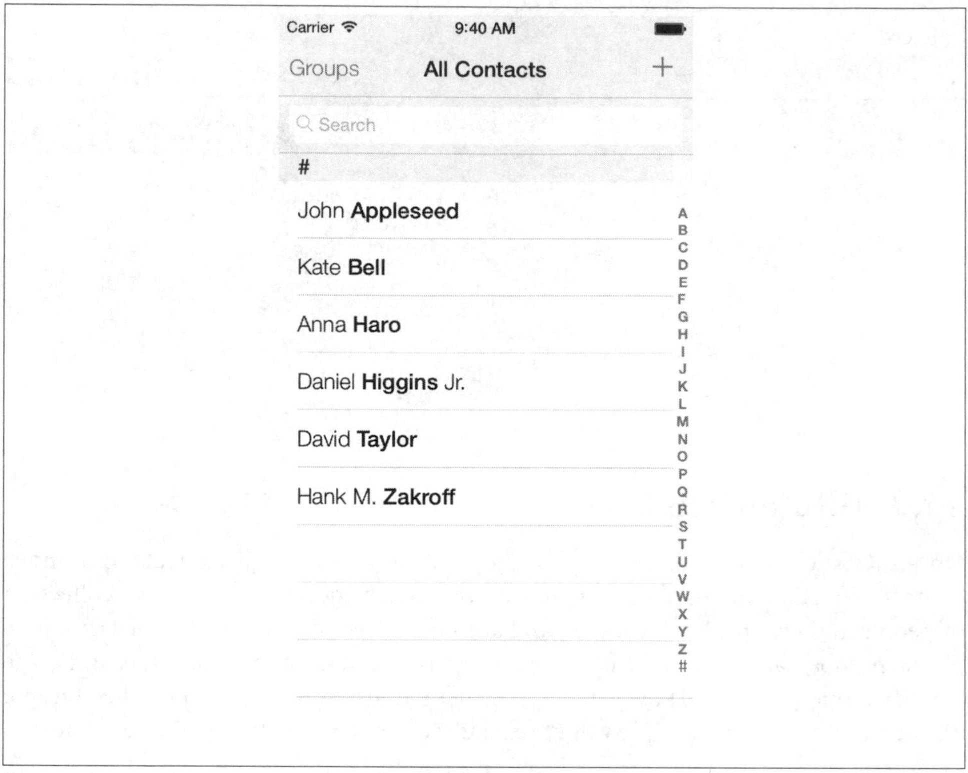


*Figure 13-1. The Contacts app on the simulator already contains prepopulated information*

The examples in this chapter don't try to handle all the different types of errors that an Address Book API could throw. We simply check whether an API succeeds or fails. In your app, however, you might need to check these errors; for this reason, the code examples retrieve the references to errors that might happen during calls to each of the Address Book methods, just for your reference.

# 13.1. Requesting Access to the Address Book

## Problem

You want to start accessing the user's address book, which requires the user to have granted your app access to the user's address book database. You want to check whether you have access so that you don't receive a runtime error when you attempt access.

## Solution

In order to find the current authorization state of your app, call the function `ABAddressBookGetAuthorizationStatus` in the Address Book framework. This function can return any of the following values:

`kABAuthorizationStatusNotDetermined`
: The user has not yet decided whether she would like to grant access to your application.

`kABAuthorizationStatusDenied`
: The user has explicitly denied your application from having access to the address book.

`kABAuthorizationStatusAuthorized`
: The user has authorized your application to have access to the address book on her device.

`kABAuthorizationStatusRestricted`
: Parental controls or other permissions configured on the iOS device prevent your app from accessing and interacting with the address book database on the device.

If you find out that the status that you received from the `ABAddressBookGetAuthorizationStatus` function is `kABAuthorizationStatusNotDetermined`, you can use the `ABAddressBookRequestAccessWithCompletion` function to ask for permission to access the user's address book database. You have to pass two parameters to this function:

*An address book reference of type* `ABAddressBookRef`
: The instance of the address book that you want to access.

*A completion block of type* `ABAddressBookRequestAccessCompletionHandler`
: After you call this function, iOS will ask the user if she wants to grant access to your application. Regardless of whether the user says yes or no, this block object will be called and you will then, through a Boolean parameter, get to know whether the answer was yes or no.

## Discussion

Starting with iOS 6, Apple is quite rightly putting restrictions on how apps can access users' personal data, such as their contact information. This is done through a user interface designed by Apple that asks the users explicitly whether they allow these apps to access certain parts of their device and data, such as their address book database. Since we are all good iOS-land citizens, we will adhere to these rules and make sure that we access the user's address book only if we have been granted permission to do so.

Regardless of what you want to do with the address book, whether to read from it or write to it, you need to make sure that you have been granted sufficient privileges. If you are not sure about whether you can access the address book, simply call the `ABAddressBookGetAuthorizationStatus` function as demonstrated in this recipe.

Here is a little example of what to do depending on what the `ABAddressBookGetAuthorizationStatus` function returns to your application. In this example, we will call the aforementioned function and just query the system about the authorization status of our app with regards to the address book database. If we are authorized to access it, fine. If we have been denied access, or if there is a system-wide restriction on address book access, we will display an alert view on the screen. If we have not yet been given access, we will ask the user for her permission to access the address book:

```
- (BOOL)            application:(UIApplication *)application
  didFinishLaunchingWithOptions:(NSDictionary *)launchOptions{

    CFErrorRef error = NULL;

    switch (ABAddressBookGetAuthorizationStatus()){
        case kABAuthorizationStatusAuthorized:{
            addressBook = ABAddressBookCreateWithOptions(NULL, &error);
            /* Do your work and once you are finished ... */
            if (addressBook != NULL){
                CFRelease(addressBook);
            }
            break;
        }
        case kABAuthorizationStatusDenied:{
            [self displayMessage:kDenied];
            break;
        }
        case kABAuthorizationStatusNotDetermined:{
            addressBook = ABAddressBookCreateWithOptions(NULL, &error);
            ABAddressBookRequestAccessWithCompletion
            (addressBook, ^(bool granted, CFErrorRef error) {
                if (granted){
                    NSLog(@"Access was granted");
                } else {
                    NSLog(@"Access was not granted");
                }
                if (addressBook != NULL){
                    CFRelease(addressBook);
                }
            });
            break;
        }
        case kABAuthorizationStatusRestricted:{
            [self displayMessage:kRestricted];
            break;
        }
    }

    self.window = [[UIWindow alloc]
```

```
                  initWithFrame:[[UIScreen mainScreen] bounds]];
    self.window.backgroundColor = [UIColor whiteColor];
    [self.window makeKeyAndVisible];
    return YES;

}
```

Now, when the user opens your app for the first time, undoubtedly, the authorization status that will come back from `ABAddressBookGetAuthorizationStatus` will be equal to `kABAuthorizationStatusNotDetermined`. At this point, we attempt to request permission using the `ABAddressBookRequestAccessWithCompletion` procedure. This will cause the user to see something similar to Figure 13-2 on her screen, and she can choose whether to grant or deny permission.

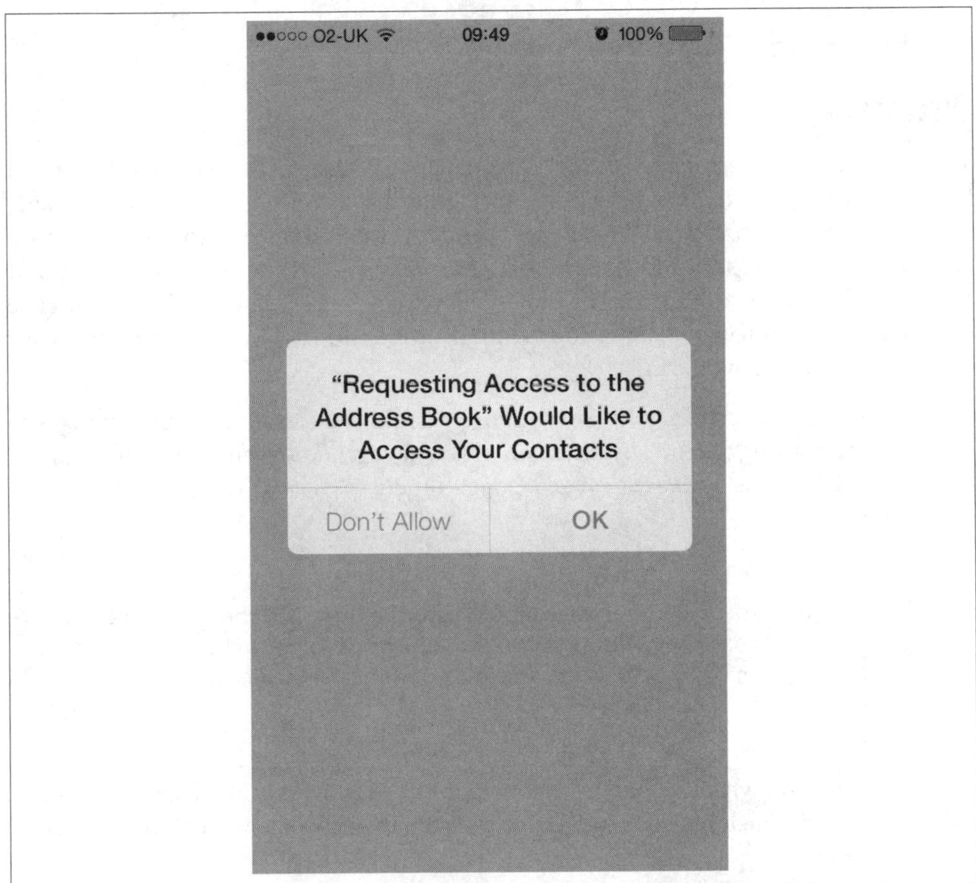


*Figure 13-2. Our app asking for permission to access the address book database*

## 13.2. Retrieving a Reference to an Address Book

### Problem

You would like to work with a user's contacts. To do this, first you need to get a reference to the user's address book database. This reference is what you use to retrieve entries, as well as to make and save changes.

### Solution

Use the `ABAddressBookCreateWithOptions` function in the Address Book framework. As the option, pass NULL and pass a reference to an error object to get any errors that may happen during the process:

```
addressBook = ABAddressBookCreateWithOptions(NULL, &error);
```

### Discussion

To get a reference to the user's address book database, you must first check whether you have permission, as discussed in Recipe 13.1. After permission is granted to your app, you can carry on to use the `ABAddressBookCreateWithOptions` function. This function returns a value of type `ABAddressBookRef` that will be `nil` if the address book cannot be accessed. You must check for `nil` values before accessing the address book reference returned by this function. Attempting to modify a `nil` address book will terminate your application with a runtime error.

After retrieving a reference to the user's address book, you can start making changes to the contacts, reading the entries, and so on. If you have made any changes to the address book, the `ABAddressBookHasUnsavedChanges` function will tell you by returning the value `YES`.

An instance of the address book database returned by the `ABAddressBookCreate` function must be released when you are finished working with it, using the `CFRelease` Core Foundation method, as demonstrated in our example code.

After determining whether changes were made to the address book database, you can either save or discard these changes using the `ABAddressBookSave` or `ABAddressBookRevert` procedure, respectively.

Here is a little example that will demonstrate this. In the implementation file of your app delegate, define an instance variable of type `ABAddressBookRef` along with the error strings that you want to display to the user should your app *not* be granted permission to the address book:

```
#import "AppDelegate.h"
#import <AddressBook/AddressBook.h>

NSString *const kDenied = @"Access to address book is denied";
NSString *const kRestricted = @"Access to address book is restricted";

ABAddressBookRef addressBook;

@implementation AppDelegate

<# Rest of your code goes here #>
```

Now we go straight into the `application:didFinishLaunchingWithOptions:` instance method of our app delegate and start checking for the status of our app to see whether we can access the address book:

```
- (BOOL)            application:(UIApplication *)application
  didFinishLaunchingWithOptions:(NSDictionary *)launchOptions{

    CFErrorRef error = NULL;

    switch (ABAddressBookGetAuthorizationStatus()){
        case kABAuthorizationStatusAuthorized:{
            addressBook = ABAddressBookCreateWithOptions(NULL, &error);
            [self useAddressBook:addressBook];
            if (addressBook != NULL){
                CFRelease(addressBook);
            }
            break;
        }
        case kABAuthorizationStatusDenied:{
            [self displayMessage:kDenied];
            break;
        }
        case kABAuthorizationStatusNotDetermined:{
            addressBook = ABAddressBookCreateWithOptions(NULL, &error);
            ABAddressBookRequestAccessWithCompletion
            (addressBook, ^(bool granted, CFErrorRef error) {
                if (granted){
                    NSLog(@"Access was granted");
                    [self useAddressBook:addressBook];
                } else {
                    NSLog(@"Access was not granted");
                }
                if (addressBook != NULL){
                    CFRelease(addressBook);
                }
            });
            break;
        }
        case kABAuthorizationStatusRestricted:{
            [self displayMessage:kRestricted];
```

```
            break;
        }
    }

    self.window = [[UIWindow alloc]
                   initWithFrame:[[UIScreen mainScreen] bounds]];
    self.window.backgroundColor = [UIColor whiteColor];
    [self.window makeKeyAndVisible];
    return YES;

}
```

You can see that if we already have or have just been granted permission to access the user's address book database, we are calling a method called `useAddressBook:`. In this method, if we have made any changes to the address book, we will save them:

```
- (void) useAddressBook:(ABAddressBookRef)paramAddressBook{
    /* Work with the address book here */

    /* Let's see whether we have made any changes to the
     address book or not, before attempting to save it */

    if (ABAddressBookHasUnsavedChanges(paramAddressBook)){
        /* Now decide if you want to save the changes to
         the address book */
        NSLog(@"Changes were found in the address book.");

        BOOL doYouWantToSaveChanges = YES;

        /* We can make a decision to save or revert the
         address book back to how it was before */
        if (doYouWantToSaveChanges){

            CFErrorRef saveError = NULL;

            if (ABAddressBookSave(paramAddressBook, &saveError)){
                /* We successfully saved our changes to the
                 address book */
            } else {
                /* We failed to save the changes. You can now
                 access the [saveError] variable to find out
                 what the error is */
            }

        } else {

            /* We did NOT want to save the changes to the address
             book so let's revert it to how it was before */
            ABAddressBookRevert(paramAddressBook);

        }
```

```
    } else {
        /* We have not made any changes to the address book */
        NSLog(@"No changes to the address book.");
    }
}
```

We created the doYouWantToSaveChanges local variable and set it to YES just to demonstrate that we can, if necessary, revert an address book whose contents have been changed (reversion is done through the ABAddressBookRevert procedure). You can add code, for instance, asking the user if he wants the changes to be saved or not, and if not, you can revert the address book to its original state.

For more information about importing the Address Book framework into your application, please refer to this chapter's Introduction.

# 13.3. Retrieving All the People in the Address Book

## Problem

You want to retrieve all the contacts in the user's address book.

## Solution

Use the ABAddressBookCopyArrayOfAllPeople function to retrieve an array of all contacts:

```
- (void) readFromAddressBook:(ABAddressBookRef)paramAddressBook{

    NSArray *arrayOfAllPeople = (__bridge_transfer NSArray *)
    ABAddressBookCopyArrayOfAllPeople(paramAddressBook);

    NSUInteger peopleCounter = 0;
    for (peopleCounter = 0;
         peopleCounter < [arrayOfAllPeople count];
         peopleCounter++){

        ABRecordRef thisPerson =
        (__bridge ABRecordRef)
        [arrayOfAllPeople objectAtIndex:peopleCounter];

        NSLog(@"%@", thisPerson);

        /* Use the [thisPerson] address book record */
    }

}
```

## Discussion

After accessing the user's address book database, we can call the ABAddressBook CopyArrayOfAllPeople function to retrieve an array of all the contacts in that address book. The return value of this function is an immutable array of type CFArrayRef. You can't work with this type of array as you would work with instances of NSArray, but you have two ways to traverse a CFArrayRef array. First, it natively supports two functions:

CFArrayGetCount
: Gets the number of items in an instance of CFArrayRef. This is similar to the count instance method of an NSArray.

CFArrayGetValueAtIndex
: Retrieves an item at a specific location of an instance of CFArrayRef. This is similar to the objectAtIndex: instance method of an NSArray.

Second, the CFArrayRef Core Foundation object is one of the objects that supports toll-free bridging to its NS counterpart, NSArray. This means that we can simply bridge this Core Foundation array and typecast it to an instance of NSArray. This works perfectly under ARC, using the __bridge_transfer keyword. That keyword decreases the reference count on the Core Foundation object, since our local array is a strong variable by default and will retain its contents without us having to do anything else. Just as a reminder, all local variables are strong variables, meaning that they will retain their contents. In this case, the ABAddressBookCopyArrayOfAllPeople function returns a Core Foundation array of all people in an address book. After we place the Core Foundation array into a local array (which will retain our Core Foundation array), we are going to have to dispose of the original Core Foundation object, before it was retained by the local variable (because of the strong local variable). Because of this, we are using __bridge_transfer to decrease the retain count on the Core Foundation array and let the strong local variable retain the toll-free array into an object of type NSArray.

The items that are put in an array of all people, retrieved by calling the ABAddressBook CopyArrayOfAllPeople function, are of type ABRecordRef. In Recipe 13.4, you will see how to access different properties of the entries, such as a person's entry, in the address book database.

## See Also

Recipe 13.2

## 13.4. Retrieving Properties of Address Book Entries

### Problem

You have retrieved a reference to an item in the address book, such as a person's entry, and you want to retrieve that person's properties, such as first and last names.

### Solution

Use the `ABRecordCopyValue` function on the person's Address Book record.

### Discussion

The records in the address book database are of type `ABRecordRef`. Each record could be either a group or a person. We have not discussed groups yet, so let's focus on people. Each person could have various types of information assigned to him, such as his first name, last name, email address, and so on. Bear in mind that many of these values are optional, and at the time of creating a new contact in the address book database, the user can simply leave out fields such as phone number, middle name, email address, URL, and so forth.

`ABRecordCopyValue` accepts an address book record and the property that has to be retrieved as its two parameters. The second parameter is the property of the record that we want to retrieve. Here are some of the common properties (all of these properties are defined as constant values in the *ABPerson.h* header file):

`kABPersonFirstNameProperty`
: This value will retrieve the first name of the given person. The return value is of type `CFStringRef`, which can be cast to `NSString` with a bridge cast, so you can do just about anything you want with the results.

`kABPersonLastNameProperty`
: This value will retrieve the last name of the given person. Like the first name property, the return value will be of type `CFStringRef`, which again can be cast to `NSString`.

`kABPersonMiddleNameProperty`
: This value will retrieve the middle name of the given person. Like the first name and the last name, the return value will be of type `CFStringRef`.

`kABPersonEmailProperty`
: This will retrieve the given person's email address. The return value in this case will be of type `ABMultiValueRef`. This is a data type that can contain multiple values inside it, like an array, but *not exactly* like an array. This type of data will be discussed next.

Some of the values that we retrieve from the ABRecordCopyValue function are straightforward, generic types, such as CFStringRef. But this function can also return more complicated values, such as the email of a contact. The email could be further broken down into home email address, work email address, and so on. Values that can be further broken down like this are called *multivalues* in the Address Book framework. Various functions allow us to work with multiple values (which are of type ABMultiValueRef):

ABMultiValueGetCount
: Returns the number of value/label pairs that are inside the multivalue.

ABMultiValueCopyLabelAtIndex
: Returns the label associated with a multivalue item at a specific index (indexes are zero-based). For instance, if the user has three email addresses, such as work, home, and test addresses, the index of the first (work) email address in the email multivalue would be 0. This function will then retrieve the label associated with that address (in this example, *work*). Please bear in mind that multivalues do not necessarily have to have labels. Make sure you check for NULL values.

ABMultiValueCopyValueAtIndex
: Returns the string value associated with a multivalue item at a specific index (indexes are zero-based). Suppose the user has work, home, and test email addresses. If we provide the index 0 to this function, it will retrieve the given contact's work email address.

All Core Foundation array indexes are zero-based, just like their Cocoa counterpart array indexes.

Now let's go ahead and write a simple method that can retrieve all the people in the address book and print out their first name, last name, and email address objects, and place it in our app delegate:

```
- (void) readFromAddressBook:(ABAddressBookRef)paramAddressBook{

    NSArray *allPeople = (__bridge_transfer NSArray *)
    ABAddressBookCopyArrayOfAllPeople(paramAddressBook);

    NSUInteger peopleCounter = 0;
    for (peopleCounter = 0;
         peopleCounter < [allPeople count];
         peopleCounter++){

        ABRecordRef thisPerson =  (__bridge ABRecordRef)
        [allPeople objectAtIndex:peopleCounter];

        NSString *firstName = (__bridge_transfer NSString *)
```

```
        ABRecordCopyValue(thisPerson, kABPersonFirstNameProperty);

        NSString *lastName = (__bridge_transfer NSString *)
        ABRecordCopyValue(thisPerson, kABPersonLastNameProperty);

        NSString *email = (__bridge_transfer NSString *)
        ABRecordCopyValue(thisPerson, kABPersonEmailProperty);

        NSLog(@"First Name = %@", firstName);
        NSLog(@"Last Name = %@", lastName);
        NSLog(@"Address = %@", email);

    }
}
```

We will obviously first ask for permission from the user whether or not we can access the device's address book database. Once permission is granted, we will call this method. I will not be repeating the code that requests for permission again, since we have already seen this code a few times in this chapter. Please refer to Recipe 13.1 for more information.

If you run this app in iOS Simulator for the latest iOS SDK, which has predefined contacts in the Contacts app, you will get the following printed to the console window:

```
First Name = Kate
Last Name = Bell
Label = _$!<Work>!$_, Localized Label =
    Work, Email = kate-bell@mac.com
Label = _$!<Work>!$_, Localized Label =
    Work, Email = www.creative-consulting-inc.com
First Name = Daniel
Last Name = Higgins
Label = _$!<Home>!$_, Localized Label =
    Home, Email = d-higgins@mac.com
First Name = John
Last Name = Appleseed
Label = _$!<Work>!$_, Localized Label =
    Work, Email = John-Appleseed@mac.com
First Name = Anna
Last Name = Haro
Label = _$!<Home>!$_, Localized Label =
    Home, Email = anna-haro@mac.com
First Name = Hank
Last Name = Zakroff
Label = _$!<Work>!$_, Localized Label =
    Work, Email = hank-zakroff@mac.com
First Name = David
Last Name = Taylor
```

It's immediately visible that the multivalue field (email) cannot be read as a plain string object. So, using the functions that we just learned, let's go ahead and implement a method to accept an object of type ABRecordRef, read that record's multivalue email field, and print the values out to the console:

```
- (void) logPersonEmails:(ABRecordRef)paramPerson{

    if (paramPerson == NULL){
        NSLog(@"The given person is NULL.");
        return;
    }

    ABMultiValueRef emails =
    ABRecordCopyValue(paramPerson, kABPersonEmailProperty);

    if (emails == NULL){
        NSLog(@"This contact does not have any emails.");
        return;
    }

    /* Go through all the emails */
    NSUInteger emailCounter = 0;

    for (emailCounter = 0;
         emailCounter < ABMultiValueGetCount(emails);
         emailCounter++){

        /* Get the label of the email (if any) */
        NSString *emailLabel = (__bridge_transfer NSString *)
        ABMultiValueCopyLabelAtIndex(emails, emailCounter);

        NSString *localizedEmailLabel = (__bridge_transfer NSString *)
        ABAddressBookCopyLocalizedLabel((__bridge CFStringRef)emailLabel);

        /* And then get the email address itself */
        NSString *email = (__bridge_transfer NSString *)
        ABMultiValueCopyValueAtIndex(emails, emailCounter);

        NSLog(@"Label = %@, Localized Label = %@, Email = %@",
              emailLabel,
              localizedEmailLabel,
              email);

    }

    CFRelease(emails);

}

- (void) readFromAddressBook:(ABAddressBookRef)paramAddressBook{

    NSArray *allPeople = (__bridge_transfer NSArray *)
    ABAddressBookCopyArrayOfAllPeople(paramAddressBook);
```

```
    NSUInteger peopleCounter = 0;
    for (peopleCounter = 0;
         peopleCounter < [allPeople count];
         peopleCounter++){

        ABRecordRef thisPerson =  (__bridge ABRecordRef)
        [allPeople objectAtIndex:peopleCounter];

        NSString *firstName = (__bridge_transfer NSString *)
        ABRecordCopyValue(thisPerson, kABPersonFirstNameProperty);

        NSString *lastName = (__bridge_transfer NSString *)
        ABRecordCopyValue(thisPerson, kABPersonLastNameProperty);

        NSLog(@"First Name = %@", firstName);
        NSLog(@"Last Name = %@", lastName);

        [self logPersonEmails:thisPerson];

    }
}
```

Calling the `CFRelease` procedure on a `NULL` value will crash your application. Make sure you check for `NULL` values before calling this Core Foundation procedure.

Label values returned by the `ABMultiValueCopyLabelAtIndex` function are rather cryptic and hard to read. Examples are *_$!<Other>!$_* and *_$!<Home>!$_*, which might be set for email addresses with labels of Other and Home. However, if you want to retrieve a plain and readable version of these labels, you can first copy the label using the `ABMultiValueCopyLabelAtIndex` function and pass the return value of this function to the `ABAddressBookCopyLocalizedLabel` function.

## See Also

Recipe 13.2; Recipe 13.3

# 13.5. Inserting a Person Entry into the Address Book

## Problem

You want to create a new person contact and insert it into the user's address book.

## Solution

Use the ABPersonCreate function to create a new person. Set the person's properties using the ABRecordSetValue function, and add the person to the address book using the ABAddressBookAddRecord function.

## Discussion

After accessing the address book database using the ABAddressBookCreate function, you can start inserting new group and person records into the database. In this recipe, we will concentrate on inserting new person records. For information about inserting new groups into the address book, please refer to Recipe 13.6.

Use the ABPersonCreate function to create a new person record. Bear in mind that calling this function is not enough to add the person record to the address book. You must save the address book for your record to appear in the database.

By calling the ABPersonCreate function, you get a Core Foundation reference to a value of type ABRecordRef. Now you can call the ABRecordSetValue function to set the various properties of a new person entry. Once you are done, you must add the new person record to the database. You can do this using the ABAddressBookAddRecord function. After doing this, you must also save any unsaved changes to the address book database in order to truly preserve your new person record. Do this by using the ABAddressBookSave function.

So let's combine all of this into a method that allows us to insert a new person entry into the address book:

```
- (ABRecordRef) newPersonWithFirstName:(NSString *)paramFirstName
                              lastName:(NSString *)paramLastName
                         inAddressBook:(ABAddressBookRef)paramAddressBook{

    ABRecordRef result = NULL;

    if (paramAddressBook == NULL){
        NSLog(@"The address book is NULL.");
        return NULL;
    }

    if ([paramFirstName length] == 0 &&
        [paramLastName length] == 0){
        NSLog(@"First name and last name are both empty.");
        return NULL;
    }

    result = ABPersonCreate();

    if (result == NULL){
        NSLog(@"Failed to create a new person.");
```

```
    return NULL;
}

BOOL couldSetFirstName = NO;
BOOL couldSetLastName = NO;
CFErrorRef setFirstNameError = NULL;
CFErrorRef setLastNameError = NULL;

couldSetFirstName = ABRecordSetValue(result,
                                     kABPersonFirstNameProperty,
                                     (__bridge CFTypeRef)paramFirstName,
                                     &setFirstNameError);

couldSetLastName = ABRecordSetValue(result,
                                    kABPersonLastNameProperty,
                                    (__bridge CFTypeRef)paramLastName,
                                    &setLastNameError);

CFErrorRef couldAddPersonError = NULL;
BOOL couldAddPerson = ABAddressBookAddRecord(paramAddressBook,
                                             result,
                                             &couldAddPersonError);

if (couldAddPerson){
    NSLog(@"Successfully added the person.");
} else {
    NSLog(@"Failed to add the person.");
    CFRelease(result);
    result = NULL;
    return result;
}

if (ABAddressBookHasUnsavedChanges(paramAddressBook)){

    CFErrorRef couldSaveAddressBookError = NULL;
    BOOL couldSaveAddressBook =
    ABAddressBookSave(paramAddressBook,
                      &couldSaveAddressBookError);

    if (couldSaveAddressBook){
        NSLog(@"Successfully saved the address book.");
    } else {
        NSLog(@"Failed to save the address book.");
    }
}

if (couldSetFirstName &&
    couldSetLastName){
    NSLog(@"Successfully set the first name \
          and the last name of the person.");
} else {
    NSLog(@"Failed to set the first name and/or \
```

```
                last name of the person.");
    }

    return result;

}
```

In our app delegate, we will first check if we have permission to access the user's address book database. We have already seen this code in Recipe 13.1, so we won't be repeating it here. Once you have access, you can then call the `createNewPersonInAddressBook:` method that we have written and pass the instance of the address book object to this method.

The `newPersonWithFirstName:lastName:inAddressBook:` method that we implemented creates a new person entry in the address book database. After invoking this function, you will see the results (as shown in Figure 13-3) in the Contacts application on iOS Simulator.

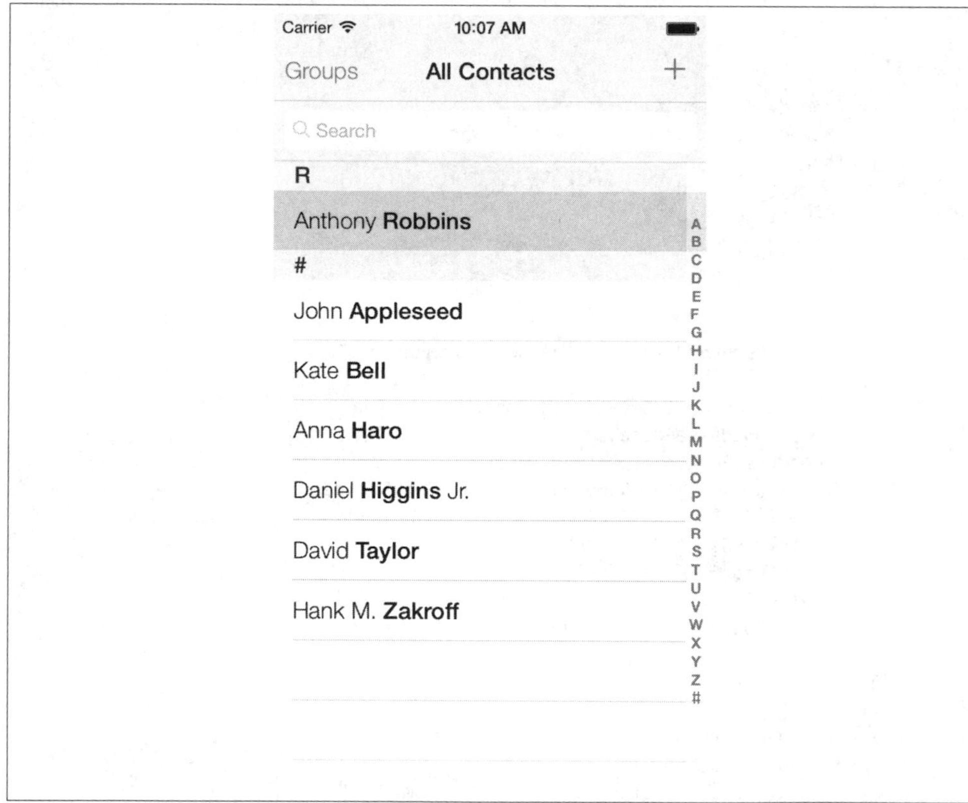


*Figure 13-3. A new person record is added to the address book*

Memory management on Core Foundation is quite different from what you might be used to when writing applications for Cocoa Touch. As this topic is beyond the scope of this book, please make sure you read the "Memory Management Programming Guide for Core Foundation" documentation on Apple's website (*http://bit.ly/1dWLlvx*).

## 13.6. Inserting a Group Entry into the Address Book

### Problem

You want to categorize your contacts into groups.

### Solution

Use the `ABGroupCreate` function.

Bear in mind that, as mentioned before, Core Foundation memory management is more complex than what Xcode's static analyzer could process. Therefore, attempting to use the LLVM compiler to compile Core Foundation code with static analysis turned on might give you a lot of warnings. You can ignore these and test the code with Instruments to make sure your code does not leak, but I encourage you to familiarize yourself with memory management in Core Foundation by reading Apple's "Memory Management Programming Guide for Core Foundation" document, as mentioned in the previous section.

### Discussion

After retrieving the reference to the address book database, you can call the `ABGroupCreate` function to create a new group entry. However, you must perform a few more operations before you can insert this group into the address book operation. The first thing you have to do is set the name of this group using the `ABRecordSetValue` function with the `kABGroupNameProperty` property, as shown in the example code.

After the name of the group is set, add it to the address book database just like you add a new person's entry—using the `ABAddressBookAddRecord` function. For more information about adding a new person's entry to the address book database, please read Recipe 13.5.

Inserting a new group with a name that already exists in the address book database will create a new group with the same name but with no group members. In later recipes, we will learn how to avoid doing this by first finding the groups in the database and making sure a group with that name doesn't already exist.

After adding the group to the address book, you also need to save the address book's contents using the `ABAddressBookSave` function.

So, with all this in mind, let's go ahead and implement a method that allows us to create a new group with any desired name in the Address Book database:

```
- (ABRecordRef) newGroupWithName:(NSString *)paramGroupName
                   inAddressBook:(ABAddressBookRef)paramAddressBook{

    ABRecordRef result = NULL;

    if (paramAddressBook == NULL){
        NSLog(@"The address book is nil.");
        return NULL;
    }

    result = ABGroupCreate();

    if (result == NULL){
        NSLog(@"Failed to create a new group.");
        return NULL;
    }

    BOOL couldSetGroupName = NO;
    CFErrorRef error = NULL;

    couldSetGroupName = ABRecordSetValue(result,
                                         kABGroupNameProperty,
                                         (__bridge CFTypeRef)paramGroupName,
                                         &error);

    if (couldSetGroupName){

        BOOL couldAddRecord = NO;
        CFErrorRef couldAddRecordError = NULL;

        couldAddRecord = ABAddressBookAddRecord(paramAddressBook,
                                                result,
                                                &couldAddRecordError);

        if (couldAddRecord){

            NSLog(@"Successfully added the new group.");
```

```
            if (ABAddressBookHasUnsavedChanges(paramAddressBook)){
                BOOL couldSaveAddressBook = NO;
                CFErrorRef couldSaveAddressBookError = NULL;
                couldSaveAddressBook =
                ABAddressBookSave(paramAddressBook,
                                  &couldSaveAddressBookError);
                if (couldSaveAddressBook){
                    NSLog(@"Successfully saved the address book.");
                } else {
                    CFRelease(result);
                    result = NULL;
                    NSLog(@"Failed to save the address book.");
                }
            } else {
                CFRelease(result);
                result = NULL;
                NSLog(@"No unsaved changes.");
            }
        } else {
            CFRelease(result);
            result = NULL;
            NSLog(@"Could not add a new group.");
        }
    } else {
        CFRelease(result);
        result = NULL;
        NSLog(@"Failed to set the name of the group.");
    }

    return result;

}

- (void) createNewGroupInAddressBook:(ABAddressBookRef)paramAddressBook{

    ABRecordRef personalCoachesGroup =
    [self newGroupWithName:@"Personal Coaches"
            inAddressBook:paramAddressBook];

    if (personalCoachesGroup != NULL){
        NSLog(@"Successfully created the group.");
        CFRelease(personalCoachesGroup);
    } else {
        NSLog(@"Could not create the group.");
    }

}
```

All we have to do now is to call the `createNewGroupInAddressBook:` method when our app delegate starts, to make sure that it works as expected. Before you attempt to call this method, though, do make sure that your app has the required permission to access the user's address book database. To read more about this, please have a look at Recipe 13.1.

After running your code, you will see results like those shown in Figure 13-4 (you might have created other groups already, so your address book might not look exactly like that shown in the figure).

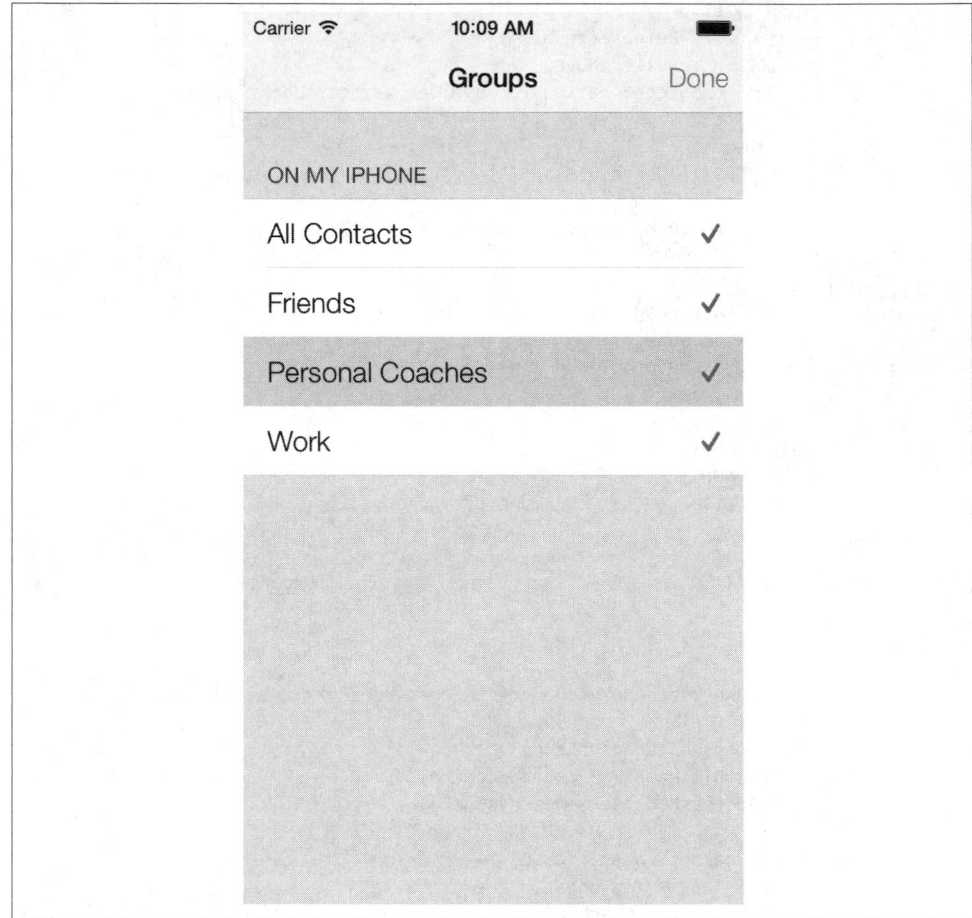


*Figure 13-4. A new group created in the address book database*

# 13.7. Adding Persons to Groups

## Problem

You want to assign a person entry in the address book to a group.

## Solution

Use the `ABGroupAddMember` function.

## Discussion

We learned to insert both person entries (in Recipe 13.5) and group entries (in Recipe 13.6) into the address book database. In those recipes we implemented two custom methods named `newPersonWithFirstName:lastName:inAddressBook:` and `newGroupWithName:inAddressBook:`. Now we want to add the person entry to the group we created and save the information to the address book database. Combining these three recipes, we can use the following code to achieve our goal:

```
- (BOOL)     addPerson:(ABRecordRef)paramPerson
               toGroup:(ABRecordRef)paramGroup
    saveToAddressBook:(ABAddressBookRef)paramAddressBook{

    BOOL result = NO;

    if (paramPerson == NULL ||
        paramGroup == NULL ||
        paramAddressBook == NULL){
        NSLog(@"Invalid parameters are given.");
        return NO;
    }

    CFErrorRef error = NULL;

    /* Now attempt to add the person entry to the group */
    result = ABGroupAddMember(paramGroup,
                              paramPerson,
                              &error);

    if (result == NO){
        NSLog(@"Could not add the person to the group.");
        return result;
    }

    /* Make sure we save any unsaved changes */
    if (ABAddressBookHasUnsavedChanges(paramAddressBook)){
        BOOL couldSaveAddressBook = NO;
        CFErrorRef couldSaveAddressBookError = NULL;
        couldSaveAddressBook = ABAddressBookSave(paramAddressBook,
                                                 &couldSaveAddressBookError);
        if (couldSaveAddressBook){
            NSLog(@"Successfully added the person to the group.");
            result = YES;
        } else {
            NSLog(@"Failed to save the address book.");
        }
    } else {
```

```
        NSLog(@"No changes were saved.");
    }

    return result;

}

- (void) addPersonsAndGroupsToAddressBook:(ABAddressBookRef)paramAddressBook{

    ABRecordRef richardBranson = [self
                                  newPersonWithFirstName:@"Richard"
                                  lastName:@"Branson"
                                  inAddressBook:paramAddressBook];

    if (richardBranson != NULL){

        ABRecordRef entrepreneursGroup = [self
                                          newGroupWithName:@"Entrepreneurs"
                                          inAddressBook:paramAddressBook];

        if (entrepreneursGroup != NULL){

            if ([self addPerson:richardBranson
                        toGroup:entrepreneursGroup
              saveToAddressBook:paramAddressBook]){

                NSLog(@"Successfully added Richard Branson \
                      to the Entrepreneurs Group");

            } else {
                NSLog(@"Failed to add Richard Branson to the \
                      Entrepreneurs group.");
            }

            CFRelease(entrepreneursGroup);
        } else {
            NSLog(@"Failed to create the Entrepreneurs group.");
        }

        CFRelease(richardBranson);
    } else {
        NSLog(@"Failed to create an entity for Richard Branson.");
    }

}
```

Once your app starts, you need to make sure it has permission to access and update the user's address book. For more information about this, please see Recipe 13.1. Once you are sure that you have permission, you can call the `addPersonsAndGroupsToAddressBook:` method and pass the instance of address book that you retrieved from the system as a parameter to this method. Once that is done, we can see that the person entry we added to the "Entrepreneurs" group and to the database is, in fact, now inside this address book group, as shown in Figure 13-5.

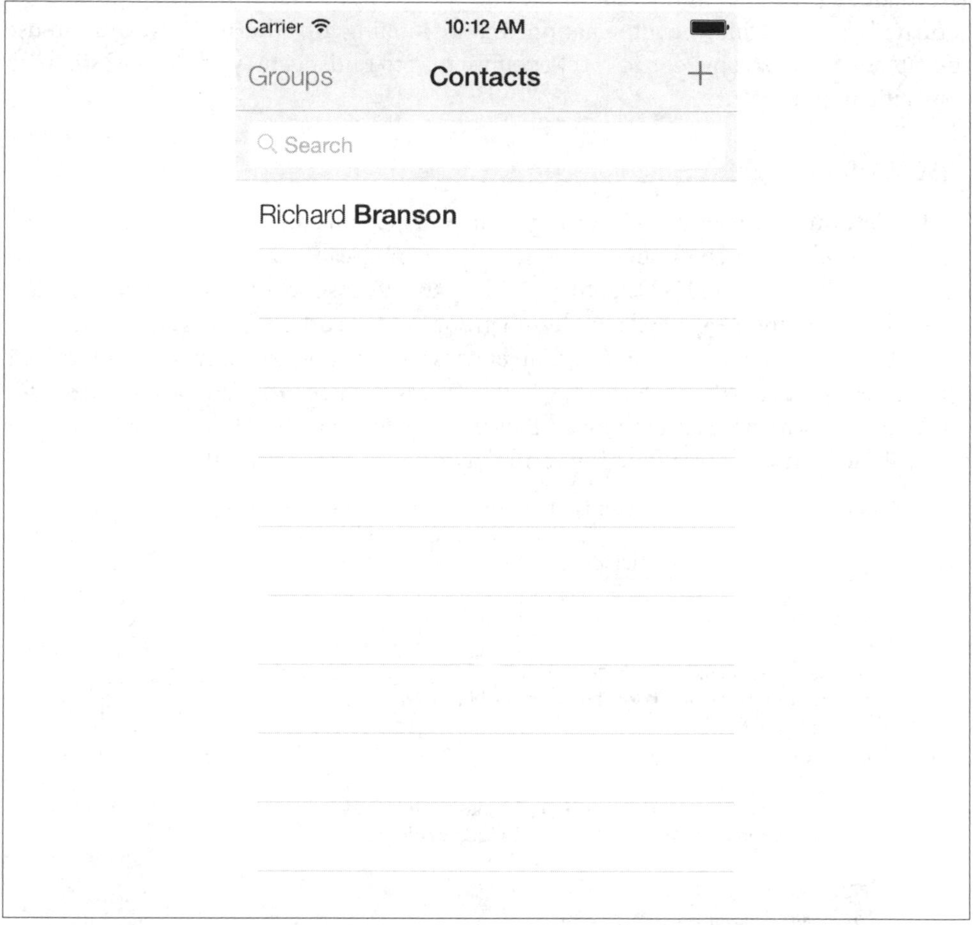


*Figure 13-5. Adding a person to a group*

## See Also

Recipe 13.6

# 13.8. Searching the Address Book

## Problem

You want to find a specific person or group in the address book database.

## Solution

Use the ABAddressBookCopyArrayOfAllPeople and ABAddressBookCopyArrayOfAllGroups functions to find all people and groups in the address book. Traverse the returned arrays to find the information you are looking for. Alternatively, you can use the ABAddressBookCopyPeopleWithName function to find an entry about a person with a specific name.

## Discussion

Up to this point, we have been inserting group and person entries into the address book without checking whether such a group or person already exists. We can use the ABAddressBookCopyArrayOfAllPeople and ABAddressBookCopyArrayOfAllGroups functions to get the array of all people and groups in the address book and search in the array to see whether the person or group entries we are about to insert into the address book already exist. When we check whether strings match, we also have to check for null strings (which we assume mean that the contacts match). Here are two methods that will make use of these functions and that can also be used in other recipes:

```
- (BOOL) doesPersonExistWithFirstName:(NSString *)paramFirstName
                             lastName:(NSString *)paramLastName
                        inAddressBook:(ABRecordRef)paramAddressBook{

    BOOL result = NO;

    if (paramAddressBook == NULL){
        NSLog(@"The address book is null.");
        return NO;
    }

    NSArray *allPeople = (__bridge_transfer NSArray *)
    ABAddressBookCopyArrayOfAllPeople(paramAddressBook);

    NSUInteger peopleCounter = 0;
    for (peopleCounter = 0;
         peopleCounter < [allPeople count];
         peopleCounter++){

        ABRecordRef person = (__bridge ABRecordRef)
        [allPeople objectAtIndex:peopleCounter];

        NSString *firstName = (__bridge_transfer NSString *)
        ABRecordCopyValue(person, kABPersonFirstNameProperty);

        NSString *lastName = (__bridge_transfer NSString *)
        ABRecordCopyValue(person, kABPersonLastNameProperty);

        BOOL firstNameIsEqual = NO;
        BOOL lastNameIsEqual = NO;
```

```
        if ([firstName length] == 0 && [paramFirstName length] == 0){
            firstNameIsEqual = YES;
        }
        else if ([firstName isEqualToString:paramFirstName]){
            firstNameIsEqual = YES;
        }

        if ([lastName length] == 0 && [paramLastName length] == 0){
            lastNameIsEqual = YES;
        }
        else if ([lastName isEqualToString:paramLastName]){
            lastNameIsEqual = YES;
        }

        if (firstNameIsEqual &&
            lastNameIsEqual){
            return YES;
        }

    }

    return result;

}
```

Similarly, we can check the existence of a group by first retrieving the array of all the groups in the address book database, using the `ABAddressBookCopyArrayOfAllGroups` function:

```
- (BOOL) doesGroupExistWithGroupName:(NSString *)paramGroupName
                       inAddressBook:(ABAddressBookRef)paramAddressBook{

    BOOL result = NO;

    if (paramAddressBook == NULL){
        NSLog(@"The address book is null.");
        return NO;
    }

    NSArray *allGroups = (__bridge_transfer NSArray *)
    ABAddressBookCopyArrayOfAllGroups(paramAddressBook);

    NSUInteger groupCounter = 0;
    for (groupCounter = 0;
         groupCounter < [allGroups count];
         groupCounter++){

        ABRecordRef group = (__bridge ABRecordRef)
        [allGroups objectAtIndex:groupCounter];

        NSString *groupName = (__bridge_transfer NSString *)
```

```
            ABRecordCopyValue(group, kABGroupNameProperty);

            if ([groupName length] == 0 && [paramGroupName length] == 0){
                return YES;
            }

            else if ([groupName isEqualToString:paramGroupName]){
                return YES;
            }

        }

        return result;

    }
```

We can use the `doesGroupExistWithGroupName:inAddressBook:` method in this way:

```
- (void) createGroupInAddressBook:(ABAddressBookRef)paramAddressBook{

    if ([self doesGroupExistWithGroupName:@"O'Reilly"
                            inAddressBook:self.addressBook]){
        NSLog(@"The O'Reilly group already exists in the address book.");
    } else {

        ABRecordRef oreillyGroup = [self newGroupWithName:@"O'Reilly"
                                            inAddressBook:self.addressBook];

        if (oreillyGroup != NULL){
            NSLog(@"Successfully created a group for O'Reilly.");
            CFRelease(oreillyGroup);
        } else {
            NSLog(@"Failed to create a group for O'Reilly.");
        }

    }

}
```

For the implementation of the `createNewGroupWithName:inAddressBook:` method, please refer to Recipe 13.6.

As we saw earlier, we have two ways of finding a person in the address book database:

- Retrieve the array of all people in the address book, using the `ABAddressBookCopyArrayOfAllPeople` function. Next, get each record inside the array and compare the first and last name properties of each person with the strings you are looking for. You can search in any of the properties assigned to that person in the address book, including first name, last name, email, phone number, and so on.

- Ask the Address Book framework to perform the search based on a composite name. This is done using the ABAddressBookCopyPeopleWithName function.

Here is an example of using the ABAddressBookCopyPeopleWithName function to search for a contact with a specific name:

```
- (BOOL) doesPersonExistWithFullName:(NSString *)paramFullName
                       inAddressBook:(ABAddressBookRef)paramAddressBook{

    BOOL result = NO;

    if (paramAddressBook == NULL){
        NSLog(@"Address book is null.");
        return NO;
    }

    NSArray *allPeopleWithThisName = (__bridge_transfer NSArray *)
    ABAddressBookCopyPeopleWithName(paramAddressBook,
                                    (__bridge CFStringRef)paramFullName);

    if ([allPeopleWithThisName count] > 0){
        result = YES;
    }

    return result;

}
```

Here is how we can use the method that we just implemented:

```
- (void) createPersonInAddressBook:(ABAddressBookRef)paramAddressBook{

    if ([self doesPersonExistWithFullName:@"Anthony Robbins"
                            inAddressBook:self.addressBook]){
        NSLog(@"Anthony Robbins exists in the address book.");
    } else {
        NSLog(@"Anthony Robbins does not exist in the address book.");

        ABRecordRef anthonyRobbins =
        [self newPersonWithFirstName:@"Anthony"
                            lastName:@"Robbins"
                       inAddressBook:self.addressBook];

        if (anthonyRobbins != NULL){
            NSLog(@"Successfully created a record for Anthony Robbins");
            CFRelease(anthonyRobbins);
        } else {
            NSLog(@"Failed to create a record for Anthony Robbins");
        }
    }

}
```

Using this function, you won't have to know the full name to be able to find a contact in the address book. You can just pass a part of the name—for instance, just the first name—in order to find all the contacts with that specific first name.

The search performed by the `ABAddressBookCopyPeopleWithName` function is case-insensitive.

# 13.9. Retrieving and Setting a Person's Address Book Image

## Problem

You want to be able to retrieve and set the images of address book entries.

## Solution

Use one of the following functions:

`ABPersonHasImageData`
: Use this function to find out if an address book entry has an image set.

`ABPersonCopyImageData`
: Use this function to retrieve the image data (if any).

`ABPersonSetImageData`
: Use this function to set the image data for an entry.

## Discussion

As mentioned in this recipe's Solution, we can use the `ABPersonCopyImageData` function to retrieve the data associated with an image of a person entry in the address book. We can use this function in a method of our own to make it more convenient to use:

```
- (UIImage *) getPersonImage:(ABRecordRef)paramPerson{

    UIImage *result = nil;

    if (paramPerson == NULL){
        NSLog(@"The person is nil.");
        return NULL;
    }

    NSData *imageData = (__bridge_transfer NSData *)
    ABPersonCopyImageData(paramPerson);
```

```
    if (imageData != nil){
        UIImage *image = [UIImage imageWithData:imageData];
        result = image;
    }

    return result;

}
```

The ABPersonSetImageData function sets the image data for a person entry in the address book. Since this function uses data, not the image itself, we need to get NSData from UIImage. If we want the data pertaining to a PNG image, we can use the UIImagePNGRepresentation function to retrieve the PNG NSData representation of the image of type UIImage. To retrieve JPEG image data from an instance of UIImage, use the UIImageJPEGRepresentation function. Here is the method that will allow you to set the image of a person entry in the address book database:

```
- (BOOL) setPersonImage:(ABRecordRef)paramPerson
         inAddressBook:(ABAddressBookRef)paramAddressBook
         withImageData:(NSData *)paramImageData{

    BOOL result = NO;

    if (paramAddressBook == NULL){
        NSLog(@"The address book is nil.");
        return NO;
    }

    if (paramPerson == NULL){
        NSLog(@"The person is nil.");
        return NO;
    }

    CFErrorRef couldSetPersonImageError = NULL;

    BOOL couldSetPersonImage =
    ABPersonSetImageData(paramPerson,
                         (__bridge CFDataRef)paramImageData,
                         &couldSetPersonImageError);

    if (couldSetPersonImage){
        NSLog(@"Successfully set the person's image. Saving...");
        if (ABAddressBookHasUnsavedChanges(paramAddressBook)){
            BOOL couldSaveAddressBook = NO;
            CFErrorRef couldSaveAddressBookError = NULL;

            couldSaveAddressBook =
            ABAddressBookSave(paramAddressBook,
                              &couldSaveAddressBookError);

            if (couldSaveAddressBook){
```

```
                NSLog(@"Successfully saved the address book.");
                result = YES;
            } else {
                NSLog(@"Failed to save the address book.");
            }
        } else {
            NSLog(@"There are no changes to be saved!");
        }
    } else {
        NSLog(@"Failed to set the person's image.");
    }

    return result;

}
```

Now let's write a simple application to demonstrate the use of these methods. In this example code, we want to achieve the following:

- Create a simple view controller with two labels and two image views.
- Attempt to retrieve a contact with the first name "Anthony" and the last name "Robbins" from our address book. If this contact doesn't exist, we will create it.
- Retrieve the previous image (if any) of the contact and display it in the first image view (the top image view).
- Set a new image for the contact, retrieved from our application bundle, and display the new image in the second image view (the bottom image view).

Let's get started. Here are the declarations of our view controller:

```
#import "ViewController.h"
#import <AddressBook/AddressBook.h>

NSString *const kDenied = @"Access to address book is denied";
NSString *const kRestricted = @"Access to address book is restricted";

@interface ViewController ()
@property (nonatomic, unsafe_unretained) ABAddressBookRef addressBook;
@property (nonatomic, strong) UILabel *labelOldImage;
@property (nonatomic, strong) UIImageView *imageViewOld;
@property (nonatomic, strong) UILabel *labelNewImage;
@property (nonatomic, strong) UIImageView *imageViewNew;
@end

@implementation  ViewController

<# Rest of your code goes here #>
```

The next stop is the `viewDidLoad` method of our view controller, where we will instantiate our labels and image views and place them on our view controller's view. We need to write our viewDidLoad method in a way that we can read a person's image from the address book and then set his image and display the new one, using the functions we've learned about in this and other recipes in this chapter:

```
- (void) changeYPositionOfView:(UIView *)paramView
                            to:(CGFloat)paramY{

    CGRect viewFrame = paramView.frame;
    viewFrame.origin.y = paramY;
    paramView.frame = viewFrame;

}

- (void) createLabelAndImageViewForOldImage{

    self.labelOldImage = [[UILabel alloc] initWithFrame:CGRectZero];
    self.labelOldImage.text = @"Old Image";
    self.labelOldImage.font = [UIFont systemFontOfSize:16.0f];
    [self.labelOldImage sizeToFit];
    self.labelOldImage.center = self.view.center;
    [self.view addSubview:self.labelOldImage];
    [self changeYPositionOfView:self.labelOldImage
                             to:80.0f];

    self.imageViewOld = [[UIImageView alloc]
                         initWithFrame:CGRectMake(0.0f,
                                                  0.0f,
                                                  100.0f,
                                                  100.0f)];
    self.imageViewOld.center = self.view.center;
    self.imageViewOld.contentMode = UIViewContentModeScaleAspectFit;
    [self.view addSubview:self.imageViewOld];
    [self changeYPositionOfView:self.imageViewOld
                             to:105.0f];

}

- (void) createLabelAndImageViewForNewImage{

    self.labelNewImage = [[UILabel alloc] initWithFrame:CGRectZero];
    self.labelNewImage.text = @"New Image";
    self.labelNewImage.font = [UIFont systemFontOfSize:16.0f];
    [self.labelNewImage sizeToFit];
    self.labelNewImage.center = self.view.center;
    [self.view addSubview:self.labelNewImage];
    [self changeYPositionOfView:self.labelNewImage
                             to:210.0f];

    self.imageViewNew = [[UIImageView alloc]
                         initWithFrame:CGRectMake(0.0f,
                                                  0.0f,
                                                  100.0f,
```

```
                                                100.0f)];
        self.imageViewNew.center = self.view.center;
        self.imageViewNew.contentMode = UIViewContentModeScaleAspectFit;
    [self.view addSubview:self.imageViewNew];
    [self changeYPositionOfView:self.imageViewNew
                             to:235.0f];

}

- (void)viewDidLoad{
    [super viewDidLoad];

    [self createLabelAndImageViewForOldImage];
    [self createLabelAndImageViewForNewImage];

}
```

The next stop would be to ask the user for permission to access the device's address book database. The best place to do this is when we know our view has appeared on the screen and that would be inside the `viewDidAppear:` instance method of our view controller. In that method, we will simply query the system to see if our app has already been authorized to access the user's address book:

```
- (ABRecordRef) getPersonWithFirstName:(NSString *)paramFirstName
                              lastName:(NSString *)paramLastName
                         inAddressBook:(ABRecordRef)paramAddressBook{

    ABRecordRef result = NULL;

    if (paramAddressBook == NULL){
        NSLog(@"The address book is null.");
        return NULL;
    }

    NSArray *allPeople = (__bridge_transfer NSArray *)
    ABAddressBookCopyArrayOfAllPeople(paramAddressBook);

    NSUInteger peopleCounter = 0;
    for (peopleCounter = 0;
         peopleCounter < [allPeople count];
         peopleCounter++){

        ABRecordRef person = (__bridge ABRecordRef)
        [allPeople objectAtIndex:peopleCounter];

        NSString *firstName = (__bridge_transfer NSString *)
        ABRecordCopyValue(person, kABPersonFirstNameProperty);

        NSString *lastName = (__bridge_transfer NSString *)
        ABRecordCopyValue(person, kABPersonLastNameProperty);

        BOOL firstNameIsEqual = NO;
```

```
        BOOL lastNameIsEqual = NO;

        if ([firstName length] == 0 &&
            [paramFirstName length] == 0){
            firstNameIsEqual = YES;
        }
        else if ([firstName isEqualToString:paramFirstName]){
            firstNameIsEqual = YES;
        }

        if ([lastName length] == 0 &&
            [paramLastName length] == 0){
            lastNameIsEqual = YES;
        }
        else if ([lastName isEqualToString:paramLastName]){
            lastNameIsEqual = YES;
        }

        if (firstNameIsEqual &&
            lastNameIsEqual){
            return person;
        }

    }

    return result;

}

- (void) updateImagesInAddressBook:(ABAddressBookRef)paramAddressBook{

    ABRecordRef anthonyRobbins = [self getPersonWithFirstName:@"Anthony"
                                                      lastName:@"Robbins"
                                                 inAddressBook:paramAddressBook];

    if (anthonyRobbins == NULL){
        NSLog(@"Couldn't find record. Creating one...");
        anthonyRobbins = [self newPersonWithFirstName:@"Anthony"
                                             lastName:@"Robbins"
                                        inAddressBook:paramAddressBook];
        if (anthonyRobbins == NULL){
            NSLog(@"Failed to create a new record for this person.");
            return;
        }
    }

    CFRetain(anthonyRobbins);

    self.imageViewOld.image = [self getPersonImage:anthonyRobbins];

    NSString *newImageFilePath =
    [[NSBundle mainBundle] pathForResource:@"Anthony Robbins"
```

```
                                                  ofType:@"jpg"];

    UIImage *newImage = [[UIImage alloc]
                         initWithContentsOfFile:newImageFilePath];

    NSData *newImageData = UIImagePNGRepresentation(newImage);

    if ([self setPersonImage:anthonyRobbins
                inAddressBook:paramAddressBook
                withImageData:newImageData]){
        NSLog(@"Successfully set this person's new image.");
        self.imageViewNew.image = [self getPersonImage:anthonyRobbins];
    } else {
        NSLog(@"Failed to set this person's new image.");
    }

    CFRelease(anthonyRobbins);

}

- (void) viewDidAppear:(BOOL)paramAnimated{
    [super viewDidAppear:paramAnimated];

    CFErrorRef error = NULL;

    switch (ABAddressBookGetAuthorizationStatus()){
        case kABAuthorizationStatusAuthorized:{
            self.addressBook = ABAddressBookCreateWithOptions(NULL, &error);
            [self updateImagesInAddressBook:self.addressBook];
            if (self.addressBook != NULL){
                CFRelease(self.addressBook);
                self.addressBook = NULL;
            }
            break;
        }
        case kABAuthorizationStatusDenied:{
            [self displayMessage:kDenied];
            break;
        }
        case kABAuthorizationStatusNotDetermined:{
            self.addressBook = ABAddressBookCreateWithOptions(NULL, &error);
            ABAddressBookRequestAccessWithCompletion
            (self.addressBook, ^(bool granted, CFErrorRef error) {
                if (granted){
                    [self updateImagesInAddressBook:self.addressBook];
                } else {
                    NSLog(@"Access was not granted");
                }
                if (self.addressBook != NULL){
                    CFRelease(self.addressBook);
                    self.addressBook = NULL;
                }
```

```
            });
            break;
        }
        case kABAuthorizationStatusRestricted:{
            [self displayMessage:kRestricted];
            break;
        }
    }

}
```

The results are shown in Figure 13-6.

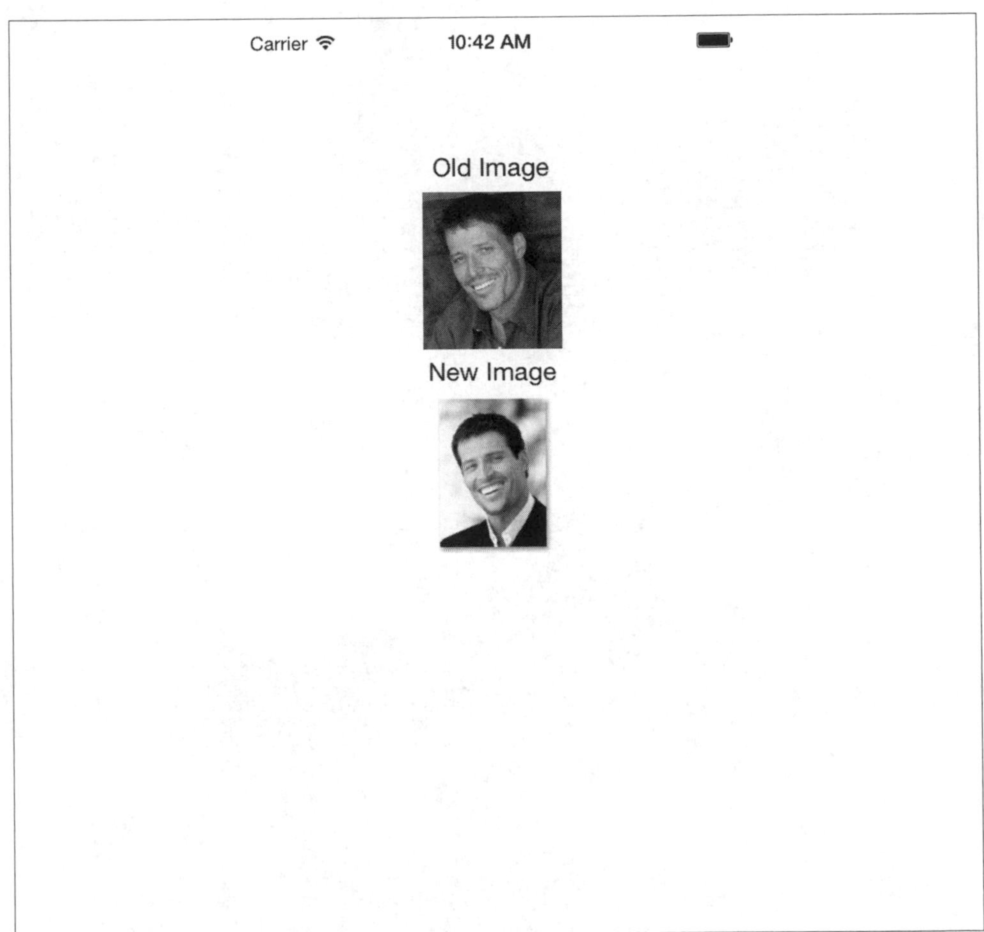


*Figure 13-6. The old image for a contact is replaced by a new one*

CHAPTER 14

# Files and Folder Management

## 14.0. Introduction

iOS is based on OS X, which itself is based on the Unix operating system. In iOS, the operating system's full directory structure is not visible to an app because each app, written by an iOS app developer, lives in its own sandbox. A sandbox environment is exactly what it sounds like: a sanctioned area where only the app that owns the sandbox can access the contents of the folder. Every app has its own sandbox folder and the sandbox folders by default have subfolders that apps can access.

When an iOS app is installed on the device, the folder structure shown in Figure 14-1 will be created for that app by the system.

*Name.app*
: Despite the odd name with the *.app* extension, this is a folder. The contents of your main bundle will all go in here. For instance, all your app icons, your app binary, your different branding images, fonts, sounds, etc., will all be placed in this folder automatically when iOS installs your app on a device. The *name* is the product name that you have set for your app. So if your app is called MyApp, the *.app* folder will be called *MyApp.app*.

*Documents/*
: This folder is the destination for all user-created content. Content that your app has populated, downloaded, or created should not be stored in this folder.

*Library/*
: You use this directory to store cached files, user preferences, and so on. Usually, this folder on its own will not have any files sitting in it. It contains other folders that will contain files.

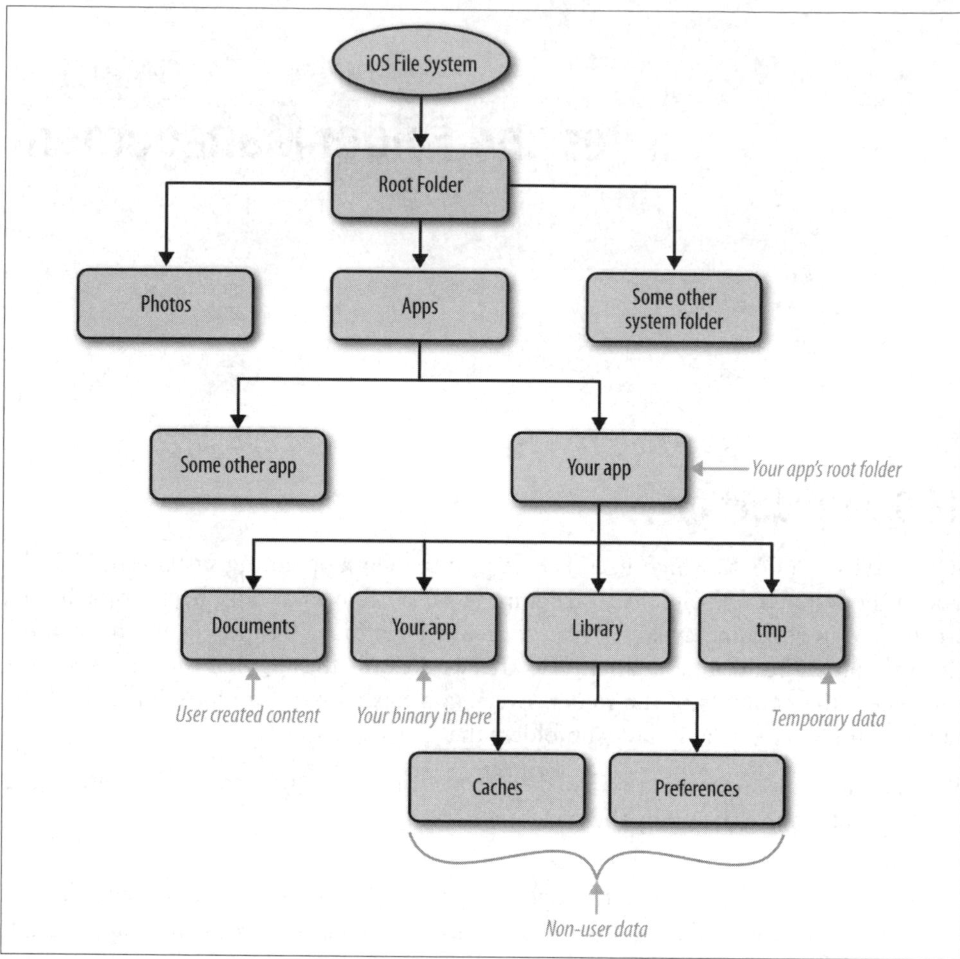


*Figure 14-1. Depiction of the iOS filesystem*

The root folder of every application contains various other folders, which I will explain here:

*Library/Caches/*
: The folder where you store data that your app can later re-create, if need be. The contents of this folder are not backed up by iOS. Also, iOS may remove the contents of this folder if the device is running out of disk space while your app is not running! So do not allow your app to rely on the contents of this folder too much; be prepared to re-create this content. Once again: the contents of this folder will not be backed up by iOS and can be deleted while your app is suspended.

For instance, if your app is relying on files and folders that are to be created on disk, this folder would not be the best place to store this data. You are better off storing such files and folders in the */tmp* folder.

*Library/Preferences/*
: As the name indicates, this folder contains the preferences that your app wants to remember between launches. We will talk about this in detail later. iOS does back up the contents of this folder.

*Library/Application Support/*
: The data that your app creates, not including the data created by the user, must be stored in this folder. It is good to know that iOS backs up the contents of this folder. This folder may not be created for you automatically, and you'll have to create it yourself if it doesn't exist. We will talk about folder creation later in this chapter.

*tmp/*
: These are temporary files that your app may create, download, and so on. The contents of this folder are not backed up by iOS. For instance, you may download a few photos from the Internet and store them in this folder in order to increase the performance of your application, so that you won't have to download the files every time the user opens your app. This folder serves exactly this purpose. Make sure that you are not storing any user-created documents or files in this folder.

Now you know the folders that iOS creates for you when your app is installed on an iOS device. The next thing you want to do is find the path of the rest of the useful folders that we just talked about, using the APIs that Apple has exposed to you (these will be explained in this chapter).

# 14.1. Finding the Paths of the Most Useful Folders on Disk

## Problem

You want to be able to find the path of some of the most useful folders that your app has access to (e.g., the folders that we talked about in this chpater's Introduction), so that you can access their content or create new content in those folders.

Programmers need to use APIs that are exposed in the iOS SDK to find the path of folders and/or files. In other words, you should never assume the path of a folder or a file. You should always make sure that you use the appropriate APIs to, for instance, find the paths that you are looking for, such as the *Documents* folder. Never, ever assume that this folder will be called *Documents* in your app's bundle. Simply use the appropriate APIs to find this path and, if you want to add or access files in the folder, attach your filenames to the end of this path.

## Solution

Use the `URLsForDirectory:inDomains:` instance method of the `NSFileManager` class.

## Discussion

The `NSFileManager` class offers a lot of file- and folder-related operations that you can do with iOS, right inside your apps, simply by making an instance of the class. I advise against using the shared file manager provided by this class through the `defaultManager` class method because it is not thread-safe. It is best to create and manage an instance of the `NSFileManager` class for yourself.

The `URLsForDirectory:inDomains:` instance method of the `NSFileManager` class allows you to search for specific directories on the iOS filesystem, mostly in your app's sandbox. There are two parameters to this method:

`URLsForDirectory:`
: This is the directory that you want to search for. Pass a value of type `NSSearchPathDirectory` enumeration to this parameter. I will talk more about this soon.

`inDomains`
: This is *where* you look for the given directory. The value to this parameter must be of type `NSSearchPathDomainMask` enumeration.

Suppose you want to find the path to your app's *Documents* folder. This is how easily you can find it:

```
NSFileManager *fileManager = [[NSFileManager alloc] init];
NSArray *urls = [fileManager URLsForDirectory:NSDocumentDirectory
                                    inDomains:NSUserDomainMask];

if ([urls count] > 0){
    NSURL *documentsFolder = urls[0];
    NSLog(@"%@", documentsFolder);
} else {
    NSLog(@"Could not find the Documents folder.");
}
```

As you can see, after creating our own instance of `NSFileManager`, we passed the `NSDocumentDirectory` value as the folder we are looking for and `NSUserDomainMask` as the domain. Let's go through some of the most important values that you can pass to each one of the parameters to the `URLsForDirectory:inDomains:` instance method of the `NSFileManager` class:

`URLsForDirectory`
: `NSLibraryDirectory`
: The library folder for the app.

`NSCachesDirectory`
: The caches folder, as explained before.

`NSDocumentDirectory`
: The documents folder.

`inDomains`
: `NSUserDomainMask`
: Specifies that the search be performed in the current user's folder. On OS X, this folder would be ~/.

Using this method, you can then find other folders such as the *caches* folder, as shown here:

```
NSFileManager *fileManager = [[NSFileManager alloc] init];
NSArray *urls = [fileManager URLsForDirectory:NSCachesDirectory
                                    inDomains:NSUserDomainMask];

if ([urls count] > 0){
    NSURL *cachesFolder = urls[0];
    NSLog(@"%@", cachesFolder);
} else {
    NSLog(@"Could not find the Caches folder.");
}
```

If you want to find the *tmp* folder, use the `NSTemporaryDirectory()` C function like so:

```
NSString *tempDirectory = NSTemporaryDirectory();
NSLog(@"Temp Directory = %@", tempDirectory);
```

When you execute this command on a device, the output will be similar to that shown here:

```
Temp Directory = /private/var/mobile/
    Applications/<# Your application ID goes here #>/tmp/
```

## See Also

Recipe 14.0, "Introduction"

# 14.2. Writing to and Reading from Files

## Problem

You want to be able to save information to disk (e.g., text, data, images, etc.).

## Solution

Cocoa classes that allow you to store information, such as `NSString`, `UIImage`, and `NSData`, all expose instance methods that allow you to store their data to disk under a given path.

## Discussion

In order to store text to disk, assuming that your text is stored in an instance of `NSString` (or the immutable version of this class), you can use the `writeToFile:atomically:encoding:error:` instance method of this class. This method works with strings that represent the destination path. Here are the different parameters:

`writeToFile`
: The path of the file to write to, as a string.

`atomically`
: A Boolean that, if set to `YES`, will first write the file to a temporary space and will then move the temporary file to the destination that you chose. This will ensure that the contents of the file will be saved to disk first and then saved to its destination, so that if iOS crashes before the file is saved to the final destination, your contents will still be saved later when the OS is back up again. It is recommended to set this value to `YES` when storing information that you don't want to lose under any circumstance while your app is running.

`encoding`
: Encoding of the text that you want to write to the path. Programmers usually use UTF8 for the encoding, using the `NSUTF8StringEncoding` constant value.

`error`
: Takes a pointer to an `NSError` object so that if the saving operation fails, you will be able to find the error that happened during the process. You can pass `nil` to this parameter if you are not interested in knowing about the errors that may occur during the saving process. Bear in mind that this function returns a Boolean value and you can simply use this value to find out whether an error has occurred.

For instance, if you have some text that you want to temporarily store in your app, and you don't want it to be backed up by iOS, you can do the following:

```
NSString *someText = @"Random string that won't be backed up.";

NSString *destinationPath =
[NSTemporaryDirectory()
 stringByAppendingPathComponent:@"MyFile.txt"];

NSError *error = nil;
BOOL succeeded = [someText writeToFile:destinationPath
                             atomically:YES
```

```
                                        encoding:NSUTF8StringEncoding
                                           error:&error];

    if (succeeded) {
        NSLog(@"Successfully stored the file at: %@", destinationPath);
    } else {
        NSLog(@"Failed to store the file. Error = %@", error);
    }
```

Also, after you are done, to make sure things went fine, you can attempt to read the same string back into memory from the destination file, using the `stringWithContentsOfFile:encoding:error:` class method of the `NSString` class. This will return back the autorelease string that is the contents of the specified file. If you want to explicitly instantiate an object of type `NSString` with the contents of the file, simply use the `initWithContentsOfFile:encoding:error:` instance method of the `NSString` class like so:

```
- (BOOL) writeText:(NSString *)paramText toPath:(NSString *)paramPath{
    return [paramText writeToFile:paramPath
                       atomically:YES
                         encoding:NSUTF8StringEncoding
                            error:nil];
}

- (NSString *) readTextFromPath:(NSString *)paramPath{
    return [[NSString alloc] initWithContentsOfFile:paramPath
                                           encoding:NSUTF8StringEncoding
                                              error:nil];
}

- (BOOL)              application:(UIApplication *)application
    didFinishLaunchingWithOptions:(NSDictionary *)launchOptions{

    NSString *filePath = [NSTemporaryDirectory()
                          stringByAppendingPathComponent:@"MyFile.txt"];

    if ([self writeText:@"Hello, World!" toPath:filePath]){

        NSString *readText = [self readTextFromPath:filePath];
        if ([readText length] > 0){
            NSLog(@"Text read from disk = %@", readText);
        } else {
            NSLog(@"Failed to read the text from disk.");
        }

    } else {
        NSLog(@"Failed to write the file.");
    }

    self.window = [[UIWindow alloc]
                   initWithFrame:[[UIScreen mainScreen] bounds]];
```

```
    self.window.backgroundColor = [UIColor whiteColor];
    [self.window makeKeyAndVisible];
    return YES;
}
```

What we have done is created two convenient methods that allow us to write text to and read text from a specified location. In our app delegate, then, we use these two methods to write some text to the *temp* folder and then read the same text back to memory in order to make sure our methods are working fine.

If you want to work with URLs encapsulated in instances of `NSURL` (or the mutable version of it), you can use the `writeToURL:atomically:encoding:error:` instance method instead.

Instances of `NSURL` can point to resources (files, directories, etc.) locally or remotely. For example, an instance of `NSURL` can represent a local file in the *Documents* folder of your app as easily as it can represent the website URL for `www.apple.com`. This class simply gives you functionality to access and work with URLs, regardless of which type of URL they are.

Other classes in foundation have methods similar to those of `NSString`. Let's take `NSArray` as an example. You can save the contents of an array using the `writeToFile:atomically:` instance method of `NSArray`. In order to read the contents of an array from disk, you can simply allocate an instance of the array and then initialize it using the `initWithContentsOfFile:` initializer of the array. Here is an example of both of these:

```
NSString *filePath = [NSTemporaryDirectory()
                      stringByAppendingPathComponent:@"MyFile.txt"];

NSArray *arrayOfNames = @[@"Steve", @"John", @"Edward"];
if ([arrayOfNames writeToFile:filePath atomically:YES]){

    NSArray *readArray = [[NSArray alloc] initWithContentsOfFile:filePath];
    if ([readArray count] == [arrayOfNames count]){
        NSLog(@"Read the array back from disk just fine.");
    } else {
        NSLog(@"Failed to read the array back from disk.");
    }
} else {
    NSLog(@"Failed to save the array to disk.");
}
```

The `writeToFile:atomically:` instance method of `NSArray` class can save only an array that contains objects of the following type:

- `NSString`
- `NSDictionary`
- `NSArray`
- `NSData`
- `NSNumber`
- `NSDate`

If you attempt to insert any other objects in the array, your data will not be saved to disk, because this method first makes sure all the objects in the array are of one of the aforementioned types. This is simply because the Objective-C runtime will not otherwise have any idea how to store your data to disk. For instance, suppose you create a class called `Person` and create a first name and last name property for the class, then instantiate an instance and add it to an array. How can an array then save your person to disk? It simply cannot do that, as it won't know what it has to save to disk. This is a problem known as *marshalling*, and is solved by iOS only for the data types just listed.

Dictionaries are also very similar to arrays and have the same way of saving their data to disk and reading data back into the dictionary. The method names are exactly the same, and the rules of saving an array also apply to dictionaries. Here is an example:

```
NSString *filePath = [NSTemporaryDirectory()
                      stringByAppendingPathComponent:@"MyFile.txt"];

NSDictionary *dict = @{
                       @"first name" : @"Steven",
                       @"middle name" : @"Paul",
                       @"last name" : @"Jobs",
                       };

if ([dict writeToFile:filePath atomically:YES]){
    NSDictionary *readDictionary = [[NSDictionary alloc]
                                    initWithContentsOfFile:filePath];

    /* Now compare the dictionaries and see if the one we read from disk
     is the same as the one we saved to disk */
    if ([readDictionary isEqualToDictionary:dict]){
        NSLog(@"The file we read is the same one as the one we saved.");
    } else {
        NSLog(@"Failed to read the dictionary from disk.");
    }
```

```
} else {
    NSLog(@"Failed to write the dictionary to disk.");
}
```

As you can see, this example writes the dictionary to disk and then reads it back from the same location. After reading, we compare the read dictionary to the one we saved to disk in order to make sure they both contain the same data.

Up to now, we have been using high-level classes such as `NSString` and `NSArray` to save our contents to disk. Now, what if we want to store a raw array of bytes to disk? That's easy too. Suppose we have an array of four characters and we want to save that to disk:

```
char bytes[4] = {'a', 'b', 'c', 'd'};
```

The easiest way of saving this raw array of bytes to disk is to encapsulate it in another high-level data structure like `NSData` and then use the relevant methods of `NSData` to write to and read from the disk. The saving and loading methods for an `NSData` are virtually the same as those for `NSArray` and `NSDictionary`. Here is an example of saving raw data to disk and reading it back from the disk:

```
NSString *filePath = [NSTemporaryDirectory()
                      stringByAppendingPathComponent:@"MyFile.txt"];

char bytes[4] = {'a', 'b', 'c', 'd'};

NSData *dataFromBytes = [[NSData alloc] initWithBytes:bytes
                                               length:sizeof(bytes)];

if ([dataFromBytes writeToFile:filePath atomically:YES]){
    NSData *readData = [[NSData alloc] initWithContentsOfFile:filePath];
    if ([readData isEqualToData:dataFromBytes]){
        NSLog(@"The data read is the same data as was written to disk.");
    } else {
        NSLog(@"Failed to read the data from disk.");
    }
} else {
    NSLog(@"Failed to save the data to disk.");
}
```

### See Also

Recipe 14.0

## 14.3. Creating Folders on Disk

### Problem

You want to be able to create folders on disk to save some of your app's files in them.

## Solution

Use the `createDirectoryAtPath:withIntermediateDirectories:attributes:error:` instance method of the `NSFileManager` class, as shown here:

```
- (BOOL)            application:(UIApplication *)application
  didFinishLaunchingWithOptions:(NSDictionary *)launchOptions{

    NSFileManager *fileManager = [[NSFileManager alloc] init];

    NSString *tempDir = NSTemporaryDirectory();
    NSString *imagesDir = [tempDir stringByAppendingPathComponent:@"images"];

    NSError *error = nil;
    if ([fileManager createDirectoryAtPath:imagesDir
               withIntermediateDirectories:YES
                                attributes:nil
                                     error:&error]){

        NSLog(@"Successfully created the directory.");

    } else {
        NSLog(@"Failed to create the directory. Error = %@", error);
    }

    self.window = [[UIWindow alloc]
                   initWithFrame:[[UIScreen mainScreen] bounds]];
    self.window.backgroundColor = [UIColor whiteColor];
    [self.window makeKeyAndVisible];
    return YES;
}
```

## Discussion

The APIs exposed by `NSFileManager` are very easy to use, and it's no surprise that you can use them to create folders on disk in a few lines. The `createDirectoryAtPath:withIntermediateDirectories:attributes:error:` method may look scary at first, but it's not that bad. I will explain the different parameters that you can pass to it:

`createDirectoryAtPath`
: The path to the folder that has to be created.

`withIntermediateDirectories`
: A Boolean parameter that, if set to `YES`, will create all the folders in the middle before it creates the final folder. For instance, if you want to create a folder named *images* in another folder named *data* inside the *tmp* folder of your app, but the *data* folder doesn't exist yet, you could easily ask to create the *tmp/data/images/* folder and set the `withIntermediateDirectories` parameter to `YES`. This will make the system create the *data* for you as well as the *images* folder.

`attributes`
: A dictionary of attributes that you can pass to the system in order to affect how your folder will be created. We won't be using these here, to keep things simple, but you can change things such as the modification date and time, the creation date and time, and other attributes of the created folder if you want to.

`error`
: This parameter accepts a pointer to an error object of type `NSObject`, which will be populated with any errors that may happen while the folder is being created. It's generally a good idea to pass an error object to this parameter, so that if the method fails (returns `NO`), you can access the error and determine what went wrong.

## See Also

Recipe 14.1

# 14.4. Enumerating Files and Folders

## Problem

You either want to enumerate folders within a folder or you want to enumerate the list of files inside a folder. The act of enumerating means that you simply want to find all the folders and/or files within another folder.

## Solution

Use the `contentsOfDirectoryAtPath:error:` instance method of the `NSFileManager` class as shown here. In this example, we are enumerating all the files, folders, and symlinks under our app's bundle folder:

```
- (BOOL)            application:(UIApplication *)application
  didFinishLaunchingWithOptions:(NSDictionary *)launchOptions{

    NSFileManager *fileManager = [[NSFileManager alloc] init];
    NSString *bundleDir = [[NSBundle mainBundle] bundlePath];

    NSError *error = nil;
    NSArray *bundleContents = [fileManager
                               contentsOfDirectoryAtPath:bundleDir
                               error:&error];

    if ([bundleContents count] > 0 &&
        error == nil){
        NSLog(@"Contents of the app bundle = %@", bundleContents);
    }
    else if ([bundleContents count] == 0 &&
             error == nil){
```

```
        NSLog(@"Call the police! The app bundle is empty.");
    }
    else {
        NSLog(@"An error happened = %@", error);
    }

    self.window = [[UIWindow alloc]
                   initWithFrame:[[UIScreen mainScreen] bounds]];
    // Override point for customization after application launch.
    self.window.backgroundColor = [UIColor whiteColor];
    [self.window makeKeyAndVisible];
    return YES;
}
```

## Discussion

In some of your iOS apps, you may need to enumerate the contents of a folder. Let me give you an example, in case this need is a bit vague right now. Imagine that the user asked you to download 10 images from the Internet and cache them in your app. You go ahead and save them, let's say, in the *tmp/images/* folder that you manually created. Now the user closes your app and reopens it, and in your UI, you want to display the list of already-downloaded files in a table view. How can you achieve this? Well, it's easy. All you have to do is enumerate the contents of the aforementioned folder using the `NSFileManager` class. As you saw in the Solution section of this recipe, the `contentsOfDirectoryAtPath:error:` instance method of the `NSFileManager` class returns an array of `NSString` objects that will represent the files, folders, and symlinks within the given folder. However, it is not easy to say which one is a folder, which one is a file, and so on. To get more fine-grained detail from the file manager, invoke the `contentsOfDirectoryAtURL:includingPropertiesForKeys:options:error:`. Let's go through the different parameters that you need to pass to this method:

`contentsOfDirectoryAtURL`
: The path of the folder that you want to inspect. This path should be provided as an instance of `NSURL`. Don't worry about it if you don't know how to construct this instance. We will talk about it soon.

`includingPropertiesForKeys`
: This is an array of properties that you would like iOS to fetch for every file, folder, or item that it finds in the given directory. For instance, you can specify that you want the creation date of the items to be returned in the results, as part of the URL instance that is returned to you (in instances of `NSURL` that you get back from the framework). Here is the list of some of the most important values that you can place in this array:

  `NSURLIsDirectoryKey`
  : Allows you to determine later whether one of the URLs returned is a directory.

`NSURLIsReadableKey`
: Allows you to determine later whether the returned URL is readable by your app's process.

`NSURLCreationDateKey`
: Returns the creation date of the item in the returned URL.

`NSURLContentAccessDateKey`
: Returns the last content access date in the returned results.

`NSURLContentModificationDateKey`
: As its name indicates, this allows you to determine the last-modified date for the returned URLs.

`options`
: Only 0 or `NSDirectoryEnumerationSkipsHiddenFiles` may be entered for this parameter. If the latter value is entered, as the name of the value shows, all hidden items will be skipped during the enumeration.

`error`
: A reference to an object that will be filled with an error should this method fail to execute its job. It's usually a good idea to provide error objects to these methods if you can. You get more control over why things fail, should they ever fail.

Now that we have more control over how the items are enumerated, let's enumerate all the items in the *.app* folder and print out the creation, last-modified, and last-accessed dates. We will also print out whether the items are hidden or not, and whether we have read access to the files or not. The last thing we'll print out will be whether the items are directories or not. Let's go:

```
- (NSArray *) contentsOfAppBundle{
    NSFileManager *manager = [[NSFileManager alloc] init];
    NSURL *bundleDir = [[NSBundle mainBundle] bundleURL];

    NSArray *propertiesToGet = @[
                                 NSURLIsDirectoryKey,
                                 NSURLIsReadableKey,
                                 NSURLCreationDateKey,
                                 NSURLContentAccessDateKey,
                                 NSURLContentModificationDateKey
                                 ];

    NSError *error = nil;
    NSArray *result = [manager contentsOfDirectoryAtURL:bundleDir
                             includingPropertiesForKeys:propertiesToGet
                                                options:0
                                                  error:&error];

    if (error != nil){
        NSLog(@"An error happened = %@", error);
```

```
    }

    return result;
}

- (NSString *) stringValueOfBoolProperty:(NSString *)paramProperty
                                 ofURL:(NSURL *)paramURL{

    NSNumber *boolValue = nil;
    NSError *error = nil;
    [paramURL getResourceValue:&boolValue
                        forKey:paramProperty
                         error:&error];
    if (error != nil){
        NSLog(@"Failed to get property of URL. Error = %@", error);
    }
    return [boolValue isEqualToNumber:@YES] ? @"Yes" : @"No";

}

- (NSString *) isURLDirectory:(NSURL *)paramURL{
    return [self stringValueOfBoolProperty:NSURLIsDirectoryKey ofURL:paramURL];
}

- (NSString *) isURLReadable:(NSURL *)paramURL{
    return [self stringValueOfBoolProperty:NSURLIsReadableKey ofURL:paramURL];
}

- (NSDate *) dateOfType:(NSString *)paramType inURL:(NSURL *)paramURL{
    NSDate *result = nil;
    NSError *error = nil;
    [paramURL getResourceValue:&result
                        forKey:paramType
                         error:&error];
    if (error != nil){
        NSLog(@"Failed to get property of URL. Error = %@", error);
    }
    return result;
}

- (void) printURLPropertiesToConsole:(NSURL *)paramURL{

    NSLog(@"Item name = %@", [paramURL lastPathComponent]);

    NSLog(@"Is a Directory? %@", [self isURLDirectory:paramURL]);

    NSLog(@"Is Readable? %@", [self isURLReadable:paramURL]);

    NSLog(@"Creation Date = %@",
          [self dateOfType:NSURLCreationDateKey inURL:paramURL]);

    NSLog(@"Access Date = %@",
```

```
        [self dateOfType:NSURLContentAccessDateKey inURL:paramURL]);

    NSLog(@"Modification Date = %@",
        [self dateOfType:NSURLContentModificationDateKey inURL:paramURL]);

    NSLog(@"-----------------------------------");
}

- (BOOL)            application:(UIApplication *)application
  didFinishLaunchingWithOptions:(NSDictionary *)launchOptions{


    NSArray *itemsInAppBundle = [self contentsOfAppBundle];
    for (NSURL *item in itemsInAppBundle){
        [self printURLPropertiesToConsole:item];
    }

    self.window = [[UIWindow alloc]
                   initWithFrame:[[UIScreen mainScreen] bounds]];
    // Override point for customization after application launch.
    self.window.backgroundColor = [UIColor whiteColor];
    [self.window makeKeyAndVisible];
    return YES;
}
```

The output of this program will be something similar to that shown here:

```
Item name = Assets.car
Is a Directory? No
Is Readable? Yes
Creation Date = 2013-06-25 16:12:53 +0000
Access Date = 2013-06-25 16:12:53 +0000
Modification Date = 2013-06-25 16:12:53 +0000
-----------------------------------
Item name = en.lproj
Is a Directory? Yes
Is Readable? Yes
Creation Date = 2013-06-25 16:12:53 +0000
Access Date = 2013-06-25 16:15:02 +0000
Modification Date = 2013-06-25 16:12:53 +0000
-----------------------------------
Item name = Enumerating Files and Folders
Is a Directory? No
Is Readable? Yes
Creation Date = 2013-06-25 16:15:01 +0000
Access Date = 2013-06-25 16:15:04 +0000
Modification Date = 2013-06-25 16:15:01 +0000
-----------------------------------
```

The important thing to note about this app is that we are using the `getResourceValue:forKey:error:` instance method of the `NSURL` class to get the value of each one of the keys that we are querying from the file manager, such as the creation and modification date. We pass these requirements to the file manager, asking it to fetch this information for us. And then, once we have our URLs, we use the aforementioned method to retrieve the different properties from the resulting URLs.

So let's have a look at the different parts of this app. I will simply explain what each one of these methods that we have written does:

*contentsOfAppBundle*
: This method searches the *.app* folder for all items (files, folders, symlinks, etc.) and returns the result as an array. All items in the array will be of type `NSURL` and contain their creation date, last modification date, and other attributes that we talked about before.

*stringValueOfBoolProperty:ofURL:*
: This method will fetch the string equivalent (`Yes` or `No`) of a Boolean property of a URL. For instance, information about whether a URL is a directory or not is stored as a binary, Boolean value. However, if we want to print this Boolean value out to the console, we need to convert it to a string. We have two query items for each URL that will return instances of `NSNumber` containing a Boolean value: `NSURLIsDirectoryKey` and `NSURLIsReadableKey`. So instead of writing this conversion code twice, methods are available to do the conversion of `NSNumber` to a string of `Yes` or `No` for us.

*isURLDirectory:*
: Takes in a URL and inspects it to see whether it is a directory. This method internally uses the `stringValueOfBoolProperty:ofURL:` method and passes the `NSURLIsDirectoryKey` key to it.

*isURLReadable:*
: Determines whether your app has read access to a given URL. This method also internally uses the `stringValueOfBoolProperty:ofURL:` method and passes the `NSURLIsReadableKey` key to it.

*dateOfType:inURL:*
: Since we are going to inspect three types of properties in each URL that will be of type `NSDate`, we have simply encapsulated the relevant code in this method, which will take the key and will return the date associated with that key in a given URL.

OK, that's about it, really. You now know how to enumerate folders and retrieve all items within the folder. You even know how to retrieve different attributes for different items.

## See Also

Recipe 14.1; Recipe 14.2

# 14.5. Deleting Files and Folders

## Problem

You have created some files and/or folders on disk and no longer need them, so you would like to delete them.

## Solution

Use the `removeItemAtPath:error:` or the `removeItemAtURL:error:` instance method of the `NSFileManager` class. The former method takes the path as a string, and the latter takes the path as a URL.

## Discussion

Deleting files and folders is perhaps one of the easiest operations that you can perform using a file manager. In iOS, you need to be mindful of where you store your files and folders in the first place, and once you have done the storage, you need to get rid of files and folders when you no longer need them. For instance, let's create five text files in the *tmp/text* folder and then delete them once we are done. In the meantime, we can enumerate the contents of the folder before and after the deletion just to make sure things are working fine. Also, as you know, the *tmp/* folder exists when your app is installed, but the *tmp/text* folder doesn't. So we need to create it first. Once we are done with the files, we will delete the folder as well:

```
/* Creates a folder at a given path */
- (void) createFolder:(NSString *)paramPath{
    NSError *error = nil;
    if ([self.fileManager createDirectoryAtPath:paramPath
                    withIntermediateDirectories:YES
                                     attributes:nil
                                          error:&error] == NO){
        NSLog(@"Failed to create folder %@. Error = %@",
              paramPath,
              error);
    }
}

/* Creates 5 .txt files in the given folder, named 1.txt, 2.txt, etc */
- (void) createFilesInFolder:(NSString *)paramPath{

    /* Create 10 files */
    for (NSUInteger counter = 0; counter < 5; counter++){
```

```
        NSString *fileName = [NSString stringWithFormat:@"%lu.txt",
                              (unsigned long)counter+1];
        NSString *path = [paramPath stringByAppendingPathComponent:fileName];
        NSString *fileContents = [NSString stringWithFormat:@"Some text"];
        NSError *error = nil;
        if ([fileContents writeToFile:path
                           atomically:YES
                             encoding:NSUTF8StringEncoding
                                error:&error] == NO){
            NSLog(@"Failed to save file to %@. Error = %@", path, error);
        }
    }

}

/* Enumerates all files/folders at a given path */
- (void) enumerateFilesInFolder:(NSString *)paramPath{

    NSError *error = nil;
    NSArray *contents = [self.fileManager contentsOfDirectoryAtPath:paramPath
                                                               error:&error];

    if ([contents count] > 0 &&
        error == nil){
        NSLog(@"Contents of path %@ = \n%@", paramPath, contents);
    }
    else if ([contents count] == 0 &&
             error == nil){
        NSLog(@"Contents of path %@ is empty!", paramPath);
    }
    else {
        NSLog(@"Failed to enumerate path %@. Error = %@", paramPath, error);
    }

}

/* Deletes all files/folders in a given path */
- (void) deleteFilesInFolder:(NSString *)paramPath{

    NSError *error = nil;
    NSArray *contents = [self.fileManager contentsOfDirectoryAtPath:paramPath
                                                               error:&error];
    if (error == nil){
        error = nil;
        for (NSString *fileName in contents){
            /* We have the file name, to delete it,
             we have to have the full path */
            NSString *filePath = [paramPath
                                  stringByAppendingPathComponent:fileName];
            if ([self.fileManager removeItemAtPath:filePath
                                             error:&error] == NO){
                NSLog(@"Failed to remove item at path %@. Error = %@",
```

```
                        fileName,
                        error);
            }
        }
    } else {
        NSLog(@"Failed to enumerate path %@. Error = %@", paramPath, error);
    }

}

/* Deletes a folder with a given path */
- (void) deleteFolder:(NSString *)paramPath{
    NSError *error = nil;
    if ([self.fileManager removeItemAtPath:paramPath error:&error] == NO){
        NSLog(@"Failed to remove path %@. Error = %@", paramPath, error);
    }
}
```

Bear in mind that the `fileManager` property, which we are using in various methods of our app delegate, is a property of the app delegate itself and is defined in this way:

```
#import "AppDelegate.h"

@interface AppDelegate ()
@property (nonatomic, strong) NSFileManager *fileManager;
@end

@implementation AppDelegate

<# Rest of your app delegate code goes here #>
```

This example code combines a lot of the things that you have learned in this chapter, from enumerating to creating to deleting files. It's all in this example. As you can see from the app's starting point, we are performing six main tasks, all of which have their associated methods to take care of them:

1. Creating the *tmp/txt* folder. We know the *tmp* folder will be created by iOS for every app, but the *txt* doesn't come already created by iOS when your app is installed on the device.
2. Creating five text files in the *tmp/txt* folder.
3. Enumerating all the files in the *tmp/txt* folder just to prove that we successfully created all five files in that folder.
4. Deleting the files that we created to prove the point of this recipe.
5. Enumerating the files again in the *tmp/txt* folder to demonstrate that the deletion mechanism worked just fine.

6. Deleting the *tmp/txt* folder, as we no longer need it. Again, as I mentioned before, be mindful of what folders and files you create on disk. Disk space doesn't grow on trees! So if you don't need your files and folders any longer, delete them.

Now you not only know how to create files and folders, but how to get rid of them when you no longer need them.

## See Also

Recipe 14.2

# 14.6. Saving Objects to Files

## Problem

You have added a new class to your project, and you would like to be able to save this object to disk as a file and then read it back from disk whenever required.

## Solution

Make sure that your class conforms to the `NSCoding` protocol and implement all the required methods of this method. Don't worry; I will walk you through this in the Discussion section of this recipe.

## Discussion

There are two really handy classes in iOS SDK for this specific purpose, which in the programming world is known as *marshalling*. They are called:

`NSKeyedArchiver`
: A class that can archive or save the contents of an object or object tree by keys. Each value in the class, let's say each property, can be saved to the archive, using a key that the programmer chooses. You will be given an archive file (we will talk more about this) and you will just save your values using keys that you choose. Just like a dictionary!

`NSKeyedUnarchiver`
: This class does the reverse of the archiver class. It simply gives you the unarchived dictionary and asks you to read the values into your object's properties.

In order for the archiver and the unarchiver to work, you need to make sure that the objects you are asking them to archive or unarchive conform to the `NSCoding` protocol. Let's start with a simple `Person` class. Here is the header file of our class:

```
#import <Foundation/Foundation.h>
```

```
@interface Person : NSObject <NSCoding>

@property (nonatomic, copy) NSString *firstName;
@property (nonatomic, copy) NSString *lastName;

@end
```

Now if you don't write any code for the implementation of this class and try to compile your code, you will see that the compiler will start to throw warnings at you saying you have not conformed to the `NSCoding` protocol and have not implemented its required methods. The methods that we have to implement are as follows:

`- (void)encodeWithCoder:(NSCoder *)aCoder`
: This method will give you a coder. You will use the coder just like you would use a dictionary. Simply store your values in it using keys that you choose.

`- (instancetype)initWithCoder:(NSCoder *)aDecoder;`
: This method gets called on your class when you try to unarchive your class using `NSKeyedUnarchiver`. Simply read your values back from the `NSCoder` instance passed to this method.

Now, using this information, let's implement our class:

```
#import "Person.h"

NSString *const kFirstNameKey = @"FirstNameKey";
NSString *const kLastNameKey = @"LastNameKey";

@implementation Person

- (void)encodeWithCoder:(NSCoder *)aCoder{
    [aCoder encodeObject:self.firstName forKey:kFirstNameKey];
    [aCoder encodeObject:self.lastName forKey:kLastNameKey];
}

- (instancetype)initWithCoder:(NSCoder *)aDecoder{
    self = [super init];
    if (self != nil){
        _firstName = [aDecoder decodeObjectForKey:kFirstNameKey];
        _lastName = [aDecoder decodeObjectForKey:kLastNameKey];
    }
    return self;
}

@end
```

You can see that the way we are using the instance of the `NSCoder` class is really similar to that of a dictionary except that, instead of `setValue:forKey:` in a dictionary, we are using `encodeObject:forKey:`, and instead of `objectForKey:` in a dictionary, we are using `decodeObjectForKey:`. All in all, very similar to the way we use dictionaries.

We are done with this class. So let's implement the archiving and unarchiving mechanism using the two aforementioned classes. Our plan is to first instantiate an object of type `Person`, archive it, get rid of it in memory, read it back from file, and see whether the unarchived value matches the value that we originally put in the class. We will be implementing this in our app delegate, because it's the easiest place to do this:

```
#import "AppDelegate.h"
#import "Person.h"

@implementation AppDelegate

- (BOOL)            application:(UIApplication *)application
  didFinishLaunchingWithOptions:(NSDictionary *)launchOptions{

    /* Define the name and the last name we are going to set in the object */
    NSString *const kFirstName = @"Steven";
    NSString *const kLastName = @"Jobs";

    /* Determine where we want to archive the object */
    NSString *filePath = [NSTemporaryDirectory()
                          stringByAppendingPathComponent:@"steveJobs.txt"];

    /* Instantiate the object */
    Person *steveJobs = [[Person alloc] init];
    steveJobs.firstName = kFirstName;
    steveJobs.lastName = kLastName;

    /* Archive the object to the file */
    [NSKeyedArchiver archiveRootObject:steveJobs toFile:filePath];

    /* Now unarchive the same class into another object */
    Person *cloneOfSteveJobs =
    [NSKeyedUnarchiver unarchiveObjectWithFile:filePath];

    /* Check if the unarchived object has the same first name and last name
     as the previously-archived object */
    if ([cloneOfSteveJobs.firstName isEqualToString:kFirstName] &&
        [cloneOfSteveJobs.lastName isEqualToString:kLastName]){
        NSLog(@"Unarchiving worked");
    } else {
        NSLog(@"Could not read the same values back. Oh no!");
    }

    /* We no longer need the temp file, delete it */
    NSFileManager *fileManager = [[NSFileManager alloc] init];
    [fileManager removeItemAtPath:filePath error:nil];

    self.window = [[UIWindow alloc]
                   initWithFrame:[[UIScreen mainScreen] bounds]];
    self.window.backgroundColor = [UIColor whiteColor];
    [self.window makeKeyAndVisible];
```

```
        return YES;
    }
```

So the archiving simply uses the `archiveRootObject:toFile` class method of the `NSKeyedArchiver` class, which takes an object and a file on which the content of the file has to be saved. Simple and easy. How about unarchiving? That is as easy as the archiving process. All you have to do is just pass the archived file path to the `unarchiveObjectWithFile:` class method of the `NSKeyedUnarchiver` class, and that class will do the rest for you.

## See Also

Recipe 14.1

# CHAPTER 15
# Camera and the Photo Library

## 15.0. Introduction

Most devices running iOS, such as the iPhone, are equipped with cameras. The most recent iPhone has two cameras, and some iPhones may only have one. Some iOS devices may not even have a camera. The `UIImagePickerController` class allows programmers to display the familiar Camera interface to their users and ask them to take a photo or shoot a video. The photos taken or the videos shot by the user with the `UIImagePickerController` class then become accessible to the programmer.

In this chapter, you will learn how to let users take photos and shoot videos from inside applications, access these photos and videos, and access the photos and videos that are placed inside the photo library on an iOS device, such as the iPod Touch and iPad.

iOS Simulator does not support the Camera interface. Please test and debug all your applications that require a Camera interface on a real iOS device with a camera.

In this chapter, we will first attempt to determine whether a camera is available on the iOS device running the application. You can also determine whether the camera allows you (the programmer) to capture videos, images, or both. To do this, make sure you have added the *MobileCoreServices.framework* framework to your target. Simply import its umbrella framework into your application like so:

```
#import "AppDelegate.h"
#import <MobileCoreServices/MobileCoreServices.h>

@implementation AppDelegate

<# Rest of your code goes here #>
```

We will then move to other topics, such as accessing videos and photos from different albums on an iOS device. These are the same albums that are accessible through the Photos application built into iOS.

Accessing photos inside albums is more straightforward than accessing videos, however. For photos, we will be given the address of the photo and we can simply load the data of the image either in an instance of `NSData` or directly into an instance of `UIImage`. For videos, we won't be given a file address on the filesystem from which to load the data of the video. Instead, we will be given an address such as this:

```
assets-library://asset/asset.MOV?id=1000000004&ext=MOV
```

For addresses such as this, we need to use the Assets Library framework. The Assets Library framework allows us to access the contents accessible through the Photos application, such as videos and photos shot by the user. You can also use the Assets Library framework to save images and videos on the device. These photos and videos will then become accessible by the as well as other applications that wish to access these contents.

To make sure the recipes in this chapter compile correctly, ensure that both the Assets Library and the Mobile Core Services frameworks are always included in your source files. You can do this by simply importing their header files into your source codes, assuming that you are using the latest version of the LLVM compiler that has support for Modules:

```
#import "AppDelegate.h"
#import <MobileCoreServices/MobileCoreServices.h>
#import <AssetsLibrary/AssetsLibrary.h>

@implementation AppDelegate

<# Rest of your code goes here #>
```

To access the data of an asset given the URL to the asset, follow these steps:

1. Allocate and initialize an object of type `ALAssetsLibrary`. The Assets Library object facilitates the bridge that you need in order to access the videos and photos accessible by the Photos application.
2. Use the `assetForURL:resultBlock:failureBlock` instance method of the Assets Library object (allocated and initialized in step 1) to access the asset. An asset could be an image, a video, or any other resource that Apple might later decide to add to the . This method works with block objects. For more information about block objects and GCD, please refer to Chapter 7.
3. Release the Assets Library object allocated and initialized in step 1.

At this point, you might be wondering: how do I access the data for the asset? The `resultBlock` parameter of the `assetForURL:resultBlock:failureBlock` instance method of the Assets Library object will need to point to a block object that accepts a single parameter of type ALAsset. ALAsset is a class provided by the Assets Library that encapsulates an asset available to Photos and any other iOS application that wishes to use these assets. For more information about storing photos and videos in the photo library, please refer to Recipes 15.4 and 15.5. If you want to learn more about retrieving photos and videos from the photo library and the Assets Library, please refer to Recipes 15.6 and 15.7.

# 15.1. Detecting and Probing the Camera

## Problem

You want to know whether the iOS device running your application has a camera that you can access. This is an important check to make before attempting to use the camera, unless you are sure your application will never run on a device that lacks one.

## Solution

Use the isSourceTypeAvailable: class method of UIImagePickerController with the UIImagePickerControllerSourceTypeCamera value, like so:

```
- (BOOL) isCameraAvailable{

    return [UIImagePickerController isSourceTypeAvailable:
            UIImagePickerControllerSourceTypeCamera];

}

- (BOOL)            application:(UIApplication *)application
  didFinishLaunchingWithOptions:(NSDictionary *)launchOptions{

    if ([self isCameraAvailable]){
        NSLog(@"Camera is available.");
    } else {
        NSLog(@"Camera is not available.");
    }

    self.window = [[UIWindow alloc] initWithFrame:
                   [[UIScreen mainScreen] bounds]];

    self.window.backgroundColor = [UIColor whiteColor];
    [self.window makeKeyAndVisible];
    return YES;
}
```

## Discussion

Before attempting to display an instance of UIImagePickerController to your user for taking photos or shooting videos, you must detect whether the device supports that interface. The isSourceTypeAvailable: class method allows you to determine three sources of data:

- The camera, by passing the UIImagePickerControllerSourceTypeCamera value to this method.
- The photo library, by passing the value UIImagePickerControllerSourceTypePhotoLibrary to this method. This browses the root folder of the *Photos* directory on the device.
- The Camera Roll folder in the *Photos* directory, by passing the UIImagePickerControllerSourceTypeSavedPhotosAlbum value to this method.

If you want to check the availability of any of these facilities on an iOS device, you must pass these values to the isSourceTypeAvailable: class method of UIImagePickerController before attempting to present the interfaces to the user.

Now we can use the isSourceTypeAvailable: and availableMediaTypesForSourceType: class methods of UIImagePickerController to determine first if a media source is available (camera, photo library, etc.), and if so, whether media types such as image and video are available on that media source:

```
- (BOOL)cameraSupportsMedia:(NSString *)paramMediaType
        sourceType:(UIImagePickerControllerSourceType)paramSourceType{

    __block BOOL result = NO;

    if ([paramMediaType length] == 0){
        NSLog(@"Media type is empty.");
        return NO;
    }

    NSArray *availableMediaTypes =
    [UIImagePickerController
     availableMediaTypesForSourceType:paramSourceType];

    [availableMediaTypes enumerateObjectsUsingBlock:
     ^(id obj, NSUInteger idx, BOOL *stop) {

         NSString *mediaType = (NSString *)obj;
         if ([mediaType isEqualToString:paramMediaType]){
             result = YES;
             *stop= YES;
         }

     }];

    return result;

}
```

```
- (BOOL) doesCameraSupportShootingVideos{

    return [self cameraSupportsMedia:(__bridge NSString *)kUTTypeMovie
                          sourceType:UIImagePickerControllerSourceTypeCamera];

}

- (BOOL) doesCameraSupportTakingPhotos{

    return [self cameraSupportsMedia:(__bridge NSString *)kUTTypeImage
                          sourceType:UIImagePickerControllerSourceTypeCamera];

}

- (BOOL)            application:(UIApplication *)application
  didFinishLaunchingWithOptions:(NSDictionary *)launchOptions{

    if ([self doesCameraSupportTakingPhotos]){
        NSLog(@"The camera supports taking photos.");
    } else {
        NSLog(@"The camera does not support taking photos");
    }

    if ([self doesCameraSupportShootingVideos]){
        NSLog(@"The camera supports shooting videos.");
    } else {
        NSLog(@"The camera does not support shooting videos.");
    }

    self.window = [[UIWindow alloc] initWithFrame:
                   [[UIScreen mainScreen] bounds]];

    self.window.backgroundColor = [UIColor whiteColor];
    [self.window makeKeyAndVisible];
    return YES;
}
```

We are typecasting the `kUTTypeMovie` and the `kUTTypeImage` values to `NSString` using `__bridge`. The reason behind this is that the two aforementioned values are of type `CFStringRef` and we need to retrieve their `NSString` representation. To help the static analyzer and the compiler and to avoid getting warnings from the compiler, it is best to do this typecasting.

Some iOS devices can have more than one camera. The two cameras might be called the front and the rear cameras. To determine whether these cameras are available, use the `isCameraDeviceAvailable:` class method of `UIImagePickerController`, like so:

```
- (BOOL) isFrontCameraAvailable{

    return [UIImagePickerController
            isCameraDeviceAvailable:UIImagePickerControllerCameraDeviceFront];

}

- (BOOL) isRearCameraAvailable{

    return [UIImagePickerController
            isCameraDeviceAvailable:UIImagePickerControllerCameraDeviceRear];

}
```

By calling these methods on an older iPhone with no rear camera, you will see that the `isFrontCameraAvailable` method returns `NO` and the `isRearCameraAvailable` method returns `YES`. Running the code on an iPhone with both front and rear cameras will prove that both methods will return `YES`, as iPhone 5 devices are equipped with both front- and rear-facing cameras.

If detecting which camera is present on a device isn't enough for your application, you can retrieve other settings using the `UIImagePickerController` class. One such setting is whether flash capability is available for a camera on the device. You can use the `isFlashAvailableForCameraDevice:` class method of `UIImagePickerController` to determine the availability of a flash capability on the rear or front camera. Please bear in mind that the `isFlashAvailableForCameraDevice:` class method of `UIImagePickerController` checks the availability of the given camera device first, before checking the availability of a flash capability on that camera. Therefore, you can run the methods we will implement on devices that do not have front or rear cameras without a need to first check if the camera is available.

```
- (BOOL) isFlashAvailableOnFrontCamera{

    return [UIImagePickerController isFlashAvailableForCameraDevice:
            UIImagePickerControllerCameraDeviceFront];

}

- (BOOL) isFlashAvailableOnRearCamera{

    return [UIImagePickerController isFlashAvailableForCameraDevice:
            UIImagePickerControllerCameraDeviceRear];

}
```

Now if we take advantage of all the methods that we wrote in this recipe and test them in your app delegate (for example), we can see the results on different devices:

```
- (BOOL)            application:(UIApplication *)application
  didFinishLaunchingWithOptions:(NSDictionary *)launchOptions{
```

```
    if ([self isFrontCameraAvailable]){
        NSLog(@"The front camera is available.");
        if ([self isFlashAvailableOnFrontCamera]){
            NSLog(@"The front camera is equipped with a flash");
        } else {
            NSLog(@"The front camera is not equipped with a flash");
        }
    } else {
        NSLog(@"The front camera is not available.");
    }

    if ([self isRearCameraAvailable]){
        NSLog(@"The rear camera is available.");
        if ([self isFlashAvailableOnRearCamera]){
            NSLog(@"The rear camera is equipped with a flash");
        } else {
            NSLog(@"The rear camera is not equipped with a flash");
        }
    } else {
        NSLog(@"The rear camera is not available.");
    }

    if ([self doesCameraSupportTakingPhotos]){
        NSLog(@"The camera supports taking photos.");
    } else {
        NSLog(@"The camera does not support taking photos");
    }

    if ([self doesCameraSupportShootingVideos]){
        NSLog(@"The camera supports shooting videos.");
    } else {
        NSLog(@"The camera does not support shooting videos.");
    }

    self.window = [[UIWindow alloc] initWithFrame:
                   [[UIScreen mainScreen] bounds]];

    self.window.backgroundColor = [UIColor whiteColor];
    [self.window makeKeyAndVisible];
    return YES;
}
```

Here are the results when we run the application on the new iPhone:

```
The front camera is available.
The front camera is not equipped with a flash
The rear camera is available.
The rear camera is equipped with a flash
The camera supports taking photos.
The camera supports shooting videos.
```

Here is the output of the same code when run on iPhone Simulator:

```
The front camera is not available.
The rear camera is not available.
The camera does not support taking photos
The camera does not support shooting videos.
```

## 15.2. Taking Photos with the Camera

### Problem

You want to ask the user to take a photo with the camera on his iOS device, and you want to access that photo once the user is done.

### Solution

Instantiate an object of type `UIImagePickerController` and present it as a modal view controller on your current view controller. Here is our view controller's declaration:

```
#import "ViewController.h"
#import <MobileCoreServices/MobileCoreServices.h>

@interface ViewController ()<UIImagePickerControllerDelegate,
                             UINavigationControllerDelegate>

@end

@implementation ViewController

<# Rest of your code goes here #>
```

The delegate of an instance of `UIImagePickerController` must conform to the `UINavigationControllerDelegate` and `UIImagePickerControllerDelegate` protocols. If you forget to include them in your source file(s), you'll get warnings from the compiler when assigning a value to the delegate property of your image picker controller. Please bear in mind that you can still assign an object to the delegate property of an instance of `UIImagePickerController` where that object does not explicitly conform to the `UIImagePickerControllerDelegate` and `UINavigationControllerDelegate` protocols, but implements the required methods in these protocols. I, however, suggest that you give a hint to the compiler that the delegate object does, in fact, conform to the aforementioned protocols in order to avoid getting compiler warnings.

In our view controller, we will attempt to display an image picker controller as a modal view controller, like so:

```
- (void)viewDidAppear:(BOOL)animated{
    [super viewDidAppear:animated];

    static BOOL beenHereBefore = NO;

    if (beenHereBefore){
```

```
        /* Only display the picker once as the viewDidAppear: method gets
         called whenever the view of our view controller gets displayed */
        return;
    } else {
        beenHereBefore = YES;
    }

    if ([self isCameraAvailable] &&
        [self doesCameraSupportTakingPhotos]){

        UIImagePickerController *controller =
        [[UIImagePickerController alloc] init];

        controller.sourceType = UIImagePickerControllerSourceTypeCamera;

        NSString *requiredMediaType = (__bridge NSString *)kUTTypeImage;
        controller.mediaTypes = [[NSArray alloc]
                                 initWithObjects:requiredMediaType, nil];

        controller.allowsEditing = YES;
        controller.delegate = self;

        [self presentViewController:controller animated:YES completion:nil];

    } else {
        NSLog(@"Camera is not available.");
    }

}
```

We are using the `isCameraAvailable` and `doesCameraSupportTakingPhotos` methods in this example. These methods are implemented and explained in Recipe 15.1.

In this example, we are allowing the user to take photos using the image picker. You must have noticed that we are setting the delegate property of the image picker to `self`, which refers to the view controller. For this, we have to make sure we have implemented the methods defined in the `UIImagePickerControllerDelegate` protocol, like so:

```
- (void)  imagePickerController:(UIImagePickerController *)picker
  didFinishPickingMediaWithInfo:(NSDictionary *)info{

    NSLog(@"Picker returned successfully.");

    NSLog(@"%@", info);

    NSString     *mediaType = info[UIImagePickerControllerMediaType];
```

```
        if ([mediaType isEqualToString:(__bridge NSString *)kUTTypeMovie]){
            NSURL *urlOfVideo = info[UIImagePickerControllerMediaURL];
            NSLog(@"Video URL = %@", urlOfVideo);
        }

        else if ([mediaType isEqualToString:(__bridge NSString *)kUTTypeImage]){

            /* Let's get the metadata. This is only for
             images. Not videos */

            NSDictionary *metadata = info[UIImagePickerControllerMediaMetadata];
            UIImage *theImage = info[UIImagePickerControllerOriginalImage];

            NSLog(@"Image Metadata = %@", metadata);
            NSLog(@"Image = %@", theImage);

        }

        [picker dismissViewControllerAnimated:YES completion:nil];

    }

    - (void)imagePickerControllerDidCancel:(UIImagePickerController *)picker{

        NSLog(@"Picker was cancelled");
        [picker dismissViewControllerAnimated:YES completion:nil];

    }
```

## Discussion

There are a couple of important things that you must keep in mind about the image picker controller's delegate. First, two delegate messages are called on the delegate object of the image picker controller. The `imagePickerController:didFinishPickingMediaWithInfo:` method gets called when the user finishes execution of the image picker (e.g., takes a photo and presses a button at the end), whereas the `imagePickerControllerDidCancel:` method gets called when the image picker's operation is cancelled.

Also, the `imagePickerController:didFinishPickingMediaWithInfo:` delegate method contains information about the item that was captured by the user, be it an image or a video. The `didFinishPickingMediaWithInfo` parameter is a dictionary of values that tell you what the image picker has captured and the metadata of that item, along with other useful information. The first thing you have to do in this method is to read the value of the `UIImagePickerControllerMediaType` key in this dictionary. The object for this key is an instance of `NSString` that could be one of these values:

`kUTTypeImage`
: For a photo that was shot by the camera

`kUTTypeMovie`
: For a movie/video that was shot by the camera

The `kUTTypeImage` and `kUTTypeMovie` values are available in the Mobile Core Services framework and are of type `CFStringRef`. You can simply typecast these values to `NSString` if needed.

After determining the type of resource created by the camera (video or photo), you can access that resource's properties using the `didFinishPickingMediaWithInfo` dictionary parameter again.

For images (`kUTTypeImage`), you can access these keys:

`UIImagePickerControllerMediaMetadata`
: This key's value is an object of type `NSDictionary`. This dictionary contains a lot of useful information about the image that was shot by the user. A complete discussion of the values inside this dictionary is beyond the scope of this chapter.

`UIImagePickerControllerOriginalImage`
: This key's value is an object of type `UIImage` containing the image that was shot by the user.

`UIImagePickerControllerCropRect`
: If editing is enabled (using the `allowsEditing` property of `UIImagePickerController`), the object of this key will contain the rectangle of the cropped area.

`UIImagePickerControllerEditedImage`
: If editing is enabled (using the `allowsEditing` property of `UIImagePickerController`), this key's value will contain the edited (resized and scaled) image.

For videos (`kUTTypeMovie`) that are shot by the user, you can access the `UIImagePickerControllerMediaURL` key in the `didFinishPickingMediaWithInfo` dictionary parameter of the `imagePickerController:didFinishPickingMediaWithInfo:` method. The value of this key is an object of type `NSURL` containing the URL of the video that was shot by the user.

After you get a reference to the `UIImage` instance that the user took with the camera, you can simply use that instance within your application.

The images shot by the image picker controller within your application are not saved to the Camera Roll by default.

## See Also

Recipe 15.1

# 15.3. Taking Videos with the Camera

## Problem

You want to allow your user to shoot a video using his iOS device, and you would like to be able to use that video from inside your application.

## Solution

Use `UIImagePickerController` with the `UIImagePickerControllerSourceTypeCamera` source type and the `kUTTypeMovie` media type:

```
- (void)viewDidAppear:(BOOL)animated{
    [super viewDidAppear:animated];

    static BOOL beenHereBefore = NO;

    if (beenHereBefore){
        /* Only display the picker once as the viewDidAppear: method gets
         called whenever the view of our view controller gets displayed */
        return;
    } else {
        beenHereBefore = YES;
    }

    if ([self isCameraAvailable] &&
        [self doesCameraSupportTakingPhotos]){

        UIImagePickerController *controller =
        [[UIImagePickerController alloc] init];

        controller.sourceType = UIImagePickerControllerSourceTypeCamera;

        controller.mediaTypes = @[(__bridge NSString *)kUTTypeMovie];

        controller.allowsEditing = YES;
        controller.delegate = self;

        [self presentViewController:controller animated:YES completion:nil];

    } else {
        NSLog(@"Camera is not available.");
    }

}
```

The isCameraAvailable and doesCameraSupportShootingVideos methods used in this sample code are implemented and discussed in Recipe 15.1.

We will implement the delegate methods of the image picker controller like so:

```
- (void) imagePickerController:(UIImagePickerController *)picker
  didFinishPickingMediaWithInfo:(NSDictionary *)info{

    NSLog(@"Picker returned successfully.");

    NSLog(@"%@", info);

    NSString     *mediaType = info[UIImagePickerControllerMediaType];

    if ([mediaType isEqualToString:(__bridge NSString *)kUTTypeMovie]){

        NSURL *urlOfVideo = info[UIImagePickerControllerMediaType];

        NSLog(@"Video URL = %@", urlOfVideo);

        NSError *dataReadingError = nil;

        NSData *videoData =
        [NSData dataWithContentsOfURL:urlOfVideo
                              options:NSDataReadingMapped
                                error:&dataReadingError];

        if (videoData != nil){
            /* We were able to read the data */
            NSLog(@"Successfully loaded the data.");
        } else {
            /* We failed to read the data. Use the dataReadingError
             variable to determine what the error is */
            NSLog(@"Failed to load the data with error = %@",
                  dataReadingError);
        }

    }

    [picker dismissViewControllerAnimated:YES completion:nil];

}

- (void)imagePickerControllerDidCancel:(UIImagePickerController *)picker{

    NSLog(@"Picker was cancelled");
    [picker dismissViewControllerAnimated:YES completion:nil];

}
```

## Discussion

Once you detect that the iOS device your application is running on supports video recording, you can bring up the image picker controller with the `UIImagePickerControllerSourceTypeCamera` source type and `kUTTypeMovie` media type to allow the users of your application to shoot videos. Once they are done, the `imagePickerController:didFinishPickingMediaWithInfo:` delegate method will get called, and you can use the `didFinishPickingMediaWithInfo` dictionary parameter to find out more about the captured video (the values that can be placed inside this dictionary are thoroughly explained in Recipe 15.2).

When the user shoots a video using the image picker controller, the video will be saved in a temporary folder inside your application's bundle, not inside the Camera Roll. The following is an example of such a URL:

> *file://localhost/private/var/mobile/Applications/< `APPID` >/tmp/capture-T0x104e20.tmp.TQ9UTr/capturedvideo.MOV*

The value *`APPID`* in the URL represents your application's unique identifier, and will clearly be different depending on your application.

As the programmer, not only can you allow your users to shoot videos from inside your application, but you can also modify how the videos are captured. You can change two important properties of the `UIImagePickerController` class in order to modify the default behavior of video recording:

`videoQuality`
: This property specifies the quality of the video. You can choose a value such as `UIImagePickerControllerQualityTypeHigh` or `UIImagePickerControllerQualityTypeMedium` for the value of this property.

`videoMaximumDuration`
: This property specifies the maximum duration of the video. This value is measured in seconds.

For instance, if we were to allow the users to record high-quality videos for up to 30 seconds, we could simply modify the values of the aforementioned properties of the instance of `UIImagePickerController` like so:

```
- (void)viewDidAppear:(BOOL)animated{
    [super viewDidAppear:animated];

    static BOOL beenHereBefore = NO;

    if (beenHereBefore){
```

```
        /* Only display the picker once as the viewDidAppear: method gets
         called whenever the view of our view controller gets displayed */
        return;
    } else {
        beenHereBefore = YES;
    }

    if ([self isCameraAvailable] &&
        [self doesCameraSupportTakingPhotos]){

        UIImagePickerController *controller =
        [[UIImagePickerController alloc] init];

        controller.sourceType = UIImagePickerControllerSourceTypeCamera;

        controller.mediaTypes = @[(__bridge NSString *)kUTTypeMovie];

        controller.allowsEditing = YES;
        controller.delegate = self;

        /* Record in high quality */
        controller.videoQuality = UIImagePickerControllerQualityTypeHigh;

        /* Only allow 30 seconds of recording */
        controller.videoMaximumDuration = 30.0f;

        [self presentViewController:controller animated:YES completion:nil];

    } else {
        NSLog(@"Camera is not available.");
    }

}
```

## See Also

Recipe 15.1

# 15.4. Storing Photos in the Photo Library

## Problem

You want to be able to store a photo in the user's photo library.

## Solution

Use the `UIImageWriteToSavedPhotosAlbum` procedure:

```
- (void) imageWasSavedSuccessfully:(UIImage *)paramImage
         didFinishSavingWithError:(NSError *)paramError
```

```
                            contextInfo:(void *)paramContextInfo{

    if (paramError == nil){
        NSLog(@"Image was saved successfully.");
    } else {
        NSLog(@"An error happened while saving the image.");
        NSLog(@"Error = %@", paramError);
    }

}

- (void)  imagePickerController:(UIImagePickerController *)picker
  didFinishPickingMediaWithInfo:(NSDictionary *)info{

    NSLog(@"Picker returned successfully.");

    NSLog(@"%@", info);

    NSString     *mediaType = info[UIImagePickerControllerMediaType];

    if ([mediaType isEqualToString:(__bridge NSString *)kUTTypeImage]){

        UIImage *theImage = nil;

        if ([picker allowsEditing]){
            theImage = info[UIImagePickerControllerEditedImage];
        } else {
            theImage = info[UIImagePickerControllerOriginalImage];
        }

        SEL selectorToCall =
        @selector(imageWasSavedSuccessfully:didFinishSavingWithError:\
                  contextInfo:);

        UIImageWriteToSavedPhotosAlbum(theImage,
                                       self,
                                       selectorToCall,
                                       NULL);

    }

    [picker dismissViewControllerAnimated:YES completion:nil];

}

- (void)imagePickerControllerDidCancel:(UIImagePickerController *)picker{

    NSLog(@"Picker was cancelled");
    [picker dismissViewControllerAnimated:YES completion:nil];

}
```

```
- (void)viewDidAppear:(BOOL)animated{
    [super viewDidAppear:animated];

    static BOOL beenHereBefore = NO;

    if (beenHereBefore){
        /* Only display the picker once as the viewDidAppear: method gets
         called whenever the view of our view controller gets displayed */
        return;
    } else {
        beenHereBefore = YES;
    }

    if ([self isCameraAvailable] &&
        [self doesCameraSupportTakingPhotos]){

        UIImagePickerController *controller =
        [[UIImagePickerController alloc] init];

        controller.sourceType = UIImagePickerControllerSourceTypeCamera;

        controller.mediaTypes = @[(__bridge NSString *)kUTTypeImage];

        controller.allowsEditing = YES;
        controller.delegate = self;

        [self presentViewController:controller animated:YES completion:nil];

    } else {
        NSLog(@"Camera is not available.");
    }

}
```

The `isCameraAvailable` and `doesCameraSupportTakingPhotos` methods used in this example are thoroughly explained in Recipe 15.1.

## Discussion

Usually after a user is done taking a photo with her iOS device, she expects the photo to be saved into her photo library. However, applications that are not originally shipped with iOS can ask the user to take a photo, using the `UIImagePickerController` class, and then process that image. In this case, the user will understand that the application we provided might not save the photo to her photo library—it might simply use it internally. For instance, if an instant messaging application allows users to transfer their photos to each other's devices, the user will understand that a photo he takes inside the application will not be saved to his photo library but will instead be transferred over the Internet to the other user.

However, if you decide you want to store an instance of `UIImage` to the photo library on the user's device, you can use the `UIImageWriteToSavedPhotosAlbum` function. This function accepts four parameters:

1. The image
2. The object that will be notified whenever the image is fully saved
3. A parameter that specifies the selector that has to be called on the target object (specified by the second parameter) when the save operation finishes
4. A context value that will get passed to the specified selector once the operation is done

Providing the second, third, and fourth parameters to this procedure is optional. If you do provide the second and third parameters, the fourth parameter still remains optional. For instance, this is the selector we have chosen in the example:

```
- (void) imageWasSavedSuccessfully:(UIImage *)paramImage
        didFinishSavingWithError:(NSError *)paramError
                     contextInfo:(void *)paramContextInfo{

    if (paramError == nil){
        NSLog(@"Image was saved successfully.");
    } else {
        NSLog(@"An error happened while saving the image.");
        NSLog(@"Error = %@", paramError);
    }

}
```

When you attempt to use the `UIImageWriteToSavedPhotosAlbum` procedure to save a photo in the user's photo library, if it's the first time your app is doing this on the device, iOS will ask the user for permission (see Figure 15-1). This will allow the user to either allow or disallow your app from storing photos in her photo library; after all, it's her device, and we should not be doing anything on it without the user's consent. If the user does give you permission, the `UIImageWriteToSavedPhotosAlbum` procedure will continue to save the image. If the user does not give you permission, our completion handler selector will still be called, but the `didFinishSavingWithError` parameter of it will be set to a valid error instance.

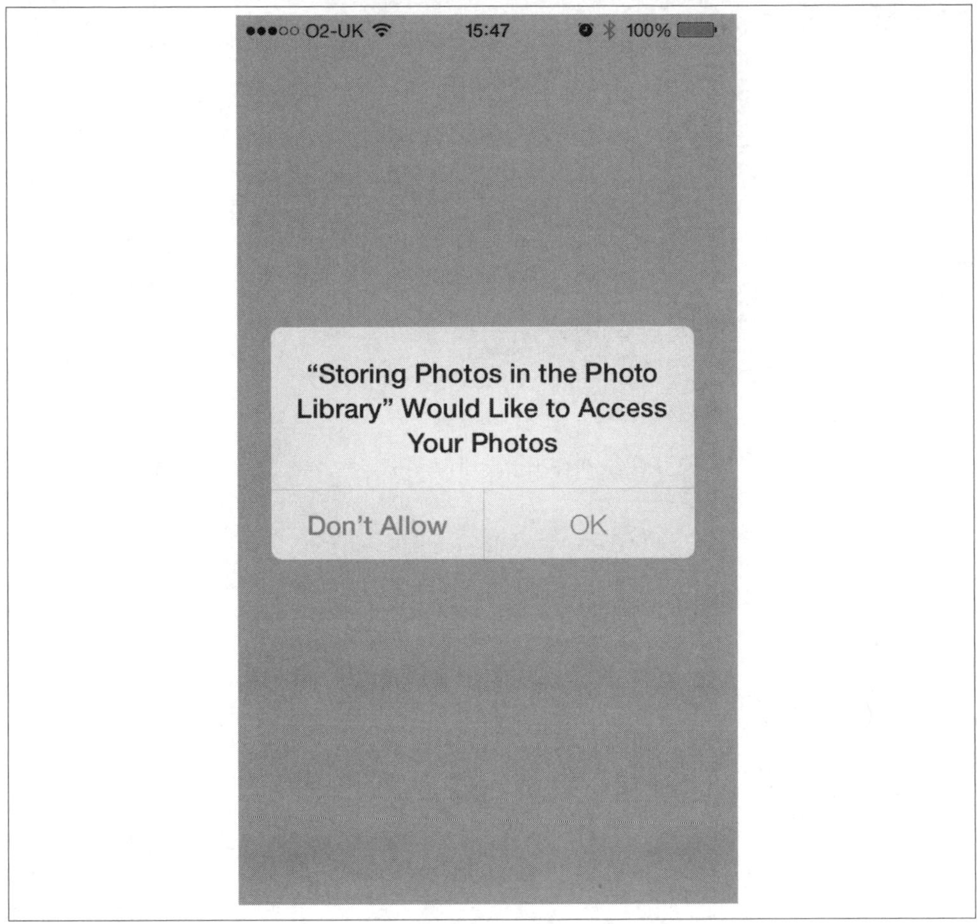


*Figure 15-1. iOS is asking the user for permission before our app can store a photo in her photo library*

Now if the user denies permission to your app, every subsequent call to the `UIImage WriteToSavedPhotosAlbum` procedure will fail until the user manually changes her device's settings (see Figure 15-2).

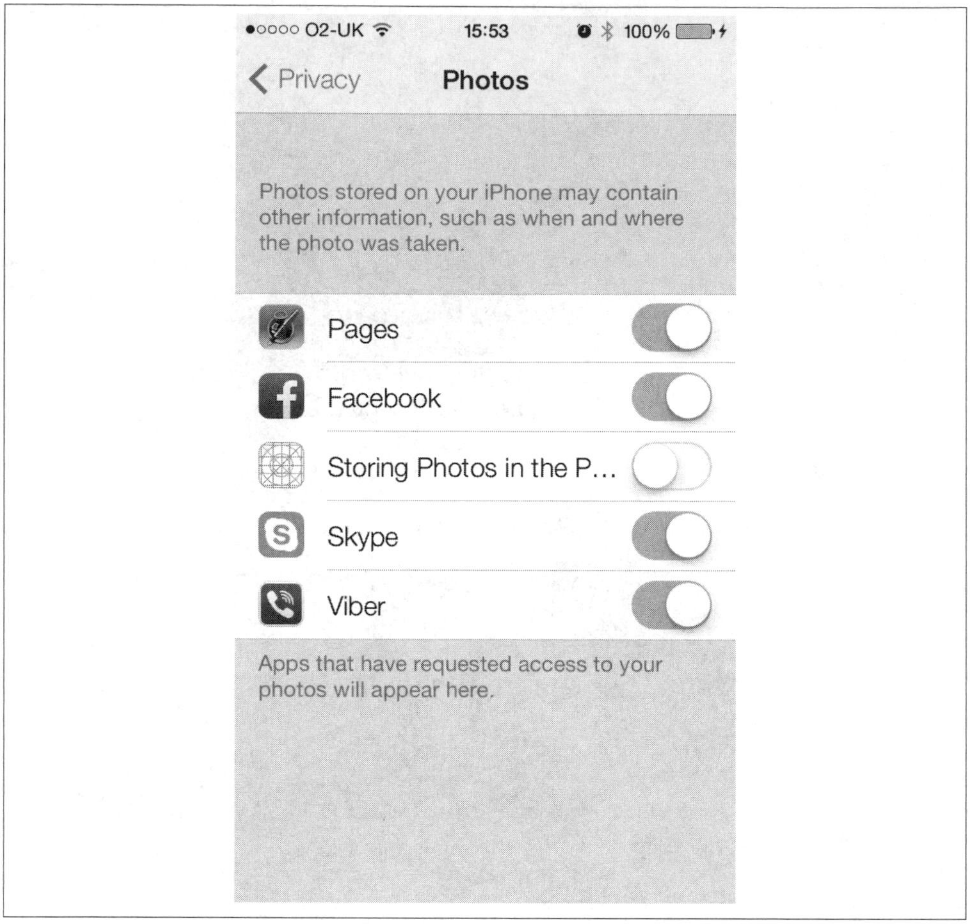

*Figure 15-2. Our app has not been given permission to access the user's photo library*

If the `error` parameter that you receive in this selector is equal to `nil`, that means the image was saved in the user's photo library successfully. Otherwise, you can retrieve the value of this parameter to determine what the issue was.

# 15.5. Storing Videos in the Photo Library

## Problem

You want to store a video accessible through a URL, such as a video in your application bundle, to the photo library.

## Solution

Use the `writeVideoAtPathToSavedPhotosAlbum:completionBlock:` instance method of `ALAssetsLibrary`:

```
#import "AppDelegate.h"
#import <AssetsLibrary/AssetsLibrary.h>

@interface AppDelegate ()
@property (nonatomic, strong) ALAssetsLibrary *assetsLibrary;
@end

@implementation AppDelegate

- (BOOL)            application:(UIApplication *)application
  didFinishLaunchingWithOptions:(NSDictionary *)launchOptions{

    self.assetsLibrary = [[ALAssetsLibrary alloc] init];

    NSURL *videoURL = [[NSBundle mainBundle] URLForResource:@"MyVideo"
                                              withExtension:@"MOV"];

    if (videoURL != nil){
        [self.assetsLibrary
         writeVideoAtPathToSavedPhotosAlbum:videoURL
         completionBlock:^(NSURL *assetURL, NSError *error) {

             if (error == nil){
                 NSLog(@"no errors happened");
             } else {
                 NSLog(@"Error happened while saving the video.");
                 NSLog(@"The error is = %@", error);
             }

         }];
    } else {
        NSLog(@"Could not find the video in the app bundle.");
    }

    return YES;
}
```

## Discussion

The Assets Library framework is a convenient bridge between developers and the photo library. As mentioned in Recipe 15.6, the iOS SDK provides you with built-in GUI components that you can use to access the contents of the photo library. However, you might sometimes require direct access to these contents. In such instances, you can use the Assets Library framework.

After allocating and initializing the Assets Library object of type `ALAssetsLibrary`, you can use the `writeVideoAtPathToSavedPhotosAlbum:completionBlock:` instance method of this object to write a video from a URL to the photo library. All you have to do is provide the URL of the video in `NSURL` form and a block object whose code will be called when the video is saved. The block object must accept two parameters of type `NSURL` and `NSError`.

If the `error` parameter is `nil`, the save process went well and you don't have to worry about anything. One of the common errors that iOS could return to you is similar to this:

```
Error Domain=ALAssetsLibraryErrorDomain Code=-3302 "Invalid data"
UserInfo=0x7923590 {NSLocalizedFailureReason=
There was a problem writing this asset because
the data is invalid and cannot be viewed or played.,
NSLocalizedRecoverySuggestion=Try with different data,
NSLocalizedDescription=Invalid data}
```

You will get this error message if you attempt to pass a URL that is not inside your application bundle. The first parameter passed to the block object provided to the `writeVideoAtPathToSavedPhotosAlbum:completionBlock:` method will point to the Assets Library URL of the stored video. A sample URL of this kind will look like this:

```
assets-library://asset/asset.MOV?id=F9B5F733-487C-
    4418-8C8D-46ABC9FEE23B&ext=MOV
```

If it's the first time your app is attempting to use the photo library on the user's device, iOS will ask the user whether to allow or disallow this operation. If the user does allow it, your call to the `writeVideoAtPathToSavedPhotosAlbum:completionBlock:` will be successful. If the user disallows the action, the error object inside your completion block will be a valid error object that you can inspect and act upon. If the user has previously disallowed your app from accessing her photo library, you won't be able to change that decision programmatically. Only she can allow access, by changing her decision in the Settings app on her device, under the Privacy section.

In Recipe 15.7, we will learn how to use such a URL to load the data for the video file into memory.

## 15.6. Retrieving Photos and Videos from the Photo Library

### Problem

You want users to be able to pick a photo or a video from their photo library and use it in your application.

## Solution

Use the `UIImagePickerControllerSourceTypePhotoLibrary` value for the source type of your `UIImagePickerController` and the `kUTTypeImage` or `kUTTypeMovie` value, or both, for the media type, like so:

```
- (BOOL) isPhotoLibraryAvailable{

    return [UIImagePickerController isSourceTypeAvailable:
            UIImagePickerControllerSourceTypePhotoLibrary];

}

- (BOOL) canUserPickVideosFromPhotoLibrary{

    return [self
            cameraSupportsMedia:(__bridge NSString *)kUTTypeMovie
            sourceType:UIImagePickerControllerSourceTypePhotoLibrary];

}

- (BOOL) canUserPickPhotosFromPhotoLibrary{

    return [self
            cameraSupportsMedia:(__bridge NSString *)kUTTypeImage
            sourceType:UIImagePickerControllerSourceTypePhotoLibrary];

}

- (void)viewDidAppear:(BOOL)animated{
    [super viewDidAppear:animated];

    static BOOL beenHereBefore = NO;

    if (beenHereBefore){
        /* Only display the picker once as the viewDidAppear: method gets
         called whenever the view of our view controller gets displayed */
        return;
    } else {
        beenHereBefore = YES;
    }

    if ([self isPhotoLibraryAvailable]){

        UIImagePickerController *controller =
        [[UIImagePickerController alloc] init];

        controller.sourceType = UIImagePickerControllerSourceTypePhotoLibrary;

        NSMutableArray *mediaTypes = [[NSMutableArray alloc] init];

        if ([self canUserPickPhotosFromPhotoLibrary]){
```

```
            [mediaTypes addObject:(__bridge NSString *)kUTTypeImage];
        }

        if ([self canUserPickVideosFromPhotoLibrary]){
            [mediaTypes addObject:(__bridge NSString *)kUTTypeMovie];
        }

        controller.mediaTypes = mediaTypes;

        controller.delegate = self;

        [self presentViewController:controller animated:YES completion:nil];

    }

}
```

For the implementation of the `cameraSupportsMedia:sourceType:` method we are using in this example, please refer to Recipe 15.1.

## Discussion

To allow your users to pick photos or videos from their photo library, you must set the `sourceType` property of an instance of `UIImagePickerController` to `UIImagePickerControllerSourceTypePhotoLibrary` before presenting them with the image picker. In addition, if you want to filter the videos or photos out of the items presented to your users once the image picker is shown, exclude the `kUTTypeMovie` or `kUTTypeImage` value (respectively) from the array of media types of the image picker (in the `mediaTypes` property).

Bear in mind that setting the `mediaTypes` property of an image picker controller to `nil` or an empty array will result in a runtime error.

After the user is done picking the image, you will get the usual delegate messages through the `UIImagePickerControllerDelegate` protocol. For more information on how you can implement the methods defined in this protocol for processing images, please refer to Recipe 15.2.

## See Also

Recipe 15.7

# 15.7. Retrieving Assets from the Assets Library

## Problem

You want to directly retrieve photos or videos from the photo library without the help of any built-in GUI components.

## Solution

Use the Assets Library framework. Follow these steps:

1. Allocate and initialize an object of type `ALAssetsLibrary`.
2. Provide two block objects to the `enumerateGroupsWithTypes:usingBlock:failureBlock:` instance method of the Assets Library object. The first block will retrieve all the groups associated with the type that we passed to this method. The groups will be of type `ALAssetsGroup`. The second block returns an error in case of failure.
3. Use the `enumerateAssetsUsingBlock:` instance method of each group object to enumerate the assets available in each group. This method takes a single parameter, a block that retrieves information on a single asset. The block that you pass as a parameter must accept three parameters, of which the first must be of type `ALAsset`.
4. After retrieving the `ALAsset` objects available in each group, you can retrieve various properties of each asset, such as their type, available URLs, and so on. Retrieve these properties using the `valueForProperty:` instance method of each asset of type `ALAsset`. The return value of this method, depending on the property passed to it, could be `NSDictionary`, `NSString`, or any other object type. We will see a few common properties that we can retrieve from each asset soon.
5. Invoke the `defaultRepresentation` instance method of each object of type `ALAsset` to retrieve its representation object of type `ALAssetRepresentation`. Each asset in the Assets Library can have more than one representation. For instance, a photo might have a PNG representation by default but a JPEG representation as well. Using the `defaultRepresentation` method of each asset of type `ALAsset`, you can retrieve the `ALAssetRepresentation` object and then use that to retrieve different representations (if available) of each asset.
6. Use the size and the `getBytes:fromOffset:length:error:` instance methods of each asset representation to load the asset's representation data. You can then write the read bytes into an `NSData` object or do whatever else you need to do in your application. Additionally, for photos, you can use the `fullResolutionImage`, `fullScreenImage`, and `CGImageWithOptions:` instance methods of each representation to retrieve images of type `CGImageRef`. You can then construct a `UIImage` from `CGImageRef` using the `imageWithCGImage:` class method of `UIImage`:

```
- (void)viewDidAppear:(BOOL)animated{
    [super viewDidAppear:animated];

    static BOOL beenHereBefore = NO;

    if (beenHereBefore){
        /* Only display the picker once as the viewDidAppear: method gets
         called whenever the view of our view controller gets displayed */
        return;
    } else {
        beenHereBefore = YES;
    }

    [self.assetsLibrary
     enumerateGroupsWithTypes:ALAssetsGroupAll
     usingBlock:^(ALAssetsGroup *group, BOOL *stop) {
         [group enumerateAssetsUsingBlock:^(ALAsset *result,
                                            NSUInteger index,
                                            BOOL *stop) {

             /* Get the asset type */
             NSString *assetType = [result
                                    valueForProperty:ALAssetPropertyType];

             if ([assetType isEqualToString:ALAssetTypePhoto]){
                 NSLog(@"This is a photo asset");
             }

             else if ([assetType isEqualToString:ALAssetTypeVideo]){
                 NSLog(@"This is a video asset");
             }

             else if ([assetType isEqualToString:ALAssetTypeUnknown]){
                 NSLog(@"This is an unknown asset");
             }

             /* Get the URLs for the asset */
             NSDictionary *assetURLs = [result
                                        valueForProperty:ALAssetPropertyURLs];

             NSUInteger    assetCounter = 0;
             for (NSString *assetURLKey in assetURLs){
                 assetCounter++;
                 NSLog(@"Asset URL %lu = %@",
                       (unsigned long)assetCounter,
                       [assetURLs valueForKey:assetURLKey]);
             }

             /* Get the asset's representation object */
             ALAssetRepresentation *assetRepresentation =
             [result defaultRepresentation];
```

```
                NSLog(@"Representation Size = %lld",
                      [assetRepresentation size]);

            }];
        }
        failureBlock:^(NSError *error) {
            NSLog(@"Failed to enumerate the asset groups.");
        }];

}
```

## Discussion

The Assets Library is broken down into groups. Each group contains assets, and each asset has properties, such as URLs and representation objects.

You can retrieve all assets of all types from the Assets Library using the `ALAssetsGroupAll` constant passed to the `enumerateGroupsWithTypes` parameter of the `enumerateGroupsWithTypes:usingBlock:failureBlock:` instance method of the Assets Library object. Here is a list of values you can pass to this parameter to enumerate different groups of assets:

`ALAssetsGroupAlbum`
: Groups representing albums that have been stored on an iOS device through iTunes.

`ALAssetsGroupFaces`
: Groups representing albums that contain face assets that were stored on an iOS device through iTunes.

`ALAssetsGroupSavedPhotos`
: Groups representing the saved photos in the photo library. These are accessible to an iOS device through the Photos application as well.

`ALAssetsGroupAll`
: All available groups in the Assets Library.

Now let's write a simple application that retrieves the data for the first image found in the Assets Library, creates a `UIImageView` out of it, and adds the image view to the view of the current view controller. This way, we will learn how to read the contents of an asset using its representation.

When the view controller displays its view, we will initialize the assets library object and then start enumerating the assets library until we find the first photo. At that time, we will use the representation of that asset (photo) to display the photo on the image view:

```
- (void)viewDidAppear:(BOOL)animated{
    [super viewDidAppear:animated];

    static BOOL beenHereBefore = NO;
```

```
if (beenHereBefore){
    /* Only display the picker once as the viewDidAppear: method gets
     called whenever the view of our view controller gets displayed */
    return;
} else {
    beenHereBefore = YES;
}

self.assetsLibrary = [[ALAssetsLibrary alloc] init];

dispatch_queue_t dispatchQueue =
dispatch_get_global_queue(DISPATCH_QUEUE_PRIORITY_DEFAULT, 0);

dispatch_async(dispatchQueue, ^(void) {

    [self.assetsLibrary
     enumerateGroupsWithTypes:ALAssetsGroupAll
     usingBlock:^(ALAssetsGroup *group, BOOL *stop) {

         [group enumerateAssetsUsingBlock:^(ALAsset *result,
                                            NSUInteger index,
                                            BOOL *stop) {

             __block BOOL foundThePhoto = NO;

             if (foundThePhoto){
                 *stop = YES;
             }

             /* Get the asset type */
             NSString *assetType =
             [result valueForProperty:ALAssetPropertyType];

             if ([assetType isEqualToString:ALAssetTypePhoto]){
                 NSLog(@"This is a photo asset");

                 foundThePhoto = YES;
                 *stop = YES;

                 /* Get the asset's representation object */
                 ALAssetRepresentation *assetRepresentation =
                 [result defaultRepresentation];

                 /* We need the scale and orientation to be able to
                  construct a properly oriented and scaled UIImage
                  out of the representation object */
                 CGFloat imageScale = [assetRepresentation scale];

                 UIImageOrientation imageOrientation =
                 (UIImageOrientation)[assetRepresentation orientation];

                 dispatch_async(dispatch_get_main_queue(), ^(void) {
```

```
                    CGImageRef imageReference =
                    [assetRepresentation fullResolutionImage];

                    /* Construct the image now */
                    UIImage     *image =
                    [[UIImage alloc] initWithCGImage:imageReference
                                                scale:imageScale
                                          orientation:imageOrientation];

                    if (image != nil){
                        UIImageView *imageView =
                        [[UIImageView alloc]
                         initWithFrame:self.view.bounds];

                        imageView.contentMode = UIViewContentModeScaleAspectFit;
                        imageView.image = image;
                        [self.view addSubview:imageView];

                    } else {
                        NSLog(@"Failed to create the image.");
                    }
                });

            }

        }];
    }
    failureBlock:^(NSError *error) {
        NSLog(@"Failed to enumerate the asset groups.");
    }];

});

}
```

We enumerate the groups and every asset in the groups. Then we find the first photo asset and retrieve its representation. Using the representation, we construct a `UIImage`, and from the `UIImage`, we construct a `UIImageView` to display that image on the view. Quite simple, isn't it?

For video files, we are dealing with a slightly different issue, as the `ALAssetRepresentation` class does not have any methods that could return an object that encapsulates the video files. For this reason, we have to read the contents of a video asset into a buffer and perhaps save it to the *Documents* folder, where it is easier for us to access later. Of course, the requirements depend on your application, but in this example code, we will go ahead and find the first video in the Assets Library and store it in the application's *Documents* folder under the name *Temp.MOV*:

```
- (NSString *) documentFolderPath{
```

```
    NSFileManager *fileManager = [[NSFileManager alloc] init];
    NSURL *url = [fileManager URLForDirectory:NSDocumentDirectory
                                     inDomain:NSUserDomainMask
                            appropriateForURL:nil
                                       create:NO
                                        error:nil];

    return url.path;

}

- (void)viewDidAppear:(BOOL)animated{
    [super viewDidAppear:animated];

    static BOOL beenHereBefore = NO;

    if (beenHereBefore){
        /* Only display the picker once as the viewDidAppear: method gets
         called whenever the view of our view controller gets displayed */
        return;
    } else {
        beenHereBefore = YES;
    }

    self.assetsLibrary = [[ALAssetsLibrary alloc] init];

    dispatch_queue_t dispatchQueue =
    dispatch_get_global_queue(DISPATCH_QUEUE_PRIORITY_DEFAULT, 0);

    dispatch_async(dispatchQueue, ^(void) {

        [self.assetsLibrary
         enumerateGroupsWithTypes:ALAssetsGroupAll
         usingBlock:^(ALAssetsGroup *group, BOOL *stop) {

             __block BOOL foundTheVideo = NO;

             [group enumerateAssetsUsingBlock:^(ALAsset *result,
                                                NSUInteger index,
                                                BOOL *stop) {

                 /* Get the asset type */
                 NSString *assetType = [result
                                        valueForProperty:ALAssetPropertyType];

                 if ([assetType isEqualToString:ALAssetTypeVideo]){
                     NSLog(@"This is a video asset");

                     foundTheVideo = YES;
                     *stop = YES;

                     /* Get the asset's representation object */
```

```
ALAssetRepresentation *assetRepresentation =
[result defaultRepresentation];

const NSUInteger BufferSize = 1024;
uint8_t buffer[BufferSize];
NSUInteger bytesRead = 0;
long long currentOffset = 0;
NSError *readingError = nil;

/* Construct the path where the video has to be saved */
NSString *videoPath =
[[self documentFolderPath]
 stringByAppendingPathComponent:@"Temp.MOV"];

NSFileManager *fileManager = [[NSFileManager alloc] init];

/* Create the file if it doesn't exist already */
if ([fileManager fileExistsAtPath:videoPath] == NO){
    [fileManager createFileAtPath:videoPath
                         contents:nil
                       attributes:nil];
}

/* We will use this file handle to write the contents
 of the media assets to the disk */
NSFileHandle *fileHandle =
[NSFileHandle
 fileHandleForWritingAtPath:videoPath];

do{

    /* Read as many bytes as we can put in the buffer */
    bytesRead =
    [assetRepresentation getBytes:(uint8_t *)&buffer
                       fromOffset:currentOffset
                           length:BufferSize
                            error:&readingError];

    /* If we couldn't read anything, we will
     exit this loop */
    if (bytesRead == 0){
        break;
    }

    /* Keep the offset up to date */
    currentOffset += bytesRead;

    /* Put the buffer into an NSData */
    NSData *readData = [[NSData alloc]
                        initWithBytes:(const void *)buffer
                        length:bytesRead];
```

```
                    /* And write the data to file */
                    [fileHandle writeData:readData];

                } while (bytesRead > 0);

                NSLog(@"Finished reading and storing the \
                      video in the documents folder");

            }

        }];

        if (foundTheVideo){
            *stop = YES;
        }

    }
    failureBlock:^(NSError *error) {
        NSLog(@"Failed to enumerate the asset groups.");
    }];

});

}
```

This is what's happening in the sample code:

- We get the default representation of the first video asset that we find in the Assets Library.
- We create a file called *Temp.MOV* in the application's *Documents* folder to save the contents of the video asset.
- We create a loop that runs as long as there is still data in the asset representation waiting to be read. The `getBytes:fromOffset:length:error:` instance method of the asset representation object reads as many bytes as we can fit into the buffer for as many times as necessary until we get to the end of the representation data.
- After reading the data into the buffer, we encapsulate the data into an object of type `NSData` using the `initWithBytes:length:` initialization method of `NSData`. We then write this data to the file we created previously using the `writeData:` instance method of `NSFileHandle`.

# 15.8. Editing Videos on an iOS Device

## Problem

You want the user of your application to be able to edit videos straight from your application.

## Solution

Use the `UIVideoEditorController` class. In this example, we will use this class in conjunction with an image picker controller. First we will ask the user to pick a video from her photo library. After she does, we will display an instance of the video editor controller and allow the user to edit the video she picked.

## Discussion

The `UIVideoEditorController` in the iOS SDK allows programmers to display a video editor interface to the users of their applications. All you have to do is provide the URL of the video that needs to be edited and then present the video editor controller as a modal view. You should not overlay the view of this controller with any other views, and you should not modify this view.

Calling the `presentModalViewController:animated:` method immediately after calling the `dismissModalViewControllerAnimated:` method of a view controller will terminate your application with a runtime error. You must wait for the first view controller to be dismissed and then present the second view controller. You can take advantage of the `viewDidAppear:` instance method of your view controllers to detect when your view is displayed. You know at this point that any modal view controllers must have disappeared.

So let's go ahead and declare the view controller and any necessary properties:

```
#import "ViewController.h"
#import <MobileCoreServices/MobileCoreServices.h>
#import <AssetsLibrary/AssetsLibrary.h>

@interface ViewController ()
<UINavigationControllerDelegate,
UIVideoEditorControllerDelegate,
UIImagePickerControllerDelegate>
@property (nonatomic, strong) NSURL *videoURLToEdit;
@property (nonatomic, strong) ALAssetsLibrary *assetsLibrary;
@end

@implementation ViewController

<# Rest of your code goes here #>
```

The next thing to do is handle different video editor delegate messages in the view controller:

```
- (void)videoEditorController:(UIVideoEditorController *)editor
     didSaveEditedVideoToPath:(NSString *)editedVideoPath{
```

```
    NSLog(@"The video editor finished saving video");
    NSLog(@"The edited video path is at = %@", editedVideoPath);
    [editor dismissViewControllerAnimated:YES completion:nil];
}

- (void)videoEditorController:(UIVideoEditorController *)editor
         didFailWithError:(NSError *)error{
    NSLog(@"Video editor error occurred = %@", error);
    [editor dismissViewControllerAnimated:YES completion:nil];
}

- (void)videoEditorControllerDidCancel:(UIVideoEditorController *)editor{
    NSLog(@"The video editor was cancelled");
    [editor dismissViewControllerAnimated:YES completion:nil];
}
```

When the view is displayed for the first time, we need to display a video picker to the user. She will then be able to pick a video from her library, and we will then proceed to allow her to edit that video:

```
- (BOOL) cameraSupportsMedia:(NSString *)paramMediaType
        sourceType:(UIImagePickerControllerSourceType)paramSourceType{

    __block BOOL result = NO;

    if ([paramMediaType length] == 0){
        NSLog(@"Media type is empty.");
        return NO;
    }

    NSArray *availableMediaTypes =
    [UIImagePickerController
     availableMediaTypesForSourceType:paramSourceType];

    [availableMediaTypes enumerateObjectsUsingBlock:
     ^(id obj, NSUInteger idx, BOOL *stop) {

         NSString *mediaType = (NSString *)obj;
         if ([mediaType isEqualToString:paramMediaType]){
             result = YES;
             *stop= YES;
         }

     }];

    return result;

}

- (BOOL) canUserPickVideosFromPhotoLibrary{
```

```
    return [self cameraSupportsMedia:(__bridge NSString *)kUTTypeMovie
                 sourceType:UIImagePickerControllerSourceTypePhotoLibrary];

}

- (BOOL) isPhotoLibraryAvailable{

    return [UIImagePickerController
            isSourceTypeAvailable:
            UIImagePickerControllerSourceTypePhotoLibrary];

}

- (void) viewDidAppear:(BOOL)animated{
    [super viewDidAppear:animated];

    static BOOL beenHereBefore = NO;

    if (beenHereBefore){
        /* Only display the picker once as the viewDidAppear: method gets
         called whenever the view of our view controller gets displayed */
        return;
    } else {
        beenHereBefore = YES;
    }

    self.assetsLibrary = [[ALAssetsLibrary alloc] init];

    if ([self isPhotoLibraryAvailable] &&
        [self canUserPickVideosFromPhotoLibrary]){

        UIImagePickerController *imagePicker =
        [[UIImagePickerController alloc] init];

        /* Set the source type to photo library */
        imagePicker.sourceType = UIImagePickerControllerSourceTypePhotoLibrary;

        /* And we want our user to be able to pick movies from the library */
        imagePicker.mediaTypes = @[(__bridge NSString *)kUTTypeMovie];

        /* Set the delegate to the current view controller */
        imagePicker.delegate = self;

        /* Present our image picker */
        [self presentViewController:imagePicker animated:YES completion:nil];

    }

}
```

We now need to know when the user is done picking a video, so let's handle various delegate methods of the image picker control:

```
- (void)    imagePickerController:(UIImagePickerController *)picker
    didFinishPickingMediaWithInfo:(NSDictionary *)info{

    NSLog(@"Picker returned successfully.");

    NSString     *mediaType = [info objectForKey:
                               UIImagePickerControllerMediaType];

    if ([mediaType isEqualToString:(NSString *)kUTTypeMovie]){
        self.videoURLToEdit = [info objectForKey:UIImagePickerControllerMediaURL];
    }

    [picker dismissViewControllerAnimated:YES completion:^{

        if (self.videoURLToEdit != nil){

            NSString *videoPath = [self.videoURLToEdit path];

            /* First let's make sure the video editor is able to edit the
             video at the path in our documents folder */
            if ([UIVideoEditorController canEditVideoAtPath:videoPath]){

                /* Instantiate the video editor */
                UIVideoEditorController *videoEditor =
                [[UIVideoEditorController alloc] init];

                /* We become the delegate of the video editor */
                videoEditor.delegate = self;

                /* Make sure to set the path of the video */
                videoEditor.videoPath = videoPath;

                /* And present the video editor */
                [self presentViewController:videoEditor
                                   animated:YES
                                 completion:nil];

                self.videoURLToEdit = nil;

            } else {
                NSLog(@"Cannot edit the video at this path");
            }

        }

    }];

}
```

```
- (void) imagePickerControllerDidCancel:(UIImagePickerController *)picker{

    NSLog(@"Picker was cancelled");
    self.videoURLToEdit = nil;
    [picker dismissViewControllerAnimated:YES completion:nil];

}
```

In the example, the user is allowed to pick any video from the photo library. Once she does, we will display the video editor controller by providing the path of the video that the video picker passes to us in a delegate method.

The video editor controller's delegate gets important messages about the state of the video editor. This delegate object must conform to the `UIVideoEditorControllerDelegate` and `UINavigationControllerDelegate` protocols. In the example, we chose the view controller to become the delegate of the video editor. Once the editing is done, the delegate object receives the `videoEditorController:didSaveEditedVideoToPath:` delegate method from the video editor controller. The path of the edited video will be passed through the `didSaveEditedVideoToPath` parameter.

Before attempting to display the interface of the video editor to your users, you must call the `canEditVideoAtPath:` class method of `UIVideoEditorController` to make sure the path you are trying to edit is editable by the controller. If the return value of this class method is `YES`, proceed to configuring and displaying the video editor's interface. If not, take a separate path, perhaps displaying an alert to your user.

## See Also

Recipe 15.6; Recipe 15.7

## CHAPTER 16
# Multitasking

## 16.0. Introduction

Multitasking enables *background execution*, which means the application can keep working as usual—running tasks, spawning new threads, listening for notifications, and reacting to events—but simply does not display anything on the screen or have any way to interact with the user. When the user presses the Home button on his device, which in previous versions of the iPhone and iPad would terminate the application, the application is now sent into the background.

When our application moves to the background (such as when the user presses the Home button) and then back to the foreground (when the user selects the application again), various messages are sent by the system and are expected to be received by an object we designate as our application delegate. For instance, when our application is sent to the background our application delegate will receive the `applicationDidEnterBackground:` method, and as the application comes back to the foreground for the user, the application delegate will receive the `applicationWillEnterForeground:` delegate message.

In addition to these delegate messages, iOS also sends notifications to the running application when it transitions the application to the background and from the background to the foreground. The notification that gets sent when the application is moved to the background is `UIApplicationDidEnterBackgroundNotification`, and the notification that gets sent when an application transitions from the background to the foreground is `UIApplicationWillEnterForegroundNotification`. You can use the default notification center to register for these notifications.

## 16.1. Detecting the Availability of Multitasking

### Problem

You want to find out whether the iOS device running your application supports multitasking.

### Solution

Call the `isMultitaskingSupported` instance method of `UIDevice`, like so:

```
- (BOOL) isMultitaskingSupported{

    BOOL result = NO;
    if ([[UIDevice currentDevice]
         respondsToSelector:@selector(isMultitaskingSupported)]){
        result = [[UIDevice currentDevice] isMultitaskingSupported];
    }
    return result;

}

- (BOOL)            application:(UIApplication *)application
  didFinishLaunchingWithOptions:(NSDictionary *)launchOptions{

    if ([self isMultitaskingSupported]){
        NSLog(@"Multitasking is supported.");
    } else {
        NSLog(@"Multitasking is not supported.");
    }

    self.window = [[UIWindow alloc] initWithFrame:
                   [[UIScreen mainScreen] bounds]];

    self.window.backgroundColor = [UIColor whiteColor];
    [self.window makeKeyAndVisible];
    return YES;
}
```

### Discussion

Your application, depending on the iOS devices it targets, can be run and executed on a variety of devices on different versions of iOS. For instance, you may be developing your app using the latest iOS SDK but set the target iOS version (the minimum version of iOS on which your app can run) to one version lower than the latest SDK version. In this case, an older device with that OS version can still run your app, but that device may not support multitasking. The golden rule in software development or even in life (not trying to be philosophical) is that if you make an assumption, you'll eventually be wrong. So never make an assumption as to which device is currently running your app, because as iOS developers, we limit our target audience by telling Xcode what the lowest iOS version is that we support. We still want to make sure anyone running a current iOS device can run our apps. So if you want to take advantage of the latest multitasking capabilities of iOS in your apps, always ensure that you check for the availability of multitasking, and if multitasking is not available, ensure that your app responds in an appropriate way and perhaps chooses an alternative route of execution.

# 16.2. Completing a Long-Running Task in the Background

## Problem

You want to borrow some time from iOS to complete a long-running task when your application is being sent to the background.

## Solution

Use the `beginBackgroundTaskWithExpirationHandler:` instance method of `UIApplication`. After you have finished the task, call the `endBackgroundTask:` instance method of `UIApplication`.

## Discussion

When an iOS application is sent to the background, its main thread is paused. The threads you create within your application using the `detachNewThreadSelector:toTarget:withObject:` class method of `NSThread` are also suspended. If you are attempting to finish a long-running task when your application is being sent to the background, you must call the `beginBackgroundTaskWithExpirationHandler:` instance method of `UIApplication` to borrow some time from iOS. The `backgroundTimeRemaining` property of `UIApplication` contains the number of seconds the application has to finish its job. If the application doesn't finish the long-running task before this time expires, iOS will terminate the application. Every call to the `beginBackgroundTaskWithExpirationHandler:` method must have a corresponding call to `endBackgroundTask:` (another instance method of `UIApplication`). In other words, if you ask for more time from iOS to complete a task, you must tell iOS when you are done with that task. Once this is done and no more tasks are requested to be running in the background, your application will be fully put into the background with all threads paused.

When your application is in the foreground, the `backgroundTimeRemaining` property of `UIApplication` is equal to the `DBL_MAX` constant, which is the largest value a value of type `double` can contain (the integer equivalent of this value is normally equal to `-1` in this case). After iOS is asked for more time before the application is fully suspended, this property will indicate the number of seconds the application has before it finishes running its task(s).

You can call the beginBackgroundTaskWithExpirationHandler: method as many times as you wish inside your application. The important thing to keep in mind is that whenever iOS returns a token or a task identifier to your application with this method, you must call the endBackgroundTask: method to mark the end of that task once you are finished running the task. Failing to do so might cause iOS to terminate your application.

While in the background, applications are not supposed to be fully functioning and processing heavy data. They are indeed only supposed to *finish* a long-running task. An example could be an application that is calling a web service API and has not yet received the response of that API from the server. During this time, if the application is sent to the background, the application can request more time until it receives a response from the server. Once the response is received, the application must save its state and mark that task as finished by calling the endBackgroundTask: instance method of UIApplication.

Let's have a look at an example. I will start by defining a property of type UIBackgroundTaskIdentifier in the app delegate. Also, let's define a timer of type NSTimer, which we will use to print a message to the console window every second when our app is sent to the background:

```
#import "AppDelegate.h"

@interface AppDelegate ()
@property (nonatomic, unsafe_unretained)
UIBackgroundTaskIdentifier backgroundTaskIdentifier;

@property (nonatomic, strong) NSTimer *myTimer;
@end

@implementation AppDelegate

<# Rest of your code goes here #>
```

Now let's move on to creating and scheduling our timer when the app gets sent to the background:

```
- (BOOL) isMultitaskingSupported{

    BOOL result = NO;
    if ([[UIDevice currentDevice]
         respondsToSelector:@selector(isMultitaskingSupported)]){
        result = [[UIDevice currentDevice] isMultitaskingSupported];
    }
    return result;

}

- (void) timerMethod:(NSTimer *)paramSender{
```

```
    NSTimeInterval backgroundTimeRemaining =
    [[UIApplication sharedApplication] backgroundTimeRemaining];

    if (backgroundTimeRemaining == DBL_MAX){
        NSLog(@"Background Time Remaining = Undetermined");
    } else {
        NSLog(@"Background Time Remaining = %.02f Seconds",
              backgroundTimeRemaining);
    }

}

- (void)applicationDidEnterBackground:(UIApplication *)application{

    if ([self isMultitaskingSupported] == NO){
        return;
    }

    self.myTimer =
    [NSTimer scheduledTimerWithTimeInterval:1.0f
                                     target:self
                                   selector:@selector(timerMethod:)
                                   userInfo:nil
                                    repeats:YES];

    self.backgroundTaskIdentifier =
    [application beginBackgroundTaskWithExpirationHandler:^(void) {
        [self endBackgroundTask];
    }];

}
```

You can see that in the completion handler for our background task, we are calling the `endBackgroundTask` method of our app delegate. This is a method that we have written, and it looks like this:

```
- (void) endBackgroundTask{

    dispatch_queue_t mainQueue = dispatch_get_main_queue();

    __weak AppDelegate *weakSelf = self;

    dispatch_async(mainQueue, ^(void) {
        AppDelegate *strongSelf = weakSelf;
        if (strongSelf != nil){
            [strongSelf.myTimer invalidate];
            [[UIApplication sharedApplication]
             endBackgroundTask:self.backgroundTaskIdentifier];
            strongSelf.backgroundTaskIdentifier = UIBackgroundTaskInvalid;
        }
    });
}
```

There are a couple of things we need to do to clean up after a long-running task:

1. End any threads or timers, whether they are foundation timers or they are created with GCD.
2. End the background task by calling the `endBackgroundTask:` method of `UIApplication`.
3. Mark our task as ended by assigning the value of `UIBackgroundTaskInvalid` to our task identifiers.

Last but not least, when our app is brought to the foreground, if we still have our background task running, we need to ensure that we get rid of it:

```
- (void)applicationWillEnterForeground:(UIApplication *)application{

    if (self.backgroundTaskIdentifier != UIBackgroundTaskInvalid){
        [self endBackgroundTask];
    }

}
```

In our example, whenever the application is put into the background, we ask for more time to finish a long-running task (in this case, for instance, our timer's code). In our time, we constantly read the value of the `backgroundTimeRemaining` property of `UIApplication` 's instance and print that value out to the console. In the `beginBackgroundTaskWithExpirationHandler:` instance method of `UIApplication`, we provided the code that will be executed just before our application's extra time to execute a long-running task finishes (usually about 5 to 10 seconds before the expiration of the task). In here, we can simply end the task by calling the `endBackgroundTask:` instance method of `UIApplication`.

When an application is sent to the background and the application has requested more execution time from iOS, before the execution time is finished, the application could be revived and brought to the foreground by the user again. If you had previously asked for a long-running task to be executed in the background when the application was being sent to the background, you must end the long-running task using the `endBackgroundTask:` instance method of `UIApplication`.

## See Also

Recipe 16.1

# 16.3. Adding Background Fetch Capabilities to Your Apps

## Problem

You want your app to be able to fetch content in the background by using the new capabilities introduced in iOS SDK.

## Solution

Add the Background Fetch capability to your app.

## Discussion

A lot of the apps that get submitted on a daily basis to the App Store have connectivity to some servers. Some fetch data, some post data, etc. For a while, in iOS, the only way for apps to fetch content in the background was to borrow some time from iOS, as you can read about in Recipe 16.2, and the apps could use that time to complete their work in the background. But this is a very active way of going about doing this. There is a passive way as well, where your app sits there and then iOS gives your app some time to do some processing in the background. So all you have to do is hook into this capability and let iOS wake your app at a quiet moment and ask it to do some processing. This is usually used for background fetches.

For instance, you may need to download some new content. Imagine the Twitter app. All you are interested in when you open that app is to see new tweets. Up until now, the only way to do this was for you to open the app and then let the app refresh the list of tweets. But now iOS is able to wake the Twitter app in the background and ask it to refresh its feed so that when you open the app, all the tweets on the screen are already up to date.

The first thing that we have to do to enable background-fetching capabilities for our app is to go to the Capabilities tab of the project settings, and under the Background Modes slice, enable the "Background fetch" item, as shown in Figure 16-1.

There are two ways your app could use background fetches. One is when your app is in the background and iOS wakes your app (without making it visible to the user) and asks it to fetch some content. The other time is when your app is not started and iOS wakes your app (again in the background), asking it to look for content to fetch. But how does iOS know which apps to wake up and which ones not to? Well, the programmer has to help iOS.

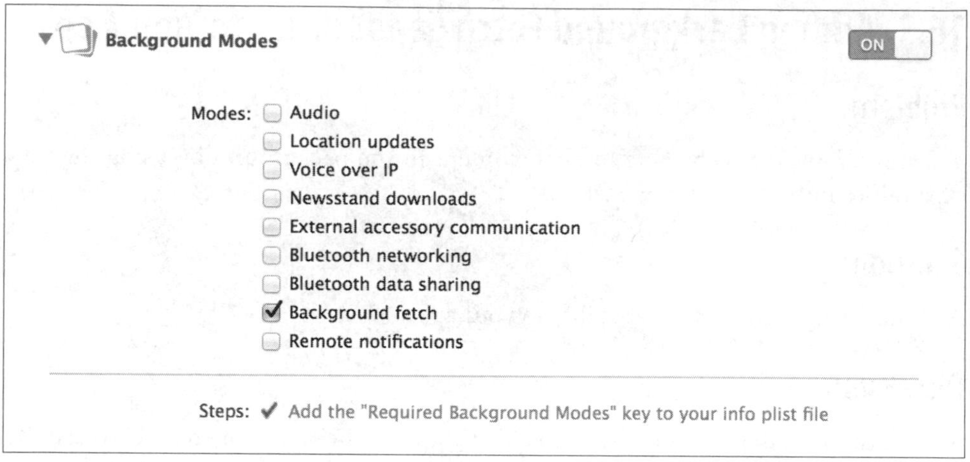

Background Modes ON

Modes: Audio
Location updates
Voice over IP
Newsstand downloads
External accessory communication
Bluetooth networking
Bluetooth data sharing
Background fetch
Remote notifications

Steps: ✔ Add the "Required Background Modes" key to your info plist file

*Figure 16-1. Enabling background fetch for our app*

The way we do that is by calling the `setMinimumBackgroundFetchInterval:` instance method of the `UIApplication` class. The parameter that you pass to this method is the interval and the frequency at which you want iOS to wake up your app in the background and ask it to fetch new data. The default value for this property is `UIApplicationBackgroundFetchIntervalNever`, meaning that iOS will never wake your app in the background. But you can set this property's value manually by passing the number of interval seconds, or you can simply pass the value of `UIApplicationBackgroundFetchIntervalMinimum` to ask iOS to put minimal effort into waking up your app by not doing the process too frequently.

```
- (BOOL)            application:(UIApplication *)application
  didFinishLaunchingWithOptions:(NSDictionary *)launchOptions{

    [application setMinimumBackgroundFetchInterval:
     UIApplicationBackgroundFetchIntervalMinimum];

    return YES;
}
```

After you've done that, you will need to implement the `application:performFetchWithCompletionHandler` instance method of your app delegate. The `performFetchWithCompletionHandler:` parameter of this method will give you a block object that you will have to call once your app is finished fetching data. This method, in general, gets called in your app delegate when iOS wants your app to fetch new content in the background, so you will have to respond to it and call the completion handler once you are done. The block object that you have to call will accept a value of type `UIBackgroundFetchResult`:

```
typedef NS_ENUM(NSUInteger, UIBackgroundFetchResult) {
    UIBackgroundFetchResultNewData,
```

```
    UIBackgroundFetchResultNoData,
    UIBackgroundFetchResultFailed
} NS_ENUM_AVAILABLE_IOS(7_0);
```

So if iOS asks your app to fetch new content and you try to fetch the data but there is no new data available, you will have to call the completion handler and pass the value of `UIBackgroundFetchResultNoData` to it. This way, iOS will know that there was no new content available for your app and can adjust its scheduling algorithm and AI in order to not call your app so frequently. iOS is very smart about this indeed. Let's imagine that you ask iOS to call your app in the background so that you can retrieve new content. If your server doesn't give you any new updates, and for a whole week of your app being woken up in the background on the user's device you could not fetch any new data and always passed `UIBackgroundFetchResultNoData` to the completion block of the aforementioned method, iOS will not wake your app as frequently. That will preserve processing power and, subsequently, battery.

For the purpose of this recipe, we are going to create a simple app that will retrieve news items from a server. To avoid overcomplicating the recipe with server code, we are going to fake the server calls. Let's first create a class named `NewsItem` that has a date and a text as its properties:

```
#import <Foundation/Foundation.h>

@interface NewsItem : NSObject

@property (nonatomic, strong) NSDate *date;
@property (nonatomic, copy) NSString *text;

@end
```

The class won't have any implementation and will only carry information through its properties. Now, back in your app delegate, define a mutable array of news items so that in our table view controller, we can hook into that array and display the news items:

```
#import <UIKit/UIKit.h>

@interface AppDelegate : UIResponder <UIApplicationDelegate>

@property (nonatomic, strong) UIWindow *window;
@property (nonatomic, strong) NSMutableArray *allNewsItems;

@end
```

Now lazily allocate this array so that it won't be allocated and initialized unless it is actually accessed by our app to preserve memory. Once the array is allocated, we will add one new item to it:

```
#import "AppDelegate.h"
#import "NewsItem.h"
```

```
@implementation AppDelegate

- (NSMutableArray *) allNewsItems{
    if (_allNewsItems == nil){
        _allNewsItems = [[NSMutableArray alloc] init];

        /* Pre-populate the array with one item */
        NewsItem *item = [[NewsItem alloc] init];
        item.date = [NSDate date];
        item.text = [NSString stringWithFormat:@"News text 1"];
        [_allNewsItems addObject:item];

    }
    return _allNewsItems;
}

<# Rest of your app delegate code will go here #>
```

We will now implement a method in our app that will fake a server call. Basically, it will toss a coin. More precisely, it will get a random integer between 0 and 1, inclusive. If that number is 1, it will pretend like there is new server content, and if that value is 0, it will pretend like there are no new server items to download. If this value turns out to be 1, then it will add a new item to the list as well:

```
- (void) fetchNewsItems:(BOOL *)paramFetchedNewItems{

    if (arc4random_uniform(2) != 1){
        if (paramFetchedNewItems != nil){
            *paramFetchedNewItems = NO;
        }
        return;
    }

    [self willChangeValueForKey:@"allNewsItems"];

    /* Generate a new item */

    NewsItem *item = [[NewsItem alloc] init];
    item.date = [NSDate date];
    item.text = [NSString stringWithFormat:@"News text %lu",
                 (unsigned long)self.allNewsItems.count + 1];
    [self.allNewsItems addObject:item];

    if (paramFetchedNewItems != nil){
        *paramFetchedNewItems = YES;
    }

    [self didChangeValueForKey:@"allNewsItems"];

}
```

The Boolean pointer parameter of this method will tell us whether there was any new content that was added to the array.

Now let's implement the background fetching mechanism of our app delegate as explained before:

```
- (void)                application:(UIApplication *)application
  performFetchWithCompletionHandler:(void (^)(UIBackgroundFetchResult))
    completionHandler{

    BOOL haveNewContent = NO;
    [self fetchNewsItems:&haveNewContent];

    if (haveNewContent){
        completionHandler(UIBackgroundFetchResultNewData);
    } else {
        completionHandler(UIBackgroundFetchResultNoData);
    }

}
```

Beautiful. In our table view controller, we will watch for changes to this array of items in the app delegate, and as soon as the array's contents are changed, we will refresh our table view. We will be smart about this, though. If our app is in the foreground, we will refresh the table view, but if our app is in the background, we will delay the refresh of the table view until the app is brought back to the foreground:

```
#import "TableViewController.h"
#import "AppDelegate.h"
#import "NewsItem.h"

@interface TableViewController ()
@property (nonatomic, weak) NSArray *allNewsItems;
@property (nonatomic, unsafe_unretained) BOOL mustReloadView;
@end

@implementation TableViewController

- (void)viewDidLoad
{
    [super viewDidLoad];

    AppDelegate *appDelegate = [UIApplication sharedApplication].delegate;
    self.allNewsItems = appDelegate.allNewsItems;

    [appDelegate addObserver:self
                  forKeyPath:@"allNewsItems"
                     options:NSKeyValueObservingOptionNew
                     context:NULL];

    [[NSNotificationCenter defaultCenter]
     addObserver:self
```

```
        selector:@selector(handleAppIsBroughtToForeground:)
        name:UIApplicationWillEnterForegroundNotification
        object:nil];
}

- (void) observeValueForKeyPath:(NSString *)keyPath
                       ofObject:(id)object
                         change:(NSDictionary *)change
                        context:(void *)context{

    if ([keyPath isEqualToString:@"allNewsItems"]){
        if ([self isBeingPresented]){
            [self.tableView reloadData];
        } else {
            self.mustReloadView = YES;
        }
    }

}

- (void) handleAppIsBroughtToForeground:(NSNotification *)paramNotification{
    if (self.mustReloadView){
        self.mustReloadView = NO;
        [self.tableView reloadData];
    }
}
```

Last but not least, we will write the required methods of our table view data source to feed the news items to the table view:

In this example code, we are dequeueing table view cells with the identifier of *Cell*. The reason that the `dequeueReusableCellWithIdentifier:forIndexPath:` method of our table view returns valid cells instead of returning `nil` is that in our storyboard file, we have already defined this identifier for the cell prototype of our table view. At runtime, our storyboard is registering this prototype cell for iOS with the given identifier, so that you can simply dequeue the cells with the given identifier without having to register the cells in advance.

```
- (NSInteger)tableView:(UITableView *)tableView
 numberOfRowsInSection:(NSInteger)section{
    return self.allNewsItems.count;
}

- (UITableViewCell *)tableView:(UITableView *)tableView
         cellForRowAtIndexPath:(NSIndexPath *)indexPath{

    static NSString *CellIdentifier = @"Cell";
```

```
    UITableViewCell *cell = [tableView
                             dequeueReusableCellWithIdentifier:CellIdentifier
                             forIndexPath:indexPath];

    NewsItem *newsItem = self.allNewsItems[indexPath.row];

    cell.textLabel.text = newsItem.text;

    return cell;
}

- (void) dealloc{
    AppDelegate *appDelegate = [UIApplication sharedApplication].delegate;
    [appDelegate removeObserver:self forKeyPath:@"allNewsItems"];
    [[NSNotificationCenter defaultCenter] removeObserver:self];
}
```

For more information about table views, please refer to Chapter 4.

So now run your app and press the Home button to send your app to the background. Go back to Xcode, and from the Debug menu, choose Simulate Background Fetch (see Figure 16-2). Now open your app again without terminating it and see whether any new content shows up in your table view. If not, it's because we put the logic in our app that, basically, tosses a coin and randomly decides whether there is new content on the server or not. This is to fake the server calls. If you don't get any new content, simply repeat the simulation of background fetch in the Debug menu until you get new content.

Up until now, we have been processing background fetch requests by iOS while our app was in the background, but what if our app has been completely terminated and is not in the background anymore? How do we simulate that situation to find out whether our app will still work? Well, it turns out that Apple has already thought about this. All you have to do is choose the Manage Schemes menu item of the Product menu in Xcode, and from there, duplicate the main scheme of your app by pressing the little (+) button and then choosing Duplicate Scheme (see Figure 16-3).

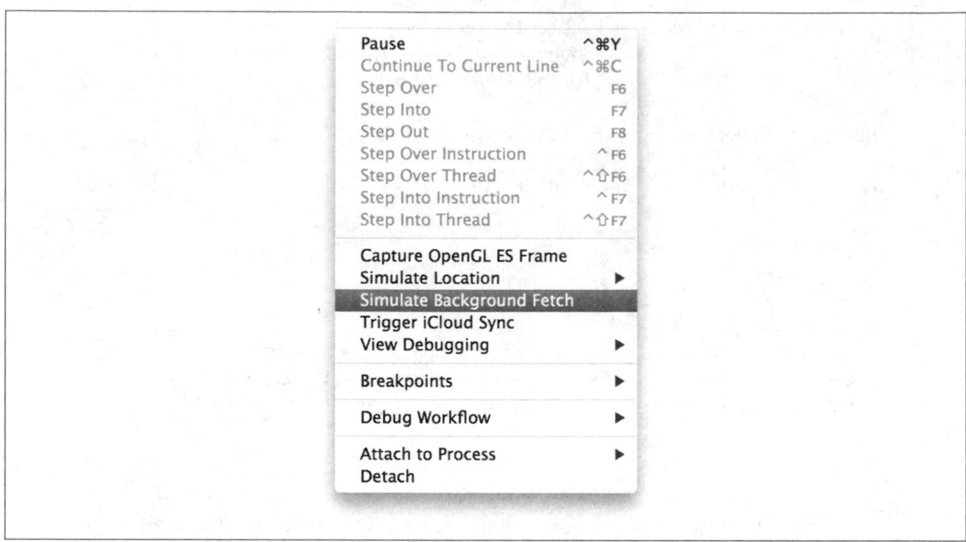


*Figure 16-2. Simulating a background fetch in Xcode*

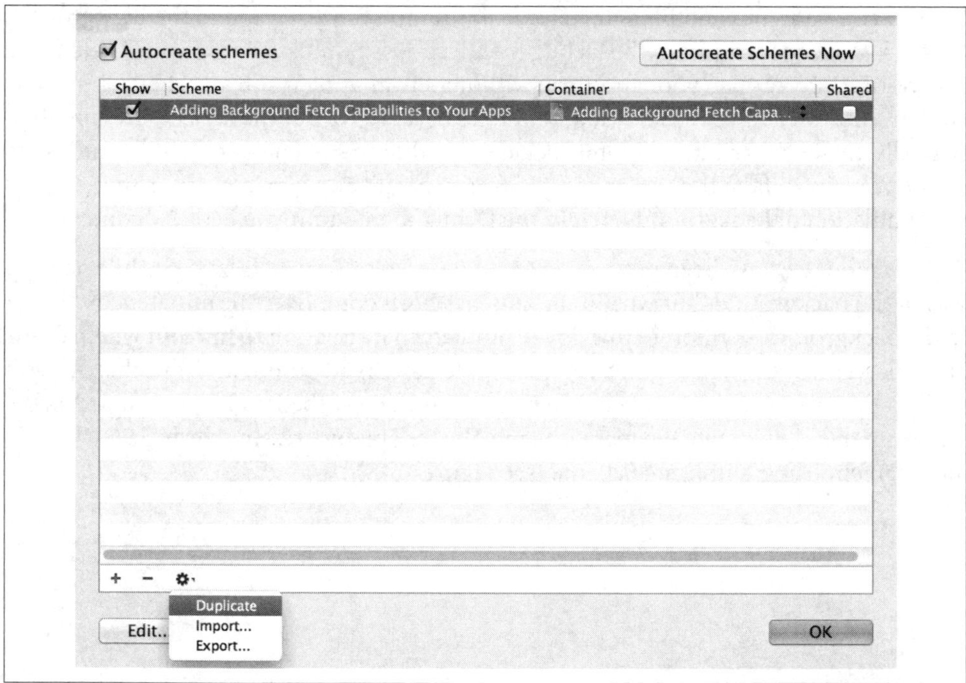


*Figure 16-3. Duplicate your scheme to enable background fetch simulations from the terminated app state*

Now a new dialog will appear in front of you, similar to that shown in Figure 16-4, and will ask you to set the various properties of the new scheme. In this dialog, enable the "Launch due to a background fetch event" item and press the OK button.

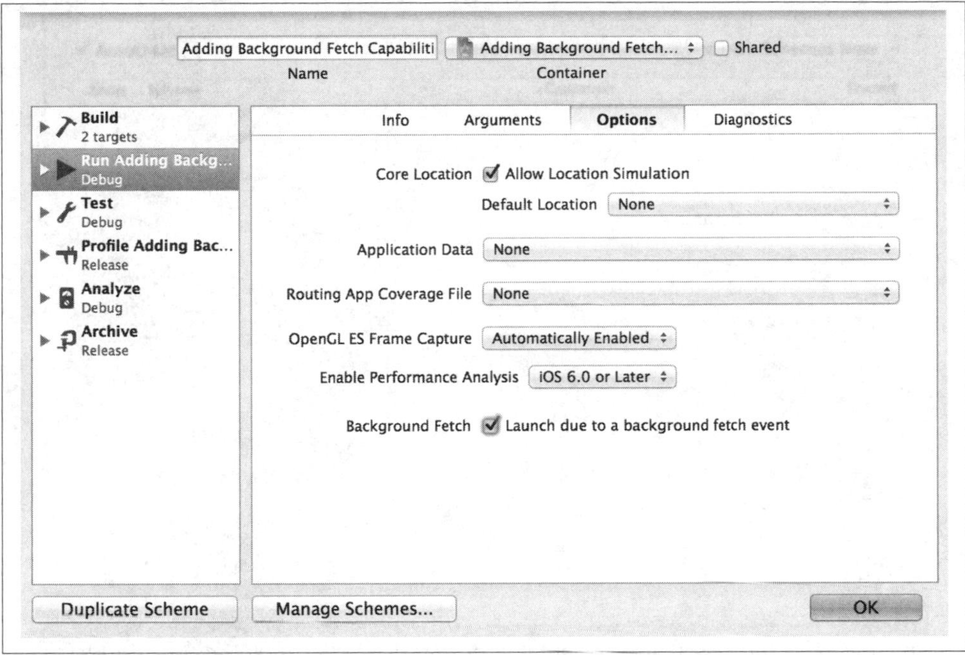


*Figure 16-4. Enabling your scheme to launch your app for background fetches*

Now you will have two schemes in the Xcode for your app (see Figure 16-5). All you have to do to launch your app for background fetches is to select the second scheme that you just created and run your app in the simulator or on the device. This will not bring your app to the foreground. Instead, it will send it a signal to fetch data in the background, and that, in turn, will invoke the `application:performFetchWithCompletionHandler:` method of your app delegate. If you have followed all the steps that were explained in this recipe, you should have a fully working app in both scenarios: when iOS wakes up your app from the background, and when your app is started afresh to fetch data in the background.

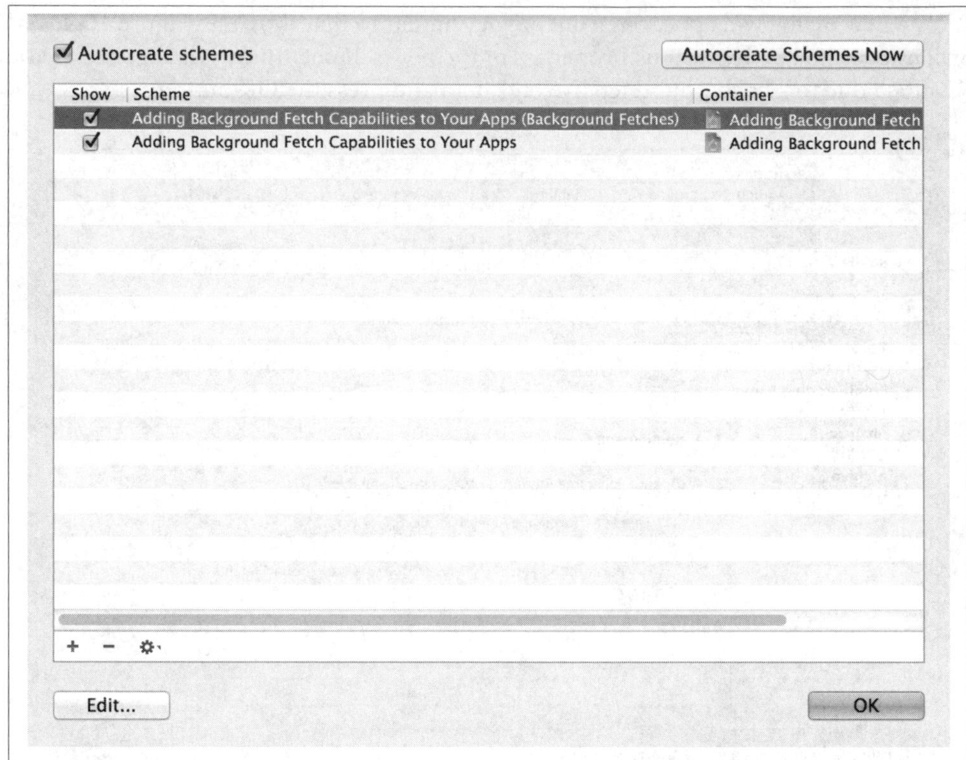


*Figure 16-5. Use the new scheme to start your app by simulating a background fetch*

## See Also

Recipe 16.2

# 16.4. Playing Audio in the Background

## Problem

You are writing an application that plays audio files (such as a music player) and you would like the audio files to be played even if your application is running in the background.

## Solution

Select your project file in the Navigator of Xcode. Then, from the Capabilities section, switch on the Background Modes subsection. After the list of background modes is given to you, tick on the Audio switch.

Now you can use the AV Foundation to play audio files, and your audio files will be played even if your application is in the background.

Please bear in mind that playing audio in the background might not work in iOS Simulator. You need to test this recipe on a real device. On the simulator, chances are that the audio will stop playing once your application is sent to the background.

## Discussion

In iOS, applications can request that their audio files continue playing even if the application is sent to the background. AV Foundation's `AVAudioPlayer` is an easy-to-use audio player that we will employ in this recipe. Our mission is to start an audio player and play a simple song, and while the song is playing, send the application to the background by pressing the Home button. If you have successfully enabled the Audio background mode (as explained in the Solution of this recipe) in our target, iOS will continue playing the music from our app's audio player, even in the background. While in the background, we should only play music and provide our music player with the data that is necessary for it to run. We should not be performing any other tasks, such as displaying new screens.

Here is the declaration of a simple app delegate that starts an `AVAudioPlayer`:

```
#import "AppDelegate.h"
#import <AVFoundation/AVFoundation.h>

@interface AppDelegate () <AVAudioPlayerDelegate>
@property (nonatomic, strong) AVAudioPlayer *audioPlayer;
@end

@implementation AppDelegate

<# Rest of your code goes here #>
```

When our app opens, we will allocate and initialize our audio player, read the contents of a file named *MySong.mp4* into an instance of `NSData`, and use that data in the initialization process of our audio player:

```
- (BOOL)            application:(UIApplication *)application
  didFinishLaunchingWithOptions:(NSDictionary *)launchOptions{

    dispatch_queue_t dispatchQueue =
    dispatch_get_global_queue(DISPATCH_QUEUE_PRIORITY_DEFAULT, 0);

    dispatch_async(dispatchQueue, ^(void) {

        NSError *audioSessionError = nil;
        AVAudioSession *audioSession = [AVAudioSession sharedInstance];
```

```
        [audioSession setActive:YES error:nil];

        if ([audioSession setCategory:AVAudioSessionCategoryPlayback
                                error:&audioSessionError]){
            NSLog(@"Successfully set the audio session.");
        } else {
            NSLog(@"Could not set the audio session");
        }

        NSBundle *mainBundle = [NSBundle mainBundle];

        NSString *filePath = [mainBundle pathForResource:@"MySong"
                                                  ofType:@"mp3"];

        NSData   *fileData = [NSData dataWithContentsOfFile:filePath];

        NSError  *error = nil;

        /* Start the audio player */
        self.audioPlayer = [[AVAudioPlayer alloc] initWithData:fileData
                                                         error:&error];

        /* Did we get an instance of AVAudioPlayer? */
        if (self.audioPlayer != nil){
            /* Set the delegate and start playing */

            self.audioPlayer.delegate = self;

            if ([self.audioPlayer prepareToPlay] &&
                [self.audioPlayer play]){
                NSLog(@"Successfully started playing...");
            } else {
                NSLog(@"Failed to play.");
            }

        } else {
            /* Failed to instantiate AVAudioPlayer */
        }
    });

    self.window = [[UIWindow alloc] initWithFrame:
                   [[UIScreen mainScreen] bounds]];

    self.window.backgroundColor = [UIColor whiteColor];
    [self.window makeKeyAndVisible];

    return YES;
}
```

In this example code, we are using AV audio sessions to silence music playback from other applications (such as the Music application) before starting to play the audio. For more information about audio sessions, please refer to Recipe 12.5. When in the background, you are not limited to playing only the current audio file. If the currently playing audio file (in the background) finishes playing, you can start another instance of `AVAudioPlayer` and play a completely new audio file. iOS will adjust the processing required for this, but there is no guarantee that while in the background, your application will be given permission to allocate enough memory to accommodate the data of the new sound file.

You've probably noticed that in our code, we are electing our app delegate to become the delegate of our audio player. We will implement the audio player delegate methods like so:

```
- (void)audioPlayerBeginInterruption:(AVAudioPlayer *)player{

    /* Audio Session is interrupted.
     The player will be paused here */

}

- (void)audioPlayerEndInterruption:(AVAudioPlayer *)player
                       withOptions:(NSUInteger)flags{

    /* Check the flags, if we can resume the audio,
     then we should do it here */

    if (flags == AVAudioSessionInterruptionOptionShouldResume){
        [player play];
    }

}

- (void)audioPlayerDidFinishPlaying:(AVAudioPlayer *)player
                       successfully:(BOOL)flag{

    NSLog(@"Finished playing the song");

    /* The flag parameter tells us if the playback was successfully
     finished or not */

    if ([player isEqual:self.audioPlayer]){
        self.audioPlayer = nil;
    } else {
        /* This isn't our audio player! */
    }

}
```

For more information about playing audio and video, please refer to Chapter 12.

Another important thing to keep in mind is that while your application is running an audio file in the background, the value returned by the `backgroundTimeRemaining` property of `UIApplication` will not be changed. In other words, an application that requests to play audio files in the background is not implicitly or explicitly asking iOS for extra execution time.

## 16.5. Handling Location Changes in the Background

### Problem

You are writing an application whose main functionality is processing location changes using Core Location. You want the application to retrieve the iOS device location changes even if the application is sent to the background.

### Solution

Select your project file in the Navigator of Xcode. Then, from the Capabilities section, switch on the Background Modes subsection. After the list of background modes is given to you, tick on the Location switch.

### Discussion

When your application is running in the foreground, you can receive delegate messages from an instance of `CLLocationManager` telling you when iOS detects that the device is at a new location. However, if your application is sent to the background and is no longer active, the location delegate messages will not be delivered normally to your application. They will instead be delivered in a batch when your application again becomes the foreground application.

If you still want to be able to receive changes in the location of the user's device while running in the background, you must enable the Location updates capability of your app, as described in the Solution section of this recipe. Once in the background, your application will continue to receive the changes in the device's location. Let's test this in a simple app with just the app delegate.

What I intend to do in this app is to keep a Boolean value in the app delegate, called *`executingInBackground`*. When the app goes to the background, I will set this value to `YES`; when the app comes back to the foreground, I will set this value to `NO`. When we get location updates from CoreLocation, we will check this flag. If this flag is set to `YES`, then we won't do any heavy calculations or any UI update because, well, our app is in the background, and as responsible programmers, we should not do heavy processing while our app is in the background. If our app is in the foreground, however, we have all the device's processing power for the normal processing that we wish to do. We also will attempt to get the best location change accuracy when our app is in the foreground; when the app is sent to the background, we will be sure to ask for less accuracy in location updates to ease the strain on the location sensors. So let's go ahead and define our app delegate:

```
#import "AppDelegate.h"
#import <CoreLocation/CoreLocation.h>

@interface AppDelegate () <CLLocationManagerDelegate>
@property (nonatomic, strong) CLLocationManager *myLocationManager;
@property (nonatomic, unsafe_unretained, getter=isExecutingInBackground)
BOOL executingInBackground;
@end

@implementation AppDelegate

<# Rest of your code goes here #>
```

Now let's go ahead and create and start our location manager when our app starts:

```
- (BOOL)            application:(UIApplication *)application
  didFinishLaunchingWithOptions:(NSDictionary *)launchOptions{

    self.myLocationManager = [[CLLocationManager alloc] init];
    self.myLocationManager.desiredAccuracy = kCLLocationAccuracyBest;
    self.myLocationManager.delegate = self;
    [self.myLocationManager startUpdatingLocation];

    self.window = [[UIWindow alloc] initWithFrame:
                   [[UIScreen mainScreen] bounds]];
    self.window.backgroundColor = [UIColor whiteColor];
    [self.window makeKeyAndVisible];
    return YES;
}
```

You can see that we have set the desired accuracy of our location manager to a high level. However, when we go to the background, we want to lower this accuracy to give iOS a bit of a rest:

```
- (void)applicationDidEnterBackground:(UIApplication *)application{
    self.executingInBackground = YES;

    /* Reduce the accuracy to ease the strain on
     iOS while we are in the background */
    self.myLocationManager.desiredAccuracy = kCLLocationAccuracyHundredMeters;
}
```

When our app is awakened from the background, we can change this accuracy back to a high level:

```
- (void)applicationWillEnterForeground:(UIApplication *)application{
    self.executingInBackground = NO;

    /* Now that our app is in the foreground again, let's increase the location
     detection accuracy */
```

```
        self.myLocationManager.desiredAccuracy = kCLLocationAccuracyBest;
    }
```

Additionally, we would like to avoid doing any intense processing when we get a new location from the location manager while our app is in the background, so we need to handle the `locationManager:didUpdateToLocation:fromLocation:` delegate method of our location manager in this way:

```
- (void)locationManager:(CLLocationManager *)manager
    didUpdateToLocation:(CLLocation *)newLocation
           fromLocation:(CLLocation *)oldLocation{

    if ([self isExecutingInBackground]){
        /* We are in the background. Do not do any heavy processing */
    } else {
        /* We are in the foreground. Do any processing that you wish */
    }

}
```

The simple rule here is that if we are in the background, we should be using the smallest amount of memory and processing power to satisfy our application's needs. So, by decreasing the accuracy of the location manager while in the background, we are decreasing the amount of processing iOS has to do to deliver new locations to our application.

Depending on the version of iOS Simulator you are testing your applications with, as well as the settings of your network connection and many other factors that affect this process, background location processing might not work for you. Please test your applications, including the source code in this recipe, on a real device.

## 16.6. Saving and Loading the State of Multitasking Apps

### Problem

You want the state of your iOS app to be saved when it is sent to the background and for the same state to resume when the application is brought to the foreground.

### Solution

Use a combination of the `UIApplicationDelegate` protocol's messages sent to your application delegate and the notifications sent by iOS to preserve the state of your multitasking apps.

## Discussion

When an empty iOS application (an application with just one window and no code written for it) is run on an iOS device with support for multitasking for the first time (not from the background), the following `UIApplicationDelegate` messages will be sent to your app delegate, in this order:

1. `application:didFinishLaunchingWithOptions:`
2. `applicationDidBecomeActive:`

If the user presses the Home button on her iOS device, your app delegate will receive these messages, in this order:

1. `applicationWillResignActive:`
2. `applicationDidEnterBackground:`

Once the application is in the background, the user can press the Home button twice and select our application from the list of background applications. (The way our app is brought to the foreground doesn't really matter. For all we know, another app might launch our app through URI schemes that we can expose in our app.) Once our application is brought to the foreground again, we will receive these messages in the application delegate, in this order:

1. `applicationWillEnterForeground:`
2. `applicationDidBecomeActive:`

In addition to these messages, we will also receive various notification messages from iOS when our application is sent to the background or brought to the foreground again.

To save and load back the state of your apps, you need to think carefully about the tasks you need to pause when going into the background and then resume when the application is brought to the foreground. Let me give you an example. As will be mentioned in Recipe 16.7, network connections can be easily resumed by the system itself, so we might not need to do anything special if we're downloading a file from the network. However, if you are writing a game, for instance, it is best to listen for the notifications iOS sends when your application is being sent to the background, and to act accordingly. In such a scenario, you can simply put the game engine into a paused state. You can also put the state of the sound engine into a paused state if necessary.

After an application is sent to the background, it has about 10 seconds to save any unsaved data and prepare itself to be brought to the foreground at any moment by the user. You can optionally ask for extra execution time if required (further information about this is available in Recipe 16.2).

Let's demonstrate saving your state with an example. Suppose we are writing a game for iOS. When our game is sent to the background, we want to do the following:

1. Put the game engine into a paused state.
2. Save the user's score to disk.
3. Save the current level's data to disk. This includes where the user is in the level, the physical aspects of the level, the camera position, and so on.

When the user opens the application again, bringing the application to the foreground, we want to do the following:

1. Load the user's score from disk.
2. Load the level the user was playing the last time from disk.
3. Resume the game engine.

Now let's say our app delegate is our game engine. Let's define a few methods in the app delegate's header file:

```
#import <UIKit/UIKit.h>

@interface AppDelegate : UIResponder <UIApplicationDelegate>

@property (nonatomic, strong) UIWindow *window;

/* Saving the state of our app */
- (void) saveUserScore;
- (void) saveLevelToDisk;
- (void) pauseGameEngine;

/* Loading the state of our app */
- (void) loadUserScore;
- (void) loadLevelFromDisk;
- (void) resumeGameEngine;

@end
```

We will proceed to place stub implementations of these methods in the implementation file of our app delegate:

```
#import "AppDelegate.h"

@implementation AppDelegate

- (void) saveUserScore{
    /* Save the user score here */
}

- (void) saveLevelToDisk{
    /* Save the current level and the user's location on map to disk */
```

```
}

- (void) pauseGameEngine{
    /* Pause the game engine here */
}

- (void) loadUserScore{
    /* Load the user's location back to memory */
}

- (void) loadLevelFromDisk{
    /* Load the user's previous location on the map */
}

- (void) resumeGameEngine{
    /* Resume the game engine here */
}

<# Rest of your code goes here #>
```

Now we need to make sure that our app is able to handle interruptions, such as incoming calls on an iPhone. On such occasions, our app won't be sent to the background but will become inactive. When the user finishes a phone call, for instance, iOS will bring our app to the active state. So when our app becomes inactive, we need to make sure we are pausing our game engine; when the app becomes active again, we can resume our game engine. We don't need to save anything to the disk when our app becomes inactive really (at least in this example), because iOS will bring our app to its previous state once it becomes active again:

```
- (void)applicationWillResignActive:(UIApplication *)application{
    [self pauseGameEngine];
}

- (void)applicationDidBecomeActive:(UIApplication *)application{
    [self resumeGameEngine];
}
```

And now, simply, when our app is sent to the background, we will save the state of our game, and when our app is back in the foreground, we will load the state back:

```
- (void)applicationDidEnterBackground:(UIApplication *)application{
    [self saveUserScore];
    [self saveLevelToDisk];
    [self pauseGameEngine];
}

- (void)applicationWillEnterForeground:(UIApplication *)application{
    [self loadUserScore];
    [self loadLevelFromDisk];
    [self resumeGameEngine];
}
```

Not every application is a game. However, you can use this technique to load and save the state of your application in the multitasking environment of iOS.

## See Also

Recipe 16.2

# 16.7. Handling Network Connections in the Background

## Problem

You are using instances of `NSURLConnection` to send and receive data to and from a web server and are wondering how you can allow your application to work in the multitasking environment of iOS without connection failures.

## Solution

Make sure you support connection failures in the block objects that you submit to your connection objects.

## Discussion

For applications that use `NSURLConnection` but do not borrow extra time from iOS when they are sent to the background, connection handling is truly simple. Let's go through an example to see how an asynchronous connection will act if the application is sent to the background and brought to the foreground again. For this, let's send an asynchronous connection request to retrieve the contents of a URL (say, Apple's home page):

```
- (BOOL)            application:(UIApplication *)application
  didFinishLaunchingWithOptions:(NSDictionary *)launchOptions{

    NSString *urlAsString = @"http://www.apple.com";
    NSURL *url = [NSURL URLWithString:urlAsString];
    NSURLRequest *urlRequest = [NSURLRequest requestWithURL:url];
    NSOperationQueue *queue = [[NSOperationQueue alloc] init];

    [NSURLConnection
     sendAsynchronousRequest:urlRequest
     queue:queue
     completionHandler:^(NSURLResponse *response,
                         NSData *data,
                         NSError *error) {

         if ([data length] > 0 &&
             error != nil){
             /* Date did come back */
         }
```

```
        else if ([data length] == 0 &&
                 error != nil){
            /* No data came back */
        }
        else if (error != nil){
            /* Error happened. Make sure you handle this properly */
        }

     }];

    self.window = [[UIWindow alloc] initWithFrame:
                   [[UIScreen mainScreen] bounds]];

    self.window.backgroundColor = [UIColor whiteColor];
    [self.window makeKeyAndVisible];
    return YES;
}
```

I advise you to replace the Apple home page URL in this example with the URL to a rather large file on the Internet. The reason is that if your app is downloading a large file, you will have more time to play with the app and send it to the background and bring it to the foreground. Whereas, if you are on a rather fast Internet connection and you are just downloading Apple's home page, chances are that the connection is going to retrieve the data for you in a second or two.

In the foreground, our application will continue downloading the file. While downloading, the user can press the Home button and send the application to the background. What you will observe is true magic! iOS will automatically put the download process into a paused state for you. When the user brings your application to the foreground again, the downloading will resume without you writing a single line of code to handle multitasking.

Now let's see what happens with synchronous connections. We are going to download a very big file on the main thread (a very bad practice—do not do this in a production application!) as soon as our application launches:

```
- (BOOL)            application:(UIApplication *)application
  didFinishLaunchingWithOptions:(NSDictionary *)launchOptions{

    /* Replace this URL with the URL of a file that is rather big in size */
    NSString *urlAsString = @"http://www.apple.com";
    NSURL *url = [NSURL URLWithString:urlAsString];
    NSURLRequest *urlRequest = [NSURLRequest requestWithURL:url];
    NSError *error = nil;

    NSData *connectionData = [NSURLConnection
                              sendSynchronousRequest:urlRequest
```

```
                                      returningResponse:nil
                                      error:&error];

    if ([connectionData length] > 0 &&
        error == nil){

    }
    else if ([connectionData length] == 0 &&
             error == nil){

    }
    else if (error != nil){

    }

    self.window = [[UIWindow alloc] initWithFrame:
                   [[UIScreen mainScreen] bounds]];

    self.window.backgroundColor = [UIColor whiteColor];
    [self.window makeKeyAndVisible];
    return YES;
}
```

If you run this application and send it to the background, you will notice that the application's GUI is sent to the background, but the application's core is never sent to the background and the appropriate delegate messages— `applicationWillResignActive:` and `applicationDidEnterBackground:` —will never be received. I have conducted this test on an iPhone.

The problem with this approach is that we are consuming the main thread's time slice by downloading files synchronously. We can fix this by either downloading the files asynchronously on the main thread, as mentioned before, or downloading them synchronously on separate threads.

Take the previous sample code, for example. If we download the same big file synchronously on a global concurrent queue, the connection will be paused when the application is sent to the background, and will resume once it is brought to the foreground again:

```
- (BOOL)            application:(UIApplication *)application
  didFinishLaunchingWithOptions:(NSDictionary *)launchOptions{

    dispatch_queue_t dispatchQueue =
    dispatch_get_global_queue(DISPATCH_QUEUE_PRIORITY_DEFAULT, 0);

    dispatch_async(dispatchQueue, ^(void) {

        /* Replace this URL with the URL of a file that is
         rather big in size */
        NSString *urlAsString = @"http://www.apple.com";
        NSURL *url = [NSURL URLWithString:urlAsString];
        NSURLRequest *urlRequest = [NSURLRequest requestWithURL:url];
```

```
        NSError *error = nil;

        NSData *connectionData = [NSURLConnection
                                  sendSynchronousRequest:urlRequest
                                  returningResponse:nil
                                  error:&error];

        if ([connectionData length] > 0 &&
            error == nil){

        }
        else if ([connectionData length] == 0 &&
                 error == nil){

        }
        else if (error != nil){

        }
    });

    self.window = [[UIWindow alloc] initWithFrame:
                   [[UIScreen mainScreen] bounds]];

    self.window.backgroundColor = [UIColor whiteColor];
    [self.window makeKeyAndVisible];
    return YES;
}
```

### See Also

Recipe 16.2

## 16.8. Opting Out of Multitasking

### Problem

You do not want your application to participate in multitasking.

### Solution

Add the `UIApplicationExitsOnSuspend` key to your application's main *.plist* file and set the value to `true`:

```
<# Some keys and values #>
<key>UIApplicationExitsOnSuspend</key>
<true/>
<# Rest of the keys and values #>
```

## Discussion

In some circumstances, you might require your iOS applications not to be multitasking (although I strongly encourage you to develop your applications to be multitasking-aware). In such cases, you can add the `UIApplicationExitsOnSuspend` key to your application's main *.plist* file. Devices on the latest iOS versions that support multitasking understand this value, and the OS will terminate an application with this key set to `true` in the application's *.plist* file. On earlier iOS versions without support for multitasking, this value will have no meaning to the operating system and will be ignored.

When such an application runs on the latest iOS, the following application delegate messages will be posted to your application:

1. `application:didFinishLaunchingWithOptions:`
2. `applicationDidBecomeActive:`

If the user presses the Home button on the device, the following messages will be sent to your application delegate:

1. `applicationDidEnterBackground:`
2. `applicationWillTerminate:`

CHAPTER 17

# Notifications

## 17.0. Introduction

Notifications are objects that can carry some data and be broadcast to multiple receivers. They are very good for decomposing work into different pieces of code, but can very easily get out of hand if you misuse them. You should understand the limitations of notifications. We will talk more about their uses in this chapter and learn when you are better off without them.

Three types of notifications are available in iOS:

*A normal notification (an instance of* `NSNotification` *class)*
: This is a simple notification that your app can broadcast to all possible receivers inside your app. iOS also broadcasts notifications of this type to your app while your app is in the foreground, informing you of various system events that are happening, such as the keyboard showing or being hidden. These notifications are great for decoupling code, in that they can allow you to cleanly separate various components in a complex iOS application.

*A local notification (an instance of* `UILocalNotification` *class)*
: This is a notification that you schedule to be delivered to your app at a specific time. Your app can receive it even if the app is in the background or not running at all, and the app is started if the notification is delivered while your app is not running. You would normally schedule a local notification if you want to ensure that your app gets woken up (granted that the user permits this action, as we will see later) at a specific time of the day.

*Push notifications*
: This is a notification that is sent to an iOS device via a server. It is called a push notification because your app doesn't have to keep polling a server for notifications. iOS maintains a persistent connection to Apple Push Notification Services servers

(APNS servers), and whenever a new push message is available, iOS will process the message and send it to the app to which the push was designated.

We will refer to normal notifications herein as notifications. The word *normal* is redundant in this context.

Local notifications are special in that they become visible to the user and the user can take action on them. Based on the user's action, your app will be notified by iOS to handle the action. On the other hand, notifications are invisible items that you can broadcast in your app and that your app has to handle. The user doesn't directly have to get involved unless you involve her as a result of receiving and processing the notification. For instance, your app may send a notification to another part of your app, which, upon receiving that notification, fires up an alert dialog. The user then has to get involved and press a button on the alert dialog to dismiss it (for instance). This is indirect involvement and is very much different from the direct involvement that local notifications demand from users.

Notifications are a big part of OS X and iOS. iOS sends system-wide notifications to all apps that are listening, and apps can send notifications as well. A system-wide, or *distributed*, notification can be delivered only by iOS.

A notification is a simple concept represented by the `NSNotification` class in the iOS SDK. A notification is posted by an object and can carry information. The object that sends the notification will identify itself to the notification center while posting the notification. The receiver of the notification can then probe the sender, perhaps using its class name, to find out more about the sender, which is called the *object* of the notification. A notification can also carry a user-info dictionary, which is a dictionary data structure that can carry extra information about the notification. If no dictionary is provided, this parameter is nil.

# 17.1. Sending Notifications

## Problem

You want to decouple parts of your app and send a notification where it can be picked up by another component in your app.

## Solution

Compose an instance of `NSNotification` and broadcast it to your app using the class's `postNotification:` method. You can get an instance of the notification center using its `defaultCenter` class method, like so:

```
#import "AppDelegate.h"

NSString *const kNotificationName = @"NotificationNameGoesHere";

@implementation AppDelegate

- (BOOL)            application:(UIApplication *)application
  didFinishLaunchingWithOptions:(NSDictionary *)launchOptions{

    NSNotification *notification = [NSNotification
                                    notificationWithName:kNotificationName
                                    object:self
                                    userInfo:@{@"Key 1" : @"Value 1",
                                               @"Key 2" : @2}];

    [[NSNotificationCenter defaultCenter] postNotification:notification];

    self.window = [[UIWindow alloc]
                   initWithFrame:[[UIScreen mainScreen] bounds]];
    self.window.backgroundColor = [UIColor whiteColor];
    [self.window makeKeyAndVisible];
    return YES;
}
```

## Discussion

A notification object is encapsulated in an instance of the `NSNotification` class. A notification object on its own is really nothing until it has been posted to the app using a notification center. A notification object has three important properties:

*Name*
: This is a string. When a listener starts listening for notifications, it has to specify the name of the notification, as we will see later in this chapter. If you are posting a notification in a class of yours, ensure that the name of that notification is well documented, and even better, that you export that string symbol in your header file. We are going to see an example of this soon in this recipe.

*Sender object*
: You can optionally specify the object that is sending the notification. Usually this will be set to `self`. But why do we need to even specify the sender of a notification? This information is useful for the parts of the app that listen for notifications. Let's say that, in one of your classes, you are sending a notification with the name of *`MyNotification`* and another class in your application is sending a notification with the exact same name. When a listener starts listening for the *`MyNotification`* notification, the receiver can specify which notification source it is interested in. So the receiver can say that it wants to receive all notifications with the name of *`MyNotification`* coming from a specific object, but not from the second object. This way, the receiver can really be in control. Even though you can leave the Sender

Object field as nil when posting a notification, it is much better to set this property to `self`, the object that is sending the notification.

*User info dictionary*
: This is a dictionary object that you can attach to your notification object. The receiver can then read this dictionary when it receives the notification. Think of this as an opportunity to pass additional information to the receivers of your notification.

## See Also

Recipe 17.0, "Introduction"

# 17.2. Listening for and Reacting to Notifications

## Problem

You want to react to a notification that is being sent either by your app or by the system.

## Solution

Listen to a particular notification by calling the `addObserver:selector:name:object:` method of the default notification center. This method has the following parameters:

`addObserver`
: The object that is going to observe a given notification. So if this is the current class, put `self` here to point to the current instance of your class.

`selector`
: The selector that will receive the notification. This selector has to have one parameter of type `NSNotification`.

`name`
: The name of the notification that you want to listen to.

`object`
: The object that is going to send you the notification. For instance, if a notification with the same name is being sent from two objects, you can narrow your target and only listen for the notification that comes from Object A instead of both Object A and Object B.

When you no longer want to receive notifications, issue the `removeObserver:` instance method of the `NSNotificationCenter` class. Make sure that you do this because the notification center retains instances of listener objects. You could encounter memory leaks or errors if the notification center retains an instance of your class after it has been released, so make sure that you remove yourself from the observers list.

## Discussion

An example can make this whole thing very easy. What we are going to do in this example is create a class named `Person` and add two properties to it: a first name and a last name, both of type `NSString`. Then in our app delegate, we are going to instantiate an object of type `Person`. Instead of setting the first name and the last name of the person, we are going to send a notification to the notification center, and in the user info dictionary of the notification, we are going to put the first name and the last name of type `NSString`. In the initialization method of our `Person` class, we are going to listen for the notification that comes from the app delegate and then extract the first name and last name from its user info dictionary and set the person's properties to those values.

So here is the header file of our app delegate:

```
#import <UIKit/UIKit.h>

/* The name of the notification that we are going to send */
extern NSString *const kSetPersonInfoNotification;
/* The first-name key in the user-info dictionary of our notification */
extern NSString *const kSetPersonInfoKeyFirstName;
/* The last-name key in the user-info dictionary of our notification */
extern NSString *const kSetPersonInfoKeyLastName;

@interface AppDelegate : UIResponder <UIApplicationDelegate>

@property (nonatomic, strong) UIWindow *window;

@end
```

And here is the implementation of our app delegate:

```
#import "AppDelegate.h"
#import "Person.h"

NSString *const kSetPersonInfoNotification = @"SetPersonInfoNotification";
NSString *const kSetPersonInfoKeyFirstName = @"firstName";
NSString *const kSetPersonInfoKeyLastName = @"lastName";

@implementation AppDelegate

- (BOOL)            application:(UIApplication *)application
  didFinishLaunchingWithOptions:(NSDictionary *)launchOptions{

    Person *steveJobs = [[Person alloc] init];

    NSNotification *notification =
    [NSNotification
     notificationWithName:kSetPersonInfoNotification
```

```
                                    object:self
                                    userInfo:@{kSetPersonInfoKeyFirstName : @"Steve",
                                               kSetPersonInfoKeyLastName : @"Jobs"}];

    /* The person class is currently listening for this notification. That class
     will extract the first name and last name from it and set its own first
     name and last name based on the userInfo dictionary of the notification. */
    [[NSNotificationCenter defaultCenter] postNotification:notification];

    /* Here is proof */
    NSLog(@"Person's first name = %@", steveJobs.firstName);
    NSLog(@"Person's last name = %@", steveJobs.lastName);

    self.window = [[UIWindow alloc]
                   initWithFrame:[[UIScreen mainScreen] bounds]];
    self.window.backgroundColor = [UIColor whiteColor];
    [self.window makeKeyAndVisible];
    return YES;
}
```

The important part is the implementation of the `Person` class (*Person.m*):

```
#import "Person.h"
#import "AppDelegate.h"

@implementation Person

- (void) handleSetPersonInfoNotification:(NSNotification *)paramNotification{

    self.firstName = paramNotification.userInfo[kSetPersonInfoKeyFirstName];
    self.lastName = paramNotification.userInfo[kSetPersonInfoKeyLastName];

}

- (instancetype) init{
    self = [super init];
    if (self != nil){

        NSNotificationCenter *center = [NSNotificationCenter defaultCenter];

        [center addObserver:self
                   selector:@selector(handleSetPersonInfoNotification:)
                       name:kSetPersonInfoNotification
                     object:[[UIApplication sharedApplication] delegate]];

    }
    return self;
}

- (void) dealloc{
    [[NSNotificationCenter defaultCenter] removeObserver:self];
}
@end
```

The value that you specify for the `object` parameter of the `addObserver:selector:name:object:` method is the object where you expect the notification to originate. If any other object sends a notification with the same name, your listener won't be asked to handle that. You would normally specify this object when you know exactly which object is going to send the notification you want to listen to. This may not always be possible, such as in a very complex application where one view controller in one tab has to listen for notifications from another view controller in another tab. In that case, the listener won't necessarily have a reference to the instance of the view controller from where the notification will be originated, so in this case you can pass `nil` for the `parameter` of the aforementioned method.

When you run this app, you will see the following printed to the console:

```
Person's first name = Steve
Person's last name = Jobs
```

So this was a notification that we sent and received from within our app. What about system notifications? We will talk about them a bit more in detail later, but for now, while in Xcode, press the Command+Shift+O key combinations (O for Open) and type in *UIWindow.h*. Once you open this header file, look for `UIKeyboardWillShowNotification` and you will find a block of code like so:

```
//Each notification includes a nil object and a userInfo
//dictionary containing the beginning and ending keyboard frame in screen
//coordinates. Use the various UIView and UIWindow convertRect facilities
//to get the frame in the desired coordinate system. Animation key/value
//pairs are only available for the "will" family of notification.
UIKIT_EXTERN NSString *const UIKeyboardWillShowNotification;
UIKIT_EXTERN NSString *const UIKeyboardDidShowNotification;
UIKIT_EXTERN NSString *const UIKeyboardWillHideNotification;
UIKIT_EXTERN NSString *const UIKeyboardDidHideNotification;
```

That is Apple's code. We wrote our code in exactly the same way. Apple is exposing the notifications that the system sends and then documenting them. You need to do something similar. When creating notifications that are sent by components from within your app, make sure that you document them and tell programmers (maybe those on your team working on the same app) what values they should be expecting from the user info of your notification, along with anything else that they should know about your notifications.

# 17.3. Listening and Reacting to Keyboard Notifications

## Problem

You are allowing the user to enter text in your UI by using a component such as a text field or a text view that requires the keyboard's presence. However, when the keyboard pops up on the screen, it obstructs a good half of your UI, rendering it useless. You want to avoid this situation.

## Solution

Listen to the keyboard notifications and move your UI components up or down, or completely reshuffle them, so that although the keyboard is obstructing the screen, what is essential to the user is still visible. For more information about the actual notifications sent by the keyboard, please refer to the Discussion section of this recipe.

## Discussion

iOS devices do not have a physical keyboard. They have a software keyboard that pops up whenever the user has to enter some text into something like a text field (`UITextField`, described further in Recipe 1.19) or a text view (`UITextView`, described further in Recipe 1.20). On the iPad, the user can even split the keyboard and move it up and down. These are some of the edge cases that you might want to take care of when designing your user interface. You can work with the UI designers in your company (if you have access to such experts) and let them know about the possibility of the user splitting the keyboard on the iPad. They will need to know about that before making the art and creatives. We will discuss that edge case in this recipe.

Let's have a look at the keyboard on the iPhone first. The keyboard can be displayed in portrait and landscape mode. In portrait, the keyboard on an iPhone looks like Figure 17-1.

The keyboard in landscape mode on an iPhone will look similar to that shown in Figure 17-2.

On the iPad, however, the keyboard is a bit different. The most obvious difference is that the keyboard is actually much bigger in size than the one on the iPhone, since the iPad screen is physically bigger. The landscape keyboard on an iPad is obviously wider, but contains the same keys as the portrait-mode keyboard. Also, the user can split the keyboard if she wants to. This gives users better control over the keyboard but introduces challenges for programmers and even more for UX and UI designers.

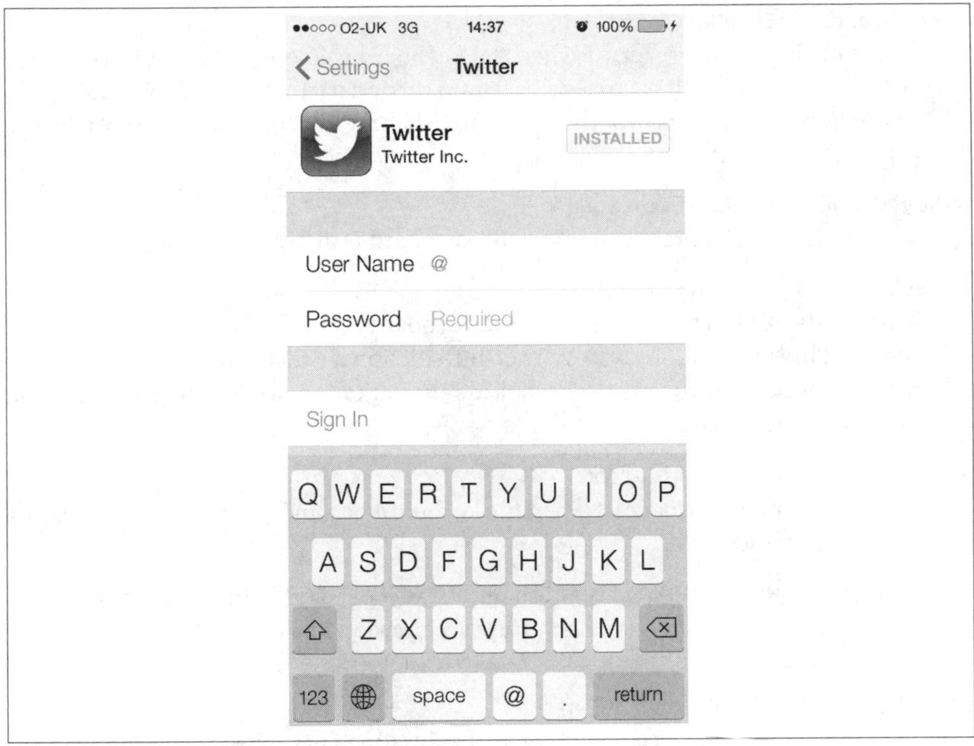


*Figure 17-1. Portrait-mode keyboard on an iPhone*

*Figure 17-2. The keyboard in landscape mode on an iPhone*

iOS broadcasts various notifications related to the display of the keyboard on the screen. Here is a list of these notifications and a brief explanation of each one:

`UIKeyboardWillShowNotification`
: This notification is broadcast when the keyboard is about to be displayed on the screen. This notification carries a user-info dictionary that contains various information about the keyboard, the animation that the keyboard uses to be displayed on the screen, and more.

`UIKeyboardDidShowNotification`
: This notification is broadcast when the keyboard is displayed on the screen.

`UIKeyboardWillHideNotification`
: This notification is broadcast when the keyboard is about to be removed from the screen. This notification carries a user-info dictionary that contains various information about the keyboard, the keyboard's animation when it is hiding, the duration of the animation, etc.

`UIKeyboardDidHideNotification`
: This notification is broadcast when the keyboard becomes fully hidden after being shown on the screen.

The `UIKeyboardWillShowNotification` and `UIKeyboardWillHideNotification` notifications carry a user-info dictionary. Here are the keys in those dictionaries that you might be interested in:

`UIKeyboardAnimationCurveUserInfoKey`
: The value of this key specifies the type of animation curve the keyboard is using to show or hide itself. This key contains a value (encapsulated in an object of type `NSValue`) of type `NSNumber` that itself contains an unsigned integer of type `NSUInteger`.

`UIKeyboardAnimationDurationUserInfoKey`
: The value of this key specifies the duration, in seconds, of the animation that the keyboard is using to show or hide itself. This key contains a value (encapsulated in an object of type `NSValue`) of type `NSNumber` that itself contains a double value of type `double`.

`UIKeyboardFrameBeginUserInfoKey`
: The value of this key specifies the frame of the keyboard before the animation happens. If the keyboard is about to be displayed, this is the frame before the keyboard appears. If the keyboard is already displayed and is about to hide, it is the frame of the keyboard as it is on the screen before it animates out of the screen. This key contains a value (encapsulated in an object of type `NSValue`) of type `CGRect`.

`UIKeyboardFrameEndUserInfoKey`
: The value of this key specifies the frame of the keyboard after the animation happens. If the keyboard is about to be displayed, this is the frame after the keyboard is animated fully displayed. If the keyboard is already displayed and is about to hide, it is the frame of the keyboard after it is fully hidden. This key contains a value (encapsulated in an object of type `NSValue`) of type `CGRect`.

The frames that get reported by iOS as the beginning and ending frames of the keyboard do not take into account the orientation of the device. You need to convert the reported `CGRect` values to a relevant orientation-aware coordinate, as we will see soon in this recipe.

Let's have a look at an example here. We are going to create a simple single-view application that runs only on the iPhone and displays an image view and a text field. The text field is going to be located at the bottom of the screen. So when the user taps on the text field to enter some text into it, the keyboard will pop up and block the text field completely. Our mission is to animate the contents of our view up to make them visible even if the keyboard is displayed on the screen. We are going to use storyboards for this app. In the view controller, we are going to fill the view with a scroll view and place the image view and a text field in the scroll view, as shown in Figure 17-3.

The superview of the image view and the text field is a scroll view that is filling the whole parent view's space.

I have already hooked the scroll view, the image view, and the text field from the storyboard into the implementation file of the view controller like so:

```
#import "ViewController.h"

@interface ViewController () <UITextFieldDelegate>
@property (weak, nonatomic) IBOutlet UIScrollView *scrollView;
@property (weak, nonatomic) IBOutlet UITextField *textField;
@property (weak, nonatomic) IBOutlet UIImageView *imageView;
@end

@implementation ViewController

...
```

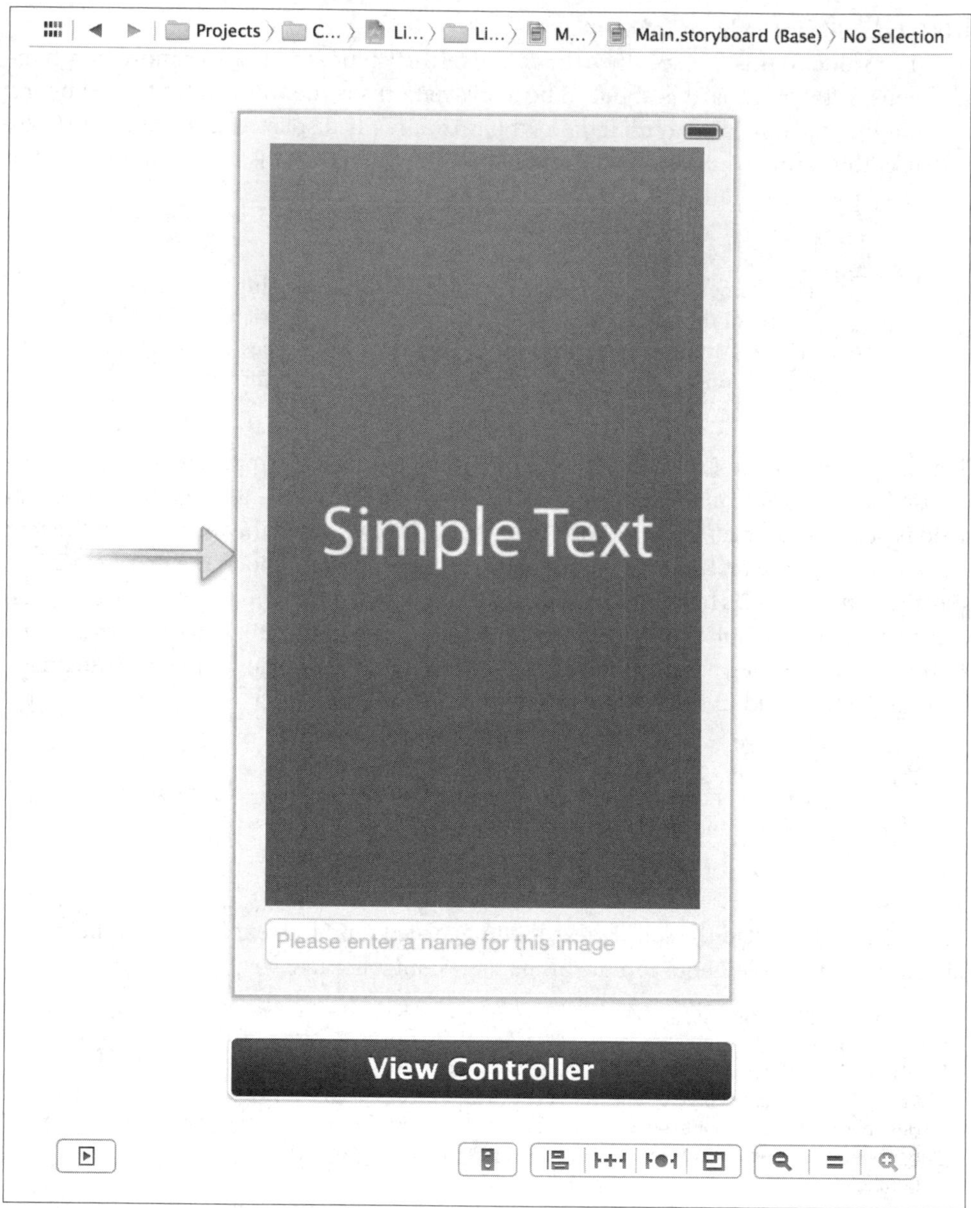


*Figure 17-3. A simple storyboard with an image view and a text field*

Now that our outlets are hooked into properties in our view controller, we can start listening to keyboard notifications:

```
- (void) viewWillAppear:(BOOL)paramAnimated{
    [super viewWillAppear:paramAnimated];
```

```
    NSNotificationCenter *center = [NSNotificationCenter defaultCenter];

    [center addObserver:self selector:@selector(handleKeyboardWillShow:)
                   name:UIKeyboardWillShowNotification object:nil];

    [center addObserver:self selector:@selector(handleKeyboardWillHide:)
                   name:UIKeyboardWillHideNotification object:nil];
}

- (void)viewWillDisappear:(BOOL)paramAnimated{
    [super viewWillDisappear:paramAnimated];
    [[NSNotificationCenter defaultCenter] removeObserver:self];
}
```

A common mistake programmers make is to keep listening for keyboard notifications when their view controller's view is not on the screen. They start listening for notifications in the `viewDidLoad` method and remove themselves as the observer in the `dealloc` method. This is a problematic approach because when your view is off the screen and the keyboard is getting displayed on some other view, you should not be adjusting any components on your view controller. Keep in mind that keyboard notifications, just like any other notification, are broadcast to all observer objects within the context of your application, so you need to take extra care that you do not react to keyboard notifications while your view is off-screen.

In the previous code snippet, we started listening for keyboard-will-show notifications on the `handleKeyboardWillShow:` instance method of our view controller, and expect the keyboard-will-hide notifications on the `handleKeyboardWillHide:` method. These methods are not coded yet. Let's start with the first method, the `handleKeyboardWillShow:`. What we have to do here is detect the height of the keyboard using the `UIKeyboardFrameEndUserInfoKey` key inside the user-info dictionary that gets sent to us for this notification, and using that value to shift up our view's contents by the height of the keyboard. The good news is that we have placed the contents of our view in a scroll view, so all we have to do is adjust the edge insets of the scroll view.

```
- (void) handleKeyboardWillShow:(NSNotification *)paramNotification{

    NSDictionary *userInfo = paramNotification.userInfo;

    /* Get the duration of the animation of the keyboard for when it
     gets displayed on the screen. We will animate our contents using
     the same animation duration */
    NSValue *animationDurationObject =
        userInfo[UIKeyboardAnimationDurationUserInfoKey];

    NSValue *keyboardEndRectObject = userInfo[UIKeyboardFrameEndUserInfoKey];
```

```
    double animationDuration = 0.0;
    CGRect keyboardEndRect = CGRectMake(0.0f, 0.0f, 0.0f, 0.0f);

    [animationDurationObject getValue:&animationDuration];
    [keyboardEndRectObject getValue:&keyboardEndRect];

    UIWindow *window = [UIApplication sharedApplication].keyWindow;

    /* Convert the frame from window's coordinate system to
     our view's coordinate system */
    keyboardEndRect = [self.view convertRect:keyboardEndRect
                                    fromView:window];

    /* Find out how much of our view is being covered by the keyboard */
    CGRect intersectionOfKeyboardRectAndWindowRect =
        CGRectIntersection(self.view.frame, keyboardEndRect);

    /* Scroll the scroll view up to show the full contents of our view */
    [UIView animateWithDuration:animationDuration animations:^{

        self.scrollView.contentInset =
        UIEdgeInsetsMake(0.0f,
                         0.0f,
                         intersectionOfKeyboardRectAndWindowRect.size.height,
                         0.0f);

        [self.scrollView scrollRectToVisible:self.textField.frame animated:NO];

    }];

}
```

Our code is quite interesting and straightforward here. The only thing that may require explanation is the `CGRectIntersection` function. What we are doing is retrieving the rectangular shape (top, left, width, and height) of the keyboard at the end of its animation when it gets displayed on the screen. Now that we have the dimensions of the keyboard, using the `CGRectIntersection` function, we can detect how much of our view is getting covered by the keyboard. So we take the frame of the keyboard and the frame of our view to find out how much of our frame's view is obscured by the frame of the keyboard. The result will be a structure of type `CGRect`, which is the rectangular area on our view that is obscured by the keyboard. Because we know the keyboard pops up from the bottom of the screen and animates up, the area of concern to us is vertical, so we retrieve the height of the intersection area and move up our contents by that much. We make the duration of our animation the same as the one used by the keyboard, so that our view and the keyboard move in sync.

The next stop is coding the `handleKeyboardWillHide:` method. This is where the keyboard will hide and no longer cover our view. So in this method, all we have to do is reset the edge insets of our scroll view, shifting everything down and back to its initial state:

```
- (void) handleKeyboardWillHide:(NSNotification *)paramSender{

    NSDictionary *userInfo = [paramSender userInfo];

    NSValue *animationDurationObject =
        [userInfo valueForKey:UIKeyboardAnimationDurationUserInfoKey];

    double animationDuration = 0.0;

    [animationDurationObject getValue:&animationDuration];

    [UIView animateWithDuration:animationDuration animations:^{
        self.scrollView.contentInset = UIEdgeInsetsZero;
    }];

}
```

Last but not least, because our view controller is the delegate of the text field, we need to ensure that the keyboard dismisses when the user presses the Return key on her keyboard after typing something into the text field:

```
- (BOOL) textFieldShouldReturn:(UITextField *)paramTextField{
    [paramTextField resignFirstResponder];

    return YES;
}
```

## See Also

Recipe 1.19; Recipe 1.20

# 17.4. Scheduling Local Notifications

## Problem

You are developing an app, such as an alarm clock or a calendar app, that needs to inform the user of an event at a specific time, even if your app is not running or is in the background.

## Solution

Instantiate an object of type `UILocalNotification`, configure it (we will see how), and schedule it using the `scheduleLocalNotification:` instance method of the `UIAppli cation` class. You can get the instance of your application object using the `sharedAp plication` class method of the `UIApplication` class.

## Discussion

A *local notification* is what gets presented to the user if your application is running in the background or not running at all. You can schedule the delivery of a local notification using the `scheduleLocalNotification:` instance method of `UIApplication`. If your app is running in the *foreground* and a scheduled local notification is fired, no alert is displayed to the user. Instead, iOS will silently, through an app delegate message, let you know that the notification was fired. Don't worry about this for now; we will go into details about all this quite soon.

You can ask iOS to deliver a local notification to the user in the future when your application is not even running. These notifications could also be recurring—for instance, every week at a certain time. However, extra care must be taken when you are specifying the *fire date* for your notifications.

The `cancelAllLocalNotifications` instance method cancels the delivery of all pending local notifications from your app.

A notification of type `UILocalNotification` has many properties. The most important properties of a local notification are the following:

`fireDate`
: This is a property of type `NSDate` that dictates to iOS when the instance of the local notification has to be fired. This is required.

`timeZone`
: This property is of type `NSTimeZone` and tells iOS in what time zone the given firedate is specified. You can get the current time zone using the `timeZone` instance method of the `NSCalendar` class, and you can get the current calendar using the `currentCalendar` class method of the aforementioned class.

`alertBody`
: This property is of type `NSString` and dictates the text that has to be displayed to the user when your notification is displayed on screen.

`hasAction`
: A Boolean property that tells iOS whether your app wants to take action when the notification happens. If you set this to `YES`, iOS displays the dialog specified by your `alertAction` property (described next) to the user. If you set this to `NO`, iOS just displays a dialog to the user indicating that the notification arrived.

`alertAction`
: If the `hasAction` property is set to `YES`, this property has to be set to a localized string that represents the action that the user can take on your local notification, should the notification be fired when the user doesn't have your app open in the foreground. iOS will subsequently display the message in the notification center or

in the lock screen. If the `hasAction` property has the value of `NO`, the `alertAction` property's value has to be nil.

`applicationIconBadgeNumber`
: If this local notification is required to change your app's icon badge number upon being fired, this property can be set to the desired badge number for your app icon. The value must be an integer. The proper way of assigning a value to this property is to set it to the current app's icon badge number, plus 1. You can get your app's current icon badge number using the `applicationIconBadgeNumber` property of `UIApplication` class.

`userInfo`
: This is an `NSDictionary` instance that can get attached to your notification and received back by your app when the notification is delivered. We usually use these dictionaries to include more information about the local notification, which can be useful for us when we have the notification delivered to our app.

The `hasAction` and `alertAction` properties combine to allow the user to swipe on your local notification in the notification center and, through that, make iOS open your app. That is how a user can take action on a local notification. This is extremely useful, especially if you are developing a calendar-like app where, for instance, you display a local notification to the user when the birthday of her friend is approaching in a few days. You can then allow her to take action on the notification. Perhaps, when she opens your app, you could even present some virtual gift options that she could send to her friend on his birthday.

The one thing that many programmers have issues with is the time zone of a local notification. Let's say the time is now 13:00 in London, the time zone is GMT+0, and your application is currently running on a user's device. You want to be able to deliver a notification at 14:00 to your user, even if your application is not running at that time. Now your user is on a plane at London's Gatwick Airport and plans to fly to Stockholm, where the time zone is GMT+1. If the flight takes 30 minutes, the user will be in Stockholm at 13:30 GMT+0 (London time) and at 14:30 GMT+1 (Stockholm time). However, when she lands, the iOS device will detect the change in the time zone of the system and will change the user's device time to 14:30. Your notification was supposed to occur at 14:00 (GMT+0), so as soon as the time zone is changed, iOS detects that the notification is due to be displayed (30 minutes earlier, in fact, with the new time zone) and will display your notification.

The issue is that your notification was supposed to be displayed at 14:00 GMT+0 or 15:00 GMT+1, and not 14:30 GMT+1. To deal with occasions such as this (which may be more common than you think, with modern travel habits), when specifying the date and time for your local notifications to be fired, you should also specify the time zone.

Let's put all this to the test and develop an app that can deliver a simple local notification 8 seconds after the user opens the app for the first time:

```
#import "AppDelegate.h"

@implementation AppDelegate

- (BOOL)            application:(UIApplication *)application
  didFinishLaunchingWithOptions:(NSDictionary *)launchOptions{

    UILocalNotification *notification = [[UILocalNotification alloc] init];

    /* Time and timezone settings */
    notification.fireDate = [NSDate dateWithTimeIntervalSinceNow:8.0];
    notification.timeZone = [[NSCalendar currentCalendar] timeZone];

    notification.alertBody =
        NSLocalizedString(@"A new item is downloaded.", nil);

    /* Action settings */
    notification.hasAction = YES;
    notification.alertAction = NSLocalizedString(@"View", nil);

    /* Badge settings */
    notification.applicationIconBadgeNumber =
        [UIApplication sharedApplication].applicationIconBadgeNumber + 1;

    /* Additional information, user info */
    notification.userInfo = @{@"Key 1" : @"Value 1",
                              @"Key 2" : @"Value 2"};

    /* Schedule the notification */
    [[UIApplication sharedApplication] scheduleLocalNotification:notification];

    self.window = [[UIWindow alloc]
                   initWithFrame:[[UIScreen mainScreen] bounds]];
    self.window.backgroundColor = [UIColor whiteColor];
    [self.window makeKeyAndVisible];
    return YES;
}
```

This is all good, but local notifications are quite useless if we don't know how to react to them and how to handle them once they are fired. Read Recipe 17.5 to find out how you can handle these notifications.

## See Also

Recipe 17.0, "Introduction"

## 17.5. Listening for and Reacting to Local Notifications

### Problem

You know how to schedule local notifications (see Recipe 17.4), but now you have to react to them when they are delivered to your app.

### Solution

Implement the `application:didReceiveLocalNotification:` method of your app delegate and read the `UIApplicationLaunchOptionsLocalNotificationKey` key of your app's launching options dictionary when the `application:didFinishLaunchingWithOptions:` method gets called on your app delegate. Read the Discussion section of this recipe for more information on why you have to handle a local notification in two places instead of just one.

### Discussion

Depending on the state of your app when a local notification is delivered and acted upon, you will have to handle it differently. Here are the different situations in which iOS may deliver a scheduled local notification to your app:

*The user has the app open in front of her while the local notification is delivered*
: In this case, the `application:didReceiveLocalNotification:` method is called when the notification is delivered.

*The user has sent the app to the background and the local notification is delivered*
: Once the user taps on the notification, iOS can launch your app. In this case, again, the `application:didReceiveLocalNotification:` method of your app delegate is called.

*The app is not open or at all active when the local notification is delivered*
: In this case, the `application:didFinishLaunchingWithOptions:` method of your app delegate is called and the `UIApplicationLaunchOptionsLocalNotificationKey` key inside the `didFinishLaunchingWithOptions` dictionary parameter of this method contains the local notification that caused your app to be woken up.

*The local notification is delivered while the user's device is locked, whether the app is active in the background or is not running at all*
: This will fire one of the previously mentioned ways of iOS opening your app, depending on whether your app was in the background or not while the user attempted to open your app using the notification.

Let's build on top of the example code that we learned about in Recipe 17.4. Regardless of the state of our app when the notification is fired, we'll handle it by displaying an alert to the user. First, we are going to put what we learned in Recipe 17.4 into a separate method so that we can just call that method and schedule a new local notification. The reason for doing this is so that when our app opens, we can check whether it opened as a result of the user tapping on a local notification in the notification center of iOS. If yes, we *won't* fire another local notification. Instead, we will act on the existing one. However, if a local notification did not open our app, we will schedule a new one. So here is the method in our app that schedules new local notifications to be delivered to our app 8 seconds after the method is called:

```
- (void) scheduleLocalNotification{

    UILocalNotification *notification = [[UILocalNotification alloc] init];

    /* Time and timezone settings */
    notification.fireDate = [NSDate dateWithTimeIntervalSinceNow:8.0];
    notification.timeZone = [[NSCalendar currentCalendar] timeZone];

    notification.alertBody =
        NSLocalizedString(@"A new item is downloaded.", nil);

    /* Action settings */
    notification.hasAction = YES;
    notification.alertAction = NSLocalizedString(@"View", nil);

    /* Badge settings */
    notification.applicationIconBadgeNumber =
        [UIApplication sharedApplication].applicationIconBadgeNumber + 1;

    /* Additional information, user info */
    notification.userInfo = @{@"Key 1" : @"Value 1",
                              @"Key 2" : @"Value 2"};

    /* Schedule the notification */
    [[UIApplication sharedApplication] scheduleLocalNotification:notification];

}
```

The method that we have written here is called `scheduleLocalNotification`. All it does, as its name suggests, is create the notification object and ask iOS to schedule it. Don't confuse our custom method named `scheduleLocalNotification` with the iOS method on `UIApplication` named `scheduleLocalNotification:` (note the colon at the end of the iOS method). You can think of our method as a handy utility method that does the hard work of scheduling a local notification by creating the notification and delegating the scheduling activity to iOS.

Now, in our `application:didFinishLaunchingWithOptions` method, we will check whether an existing notification was the reason our app opened in the first place. If yes, we will act upon the existing local notification. If no, we will schedule a new one:

```
- (BOOL)            application:(UIApplication *)application
  didFinishLaunchingWithOptions:(NSDictionary *)launchOptions{
```

```
    if (launchOptions[UIApplicationLaunchOptionsLocalNotificationKey] != nil){
        UILocalNotification *notification =
        launchOptions[UIApplicationLaunchOptionsLocalNotificationKey];
        [self application:application didReceiveLocalNotification:notification];
    } else {
        [self scheduleLocalNotification];
    }

    self.window = [[UIWindow alloc]
                   initWithFrame:[[UIScreen mainScreen] bounds]];
    self.window.backgroundColor = [UIColor whiteColor];
    [self.window makeKeyAndVisible];
    return YES;
}
```

In the preceding code, when an existing local notification caused our app to get launched, we redirected the local notification to the `application:didReceiveLocalNotification:` method, where we acted upon the existing notification and displayed an alert to the user. Here is our simple implementation of the aforementioned method:

```
- (void)            application:(UIApplication *)application
    didReceiveLocalNotification:(UILocalNotification *)notification{

    NSString *key1Value = notification.userInfo[@"Key 1"];
    NSString *key2Value = notification.userInfo[@"Key 2"];

    if ([key1Value length] > 0 &&
        [key2Value length] > 0){

        UIAlertView *alert =
        [[UIAlertView alloc] initWithTitle:nil
                                   message:@"Handling the local notification"
                                  delegate:nil
                         cancelButtonTitle:@"OK"
                         otherButtonTitles:nil];
        [alert show];

    }

}
```

Give it a go now. You can try different combinations. Open the app and then keep it in the foregorund, send it to the background, or even close it permanently. Take a look at how the app behaves in the various conditions that you put it in.

## See Also

Recipe 17.0, "Introduction"; Recipe 17.4

## 17.6. Handling Local System Notifications

### Problem

When your application is brought to the foreground, you want to be able to get notifications about important system changes, such as the user's locale changes.

### Solution

Simply listen to one of the many system notifications that iOS sends to waking applications. Some of these notifications are listed here:

`NSCurrentLocaleDidChangeNotification`
: This notification is delivered to applications when the user changes her locale; for instance, if the user switches her iOS device's language from English to Spanish in the Settings page of the device.

`NSUserDefaultsDidChangeNotification`
: This notification is fired when the user changes the application's settings in the Settings page of the iOS device (if any settings are provided to the user).

`UIDeviceBatteryStateDidChangeNotification`
: This notification gets sent whenever the state of the battery of the iOS device is changed. For instance, if the device is plugged into a computer when the application is in the foreground, and then unplugged when in the background, the application will receive this notification (if the application has registered for this notification). The state can then be read using the `batteryState` property of an instance of `UIDevice`.

`UIDeviceProximityStateDidChangeNotification`
: This notification gets sent whenever the state of the proximity sensor changes. The last state is available through the `proximityState` property of an instance of `UIDevice`.

### Discussion

When your application is in the background, a lot of things could happen! For instance, the user might suddenly change the language of her iOS device through the Settings page from English to Spanish. Applications can register themselves for such notifications. These notifications will be coalesced and then delivered to a waking application.

Let me explain what I mean by the term *coalesced*. Suppose your application is in the foreground and you have registered for `UIDeviceOrientationDidChangeNotification` notifications. Now the user presses the Home button and your application gets sent to the background. The user then rotates the device from portrait to landscape right, back to portrait, and then to landscape left. When the user brings your application to the foreground, you will receive only *one* notification of type `UIDeviceOrientationDidChangeNotification`. This is coalescing. All the other orientations that happened along the way before your application opens are not important (since your application isn't on the screen) and the system will not deliver them to your application. However, the system will deliver at least one notification for each aspect of the system, such as orientation, and you can then detect the most up-to-date orientation of the device.

Here is the implementation of a simple view controller that takes advantage of this technique to determine changes in orientation:

```
#import "ViewController.h"

@implementation ViewController

- (void) orientationChanged:(NSNotification *)paramNotification{
    NSLog(@"Orientation Changed");
}

- (void)viewDidAppear:(BOOL)paramAnimated{

    [super viewDidAppear:paramAnimated];

    /* Listen for the notification */
    [[NSNotificationCenter defaultCenter]
     addObserver:self
     selector:@selector(orientationChanged:)
     name:UIDeviceOrientationDidChangeNotification
     object:nil];

}

- (void) viewDidDisappear:(BOOL)paramAnimated{
    [super viewDidDisappear:paramAnimated];

    /* Stop listening for the notification */
    [[NSNotificationCenter defaultCenter]
     removeObserver:self
     name:UIDeviceOrientationDidChangeNotification
     object:nil];

}

@end
```

Run the application on the device now. After the view controller is displayed on the screen, press the Home button to send the application to the background. Now try changing the orientation of the device a couple of times, and then relaunch the application. Observe the results, and you will see that initially when your application opens, at most, one notification has been sent to the `orientationChanged:` method. You might get a second call, though, if your view hierarchy supports orientation changes.

Now let's say that your application exposes a settings bundle to the user. You want to get notified of the changes the user has made to your application's settings (while the application was in the background) as soon as your application is brought to the foreground. To do this, you should register for the `NSUserDefaultsDidChangeNotification` notification.

Applications written for iOS can expose a bundle file for their settings. These settings are available to users through the Settings application on their device. To get a better understanding of how this works, let's create a settings bundle:

1. In Xcode, choose File → New File.
2. Make sure the iOS category is selected on the left.
3. Choose the Resources subcategory.
4. Choose Settings Bundle as the file type and click Next.
5. Set the filename as *Settings.bundle.*
6. Click Save.

Now you have a file in Xcode named *Settings.bundle*. Leave this file as it is, without modifying it. Press the Home button on the device and go to the device's Settings application. If you have named your application "Foo" you will see "Foo" in the Settings application, as shown in Figure 17-4 (the name of the sample application I created is "Handling Local System Notifications").

Tap on your application's name to see the settings your application exposes to the user. What we want to know is when the user changes these settings, so that we can adjust our application's internal state if required. Let's go ahead and start listening for the `NSUserDefaultsDidChangeNotification` notification in our app delegate. When our app terminates, obviously, we will remove our app delegate from the notification chain:

```
#import "AppDelegate.h"

@implementation AppDelegate

- (void) handleSettingsChanged:(NSNotification *)paramNotification{

    NSLog(@"Settings changed");
    NSLog(@"Notification Object = %@", paramNotification.object);

}

- (BOOL)            application:(UIApplication *)application
  didFinishLaunchingWithOptions:(NSDictionary *)launchOptions{

    [[NSNotificationCenter defaultCenter]
         addObserver:self
         selector:@selector(handleSettingsChanged:)
```

```
            name:NSUserDefaultsDidChangeNotification
            object:nil];

    return YES;
}

- (void)applicationWillTerminate:(UIApplication *)application{
    [[NSNotificationCenter defaultCenter] removeObserver:self];
}
```

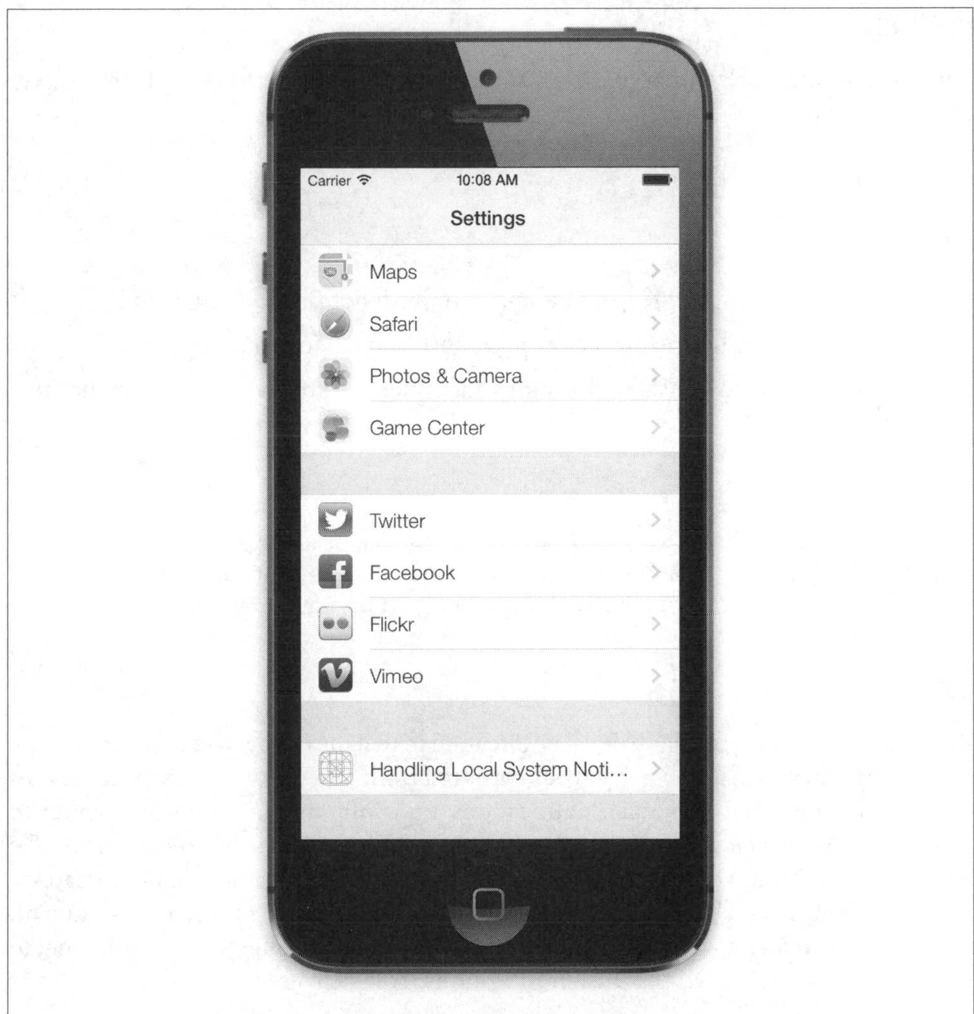


*Figure 17-4. Our Settings.bundle displayed in the Settings app on iOS Simulator*

Now try to change some of these settings while your application is running in the background. After you are done, bring the application to the foreground, and you will see that only one `NSUserDefaultsDidChangeNotification` notification will be delivered to your application. The object attached to this notification will be of type `NSUserDefaults` and will contain your application's settings `user defaults`.

# 17.7. Setting Up Your App for Push Notifications

## Problem

You want to configure your application so that you can push notifications from a server to various devices.

## Solution

Follow these steps:

1. Set up a provision profile for your app with push notifications enabled.
2. In your app, register the device for push notifications for your app.
3. Collect the device's push notifications identifier for your app and send that to a server.

In this recipe, we are going to discuss setting up and registering your app for push notifications. We are not going to talk about the server side of things yet. We will discuss that part in another recipe.

## Discussion

Push notifications are similar to local notification in that they allow you to communicate something with the user even when your app is not running. Although local notifications are scheduled by your app, push notifications are configured and sent by a server to Apple, and Apple will push the notifications to various devices around the world. The server part of things needs to be done by us. We then compose the push notifications and send them to Apple Push Notification Services servers (or APNS, as it is known). APNS will then attempt to deliver our push notifications through a secure channel to devices that we designated the push notifications to be delivered to.

For iOS apps to be able to receive push notifications, they have to have a valid provision profile that has push notifications enabled. To configure your profile properly, follow these steps:

I am assuming that you have already set up your development and distribution certificates in your developer portal. You can use Xcode's new Accounts settings to automatically configure your certificates. Simply go to Xcode's Preferences and then open the Accounts pane. Add your Apple ID in the Accounts list and allow Xcode to configure your certificates for you.

1. Log into the iOS Dev Center (*http://bit.ly/19h9aLw*).
2. Navigate to the Certificates, Identifiers & Profiles section on the righthand side.
3. In the Identifiers section, create a new App ID for yourself with a valid Explicit App ID such as *`com.pixolity.ios.cookbook.PushNotificationApp`*. Note that this is the reverse domain style name that I've picked for this example app. Pick a reverse domain-style App ID that makes sense to you or your organization.
4. Under the App Services section of the new App ID page, ensure that you've enabled the Push Notifications box as shown in Figure 17-5.

App Services

Select the services you would like to enable in your app. You can edit your choices after this App ID has been registered.

Enable Services: Data Protection
Complete Protection
Protected Unless Open
Protected Until First User Authentication
Game Center
iCloud
In-App Purchase
Inter-App Audio
Passbook
Push Notifications

Cancel Continue

*Figure 17-5. Enabling push notifications for an App ID*

5. Once you are happy with the configuration of your App ID (see Figure 17-6), submit the App ID to Apple.
6. After you have set all your App ID configurations, generate your App ID and then navigate to the Provisioning Profiles section of the iOS portal.
7. Create a Development provision profile for your app. You can create the Ad Hoc and the App Store versions later, but for now you just need the Development provision profile to get started. The process is the same for Ad Hoc and App Store profiles, so don't worry. You can simply come back to this step when you are ready to submit your app to the App Store, and you will be able to generate the Ad Hoc and the App Store profiles.

   Ensure that your new development provision profile is linked to the App ID that you generated earlier. This is the first question that you will be asked when generating the provision profile.

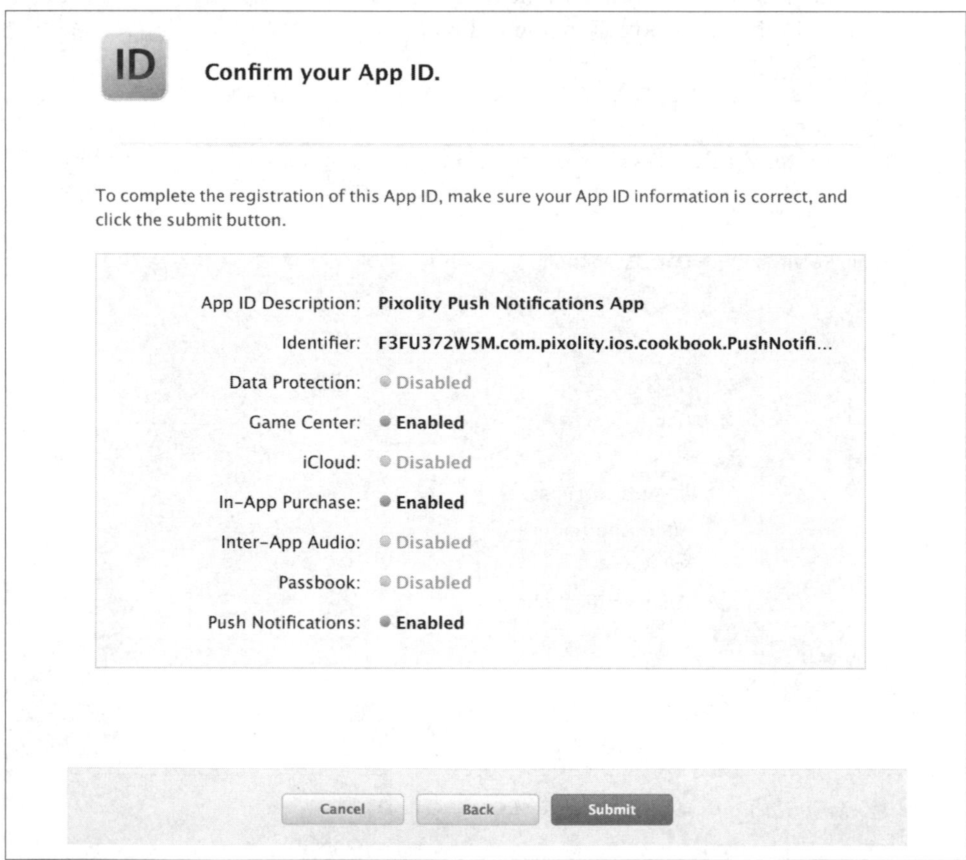


*Figure 17-6. Creating an App ID with push notifications*

8. Once your profile is ready, download it and drag and drop it into iTunes on your computer in order to install it. Avoid double-clicking on the profile to install it. Doing so will change the name of the installed profile's filename to the MD5 hash name of the profile, which is very difficult to identify on disk. If you drag and drop the profile in iTunes, iTunes will install the profile with its original name.
9. In your app's build settings in Xcode, simply select to build with the provision profile that you just created. Ensure that you are using this profile for Development and use the App Store or Ad Hoc profile that you'll create later for the Release scheme.
10. Drag and drop your provision profile into a text editor, such as TextEdit, on OS X and find the `Entitlements` key in there. The entire section in my provision profile looks like this:

```
<key>Entitlements</key>
<dict>
    <key>application-identifier</key>
    <string>F3FU372W5M.com.pixolity.ios.cookbook.PushNotificationApp</string>
    <key>aps-environment</key>
    <string>development</string>
    <key>get-task-allow</key>
    <true/>
    <key>keychain-access-groups</key>
    <array>
        <string>F3FU372W5M.*</string>
    </array>
</dict>
```

11. Create a new plist in your Xcode project and name it *Entitlements.plist*. Right-clic that file in Xcode and select Open As and then Source Code. Your file's contents will initially look like this:

```
<plist version="1.0">
<dict/>
</plist>
```

12. Put the entitlements of your provision profile right into the *Entitlements.plist* file so that its contents will look like this:

```
<plist version="1.0">
<dict>
    <key>application-identifier</key>
    <string>F3FU372W5M.com.pixolity.ios.cookbook.PushNotificationApp</string>
    <key>aps-environment</key>
    <string>development</string>
    <key>get-task-allow</key>
    <true/>
    <key>keychain-access-groups</key>
    <array>
```

```
        <string>F3FU372W5M.*</string>
    </array>
</dict>
</plist>
```

The values shown here in our code snippets relate to the profiles that *I* have created. The profile that you'll create will have different values and certainly will have a different App ID, so follow the previous steps to create your App ID and profile properly, then grab the entitlements for *your* profile and place them in the *Entitlements.plist* file in your project.

13. Now go to the build settings of your project, and in the Code Signing Entitlements section, enter the value of *$(SRCROOT)/$(TARGET_NAME)/Entitlements.plist* if you created your entitlements file under your project's target folder, or enter *$(SRCROOT)/Entitlements.plist* if you created the entitlements file under the root folder of your source codes. If you are confused, simply try these two values, and after setting them, try to build your project. If Xcode complains that it cannot find the entitlements file, try the other value, and it should work. The Code Signing Entitlements build setting requires the relative path of the entitlements file from the root folder of your source code. So if you have placed this file into another folder, you'll have to manually calculate the path to the file and feed it to this field.
14. Build your project and make sure no error is thrown by Xcode. If you are getting an error, it is probably because you have not set the proper provision profile to use or you have entered the wrong path for the Code Signing Entitlements in your build settings.
15. In your app delegate, invoke the `registerForRemoteNotificationTypes:` method of your `UIApplication` and pass the values `UIRemoteNotificationTypeAlert`, `UIRemoteNotificationTypeBadge` and `UIRemoteNotificationTypeSound` to that method, as you can see here:

```
- (BOOL)            application:(UIApplication *)application
  didFinishLaunchingWithOptions:(NSDictionary *)launchOptions{

    [[UIApplication sharedApplication] registerForRemoteNotificationTypes:
     UIRemoteNotificationTypeAlert |
     UIRemoteNotificationTypeBadge |
     UIRemoteNotificationTypeSound];

    self.window = [[UIWindow alloc]
                   initWithFrame:[[UIScreen mainScreen] bounds]];
    self.window.backgroundColor = [UIColor whiteColor];
    [self.window makeKeyAndVisible];
    return YES;
}
```

This will ensure that your app is registered to receive push notifications that can carry alert messages, badge number modifications to your app icon, and also sounds. Don't worry about this for now. Just register your app for push notifications, as shown before. Once you do this, iOS will send a push notification registration request to APNS. Upon doing this, iOS will first ask the user for permission to register your app for push notifications. The UI of that permission request by iOS will look like Figure 17-7.

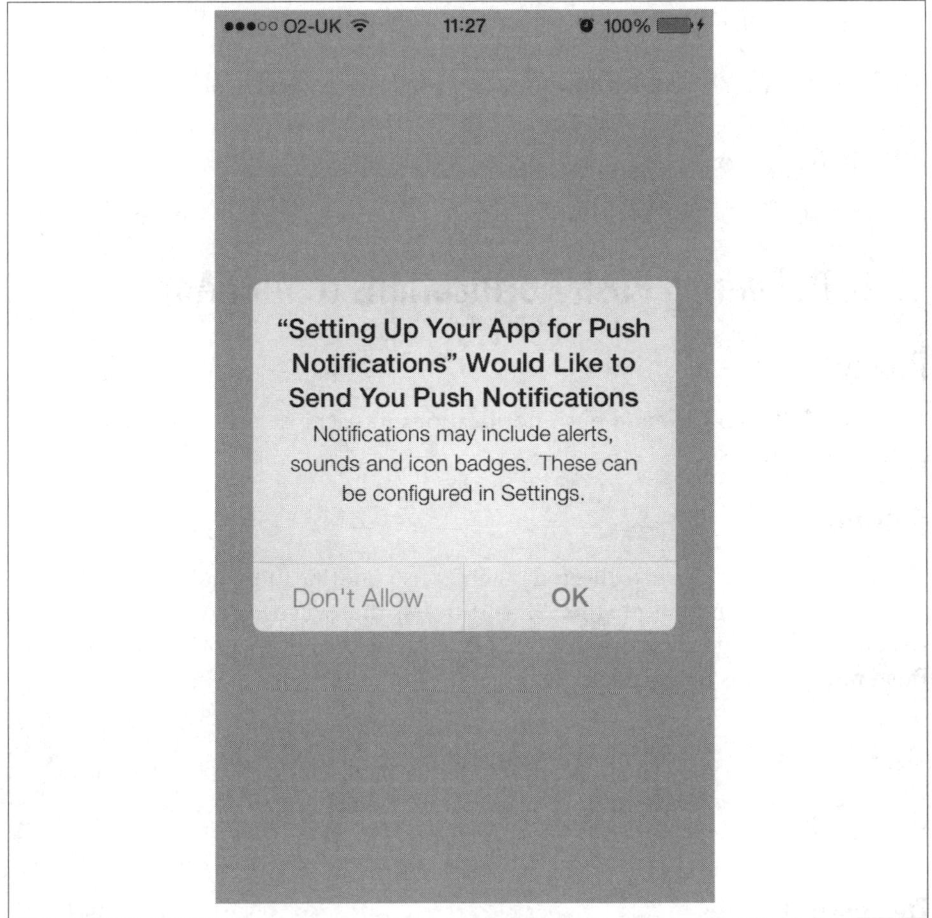


*Figure 17-7. iOS displaying a push notifications permission request screen to the user*

16. Now implement the `application:didRegisterForRemoteNotificationsWithDeviceToken:` method of your app delegate. This method is called when iOS

successfully registers this device with the APNS and assigns a token to it. This token is only for this app and only for this device.

17. Next, implement the `application:didFailToRegisterForRemoteNotifications WithError:` method of your app delegate. This method is called if iOS fails to register your app for push notifications. This could happen if your profile is set up incorrectly or the device doesn't have an Internet connection, among many other reasons. The `didFailToRegisterForRemoteNotificationsWithError` parameter will give you an error of type `NSError` that you can analyze to find out the source of the problem.

That was all you needed to know to set up your app to receive push notifications.

### See Also

Recipe 17.0, "Introduction"

## 17.8. Delivering Push Notifications to Your App

### Problem

You want to be able to send push notifications to users' devices that are registered for push notifications.

### Solution

Ensure that you have collected their push notification token identifiers (see Recipe 17.7). Then generate the SSL certificates that will be used by your web services to send push notifications to devices. Once done, create a simple web service to send push notifications to registered devices.

This recipe is a follow-up to Recipe 17.7. Ensure that you have read and understood that recipe before proceeding with this one.

### Discussion

In order to be able to communicate with the APNS, your web services need to do *handshaking* with the APNS using an Apple-issued SSL certificate. To generate this certificate, follow these steps:

1. Log into the iOS Dev Center (*http://bit.ly/19h9aLw*).
2. Navigate to the Certificates, Identifiers & Profiles section on the righthand side.

3. In the App IDs section, find the App ID for your app that has push notifications set up for it, select that App ID, and press the Settings button to configure it, as shown in Figure 17-8.

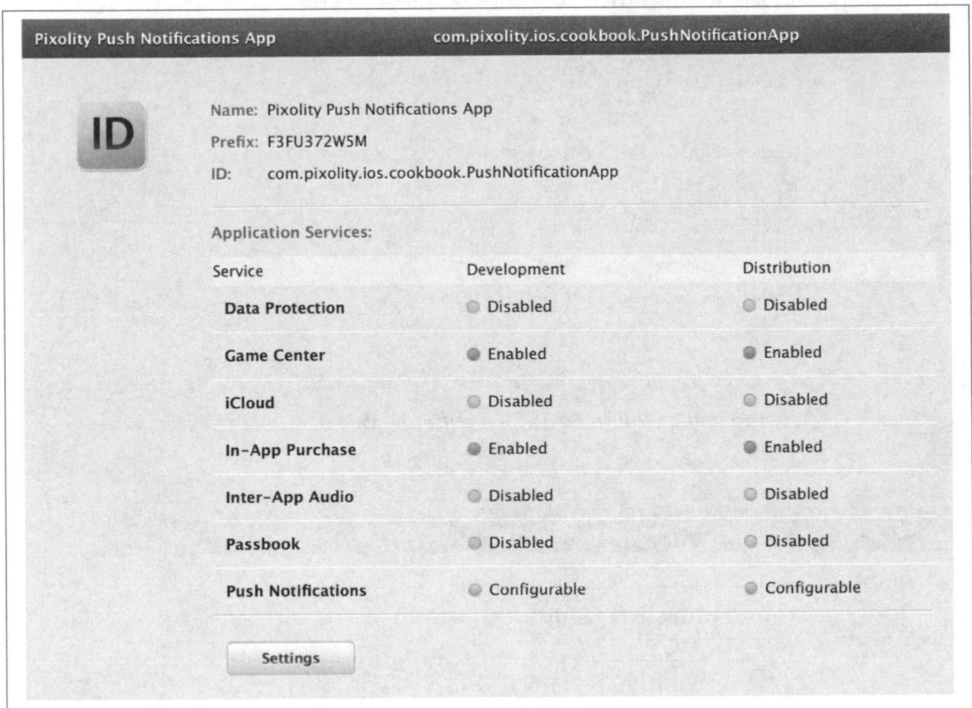


*Figure 17-8. Modifying the settings of an existing App ID*

4. In the Push Notifications section of the settings, under the Development SSL Certificate section, press the Create Certificate button (see Figure 17-9) and follow the guidance that Apple will provide you to create your certificate. We are creating the Development push notification SSL certificate for now, because we are solely focusing on the development part. Later, when you are ready to ship your app to the App Store, simply go through a similar process to create the Distribution version of the SSL certificates.
5. Once your certificate is ready (see Figure 17-10), download it onto your computer and double-click it to import it into your keychain.

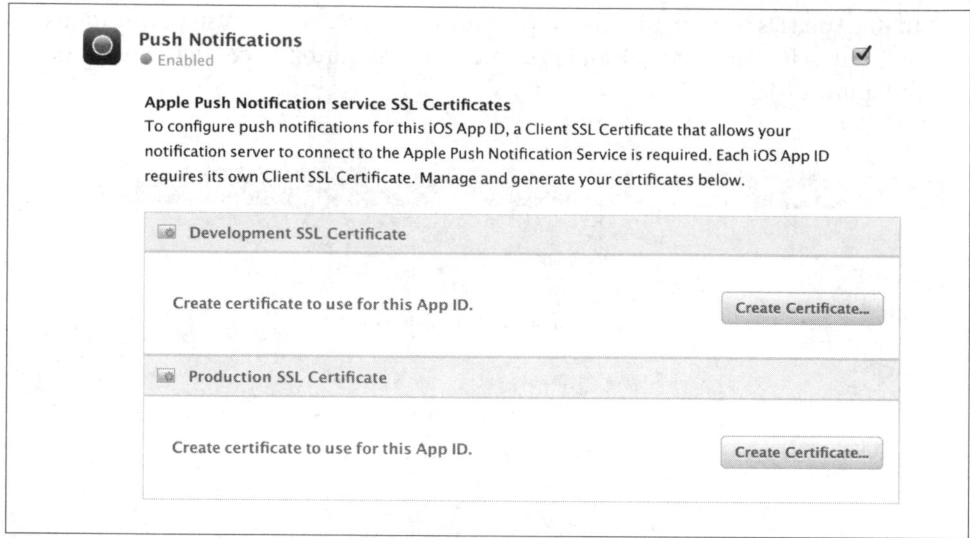


*Figure 17-9. Creating a Development SSL Certificate for push notifications*

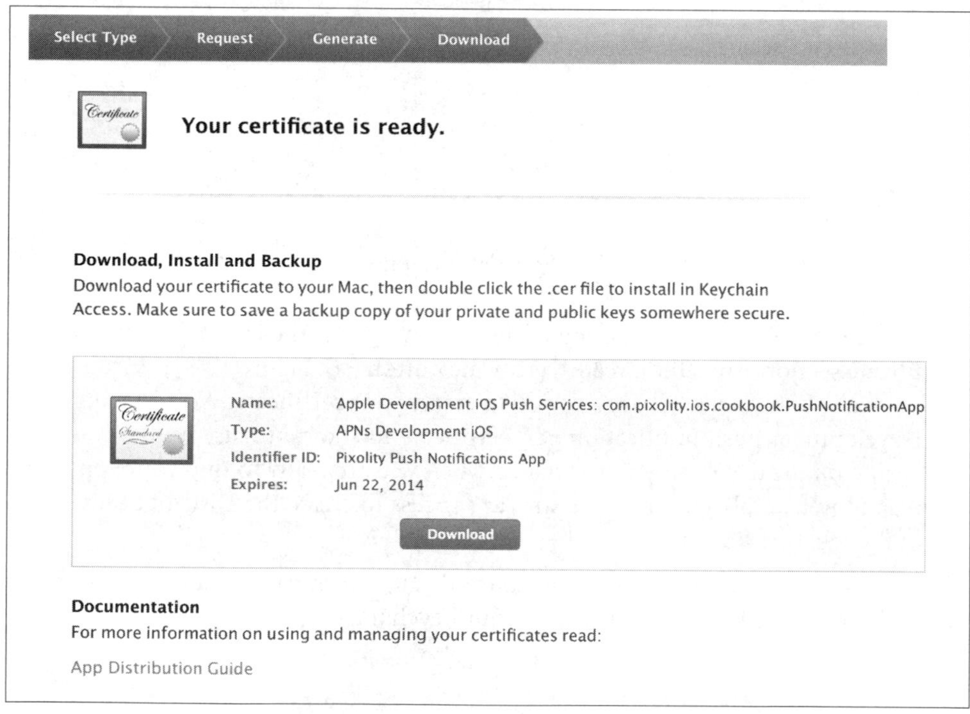


*Figure 17-10. Development APNS SSL certificate is ready to download*

6. Now open Keychain Access on OS X and go to the Login keychain (if that's your default keychain). Under the My Certificates section, find the certificate that you just imported into the keychain and expand it by clicking the little arrow button to its lefthand side, in order to reveal the associated private key for that certificate (see Figure 17-11).

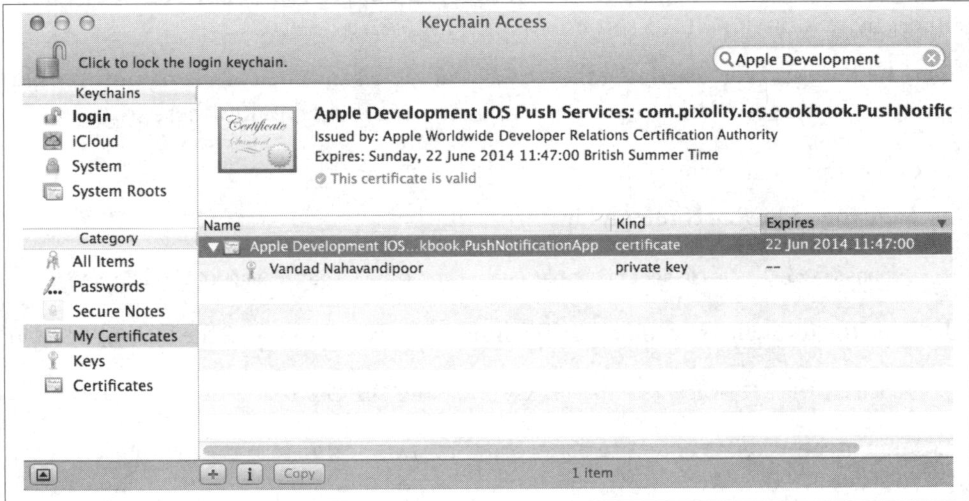


*Figure 17-11. The push notifications development certificate and its private key*

7. Right-click the certificate and export it as a *.cer* certificate file (as opposed to a *.p12* file) and give it the name of *PushCertificate.cer*.
8. Right-click the private key and export it as a *.p12* file (as opposed to a certificate file) and give it the name of *PushKey.p12*. You will be asked to specify a password for the private key. Make sure that you give it a password that you'll be able to remember later.

Great stuff. Now, for the purpose of this recipe and for the sake of simplicity, we are going to use PHP to send a simple push notification to our device, which has already been set up for push notifications in Recipe 17.7. Since setting up PHP on an Apache server is not really the topic of this book, we are going to take a shortcut and use MAMP (*http://www.mamp.info*). MAMP will install Apache and PHP on your machine if you don't already have them, so follow the instructions on the MAMP website. Once you install MAMP, the root folder of your PHP files will be at */Applications/MAMP/htdocs/*. In case the folder changes in a future installation, open MAMP and navigate to the Preferences section, and then navigate to Apache. You can then find the root folder of Apache there.

For our PHP script to be able to communicate with APNS, we need to feed it the SSL certificate that we generated earlier in the iOS development portal. This is why we extracted the *.cer* certification and the *.p12* private key files, which we now need to feed to our PHP script. The way this works is that we will use the *openssl* in Terminal to combine the certificate and the *.p12* private key into a PEM file. A discussion about PEM files lies outside the scope of this book. In fact, you could write a whole book on this subject. I will, however, let you know that you can get more information about the subject by reading RFC 1421 (*http://www.ietf.org/rfc/rfc1421.txt*).

To create the PEM file, assuming that the *PushKey.p12* and the *PushCertificate.cer* files are exported on your desktop as you were instructed earlier, follow these steps:

1. Open Terminal in your OS X.
2. Type the following command in Terminal:

   ```
   openssl x509 -in PushCertificate.cer -inform der -out PushCertificate.pem
   ```

3. Type the following command in Terminal to convert your *.p12* file into a PEM file:

   ```
   openssl pkcs12 -nocerts -in PushKey.p12 -out PushKey.pem
   ```

4. You will be asked to enter the password that you specified for this private key when you exported it from Keychain Access. Also, once the importing password is checked and verified, you will be asked by OpenSSL to specify a passphrase for the resulting PEM file. The password needs to be at least four characters. Go ahead with that and ensure that you'll remember this password for later.
5. Now you have two PEM files on your desktop: *PushCertificate.pem* and *PushKey.pem*. You need to combine the two into a single PEM file, the format recognized by PHP. Use the following command to accomplish this task:

   ```
   cat PushCertificate.pem PushKey.pem > PushCertificateAndKey.pem
   ```

6. Now let's test if we can connect to the sandbox (test version, for development purposes) APNS server using the generated *.pem* files. So issue the following command in Terminal:

   ```
   openssl s_client -connect gateway.sandbox.push.apple.com:2195 \
       -cert PushCertificate.pem -key PushKey.pem
   ```

If everything goes well, you will be asked to enter the passphrase for your private key file. Remember it? OK, then, enter that here. If your connection is successful, you will see OpenSSL waiting for some input characters from you before closing the connection. Type in something random and press the Enter key. The connection is then closed. This means that your connection to the APNS server is successful with the given certificate and private key.

It is now time to set up a simple PHP script to push a simple notification to our device. But before we move forward any further, we need to get our device's push notification token in a format that can be understood by PHP. iOS encapsulates the push notification token in an instance of `NSData`, but PHP has no notion of what that means. We need to convert that token into a string that we can use in our PHP script. To do that, we will read every byte in the token and convert that byte into its hexadecimal-string representation:

```
- (void)                                application:(UIApplication *)application
 didRegisterForRemoteNotificationsWithDeviceToken:(NSData *)deviceToken{

    /* Each byte in the data will be translated to its hex value like 0x01 or
     0xAB excluding the 0x part, so for 1 byte, we will need 2 characters to
     represent that byte, hence the * 2 */
    NSMutableString *tokenAsString = [[NSMutableString alloc]
                                      initWithCapacity:deviceToken.length * 2];

    char *bytes = malloc(deviceToken.length);
    [deviceToken getBytes:bytes];

    for (NSUInteger byteCounter = 0;
         byteCounter < deviceToken.length;
         byteCounter++){

        char byte = bytes[byteCounter];
        [tokenAsString appendFormat:@"%02hhX", byte];
    }

    free(bytes);

    NSLog(@"Token = %@", tokenAsString);

}
```

Run your app and see that the device token will get printed to the console like so:

```
Token = 05924634A8EB6B84437A1E8CE02E6BE6683DEC83FB38680A7DFD6A04C6CC586E
```

Take note of this device token, because we are going to use it in our PHP script:

```
<?php

/* We are using the sandbox version of the APNS for development. For production
 environments, change this to ssl://gateway.push.apple.com:2195 */
$apnsServer = 'ssl://gateway.sandbox.push.apple.com:2195';

/* Make sure this is set to the password that you set for your private key
 when you exported it to the .pem file using openssl on your OS X */
$privateKeyPassword = '1234';

/* Put your own message here if you want to */
$message = 'Welcome to iOS 7 Push Notifications';

/* Pur your device token here */
$deviceToken =
    '05924634A8EB6B84437A1E8CE02E6BE6683DEC83FB38680A7DFD6A04C6CC586E';

/* Replace this with the name of the file that you have placed by your PHP
 script file, containing your private key and certificate that you generated
 earlier */
$pushCertAndKeyPemFile = 'PushCertificateAndKey.pem';

$stream = stream_context_create();

stream_context_set_option($stream,
                          'ssl',
                          'passphrase',
                          $privateKeyPassword);

stream_context_set_option($stream,
                          'ssl',
                          'local_cert',
                          $pushCertAndKeyPemFile);

$connectionTimeout = 20;
$connectionType = STREAM_CLIENT_CONNECT | STREAM_CLIENT_PERSISTENT;
$connection = stream_socket_client($apnsServer,
                                   $errorNumber,
                                   $errorString,
                                   $connectionTimeout,
                                   $connectionType,
                                   $stream);

if (!$connection){
    echo "Failed to connect to the APNS server. Error no = $errorNumber<br/>";
    exit;
} else {
    echo "Successfully connected to the APNS. Processing...</br>";
}
```

```
$messageBody['aps'] = array('alert' => $message,
                            'sound' => 'default',
                            'badge' => 2,
                            );

$payload = json_encode($messageBody);

$notification = chr(0) .
                pack('n', 32) .
                pack('H*', $deviceToken) .
                pack('n', strlen($payload)) .
                $payload;

$wroteSuccessfully = fwrite($connection, $notification, strlen($notification));

if (!$wroteSuccessfully){
    echo "Could not send the message<br/>";
}
else {
    echo "Successfully sent the message<br/>";
}

fclose($connection);
```

Go through this script, even if you are not a PHP programmer, and read the comments. Ensure that you replace the values in the PHP script with the correct values for you. For instance, the device token used here is for my personal device. Use the device token that you retrieved for your own device earlier in this recipe. The passphrases and the *.pem* file locations may be different for you. What I've done in this recipe to make sure things are easier is to place my PHP script in the same folder where I've placed my private key and certificate *.pem* file (*PushCertificateAndKey.pem*) so that I can access the *.pem* file using a simple filename.

If you've done everything right and followed the advice of this recipe, you should now be able to open your PHP script in a web browser and see the notifications appear on your device. The script sends the notification to the APNS server, which delivers it to the device. When the push notification is delivered to the app, assuming it is displaying the lock screen, you will see something on the device similar to that shown in Figure 17-12.

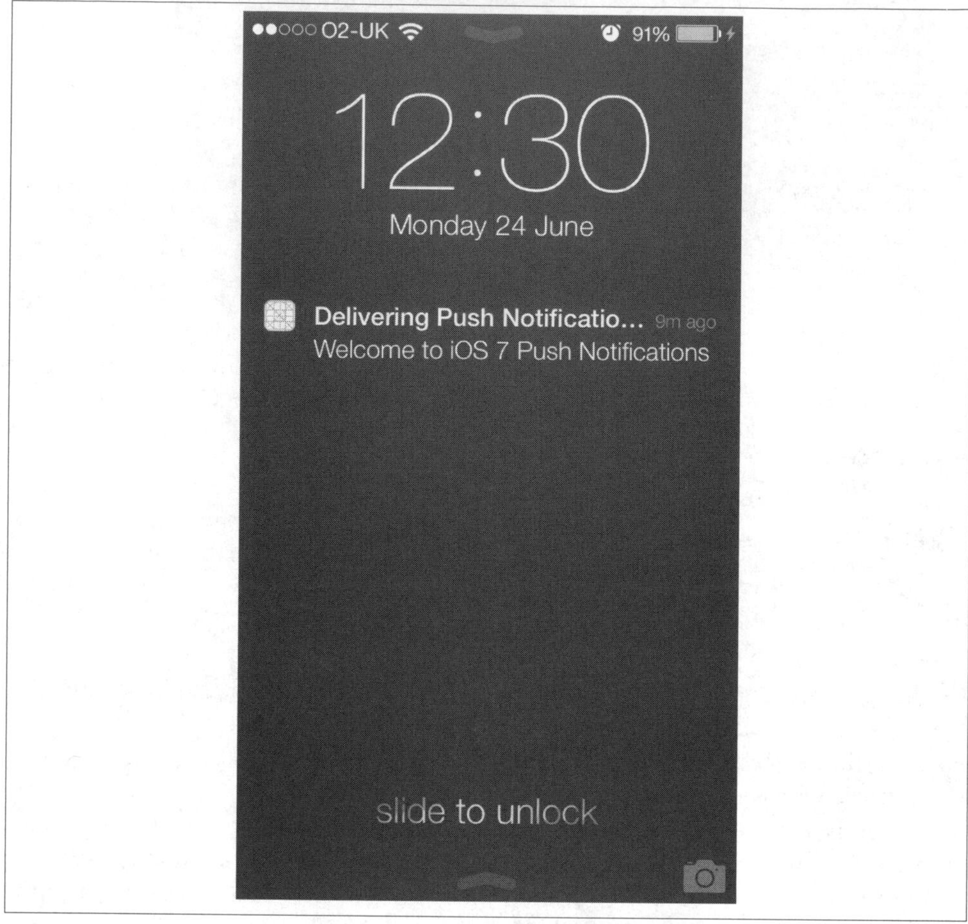


*Figure 17-12. A push notification displayed on the lock screen*

## See Also

Recipe 17.7

# 17.9. Reacting to Push Notifications

## Problem

You have been able to deliver push notifications to your app after reading Recipe 17.8 but don't know how to react to them in your app.

## Solution

Implement the `application:didReceiveRemoteNotification:` method of your app delegate.

## Discussion

The `application:didReceiveRemoteNotification:` method of your app delegate gets called whenever a push notification is delivered to iOS and the user acts upon it in a way that opens your app. This method gets called if your app is either in the foreground or the background, but not completely terminated. For instance, the user can ignore the push notification. In that case, the aforementioned method will not get called. If the user presses the push notification, which in turn opens your app, iOS will open your app and bring it to the foreground, after which the aforementioned method will get called on your app delegate.

If your app is fully terminated and not in the background, the push notification that triggers your app to wake up will be encapsulated by iOS in the launch options that will be passed to the `application:didFinishLaunchingWithOptions:` method of your app delegate. To retrieve the notification object, simply query the `didFinishLaunchingWithOptions` parameter of this method (which is of type `NSDictionary`) and look for the `UIApplicationLaunchOptionsRemoteNotificationKey` key. The value of this key will be the push notification object that started your app.

The `didReceiveRemoteNotification` parameter of this property carries a dictionary of type `NSDictionary`. This dictionary will contain a root object called `aps`, and under this object, you will have a dictionary with the following keys, depending on how the server created the push notification (the server may not send all of these at once):

`badge`
: The value of this key is a number indicating the badge number that has to be set for your app's icon.

`alert`
: The message inside the push notification, of type `String`. The server may decide to send you a modified version of this key's value, which itself will be a dictionary containing the keys `body` and `show-view`. If this modified version of the alert is sent to you, the `body` key will contain the actual text of the body of the alert, and the `show-view` key will contain a Boolean value indicating whether the action button of the notification should be displayed to the user. The Action button allows the user to tap the notification in the notification center in order to open your app.

`sound`
: This is a string indicating the name of the sound file that your app needs to play.

`content-available`
: The value of this key is a number. If set to 1, it indicates that there is new content available for the application to download from the server. The server can send this to your app to request that it fetches from the server to retrieve a list of new items. Your app doesn't have to comply. Rather, this is a protocol between the server and the client, and you can use it if it makes sense in your app.

## See Also

Recipe 17.8

# CHAPTER 18
# Core Data

## 18.0. Introduction

Core Data is a powerful framework on the iOS SDK that allows programmers to store and manage data in an object-oriented way. Traditionally, programmers had to store their data on disk using the archiving capabilities of Objective-C, or write their data to files and manage them manually. With the introduction of Core Data, programmers can simply interact with its object-oriented interface to manage their data efficiently. In this chapter, you will learn how to use Core Data to create the model of your application (in the model-view-controller software architecture).

Core Data interacts with a persistent store at a lower level that is not visible to the programmer. iOS decides how the low-level data management is implemented. All the programmer must know is the high-level API she is provided with. But understanding the structure of Core Data and how it works internally is very important. Let's create a Core Data application to understand this a bit better.

With the new LLVM compiler, all you have to do in order to include Core Data into your project is to include the umbrella header file, like so:

```
#import "AppDelegate.h"
#import <CoreData/CoreData.h>

@implementation AppDelegate

<# Rest of your code goes here #>
```

To be able to work with Core Data, you need to understand that a Core Data stack is based on the following concepts:

*Persistent store*
: The object that represents the actual data base on disk. We never use this object directly.

*Persistent store coordinator*
: The object that coordinates reading and writing of information from and to the persistent store. The coordinator is the bridge between the managed object context and the persistent store.

*Managed object model (MOM)*
: This is a simple file on disk that will represent our data model. Think about it as your database schema.

*Managed object*
: This class represents an entity that we want to store in Core Data. Traditional database programmers would know such entities as *tables*. A managed object is of type `NSManagedObject`, and its instances are placed on managed object contexts. They adhere to the schema dictated by the managed object model, and they get saved to a persistent store through a persistent store coordinator.

*Managed object context (MOC)*
: This is a virtual board. That sounds strange, right? But let me explain. We create Core Data objects in memory and set their properties and play with them. All this playing is done on a managed object context. The context keeps track of all the things that we are doing with our managed objects and even allows us to undo those actions. Think of your managed objects on a context as toys that you have brought on a table to play with. You can move them around, break them, move them out of the table, and bring new toys in. That table is your managed object context, and you can save its state when you are ready. When you save the state of the managed object context, this save operation will be communicated to the persistent store coordinator to which the context is connected, upon which the persistent store coordinator will store the information to the persistent store and subsequently to disk.

To add Core Data to your project and start using all the cool features that it has to offer, simply create a project and when asked whether to add Core Data to it or not, check the relevant box, as shown in Figure 18-1.

Once you create your project with Core Data, your app delegate will have some new properties:

```
NSManagedObjectContext *managedObjectContext;
NSManagedObjectModel *managedObjectModel;
NSPersistentStoreCoordinator *persistentStoreCoordinator;
```

You should already know these from the description earlier in this chapter. The context is our playing table, the model is the schema of our data base and the coordinator is the object that will help us save our context to disk. Plain and easy. OK then, let's get started with the rest of this chapter now.

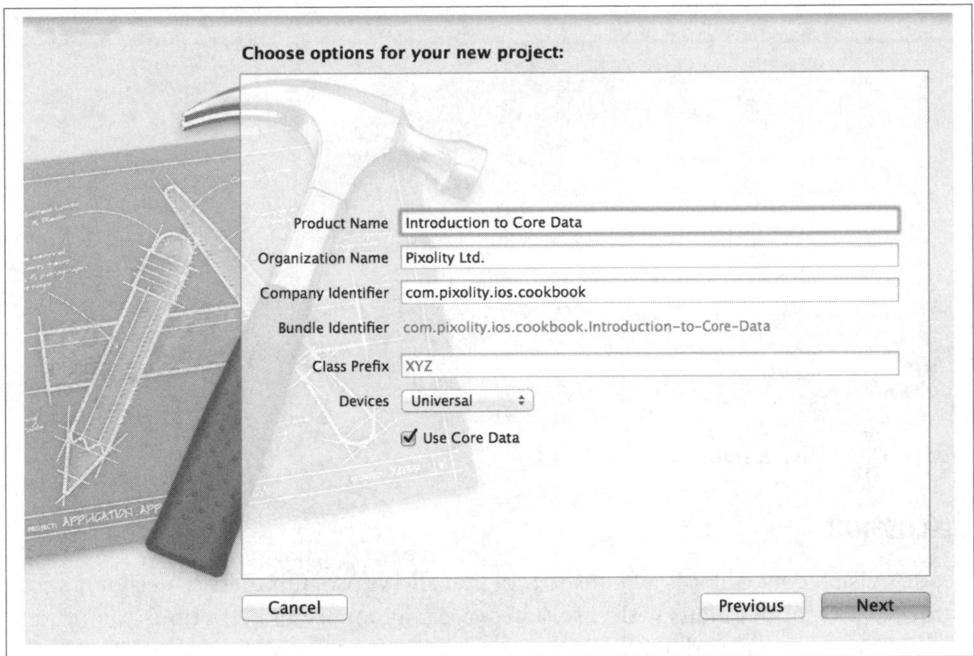


*Figure 18-1. Adding Core Data to a new Xcode project*

# 18.1. Creating a Core Data Model with Xcode

## Problem

You want to visually design the data model of your iOS application using Xcode.

## Solution

Follow the instructions in this chapter's Introduction to create a Core Data project. Then find the file with the extension of *xcdatamodel* in your application bundle in Xcode and click it to open the visual data editor, as shown in Figure 18-2.

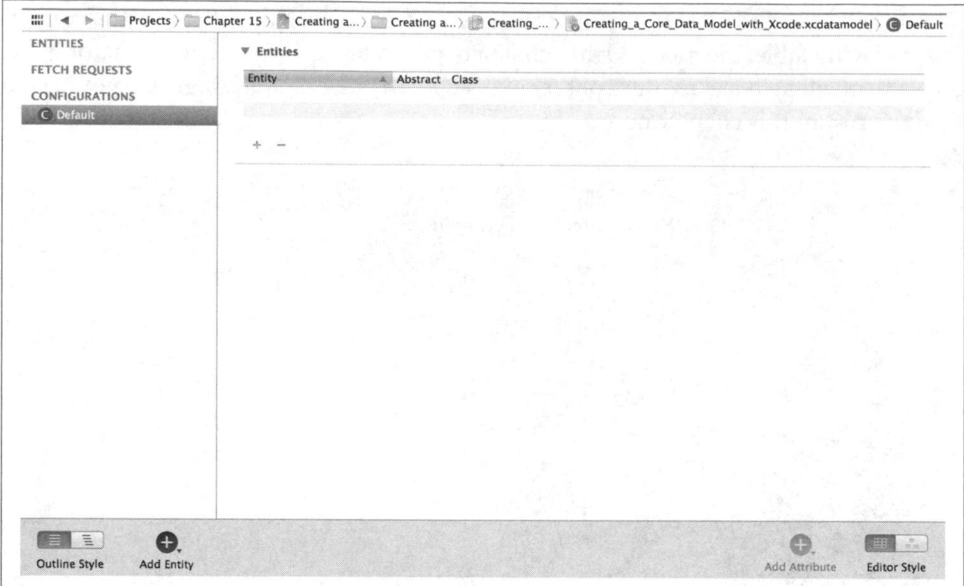


*Figure 18-2. Visual data editor in Xcode*

## Discussion

Xcode's visual data editor is a fantastic tool that allows programmers to design the data model of their applications with ease. There are two important definitions you need to learn before you can work with this tool:

*Entity*
: Corresponds to a table in a database

*Attribute*
: Corresponds to a column in a table

Entities will later become objects (managed objects) when we generate the code based on our object model. This is explained in Recipe 18.2. For now, in this recipe, we will concentrate on creating the data model in this tool.

In the editor, find the + button at the bottom. Click and hold on this button and then select Add Entity from the menu that will appear, as shown in Figure 18-3.

Your new entity will be created and will be in a state where you can immediately rename it after creation. Change the name of this entity to `Person`, as shown in Figure 18-4.

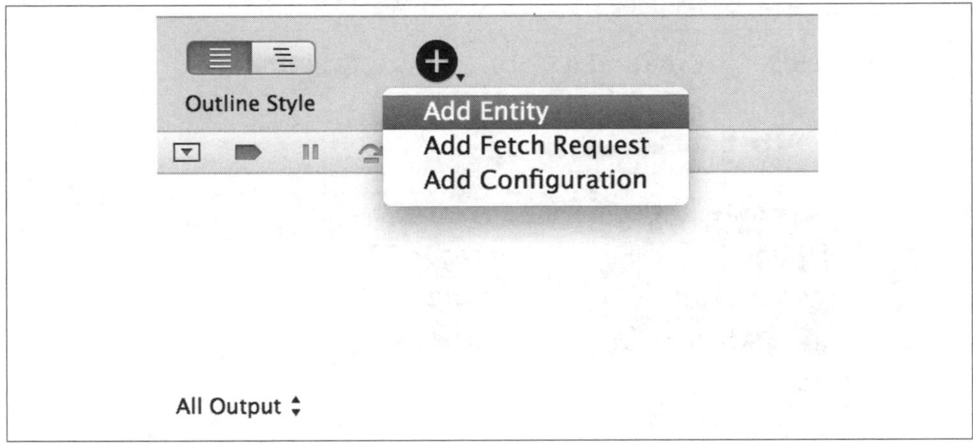


*Figure 18-3. Adding a new entity to our data model*

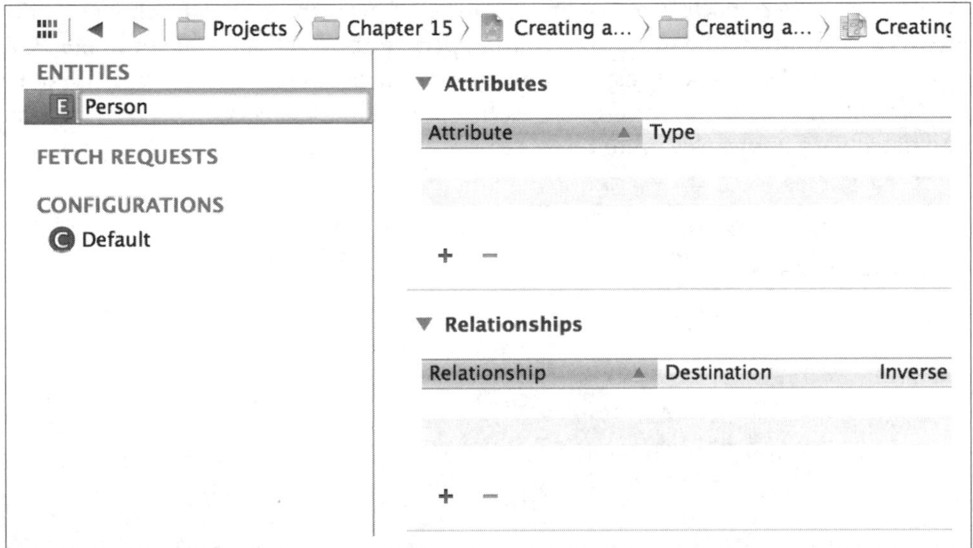


*Figure 18-4. Changing the name of the new entity to Person*

Select the `Person` entity, then select the + button in the Attributes pane and create the following three attributes for it (the results are shown in Figure 18-5).

- `firstName` (of type `String`).
- `lastName` (of type `String`).
- `age` (of type `Integer 32`).

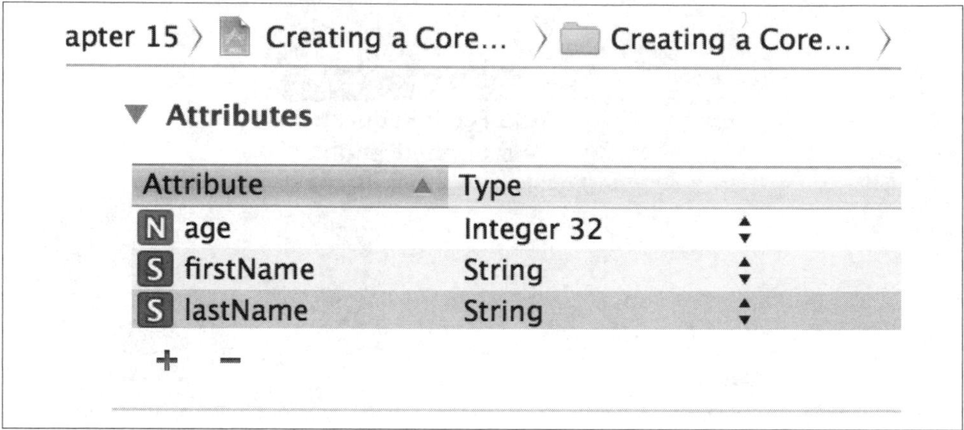


*Figure 18-5. We have added three attributes to the Person entity*

While you are in the data model editor, from the View menu in Xcode, choose Utilities → Show Utilities. The utilities pane will open on the righthand side of Xcode. On top, choose the Data Model Inspector button and make sure that you have clicked on the `Person` entity that we just created. At this point, the Data Model inspector will be populated with items relevant to the `Person` entity, as shown in Figure 18-6.

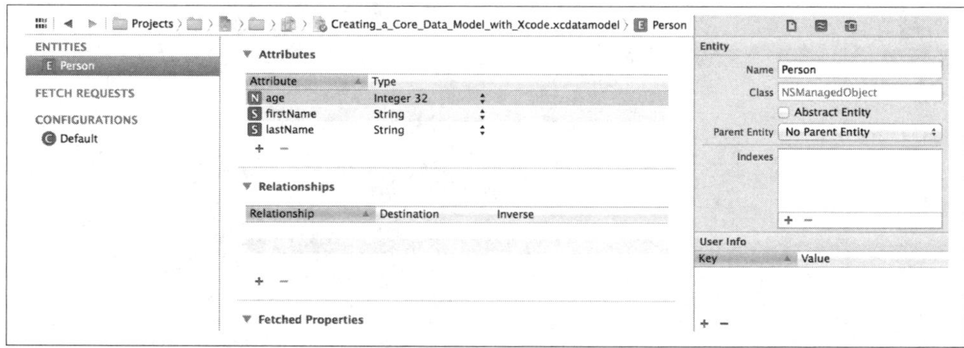


*Figure 18-6. The Data Model Inspector shown on the right side of the Xcode window*

Now click the `firstName`, `lastName`, and `age` attributes of the Person entity. Make sure the `firstName` and the `lastName` attributes are *not optional* by unticking the `Optional` checkbox and make sure the `age` field is optional by ticking the `Optional` checkbox.

OK, we are done creating the model. Choose File → Save to make sure your changes are saved. To learn how to generate code based on the managed object you just created, refer to Recipe 18.2.

# 18.2. Generating Class Files for Core Data Entities

## Problem

You followed the instructions in Recipe 18.1 and you want to know how to create code based on your object model.

## Solution

Follow these steps:

1. In Xcode, find the file with the *xcdatamodel* extension that was created for your application when you created the application itself in Xcode. Click the file, and you should see the editor on the righthand side of the Xcode window.
2. Select the `Person` entity that we created earlier (see Recipe 18.1).
3. Select File → New File in Xcode.
4. In the New File dialog, make sure you have selected iOS as the main category and Core Data as the subcategory. Then choose the `NSManagedObject subclass` item from the righthand side of the dialog and press Next, as shown in Figure 18-7.

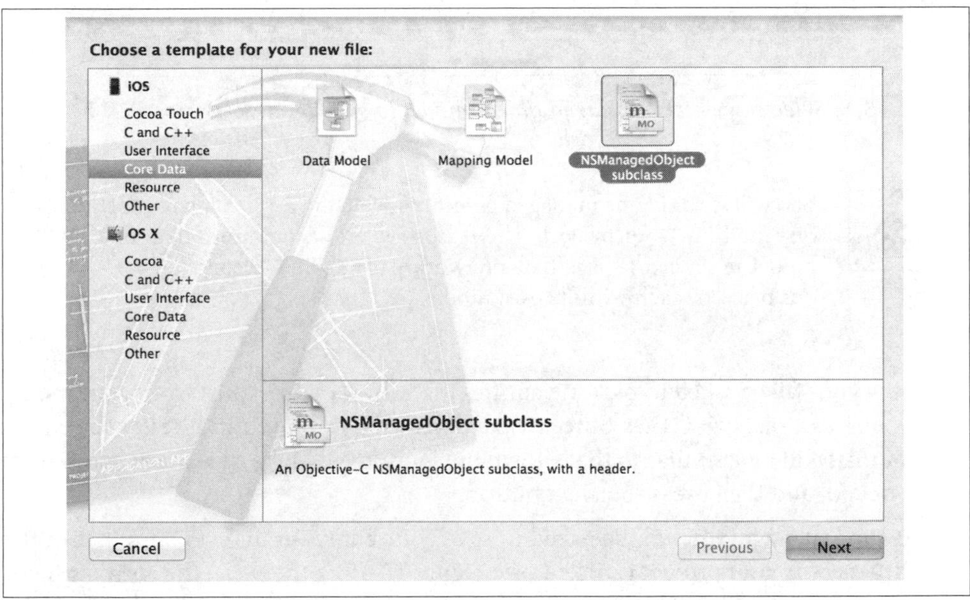


*Figure 18-7. Creating a managed object subclass in Xcode*

5. On the next screen, choose the managed object model that you want to save to disk and ensure it is ticked. Once you are done, press the Next button (see Figure 18-8).

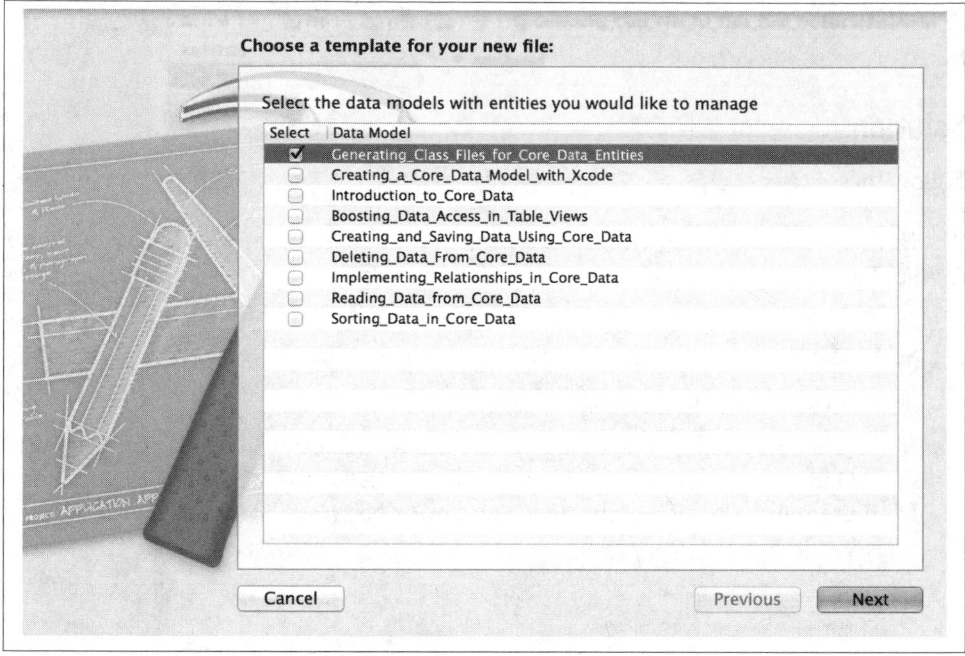


*Figure 18-8. Selecting which managed object model to save on disk*

You will see only one managed object model in the list if you have only one model in your project. The reason we are seeing more than one model in Figure 18-8 is that my workspace in Xcode contains various projects, each with its own model.

6. Now you will be asked to pick the entities that you want to export from your model on disk as Objective-C files. Since we have created only one entity, the `Person` entity, your list will look similar to that shown in Figure 18-9. Make sure the `Person` entity is ticked, and then press the Next button.
7. At the last stage, you will be asked to save your entity on disk. Ensure that in the Targets box, your project is ticked (see Figure 18-10); otherwise, the entity will not be available to different source files in your code. Once you are happy, press the Create button.

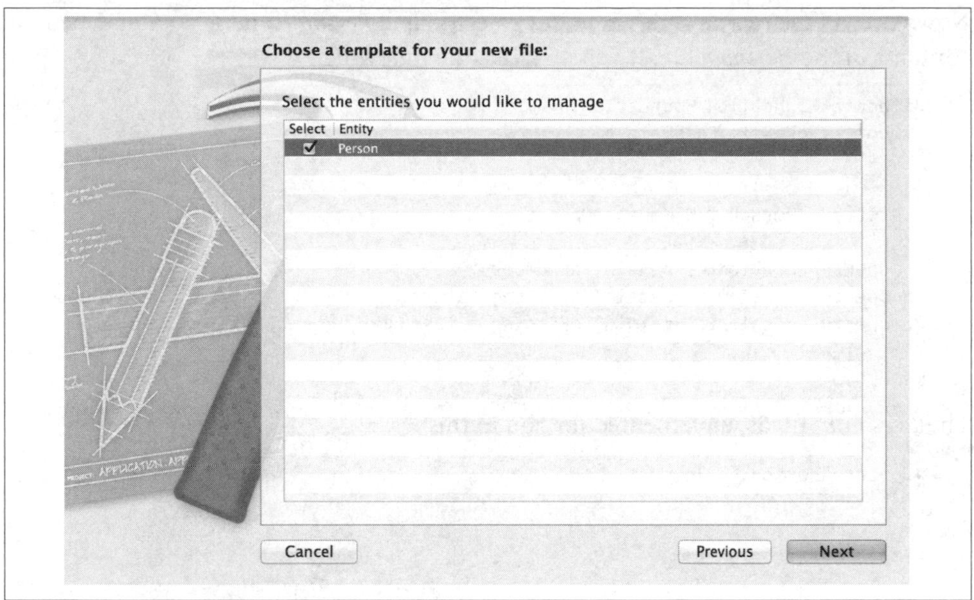


*Figure 18-9. Exporting the Person entity to disk as a managed object*

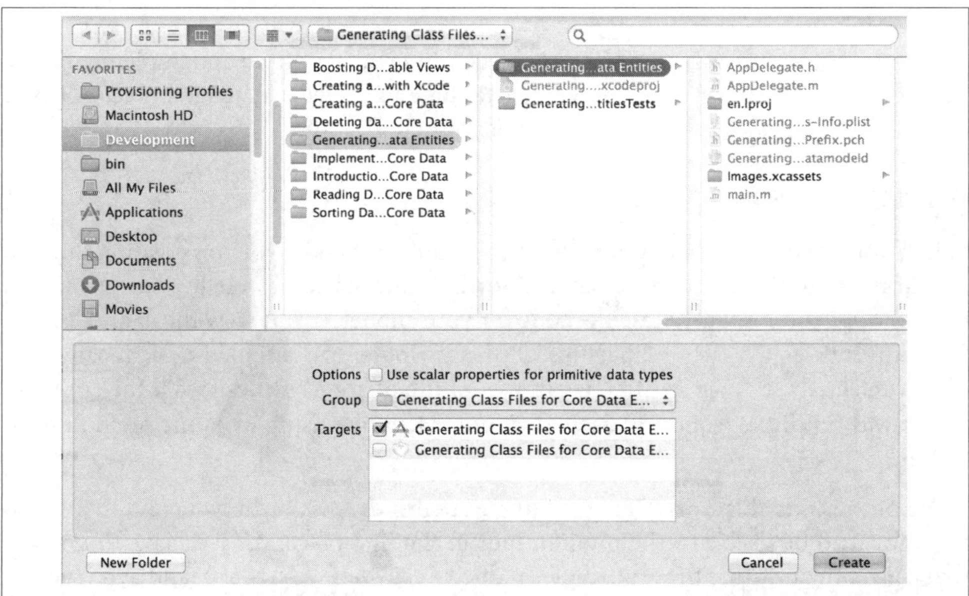


*Figure 18-10. Saving our entity on disk*

Now you will see two new files in your project, called *Person.h* and *Person.m*. Open the contents of the *Person.h* file. It will look like the following:

```
#import <Foundation/Foundation.h>
#import <CoreData/CoreData.h>


@interface Person : NSManagedObject

@property (nonatomic, retain) NSNumber * age;
@property (nonatomic, retain) NSString * firstName;
@property (nonatomic, retain) NSString * lastName;

@end
```

The *Person.m* file is implemented for you in this way:

```
#import "Person.h"


@implementation Person

@dynamic age;
@dynamic firstName;
@dynamic lastName;

@end
```

There you go! We turned our managed object into a real definition and implementation. In Recipe 18.3, you will learn how to instantiate and save a managed object of type `Person` into the managed object context of your application.

## Discussion

When you create your data model using the editor in Xcode, you are creating the data relationships, entities, attributes, and so forth. However, to be able to use your model in your app, you must generate the code for your model. If you view the *.h* and *.m* files for your entities, you will realize that all the attributes are assigned dynamically. You can even see the `@dynamic` directive in the *.m* file of your entities to tell the compiler that it will fulfill the request of each attribute at runtime using dynamic method resolution.

None of the code that Core Data runs on your entities is visible to you, and there is no need for it to be visible to the programmer in the first place. All you have to know is that a `Person` entity has three attributes named `firstName`, `lastName`, and `age`. You can assign values to these attributes (if they are read/write properties), and you can save to and load them from the context, as we'll see in Recipe 18.3.

# 18.3. Creating and Saving Data Using Core Data

## Problem

You have already created a managed object, and you want to instantiate it and insert that instance into your app's Core Data context.

## Solution

Follow the instructions in Recipe 18.1 and Recipe 18.2. Now you can use the `insertNewObjectForEntityForName:inManagedObjectContext:` class method of `NSEntityDescription` to create a new object of a type specified by the first parameter of this method. Once the new entity (the managed object) is created, you can modify it by changing its properties. After you are done, save your managed object context using the `save:` instance method of the managed object context.

I'll assume that you have created a universal application in Xcode with the name *Creating and Saving Data Using Core Data*; now, follow these steps to insert a new managed object into the context:

1. Find the implementation file of your app delegate.
2. Import the *Person.h* file into the app delegate's implementation file:

`Person` is the entity we created in Recipe 18.1.

```
#import "AppDelegate.h"
#import "Person.h"

@implementation AppDelegate

@synthesize managedObjectContext = _managedObjectContext;
@synthesize managedObjectModel = _managedObjectModel;
@synthesize persistentStoreCoordinator = _persistentStoreCoordinator;

<# Rest of your app delegate code goes here #>
```

3. In the `application:didFinishLaunchingWithOptions:` method of your shared application delegate, write this code:

```
- (BOOL)            application:(UIApplication *)application
  didFinishLaunchingWithOptions:(NSDictionary *)launchOptions{
```

```
    Person *newPerson = [NSEntityDescription
                         insertNewObjectForEntityForName:@"Person"
                         inManagedObjectContext:self.managedObjectContext];

    if (newPerson != nil){

        newPerson.firstName = @"Anthony";
        newPerson.lastName = @"Robbins";
        newPerson.age = @51;

        NSError *savingError = nil;

        if ([self.managedObjectContext save:&savingError]){
            NSLog(@"Successfully saved the context.");
        } else {
            NSLog(@"Failed to save the context. Error = %@", savingError);
        }

    } else {
        NSLog(@"Failed to create the new person.");
    }

    self.window = [[UIWindow alloc] initWithFrame:
                   [[UIScreen mainScreen] bounds]];

    self.window.backgroundColor = [UIColor whiteColor];
    [self.window makeKeyAndVisible];
    return YES;
}
```

## Discussion

Previous recipes showed how to create entities and generate code based on them using the editor in Xcode. The next thing we need to do is start using those entities and instantiate them. For this, we use `NSEntityDescription` and call its `insertNewObjectForEntityForName:inManagedObjectContext:` class method. This will look up the given entity (specified by its name as `NSString`) in the given managed object context. If the entity is found, the method will return a new instance of that entity. This is similar to creating a new row (managed object) in a table (entity) in a database (managed object context).

> Attempting to insert an unknown entity into a managed object context will raise an exception of type `NSInternalInconsistencyException`.

After inserting a new entity into the context, we must save the context. This will flush all the unsaved data of the context to the persistent store. We can do this using the `save:`

instance method of our managed object context. If the BOOL return value of this method is YES, we can be sure that our context is saved. In Recipe 18.4, you will learn how to read the data back to memory.

# 18.4. Reading Data from Core Data

## Problem

You want to be able to read the contents of your entities (tables) using Core Data.

## Solution

Use an instance of NSFetchRequest:

```
- (BOOL) createNewPersonWithFirstName:(NSString *)paramFirstName
                             lastName:(NSString *)paramLastName
                                  age:(NSUInteger)paramAge{

    BOOL result = NO;

    if ([paramFirstName length] == 0 ||
        [paramLastName length] == 0){
        NSLog(@"First and Last names are mandatory.");
        return NO;
    }

    Person *newPerson = [NSEntityDescription
                         insertNewObjectForEntityForName:@"Person"
                         inManagedObjectContext:self.managedObjectContext];

    if (newPerson == nil){
        NSLog(@"Failed to create the new person.");
        return NO;
    }

    newPerson.firstName = paramFirstName;
    newPerson.lastName = paramLastName;
    newPerson.age = @(paramAge);

    NSError *savingError = nil;

    if ([self.managedObjectContext save:&savingError]){
        return YES;
    } else {
        NSLog(@"Failed to save the new person. Error = %@", savingError);
    }

    return result;

}
```

```
- (BOOL)            application:(UIApplication *)application
  didFinishLaunchingWithOptions:(NSDictionary *)launchOptions{

    [self createNewPersonWithFirstName:@"Anthony"
                              lastName:@"Robbins"
                                   age:51];

    [self createNewPersonWithFirstName:@"Richard"
                              lastName:@"Branson"
                                   age:61];

    /* Tell the request that we want to read the
     contents of the Person entity */
    /* Create the fetch request first */
    NSFetchRequest *fetchRequest = [[NSFetchRequest alloc]
                                    initWithEntityName:@"Person"];

    NSError *requestError = nil;

    /* And execute the fetch request on the context */
    NSArray *persons =
    [self.managedObjectContext executeFetchRequest:fetchRequest
                                             error:&requestError];

    /* Make sure we get the array */
    if ([persons count] > 0){

        /* Go through the persons array one by one */
        NSUInteger counter = 1;
        for (Person *thisPerson in persons){

            NSLog(@"Person %lu First Name = %@",
                  (unsigned long)counter,
                  thisPerson.firstName);

            NSLog(@"Person %lu Last Name = %@",
                  (unsigned long)counter,
                  thisPerson.lastName);

            NSLog(@"Person %lu Age = %ld",
                  (unsigned long)counter,
                  (unsigned long)[thisPerson.age unsignedIntegerValue]);

            counter++;
        }

    } else {
        NSLog(@"Could not find any Person entities in the context.");
    }

    self.window = [[UIWindow alloc] initWithFrame:
```

```
                    [[UIScreen mainScreen] bounds]];

    self.window.backgroundColor = [UIColor whiteColor];
    [self.window makeKeyAndVisible];
    return YES;
}
```

In this code, we are using a counter variable inside a fast-enumeration block. The reason we need the counter in this fast-enumeration is for use in `NSLog` debugging messages that we are printing in order to see the index of the current enumerated person object in the array. An alternative to this solution would have been to use a classic for-loop with a counter variable.

For more information about fetch requests, please refer to this recipe's Discussion.

## Discussion

For those of you who are familiar with database terminology, a *fetch request* is similar to a `SELECT` statement. In the `SELECT` statement, you specify which rows, with which conditions, have to be returned from which table. With a fetch request, we do the same thing. We specify the entity (table) and the managed object context (the database layer). We can also specify sort descriptors for sorting the data we read. But first we'll focus on reading the data to make it simpler.

To be able to read the contents of the `Person` entity (we created this entity in Recipe 18.1 and turned it into code in Recipe 18.2), we must set the target entity name, in this case *Person*, in the fetch request by using the `initWithEntityName:` method. Once the fetch request is constructed successfully, all that's left to do is execute the fetch request as we saw in this recipe's Solution.

The return value of the `executeFetchRequest:error:` instance method of `NSManagedObjectContext` is either `nil` (in case of an error) or an array of `Person` managed objects. If no results are found for the given entity, the returned array will be empty.

## See Also

Recipe 18.1; Recipe 18.2

# 18.5. Deleting Data from Core Data

## Problem

You want to delete a managed object (a row in a table) from a managed object context (your database).

## Solution

Use the `deleteObject:` instance method of `NSManagedObjectContext`:

```
- (BOOL)            application:(UIApplication *)application
  didFinishLaunchingWithOptions:(NSDictionary *)launchOptions{

    [self createNewPersonWithFirstName:@"Anthony"
                              lastName:@"Robbins"
                                   age:51];

    [self createNewPersonWithFirstName:@"Richard"
                              lastName:@"Branson"
                                   age:61];

    /* Create the fetch request first */
    NSFetchRequest *fetchRequest = [[NSFetchRequest alloc]
                                    initWithEntityName:@"Person"];

    NSError *requestError = nil;

    /* And execute the fetch request on the context */
    NSArray *persons =
    [self.managedObjectContext executeFetchRequest:fetchRequest
                                             error:&requestError];

    /* Make sure we get the array */
    if ([persons count] > 0){

        /* Delete the last person in the array */
        Person *lastPerson = [persons lastObject];

        [self.managedObjectContext deleteObject:lastPerson];

        NSError *savingError = nil;
        if ([self.managedObjectContext save:&savingError]){
            NSLog(@"Successfully deleted the last person in the array.");
        } else {
            NSLog(@"Failed to delete the last person in the array.");
        }

    } else {
        NSLog(@"Could not find any Person entities in the context.");
    }
```

```
    self.window = [[UIWindow alloc] initWithFrame:
                   [[UIScreen mainScreen] bounds]];

    self.window.backgroundColor = [UIColor whiteColor];
    [self.window makeKeyAndVisible];
    return YES;
}
```

In this example code, we are using the createNewPersonWithFirstName:lastName:age: method that we coded in Recipe 18.4.

## Discussion

You can delete managed objects (records of a table in a database) using the deleteObject: instance method of NSManagedObjectContext.

This method doesn't return an error to you in any of its parameters, nor does it return a BOOL value, so you really have no good way of knowing whether an object was successfully deleted using the managed object context. The best way to determine this is to use that managed object's isDeleted method.

With this information, let's change the code that we wrote previously in this recipe:

```
- (BOOL)            application:(UIApplication *)application
  didFinishLaunchingWithOptions:(NSDictionary *)launchOptions{

    [self createNewPersonWithFirstName:@"Anthony"
                              lastName:@"Robbins"
                                   age:51];

    [self createNewPersonWithFirstName:@"Richard"
                              lastName:@"Branson"
                                   age:61];

    /* Create the fetch request first */
    NSFetchRequest *fetchRequest = [[NSFetchRequest alloc]
                                    initWithEntityName:@"Person"];

    NSError *requestError = nil;

    /* And execute the fetch request on the context */
    NSArray *persons =
    [self.managedObjectContext executeFetchRequest:fetchRequest
                                             error:&requestError];

    /* Make sure we get the array */
    if ([persons count] > 0){
```

```
            /* Delete the last person in the array */
            Person *lastPerson = [persons lastObject];

            [self.managedObjectContext deleteObject:lastPerson];

            if ([lastPerson isDeleted]){
                NSLog(@"Successfully deleted the last person...");

                NSError *savingError = nil;
                if ([self.managedObjectContext save:&savingError]){
                    NSLog(@"Successfully saved the context.");
                } else {
                    NSLog(@"Failed to save the context.");
                }

            } else {
                NSLog(@"Failed to delete the last person.");
            }

        } else {
            NSLog(@"Could not find any Person entities in the context.");
        }

        self.window = [[UIWindow alloc] initWithFrame:
                       [[UIScreen mainScreen] bounds]];

        self.window.backgroundColor = [UIColor whiteColor];
        [self.window makeKeyAndVisible];
        return YES;
    }
```

Once you run the app, you will get results similar to this printed to the console window:

```
Successfully deleted the last person...
Successfully saved the context.
```

# 18.6. Sorting Data in Core Data

## Problem

You want to sort the managed objects (records) that you fetch from a managed object context (database).

## Solution

Create instances of `NSSortDescriptor` for each attribute (column, in the database world) of an entity that has to be sorted. Add the sort descriptors to an array and assign the array to an instance of `NSFetchRequest` using the `setSortDescriptors:` instance method. In this example code, `Sorting_Data_in_Core_DataAppDelegate` is the class that represents the app delegate in a universal app. To understand how the `Person` entity is created, please refer to Recipes 18.1 and 18.2:

```
- (BOOL)            application:(UIApplication *)application
  didFinishLaunchingWithOptions:(NSDictionary *)launchOptions{

    [self createNewPersonWithFirstName:@"Richard"
                              lastName:@"Branson"
                                   age:61];

    [self createNewPersonWithFirstName:@"Anthony"
                              lastName:@"Robbins"
                                   age:51];

    /* Create the fetch request first */
    NSFetchRequest *fetchRequest = [[NSFetchRequest alloc]
                                    initWithEntityName:@"Person"];

    NSSortDescriptor *ageSort =
    [[NSSortDescriptor alloc] initWithKey:@"age"
                                ascending:YES];

    NSSortDescriptor *firstNameSort =
    [[NSSortDescriptor alloc] initWithKey:@"firstName"
                                ascending:YES];

    fetchRequest.sortDescriptors = @[ageSort, firstNameSort];

    NSError *requestError = nil;

    /* And execute the fetch request on the context */
    NSArray *persons =
    [self.managedObjectContext executeFetchRequest:fetchRequest
                                             error:&requestError];

    for (Person *person in persons){

        NSLog(@"First Name = %@", person.firstName);
        NSLog(@"Last Name = %@", person.lastName);
        NSLog(@"Age = %lu", (unsigned long)[person.age unsignedIntegerValue]);

    }

    self.window = [[UIWindow alloc] initWithFrame:
                   [[UIScreen mainScreen] bounds]];

    self.window.backgroundColor = [UIColor whiteColor];
    [self.window makeKeyAndVisible];
    return YES;
}
```

## Discussion

An instance of NSFetchRequest can carry with itself an array of NSSortDescriptor instances. Each sort descriptor defines the attribute (column) on the current entity that has to be sorted and whether the sorting has to be ascending or descending. For instance, the Person entity we created in Recipe 18.1 has firstName, lastName, and age attributes. If we want to read all the persons in a managed object context and sort them from youngest to oldest, we would create an instance of NSSortDescriptor with the age key and set it to be ascending:

```
NSSortDescriptor *ageSort =
[[NSSortDescriptor alloc] initWithKey:@"age"
                            ascending:YES];
```

You can assign more than one sort descriptor to one fetch request. The order in the array determines the order in which descriptors are provided. In other words, The output is sorted according to the first descriptor of the array, and within that order, entries are sorted according to the second descriptor of the array, etc.

## See Also

Recipe 18.4

# 18.7. Boosting Data Access in Table Views

## Problem

In an application that uses table views to present managed objects to the user, you want to be able to fetch and present the data in a more fluid and natural way than managing your data manually.

## Solution

Use fetched results controllers, which are instances of NSFetchedResultsController.

In this recipe, we are going to use storyboards to reduce the time that it takes to develop the sample application in the Discussion section. For more information about storyboards, please refer to Chapter 6).

## Discussion

Fetched results controllers work in the same way as table views. Both have sections and rows. A fetched results controller can read managed objects from a managed object context and separate them into sections and rows. Each section is a group (if you specify it), and each row in a section is a managed object. You can then easily map this data to a table view and display it to the user. There are a few very important reasons why you might want to modify your application to use fetched results controllers:

- After a fetched results controller is created on a managed object context, any change (insertion, deletion, modification, etc.) will immediately be reflected on the fetched results controller as well. For instance, you could create your fetched results controller to read the managed objects of the `Person` entity. Then in some other place in your application, you might insert a new `Person` managed object into the context (the same context the fetched results controller was created on). Immediately, the new managed object will become available in the fetched results controller. This is just magical!
- With a fetched results controller, you can manage cache more efficiently. For instance, you can ask your fetched results controller to keep only *N* number of managed objects in memory per controller instance.
- Fetched results controllers are exactly like table views in the sense that they have sections and rows, as explained before. You can use a fetched results controller to present managed objects in the GUI of your application with table views with ease.

Here are some of the important properties and instance methods of fetched results controllers (all are objects of type `NSFetchedResultsController`):

`sections` *(property, of type* `NSArray`*)*
: A fetched results controller can group data together using a key path. The designated initializer of the `NSFetchedResultsController` class accepts this grouping filter through the `sectionNameKeyPath` parameter. The `sections` array will then contain each grouped section. Each object in this array conforms to the `NSFetchedResultsSectionInfo` protocol.

`objectAtIndexPath:` *(instance method, returns a managed object)*
: Objects fetched with a fetched results controller can be retrieved using their section and row index. Each section's rows are numbered 0 through *N*-1, where *N* is the total number of items in that section. An index path object comprises a section and row index and perfectly matches the information needed to retrieve objects from a fetched results controller. The `objectAtIndexPath:` instance method accepts index paths. Each index path is of type `NSIndexPath`. If you need to construct a table view cell using a managed object in a fetched results controller, simply pass the index path object in the `cellForRowAtIndexPath` parameter of the `tableView:cellForRowAtIndexPath:` delegate method of a table view. If you want to construct an

index path yourself anywhere else in your application, use the `indexPathForRow:inSection:` class method of `NSIndexPath`.

`fetchRequest` *(property, of type* `NSFetchRequest`*)*
: If at any point in your application you believe you have to change the fetch request object for your fetched results controllers, you can do so using the `fetchRequest` property of an instance of `NSFetchedResultsController`. This is useful, for example, if you want to change the sort descriptors (refer to Recipe 18.6 for information about this) of the fetch request object after you have allocated and initialized your fetched results controllers.

A fetched results controller also tracks the changes that happen in the context that it is bound to. For instance, let's say you have created your fetched results controller on View Controller A, and on View Controller B you are deleting an object from your context. As soon as you do that on View Controller B, your first view controller that owns the fetched results controller will get notified, assuming that View Controller A is the delegate of the fetched results controller. This is great and will come in handy. Imagine the situation where you are developing an app and your app displays two view controllers to the user. The root view controller is a table view controller that lists all the user's contacts, and the second view controller allows the user to add a new contact. As soon as the user presses the Save button on the second view controller and goes back to the list of her contacts, the list is already updated because of the delegation mechanism of the fetched results controller.

In the previously described application, you would declare your table view controller that lists all the user's contacts in this way:

```
#import "PersonsListTableViewController.h"
#import "AppDelegate.h"
#import "Person.h"
#import "AddPersonViewController.h"

static NSString *PersonTableViewCell = @"PersonTableViewCell";

@interface PersonsListTableViewController ()
<NSFetchedResultsControllerDelegate>

@property (nonatomic, strong) UIBarButtonItem *barButtonAddPerson;
@property (nonatomic, strong) NSFetchedResultsController *frc;

@end
```

The bar button declared in the code will be a simple + button on the navigation bar that allows the user to go to the Add Person view controller, where he will be able to add a new contact to our managed object context. The fetched results controller will also be used to actually fetch the persons from context and assist us in displaying them on our table view.

This is how we construct our fetched results controller:

```
/* Create the fetch request first */
NSFetchRequest *fetchRequest = [[NSFetchRequest alloc]
                                initWithEntityName:@"Person"];

NSSortDescriptor *ageSort =
[[NSSortDescriptor alloc] initWithKey:@"age"
                            ascending:YES];

NSSortDescriptor *firstNameSort =
[[NSSortDescriptor alloc] initWithKey:@"firstName"
                            ascending:YES];

fetchRequest.sortDescriptors = @[ageSort, firstNameSort];

self.frc =
[[NSFetchedResultsController alloc]
 initWithFetchRequest:fetchRequest
 managedObjectContext:[self managedObjectContext]
 sectionNameKeyPath:nil
 cacheName:nil];

self.frc.delegate = self;
NSError *fetchingError = nil;
if ([self.frc performFetch:&fetchingError]){
    NSLog(@"Successfully fetched.");
} else {
    NSLog(@"Failed to fetch.");
}
```

You can see that the fetched results controller is choosing the current table view controller as its own delegate. The delegate of the fetched results controller has to conform to the `NSFetchedResultsControllerDelegate` protocol. Here are some of the most important methods in this protocol:

`controllerWillChangeContent:`
: Gets called on the delegate to let it know that the context that is backing the fetched results controller has changed and that the fetched results controller is about to change its contents to reflect that. We usually use this method to prepare our table view for updates by calling the `beginUpdates` method on it.

`controller:didChangeObject:atIndexPath:forChangeType:newIndexPath:`
: Gets called on the delegate to inform the delegate of specific changes made to an object on the context. For instance, if you delete an object from the context, this method gets called, and its `forChangeType` parameter will contain the value `NSFetchedResultsChangeDelete`. Alternatively, if you insert a new object into the context, this parameter will contain the value `NSFetchedResultsChangeInsert`.

This method also gets called on your fetched results controller's delegate method when a managed object is updated, after the context is saved using the `save:` method of the context.

`controllerDidChangeContent:`
: Gets called on the delegate to inform it that the fetched results controller was refreshed and updated as a result of an update to a managed object context. Generally, programmers issue an `endUpdates` call on their table view within this method to ask the table view to process all the updates that they submitted after a `beginUpdates` method.

Here is a typical implementation of the aforementioned methods in the app whose concept was explained earlier:

```
- (void) controllerWillChangeContent:(NSFetchedResultsController *)controller{
    [self.tableView beginUpdates];
}

- (void) controller:(NSFetchedResultsController *)controller
    didChangeObject:(id)anObject
        atIndexPath:(NSIndexPath *)indexPath
      forChangeType:(NSFetchedResultsChangeType)type
       newIndexPath:(NSIndexPath *)newIndexPath{

    if (type == NSFetchedResultsChangeDelete){
        [self.tableView
         deleteRowsAtIndexPaths:@[indexPath]
         withRowAnimation:UITableViewRowAnimationAutomatic];
    }

    else if (type == NSFetchedResultsChangeInsert){
        [self.tableView
         insertRowsAtIndexPaths:@[newIndexPath]
         withRowAnimation:UITableViewRowAnimationAutomatic];
    }

}

- (void) controllerDidChangeContent:(NSFetchedResultsController *)controller{
    [self.tableView endUpdates];
}
```

Now, obviously, we also talked about providing information to a table view using various methods of the fetched results controller, such as the `objectAtIndexPath:` method. A simple implementation of this method in a table view could look like this:

```
- (NSInteger)tableView:(UITableView *)tableView
 numberOfRowsInSection:(NSInteger)section{

    id <NSFetchedResultsSectionInfo> sectionInfo =
        self.frc.sections[section];
```

```
        return sectionInfo.numberOfObjects;

    }

    - (UITableViewCell *)tableView:(UITableView *)tableView
            cellForRowAtIndexPath:(NSIndexPath *)indexPath{

        UITableViewCell *cell = nil;

        cell = [tableView dequeueReusableCellWithIdentifier:PersonTableViewCell
                                                forIndexPath:indexPath];


        Person *person = [self.frc objectAtIndexPath:indexPath];

        cell.textLabel.text =
        [person.firstName stringByAppendingFormat:@" %@", person.lastName];

        cell.detailTextLabel.text =
        [NSString stringWithFormat:@"Age: %lu",
         (unsigned long)[person.age unsignedIntegerValue]];

        return cell;
    }
```

In this code, we are telling our table view controller to display as many cells as there are instances of managed objects in our fetched results controller. While displaying each cell, we retrieve the `Person` managed object from the fetched results controller and configure our cell accordingly. Our table view controller, with no items in the managed object context, could look like Figure 18-11.

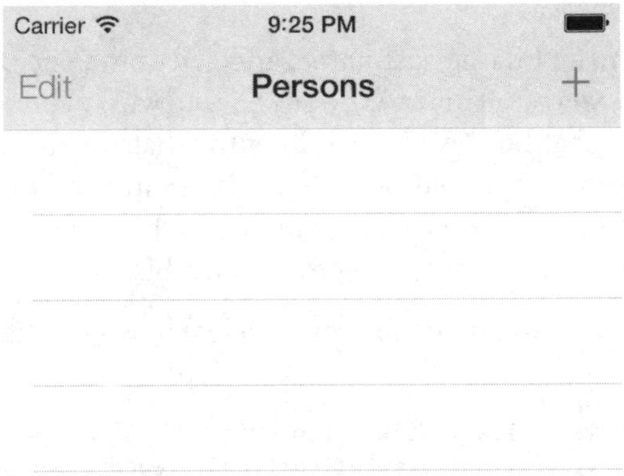

*Figure 18-11. An empty table view backed by a fetched results controller*

Now in the second view controller, where the user is allowed to add a new Person instance to the managed object context, we will use the following method:

```
- (void) createNewPerson:(id)paramSender{

    AppDelegate *appDelegate = [[UIApplication sharedApplication] delegate];

    NSManagedObjectContext *managedObjectContext =
        appDelegate.managedObjectContext;

    Person *newPerson =
    [NSEntityDescription insertNewObjectForEntityForName:@"Person"
                                  inManagedObjectContext:managedObjectContext];

    if (newPerson != nil){

        newPerson.firstName = self.textFieldFirstName.text;
        newPerson.lastName = self.textFieldLastName.text;
        newPerson.age = @([self.textFieldAge.text integerValue]);

        NSError *savingError = nil;

        if ([managedObjectContext save:&savingError]){
            [self.navigationController popViewControllerAnimated:YES];
        } else {
            NSLog(@"Failed to save the managed object context.");
        }

    } else {
        NSLog(@"Failed to create the new person object.");
    }

}
```

This method reads the first name, last name, and age of the person to be created from three text fields on the view controller. We don't have to worry about the implementation of those text fields, as that has nothing to do with what we are trying to learn in this recipe. After this method gets called, we call the save: method on our managed object context. This will in turn trigger the change in our fetched results controller in the first table view controller, which in turn will refresh the table view.

One last thing is how we can allow the user to delete items on the first table view controller:

```
- (void)     tableView:(UITableView *)tableView
    commitEditingStyle:(UITableViewCellEditingStyle)editingStyle
     forRowAtIndexPath:(NSIndexPath *)indexPath{

    Person *personToDelete = [self.frc objectAtIndexPath:indexPath];

    [[self managedObjectContext] deleteObject:personToDelete];
```

```
        if ([personToDelete isDeleted]){
            NSError *savingError = nil;
            if ([[self managedObjectContext] save:&savingError]){
                NSLog(@"Successfully deleted the object");
            } else {
                NSLog(@"Failed to save the context with error = %@", savingError);
            }
        }

    }
```

This code won't even touch the fetched results controller directly, but it deletes the selected person from the managed object context, which will refresh the fetched results controller, that in turn refreshing the table view. To learn more about table views, please refer to Chapter 4. The interface of our table view controller in deletion mode could look like that shown in Figure 18-12.

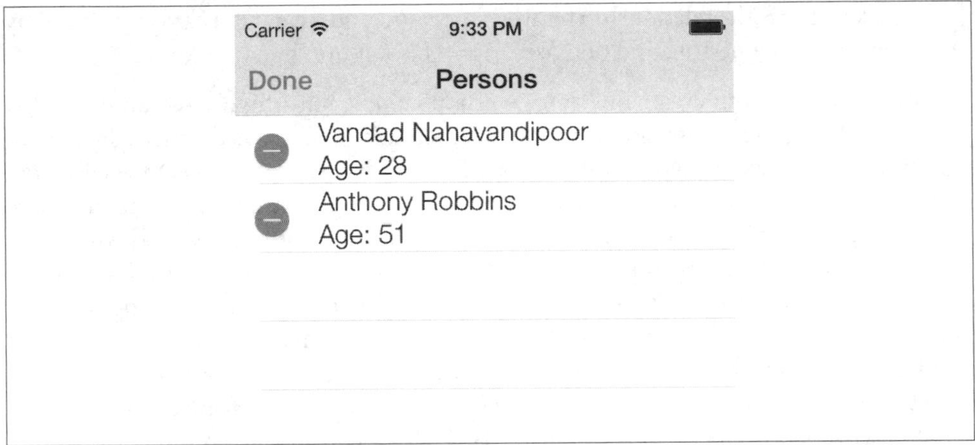


*Figure 18-12. Deletion mode of a table view controller that uses a fetched results controller*

# 18.8. Implementing Relationships in Core Data

## Problem

You want to be able to link your managed objects to each other: for instance, linking a `Person` to the `Home` he lives in.

## Solution

Use inverse relationships in the model editor.

## Discussion

Relationships in Core Data can be one-to-one, inverse one-to-many, or inverse many-to-many. Here is an example of each type of relationship:

*One-to-one relationship*
: An example is the relationship between a person and her nose. Each person can have only one nose, and each nose can belong to only one person.

*Inverse one-to-many relationship*
: An example is the relationship between an employee and his manager. The employee can have only one direct manager, but his manager can have multiple employees working for her. Here, the relationship of the employee with the manager is one-to-one, but from the manager's perspective, the relationship is one (manager) to many (employees); hence the word *inverse*.

*Inverse many-to-many relationship*
: An example is the relationship between a person and a car. One car can be used by more than one person, and one person can have more than one car.

In Core Data, you can create one-to-one relationships, but I highly recommend that you avoid doing so because, going back to the example in the preceding list, the person will know what nose she has, but the nose will not know who it belongs to. Please note that this is a different one-to-one model than what you might have seen in other database management systems where Object A and Object B will be linked together when they have a one-to-one relationship. In a Core Data one-to-one relationship, Object A will know about Object B, but not the other way around. In an object-oriented programming language such as Objective-C, it is always best to create inverse relationships so that child elements can refer to parent elements of that relationship. In a one-to-many relationship, the object that can have associations with many other objects will retain a set of those objects. The set will be of type `NSSet`. However, in a one-to-one relationship, objects on both sides of the fence keep a reference to one another using the proper class names of one another since, well, the relationship is one-to-one and an instance of one object in another object can easily be represented with the class name of that object.

Let's go ahead and create a data model that takes advantage of an inverse one-to-many relationship:

1. In Xcode, find the *xcdatamodel* file that was created for you when you started your Core Data project, as shown earlier in this chapter's Introduction (refer to Recipe 18.1 to create such a project).
2. Open the data model file in the editor by clicking on it.
3. Remove any entities that were created for you previously by selecting them and pressing the Delete key on your keyboard.

4. Create a new entity and name it **`Employee`**. Create three attributes for this entity, named **`firstName`** (of type `String`), **`lastName`** (of type `String`), and **`age`** (of type `Integer 32`), as shown in Figure 18-13.

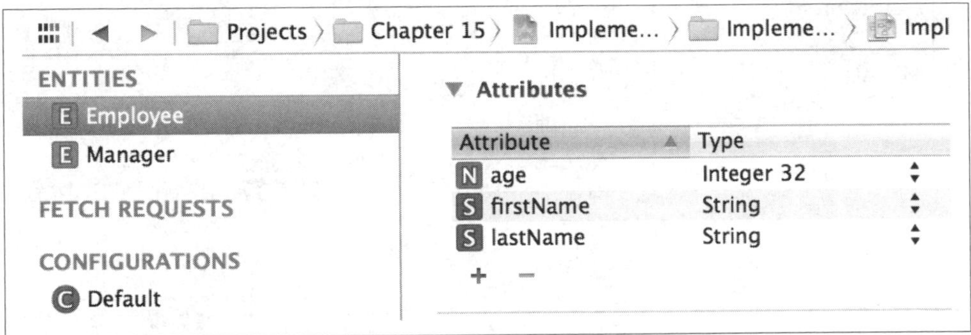


*Figure 18-13. The Employee entity with three attributes*

5. Create another entity named **`Manager`** with the same attributes you created for the `Employee` entity (`firstName` of type `String`, `lastName` of type `String`, and `age` of type `Integer 32`). See Figure 18-14.

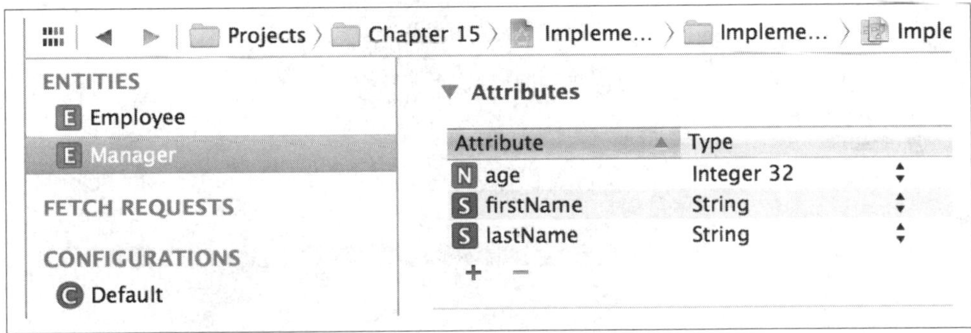


*Figure 18-14. The Manager entity with three attributes*

6. Create a new relationship for the `Manager` entity by first selecting the Manager entity in the list and then pressing the + button in the bottom of the Relationships box (see Figure 18-15).

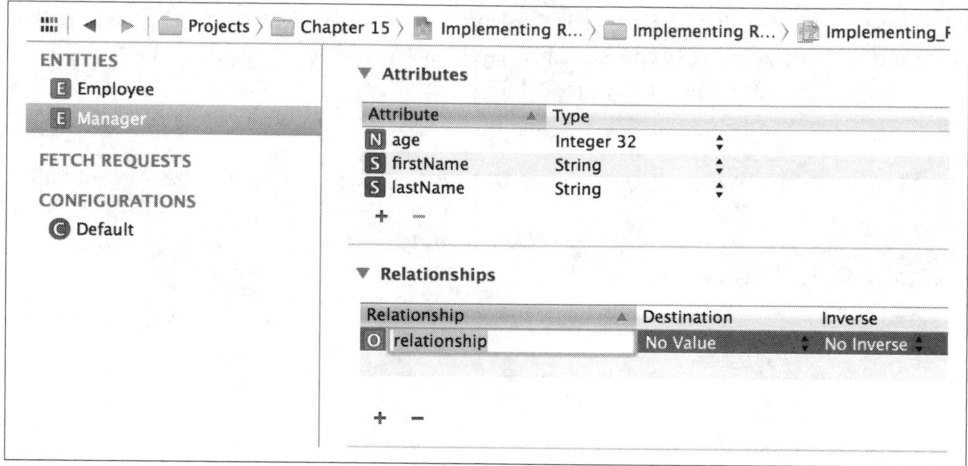


*Figure 18-15. We have added a new relationship to the Manager entity*

7. Set the name of the new relationship to **`employees`** (see Figure 18-16).

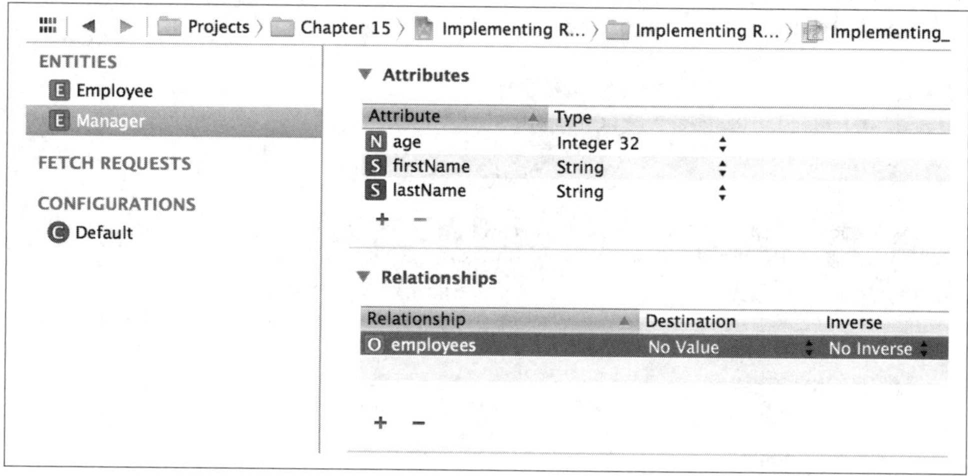


*Figure 18-16. Changing the name of the new Manager-to-Employees relationship*

8. Select the `Employee` entity and create a new relationship for it. Name the relationship **`manager`** (see Figure 18-17).

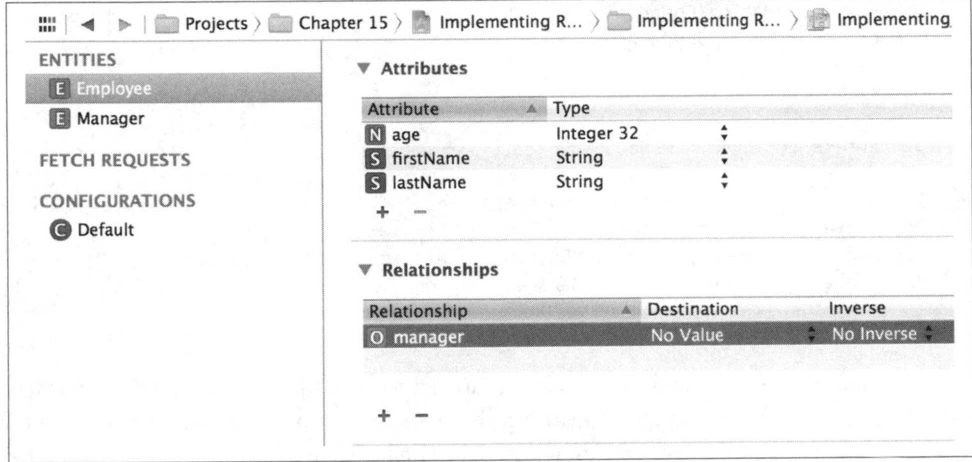


*Figure 18-17. Changing the name of the new Employee-to-Manager relationship*

9. Choose the `Manager` entity, and then select the `employees` relationship for the `Manager`. In the Relationships box, choose Employee in the Destination drop-down menu (because we want to connect a `Manager` to an `Employee` entity through this relationship), set the Inverse box's value to `manager` (because the `manager` relationship of the `Employee` will link an employee to her `Manager`), and tick the To-Many Relationship box in Data Model inspector (see Recipe 18.1). The results are shown in Figure 18-18.

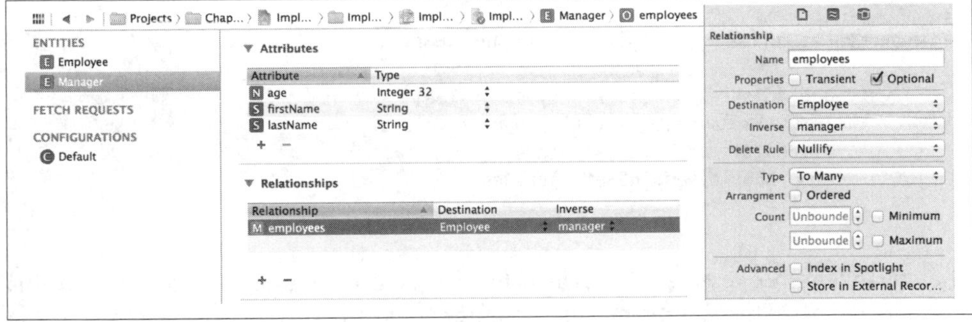


*Figure 18-18. The Manager inverse relationship established with employees*

10. Select both your `Employee` and `Manager` entities, select File → New File, and create the managed object classes for your model, as described in Recipe 18.2.

After creating the inverse one-to-many relationship, open the *.h* file of your `Employee` entity:

```
#import <Foundation/Foundation.h>
#import <CoreData/CoreData.h>

@class Manager;

@interface Employee : NSManagedObject

@property (nonatomic, retain) NSNumber * age;
@property (nonatomic, retain) NSString * firstName;
@property (nonatomic, retain) NSString * lastName;
@property (nonatomic, retain) Manager *manager;

@end
```

You can see that a new property has been added to this file. The property is named `manager` and its type is `Manager`, meaning that from now on, if we have a reference to any object of type `Employee`, we can access its `manager` property to access that specific employee's `Manager` object (if any). Let's have a look at the *.h* file of the `Manager` entity:

```
#import <Foundation/Foundation.h>
#import <CoreData/CoreData.h>

@class Employee;

@interface Manager : NSManagedObject

@property (nonatomic, retain) NSNumber * age;
@property (nonatomic, retain) NSString * firstName;
@property (nonatomic, retain) NSString * lastName;
@property (nonatomic, retain) NSSet *employees;
@end

@interface Manager (CoreDataGeneratedAccessors)

- (void)addEmployeesObject:(Employee *)value;
- (void)removeEmployeesObject:(Employee *)value;
- (void)addEmployees:(NSSet *)values;
- (void)removeEmployees:(NSSet *)values;

@end
```

The `employees` property is also created for the `Manager` entity. The data type of this object is `NSSet`. This simply means the `employees` property of any instance of the `Manager` entity can contain 1 to *N* number of `Employee` entities (a one-to-many relationship: one manager, many employees).

Another type of relationship that you might want to create is a many-to-many relationship. Going back to the `Manager` to `Employee` relationship, with a many-to-many relationship, any manager could have *N* number of employees, and one employee could have *N* number of managers. To do this, follow the same instructions for creating a one-to-many relationship, but select the `Employee` entity and then the `manager` relationship.

Change this name to `managers` and tick the To-Many Relationship box, as shown in Figure 18-19. Now the arrow has double arrowheads on both sides.

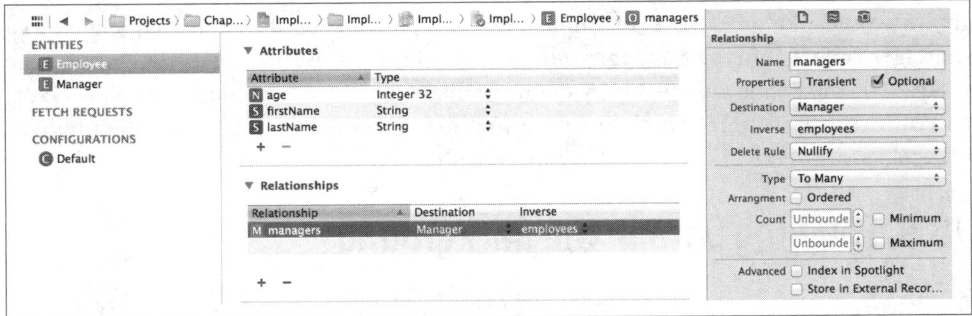


*Figure 18-19. Creating a Many-to-Many relationship between the Manager and Employee entities*

Now if you open the *Employee.h* file, the contents will be different:

```
#import <Foundation/Foundation.h>
#import <CoreData/CoreData.h>

@class Manager;

@interface Employee : NSManagedObject

@property (nonatomic, retain) NSNumber * age;
@property (nonatomic, retain) NSString * firstName;
@property (nonatomic, retain) NSString * lastName;
@property (nonatomic, retain) NSSet *managers;
@end

@interface Employee (CoreDataGeneratedAccessors)

- (void)addManagersObject:(Manager *)value;
- (void)removeManagersObject:(Manager *)value;
- (void)addManagers:(NSSet *)values;
- (void)removeManagers:(NSSet *)values;

@end
```

You can see that the `managers` property of the `Person` entity is now a set. Since the relationship from the employee to her managers is a set and so is the relationship from the manager to the employees, this creates a many-to-many relationship in Core Data.

In your code, for a one-to-many relationship, you can simply create a new `Manager` managed object (read how you can insert objects to a managed object context in Recipe 18.3), save it to the managed object context, and then create a couple of `Employee` managed objects and save them to the context as well. Now, to associate the manager with an employee, set the value of the manager property of an instance of Employee to an instance of the Manager managed object. Core Data will then create the relationship for you.

If you would like to retrieve all employees (of type Employee) that are associated to a manager object (of type Manager), all you have to do is use the allObjects instance method of the employees property of our manager object. This object is of type NSSet, so you can use its allObjects instance method to retrieve the array of all employee objects associated with a particular manager object.

## 18.9. Fetching Data in the Background

### Problem

You want to perform fetches in your Core Data Stack, all in the background. This is great if you want to ensure that you have a responsive user interface.

### Solution

Before performing background fetches, create a new managed object context with the concurrency type of NSPrivateQueueConcurrencyType. Then use the performBlock: method of your new background context to perform your fetches in the background. Once you are done and are ready to use your fetched objects in your UI, go back to the UI thread using dispatch_async (see Recipe 7.4) and for every object that you fetched in the background, issue the objectWithID: method on your main context. This will bring those background-fetched objects to your foreground context, ready to be used in your UI thread.

### Discussion

Fetching on the main thread is not a good idea unless you have a very limited number of items in your Core Data stack, because a fetch generally issues a search call to Core Data. It then has to fetch some data for you, usually using a predicate. To make your UI more responsive, it's best that you issue your fetches on a background context.

You can have as many contexts as you want in your app, but there is one golden rule here. You cannot pass managed objects between contexts on different threads, because the objects are not thread safe. That means that if you fetch objects on a background context, you cannot use them on the main thread. The correct way of passing managed objects between threads is to fetch them on a background thread, and then bring them into the main context (running on the main thread) using the objectWithID: method of your main context. This method accepts an object of type NSManagedObjectID, so in your background thread, instead of actually fetching the full managed objects, just fetch their persistent IDs and then pass those IDs to the main context to get the full object for you. This means that you do your actual searches and fetches in the background, grab the IDs of the objects that you found, and then pass those IDs to the main context for retrieval. This way, the main context will get a persistent ID to the objects, and the retrieval of those objects from the persistent store will be much faster than actually doing your whole search on the main context.

For the purpose of this recipe, I'm going to assume that you've already created a managed object model object named `Person` similar to that shown in Figure 18-20:

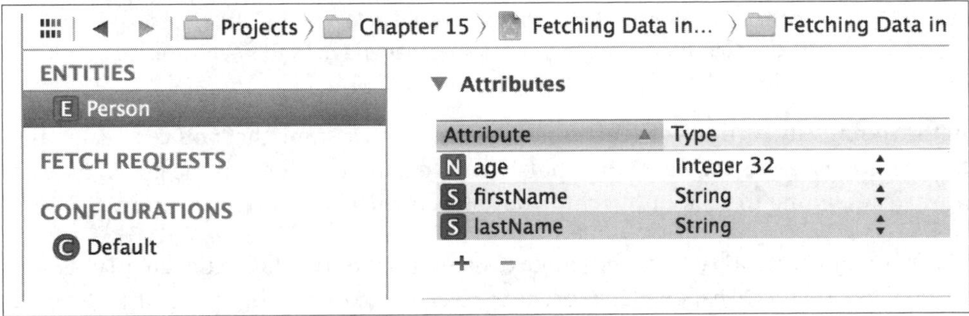


*Figure 18-20. Our simple Core Data model for this recipe*

With this model, before attempting to fetch anything from the stack, I'm going to populate the stack with 1,000 `Person` objects like so:

```
- (void) populateDatabase{

    for (NSUInteger counter = 0; counter < 1000; counter++){
        Person *person =
        [NSEntityDescription
         insertNewObjectForEntityForName:NSStringFromClass([Person class])
         inManagedObjectContext:self.managedObjectContext];

        person.firstName = [NSString stringWithFormat:@"First name %lu",
                            (unsigned long)counter];

        person.lastName = [NSString stringWithFormat:@"Last name %lu",
                           (unsigned long)counter];
        person.age = @(counter);
    }

    NSError *error = nil;
    if ([self.managedObjectContext save:&error]){
        NSLog(@"Managed to populate the database.");
    } else {
        NSLog(@"Failed to populate the database. Error = %@", error);
    }

}
```

Note how I am using the `NSStringFromClass` to change the name of the `Person` class into a string and then instantiate objects of that type. Some programmers prefer just to type `"Person"` as a literal string, but the problem with hardcoding your string in such a manner is that, if you change your mind later and want to change the name of the `Per son` in your Core Data stack, the hardcoded string will stay there and you may get crashes in your app at *runtime* as the model object named `Person` no longer exists. But if you use the aforementioned function to change the name of a class to a string, if that class's name is changed, or that class doesn't exist anymore, you'll get *compile-time* errors; and before you ship your app, you'll know that you have to fix those errors.

Before going any further with this recipe, I'm going to assume that you've already used the method that we just wrote to populate your database. So here is the general idea of how we are going to go about fetching our objects on a background context:

1. We will create a background context using the `initWithConcurrencyType:` initializer of the `NSManagedObjectContext` class and pass the value of `NSPrivate QueueConcurrencyType` to this method. This will give us a context that has its own private dispatch queue, so if you call the `performBlock:` block on the context, the block will be executed on a private background queue.
2. We are then going to set the value of the `persistentStoreCoordinator` property of our background context to the instance of our persistent store coordinator. This will bind our background context with our persistent store coordinator so that if you issue a fetch on the background context, it will be able to fetch the data right from disk or wherever the coordinator is storing the data.
3. We'll issue a `performBlock:` call on our background context and then issue a fetch request to look for all persons in the Core Data stack whose ages are between 100 and 200. Remember that the point of this exercise is not how realistic the data is. We are just trying to demonstrate a background fetch. When constructing the fetch request, we are going to set its `resultType` property's value to `NSManagedObjectI DResultType`. This will ensure that the results that come back from making this fetch request are not actual managed objects, but just the object IDs. As explained before, we don't want to fetch managed objects because they are fetched on the background context and therefore can't be used on the main thread. So we will fetch their IDs on the background context and then turn those IDs into real managed objects on the main context, after which the objects can be used on the main thread.

This is how we will construct our fetch request:

```
- (NSFetchRequest *) newFetchRequest{

    NSFetchRequest *request = [[NSFetchRequest alloc]
                               initWithEntityName:
                               NSStringFromClass([Person class])];

    request.fetchBatchSize = 20;
    request.predicate =
    [NSPredicate predicateWithFormat:@"(age >= 100) AND (age <= 200)"];

    request.resultType = NSManagedObjectIDResultType;
    return request;

}
```

And this is how we will go about creating our background context and then issue the fetch request on it:

```
- (BOOL)            application:(UIApplication *)application
  didFinishLaunchingWithOptions:(NSDictionary *)launchOptions{

    __weak NSManagedObjectContext *mainContext = self.managedObjectContext;
    __weak AppDelegate *weakSelf = self;
    __block NSMutableArray *mutablePersons = nil;

    /* Set up the background context */
    NSManagedObjectContext *backgroundContext =
    [[NSManagedObjectContext alloc]
     initWithConcurrencyType:NSPrivateQueueConcurrencyType];

    backgroundContext.persistentStoreCoordinator =
    self.persistentStoreCoordinator;

    /* Issue a block on the background context */
    [backgroundContext performBlock:^{

        NSError *error = nil;
        NSArray *personIds = [backgroundContext
                              executeFetchRequest:[weakSelf newFetchRequest]
                              error:&error];

        if (personIds != nil && error == nil){
            mutablePersons = [[NSMutableArray alloc]
                              initWithCapacity:personIds.count];

            /* Now go on the main context and get the objects on that
             context using their IDs */
            dispatch_async(dispatch_get_main_queue(), ^{
                for (NSManagedObjectID *personId in personIds){
                    Person *person = (Person *)[mainContext
                                                objectWithID:personId];
```

```
                [mutablePersons addObject:person];
            }
            [weakSelf processPersons:mutablePersons];
        });
    } else {
        NSLog(@"Failed to execute the fetch request.");
    }
}];

self.window = [[UIWindow alloc]
               initWithFrame:[[UIScreen mainScreen] bounds]];

self.window.backgroundColor = [UIColor whiteColor];
[self.window makeKeyAndVisible];
return YES;
}
```

This code collects all the managed objects in an array and then calls the `processPersons:` method on our app delegate to process the results in the array. We will develop this method like so:

```
- (void) processPersons:(NSArray *)paramPersons{
    for (Person *person in paramPersons){
        NSLog(@"First name = %@, last name = %@, age = %ld",
              person.firstName,
              person.lastName,
              (long)person.age.integerValue);
    }
}
```

## See Also

Recipe 7.4; Recipe 18.4; Recipe 18.6

# 18.10. Using Custom Data Types in Your Core Data Model

## Problem

You believe the choice of data types provided by Core Data doesn't suit your needs. You may need to use more data types, such as `UIColor`, in your model objects, but Core Data doesn't offer that data type out of the box.

## Solution

Use transformable data types.

## Discussion

Core Data allows you to create properties on your model objects and assign data types to those properties. Your choice is quite limited: a data type can be used in Core Data only if it can be turned into an instance of `NSData` and back again. By default, there are a number of popular classes, such as `UIColor`, that you cannot use for your properties. So what is the way around it? The answer is *transformable properties*. Let me explain the concept to you first.

So let's say that we want to create a model object in Core Data and name that model object `Laptop`. This object is going to have two properties: a `model` of type `String` and a `color` that we want to be of type `UIColor`. Core Data does not offer that data type, so we have to create a subclass of the `NSValueTransformer` class. Let's name our class `ColorTransformer`. Here are the things you have to do in the implementation of your class:

1. Override the `allowsReverseTransformation` class method of your class and return `YES` from it. This will tell Core Data that you can turn colors into data and data back into colors.
2. Override the `transformedValueClass` class method of your class and return the class name of `NSData` from it. The return value of this class method tells Core Data what class you are transforming your custom value to. In this case, you are turning `UIColor` to `NSData`, so we need to return the class name of `NSData` from this method.
3. Override the `transformedValue:` instance method of your transformer. In your method, take the incoming value (which will in this case be an instance of `UIColor`), transform it to `NSData`, and return that data back from this method.
4. Override the `reverseTransformedValue:` instance method of your transformer to do the opposite: take the incoming value, which will be data, and transform it to color.

Given this information, we are going to proceed to implementing our transformer as follows. We store a color as data simply by taking it apart into integer components and storing them in an array:

```
#import <UIKit/UIKit.h>
#import "ColorTransformer.h"

@implementation ColorTransformer

+ (BOOL) allowsReverseTransformation{
    return YES;
}

+ (Class) transformedValueClass{
    return [NSData class];
```

```
}

- (id) transformedValue:(id)value{

    /* Transform color to data */

    UIColor *color = (UIColor *)value;

    CGFloat red, green, blue, alpha;
    [color getRed:&red green:&green blue:&blue alpha:&alpha];
    CGFloat components[4] = {red, green, blue, alpha};
    NSData *dataFromColors = [[NSData alloc] initWithBytes:components
                                                    length:sizeof(components)];
    return dataFromColors;

}

- (id) reverseTransformedValue:(id)value{

    /* Transform back from data to color */

    NSData *data = (NSData *)value;
    CGFloat components[4] = {0.0f, 0.0f, 0.0f, 0.0f};
    [data getBytes:components length:sizeof(components)];

    UIColor *color = [UIColor colorWithRed:components[0]
                                     green:components[1]
                                      blue:components[2]
                                     alpha:components[3]];

    return color;

}

@end
```

Now let's go to our data model to create the `Laptop` managed object and create its attributes/properties. Ensure that the `color` attribute is transformable, and while this attribute is selected, press Alt+Command+3 on your keyboard to open the Model Inspector for this attribute. In the `name` field of the transformable class, enter the name of your custom transformer, in this case, `ColorTransformer`, as shown in Figure 18-21.

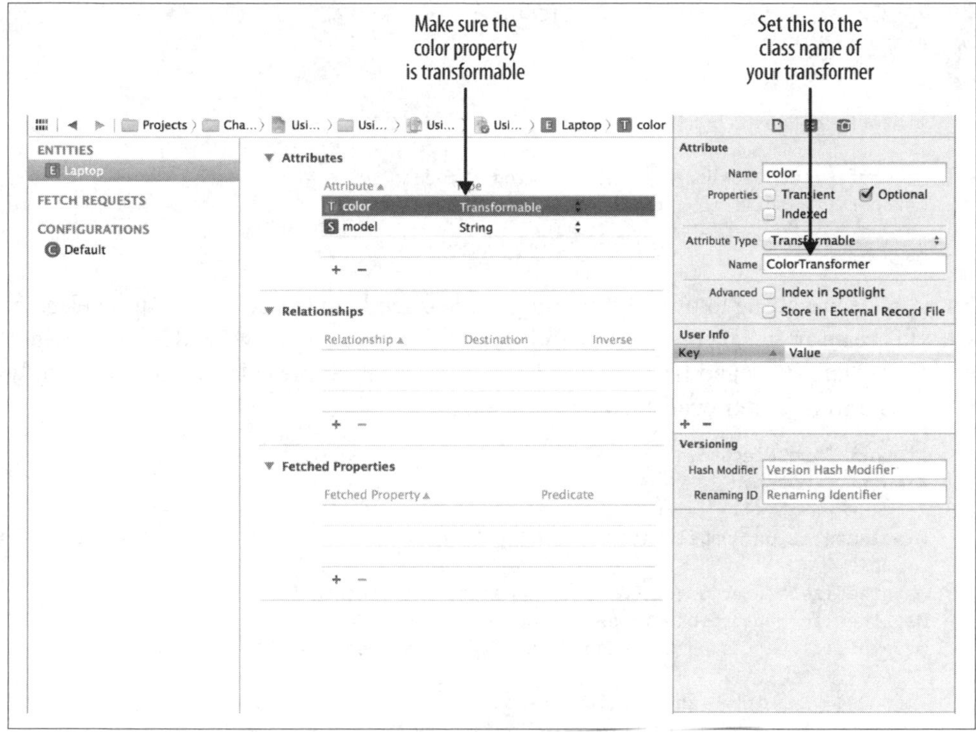


*Figure 18-21. Setting up our model with a transformable attribute*

Now use the technique that you learned in Recipe 18.2 to generate the class file for the `Laptop` managed object. After doing that, go into the header file of this managed object and you'll notice that the `color` attribute of your class is of type `id`.

```
#import <Foundation/Foundation.h>
#import <CoreData/CoreData.h>


@interface Laptop : NSManagedObject

@property (nonatomic, retain) NSString * model;
@property (nonatomic, retain) id color;

@end
```

This is good, but to make it better and help the compiler catch issues for us if we assign values of the incorrect type to this property, let's manually change this data type to `UIColor`:

```
#import <Foundation/Foundation.h>
#import <CoreData/CoreData.h>
```

```
/* Make sure to import this as UIColor is in UIKit */
#import <UIKit/UIKit.h>


@interface Laptop : NSManagedObject

@property (nonatomic, retain) NSString * model;
@property (nonatomic, retain) UIColor *color;

@end
```

So now we are going to put all the things we learned here to use. In our app delegate, we will create an instance of `Laptop` and set its color to red. Then we will insert that into our Core Data stack and try to read it back to see whether the color could successfully be saved and then retrieved back from the database:

```
#import "AppDelegate.h"
#import "Laptop.h"

@implementation AppDelegate

@synthesize managedObjectContext = _managedObjectContext;
@synthesize managedObjectModel = _managedObjectModel;
@synthesize persistentStoreCoordinator = _persistentStoreCoordinator;

- (BOOL)            application:(UIApplication *)application
  didFinishLaunchingWithOptions:(NSDictionary *)launchOptions{

    self.window = [[UIWindow alloc]
                   initWithFrame:[[UIScreen mainScreen] bounds]];
    self.window.backgroundColor = [UIColor whiteColor];
    [self.window makeKeyAndVisible];

    /* Save the laptop with a given color first */
    Laptop *laptop =
    [NSEntityDescription
     insertNewObjectForEntityForName:NSStringFromClass([Laptop class])
     inManagedObjectContext:self.managedObjectContext];

    laptop.model = @"model name";
    laptop.color = [UIColor redColor];

    NSError *error = nil;
    if ([self.managedObjectContext save:&error] == NO){
        NSLog(@"Failed to save the laptop. Error = %@", error);
    }

    /* Now find the same laptop */
    NSFetchRequest *fetch =
    [[NSFetchRequest alloc]
     initWithEntityName:NSStringFromClass([Laptop class])];
    fetch.fetchLimit = 1;
```

```
    fetch.predicate = [NSPredicate predicateWithFormat:@"color == %@",
                       [UIColor redColor]];

    error = nil;
    NSArray *laptops = [self.managedObjectContext
                        executeFetchRequest:fetch
                        error:&error];

    /* Check for 1 because out fetch limit is 1 */
    if (laptops.count == 1 && error == nil){

        Laptop *fetchedLaptop = laptops[0];

        if ([fetchedLaptop.color isEqual:[UIColor redColor]]){
            NSLog(@"Right colored laptop was fetched");
        } else {
            NSLog(@"Could not find the laptop with the given color.");
        }

    } else {
        NSLog(@"Could not fetch the laptop with the given color. \
              Error = %@", error);
    }

    return YES;
}
```

## See Also

Recipe 18.1

# CHAPTER 19
# Dates, Calendars, and Events

## 19.0. Introduction

The Event Kit and Event Kit UI frameworks allow iOS developers to access the Calendar database on an iOS device. You can insert, read, and modify events using the Event Kit framework. The Event Kit UI framework allows you to present built-in SDK GUI elements that allow the user to manipulate the Calendar database manually. In this chapter, we will focus on the Event Kit framework first and then learn about the Event Kit UI framework.

With the Event Kit framework, a programmer can modify the user's Calendar database without him knowing. However, this is not a very good practice. In fact, Apple prohibits programmers from doing so and asks us to always notify users about any changes that the program might make to the Calendar database. Here is a quote from Apple:

> If your application modifies a user's Calendar database programmatically, it must get confirmation from the user before doing so. An application should never modify the Calendar database without specific instruction from the user.

iOS comes with a built-in Calendar app that can work with different types of calendars, such as local, CalDAV, and so forth. In this chapter, we will be working with different types of calendars as well. To make sure you are prepared to run the code in some of the recipes in this chapter, please create an iCloud account and log into that account using your iOS device.

If you don't already have an iCloud account, you can create one using your iOS device again or using your Mac. To create an iCloud account on your Mac (which is a little easier), you will need to:

1. Open System Preferences.
2. Head over to the iCloud item, as shown in Figure 19-1.

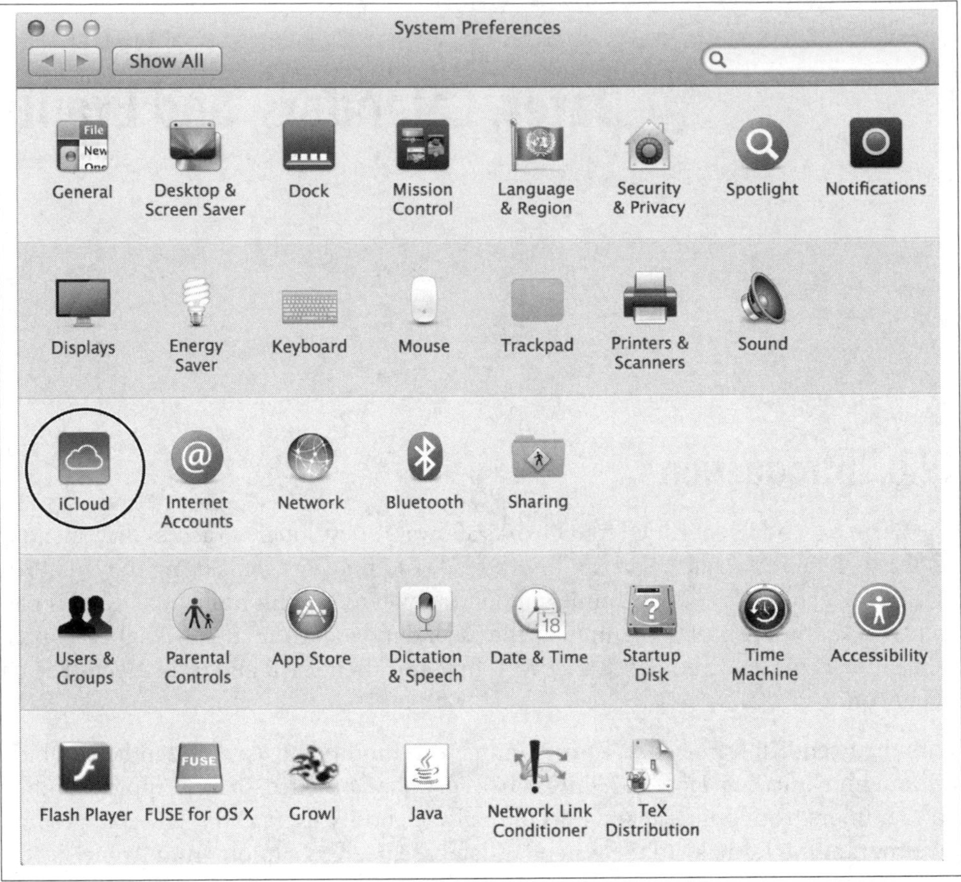


*Figure 19-1. Find and press the iCloud icon in your System Preferences*

3. You will be presented with a screen that asks you to log in with your existing iCloud account. Assuming that you don't already have one, you will need to select the "Create an Apple ID..." option on the screen, which shows as a link (see Figure 19-2).
4. Follow the on-screen instructions until you have your iCloud account. After signing into your iCloud account in System Preferences, you will see an interface similar to that shown in Figure 19-3.

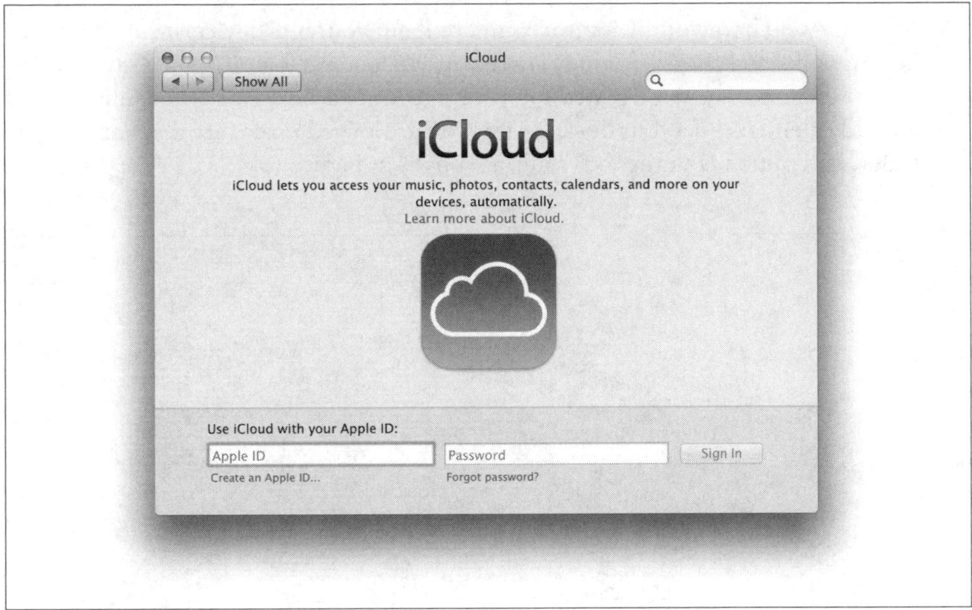


*Figure 19-2. System asking you to log into iCloud*

*Figure 19-3. Logged into an iCloud account on OS X*

5. Now that you have your iCloud account, pull out your iOS device, head over to the Settings app, and choose iCloud. There you can log into your iCloud account using the credentials that you created for your account earlier. This will bring all your iCloud calendars into your device. After you are logged in, ensure that your iCloud Calendars option is in the "on" state, as shown in Figure 19-4.

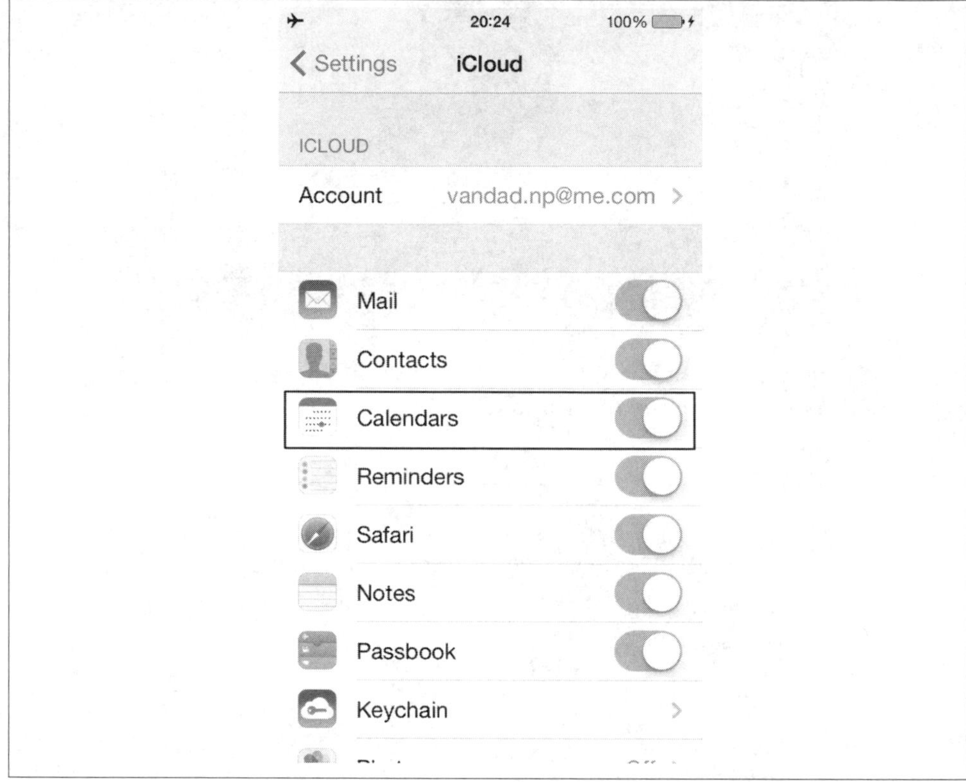


*Figure 19-4. iCloud Calendars needs to be enabled on your device*

That was all you needed to know in order to set your iOS device up with an iCloud account and enable calendar support on it. Now if you open the Calendar app on your device and head to the Calendars section of the app, you will see an interface similar to that shown in Figure 19-5. That is a confirmation that your iCloud account has been set up properly and that you have been given, with your iCloud account, a series of calendars that you can just use out of the box.

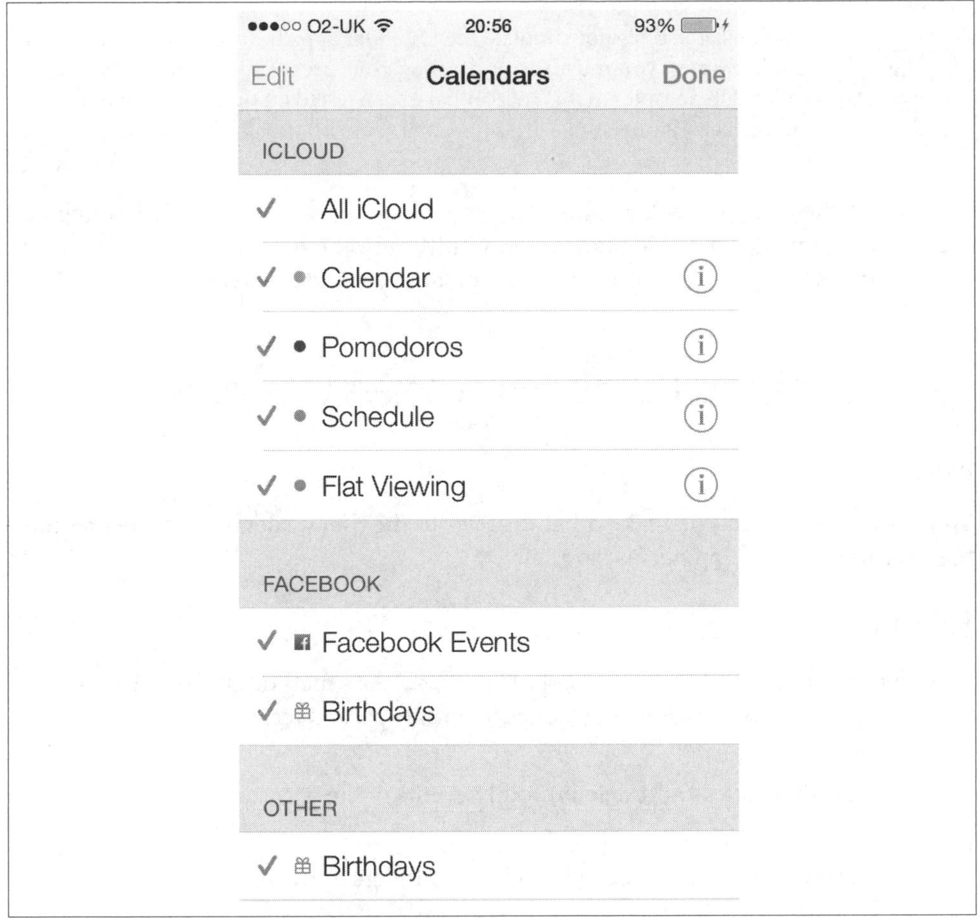


*Figure 19-5. iCloud Calendars are enabled in the Calendar app on an iOS device*

To run the example code in this chapter, you must add the Event Kit framework, and in some cases the Event Kit UI framework, to your application. Using the Modules feature in the new LLVM compiler, all you have to do to include these two frameworks into your projects is to import their appropriate umbrella headers into your source code, like so:

```
#import "AppDelegate.h"
#import <EventKit/EventKit.h>
#import <EventKitUI/EventKitUI.h>

@implementation AppDelegate

<# Rest of your code goes here #>
```

iOS Simulator does not simulate the Calendar app. To test the recipes in this chapter, you must run and debug your program on a real iOS device. All examples in this chapter have been tested on the new iPhone and the new iPad.

In most of the example code in this chapter, we will focus on manually reading and manipulating events in a calendar. If you want to use the built-in iOS capabilities to allow your users to quickly access their calendar events, please refer to Recipes 19.10 and 19.11.

# 19.1. Requesting Permission to Access Calendars

## Problem

You want to add events or make other changes to the user's calendar, but this requires the user to give your app permission.

## Solution

Invoke the `authorizationStatusForEntityType:` class method of the `EKEventStore` class and pass one of the following values to it as its parameter:

`EKEntityTypeEvent`
: Permission to access/add/delete/modify events in the user's calendars.

`EKEntityTypeReminder`
: Permission to access/add/delete/modify reminders in the user's calendars.

The method returns one of the following values:

`EKAuthorizationStatusAuthorized`
: Your app is authorized to access the given type of items (events or reminders).

`EKAuthorizationStatusDenied`
: The user has previously denied your app's access to the event store, and this remains in force.

`EKAuthorizationStatusNotDetermined`
: Your app has not attempted to access the event store before, so the user has not been asked to grant or reject permission. In this case, you need to ask for permission from the user to access the event store on her device using the `requestAccessToEntityType:completion:` instance method of the `EKEventStore` class.

`EKAuthorizationStatusRestricted`
: Due to some other restrictions on the device, such as parental controls, your app cannot access the event store on the device.

Here is a code snippet that will handle all these cases for us:

```
- (BOOL)            application:(UIApplication *)application
  didFinishLaunchingWithOptions:(NSDictionary *)launchOptions{

    EKEventStore *eventStore = [[EKEventStore alloc] init];

    switch ([EKEventStore
             authorizationStatusForEntityType:EKEntityTypeEvent]){

        case EKAuthorizationStatusAuthorized:{
            [self extractEventEntityCalendarsOutOfStore:eventStore];
            break;
        }
        case EKAuthorizationStatusDenied:{
            [self displayAccessDenied];
            break;
        }
        case EKAuthorizationStatusNotDetermined:{
            [eventStore
             requestAccessToEntityType:EKEntityTypeEvent
             completion:^(BOOL granted, NSError *error) {
                 if (granted){
                     [self extractEventEntityCalendarsOutOfStore:eventStore];
                 } else {
                     [self displayAccessDenied];
                 }
            }];
            break;
        }
        case EKAuthorizationStatusRestricted:{
            [self displayAccessRestricted];
            break;
        }

    }

    self.window = [[UIWindow alloc] initWithFrame:
                   [[UIScreen mainScreen] bounds]];

    self.window.backgroundColor = [UIColor whiteColor];
    [self.window makeKeyAndVisible];
    return YES;
}
```

This code snippet uses some methods whose implementation will be described in the Discussion section of this recipe.

## Discussion

The more Apple works on iOS, the more it pays attention to the user's privacy. So it is no shock that apps that want to access the user's event store, which contains all the calendars that have events and reminders, have to ask the user for permission first. In fact, if you don't ask for permission and then attempt to access the user's calendars, iOS will block the execution of your app and will display a dialog to the user asking for permission. This dialog looks similar to the one shown in Figure 19-6.

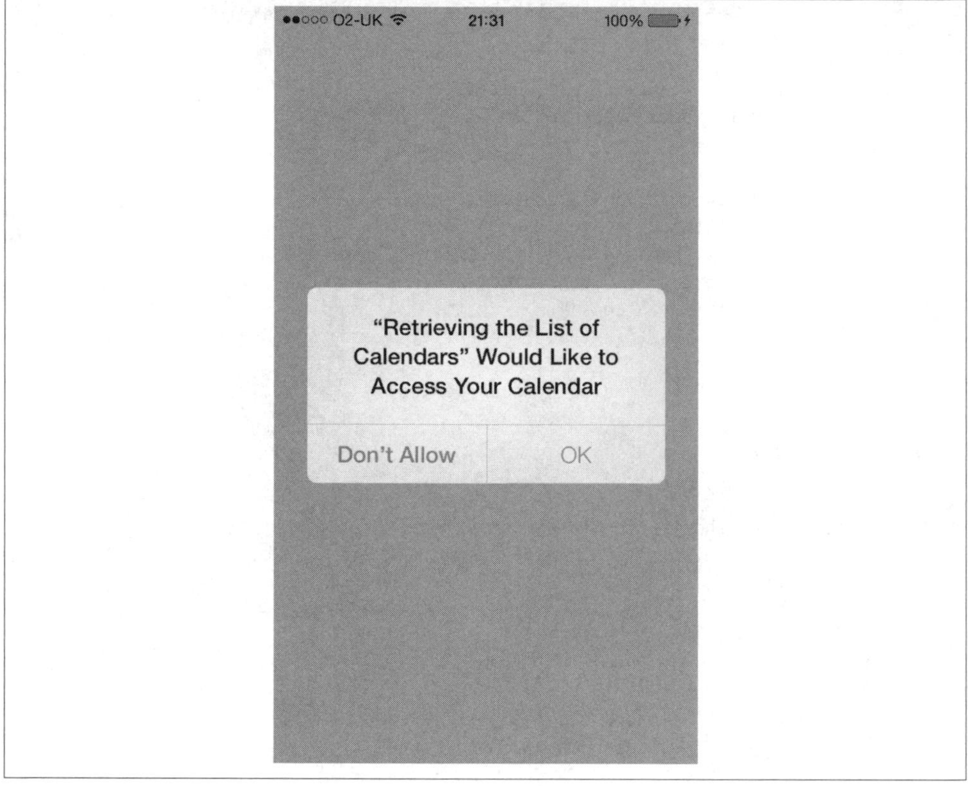


*Figure 19-6. Asking the user to grant or reject permission to an app wanting to access the event store on her device*

Now as good citizens of the iOS land, it's best that we ask the Event Kit framework for permission to access the user's event store *before* attempting to make the requests. The `requestAccessToEntityType:completion:` instance method of the `EKEventStore` class is the best way to do that. The `requestAccessToEntityType` parameter can be either `EKEntityTypeEvent` or `EKEntityTypeReminder`, depending on whether you want to access the events or the reminders, respectively, and the `completion` parameter needs to be a block object of the following type:

```
typedef void(^EKEventStoreRequestAccessCompletionHandler)
    (BOOL granted, NSError *error);
```

When you call this method, iOS asks the user to grant permission to your app to access the event store on her iOS device. Depending on her decision, your app may or may not get access. You can find that out by reading the value of the `granted` Boolean parameter of the `completion` block. If this value is `NO`, you can then read the value of the `error` parameter to determine what went wrong.

In the Solution section code snippet, we are calling some instance methods that are supposed to display an error message to the user for the `EKAuthorizationStatusDenied` and the `EKAuthorizationStatusRestricted` return values of the `authorizationStatusForEntityType:` class method of the `EKEventStore` class. The implementation of these two methods is extremely simple:

```
- (void) displayMessage:(NSString *)paramMessage{
    UIAlertView *alertView = [[UIAlertView alloc] initWithTitle:nil
                                                        message:paramMessage
                                                       delegate:nil
                                              cancelButtonTitle:nil
                                              otherButtonTitles:@"OK", nil];
    [alertView show];
}

- (void) displayAccessDenied{
    [self displayMessage:@"Access to the event store is denied."];
}

- (void) displayAccessRestricted{
    [self displayMessage:@"Access to the event store is restricted."];
}
```

The methods just display an alert to the user letting her know that your app cannot access the event store because it is being denied access. Now under the `EKAuthorizationStatusNotDetermined` status, if the `granted` value is `YES`, we call the `extractEventEntityCalendarsOutOfStore:` instance method of our class. This is a method that will take the instance of our event store and then try to use its `calendarsForEntityType:` instance method to get a list of calendars for that specific event type. The parameter to this method again can be either `EKEntityTypeEvent` or `EKEntityTypeReminder`, and the return value that comes back from this method will be an array of calendars that can handle events or reminders, respectively. The objects in the returned array will be of type `EKCalendar`.

Instances of `EKCalendar` represent a calendar, as their name shows, in the user's event store. As you saw in Figure 19-5, the user may have different accounts on her device and under each account, she may have different calendars. For instance, you can create multiple calendars under your iCloud account. Each instance of the `EKCalendar` class will represent one calendar object on the user's device.

Instances of the `EKCalendar` class have some interesting properties, such as the following:

`title`
: A string value that is set to the title of the calendar, such as "Birthdays."

`type`
: The type of the calendar. This value is of type `EKCalendarType` and can be equal to `EKCalendarTypeLocal`, `EKCalendarTypeCalDAV`, etc. This is the type of the calendar. For instance, iCloud calendars can be CalDAV calendars, so by querying this value, you can find out what type of calendar object you are dealing with. The type of the calendar will in turn tell you what you can do and not do with that calendar.

`CGColor`
: This is the color of the calendar. This is a Core Graphics color, and you can convert it to `UIColor` by using the `colorWithCGColor:` class method of the `UIColor` class.

`allowsContentModifications`
: This property will tell you if the current calendar allows you to make any modifications to it. A modification could be an insertion, a deletion, or a simple change of an existing event or reminder in that calendar.

As you saw earlier, the `application:didFinishLaunchingWithOptions:` method of our app delegate was calling the `extractEventEntityCalendarsOutOfStore:` instance method of our class. Using what you have learned about calendar objects, you can now understand the implementation of this method:

```
- (void) extractEventEntityCalendarsOutOfStore:(EKEventStore *)paramStore{

    NSArray *calendarTypes = @[
                               @"Local",
                               @"CalDAV",
                               @"Exchange",
                               @"Subscription",
                               @"Birthday",
                               ];

    NSArray *calendars = [paramStore
                          calendarsForEntityType:EKEntityTypeEvent];

    NSUInteger counter = 1;
    for (EKCalendar *calendar in calendars){
        /* The title of the calendar */
        NSLog(@"Calendar %lu Title = %@",
              (unsigned long)counter, calendar.title);

        /* The type of the calendar */
        NSLog(@"Calendar %lu Type = %@",
              (unsigned long)counter,
              calendarTypes[calendar.type]);
```

```
        /* The color that is associated with the calendar */
        NSLog(@"Calendar %lu Color = %@",
              (unsigned long)counter,
              [UIColor colorWithCGColor:calendar.CGColor]);

        /* And whether the calendar can be modified or not */
        if ([calendar allowsContentModifications]){
            NSLog(@"Calendar %lu can be modified.",
                  (unsigned long)counter);
        } else {
            NSLog(@"Calendar %lu cannot be modified.",
                  (unsigned long)counter);
        }
        counter++;
    }
}
```

Once you run this code on your device, depending on how many calendars you have already set up on your iCloud account and other calendars that may have been linked to your computer, you will get results similar to those shown here, printed to your console:

```
Calendar 1 Title = vandad.np@gmail.com
Calendar 1 Type = CalDAV
Calendar 1 Color = UIDeviceRGBColorSpace 0.160784 0.321569 0.639216 1
Calendar 1 can be modified.
Calendar 4 Title = Sportives
Calendar 4 Type = CalDAV
Calendar 4 Color = UIDeviceRGBColorSpace 0.694118 0.266667 0.054902 1
Calendar 4 can be modified.
Calendar 5 Title = Concerts
Calendar 5 Type = CalDAV
Calendar 5 Color = UIDeviceRGBColorSpace 0.184314 0.388235 0.0352941 1
Calendar 5 can be modified.
Calendar 6 Title = Schedule
Calendar 6 Type = CalDAV
Calendar 6 Color = UIDeviceRGBColorSpace 0.964706 0.309804 0 1
Calendar 6 can be modified.
Calendar 7 Title = Flat Viewing
Calendar 7 Type = CalDAV
Calendar 7 Color = UIDeviceRGBColorSpace 0.266667 0.654902 0.0117647 1
Calendar 7 can be modified.
```

## See Also

Recipe 19.0, "Introduction"

# 19.2. Retrieving Calendar Groups on an iOS Device

## Problem

The user has different calendar accounts, such as an iCloud account and a separate CalDAV account, and a calendar named *Calendar* under both of these accounts. You want to create an event under the calendar appropriately titled "Calendar" that belongs to the user's iCloud account, and not the other accounts that she may have on her iOS device.

## Solution

Find the event sources that are present in the user's event store by going through the `sources` array property in an instance of `EKEventStore`. This array will contain objects of type `EKSource`, each of which represents a group of calendars in the event store on the user's device.

## Discussion

Let's not make anything complicated here. To make a long story short, users can have different accounts (iCloud, Exchange, etc.). Each of these accounts, if they support calendars, is treated as an *event source*. An event source will then contain calendars.

To find a specific calendar with a given title, you first have to find that calendar in the correct event source. For instance, the following code snippet attempts to find the event source titled *iCloud* on the user's device:

```
- (void) findIcloudEventSource{

    EKSource *icloudEventSource = nil;

    EKEventStore *eventStore = [[EKEventStore alloc] init];
    for (EKSource *source in eventStore.sources){

        if (source.sourceType == EKSourceTypeCalDAV &&
            [source.title caseInsensitiveCompare:@"iCloud"]){
            icloudEventSource = source;
            break;
        }
    }

    if (icloudEventSource != nil){
        NSLog(@"The iCloud event source was found = %@", icloudEventSource);
    } else {
        NSLog(@"Could not find the iCloud event source");
    }

}
```

By following the instructions in Recipe 19.1, ensure that you have already asked the user for permission to access the calendars on her device.

If you look closely, we are also checking the type of the event source. This is because we know that iCloud calendars are CalDAV; hence, finding the source not only by the title "iCloud," but also by its type gives us more precision in pinpointing the correct event source.

Once you find your target `EKSource` event source, you can enumerate and go through the different calendar objects that it holds by invoking the `calendarsForEntityType:` instance method on it. As its parameter, pass `EKEntityTypeEvent` to look for calendars that support events, or `EKEntityTypeReminder` to look for calendars that support reminders. Bear in mind that the return value of the aforementioned method is of type `NSSet`, not an array. But you can enumerate the items in that set just like you would an array:

```
- (void) findIcloudEventSource{

    EKSource *icloudEventSource = nil;

    EKEventStore *eventStore = [[EKEventStore alloc] init];
    for (EKSource *source in eventStore.sources){

        if (source.sourceType == EKSourceTypeCalDAV &&
            [source.title caseInsensitiveCompare:@"iCloud"]){
            icloudEventSource = source;
            break;
        }
    }

    if (icloudEventSource != nil){
        NSLog(@"The iCloud event source was found = %@", icloudEventSource);

        NSSet *calendars = [icloudEventSource
                            calendarsForEntityType:EKEntityTypeEvent];

        for (EKCalendar *calendar in calendars){
            NSLog(@"Calendar = %@", calendar);
        }

    } else {
        NSLog(@"Could not find the iCloud event source");
    }

}
```

## See Also

Recipe 19.1

# 19.3. Adding Events to Calendars

## Problem

You would like to be able to create new events in users' calendars.

## Solution

Find the calendar you want to insert your event into (please refer to Recipe 19.1 and Recipe 19.2). Create an object of type `EKEvent` using the `eventWithEventStore:` class method of `EKEvent` and save the event into the user's calendar using the `saveEvent:span:error:` instance method of `EKEventStore`:

```
- (BOOL)     createEventWithTitle:(NSString *)paramTitle
                        startDate:(NSDate *)paramStartDate
                          endDate:(NSDate *)paramEndDate
                       inCalendar:(EKCalendar *)paramCalendar
                     inEventStore:(EKEventStore *)paramStore
                            notes:(NSString *)paramNotes{

    BOOL result = NO;

    /* If a calendar does not allow modification of its contents
     then we cannot insert an event into it */
    if (paramCalendar.allowsContentModifications == NO){
        NSLog(@"The selected calendar does not allow modifications.");
        return NO;
    }

    /* Create an event */
    EKEvent *event = [EKEvent eventWithEventStore:paramStore];
    event.calendar = paramCalendar;

    /* Set the properties of the event such as its title,
     start date/time, end date/time, etc. */
    event.title = paramTitle;
    event.notes = paramNotes;
    event.startDate = paramStartDate;
    event.endDate = paramEndDate;

    /* Finally, save the event into the calendar */
    NSError *saveError = nil;

    result = [paramStore saveEvent:event
                              span:EKSpanThisEvent
                             error:&saveError];
```

```
    if (result == NO){
        NSLog(@"An error occurred = %@", saveError);
    }

    return result;

}
```

As you can see, this method expects a calendar object and an event store to create the event in. In Recipe 19.2, we learned how to find event sources and the calendars that are associated with those sources. We are therefore going to create some handy methods that can search in all the available event sources, and all the available calendars in those sources, for the specific calendar we are looking for. So here are our methods:

```
- (EKSource *) sourceInEventStore:(EKEventStore *)paramEventStore
                        sourceType:(EKSourceType)paramType
                       sourceTitle:(NSString *)paramSourceTitle{

    for (EKSource *source in paramEventStore.sources){

        if (source.sourceType == paramType &&
            [source.title
             caseInsensitiveCompare:paramSourceTitle] == NSOrderedSame){
            return source;
        }
    }
    return nil;

}

- (EKCalendar *) calendarWithTitle:(NSString *)paramTitle
                              type:(EKCalendarType)paramType
                          inSource:(EKSource *)paramSource
                      forEventType:(EKEntityType)paramEventType{

    for (EKCalendar *calendar in [paramSource
                                  calendarsForEntityType:paramEventType]){
        if ([calendar.title
             caseInsensitiveCompare:paramTitle] == NSOrderedSame &&
            calendar.type == paramType){
            return calendar;
        }
    }

    return nil;

}
```

The `sourceInEventStore:sourceType:sourceTitle:` is able to find an event source with a given type and title. For instance, you can find the iCloud event source by passing `EKSourceTypeCalDAV` as the type and iCloud as the title and you will get the event source, if it is present on the device. After you have the event source, use the `calendarWithTitle:type:inSource:forEventType:` method to get a specific calendar inside a given event source. So if you want to find an iCloud calendar titled *`Calendar`*, assuming that you've already found the event source, pass `EKCalendarTypeCalDAV` as the type of the calendar and `EKEntityTypeEvent` as the event type.

Once you have these handy methods at your disposal, you can create a new event as shown here:

```
- (void) insertEventIntoStore:(EKEventStore *)paramStore{

    EKSource *icloudSource = [self sourceInEventStore:paramStore
                                           sourceType:EKSourceTypeCalDAV
                                          sourceTitle:@"iCloud"];

    if (icloudSource == nil){
        NSLog(@"You have not configured iCloud for your device.");
        return;
    }

    EKCalendar *calendar = [self calendarWithTitle:@"Calendar"
                                              type:EKCalendarTypeCalDAV
                                          inSource:icloudSource
                                      forEventType:EKEntityTypeEvent];

    if (calendar == nil){
        NSLog(@"Could not find the calendar we were looking for.");
        return;
    }

    /* The event starts from today, right now */
    NSDate *startDate = [NSDate date];

    /* And the event ends this time tomorrow.
     24 hours, 60 minutes per hour and 60 seconds per minute
     hence 24 * 60 * 60 */
    NSDate *endDate = [startDate
                       dateByAddingTimeInterval:24 * 60 * 60];

    /* Create the new event */
    BOOL createdSuccessfully = [self createEventWithTitle:@"My Concert"
                                                startDate:startDate
                                                  endDate:endDate
                                               inCalendar:calendar
                                             inEventStore:paramStore
                                                    notes:nil];

    if (createdSuccessfully){
        NSLog(@"Successfully created the event.");
```

```
        } else {
            NSLog(@"Failed to create the event.");
        }

}
```

## Discussion

To programmatically create a new event in a calendar on an iOS device, we must do the following:

1. Allocate and initialize an instance of `EKEventStore`.
2. Find the calendar we want to save the event to (please refer to Recipe 19.2). We must make sure the target calendar supports modifications by checking that the calendar object's `allowsContentModifications` property is `YES`. If it is not, you must choose a different calendar or forgo saving the event.
3. Once you find your target calendar, create an event of type `EKEvent` using the `eventWithEventStore:` class method of `EKEvent`.
4. Set the properties of the new event such as its `title`, `startDate`, and `endDate`.
5. Associate your event with the calendar that you found in step 2 using the `calendars` property of an instance of `EKEvent`.
6. Once you are done setting the properties of your event, add that event to the calendar using the `saveEvent:span:error:` instance method of `EKEventStore`. The return value of this method (a `BOOL` value) indicates whether the event was successfully inserted into the Calendar database. If the operation fails, the `NSError` object passed to the `error` parameter of this method will contain the error that has occurred in the system while inserting this event.

If you attempt to insert an event without specifying a target calendar, or if you insert an event into a calendar that cannot be modified, the `saveEvent:span:error:` instance method of `EKEventStore` will fail with an error similar to this:

```
Error Domain=EKErrorDomain Code=1 "No calendar has been set."
UserInfo=0x15d860 {NSLocalizedDescription=No calendar has been set.}
```

Running our code on an iOS device, we will see an event created in the Calendar database, as shown in Figure 19-7.

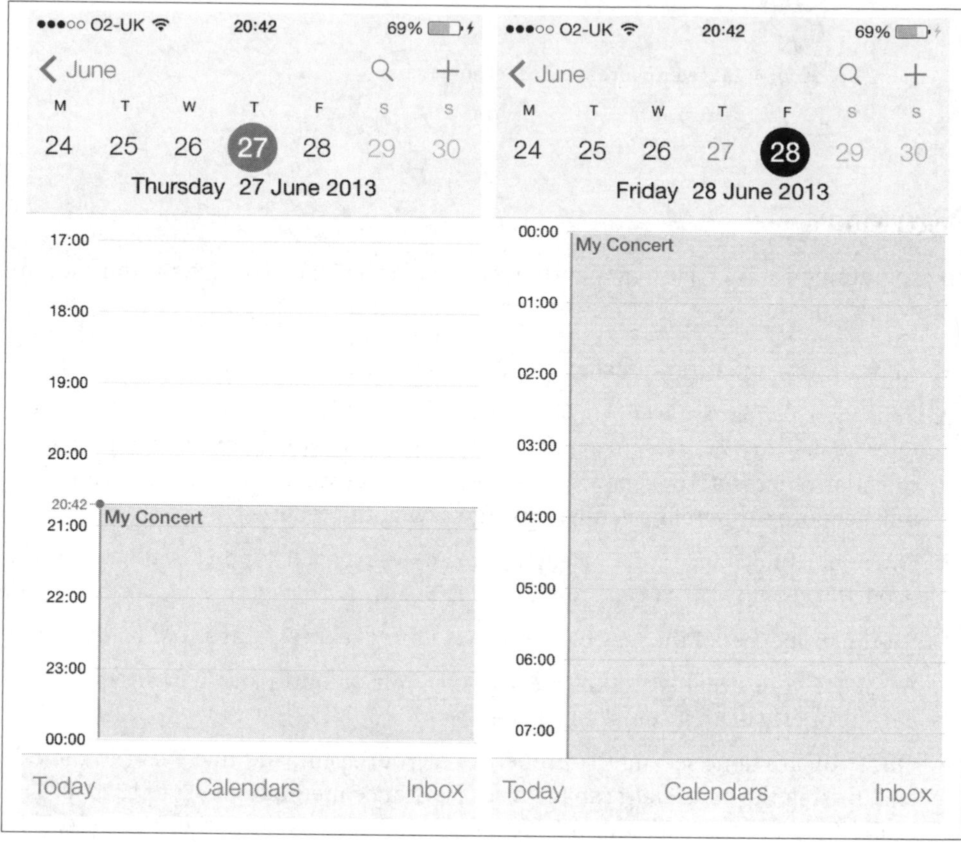


*Figure 19-7. Programmatically adding an event to a calendar*

iOS syncs online calendars with the iOS calendar. These calendars could be Exchange, CalDAV, and other common formats. Creating an event on a CalDAV calendar on an iOS device will create the same event on the server. The server changes are also reflected in the iOS Calendar database when the Calendar database is synced with the server.

## See Also

Recipe 19.1

# 19.4. Accessing the Contents of Calendars

## Problem

You want to retrieve events of type `EKEvent` from a calendar of type `EKCalendar` on an iOS device.

## Solution

Follow these steps:

1. Instantiate an object of type `EKEventStore`.
2. Using the techniques that you learned earlier in this chapter, find the calendar object that you want to inspect and read from.
3. Determine the time and date where you want to start the search in the calendar and the time and date where the search must stop.
4. Pass the calendar object (found in step 2), along with the two dates you found in step 3, to the `predicateForEventsWithStartDate:endDate:calendars:` instance method of `EKEventStore`.
5. Pass the predicate created in step 4 to the `eventsMatchingPredicate:` instance method of `EKEventStore`. The result of this method is an array of `EKEvent` objects (if any) that fell between the given dates (step 3) in the specified calendar (step 2).

This code illustrates the preceding steps:

```
- (void) readEvents{

    /* Instantiate the event store */
    EKEventStore *eventStore = [[EKEventStore alloc] init];

    EKSource *icloudSource = [self sourceInEventStore:eventStore
                                           sourceType:EKSourceTypeCalDAV
                                          sourceTitle:@"iCloud"];

    if (icloudSource == nil){
        NSLog(@"You have not configured iCloud for your device.");
        return;
    }

    EKCalendar *calendar = [self calendarWithTitle:@"Calendar"
                                               type:EKCalendarTypeCalDAV
                                           inSource:icloudSource
                                       forEventType:EKEntityTypeEvent];

    if (calendar == nil){
        NSLog(@"Could not find the calendar we were looking for.");
        return;
    }

    /* The start date will be today */
    NSDate *startDate = [NSDate date];

    /* The end date will be 1 day from today */
    NSDate *endDate = [startDate dateByAddingTimeInterval:24 * 60 * 60];
```

```
    /* Create the predicate that we can later pass to the
     event store in order to fetch the events */
    NSPredicate *searchPredicate =
    [eventStore predicateForEventsWithStartDate:startDate
                                        endDate:endDate
                                      calendars:@[calendar]];

    /* Make sure we succeeded in creating the predicate */
    if (searchPredicate == nil){
        NSLog(@"Could not create the search predicate.");
        return;
    }

    /* Fetch all the events that fall between
     the starting and the ending dates */
    NSArray *events = [eventStore eventsMatchingPredicate:searchPredicate];

    /* Go through all the events and print their information
     out to the console */
    if (events != nil){

        NSUInteger counter = 1;
        for (EKEvent *event in events){

            NSLog(@"Event %lu Start Date = %@",
                  (unsigned long)counter,
                  event.startDate);

            NSLog(@"Event %lu End Date = %@",
                  (unsigned long)counter,
                  event.endDate);

            NSLog(@"Event %lu Title = %@",
                  (unsigned long)counter,
                  event.title);

            counter++;
        }

    } else {
        NSLog(@"The array of events for this start/end time is nil.");
    }

}
```

This code is using the methods that we learned in Recipe 19.3 to find an iCloud calendar. I highly encourage you to review that recipe if you have not already done so or if you are having difficulty understanding how this code works.

## Discussion

As mentioned in this chapter's Introduction, an iOS device can be configured with different types of calendars using CalDAV (for iCloud, etc.), Exchange, and so on. Each calendar that is accessible by the Event Kit framework is encompassed within an `EKCalendar` object. You can fetch events inside a calendar in different ways, but the easiest way is to create and execute a specially formatted specification of dates and times, called a *predicate*, inside an event store.

A predicate of type `NSPredicate` that we can use in the Event Kit framework can be created using the `predicateForEventsWithStartDate:endDate:calendars:` instance method of an `EKEventStore`. The parameters to this method are the following:

`predicateForEventsWithStartDate`
: The starting date and time from when the events have to be fetched.

`endDate`
: The ending date up until which the events will be fetched.

`calendars`
: The array of calendars to search for events between the starting and ending dates.

Be sure to ask the user for her permission before attempting to access events or any other objects in her calendars. You can learn more about this in Recipe 19.1.

## See Also

Recipe 19.1

# 19.5. Removing Events from Calendars

## Problem

You want to be able to delete a specific event or series of events from users' calendars.

## Solution

Use the `removeEvent:span:commit:error:` instance method of `EKEventStore`.

## Discussion

The `removeEvent:span:commit:error:` instance method of `EKEventStore` can remove an instance of an event or all instances of a recurring event. For more information about recurring events, please refer to Recipe 19.6. In this recipe, we will only remove an instance of the event and not the other instances of the same event in the calendar.

The parameters that we can pass to this method are the following:

`removeEvent`
: This is the `EKEvent` instance to be removed from the calendar.

`span`
: This is the parameter that tells the event store whether we want to remove only this event or all the occurrences of this event in the calendar. To remove only the current event, specify the `EKSpanThisEvent` value for the `removeEvent` parameter. To remove all occurrences of the same event from the calendar, pass the `EKSpanFutureEvents` value for the parameter.

`commit`
: A Boolean value that tells the event store if the changes have to be saved on the remote/local calendar immediately or not.

`error`
: This parameter can be given a reference to an `NSError` object that will be filled with the error (if any), when the return value of this method is `NO`.

To demonstrate this, let's use the event creation method that we implemented in Recipe 19.3. What we can do then is to create an event in our iCloud calendar and after it has been created, attempt to delete it from the event store:

```
- (void) deleteEventInStore:(EKEventStore *)paramEventStore{

    EKSource *icloudSource = [self sourceInEventStore:paramEventStore
                                           sourceType:EKSourceTypeCalDAV
                                          sourceTitle:@"iCloud"];

    if (icloudSource == nil){
        NSLog(@"You have not configured iCloud for your device.");
        return;
    }

    EKCalendar *calendar = [self calendarWithTitle:@"Calendar"
                                              type:EKCalendarTypeCalDAV
                                          inSource:icloudSource
                                      forEventType:EKEntityTypeEvent];

    if (calendar == nil){
        NSLog(@"Could not find the calendar we were looking for.");
        return;
    }

    /* Create the event first */
    /* The event starts from today, right now */
    NSDate *startDate = [NSDate date];

    /* And the event ends this time tomorrow.
     24 hours, 60 minutes per hour and 60 seconds per minute
     hence 24 * 60 * 60 */
```

```
    NSDate *endDate = [startDate
                       dateByAddingTimeInterval:24 * 60 * 60];

    NSString *eventTitle = @"My Event";

    BOOL createdSuccessfully = [self createEventWithTitle:eventTitle
                                                startDate:startDate
                                                  endDate:endDate
                                               inCalendar:calendar
                                             inEventStore:paramEventStore
                                                    notes:nil];

    if (createdSuccessfully == NO){
        NSLog(@"Could not create the event.");
    }

    BOOL removedSuccessfully = [self removeEventWithTitle:eventTitle
                                                startDate:startDate
                                                  endDate:endDate
                                             inEventStore:paramEventStore
                                               inCalendar:calendar
                                                    notes:nil];

    if (removedSuccessfully){
        NSLog(@"Successfully created and deleted the event");
    } else {
        NSLog(@"Failed to delete the event.");
    }

}
```

The `sourceInEventStore:sourceType:sourceTitle:` and `calendarWithTitle:type:inSource:forEventType:` methods that we are using in this example code were described in Recipe 19.3. So I suggest you have a look at that recipe before proceeding with this one. In this code, after finding our target calendar, we are creating a dummy event in the calendar using the method described in Recipe 19.3. After that, we attempt to remove that event. The method that allows us to remove an existing event is coded this way:

```
- (BOOL)     removeEventWithTitle:(NSString *)paramTitle
                        startDate:(NSDate *)paramStartDate
                          endDate:(NSDate *)paramEndDate
                     inEventStore:(EKEventStore *)paramEventStore
                       inCalendar:(EKCalendar *)paramCalendar
                            notes:(NSString *)paramNotes{

    BOOL result = NO;

    /* If a calendar does not allow modification of its contents
     then we cannot insert an event into it */
    if (paramCalendar.allowsContentModifications == NO){
        NSLog(@"The selected calendar does not allow modifications.");
```

```
        return NO;
    }


    NSPredicate *predicate =
    [paramEventStore predicateForEventsWithStartDate:paramStartDate
                                             endDate:paramEndDate
                                           calendars:@[paramCalendar]];

    /* Get all the events that match the parameters */
    NSArray *events = [paramEventStore eventsMatchingPredicate:predicate];

    if ([events count] > 0){

        /* Delete them all */
        for (EKEvent *event in events){
            NSError *removeError = nil;
            /* Do not commit here, we will commit in batch after we have
             removed all the events that matched our criteria */
            if ([paramEventStore removeEvent:event
                                        span:EKSpanThisEvent
                                      commit:NO
                                       error:&removeError] == NO){
                NSLog(@"Failed to remove event %@ with error = %@",
                      event,
                      removeError);
            }
        }

        NSError *commitError = nil;
        if ([paramEventStore commit:&commitError]){
            result = YES;
        } else {
            NSLog(@"Failed to commit the event store.");
        }

    } else {
        NSLog(@"No events matched your input.");
    }

    return result;

}
```

Since this method takes, as parameters, the calendar and the event store that the deletion has to occur on, it really has to do minimal processing. It just takes the start and end dates that we provide and creates a predicate to find the event that we are asking it to delete. After the event is found, it invokes the `removeEvent:span:commit:error:` instance method of the event store. This method, as explained previously, can delete a single event or an occurrence of events. For instance, you may have set an alarm on your device to wake you up every day at 6 o'clock in the morning. This is a recurring event. With what you learned here, you can delete *one* of the occurrences of that event but not all of them. But don't worry, we will soon learn about deleting recurring events in this chapter.

In this example, we are not committing the deletion of every event one by one. We are simply setting the `commit` parameter of the `removeEvent:span:commit:error:` method to `NO`. After we are done, we are invoking the `commit:` method of the event store explicitly. The reason for this is that we don't really want to commit every single deletion. That would create a lot of overhead. We can delete as many events as we need to and then commit them all in one batch.

## See Also

Recipe 19.1; Rccipe 19.4

# 19.6. Adding Recurring Events to Calendars

## Problem

You want to add a recurring event to a calendar.

## Solution

In this example, we are creating an event that occurs on the same day, every month, for an entire year. The steps are as follows:

1. Create an instance of `EKEventStore`.
2. Find a modifiable calendar inside the event store, as we saw in Recipe 19.3.
3. Create an object of type `EKEvent` (for more information, refer to Recipe 19.3).

4. Set the appropriate values for the event, such as its `startDate` and `endDate` (for more information, refer to Recipe 19.3).
5. Instantiate an object of type `NSDate` that contains the exact date when the recurrence of this event ends. In this example, this date is one year from today's date.
6. Use the `recurrenceEndWithEndDate:` class method of `EKRecurrenceEnd` and pass the `NSDate` you created in step 5 to create an object of type `EKRecurrenceEnd`.
7. Allocate and then instantiate an object of type `EKRecurrenceRule` using the `ini tRecurrenceWithFrequency:interval:end:` method of `EKRecurrenceRule`. Pass the recurrence end date that you created in step 6 to the `end` parameter of this method. For more information about this method, please refer to this recipe's Discussion.
8. Assign the recurring event that you created in step 7 to the `recurringRule` property of the `EKEvent` object that was created in step 3.
9. Invoke the `saveEvent:span:error:` instance method with the event (created in step 3) as the `saveEvent` parameter and the value `EKSpanFutureEvents` for the `span` parameter. This will create our recurring event for us.

The following code illustrates these steps:

```
- (BOOL) createRecurringEventInStore:(EKEventStore *)paramStore
                          inCalendar:(EKCalendar *)paramCalendar{

    /* Create an event */
    EKEvent *event = [EKEvent eventWithEventStore:paramStore];

    /* Create an event that happens today and happens
     every month for a year from now */

    NSDate *eventStartDate = [NSDate date];

    /* The event's end date is one hour from the moment it is created */
    NSTimeInterval NSOneHour = 1 * 60 * 60;
    NSDate *eventEndDate = [eventStartDate dateByAddingTimeInterval:NSOneHour];

    /* Assign the required properties, especially
     the target calendar */
    event.calendar = paramCalendar;
    event.title = @"My Event";
    event.startDate = eventStartDate;
    event.endDate = eventEndDate;

    /* The end date of the recurring rule
     is one year from now */
    NSTimeInterval NSOneYear = 365 * 24 * 60 * 60;
    NSDate *oneYearFromNow = [eventStartDate
                              dateByAddingTimeInterval:NSOneYear];
```

```
    /* Create an Event Kit date from this date */
    EKRecurrenceEnd *recurringEnd =
    [EKRecurrenceEnd recurrenceEndWithEndDate:oneYearFromNow];

    /* And the recurring rule. This event happens every
     month (EKRecurrenceFrequencyMonthly), once a month (interval:1)
     and the recurring rule ends a year from now (end:RecurringEnd) */

    EKRecurrenceRule *recurringRule =
    [[EKRecurrenceRule alloc]
     initRecurrenceWithFrequency:EKRecurrenceFrequencyMonthly
     interval:1
     end:recurringEnd];

    /* Set the recurring rule for the event */
    event.recurrenceRules = @[recurringRule];

    NSError *saveError = nil;

    /* Save the event */
    if ([paramStore saveEvent:event
                         span:EKSpanFutureEvents
                        error:&saveError]){
        NSLog(@"Successfully created the recurring event.");
        return YES;
    } else {
        NSLog(@"Failed to create the recurring event %@", saveError);
    }
    return NO;

}
```

In this code, we are using some of the methods and code snippets that we learned in Recipe 19.3. Have a look at the aforementioned recipe if you are unfamiliar with adding nonrecurring events to a calendar object.

Once you run this code on your device and go to the Calendar app and tap on the created event, you will see something similar to that shown in Figure 19-8.

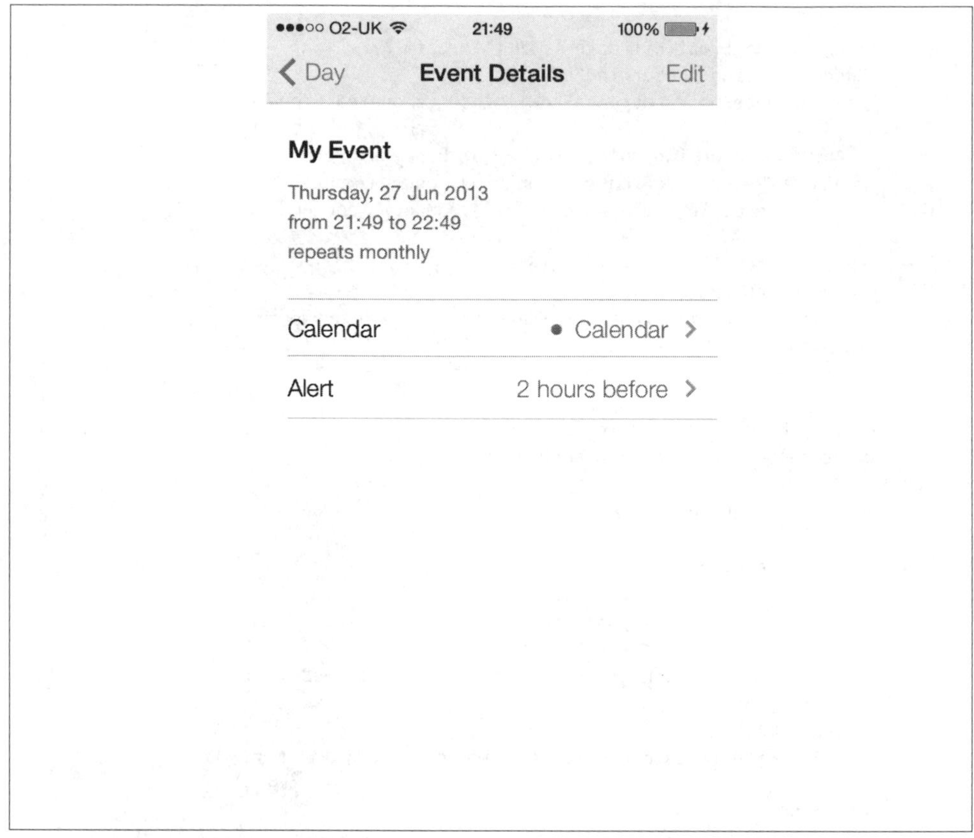


*Figure 19-8. A recurring event has been added to a calendar*

## Discussion

A recurring event is an event that happens more than once. We can create a recurring event just like a normal event. Please refer to Recipe 19.3 for more information about inserting normal events into the Calendar database. The only difference between a recurring event and a normal event is that you apply a recurring rule to a recurring event. A recurring rule tells the Event Kit framework how the event has to occur in the future.

We create a recurring rule by instantiating an object of type `EKRecurrenceRule` using the `initRecurrenceWithFrequency:interval:end:` initialization method. Here are the parameters for this method:

`initRecurrenceWithFrequency`
: Specifies whether you want the event to be repeated daily (`EKRecurrenceFrequencyDaily`), weekly (`EKRecurrenceFrequencyWeekly`), monthly (`EKRecurrenceFrequencyMonthly`), or yearly (`EKRecurrenceFrequencyYearly`).

`interval`
: A value greater than zero that specifies the interval between each occurrence's start and end period. For instance, if you want to create an event that happens every week, specify the `EKRecurrenceFrequencyWeekly` value with an `interval` of `1`. If you want this event to happen every other week, specify `EKRecurrenceFrequencyWeekly` with an `interval` of `2`.

`end`
: A date of type `EKRecurrenceEnd` that specifies the date when the recurring event ends in the specified calendar. This parameter is not the same as the event's end date (the `endDate` property of `EKEvent`). The end date of an event specifies when that specific event ends in the calendar, whereas the `end` parameter of the `initRecurrenceWithFrequency:interval:end:` method specifies the final occurrence of the event in the database.

By editing this event (see Figure 19-9) in the Calendar application on an iOS device, you can see that the event is truly a recurring event that happens every month, on the same day the event was created, for a whole year.

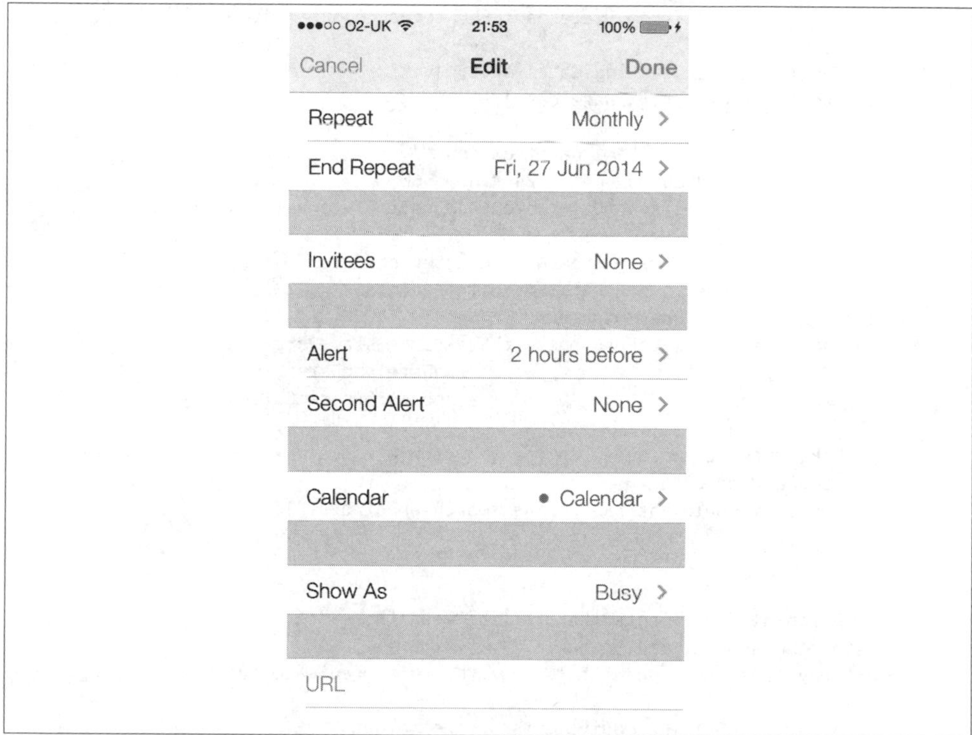


*Figure 19-9. Editing a recurring event in the Calendar app on an iOS device*

## See Also

Recipe 19.3

# 19.7. Retrieving the Attendees of an Event

## Problem

You want to retrieve the list of attendees for a specific event.

## Solution

Use the `attendees` property of an instance of `EKEvent`. This property is of type `NSAr ray` and includes objects of type `EKParticipant`.

The example code that follows will retrieve all the events that happen today (whatever the day may be) and print out useful event information, including the attendees of that event, to the console window:

```
- (void) enumerateTodayEventsInStore:(EKEventStore *)paramStore
                            calendar:(EKCalendar *)paramCalendar{

    /* Construct the starting date for today */
    NSDate *startDate = [NSDate date];

    /* The end date will be 1 day from now */
    NSTimeInterval NSOneDay = 1 * 24 * 60 * 60;
    NSDate *endDate = [startDate dateByAddingTimeInterval:NSOneDay];

    /* Create the predicate that we can later pass to
     the event store in order to fetch the events */
    NSPredicate *searchPredicate =
    [paramStore predicateForEventsWithStartDate:startDate
                                        endDate:endDate
                                      calendars:@[paramCalendar]];

    /* Make sure we succeeded in creating the predicate */
    if (searchPredicate == nil){
        NSLog(@"Could not create the search predicate.");
        return;
    }

    /* Fetch all the events that fall between the
     starting and the ending dates */
    NSArray *events = [paramStore eventsMatchingPredicate:searchPredicate];

    /* Array of NSString equivalents of the values
     in the EKParticipantRole enumeration */
    NSArray *attendeeRole = @[
                              @"Unknown",
```

```
                                   @"Required",
                                   @"Optional",
                                   @"Chair",
                                   @"Non Participant",
                                   ];

/* Array of NSString equivalents of the values
 in the EKParticipantStatus enumeration */
NSArray *attendeeStatus = @[
                                     @"Unknown",
                                     @"Pending",
                                     @"Accepted",
                                     @"Declined",
                                     @"Tentative",
                                     @"Delegated",
                                     @"Completed",
                                     @"In Process",
                                     ];

/* Array of NSString equivalents of the values
 in the EKParticipantType enumeration */
NSArray *attendeeType = @[
                                   @"Unknown",
                                   @"Person",
                                   @"Room",
                                   @"Resource",
                                   @"Group"
                                   ];

/* Go through all the events and print their information
 out to the console */
if (events != nil){

    NSUInteger eventCounter = 0;
    for (EKEvent *thisEvent in events){

        eventCounter++;

        NSLog(@"Event %lu Start Date = %@",
              (unsigned long)eventCounter,
              thisEvent.startDate);

        NSLog(@"Event %lu End Date = %@",
              (unsigned long)eventCounter,
              thisEvent.endDate);

        NSLog(@"Event %lu Title = %@",
              (unsigned long)eventCounter,
              thisEvent.title);

        if (thisEvent.attendees == nil ||
            [thisEvent.attendees count] == 0){
```

```
                NSLog(@"Event %lu has no attendees",
                      (unsigned long)eventCounter);
                continue;
            }

            NSUInteger attendeeCounter = 1;
            for (EKParticipant *participant in thisEvent.attendees){

                NSLog(@"Event %lu Attendee %lu Name = %@",
                      (unsigned long)eventCounter,
                      (unsigned long)attendeeCounter,
                      participant.name);

                NSLog(@"Event %lu Attendee %lu Role = %@",
                      (unsigned long)eventCounter,
                      (unsigned long)attendeeCounter,
                      attendeeRole[participant.participantRole]);

                NSLog(@"Event %lu Attendee %lu Status = %@",
                      (unsigned long)eventCounter,
                      (unsigned long)attendeeCounter,
                      attendeeStatus[participant.participantStatus]);

                NSLog(@"Event %lu Attendee %lu Type = %@",
                      (unsigned long)eventCounter,
                      (unsigned long)attendeeCounter,
                      attendeeType[participant.participantType]);

                NSLog(@"Event %lu Attendee %lu URL = %@",
                      (unsigned long)eventCounter,
                      (unsigned long)attendeeCounter,
                      participant.URL);

                attendeeCounter++;

            }

        }

    } else {
        NSLog(@"The array of events is nil.");
    }

}
```

In this code snippet, we are using vocabulary such as *stores*. If you are not familiar with what stores are and how you can retrieve calendar objects, please have a read through Recipe 19.2 before proceeding with this recipe.

## Discussion

Different types of calendars, such as iCloud (CalDAV), can include participants in an event. iOS allows users to add participants to a calendar on the server, although not to the calendar on the iOS device. You can do this using iCloud, for instance.

Once the user adds participants to an event, you can use the `attendees` property of an instance of `EKEvent` to access the participant objects of type `EKParticipant`. Each participant has properties such as the following:

`name`
: This is the name of the participant. If you just specified the email address of a person to add him to an event, this field will be that email address.

`URL`
: This is usually the "mailto" URL for the attendee.

`participantRole`
: This is the role the attendee plays in the event. Different values that can be applied to this property are listed in the `EKParticipantRole` enumeration.

`participantStatus`
: This tells us whether this participant has accepted or declined the event request. This property could have other values, all specified in the `EKParticipantStatus` enumeration.

`participantType`
: This is of type `EKParticipantType`, which is an enumeration and, as its name implies, specifies the type of participant, such as group (`EKParticipantTypeGroup`) or individual person (`EKParticipantTypePerson`).

## See Also

Recipe 19.3; Recipe 19.4

# 19.8. Adding Alarms to Calendars

## Problem

You want to add alarms to the events in a calendar.

## Solution

Use the `alarmWithRelativeOffset:` class method of `EKAlarm` to create an instance of `EKAlarm`. Add the alarm to an event using the `addAlarm:` instance method of `EKEvent`, like so:

```
- (void) addAlarmToCalendar:(EKCalendar *)paramCalendar
                    inStore:(EKEventStore *)paramStore{

    /* The event starts 60 seconds from now */
    NSDate *startDate = [NSDate dateWithTimeIntervalSinceNow:60.0];

    /* And end the event 20 seconds after its start date */
    NSDate *endDate = [startDate dateByAddingTimeInterval:20.0];

    EKEvent *eventWithAlarm = [EKEvent eventWithEventStore:paramStore];

    eventWithAlarm.calendar = paramCalendar;
    eventWithAlarm.startDate = startDate;
    eventWithAlarm.endDate = endDate;

    /* The alarm goes off 2 seconds before the event happens */
    EKAlarm *alarm = [EKAlarm alarmWithRelativeOffset:-2.0];

    eventWithAlarm.title = @"Event with Alarm";
    [eventWithAlarm addAlarm:alarm];

    NSError *saveError = nil;

    if ([paramStore saveEvent:eventWithAlarm
                         span:EKSpanThisEvent
                        error:&saveError]){
        NSLog(@"Saved an event that fires 60 seconds from now.");
    } else {
        NSLog(@"Failed to save the event. Error = %@", saveError);
    }

}
```

For information about event stores and calendars and the way to retrieve instances to them, please see Recipe 19.2.

## Discussion

An event of type `EKEvent` can have multiple alarms. Simply create the alarm using either the `alarmWithAbsoluteDate:` or `alarmWithRelativeOffset:` class method of `EKAlarm`. The former method requires an absolute date and time (you can use the `CFAbsoluteTimeGetCurrent` function to get the current absolute time), whereas the latter method requires a number of seconds relative to the start date of the event when the alarm must be fired. For instance, if the event is scheduled for today at 6:00 a.m., and we go ahead and create an alarm with the relative offset of –60 (which is counted in units of seconds), our alarm will be fired at 5:59 a.m. the same day. Only zero and negative numbers are allowed for this offset. Positive numbers will automatically be changed to zero by iOS. Once an alarm is fired, iOS will display the alarm to the user, as shown in Figure 19-10.

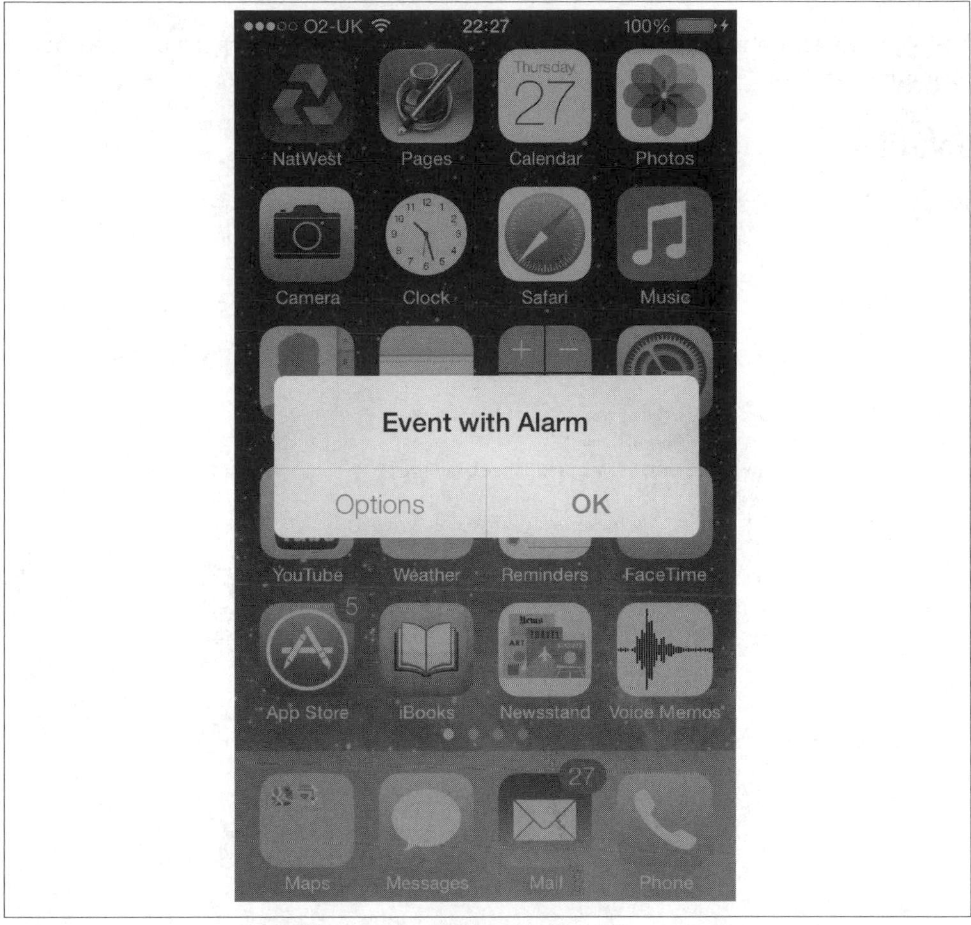


*Figure 19-10. iOS displaying an alert on the screen when an alarm is fired*

You can use the `removeAlarm:` instance method of `EKEvent` to remove an alarm associated with that event instance.

## See Also

Recipe 19.1

## 19.9. Handling Event Changed Notifications

### Problem

You want to get notified in your application when the user changes the contents of the Calendar database.

### Solution

Register for the `EKEventStoreChangedNotification` notification:

```
- (void) eventsChanged:(NSNotification *)paramNotification{

    NSMutableArray *invalidatedEvents = [[NSMutableArray alloc] init];

    NSLog(@"Refreshing array of events...");

    for (EKEvent *event in self.eventsForOneYear){
        if ([event refresh] == NO){
            [invalidatedEvents addObject:event];
        }
    }

    if ([invalidatedEvents count] > 0){
        [self.eventsForOneYear removeObjectsInArray:invalidatedEvents];
    }

}

- (void) handleNotificationsInStore:(EKEventStore *)paramStore{

    EKSource *icloudSource = [self sourceInEventStore:paramStore
                                           sourceType:EKSourceTypeCalDAV
                                          sourceTitle:@"iCloud"];

    if (icloudSource == nil){
        NSLog(@"You have not configured iCloud for your device.");
        return;
    }

    EKCalendar *calendar = [self calendarWithTitle:@"Calendar"
                                              type:EKCalendarTypeCalDAV
                                          inSource:icloudSource
                                      forEventType:EKEntityTypeEvent];

    if (calendar == nil){
        NSLog(@"Could not find the calendar we were looking for.");
        return;
    }

    NSTimeInterval NSOneYear = 1 * 365 * 24 * 60 * 60;
```

```
    NSDate *startDate = [NSDate date];
    NSDate *endDate = [startDate dateByAddingTimeInterval:NSOneYear];

    NSPredicate *predicate =
    [paramStore predicateForEventsWithStartDate:startDate
                                        endDate:endDate
                                      calendars:@[calendar]];

    NSArray *events = [paramStore eventsMatchingPredicate:predicate];

    self.eventsForOneYear = [[NSMutableArray alloc] initWithArray:events];

    [[NSNotificationCenter defaultCenter]
     addObserver:self
     selector:@selector(eventsChanged:)
     name:EKEventStoreChangedNotification
     object:nil];

}
```

In this code snippet, we are using some of the methods that we have already programmed in earlier recipes in this chapter. For more information about these methods, please refer to Recipe 19.2.

## Discussion

Multitasking is possible on iOS. Imagine you have fetched a series of events from `EKEventStore` into an array and you allow your user to work with them (edit them, add to them, and remove from them). The user could simply switch from your application to the Calendar application and delete the same event she is trying to delete in your application. Such a sequence of activities will generate an `EKEventStoreChangedNotification` notification that you can choose to receive.

The `EKEventStoreChangedNotification` notification will be sent to your application (at least, if you subscribe to this notification) even if your application is in the foreground. Because of this, you must make sure you treat this notification differently depending on whether your application is in the background or the foreground. Here are a couple of things to consider:

- If you receive the `EKEventStoreChangedNotification` notification while your application is in the foreground, it is best to implement a mechanism to find out whether the changes to the event store originated inside your own application or came from someone else outside the application. If they came from outside the application, you must make sure you are retaining the latest version of the events in the store, and not the old events. If for any reason you copied one of the events in the event store and kept the copy somewhere, you must call the `refresh` instance method of that event of type `EKEvent`. If the return value of this method is `YES`, you can keep the object in memory. If the return value is `NO`, you must dispose of the object, because someone outside your application has deleted or somehow invalidated the event.

- If you receive the `EKEventStoreChangedNotification` notification while your application is in the background, according to documentation from Apple, your application should not attempt to do any GUI-related processing and should, in fact, use as little processing power as possible. You must therefore refrain from adding new screens to, or modifying in any way, the GUI of your application.
- If you receive the `EKEventStoreChangedNotification` notification while your application is in the background, you must make note of it inside the application (perhaps store this in a property of type `BOOL`) and react to this change when the application is brought to the foreground again. Normally, if you receive any notification about a change to an event while you are in the background, you should retrieve all events stored in the application when you return to the foreground.

Coalescing is not enabled on the `EKEventStoreChangedNotification` event store notification. In other words, you can receive multiple notifications of the same type if a single event changes in the Calendar database. It is up to you to determine how and when you need to refetch your retained events.

# 19.10. Presenting Event View Controllers

## Problem

You want to use the built-in iOS SDK view controllers to display the properties of an event in the Calendar database.

## Solution

Create an instance of `EKEventViewController` and push it into a navigation controller or present it as a modal view controller on another view controller.

## Discussion

Users of iOS devices are already familiar with the interface they see on the Calendar application. When they select an event, they can see that event's properties and they might be allowed to modify the event. To present a view to a user using built-in iOS SDK event view controllers, we can instantiate an object of type `EKEventViewController` and assign an event of type `EKEvent` to its event property. Once that's done, we can push the event view controller into our navigation controller and let iOS take care of the rest.

We want to find an event (any event) in any of the calendars available on an iOS device, from one year ago to now. We will use `EKEventViewController` to present that event to the user. Here is the declaration of our view controller:

```
#import "ViewController.h"
#import <EventKit/EventKit.h>
#import <EventKitUI/EventKitUI.h>

@interface ViewController () <EKEventViewDelegate>
@property (nonatomic, strong) EKEventStore *eventStore;
@end

@implementation ViewController
```

Now in the `viewDidAppear:` method of our view controller, let's go ahead and display the instance of `EKEventViewController` on the first event we find in any of the calendars on the device, from a year ago:

```
- (void) displayEventViewController{

    EKSource *icloudSource = [self sourceInEventStore:self.eventStore
                                           sourceType:EKSourceTypeCalDAV
                                          sourceTitle:@"iCloud"];

    if (icloudSource == nil){
        NSLog(@"You have not configured iCloud for your device.");
        return;
    }

    NSSet *calendars = [icloudSource
                        calendarsForEntityType:EKEntityTypeEvent];

    NSTimeInterval NSOneYear = 1 * 365 * 24.0f * 60.0f * 60.0f;
    NSDate *startDate = [[NSDate date] dateByAddingTimeInterval:-NSOneYear];
    NSDate *endDate = [NSDate date];

    NSPredicate *predicate =
    [self.eventStore predicateForEventsWithStartDate:startDate
                                             endDate:endDate
                                           calendars:calendars.allObjects];

    NSArray *events = [self.eventStore eventsMatchingPredicate:predicate];

    if ([events count] > 0){
        EKEvent *event = events[0];
        EKEventViewController *controller = [[EKEventViewController alloc] init];
        controller.event = event;
        controller.allowsEditing = NO;
        controller.allowsCalendarPreview = YES;
```

```
        controller.delegate = self;

        [self.navigationController pushViewController:controller
                                             animated:YES];
    }


}

- (void) viewDidAppear:(BOOL)animated{
    [super viewDidAppear:animated];


    static BOOL beenHereBefore = NO;

    if (beenHereBefore){
        return;
    } else {
        beenHereBefore = YES;
    }

    self.eventStore = [[EKEventStore alloc] init];

    switch ([EKEventStore
             authorizationStatusForEntityType:EKEntityTypeEvent]){

        case EKAuthorizationStatusAuthorized:{
            [self displayEventViewController];
            break;
        }
        case EKAuthorizationStatusDenied:{
            [self displayAccessDenied];
            break;
        }
        case EKAuthorizationStatusNotDetermined:{
            [self.eventStore
             requestAccessToEntityType:EKEntityTypeEvent
             completion:^(BOOL granted, NSError *error) {
                 if (granted){
                     [self displayEventViewController];
                 } else {
                     [self displayAccessDenied];
                 }
             }];
            break;
        }
        case EKAuthorizationStatusRestricted:{
            [self displayAccessRestricted];
            break;
        }

    }
```

```
}
```

Last but not least, as you can see in the code, we have become the delegate object of the event view controller, so let's make sure we are handling the delegate methods if required:

```
- (void)eventViewController:(EKEventViewController *)controller
      didCompleteWithAction:(EKEventViewAction)action{

    switch (action){

        case EKEventViewActionDeleted:{
            NSLog(@"User deleted the event.");
            break;
        }
        case EKEventViewActionDone:{
            NSLog(@"User finished viewing the event.");
            break;
        }
        case EKEventViewActionResponded:{
            NSLog(@"User responsed to the invitation in the event.");
            break;
        }

    }

}
```

Once we run this application on an iOS device, we can see the built-in event view controller displaying the contents of the event that we have found (see Figure 19-11).

*Figure 19-11. The built-in iOS event view controller*

Different properties of an instance of `EKEventViewController` that we can use to change the behavior of this object are as follows:

`allowsEditing`
: If this property's value is set to `YES`, the Edit button will appear on the navigation bar of the event view controller, allowing the user to edit the event. This happens only on modifiable calendars and only for events that have been created by the user on this device. For instance, if you create an event on the Web using Google Calendar and the event appears in your iOS device, you are not allowed to edit that event.

`allowsCalendarPreview`
: If this property's value is set to `YES` and the event the user is viewing is an invitation, the user will be given the option to view this current event in a calendar with other events that have been scheduled on the same date.

`event`
: This property must be set before presenting the event view controller. This will be the event that the event view controller will display to the user.

When you push the event view controller, the Back button will appear with the title "Back" by default, so you do not have to change it manually. However, if you decide to change the Back button, you can do so by assigning a new object of type `UIBarButtonItem` to the `backBarButtonItem` property of your navigation item. In our example code, we can modify the `pushController:` method to give our root view controller a custom Back button before pushing the event view controller.

```
- (void) displayEventViewController{

    EKSource *icloudSource = [self sourceInEventStore:self.eventStore
                                           sourceType:EKSourceTypeCalDAV
                                          sourceTitle:@"iCloud"];

    if (icloudSource == nil){
        NSLog(@"You have not configured iCloud for your device.");
        return;
    }

    NSSet *calendars = [icloudSource
                        calendarsForEntityType:EKEntityTypeEvent];

    NSTimeInterval NSOneYear = 1 * 365 * 24.0f * 60.0f * 60.0f;
    NSDate *startDate = [[NSDate date] dateByAddingTimeInterval:-NSOneYear];
    NSDate *endDate = [NSDate date];

    NSPredicate *predicate =
    [self.eventStore predicateForEventsWithStartDate:startDate
                                             endDate:endDate
                                           calendars:calendars.allObjects];

    NSArray *events = [self.eventStore eventsMatchingPredicate:predicate];
```

```
    if ([events count] > 0){
        EKEvent *event = events[0];
        EKEventViewController *controller = [[EKEventViewController alloc] init];
        controller.event = event;
        controller.allowsEditing = YES;
        controller.allowsCalendarPreview = YES;
        controller.delegate = self;

        self.navigationItem.backBarButtonItem =
        [[UIBarButtonItem alloc] initWithTitle:@"Go Back"
                                         style:UIBarButtonItemStylePlain
                                        target:nil
                                        action:nil];

        [self.navigationController pushViewController:controller
                                             animated:YES];
    }

}
```

The results of this modification are depicted in Figure 19-12 (please note that in this example, editing is enabled for the event view controller).

*Figure 19-12. An edit view controller with editing enabled and a custom Back button*

## See Also

Recipe 19.11

## 19.11. Presenting Event Edit View Controllers

### Problem

You want to allow your users to edit (insert, delete, and modify) events in the Calendar database from inside your application, using built-in SDK view controllers.

### Solution

Instantiate an object of type `EKEventEditViewController` and present it on a navigation controller.

### Discussion

An instance of the `EKEventEditViewController` class allows us to present an event edit view controller to the user. This view controller, depending on how we set it up, can allow the user to either edit an existing event or create a new event. If you want this view controller to edit an event, set the `event` property of this instance to an event object. If you want the user to be able to insert a new event into the system, set the `event` property of this instance to `nil`.

The `editViewDelegate` property of an instance of `EKEventEditViewController` is the object that will receive delegate messages from this view controller telling the programmer about the action the user has taken. One of the most important delegate messages your delegate object must handle (a required delegate selector) is the `eventEditViewController:didCompleteWithAction:` method. This delegate method will be called whenever the user dismisses the event edit view controller in one of the possible ways indicated by the `didCompleteWithAction` parameter. This parameter can have values such as the following:

`EKEventEditViewActionCanceled`
: The user pressed the Cancel button on the view controller.

`EKEventEditViewActionSaved`
: The user saved (added/modified) an event in the Calendar database.

`EKEventEditViewActionDeleted`
: The user deleted an event from the Calendar database.

Please make sure to dismiss the event edit view controller after receiving this delegate message, if you are displaying the edit view controller as a modal view controller.

So let's go ahead and define our view controller:

```
#import "ViewController.h"
#import <EventKitUI/EventKitUI.h>
#import <EventKit/EventKit.h>
```

```
@interface ViewController () <EKEventEditViewDelegate>
@property (nonatomic, strong) EKEventStore *eventStore;
@end

@implementation ViewController
```

Now let's try to find the first event from a year ago (whatever event that might be) and allow the user to edit that event by displaying an edit event view controller:

```
- (void)eventEditViewController:(EKEventEditViewController *)controller
          didCompleteWithAction:(EKEventEditViewAction)action{

    switch (action){

        case EKEventEditViewActionCanceled:{
            NSLog(@"Cancelled");
            break;
        }
        case EKEventEditViewActionSaved:{
            NSLog(@"Saved");
            break;
        }
        case EKEventEditViewActionDeleted:{
            NSLog(@"Deleted");
            break;
        }

    }

    [self.navigationController dismissViewControllerAnimated:YES
                                                   completion:nil];

}

- (void) displayEventEditController{

    EKSource *icloudSource = [self sourceInEventStore:self.eventStore
                                           sourceType:EKSourceTypeCalDAV
                                          sourceTitle:@"iCloud"];

    if (icloudSource == nil){
        NSLog(@"You have not configured iCloud for your device.");
        return;
    }

    NSSet *calendars = [icloudSource
                        calendarsForEntityType:EKEntityTypeEvent];

    NSTimeInterval NSOneYear = 1 * 365 * 24.0f * 60.0f * 60.0f;
    NSDate *startDate = [[NSDate date] dateByAddingTimeInterval:-NSOneYear];
    NSDate *endDate = [NSDate date];
```

```
    NSPredicate *predicate =
    [self.eventStore predicateForEventsWithStartDate:startDate
                                             endDate:endDate
                                           calendars:calendars.allObjects];

    NSArray *events = [self.eventStore eventsMatchingPredicate:predicate];

    if ([events count] > 0){
        EKEvent *event = events[0];

        EKEventEditViewController *controller =
        [[EKEventEditViewController alloc] init];

        controller.event = event;
        controller.editViewDelegate = self;

        [self.navigationController presentViewController:controller
                                                animated:YES
                                              completion:nil];

    }

}
```

In this code we are using other methods that we have already developed in various other recipes in this chapter. For more information, please refer to Recipe 19.1 and Recipe 19.2.

Depending on the event that is found on the device, the user will see something similar to Figure 19-13.

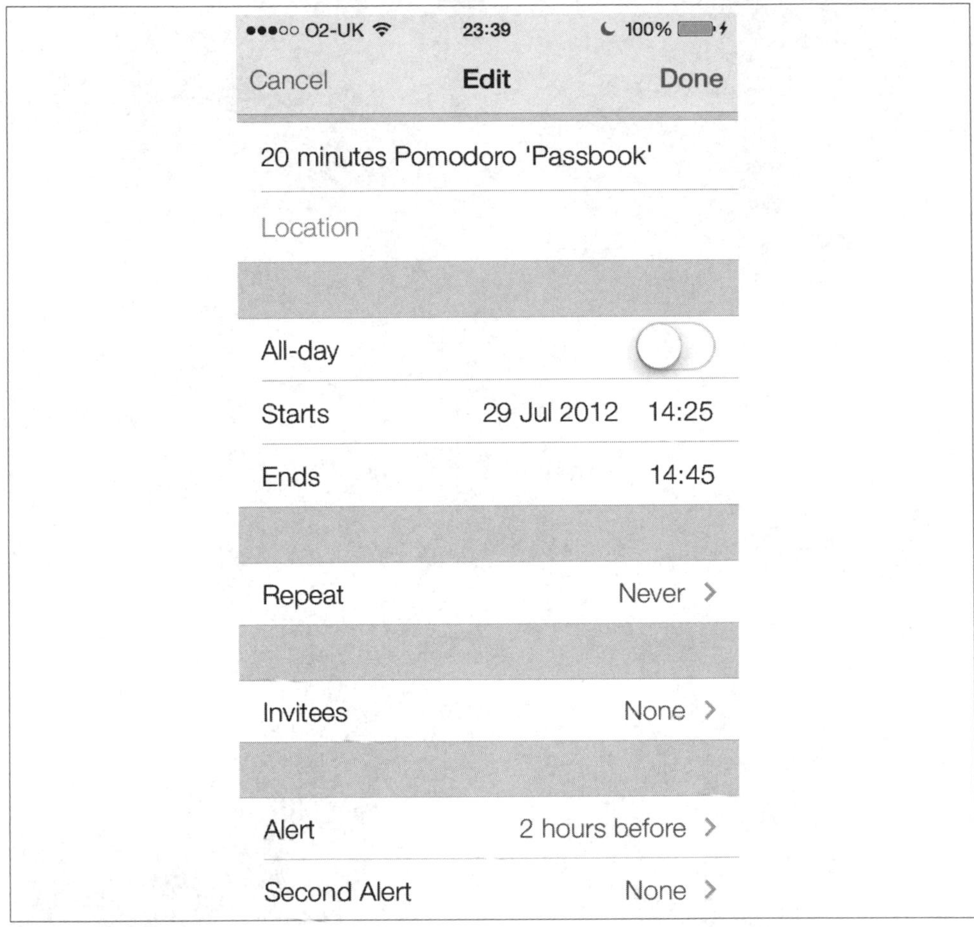


*Figure 19-13. An edit event view controller displaying an event*

## See Also

Recipe 19.10

CHAPTER 20

# Graphics and Animations

## 20.0. Introduction

You've certainly seen applications with beautiful graphics effects on iOS devices. And you've probably also encountered impressive animations in games and other apps. Working together, the iOS runtime and Cocoa programming frameworks make possible an amazing variety of graphics and animation effects with relatively simple coding. The quality of these graphics and animations depends partly, of course, on the aesthetic sensitivities of the programmer and artistic collaborators. But in this chapter, you'll see how much you can accomplish with modest programming skills.

I'll dispense with conceptual background, preferring to introduce ideas such as color spaces, transformation, and the graphics context as we go along. I'll just mention a few basics before leaping into code.

In Cocoa Touch, an app is made up of *windows* and *views*. An app with a UI has at least one window that contains, in turn, one or more views. In Cocoa Touch, a window is an instance of `UIWindow`. Usually, an app will open to the main window and the programmer will then add views to the window to represent different parts of the UI: parts such as buttons, labels, images, and custom controls. All these UI-related components are handled and drawn by UIKit.

Some of these things might sound relatively difficult to understand, but I promise you that as we proceed through this chapter, you will understand them step by step with the many examples I will give.

Apple has provided developers with powerful frameworks that handle graphics and animations in iOS and OS X. Here are some of these frameworks and technologies:

*UIKit*
: The high-level framework that allows developers to create views, windows, buttons, and other UI related components. It also incorporates some of the low-level APIs into an easier-to-use high-level API.

*Quartz 2D*
: The main engine running under the hood to facilitate drawing in iOS; UIKit uses Quartz.

*Core Graphics*
: A framework that supports the graphics context (more on this later), loading images, drawing images, and so on.

*Core Animation*
: A framework that, as its name implies, facilitates animations in iOS.

When drawing on a screen, one of the most important concepts to grasp is the relation between points and pixels. I'm sure you're familiar with pixels, but what are *points*? They're the device-independent counterpart of pixels. Simply put, when writing your iOS apps and asked to provide a width/height or any other measurements like these, iOS reads your provided values as points, instead of pixels. For instance, if you want to fill the whole screen on an iPhone 5, you will say that you want a width of 320 and height of 568. However, we all know that the actual screen resolution of an iPhone 5 is 640 by 1136. This is the beauty of points: they take *content scale factor* into account.

Let me clarify what content scale factor is. It's a simple floating point number that allows iOS to calculate the actual number of pixels on the screen by looking at the logical number of points that it can render on that screen. On an iPhone 5, the content scale factor is 2.0, which tells iOS to multiply 320 by 2 to get the actual number of pixels that the device can render horizontally and to multiply 568 by 2 to get the number of pixels that the device can render vertically.

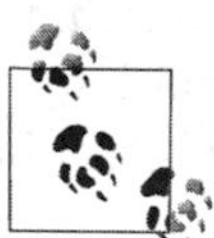

The origin point of the screen on an iOS device is the top-left corner. Screens whose drawing origin is on the top-left corner are also referred to as upper left origin, or ULO, screens. This means that point (0, 0) is the topmost and leftmost point on the screen, and that positive values of the x-axis extend toward the right, while positive values of the *y*-axis extend toward the bottom. In other words, an *x* position of 20 is farther right on the screen than a position of 10 is. On the *y*-axis, point 20 is farther down than point 10.

In this chapter, we will be using view objects of type `UIView` to draw shapes, strings, and everything else that's visible on the screen.

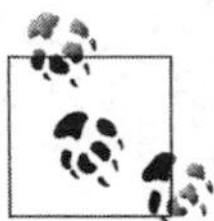

I assume you have the latest Xcode from Apple. If not, open App Store on your OS X installation and search for and download Xcode.

In order to be able to incorporate some of these code snippets in an application, I will first show you the required steps to create a new project in Xcode and subclass `UIView`, where we can place the code:

1. Open Xcode.
2. From the File menu, select New → Project.
3. On the left side of the screen, make sure the iOS category is selected. Select Application under that category (see Figure 20-1).
4. On the right side of the screen, select single-view application, and press Next (see Figure 20-1).

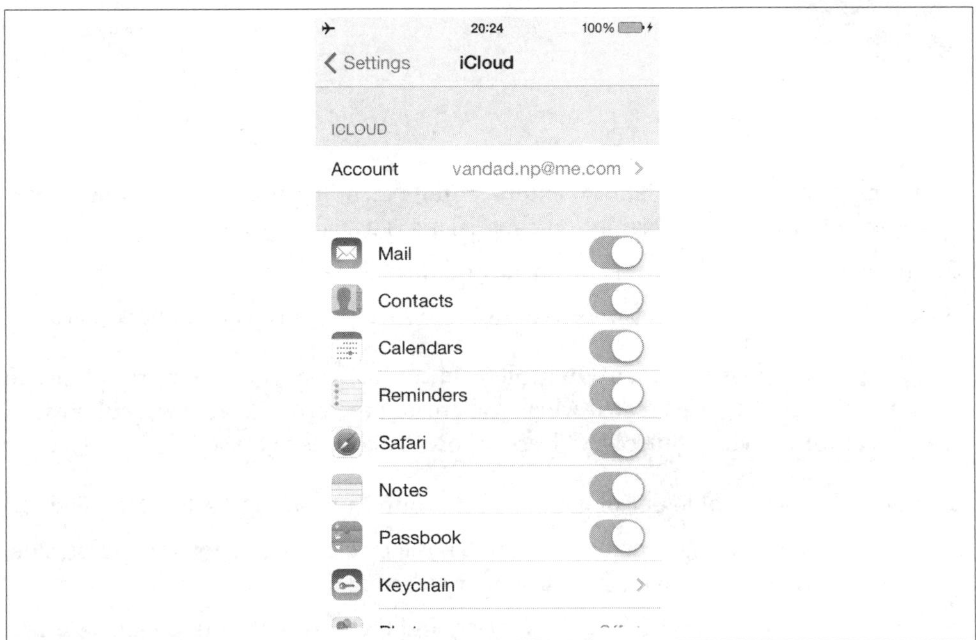


*Figure 20-1. Creating a single-view application for iOS in Xcode*

5. In the Product Name box (Figure 20-2), select a name for your project.

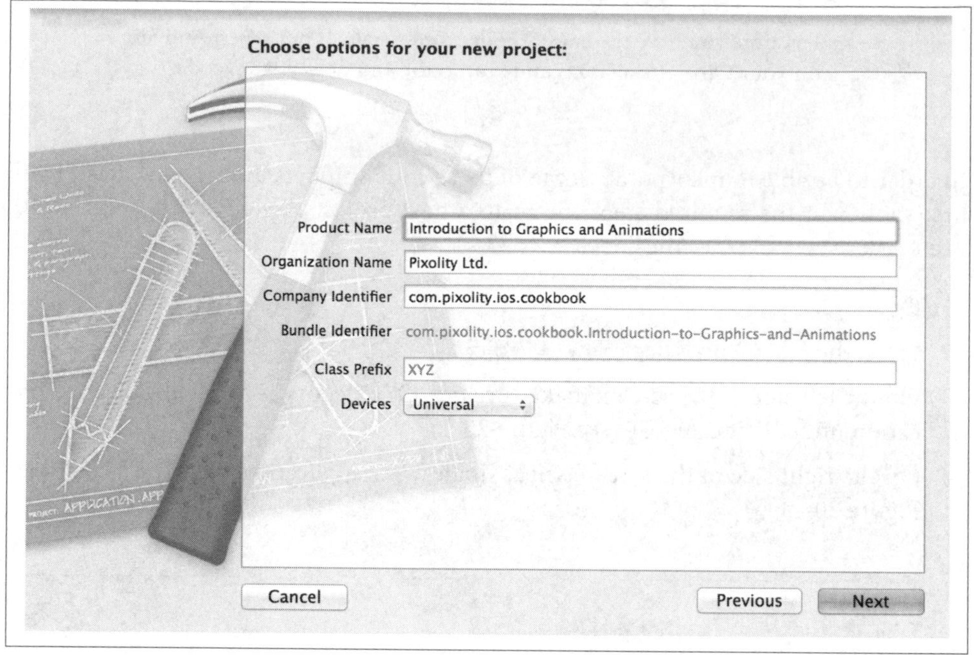


*Figure 20-2. Setting the options for a new project in Xcode*

6. In the Company Identifier box, enter a bundle identifier prefix, which will be prepended to the Product Name you chose. This is usually `com.company`.
7. In the Device Family, select Universal, and then press Next.
8. On the next screen, select where you want to save your project and press Create.

Now your Xcode project is open. On the left side of Xcode, expand your project files to see all the files that Xcode created when you created the project. Now we will create a view object for the view controller. Please follow these steps to do so:

1. Right-click the root folder of your project group in Xcode and select New File....
2. In the New File dialog box, make sure iOS is selected as the category on the left side, and select Cocoa Touch as the subcategory (see Figure 20-3).
3. On the right side, select Objective-C class, and then press Next (see Figure 20-3).
4. On the next screen (Figure 20-4), make sure that the Subclass box has *`UIView`* written inside it, and set your class name to **`View`**. Proceed to saving your file on disk.

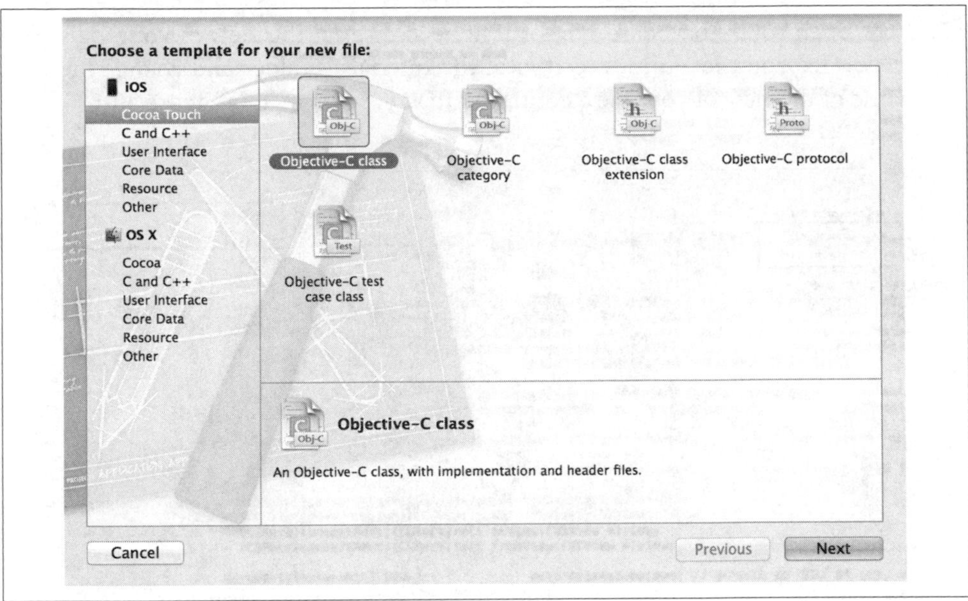


*Figure 20-3. Creating a new Objective-C class in Xcode*

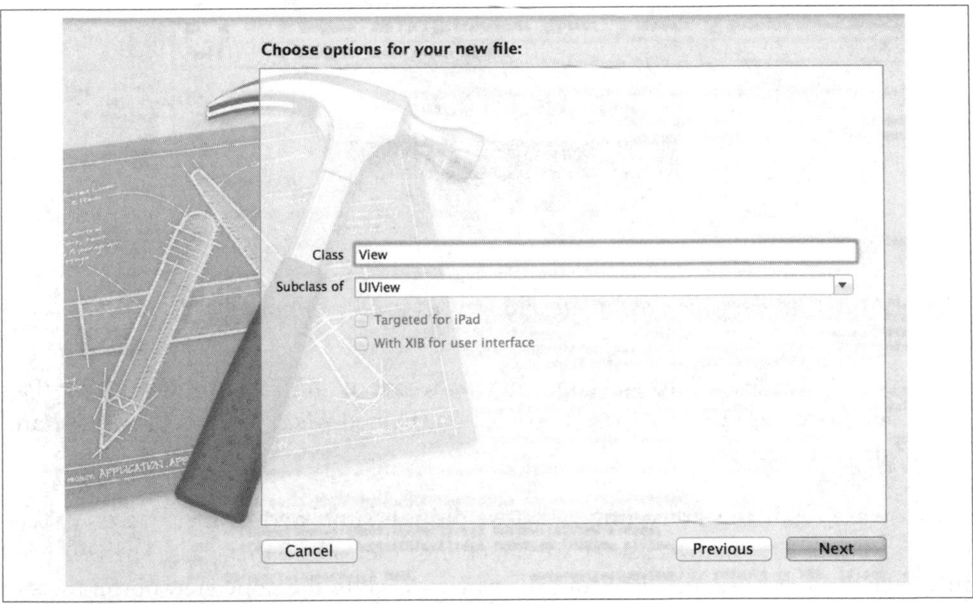


*Figure 20-4. Creating a subclass of UIView*

5. Now open your storyboard file for iPhone and select the view of your view controller. Expand the Utilities section of the Interface Builder and change the class name of the view of your view controller to `View`, as shown in Figure 20-5.

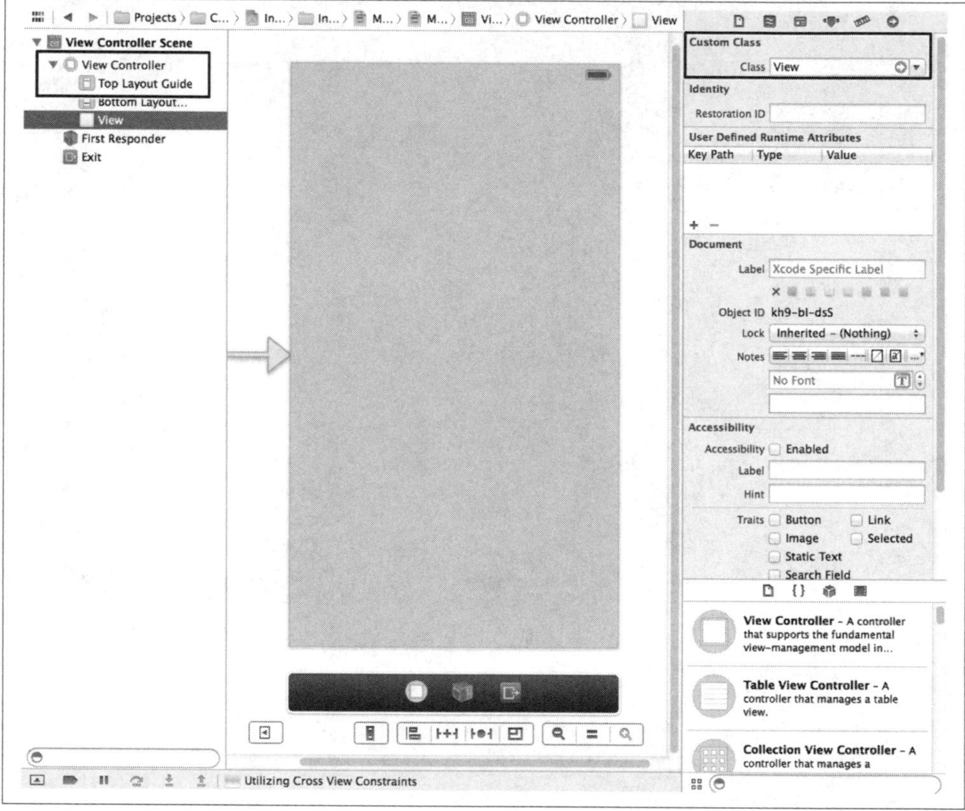


*Figure 20-5. Changing the class name of a view controller in storyboard*

6. Since we created a universal app, you will need to do the same thing for your iPad storyboard file. Usually these two files are named *Main_iPhone.storyboard* and *Main_iPad.storyboard*.

Now we are ready to start coding. What we did was simply create a view class of type `UIView` so that later in this chapter, we can change the code in that class. Then we used Interface Builder to set the view controller's view class to the same view object that we created. This means that the view controller's view will now be an instance of the `View` class that we created.

You have probably already looked at the contents of the view object that Xcode generated. One of the most important methods inside this object is `drawRect:`. Cocoa Touch automatically calls this method whenever it is time to draw the view and uses it to ask the view object to draw its contents on the graphical context that Cocoa Touch automatically prepares for the view. A graphical context can be thought of as a canvas, offering an enormous number of properties, such as pen color, pen thickness, etc. Given the context, you can start *painting* straight away inside the `drawRect:` method, and Cocoa Touch will make sure that the attributes and properties of the context are applied to your drawings. We will talk about this more later, but for now, let's move on to more interesting subjects.

# 20.1. Enumerating and Loading Fonts

## Problem

You want to use fonts that come preinstalled on an iOS device in order to render some text on the screen.

## Solution

Use the `UIFont` class.

## Discussion

Fonts are fundamental to displaying text on a graphical user interface. The UIKit framework provides programmers with high-level APIs that facilitate the enumerating, loading, and use of fonts. Fonts are encapsulated in the `UIFont` class in Cocoa Touch. Each iOS device comes with built-in system fonts. Fonts are organized into *families*, and each family contains *faces*. For instance, Helvetica is a font family, and Helvetica *Bold* is one of the faces of the Helvetica family. To be able to load a font, you must know the font's face (that is, its name)—and to know the face, you have to know the family. So first, let's enumerate all the font families that are installed on the device, using the `familyNames` class method of the `UIFont` class:

```
- (void) enumerateFonts{

  for (NSString *familyName in [UIFont familyNames]){
    NSLog(@"Font Family = %@", familyName);
  }

}
```

Running this program in iOS Simulator, I get results similar to this:

```
Font Family = Thonburi
Font Family = Academy Engraved LE
```

```
Font Family = Snell Roundhand
Font Family = Avenir
Font Family = Marker Felt
Font Family = Geeza Pro
Font Family = Arial Rounded MT Bo
Font Family = Trebuchet MS
...
```

After getting the font families, we can enumerate the font names inside each family. We'll use the `fontNamesForFamilyName:` class method of the `UIFont` class and get back an array of font names for the family name that we pass as a parameter:

```
- (void) enumerateFonts{

    for (NSString *familyName in [UIFont familyNames]){
        NSLog(@"Font Family = %@", familyName);
        for (NSString *fontName in
             [UIFont fontNamesForFamilyName:familyName]){
            NSLog(@"\t%@", fontName);

        }
    }

}
```

Running this code in iOS Simulator gives me the following results:

```
Font Family = Thonburi Thonburi-Bold Thonburi
Font Family = Academy Eng AcademyEngravedLetPla
Font Family = Snell Round SnellRoundhand-Bold SnellRoundhand-Black SnellRoundhand
    ...
```

So as you can see, *Thonburi* is the font family and *Thonburi-Bold* is one of the font names in this family. Now that we know the font name, we can load the fonts into objects of type `UIFont` using the `fontWithName:size:` class method of the `UIFont` class:

```
__unused UIFont *font = [UIFont fontWithName:@"Thonburi-Bold"
                                        size:12.0f];
```

If the result of the `fontWithName:size:` class method of the `UIFont` class is `nil`, the given font name could not be found. Make sure that the font name you have provided is available in the system by first enumerating all the font families and then all font names available in each family.

You can also use the `systemFontOfSize:` instance method of the `UIFont` class (or its bold alternative, `boldSystemFontOfSize:`) to load local system fonts, whatever they might be, from the device that is running your code. The default system font for iOS devices is Helvetica.

After you have loaded fonts, you can proceed to Recipe 20.2, where we will use the fonts that we loaded here in order to draw text on a graphical context.

## See Also

Recipe 20.2

# 20.2. Drawing Text

## Problem

You want to be able to draw text on the screen of an iOS device.

## Solution

Use the `drawAtPoint:withFont:` method of `NSString`.

## Discussion

To draw text, we can use some really handy methods built into the `NSString` class, such as `drawAtPoint:withAttributes:`. Before we proceed further, make sure that you have followed the instructions in this chapter's Introduction. You should now have a view object, subclassed from `UIView`, named `View`. Open that file. If the `drawRect:` instance method of the view object is commented out, remove the comments until you have that method in your view object:

```
#import "View.h"

@implementation View

- (id)initWithFrame:(CGRect)frame
{
    self = [super initWithFrame:frame];
    if (self) {
        // Initialization code
    }
    return self;
}

- (void)drawRect:(CGRect)rect{

}

@end
```

The `drawRect:` method is where we'll do the drawing, as mentioned before. Here we can start loading the font, and then draw a simple string on the screen at point 40 on the *x*-axis and 180 on the *y*-axis (Figure 20-6):

```
- (void)drawRect:(CGRect)rect{

    UIFont *helveticaBold =  [UIFont fontWithName:@"HelveticaNeue-Bold"
                                             size:40.0f];

    NSString *myString = @"Some String";

    [myString drawAtPoint:CGPointMake(40, 180)
           withAttributes:@{
                            NSFontAttributeName : helveticaBold
                            }];

}
```

In this code, we are simply loading a bold Helvetica font at size 40, and using it to draw the text `Some String` at point (40, 180).

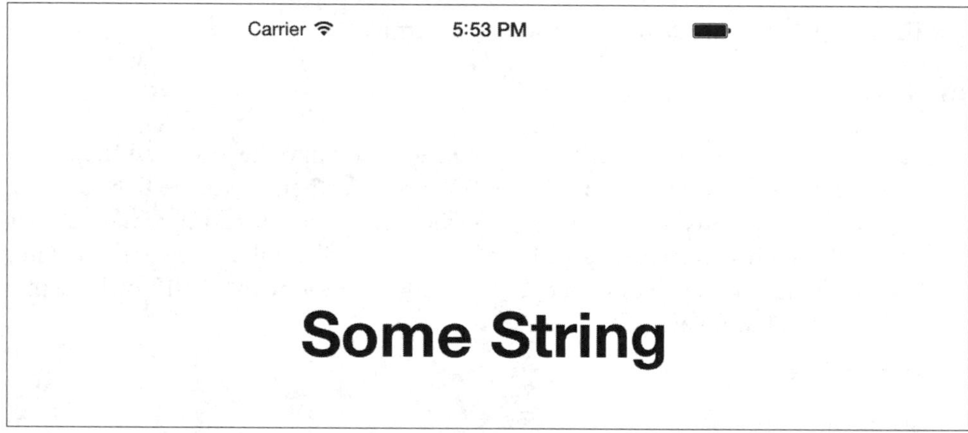


*Figure 20-6. A random string drawn on the graphical context of a view*

## 20.3. Constructing, Setting, and Using Colors

### Problem

You want to be able to obtain references to color objects in order to use them while you are drawing various forms on a view, such as text, rectangles, triangles, and line segments.

### Solution

Use the `UIColor` class.

## Discussion

UIKit provides programmers with a high-level abstraction of colors, encapsulated in the `UIColor` object. This class has a few really handy class methods, such as `redColor`, `blueColor`, `brownColor`, and `yellowColor`. However, if the color you are looking for isn't one of the explicitly named `UIColor` methods, you can always use the `colorWithRed:green:blue:alpha:` class method of `UIColor` class to load the color that you are looking for. The return value of this class method is a value of type `UIColor`. Here are the parameters of this method:

`red`
: The amount of red to use in the color. This value can be anything between `0.0f` to `1.0f`, where `0.0f` omits all red and `1.0f` makes the red component as dark as possible.

`green`
: The amount of green to mix with the red in the color. This value also ranges from `0.0f` to `1.0f`.

`blue`
: The amount of blue to mix with the red and green in the color. This value also ranges from `0.0f` to `1.0f`.

`alpha`
: The opaqueness of the color. This value can range from `0.0f` to `1.0f`, with `1.0f` making the color completely opaque and `0.0f` making the color completely transparent (in other words, invisible).

After you have an object of type `UIColor`, you can use its `set` instance method to make the current graphics context use that color for subsequent drawing.

You can use the `colorWithRed:green:blue:alpha:` class method of the `UIColor` class to load primary colors like red by simply passing `1.0f` as the `red` parameter and `0.0f` for the `green` and `blue` parameters. The `alpha` is up to you.

We will be using instance methods of the `NSString` class to draw text on the current graphics context, as we shall soon discuss. Now let's load a magenta color into an object of type `UIColor` and then draw the text `I Learn Really Fast` on the view's graphical context using a bold Helvetica font of size 30 (see Recipe 20.1 for loading fonts):

```
- (void)drawRect:(CGRect)rect{

    /* Load the color */
    UIColor *magentaColor =[UIColor colorWithRed:0.5f
                                           green:0.0f
```

```
                                                  blue:0.5f
                                                  alpha:1.0f];

    /* Set the color in the graphical context */
    [magentaColor set];

    /* Load the font */
    UIFont *helveticaBold = [UIFont fontWithName:@"HelveticaNeue-Bold"
                                            size:30.0f];

    /* Our string to be drawn */
    NSString *myString = @"I Learn Really Fast";

    /* Draw the string using the font. The color has
     already been set */
    [myString drawAtPoint:CGPointMake(25, 190)
           withAttributes:@{
                            NSFontAttributeName : helveticaBold
                            }];

}
```

The results are shown in Figure 20-7.

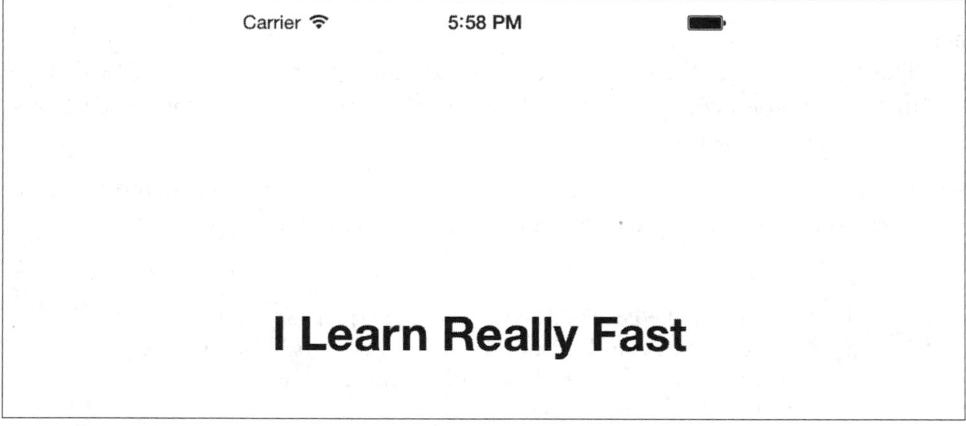


*Figure 20-7. String drawn with a color on a graphical context*

We can also use the `drawWithRect:options:attributes:context:` instance method of the `NSString` class to draw text inside a rectangular space. The text will get stretched to fit into that rectangle. UIKit will even wrap the text if it doesn't fit horizontally within the given rectangle. Rectangular bounds are encapsulated in `CGRect` structures. You can use the `CGRectMake` function to create the bounds of a rectangle:

```
- (void)drawRect:(CGRect)rect{

    /* Load the color */
```

```
    UIColor *magentaColor = [UIColor colorWithRed:0.5f
                                            green:0.0f
                                             blue:0.5f
                                            alpha:1.0f];

    /* Set the color in the graphical context */
    [magentaColor set];

    /* Load the font */
    UIFont *helveticaBold = [UIFont boldSystemFontOfSize:30];

    /* Our string to be drawn */
    NSString *myString = @"I Learn Really Fast";

    /* Draw the string using the font. The color has
     already been set */

    [myString drawWithRect:CGRectMake(100,  /* x */
                                      120,  /* y */
                                      100,  /* width */
                                      200)
                   options:NSStringDrawingUsesLineFragmentOrigin
                attributes:@{
                             NSFontAttributeName : helveticaBold
                             }
                   context:nil];

}
```

The `CGRectMake` function takes four parameters:

`x`
: The *x* position of the origin point of the rectangle in relation to the graphics context. In iOS, this is the number of points heading right, starting from the left side of the rectangle.

`y`
: The *y* position of the origin point of the rectangle in relation to the graphics context. In iOS, this is the number of points heading down, starting from the top of the rectangle.

`width`
: The width of the rectangle in points.

`height`
: The height of the rectangle in points.

The output is shown in Figure 20-8.

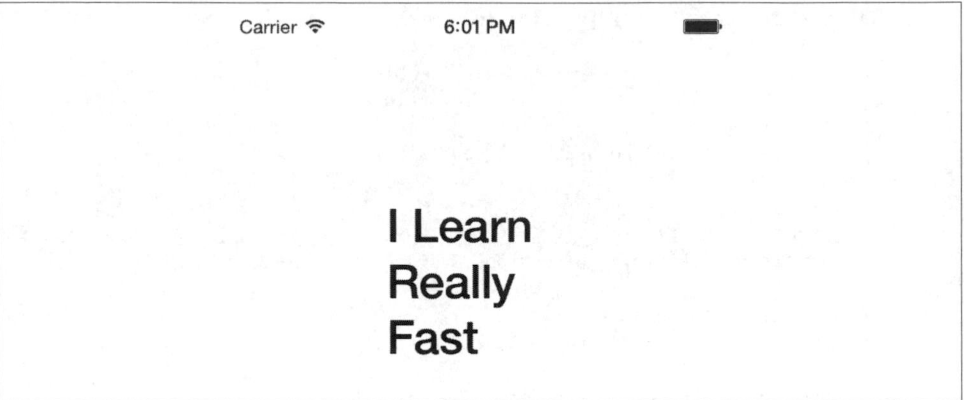


*Figure 20-8. Drawing a string in a rectangular space*

`UIColor` is really a UIKit wrapper around the Core Graphics class `CGColor`. When we get as low level as Core Graphics, we suddenly gain more control over how we use the color objects, and we can even determine the components from which the color is made. Let's say some other code passed you an object of type `UIColor`, and you want to detect its `red`, `green`, `blue`, and `alpha` components. To get the components that make up a `UIColor` object, follow these steps:

1. Use the `CGColor` instance method of the instance of the `UIColor` class. This will give us a color object of type `CGColorRef`, which is a Core Graphics Color Reference object.
2. Use the `CGColorGetComponents` function to get the components that construct the color object.
3. Use the `CGColorGetNumberOfComponents` function to determine the number of components that were used to construct the color (red + green + etc.) if need be.

Here is an example:

```
- (void) drawRect:(CGRect)rect{

    /* Load the color */
    UIColor *steelBlueColor = [UIColor colorWithRed:0.3f
                                              green:0.4f
                                               blue:0.6f
                                              alpha:1.0f];

    CGColorRef colorRef = steelBlueColor.CGColor;

    const CGFloat *components = CGColorGetComponents(colorRef);

    NSUInteger componentsCount = CGColorGetNumberOfComponents(colorRef);
```

```
        NSUInteger counter = 0;
        for (counter = 0;
             counter < componentsCount;
             counter++){
            NSLog(@"Component %lu = %.02f",
                  (unsigned long)counter + 1,
                  components[counter]);
        }

    }
```

The output that we get in the console window after running this code is:

```
Component 1 = 0.30
Component 2 = 0.40
Component 3 = 0.60
Component 4 = 1.00
```

## See Also

Recipe 20.1

# 20.4. Drawing Images

## Problem

You want to be able to draw images on the screen of an iOS device.

## Solution

Use the `UIImage` class to load an image and then use the `drawInRect:` method of the image to draw it on a graphics context.

## Discussion

UIKit helps you draw images with ease. All you have to do is load your images in instances of type `UIImage`. The `UIImage` class provides various class and instance methods to load your images. Here are some of the important ones in iOS:

`imageNamed:` *class method*
: Loads the image (and caches the image if it can load it properly). The parameter to this method is the name of the image in the bundle, such as *Tree Texture.png*.

`imageWithData:` *class method*
: Loads an image from the data encapsulated in an instance of an `NSData` object that was passed as the parameter to this method.

`initWithContentsOfFile:` *instance method (for initialization)*
Uses the given parameter as the path to an image that has to be loaded and used to initialize the image object.

This path should be the full path to the image in the app bundle.

`initWithData:` *instance method (for initialization)*
Uses the given parameter of type `NSData` to initialize the image. This data should belong to a valid image.

Please follow these steps to add an image to your Xcode project:

1. Find where the image is located in your computer.
2. Drag and drop the image into your image category, usually named *images.xcassets*. Xcode will do the rest for you.

You can retrieve Xcode's icon by following these steps:

1. Find the Xcode app in the Finder.
2. Press Command+I on Xcode in the Finder to get information on it.
3. Click the icon in the upper left of the Xcode Info window.
4. Press Command+C to copy it.
5. Open the Preview app.
6. Hit Command+V to paste the Xcode icon into a new image.
7. You will now have an ICNS file with five separate pages. Save it as a PDF, and then delete all but the highest-resolution icon (page 1).

We will be drawing this image on a graphics context to demonstrate how to draw images in this section of the book. I've already found the file, and dragged and dropped that image into my iOS app. Now I have an image called *Xcode.png* in my app project's asset category. The image is shown in Figure 20-9.

*Figure 20-9. Xcode's icon, found in your Xcode app*

Here is the code for *loading* an image:

```
- (void)drawRect:(CGRect)rect{

    UIImage *image = [UIImage imageNamed:@"Xcode"];

    if (image != nil){
        NSLog(@"Successfully loaded the image.");
    } else {
        NSLog(@"Failed to load the image.");
    }

}
```

If you have the *Xcode* image in your app bundle, running this code will print `Successfully loaded the image.` in the console. If you don't have the image, `Failed to load the image.` will get printed. For the remainder of this section, I assume you have this image in your project's asset category. Feel free to place other images in your app and refer to those images instead of *Xcode.png*, which I will be using in example code.

The two easiest ways to draw an image of type `UIImage` on a graphics context are:

`drawAtPoint:` *instance method of* `UIImage` *class*
: Draws the image at its original size at the given point. Construct the point using the `CGPointMake` function.

`drawInRect:` *instance method of* `UIImage` *class*
: Draws the image in the given rectangular space. To construct this rectangular space, use the `CGRectMake` function:

```
- (void)drawRect:(CGRect)rect{

    /* Assuming the image is in your app bundle and we can load it */
    UIImage *xcodeIcon = [UIImage imageNamed:@"Xcode"];

    [xcodeIcon drawAtPoint:CGPointMake(0.0f,
                                       20.0f)];

    [xcodeIcon drawInRect:CGRectMake(50.0f,
                                     10.0f,
                                     40.0f,
                                     35.0f)];

}
```

The `drawAtPoint:` call shown in this code snippet will draw the image at its full size at point (0, 20), and the `drawInRect:` call will draw the image at point (50, 10) at 40×35 points, as shown in Figure 20-10.

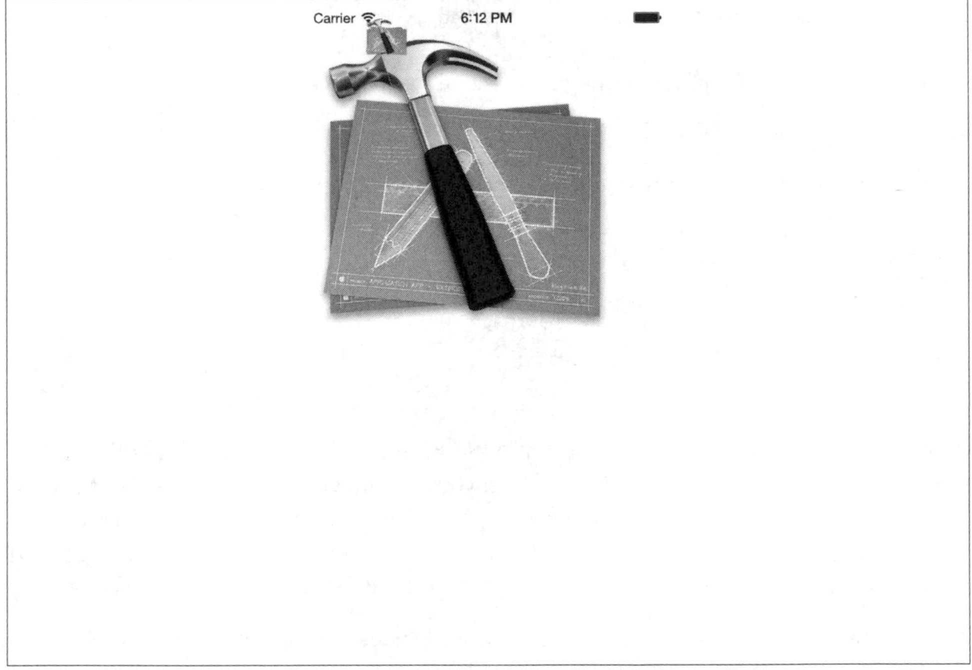


*Figure 20-10. Drawing an image on a graphics context can be accomplished with two different methods*

Aspect ratio is the ratio between the width and the height of an image (or a computer screen). Let's assume you have an image that is 100×100 pixels. If you draw this image at point (0, 0) with a size of (100, 200), you can immediately see on the screen that the image is stretched in height (200 pixels instead of 100). The `drawInRect:` instance method of `UIImage` leaves it up to you how you want to draw your images. In other words, it is *you* who has to specify the *x*, *y*, width, and height of your image as it appears on the screen.

## See Also

Recipe 15.6

# 20.5. Constructing Resizable Images

## Problem

You want to be able to save some memory and disk space by creating resizable images for your UI components. You may also want to be able to create different sizes of the same UI component, such as a button, using only a single background image.

Resizable images refer to simple PNG or JPEG images that can be loaded into an instance of `UIImage`.

## Solution

Create a resizable image using the `resizableImageWithCapInsets:` instance method of the `UIImage` class.

## Discussion

Resizable images may sound a bit strange at first, but they make sense when you understand the different display needs of your app. For instance, you may be working on an iOS app where you want to provide a background image for your buttons. The bigger the text in the button, the wider the button. So you now have two options on how you want to provide the background images of your buttons:

- Create one image per size of button. This will add to the size of your bundle, consume more memory, and require much more work from you. In addition, any change to the text requires a new image to make the button fit.

- Create one resizable image and use that throughout the app for all the buttons.

Without a doubt, the second option is much more appealing. So what are resizable images? They are simply images that are divided into two virtual areas:

- An area that will not be stretched.
- An area that will be stretched to fit any size.

As you can see in Figure 20-11, we have created an image for a button. After a better look at the image, you can clearly see that it is made out of a gradient. The area that I have drawn a rectangle around is the area that can be cut out of the image. You might be wondering why. Have a closer look! If I cut that area and made it only 1 pixel wide and as tall as it is now, I could, in my app, put as many of those vertical slices that I cut together to form the same area that is highlighted in this photo. See Figure 20-12.

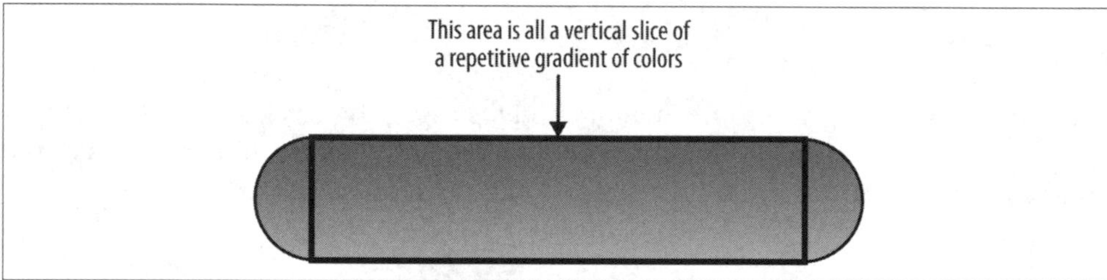


*Figure 20-11. An image with a redundant area is a great candidate for a resizable image*

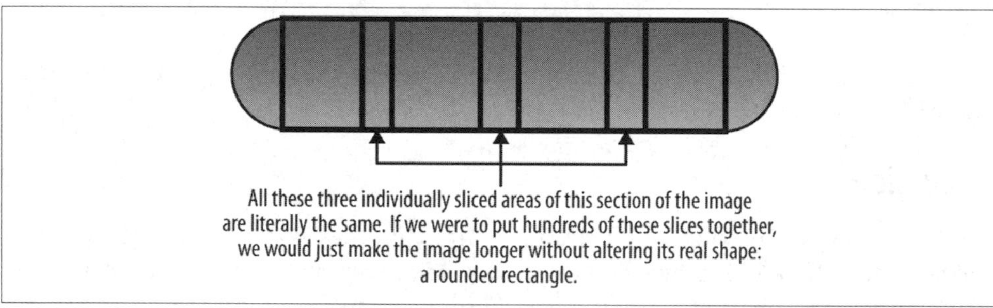


*Figure 20-12. Individual slices of the center section of the image are all the same*

So how can one make this image smaller and still be able to construct a button out of it? The answer is simple. In this case, where the image is consistently the same across the length of the image, we will simply cut the center of it into a slice that is 1 point wide while keeping it as tall as it is right now. Figure 20-13 shows what our image will look like after this operation.

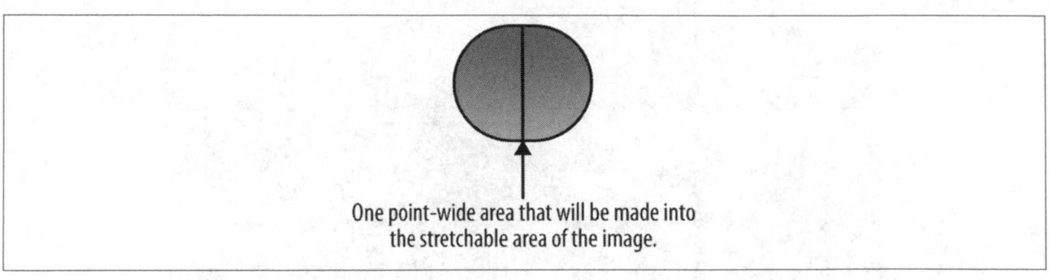
One point-wide area that will be made into
the stretchable area of the image.

*Figure 20-13. The resizable area of the image is made into a 1-point-wide area*

Now comes the interesting part! How can we tell the iOS SDK which part of the image to keep intact and which part to stretch? It turns out that iOS SDK has already taken care of this. First, load your image into memory using the `UIImage` APIs that you learned in this chapter. After constructing an instance of `UIImage` with an image that you know you can stretch, transform the image instance into a resizable image using the `resizableImageWithCapInsets:` instance method of the same instance. The parameter that this method takes is of type `UIEdgeInsets`, which is itself defined in this way:

```
typedef struct UIEdgeInsets {
    CGFloat top, left, bottom, right;
} UIEdgeInsets;
```

Edge insets are there to allow us to create what Apple calls *nine-part images*. A nine-part image is an image that has the following nine components:

- Upper-left corner
- Top edge
- Upper-right corner
- Right edge
- Lower-right corner
- Bottom edge
- Lower-left corner
- Left edge
- Center

Figure 20-14 illustrates this concept much better than words can.

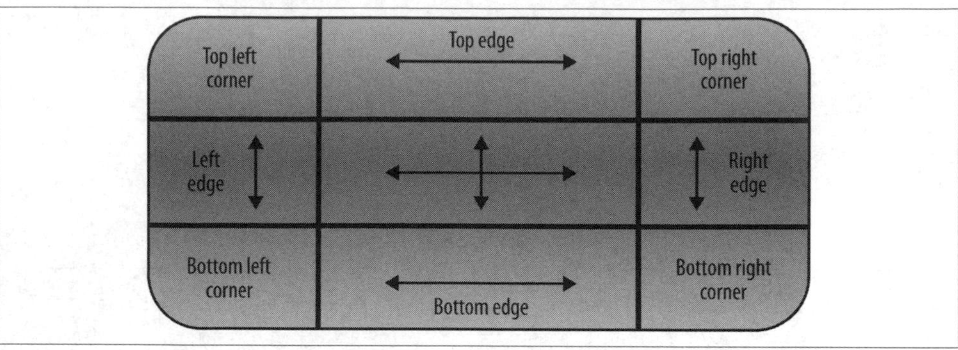


*Figure 20-14. Illustration of a nine-part image*

The purpose of storing an image as a nine-part image is that programmers can resize it vertically and horizontally to pretty much any size they want. When the programmer requires the image to be resized, some of these components will stay unchanged and some will be resized. The parts that stay unchanged are the corners, which aren't resized at all. The other parts of the image will be resized as follows:

*Top edge*
: This part of the image will be resized in its width but not in its height.

*Right edge*
: This part of the image will be resized in its height but not in its width.

*Bottom edge*
: This part of the image, just like the top edge, will be resized in its width, but not in its height.

*Left edge*
: Just like the right edge, this part of the image will be resized in its height, but not in its width.

*Center*
: Will be resized in both its width and its height.

The top, left, bottom, and right values of the inset mark the area that you don't want to stretch. For instance, if you specified the value of 10 for the left, 11 for the top, 14 for the right, and 5 for the bottom, you are telling iOS to put a vertical *line* on the image at 10 points from the left, a horizontal line at 11 points from the top, another vertical line at 14 points from the right, and a final horizontal line at 5 points from the bottom. The rectangular area *trapped* between these virtual lines is the resizable area of the image and the area outside this rectangle is not stretched. This may sound a bit confusing, but imagine a rectangle (your image) and then you draw another rectangle inside it. The inner rectangle is resizable but the outer rectangle stays intact. I think looking at a picture demonstrating these values will clarify this (Figure 20-15).

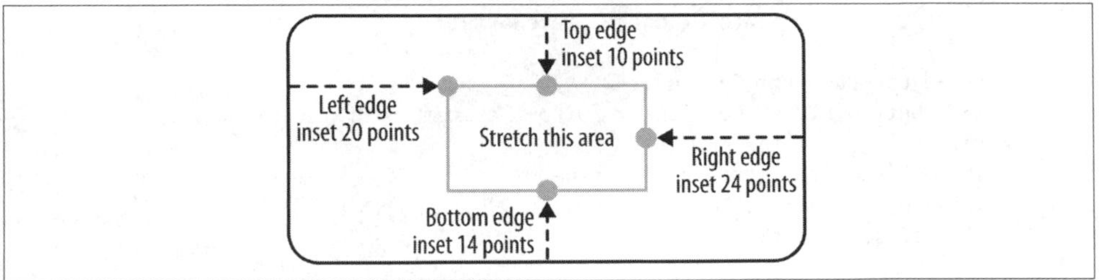


*Figure 20-15. The stretchable portion of the image is defined by the edge insets*

The left and right distances are really the same in Figure 20-15. So are the top and the bottom distances. I have just set them to different values to make the edge inset construction a bit more straightforward and easier to understand. If all the values were the same, when we construct the edge insets later you may ask: which one is which?!

For an image like Figure 20-15, we should construct the edge inset like so:

```
UIEdgeInsets edgeInsets;
edgeInsets.left = 20.0f;
edgeInsets.top = 10.0f;
edgeInsets.right = 24.0f;
edgeInsets.bottom = 14.0f;
```

OK, now let's go back to our example code. What we are trying to do here is use the stretchable image that we created in Figure 20-13 for a real application. We will create a button and place it at the center of our only view controller's view. The button's text will read "Stretched Image on Button" and its size will be 200 points wide and 44 points tall. Here is our code:

```
#import "ViewController.h"

@interface ViewController ()
@property (nonatomic, strong) UIButton *button;
@end

@implementation ViewController

- (void)viewDidLoad{
    [super viewDidLoad];

    /* Instantiate the button */
    self.button = [UIButton buttonWithType:UIButtonTypeCustom];
    [self.button setFrame:CGRectMake(0.0f, 0.0f, 200.0f, 44.0f)];

    /* Set the title of the button */
```

```
        [self.button setTitle:@"Stretched Image on Button"
                     forState:UIControlStateNormal];

        /* Adjust the font for our text */
        self.button.titleLabel.font = [UIFont systemFontOfSize:15.0f];

        /* Construct the stretchable image */
        UIImage *image = [UIImage imageNamed:@"Button"];
        UIEdgeInsets edgeInsets;
        edgeInsets.left = 14.0f;
        edgeInsets.top = 0.0f;
        edgeInsets.right = 14.0f;
        edgeInsets.bottom = 0.0f;
        image = [image resizableImageWithCapInsets:edgeInsets];

        /* Set the background image of the button */
        [self.button setBackgroundImage:image forState:UIControlStateNormal];

        [self.view addSubview:self.button];
        self.button.center = self.view.center;

    }

    @end
```

Now if you run the app, you will see something similar to Figure 20-16.

## See Also

Recipe 20.4

# 20.6. Drawing Lines

## Problem

You simply want to be able to draw lines on a graphics context.

## Solution

Retrieve the handle to your graphics context and then use the `CGContextMoveToPoint` and the `CGContextAddLineToPoint` functions to draw your line.

## Discussion

When we talk about drawing shapes in iOS or OS X, we are implicitly talking about *paths*. What are paths, you may ask? A path is constructed from one or more series of points drawn on a screen. There is a big difference between paths and lines. A path can contain many lines, but a line cannot contain many paths. Think of paths as series of points—it's as simple as that.

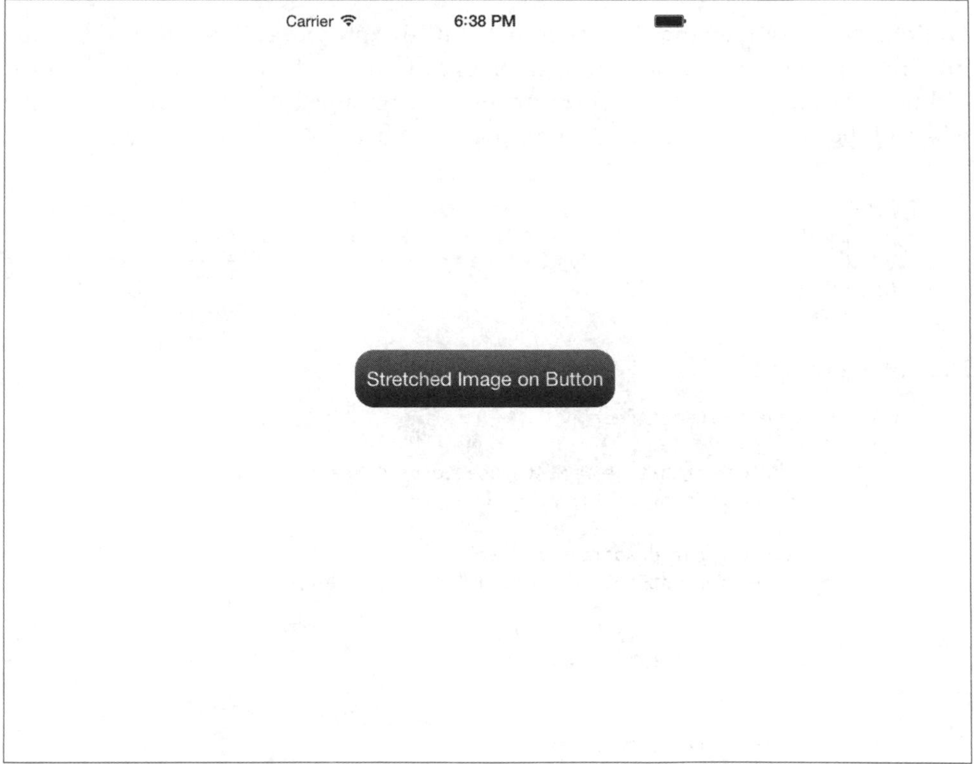


*Figure 20-16. A button is displayed on the screen with a stretchable background image*

Lines have to be drawn using paths. Specify the start and end points, and then ask Core Graphics to fill that path for you. Core Graphics realizes that you have created a line on that path and will paint that path for you using the color that you specified (see Recipe 20.3).

We will be talking about paths in more depth later (see Recipe 20.7), but for now let's focus on using paths to create straight lines. To do this, follow these steps:

1. Choose a color on your graphics context (see Recipe 20.3).
2. Retrieve the handle to the graphics context, using the `UIGraphicsGetCurrentContext` function.
3. Set the starting point for your line using the `CGContextMoveToPoint` procedure.
4. Move your pen on the graphics context using the `CGContextAddLineToPoint` procedure to specify the ending point of your line.

5. Create the path that you have laid out using the `CGContextStrokePath` procedure. This procedure will draw the path using the current color that has been set on the graphics context.

Optionally, you can use the `CGContextSetLineWidth` procedure to set the width of the lines that you are drawing on a given graphics context. The first parameter to this procedure is the graphics context that you are drawing on, and the second parameter is the width of the line, expressed as a floating-point number (`CGFloat`).

In iOS, the line width is measured in logical points.

Here is an example:

```
- (void)drawRect:(CGRect)rect{

    /* Set the color that we want to use to draw the line */
    [[UIColor brownColor] set];

    /* Get the current graphics context */
    CGContextRef currentContext = UIGraphicsGetCurrentContext();

    /* Set the width for the line */
    CGContextSetLineWidth(currentContext,
                          5.0f);

    /* Start the line at this point */
    CGContextMoveToPoint(currentContext,
                         50.0f,
                         10.0f);

    /* And end it at this point */
    CGContextAddLineToPoint(currentContext,
                            100.0f,
                            200.0f);

    /* Use the context's current color to draw the line */
    CGContextStrokePath(currentContext);

}
```

Running this code in iOS Simulator will show you results similar to Figure 20-17.

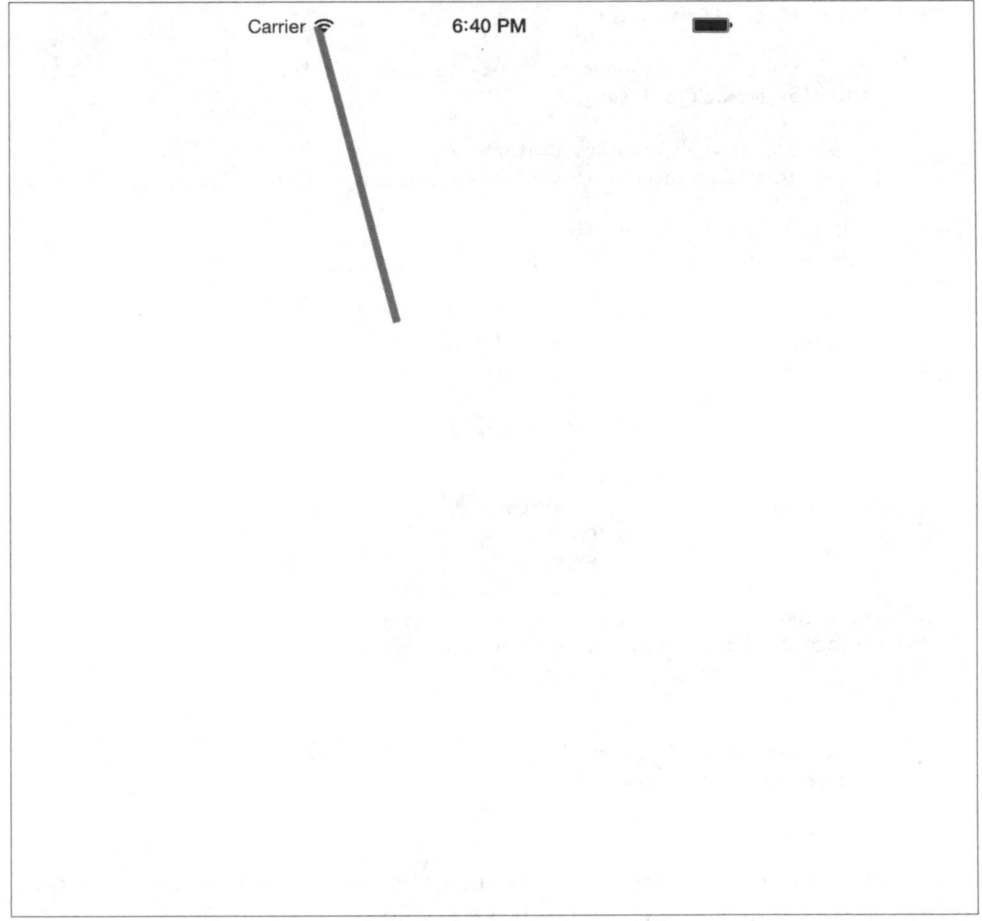


*Figure 20-17. Drawing a line on a current graphics context*

Let me show you another example. As mentioned earlier, the `CGContextAddLineToPoint` procedure specifies the end point of the current line. Now what if we have already drawn a line from point (20, 20) to point (100, 100), and want to draw a line from (100, 100) to (300, 100)? You might think that after drawing the first line, we have to move the pen to point (100, 100) using the `CGContextMoveToPoint` procedure, and then draw the line to point (300, 100) using the `CGContextAddLineToPoint` procedure. While that will work, there is a more efficient way to do this. After you call the `CGContextAddLineToPoint` procedure to specify the ending point of your current line, your pen's position will change to what you pass to this method. In other words, after you issue a method using the pen, it leaves the pen's position at the ending point of whatever it drew. So to draw another line from the current ending point to another point, all you have to do is call the `CGContextAddLineToPoint` procedure again with another ending point. Here is an example:

```
- (void)drawRect:(CGRect)rect{

    /* Set the color that we want to use to draw the line */
    [[UIColor brownColor] set];

    /* Get the current graphics context */
    CGContextRef currentContext = UIGraphicsGetCurrentContext();

    /* Set the width for the lines */
    CGContextSetLineWidth(currentContext,
                          5.0f);

    /* Start the line at this point */
    CGContextMoveToPoint(currentContext,
                         20.0f,
                         20.0f);

    /* And end it at this point */
    CGContextAddLineToPoint(currentContext,
                            100.0f,
                            100.0f);

    /* Extend the line to another point */
    CGContextAddLineToPoint(currentContext,
                            300.0f,
                            100.0f);

    /* Use the context's current color to draw the lines */
    CGContextStrokePath(currentContext);

}
```

The results are shown in Figure 20-18. You can see that both lines are successfully drawn without us having to move the pen for the second line.

The point where two lines meet is, not surprisingly, called a join. With Core Graphics, you can specify what type of join you want to have between lines that are connected to each other. To make your choice, you must use the `CGContextSetLineJoin` procedure. It takes two parameters: a graphics context on which you are setting the join type, and the join type itself, which must be of type `CGLineJoin`. `CGLineJoin` is an enumeration of the following values:

`kCGLineJoinMiter`
: Joins will be made out of sharp corners. This is the default join type.

`kCGLineJoinBevel`
: Joins will be squared off on the corner.

`kCGLineJoinRound`
: As the name implies, this makes round joins.

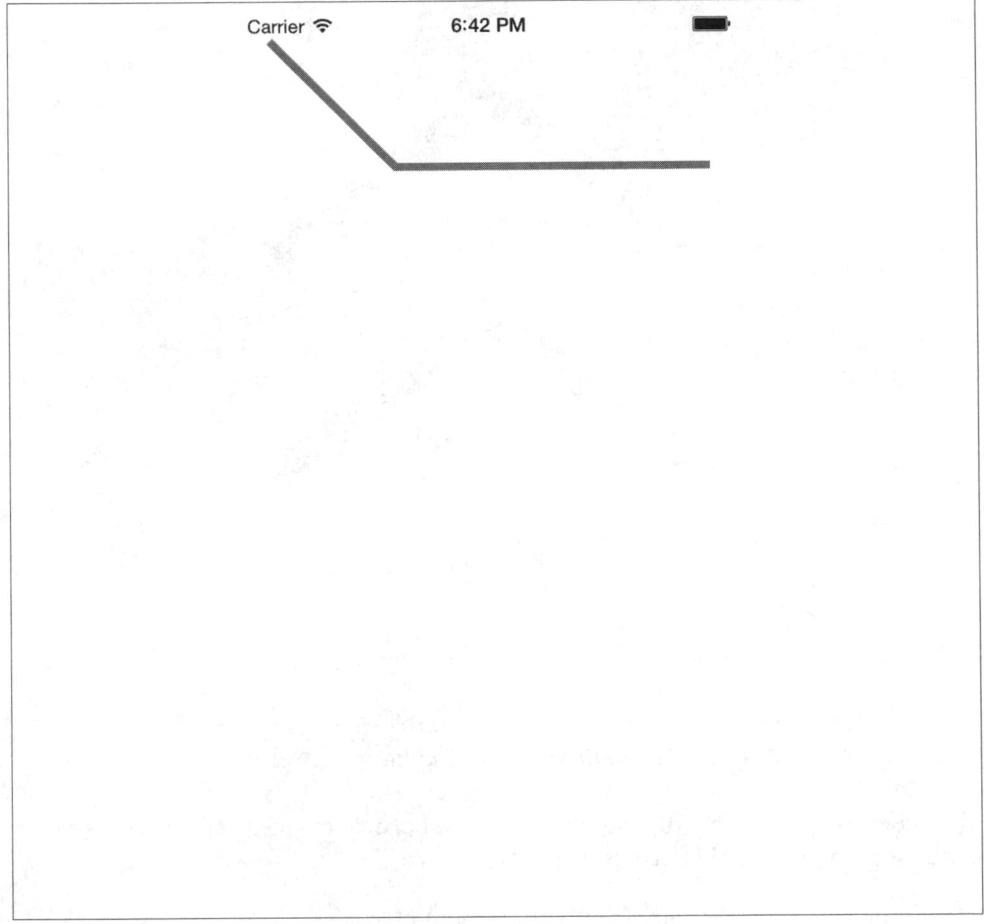


*Figure 20-18. Drawing two lines at once*

Let's have a look at an example. Let's say we want to write a program that can draw "rooftops" on a graphics context (three of them, one for each join type), and also draws text below each rooftop describing the type of join it is using. Something similar to Figure 20-19 will be the result.

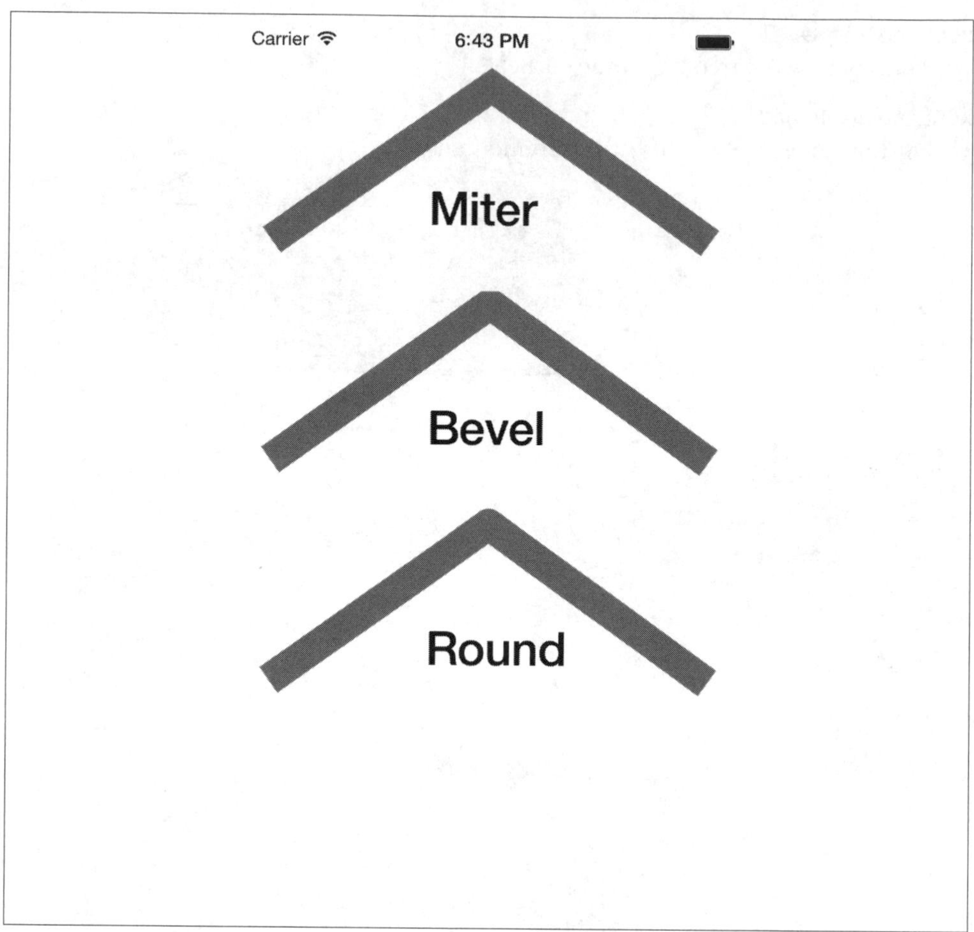


*Figure 20-19. Three types of line joins in Core Graphics*

To accomplish this, I've written a method named `drawRooftopAtTopPointof:textToDisplay:lineJoin:`, which takes three parameters:

1. A point at which the top of the rooftop should be placed.
2. The text to display inside the rooftop.
3. The join type to be used.

The code is as follows:

```
- (void) drawRooftopAtTopPointof:(CGPoint)paramTopPoint
                   textToDisplay:(NSString *)paramText
                        lineJoin:(CGLineJoin)paramLineJoin{

    /* Set the color that we want to use to draw the line */
```

```
    [[UIColor brownColor] set];

    /* Get the current graphics context */
    CGContextRef currentContext = UIGraphicsGetCurrentContext();

    /* Set the line join */
    CGContextSetLineJoin(currentContext,
                         paramLineJoin);

    /* Set the width for the lines */
    CGContextSetLineWidth(currentContext,
                          20.0f);

    /* Start the line at this point */
    CGContextMoveToPoint(currentContext,
                         paramTopPoint.x - 140,
                         paramTopPoint.y + 100);

    /* And end it at this point */
    CGContextAddLineToPoint(currentContext,
                            paramTopPoint.x,
                            paramTopPoint.y);

    /* Extend the line to another point to
     make the rooftop */
    CGContextAddLineToPoint(currentContext,
                            paramTopPoint.x + 140,
                            paramTopPoint.y + 100);

    /* Use the context's current color to draw the lines */
    CGContextStrokePath(currentContext);

    /* Draw the text in the rooftop using a black color */
    [[UIColor blackColor] set];

    /* Now draw the text */
    CGPoint drawingPoint = CGPointMake(paramTopPoint.x - 40.0f,
                                       paramTopPoint.y + 60.0f);
    UIFont *font = [UIFont boldSystemFontOfSize:30.0f];

    [paramText drawAtPoint:drawingPoint
            withAttributes:@{NSFontAttributeName : font}];

}
```

Now let's call this method in the `drawRect:` instance method of the view object where we have a graphics context:

```
- (void)drawRect:(CGRect)rect{

    [self drawRooftopAtTopPointof:CGPointMake(160.0f, 40.0f)
                    textToDisplay:@"Miter"
                         lineJoin:kCGLineJoinMiter];
```

```
        [self drawRooftopAtTopPointof:CGPointMake(160.0f, 180.0f)
                        textToDisplay:@"Bevel"
                             lineJoin:kCGLineJoinBevel];

        [self drawRooftopAtTopPointof:CGPointMake(160.0f, 320.0f)
                        textToDisplay:@"Round"
                             lineJoin:kCGLineJoinRound];

    }
```

## See Also

Recipe 20.3; Recipe 20.7

# 20.7. Constructing Paths

## Problem

You want to be able to draw any shape that you wish on a graphics context.

## Solution

Construct and draw paths.

## Discussion

A series of points placed together can form a shape. A series of shapes put together builds a path. Paths can easily be managed by Core Graphics. In Recipe 20.6, we worked indirectly with paths using `CGContext` functions. But Core Graphics also has functions that work directly with paths, as we shall soon see.

Paths belong to whichever graphics context they are drawn on. Paths do not have boundaries or specific shapes, unlike the shapes we draw on them. But paths do have bounding boxes. Please bear in mind that boundaries are not the same as bounding boxes. Boundaries are limits above which you cannot draw on a canvas, while the bounding box of a path is the smallest rectangle that contains all the shapes, points, and other objects that have been drawn on that specific path. Think of paths as stamps, and think of your graphics context as the envelope. Your envelope could be the same every time you mail something to your friend, but what you put on that context (the stamp or the path) can be different.

After you finish drawing on a path, you can then draw that path on the graphics context. Developers familiar with game programming know the concept of *buffers*, which draw their scenes and, at appropriate times, *flush* the images onto the screen. Paths are those buffers. They are like blank canvases that can be drawn on graphics contexts when the time is right.

The first step in directly working with paths is to create them. The method creating the path returns a handle that you use whenever you want to draw something on that path, passing the handle to Core Graphics for reference. After you create the path, you can add different points, lines, and shapes to it and then draw the path. You can either fill the path or paint it with a stroke on a graphics context. Here are the methods you have to work with:

`CGPathCreateMutable` *function*
: Creates a new mutable path of type `CGMutablePathRef` and returns its handle. We should dispose of this path once we are done with it, as you will soon see.

`CGPathMoveToPoint` *procedure*
: Moves the current pen position on the path to the point specified by a parameter of type `CGPoint`.

`CGPathAddLineToPoint` *procedure*
: Draws a line segment from the current pen position to the specified position (again, specified by a value of type `CGPoint`).

`CGContextAddPath` *procedure*
: Adds a given path (specified by a path handle) to a graphics context, ready for drawing.

`CGContextDrawPath` *procedure*
: Draws a given path on the graphics context.

`CGPathRelease` *procedure*
: Releases the memory allocated for a path handle.

`CGPathAddRect` *procedure*
: Adds a rectangle to a path. The rectangle's boundaries are specified by a `CGRect` structure.

There are three important drawing methods that you can ask the `CGContextDrawPath` procedure to perform:

`kCGPathStroke`
: Draws a line (stroke) to mark the boundary or edge of the path, using the currently selected stroke color.

`kCGPathFill`
: Fills the area surrounded by the path with the currently selected fill color.

`kCGPathFillStroke`
: Combines stroke and fill. Uses the currently selected fill color to fill the path and the currently selected stroke color to draw the edge of the path. We'll see an example of this method in the following section.

Let's have a look at an example. We will draw a blue line from the top-left to the bottom-right corner, and another from the top-right to the bottom-left corner, to create a gigantic X across the screen.

For this example, I have removed the status bar from the application in iOS Simulator. If you don't want to bother doing this, please continue to the example code. With a status bar, the output of this code will be only slightly different from the screenshot I'll show. To hide the status bar, find the *Info.plist* file in your Xcode project and add a key to it named `UIStatusBarHidden` with the value of `YES`, as shown in Figure 20-20. This will force your app's status bar to be hidden when it opens.

Projects 〉 Chapter 17 〉 Constructing Paths 〉 Constructing Paths 〉 Supporting Files 〉 Cor

| Key | Type | Value |
|---|---|---|
| ▼ Information Property List | Dictionary | (17 items) |
| Localization native development r... | String | en |
| Bundle display name | String | ${PRODUCT_NAME} |
| Executable file | String | ${EXECUTABLE_NAME} |
| Status bar is initially hidden | Boolean | YES |
| Bundle identifier | String | com.pixolity.ios.cookbook.${PRODUCT_NAME:rfc1034identifier} |
| InfoDictionary version | String | 6.0 |
| Bundle name | String | ${PRODUCT_NAME} |
| Bundle OS Type code | String | APPL |
| Bundle versions string, short | String | 1.0 |
| Bundle creator OS Type code | String | ???? |
| Bundle version | String | 1.0 |
| Application requires iPhone envir... | Boolean | YES |
| Main storyboard file base name | String | Main_iPhone |
| Main storyboard file base name (iPad) | String | Main_iPad |
| ▶ Required device capabilities | Array | (1 item) |
| ▶ Supported interface orientations | Array | (3 items) |
| ▶ Supported interface orientations (... | Array | (4 items) |

*Figure 20-20. Hiding the status bar in an iOS app using the Info.plist file*

```
- (void)drawRect:(CGRect)rect{

    /* Create the path */
    CGMutablePathRef path = CGPathCreateMutable();

    /* How big is our screen? We want the X to cover
     the whole screen */
```

```
    CGRect screenBounds = [[UIScreen mainScreen] bounds];

    /* Start from top-left */
    CGPathMoveToPoint(path,
                      NULL,
                      screenBounds.origin.x,
                      screenBounds.origin.y);

    /* Draw a line from top-left to bottom-right of the screen */
    CGPathAddLineToPoint(path,
                         NULL,
                         screenBounds.size.width,
                         screenBounds.size.height);

    /* Start another line from top-right */
    CGPathMoveToPoint(path,
                      NULL,
                      screenBounds.size.width,
                      screenBounds.origin.y);

    /* Draw a line from top-right to bottom-left */
    CGPathAddLineToPoint(path,
                         NULL,
                         screenBounds.origin.x,
                         screenBounds.size.height);

    /* Get the context that the path has to be drawn on */
    CGContextRef currentContext = UIGraphicsGetCurrentContext();

    /* Add the path to the context so we can
     draw it later */
    CGContextAddPath(currentContext,
                     path);

    /* Set the blue color as the stroke color */
    [[UIColor blueColor] setStroke];

    /* Draw the path with stroke color */
    CGContextDrawPath(currentContext,
                      kCGPathStroke);

    /* Finally release the path object */
    CGPathRelease(path);

}
```

The NULL parameters getting passed to procedures such as `CGPathMoveToPoint` represent possible transformations that can be used when drawing the shapes and lines on a given path. For information about transformations, refer to Recipes 20.11, 20.12, and 20.13.

You can see how easy it is to draw a path on a context. All you really have to remember is how to create a new mutable path (`CGPathCreateMutable`), add that path to your graphics context (`CGContextAddPath`), and draw it on a graphics context (`CGContextDrawPath`). If you run this code, you will get an output similar to that shown in Figure 20-21.

*Figure 20-21. Drawing on a graphics context using paths*

## See Also

Recipe 20.6; Recipe 20.11; Recipe 20.12; Recipe 20.13

# 20.8. Drawing Rectangles

## Problem

You want to be able to draw rectangles on a graphics context.

## Solution

Use the `CGPathAddRect` to add a rectangle to a path and then draw that path on a graphics context.

## Discussion

As we learned in Recipe 20.7, you can construct and use paths quite easily. One of the procedures that you can use on paths in Core Graphics is `CGPathAddRect`, which lets you draw rectangles as part of paths. Here is an example:

```
- (void)drawRect:(CGRect)rect{

    /* Create the path first. Just the path handle. */
    CGMutablePathRef path = CGPathCreateMutable();

    /* Here are our rectangle boundaries */
    CGRect rectangle = CGRectMake(10.0f,
                                  30.0f,
                                  200.0f,
                                  300.0f);

    /* Add the rectangle to the path */
    CGPathAddRect(path,
                  NULL,
                  rectangle);

    /* Get the handle to the current context */
    CGContextRef currentContext = UIGraphicsGetCurrentContext();

    /* Add the path to the context */
    CGContextAddPath(currentContext,
                     path);

    /* Set the fill color to cornflower blue */
    [[UIColor colorWithRed:0.20f
                     green:0.60f
                      blue:0.80f
                     alpha:1.0f] setFill];

    /* Set the stroke color to brown */
    [[UIColor brownColor] setStroke];

    /* Set the line width (for the stroke) to 5 */
    CGContextSetLineWidth(currentContext,
                          5.0f);

    /* Stroke and fill the path on the context */
    CGContextDrawPath(currentContext,
                      kCGPathFillStroke);

    /* Dispose of the path */
    CGPathRelease(path);

}
```

Here we are drawing a rectangle on the path, filling it with cornflower blue, and stroking the edges of the rectangle with brown. Figure 20-22 shows how the output will look when we run the program.

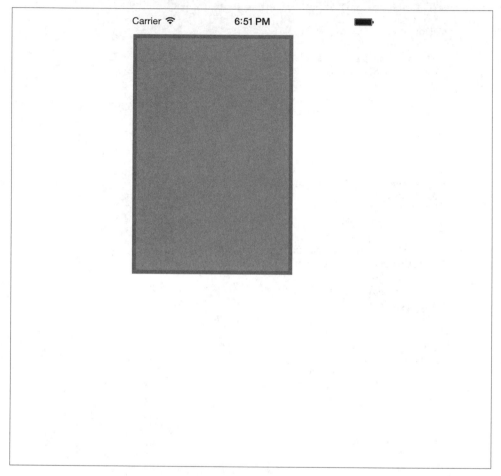


*Figure 20-22. Drawing a rectangle using paths*

If you have multiple rectangles to draw, you can pass an array of `CGRect` objects to the `CGPathAddRects` procedure. Here is an example:

```
- (void)drawRect:(CGRect)rect{

    /* Create the path first. Just the path handle. */
    CGMutablePathRef path = CGPathCreateMutable();

    /* Here are our first rectangle boundaries */
    CGRect rectangle1 = CGRectMake(10.0f,
```

```
                                         30.0f,
                                         200.0f,
                                         300.0f);

    /* And the second rectangle */
    CGRect rectangle2 = CGRectMake(40.0f,
                                   100.0f,
                                   90.0f,
                                   300.0f);

    /* Put both rectangles into an array */
    CGRect rectangles[2] = {
        rectangle1, rectangle2
    };

    /* Add the rectangles to the path */
    CGPathAddRects(path,
                   NULL,
                   (const CGRect *)&rectangles,
                   2);

    /* Get the handle to the current context */
    CGContextRef currentContext = UIGraphicsGetCurrentContext();

    /* Add the path to the context */
    CGContextAddPath(currentContext,
                     path);

    /* Set the fill color to cornflower blue */
    [[UIColor colorWithRed:0.20f
                     green:0.60f
                      blue:0.80f
                     alpha:1.0f] setFill];

    /* Set the stroke color to black */
    [[UIColor blackColor] setStroke];

    /* Set the line width (for the stroke) to 5 */
    CGContextSetLineWidth(currentContext,
                          5.0f);

    /* Stroke and fill the path on the context */
    CGContextDrawPath(currentContext,
                      kCGPathFillStroke);

    /* Dispose of the path */
    CGPathRelease(path);

}
```

Figure 20-23 shows how the output of this code will look when run in iOS Simulator. The parameters that we pass to the `CGPathAddRects` procedure are (in this order):

1. The handle to the path where we will add the rectangles.
2. The transformation, if any, to use on the rectangles. (For information about transformations, refer to Recipes 20.11, 20.12, and 20.13.)
3. A reference to the array holding the `CGRect` rectangles.
4. The number of rectangles in the array that we passed in the previous parameter. It is very important that you pass exactly as many rectangles as you have in your array, to avoid unknown behavior by this procedure.

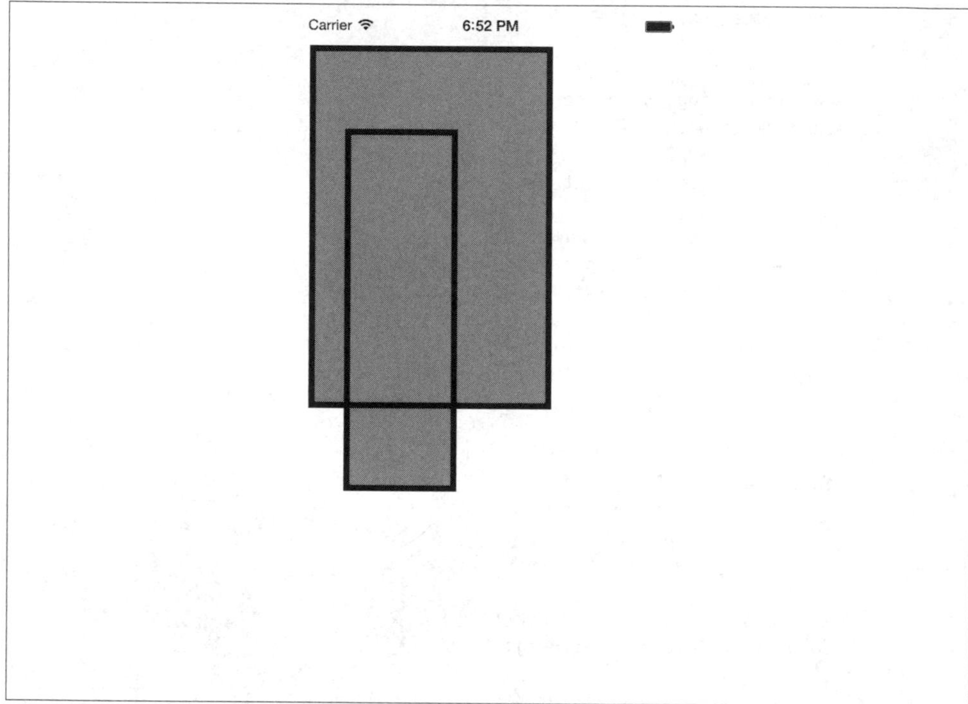


*Figure 20-23. Drawing multiple rectangles at once*

## See Also

Recipe 20.7; Recipe 20.11; Recipe 20.12; Recipe 20.13

# 20.9. Adding Shadows to Shapes

## Problem

You want to be able to apply shadows to shapes that you draw on graphic contexts.

## Solution

Use the `CGContextSetShadow` procedure.

## Discussion

It is easy to draw shadows using Core Graphics. The graphics context is the element that bears the shadow. What that means is that you need to apply the shadow to the context, draw the shapes that need the shadow, and then remove the shadow from the context (or set a new context). We will see an example of this soon.

In Core Graphics, we can use two procedures to apply a shadow to a graphics context:

`CGContextSetShadow` *procedure*
: This procedure, which creates black or gray shadows, accepts three parameters:

    - The graphics context on which the shadow has to be applied.
    - The offset, specified by a value of type `CGSize`, from the right and the bottom part of each shape where the shadow has to be applied. The greater the *x* value of this offset is, the farther to the right of each shape the shadow will extend. The greater the *y* value of this offset is, the lower the shadow will extend.
    - The blur value that has to be applied to the shadow, specified as a floating-point value (`CGFloat`). Specifying `0.0f` will cause the shadow to be a solid shape. The higher this value goes, the more blurred the shadow will get. We will see an example of this soon.

`CGContextSetShadowWithColor` *procedure*
: This procedure accepts the exact same parameters as `CGContextSetShadow`, with one addition. This fourth parameter, of type `CGColorRef`, sets the color of the shadow.

At the beginning of this section, I mentioned that the graphics context retains its shadow properties until we explicitly remove the shadow. Let me make that point clearer by showing you an example. Let us go ahead and write code that allows us to draw two rectangles, the first one with a shadow and the second one without a shadow. We will draw the first one in this way:

```
- (void) drawRectAtTopOfScreen{

    /* Get the handle to the current context */
    CGContextRef currentContext = UIGraphicsGetCurrentContext();

    CGContextSetShadowWithColor(currentContext,
                                CGSizeMake(10.0f, 10.0f),
                                20.0f,
                                [[UIColor grayColor] CGColor]);
```

```
    /* Create the path first. Just the path handle. */
    CGMutablePathRef path = CGPathCreateMutable();

    /* Here are our rectangle boundaries */
    CGRect firstRect = CGRectMake(55.0f,
                                  60.0f,
                                  150.0f,
                                  150.0f);

    /* Add the rectangle to the path */
    CGPathAddRect(path,
                  NULL,
                  firstRect);

    /* Add the path to the context */
    CGContextAddPath(currentContext,
                     path);

    /* Set the fill color to cornflower blue */
    [[UIColor colorWithRed:0.20f
                     green:0.60f
                      blue:0.80f
                     alpha:1.0f] setFill];

    /* Fill the path on the context */
    CGContextDrawPath(currentContext,
                      kCGPathFill);

    /* Dispose of the path */
    CGPathRelease(path);

}

- (void) drawRect:(CGRect)rect{
    [self drawRectAtTopOfScreen];
}
```

If we call this method in the `drawRect:` instance method of the view object, we will see the rectangle drawn on the screen with a nice shadow just like we wanted it, as shown in Figure 20-24.

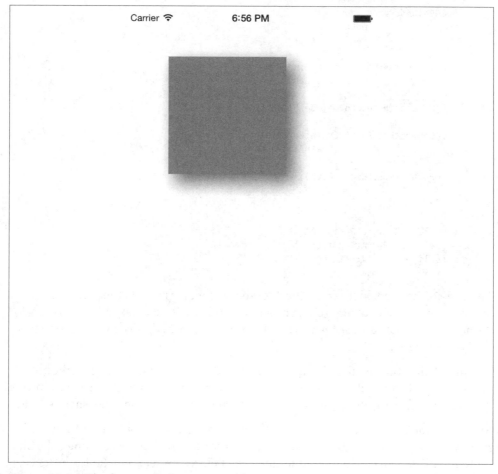


*Figure 20-24. Shadow applied to a rectangle*

Now let's go ahead and draw a second rectangle after the first one. We won't ask for a shadow, but we'll leave the shadow property of the graphics context as it was for the first rectangle:

```
- (void) drawRectAtBottomOfScreen{

    /* Get the handle to the current context */
    CGContextRef currentContext = UIGraphicsGetCurrentContext();

    CGMutablePathRef secondPath = CGPathCreateMutable();

    CGRect secondRect = CGRectMake(150.0f,
                                   250.0f,
                                   100.0f,
                                   100.0f);
```

```
    CGPathAddRect(secondPath,
                  NULL,
                  secondRect);

    CGContextAddPath(currentContext,
                     secondPath);

    [[UIColor purpleColor] setFill];

    CGContextDrawPath(currentContext,
                      kCGPathFill);

    CGPathRelease(secondPath);

}

- (void)drawRect:(CGRect)rect{
    [self drawRectAtTopOfScreen];
    [self drawRectAtBottomOfScreen];
}
```

The `drawRect:` method first calls the `drawRectAtTopOfScreen` method, and right after that calls the `drawRectAtBottomOfScreen` method. We haven't asked for a shadow for the `drawRectAtBottomOfScreen` rectangle, yet if you run the app, you will see something similar to Figure 20-25.

It's immediately obvious that the shadow is applied to the second rectangle at the bottom of the screen. To avoid this, we will save the state of the graphics context *before* applying the shadow effect and then restore the state when we want to remove the shadow effect.

Broadly speaking, saving and restoring the state of a graphics context is not limited to shadows only. Restoring the state of a graphics context restores everything (fill color, font, line thickness, etc.) to the values they had before you set them. So for instance, if you applied fill and stroke colors in the meantime, those colors will be reset.

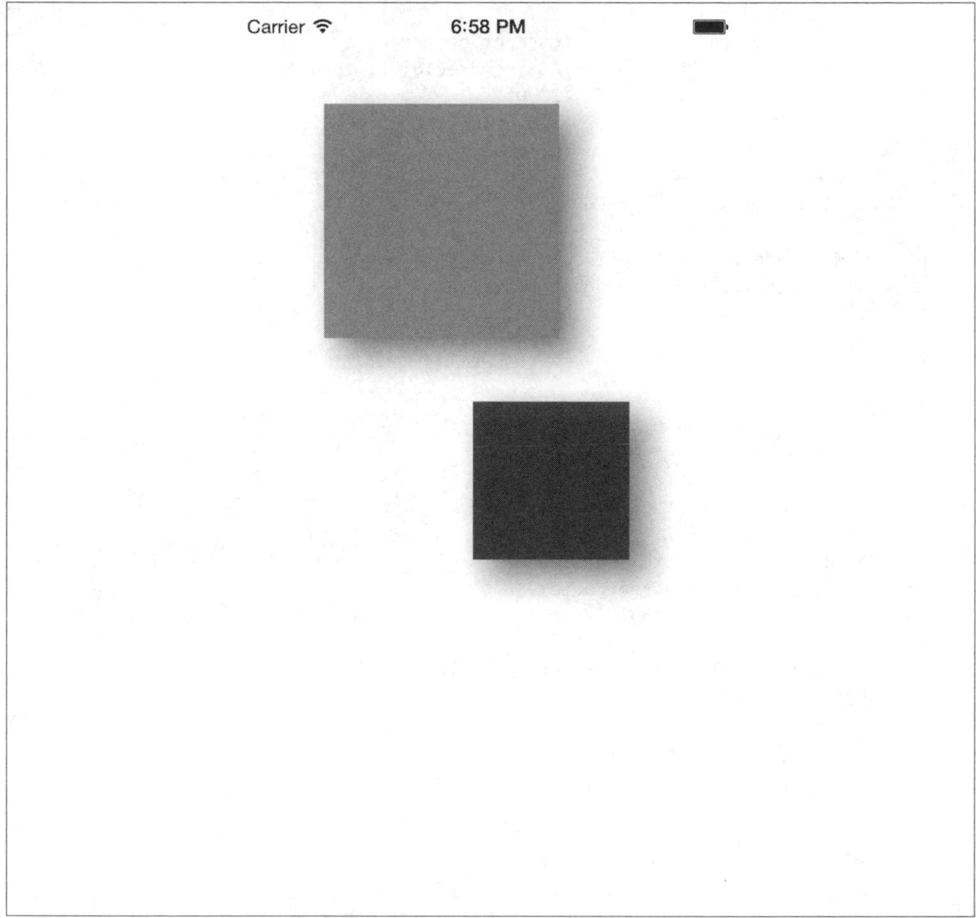


*Figure 20-25. A shadow is unintentionally applied to the second rectangle*

You can save the state of a graphics context through the `CGContextSaveGState` procedure and restore the previous state through the `CGContextRestoreGState` procedure. So if we modify the `drawRectAtTopOfScreen` procedure by saving the state of the graphics context before applying the shadow, and restore that state after drawing the path, we will have different results, shown in Figure 20-26:

```
- (void) drawRectAtTopOfScreen{

    /* Get the handle to the current context */
    CGContextRef currentContext = UIGraphicsGetCurrentContext();

    CGContextSaveGState(currentContext);
```

```
    CGContextSetShadowWithColor(currentContext,
                                CGSizeMake(10.0f, 10.0f),
                                20.0f,
                                [[UIColor grayColor] CGColor]);

    /* Create the path first. Just the path handle. */
    CGMutablePathRef path = CGPathCreateMutable();

    /* Here are our rectangle boundaries */
    CGRect firstRect = CGRectMake(55.0f,
                                  60.0f,
                                  150.0f,
                                  150.0f);

    /* Add the rectangle to the path */
    CGPathAddRect(path,
                  NULL,
                  firstRect);

    /* Add the path to the context */
    CGContextAddPath(currentContext,
                     path);

    /* Set the fill color to cornflower blue */
    [[UIColor colorWithRed:0.20f
                     green:0.60f
                      blue:0.80f
                     alpha:1.0f] setFill];

    /* Fill the path on the context */
    CGContextDrawPath(currentContext,
                      kCGPathFill);

    /* Dispose of the path */
    CGPathRelease(path);

    /* Restore the context to how it was
     when we started */
    CGContextRestoreGState(currentContext);

}
```

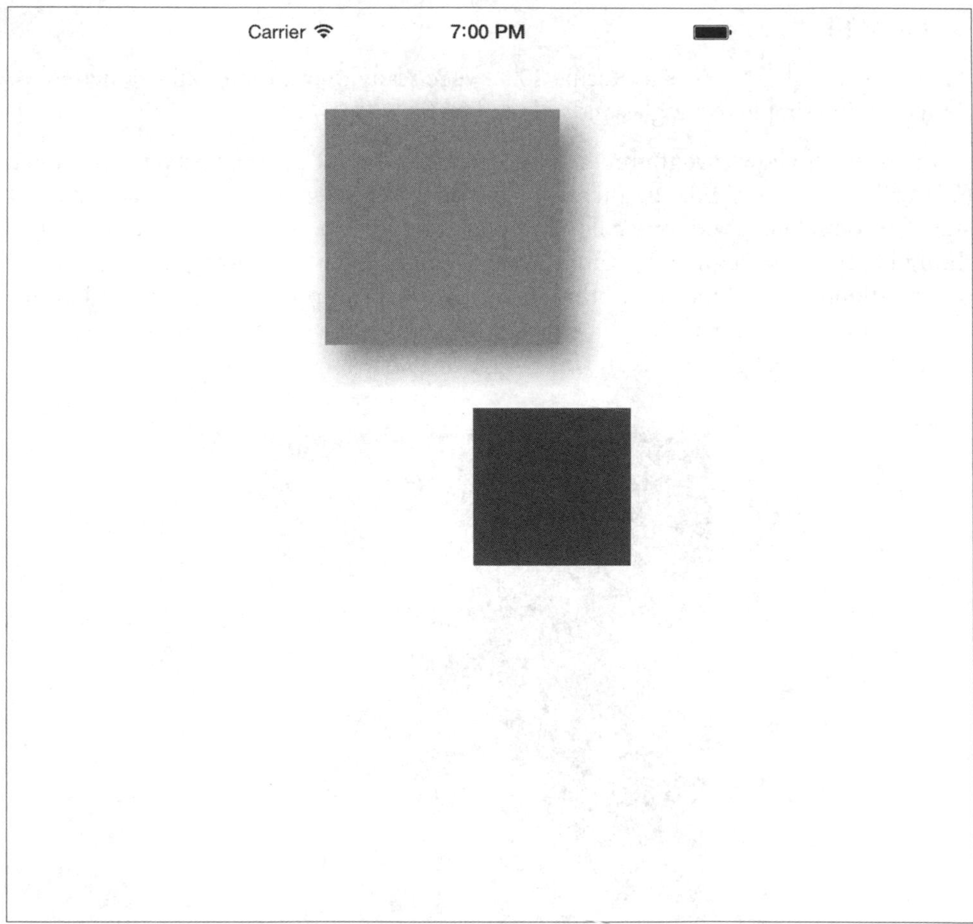


*Figure 20-26. Saving the state of the graphics context for accurate shadows*

## 20.10. Drawing Gradients

### Problem

You want to draw gradients on graphics contexts, using different colors.

### Solution

Use the `CGGradientCreateWithColor` function.

## Discussion

After learning about colors in Recipe 20.3, we're ready to put these skills to better use than drawing simple rectangles and colorful text!

Core Graphics allows programmers to create two types of gradients: axial and radial. (We will discuss only axial gradients in this book.) Axial gradients are gradients that start from one point with one color and end at another point with another color (although they can start and stop with the same color, which does not make them much of a gradient). "Axial" means relating to an axis. The two points (start and end point) create a line segment, which will be the axis on which the gradient will be drawn. An example of an axial gradient is shown in Figure 20-27.

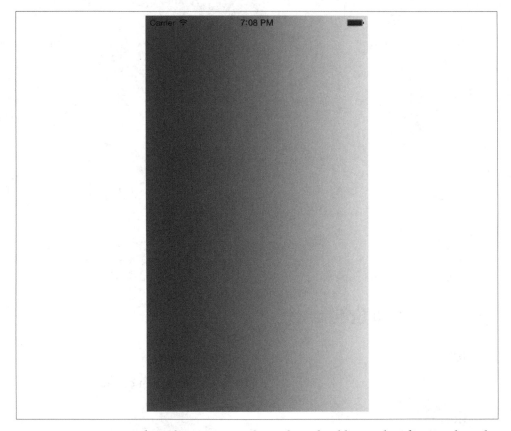


*Figure 20-27. An axial gradient starting from the color blue and ending in the color green*

In order to create an axial gradient, you must call the `CGGradientCreateWithColorComponents` function. The return value of this function will be the new gradient of type `CGGradientRef`. This is the handle to the gradient. Once you are done with the gradient, you *must* call the `CGGradientRelease` procedure, passing the handle to the gradient that you had previously retrieved from `CGGradientCreateWithColorComponents`.

The `CGGradientCreateWithColorComponents` function takes four parameters:

*A color space*
: This is a container for a range of colors and must be of type `CGColorSpaceRef`. For this parameter, we can just pass the return value of the `CGColorSpaceCreateDeviceRGB` function, which will give us an RGB color space.

*An array of color components (for details, see Recipe 20.3)*
: This array has to contain red, green, blue, and alpha values, all represented as `CGFloat` values. The number of elements in the array is tightly linked to the next two parameters. Essentially, you have to include enough values in this array to specify the number of locations in the fourth parameter. So if you ask for two locations (the start and end point), you have to provide two colors in the array here. And since each color is made out of red, green, blue, and alpha, this array has to have 2×4 items: four for the first color and four for the second. Don't worry if you didn't get all this; you will eventually understand it through the examples that follow in this section.

*Locations of colors in the array of colors*
: This parameter controls how quickly the gradient shifts from one color to another. The number of elements must be the same as the value of the fourth parameter. If we ask for four colors, for example, and we want the first color to be the starting color and the last color to be the ending color in the gradient, we have to provide an array of two items of type `CGFloats`, with the first item set to `0.0f` (as in the *first* item in the array of colors) and the second item set to `3.0f` (as in the *fourth* item in the array of colors). The values of the two intermediate colors determine how the gradient actually inserts colors to get from the start to the end. Again, don't worry if this is too difficult to grasp. I will give you many examples to help you fully understand the concept.

*Number of locations*
: This specifies how many colors and locations we want.

Let's have a look at an example. Suppose we want to draw the same gradient we saw in Figure 20-27. Here's how:

1. Pick the start and end points of the gradient—the axis along which it will shift. In this case, I've chosen to move from left to right. Think of this as changing color as you move along a hypothetical horizontal line. Along that line, we will spread the colors so that every perpendicular line to this horizontal line contains only one color. In this case, the perpendicular lines would be every vertical line in

Figure 20-27. Look at those vertical lines closely. Every single one contains only one color, which runs all the way from the top to the bottom. That's how axial gradients work. OK, that's enough theory—let's go to the second step.

2. Now we have to create a color space to pass to the first parameter of the `CGGradientCreateWithColorComponents` function, as mentioned before:

```
CGColorSpaceRef colorSpace =
CGColorSpaceCreateDeviceRGB();
```

We will release this color space once we are done with it.

3. Select blue as the starting point (left) and green as the ending point (right), according to the colors chosen in Figure 20-27. The names I've selected (`startColorComponents` and `endColorComponents`) are arbitrarily chosen to help us remember what we're doing with each color. We'll actually use array positions to specify which one is the start and which one is the end:

```
UIColor *startColor = [UIColor blueColor];
CGFloat *startColorComponents =
    (CGFloat *)CGColorGetComponents([startColor CGColor]);

UIColor *endColor = [UIColor greenColor];

CGFloat *endColorComponents =
    (CGFloat *)CGColorGetComponents([endColor CGColor]);
```

If you don't remember the concept behind color components, I suggest that you look at Recipe 20.3 before you continue reading these instructions.

4. After retrieving the components of each color, we place them all in one flat array to pass to the `CGGradientCreateWithColorComponents` function:

```
CGFloat colorComponents[8] = {

    /* Four components of the orange color (RGBA) */
    startColorComponents[0],
    startColorComponents[1],
    startColorComponents[2],
    startColorComponents[3], /* First color = orange */
```

```
        /* Four components of the blue color (RGBA) */
        endColorComponents[0],
        endColorComponents[1],
        endColorComponents[2],
        endColorComponents[3], /* Second color = blue */

    };
```

5. Because we have only two colors in this array, we need to specify that the first is positioned at the very beginning of the gradient (position 0.0) and the second at the very end (position 1.0). So let's place these indices in an array to pass to the `CGGradientCreateWithColorComponents` function:

```
    CGFloat colorIndices[2] = {
        0.0f, /* Color 0 in the colorComponents array */
        1.0f, /* Color 1 in the colorComponents array */
    };
```

6. Now all we have to do is actually call the `CGGradientCreateWithColorComponents` function with all these values that we generated:

```
    CGGradientRef gradient = CGGradientCreateWithColorComponents
    (colorSpace,
     (const CGFloat *)&colorComponents,
     (const CGFloat *)&colorIndices,
     2);
```

7. Fantastic! Now we have the gradient object in the `gradient` variable. Before we forget, we have to release the color space that we created using the `CGColorSpaceCreateDeviceRGB` function:

```
    CGColorSpaceRelease(colorSpace);
```

Now we'll use the `CGContextDrawLinearGradient` procedure to draw the axial gradient on a graphics context. This procedure takes five parameters:

*Graphics context*
: Specifies the graphics context on which the axial gradient will be drawn.

*Axial gradient*
: The handle to the axial gradient object. We created this gradient object using the `CGGradientCreateWithColorComponents` function.

*Start point*
: A point on the graphics context, specified by a `CGPoint`, that indicates the start point of the gradient.

*End point*
: A point on the graphics context, specified by a `CGPoint`, that indicates the end point of the gradient.

*Gradient drawing options*
: Specifies what happens if your start or end point isn't at the edge of the graphical context. You can use your start or end color to fill the space that lies outside the gradient. Specify one of the following values for this parameter:

  `kCGGradientDrawsAfterEndLocation`
  : Extends the gradient to all points after the ending point of the gradient

  `kCGGradientDrawsBeforeStartLocation`
  : Extends the gradient to all points before the starting point of the gradient

  `0`
  : Does not extend the gradient in any way

To extend colors on both sides, specify both the "after" and "before" parameters as a logical OR (using the | operator). We'll see an example later:

```
CGPoint startPoint, endPoint;

CGRect screenBounds = [[UIScreen mainScreen] bounds];

startPoint = CGPointMake(0.0f,
                         screenBounds.size.height / 2.0f);

endPoint = CGPointMake(screenBounds.size.width,
                       startPoint.y);

CGContextDrawLinearGradient (currentContext,
                             gradient,
                             startPoint,
                             endPoint,
                             0);

CGGradientRelease(gradient);
```

The gradient handle we are releasing at the end of this code was created in another code block in an earlier example.

The output of this code will obviously look similar to Figure 20-27. Because we started the gradient from the leftmost point of the view and stretched it all the way to the rightmost point, we couldn't take advantage of all the values that could be passed to the final *gradient drawing options* parameter of the `CGContextDrawLinearGradient` procedure. Let's remedy that, shall we? How about we draw a gradient that looks similar to that shown in Figure 20-28?

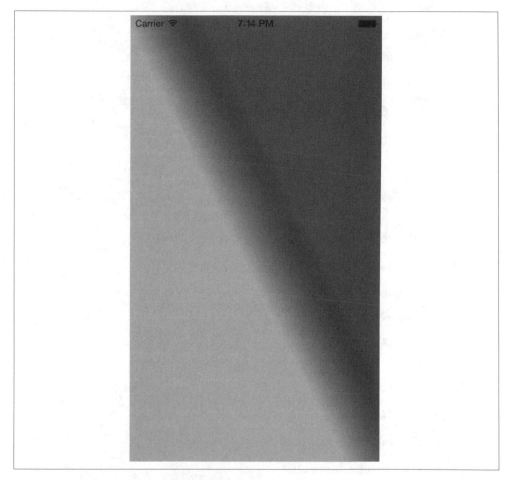


*Figure 20-28. An axial gradient with start and end point color extensions*

We will use the same procedure explained earlier in this section to code the result:

```
- (void)drawRect:(CGRect)rect{

    CGContextRef currentContext = UIGraphicsGetCurrentContext();

    CGContextSaveGState(currentContext);

    CGColorSpaceRef colorSpace =
    CGColorSpaceCreateDeviceRGB();

    UIColor *startColor = [UIColor orangeColor];
```

```
CGFloat *startColorComponents =
(CGFloat *)CGColorGetComponents([startColor CGColor]);

UIColor *endColor = [UIColor blueColor];
CGFloat *endColorComponents =
(CGFloat *)CGColorGetComponents([endColor CGColor]);

CGFloat colorComponents[8] = {

    /* Four components of the orange color (RGBA) */
    startColorComponents[0],
    startColorComponents[1],
    startColorComponents[2],
    startColorComponents[3], /* First color = orange */


    /* Four components of the blue color (RGBA) */
    endColorComponents[0],
    endColorComponents[1],
    endColorComponents[2],
    endColorComponents[3], /* Second color = blue */

};

CGFloat colorIndices[2] = {
    0.0f, /* Color 0 in the colorComponents array */
    1.0f, /* Color 1 in the colorComponents array */
};

CGGradientRef gradient = CGGradientCreateWithColorComponents
(colorSpace,
 (const CGFloat *)&colorComponents,
 (const CGFloat *)&colorIndices,
 2);

CGColorSpaceRelease(colorSpace);

CGPoint startPoint, endPoint;

startPoint = CGPointMake(120,
                         260);

endPoint = CGPointMake(200.0f,
                       220);

CGContextDrawLinearGradient (currentContext,
                             gradient,
                             startPoint,
                             endPoint,
                             kCGGradientDrawsBeforeStartLocation |
                             kCGGradientDrawsAfterEndLocation);
```

```
    CGGradientRelease(gradient);

    CGContextRestoreGState(currentContext);

}
```

It might be difficult to understand how mixing `kCGGradientDrawsBeforeStartLocation` and `kCGGradientDrawsAfterEndLocation` values passed to the `CGContextDrawLinearGradient` procedure is creating a diagonal effect like that shown in Figure 20-28. So let's remove those values and set the parameter of the `CGContextDrawLinearGradient` procedure to `0`, as we had it before. Figure 20-29 shows what the results will be.

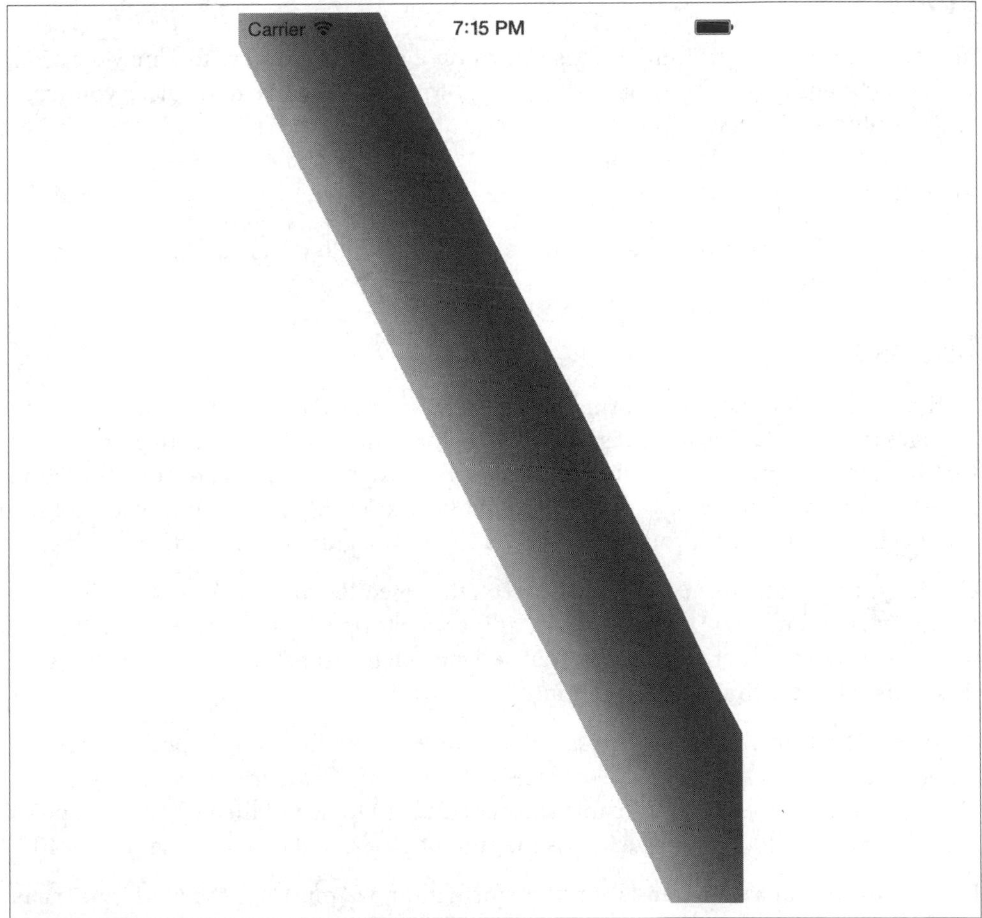


*Figure 20-29. Axial gradient without stretched colors*

It's easy to conclude that the gradient in Figure 20-29 is the same gradient shown in Figure 20-28. However, the gradient in Figure 20-28 extends the start and end points' colors all the way across the graphics context, which is why you can see the whole screen covered with color.

## See Also

Recipe 20.3

# 20.11. Moving Shapes Drawn on Graphic Contexts

## Problem

You want to move everything that is drawn on a graphics context to a new location, without changing your drawing code—or you would simply like to displace your context's contents with ease.

## Solution

Use the `CGAffineTransformMakeTranslation` function to create an affine translation transformation.

## Discussion

Recipe 20.8 mentioned transformations. These are exactly what the name suggests: changes to the way a graphic is displayed. Transformations in Core Graphics are objects that you apply to shapes before they get drawn. For instance, you can create a translation transformation. Translating what? you might be asking. A translation transformation is a mechanism by which you can *displace* a shape or a graphics context.

Other types of transformations include rotation (see Recipe 20.13) and scaling (see Recipe 20.12). These are all examples of *affine* transformations, which map each point in the origin to another point in the final version. All the transformations we discuss in this book will be affine transformations.

A translation transformation *translates* the current position of a shape on a path or graphics context to another relative place. For instance, if you draw a point at location (10, 20), apply a translation transformation of (30, 40) to it, and then draw it, the point will be drawn at (40, 60), because 40 is the sum of 10+30 and 60 is the sum of 20+40.

In order to create a new translation transformation, we must use the `CGAffineTransformMakeTranslation` function, which will return an affine transformation of type `CGAffineTransform`. The two parameters to this function specify the *x* and the *y* translation in points.

In Recipe 20.8, we saw that the `CGPathAddRect` procedure accepts, as its second parameter, a transformation object of type `CGAffineTransform`. To displace a rectangle from its original place to another, you can simply create an affine transformation specifying the changes you want to make in the *x* and *y* coordinates and pass the transformation to the second parameter of the `CGPathAddRect` procedure as shown here:

```
- (void)drawRect:(CGRect)rect{

    /* Create the path first. Just the path handle. */
    CGMutablePathRef path = CGPathCreateMutable();

    /* Here are our rectangle boundaries */
    CGRect rectangle = CGRectMake(10.0f,
                                  30.0f,
                                  200.0f,
                                  300.0f);

    /* We want to displace the rectangle to the right by
     100 points but want to keep the y position
     untouched */
    CGAffineTransform transform = CGAffineTransformMakeTranslation(100.0f,
                                                                   0.0f);

    /* Add the rectangle to the path */
    CGPathAddRect(path,
                  &transform,
                  rectangle);

    /* Get the handle to the current context */
    CGContextRef currentContext =
    UIGraphicsGetCurrentContext();

    /* Add the path to the context */
    CGContextAddPath(currentContext,
                     path);

    /* Set the fill color to cornflower blue */
    [[UIColor colorWithRed:0.20f
                     green:0.60f
                      blue:0.80f
                     alpha:1.0f] setFill];

    /* Set the stroke color to brown */
    [[UIColor brownColor] setStroke];

    /* Set the line width (for the stroke) to 5 */
    CGContextSetLineWidth(currentContext,
                          5.0f);

    /* Stroke and fill the path on the context */
    CGContextDrawPath(currentContext,
                      kCGPathFillStroke);
```

```
    /* Dispose of the path */
    CGPathRelease(path);

}
```

Figure 20-30 shows the output of this block of code when placed inside a view object.

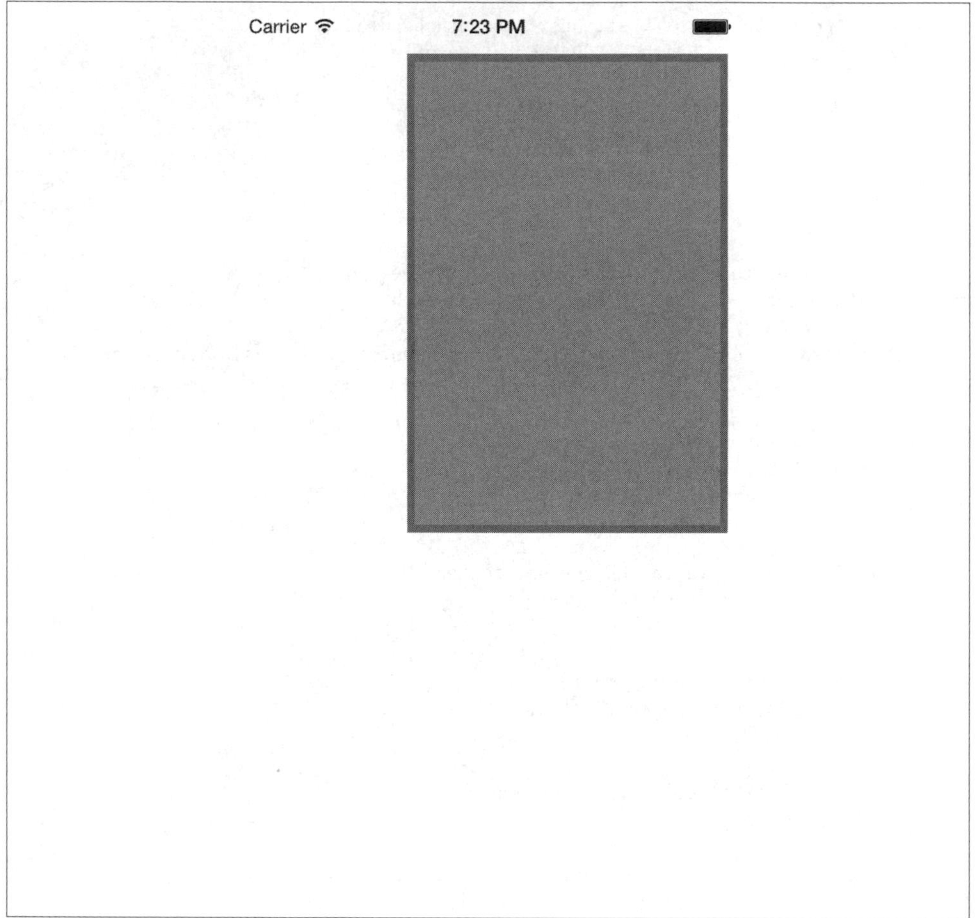


*Figure 20-30. A rectangle with an affine translation transformation*

Compare Figure 20-30 with Figure 20-22. Can you see the difference? Check the source code for both figures and you'll see that the *x* and *y* points specified for both rectangles in both code blocks are the same. It is just that in Figure 20-30, we have applied an affine translation transformation to the rectangle when we added it to the path.

In addition to applying transformations to shapes that get drawn to a path, we can apply transformations to graphics contexts using the `CGContextTranslateCTM` procedure. This applies a translation transformation on the current transformation matrix (CTM). The current transformation matrix, although its name might be complex, is quite simple to understand. Think of CTM as how your graphics context's center is set up and how each point that you draw gets projected onto the screen. For instance, when you ask Core Graphics to draw a point at (0, 0), Core Graphics finds the center of the screen by looking at the CTM. The CTM will then do some calculations and tell Core Graphics that point (0, 0) is indeed at the top-left corner of the screen. Using procedures such as `CGContextTranslateCTM`, you can change how CTM is configured and subsequently force every shape drawn on the graphics context to be shifted to another place on the canvas. Here is an example where we achieve the exact same effect we saw in Figure 20-30 by applying a translation transformation to the CTM instead of directly to the rectangle:

```
- (void)drawRect:(CGRect)rect{

    /* Create the path first. Just the path handle. */
    CGMutablePathRef path = CGPathCreateMutable();

    /* Here are our rectangle boundaries */
    CGRect rectangle = CGRectMake(10.0f,
                                  30.0f,
                                  200.0f,
                                  300.0f);

    /* Add the rectangle to the path */
    CGPathAddRect(path,
                  NULL,
                  rectangle);

    /* Get the handle to the current context */
    CGContextRef currentContext = UIGraphicsGetCurrentContext();

    /* Save the state of the context to revert
     back to how it was at this state, later */
    CGContextSaveGState(currentContext);

    /* Translate the current transformation matrix
     to the right by 100 points */
    CGContextTranslateCTM(currentContext,
                          100.0f,
                          0.0f);

    /* Add the path to the context */
    CGContextAddPath(currentContext,
                     path);

    /* Set the fill color to cornflower blue */
    [[UIColor colorWithRed:0.20f
                     green:0.60f
```

```
                        blue:0.80f
                       alpha:1.0f] setFill];

    /* Set the stroke color to brown */
    [[UIColor brownColor] setStroke];

    /* Set the line width (for the stroke) to 5 */
    CGContextSetLineWidth(currentContext,
                          5.0f);

    /* Stroke and fill the path on the context */
    CGContextDrawPath(currentContext,
                      kCGPathFillStroke);

    /* Dispose of the path */
    CGPathRelease(path);

    /* Restore the state of the context */
    CGContextRestoreGState(currentContext);

}
```

After running this program, you will notice that the results are exactly like those shown in Figure 20-30.

## See Also

Recipe 20.8; Recipe 20.12; Recipe 20.13

# 20.12. Scaling Shapes Drawn on Graphic Contexts

## Problem

You want to scale shapes on your graphics context up and down dynamically.

## Solution

Create an affine scale transformation using the `CGAffineTransformMakeScale` function.

## Discussion

Recipe 20.11 explained what a transformation is and how to apply it to shapes and graphics contexts. One of the transformations that you can apply is scaling. You can easily ask Core Graphics to scale a shape, such as a circle, to 100 times its original size.

To create an affine scale transformation, use the `CGAffineTransformMakeScale` function, which returns a transformation object of type `CGAffineTransform`. If you want to apply a scale transformation directly to a graphics context, use the `CGContextScaleCTM` procedure to scale the current transformation matrix (CTM). For more information about CTM, see Recipe 20.11.

Scale transformation functions take two parameters: one to scale the *x*-axis and the other to scale the *y*-axis. Take another look at the rectangle in Figure 20-22. If we want to scale this rectangle to half its normal length and width, shown in Figure 20-22, we can simply scale the *x*- and the *y*- axis by 0.5 (half their original value), as shown here:

```
/* Scale the rectangle to half its size */
CGAffineTransform transform =
CGAffineTransformMakeScale(0.5f, 0.5f);

/* Add the rectangle to the path */
CGPathAddRect(path,
              &transform,
              rectangle);
```

Figure 20-31 shows what we will see after applying the scale transformation to the code we wrote in Recipe 20.8.

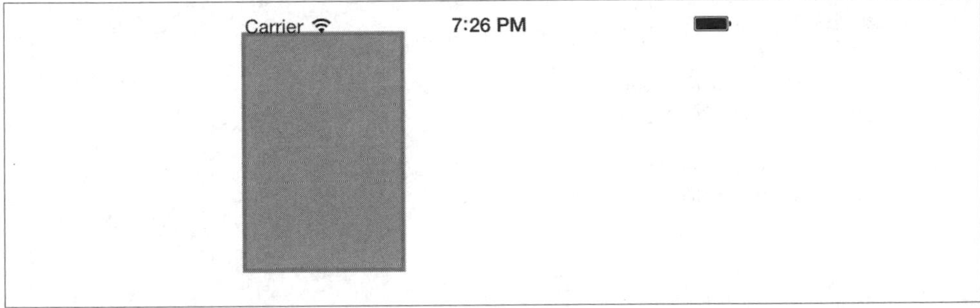


*Figure 20-31. Scaling a rectangle*

In addition to the `CGAffineTransformMakeScale` function, you can use the `CGContextScaleCTM` procedure to apply a scale transformation to a graphics context. The following code will achieve the exact same effect as the previous example, as you can see in Figure 20-31:

```
- (void)drawRect:(CGRect)rect{

    /* Create the path first. Just the path handle. */
    CGMutablePathRef path = CGPathCreateMutable();

    /* Here are our rectangle boundaries */
    CGRect rectangle = CGRectMake(10.0f,
                                  30.0f,
                                  200.0f,
                                  300.0f);
```

```
    /* Add the rectangle to the path */
    CGPathAddRect(path,
                  NULL,
                  rectangle);

    /* Get the handle to the current context */
    CGContextRef currentContext = UIGraphicsGetCurrentContext();

    /* Scale everything drawn on the current
     graphics context to half its size */
    CGContextScaleCTM(currentContext,
                      0.5f,
                      0.5f);

    /* Add the path to the context */
    CGContextAddPath(currentContext,
                     path);

    /* Set the fill color to cornflower blue */
    [[UIColor colorWithRed:0.20f
                     green:0.60f
                      blue:0.80f
                     alpha:1.0f] setFill];

    /* Set the stroke color to brown */
    [[UIColor brownColor] setStroke];

    /* Set the line width (for the stroke) to 5 */
    CGContextSetLineWidth(currentContext,
                          5.0f);

    /* Stroke and fill the path on the context */
    CGContextDrawPath(currentContext,
                      kCGPathFillStroke);

    /* Dispose of the path */
    CGPathRelease(path);

}
```

## See Also

Recipe 20.11

# 20.13. Rotating Shapes Drawn on Graphic Contexts

## Problem

You want to be able to rotate the contents that you have drawn on a graphics context without changing your drawing code.

## Solution

Use the `CGAffineTransformMakeRotation` function to create an affine rotation transformation.

## Discussion

I strongly suggest that you read the material in Recipes 20.11 and in 20.12 before proceeding with this section. To avoid redundancy, I have tried to keep material that has been taught in earlier sections out of later sections.

Just like scaling and translation, you can apply rotation translation to shapes drawn on paths and graphics contexts. You can use the `CGAffineTransformMakeRotation` function and pass the rotation value in radians to get back a rotation transformation of type `CGAffineTransform`. You can then apply this transformation to paths and shapes. If you want to rotate the whole context by a specific angle, you must use the `CGContextRotateCTM` procedure.

Let's rotate the same rectangle we had in Figure 20-22 45 degrees clockwise (see Figure 20-32). The values you supply for rotation must be in radians. Positive values cause clockwise rotation, while negative values cause counterclockwise rotation:

```
/* Rotate the rectangle 45 degrees clockwise */
CGAffineTransform transform =
CGAffineTransformMakeRotation((45.0f * M_PI) / 180.0f);

/* Add the rectangle to the path */
CGPathAddRect(path,
              &transform,
              rectangle);
```

As we saw in Recipe 20.12, we can also apply a transformation directly to a graphics context using the `CGContextRotateCTM` procedure.

## See Also

Recipe 20.11; Recipe 20.12

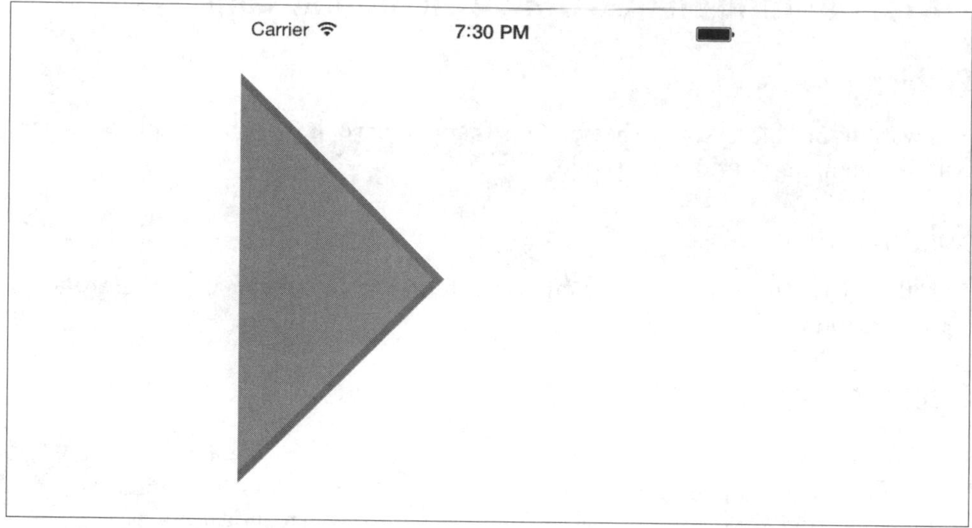

*Figure 20-32. Rotating a rectangle*

## 20.14. Animating and Moving Views

### Problem

You want to animate the displacement of views.

### Solution

Use the animation methods of `UIView` while displacing your views.

### Discussion

There are various ways of performing animations in iOS: capabilities are provided at a relatively low level, but also at a higher level. The highest level we can get is through UIKit, which is what we will be discussing in this section. UIKit includes some low-level Core Animation functionalities and presents us with a really clean API to work with.

The starting point for performing animations in UIKit is to call the `beginAnimations:context:` class method of the `UIView` class. Its first parameter is an optional name that you choose for your animation, and the second is an optional context that you can retrieve later to pass to delegate methods of the animations. We will talk about these shortly.

After you start an animation with the `beginAnimations:context:` method, it won't actually take place until you call the `commitAnimations` class method of `UIView` class.

The calculation you perform on a view object (such as moving it) between calling `beginAnimations:context:` and `commitAnimations` will be animated after the `commitAnimations` call. Let's have a look at an example.

As we saw in Recipe 20.4, I included in my assets category an image called *Xcode.png*. This is Xcode's icon, which I found by searching in Google Images (see Figure 20-9). Now, in my view controller (see this chapter's Introduction), I want to place this image in an image view of type `UIImageView` and then move that image view from the top-left corner of the screen to the bottom-right corner.

Here are the steps that complete this task:

1. Open the *.m* file of your view controller.
2. Define an instance of `UIImageView` as a property of the view controller, and call it `xcodeImageView`, like so:

```
#import "ViewController.h"

@interface ViewController ()
@property (nonatomic, strong) UIImageView *xcodeImageView;
@end
```

3. Load the *Xcode.png* image into an instance of `UIImage` when your view is loaded:

```
- (void) viewDidLoad{
    [super viewDidLoad];

    UIImage *xcodeImage = [UIImage imageNamed:@"Xcode"];

    self.xcodeImageView = [[UIImageView alloc]
                           initWithImage:xcodeImage];

    /* Just set the size to make the image smaller */
    [self.xcodeImageView setFrame:CGRectMake(0.0f,
                                             30.0f,
                                             100.0f,
                                             100.0f)];

    self.view.backgroundColor = [UIColor whiteColor];
    [self.view addSubview:self.xcodeImageView];

}
```

4. Figure 20-33 shows how the view will look when we run the program in iOS Simulator.

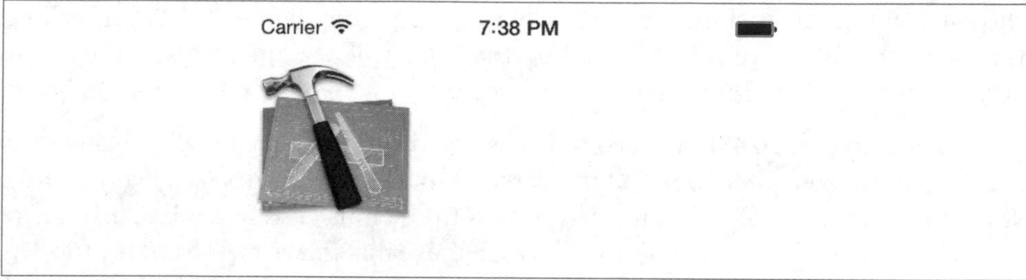


*Figure 20-33. Adding an image view to a view object*

5. Now when the view appears on the screen, in the `viewDidAppear:` instance method of the view controller, we will start the animation block for the image view and start an animation that moves the image from its initial location at the top-left corner of the screen to the bottom-right corner. We will make sure this animation happens over a five-second time period:

```
- (void) viewDidAppear:(BOOL)paramAnimated{

    [super viewDidAppear:paramAnimated];

    /* Start from top left corner */
    [self.xcodeImageView setFrame:CGRectMake(0.0f,
                                             30.0f,
                                             100.0f,
                                             100.0f)];

    [UIView beginAnimations:@"xcodeImageViewAnimation"
                    context:(__bridge void *)self.xcodeImageView];

    /* 5 seconds animation */
    [UIView setAnimationDuration:5.0f];

    /* Receive animation delegates */
    [UIView setAnimationDelegate:self];

    [UIView setAnimationDidStopSelector:
     @selector(imageViewDidStop:finished:context:)];

    CGRect endRect;
    endRect.origin.x = self.view.bounds.size.width - 100;
    endRect.origin.y = self.view.bounds.size.height - 100;
    endRect.size = CGSizeMake(100.0f, 100.0f);

    /* End at the bottom right corner */
    [self.xcodeImageView setFrame:endRect];
```

```
    [UIView commitAnimations];

}
```

6. Provide the implementation for a `imageViewDidStop:finished:context:` delegate method for your view controller so that it gets called by UIKit when the animation finishes. This is optional, and for this example I will just log some messages to prove that the method was called. Later examples will show how you can use the method to kick off other activity the moment the animation is finished:

```
- (void)imageViewDidStop:(NSString *)paramAnimationID
               finished:(NSNumber *)paramFinished
                context:(void *)paramContext{

    NSLog(@"Animation finished.");

    NSLog(@"Animation ID = %@", paramAnimationID);

    UIImageView *contextImageView = (__bridge UIImageView *)paramContext;
    NSLog(@"Image View = %@", contextImageView);

}
```

Now if you run the app, you will notice that as soon as your view gets displayed, the image shown in Figure 20-33 will start moving toward the bottom-right corner, as shown in Figure 20-34, over a period of five seconds.

Also, if you look at the output printed to the console, you will see something similar to this if you wait for the animation to finish:

```
Animation finished.
Animation ID = xcodeImageViewAnimation
Image View = <UIImageView: 0x8eaee20;
    frame = (220 468; 100 100); opaque = NO;
    userInteractionEnabled = NO;
    layer = <CALayer: 0x8eaef10>>
```

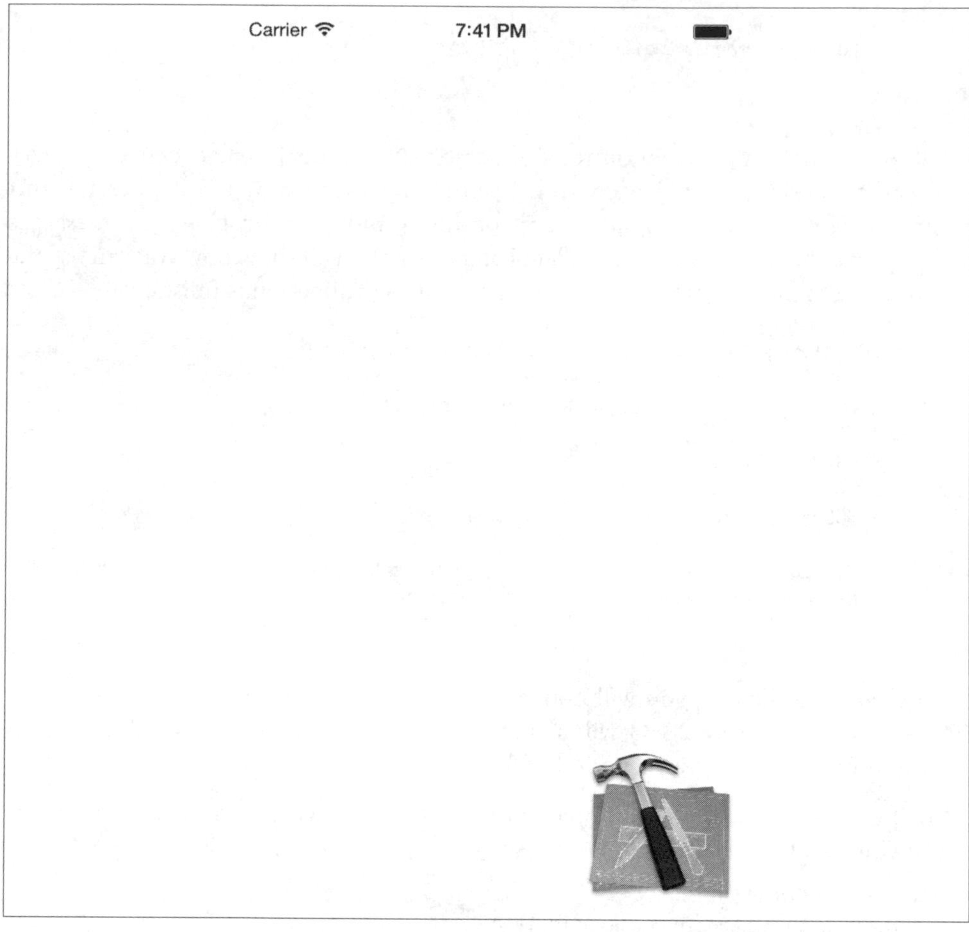


*Figure 20-34. The image is animated to the bottom-right corner of the screen*

Now let's go through some of the concepts and how we actually animated this image view. Here are the important class methods of `UIView` that you should know about when performing animations using UIKit:

`beginAnimations:context:`
: Starts an animation block. Any animatable property change that you apply to views after calling this class method will be animated after the animation is committed.

`setAnimationDuration:`
: Sets the duration of the animation in seconds.

`setAnimationDelegate:`
: Sets the object that will receive delegate objects for various events that could happen before, during, or after the animation. Setting a delegate object will *not* immediately

start firing animation delegates. You must also use different setter class methods on the view object to tell UIKit which selectors in your delegate object have to receive which delegate messages.

`setAnimationDidStopSelector:`
: Sets the method in the delegate object that has to be called when the animation finishes. This method has to accept three parameters in this order:

    1. An animation identifier of type `NSString`: this will contain the animation identifier passed to the `beginAnimations:context:` class method of `UIView` when the animation was started.
    2. A "finished" indicator, of type `NSNumber`: this parameter contains a Boolean value inside the `NSNumber`, which the runtime sets to `YES` if it could fully finish the animation before it was stopped by the code. If this value is set to `NO`, it means the animation was interrupted before it was completed.
    3. A context of type `void *`: this is the context that was passed to the `beginAnimations:context:` class method of `UIView` when the animation was started.

`setAnimationWillStartSelector:`
: Sets the selector that has to be called in the delegate object when the animation is about to start. The selector passed to this class method has to have two parameters, in this order:

    1. An animation identifier of type `NSString`: the runtime sets this to the animation identifier passed to the `beginAnimations:context:` class method of `UIView` when the animation was started.
    2. A context of type `void *`: this is the context that was passed to the `beginAnimations:context:` class method of `UIView` when the animation was started.

`setAnimationDelay:`
: Sets a delay (in seconds) for the animation before it starts. If this value is set to `3.0f`, for instance, the animation will start three seconds after it has been committed.

`setAnimationRepeatCount:`
: Sets the number of times an animation block has to repeat its animation.

Now that we know some of the most useful `UIView` class methods that help us animate views, let's look at another animation. In this example code, I want to have two image views (both displaying the same image) appear on the screen at the same time: one at the top-left corner and the other at the bottom-right corner, as shown in Figure 20-35.

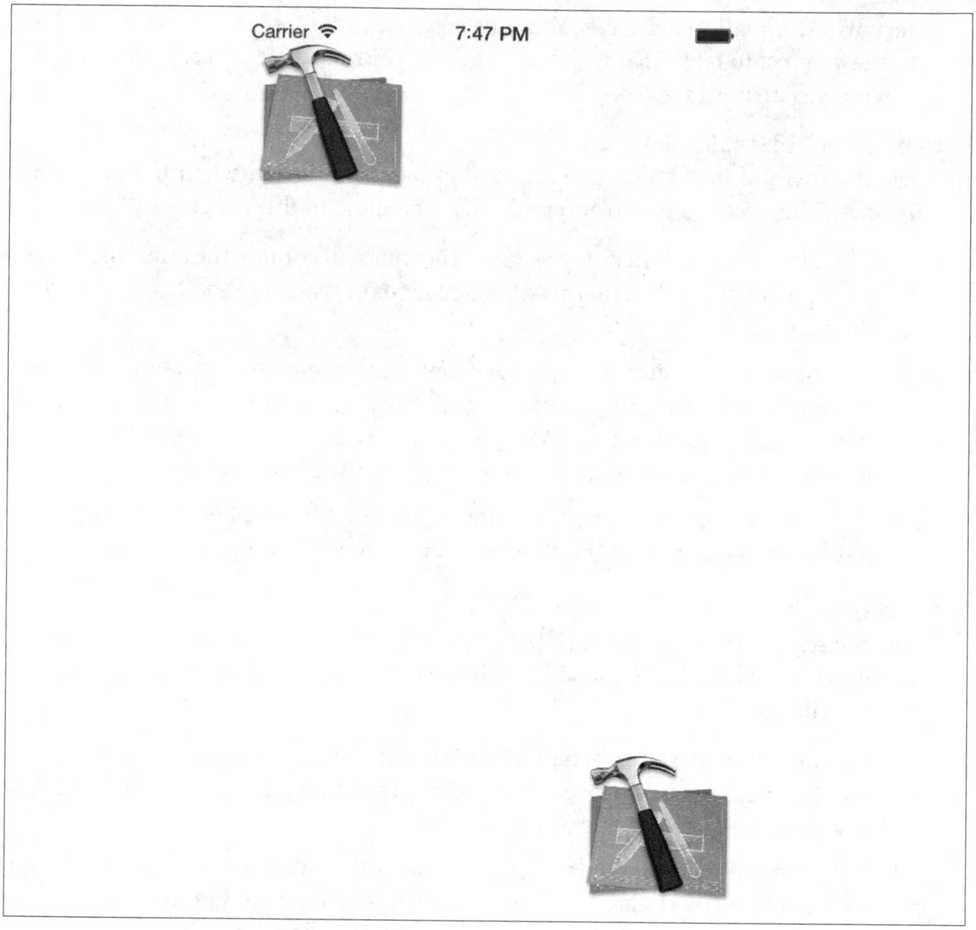

*Figure 20-35. The starting position of the animation*

In this section, I will call the top-left image *image 1* and the bottom-right image *image 2*.

In this code, we are going to create two images, as mentioned, in the top-left and bottom-right corners. Next, we want image 1 to start moving toward image 2 over a three-second period, and then fade away. While image 1 is approaching image 2, we want image 2 to start its animation and move toward the top-left corner of the screen, where image 1 used to be. We also want image 2 to complete its animation over a three-second time period and fade away at the end. This will look *really* cool when you run it on a device or on iOS Simulator. Let me show you how to code it:

1. On the top of the *.m* file of your view controller, define two image views:

```
@interface ViewController ()
@property (nonatomic, strong) UIImageView *xcodeImageView1;
@property (nonatomic, strong) UIImageView *xcodeImageView2;
@end

@implementation ViewController
```

2. In the `viewDidLoad` instance method of your view controller, initialize both of the image views and place them on your view:

```
- (CGRect) bottomRightRect{
    CGRect endRect;
    endRect.origin.x = self.view.bounds.size.width - 100;
    endRect.origin.y = self.view.bounds.size.height - 100;
    endRect.size = CGSizeMake(100.0f, 100.0f);
    return endRect;
}

- (void) viewDidLoad{
    [super viewDidLoad];

    UIImage *xcodeImage = [UIImage imageNamed:@"Xcode"];

    self.xcodeImageView1 = [[UIImageView alloc]
                            initWithImage:xcodeImage];

    self.xcodeImageView2 = [[UIImageView alloc]
                            initWithImage:xcodeImage];

    /* Just set the size to make the images smaller */
    [self.xcodeImageView1 setFrame:CGRectMake(0.0f,
                                              0.0f,
                                              100.0f,
                                              100.0f)];

    [self.xcodeImageView2 setFrame:[self bottomRightRect]];


    self.view.backgroundColor = [UIColor whiteColor];
    [self.view addSubview:self.xcodeImageView1];
    [self.view addSubview:self.xcodeImageView2];

}
```

3. Implement an instance method called `startTopLeftImageViewAnimation` for your view controller. This method, as its name suggests, will carry out the animation for

image 1, moving it from the top-left corner of the screen to the bottom-right corner while fading it out. Fading is accomplished simply by setting the alpha value to 0:

```
- (void) startTopLeftImageViewAnimation{

    /* Start from top left corner */
    [self.xcodeImageView1 setFrame:CGRectMake(0.0f,
                                              0.0f,
                                              100.0f,
                                              100.0f)];

    [self.xcodeImageView1 setAlpha:1.0f];

    [UIView beginAnimations:@"xcodeImageView1Animation"
                    context:(__bridge void *)self.xcodeImageView1];

    /* 3 seconds animation */
    [UIView setAnimationDuration:3.0f];

    /* Receive animation delegates */
    [UIView setAnimationDelegate:self];

    [UIView setAnimationDidStopSelector:
     @selector(imageViewDidStop:finished:context:)];

    /* End at the bottom right corner */
    [self.xcodeImageView1 setFrame:[self bottomRightRect]];

    [self.xcodeImageView1 setAlpha:0.0f];

    [UIView commitAnimations];

}
```

4. When the animation for any of these image views stops, we intend to remove those image views from their parent views, as they are not useful anymore. As we saw in the `startTopLeftImageViewAnimation` method, we passed a delegate selector to the `setAnimationDidStopSelector:` class method of `UIView`, and this selector will get called when the animations for image 1 (as we saw before) and for image 2 (as we will soon see) stop. Here is the implementation for this delegate selector:

```
- (void)imageViewDidStop:(NSString *)paramAnimationID
                finished:(NSNumber *)paramFinished
                 context:(void *)paramContext{

    UIImageView *contextImageView = (__bridge UIImageView *)paramContext;
    [contextImageView removeFromSuperview];

}
```

5. We also need a method that will animate image 2. There is a little difference between how I've written the animation method for image 2 as compared to that for image 1. I want to be able to start image 2's animation *almost* as image 1 is finishing its animation. So if image 1 performs its animation in three seconds, I want image 2 to start its animation at second 2.0 in image 1's animation, so that I can see image 2 starting to animate before image 1 gets to the bottom-right corner of the screen and fades away. To accomplish this, I am starting both animations at the same time, but the animation for image 2 will include a two-second delay at the beginning. So if I start both animations at 1 p.m., image 1 will start its animation at 13:00:00 and finish it at 13:00:03, while image 2 starts at 13:00:02 and finishes at 13:00:05. Here is how we will animate image 2:

```
- (void) startBottomRightViewAnimationAfterDelay:(CGFloat)paramDelay{

    /* Start from bottom right corner */
    [self.xcodeImageView2 setFrame:[self bottomRightRect]];

    [self.xcodeImageView2 setAlpha:1.0f];

    [UIView beginAnimations:@"xcodeImageView2Animation"
                    context:(__bridge void *)self.xcodeImageView2];

    /* 3 seconds animation */
    [UIView setAnimationDuration:3.0f];

    [UIView setAnimationDelay:paramDelay];

    /* Receive animation delegates */
    [UIView setAnimationDelegate:self];

    [UIView setAnimationDidStopSelector:
     @selector(imageViewDidStop:finished:context:)];

    /* End at the top left corner */
    [self.xcodeImageView2 setFrame:CGRectMake(0.0f,
                                              0.0f,
                                              100.0f,
                                              100.0f)];

    [self.xcodeImageView2 setAlpha:0.0f];

    [UIView commitAnimations];

}
```

6. Last but not least, we have to fire both the `startTopLeftImageViewAnimation` and the `startBottomRightViewAnimationAfterDelay:` methods at the same time when the view becomes visible:

```
- (void) viewDidAppear:(BOOL)paramAnimated{

    [super viewDidAppear:paramAnimated];
    [self startTopLeftImageViewAnimation];
    [self startBottomRightViewAnimationAfterDelay:2.0f];

}
```

# 20.15. Animating and Scaling Views

## Problem

You want to be able to animate the scaling up or down of your views.

## Solution

Create a scale affine transformation for your view and use the `UIView` animation methods to animate the scale transformation.

## Discussion

I highly recommend that you read Recipe 20.14 before proceeding with this section of the book.

In order to scale a view while animating it, you can either apply a scale transformation to it within an animation block (see Recipe 20.12), or just increase the view's width and/or height.

Let's have a look at scaling an image view by applying a scale transformation to it:

```
- (void) viewDidAppear:(BOOL)paramAnimated{
    [super viewDidAppear:paramAnimated];

    /* Place the image view at the center of the view of this view controller */
    self.xcodeImageView.center = self.view.center;

    /* Make sure no translation is applied to this image view */
    self.xcodeImageView.transform = CGAffineTransformIdentity;

    /* Begin the animation */
    [UIView beginAnimations:nil
                    context:NULL];

    /* Make the animation 5 seconds long */
    [UIView setAnimationDuration:5.0f];
```

```
    /* Make the image view twice as large in
     width and height */
    self.xcodeImageView.transform = CGAffineTransformMakeScale(2.0f,
                                                               2.0f);

    /* Commit the animation */
    [UIView commitAnimations];

}
```

This code uses an affine scale transformation to scale the image view to become twice as big as it originally was. The best thing about applying scale transformations to a view is that the width and height are scaled using the center of the view as the center of the scaling. Suppose that the center of your view is at point (100, 100) on the screen, and you scale your view to be twice as big in width and height. The resulting view will have its center remain at point (100, 100) on the screen, while being twice as big in each direction. If you were to scale a view by increasing its frame's width and height explicitly, you would end up with the final view being located somewhere else on the screen. That's because when changing the frame of the image view to scale the width and height, you are also changing the value of the *x* and the *y* of the frame, whether you want to or not. Because of that, your image view will not be scaled up from its center. Fixing this issue is outside the scope of this book, but feel free to play with it for a while, and maybe you will find the solution. One hint that I *will* give you is that you can run two animations at the same time in parallel: one for changing the width and height, and the other for changing the center of the image view!

### See Also

Recipe 20.12; Recipe 20.14

## 20.16. Animating and Rotating Views

### Problem

You want to animate the rotation of your views.

### Solution

Create a rotation affine transform and use the animation methods of `UIView` to animate the rotation.

## Discussion

I highly recommend that you read Recipe 20.14 before proceeding with this section of the book.

In order to rotate a view while animating it, you must apply a rotation transformation to it while in an animation block (see Recipe 20.12). Let's have a look at some sample code that will make this clearer. Let's say we have an image named *Xcode.png* (see Figure 20-9), and we want to display it in the center of the screen. After the image is displayed, we want to rotate it 90 degrees over a five-second time period and then rotate it back to its original orientation. So when the view appears on the screen, let's rotate the image view 90 degrees clockwise:

```
- (void) viewDidAppear:(BOOL)paramAnimated{
    [super viewDidAppear:paramAnimated];

    self.xcodeImageView.center = self.view.center;

    /* Begin the animation */
    [UIView beginAnimations:@"clockwiseAnimation"
                    context:NULL];

    /* Make the animation 5 seconds long */
    [UIView setAnimationDuration:5.0f];

    [UIView setAnimationDelegate:self];

    [UIView setAnimationDidStopSelector:
     @selector(clockwiseRotationStopped:finished:context:)];

    /* Rotate the image view 90 degrees */
    self.xcodeImageView.transform =
    CGAffineTransformMakeRotation((90.0f * M_PI) / 180.0f);

    /* Commit the animation */
    [UIView commitAnimations];

}
```

We've chosen the `clockwiseRotationStopped:finished:context:` selector to get called when the clockwise rotation animation finishes. In that method, we will be rotating the image view counterclockwise back to 0 degrees (where it originally was) over a five-second time period:

```
- (void)clockwiseRotationStopped:(NSString *)paramAnimationID
                        finished:(NSNumber *)paramFinished
                         context:(void *)paramContext{
```

```
    [UIView beginAnimations:@"counterclockwiseAnimation"
                    context:NULL];

    /* 5 seconds long */
    [UIView setAnimationDuration:5.0f];

    /* Back to original rotation */
    self.xcodeImageView.transform = CGAffineTransformIdentity;

    [UIView commitAnimations];

}
```

As you saw in Recipe 20.14, Recipe 20.15, and in this section, there are many ways to animate views (direct or indirect subclasses of `UIView`) and many properties that you can modify while carrying out your animations. Be creative and inspect other properties in `UIView` that you might have not previously known about. You may also want to take a look at the documentation for `UIView` in Xcode Organizer.

### See Also

Recipe 20.13; Recipe 20.14; Recipe 20.15

## 20.17. Capturing a Screenshot of Your View into an Image

### Problem

You want to capture the contents of a view object within your app into an image and perhaps save that image to disk or perform another action with it, such as allowing the user to share it to her favorite social media network (see Recipe 11.11).

### Solution

Follow these steps:

1. Use the `UIGraphicsBeginImageContextWithOptions` function to create a new image context. This new context will become the current context that subsequent painting will happen on.
2. Invoke the `drawViewHierarchyInRect:` method of your `UIView` and, as a parameter to this method, pass the boundaries of the view that you want drawn into the current context.
3. Invoke the `UIGraphicsGetImageFromCurrentImageContext` method, whose return value is an image representation of the current context. This is an image of type `UIImage`.

4. Convert your image instance into data using the `UIImagePNGRepresentation` function. This function will give you an object of type `NSData`.
5. Last but not least, issue the `writeToUrl:atomically:` instance method of your data object to write the image data to a location on disk, if that's what you wish to do. Alternatively, you can perform any type of operation that you want with the image once you have it as an instance of `UIImage`.

## Discussion

Sometimes, programmers need to take a screenshot of the device's screen, programmatically. One use case is when you've written a drawing app and you would like the user to be able to save her drawing into a file, perhaps on iCloud, so that she can retrieve it later.

Before saving or sharing an image this way, it must be drawn into an *image context*. An image context is invisible to us, because we won't even get a handle to it. However, any drawing methods you call will affect the current image context. Think of image contexts as invisible drawing canvases. They become visible only when you draw on them. You get their image representation using the `UIGraphicsGetImageFromCurrentImageContext` function.

Using the new SDK, all you have to do to draw the contents of a view into the current context is issue the `drawViewHierarchyInRect:` method on that view.

So let's put what we learned to use. In this code snippet, we are going to place some components on our view (using storyboards, described in Chapter 6). What you place on your storyboard is not relevant. What we want to do, however, is capture the contents of our view controller's view into an image and then store that image in the Documents folder on disk:

```
- (void) viewDidAppear:(BOOL)animated{
    [super viewDidAppear:animated];

    /* Capture the screenshot */
    UIGraphicsBeginImageContextWithOptions(self.view.bounds.size, YES, 0.0f);
    if ([self.view drawViewHierarchyInRect:self.view.bounds]){
        NSLog(@"Successfully draw the screenshot.");
    } else {
        NSLog(@"Failed to draw the screenshot.");
    }
    UIImage *screenshot = UIGraphicsGetImageFromCurrentImageContext();
    UIGraphicsEndImageContext();

    /* Save it to disk */
    NSFileManager *fileManager = [[NSFileManager alloc] init];
    NSURL *documentsFolder = [fileManager URLForDirectory:NSDocumentDirectory
                                                 inDomain:NSUserDomainMask
```

```
                                            appropriateForURL:nil
                                                       create:YES
                                                        error:nil];
    NSURL *screenshotUrl = [documentsFolder
                            URLByAppendingPathComponent:@"screenshot.png"];

    NSData *screenshotData = UIImagePNGRepresentation(screenshot);

    if ([screenshotData writeToURL:screenshotUrl atomically:YES]){
        NSLog(@"Successfully saved screenshot to %@", screenshotUrl);
    } else {
        NSLog(@"Failed to save screenshot.");
    }

}
```

Our code starts by creating a new image context and getting its image representation using `UIGraphicsGetImageFromCurrentImageContext`. Once we have the image representation, we use `NSFileManager` to find the path of the Documents folder of our app on disk (see Recipe 14.1). Last but not least, we get the data representation of our screenshot image using the `UIImagePNGRepresentation` function so that we can store it on disk. The `UIImage` class doesn't allow us to save its contents on disk. We need to get the PNG or the JPEG representation of the image, using the `UIImageJPEGRepresentation` function, to get the data that represents that image for that format (PNG/JPEG). Once we have the data, we can save it to disk or perform other operations on it.

## See Also

Recipe 11.11; Chapter 6

# CHAPTER 21
# Core Motion

## 21.0. Introduction

iOS devices are usually equipped with accelerometer hardware. Some iOS devices might also include a gyroscope, such as the new iPhone and the new iPad. Before attempting to use either the accelerometer or the gyroscope in your iOS applications, you must check the availability of these sensors on the iOS device on which your app runs. Recipes 21.1 and 21.2 include techniques you can use to detect the availability of the accelerometer and gyroscope. With a gyroscope, iOS devices are able to detect motion in six axes.

Let's go through a situation that will show you the value of the gyroscope. The accelerometer cannot detect the rotation of the device around its vertical axis if you are holding the device perfectly still in your hands, sitting in a computer chair, and rotating your chair in a clockwise or counterclockwise fashion. From the standpoint of the floor or the Earth, the device is rotating around the vertical axis, but it's not rotating around its own *y*-axis which is the vertical center of the device. So, the accelerometer does not detect any motion.

However, the gyroscope included in some iOS devices allows us to detect such movements. This allows more fluid and flawless movement detection routines. This is typically useful in games, where the developers need to know not only whether the device is moving on the *x*-, *y*-, and *z*-axes (information they can get from the accelerometer), but also whether it is changing in relation to the Earth along these directions, which requires a gyroscope.

Programmers can use the Core Motion framework to access both the accelerometer data and the gyroscope data (if available). All recipes in this chapter make use of the Core Motion framework. With the new features in the LLVM compiler, all you have to do in order to link your app with a system framework is to simply import that framework on top of your header/implementation files and the compiler will do the actual importing of the framework into your app for you.

iOS Simulator does not simulate the accelerometer or the gyroscope hardware. However, you can generate a *shake* with iOS Simulator using Hardware → Shake Gesture (see Figure 21-1).

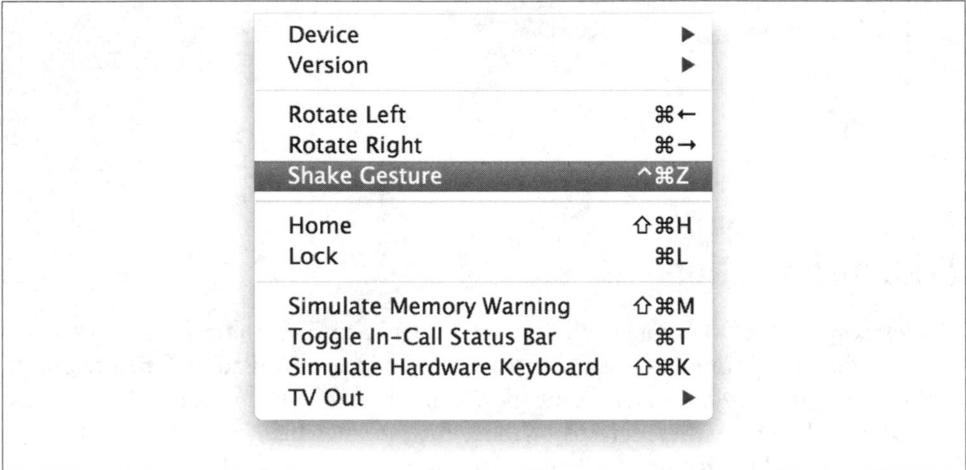


*Figure 21-1. The Shake Gesture option in iOS Simulator*

# 21.1. Detecting the Availability of an Accelerometer

## Problem

In your program, you want to detect whether the accelerometer hardware is available.

## Solution

Use the `isAccelerometerAvailable` method of `CMMotionManager` to detect the accelerometer hardware. The `isAccelerometerActive` method can also be used to detect whether the accelerometer hardware is currently sending updates to the program.

Let's first make sure we have imported the required header files:

```
#import "AppDelegate.h"
#import <CoreMotion/CoreMotion.h>

@implementation AppDelegate
```

Next, go on to detect the availability of an accelerometer in the implementation file of our app delegate:

```
- (BOOL)            application:(UIApplication *)application
  didFinishLaunchingWithOptions:(NSDictionary *)launchOptions{

    CMMotionManager *motionManager = [[CMMotionManager alloc] init];

    if ([motionManager isAccelerometerAvailable]){
        NSLog(@"Accelerometer is available.");
    } else{
        NSLog(@"Accelerometer is not available.");
    }

    if ([motionManager isAccelerometerActive]){
        NSLog(@"Accelerometer is active.");
    } else {
        NSLog(@"Accelerometer is not active.");
    }

    self.window = [[UIWindow alloc] initWithFrame:
                   [[UIScreen mainScreen] bounds]];

    self.window.backgroundColor = [UIColor whiteColor];
    [self.window makeKeyAndVisible];
    return YES;
}
```

Accelerometer hardware might be available on the iOS device running your program. This, however, does not mean the accelerometer hardware is sending updates to your program. If the accelerometer or gyroscope *is* sending updates to your program, we say it is *active* (which requires you to define a delegate object, as we will soon see).

If you run this code on iOS Simulator, you will get values similar to these in the console window:

```
Accelerometer is not available.
Accelerometer is not active.
```

Running the same code on the new iPhone, you will get values similar to these:

```
Accelerometer is available.
Accelerometer is not active.
```

## Discussion

An iOS device could have a built-in accelerometer. As we don't yet know which iOS devices might have accelerometer hardware built in and which ones won't, it is best to test the availability of the accelerometer before using it.

You can detect the availability of this hardware by instantiating an object of type `CMMotionManager` and accessing its `isAccelerometerAvailable` method. This method is of type `BOOL` and returns `YES` if the accelerometer hardware is available and `NO` if not.

In addition, you can detect whether the accelerometer hardware is currently sending updates to your application (whether it is active) by issuing the `isAccelerometerActive` method of `CMMotionManager`. You will learn about retrieving accelerometer data in Recipe 21.3.

## See Also

Recipe 21.3

# 21.2. Detecting the Availability of a Gyroscope

## Problem

You want to find out whether the current iOS device that is running your program has gyroscope hardware available.

## Solution

Use the `isGyroAvailable` method of an instance of `CMMotionManager` to detect the gyroscope hardware. The `isGyroActive` method is also available if you want to detect whether the gyroscope hardware is currently sending updates to your program (in other words, whether it is active):

```
#import "AppDelegate.h"
#import <CoreMotion/CoreMotion.h>

@implementation AppDelegate

- (BOOL)            application:(UIApplication *)application
  didFinishLaunchingWithOptions:(NSDictionary *)launchOptions{

    CMMotionManager *motionManager = [[CMMotionManager alloc] init];

    if ([motionManager isGyroAvailable]){
        NSLog(@"Gryro is available.");
    } else {
        NSLog(@"Gyro is not available.");
    }

    if ([motionManager isGyroActive]){
        NSLog(@"Gryo is active.");
    } else {
        NSLog(@"Gryo is not active.");
    }

    self.window = [[UIWindow alloc] initWithFrame:
                   [[UIScreen mainScreen] bounds]];
```

```
        self.window.backgroundColor = [UIColor whiteColor];
        [self.window makeKeyAndVisible];
        return YES;
    }
```

iOS Simulator does not have gyroscope simulation in place. If you run this code on the simulator, you will receive results similar to these in the console window:

```
Gyro is not available.
Gyro is not active.
```

If you run this code on an iOS device with a gyroscope, such as the new iPhone, the results could be different:

```
Gyro is available.
Gyro is not active.
```

## Discussion

If you plan to release an application that makes use of the gyroscope, you must make sure other iOS devices without this hardware can run your application. If you are using the gyroscope as part of a game, for instance, you must make sure other iOS devices that are capable of running your application can play the game, although they might not have a gyroscope installed. Not all iOS devices have a gyroscope. This recipe shows you how to determine whether a device has a gyroscope.

To achieve this, you must first instantiate an object of type `CMMotionManager`. After this, you must access the `isGyroAvailable` method (of type `BOOL`) and see whether the gyroscope is available on the device running your code. You can also use the `isGyroActive` method of the `CMMotionManager` instance to find out whether the gyroscope is currently sending your application any updates. For more information about this, please refer to Recipe 21.5.

## See Also

Recipe 21.5

# 21.3. Retrieving Accelerometer Data

## Problem

You want to ask iOS to send accelerometer data to your application.

## Solution

Use the `startAccelerometerUpdatesToQueue:withHandler:` instance method of `CMMotionManager`. Here is our view controller that utilizes `CMMotionManager` to get accelerometer updates:

```
#import "ViewController.h"
#import <CoreMotion/CoreMotion.h>

@interface ViewController ()
@property (nonatomic, strong) CMMotionManager *motionManager;
@end

@implementation ViewController
```

We will now implement our view controller and take advantage of the `startAccelerometerUpdatesToQueue:withHandler:` method of the `CMMotionManager` class:

```
- (void)viewDidLoad{
    [super viewDidLoad];

    self.motionManager = [[CMMotionManager alloc] init];

    if ([self.motionManager isAccelerometerAvailable]){
        NSOperationQueue *queue = [[NSOperationQueue alloc] init];
        [self.motionManager
         startAccelerometerUpdatesToQueue:queue
         withHandler:^(CMAccelerometerData *accelerometerData, NSError *error) {
             NSLog(@"X = %.04f, Y = %.04f, Z = %.04f",
                   accelerometerData.acceleration.x,
                   accelerometerData.acceleration.y,
                   accelerometerData.acceleration.z);
         }];
    } else {
        NSLog(@"Accelerometer is not available.");
    }

}
```

## Discussion

The accelerometer reports three-dimensional data (three axes) that iOS reports to your program as *x*, *y*, and *z* values. These values are encapsulated in a `CMAcceleration` structure:

```
typedef struct { double x; double y; double z;
} CMAcceleration;
```

If you hold your iOS device in front of your face with the screen facing you in portrait mode:

- The *x*-axis runs from left to right at the horizontal center of the device, with values ranging from -1 to +1 from left to right.
- The *y*-axis runs from bottom to top at the vertical center of the device, with values ranging from -1 to +1 from bottom to top.
- The *z*-axis runs from the back of the device, through the device toward you, with values ranging from -1 to +1 from back to front.

The best way to understand the values reported from the accelerometer hardware is by taking a look at a few examples. Here is one: let's assume you have your iOS device facing you with the bottom of the device pointing to the ground and the top pointing up. If you hold it perfectly still without tilting it in any specific direction, the values you have for the *x*-, *y*-, and *z*-axes at this moment will be (x: 0.0, y: −1.0, z: 0.0). Now try the following while the screen is facing you and the bottom of the device is pointing to the ground:

1. Turn the device 90 degrees clockwise. The values you have at this moment are (x: +1.0, y: 0.0, z: 0.0).
2. Turn the device a further 90 degrees clockwise. Now the top of the device must be pointing to the ground. The values you have at this moment are (x: 0.0, y: +1.0, z: 0.0).
3. Turn the device a further 90 degrees clockwise. Now the top of the device must be pointing to the left. The values you have right now are (x: -1.0, y: 0.0, z: 0.0).
4. Finally, if you rotate the device a further 90 degrees clockwise, where the top of the device once again points to the sky and the bottom of the device points to the ground, the values will be as they were originally (x: 0.0, y: -1.0, z: 0.0).

So, from these values, we can conclude that rotating the device around the *z*-axis changes the *x* and *y* values reported by the accelerometer, but not the *z* value.

Let's conduct another experiment. Hold the device again so it's facing you with its bottom pointing to the ground and its top pointing to the sky. The values that a program will get from the accelerometer, as you already know, are (x: 0.0, y: -1.0, z: 0.0). Now try these movements:

1. Tilt the device backward 90 degrees around the *x*-axis so that its top will be pointing backward. In other words, hold it as though it is sitting face-up on a table. The values you get at this moment will be (x: 0.0, y: 0.0, z: -1.0).
2. Now tilt the device backward 90 degrees again so that its back is facing you, its top is facing the ground, and its bottom is facing the sky. The values you get at this moment will be (x: 0.0, y: 1.0, z: 0.0).

3. Tilt the device backward 90 degrees so that it's facing the ground with its back facing the sky and its top pointing toward you. The reported values at this moment will be (x: 0.0, y: 0.0, z: 1.0).
4. And finally, if you tilt the device one more time in the same direction, so the device is facing you and its top is facing the sky, the values you get will be the same values you started with.

Therefore, we can observe that rotating the device around the *x*-axis changes the values of the *y*- and *z*-axes, but not *x*. I encourage you to try the third type of rotation—around the y-axis (pointing from top to bottom)—and observe the changes in the values reported for the *x*- and the *z*-axes.

To be able to receive accelerometer updates, you have two options:

- The `startAccelerometerUpdatesToQueue:withHandler:` instance method of `CMMotionManager`.

  This method will deliver accelerometer updates on an operation queue (of type `NSOperationQueue`) and will require a basic knowledge of blocks that are used extensively in Grand Central Dispatch (GCD). For more information about blocks, please refer to Chapter 7.

- The `startAccelerometerUpdates` instance method of `CMMotionManager`.

  Once you call this method, the accelerometer (if available) will start updating accelerometer data in the motion manager object. You need to set up your own thread to continuously read the value of the `accelerometerData` property (of type `CMAccelerometerData`) of `CMMotionManager`.

In this recipe, we are using the first method (with blocks). I highly recommend that you first read Chapter 7 before proceeding with this recipe. The block we provide to the `startAccelerometerUpdatesToQueue:withHandler:` instance method of `CMMotionManager` must be of type `CMAccelerometerHandler`:

```
typedef void (^CMAccelerometerHandler)(
                                       CMAccelerometerData *accelerometerData,
                                       NSError *error);
```

In other words, we must accept two parameters on the block. The first one must be of type `CMAccelerometerData`, and the second must be of type `NSError`, as implemented in our example code.

## See Also

Recipe 21.1

# 21.4. Detecting Shakes on an iOS Device

## Problem

You want to know when the user shakes an iOS device.

## Solution

Use the `motionEnded:withEvent:` method of any object in your application that is of type `UIResponder`. This could be your view controller(s) or even your main window object.

## Discussion

The `motionEnded:withEvent:` method of a responder object gets called whenever a motion has been captured by iOS. The simplest implementation of this method is this:

```
- (void) motionEnded:(UIEventSubtype)motion withEvent:(UIEvent *)event{
    /* Handle the motion */
}
```

The `motion` parameter, as you can see, is of type `UIEventSubtype`. One of the values of type `UIEventSubtype` is `UIEventSubtypeMotionShake`, which is what we are interested in. As soon as we detect this event, we know that the user has shaken her iOS device. Now go to the implementation of your view controller and handle the `motionEnded:withEvent:` method:

```
- (void) motionEnded:(UIEventSubtype)motion withEvent:(UIEvent *)event{
    if (motion == UIEventSubtypeMotionShake){
        UIAlertView *alert =
        [[UIAlertView alloc] initWithTitle:@"Shake"
                                   message:@"The device is shaken"
                                  delegate:nil
                         cancelButtonTitle:@"OK" otherButtonTitles:nil];
        [alert show];
    }
}
```

If you now simulate a shake event even if you are on iOS Simulator (see this chapter's Introduction), you will see that our window prints the text "Detected a shake" to the console window.

# 21.5. Retrieving Gyroscope Data

## Problem

You want to be able to retrieve information about the device's motion from the gyroscope hardware on an iOS device.

## Solution

Follow these steps:

1. Find out whether the gyroscope hardware is available on the iOS device. Please refer to Recipe 21.2 for directions on how to do this.
2. If the gyroscope hardware is available, make sure it is not already sending you updates. Please refer to Recipe 21.2 for directions.
3. Use the `setGyroUpdateInterval:` instance method of `CMMotionManager` to set the number of updates you want to receive per second. For instance, for 20 updates per second (one second), set this value to 1.0/20.0.
4. Invoke the `startGyroUpdatesToQueue:withHandler:` instance method of `CMMotionManager`. The queue object could simply be the main operation queue (as we will see later), and the handler block must follow the `CMGyroHandler` format.

The following code implements these steps:

```
- (BOOL)            application:(UIApplication *)application
  didFinishLaunchingWithOptions:(NSDictionary *)launchOptions{

    CMMotionManager *manager = [[CMMotionManager alloc] init];

    if ([manager isGyroAvailable]){

        if ([manager isGyroActive] == NO){

            [manager setGyroUpdateInterval:1.0f / 40.0f];

            NSOperationQueue *queue = [[NSOperationQueue alloc] init];

            [manager
             startGyroUpdatesToQueue:queue
             withHandler:^(CMGyroData *gyroData, NSError *error) {

                 NSLog(@"Gyro Rotation x = %.04f", gyroData.rotationRate.x);
                 NSLog(@"Gyro Rotation y = %.04f", gyroData.rotationRate.y);
                 NSLog(@"Gyro Rotation z = %.04f", gyroData.rotationRate.z);

             }];
        } else {
```

```
            NSLog(@"Gyro is already active.");
        }

    } else {
        NSLog(@"Gyro isn't available.");
    }

    self.window = [[UIWindow alloc] initWithFrame:
                   [[UIScreen mainScreen] bounds]];

    self.window.backgroundColor = [UIColor whiteColor];
    [self.window makeKeyAndVisible];
    return YES;
}
```

## Discussion

With `CMMotionManager`, application programmers can attempt to retrieve gyroscope updates from iOS. You must first make sure the gyroscope hardware is available on the iOS device on which your application is running (please refer to Recipe 21.2). After doing so, you can call the `setGyroUpdateInterval:` instance method of `CMMotionManager` to set the number of updates you would like to receive per second on updates from the gyroscope hardware. For instance, if you want to be updated *N* times per second, set this value to 1.0/*N*.

After you set the update interval, you can call the `startGyroUpdatesToQueue:withHandler:` instance method of `CMMotionManager` to set up a handler block for the updates. For more information about blocks, please refer to Chapter 7. Your block object must be of type `CMGyroHandler`, which accepts two parameters:

`gyroData`
: The data that comes from the gyroscope hardware, encompassed in an object of type `CMGyroData`. You can use the `rotationRate` property of `CMGyroData` (a structure) to get access to the *x*, *y*, and *z* values of the data, which represent all three Euler angles known as roll, pitch, and yaw, respectively. You can learn more about these by reading about flight dynamics.

`error`
: An error of type `NSError` that might occur when the gyroscope is sending us updates.

If you do not wish to use block objects, you must call the `startGyroUpdates` instance method of `CMMotionManager` instead of the `startGyroUpdatesToQueue:withHandler:` instance method and set up your own thread to read the gyroscope hardware updates posted to the `gyroData` property of the instance of `CMMotionManager` you are using.

## See Also

Recipe 21.2

CHAPTER 22

# iCloud

## 22.0. Introduction

iCloud is Apple's cloud infrastructure. A cloud is a name given to a service that stores information on a centralized location, where the user cannot physically access the disk/memory that stores the information. For instance, an iCloud storage space could be allocated by Apple in California, and all iPhone devices in New York could have all their iCloud traffic go to the California iCloud data center.

The purpose of using iCloud, from a programmer's perspective, is to give his users the ability to seamlessly have their apps' data transferred from one machine to another. Let's have a look at a real-life example of when iCloud would come in very handy: imagine that you have developed an app called Game XYZ. Sarah is a hypothetical user of your game, and she has purchased it through the App Store. Your game is a universal app and hence can be run on both the iPhone and the iPad. It just so happens that Sarah has an iPad and an iPhone and has installed your game on both her devices. She is playing your game at the office and is at level 12. She goes back home and picks up her iPad to play some more, only to discover that the game starts from level 1 on her iPad because she was playing on her iPhone all along. This is definitely not a pretty situation. What is better is for your game to be intelligent enough to save its state and resume that state when your users restart the game, regardless of which device they have been running it on. To handle this situation, you could use iCloud to store Sarah's game state on her iPhone and let iCloud synchronize this data to the data centers that are maintained by Apple. When she picks her iPad up, you could use your app to contact iCloud and find out if there is a recent game state saved for Sarah. If yes, then you can load that state for her to give her the feeling that she really didn't even leave your game. She just switched devices. This is a bit more work for you, but in the end you will get really happy customers.

Before being able to use iCloud services, you first need to enable your app for iCloud. This requires creating the correct provisioning profiles in iOS Provisioning Portal and then enabling the correct entitlements in your project. You can read more about this in Recipe 22.1.

I use the terms "folder" and "directory" interchangeably throughout this chapter.

# 22.1. Setting Up Your App for iCloud

## Problem

You want to start using iCloud in your apps, and you would like to know how you should set up your Xcode project.

## Solution

At a high level, these are the steps you need to follow to enable iCloud storage in your app:

1. Create a new App ID that has iCloud enabled in it.
2. Create a new development provision profile that is linked to that App ID and download and install that profile onto your computer.
3. Create a new app in Xcode and set the provision profile for that app to the profile that you just created.
4. In the Capabilities tab in Xcode, flick the iCloud switch on.

Your app is now set up for iCloud. In the Discussion section, we will talk more about the details of these steps and the things that could go wrong during the setting up process.

## Discussion

In the Solution section, we had a brief look at the high-level steps required to set your app up for iCloud. Here we are going to look at the details with illustrations. So let's get started.

1. Create an app in Xcode and set its bundle identifier using a reverse-domain style: for instance, *com.pixolity.ios.cookbook.icloudapp*. Remember that this is the reverse domain style bundle identifier that *I* have chosen for my app. Usually you would take the domain name of your website and just reverse that and append the identifier of your app to the results.
2. Using the iOS Provisioning Portal, create a new App ID for your app. Enable iCloud for that App ID by selecting it in the portal, enabling the checkbox for iCloud, and saving your changes (see Figure 22-1).

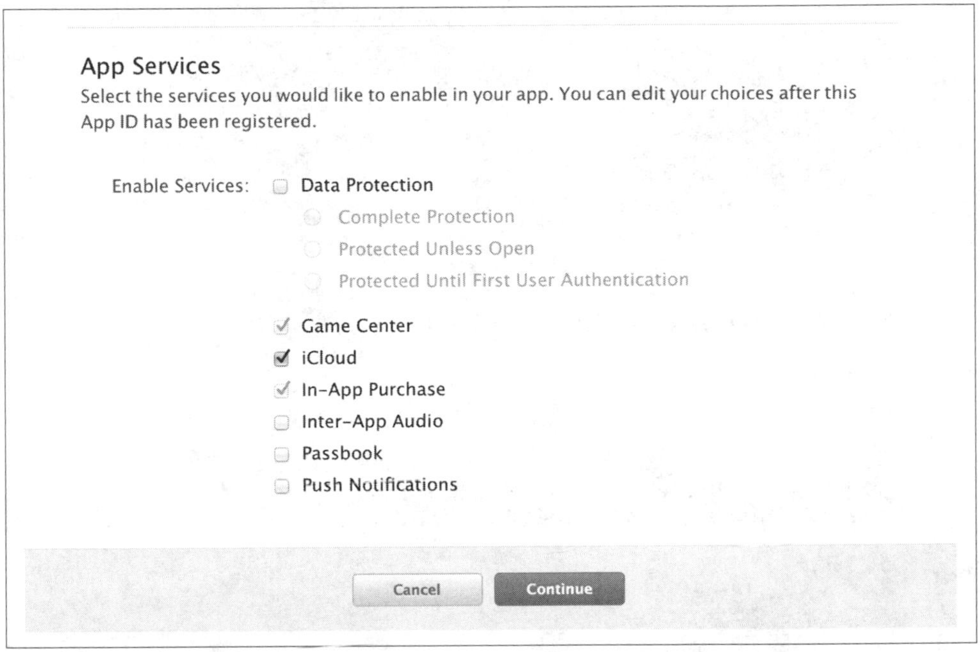

*Figure 22-1. Enabling iCloud access for your App ID*

3. After your App ID is created (as shown in Figure 22-2), navigate to the Provisioning Profiles section of the portal, and create a new development provision profile that is linked to the App ID that you created earlier.
4. Once you are done creating the profile (see Figure 22-3), download the profile and drag and drop it into iTunes for iTunes to install the profile on your Mac.

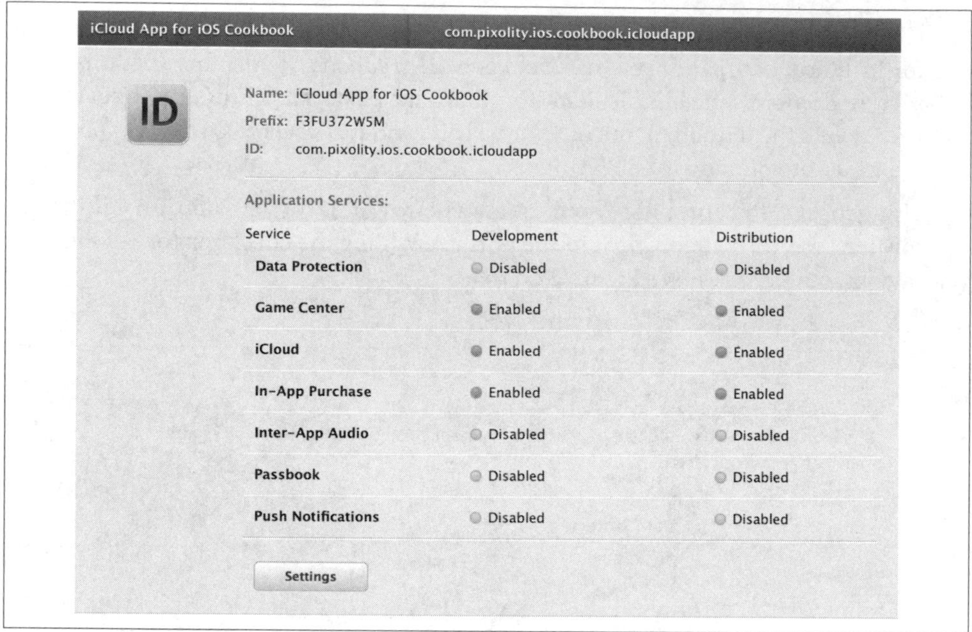


*Figure 22-2. Your App ID successfully set up for iCloud*

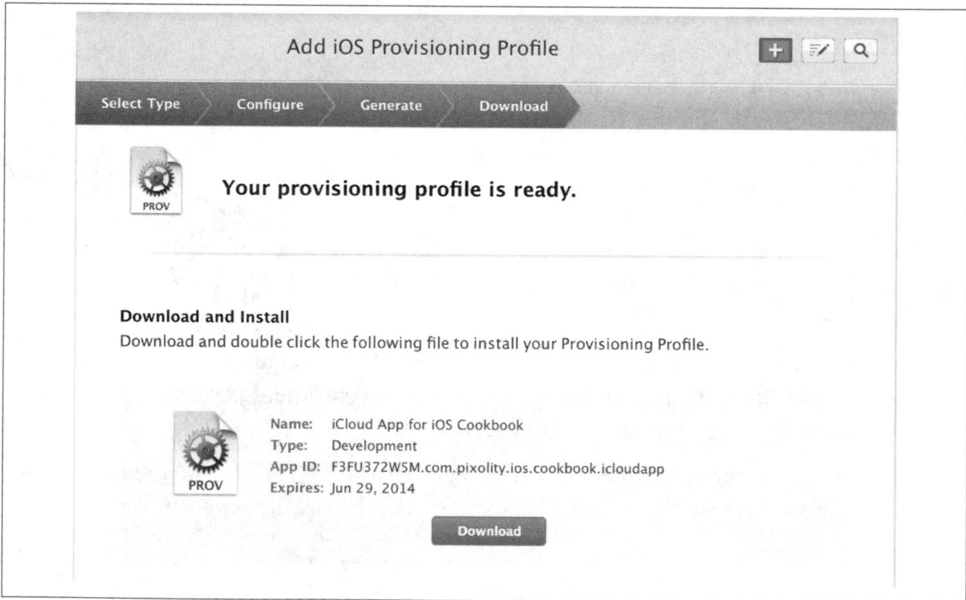


*Figure 22-3. Download and install your new iCloud-enabled profile*

5. In Xcode, create a new app and change your bundle ID to that which you specified for your App ID before. If you forget this step, your app won't be able to use the new profile.
6. In Xcode, press Command+0 if the navigator on the lefthand side is not showing. After you see the navigator, choose your project from the list by clicking on it and then choose your target. In the build settings of your target, set the correct provision profile (the one that you just created and downloaded) for your app.
7. Navigate away from the Build Settings tab and move to the Capabilities tab and flick the iCloud switch on, as shown in Figure 22-4.

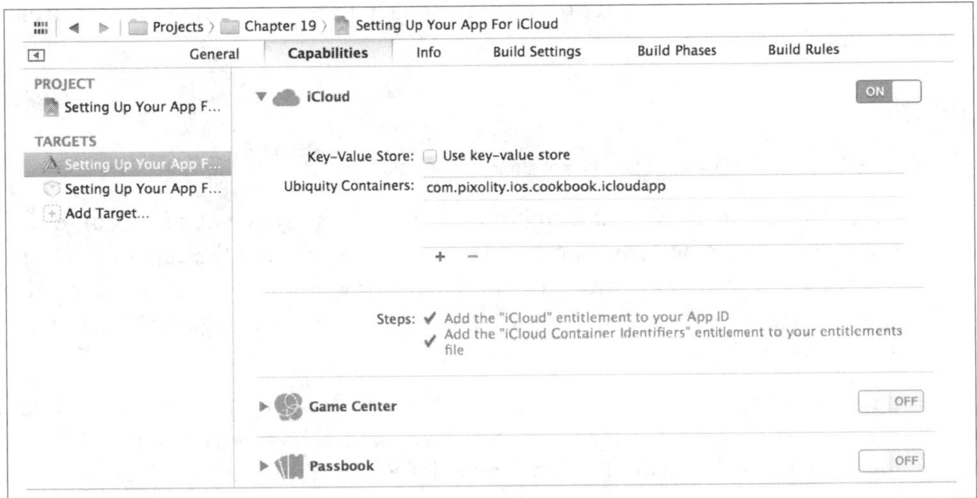


*Figure 22-4. Enabling iCloud capabilities for your app*

Now attempt to compile your app. If you get an error from the compiler telling you that your app entitlements file could not be found, check the Code Signing Entitlements path that Xcode has set for your app in the Build Settings tab of your target. Usually you can fix this issue by changing the default path that Xcode has given you and prepend `$(SRCROOT)/$(TARGET_NAME)/` to the entitlements filename. For instance, the default entitlements file that Xcode assigned to my project was set up in Build Settings as `Setting Up Your App For iCloud.entitlements`, and with that I was getting a compilation error. But after I changed that value to `$(SRCROOT)/$(TARGET_NAME)/Setting Up Your App For iCloud.entitlements`, Xcode was happy and so was I. This in fact seems like an issue in Xcode that I'm hoping Apple will fix at some point.

Now compile your app. If you are able to compile it successfully, that means your app is set up for iCloud. If you are getting errors, have a look at the errors console to find out more about the issues. Typically, the issues are related to an invalid profile or missing entitlements, so read the steps discussed earlier in this recipe and ensure that you follow them one by one.

# 22.2. Storing and Synchronizing Dictionaries in iCloud

## Problem

You want to store key-value data in dictionary form in iCloud and seamlessly read and write to this centralized and synchronized dictionary from various devices and from various iCloud accounts.

## Solution

Use the `NSUbiquitousKeyValueStore` class.

The data that you store in iCloud using the `NSUbiquitousKeyValueStore` is uniquely created in iCloud using the provision profile with which you sign the app and the end user's iCloud account. In other word, you simply store values in iCloud using the `NSUbiquitousKeyValueStore` class, not worrying if one user's data is going to clash with another user's data. iCloud does that separation for you.

In Recipe 22.1, we used the Capabilities tab of our target settings to enable iCloud for our app. However, to use the `NSUbiquitousKeyValueStore` class, we need to enable the key-value store for iCloud as well. This can be done from the same Capabilities tab of your target settings. Once you are in the Capabilities tab, expand the iCloud section if it's not already expanded, and then ensure that the *Use key-value store* option is ticked, as shown in Figure 22-5.

## Discussion

The `NSUbiquitousKeyValueStore` class works very similar to the `NSUserDefaults` class. It can store string, Boolean, integer, float and other values. Each one of the values has to have a key associated with it. You will then be able to read the values by passing the keys to this class. The difference between the `NSUbiquitousKeyValueStore` and the `NSUserDefaults` class is that the former synchronizes its dictionary data with iCloud, whereas the latter only stores the dictionary locally to a *.plist* file—this data will be deleted once the app gets deleted from the user's device.

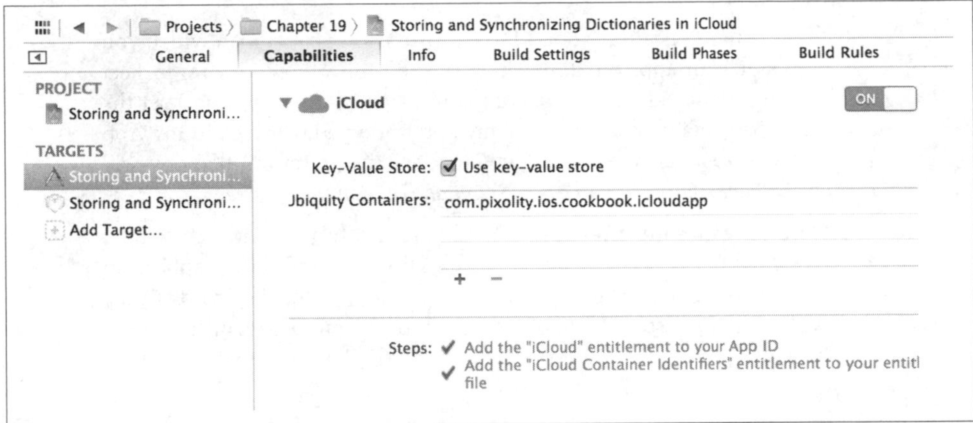


*Figure 22-5. Enabling the iCloud key-value store for our app*

Before you can use the `NSUbiquitousKeyValueStore` class to store key-value data in iCloud, you must set up the appropriate entitlements for your project. Please refer to Recipe 22.1 to learn how to do this.

An instance of your application uses a unique identifier to store data in iCloud. This unique identifier is made up of three key pieces:

*Team ID*
: This is the unique identifier for your iOS Developer Program. When you sign up for iOS Developer Program, Apple will automatically generate a unique identifier for your account. To retrieve this identifier, simply log into Developer Center (*http://bit.ly/Qdj3FC*) and then select Your Account from the top menu items. Then choose Account Summary from the menus on the left. On the screen to the right, your Team ID is displayed under the *Developer Account Summary* section. No two iOS Developer accounts can have the same Team ID.

*Reverse domain-style of company identifier*
: This string is usually in the form of *`com.COMPANYNAME`*, where *`COMPANYNAME`* is the name of your company and *`APPNAME`* is the name of your app. For instance, my company name is `Pixolity`, so my reverse domain style of company identifier will be *`com.pixolity`*.

*App identifier and optional suffix*
: This is the string that gets attached as the suffix to the Reverse domain-style of company identifier.

The Team ID is always bound to the provision profile with which you will sign your app. You do *not* have to enter this value into your project settings. For instance, if my company name is *`Pixolity`* and I set the reverse domain style name for my app to *`com.pixolity`* and my App ID to *`icloudapp`*, the name that iCloud will use in the entitlements will be *`$(TeamIdentifierPrefix)$(CFBundleIdentifier)`*.

The `$(TeamIdentifierPrefix)` value is the Team ID, which will be resolved to my actual Team ID when Xcode compiles my application and signs it with a provision profile. The `$(CFBundleIdentifier)` value will be resolved, at compile time, to the bundle identifier of my target.

Now that we are sure we have set up the project properly and entitlements are set up as well, then we can move on to using the `NSUbiquitousKeyValueStore` class to store keys and values in iCloud. There are various methods that `NSUbiquitousKeyValueStore` class exposes to us in order for us to save the values in iCloud. Some of these methods are listed and explained here:

`setString:forKey:`
: Sets a string value for the given key. The string must be of type `NSString`. Obviously, classes that subclass `NSString`, such as `NSMutableString` can also be stored in iCloud using this method.

`setArray:forKey:`
: Sets an array value for the given key. The array can be either a mutable or an immutable array.

`setDictionary:forKey:`
: Sets a mutable or an immutable dictionary for the given key.

`setBool:forKey:`
: Sets method, NSUbiquitousKeyValueStore a Boolean value of type `BOOL` for the given key.

`setData:forKey:`
: Sets a mutable or an immutable data for the given key.

None of these methods will actually do the saving for you. If you are done setting the values, then you must call the `synchronize` method of `NSUbiquitousKeyValueStore` for your settings to be flushed first to iOS and then synchronized with iCloud.

All the work that we do with the `NSUbiquitousKeyValueStore` is done through the `defaultStore` class method of this class. This class method will return an instance of the `NSUbiquitousKeyValueStore` class, which is ready for us to use.

Obviously, after setting the values for keys, we are going to want to retrieve those values at some point during the runtime of the app. We can do this using some of the methods that the `NSUbiquitousKeyValueStore` provides us with. Some of these methods are listed here:

`stringForKey:`
: Returns the string associated with the given key, or `nil` if that key cannot be found. This will be an immutable string even if you used this key to store a mutable string in iCloud.

`arrayForKey:`
: Returns the array associated with the given key, or `nil` if that key cannot be found. This will be an immutable array even if the original array you stored in iCloud for this key was mutable.

`dictionaryForKey:`
: Returns the dictionary associated with the given key, or `nil` if that key cannot be found. The dictionary returned by this method will be immutable even if the original dictionary you stored into iCloud for this key was mutable.

`boolForKey:`
: Returns the Boolean value of type `BOOL` associated with the given key, or `nil` if that key cannot be found.

`dataForKey:`
: Returns the data of type `NSData` associated with the given key, or `nil` if that key cannot be found. The data returned by this method will be immutable even if the original data stored in iCloud for this key was mutable.

So let's have a look at how we can perhaps use this class in the apps. As you already know, iCloud's power really proves handy when you are sharing data between two or more devices for the same user. For instance, if the user starts reading a book on his iPhone, and then picks up his iPad, the app that presents the book sees the last page the user was at and opens the book right there. In effect, we have two devices pretending to be one, for the sake of usability for the end user. For this example, we will store a string and a Boolean value into iCloud using the `NSUbiquitousKeyValueStore` class. We will place a check to see if those values had already been stored in iCloud; if yes, we will read their value. I can then build this app, run it on my iPhone and then on my iPad, and see what happens:

```
- (BOOL)            application:(UIApplication *)application
  didFinishLaunchingWithOptions:(NSDictionary *)launchOptions{

    NSUbiquitousKeyValueStore *kvoStore =
    [NSUbiquitousKeyValueStore defaultStore];

    NSString *stringValue = @"My String";
    NSString *stringValueKey = @"MyStringKey";

    BOOL boolValue = YES;
    NSString *boolValueKey = @"MyBoolKey";

    BOOL mustSynchronize = NO;

    if ([[kvoStore stringForKey:stringValueKey] length] == 0){
        NSLog(@"Could not find the string value in iCloud. Setting...");
        [kvoStore setString:stringValue
                     forKey:stringValueKey];
        mustSynchronize = YES;
    } else {
        NSLog(@"Found the string in iCloud, getting...");
        stringValue = [kvoStore stringForKey:stringValueKey];
    }

    if ([kvoStore boolForKey:boolValueKey] == NO){
        NSLog(@"Could not find the boolean value in iCloud. Setting...");
        [kvoStore setBool:boolValue
                   forKey:boolValueKey];
        mustSynchronize = YES;
    } else {
        NSLog(@"Found the boolean in iCloud, getting...");
        boolValue = [kvoStore boolForKey:boolValueKey];
    }

    if (mustSynchronize){
        if ([kvoStore synchronize]){
            NSLog(@"Successfully synchronized with iCloud.");
        } else {
            NSLog(@"Failed to synchronize with iCloud.");
        }
    }

    self.window = [[UIWindow alloc]
                   initWithFrame:[[UIScreen mainScreen] bounds]];
    self.window.backgroundColor = [UIColor whiteColor];
    [self.window makeKeyAndVisible];
    return YES;
}
```

After setting up the correct provision profiles, enabling entitlements for this project, and running this app on an iOS device that has already been set up with an iCloud account, we can observe these results printed to the console screen:

```
Could not find the string value in iCloud. Setting...
Could not find the boolean value in iCloud. Setting...
Successfully synchronized with iCloud.
```

Now I will leave my device sitting here for a minute or two just to make sure that iCloud has enough time to synchronize my data with the cloud. I will then run the same code on another device that has been linked to the same iCloud account as the first device to see what happens:

```
Found the string in iCloud, getting...
Found the boolean in iCloud, getting...
```

Fantastic. This demonstrates that iCloud is indeed synchronizing the data for multiple iOS devices that are hooked to the same iCloud account.

# 22.3. Creating and Managing Folders for Apps in iCloud

## Problem

You want to store specific files into specific folders within the user's iCloud storage for your app.

## Solution

Follow these steps:

1. Make sure your app is set up to use iCloud (see Recipe 22.1)
2. Select your project file in Xcode and select the Summary tab.
3. Select the entitlements file that Xcode created for you by clicking on it, as we saw in Recipe 22.1, and look at the first value under the `com.apple.developer.ubiquity-container-identifiers` section. This value is simply equal to `$(TeamIdentifierPrefix)` plus your bundle ID, so make a note of that. For my app for this recipe, the value of this key is equal to `$(TeamIdentifierPrefix)com.pixolity.ios.cookbook.icloudapp`. We are going to use this full value in the next steps.
4. In your app delegate, place the string that you copied from the iCloud Containers list, into a string. Prefix this string with your Team ID (see Recipe 22.2 on how to find your Team ID).
5. Now instantiate an object of type `NSFileManager` and pass the path that you created in the previous two steps to the `URLForUbiquityContainerIdentifier:` method of this class. The value of this method will be the *local* address for iCloud storage on the device that is running your app. Let's call this path *Root iCloud Path*.
6. Append the folder name that you want to create to the Root iCloud Path (see previous step). Keep the resulting path in a string or an instance of `NSURL`.

7. Invoke the `fileExistsAtPath:isDirectory:` method of your file manager. If this method returns `NO`, then go on to create the folder using the `createDirectoryAtPath:withIntermediateDirectories:attributes:error:`method of the file manager. If the return value of the `fileExistsAtPath:isDirectory:` method is `YES`, check whether the Boolean value that comes out of the `isDirectory` parameter is `NO`. If it is `NO`, then you must create your folder again as instructed, because the path that was found by the `fileExistsAtPath:isDirectory:` method was not a directory, but rather a file.

## Discussion

One of the things that can make iCloud *sound* complicated to developers is that they assume, since it is a cloud storage, that they have to deal with URLs outside their apps or URLs on the Internet. Well, this is not true. With iCloud, the URLs that you deal with are actually iOS-related. By that, I mean that the URLs are local to the device connected to iCloud. iCloud will then synchronize these local URLs and their data with the iCloud storage hosted by Apple in the cloud. The developer doesn't really have to worry about this part, unless there are conflicts that need to be resolved because two devices running your app and using the same iCloud account simultaneously modified a resource that cannot automatically be merged. We will talk about this later; let's just focus on creating folders in iCloud for now.

So let's now implement what we learned in the Solution section of this chapter:

```
- (BOOL)            application:(UIApplication *)application
  didFinishLaunchingWithOptions:(NSDictionary *)launchOptions{

    NSFileManager *fileManager = [[NSFileManager alloc] init];

    NSString *teamID = <# Put your team ID here #>;

    NSString *bundleId = [[NSBundle mainBundle] bundleIdentifier];

    NSString *rootFolderIdentifier = [NSString stringWithFormat:
                                      @"%@.%@",
                                      teamID, bundleId];

    NSURL *containerURL =
    [fileManager URLForUbiquityContainerIdentifier:rootFolderIdentifier];

    NSString *documentsDirectory =
    [[containerURL path]
     stringByAppendingPathComponent:@"Documents"];

    BOOL isDirectory = NO;
    BOOL mustCreateDocumentsDirectory = NO;
```

```
    if ([fileManager fileExistsAtPath:documentsDirectory
                          isDirectory:&isDirectory]){
        if (isDirectory == NO){
            mustCreateDocumentsDirectory = YES;
        }
    } else {
        mustCreateDocumentsDirectory = YES;
    }

    if (mustCreateDocumentsDirectory){
        NSLog(@"Must create the directory.");

        NSError *directoryCreationError = nil;

        if ([fileManager createDirectoryAtPath:documentsDirectory
                   withIntermediateDirectories:YES
                                    attributes:nil
                                         error:&directoryCreationError]){
            NSLog(@"Successfully created the folder.");
        } else {
            NSLog(@"Failed to create the folder with error = %@",
                  directoryCreationError);
        }

    } else {
        NSLog(@"This folder already exists.");
    }

    self.window = [[UIWindow alloc] initWithFrame:
                   [[UIScreen mainScreen] bounds]];

    self.window.backgroundColor = [UIColor whiteColor];
    [self.window makeKeyAndVisible];
    return YES;
}
```

The Container Identifier that Xcode sets up by default for your application is made out of a Team ID and a Bundle Identifier. If you want, you can simply change this. One of the great features of iCloud for developers is that the container identifiers that you specify for your app's iCloud storage don't have to necessarily be linked in any way to your app or your app's bundle identifier. If you believe the default identifier is confusing, just change it to something that makes more sense to you and your team.

What we can do now is to wrap the code into a method for reuse:

```
- (BOOL) createIcloudDirectory:(NSString *)paramDirectory
           recursiveCreation:(BOOL)paramRecursiveCreation
```

```
                    teamID:(NSString *)paramTeamID
          iCloudContainer:(NSString *)paramContainer
                finalPath:(NSString **)paramFinalPath{

    BOOL result = NO;

    NSFileManager *fileManager = [[NSFileManager alloc] init];

    NSString *rootFolderIdentifier = [NSString stringWithFormat:
                                      @"%@.%@", paramTeamID, paramContainer];

    NSURL *containerURL =
    [fileManager URLForUbiquityContainerIdentifier:rootFolderIdentifier];

    NSString *documentsDirectory =
    [[containerURL path]
     stringByAppendingPathComponent:@"Documents"];

    if (paramFinalPath != nil){
        *paramFinalPath = documentsDirectory;
    }

    BOOL isDirectory = NO;
    BOOL mustCreateDocumentsDirectory = NO;

    if ([fileManager fileExistsAtPath:documentsDirectory
                          isDirectory:&isDirectory]){
        if (isDirectory == NO){
            mustCreateDocumentsDirectory = YES;
        }
    } else {
        mustCreateDocumentsDirectory = YES;
    }

    if (mustCreateDocumentsDirectory){
        NSLog(@"Must create the directory.");

        NSError *directoryCreationError = nil;

        if ([fileManager createDirectoryAtPath:documentsDirectory
                   withIntermediateDirectories:paramRecursiveCreation
                                    attributes:nil
                                         error:&directoryCreationError]){
            result = YES;
            NSLog(@"Successfully created the folder.");
        } else {
            NSLog(@"Failed to create the folder with error = %@",
                  directoryCreationError);
        }

    } else {
        NSLog(@"This folder already exists.");
```

```
        result = YES;
    }

    return result;

}

- (BOOL)            application:(UIApplication *)application
  didFinishLaunchingWithOptions:(NSDictionary *)launchOptions{

    NSString *teamID = <# Put your team ID here #>;

    NSString *containerID = [[NSBundle mainBundle] bundleIdentifier];

    NSString *documentsDirectory = nil;

    if ([self createIcloudDirectory:@"Documents"
                  recursiveCreation:YES
                             teamID:teamID
                    iCloudContainer:containerID
                          finalPath:&documentsDirectory]){
        NSLog(@"Successfully created the directory in %@", documentsDirectory);
    } else {
        NSLog(@"Failed to create the directory.");
    }

    self.window = [[UIWindow alloc] initWithFrame:
                   [[UIScreen mainScreen] bounds]];

    self.window.backgroundColor = [UIColor whiteColor];
    [self.window makeKeyAndVisible];
    return YES;
}
```

The `finalPath` parameter in the new method is an out parameter, meaning that it can store the final path of the directory that you created into an output string, should you need it for any other method (or anywhere in your app).

OK, now that we have this method, we can go ahead and save a resource into the Documents folder for the current user's iCloud storage for the app:

```
- (BOOL)            application:(UIApplication *)application
  didFinishLaunchingWithOptions:(NSDictionary *)launchOptions{

    NSString *teamID = <# Put your team ID here #>;

    NSString *containerID = [[NSBundle mainBundle] bundleIdentifier];

    NSString *documentsDirectory = nil;
```

```
    if ([self createIcloudDirectory:@"Documents"
                 recursiveCreation:YES
                            teamID:teamID
                   iCloudContainer:containerID
                         finalPath:&documentsDirectory]){

        NSLog(@"Successfully created the directory in %@",
              documentsDirectory);

        NSString *stringToSave = @"My String";

        NSString *pathToSave =
        [documentsDirectory
         stringByAppendingPathComponent:@"MyString.txt"];

        NSError *savingError = nil;

        if ([stringToSave writeToFile:pathToSave
                           atomically:YES
                             encoding:NSUTF8StringEncoding
                                error:&savingError]){
            NSLog(@"Successfully saved the string in iCloud.");
        } else {
            NSLog(@"Failed to save the string with error = %@", savingError);
        }


    } else {
        NSLog(@"Failed to create the directory.");
    }

    self.window = [[UIWindow alloc] initWithFrame:
                   [[UIScreen mainScreen] bounds]];

    self.window.backgroundColor = [UIColor whiteColor];
    [self.window makeKeyAndVisible];
    return YES;
}
```

Saving a file in a cloud URL does not explicitly tell iOS that the file has to be placed in cloud storage. We will learn about saving files in cloud storage in Recipe 22.5.

If you run this app on an iPhone that has been set up to back up data and files to an iCloud account, you can go to the Settings app and select the iCloud option in the list. In the iCloud screen, select Storage & Backup. Once in the Storage & Backup screen, under the DOCUMENTS & DATA section, find and select the name of your app, as shown in Figure 22-6.

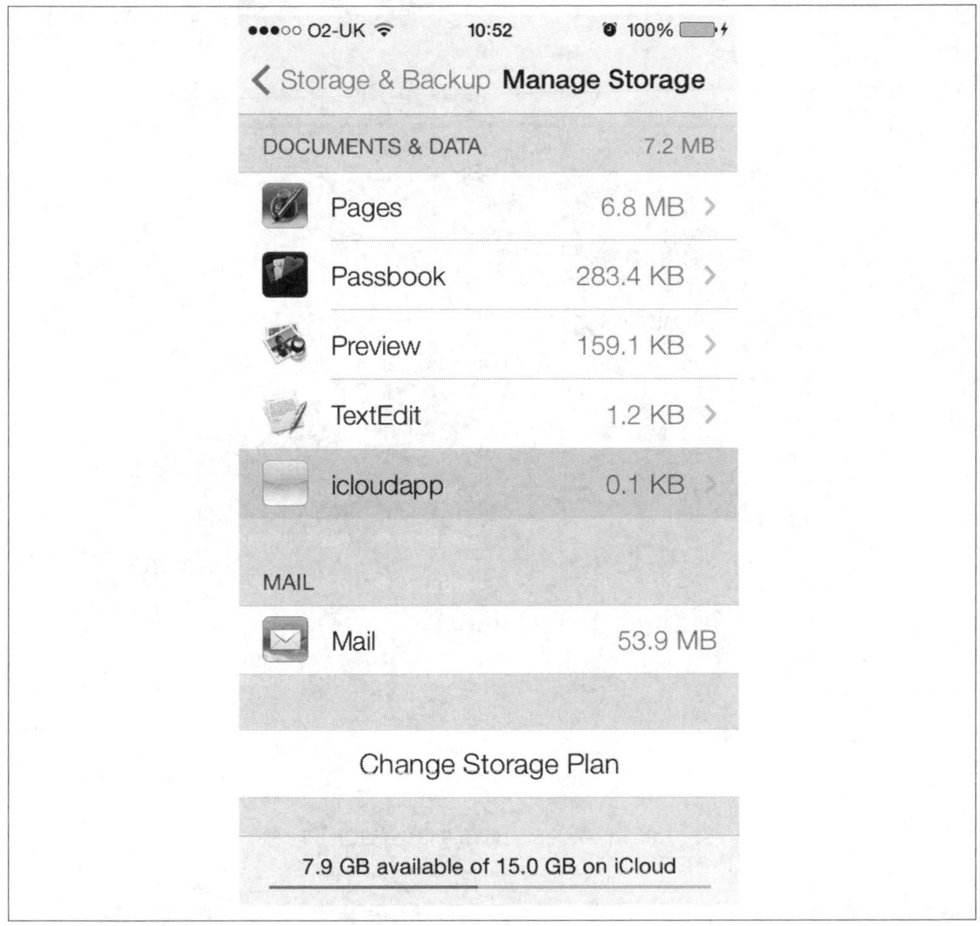


*Figure 22-6. Selecting your app in the list of apps that store data to iCloud*

Now you should be able to see the file that we created earlier in the list, as shown in Figure 22-7.

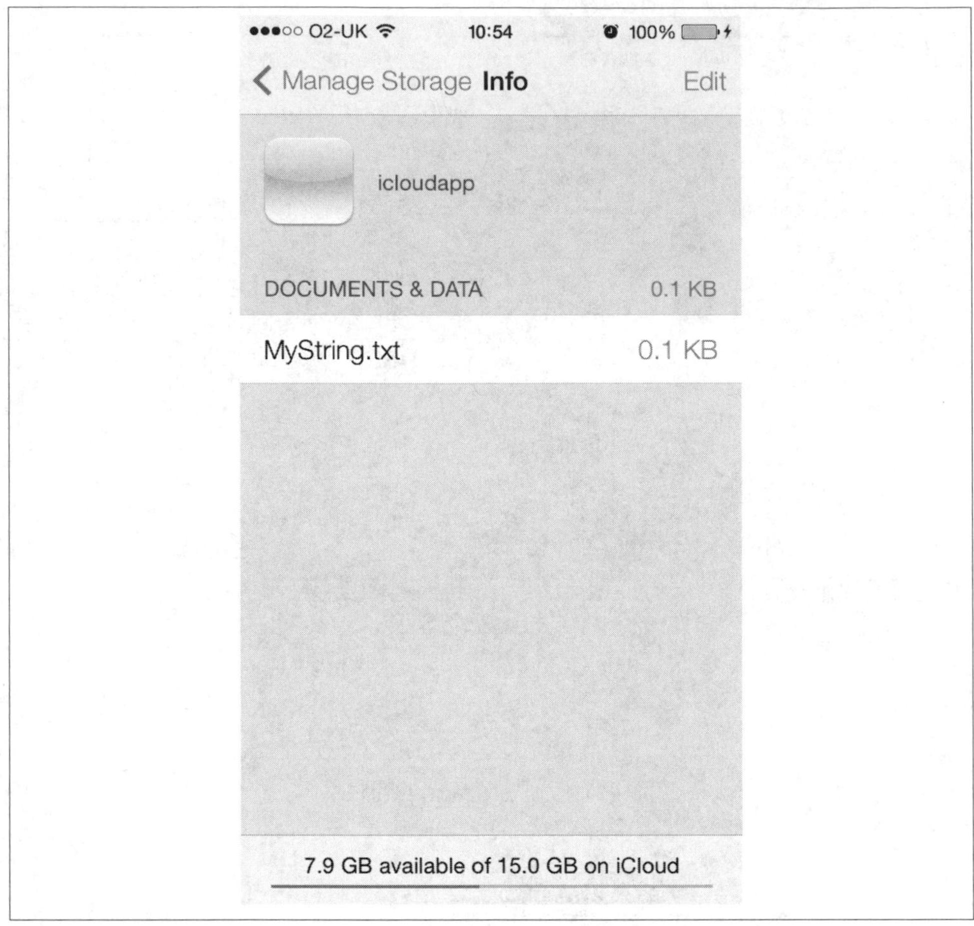


*Figure 22-7. Our file is indeed saved in iCloud*

## See Also

Recipe 22.1; Recipe 22.2; Recipe 22.5

# 22.4. Searching for Files and Folders in iCloud

## Problem

You want to search for files and/or folders inside the current iCloud user's cloud space allocated for your app.

## Solution

Use the `NSMetadataQuery` class.

## Discussion

OS X developers are probably familiar with the `NSMetadataQuery` class. This class allows developers to query Spotlight items, whether they are files or folders. In iOS, we will use this class to search for files and folders in the iCloud space assigned to the app for the current user, if she has set up iCloud for the iOS device on which the app is running.

To set up a metadata query, there are three very important things that we need to do:

1. We need to set the predicate of the metadata query. The predicate is the *search criteria* of the query. This predicate will tell the query what items we are searching for.
2. We also need to set the query's search scope. In order to search in the user's iCloud Documents folder, we set this scope to `NSMetadataQueryUbiquitousDocumentsScope`. Otherwise, you can use the `NSMetadataQueryUbiquitousDataScope`, which represents the Data folder in iCloud, a folder your app can use to store data related to the user-created documents. Remember that the files you store in the user's iCloud should not be your app's temporary files or any other files that your app can retrieve in some other way if those files weren't present in the user's iCloud storage. Things that you store in the user's iCloud storage should be the user's creations.
3. After we start the query, we shall start listening for the `NSMetadataQueryDidFinishGatheringNotification` notification. This notification gets called when the query has finished its search. In the method that handles this notification, we can then look through the results the query gathered for us and determine if any of those files/folders are the ones we're looking for.

The `setPredicate:` instance method of `NSMetadataQuery` class allows us to set the predicate of the query. The predicate must be of type `NSPredicate`. We will use the `predicateWithFormat:` class method of `NSPredicate` class to initialize the predicate. Remember, the predicate will tell the query what to search for. The `predicateWithFormat:` accepts a format string in the following format:

```
QUERY_ITEM COMPARISON_CRITERIA PATTERN
```

The *`QUERY_ITEM`* part of the format of the predicate can be any of the `NSMetadataItem` constant values. For instance, we can use the `NSMetadataItemFSNameKey` constant value to tell the predicate that the search pattern targets the filesystem name of the items in the cloud. Since the format provided to the `predicateWithFormat:` method can be a variable number of arguments, with the first argument dictating the format of the rest of the arguments, you can pass `%K` as the *`QUERY_ITEM`*. For instance, the following two predicates are basically the same in terms of how they will supply an input to the metadata query:

```
NSPredicate *predicate = [NSPredicate predicateWithFormat:@"%K like %@",
                          NSMetadataItemFSNameKey,
                          @"*"];

NSPredicate *samePredicate = [NSPredicate predicateWithFormat:
                              @"NSMetadataItemFSNameKey like %@",
                              @"*"];
```

The *`COMPARISON_CRITERIA`* part of the format of the predicate can be any of the following values:

>
: To indicate that you are searching for query items that are, in value, bigger than your criteria patterns. For instance, you can search in the Documents folder in the iCloud container of an app for all files whose size is bigger than X kilobytes, where X is defined by you.

<
: This comparison criteria is similar to the previous criteria. This criteria looks for items in the iCloud container of an app whose size (as an example) is smaller than the file size that you have specified in the pattern.

*like*
: This comparison criteria is used for searching for filenames and display names of files. You can even use wildcards with this criteria; for instance, looking for all files whose names start with a specific character.

We can go on and on about this, but I suggest we dive into the development piece to get a better understanding of how metadata queries work. For this example, here is what we will do:

1. When the app loads (in the app delegate), we will simply search for *all* files in the app's iCloud container.
2. We will then log the names of all the files that we found to the console, using `NSLog`.
3. At the end of every search, we will create a new file whose name is generated randomly using a random integer. We will then make sure that file doesn't already exist in the iCloud container for the app. If it doesn't, we will save it to the iCloud container. Simple, isn't it? This way, whenever the app opens up, we are creating a new file to the user's iCloud storage.

Storing unnecessary files in users' iCloud storage is a really bad practice. Make sure, as stated before, that you use iCloud only to store files that have been directly created by your user, such as documents or creative images. For this example, since we need to find files/folders in the user's iCloud container to prove that the solution works, we need to at least have something stored in the iCloud container for the app.

Although we are going to learn about storing files in iCloud in Recipe 22.5, for the sake of this recipe, we will use another, easier method to store files into iCloud. We will accomplish this using the `setUbiquitous:itemAtURL:destinationURL:error:` instance method of `NSFileManager`. Here are the parameters that we will pass to this method:

`setUbiquitous`
: This is a Boolean value that you set to `YES` if you want to move a file to iCloud.

`itemAtURL`
: The parameter passed to this method is the `NSURL` pointing to the file in your app's bundle that needs to be moved to iCloud.

`destinationURL`
: This is the URL of where the source file has to be copied in the user's iCloud storage. This URL must be an iCloud URL.

`error`
: A pointer to an `NSError` object that will get set to an error, if one occurs during the process.

So let's go ahead and create an empty application and then define our metadata query property that we will use for searching in the app's iCloud container:

```
#import "AppDelegate.h"

@interface AppDelegate ()
@property (nonatomic, strong) NSMetadataQuery *metadataQuery;
@end

@implementation AppDelegate

<# Rest of your code goes here #>
```

When the app delegate is started, we shall start the query and search for all files in the Documents directory of the app's iCloud container:

```
- (BOOL)            application:(UIApplication *)application
  didFinishLaunchingWithOptions:(NSDictionary *)launchOptions{

    /* Listen for a notification that gets fired when the metadata query
     has finished finding the items we were looking for */
```

```
    [[NSNotificationCenter defaultCenter]
     addObserver:self
     selector:@selector(handleMetadataQueryFinished:)
     name:NSMetadataQueryDidFinishGatheringNotification
     object:nil];

    /* Create our query now */
    self.metadataQuery = [[NSMetadataQuery alloc] init];
    NSArray *searchScopes = [[NSArray alloc] initWithObjects:
                             NSMetadataQueryUbiquitousDocumentsScope, nil];
    [self.metadataQuery setSearchScopes:searchScopes];
    NSPredicate *predicate = [NSPredicate predicateWithFormat:
                              @"%K like %@",
                              NSMetadataItemFSNameKey,
                              @"*"];
    [self.metadataQuery setPredicate:predicate];
    if ([self.metadataQuery startQuery]){
        NSLog(@"Successfully started the query.");
    } else {
        NSLog(@"Failed to start the query.");
    }

    self.window = [[UIWindow alloc]
                   initWithFrame:[[UIScreen mainScreen] bounds]];
    self.window.backgroundColor = [UIColor whiteColor];
    [self.window makeKeyAndVisible];
    return YES;
}
```

In this code, we have elected the `handleMetadataQueryFinished:` instance method of the app delegate (yet to be implemented) as the method that the query will call whenever it has finished searching inside the Documents folder of the app's iCloud container. Let's go and implement this method. What we want to do in this method is to look for all the files that the metadata query found (if any), and then list them by printing them out to the console. After this, we will create a new random file and place it in the app's iCloud container. Here are the steps that we have to take in order to achieve this:

1. Generate a URL for a new random file in the app's iCloud container. For this, we first need to find the app's iCloud container URL.
2. If the URL for this new random file already exists in the results returned by the metadata query, we will ignore the whole operation.
3. If a file with the exact same name as the new random file has *not* been created in the Documents directory of the app's iCloud container, we will save a file with the same name to the app's Documents directory in the app's sandbox on the device.
4. After the file has been created in the app's sandbox, we will set it to ubiquitous, where the file will be moved to iCloud and will automatically be deleted from the app's sandbox.

As described before, we are going to have to store a file into the app's Documents folder, on the app's sandbox, and in iCloud. Therefore, we need to have some methods that give us these URLs. First we will start with a method that will return the URL for the app's Documents folder in iCloud:

```
- (NSURL *) urlForDocumentsFolderIniCloud{

    NSURL *result = nil;

    NSString *teamID = <# Put your team ID here #>;

    NSString *containerID = [[NSBundle mainBundle] bundleIdentifier];

    NSString *teamIDAndContainerID = [[NSString alloc] initWithFormat:@"%@.%@",
                                      teamID, containerID];

    NSFileManager *fileManager = [[NSFileManager alloc] init];

    NSURL *appiCloudContainerURL =
    [fileManager URLForUbiquityContainerIdentifier:teamIDAndContainerID];

    result = [appiCloudContainerURL URLByAppendingPathComponent:@"Documents"
                                                    isDirectory:YES];

    if ([fileManager fileExistsAtPath:[result path]] == NO){

        /* The Documents directory does NOT exist in our app's iCloud
         container; attempt to create it now */

        NSError *creationError = nil;
        BOOL created = [fileManager createDirectoryAtURL:result
                             withIntermediateDirectories:YES
                                              attributes:nil
                                                   error:&creationError];

        if (created){
            NSLog(@"Successfully created the Documents folder in iCloud.");
        } else {
            NSLog(@"Failed to create the Documents folder in \
                  iCloud. Error = %@", creationError);
            result = nil;
        }

    } else {
        /* the Documents directory already exists in our app's
         iCloud container; we don't have to do anything */
    }

    return result;

}
```

Now we will use this method to determine the URL of the random file in the Documents folder in the iCloud container for the app:

```
- (NSURL *) urlForRandomFileInDocumentsFolderInIcloud{

    NSURL *result = nil;

    NSUInteger randomNumber = arc4random() % NSUIntegerMax;

    NSString *randomFileName = [[NSString alloc] initWithFormat:@"%lu.txt",
                                (unsigned long)randomNumber];

    /* Check in the metadata query if this file already exists */
    __block BOOL fileExistsAlready = NO;
    [self.metadataQuery.results enumerateObjectsUsingBlock:
     ^(NSMetadataItem *item, NSUInteger idx, BOOL *stop) {
         NSString *itemFileName =
            [item valueForAttribute:NSMetadataItemFSNameKey];
         if ([itemFileName isEqualToString:randomFileName]){
             NSLog(@"This file already exists. Aborting...");
             fileExistsAlready = YES;
             *stop = YES;
         }
     }];

    if (fileExistsAlready){
        return nil;
    }

    result = [[self urlForDocumentsFolderIniCloud]
              URLByAppendingPathComponent:randomFileName];

    return result;

}
```

Now that we have the URL for the random file (yet to be created) in iCloud, we also need to write a method that we can use to get the URL for the same file in the app bundle. Since we created this random filename in the `urlForRandomFileInDocumentsFolderIniCloud` method, the new method won't know about this name, and thus we need to pass the filename to the method as a parameter:

```
- (NSURL *) urlForRandomFileInDocumentsFolderForFileWithName
          :(NSString *)paramFileName{

    NSFileManager *fileManager = [[NSFileManager alloc] init];
    NSURL *documentsUrl = [fileManager URLForDirectory:NSDocumentDirectory
                                              inDomain:NSUserDomainMask
                                     appropriateForURL:Nil
                                                create:YES
                                                 error:nil];
```

```
    return [documentsUrl URLByAppendingPathComponent:paramFileName];

}
```

Next, we have to implement a method that we will soon use to enumerate through the metadata items returned by the metadata query:

```
- (void) enumerateMetadataResults:(NSArray *)paramResults{

    [paramResults enumerateObjectsUsingBlock:
     ^(NSMetadataItem *item, NSUInteger index, BOOL *stop) {

         NSString *itemName = [item valueForAttribute:NSMetadataItemFSNameKey];
         NSURL *itemURL = [item valueForAttribute:NSMetadataItemURLKey];
         NSNumber *itemSize = [item valueForAttribute:NSMetadataItemFSSizeKey];

         NSLog(@"Item name = %@", itemName);
         NSLog(@"Item URL = %@", itemURL);
         NSLog(@"Item Size = %llu",
               (unsigned long long)[itemSize unsignedLongLongValue]);

     }];

}
```

Last but not least, we will implement the `handleMetadataQueryFinished:` method, which will get called by the notification center when the metadata query finishes searching for the query:

```
- (void) handleMetadataQueryFinished:(id)paramSender{

    NSLog(@"Search finished");

    if ([[paramSender object] isEqual:self.metadataQuery] == NO){
        NSLog(@"An unknown object called this method. Not safe to proceed.");
        return;
    }

    /* Stop listening for notifications as we are not expecting
     anything more */
    [[NSNotificationCenter defaultCenter] removeObserver:self];

    /* We are done with the query, let's stop the process now */
    [self.metadataQuery disableUpdates];
    [self.metadataQuery stopQuery];

    [self enumerateMetadataResults:self.metadataQuery.results];

    if ([self.metadataQuery.results count] == 0){
        NSLog(@"No files were found.");
    }

    NSURL *urlForFileIniCloud =
```

```
[self urlForRandomFileInDocumentsFolderInIcloud];

if (urlForFileIniCloud == nil){
    NSLog(@"Cannot create a file with this URL. URL is empty.");
    return;
}

NSString *fileName = [[[urlForFileIniCloud path]
                        componentsSeparatedByString:@"/"] lastObject];

NSURL *urlForFileInAppSandbox =
[self urlForRandomFileInDocumentsFolderForFileWithName:fileName];

NSString *fileContent =
[[NSString alloc] initWithFormat:@"Content of %@",
 [[self urlForRandomFileInDocumentsFolderInIcloud] path]];

/* Save the file temporarily in the app bundle and then move
 it to the cloud */
NSError *writingError = nil;
BOOL couldWriteToAppSandbox =
[fileContent writeToFile:[urlForFileInAppSandbox path]
              atomically:YES
                encoding:NSUTF8StringEncoding
                   error:&writingError];

/* If cannot save the file, just return from method because it
 won't make any sense to continue as we, ideally, should have
 stored the file in iCloud from the app sandbox but here, if an
 error has occurred, we cannot continue */
if (couldWriteToAppSandbox == NO){
    NSLog(@"Failed to save the file to app sandbox. Error = %@",
          writingError);
    return;
}

NSFileManager *fileManager = [[NSFileManager alloc] init];

/* Now move the file to the cloud */
NSError *ubiquitousError = nil;
BOOL setUbiquitousSucceeded =
[fileManager setUbiquitous:YES
                 itemAtURL:urlForFileInAppSandbox
            destinationURL:urlForFileIniCloud
                     error:&ubiquitousError];

if (setUbiquitousSucceeded){
    NSLog(@"Successfully moved the file to iCloud.");
    /* The file has been moved from App Sandbox to iCloud */
} else {
    NSLog(@"Failed to move the file to iCloud with error = %@",
          ubiquitousError);
```

```
        }

    }
```

You can now go ahead and run the app and see for yourself. Once you open and close the app a few times, you will be able to see something similar to Figure 22-8 in the Settings app on your iOS device.

Our app creates a new file only when the metadata query finishes. The metadata query gets fired when our app delegate is started by iOS. Therefore, if you simply open the app and press the Home button on your iOS device, and then open the app again, the app might not create a new file since the app was simply sent to the background instead of being terminated and reopened. To make sure the app creates a new file every time you open it, before opening the app, close it manually from the apps bar in iOS by double-pressing the Home button and closing the app from the list of running apps.

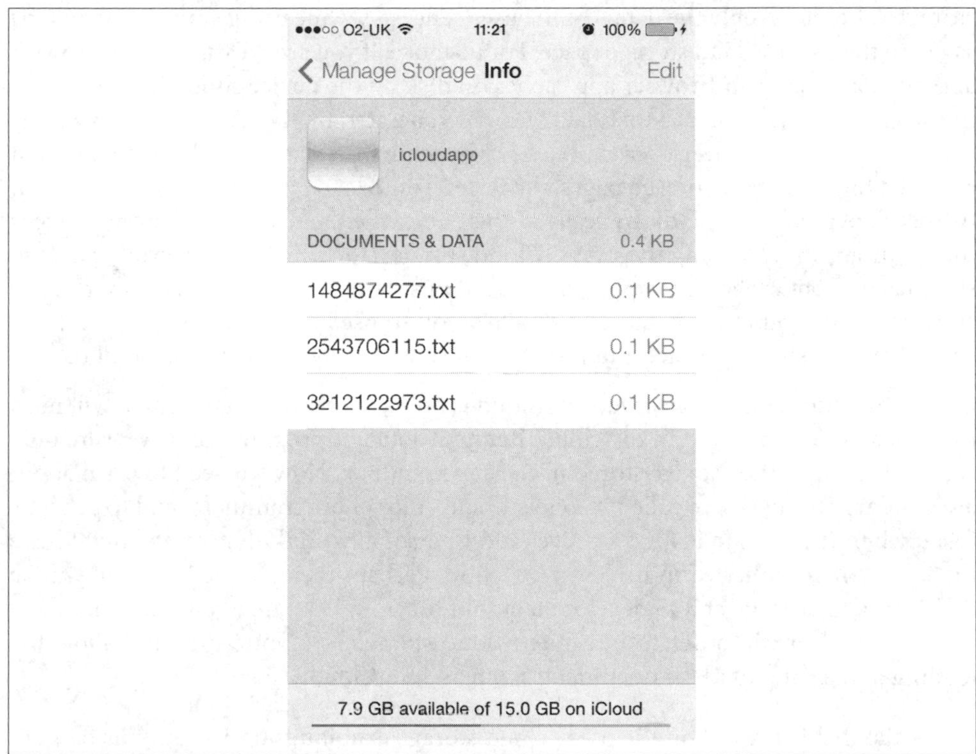


*Figure 22-8. The list of random files that the app has created in iCloud*

## See Also

Recipe 22.5

## 22.5. Storing User Documents in iCloud

### Problem

You want to allow your users to create documents in your app, and you want to have those documents present on all devices that the user owns.

### Solution

Use `UIDocument`.

### Discussion

Although a user can have many files of different types stored on her device by different apps, each app has to be considerate of the amount of data that it puts in the user's iCloud storage. Therefore, only the data that the user generates while using your app should be saved to the user's iCloud storage space. For instance, if you are creating a web-browser app, the data that your browser app caches on disk on the device should not be stored in the cloud. Why? Because that data was not generated by the user. Your app simply was trying to give a better user experience by caching the data so that the next time it accessed the same series of web pages, the pages would load faster. If you look at it from the user's perspective, she didn't really ask you to cache the data. What's even worse is that your app is now using the user's iCloud storage (for which she probably paid) to store cached data. That is simply wrong. You must tell the user what data your app is storing in the cloud, and if she doesn't allow you to use her cloud storage space, you should avoid using that space and just store the data locally in your app's sandbox.

One of the most confusing aspects of iCloud is how you, as the programmer, will need to manage the data stored in the cloud. Before iCloud, as programmers, we were only concerned about the data we stored in the app's sandbox. Now we need to learn about a secondary storage space called iCloud storage. A lot of programmers tend to get confused when it comes to iCloud storage, and I personally think that Apple might have made it a bit complicated in its documentation. Perhaps this is something that will be solved at a later stage of iOS development, but for now, here are a few key points you will need to learn in order to integrate iCloud storage into your apps and allow the loading and saving of users' documents from and to iCloud:

1. A file that is present on the user's cloud storage is ubiquitous. Ubiquitous files are files that are stored outside an app's sandbox. We will talk about these more, but for now, remember that a ubiquitous file is a file that is no longer present in the app's sandbox, but rather in the cloud.
2. We have to subclass the `UIDocument` class in order to manage users' documents. Each document will be given a ubiquitous URL to load its contents from. In the

subclass, all we really have to do is implement two very important methods that will allow iOS to pass data to us (when iOS reads the data from iCloud) and for us to be able to pass data to iOS to store on iCloud.

3. Your ubiquitous files do *not* necessarily have to be in your app sandbox. If you want to store a file in iCloud, you will simply retrieve a direct URL to the iCloud folder (more on this later) and place your files there.
4. Before you go and create files in the user's iCloud storage, you must first query the iCloud storage to see if that file already exists or not.
5. Each app has an identifier; iCloud uses that identifier to separate the iCloud files for that app from files from other apps present on users' iOS devices. If you use the same app identifier across multiple apps, all those apps will be able to share one another's iCloud storage space. This can be good if you are developing a "lite" version of your app and you want the full version to be able to access the iCloud storage of the "lite" version of your app and vice versa.
6. You can search for files in your app's iCloud storage for the current user, using the `NSMetadataQuery` class (refer to Recipe 22.4 for more information).

In this recipe, we would like to write an app that simply creates a document for the user (text file) and allows him to edit that document. In the background, we will save that document to iCloud so that if he has another iOS device set up with the same iCloud credentials (username and password), he can see the most up-to-date version of the file, regardless of which iOS device he is editing it on. Here is the checklist for this app:

1. We need to set up the appropriate provision profiles for the app, as well as entitlements (see Recipe 22.1 for more information).
2. Now we have to give the document a name (for now, let's call the document file *UserDocument.txt*).
3. When the app opens (whether it is for the first time or not), we will fire up a metadata query and try to find the file in the user's iCloud storage. If that file already exists, we will retrieve its URL. If that file doesn't exist, we will create an empty/dummy file in that URL.
4. Now that we have the URL for the document file in the user's iCloud storage, we will open that document into the instance of the subclass of `UIDocument`. We will learn about this in a minute.

Something that can confuse any programmer is using the `UIDocument` class—but to be perfectly honest, if you want to start with the basics, there are only four things you need to learn about this class:

1. You must always subclass this class. This class itself doesn't know how to load its contents or how to pass its contents as data to iOS to store in the cloud.

2. You must initialize this class with the URL of a file. In this recipe, we will pass the URL of a file in the user's cloud storage to the designated initializer of this class.
3. In your subclass, you must override the `contentsForType:error:` instance method of `UIDocument`. The return value of this method can be an `NSData` snapshot of the document you are managing. For instance, if it is a text file whose URL you passed to the initializer of your document class, then you must simply convert that text (presumably in the form of `NSString`) to `NSData` and return that data as the return value of this method. iOS calls this method in your document whenever it needs to store that data to the cloud or needs to read that content to present it to the user.
4. You must override the `loadFromContents:ofType:error:` instance method of your `UIDocument` subclass. In this method, iOS passes you the data (that perhaps was read from the cloud storage), and you must read that data into text (if text is what your document manages).

So, assuming that we have already set up the app with iCloud (see Recipe 22.1), we will go ahead and start subclassing `UIDocument`. In this recipe, we want to create a Documents folder in the user's iCloud storage for the app (if this folder doesn't exist yet). We will then read from/store a file named *UserDocument.txt* in this folder. Follow these steps to subclass the `UIDocument` class:

1. In Xcode, select File → New → New File... from the menus.
2. In the New File dialog, make sure the Cocoa Touch subcategory of the iOS category is selected on the lefthand side. Then select the Objective-C class item on the right-hand side of the dialog and press the Next button (see Figure 22-9).
3. On the next screen, name your new class `CloudDocument` and make sure you are subclassing `UIDocument`, as shown in Figure 22-10. Once you are done, press the Next button.
4. In the next dialog, select where you wish to save the new class and press the Create button.

Now that we have the `UIDocument` subclass, we need to see how we can initialize it. The designated initializer of `UIDocument` class is the `initWithFileURL:` method. However, we need to change this a bit, as we are going to need a delegate object as well. Why do we need a delegate object? you might be asking. We want to let the delegate object know whenever iOS downloads a newer version of the document from iCloud. Imagine this scenario: the user has two iOS devices running your app, and she has already set up those devices with her iCloud credentials. Now she opens your app on her iPhone and starts writing some text into the text view. She leaves the app and goes to run some errands. She comes back and picks up her *iPad* (as opposed to her iPhone, which she originally used to write content in the app), and sees that the app picked up the latest version of the document and shows that content. Remember that the app is still present

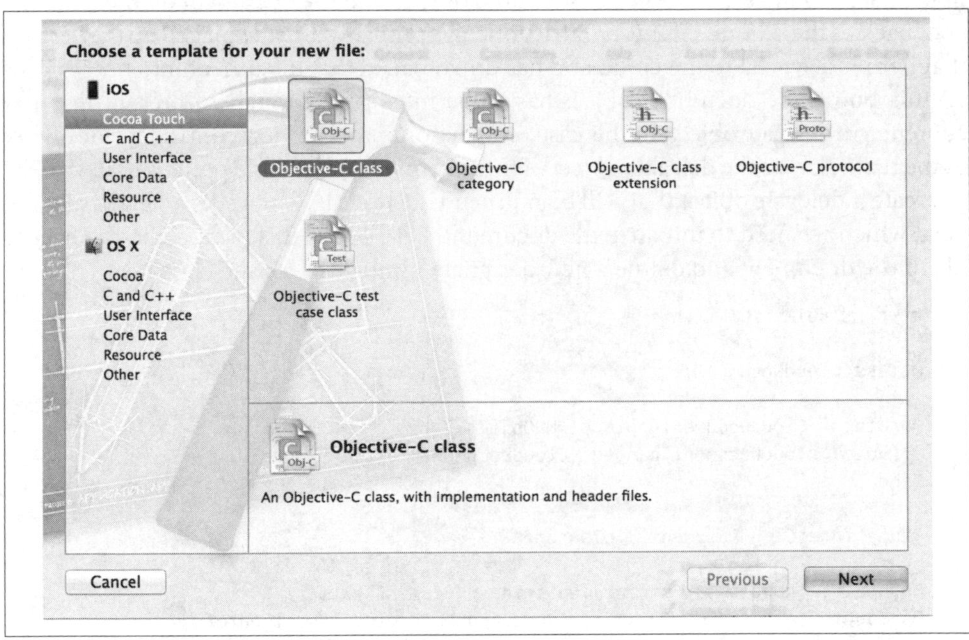


*Figure 22-9. Beginning to create a new document class*

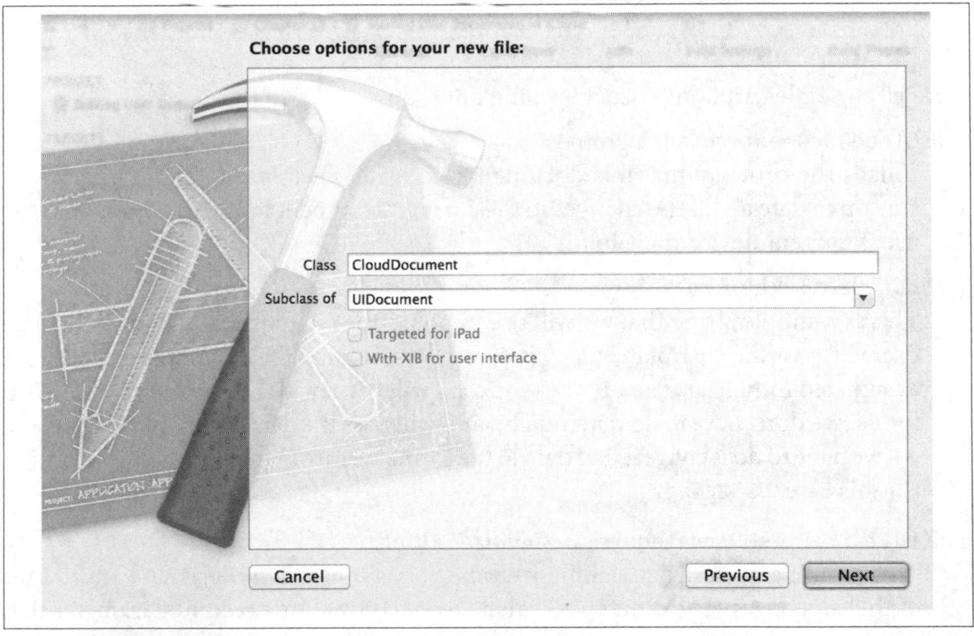


*Figure 22-10. Subclassing UIDocument*

in the background on her iPhone. She adds some text to the document on the iPad and goes back to the iPhone. At this point, iCloud has probably already picked up the version that her iPad synced to the cloud and has downloaded that document into her iPhone. At this point, the document object has to be intelligent enough to present the new content to a delegate object. In this case, we can nominate the view controller (the owner of the text view) as the delegate object of the document. The whole point is that we need to create a delegate object that will be notified whenever iCloud gives a new version of data, which we need to initialize the document. Let's define this protocol in the header file of the document and define a new designated initializer for the class:

```
#import <UIKit/UIKit.h>

@class CloudDocument;

@protocol CloudDocumentProtocol<NSObject>
- (void) cloudDocumentChanged:(CloudDocument *)paramSender;
@end

@interface CloudDocument : UIDocument

@property (nonatomic, strong) NSString *documentText;
@property (nonatomic, weak) id<CloudDocumentProtocol> delegate;

/* Designated Initializer */
- (id) initWithFileURL:(NSURL *)paramURL
              delegate:(id<CloudDocumentProtocol>)paramDelegate;

@end
```

Here is a brief description of what is going on in this header file:

*The* `CloudDocumentProtocol` *protocol*
: This is the protocol that this document's delegate object has to adapt in order to stay up to date about the changes to the current document that are brought into the user's current device via iCloud.

*The* `documentText` *string*
: This is a simple string that we will use to house the content of the document. The user will pass the URL of the file that we need to initialize the document to the class's designated initializer. The `UIDocument` class will then read the contents of that URL for us (we don't have to do it manually) and will pass the data of that file to the class. All we have to do is convert that data to the format we are managing in the document (in this case, `NSString`).

*The* `initWithFileURL:delegate:` *designated initializer*
: This is the class's designated initializer, and very similar to the designated initializer of the superclass. The difference is that we are asking for a second parameter that will be the delegate of an instance of the class. We will keep the delegate object

updated whenever new content is downloaded by iOS from iCloud for the document we are managing.

We will follow that with the implementation of the class's designated initializer:

```
#import "CloudDocument.h"

@implementation CloudDocument

- (id) initWithFileURL:(NSURL *)paramURL
              delegate:(id<CloudDocumentProtocol>)paramDelegate{

    self = [super initWithFileURL:paramURL];

    if (self != nil){

        if (paramDelegate == nil){
            NSLog(@"Warning: no delegate is given.");
        }

        _delegate = paramDelegate;
    }

    return self;

}

- (id) initWithFileURL:(NSURL *)paramURL{
    return [self initWithFileURL:paramURL
                        delegate:nil];
}
```

As described before, we shall now implement the `contentsForType:error:` instance method of the class. This method gets called whenever iOS decides to read the contents of the document that the instance of the class is managing. For instance, iOS might ask the instance to say what contents it is managing so that iOS can store that content on iCloud. In this method, we will simply convert the string to an instance of `NSData` and return it:

```
- (id) contentsForType:(NSString *)typeName
                 error:(NSError *__autoreleasing *)outError{

    if ([self.documentText length] == 0){
        self.documentText = @"New Document";
    }

    return [self.documentText dataUsingEncoding:NSUTF8StringEncoding];
}
```

We are setting a default text for the document if the text that we are managing at the moment is empty, so that when the user first creates a new document (our app creates the document for the user), the text won't be empty and the user at least sees something on the screen.

Moving on to the implementation of the `loadFromContents:ofType:error:` instance method of the document class now, we shall simply read the content that is passed to us as the first parameter of this method and turn it into the text that the document instance is managing. This method gets called when iOS reads the contents of the URL with which the instance of the class gets initialized. So we will take the data and turn it into a string in this example. In addition to that, we also let the delegate object know (if one is set) that the text the instance is managing has changed:

```
- (BOOL) loadFromContents:(id)contents
                   ofType:(NSString *)typeName
                    error:(NSError *__autoreleasing *)outError{

    NSData *data = (NSData *)contents;

    if ([data length] == 0){
        self.documentText = @"New Document";
    } else {
        self.documentText = [[NSString alloc]
                             initWithData:data
                             encoding:NSUTF8StringEncoding];
    }

    if ([_delegate respondsToSelector:@selector(cloudDocumentChanged:)]){
        [_delegate cloudDocumentChanged:self];
    }

    return YES;

}
```

In this method, we will notify the delegate object that the contents of the document have changed, to give the delegate object a chance to update things, such as the UI.

That was really all we had to implement in the document class. The rest of the heavy lifting has to happen in the view controller. The first thing that we need to do in the view controller is to find the iCloud path of the *UserDocument.txt* file we are creating for the user. For this, as we learned in Recipe 22.3, we will use the `URLForUbiquityContainerIdentifier:` instance method of `NSFileManager`. Also, as we learned in Recipe 22.3, we will create a Documents directory in the app's root iCloud directory if one doesn't exist. Let's begin with a method that returns the URL for the Documents directory in iCloud for the app and creates the directory if it doesn't exist already:

```
- (NSURL *) urlForDocumentsDirectoryInIcloud{

    NSURL *result = nil;

    NSString *teamID = @"F3FU372W5M";

    NSString *containerID = [[NSBundle mainBundle] bundleIdentifier];

    NSString *teamIdAndContainerId = [NSString stringWithFormat:@"%@.%@",
                                      teamID,
                                      containerID];

    NSFileManager *fileManager = [[NSFileManager alloc] init];

    NSURL *iCloudURL = [fileManager
                        URLForUbiquityContainerIdentifier:teamIdAndContainerId];

    NSURL *documentsFolderURLIniCloud =
    [iCloudURL URLByAppendingPathComponent:@"Documents"
                               isDirectory:YES];

    /* If it doesn't exist, create it */
    if ([fileManager
         fileExistsAtPath:[documentsFolderURLIniCloud path]] == NO){
        NSLog(@"The documents folder does NOT exist in iCloud. Creating...");
        NSError *folderCreationError = nil;

        BOOL created = [fileManager
                        createDirectoryAtURL:documentsFolderURLIniCloud
                        withIntermediateDirectories:YES
                        attributes:nil
                        error:&folderCreationError];

        if (created){
            NSLog(@"Successfully created the Documents folder in iCloud.");
            result = documentsFolderURLIniCloud;
        } else {
            NSLog(@"Failed to create the Documents folder in iCloud. \
                  Error = %@", folderCreationError);
        }
    } else {
        NSLog(@"The Documents folder already exists in iCloud.");
        result = documentsFolderURLIniCloud;
    }

    return result;

}
```

We will use the URL returned by the `urlForDocumentsDirectoryInIcloud` method to create the URL for the *UserDocument.txt* that the app wants to create/edit/manage:

```
- (NSURL *) urlForFileInDocumentsDirectoryIniCloud{

    return [[self urlForDocumentsDirectoryInIcloud]
            URLByAppendingPathComponent:@"UserDocument.txt"];

}
```

Now let's go to the declaration of our view controller and define the appropriate instance variables. We need:

1. An instance of the `CloudDocument` class that will manage the document in the cloud.
2. An instance of the `UITextView` class that we will use to allow the user to enter his text, which we will sync to iCloud as he types.
3. An instance of the `NSMetadataQuery` class that we will use to find the existing document in the cloud, if one exists.

```
#import "ViewController.h"
#import "CloudDocument.h"

@interface ViewController () <CloudDocumentProtocol, UITextViewDelegate>
@property (nonatomic, strong) CloudDocument *cloudDocument;
@property (nonatomic, strong) UITextView *textViewCloudDocumentText;
@property (nonatomic, strong) NSMetadataQuery *metadataQuery;
@end

@implementation ViewController

<# Rest of your view controller's code goes here #>
```

Now that we have the text view declared, let's instantiate it:

```
- (void) setupTextView{
    /* Create the text view */

    CGRect textViewRect = CGRectMake(20.0f,
                                     20.0f,
                                     self.view.bounds.size.width - 40.0f,
                                     self.view.bounds.size.height - 40.0f);

    self.textViewCloudDocumentText = [[UITextView alloc] initWithFrame:
                                      textViewRect];

    self.textViewCloudDocumentText.delegate = self;
    self.textViewCloudDocumentText.font = [UIFont systemFontOfSize:20.0f];
    [self.view addSubview:self.textViewCloudDocumentText];
}
```

We will be using this method in the viewDidLoad method of the view controller, which will be discussed soon. Now let's start implementing a method that will allow the view controller to react to keyboard notifications. As was discussed in Recipe 17.3, when the user starts to change the text in the text view, the keyboard will pop up (if a Bluetooth keyboard isn't set up) and the keyboard will cover almost half of the iPhone screen. So in this case, we need to change the content inset of the text view. We start by listening to keyboard notifications:

```
- (void) listenForKeyboardNotifications{

    /* As we have a text view, when the keyboard shows on screen, we want to
     make sure our textview's content is fully visible so start
     listening for keyboard notifications */
    [[NSNotificationCenter defaultCenter]
     addObserver:self
     selector:@selector(handleKeyboardWillShow:)
     name:UIKeyboardWillShowNotification
     object:nil];

    [[NSNotificationCenter defaultCenter]
     addObserver:self
     selector:@selector(handleKeyboardWillHide:)
     name:UIKeyboardWillHideNotification
     object:nil];
}
```

The next thing to take care of is to search for existing user documents when the view controller's view is loaded (in the viewDidLoad method). If a document exists in the cloud, then we will load that; if not, we will create a new document:

```
- (void) startSearchingForDocumentIniCloud{
    /* Start searching for existing text documents */
    self.metadataQuery = [[NSMetadataQuery alloc] init];

    NSPredicate *predicate = [NSPredicate predicateWithFormat:@"%K like %@",
                              NSMetadataItemFSNameKey,
                              @"*"];

    [self.metadataQuery setPredicate:predicate];
    NSArray *searchScopes = [[NSArray alloc] initWithObjects:
                             NSMetadataQueryUbiquitousDocumentsScope,
                             nil];
    [self.metadataQuery setSearchScopes:searchScopes];

    NSString *metadataNotification =
    NSMetadataQueryDidFinishGatheringNotification;

    [[NSNotificationCenter defaultCenter]
     addObserver:self
     selector:@selector(handleMetadataQueryFinished:)
     name:metadataNotification
```

```
         object:nil];

     [self.metadataQuery startQuery];
}
```

Let's utilize all these methods in the view controller:

```
- (void)viewDidLoad{
    [super viewDidLoad];
    [self listenForKeyboardNotifications];
    self.view.backgroundColor = [UIColor brownColor];
    [self setupTextView];
    [self startSearchingForDocumentIniCloud];
}
```

In the `startSearchingForDocumentIniCloud` method, we started listening for `NSMetadataQueryDidFinishGatheringNotification` notifications on the `handleMetadataQueryFinished:` method. We need to have a look at the implementation of this method. The way we have to implement this method is to first find out if the metadata query could find any existing iCloud documents. If yes, then we will look for the specific document that the app creates for the user, which is called *UserDocument.txt*. If this file is found in the user's cloud space, then we will open that document. If not, we will create it:

```
- (void) handleMetadataQueryFinished:(NSNotification *)paramNotification{

    /* Make sure this is the metadata query that we were expecting... */
    NSMetadataQuery *senderQuery = (NSMetadataQuery *)[paramNotification object];

    if ([senderQuery isEqual:self.metadataQuery] == NO){
        NSLog(@"Unknown metadata query sent us a message.");
        return;
    }

    [self.metadataQuery disableUpdates];

    /* Now we stop listening for these notifications because we don't really
     have to, any more */
    NSString *metadataNotification =
    NSMetadataQueryDidFinishGatheringNotification;

    [[NSNotificationCenter defaultCenter] removeObserver:self
                                                    name:metadataNotification
                                                  object:nil];
    [self.metadataQuery stopQuery];

    NSLog(@"Metadata query finished.");


    /* Let's find out if we had previously created this document in the user's
     cloud space because if yes, then we have to avoid overwriting that
     document and just use the existing one */
```

```
__block BOOL documentExistsIniCloud = NO;
NSString *FileNameToLookFor = @"UserDocument.txt";

NSArray *results = self.metadataQuery.results;

[results
 enumerateObjectsUsingBlock:^(id obj, NSUInteger idx, BOOL *stop) {
     NSMetadataItem *item = (NSMetadataItem *)obj;
     NSURL *itemURL = [item valueForAttribute:NSMetadataItemURLKey];
     NSString *lastComponent = [[itemURL pathComponents] lastObject];
     if ([lastComponent isEqualToString:FileNameToLookFor]){
         if ([itemURL
              isEqual:[self urlForFileInDocumentsDirectoryIniCloud]]){
             documentExistsIniCloud = YES;
             *stop = YES;
         }
     }
 }];

NSURL *urlOfDocument = [self urlForFileInDocumentsDirectoryIniCloud];
self.cloudDocument = [[CloudDocument alloc] initWithFileURL:urlOfDocument
                                                   delegate:self];

__weak ViewController *weakSelf = self;

/* If the document exists, open it */
if (documentExistsIniCloud){
    NSLog(@"Document already exists in iCloud. Loading it from there...");
    [self.cloudDocument openWithCompletionHandler:^(BOOL success) {
        if (success){
            ViewController *strongSelf = weakSelf;
            NSLog(@"Successfully loaded the document from iCloud.");
            strongSelf.textViewCloudDocumentText.text =
            strongSelf.cloudDocument.documentText;
        } else {
            NSLog(@"Failed to load the document from iCloud.");
        }
    }];

} else {
    NSLog(@"Document does not exist in iCloud. Creating it...");

    /* If the document doesn't exist, ask the CloudDocument class to
     save a new file on that address for us */
    [self.cloudDocument
     saveToURL:[self urlForFileInDocumentsDirectoryIniCloud]
     forSaveOperation:UIDocumentSaveForCreating
     completionHandler:^(BOOL success) {
         if (success){
             NSLog(@"Successfully created the new file in iCloud.");
             ViewController *strongSelf = weakSelf;
```

```
                strongSelf.textViewCloudDocumentText.text =
                strongSelf.cloudDocument.documentText;

            } else {
                NSLog(@"Failed to create the file.");
            }
        }];

    }

}
```

What is left now is to listen for changes in the text view—once the changes have been applied by the user, we will try to save them into the document. We do this by implementing the `textViewDidChange:` delegate method of the `UITextViewDelegate` protocol:

```
- (void) textViewDidChange:(UITextView *)textView{
    self.cloudDocument.documentText = textView.text;
    [self.cloudDocument updateChangeCount:UIDocumentChangeDone];
}
```

With this method, we let the document know that the user has updated the contents of the text in the text view. We call the `updateChangeCount:` instance method of `UIDocument` to get the document to reflect those changes to the cloud. We also have to implement the `cloudDocumentChanged:` delegate method of the `CloudDocumentProtocol` protocol, and change the text inside the text view when the text in the document changes. This method will get called, for instance, when the user opens the app in two devices with the same iCloud credentials changes the document in one device, and leaves the document open in the other device. The second device's iCloud daemon will then retrieve the latest version of the document from the cloud, and the document class will call the `cloudDocumentChanged:` delegate message to give us a chance to update the UI:

```
- (void) cloudDocumentChanged:(CloudDocument *)paramSender{
    self.textViewCloudDocumentText.text = paramSender.documentText;
}
```

Before we forget, we also have to implement the keyboard notification handlers:

```
- (void) handleKeyboardWillShow:(NSNotification *)paramNotification{

    NSDictionary *userInfo = [paramNotification userInfo];

    NSValue *animationDurationObject =
    [userInfo valueForKey:UIKeyboardAnimationDurationUserInfoKey];

    NSValue *keyboardEndRectObject =
    [userInfo valueForKey:UIKeyboardFrameEndUserInfoKey];

    double animationDuration = 0.0;
    CGRect keyboardEndRect = CGRectMake(0.0f, 0.0f, 0.0f, 0.0f);
```

```
    [animationDurationObject getValue:&animationDuration];
    [keyboardEndRectObject getValue:&keyboardEndRect];

    UIWindow *window = [[[UIApplication sharedApplication] delegate] window];

    /* Convert the frame from window's coordinate system to
     our view's coordinate system */
    keyboardEndRect = [self.view convertRect:keyboardEndRect
                                    fromView:window];

    [UIView animateWithDuration:animationDuration animations:^{
        CGRect intersectionOfKeyboardRectAndWindowRect =
        CGRectIntersection(self.view.frame, keyboardEndRect);

        CGFloat bottomInset =
        intersectionOfKeyboardRectAndWindowRect.size.height;

        self.textViewCloudDocumentText.contentInset =
        UIEdgeInsetsMake(0.0f,
                         0.0f,
                         bottomInset,
                         0.0f);
    }];

}

- (void) handleKeyboardWillHide:(NSNotification *)paramNotification{

    if (UIEdgeInsetsEqualToEdgeInsets
        (self.textViewCloudDocumentText.contentInset,
         UIEdgeInsetsZero)){
            /* Our text view's content inset is intact so no need to
             reset it */
            return;
        }

    NSDictionary *userInfo = [paramNotification userInfo];

    NSValue *animationDurationObject =
    [userInfo valueForKey:UIKeyboardAnimationDurationUserInfoKey];

    double animationDuration = 0.0;

    [animationDurationObject getValue:&animationDuration];

    [UIView animateWithDuration:animationDuration animations:^{
        self.textViewCloudDocumentText.contentInset = UIEdgeInsetsZero;
    }];

}
```

Go ahead and run this app on a device. It is actually better if you can run the same app on two iOS devices with the same iCloud credentials, and then update the document on one device and wait for the second device to automatically update its contents from the cloud.

After you execute any iCloud-related command to iOS, the operating system will do the work for you immediately and return the results either synchronously or asynchronously. But that doesn't mean that the updates have really happened then and there. In fact, iOS may batch all those updates that you request of it and perform them at a later time, perhaps even when your app is not running in the foreground. If iCloud operations for your app are pending in this manner when the user attempts to delete your app from her device, she will get an alert from iOS letting her know that if she deletes your app, all pending changes will be discarded (see Figure 22-11).

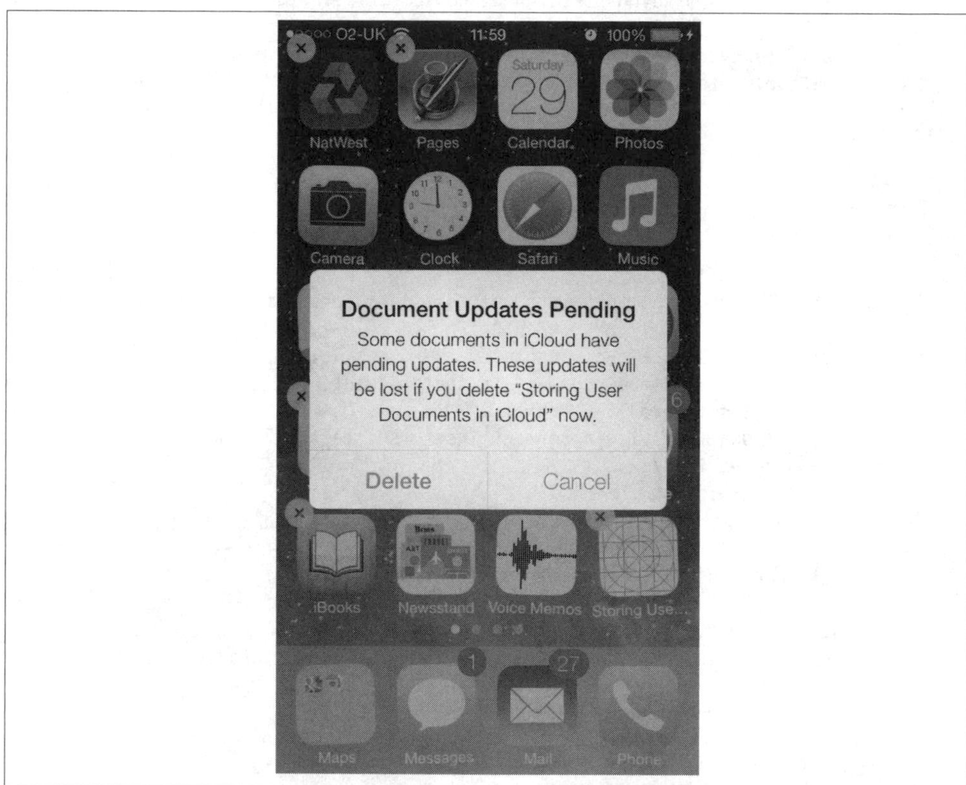


*Figure 22-11. User deleting an app with pending iCloud operations*

In edge cases like this, your user may end up deleting the app and consequently losing the pending changes. But apart from this unusual situation, you can be sure that the commands that you issue to iCloud will be carried out in due time and all these operations will be transparent to you and the user.

### See Also

Recipe 17.3; Recipe 22.1; Recipe 22.3

## 22.6. Managing the State of Documents in iCloud

### Problem

You want to be able to detect conflicts and other issues that could occur as a result of syncing documents to iCloud.

### Solution

Start listening to the `UIDocumentStateChangedNotification` notification.

I highly recommend reading Recipe 22.5 before proceeding with this recipe, as the material described here highly relies on what was taught in that section.

### Discussion

The `UIDocumentStateChangedNotification` notification gets sent when the state of an iCloud document (of type `UIDocument`) is changed. The object carried by this notification is the instance of the `UIDocument` whose state was changed. You can listen to this notification and then analyze the `documentState` property of your iCloud document; this property is of type `UIDocumentState` and can be a mixture of these values:

`UIDocumentStateNormal`
: Things are normal, and no conflicts have occurred in the document.

`UIDocumentStateClosed`
: This means that the document has not yet been opened, or was open and has just been closed. You might want to disallow the user from editing the document while the document is in this state. Apple recommends that you do not display alert views to your users, but instead, perhaps, display graphical components on the screen to indicate to the user that editing has been disabled.

`UIDocumentStateInConflict`
: This state indicates that a conflict has happened in the document. For instance, the same document could had been edited by two or more people at the same time, causing a conflict. In such cases, you will have two options. Either fix the conflict

programmatically for the user or prompt the user to choose which version of that document she wants to keep.

`UIDocumentStateSavingError`
: This document state indicates that an error has occurred in saving the document to iCloud. You *might* want to allow the user to continue editing the document while the document is in this state but there is no guarantee as to whether the user changes will be saved to iCloud or not. Obviously, you might want to implement some smart mechanisms in your apps that will temporarily store the contents of the document in the app bundle while the document is in this state, and reflect those changes to iCloud at a later time. The solution is up to you. Alternatively, you might want to let your users know that an error has happened to the document and that there is a possibility of data loss.

`UIDocumentStateEditingDisabled`
: This state indicates that editing has been disabled on the document because of an error. It is best in this case to disallow the user from editing the document.

As explained before, the `documentState` property of `UIDocument` can be a mixture of the aforementioned values.

To demonstrate how we can take advantage of the `UIDocumentStateChangedNotification` notification, let's build on top of the example code in Recipe 22.5 and change the `viewDidLoad` method of the view controller to subscribe to this notification:

```
- (void) listenForDocumentStateChangesNotification{

    /* Start listening for the Document State Changes notification */
    [[NSNotificationCenter defaultCenter]
     addObserver:self
     selector:@selector(handleDocumentStateChanged:)
     name:UIDocumentStateChangedNotification
     object:nil];

}

- (void)viewDidLoad{
    [super viewDidLoad];

    [self listenForDocumentStateChangesNotification];
    [self listenForKeyboardNotifications];
    self.view.backgroundColor = [UIColor brownColor];
    [self setupTextView];
    [self startSearchingForDocumentIniCloud];
}
```

We have elected the `handleDocumentStateChanged:` method of the view controller to listen for the `UIDocumentStateChangedNotification` notification. Now let's go ahead and implement this method:

```
- (void) handleDocumentStateChanged:(NSNotification *)paramNotification{

    NSLog(@"Document state has changed");
    NSLog(@"Notification Object = %@", [paramNotification object]);

    NSLog(@"Notification Object Class = %@",
          NSStringFromClass([[paramNotification object] class]));

    CloudDocument *senderDocument = (CloudDocument *)paramNotification.object;
    NSLog(@"Document State = %d", senderDocument.documentState);


    /* Since we don't yet know how to solve conflicts, we will disallow
     the user from editing the document if an error of any sort has happened.
     Later when we will learn about handling conflicts, we will handle
     these issues more gracefully */

    if (senderDocument.documentState & UIDocumentStateInConflict){
        NSLog(@"Conflict found in the document.");
        self.textViewCloudDocumentText.editable = NO;
    }
    if (senderDocument.documentState & UIDocumentStateClosed){
        NSLog(@"Document is closed.");
        self.textViewCloudDocumentText.editable = NO;
    }
    if (senderDocument.documentState & UIDocumentStateEditingDisabled){
        NSLog(@"Editing is disabled on this document.");
        self.textViewCloudDocumentText.editable = NO;
    }
    if (senderDocument.documentState & UIDocumentStateNormal){
        NSLog(@"Things are normal. We are good to go.");
        self.textViewCloudDocumentText.editable = YES;
    }
    if (senderDocument.documentState & UIDocumentStateSavingError){
        NSLog(@"A saving error has happened.");
        self.textViewCloudDocumentText.editable = NO;
    }

}
```

As you can see, we are using if statements instead of else-if statements in this example, simply because the state of a cloud document can be more than one of the aforementioned values at the same time. Therefore, we have to be able to handle them in conjunction.

## See Also

Recipe 22.5

# CHAPTER 23
# Pass Kit

## 23.0. Introduction

We're all familiar with coupons and tickets. For instance, you may go to a coffee shop that gives you a loyalty card that offers you a free cup of coffee after you have accumulated some number of stamps for previous coffee purchases. We also use coupons when we shop. You can buy X amount of food and the shop may give you a coupon to spend when you next shop there.

Figure 23-1 depicts what a simple railway ticket (presented as a pass) looks like in Passbook on a real iOS device.

iOS apps can use the Passbook framework to interact with passes as well. Going back to the coffee shop example, the app for this coffee shop may allow him to top up his loyalty card with cash to allow him to take advantage of other cool things that the shop has to offer, such as WiFi access across the country. So, when the user opens the app, it will detect a pass in his Passbook database related to the coffee shop, allow the user to top the pass up right there on his phone, and then contact a barista to say that the pass installed on the device has been topped up with cash.

Pass Kit is how Apple represents this type of transaction digitally. So let's get our terminology right before we dig any deeper:

*Pass Kit*
: The framework Apple provides to developers to allow digitally signed passes to be delivered to compatible iOS devices running iOS 6 or later.

*Passbook*
: The client application on iOS 7 devices able to store, handle, and manage passes created by developers.

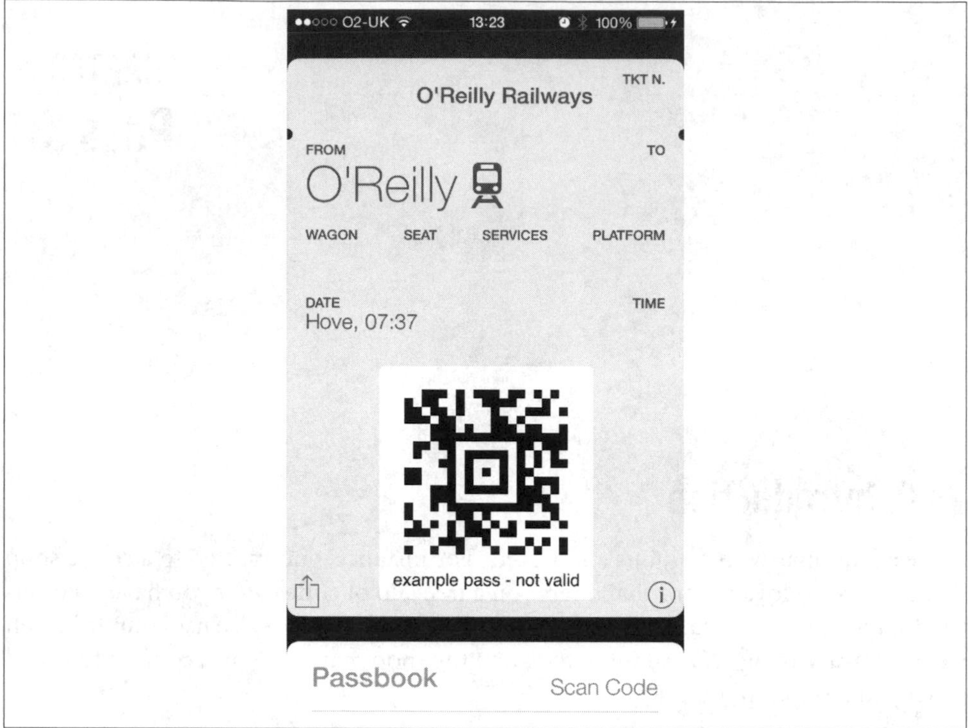


*Figure 23-1. A railway ticket presented as a pass in Passbook on an iOS device*

Therefore, we as developers will be using Pass Kit to create digitally signed passes and deliver them to our users. Our users will use Passbook on their devices to interact with the passes we create for them. Of course, this allows us developers to deliver coupons, rail passes, public transportation tickets, loyalty cards, and so on to our users in the form of digitally signed passes instead of the traditional, paper-based approach where people have to carry multiple cards in their wallets. Passbook on iOS devices is the place where all this content can be stored in a single place, without users having to carry all these passes.

Before attempting to use new technology, you should get a grasp of the big picture: the high-level design of the technology and how it enables us to achieve our goals. For Pass Kit, I have broken this big picture down into small steps so that you can learn how you can use it to deliver digitally signed passes to your users:

1. The developer creates a certificate and its corresponding private key using Apple's Provisioning Portal.
2. The developer then creates a series of files that will represent the pass that the user will be given later.

3. The developer signs the created pass with the certificate that she created at the first step.
4. The developer delivers the pass to the user through various means of delivery.
5. The user will see the pass and will have the opportunity to add that pass to her device.
6. Once the pass is added to the user's device, Passbook will retain it for future use until the user decides to delete the pass.

I know that it can be difficult to understand the big picture simply by reading a few paragraphs of text. Figure 23-2 shows the sequence in more detail.

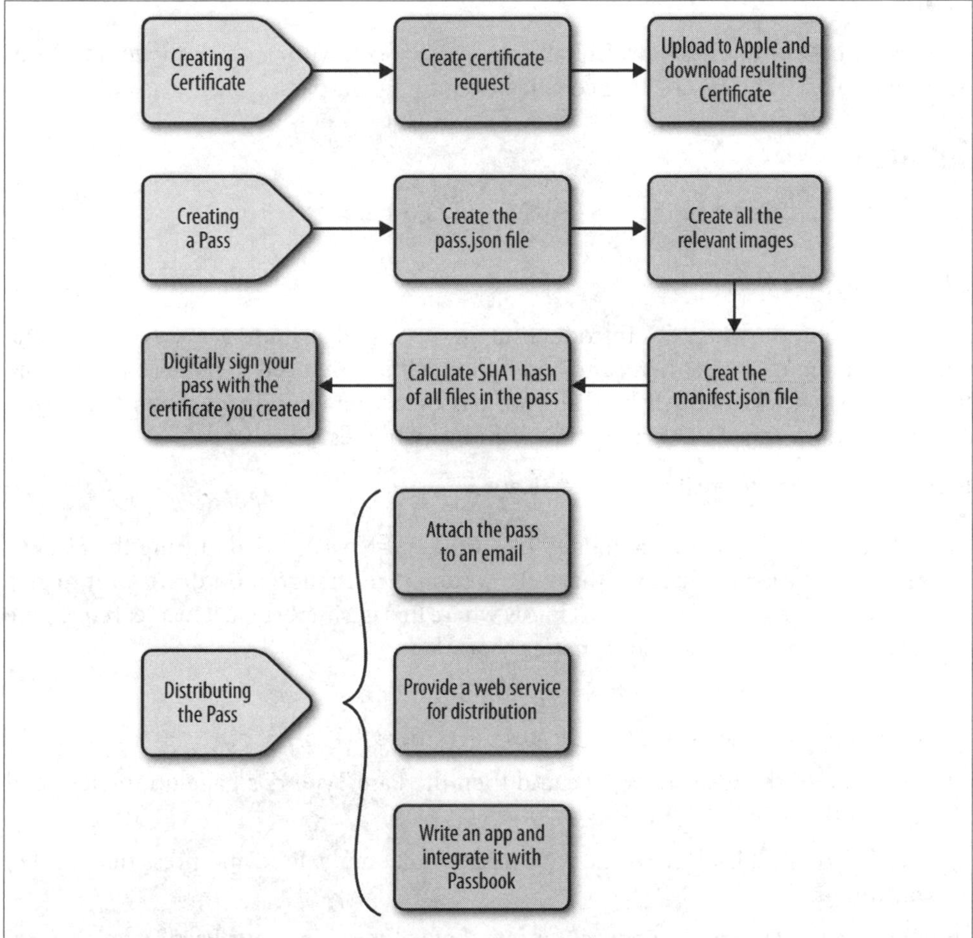


*Figure 23-2. Creating and distributing digitally signed passes to users, iOS 6 and above*

The recipes in this chapter will thoroughly explain the details of this process. A few bits and pieces related to Pass Kit as a technology—keeping your pass up to date and learning how to push updates from a server—require you to know a bit about server-side development. For the sake of simplicity, we won't be covering those parts in this chapter and instead will be focusing on creating passes. Once you know how to create a pass, you can distribute it in a variety of ways, two of which are explained in this chapter. However, parts that are not relevant to iOS, such as those that require server-side development knowledge, are skipped in this chapter for this reason.

# 23.1. Creating Pass Kit Certificates

## Problem

You have decided to distribute digitally signed passes to your users and would like to begin with the first step, creating certificates to sign your passes with.

## Solution

Create your certificates in the iOS Provisioning Portal.

## Discussion

As explained in this chapter's Introduction, in order to distribute passes to your users, you need to digitally sign them, and before doing that, you need to request a certificate from Apple that will uniquely bind all your passes to your developer account. That way, Apple knows which passes are legitimate and which ones are not.

Follow these steps to create your certificate:

1. Navigate your browser to the iOS Dev Center. I have avoided putting the URL to the iOS Dev Center here, as this URL is subject to change and I don't want to give you the wrong URL. If you don't know where this is, simply type it in a search engine and I bet you will find it in a matter of seconds.
2. If you are not logged in already, log in now.
3. Once logged in, go to the Certificates, Identifiers & Profiles page.
4. Navigate to the Identifiers page and then the Pass Type IDs page on the lefthand side of the screen.
5. When you first land there, the page might look empty. Find and press the plus (+) button on the screen.
6. Now, in the Description box, enter text that will describe your Pass Type ID.
7. In the Identifier box, enter a reverse-domain-style identifier of your pass. For instance, if your App ID is *com.pixolity.testingpasskit*, then for passes that integrate

with that app you can use *pass.pixolity.ios.cookbook.testingpasses*. The pass identifier is really something that should make sense to you and your application. However, the practice is that the whole identifier name should start with *pass.* and then you use whatever you wish for the rest of the identifier. Figure 23-3 demonstrates how you can fill in the details in this page.

Register a pass type identifier (Pass Type ID) for each kind of pass you create (i.e. gift cards). Registering your Pass Type IDs lets you generate Apple-issued certificates which are used to digitally sign and send updates to your passes, and allow your passes to be recognized by Passbook.

Pass Type ID Description

Description: Testing Passbook in iOS

You cannot use special characters such as @, &, *, ', "

Identifier

Enter a unique identifier for your Pass Type ID, starting with the string 'pass'

ID: pass.pixolity.ios.cookbook.testingpasses

We recommend using a reverse-domain name style string (i.e., com.domainname.appname).

Cancel Continue

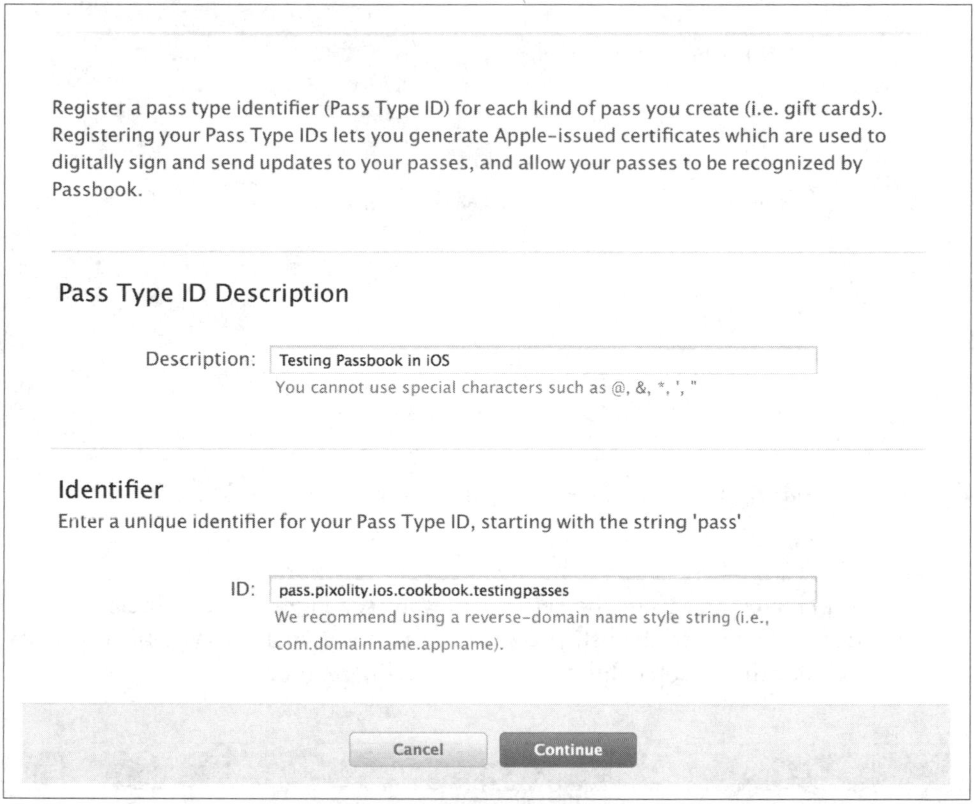

*Figure 23-3. Filling in the details of a simple Pass Type ID*

Once you are done populating the details in this page, press the Continue button. You will then be presented with the overview of your pass. If you are happy with the information that you entered in the previous page, simply press the Register button (see Figure 23-4). Now you have a Pass Type ID. However, this Pass Type ID is not linked to any certificate. So now you have to associate your Pass Type ID to a certificate. That's also easy. Follow these steps to create the certificate and associate it with your Pass Type ID.

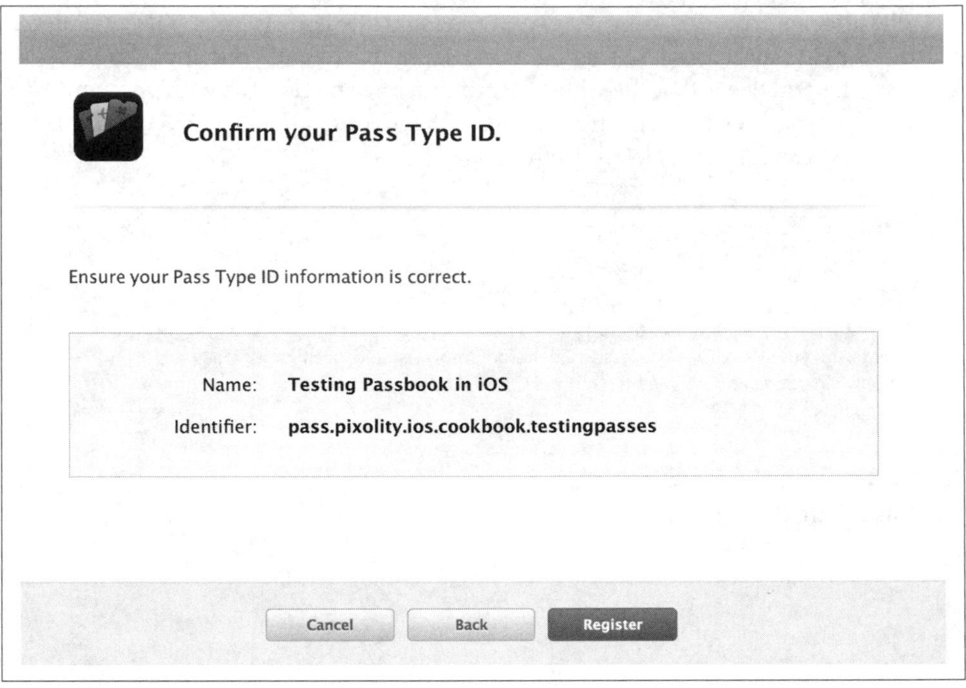


*Figure 23-4. Confirm your Pass Type ID if you are happy with all the settings*

1. In the Pass Type IDs section of the iOS Provisioning Portal, find the Pass Type ID that you created and press the Settings button (see Figure 23-5). Under the Pass Certificates column of the list, you can see that for your Pass Type ID, it will say *None*. Under the Action column, select the Configure link.

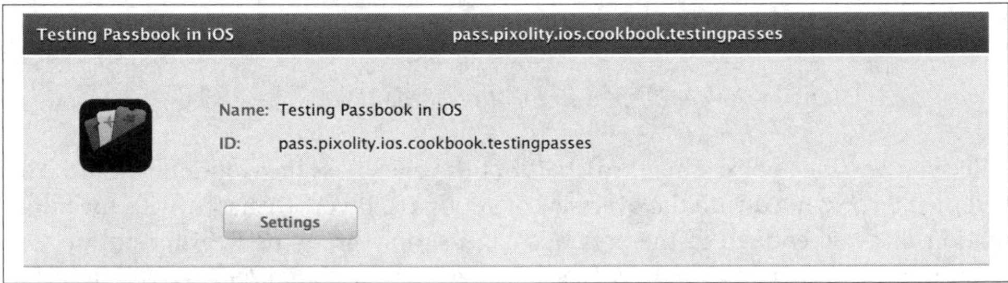


*Figure 23-5. Setting up our Pass Type ID*

2. After you select your Pass Type ID in the portal, you will be able to create a certificate for it (see Figure 23-6). Simply press the Create Certificate button.

*Figure 23-6. Ready to create a certificate for our Pass Type ID*

3. You will now be instructed to create a certificate signing request using Keychain Access on your Mac (Figure 23-7). Follow the instructions on the screen, and once you have created your certificate signing request, press the Continue button on the screen.

It is possible to create the certificate signing request on a non-Mac machine. In order to do so, you need to make sure that Open SSL is installed on that machine. The instructions on how to generate these certificates on non-Mac machines are outside the scope of this book, but if you are interested, a simple web search will help you understand the process on those machines.

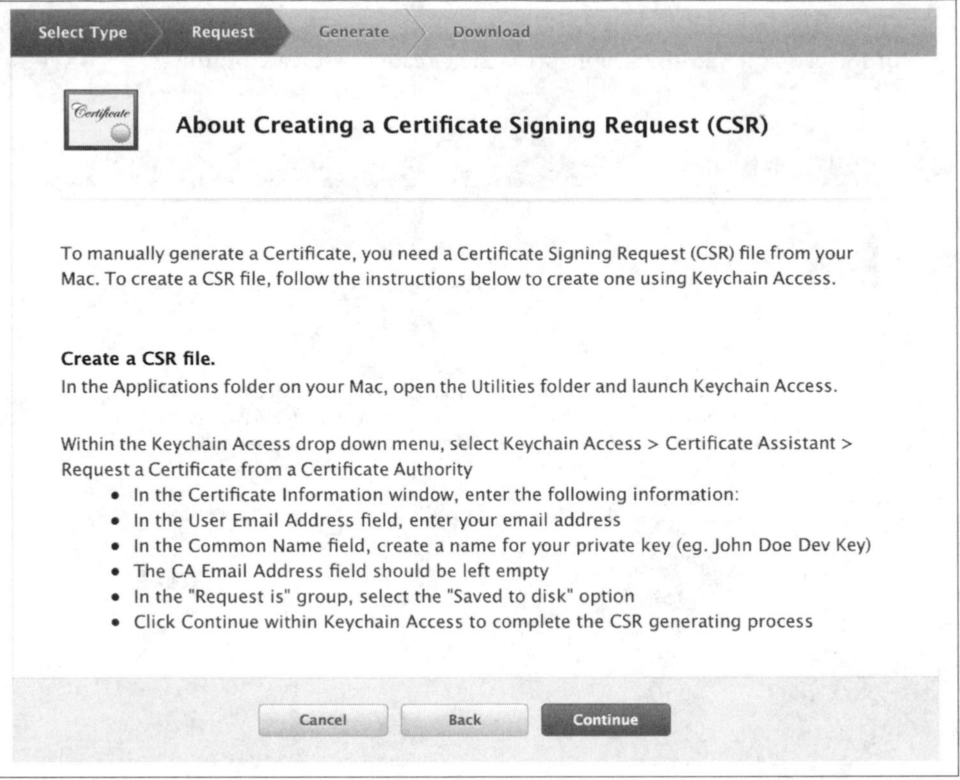


*Figure 23-7. Follow the on-screen instructions to create a certificate signing request*

The certificate requests that you create on your computer using Keychain Access will also create a private key that is associated with that certificate. Apple recommends that you back up your keychain database every now and then so that you won't lose your private keys, as Apple will not be saving your private keys on the iOS Provisioning Portal. If you are moving to a new computer, you need to move your private keys with you manually. That's why they are called private keys. Exporting private keys is simple: right-click your private key and press the Export menu item.

4. Now you will be asked on your browser to upload the certificate signing request to Apple in order to retrieve your certificate. The private key was created on your computer the moment you created the certificate signing request. The certificate that Apple will issue you at the end of this process will match your private key. So now select the Choose File button in this screen in order to select the certificate signing request that the keychain created for you (see Figure 23-8) and once done, press the Generate button.

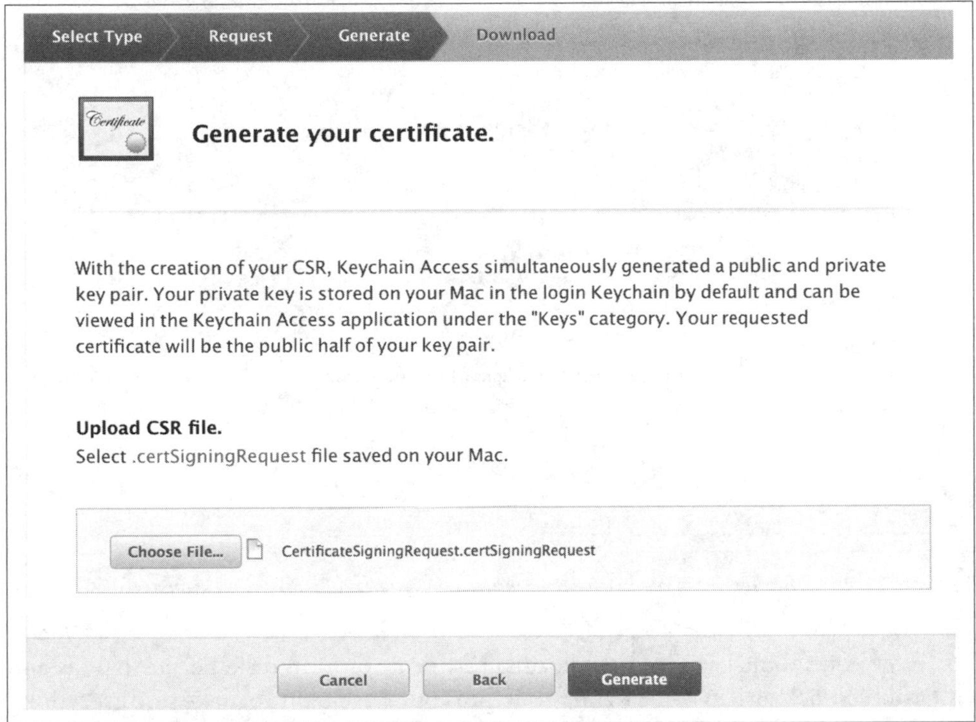


*Figure 23-8. Uploading the certificate signing request to Apple to get a certificate back*

5. After the certificate has been generated, you will be presented with a screen similar to Figure 23-9. Press the Download button on this screen to download the generated certificate.

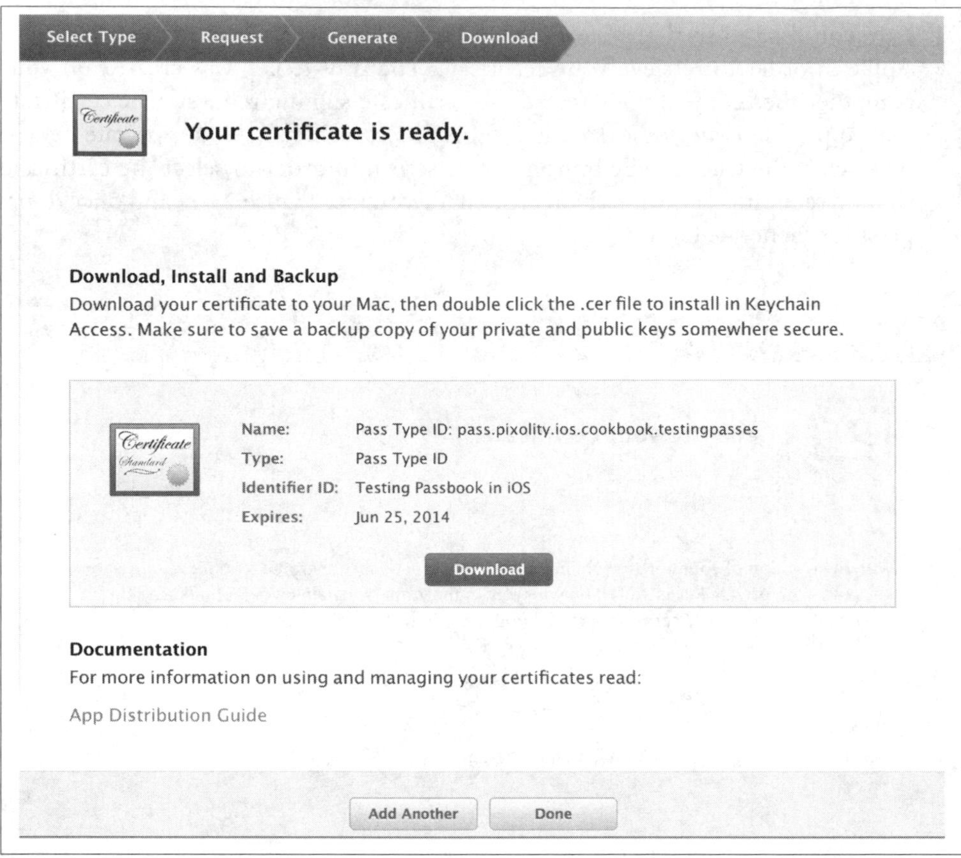


*Figure 23-9. Apple letting you know that your certificate was created successfully*

6. Now you should have the downloaded certificate on your disk. Locate that file and double-click on it in order to import it into your Keychain. To make sure everything worked successfully, open Keychain Access on your computer and navigate to the Login section and then the My Certificate subsection. Now on the righthand side of the screen, confirm that your certificate is present and that it is associated with a private key, as shown in Figure 23-10.

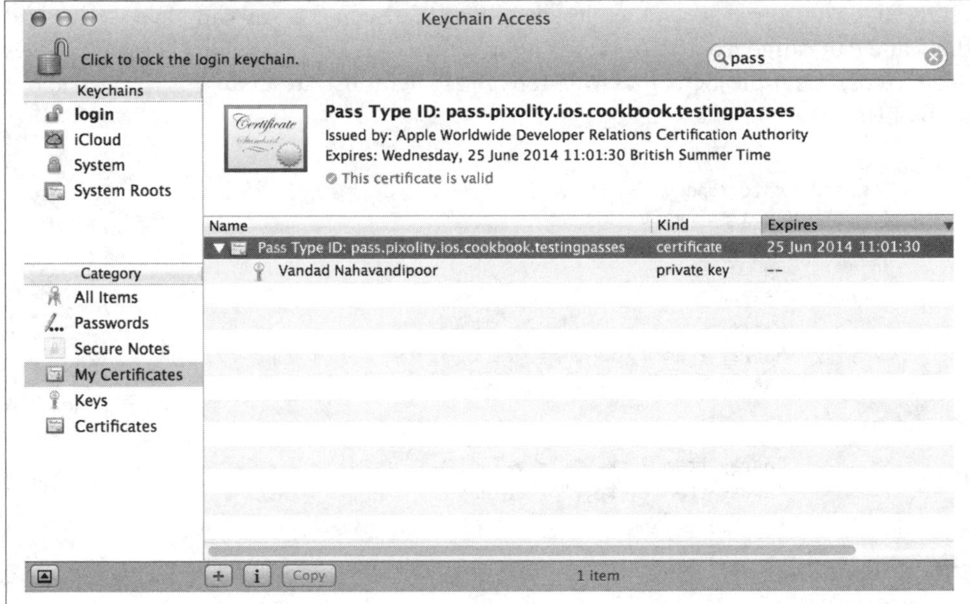


*Figure 23-10. The Apple-generated certificate is correctly associated with a private key*

You are now done creating your certificate and ready to sign your passes, ready to be sent to iOS devices.

## See Also

Recipe 23.0, "Introduction"

# 23.2. Creating Pass Files

## Problem

You want to create a pass file that represents the data that you want your users to hold in their iOS devices.

## Solution

Create a *pass.json* file and populate it with appropriate keys and values.

## Discussion

Apple has chosen JSON files to represent passes for Pass Kit. JSON stands for *JavaScript Object Notation* and is extensively used in web applications and services. However, as an iOS developer, you don't necessarily have to know about JSON files.

JSON files are simple key-value files, just like a dictionary. A key can have a value and the value can range from a simple string to a dictionary that contains keys and values itself. Here is a simple JSON that will pretty much demonstrate all there is to know about JSON files:

```
{
    "key 2 - dictionary" =     {
        "key 2.1" = "value 2.1";
        "key 2.2" = "value 2.2";
    };
    "key 3 - array" =     (
                {
            "array item 1, key1" = value;
            "array item 1, key2" = value;
        },
                {
            "array item 2, key1" = value;
            "array item 2, key2" = value;
        }
    );
    key1 = value1;
}
```

You can see that dictionaries are represented with square brackets and arrays with curly brackets. Other values are just simple key value pairs. If we were to represent this same JSON object with a normal `NSDictionary`, this is what the resulting code would be:

```
NSDictionary *json = @{
                       @"key1" : @"value1",
                       @"key 2 - dictionary" : @{
                               @"key 2.1" : @"value 2.1",
                               @"key 2.2" : @"value 2.2",
                               },
                       @"key 3 - array" : @[
                               @{
                                   @"array item 1, key1" : @"value",
                                   @"array item 1, key2" : @"value"
                                   },
                               @{
                                   @"array item 2, key1" : @"value",
                                   @"array item 2, key2" : @"value"
                                   }
                               ]
                       };
```

For more information about JSON, you can refer to JSON.org (*http://www.json.org*). Let's move on to creating our pass files. A pass file, as mentioned before, is a simple JSON file. Don't confuse pass files with passes. A pass is a collection of files, including the *pass.json* file, that will, as a whole, represent the digitally signed pass that users can install on their devices. A pass file is a file that explains how the pass should appear on the device.

The *pass.json* file can be constructed using high- and low-level keys. High-level keys are the keys that will be immediately visible in the top hierarchy of the *pass.json* file. The low-level keys will appear as children of the high-level keys. Don't worry if this sounds confusing for now. I know I was confused when I first heard about this, but if you read on, I promise it will all click eventually.

Let's start by creating a *pass.json* in Xcode. I should warn you that Xcode is unfortunately not the best editor for JSON files; however, it is our primary IDE, so we will stick with it. Follow these steps to create a *pass.json* file:

1. Create an empty iOS project in Xcode by choosing File → New → Project...
2. On the lefthand side of the New Project dialog, make sure you are under the iOS category. Then choose Other and on the righthand side, choose Empty, as shown in Figure 23-11. Once done, press the Next button.

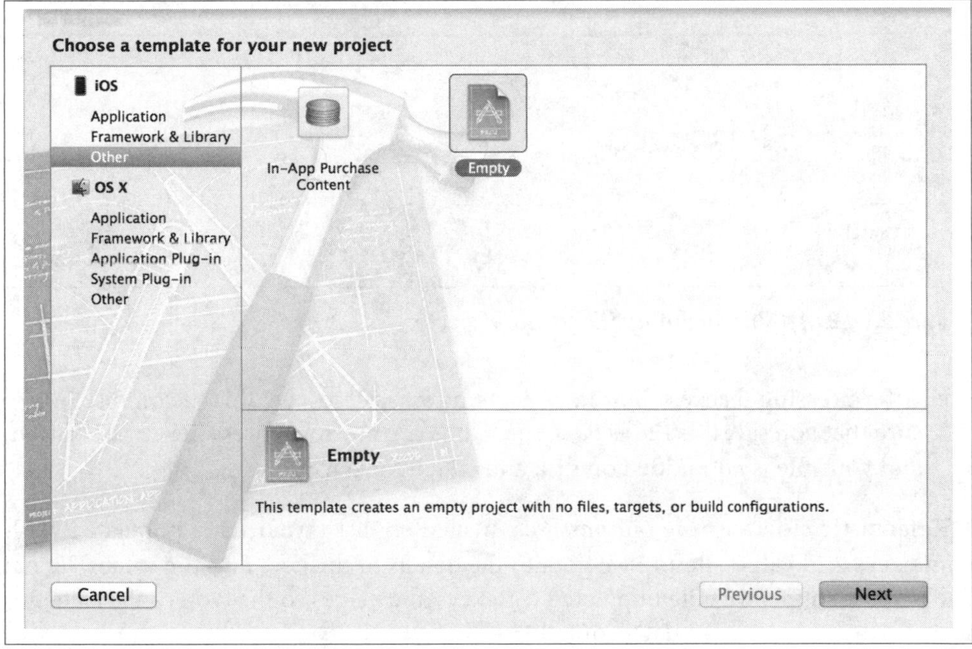


*Figure 23-11. Creating an empty iOS project*

3. Now, give your project a name under the Product Name box and once done, press the Next button. Now you get the chance to save your file on disk. Once you have successfully chosen the path to save the project, you are ready to create the *pass.json* file.
4. In your new empty project, in Xcode, choose File → New → File...

5. In the New File dialog, make sure you are under the iOS category, and then choose Other. On the righthand side, choose Empty, as shown in Figure 23-12. Once you are done, press the Next button.

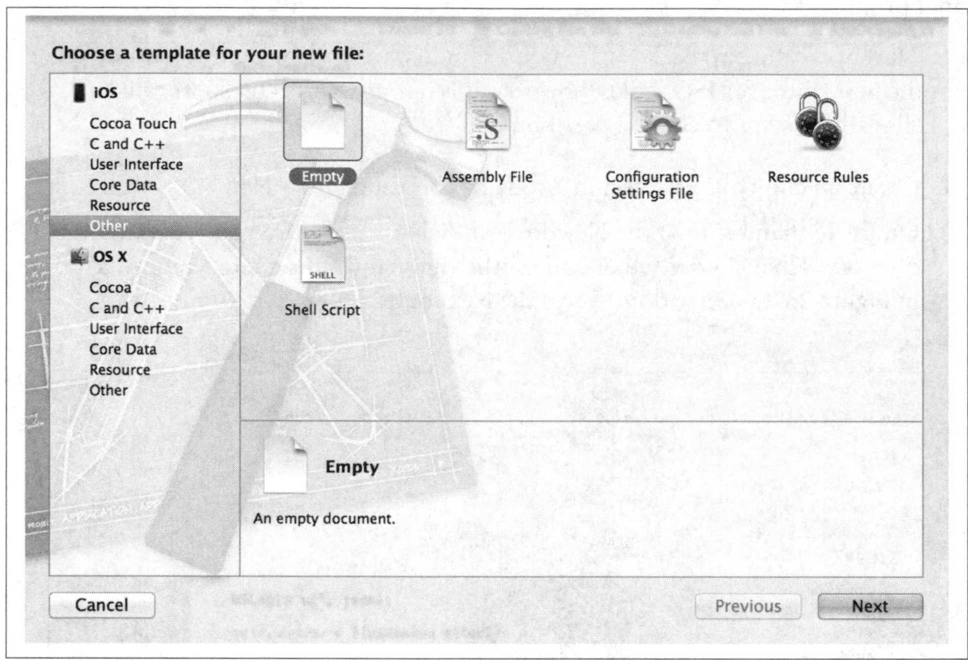


*Figure 23-12. Adding an empty file to our project*

6. After pressing the Next button, you are now asked to save this file on disk. Make sure that you save this file as *pass.json*. Once you are done, press the Create button, and your file is now added on disk and added to your project.

OK, fantastic: now we have our *pass.json* created on disk. We need to populate it with some keys and values. Before we go into the details of the keys and the values, let me show you a simple pass file populated with keys and values so that you can get a better idea of what a pass file actually contains:

```
{
  "formatVersion" : 1,
  "passTypeIdentifier" : "<# Put your Pass Type ID here #>",
  "serialNumber" : "p69f2J",
  "teamIdentifier" : "<# Put your team ID here #>",
  "description" : "Train Ticket Example",
  "locations" : [
    {
      "longitude" : -0.170867,
```

```
        "latitude" : 50.834948
      }
    ],
    "barcode" : {
      "message" : "1234567890",
      "format" : "PKBarcodeFormatPDF417",
      "messageEncoding" : "iso-8859-1"
    },
    "organizationName" : "O'Reilly Railways",
    "logoText" : "O'Reilly Railways",
    "foregroundColor" : "rgb(255, 255, 255)",
    "backgroundColor" : "rgb(100, 100, 100)",
    "boardingPass" : {
      "transitType" : "PKTransitTypeTrain",
      "primaryFields" : [
        {
          "key" : "departure",
          "label" : "Departs From",
          "value" : "Hove, 07:37",
        },
        {
          "key" : "departurePlatform",
          "label" : "Departs from Platform",
          "value" : "2",
        }
      ],
      "auxiliaryFields" : [
        {
          "key" : "arrival",
          "label" : "Arrives At",
          "value" : "London Bridge, 08:41"
        },
        {
          "key" : "arrivalPlatform",
          "label" : "Arrives at Platform",
          "value" : "13"
        }
      ],
      "backFields" : [
        {
          "key" : "oreillyRailways",
          "label" : "O'Reilly Railways",
          "value" : "For more information, visit www.oreilly.com"
        },
        {
          "key" : "termsAndConditions",
          "label" : "Terms and Conditions",
          "value" : "To be filled later"
        }
      ]
    }
  }
```

I have intentionally left the `teamIdentifier` and `passTypeIdentifier` keys' values empty. You need to make sure that you populate the values of these keys to something that you have set up in your provisioning portal as a Pass Type ID. It is imperative that you fill the values of these keys with accurate information.

Fantastic. Now we have our *pass.json* ready to be included in our digitally signed pass. Remember, a pass is more than just the *pass.json* file. We need to include a handful of images and a manifest file that will list all the files included in our pass.

Here are some of the most important keys that you can place in the *pass.json* file:

`formatVersion`
: This key specifies the version of the pass format. Please set this value to the constant value of *1*.

`passTypeIdentifier`
: This is the identifier of the pass that you created in the iOS Provisioning Portal before, minus your team ID. For instance, if my full Pass Type ID is *TEAMID.pass.pixolity.testingpasskit*, I will set the value of the pass identifier to *pass.pixolity.testingpasskit*.

`teamIdentifier`
: This is your team identifier. To find this value, simply navigate to the main page of iOS Dev Center, and then navigate to Member Center. Choose Your Account and then Organization Profile. You should now be able to see a field that reads *Company/Organization ID*. That is your Team ID. Simply copy and paste that value in this key in your *pass.json* file.

`description`
: A short description of what this pass is for. Accessibility in iOS will use this description.

`organizationName`
: This is the name of your company.

`serialNumber`
: A unique serial number for your pass. You can make this up as you go. It should make sense to you and your organization. Note that if two or more passes are using the same pass type identifier, their serial numbers *cannot* be the same.

`barcode`
: A barcode for your pass. It is highly recommended that you include barcode information with your digital passes. The keys that you can enter in this dictionary are explained here:

  `message`
  : The message to be encoded within your barcode.

  `format`
  : The format of your barcode. The value of this key must be `PKBarcodeFormatText`, `PKBarcodeFormatQR`, `PKBarcodeFormatPDF417`, or `PKBarcodeFormatAztec`. A discussion of barcode formats is outside the scope of this book, so we won't go into details about barcodes and what each format means.

  `messageEncoding`
  : The encoding that you want to use for your barcode. Leave the value of this key at `iso-8859-1`.

`logoText`
: This text will appear next to the logo of your pass in the Passbook app on the device.

`foregroundColor`
: The foreground color of your pass. This value is specified in red, green, and blue values, each ranging from 0 to 255 inclusive. Wrap the value inside an `rgb()` function. For instance, for pure red color, specify `rgb(255, 0, 0)`, or for white, specify `rgb(255, 255, 255)`.

`backgroundColor`
: This is the background color of your pass, specified in the same format as the `foregroundColor`.

Once you are done setting the values for these keys, you can now specify what type of pass you are creating. You can do this by putting one of the following keys in your pass's top-level keys, just like all the previously mentioned keys:

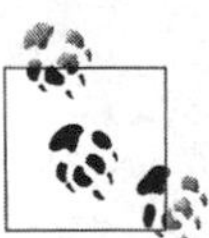

The following keys in your *pass.json* will contain a dictionary of values (keys and values) that will specifically dictate what the pass is for and what values it contains.

`eventTicket`
: This tells Passbook that your pass is for an event, such as a concert.

`coupon`
: This tells Passbook that your pass is a coupon. For instance, the user can use a pass like this to get some items more cheaply in the store that issued the pass.

`storeCard`
: This tells Passbook that your pass is a store card (e.g., a loyalty card that you can use in a store to collect points).

`boardingPass`
: This tells Passbook that your pass is a boarding pass (e.g., for plane, train, or bus travel).

`generic`
: A pass that doesn't fit into any of the aforementioned categories.

Once you have included one of these pass types as a key into your *pass.json*, it is now time to specify the keys and values for the pass type dictionary (which we just talked about). Each pass type dictionary can contain the following keys:

`transitType`
: This key is required only inside the `boardingPass` dictionary; otherwise, you can just ignore this key. The possible values for this key are `PKTransitTypeAir`, `PKTransitTypeBus`, `PKTransitTypeTrain`, `PKTransitTypeBoat`, and `PKTransitTypeGeneric`. All of these are self-explanatory.

`headerFields`
: The visible part of the top of the pass in Passbook on the device. Make sure you don't put too much information here, as these values are always visible to the user even when all passes are stacked on top of each other in the Passbook app on the device.

`primaryFields`
: The most important information about your pass, which will be displayed on the front side of the pass. For instance, for a boarding pass at an airport, the gate, seat number, and airline name may be the most important pieces of information to display. For another type of pass, these values may be different.

`secondaryFields`
: Less important information about the pass, also displayed on the front side of the pass. Again, for a boarding pass at an airport, the secondary fields might be the boarding time, boarding date, and aircraft type.

`auxiliaryFields`
: The least important information to be displayed on the front side of the pass. Again, going back to our example of a boarding pass at an airport, this might be the expected arrival time.

`backFields`
: The values to display on the back of the pass.

All the aforementioned keys have dictionaries as their values, and those dictionaries can contain any of the following keys:

`label`
: The value of the field that has to be displayed on the pass (back or front of the pass, depending on the key that it has been added to).

`key`
: The key that your app can use to read the value of this field.

`value`
: The value of this field.

`textAlignment`
: An optional key that can describe the alignment of the label visually on the pass. You can specify any of the following values for this field (these values are really self-explanatory):

  - PKTextAlignmentRight
  - PKTextAlignmentCenter
  - PKTextAlignmentLeft
  - PKTextAlignmentNatural
  - PKTextAlignmentJustified

Phew! Those are a lot of keys and values to remember. Don't worry, though, you'll get used to them after some time! So let's create a simple *pass.json* now. I believe if we put our requirements down first and then tackle the creation of the pass file itself, it will be much easier to map what we've learned so far to how we create the *pass.json* file. So here is what we'll do for an example:

- The type of pass is a train boarding pass.
- The train departs from a city called Hove in the United Kingdom at 07:37. The platform from which the train departs at Hove is Platform 2.
- The train will arrive into London Bridge station in London at 08:41 on Platform 13.
- The ticket is valid for all trains operated by a made-up company named O'Reilly Railways.

Before we move on, though, we need to go through the `locations` array in our *pass.json* file. This key is an array in which every element has two keys I will describe in a moment. But the cool thing about this key is that it can describe the geolocations where the pass that you are creating belongs. When the pass is imported in the Passbook app on the user's device, iOS will display a message on the user's screen with the details of your pass, telling the user that your pass is relevant at the current location where the user is. Think of it this way: in our example, the user has to display the train ticket at the ticket barriers every time she reaches the train station at Hove (the departure city). So you can put the location of the departure train station in the pass (under the `locations` key) so that iOS will automatically display the pass on the screen when the user reaches the train station. You can do the same thing for the destination train station because when the user is coming back home to the Hove train station via London Bridge, London Bridge will be the departing station. It's just the other way around. If you go from point A to B, A is the source and B is the destination. Once you come back, B is the source and A is the destination. So you can put the location of both point A and B, or even some other points where your pass is relevant, inside the `locations` array. Here are the keys that every location can contain:

`longitude`
: The longitude of the location. This value is of type `double`. Do not put quotation marks around this value.

`latitude`
: The latitude of the location. This value is of type `double`. Do not put quotation marks around this value.

## See Also

Recipe 23.2; Recipe 23.0, "Introduction"

# 23.3. Providing Icons and Images for Passes

## Problem

You want to make sure that your pass will be branded according to your company's style, or give your pass a distinct flavor or image.

## Solution

Create backgrounds, icons, and logos and embed them inside your digitally signed pass.

## Discussion

A pass can contain different images:

*Background (background.png, background@2x.png, and background-568@2x.png)*
: The background image of the pass. Not all passes can have background images.

*Logo (logo.png and logo@2x.png)*
: The logo that will appear on the upper-left corner of the pass, depending on which type of pass it is.

*Icon (icon.png and icon@2x.png)*
: The icon for the pass. Not all passes can have icons. We will have a look at creating icons for passes in this chapter.

*Thumbnail (thumbnail.png and thumbnail@2x.png)*
: The thumbnail image that will be visible when the passes are stacked on top of each other.

All images, as you can see from the filenames, have to come in the non-Retina and the Retina flavors. Apple doesn't strictly say that this is a must, but don't we all as developers value our customers? Retina displays are so popular now that they are becoming industry standard, so please do provide the Retina images for your passes.

Now that we know the image filenames, let's move on to the image dimensions. In the following, I list only the Retina images, so to get the dimensions of the non-Retina images, please divide the image width and height in half:

*background@2x.png*
: 640 pixels wide and 960 pixels tall

*background-568@2x.png*
: 640 pixels wide and 1136 pixels tall, for iPhone 5

*logo@2x.png*
: 60 pixels wide and 60 pixels tall

*icon@2x.png*
: 58 pixels wide and 29 pixels tall

*thumbnail@2x.png*
: 200 pixels wide and 200 pixels tall

For the purposes of this recipe, I have created all these images in a very simple way. Figure 23-13 shows them together on one canvas.

The figure is for demonstration purposes and just to show you how many images you have to prepare for one pass. You do *not* have to create such an image where all your images appear on one canvas.

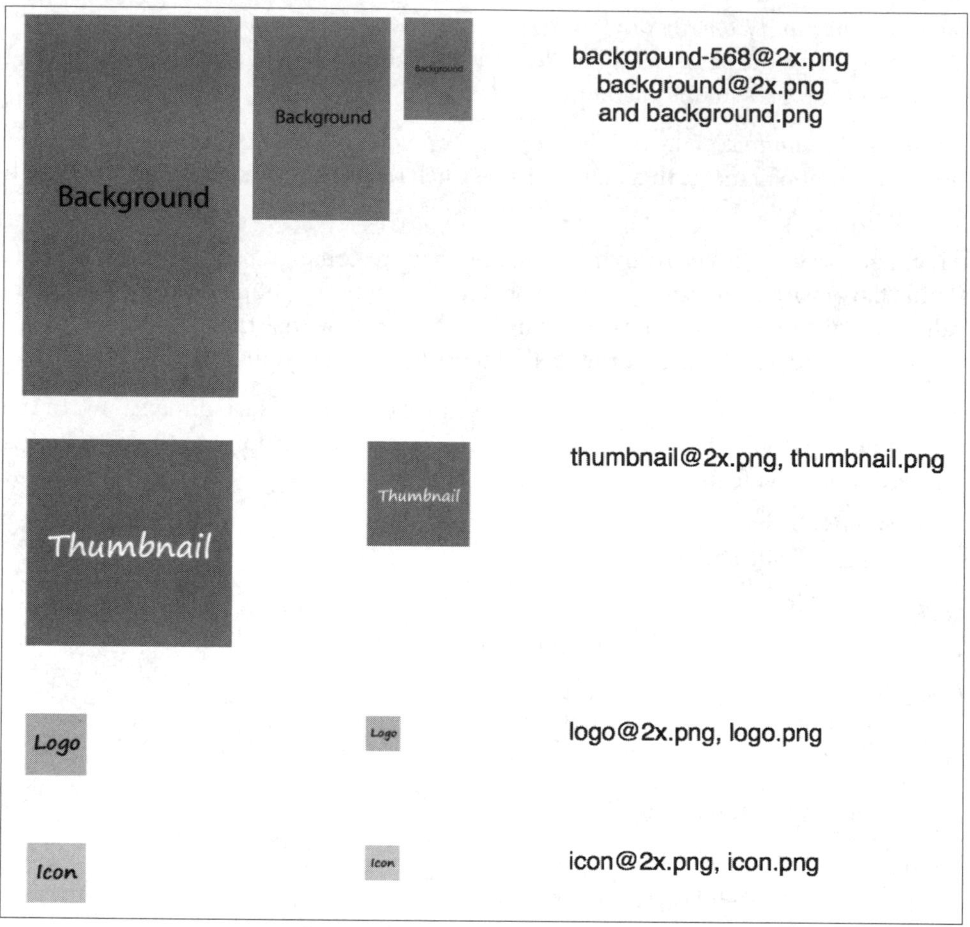


*Figure 23-13. All pass images on one canvas*

Now that your images are ready, place them in the same folder where you have placed your *pass.json* file. We will move on to the next stage now, which is preparing our manifest file.

## See Also

Recipe 23.2

## 23.4. Preparing Your Passes for Digital Signature

### Problem

You want to prepare your passes for digital signature. This is the step that you have to take before you are able to digitally sign your passes.

### Solution

Create a file named *manifest.json* in the same folder where you placed your *pass.json* and your pass images. The manifest file will be a JSON file. Its root object is a dictionary. The keys to the dictionary are the names of the files (all your images, plus the *pass.json* file). The value of each key is the SHA1 hash of the file.

### Discussion

Simply create the *manifest.json* file with the keys for all your images and leave the values empty for now. Your *manifest.json* file's contents should look similar to what's shown here:

```
{
    "background.png"          :   "",
    "background@2x.png"       :   "",
    "background-568@2x.png"   :   "",
    "icon.png"                :   "",
    "icon@2x.png"             :   "",
    "logo.png"                :   "",
    "logo@2x.png"             :   "",
    "pass.json"               :   "",
    "thumbnail.png"           :   "",
    "thumbnail@2x.png"        :   ""
}
```

Now off to do the interesting part. We have to calculate the SHA1 hashes of all these files. Remember that every time you change the files from now on (for instance, if you find an issue with the *pass.json* file), you will have to recalculate the SHA1 hash and place the new SHA1 value in the *manifest.json* file. In order to calculate the SHA1 hash of any file in OS X, simply follow these steps:

1. Open up Terminal and navigate to the folder where the target file sits, using the `cd` command.
2. Issue an *openssl* command in Terminal. Pass `sha1` as the first argument and the filename as the second argument to this command.

For instance, in my project folder, I have a folder called *pass* and I have placed my *pass.json* and my almost-empty *manifest.json* files in there along with the images (background, logo, etc.). Now in Terminal, I shall calculate the SHA1 hashes of all these files and place them in the manifest file. So the following listing shows my *openssl* command on the first line, and the output with all the hashes on the rest of the lines.

```
openssl sha1 *.png *.json
SHA1(background-568h@2x.png)= e2aaf36f4037b2a4008240dc2d13652aad6a15bb
SHA1(background.png)= b21a92dedb89f8b731adabc299b054907de2347d
SHA1(background@2x.png)= 6abab0f77fd89f1a213940fd5c36792b4cc6b264
SHA1(icon.png)= ed698ab24c5bd7f0e7496b2897ec054bbd426747
SHA1(icon@2x.png)= 90381c84cfea22136c951ddb3b368ade71f49eef
SHA1(logo.png)= c3bd8c5533b6c9f500bbadbdd957b9eac8a6bfe9
SHA1(logo@2x.png)= 1a56a5564dec5e8742ad65dc47aa9bd64c39222f
SHA1(thumbnail.png)= 58883d22196eb73f33ea556a4b7ea735f90a6213
SHA1(thumbnail@2x.png)= 0903df90165ef1a8909a15b4f652132c27368560
SHA1(manifest.json)= 894f795b991681de8b12101afb8c2984bf8d0f65
SHA1(pass.json)= c5acddbab742f488867c34882c55ca14efff0de9
```

We calculated the SHA1 of all files, including the SHA1 of the *manifest.json*. However, we are not going to need the SHA1 of *manifest.json* because it holds the hashes for all the other files and doesn't have to hold its own. So just ignore the SHA1 of this file.

What we have to do now is to populate the *manifest.json* with the SHA1 values of the rest of the files that we just calculated:

```
{
    "background.png"          :    "b21a92dedb89f8b731adabc299b054907de2347d",
    "background@2x.png"       :    "6abab0f77fd89f1a213940fd5c36792b4cc6b264",
    "background-568@2x.png"   :    "e2aaf36f4037b2a4008240dc2d13652aad6a15bb",
    "icon.png"                :    "ed698ab24c5bd7f0e7496b2897ec054bbd426747",
    "icon@2x.png"             :    "90381c84cfea22136c951ddb3b368ade71f49eef",
    "logo.png"                :    "c3bd8c5533b6c9f500bbadbdd957b9eac8a6bfe9",
    "logo@2x.png"             :    "1a56a5564dec5e8742ad65dc47aa9bd64c39222f",
    "pass.json"               :    "c5acddbab742f488867c34882c55ca14efff0de9",
    "thumbnail.png"           :    "58883d22196eb73f33ea556a4b7ea735f90a6213",
    "thumbnail@2x.png"        :    "0903df90165ef1a8909a15b4f652132c27368560"
}
```

All is good now. We can move on to the next step, which is the signature of our pass.

## See Also

Recipe 23.1

## 23.5. Signing Passes Digitally

### Problem

You have prepared your *pass* folder with the manifest and the *pass.json* and all the images, and now you want to be able to digitally sign the pass folder and its content to create your pass file, ready to be distributed.

### Solution

Use OpenSSL to sign your passes.

### Discussion

Every pass has to be signed using the certificate that we created in Recipe 23.1. We will use *openssl* again in Terminal in order to sign our passes. Before you continue reading, make sure that you have created a folder named *pass* and place your *pass.json*, *manifest.json* and all your images in this folder. The folder name doesn't necessarily have to be called *pass*. However, to make sure you can follow through the steps in this recipe and the rest of this chapter, it's best to do what I've done and put the files in a folder named *pass* so you can follow along more easily.

Some of you may be a bit confused as to what keys are which and what certificates do what. I hope I can make it a bit more clear here. When you request a new certificate in the iOS Provisioning Portal, the keychain creates a private key on your computer along with a certificate signing request (CSR) file. The certificate will be generated by Apple. When you download the certificate, its file extension will be *.cer*. This is just the certificate! When you import this certificate into your keychain, The keychain will automatically associate the certificate with the private key that it created before. Now if you export the certificate from the keychain, the resulting file will be of type *.p12*, which contains both the certificate and the private key for the certificate.

Before we can dive into the signing process, we will need to export our certificate from Keychain Access. Keep in mind that the certificate that you downloaded from iOS Provisioning Profile is not the same certificate that you will now export from Keychain Access, so make sure that you follow these steps to export your Pass Type ID certificate from your keychain:

1. Open up Keychain Access on your Mac.

2. On the upper-left side of the window under Keychains, make sure that you have selected the Login keychain.
3. Under the Category section on the left side, choose My Certificates.
4. Locate your Pass Type ID certificate on the righthand side of the screen and then right-click it.
5. Now choose the Export option, as shown in Figure 23-14, and proceed to export your certificate to disk as a *.p12* file. Do not save the certificate in the *pass* folder. Keep the certificate outside that folder.

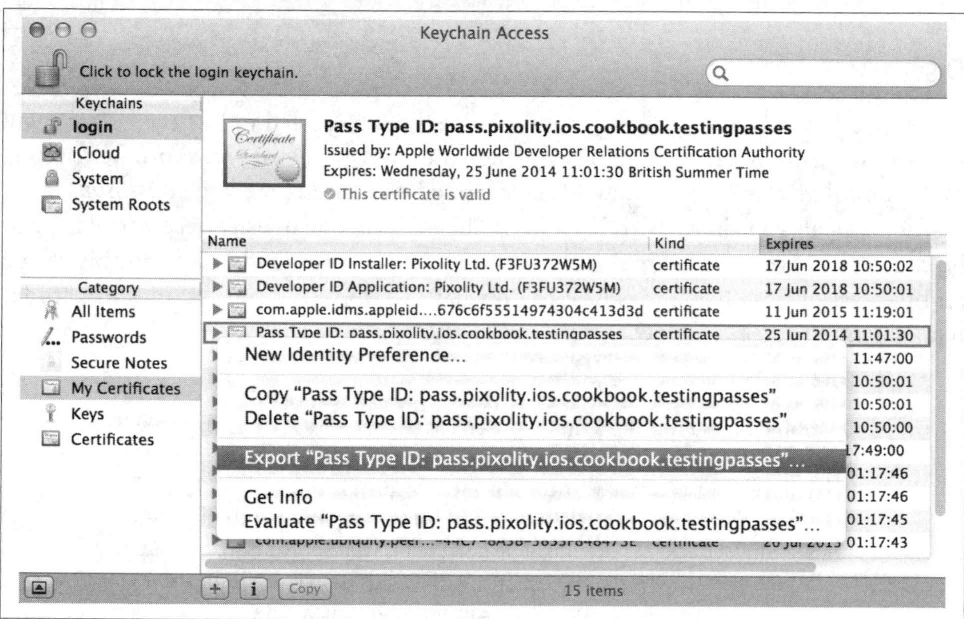


*Figure 23-14. Exporting our Pass Type ID certificate from Keychain Access*

6. After you attempt to export your certificate, you will be asked for two pieces of information: a password that you need to set on your certificate and the password of your OS X user, who owns the Keychain Access. The first password is on the certificate, which will make sure the certificate cannot be imported into any random machine if the user doesn't have the password. The second password makes sure the person who is exporting your certificate from your keychain really has permission to do so. For instance, if you leave your computer on and unlocked and your friend attempts to export a certificate from your keychain, he or she will have to enter your user account's password in order to do so. It's always good practice to make sure different accounts on the system have different passwords. For instance, if you and your brother both use the same Mac, you need to make sure that your

account's password is something unique to your account. If you and your brother have the same password on both your accounts on the same Mac, that defies the whole purpose of security on your Mac.

Make sure that you *do not* save the certificate inside the *pass* folder. You should not ship your certificate inside your pass.

Now that you have exported your certificate, you have ended up with a file that is probably named *Certificates.p12*. Now it is time to split this file into the certificate part and the private key. As you may know, when you export a certificate from Keychain Access, the resulting *.p12* file contains both the certificate and the private key. However, when you use OpenSSL to sign your pass, you will need to pass the private key and the certificate separately. So to retrieve the private key and the certificate from your *Certificates.p12* file that we just exported from Keychain Access, follow these steps:

1. Open up Terminal if it's not open already.
2. Navigate to the folder where you saved the exported certificate `.p12` file.
3. In order to get the certificate out, issue the following command:

```
openssl pkcs12 -in "NAME OF YOUR .P12 CERTIFICATE FILE" -clcerts \
-nokeys -out "NAME OF THE OUTPUT CERTIFICATE"
```

For instance, the certificate and private key file exported from my keychain is named *Certificates.p12* and I want to export the certificate out of it, under the name *exported-certificate*. To do this, I have to issue the following command in Terminal:

```
openssl pkcs12 -in "Certificates.p12" -clcerts -nokeys \
    -out "exported-certificate"
```

Once you issue this command, you will be asked to assign your exported certificate a password. For this example, I am setting the password as *123*, but please give yours a better password.

4. In order to export the private key out of the keychain-exported certificate, you will need to issue the following command in Terminal:

```
openssl pkcs12 -in "NAME OF YOUR .P12 CERTIFICATE FILE" \
-nocerts -out "NAME OF THE OUTPUT KEY"
```

I will name the exported private key *exported-key*, but feel free to choose another name if you want to:

```
openssl pkcs12 -in "Certificates.p12" -nocerts -out "exported-key"
```

Again, you will be asked to enter passwords for your key. I have set mine up with the password of *1234* so that I can easily remember it, and it's the same password I have set up for my certificate. In an organization where you need to make sure things are done in a secure way, of course, you wouldn't want to choose this type of password. Choose something that makes sense for you, and make sure the passwords that you choose for different certificates/keys that you export are distinct for maximum protection.

Fantastic. Now we have our exported certificate and private key files. We can now move on to signing our pass with these files. Follow these steps in order to do so:

1. If you haven't already, place all the files related to the pass (*pass.json*, *manifest.json*, and all the relevant images) inside a folder called *pass*. You can name this folder anything you want, but for the purpose of clarity in this recipe, it's best that the folder name that you create be the same folder that I have here. That way, it will be easier for all of us to know which folder we are in and what we are doing in Terminal.
2. Use the `cd` command to change the current working directory to the *pass* directory where all your pass files exist.
3. Execute the *rm -f .DS_Store* command to make sure no unnecessary OS X hidden system files are present in your *pass* folder. You need to make sure all the files in this folder are listed in the *manifest.json* along with their SHA1 hashes. If any other files, hidden or not, creep into this folder without being listed in the manifest file, the resulting pass will be invalid and not readable by Passbook on iOS devices or the simulator.
4. Issue the following command in Terminal in order to generate a *signature* file inside your *pass* folder:

```
openssl smime -binary -sign -signer "PATH TO YOUR EXPORTED CERTIFICATE" \
-inkey "PATH TO YOUR EXPORTED PRIVATE KEY" -in manifest.json \
-out signature -outform DER
```

This command has to be issued inside the *pass* folder where all your pass assets exist. The exported certificate and private key are the certificate and the private key that you extracted from the keychain-exported certificate. Avoid providing the actual keychain-exported certificate to this command. Before this, we learned how to extract the real certificate and the private key out of the keychain-exported `.p12`

file, so you may want to have a look at that again to make sure things are going as planned.

As part of the last step, you will be asked to provide the password for your private key. Do you remember it? That is the password you set when you were extracting the private key from the keychain-exported certificate. This command has now created a file named *signature* in the *pass* folder. We are almost done; all we have to do now is to compress the *pass* directory into a ZIP file with the extension of *.pkpass*. In order to do that, follow these steps:

1. Open up Terminal and using the `cd` command, navigate to your *pass* folder.
2. Issue the following command in order to zip your *pass* folder into a file called *pass.pkpass* in the current folder:

```
zip -r pass.pkpass . -x '.DS_Store'
```

This will zip up all the pass files into the *pass.pkpass* and, again, makes sure that a file named *.DS_Store* will not be included in the output archive.

### See Also

Recipe 23.4; Recipe 23.1

## 23.6. Distributing Passes Using Email

### Problem

You want to be able to send your digitally signed passes to people using their email addresses.

### Solution

Simply send the passes as attachments in your email.

### Discussion

The pass that you signed and packaged up in Recipe 23.5 is now ready to be distributed. One of the easiest ways of distributing passes is through email. Follow these steps to distribute your pass through email using the Mail.app on your installation of OS X:

1. Open up Mail.app on your installation of OS X.
2. From the File menu, choose New Message.
3. Enter the email address of the person to whom you want to send the pass.

4. Enter a title for your email.
5. Enter the message for your email and simply drag and drop the *pass.pkpass* file, which you prepared in Recipe 23.5, into the message of your email at the end, as shown in Figure 23-15.

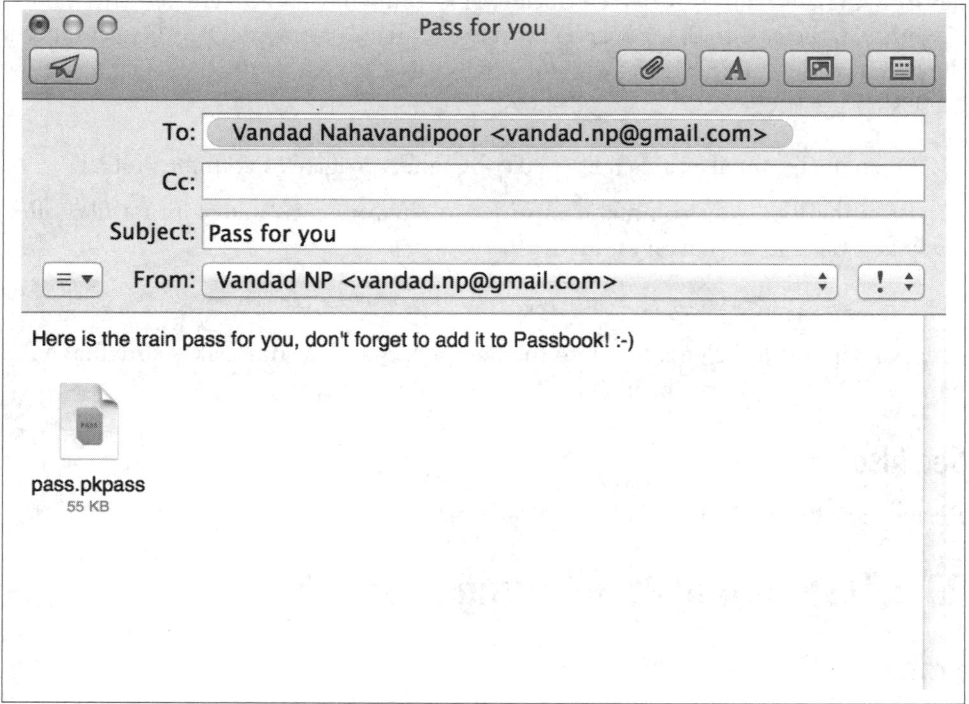


*Figure 23-15. Distributing digitally signed passes using Mail.app on OS X*

6. Now send the email.

OS X Mavericks has added the ability for users to be able to see passes right in the Mail app. Since Passbook is integrated with iCloud, you can now tap on the pass in your email on OS X Mavericks and send it right to your iOS device(s) that have Passbook for iCloud enabled in the iCloud settings of their devices (see Figure 23-16).

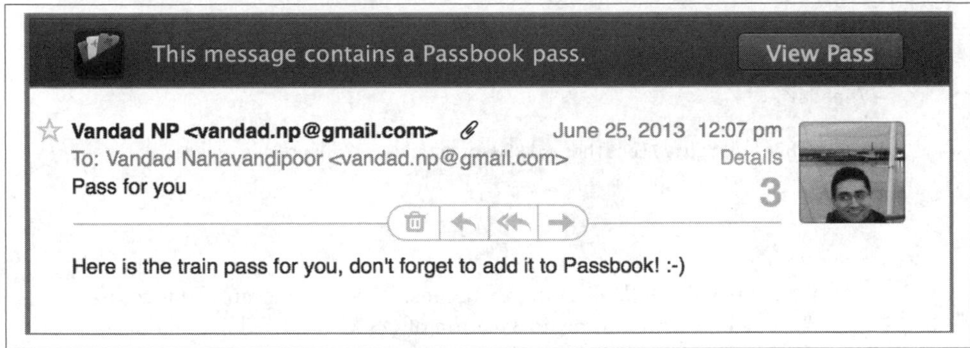


*Figure 23-16. OS X Mavericks displays passes right in the Mail app*

Now the user has the ability to tap on the pass attached to the email. This will cause Passbook to pop up and display the pass in its interface, allowing the user to add the pass to Passbook, right on the device.

### See Also

Recipe 23.7

## 23.7. Distributing Passes Using Web Services

### Problem

You want users to be able to download your digitally signed passes right from your website.

### Solution

In your web pages, create hyperlinks to your *.pkpass* passes. When users view the web pages on their devices, they can simply tap on those links. Once they tap on the link, Safari will detect that the link leads to a *.pkpass* file and will hand the link to Passbook, which will display the pass on the website and allow the users to add your passes to their Passbooks.

### Discussion

Safari on iOS does not handle direct downloading of *.pkpass* pass files. In order to let your users download the *.pkpass* passes, you need to create web pages with hyperlinks in them that point to the *.pkpass* files. A simple HTML code file that serves a *pass.pkpass* to the user is displayed here:

```
<html>
    <header>
        <title>Passbook Site</title>
    </header>
    <body>
        <a href="http://localhost:8888/pass.pkpass">Download your pass here</a>
    </body>
</html>
```

I have put the link as *localhost* because I'm running an instance of Apache web server on my installation of OS X. You need to make sure the link in this HTML file makes sense in your web development environment.

Now when the user opens this link in Safari on her device, she will see something similar to Figure 23-17.

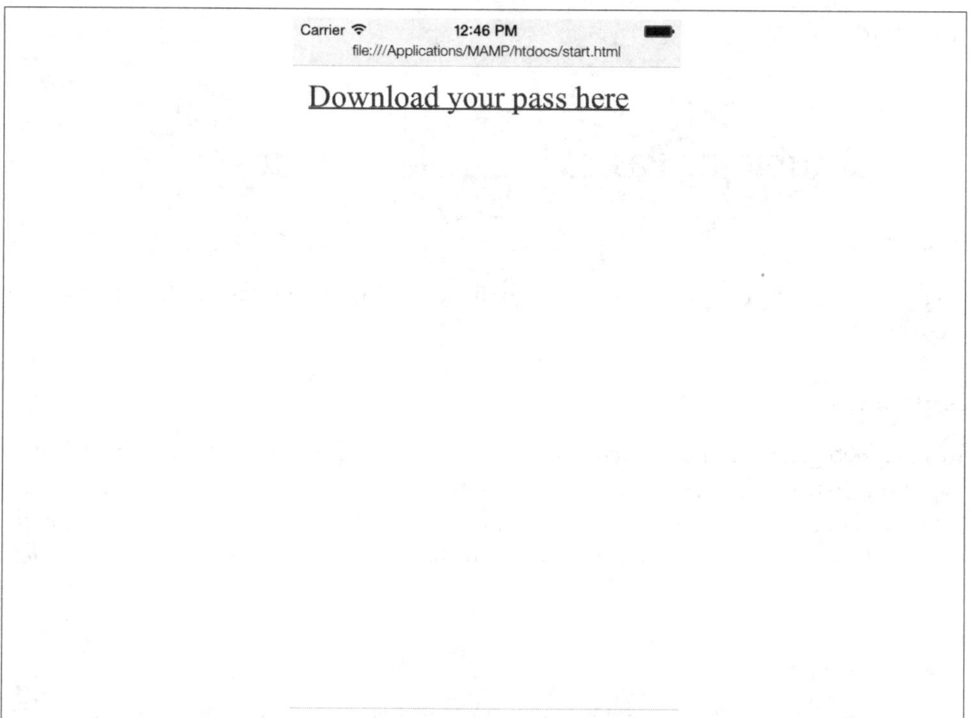


*Figure 23-17. Viewing our website in Safari on iOS Simulator*

When the user taps on the link, Passbook will pop up and display its familiar UI to the user, allowing her to add your pass to her device's Passbook.

## See Also

Recipe 23.6

# 23.8. Enabling Your iOS Apps to Access Passes on iOS Devices

## Problem

You want to deploy your Passbook-enabled app to iOS devices and you want to make sure that your app can read the digitally signed passes that you have pushed into those devices.

## Solution

Create an appropriate provision profile for your app, linked to an App ID that has Passes access enabled for it.

## Discussion

You need to sign your apps with an appropriate provisioning profile that has been created in the same portal that your Pass Type IDs were created in, in order to be able to read our own passes from the Passbook app on users' devices. The whole process is depicted in Figure 23-18.

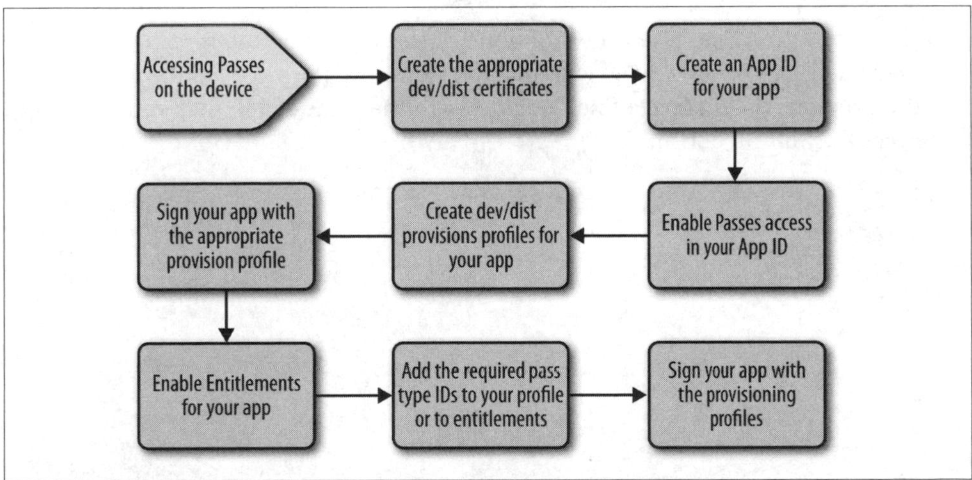


*Figure 23-18. The process of enabling an iOS app to access passes on an iOS device*

So let's begin! Here I assume that you already have a dev/dist certificate. We'll create an App ID for the Pass Type ID that we created in Recipe 23.1 and then move on to create the appropriate provisioning profile for that App ID. Here we go:

1. Navigate to iOS Dev Center in your browser, and log in if you are not logged in already.
2. Navigate to the Certificates, Identifiers & Profiles section
3. Navigate to the Identifiers section and then the App IDs section and press the plus (+) button.
4. In the Description box, describe your App ID; something that is meaningful to you and your team or organization.
5. Leave the Bundle Seed ID as Use Team ID.
6. In the Bundle Identifier (App ID Suffix), enter the reverse domain style name of your bundle ID. For me, for the pass with an ID of *pass.pixolity.testingpasskit*, I have set the bundle identifier of my App ID to *com.pixolity.testingpasskit*.
7. Ensure that the Explicit App ID box is checked and enter the full reverse-domain-style bundle identifier of the app that you want to create. I have set this value to *`com.pixolity.ios.cookbook.testingpasses`*, and my Pass Type ID from before was set to *`pass.pixolity.ios.cookbook.testingpasses`*. You don't have to match your Pass Type ID with your bundle identifier, but it really does help you find which App ID matches which Pass Type ID in the future.
8. In the App Services section of the page, make sure you have ticked the Passbook box to enable access to Passbook in your app.
9. Once you are done, press the Continue button. On the next screen, you will be presented (see Figure 23-19) with the overview of all the values that you entered in the previous page. Have a final look through the values, and once you are happy, press the Submit button.

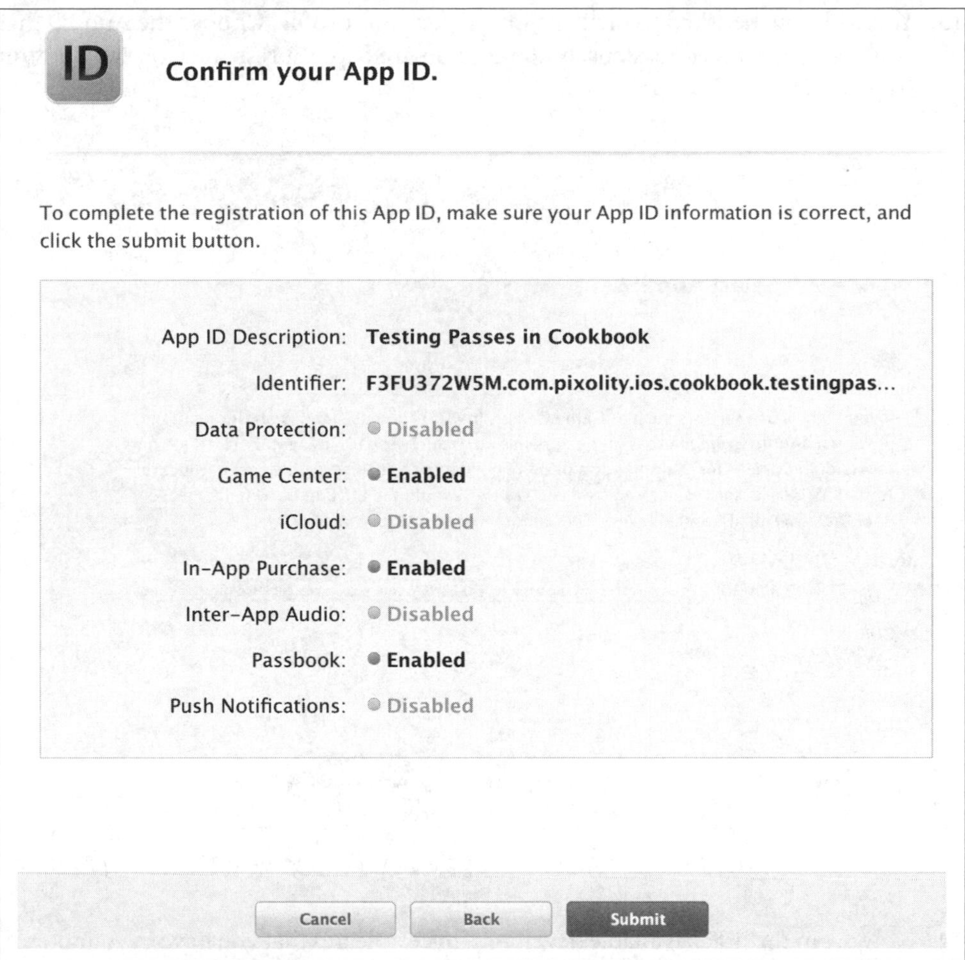


*Figure 23-19. Overview of a new App ID to integrate with Passbook*

10. Now that we have enabled Passes for our App ID, it is time to create our provisioning profile. Head to the Provisioning Profiles section of the iOS Provisioning Profile now.
11. We are going to create a developer provisioning profile as opposed to an Ad Hoc build, so in the Provisioning section, under the Development section, press the plus (+) button.
12. In the screen that appears, select the *iOS App Development* item and press the Continue button.

13. You will now be asked to pick an App ID for your profile. Choose the App ID that you created in previous steps, and once you are happy, press the Continue button (see Figure 23-20).

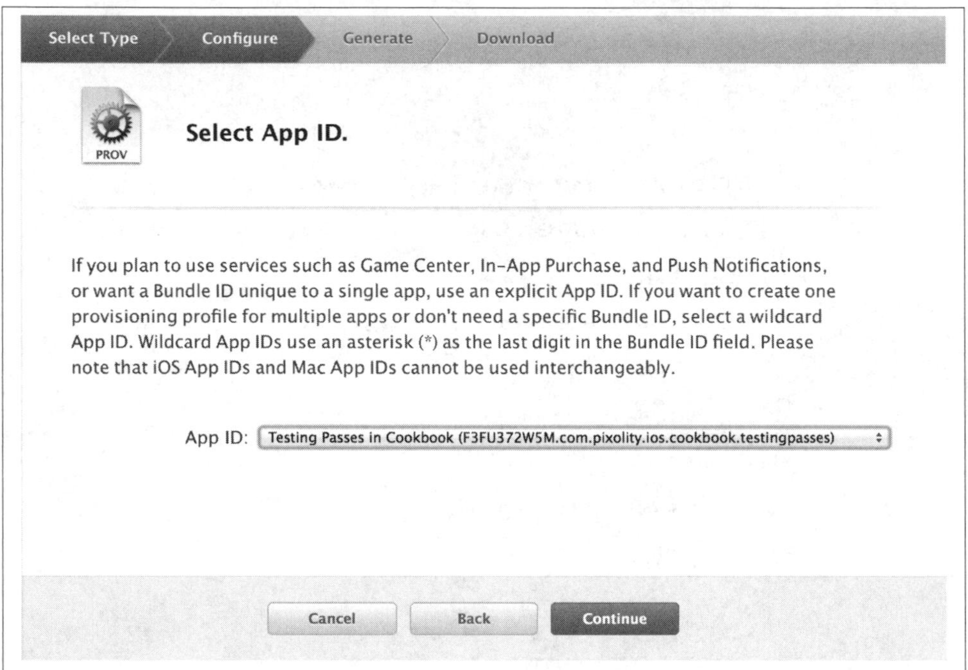


*Figure 23-20. Selecting the correct App ID for the new development provision profile*

14. Now, from the list of available development certificates that you have in your portal, choose one or a few certificates to associate your profile with. Usually you would associate a profile with one certificate, but in a portal where there are multiple developers, each with its own development certificate, it may make sense to create a provision profile that is associated with more than one certificate. Once you have made your choice, press the Continue button.
15. Now, from the list of registered devices, select the ones that will be included in your profile. Once you are satisfied with your selection, press the Continue button.
16. On the next screen, you are asked to give a name to your profile. Give a name that makes sense to you, and press the Generate button.
17. Once your profile is generated, press the Download button to download it onto your device (see Figure 23-21). After the download is complete, drag and drop that profile onto iTunes for it to install the profile on your device.

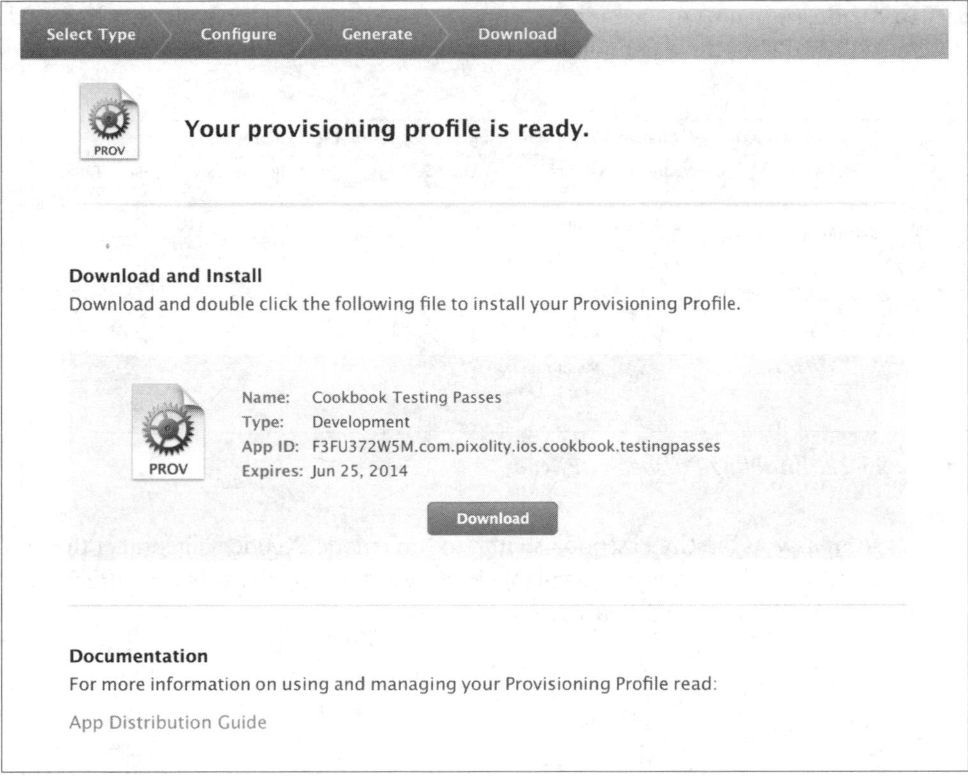


*Figure 23-21. Your Passbook profile is ready for download*

There are various ways of installing a provisioning profile on your OS X installation. The best and fastest way is to drag and drop the profile into iTunes. You can also use Xcode to install the profile. Whatever method you choose, make sure that you *avoid* double-clicking on the profile in order to install it. Double-clicking will install your profile with a really cryptic name on your disk, and later it will be very difficult to distinguish which profile is which. To keep your disk clean, use iTunes or Xcode to install your provisioning profiles. You can view all installed provisioning profiles on your disk in the file *~/Library/MobileDevice/Provisioning Profiles/*.

18. Now open your project in Xcode. In the Build Settings tab of your target app, choose the provisioning profile that you just created for Debug-only builds. You can do the same thing for Ad Hoc builds, but under the Release scheme in Build Settings.

19. In Xcode, right next to the Build Settings tab, choose Capabilities and flip the switch to "on" mode for the Passbook item (see Figure 23-22).

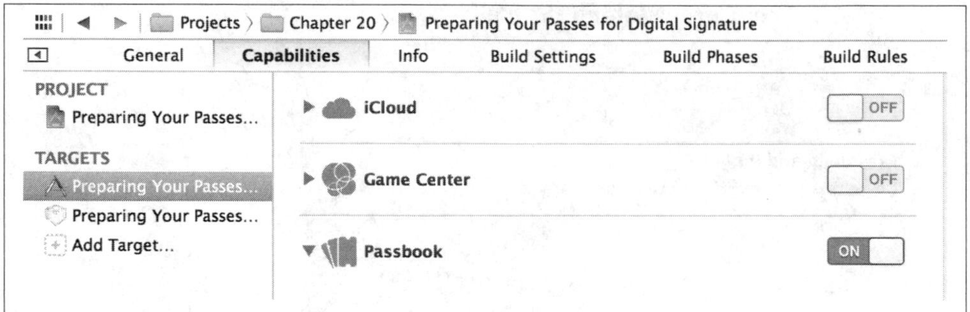


*Figure 23-22. Enabling Passbook in Xcode*

20. As soon as you flip the Passbook switch to "on" mode, Xcode will contact the Dev Center and will fetch all your available Pass Type IDs. In the list (see Figure 23-23), choose the Pass Type ID that you created earlier.

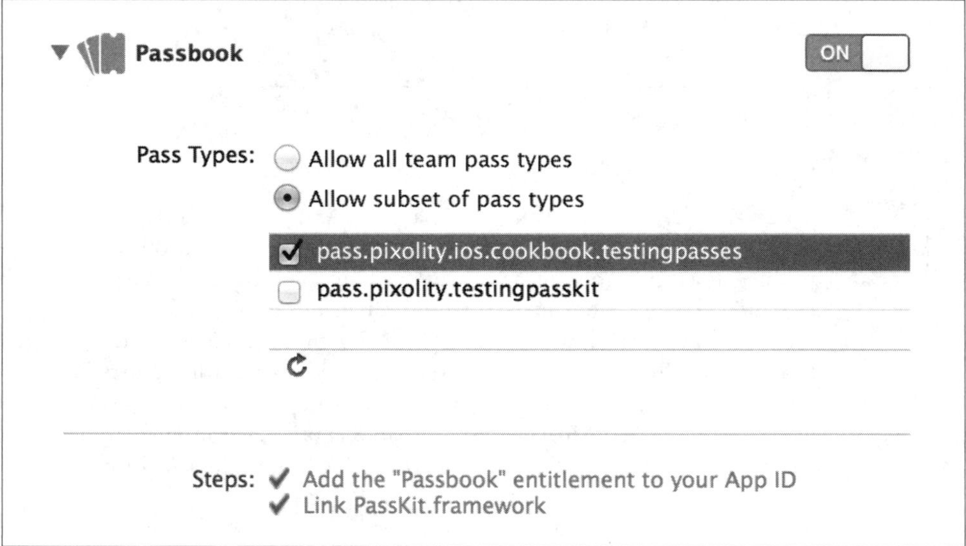


*Figure 23-23. Choosing the correct Pass Type ID in Xcode*

And with this task, we are all done setting up Pass Kit! All we need is to write an app that can access passes on the device. The app will be described in Recipe 23.9.

## See Also

Recipe 23.6; Recipe 23.7

# 23.9. Interacting with Passbook Programmatically

## Problem

You want to be able to interact with the installed passes on a user's device programmatically.

## Solution

Include the PassKit.framework into your project and use the `PKPassLibrary` to find the passes that you are interested in. Passes will be of type `PKPass`, so using this class you can retrieve information about your passes.

## Discussion

As a prerequisite to this recipe, please make sure that you have read Recipe 23.8 and now have an Xcode iOS project that has the appropriate provisioning profile to access your passes in the user's Passbook library.

Apple has provided the PassKit.framework for iOS developers. Using this framework, you can interact with passes that the user has installed on her devices. To be able to use this framework using the latest LLVM compiler, all you have to do is import the relevant umbrella header into your project like so:

```
#import "AppDelegate.h"
#import <PassKit/PassKit.h>

<# Rest of your code goes here #>
```

The next thing that we are going to do is declare a private property of type `PKPassLibrary` in the implementation file of our app delegate. The aforementioned class in PassKit.framework will allow you to interact with the passes that have been added to the device. While you are at it, you will also need to know the keys in the *pass.json* file that you created in Recipe 23.2 in order to be able to read values such as the departure platform and departure city. So declare these keys as well, all in the implementation file of your app delegate:

```
#import "AppDelegate.h"
#import <PassKit/PassKit.h>
```

```
@interface AppDelegate ()
@property (nonatomic, strong) PKPassLibrary *passLibrary;
@end

NSString *PassIdentifier          = @"pass.pixolity.testingpasskit";
NSString *PassSerialNumber        = @"p69f2J";

NSString *DepartureKey            = @"departure";
NSString *DeparturePlatformKey    = @"departurePlatform";
NSString *Arrival                 = @"arrival";
NSString *ArrivalPlatform         = @"arrivalPlatform";

@implementation AppDelegate

<# Rest of your code goes here #>
```

Fantastic! After you are done with that, you need to start accessing the Passbook library on the device. But wait a minute: what if the device doesn't have Passbook installed on it? You have to first check whether Passbook is available on the device. Do that using the `isPassLibraryAvailable` class method of the `PKPassLibrary` class.

The next thing you need to do is instantiate your `passLibrary` property of type `PKPassLibrary` and then use the `passWithPassTypeIdentifier:serialNumber:` instance method of the pass library to find the pass that you are looking for. So now you know why we have also defined our pass identifier and its serial number among the keys to different fields within the pass. The aforementioned method will return an object of type `PKPass` that will represent your pass object. Once you have this pass object, you can read the values from its different keys.

Default keys, such as organization name and serial number, are mapped to properties for you by Apple in the `PKPass` class itself. However, if you want to access the values within `primaryFields` or other similar places, you will need to use the `localizedValueForFieldKey:` instance method of the `PKPass` class and pass your keys to this method to get the values associated with those keys. So here is a little code snippet that can read the departure and arrival city and platforms from the pass that we created in Recipe 23.2:

This is inside the implementation file of our app delegate.

```
#import "AppDelegate.h"
#import <PassKit/PassKit.h>

@interface AppDelegate ()
@property (nonatomic, strong) PKPassLibrary *passLibrary;
@end
```

```
NSString *PassIdentifier          = @"pass.pixolity.testingpasskit";
NSString *PassSerialNumber        = @"p69f2J";

NSString *DepartureKey            = @"departure";
NSString *DeparturePlatformKey    = @"departurePlatform";
NSString *Arrival                 = @"arrival";
NSString *ArrivalPlatform         = @"arrivalPlatform";

@implementation AppDelegate

- (void) displayPassInformation:(PKPass *)paramPass{

    if (paramPass == nil){
        NSLog(@"The given pass is nil.");
        return;
    }

    NSLog(@"Departs From = %@",
          [paramPass localizedValueForFieldKey:DepartureKey]);
    NSLog(@"Departure Platform = %@",
          [paramPass localizedValueForFieldKey:DeparturePlatformKey]);

    NSLog(@"Arrives at = %@",
          [paramPass localizedValueForFieldKey:Arrival]);
    NSLog(@"Arrival Platform = %@",
          [paramPass localizedValueForFieldKey:ArrivalPlatform]);

}

- (BOOL)                application:(UIApplication *)application
      didFinishLaunchingWithOptions:(NSDictionary *)launchOptions{

    if ([PKPassLibrary isPassLibraryAvailable]){
        self.passLibrary = [[PKPassLibrary alloc] init];

        PKPass *pass =
        [self.passLibrary passWithPassTypeIdentifier:PassIdentifier
                                        serialNumber:PassSerialNumber];
        [self displayPassInformation:pass];

    } else {
        /* Take another action here perhaps */
        NSLog(@"The pass library is not available.");
    }

    self.window = [[UIWindow alloc]
                   initWithFrame:[[UIScreen mainScreen] bounds]];

    // Override point for customization after application launch.
    self.window.backgroundColor = [UIColor whiteColor];
    [self.window makeKeyAndVisible];
```

```
    return YES;
}
```

The pass identifier and serial number provided are for the pass that I created using my certificate. Your serial number may be the same, but the pass identifier will certainly be different, and will be something that makes more sense for you and your provisioning portal/organization.

## See Also

Recipe 23.2

# Index

## Symbols



## A



*We'd like to hear your suggestions for improving our indexes. Send email to index@oreilly.com.*

## B



## C

## D

## E

## F

## G



## H

## I

## J



## K

## N

## O



## P

## Q



## R

## S

## T

## U

## V

## W



## X

## About the Author

**Vandad Nahavandipoor** has developed software using Cocoa, Cocoa Touch, Assembly and C for many years. He has worked with some of the world's biggest brands, such as Visa, U.S. Bank and HSBC to deliver mobile applications to millions of customers around the world. He has always had a passion for teaching and used to make a living by teaching programming when he was only 17 years old. In programming, his main focus is optimization and delivering high performance applications to users. His hobbies are playing the guitar, practicing the piano, and road cycling.

## Colophon

The cover image for *iOS 7 Programming Cookbook* is the Cowan's shrew tenrec (*Microgale cowani*). One of 20 known species of *Microgale* native to Madagascar, Cowan's shrew tenrec is 4 to 6 inches in length and weighs less than an ounce, with a tail smaller than its body. Because it has poor eyesight, the shrew tenrec instead uses its stiff, sensitive whiskers and a keen sense of smell to navigate the dense tropical rainforests of eastern Madagascar. The tenrecs are one of the few mammals that retain a cloaca, a single urogenital opening that was characteristic of the earliest known mammals and the modern day platypus and marsupials.

An insectivore like many tenrecs, Cowan's shrew tenrec is also known to eat small mammals and earthworms. Its natural predators include larger tenrecs and Madagascan red owls, although it can evade most predators by hiding in the leafy underbrush of the forest floor, where it also forages for insects.

Some speculate that the tenrecs migrated to Madagascar from Africa through oceanic dispersal, or rafting over, after the island had broken off from the continent 165 million years ago. The earliest known tenrecs appeared on the island some 60 million years ago and have evolved into widely diversified species, having arrived at a time when there were no other mammals. Thus, with little to no competition, they came to dominate their ecological niche. Most African tenrecs have disappeared and are known only through fossils. The larger tenrecs of Madagascar evolved into quill-bearing mammals similar to hedgehogs, while the smaller tenrecs look like shrews or moles; however, tenrecs are not related to any of those other animals.

The cover image is from a loose page, origin unknown. The cover fonts are URW Typewriter and Guardian Sans. The text font is Adobe Minion Pro; the heading font is Adobe Myriad Condensed; and the code font is Dalton Maag's Ubuntu Mono.

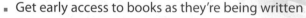